OCEAN OF ATTAINMENTS

Studies in Indian and Tibetan Buddhism

This peer-reviewed series was conceived to provide a forum for publishing outstanding new contributions to scholarship on Indian and Tibetan Buddhism and also to make accessible seminal research not widely known outside a narrow specialist audience, including translations of appropriate monographs and collections of articles from other languages. The series strives to shed light on the Indic Buddhist traditions by exposing them to historical-critical inquiry, illuminating through contextualization and analysis these traditions' unique heritage and the significance of their contribution to the world's religious and philosophical achievements.

Members of the Editorial Board:

Tom Tillemans (co-chair), Emeritus, University of Lausanne
Leonard van der Kuijp (co-chair), Harvard University
Shrikant Bahulkar, Bhandarkar Oriental Research Institute
José Cabezón, University of California, Santa Barbara
Georges Dreyfus, Williams College, Massachusetts
Vincent Eltschinger, École Pratique des Hautes Études
Janet Gyatso, Harvard University
Paul Harrison, Stanford University
Toni Huber, Humboldt University, Berlin
Pascale Hugon, Austrian Academy of the Sciences
Shoryu Katsura, Ryukoku University, Kyoto
Kataoka Kei, Kyushu University, Fukuoka
Thupten Jinpa Langri, Institute of Tibetan Classics, Montreal
Chenkuo Lin, National Chengchi University, Taipei
Hong Luo, Peking University
Cristina Scherrer-Schaub, University of Lausanne
Ernst Steinkellner, Emeritus, University of Vienna
Jan Westerhoff, Oxford University
Jeson Woo, Dongguk University, Seoul
Shaoyong Ye, Peking University
Chizoku Yoshimizu, Tsukuba University

STUDIES IN INDIAN AND TIBETAN BUDDHISM

OCEAN OF ATTAINMENTS

The Creation Stage of the Guhyasamāja Tantra according to Khedrup Jé

Translated by Yael Bentor and Penpa Dorjee
Edited and introduced by Yael Bentor

Wisdom

Wisdom Publications
132 Perry Street
New York, NY 10014 USA
wisdomexperience.org

Library of Congress Cataloging-in-Publication Data
Names: Dge-legs-dpal-bzang-po, Mkhas-grub-rje, 1385–1438, author. | Bentor, Yael, 1951– translator. | Penpā Dorjee, translator.
Title: Ocean of attainments: the creation stage of the Guhyasamāja Tantra according to Khedrup Jé / Yael Bentor and Penpa Dorjee.
Other titles: Rgyud thams cad kyi rgyal po Dpal Gsang ba 'dus pa'i bskyed rim Dngos grub rgya mtsho zhes bya ba bzhugs so. English.
Description: First edition. | New York: Wisdom Publications, 2024. | Series: Studies in Indian and Tibetan Buddhism | Includes bibliographical references and index.
Identifiers: LCCN 2023028702 (print) | LCCN 2023028703 (ebook) | ISBN 9781614298304 (hardcover) | ISBN 9781614298533 (ebook)
Subjects: LCSH: Tripiṭaka. Sūtrapiṭaka. Tantra. Guhyasamājatantra—Commentaries. | Dge-legs-dpal-bzang-po, Mkhas-grub-rje, 1385–1438. Rgyud thams cad kyi rgyal po Dpal Gsang ba 'dus pa'i bskyed rim Dngos grub rgya mtsho zhes bya ba bzhugs so. | Tantric Buddhism. | BISAC: RELIGION / Buddhism / Tibetan | RELIGION / Buddhism / Sacred Writings
Classification: LCC BQ2152.E5 D4413 2024 (print) | LCC BQ2152.E5 (ebook) | DDC 294.3/823—dc23/eng/20231002
LC record available at https://lccn.loc.gov/2023028702
LC ebook record available at https://lccn.loc.gov/2023028703

ISBN 978-1-61429-830-4 ebook ISBN 978-1-61429-853-3

28 27 26 25 24
5 4 3 2 1

Cover and interior design by Gopa & Ted 2. Typeset by Tim Holtz.

Printed on acid-free paper that meets the guidelines for permanence and durability of the Production Guidelines for Book Longevity of the Council on Library Resources.

Printed in Canada.

Contents

List of Illustrations vii

Outline of the Introductory Essay ix

Preface xiii

Introductory Essay

1. The Creation Stage and Deity Yoga 3
2. Tsongkhapa, Khedrup Jé, and Polemical Literature 41
3. The Guhyasamāja Sādhana 49
4. Meditation on Emptiness in the Creation Stage 59
5. Correspondences between the Meditation, Cosmos, and Person 81
6. Meditation on the Celestial Mansion 97
7. Generation of the Specially Visualized Deities and Their Deeds 113
8. The Core of the Practice 121
9. Concluding Practices: The Supreme Kings 221
10. The Preliminary Rituals 237
11. The Aftermath 249

Translation

Homage and Introduction 257

Part 1. The First Yoga: Preliminary Stages

1. Preparatory Steps 289
2. Establishing Favorable Conditions 295

3. Averting Unfavorable Conditions 309

PART 2. THE FIRST YOGA: THE ACTUAL MEDITATION

4. Meditating on the Ground of Wisdom 337
5. Meditation on the Celestial Mansion 367
6. Meditation on the Specially Visualized Deities 431
7. The Significance of Purification by Means of the Creation Stage 459
8. The Deeds of the Specially Visualized Deities and Their Gathering into the Body 477
9. The Yoga of Taking Death as the Dharmakāya 483
10. The Yoga of Taking the Intermediate State as the Saṃbhogakāya 499
11. The Yoga of Taking Birth as the Nirmāṇakāya 527
12. How to Meditate on the Body Maṇḍala 547
13. Blessing the Three Doors and Meditating on the Triple Sattvas 583
14. The Yoga with the Consort 603

PART 3. CONCLUDING

15. The Supreme King of Maṇḍalas 625
16. The Supreme King of Deeds 653
17. Epilogue 689

Topic Outline 725
Abbreviations 731
Bibliography 733
Index 763
About the Authors 797

Illustrations

Diagrams

1. A sideview of the maṇḍala's wall and portal with labels 105

2. Locations of the deities in the celestial palace 109

3. The main lines of the maṇḍala 110

Plates

1. A wooden model of the Guhyasamāja maṇḍala, Gyümé Monastery

2. The Guhyasamāja maṇḍala in color from Rongtha

3. The prong and stairway in the western direction, Gyümé Monastery

4. A corner side view of the Guhyasamāja maṇḍala, Gyümé Monastery

5. The western side of the Guhyasamāja maṇḍala, Gyümé Monastery

6. A closeup of part of the western side of the Guhyasamāja maṇḍala, Gyümé Monastery

7. A closer view of the upper part of the wall of the Guhyasamāja maṇḍala, Gyümé Monastery

8. The wooden model of the Guhyasamāja maṇḍala, with its roof removed, Gyümé Monastery

9. The roof of the wooden model taken off and inverted, Gyümé Monastery

10. The three outer rings of the Guhyasamāja maṇḍala in the southern direction, Gyümé Monastery

Outline of the Introductory Essay

1. The Creation Stage and Deity Yoga 3
Is the Visualization Contrived? 9
The Yoga of Nondual Profundity and Manifestations 13
Jñānapāda School 14
Mental Overload or Mental Deprivation? 19
Authenticating the Reality of the Maṇḍala 21
Causes That Accord with the Fruit 23
The Illusion-Like Nature of the Special Appearances 24
Relinquishing Ordinary Appearances and Attitudes 26
Divine Identity or Pride 27
Taking the Fruit as the Path 29
Becoming the Five Tathāgatas of the Guhyasamāja Maṇḍala 30
Ripening the Mental Continuum of the Yogi for Realization during the Completion Stage 31
Relinquishing Ordinary Appearances and Attaining Clear Appearances 33
The Nature of the Transformation of the Ordinary Body into a Buddha's Body 38

2. Tsongkhapa, Khedrup Jé, and Polemical Literature 41

3. The Guhyasamāja Sādhana 49
The Relationship between the *Guhyasamāja Tantra* and Its Sādhanas 49
The Guhyasamāja Sādhanas of the Ārya School 51
Dissimilarities among Guhyasamāja Sādhanas of the Ārya School 55

The Framework of the *Guhyasamāja Sādhana* 56

4. Meditation on Emptiness in the Creation Stage 59

Gorampa's Critique 62

Straddling Emptiness and Nothingness 72

Prāsaṅgika and Yogācāra Meditations on the Verse of Emptiness 73

The Goal of the Meditation on Emptiness 77

The Empty Visualization 79

5. Correspondences between the Meditation, Cosmos, and Person 81

The Meaning of the Correspondences between the Meditation, Cosmos, and Person 81

Correspondences with Macrocosmic Events 86

Correspondences with Microcosmic Events 93

6. Meditation on the Celestial Mansion 97

Meditation on the Enclosures, the Source of Phenomena, and the Lotus 97

The Fire and Vajra Enclosures 97

Meditation on the Source of Phenomena 98

Meditation on the Lotus 99

Meditation on the Four Disks 100

The Merging of the Four Disks into the Crossed Vajra 102

The Celestial Mansion and the Relationship between Its Two- and Three-Dimensional Depictions 103

The Inner Mansion 108

7. Generation of the Specially Visualized Deities and Their Deeds 113

Meditation on the Specially Visualized Deities 113

The Deeds of the Specially Visualized Deities 115

Withdrawing the Specially Visualized Deities into the Body 117

Is the "Withdrawal of the Specially Visualized Deities into the Body" Part of the Core Practice? 118

8. The Core of the Practice 121

(1) The Yoga of Taking Death, Intermediate State, and Rebirth as the Path That Leads to the Three Buddha's Bodies 121

(2) Dissolution of the Specially Visualized Deities into Clear Light: The Yoga of Taking Death on the Path That Leads to the Dharmakāya 121

Meditation on Emptiness in the Microcosmic Context 127

(3) The Yoga of Taking the Intermediate State on the Path That Leads to the Saṃbhogakāya 129

The Moon and Mind Only 130

Awakening in This Body 136

The Five Manifest Awakenings 139

Disagreements about the Meditation on the First Lord 141

(4) The Yoga of Taking Rebirth on the Path That Leads to the Nirmāṇakāya 146

Which Rebirth Is Purified? 146

Rebirth as Human Beings 149

Correspondence to the Grounds of Purification 150

Where Does Akṣobhya Come From? 157

(5) Meditation on the Body Maṇḍala 159

A True Transformation? 161

Meditation on the Body as the Celestial Mansion 164

Disagreements among Geluk Scholars 166

Meditation on the Respective Parts of the Body as the Deities of the Maṇḍala 169

Disagreements between Tsongkhapa and Khedrup Jé on This Meditation 170

Is the Body Maṇḍala Uncontrived? 173

Disagreements with Sakya Scholars 177

(6) Blessing the Body, Speech, and Mind 187

(7) Meditation on the Triple Sattvas 189

(8) Sealing with the Lord of the Tathāgata Family 193

(9) The Yoga with the Consort 193

Can Women Attain Enlightenment through Vajrayāna Practices? 193

By That Very Passion They Are Released 197

The Rarity of Meeting the Required Conditions 199

The Purpose of the Union with the Consort 202
(10) The Samādhis in the First Chapter of the *Guhyasamāja Tantra* and Enacting Past Events 203
The Relationship between the Past Events and the Sādhana 205
Completion of the Four Yogas 213
Disputes 216
The Supreme King of Maṇḍalas 218
Conclusion 220

9. Concluding Practices: The Supreme Kings 221
The Supreme King of Maṇḍalas 223
The "Seven Steps" 224
Examining Uncertainties 227
The Supreme King of Deeds 230
The Yoga Pertaining to the Actual Meditation Session 230
The Yoga Pertaining to the Periods between Meditative Sessions 235

10. The Preliminary Rituals 237
The Preparatory Steps 235
Establishing Favorable Conditions 241
Averting Unfavorable Conditions 245

11. The Aftermath 249
Dissolution of the Principal Deities into Clear Light 249
Arising in Response to the Invocation with a Song 250
Praises, Offerings, and Tasting the Nectar 251
Final Dissolution of the Visualization 252

Preface

As a graduate student in Tibetan studies in the eighties of the previous century, I dreamed I would do my doctoral fieldwork in Gyümé (Tib. Rgyud smad) Monastery in Hunsur, Karnataka. I was planning a dissertation about tantric rituals and meditations, topics Gyümé Monastery was dedicated to. But there were several impediments, including the special permit required of foreign citizens, the delays in obtaining that permit, and the absence of female accommodation in the monastery. As it turned out, I spent most of my fieldwork in Bodha, Kathmandu, studying consecrations of stūpas or images and enjoyed every moment in doing this.

My dreams about Gyümé Monastery came true much later at the beginning of 2020, just before COVID entered our lives. This could not have happened without my coauthor Professor Penpa Dorjee of the Central Institute of Higher Tibetan Studies in Sarnath. Already in 2019 our translation had been completed, apart from certain passages in the fifth chapter on the celestial mansion of the maṇḍala that make use of often obscure architectural references. We spent two weeks in Gyümé Monastery meeting daily with Geshé Lozang Rapjor (Tib. Blo bzang rab 'byor), who patiently explained to us all the relevant passages. Without his help we could not have brought this book to completion. Most of the illustrations seen here were taken by Penpa Dorjee when Geshé Lozang Rapjor kindly admitted us to the special halls where the three-dimensional maṇḍalas were kept.

In 2019 we published a translation of a *précis* of the work translated here. This distillation, composed by Panchen Losang Chökyi Gyaltsen (Blo bzang chos kyi rgyal mtshan, 1570–1662), was titled *The Essence of the Ocean of Attainments*, and like the present volume, it was rendered in English by Yael Bentor and Penpa Dorjee and published by Wisdom. Though we published that volume first, we worked on the two translations side by side, as the two works share a similar outline. The final concluding section, part 3 of the present volume, is much longer in Khedrup's work, and so took longer to finish.

In the period since 2019 a number of important publications related to the subject of this book saw light but unfortunately too late to substantially incorporate here. I highly recommend reading the translation below alongside the excellent translation of Tsongkhapa's *Sādhana* by Artemus B. Engle, with the Tibetan on facing pages, in the book *Guhyasamāja Practice in the Ārya Nāgārjuna System* (Engle 2019, 515–693). An earlier partial English translation of this work appeared in Thurman 1995. This is the sādhana of the Guhyasamāja that Khedrup Jé explains in the present book. I urge the interested reader to delve into the first and major part of this book, this being a translation of the illuminating explanations by Gyümé Khensur Lobsang Jampa on the practice of the sādhana. The minute differences in the practice between Khedrup Jé and current Geluk lamas will not create any difficulty.

Another masterful contribution published in 2019 is *Tsongkhapa: A Buddha in the Land of Snows*, by Thupten Jinpa. This book includes a chapter on Tsongkhapa as a yogi of Guhyasamāja. In the year 2020 appeared a translation of the first twelve chapters of the *Guhyasamāja Tantra* along with Candrakīrti's commentary, the *Illuminating Lamp* (Campbell 2020). In the same year an important commentarial tantra of the *Guhyasamāja Tantra*, entitled *Vajra Garland Tantra*, was published (Kittay 2020). In 2022 a new and marvelous translation of the *Vimalakīrti Nirdeśa* entered the world (Gomez and Harrison 2022).

I can also highly recommend the excellent translation of Tsongkhapa's *A Lamp to Illuminate the Five Stages* by Gavin Kilty (Kilty 2013). The first two chapters provide explanations of the unexcelled tantras and in particular the *Guhyasamāja Tantra*. The same work was translated also in Thurman 2010.

A Note on the Translation

Ocean of Attainments (*Bskyed rim dngos grub rgya mtsho*) has been translated here from Tibetan, the language of Khedrup Jé. Yet the work contains copious citations of scriptures translated into Tibetan from Sanskrit and other Indian languages, a great number of which are fortunately available to us in Sanskrit as well. A great effort has been made to provide references to the Sanskrit original scriptures. At times, however, for a variety of reasons, the Tibetan translations in their forms quoted in our text differ from the Sanskrit available to us. Moreover, once in a while the differences in meaning of the Sanskrit and Tibetan are crucial for the arguments presented in this work. In such cases the variant readings are listed in the notes, but for the sake of reducing the number of notes all variants are listed in the first note to each quotation. Critical readers are therefore advised to read the notes carefully in order to appreciate the choices made in the translation. Nevertheless, the main goal in this book is to present Tibetan rather than Indian understanding of the Guhyasamāja sādhana.

Folio numbers in brackets in the translation reference the Tibetan source text of the *Bskyed rim dngos grub rgya mtsho* found in the Old Zhol edition of Khedrup Je's collected works, volume *ja*, reproduced in 1982 in New Delhi by Gurudeva.

The reader may wonder why quotations do not appear in an indented format. The reason is that quoting canonical authorities is only one aspect of a complex process of presentation. According to numerous Tibetan works, a proper discourse should consist of both scriptural authorities and reasoning, and within the Geluk school reasoning is no less important than citations. Hence allowing quotations a central position on a page while keeping reasoning in a less prominent position does not do justice to the Tibetan Geluk author of this book.

Two types of second-person pronouns are used in the translation. The small-case "you" addresses the recipients to whom Khedrup Jé offers the instructions on the Guhyasamāja sādhana—in other words the audience of this work—while the small-caps "YOU" addresses opponents who had raised positions not favored by Khedrup Jé and his lineage. Small caps are also used to denote references to unnamed opponents such as SOME, SOME PEOPLE, CERTAIN LAMAS, SOME TIBETAN LAMAS, EARLIER LAMAS, and LATER LAMAS.

For the sake of clarity and ease of reference, I have inserted subsections and supplementary titles in the translation. Titles not found in the original Tibetan are enclosed in brackets.

The English translation of *Ocean of Attainments* by Khedrup Jé is the fruit of a joint work with Penpa Dorjee. However, the responsibility for any mistakes that might be found in this introduction, in the notes, and in my editing of the English translation is mine and mine alone.

Acknowledgments

This book could not have been written without the people who assisted me in my work. First and foremost I am exceedingly grateful to Professor Penpa Dorjee, the co-translator, for making our joint effort such a great pleasure. Over several years we met in the summers to read together both Khedrup Jé's lengthy *Ocean of Attainments*, translated here and its summary, the *Essence of the Ocean of Attainments* by Panchen Losang Chökyi Gyaltsen (Bentor and Dorjee 2019). During this period I became acquainted with his wife Tashi and his children, as well as their extended families, all of whom I would like to thank here. I am very much obliged to Dr. Thupten Jinpa for clarifying plenty of obscure points in our special meeting in Montréal as well as over the years since. Special thanks are due to Geshe Lozang Rapjor from Gyümé Monastery, who clarified architectural terms related to maṇḍalas. I would like to thank Wisdom Publications and its staff for bringing this book to light. Last but not least, I would like to thank my husband, Dan Martin, my life companion in things Tibetan and beyond.

Yael Bentor

Introductory Essay

1. The Creation Stage and Deity Yoga

THE WORK TRANSLATED HERE is entitled *Ocean of Attainments: The Creation Stage of the Glorious Guhyasamāja, King of All Tantras.*[1] Composed by Khedrup Jé Gelek Palsang,[2] one of Tsongkhapa Losang Drakpa's[3] most prominent disciples. Its subject is the creation stage,[4] a quintessential Buddhist tantric meditation that together with the completion stage[5] comprises the tantric path of the unexcelled mantra. The *Guhyasamāja Tantra*, here referred to as the "king of all tantras," is one of the tantras of the unexcelled mantra; it is revered in Tibet, especially by the Geluk school, for its hermeneutic methods, which are in turn applied to other tantras.

In the colophon, Khedrup Jé does not specify the date of his *Ocean of Attainments*, but he does note that it was written in Palkhor Dechen.[6] We know that Khedrup Jé served as the abbot of this monastery from 1421 to 1427.[7] In 1426, Ngorchen Kunga Sangpo[8] wrote his two works on the Hevajra body maṇḍala,[9] and in them he cites passages on the body maṇḍala from Khedrup Jé's *Ocean of Attainments* at length. Thus it seems clear that Khedrup Jé completed this work between 1421 and 1426.

I begin with an introduction to the subject matter: the creation stage, the author—Khedrup Jé—and the *Guhyasamāja Sādhana* itself.

1. Mkhas grub rje, *Bskyed rim dngos grub rgya mtsho = Rgyud thams cad kyi rgyal po dpal gsang ba 'dus pa'i bskyed rim dngos grub rgya mtsho*.

2. Mkhas grub rje Dge legs dpal bzang (1385–1438).

3. Tsong kha pa Blo bzang grags pa (1357–1419), considered the founder of the Geluk (*dge lugs*) school.

4. The creation, visualization, or generation stage, Tib. *bskyed rim*, Skt. *utpattikrama*.

5. Tib. *rdzogs rim*, Skt. *niṣpannakrama* or *utpannakrama*.

6. Dpal 'khor sde chen or Dpal 'khor chos sde.

7. According to Jackson 2007, 355.

8. Ngor chen Kun dga' bzang po (1382–1456).

9. Ngor chen, *Smra ba ngan 'joms*, work 49, and *Lta ba ngan sel*, work 50.

In practicing the creation stage, meditators visualize themselves as awakened beings at the center of the embellished celestial mansion of the maṇḍala. In this visualization, they are surrounded in all directions by other male and female buddhas, bodhisattvas, vajra ladies, and so forth, abiding on their thrones. The core of the practice is visualization, and thus this meditation—perhaps even more so than many other meditations—presumes the creative power of the mind. Visualizations form the basis not only of the creation stage and deity yoga but of all tantric practices and rituals, since no tantric practice or ritual takes place in mundane existence.

Let us take, for example, the ritual of making offerings to the buddhas, a preliminary step in most Buddhist practices. Often, these offerings are represented by eight bowls of water, but even such representations are optional. The buddhas are not actually offered material flowers, incense, food, and music, but rather magnificent fields of flowers, food, music, and so forth that are produced by the mind and which cannot be apprehended by ordinary witnesses of the ritual. Likewise, the buddhas and bodhisattvas who are the recipients of these offerings cannot be seen by the casual observer. The entire ritual takes place in the minds of the yogis visualizing it.

In a similar vein, tantric aspirants visualize themselves as awakened beings, not only on their meditation mats but also in the world of ordinary appearance. They aspire to continue to function in the world as awakened beings, and so they think of themselves as buddhas, act and speak as buddhas, and teach others how to become buddhas. They behave as though they have already attained the goal of their practice; in tantric terminology, they take the fruit as the path. Since they perceive themselves as buddhas, they even make offerings to themselves as buddhas. This actualization of Buddhist teachings and the bodhisattva ideal has a significant impact on tantric aspirants. The practice serves to transform their mental state and open it to a new reality while altering their mode of participation in the world. At the same time, as we will see, yogis remain aware of their ordinary surroundings.

In this process, aspirants not only see themselves as an awakened being or a buddha; they also develop a strong identification with that buddha, known as "divine pride,"[10] and a "vivid appearance"[11] of their entire visualization. At the same time, they are taught to regard their visualization as "illusion-like"[12] and devoid of intrinsic existence. At the end of a meditative session, they

10. Tib. *nga rgyal*, Skt. *ahaṃkāra*.

11. Tib. *gsal snang*.

12. Tib. *sgyu ma lta bu*, Skt. *māyopama*.

dissolve the entire visualization into clear-light-emptiness, only to arise from the meditation with a conventional, but altered, identity.

By visualizing themselves as awakened beings, aspirants endeavor to attain the rūpakāya; by meditating on their visualization as illusion-like and empty of intrinsic nature, they aim at actualizing the dharmakāya. The realization of the dharmakāya—the true nature of all phenomena—is a goal for the sake of the aspirant's own awakening, but impossible to attain without at the same time achieving the Mahāyāna ideal of the bodhisattva, compassion—assisting other sentient beings to attain enlightenment. Therefore aspirants arise again in the world as awakened beings in the form of rūpakāyas.

One of the goals of the creation stage is the deconstruction of conceptual thinking and the attainment of altered mental states that are not conditioned by ordinary mental activity. Toward this end, aspirants dissolve their ordinary world and recreate it as a maṇḍala inhabited by awakened beings. In this way, they begin to grasp the workings of their ordinary mind and therefore the illusory nature of all appearances. They come to recognize conceptualization as conceptualization, and thus they begin to understand how their ordinary world came into being, why it appears to them the way it does, and why they perceive things as they do. They come to know how their minds work, and they can then apply these insights not only to their ordinary world but to their visualized maṇḍalic world.

The use of the conceptualization involved in visualization for the sake of overcoming conceptualization is an application of a basic tantric technique known as employing one's "enemy" to overcome that "enemy." A well-known expression of this notion is found in the *Hevajra Tantra*: "By passion beings are bound and by that very passion they are released."[13] The same chapter of the *Hevajra Tantra* provides an explanation of tantric visualization: "By means of the yoga of the creation stage, aspirants must meditate on the proliferations of mental constructs. Once they have made the proliferations dream-like, they should use this very proliferation to deproliferate."[14] Yogis who practice the creation stage first meditate on mental proliferation[15] by visualizing themselves as the maṇḍala and the awakened beings residing within it. Then, as they come to understand that this mental visualization is a dream-like illusion, they comprehend the nature of all mental elaborations. In this way,

13. *Brtag gnyis*, *Hevajra Tantra*, Tōh 418, 16a4–5; Snellgrove 1959, II.ii.51.

14. *Brtag gnyis*, *Hevajra Tantra*, Tōh 418, 15a7; Snellgrove 1959, II.ii.29.

15. Tib. *spros pa*, Skt. *prapañca*.

deproliferation[16] is accomplished by means of proliferation. Just as, upon awakening from sleep, one understands a dream as a product of the mind, meditators in the creation stage grasp the dream-like nature of their visualizations.

Although they are initially created by proliferations of mental constructs, visions seen during the creation stage are in a sense "more than real," that is, more real than any other saṃsāric appearance. The visions, after all, depict the buddhas and other awakened beings who dwell in the maṇḍala. Aspirants cannot completely discard these visions; they know precisely how the visions appeared, since they themselves created them. At the same time, these visions are considered "reality" as it appears to the awakened eye, and they constitute the transformed reality that is a central goal of tantric practice.

Nevertheless, Indian and Tibetan works differ considerably as to the extent of the creative power they are willing to grant to a mind engaged in meditation. Moreover, they vary in the degree to which they accept the reality of the yogis' visions of themselves as awakened beings. Still, these different approaches do not necessarily typify the general perspectives of different Indian and Tibetan scholars, but rather may reflect the various contexts in which a single scholar is writing.

Among Tibetan scholars, there is a range of opinions. At one end, we find the position that the yogis in fact see themselves as they are, since awakening is their true nature; at the other, we see attitudes that limit the visualizations' scope, claiming that the yogis merely meditate on themselves as having an appearance similar to the rūpakāya of the Buddha. For them, if mere visualization were to be regarded as the creation of a true reality, it would be like a beggar claiming to be a king. Most Tibetan scholars, however, position themselves somewhere between these two extremes.

It is worth mentioning that although I use the term "the yogis visualize themselves as the deity" in accordance with Tibetan scholars, this characterization is certainly not accurate. It is not themselves that yogis visualize as deities, and therefore they are not like beggars claiming to be kings. Yogis first dissolve their ordinary existence into emptiness and only then create a deity out of emptiness—the potential or ground for everything.[17] Thus, because the deity is born from emptiness, it is regarded as more real. As we have seen, the appearance of the buddha in the center of the maṇḍala is even more than real.

Additionally, it is important to bear in mind that when tantric Buddhism evolved in India, the predominant philosophical systems were the Yogācāra

16. Tib. *spros med bya*, Skt. *niḥprapañcayet*.

17. See the section "Meditation on Emptiness in the Creation Stage" below.

school and the Yogācāra-Madhyamaka.[18] Therefore the profound impact of these systems on Vajrayāna is not surprising. Moreover, from among all the Buddhist approaches, Mind Only[19] is best suited to explain the creation stage. Indeed, we find that Indian scholars writing on the creation stage often use the terminology of Mind Only. These include not only Ratnākaraśānti but also scholars classified as belonging to the Ārya school—in other words, to the tradition of Ārya Nāgārjuna, which purportedly follows the theories of Madhyamaka. Among these scholars are the Candrakīrti, who composed the *Vajrasattva Sādhana*,[20] and the two commentators on Nāgārjuna's *Five Stages*,[21] Muniśrībhadra and Bhavyakīrti, all of whom use the terms of the Mind Only school in their works on the "Ārya tradition" of the Guhyasamāja.[22]

In Tibet as well, as late as the fourteenth century, Butön Rinchen Drup[23] deployed this terminology in his tantric works alongside Madhyamaka vocabulary.[24] Once the Madhyamaka school reached a prominent position among most Tibetan scholars, however, it became difficult to explain the workings of the creation stage on the basis of the philosophy of Mind Only. Hence, while most Buddhist traditions emphasize the creative power of the mind, they do so only in a limited fashion.

The historical development of the tantric path to enlightenment provides another reason for the relegation of the creation stage to an inferior position. When the creation stage first developed in India, it is likely that it was an independent practice aimed at reaching buddhahood. Later, perhaps at the time of Jñānapāda,[25] the completion stage was added to the creation stage to create what is considered in the tradition as a complete tantric path. As is typical of such developments, the later practice became the predominant one, relegating

18. See the chapter entitled "The Yogācāra-Madhyamaka Synthesis" in Ruegg 1981.

19. Tib. *sems tsam*, Skt. *cittamātra*.

20. Candrakīrti, *Rdo rje sems dpa'i sgrub thabs*, *Vajrasattva Sādhana*, Tōh 1814, 199a5; Luo and Tomabechi 2009, 15.7–8 and 47.17.

21. Nāgārjuna, *Rim lnga*, *Pañcakrama*, Tōh 1802.

22. Muniśrībhadra, *Rim pa lnga'i don mdor bshad pa*, *Pañcakramārthaṭippaṇī*, Tōh 1813, 159a4–5; Jiang and Tomabechi 1996, 17.1. Bhavyakīrti, *Rim pa lnga'i dka' 'grel*, *Pañcakramapañjikā*, Tōh 1838, 2b2–3.

23. Bu ston Rin chen grub (1290–1364).

24. Bu ston, *Mdor byas 'grel chen*, 34a4–b1; an English translation in Yoshimizu 1987, 26.

25. Kikūya 2010, 134; Tanemura 2015, 329. See also Tsong kha pa, *Rim lnga gsal sgron*, 25a1–2. Another early source for the division of the practice into the two stages is *Guhyasamāja Tantra*, chap. 18, verse 84, as noted by Matsunaga 1978, 119. For more on the life and thought of Jñānapāda (active ca. 770–820), see Dalton and Szántó 2019 and Dalton 2019.

the creation stage to the margins as preliminary to or prerequisite for the completion stage—much as Christianity regards its predecessor, the old covenant, as a plan directed to prepare for the coming of Christ.

In the second stage, the completion stage, visualizations retain their importance; however, the stage's goals are achieved through actual bodily transformations, albeit mainly transformations of the subtle body, which is made of cakras, winds,[26] and drops. Practices of the completion stage include the yoga of the winds, the penetration of the vital points in the body,[27] the power of great bliss, and so forth. In this stage, which has its antecedents in Indian yogic practices, a nonconceptual mind is achieved when all the winds and minds of the so-called subtle body dissolve into the heart cakra.

Notably, the creation stage was not entirely disregarded. First of all, as this stage is considered preliminary or prerequisite, the actual practice of the tantric path must always begin with it. The fact that the creation stage incorporates multiple Mahāyāna notions also contributes to its enduring status. However, in the later model, the goal of the tantric path is attained only at the culmination of the completion stage, not during the creation stage itself. The creation stage nonetheless remains indispensable to the tantric path, as without first practicing it buddhahood cannot be attained. Moreover, we find an emphasis on the "union of the two stages,"[28] which is required to reach enlightenment.

One of the reasons that the creation stage is said to be merely preparatory is that it is based on visualization. Since visualization involves mental contrivance, the deity's body that arises from it is also contrived; therefore, only the subsequent steps of the path, which do not involve mental creations, can bring about true divine bodies. Thus the creation stage has come to be called "contrived" or "conceptual," while the completion stage is known as "nonconceptual yoga," "noncontrived yoga," "innate yoga," and so forth. Still, the two stages are considered to constitute a single sequence.

Here we come to a crucial point: the attitude we find in Tibetan writings on the creation stage is twofold. In certain contexts, the creation stage is regarded as a mere preliminary to the later stages of the tantric path, but in other contexts it is regarded as a practice that can achieve soteriological goals of its own accord.

As an example, when Tsongkhapa describes the entire tantric path, comprised of both the creation and completion stages, he asserts that the creation stage is a method contrived by the mind, while the completion stage is not;

26. Tib. *lung*, Skt. *prāṇa*.

27. Tib. *lus la gnad du bsnun pa*.

28. Tib. *rim gnyis zung 'jug*.

therefore, only the latter practice can bring about a result that is not conceptualized by the mind.[29] Tsongkhapa then cites the verses from the *Hevajra Tantra* mentioned above on using proliferation to deproliferate.[30] In this context of the entire tantric path, his aim is to demonstrate that conceptualization should be used to overcome conceptualization not in the creation stage, but rather in the completion stage, because the creation stage cannot lead to a true transformation.

Conversely, in the very same work, when Tsongkhapa discusses the creation stage on its own terms, he has a different purpose in mind and therefore interprets the very same verses of the *Hevajra Tantra* in a different way.[31] In this context, meditators on the creation stage can certainly achieve the final goal by using conceptualization to overcome conceptualization not only within the completion stage but specifically within the creation stage itself. Notably, the aforementioned verse of the *Hevajra Tantra* speaks explicitly about the creation stage, implying that this stage itself can bring the yogis to de-proliferate. Therefore we turn now to the varied and often opposing positions of several Indian and Tibetan scholars dating from the eighth century and up to our time on the nature of the visualizations during the creation stage.

Is the Visualization Contrived?

Notwithstanding the waning status of the creation stage, it has still retained its capacity to achieve a mind apprehending nonduality, one of the characteristics of the goal of the entire path. Such an equivocal approach should not surprise us, since it is also found in relation to several types of meditation.

We will look first at three works from the Indian subcontinent: Indrabhūti's *Jñānasiddhi*, dated to the eighth or ninth centuries;[32] Puṇḍarīka's *Stainless*

29. Tsong kha pa, *Sngags rim chen mo*, 456.

30. Tsong kha pa, *Sngags rim chen mo*, 459.

31. Tsong kha pa, *Sngags rim chen mo*, 493.

32. Indrabhūti, *Ye shes grub pa*, *Jñānasiddhi*, chap. 2, vv. 13–18, Tōh 2219, 41a4–7; Sanskrit and Tibetan in Samdhong and Dwivedi et al. 1987, 104 and 164. An English translation in Krug 2018, 241–242. This chapter is entitled "Refuting Meditation on Forms," Tib. *gzugs su bsgom pa dgag pa*, Skt. *rūpabhāvanāniṣedha*. For the dating see Gerloff and Schott 2020, 241.

Light, dated to the eleventh century;[33] and Ratnarakṣita's *Padminī*, dated to the twelfth or thirteenth centuries.[34] While Indrabhūti and Ratnarakṣita clearly recognize the soteriological value of the creation stage, they introduce positions of real or imagined opponents in order to refute them. These opponents raise the following arguments: Deity yoga is a conceptual meditation, because yogis are overburdened by numerous details of colors, shapes, numbers, and so forth. The deities are constructed and therefore impermanent as a pot and as such are limited to a particular place and time, while deities are omnipresent. Since visualized deities are lacking qualities such as the super-knowledges, how can they lead yogis to buddhahood? Mental elaboration cannot even achieve a single-pointed samādhi. Contrived thoughts are false because they arise from clinging to unreal objects.

We know that Ratnarakṣita was familiar with the *Jñānasiddhi*, since he cites it in other contexts in the same chapter. His arguments clearly follow the *Jñānasiddhi* and echo the positions of the opponents in the *Stainless Light*. By relying on Dharmakīrti, a subject that will be elaborated below,[35] Ratnarakṣita concludes that, whether real or not, visualized deities can be seen by yogis nonconceptually with all their various aspects appearing simultaneously, when the meditation is powerful. While the opponent in the *Jñānasiddhi* argues that meditation on forms is futile, Ratnarakṣita replies that when yogis visualize the deities, they do not meditate merely on their forms, but rather on nondual union[36] of forms and emptiness, another topic we will return to below. According to Ratnarakṣita, while a pot is indeed neither pervasive nor omnipresent, this is not because it has a form but because it arises through bifurcation into subject and object. Deities, on the other hand, arise from aspiration prayers based on great compassion inseparable from emptiness. Therefore they can take every form and act to benefit others.

These discussions continued among Tibetan scholars as well. For example,

33. Puṇḍarīka, *Dri ma med pa'i 'od*, *Vimalaprabhā*, Tōh 1347, *da*, 227b7–230b1; Dwivedi and Bahulkar 1994, 67–69; See also Wallace 2001, 199. The relevant lines are found in the commentary on the *Kālacakra Tantra*, 5.127, which "probably existed as a separate and complete didactic text." See Sferra 2005, 266.

34. Ratnarakṣita, *Padma can*, *Padminī*, Tōh 1420, 41b2–3; Tanemura, Kano, and Kuranishi 2017, §13.2.1.1.2, 22–23. This chapter is a commentary on chapter thirteen in the *Sdom 'byung*, *Saṃvarodaya Tantra*, Tōh 373, dedicated to the creation stage.

35. Dharmakīrti, *Tshad ma rnam 'grel*, *Pramāṇavārttika*, *Pratyakṣa*, Tōh 4210, 129a6–7; Miyasaka 1971–1972, v. 285. See the section "Relinquishing Ordinary Appearances and Attaining Clear Appearances" below.

36. Tib. *zung 'jug gnyis su med pa*, Skt. *yuganaddha*.

Barawa Gyeltsen Palsangpo[37] cites and refutes the position of the opponent in the *Stainless Light*.[38] According to Barawa, deity yoga is uncontrived because it has the potential for actualizing its goal.[39] As he adheres to the *tathāgatagarbha* theory, for him all sentient beings have the potential to attain enlightenment.

Yet another essential question asked in our texts is whether yogis meditating on themselves as deities do so with wrong cognitions.[40] The opponent in Indrabhūti's *Jñānasiddhi*[41] argues that when yogis who are not deities meditate as if they were, their cognitions are wrong. On the basis of a wrong meditation, yogis will never become buddhas, just as a destitute man who, for a billion eons, entertains the thought "I am a king" will never become a king, because his meditation is based on a mistaken thought. Indrabhūti's[42] own position, however, is that through meditative absorption, "may I be such," the yogis' concentrations become lucid and the deities are seen as clearly as if they were in paintings in front of them. Likewise, in his commentary on a Guhyasamāja sādhana, Muniśrībhadra says: When you know all the variety of the ordinary world to be in fact the maṇḍala, how could your mind be wrong?[43]

According to Barawa, yogis, in fact, do not visualize their ordinary forms as deities, hence their cognitions are not mistaken.[44] This is because prior to the visualization of the deities, they dissolve all appearances into emptiness through the mantra *svabhāva* or *śūnyatā*.[45] Only then, from within the continuum of emptiness, do they visualize the deities arising from their seed syllables and so forth. In his public talks, the Fourteenth Dalai Lama provides a similar reply, framed in Prāsaṅgika terms. The Dalai Lama emphasizes that when yogis dissolve, on the level of their minds, the ordinary existence of

37. 'Ba' ra ba Rgyal mtshan dpal bzang po (1310–91).

38. 'Ba' ra ba, *Bskyed rim zab don*, 2a4, 5b6, 6a2–4, 6b1.

39. 'Ba' ra ba's final conclusion is that the creation stage is both contrived and uncontrived, without any contradiction between the two.

40. Tib. *log pa'i rtog pa*, Skt. *mithyākalpana*.

41. Indrabhūti, *Ye shes grub pa*, *Jñānasiddhi*, chap. 2, vv. 8–9, Tōh 2219, 41a1–2; Sanskrit and Tibetan in Samdhong and Dwivedi et al. 1987, 103 and 163.

42. Indrabhūti, *Ye shes grub pa*, *Jñānasiddhi*, chap. 2, vv. 20–21, Tōh 2219, 41b1–2; Sanskrit and Tibetan in Samdhong and Dwivedi et al. 1987, 104–105 and 165.

43. Muniśrībhadra, *Rim pa lnga'i don mdor bshad pa*, *Pañcakramaṭippaṇī*, Tōh 1813, 167b1; Jiang and Tomabechi 1996, 34; The first part of this work is a commentary on Nāgārjuna, *Mdor byas*, *Piṇḍīkrama Sādhana*, Tōh 1796; de La Vallée Poussin 1896 and Tripathi 2001.

44. 'Ba' ra ba, *Bskyed rim zab don*, 7a5–b2.

45. *Oṃ svabhāva śuddhāḥ sarvadharmāḥ svabhāva śuddho 'haṃ* and *Oṃ śūnyatā jñāna vajra svabhāva ātmako 'haṃ*.

themselves and their environment into emptiness with the *śūnyatā* mantra, they change the bases of imputation, because when they habituate to the thought "I am a deity," the referent for "I" is not their ordinary selves but the deity that has arisen from emptiness. Therefore their cognitions are not wrong; rather, the claim that yogis meditate on their ordinary existence as deities is wrong.

The issue of the mind meditating on deity yoga being a wrong cognition is not only philosophical in nature but psychological as well. If, while meditating on themselves as Vajradhara, yogis' experience confirms that their bodies are in no way adorned with the major and minor marks of the Buddha and their minds are unable to realize the nature of all phenomena, they surely feel that they are pretending to be someone other than who they are. Those who accept the *tathāgatagarbha* view might explain that this feeling results from the yogis' habituation to conceive themselves and their environment as impure, while their true nature is pure. Yet these yogis still require a method to dissolve the discrepancy. One remedy offered to yogis engaged in deity yoga is to invite the real deity in the form of the jñānasattva into themselves, visualized as the samayasattva. This visualization is included in a large variety of sādhanas.

Another way to address the dis-ease yogis experience while "pretending" to be something they are not is to point out that self-deception is a part of the tantric approach called "taking the goal in the path." In order to become buddhas, yogis purposely meditate on themselves as buddhas already during the path. For example, Drakpa Shedrup[46] maintains that as long as yogis are aware of being self-deceived—though they meditate on something not present as if it is present—their cognitions are not mistaken.[47] In other words, in meditating on the creation stage, yogis intentionally engage in self-deception, while being aware of this. Another point Drakpa Shedrup makes is that although the deities are not real, it is not inconsistent to identify with the deities as if they are real for a short time. This is because if yogis block their clinging to ordinary appearances in this way, they will focus on the supreme appearances of the celestial mansion and the deities dwelling there, and thereby attain extraordinary goals. Drakpa Shedrup's conclusion has wider implications. He explains that the special wish for the deity to be real is inconceivable, that is to say, beyond the reach of human intellect, hence it cannot be refuted by mere rational reasoning. In other words, no logical discussion can lead us to an understanding of deity yoga.

46. Grags pa bshad sgrub (1675–1748).

47. Grags pa bshad sgrub, *Rdo rje 'jigs byed bskyed rim*, 151–153.

In his own explanations, Tsongkhapa follows Jñānapāda, who maintains that meditators on the creation stage are endowed with the yoga of nondual profundity and manifestations. We turn now to this unique yoga.

The Yoga of Nondual Profundity and Manifestations

According to Tsongkhapa, the creation stage is not just simple visualization, but rather a type of yoga called "deity yoga."[48] This is the defining characteristic of the Mantra Vehicle, making it superior to the method of the Pāramitā Vehicle. While deity yoga is practiced in all four classes of tantra,[49] the creation stage or the deity yoga of the unexcelled tantra is superior to the deity yoga of the lower tantras. The deity yoga of the creation stage is a unique practice that indivisibly unites the meditation on emptiness with the visualization of the maṇḍala and its deities in a single mind. Tsongkhapa describes how to meditate on this yoga of nondual profundity and manifestation[50] in his *Great Treatise on the Stages of the Mantric Path*:

> Once you have meditated on the circle of deities, you should take the deities as the focus of your visualization, and allow the subjective aspect of your mind—in its mode of apprehension that understands the meaning of appearances without intrinsic nature—to be absorbed in emptiness, while the objective aspect of your mind arises as the maṇḍala with its celestial mansion and deities.[51]

Tsongkhapa stresses that the yogi's mind meditates simultaneously on emptiness and manifestations, or appearances. He does not speak here about nonduality of form and emptiness in general, but specifically in relation to the meditating mind. Form and emptiness, or manifestation and profundity, are united indivisibly in a single cognition.[52] He explains how a single mind can be absorbed in both the meditation on the absence of intrinsic nature and the

48. Tib. *lha'i rnal 'byor*, Skt. *devatāyoga*. See Tsong kha pa, *Sngags rim chen mo*, 22–24; an English translation in Hopkins 1977, 119–122.

49. Here Tsong kha pa differs from Ngor chen, who maintains that there is no deity yoga or divine identification in the kriyā tantras. See Ngor chen, *Spyod pa'i rgyud spyi'i rnam gzhag*, 69b4–5, and *Bya rgyud spyi'i rnam bshad*, 105b6–106a1.

50. Tib. *zab gsal gnyis med kyi rnal 'byor*.

51. Tsong kha pa, *Sngags rim chen mo*, 493. For another English translation see Yarnall 2013, 195.

52. Tib. *shes pa gcig*.

visualization of the maṇḍala wheel. While the subjective aspect of the mind that understands the absence of intrinsic nature is absorbed in emptiness, the objective aspect of this mind arises as the maṇḍala, with its celestial mansion and deities. In other words, one aspect of the very mind that realizes emptiness arises as a special appearance of the celestial mansion and the deities therein. Hence, this mind, endowed with nondual profundity and manifestation, is capable of achieving a soteriological goal.

In *Ocean of Attainments*, Khedrup Jé follows Tsongkhapa's explanation.[53] Like Tsongkhapa, he argues that this is another reason that the meditation on emptiness in the Mantra Vehicle is superior to that of the Pāramitā Vehicle:

> Hence, in terms of its effectiveness as an antidote to grasping at true existence, the mind that takes the circle of deities for its focus and apprehends the absence of its intrinsic existence is a hundred times superior to a mind that takes a sprout for its focus and apprehends there an absence of intrinsic existence. Therefore you should use this human opportunity in a beneficial way by striving hard on a path such as this, whereby a single mind arises in the unique nature of the two accumulations, endowed with the full power to eradicate saṃsāra.[54]

This is the yoga of nondual profundity and manifestation, in which the subjective aspect of the mind focuses on the realization of emptiness while its objective aspect arises as the maṇḍala with its deities.

Jñānapāda School

Tsongkhapa expands on a notion developed by Jñānapāda, the "founder" and namesake of a Guhyasamāja school.[55] Jñānapāda explains the working of the creation stage by drawing upon the notion of the "profound"[56] and "sub-

53. Mkhas grub rje, *Bskyed rim dngos grub rgya mtsho*, 36b2–37b3.

54. Mkhas grub rje, *Bskyed rim dngos grub rgya mtsho*, 37a3–5.

55. Jñānapāda is also mentioned above as perhaps the earliest witness to the integration of the creation and completion stage. He was active from the late eighth to early ninth centuries.

56. Tib. *zab*, Skt. *gambhīra*.

lime," or "vast,"[57] mind as antithetical to conceptual thoughts.[58] Jñānapāda was no doubt aware that his terminological choice alludes to nontantric works, including the *Mahāyānasūtrālaṃkāra*[59] and the *Pramāṇavārttika*.

According to Jñānapāda's *Samantabhadra Sādhana*, a mind endowed with a profound and sublime nature[60] is an antidote to ordinary conceptual thoughts,[61] the source of saṃsāric suffering.[62] This is because "conceptual thoughts will not appear to [the mind] endowed with a profound and sublime nature."[63] In the present context, the mind endowed with a profound and sublime nature is the mind that visualizes the maṇḍala with its celestial mansion and deities, and this mind dispels conceptual thoughts.[64]

In the next verse, Jñānapāda discusses how such a mind is capable of

57. Tib. *rgya che ba*, Skt. *udāra*. While the meaning of the Tibetan term is vast, the Sanskrit *udāra* means sublime. In other words, while the Sanskrit term alludes to a two-dimensional line, from the deepest low to the utmost high, the Tibetan term refers to a three-dimensional picture, deep vertically and extensive horizontally. But since the works I refer to here are Indian works written in Sanskrit, I will use the translation "sublime" in this context.

58. See Jñānapāda, *Bdag sgrub pa la 'jug pa*, Ātmasādhanāvatāra, Tōh 1860, 54a5–6 and 54b1–3, a treatise on the creation stage. In the *Pramāṇavārttika*, the pair "profound" and "sublime" is associated with the relinquishing of conceptualization: "Homage to him who is universally good, whose manifestations are divested of the snares of conceptualization and are profound and lofty [sublime]..." translated by Hayes and Gillon 1991, 2. Dharmakīrti, *Tshad ma rnam 'grel, Pramāṇavārttika, Svārthānumāna*, Tōh 4210, 94b1–2; Sanskrit and Tibetan editions in Miyasaka 1971–1972, v. 1.

59. According to the *Mahāyānasūtrālaṃkāra*, chap. 1, v. 13, the sublime and the profound bring about nonconceptuality: "From the sublime and the profound arise ripening and nonconceptuality. Thus both have been taught. This method is [found] in this supreme [pair]." A Sanskrit edition and a French translation in Lévi 1907, 5 and 13. Jñānapāda cites these lines in his *Bdag sgrub pa la 'jug pa*, Ātmasādhanāvatāra, Tōh 1860, 54a6.

60. See Jñānapāda, *Kun bzang sgrub thabs, Samantabhadra Sādhana*, vv. 158–159, Tōh 1855, 35b6–7. The Sanskrit terms can be found in Szántó, work in progress. Furthermore, Szántó points out that this verse is quoted in Abhayākaragupta's *'Jigs pa med pa'i gzhung 'grel, Abhayapaddhati*, Tōh 1654, that has been preserved in Sanskrit. For a Sanskrit edition and an English translation, see Luo 2010, 5.

61. Tib. *tha mal rnam rtog*, Skt. *prākṛtavikalpa*.

62. Tib. *srid pa'i sdug bsngal*, Skt. *bhavaduḥkha*.

63. Jñānapāda, *Kun bzang sgrub thabs, Samantabhadra Sādhana*, v. 159, Tōh 1855, 35b7.

64. See Thagana, *Kun bzang sgrub thabs 'grel ba, Samantabhadrasādhanavṛtti*, Tōh 1868, 229b3–5; and Vaidyapāda, *Yan lag bzhi pa'i sgrub thabs kun tu bzang mo'i rnam par bshad pa, Caturaṅgasādhanasamantabhadrīṭīkā*, Tōh 1872, 176b7–177a2.

overcoming conceptual thoughts.[65] What Jñānapāda seems to be saying[66] is that when an antidote occurs once, it will advance and increase through practice, and finally become capable of blocking its opposite entirely. In other words, when a mind endowed with a profound and sublime nature is cultivated to an extreme degree, it will gain the capacity to wholly eradicate ordinary conceptualizations. It should be emphasized that this goal is achieved only after prolonged habituation. Jñānapāda does not explain why a mind endowed with a profound and sublime nature that visualizes the maṇḍala circle would be guaranteed to transcend ordinary conceptualization and liberate yogis from saṃsāra. To understand this, we need to rely on Indian commentaries on Jñānapāda's *Samantabhadra Sādhana*.

All these commentaries resort to the *Pramāṇasiddhi* chapter in the *Pramāṇavārttika*[67] to explain the verses in question.[68] According to Dharmakīrti, by engaging in selflessness, the mind prevents the opposite of selflessness, thus eradicating the roots of grasping at the self. As Cristina Pecchia explains: "For the contrary of the view of selflessness can no longer maintain its grip on a mind whose epistemic condition is defined by selflessness."[69] Additionally, these commentaries explain that ordinary conceptual thoughts

65. Jñānapāda, *Kun bzang sgrub thabs, Samantabhadra Sādhana*, v. 160, Tōh 1855, 35b7–36a1.

66. The Tibetan translation of this verse is unclear and, unfortunately, we do not have access to the Sanskrit, although the manuscript is stored in Lhasa. I rely here on Harunaga Isaacson's kind explanation in Vienna on May 16, 2019, of Samantabhadra's commentary on this verse in Sanskrit.

67. Dharmakīrti, *Tshad ma rnam 'grel, Pramāṇavārttika, Pramāṇasiddhi*, Tōh 4210, 115a7–b7; Sanskrit and Tibetan editions in Miyasaka 1971–1972, vv. 205cd–217ab; a Sanskrit edition and an English translation in Pecchia 2015, vv. 205–216.

68. Vaidyapāda alludes to the *Pramāṇasiddhi*, vv. 212cd–213ab in Miyasaka 1971–1972; see his *Yan lag bzhi pa'i sgrub thabs kun tu bzang mo'i rnam par bshad pa, Caturaṅgasādhanasamantabhadrīṭīkā*, Tōh 1872, 177a4. Phalavajra cites the *Pramāṇasiddhi*, vv. 208cd–211ab in Miyasaka 1971–1972; see his *Kun tu bzang po'i sgrub pa'i thabs kyi 'grel pa, Samantabhadrasādhanavṛtti*, Tōh 1867, 185b3–4. Samantabhadra cites the *Pramāṇasiddhi*, vv. 211cd–213ab in Miyasaka 1971–1972; see his *Snying po snye ma, Sāramañjarī*, Tōh 1869 [only in the Sanskrit, see Szántó, work in progress, 160.2]. Ratnākaraśānti cites the *Pramāṇasiddhi*, vv. 210cd–211ab in Miyasaka 1971–1972; see his *Gsang ba 'dus pa'i dkyil 'khor gyi cho ga'i 'grel pa, Guhyasamāja Maṇḍalavidhiṭīkā*, Tōh 1871, 127b2.

69. Pecchia 2015, 240. Here she explains Dharmakīrti's lines in *Pramāṇasiddhi*, vv. 210cd–211ab in Miyasaka 1971–1972; v. 210 in Pecchia 2015, 240 and in Franco 2017, 341. The latter paraphrases the verse in the following words: "The nature of the mind which is truthful and free from afflictions is not sublated by the opposites (i.e., by errors and defilements) even if one makes an effort, because the mind takes sides with them (i.e., with truth and purity)." English translations in Dunne 2004, 369–370, and Yaita 1988, 436.

typical of saṃsāric suffering are identified with grasping at "I and mine,"[70] while the mind that visualizes the maṇḍala circle is equated with the wisdom that realizes no-self. Therefore the mind engaged in the maṇḍala circle, which is endowed with the inconceivable nature, the all-good,[71] is capable of bringing about the irreversible cessation of conceptual thoughts and saṃsāric suffering.

The example Dharmakīrti uses to explain why grasping at the self will not recur is the false perception of a rope as a snake.[72] Vaidyapāda, one of the earlier commentators on the *Samantabhadra Sādhana*, offers this very simile to illustrate how the mind that visualizes the maṇḍala circle entirely blocks saṃsāric suffering.[73]

These commentators also follow Dharmakīrti's view of the unique nature of this particular antidote.[74] In the *Pramāṇasiddhi*, Dharmakīrti contrasts the antidote that can achieve an irreversible transformation with antidotes such

70. Tib. *bdag dang bdag gi*, Skt. ātmātmīya. See Samantabhadra, *Snying po snye ma, Sāramañjarī*, Tōh 1869, 43b7; Vaidyapāda, *Yan lag bzhi pa'i sgrub thabs kun tu bzang mo'i rnam par bshad pa, Caturaṅga Sādhana Samantabhadrīṭīkā*, Tōh 1872, 176b5; Phalavajra, *Kun tu bzang po'i sgrub pa'i thabs kyi 'grel pa, Samantabhadra Sādhana Vṛtti*, Tōh 1867, 185a7; Thagana, *Kun bzang sgrub thabs 'grel ba, Samantabhadrasādhanavṛtti*, Tōh 1868, 229b2–3; and Ratnākaraśānti, *Gsang ba 'dus pa'i dkyil 'khor gyi cho ga'i 'grel pa, Guhyasamāja Maṇḍalavidhiṭīkā*, Tōh 1871, 127a6.

71. See respectively, Samantabhadra, *Snying po snye ma, Sāramañjarī*, Tōh 1869, 43b6 (Tib. *bsam kyis mi khyab pa*, Skt. *acintya*); Vaidyapāda, *Yan lag bzhi pa'i sgrub thabs kun tu bzang mo'i rnam par bshad pa, Caturaṅga Sādhana Samantabhadrīṭīkā*, Tōh 1872, 176b4 (Tib. *bsam gyis mi khyab pa*); and Phalavajra, *Kun tu bzang po'i sgrub pa'i thabs kyi 'grel pa, Samantabhadra Sādhana Vṛtti*, Tōh 1867, 185a7 (Tib. *kun tu bzang po*).

72. Dharmakīrti, *Tshad ma rnam 'grel, Pramāṇavārttika, Pramāṇasiddhi*, Tōh 4210, 115b1–2; Sanskrit and Tibetan editions in Miyasaka 1971–1972, v. 208; a Sanskrit edition and an English translation in Pecchia 2015, 230, v. 207; see also Franco 2017, 341. Yet this metaphor is found in texts that precede Dharmakīrti, including the *Lang kar gshegs pa'i theg pa chen po'i mdo, Laṅkāvatāra Sūtra*, Tōh 107, Nanjio 1923, *Sagāthaka*, v. 498; Asaṅga, *Theg pa chen po bsdus pa, Mahāyānasaṃgraha*, Tōh 4048, Lamotte 1938–1939, III.8; and Vasubandhu, *Kośabhāṣya*, Tōh 4090, on chap. 6, v. 58.

73. Vaidyapāda, *Yan lag bzhi pa'i sgrub thabs kun tu bzang mo'i rnam par bshad pa, Caturaṅga Sādhana Samantabhadrīṭīkā*, Tōh 1872, 177b1.

74. Vaidyapāda, *Yan lag bzhi pa'i sgrub thabs kun tu bzang mo'i rnam par bshad pa, Caturaṅga Sādhana Samantabhadrīṭīkā*, Tōh 1872, 177a4: "This is unlike kindness and so forth"; Samantabhadra, *Snying po snye* ma, *Sāramañjarī*, Tōh 1869, 44a7–b1; and Ratnākaraśānti, *Gsang ba 'dus pa'i dkyil 'khor gyi cho ga'i 'grel pa, Guhyasamāja Maṇḍalavidhiṭīkā*, Tōh 1871, 127b4–5: "It fully annihilates."

as benevolent love,[75] taken to be an antidote to aversion.[76] The latter type of antidote cannot completely eliminate afflictions such as aversion, because it still has at its root the notion of an existing self. The mind endowed with the inconceivable nature of the maṇḍala circle, by contrast, is singularly capable of stopping conceptual thoughts and saṃsāric suffering, as a result of its nondual profound and sublime essence.

Thus, on the basis of Dharmakīrti's theories, Jñānapāda and his commentators hold that the mind visualizing the maṇḍala is capable of achieving a soteriological transformation, such as putting an end to saṃsāric suffering, because it is characterized by nondual profundity and sublimity.[77] For the Jñānapāda school, the nondual profound and sublime nature of the mind is one of the features that makes the Mantra Vehicle superior to the Pāramitā Vehicle.[78]

To conclude, Jñānapāda describes a contradictory event or an antidote that occurs *once*. After this single occurrence, through gradual practice, yogis intensify their experience of the mind endowed with the profound and sublime until they are finally able to totally block its opposite: conceptual thoughts—just as the mind that engages in selflessness cannot but prevent the opposite of selflessness in Dharmakīrti's explanation. The rope that can no longer be seen as a snake, the example used for the irreversible cessation of conceptual thoughts and the attainment of the mind endowed with nondual profound and sublime essence, certainly indicates a single instantaneous transformation. Still, it seems that the process Jñānapāda delineates is not sudden, but

75. Tib. *byams pa*, Skt. *maitrī*.

76. Tib. *zhe sdang*, Skt. *dveṣa*. Dharmakīrti, *Tshad ma rnam 'grel*, *Pramāṇavārttika*, *Pramāṇasiddhi*, Tōh 4210, vv. 212cd–213ab in Miyasaka 1971–1972; v. 212 in Pecchia 2015, 245, and Franco 2017, 342.

77. As we would expect, the commentators on the *Samantabhadra Sādhana* associate the two poles indivisibly united in this mind with emptiness (Tib. *stong pa nyid*, Skt. *śūnyatā*) and compassion (Tib. *snying rje*, Skt. *karuṇā*), wisdom (Tib. *shes rab*, Skt. *prajñā*) and method (Tib. *thabs*, Skt. *upāya*), as well as profound (Tib. *zab mo*, Skt. *gambhīra*) and manifest (Tib. *gsal ba*). See respectively Vaidyapāda, *Yan lag bzhi pa'i sgrub thabs kun tu bzang mo'i rnam par bshad pa*, *Caturaṅga Sādhana Samantabhadrīṭīkā*, Tōh 1872, 176b7 and 177a4; Thagana, *Kun bzang sgrub thabs 'grel ba*, *Samantabhadra Sādhana Vṛtti*, Tōh 1868, 229b4–5.

78. See Jñānapāda, *Kun bzang sgrub thabs*, *Samantabhadra Sādhana*, vv. 158–161, Tōh 1855, 35b6–36a1, with the commentaries by Vaidyapāda, *Yan lag bzhi pa'i sgrub thabs kun tu bzang mo'i rnam par bshad pa*, *Caturaṅga Sādhana Samantabhadrīṭīkā*, Tōh 1872, 177b2, and by Thagana, *Kun bzang sgrub thabs 'grel ba*, *Samantabhadra Sādhana Vṛtti*, Tōh 1868, 230a4–5.

rather requires prolonged cultivation of the mind before it can reach its utmost stage and eliminate ordinary conceptual thoughts entirely.

What enables yogis to reach this stage is the antidote that, although devoid of any basis or ground,[79] is endowed with nondual nature and therefore differs from ordinary antidotes such as benevolent love. In this way, a mind endowed with nondual profound and sublime essence that meditates on the maṇḍala can annihilate conceptual thoughts and thus achieve a soteriological goal.

It is worth bearing in mind that tantric authors writing on the creation stage, especially members of Jñānapāda schools and their followers, based their method on the theoretical approach of Dharmakīrti. Even so, it remains for us to explore if and when the views of these tantric scholars diverge from those of Dharmakīrti. In any case, a better understanding of tantric theories on the creation stage requires that we take into account the great Buddhist treatises on logic.

Mental Overload or Mental Deprivation?

As we have seen, according to Jñānapāda, the antidote that occurs once initiates a gradual process. The term translated here as "once," *sakṛt*,[80] is in fact ambiguous; it can mean either "once" or "simultaneously."[81] Indeed, in certain Tibetan translations of commentaries on Jñānapāda's *Samantabhadra Sādhana*, this term was understood as simultaneously,[82] but Ratnākaraśānti disagreed with them.[83] For him, it is not the case that ordinary appearances are prevented from arising in the yogi's mind simply because this mind is submerged in maṇḍala visualization.

According to Ratnākaraśānti: "Conceptual thoughts do not appear because the mind endowed with the aspect of the maṇḍala engages in dispelling all false conceptualizations, not because they do not appear simultaneously."[84]

79. Tib. *dmigs pa med pa*, Skt. *nirālambanā*.

80. According to Szántó's edition (work in progress) of the *Snying po snye ma*, *Sāramañjarī*, Tōh 1869, by Samantabhadra, the Sanskrit here is *sakṛt*: *sa* + *kṛt*, which is equally ambiguous; it means either "once" or "simultaneously."

81. In Tibetan *lan cig* and *lhan cig*.

82. Tibetan *lhan cig*. See Vaidyapāda, *Yan lag bzhi pa'i sgrub thabs kun tu bzang mo'i rnam par bshad pa*, *Caturaṅga Sādhana Samantabhadrīṭīkā*, Tōh 1872, 177a5 and Phalavajra, *Kun tu bzang po'i sgrub pa'i thabs kyi 'grel pa*, *Samantabhadra Sādhana Vṛtti*, Tōh 1867, 185b5.

83. Ratnākaraśānti, ca. 970–1045. Seton 2018, 366.

84. Ratnākaraśānti, *Gsang ba 'dus pa'i dkyil 'khor gyi cho ga'i 'grel pa*, *Guhyasamāja Maṇḍalavidhiṭīkā*, Tōh 1871, 127a7–b1.

"They" here refers to conceptual thoughts and the visualization of the maṇḍala. In other words, it is not that false conceptualizations cannot appear at the same time as the maṇḍala. Rather, Ratnākaraśānti emphasizes, a mind absorbed in maṇḍala visualization cannot help but dispel false conceptualizations, because it is "endowed with a profound and sublime nature" capable of eliminating the conceptual thoughts that bring about saṃsāric suffering. For him, such a mind is capable of "complete transformation of the basis"[85] of the essence of the mental continuum, equivalent to the ultimate truth.

Ratnākaraśānti supports his argument by comparing the mind endowed with the form of the maṇḍala to the meditative absorption in infinite space.[86] He concludes that, while the latter meditation cannot avert saṃsāric suffering, the mind endowed with "a profound and sublime nature" can do so.[87] After citing Ratnākaraśānti's explanation, Tsongkhapa concludes:

> Thus Śāntipa [Ratnākaraśānti] clearly distinguishes between two methods of meditation: (1) The meditative absorption in infinite space does not turn the mind away from selflessness, and so this meditation does not prevent self-grasping. Therefore, even if yogis meditate on infinite space, they will not be liberated from saṃsāra. (2) The mind endowed with the aspect of the maṇḍala circle engages in selflessness and blocks the object grasped at as a self. Therefore this mind is able to counteract self-grasping.[88]

Here, the counteraction of self-grasping is synonymous with liberation from saṃsāra.

This comparison brings us to a fundamental feature of the creation stage. While the meditative absorption in infinite space reduces mental content to a bare minimum, the creation stage inflates it with incredible elaborations. This very difference also pertains to the closely related *kṛtsna*[89] meditation, the single-pointed concentration of śamatha practice, and absorptions[90]

85. Tib. *gnas yongs su gyur pa*, Skt. *āśrayaparāvṛtti*.

86. Tib. *nam mkha' mtha' yas skye mched*, Skt. *ākāśānantyāyatana*.

87. Ratnākaraśānti, *Gsang ba 'dus pa'i dkyil 'khor gyi cho ga'i 'grel pa*, *Guhyasamāja Maṇḍalavidhiṭīkā*, Tōh 1871, 127b3–5.

88. Tsong kha pa, *Sngags rim chen mo*, 492. Mkhas grub rje follows Tsong kha pa's explanation verbatim. See his *Bskyed rim dngos grub rgya mtsho*, 35b4–5.

89. Tib. *zad par gyi skye mched*, Skt. *kṛtsna* or *kṛtsnāyatana*, Pāli *kasiṇa*. See Ñāṇamoli, Bhikkhu 2010, part 2, chapters 4–5.

90. Tib. *snyoms par 'jug pa*, Skt. *samāpatti*.

in the formless realm.[91] For Ratnākaraśānti, then, mental overload is more effective than mental deprivation. Hence, the mind meditating on an embellished maṇḍala—inhabited by numerous ornamented deities holding various emblems—can better achieve a transformation of soteriological significance than a mind emptied of any content. This brings us to revisit Dharmakīrti.

Authenticating the Reality of the Maṇḍala

For Dharmakīrti, meditations on *kṛtsna* and the loathsome[92] are nonconceptual because they are created through the power of meditation.[93] This is despite the fact that in these meditations, the objects are unreal.[94] At the same time, in his *Pramāṇaviniścaya*,[95] Dharmakīrti defines direct perception[96] as nonconceptual and nonerroneous.[97] As Eltschinger notes, cognitions meditating on the *kṛtsna* and the loathsome meet the first defining condition of a direct perception but not the second. Although nonconceptual, these cognitions are erroneous because their objects are imaginary and not real; hence, they are not reliable or valid.[98]

As we saw above, the mind endowed with a profound and sublime nature that visualizes the maṇḍala circle is free of conceptualization. Can this mind, however, be taken as nonerroneous or valid, and therefore qualify for Dharmakīrti's definition of direct perception? Dharmakīrti's concern in the aforementioned discussions of the meditations on *kṛtsna* and direct perception is the nonconceptual and direct perception of the four noble truths, the classic example of direct perception.

Yet Samantabhadra, another early commentator on Jñānapāda's

91. Tib. *gzugs med pa'i khams*, Skt. *ārūpyadhātu*.

92. Tib. *mi gtsang*, Skt. *aśubha*, translated into English also as foulness. See Ñāṇamoli, Bhikkhu 2010, part 2, chapter 6.

93. Dharmakīrti, *Tshad ma rnam 'grel*, *Pramāṇavārtika*, *Pratyakṣa*, Tōh 4210, 129a6; Sanskrit and Tibetan editions in Miyasaka 1971–1972, v. 284; English translations in Dunne 2006, 516, and Eltschinger 2009, 194. Cited in Tsong kha pa, *Sngags rim chen mo*, 442.

94. Tib. *yang dag min pa*, Skt. *abhūta*.

95. As Eli Franco 2017, 119–121, points out, Dharmakīrti does so only in his *Tshad ma rnam par nges pa*, *Pramāṇaviniścaya*, Tōh 4211 (see note 97), while in the *Pramāṇavārtika*, he still keeps Dignāga's definition as nonconceptual alone.

96. Tib. *mngon sum*, Skt. *pratyakṣa*.

97. Tib. *ma 'khrul pa*, Skt. *abhrānta*. *Tshad ma rnam par nges pa*, *Pramāṇaviniścaya*, Tōh 4211, Steinkellner 2007, 7.7. See also Eltschinger 2009, 192.

98. Tib. *tshad ma*, Skt. *pramāṇa*. Eltschinger 2009, 195–196.

Samantabhadra Sādhana, mentions a nonconceptual and valid mind in relation to the mind endowed with a profound and sublime nature that visualizes the maṇḍala circle. Samantabhadra concludes his explanation of Jñānapāda's verse cited above—"conceptual thoughts will not appear to [the mind] endowed with a profound and sublime nature"—by saying: "That experience itself is valid (*pramāṇa*)."[99] The context of this statement is unclear, if not outright obscure. Can we entertain the possibility that what Samantabhadra has in mind is Dharmakīrti's definition of direct perception as nonconceptual and valid? In other words, I suggest that Samantabhadra is explaining that the mind endowed with a profound and sublime nature that visualizes the maṇḍala circle is a direct perception as defined by Dharmakīrti.

We have seen various attitudes toward visions of the maṇḍala with its deities. In certain contexts they are described as mere conceptualizations contrived by the mind that as such cannot achieve a soteriological end, while in other instances they are regarded as the fruit of a nondual mind that, by unifying emptiness and appearance, is capable of achieving a soteriological transformation. On the one hand, the yogis are aware that they themselves have generated these visions and know how they have created them. On the other hand, these visions are magnificent displays[100] of buddha fields,[101] created through the powers of samādhis; they cannot be delusions, but rather are more real than ordinary reality, displaying as they do the world as it appears to enlightened beings.

It is perhaps in order to confirm the reality of the maṇḍala that Samantabhadra describes the mind that visualizes the maṇḍala not only as nonconceptual but also valid (*pramāṇa*). In this way, Samantabhadra sanctions "reality" as it appears to the awakened eye through Buddhist philosophical terminology.

Tsongkhapa also turns to Dharmakīrti in order to establish the authenticity of the mind endowed with nondual profundity and manifestation. Immediately after his explanation of Ratnākaraśānti's interpretation cited above, Tsongkhapa says:

> The wisdom-realizing-selflessness overcomes self-grasping by countering it, since self-grasping is a mistaken apprehension, while wisdom-realizing-emptiness is not. Furthermore, determining

99. Tib. *nyams su myong ba nyid tshad ma yin*, Skt. *anubhava eva pramāṇam*. Samantabhadra, *Snying po snye ma*, *Sāramañjarī*, Tōh 1869, 44a2–3; Szántó, work in progress, 159.1.

100. Tib. *bkod pa*, Skt. *vyūha*.

101. Tib. *sangs rgyas kyi zhing*, Skt. *buddhakṣetra*.

> whether or not an apprehension is erroneous depends on whether or not there is supportive-valid-cognition proving that what has been apprehended is actually so. As the master logician Dharmakīrti said: "Of the [two], it is the one supported by valid cognition that invalidates the other."[102]

Causes That Accord with the Fruit

According to Jñānapāda, a mind endowed with a profound and sublime nature can attain its fruit because it is granted the same nature as the fruit—in other words, it cultivates causes that accord with the result.[103] For Tsongkhapa, this point is of utmost importance. At the beginning of his *Great Treatise on the Stages of the Mantric Path*, Tsongkhapa explains that such a profound and sublime nature accords with the fruit of the path, the two kinds of Buddha kāyas. The profound nature of the mind brings about the dharmakāya and wisdom, while the sublime brings about the rūpakāya, which is the method that can act for the sake of others. In this way, yogis on the Mantra Vehicle engage in causes that are compatible with the goal and are therefore efficacious.[104]

According to Tsongkhapa, while the Pāramitā Vehicle offers meditations on suchness that accord with dharmakāya, it offers no meditations that are similar to a rūpakāya; hence, it lacks causes that accord with the goal of the rūpakāya. On the other hand, the deity yoga offered in the Mantra Vehicle does accord with rūpakāya, so that the Mantra Vehicle alone provides a method for attaining both dharmakāya and rūpakāya, the goals of the path. Tsongkhapa points out that when the path is described in terms of wisdom and method, both the Pāramitā and the Mantra Vehicles specify that the path of wisdom is meditation on emptiness. However, the method of the other five pāramitās has no cause that can lead directly to the rūpakāya. By contrast, the meditation on the deity during the creation stage and the practice of the illusory body during the completion stage accord in their nature with the fruit

102. Tsong kha pa, *Sngags rim chen mo*, 492. Once more Mkhas grub rje follows Tsong kha pa's explanation almost verbatim. See his *Bskyed rim dngos grub rgya mtsho*, 35b5–36a1. The Dharmakīrti passage is from the *Tshad ma rnam 'grel, Pramāṇavārttika, Parārthānumāna*, Tōh 4210, 143a5–6; Sanskrit and Tibetan editions in Miyasaka 1971–1972, v. 99cd; a Sanskrit edition and an English translation in Tillemans 2000, 138–139. The "other" is the one that is not supported by a valid cognition.

103. Jñānapāda, *Bdag sgrub pa la 'jug pa, Ātmasādhanāvatāra*, Tōh 1860, 54b1–3.

104. Tsong kha pa, *Sngags rim chen mo*, 20–42; an English translation in Hopkins 1977, 115–150.

and are therefore effective. For Tsongkhapa, it is this specific characteristic of the mantric path that makes it superior to the path of the *pāramitās*.[105]

In the chapter on the creation stage in his *Great Treatise on the Stages of the Mantric Path*, Tsongkhapa expands on Jñānapāda's notion of the mind endowed with a profound and sublime nature, or with the inconceivable nature of the maṇḍala circle.[106] Tsongkhapa explains that this mind meditates simultaneously on emptiness and appearances within a single cognition by means of the yoga of nondual profundity and manifestation as described above.

The Illusion-Like Nature of the Special Appearances

It is clear now why Tsongkhapa rejects the position that yogis of the creation stage only need to meditate on the visualization of the maṇḍala with its deities, the appearance aspect, while the meditation on emptiness takes place mainly during the completion stage.[107] Yogis of the creation stage for the most part do not meditate solely on emptiness, though during certain steps of the creation stage they certainly do so by visualizing the dissolution of dualistic appearances and meditating on suchness or emptiness.[108] By virtue of these moments of meditation on suchness, when yogis visualize the maṇḍala and its deities throughout the creation stage, their visualization is infused with meditation on emptiness.

If it were not so, the yogis would simply be replacing one conceptualization with another. Instead of the mistaken appearance of their ordinary reality, seen through their own mental proliferations, they perceive the appearance of the maṇḍalas created by their minds. In non-tantric meditation, too, as Tsongkhapa explains in his *Short Treatise on the Stage of the Path*,[109] aspirants absorb themselves in meditation on emptiness in order to realize that things are empty of intrinsic nature. When they subsequently arise from their meditation and view the diversity of appearances, these appearances arise as illusion-like—that is, while they are visible to the eye, they are devoid of

105. Tsong kha pa, *Sngags rim chen mo*, 20–42; an English translation in Hopkins 1977, 115–150.

106. Tsong kha pa, *Sngags rim chen mo*, 493.

107. Tsong kha pa, *Sngags rim chen mo*, 489; Mkhas grub rje, *Bskyed rim dngos grub rgya mtsho*, 32a2–3.

108. For example, during the purification into the ground of wisdom or the dissolution of the specially visualized deities into clear light.

109. Tsong kha pa, *Lam rim chung ba*, 180b3–185a1; Hopkins 2008a, 75–85.

intrinsic nature. Likewise, in the creation stage, yogis first meditate on emptiness; when they visualize the maṇḍala immediately afterward, as long as the impact of their equipoise on emptiness remains, their visualization arises as an illusion-like circle of deities.

Scholars of the Indian subcontinent also instruct tantric aspirants not to visualize the maṇḍala as a concrete reality. According to Ratnarakṣita: "You ought not meditate on a mere form but rather on the attainment of the Blessed One, who is endowed with the supreme of all forms, and whose nature is emptiness that is one taste with great bliss. You ought to meditate on dharmatā,[110] which cannot be separated from the wheel of forms."[111] Likewise, Tsongkhapa cites Nāgārjuna on this point: "But why explain so much when the Vajrayāna teaches that, in actuality, whatever the yogi focuses on should be conceived of as only illusion?"[112] Among the purposes of the meditation on emptiness in the creation stage, Dīpaṅkaraśrījñāna mentions "realizing that the entire maṇḍala of the celestial mansion and its deities are emanations of emptiness."[113] After citing this line, Tsongkhapa explains that once the yogi has thoroughly established an understanding of emptiness and meditated on it, the entire appearance aspect of the maṇḍala arises as a playful display of illusion.[114]

Hence, although during the creation stage yogis strive to achieve a perfect and highly detailed visualization of a celestial mansion with thirty-two male and female buddhas and bodhisattvas dwelling inside, these special appearances of the maṇḍala would not appear illusion-like were they not preceded by the meditation on emptiness.

Luis Gómez has highlighted an important difference between ordinary magicians and wonder-worker bodhisattvas.[115] While the former seek to deceive their audience, the latter aim to alert their disciples to the fact that they are constantly deceived by ordinary perceptions. Accomplished tantric

110. Tib. *chos nyid.*

111. Ratnarakṣita, *Padma can, Padminī,* Tōh 1420, 42b1–2; Tanemura, Kano, and Kuranishi 2017, 9.74–76.

112. Tsong kha pa, *Sngags rim chen mo,* 490. See also Mkhas grub rje, *Bskyed rim dngos grub rgya mtsho,* 38b3. The Nāgārjuna quotation is found in *Rim lnga, Pañcakrama,* chap. 3, v. 33, Tōh 1802, 53a2–5; Sanskrit and Tibetan in Mimaki and Tomabechi 1994; Sanskrit and French translation in Tomabechi 2006, 160–161.

113. Dīpaṅkaraśrījñāna, *Mngon par rtogs pa rnam par 'byed pa, Abhisamayavibhaṅga,* Tōh 1490, 189b1–2.

114. Tib. *sgyu ma'i rnam rol.* Tsong kha pa, *'Dod 'jo,* 52b2–4. See also Tsong kha pa, *Sngags rim chen mo,* 500.

115. Gómez 1977, 229.

yogis realize on their own how their visualizations work, and therefore know that their ordinary and maṇḍalic worlds alike are illusory.

The illusory nature of the visualization during the creation stage is not unique to the Geluk tradition. According to Kongtrul Yönten Gyatso:[116] "In the creation stage, aspirants abandon ordinary appearances and attitudes, as well as grasping at things as though they are real. These are countered by means of clear appearances, pride, and regarding things as illusory."[117] Hence, we will now turn to the topic of relinquishing ordinary appearances and attitudes.

Relinquishing Ordinary Appearances and Attitudes

According to Tsongkhapa:

> The meditation in which yogis visualize the special appearance of the maṇḍala, with its celestial mansion and deities, in order to shed ordinary appearances and attitudes is a feature exclusive to the Mantra Vehicle.[118]

The meditation on the maṇḍala serves as an antidote[119] to both ordinary appearances[120] and attitudes.[121] By habituating themselves to the appearance of the environment, which arises as the celestial mansion of the maṇḍala, and the appearance of the inhabitants, which arises as the deities dwelling in it, yogis avert ordinary appearances and attain pure vision or vivid appearance[122] of the maṇḍala. Likewise, by habituating themselves to the divine pride of being Akṣobhya or Vairocana, they shed their ordinary identity and attitudes and gain the divine pride[123] of being the deity, or identification with the deity. In this way, the ordinary, subjective mode of apprehension of the yogis transforms into maṇḍalic reality.

116. Kong sprul Yon tan rgya mtsho (1813–1899).

117. Kong sprul, *Shes bya kun khyab*, vol. 3, 165; for another translation, see Guarisco and McLeod 2008, 60.

118. Tsong kha pa, *Sngags rim chen mo*, 462.

119. Tib. *gnyen po*.

120. Tib. *tha mal pa'i snang ba*.

121. Tib. *tha mal pa'i zhen pa*.

122. Tib. *gsal snang*.

123. Tib. *nga rgyal*, Skt. *ahaṃkāra*.

For Tsongkhapa, the main goal of the creation stage is identification with the maṇḍala and its deities as an antidote to ordinary identity, while meditation on the special appearances of the maṇḍala in order to avert ordinary appearances is subsidiary.[124] We will now examine the first of these.

Divine Identity or Pride

During the sādhana, yogis often meditate on divine identity. Khedrup Jé explains that as an antidote to ordinary attitudes, yogis should:

> meditate on the celestial mansion and its deities while maintaining a most powerful and pure divine identity with the resolve: "I am the actual deity so-and-so, endowed with a pure buddha field, with the body of the Buddha, and with the virtues of a mind that has abandoned all obscurations and knows all knowable objects."[125]

At the beginning of the sādhana's core practices, yogis meditate on the divine identity of the dharmakāya. Khedrup Jé describes this meditation:

> Therefore, in this context as well, when you meditate on emptiness, you should maintain the divine identity of the dharmakāya—indivisible emptiness and wisdom. Then, from within the continuing state of the dharmakāya, you should arise in the appearance of the maṇḍala of the rūpakāya—with its celestial mansion and deities—by recalling your wishing prayer to act for the sake of the disciples. You do so by visualizing that the objective aspect of the wisdom of the dharmakāya arises as the maṇḍala of the celestial mansion and its deities.[126]

As in the yoga of nondual profundity and manifestations described above, while the subjective aspect of the mind maintains the divine identity of the dharmakāya—indivisible emptiness and wisdom—its objective aspect arises as the rūpakāya—the maṇḍala with its celestial mansion and deities.

The meditation on emptiness while maintaining a divine identity in the

124. Tsong kha pa, *Sngags rim chen mo*, 462–463. Other Tibetan scholars agree. See for example Bstan pa'i nyi ma, *Bskyed rim gyi zin bris*, 40b3–4.

125. Mkhas grub rje, *Bskyed rim dngos grub rgya mtsho*, 181b3–5.

126. Mkhas grub rje, *Bskyed rim dngos grub rgya mtsho*, 42b3–5, and Tsong kha pa, *Sngags rim chen mo*, 500.

creation stage is different from the meditation on emptiness and selflessness in the Pāramitā Vehicle. There the goal of the meditation on selflessness is to eradicate the root of self-grasping by means of the super-mundane path, or at least to weaken its root through the mundane path.[127] The emphasis in the Mantra Vehicle is neither on the elimination of inherent existence nor on nonaffirming negation, though these features are certainly present. The meditation here is characterized by a positive and subjective aspect of identification with the dharmakāya that will give rise to the rūpakāya. Norsang Gyatso[128] explains this by raising the following quandary:

> Regarding the method of meditation on emptiness here, is it sufficient merely to abide in absorption on nonaffirming negation of emptiness, that is to say, in merely refuting the object of negation, as in the meditation of the Pāramitā Vehicle?

[Reply:]

> It is insufficient, because in this context, having sustained a powerful discernment of the view of emptiness for not a short time, still within this continuing state, you certainly need to maintain divine identity with the resolution: "I am the embodiment of the dharmakāya of the indivisible objective emptiness and subjective wisdom."[129]

Thus the identification with the dharmakāya of the deity during the creation stage is one of the significant differences between the meditation on emptiness in the Pāramitā and Mantra Vehicles, and its implications are far-reaching.

The identification with the dharmakāya, or maintaining its divine pride, has a much greater impact on the subject—the yogis themselves—than meditation on the absence of inherent existence of all phenomena. The yogis maintain the divine identity of the dharmakāya by meditating on the mantra of emptiness: *oṃ śūnyatā jñāna vajra svabhāva ātmako 'haṃ*. Most mantras on divine identity end with *ahaṃ*, I; they do not refer to external emptiness but to the yogi. Tsongkhapa explains:

127. Tsong kha pa, *Sngags rim chen mo*, 463.

128. Nor bzang rgya mtsho (1423–1513).

129. Nor bzang rgya mtsho, *Gsang ba 'dus pa'i bskyed rim gyi don gsal bar byed pa'i sgron me*, 36b4–6.

> In the context of this tantra, it is insufficient for the yogis to merely apply their minds to the meaning of emptiness. *Ahaṃ* means "maintaining divine pride or identity." Therefore, in this [Mantra] Vehicle from now on, yogis need to maintain the identity of both the dharmakāya and rūpakāya; at this point, they maintain the identity of the dharmakāya.[130]

Tsongkhapa stresses that the main purpose of the meditation on emptiness here is to maintain the identity of the dharmakāya; unless yogis realize this, they will not be able to maintain the identity of the rūpakāya later on. In order to attain the Buddha's kāyas, the path has to accord with both the rūpakāya and dharmakāya, and here the latter is taken on the path.[131]

The mantra *oṃ śūnyatā jñāna vajra svabhāva ātmako 'haṃ* is found at the beginning of the third chapter of the *Guhyasamāja Tantra*, just before the visualization of the maṇḍala with its deities.[132] In his commentary, Tsongkhapa explains that *śūnyatā* (emptiness) here refers to the object, while *jñāna* (pristine wisdom) refers to the subject, and *vajra* means that these two are as indivisible as water poured into water.[133] Thus the first part of the mantra, *śūnyatā jñāna vajra*, refers to the indivisible objective emptiness and subjective wisdom. In other words, the wisdom-mind that meditates on emptiness is indivisible from the emptiness on which it meditates. *Svabhāva* is nature in the sense of pure nature, *ātmako* is consisting or being, and *ahaṃ* is I. Thus *svabhāva ātmako 'haṃ* means "[being pure by] nature, that am I,"[134] and the meaning of the entire mantra is "Consisting of invisible emptiness, [pure by] nature, and the wisdom which is its subject, that am I."

Taking the Fruit as the Path

According to Tsongkhapa, as we saw above, the tantric path is endowed with the two main causes that accord with the fruit—the dharmakāya and the rūpakāya. Meditation on emptiness, or the profound nature, is the cause that accords with the dharmakāya and thus leads to the fruit of the dharmakāya; the visualization of the maṇḍala with its deities, or the manifestation aspect,

130. Tsong kha pa, *Sgron gsal mchan*, 98b5–6.

131. Tsong kha pa, *Sngags rim chen mo*, 500.

132. *Gsang 'dus*, chap. 3, Tōh 442; Zhol 6b6; Stog 10b4–5; Dunh 9b1–2; Fremantle 1971, 196; Matsunaga 1978, 11.

133. Tsong kha pa, *Sgron gsal mchan*, chap. 3, 98b3–5.

134. Tsong kha pa, *Bskyed rim zin bris*, 22a2–3.

is the cause that accords with the rūpakāya. Another important principle of the tantric path is taking on the path the Buddha's bodies at the time of their fruition. Khedrup Jé explains:

> In the Mantra Vehicle you should take the fruit as the path by meditating, beginning in the present moment, on the state of the Buddha. For this reason, the Mantra Vehicle is called the fruit vehicle.[135]

At the time of fruition, yogis will attain the dharmakāya; this dharmakāya will then arise in the aspect of the rūpakāya through the power of prior aspirations and through generating the mind for the sake of the disciples. During the creation stage, yogis take the dharmakāya on the path by meditating on emptiness, then take the rūpakāya on the path by meditating on the appearance of the deities.

Becoming the Five Tathāgatas of the Guhyasamāja Maṇḍala

At which point during the sādhana do the yogis maintain the divine identity of the rūpakāya or of the saṃbhogakāya and nirmāṇakāya? Put differently, who is Guhyasamāja, and do the yogis transform into Guhyasamāja by meditating on the sādhana? The answer is that the principal deity during the creation stage of the Guhyasamāja is not a single entity but a dynamic figure that takes the forms of different deities, including Vajradhara, Akṣobhya, and Vajrasattva.

The first deity whose divine pride or divine identity the yogis adopt during the main section of the sādhana is Vajradhara,[136] the lord of the specially visualized deities.[137] Together with the specially visualized deities, Vajradhara dissolves into clear light, after which the yogis maintain the divine identity of the dharmakāya as described. When the yogis arise as the First Lord[138] in the following step of the practice, they maintain the divine identity of Vajradhara once more.[139]

The yogis successively transform into the five tathāgatas of the maṇḍala toward the end of the core practices of the sādhana during the step of blessing

135. Mkhas grub rje, *Bskyed rim dngos grub rgya mtsho*, 42b3.

136. Vajradhara belongs to the sixth tathāgata family; he is not one of the five tathāgatas of the Guhyasamāja maṇḍala. See Mkhas grub rje, *Bskyed rim dngos grub rgya mtsho*, 70b4.

137. Tib. *lhag mos kyi lha*. Tsong kha pa, *Gsang mngon*, 31a5.

138. Tib. *dang po mgon po*, Skt. *ādinātha*.

139. Mkhas grub rje, *Bskyed rim dngos grub rgya mtsho*, 104b6.

of the body, speech, and mind, and then during the yoga with the consort. They do so by meditating on mantras found at the beginning of the sixth chapter of the *Guhyasamāja Tantra*. Although there might seem to be no special connection between these two steps of the sādhana, separated as they are by the meditation on the triple sattvas, they are linked by the mantras found together in the *Guhyasamāja Tantra*.

While reciting the mantras, the yogis turn into each of the five tathāgatas of the maṇḍala by maintaining their divine pride. During the blessing of the body, speech, and mind, the yogis become Vajra Body Vairocana, Vajra Speech Amitābha, and Vajra Mind Akṣobhya respectively. Then, once again, they maintain the divine identity of Vajradhara, the indivisible three vajras. During the yoga with the consort, the yogis maintain divine identification of Ratnasaṃbhava and Amoghasiddhi. In order to experience great bliss, they become once more Vajradharas. The five mantras are:

Oṃ sarva tathāgata kāya vajra svabhāva ātmako 'haṃ.
Oṃ sarva tathāgata vāk vajra svabhāva ātmako 'haṃ.
Oṃ sarva tathāgata citta vajra svabhāva ātmako 'haṃ.
Oṃ sarva tathāgata anurāgana vajra svabhāva ātmako 'haṃ.
Oṃ sarva tathāgata pūjā vajra svabhāva ātmako 'haṃ.

Ripening the Mental Continuum of the Yogi for Realization during the Completion Stage

At times the creation stage is regarded as an independent practice capable of achieving important soteriological goals. We have seen how Jñānapāda and Tsongkhapa, among others, sometimes describe the creation stage in terms of a mind that apprehends nonduality; in doing so, they momentarily set aside the restraints they have themselves imposed on the creation stage. Yet, though indispensable, the creation stage is regarded as only the first stage in the tantric path to buddhahood. As such, its main role is to ripen[140] the yogi for the completion stage, during which the actual transformations take place before the fruit is attained.[141] The creation stage ripens the yogi for the completion stage by building a foundation of virtue,[142] habituating the yogi to the three bodies,

140. Tib. *smin pa*, Skt. *vipāka*.

141. See Tsong kha pa, *Sngags rim chen mo*, 471–472; and Mkhas grub rje, *Bskyed rim dngos grub rgya mtsho*, 1b6–2a1.

142. Developing roots of virtue, Tib. *dge rtsa*, Skt. *kuśulamūla*.

cultivating the wisdom that realizes emptiness, and making the elements of the subtle body serviceable. As Khedrup Jé explains:

> It is the completion stage that purifies all the seeds of appearance and attitude that proceed from ordinary birth, death, and the intermediate state and actually transforms them into the three bodies. For only during the completion stage do the aspects of birth, death, and the intermediate state of the time of the ground[143] arise in the inner continuum in actuality as they are. Prior to this, during the creation stage, aspects akin to birth, death, and the intermediate state of the time of the ground are perceived by the mind, but no actual transformation occurs. Though birth, death, and the intermediate state have not yet actually turned into the genuine three bodies of the buddhas, the aspects that resemble the three bodies in the mind of the meditator on the creation stage—the same ones that correspond to the aspects of the completion stage—effectuate ripening for the completion stage by suppressing the manifestation of appearances and attitudes of ordinary birth, death, and the intermediate state.[144]

Not only does the entire creation stage ripen the yogi for the perfect completion stage to arise, each step of the sādhana has its own fruit during the completion stage. Tsongkhapa often specifies this, particularly in his *Fulfilling the Bee's Hopes*.[145] For example, the meditation on emptiness during the creation stage readies the yogi's mental continuum for the clear light of the completion stage; the visualization of the First Lord prepares for the arising of the illusory bodies after the three isolations; the recitation of the mantra serves to ripen the continuum of speech isolation of the meditator on the completion stage; and so forth.

143. Tib. *gzhi dus*. This refers to ordinary birth, death, and the intermediate state of the yogis before they begin to practice the sādhana. A successful completion of the practice will transform these three ordinary conditions into the three bodies of the Buddha. See the section "Correspondences with Microcosmic Events" below.

144. Mkhas grub rje, *Bskyed rim dngos grub rgya mtsho*, 12a2–4.

145. Tsong kha pa, *Bung ba'i re skong*, 18a1–3, 19b5–6, 22b3–4.

Relinquishing Ordinary Appearances and Attaining Clear Appearances

As we have seen, the meditation on the maṇḍala serves as an antidote to ordinary appearances and attitudes. We have discussed the vital importance attributed by scholars of the creation stage to the maintenance of divine pride as an antidote to ordinary identity. Now we will turn to the meditation on the special appearances of the maṇḍala, intended to cast off ordinary appearances.

Since the special appearances of the maṇḍala stand in contrast to ordinary appearances perceived by ordinary people, the creation stage serves to offset ordinary appearances. Nevertheless, the elimination of ordinary appearances from the meditating mind does not imply the dissipation of external objects. As Tsongkhapa explains: "The ordinary appearances that should be abandoned are not the world and its inhabitants as they appear to the sensory consciousness, but the ordinary world and its inhabitants as they appear to the mental consciousness."[146]

Visualizations take place on the level of the mental consciousness. The five sensory consciousnesses engage in direct experiences of their respective objects at any given moment without conceptually recognizing the things they observe. The mental consciousness, by contrast, processes the direct experiences of the five sensory consciousnesses as its own creation using mental images or generalities. Simply put, the five sensory consciousnesses cannot engage in visualization, whereas the mental consciousness that visualizes the deity does not engage with "real" external objects. Hence, the visualization of the maṇḍala and sensory perception take place on different planes. This implies that yogis meditating on the creation stage do not lose their grip on ordinary reality.

Śamatha and *kṛtsna* meditations also take place on the level of mental consciousness, but the superiority of the creation stage, in spite of certain similarities, has been discussed above. Yet, as we have seen, the mind endowed with a profound and sublime nature must be cultivated to an extreme point before it can wholly eradicate ordinary conceptualizations. Still, there is no consensus among Tibetan scholars as to how and when ordinary appearances no longer arise in the mind. Moreover, the same scholar may express somewhat different positions in different contexts.

Khedrup Jé explains how, by meditating on emptiness, yogis can block ordinary appearances from appearing to their cognition:

146. Tsong kha pa, *Sngags rim chen mo*, 463.

> Therefore you must prevent the ordinary appearance from arising in your cognition. Still, you cannot stop ordinary appearances by meditating on them as mere nothingness. Rather, when you withdraw the cognition that engages with the conventional world of ordinary appearances and set your mind on emptiness—the ultimate truth—ordinary appearances cease to arise within the sphere of your cognition. This is one of the reasons for meditating on emptiness. You should understand the distinction between preventing ordinary appearances from arising within the sphere of cognition and actually stopping their existence.[147]

When Tsongkhapa discusses the creation stage in the context of its role in the full path to buddhahood, he explains that ordinary appearances cannot manifest in the mental consciousness at the same time as the special appearances of the maṇḍala and its deities. We saw above that in a different context—the yoga of nondual profundity and manifestation, which indivisibly unites the visualization of the maṇḍala with the meditation on emptiness—Tsongkhapa sided with Ratnākaraśānti's opposing position.[148] Here, Tsongkhapa elaborates on another verse by Dharmakīrti:

> When yogis, who have increased their habituation, are absorbed in equipoise on deity yoga, other appearances do not arise to their eye-consciousness and so forth. This is because their mental consciousness is intensely engaged in the object [of the maṇḍala and its deities], and therefore the power of the immediately preceding condition[149] for the arising of the eye-consciousness and so forth diminishes. Hence, for a while, these [eye-consciousness and so forth] do not arise, and therefore further appearances of color and so forth do not arise. However, these appearances are not stopped by the creation stage. As the Lord of Reasoning [Dharmakīrti] explains: "For a consciousness that is intent on something becomes incapable of apprehending another object." Therefore, when you gain the power to block ordinary appearances from your mental consciousness by means of special appearances, you attain the goal.

147. Mkhas grub rje, *Bskyed rim dngos grub rgya mtsho*, 42a2–3.

148. Tsong kha pa, *Sngags rim chen mo*, 491–492. The Dharmakīrti passage is in *Tshad ma rnam 'grel, Pramāṇavārttika, Pramāṇasiddhi*, Tōh 4210, 111b6–7; Sanskrit and Tibetan editions in Miyasaka 1971–1972, v. 112cd; English translations in Jackson 1992, 294, v. 112, and Coghlan and Zarpani 2011, 114.

149. Tib. *de ma thag rkyen*, Skt. *samanantarapratyaya*, a former moment of consciousness.

Tsongkhapa immediately continues:

> Likewise, although yogis will not become deities in actuality by means of the creation stage, when a genuine identity of the deity arises the goal is attained.[150]

Thus the practice of divine identity can lead to higher attainments than the practice of the special appearances of the maṇḍala and the deities dwelling there.

Khedrup Jé describes how yogis:

> should meditate on the appearance of the maṇḍala as an antidote to ordinary appearances. At first, while meditating on the sādhana stage by stage, stabilize your mind so that it will not be distracted even slightly by other objects, and then slowly visualize each pure appearance at the right stage until a clear generic image arises in your mind. Then, after meditating on the sādhana in this way stage by stage, maintain a stabilized meditation. This is the position held by most scholar-yogis in the land of India. Accordingly, visualize the generic image of the complete maṇḍala wheel with its celestial mansion and deities; focus single-pointedly[151] on it, systematically applying mindfulness and alertness; and then instantaneously visualize the entire maṇḍala, practicing "clear appearance" stage by stage. If you know how to maintain this, it will be exceedingly powerful.[152]

Here, the yogis practice the visualization of the generic image of the maṇḍala again and again, beginning with the visualization of the principal deity with one face and two arms, until they gain a clear appearance and their minds are stable. They focus on the part that appears clearly, then gradually add the other parts. Once the appearance of the principal deity, with all his faces and arms, is clear and their minds are stable, they add the other deities one by one, until their minds are stable in the clear appearance of the entire maṇḍala of the celestial mansion and its deities and they are able to instantaneously visualize the entire maṇḍala.

Eventually, the maṇḍala will appear to the minds of the yogis not as a generic image, but *as* a direct perception:

150. Tsong kha pa, *Sngags rim chen mo*, 464.

151. Tib. *rtse gcig tu dmigs te.*

152. Mkhas grub rje, *Bskyed rim dngos grub rgya mtsho*, 182a1–4.

> Merely by visualizing the maṇḍala wheel, it will appear to your mind clearly as a direct perception in the very same way that you visualized it; and merely by meditating on divine identity, you will maintain a genuine divine identity with the resolve: "I am actually this particular deity." Thus you will engage naturally in both [the clear appearance of the maṇḍala wheel and divine identity] without exertion until the end of the session.[153]

Over the course of time, says Khedrup Jé:

> Merely by meditating on deity yoga, the appearances of the impure world and its inhabitants that arise in your mind, and your attitudes toward them, will be transformed into pure appearances and attitudes, clear and intense; and you will be able to keep these pure appearances and attitudes stable naturally for a very long time without exertion. This is what it means to block ordinary appearances and attitudes through the creation stage.[154]

Khedrup Jé reminds the yogis that while they engage in the practice of clear appearance and identification with the deities, they should not neglect their meditation on emptiness.[155] At the same time, they should cultivate the understanding that while the maṇḍala appears, it is empty of intrinsic existence and therefore arises as illusion-like. Moreover, the objective aspect of the wisdom-mind—indivisible from emptiness—arises in the form of the maṇḍala.[156]

However, even when they are able to block ordinary appearances and attitudes and attain a clear, instantaneous appearance of the maṇḍala, up to the white and black of the deities' eyes, this does not mean yogis have mastered the creation stage. When they achieve this clear appearance, accompanied by the apprehension in which they sense themselves transformed into the actual identity of the deity for as long as they wish and without the interference of ordinary thought, they attain the stage called "attaining a stable mind" in the creation stage.[157] In order to complete the creation stage and become qualified

153. Mkhas grub rje, *Bskyed rim dngos grub rgya mtsho*, 182b6–183a2.

154. Mkhas grub rje, *Bskyed rim dngos grub rgya mtsho*, 183a2–3.

155. See the sections "Meditation on Emptiness in the Creation Stage" and "Meditation on Emptiness in the Microcosmic Context" below.

156. Mkhas grub rje, *Bskyed rim dngos grub rgya mtsho*, 183a5–6.

157. Tib. *sems brtan pa*. Mkhas grub rje, *Bskyed rim dngos grub rgya mtsho*, 184a3–4. Actual stable mind is attained only during the completion stage.

to practice the completion stage, yogis must attain the stage called "attainment of perfect mastery of wisdom."[158] Still, once the yogis have completed the sādhana, as long as the yogis persevere in their meditation on deity yoga, they need not practice for more than one year.[159]

Although the maṇḍala does not exist in actuality as it is meditated upon, it arises directly, clearly, and nonconceptually to the mental consciousness of advanced yogis. As noted above,[160] according to Dharmakīrti, unreal objects such as the loathsome and the *kṛtsna*, "when manifest through the powers of meditation, are clear and nonconceptual."[161] Tsongkhapa cites another relevant verse from the *Pratyakṣa* chapter of the *Pramāṇavārtika*: "Therefore, whatever you intensely meditate on, whether real or not, will bear the fruit of a clear and nonconceptual cognition when your meditation becomes powerful."[162]

This brings us to an important point: Although when yogis begin meditating on deity yoga, their mental continuums are engaged in conceptual meditation, their mental continuums can become *nonconceptual* by means of their *conceptual* meditation.[163] We may recall the verse of the *Hevajra Tantra*: "By means of the yoga of the creation stage, aspirants must meditate on the proliferations of mental constructs. Once they have made the proliferations dreamlike, they should use this very proliferation to deproliferate."[164]

158. See Mkhas grub rje, *Bskyed rim dngos grub rgya mtsho*, 184a5. This is the fourth level of four: beginner level, the initial dawning of wisdom, attainment of initial mastery of wisdom, and the attainment of perfect mastery of wisdom. Tib. *las dang po pa* or *dang po'i las*, *ye shes cung zad babs pa*, *ye shes la cung zad dbang thob pa* or *ye shes dbang ba cung zad 'thob pa*, and *ye shes la yang dag par dbang thob pa* or *yang dag ye shes dbang thob pa*. These stages are found in Mar me mdzad bzang po, Dīpaṅkarabhadra, *Gsang ba 'dus pa'i dkyil 'khor gyi cho ga = Dkyil chog bzhi rgya lnga bcu pa*, *Guhyasamājamaṇḍala Vidhi*, Tōh 1865, 74b2–4; Klein-Schwind 2008, vv. 133–136; and its commentary by Ratnākaraśānti, *Gsang ba 'dus pa'i dkyil 'khor gyi cho ga'i 'grel pa*, *Guhyasamāja Maṇḍalavidhiṭīkā*, Tōh 1871, 87a4–b3. See Tsong kha pa, *Sngags rim chen mo*, chap. 12, 464–469.

159. Tsong kha pa, *Sngags rim chen mo*, 473, Mkhas grub rje, *Bskyed rim dngos grub rgya mtsho*, 184b1–185a2.

160. See the section "Authenticating the Reality of the Maṇḍala."

161. Dharmakīrti, *Tshad ma rnam 'grel*, *Pramāṇavārttika*, *Pratyakṣa*, Tōh 4210, 129a6; Miyasaka 1971–1972, v. 284.

162. Tsong kha pa, *Sngags rim chen mo*, 470. The Dharmakīrti passage is found in *Tshad ma rnam 'grel*, *Pramāṇavārttika*, *Pratyakṣa*, Tōh 4210, 129a6–7; Miyasaka 1971–1972, v. 285. My translation is based on the English translation in Isaacson and Sferra 2014, 267.

163. Mkhas grub rje, *Bskyed rim dngos grub rgya mtsho*, 185a4–b2.

164. *Brtag gnyis*, Tōh 418, 15a7; Snellgrove 1959, II.ii.29.

Another example supplied by Dharmakīrti is cited by Tsongkhapa and Khedrup Jé: "Those who are deranged by desire, grief, or fear, or by dreams of thieves and so forth see these distressing objects that are unreal as if they were right in front of them."[165] That is to say, fear of robbers or desire for a loved one can render an imaginary object vivid and therefore nonconceptual. According to Tsongkhapa, this means that for a clear appearance to arise, yogis need not first attain a stable mind, nor must they habituate to each and every part of the visualization.[166]

Once again, in certain contexts the creation stage is described as a method contrived by the mind that results in a contrived cognition of the maṇḍala, in contrast to the completion stage, where nonconceptualized realizations can be achieved. But in the present context, clear and nonconceptual cognition is already achieved in the meditation on the creation stage.

We have seen how conceptual meditation can become nonconceptual. Now we will turn to the question of how impure bodies can become pure.

The Nature of the Transformation of the Ordinary Body into a Buddha's Body

According to the *Guhyasamāja* and other tantras, the transformation of the ordinary body into a buddha's body is made possible through special links that are thought to exist between the impure psycho-physical elements of the human body and their purified aspects in the forms of the deities of the maṇḍala. The *Guhyasamāja Tantra* relates the body's components to the five buddhas of the maṇḍala and so forth: "The five aggregates are proclaimed as the five buddhas, the vajra sense bases[167] as the supreme maṇḍala of bodhisattvas."[168] Importantly, the five aggregates are not explicitly equated here with the five buddhas; rather, they are proclaimed[169] as buddhas. Hence, there is a certain ambiguity regarding the nature of these

165. Tsong kha pa, *Sngags rim chen mo*, 470; Mkhas grub rje, *Bskyed rim dngos grub rgya mtsho*, 185b1; Dharmakīrti, *Tshad ma rnam 'grel, Pramāṇavārttika, Pratyakṣa*, Tōh 4210, 129a5; Sanskrit and Tibetan editions in Miyasaka 1971–1972, v. 282; English translations in Dunne 2006, 516, Eltschinger 2009, 193, and Yarnall 2013, 155.

166. Tsong kha pa, *Sngags rim chen mo*, 470.

167. Tib. *skyed mched*, Skt. *āyatana*.

168. *Gsang 'dus*, chap. 17, v. 50, Tōh 442; Zhol 44a6–7; Stog 82b5; Fremantle 1971, 388; Matsunaga 1978, 109.

169. Tib. *rab tu bsgrags*, Skt. *prakīrtita*.

relations and the extent to which the aggregates and the buddhas may be regarded as identical.

On the one hand, numerous Buddhist tantras understand the psycho-physical elements of the human body and the deities of the maṇḍala as completely identical. Thus, in commenting on the above-cited verses of the *Guhyasamāja Tantra* in his *Illuminating Lamp*, Candrakīrti emphasizes the equivalence of the aggregates and the buddhas: The five tathāgatas are the nature of the five aggregates, the five physical elements are the nature of the four mothers, the sense bases the nature of the bodhisattvas, and so forth.[170] Similarly, some mother tantras, including the *Hevajra* and *Saṃvarodaya* tantras,[171] contain a whole chapter on the equivalence of bodily constituents and the deities of the maṇḍala (in fact called purity).[172] On the other hand, it seems that a certain transition from the impure to the pure stage must be acknowledged. Āryadeva, for his part, glosses the above line of the *Guhya-samāja Tantra* as follows:

> It is taught that the aggregates, sensory spheres, and sense bases, which since time without beginning have abided with the identity of the ordinary, now have the nature of being produced from tiny particles of all tathāgatas.[173]

Here, a distinction is made between the state of things in the past and in the present, but the nature of the shift from the former to the latter remains unclear. Such ambiguities often play an important role in debates among Indian and Tibetan Buddhist scholars, where each party accuses the other of falling into one or another of the extremes rather than straddling both.

170. Candrakīrti, *Sgron gsal, Pradīpoddyotana*, Tōh 1785, 186a2–3; Chakravarti 1984, 214.

171. See the *Brtag gnyis*, part 1, chap. 9, Tōh 417; and *Sdom 'byung*, chap. 4, Tōh 373.

172. Tib. *rnam par dag pa*, Skt. *viśuddhi*.

173. Āryadeva, *Spyod bsdus, Caryāmelāpakapradīpa*, chap. 2, Tōh 1803, 61a6; Sanskrit, Tibetan, and English translation in Wedemeyer 2007, A: 7b; Sanskrit and Tibetan in Pandey 2000, 8 and 169–170.

2. Tsongkhapa, Khedrup Jé, and Polemical Literature

BEFORE BEGINNING THIS SECTION, I would like to highlight two essential points. First, Khedrup Jé's *Ocean of Attainments* is known as a polemical work.[174] However, my purpose here is not to study polemics for their own sake, but rather to use them to better understand the formation of tantric traditions in Tibet during the twelfth to fifteenth centuries. Second, although *Ocean of Attainments* contains various arguments against unnamed scholars, its goal is not only to attack other systems but to explain the author's own interpretation of the *Guhyasamāja Sādhana* according to the Ārya tradition.[175]

The reverence of Khedrup Jé toward his teacher Tsongkhapa Losang Drakpa is evident throughout his *Ocean of Attainments*; most positions expressed in it—though not all—are those of Tsongkhapa.[176] The fourteenth and fifteenth centuries were central to the systematization of tantric traditions in Tibet. This was the epoch in which Tibetan Buddhist thought and practice coalesced, the peak of exegetical writing activity. In this period, Tibetan scholars gained the confidence to assert their own interpretations of the Buddhist culture imported from India, and to form their own styles of Tibetan Buddhism.

In addition to Tsongkhapa, polymaths in other schools, including Ngorchen Kunga Sangpo and Longchen Rapjampa,[177] attempted to formulate coherent systems on the basis of a large variety of scriptural sources. A perfectly systematic presentation required that these scholars include multiple disputations in their works and distance themselves from the methods of several of their Indian and Tibetan predecessors. Moreover, the uniform structures created

174. On polemical literature in Tibet, see, for example, Lopez 1996, Martin 2001, Cabezón and Dargyay 2007, Hugon 2012, and Viehbeck 2014.

175. Tib. *'phags lugs*.

176. Some of the points of disagreement will be noted below.

177. Klong chen rab 'byams pa (1308–1363/4).

by these different scholars could not be identical, though there is evidence that some of them read one another's works.[178]

Though the tradition of the *Guhyasamāja Tantra* is known to members of all Tibetan Buddhist schools, the sādhana manuals for the actual meditations used by the different schools are not identical. Furthermore, there are numerous variations on the practice of the Guhyasamāja even among the Indian Tantric works in Sanskrit. Tibetan masters were aware of the troubling fact that the three well-accepted scriptural authorities for the practice of the creation stage of the Guhyasamāja according to the Ārya tradition[179] do not prescribe one and the same practice, and that even the two works attributed to Nāgārjuna do not describe identical meditations. This clearly suggests that the task of Tibetan lamas who sought to establish a systematized and reasoned method of this practice—one well supported by scriptural authorities—would not be an easy one. It is not surprising, then, that a variety of solutions were offered, not always in accord with one another.

Tibetan scholars of different schools who compiled their own manuals for the meditation on the creation stage of the Guhyasamāja did so not only on the basis of Indian works found in the Tibetan canon and the tradition they received from their own teachers, but also through the use of reasoning. Reasoning was important for justifying their choices among the diverse possibilities. Some scholars composed explanatory works on the practice in which they presented reasoned arguments to support their own system and reject the interpretations of others.

However, the refutations of the positions of other scholars in these explanatory works are often not as straightforward as we might like them to be, partly because in accordance with the Tibetan tradition, earlier Tibetan lamas are not explicit about the identities of the writers whom they criticize. It was permissible to mention the names of writers belonging to certain groups commonly accepted as heretical, but the more interesting discussions are among scholars of the same tradition. Occasionally, Tibetan lamas supply certain hints as to the identity of their opponents; however, not a few of the keys to identification have long since been lost to the Tibetan tradition. At other times, Tibetan lamas cite opponents' positions in sufficient detail for those who might wish to identify them to do so. Apparently, lamas of the time or soon after could still tell who these opponents were; however, later generations

178. See Bentor 2017a.

179. These are the *Mdor byas*, *Piṇḍīkrama Sādhana* or *Piṇḍīkṛta Sādhana*, and the *Mdo bsre*, *Sādhanasūtramelāpaka* by Nāgārjuna, as well as the *Rnam gzhag rim pa*, *Samājasādhanavyavastholi* by Nāgabuddhi.

took less interest in their specific identities. Regardless, in most of these works, no names are mentioned.

Thus, in this process of systematization, any criticism of a former lama within one's own school was vigilantly concealed. This forces us to read the writings of the criticized and criticizing lamas attentively in order to discover their points of disagreement. A careful, comparative reading of different works on the same subject makes the convoluted affiliations apparent and sheds light on the reasons for the differing approaches. Such an investigation enables twenty-first-century readers not only to understand the points of dispute but also to further investigate the ways in which members of one tradition defend the positions of their own former lamas when criticized by another school. In this way, we can follow the fascinating dynamics of the coalescence of classical systems of Tibetan Buddhism.

For Tsongkhapa, the great systematizer, all aspects of Buddhism had to work together—sūtra with tantra, creation stage with completion stage, and so on—and all of them needed to work according to reason. In order to turn all aspects of Buddhism in his writings into one coherent whole, he had no choice but to modify to various extents the traditions that preceded him. We will investigate how Tsongkhapa formed the method that eventually became the tradition of the creation stage of the *Guhyasamāja Tantra* as understood and practiced by the Geluk school.

In his various writings on the creation stage, Tsongkhapa explains and defends his position regarding the practice of this meditation by supplying numerous scriptural authorities and reasonings, meanwhile arguing against certain traditions of other Tibetan lamas. These arguments reveal how and why Tsongkhapa saw the creation stage differently from other writers. Although Tsongkhapa does not identify his opponents by name, we are able to identify the targets of his barbs when he directly quotes or very closely paraphrases their opinions. But Tsongkhapa did not always write explicitly against his close teachers in the lineage of the *Guhyasamāja Tantra*.[180] At times, Khedrup Jé hints further at the identities of the adversaries—for instance, by quoting them at length. For this reason, and because its orderly structure corresponds to the sequence of the practice, Khedrup Jé's *Ocean of Attainments* is a valuable framework for our discussion.

In *Ocean of Attainments*, Khedrup Jé gathered a number of Tsongkhapa's explanations of the creation stage of the Guhyasamāja. These explanations are scattered throughout Tsongkhapa's numerous works on the path of mantra or Vajrayāna in general, on the cycle of the *Guhyasamāja Tantra*, and on

180. For Tsong kha pa's lineage of the Guhyasamāja, see Tsong kha pa, *Mtha' gcod*, 38b2–39a3.

the creation stage. Khedrup Jé paid special attention to cases in which Tsongkhapa disagreed with the positions of others and arranged these explanations and disapprovals according to the steps of the creation stage.

Due to Khedrup Jé's emphasis on disagreements, *Ocean of Attainments* contains more than one hundred points of dispute with SOME PEOPLE[181] and they are at times severely criticized. Yet only a minority of these attacks are the original criticism of Khedrup Jé himself. The vast majority of the points of dispute can be found in the writings of Tsongkhapa and of the Indian and Tibetan authors who preceded him.

The points of dispute amassed by Khedrup Jé in his *Ocean of Attainments* are a convenient basis for our attempt to better understand the formation of coherent tantric traditions in Tibet in the fourteenth to fifteenth centuries, with special attention given to the Sakya and Geluk schools.

One of my major tasks in this book has been to identify the numerous unnamed opponents mentioned in the text. It is often easier to locate disagreements between scholars belonging to different schools and in this way to track down innovations, since Tibetan scholars may point to controversial issues in their criticisms of other schools. However, as has already been observed, some of the most severe criticisms are directed toward authors who explain the practice of the *Guhyasamāja Tantra* according to the Ārya tradition, the tradition to which Tsongkhapa and Khedrup Jé belong. In fact, as we will see, most of the unnamed opponents appear in the lists of transmissions received[182] of these Geluk scholars, and even in the lineage prayer in the very sādhana of the Guhyasamāja used by members of the Geluk school. This is not something that most would normally expect.

In lieu of names, the scholars under attack are referred to as "some people," "early lamas," "early Tibetan lamas," "some lamas of the Tibetan Guhyasamāja," "some unlearned Tibetans," "some later lamas," "some lamas," and so on.[183] Thus, though nameless, they are called by a variety of designations that often provide hints as to their identities.

On the whole, Tsongkhapa and Khedrup Jé disagree with four major opponents in the context of the creation stage of the Guhyasamāja: Gö Khukpa

181. Tib. *kha cig*.

182. Tib. *gsan yig*.

183. Tib. *kha cig*, *bla ma snga ma*, *bod kyi bla ma snga ma*, *bod kyi 'dus pa'i bla ma kha cig*, *bod kyi ma sbyangs pa kha cig*, *phyis kyi bla ma kha cig*, and *bla ma kha cig*.

Lhetsé,[184] Butön Rinchen Drup, Rendawa Shönu Lodrö,[185] and Ngorchen Kunga Sangpo. Occasionally, members of the Ngok[186] tradition[187] are also criticized. Gö Khukpa Lhetsé, who composed the *Quintessential Elucidation of the Guhyasamāja Practice*,[188] one of the early important works on the Guhyasamāja—is at times referred to as one of the "early lamas."[189] Butön Rinchen Drup—especially his commentary on Nāgārjuna's *Concise Sādhana*,[190] one of the main sādhanas of the creation stage of the Guhyasamāja—is often dubbed "one of the later lamas." Thus these designations are not arbitrary.

At the same time, Tsongkhapa also names Gö Khukpa Lhetsé as one of the "Tibetans who were learned in the Guhyasamāja"[191] or as "some former spiritual teachers,"[192] and Khedrup Jé also calls him one of the "early and later Tibetans who were learned in the Guhyasamāja."[193] Gö Khukpa Lhetsé passed away long before Tsongkhapa was born, while Butön died seven years after Tsongkhapa's birth, so he never met either scholar. The relations between Tsongkhapa and Rendawa, who criticized each other, were more complex.

Rendawa was one of Tsongkhapa's most important teachers of the theory and practice of the *Guhyasamāja Tantra*. By the year 1390, Rendawa had probably already written his famous commentary on the *Guhyasamāja Tantra*,[194] which he taught to his disciples, including Tsongkhapa and Khedrup Jé. In

184. 'Gos Khug pa lhas btsas (eleventh century) played a role in the translation and revision of the *Guhyasamāja Tantra* (for details see the colophon at the end of the seventeenth chapter of the *Guhyasamāja Tantra*). He is the author of *Gsang 'dus stong thun*, one of the earliest Tibetan treatises on the central practices of the Guhyasamāja. For a sketch of his life and works, see Ko zhul and Rgyal ba 1992, 346–347. See also Tsong kha pa, *Rim lnga gsal sgron*, 34a2–b2; Kilty 2013, 75; and the *Blue Annals*, Roerich 1979, 360–361.

185. Red mda' ba Gzhon nu blo gros (1348–1412).

186. Rngog or Rdog.

187. Collected in Gser sdings pa Gzhon nu 'od, *Slob brgyud dang bcas pa'i gsung 'bum*.

188. 'Gos Khug pa lhas btsas, *Gsang 'dus stong thun*, 13b3–4.

189. For example, Mkhas grub rje, *Bskyed rim dngos grub rgya mtsho*, 82b6, 102b2, 105b1, 111a6, and 115a5.

190. Bu ston, *Gsang ba 'dus pa'i sgrub thabs mdor byas kyi rgya cher bshad pa bskyed rim gsal byed*.

191. Tib. *bod kyi 'dus pa la sbyangs pa rnams*. Tsong kha pa, *Rnam gzhag rim pa'i rnam bshad*, 46a4.

192. Tib. *sngon dus kyi bshes gnyen kha cig*. Tsong kha pa, *Rnam gzhag rim pa'i rnam bshad*, 27b2.

193. Tib. *bod kyi 'dus pa la sbyangs pa snga phyi gzhan dag*. Mkhas grub rje, *Bskyed rim dngos grub rgya mtsho*, 81a2.

194. Red mda' ba, *Gsang ba 'dus pa'i 'grel pa sgron ma gsal ba dang bcas pa'i bshad sbyar yid kyi mun sel*.

the winter of 1401–1402,[195] it was Tsongkhapa who taught the *Illuminating Lamp* to Rendawa. Soon after, in 1404,[196] while Rendawa was in a strict retreat in western Tibet, Tsongkhapa wrote a work[197] in which he criticized Rendawa, among others. Later still, Rendawa wrote a reply[198] that in turn provoked a fierce response by Tsongkhapa's disciple, Khedrup Jé.[199]

Gö, Butön, and Rendawa, as well as members of the Ngok family and Serdingpa Shönu Ö,[200] appear in the lineage of Tsongkhapa's teachers of the Guhyasamāja in his own *Record of Teachings Received*[201] and *Precious Sprout.*[202] These lamas, moreover, are included in the lineage prayers at the opening of the Guhyasamāja sādhana used by the Geluk school, and are among the recipients of the offering made toward the end of the practice.[203] Hence, some of the same teachers that Tsongkhapa and Khedrup Jé worshipped while meditating on the Guhyasamāja sādhana are those whom they sharply criticize in their treatises on the practice.

The dispute between Khedrup Jé and Ngorchen Kunga Sangpo is especially well known.[204] Indeed, to indicate his target, the title Khedrup Jé chose for his composition, *Ocean of Attainments,* is identical to the poetic name of Ngorchen's Guhyasamāja sādhana,[205] a fact that did not escape the attention of the Sakya scholars. As we will see, in the *Ocean of Attainments* Khedrup Jé replies to criticism made by Ngorchen against Tsongkhapa in Ngorchen's own *Ocean of Attainments,* as well in other works.

Debates between early Geluk and contemporaneous Sakya scholars arose not only because of disagreements between these two groups. At times, Sakya scholars were in complete accord with Tsongkhapa and his disciples on a particular subject, but felt an obligation to defend the five forefathers of the Sakya

195. For this and the following dates, see Roloff 2009, 289–296.

196. See Tshe tan zhabs drung 1982, 211; Jinpa 2019, 387.

197. Tsong kha pa, *Rnam gzhag rim pa'i rnam bshad.*

198. Red mda' ba, *Bla ma bsgrub pa dpal zhus lan.*

199. Mkhas grub rje, *Bskyed rim dngos grub rgya mtsho.*

200. Gser sdings pa Gzhon nu 'od (probably late twelfth century).

201. *Gsan yig,* 3a6–5a6.

202. Tsong kha pa, *Mtha' gcod rin chen myu gu,* 39a5–b6.

203. Tsong kha pa, *Gsang mngon,* 5b1–5 and 70b4–71b1.

204. van der Kuijp 1985a and 1985c; Davidson 1991, 221–222; Heimbel 2017b; and Bentor 2017b.

205. Ngor chen, *Gsang ba 'dus pa'i dkyil 'khor gyi sgrub pa'i thabs dngos grub rgya mtsho,* work 106.

tradition against Geluk criticism. The contemporary Sakya scholars might have also disagreed with their forefathers on that topic, yet still perceived these disapprovals as attacks on their own Sakya school. Moreover, since the contemporary Sakya scholars could not openly express their differences with the founders of their tradition, they found themselves in an uncomfortable position. We will look at several situations of this kind.

Yet not all the opponents were Tibetan teachers. There were also inherited opponents, to use the terminology of Pascale Hugon,[206] who were already criticized by earlier Tibetans as well as by Indic scholars. In other words, the attacks against the inherited opponents were not new, but rather ongoing criticism maintained by the tradition. Thus, in our context, these are not original positions raised by Tsongkhapa in his own writings but earlier points of dispute collected by Khedrup Jé in his *Ocean of Attainments.*

Another type of opponent in these works is a rhetorical assertion made to clarify a point. The celebrated Buddhist culture of oral debate made its way into written works, which raised such queries and provided answers. At times, these queries took on a life of their own, assuming the form of an actual, anonymous person known as "someone."

In the following chapters, we will delve into some of the more important topics on which Tsongkhapa differed from earlier Tibetan lamas, as well as certain modifications introduced by Tsongkhapa in his *Guhyasamāja Sādhana* in order to create the coherent system of Buddhist thought that he saw as most fundamental. We should note that Tsongkhapa was certainly an innovator within the constraints allotted by the Tibetan tradition. However, we should not lose sight of the lengthy process of coalescence during the classical period of the Tibetan tradition before him.

Among the scholars of the Guhyasamāja sādhanas of the Ārya tradition who preceded Tsongkhapa was Butön Rinchen Drup. Butön lived between two eras: the end of the translation of Buddhist works from Indian languages, and the beginning of the systematization and development of the unique Tibetan Buddhist tradition, to which he contributed significantly. There is no doubt that Butön laid the ground for a consistent system linking the grounds, path, and fruit of the Guhyasamāja sādhanas. But Butön was perhaps too early in the coalescence of the Tibetan tradition. Tsongkhapa, who lived about two generations later, was able to take another groundbreaking step that brought the system of the Guhyasamāja sādhanas to a new level of coherence.

In the introduction to his *Ocean of Attainments,* Khedrup Jé states his purpose in composing this work:

206. See Hugon 2012 on inherited opponents and new opponents.

> My glorious holy teacher [Tsongkhapa]—the essence of Vajradhara—explained how to practice on the path of the glorious *Guhyasamāja Tantra*...[207] But since Tsongkhapa did not compose a work that analyzes in detail the reasons and so forth why each and every step of the sādhana should be practiced in a particular way, so that those with inferior minds will be made to understand, the arrogant ones who claim that they have superior intellect will lose all their doubts, the fortunate ones will develop their comprehension, and so that I too will not forget the teachings of my venerable lama, I will explain the reasons for each and every step of the sādhana, and the order of the visualizations, adorned with transmitted instruction.[208]

207. Here Mkhas grub rje expands on some of Tsong kha pa's writings.

208. Mkhas grub rje, *Bskyed rim dngos grub rgya mtsho*, 4b3–6.

3. The Guhyasamāja Sādhana

The Relationship between the Guhyasamāja Tantra *and Its Sādhanas*

In his book *The Buddhist Tantras,* Alex Wayman asks: "The final point is whether anyone, just by reading a tantra (say the *Guhyasamāja Tantra*) knows what the work is talking about, and how its procedures, say of initiation, are actually conducted."[209] In reviewing this book, Reginald Ray was of the opinion that "[t]he Tantras embody what the practitioners actually do... [O]ur understanding of the Vajrayāna cult itself must always be based on a study and interpretation of the Tantras themselves."[210] Ten years before them, Matsunaga pointed out that the fact that six explanatory tantras of the *Guhyasamāja Tantra* appeared not long after the appearance of the *Guhyasamāja Tantra* may indicate that there were already gaps between the practice and the text of the tantra at that time.[211]

The great differences between the *Guhyasamāja Tantra* and its practices did not escape the attention of traditional authors in Tibet. In his commentary on the *Vajrajñānasamuccaya Tantra,* Tsongkhapa offers an explanation for the relations between the *Guhyasamāja Root Tantra,* its explanatory tantras, and its practice:

> Query: While the *Guhyasamāja Root Tantra* could have explicitly taught the practice, it does not do so. So why do the explanatory tantras teach it?
>
> Reply: The *Guhyasamāja Root Tantra* conceals the practice and does not teach it explicitly so that you will need to rely on its explanatory tantras, and also so that in [relying on the explanatory tantras] you will depend on a guru who knows to explain by correlating [the explanatory tantras] with the *Guhyasamāja Root Tantra.* This is in

209. Wayman 1973, 62.

210. Ray 1974, 123.

211. Matsunaga 1964, 25.

> order to prevent you from engaging in the tantra independently without properly venerating your guru, because pleasing your guru in every way for a long time is the basis for accomplishments in the Mantra Vehicle.[212]

Khedrup Jé provides a similar explanation:

> To ensure that you will rely on a master, Vajradhara[213] concealed various portions of the creation stage in the *Guhyasamāja Tantra* and did not teach them explicitly. Neither did he teach various parts of the practice in a single section of the tantra but scattered them randomly throughout the tantra from beginning to end. Therefore you should learn the meaning of the creation stage [...] through the transmitted instruction of the guru, who has followed explanatory tantras, such as the *Later Tantra*,[214] the *Vajra Garland Tantra*,[215] and so forth.[216]

These early Geluk authors acknowledge the disparity between the *Guhyasamāja Tantra*, the explanatory tantras, and the practice. The explanatory tantras serve as a bridge between the *Guhyasamāja Tantra* and the practice; still another imperative mediator for the yogi is the guru, who is informed by the transmitted instructions of the lineage. On the one hand, gurus are bound by the tradition, but on the other, they are given a certain amount of freedom in their explanations of the practice. It is not surprising, then, that both the *Guhyasamāja Tantra* and its sādhanas continued to evolve in India, and that the Tibetan Tengyur contains multiple different practice manuals, or sādhanas, for the *Guhyasamāja Tantra*. The differences among these sādhanas were acknowledged by the tradition itself—at least in the Tibetan canon—since they, as well as other treatises on the *Guhyasamāja Tantra*, are arranged according to different schools of the *Guhyasamāja Tantra*. Though the total

212. Tsong kha pa, *Ye rdor ṭīkā*, 47a2–4.

213. Vajradhara, Rdo rje 'chang, is considered to be the teacher (*ston pa*) of the *Guhyasamāja Tantra*.

214. The *Rgyud phyi ma*, *Uttara Tantra*, Tōh 443, one of the explanatory tantras of the *Guhyasamāja Tantra*, which at times is taken to be the eighteenth chapter of the *Guhyasamāja Tantra*.

215. This is *Rgyud rdo rje phreng ba*, *Vajramālā Tantra*, Tōh 445. An English translation in Kittay 2011.

216. Mkhas grub rje, *Bskyed rim dngos grub rgya mtsho*, 13b5–6.

number of Indian schools of the *Guhyasamāja* is uncertain, two of the more famous among them are the Jñānapāda and Ārya Schools.[217]

This situation created a difficulty: If there is more than one way to engage in the practice of a given tantra, how can the authenticity and authority of a given sādhana manual be determined? On what grounds were the early Indian sādhanas of the *Guhyasamāja Tantra* composed? Moreover, which of these numerous sādhanas is authentic? This fluidity of development is also signaled by the fact that sādhanas were written not only by Indian gurus but also by Tibetan lamas. During most of the second millennium CE, Tibetan aspirants engaged in Guhyasamāja sādhanas written by members of their own school or subschool. It is thus not surprising that Tibetan lamas during the fifteenth century could not agree on how to practice the Guhyasamāja sādhana.

The Guhyasamāja Sādhanas of the Ārya School

As Khedrup Jé writes about the sādhana of the Ārya school, we will limit our survey of Guhyasamāja sādhanas to this school alone. It is worth noticing that, back in the 1960s, Matsunaga suggested that the explanatory tantras of the *Guhyasamāja* were composed by members of the Ārya school in order to provide canonical authority to their own sādhanas.[218] This school carries the name of its founder, Ārya Nāgārjuna, who composed two Guhyasamāja sādhanas: the *Concise Sādhana*[219] and the *Sādhana Incorporating the Scripture*.[220] Though these two works, attributed to the same author, might be expected to prescribe one and the same practice, this is not the case, as already mentioned. Given that the disparities between Indian sādhanas were such that even sādhanas written by the same master were incompatible, it is hardly surprising that different traditions for the practice of the Guhyasamāja developed in Tibet.

Nāgārjuna's *Concise Sādhana* is the basic sādhana of the Ārya tradition of the Guhyasamāja, written in verses and thus suitable for recitation. Yet it has not been used in the actual practice in Tibet for hundreds of years; only manuals written by Tibetan authors have been used. Verses from the *Guhyasamāja Tantra* are incorporated in the *Concise Sādhana*, though without being marked as such. The *Sādhana Incorporating the Scripture*, on the other hand, explicitly identifies specific lines in the *Guhyasamāja Tantra* that

217. See Tanemura 2015, 328.

218. Matsunaga 1964, 25.

219. Nāgārjuna, *Mdor byas*, *Piṇḍīkrama Sādhana* or *Piṇḍīkṛta Sādhana*, Tōh 1796; de La Vallée Poussin 1896 and Tripathi 2001.

220. Nāgārjuna, *Mdo bsre*, *Sādhanasūtramelāpaka*, Tōh 1797.

pertain to individual steps of the practice, as its name indicates. These lines, Khedrup Jé informs us, are concealed and scattered randomly throughout the tantra. By revealing these hidden connections, not only does Nāgārjuna clarify the relation between the tantra and the practice, but he also demonstrates the authenticity of the sādhana. Since it is based on the *Guhyasamāja Tantra*, the practice is genuine.

Yet which of the two sādhanas by Nāgārjuna is genuine? Tibetan writings offer different ways of dealing with such variance. In his attempt to create a consistent and harmonious system, Tsongkhapa mostly ignores the disparities between the two works of Nāgārjuna. He notes that these two authoritative works have different roles. While the *Concise Sādhana* instructs on the actual meditations, the *Sādhana Incorporating the Scripture* establishes the scriptural authority for these meditations in the *Guhyasamāja Tantra*.[221] In his various works on the practice of the Guhyasamāja, Tsongkhapa cites and refers to both of Nāgārjuna's sādhanas. No doubt he recognized the incompatibilities but chose not to highlight them.

The Sakya scholar Ngorchen Kunga Sangpo likewise made significant efforts to formulate a coherent structure. However, he devoted a short work to what he calls "slight differences" between Nāgārjuna's two sādhanas.[222] In this treatise, appended to his own sādhana of the Guhyasamāja,[223] Ngorchen points out slightly different methods[224] in the "higher yoga,"[225] the third of the four yogas that build the practice according to Nāgārjuna's two sādhanas. After discussing these differences, Ngorchen concludes:

> Therefore it seems that the later lamas,[226] who wrote many inadequate explanations by only taking into account one method of the "higher yoga," did not investigate this matter in detail.[227]

Tsongkhapa is likely included among these "later lamas." Ngorchen's work is dated to 1423, four years after Tsongkhapa's death and just before or at the

221. Tsong kha pa, *Rnam gzhag rim pa'i rnam bshad*, 4a6–b2.

222. Ngor chen, *Shin tu rnal 'byor gyi khyad par sgrub thabs kyi yan lag tu bris pa*, work 107, 204b2–206a5.

223. Ngor chen, *Gsang ba 'dus pa'i dkyil 'khor gyi sgrub pa'i thabs dngos grub rgya mtsho*, work 106, 184a1–204b2.

224. Tib. *tshul cung zad mi 'dra ba gnyis*.

225. Tib. *shin tu rnal 'byor*, Skt. *atiyoga*.

226. Tib. *phyis kyi bla ma rnams*.

227. Ngor chen, *Shin tu rnal 'byor gyi khyad par sgrub thabs kyi yan lag tu bris pa*, 206a5.

same time that Khedrup Jé composed the work translated here.[228] The divergence between Nāgārjuna's two sādhanas will be described below; first, we must address additional sādhanas of the Ārya school of the Guhyasamāja.

The *Vajrasattva Sādhana*[229] by Candrakīrti was another important Guhyasamāja sādhana of the Ārya tradition, written, according to tradition, by the famous disciple of the author of the first basic sādhana. Two Indian masters, Tathāgatarakṣita and Līlavajra, wrote commentaries on it.[230] In his commentary on the *Concise Sādhana*, Muniśrībhadra[231] acknowledges that this work was written by Candrakīrti.[232] The authenticity of the *Vajrasattva Sādhana* has nevertheless been debated.

According to Rendawa Shönu Lodrö, a teacher of both Tsongkhapa and Khedrup Jé, the author of the *Vajrasattva Sādhana* is not the renowned Candrakīrti but another person of the same name. Rendawa asks: "While Ārya Nāgārjuna himself wrote a very clear sādhana such as the *Concise Sādhana*, how is it possible that Glorious Candrakīrti did nothing other than putting it into prose?"[233] Rendawa is here referring to the fact that whereas the *Concise Sādhana* is written in verses conducive to recitation, the *Vajrasattva Sādhana*'s prescriptions are written in prose. Likewise, Ngorchen Kunga Sangpo maintains that the *Vajrasattva Sādhana* was written by a second Candrakīrti.[234]

Candrakīrti's *Vajrasattva Sādhana* is more than just a sādhana. Not only does it offer instruction on the practice, it also identifies specific lines of the

228. As noted, Mkhas grub rje's work includes criticism against Ngor chen.

229. Candrakīrti, *Rdo rje sems dpa'i sgrub thabs*, *Vajrasattva Sādhana*, Tōh 1814, 195b6–204b6; Sanskrit and Tibetan editions in Luo and Tomabechi 2009.

230. Tathāgatarakṣita, *Rdo rje sems dpa'i sgrub pa'i thabs kyi bshad pa*, *Vajrasattvasādhanavyākhyā*, Tōh 1835, 280b2–285b4. Līlavajra, *Rdo rje sems dpa'i sgrub thabs kyi 'grel pa*, *Vajrasattvasādhananibandha*, Tōh 1815, 204b6–209a3.

231. *Rim pa lnga'i don mdor bshad pa*, *Pañcakramaṭippaṇī*, Tōh 1813, 152b3; Jiang and Tomabechi 1996, 11.

232. As Toru Tomabechi pointed out to me on April 22, 2016, at Taisho University, in his commentary on the *Pradīpoddyotana*, Bhavyakīrti explains that the sādhana referred to in the line *sādhanopayikāyāṃ kṛta eva*, *sgrub pa'i thabs su byas pa nyid* (in Tōh 1785, 21b4, Chakravarti 1984, 37) could be either the *Piṇḍīkrama* or Candrakīrti's own work (presumably the *Vajrasattva Sādhana*), *Rab tu sgron gsal*, *Prakāśikā*, Tōh 1793, 139a3–4. Hence, there is an indication by another Indian master that Candrakīrti could be the author of the *Vajrasattva Sādhana*.

233. Red mda' ba, *Bla ma bsgrub pa dpal bas zhus pa'i lan*, Kathmandu, 51a4–5; TBRC, 306b.

234. Ngor chen, *Shin tu rnal 'byor gyi khyad par sgrub thabs kyi yan lag tu bris pa*, 206a3.

Guhyasamāja Tantra that serve as scriptural authority for each step, similar to the *Sādhana Incorporating the Scripture*. The Sakya scholar Amyé Shap[235] finds incompatibilities between the *Vajrasattva Sādhana* and the *Sādhana Incorporating the Scripture* with regard to scriptural attribution for stages of the meditation in the *Guhyasamāja Tantra*. Hence, he argues that the *Vajrasattva Sādhana* could not have been written by the well-known Candrakīrti, and that the attribution of this text to him in the colophon is a mistake. Amyé Shap does not dispute the Indic origin of this sādhana, but in following the *Record of Teachings Received* of Sakya Paṇḍita,[236] he maintains that the *Vajrasattva Sādhana* was composed by Prajñākaragupta.[237]

On the other hand, the early Geluk scholars do not doubt the authorship of the well-known Candrakīrti.[238] Khedrup Jé objects to Rendawa's position that the *Vajrasattva Sādhana* is merely a prosified version of the *Concise Sādhana* and argues against the claim that anything of value in the *Vajrasattva Sādhana* is likewise already present in Nāgārjuna's sādhanas. According to Khedrup Jé, the *Vajrasattva Sādhana* contains many specific points not found in Nāgārjuna's two sādhanas, as well as a variety of explanations on how to apply the steps of the meditation to the *Guhyasamāja Tantra*. Moreover, he says, there is no indication whatsoever that it was not written by Candrakīrti.[239]

It is interesting to note that, although for both Tsongkhapa and Khedrup Jé a sādhana by Candrakīrti must belong to the Ārya school of the Guhyasamāja, whose theoretical grounds are Prāsaṅgika Madhyamaka, in none of these arguments is a reference made to the line in the *Vajrasattva Sādhana* that instructs the yogi to meditate on Mind Only.[240]

The last of the four basic texts of the Ārya tradition of the Guhyasamāja is *Formulating the Sādhana*[241] by Nāgabuddhi.[242] By and large, its authenticity

235. A myes zhabs Ngag dbang kun dga' bsod nams (1597–1659/60), *Gsang 'dus chos byung*, 18a2–5.

236. Rin chen dpal, *Dpal ldan Sa skya Paṇḍita'i rnam thar*, 45b6.

237. Shes rab 'byung gnas sbas pa.

238. See Tsong kha pa, *Mtha' gcod*, 36a3–6; and *Rim lnga gsal sgron*, chap. 1, 30b1–4; an English translation in Kilty 2013, 66–67.

239. Mkhas grub rje, *Bskyed rim dngos grub rgya mtsho*, 14a3–4.

240. Candrakīrti, *Rdo rje sems dpa'i sgrub thabs*, *Vajrasattva Sādhana*, Tōh 1814, 199a5; Sanskrit and Tibetan editions in Luo and Tomabechi 2009, 15.7 and 47.17. See the section "The Moon and Mind Only" below.

241. Nāgabuddhi, *Rnam par gzhag rim*, *Vyavastholi*, Tōh 1809, 121a5–131a5; Sanskrit and Tibetan editions in Tanaka 2016. The term *oli* is a Middle Indic form of āvali, an equivalent of *krama*, and *vyavastholi* corresponds to the Tibetan *rnam gzhag rim pa*. See Szántó 2016, 440.

242. On the names Nāgabuddhi/Nāgabodhi, see van der Kuijp 2007 and Sinclair 2016.

is accepted by Tibetan authors, though their interpretations of this work differ. *Formulating the Sādhana* is not a mere sādhana; it also portrays parallels between steps of the meditation and events that occur periodically in both the cosmos and the individual. In other words, *Formulating the Sādhana* refers to the creations and destructions of the world, as well as birth, death, and the intermediate state during the lives of sentient beings. These macro- and microcosmic parallels imbue the steps of the sādhana with new meanings in relation to the cosmic whole and the particular individual.

To give examples of the parallels *Formulating the Sādhana* draws with cosmological events: It relates the meditation on emptiness at the beginning of the main part of the sādhana to the destruction of the universe by the seven suns that burn the entire three realms.[243] Then it correlates the visualization of the celestial mansion of the maṇḍala to the cyclical creation of the universe. With regard to the individual, *Formulating the Sādhana* links death and the intermediate state to the death of the first people in the eon, and the issuing intermediate state with a special reference to the bodhisattva who had only one birth remaining before reaching awakening. Still, these parallels are not always as straightforward as we would wish, and thus they open the door for different readings. For this reason, Tibetan masters once again vary in their understanding of the new meanings acquired by the individual steps of the sādhana through their connections to specific macro- and microcosmic events.

Dissimilarities among Guhyasamāja Sādhanas of the Ārya School

Before parallels can be drawn between individual steps of the sādhana and further elements, these steps and their sequence must be established. However, the four basic sādhanas that are regarded as the authoritative manuals of the Ārya tradition do not prescribe identical practices. The differences are not always minor; for instance, these sādhanas diverge with regard to the identity of the principal deities[244] at the center of the maṇḍala visualized during the main part of the practice,[245] consisting of the four yogas.[246] In Nāgārjuna's

243. Nāgabuddhi, *Rnam gzhag rim pa*, *Vyavastholi*, chap. 1, Tōh 1809, 121b4–5; Tanaka 2016, 80–81.

244. Tib. *gtso bo*.

245. Tib. *dngos gzhi*.

246. These are yoga, subsequent yoga, higher yoga, and great yoga; Tib. *rnal 'byor*, *rjes su rnal 'byor*, *shin tu rnal 'byor*, and *rnal 'byor chen po*; Skt. *yoga*, *anuyoga*, *atiyoga*, and *mahāyoga*.

Concise Sādhana, yogis first visualize themselves as the First Lord,[247] and later this deity transforms into Vajrasattva;[248] thus, two deities are visualized altogether. In the second sādhana by Nāgārjuna, the *Sādhana Incorporating the Scripture*, the yogi arises as Vajradhara from the beginning of the main part.[249] However, we are told that, because at first the nature of Vajradhara's body is wisdom and as such he cannot act for the sake of sentient beings, he transforms into a visible body later in the sādhana. The *Vajrasattva Sādhana* and *Formulating the Sādhana*, by contrast, offer no hint of two deities or of two aspects of the same deity.[250] Furthermore, unlike the other sādhanas, the *Vajrasattva Sādhana* explicitly links three consecutive steps of the practice to the attainment of the three bodies of the Buddha. Tibetan scholars, however, debate the demarcations between these steps.

The Framework of the Guhyasamāja Sādhana

Various frameworks for the Guhyasamāja sādhana are found in Indian Buddhist tantras and treatises. Tsongkhapa's *Guhyasamāja Sādhana* and Khedrup Jé's *Ocean of Attainments* are structured on the basis of the three samādhis; these are the First Yoga,[251] the Supreme King of Maṇḍalas,[252] and the Supreme King of Deeds.[253] The goal of the entire sādhana is the attainment of the yogi's own awakening and assisting other sentient beings to attain awakening. The First Yoga is not merely a preparatory yoga but contains the core of the practice. Its purpose is the eventual attainment of buddhahood through the transformation of the yogi's ordinary existence into the three buddha bodies. The two samādhis that follow are practices for the sake of other sentient beings.

The First Yoga consists of three parts: the core practices aimed at the awakening of the yogis, practices that precede the core, and practices that follow it. *Ocean of Attainments* opens with Khedrup Jé's general observations on the

247. Tib. *dang po mgon po*, Skt. *ādinātha*. *Mdor byas*, *Piṇḍīkrama Sādhana*, Tōh 1796, 3b7–4a3, L 51–54.

248. Nāgārjuna, *Mdor byas*, *Piṇḍīkrama Sādhana*, Tōh 1796, 3b5–5b,2 L 46–93.

249. Nāgārjuna, *Mdo bsre*, *Sādhanasūtramelāpaka*, Tōh 1797, 12a5–13b2.

250. Candrakīrti, *Rdo rje sems dpa'i sgrub thabs*, *Vajrasattva Sādhana*, Tōh 1814, D 199a3–201b5, Luo and Tomabechi 2009, 15.3–23.8 and 47.11–56.18; and Nāgabuddhi, *Rnam gzhag rim pa*, *Vyavastholi*, chap. 1, Tōh 1809, 121a5–125a1; Tanaka 2016, 79–81.

251. Tib. *dang po sbyor ba*, Skt. *ādiyoga*.

252. Tib. *dkyil 'khor rgyal mchog*, Skt. *maṇḍalarājāgrī*.

253. Tib. *las kyi rgyal mchog*, Skt. *karmarājāgrī*.

Guhyasamāja Sādhana and continues with the First Yoga, to which Khedrup Jé devotes about two-thirds of the work's length.

In the translation below, additional frameworks for the sādhana are found. We have just encountered the division into four yogas found in the *Concise Sādhana* and the *Sādhana Incorporating the Scripture* by Nāgārjuna, as well as in the *Vajrasattva Sādhana* by Candrakīrti. The scriptural authority for this is found in the *Vajra Garland Tantra*.[254] The *Guhyasamāja*[255] and the *Later* tantras[256] divide the sādhana into four stages of familiarization and achievement: (1) familiarization, (2) approaching achievement, (3) achievement, and (4) great achievement.[257] This classification is used in the Jñānapāda school.[258]

Regarding the relation between the frameworks of the three samādhis and these two fourfold systems, the four yogas and the four stages of familiarization and achievement: Both fourfold systems correspond to the First Yoga alone and not to the Supreme King of Maṇḍalas and the Supreme King of Deeds. The *Vajra Garland Tantra*[259] mentions another framework that covers the entire sādhana, including the Supreme King of Maṇḍalas and the Supreme King of Deeds. On this basis, Tsongkhapa divides his sādhana into forty-nine essential points that cover the entire sādhana.[260] Khedrup Jé explains these four different frameworks of the sādhana and the relations among them at the end of *Ocean of Attainments*.[261]

254. *Rgyud rdo rje phreng ba*, *Vajramālā Tantra*, chap. 65, Tōh 445, 272a1–2.

255. *Gsang 'dus*, chap. 12, Tōh 442; Zhol 19a5–7; Stog 32b5–7; Fremantle 1971, vv. 61–64; Matsunaga 1978, vv. 60–63ab.

256. *Rgyud phyi ma*, *Uttara Tantra*, Tōh 443, 154a3; Matsunaga 1978, v. 136.

257. Tib. *bsnyen*, *nye sgrub*, *sgrub pa*, and *sgrub chen*; Skt. *sevā*, *upasādhana*, *sādhana*, and *mahāsādhana*.

258. Jñānapāda, *Yan lag bzhi pa'i sgrub thabs kun tu bzang mo*, *Caturaṅgasādhanasamantabhadrī*, Tōh 1856—a prose translation of the *Kun bzang sgrub thabs*, *Samantabhadra Sādhana*—has these four stages in its title. In his commentary on this work, Vaidyapāda applies these four stages. See his *Yan lag bzhi pa'i sgrub thabs kun tu bzang mo'i rnam par bshad pa*, *Caturaṅgasādhanasamantabhadrīṭīkā*, Tōh 1872.

259. *Rgyud rdo rje phreng ba*, *Vajramālā Tantra*, chap. 35, Tōh 445, 245a6–7.

260. Tib. *de nyid zhe dgu*.

261. Mkhas grub rje, *Bskyed rim dngos grub rgya mtsho*, 177b5–180b5; based on Tsong kha pa, *Bung ba'i re skong*, 1b4–4b2.

4. Meditation on Emptiness in the Creation Stage

THE EFFECTIVENESS of the meditation on the sādhana depends not only on tantric methods but also on general nontantric Mahāyāna practices, including bodhicitta, the mind for enlightenment,[262] and meditation on emptiness. All things animate or inanimate that take part in the sādhana, such as offerings, for example, must first shed their ordinary existence and arise in their special form out of the continuum of emptiness by means of visualization.

There are two major meditations on emptiness during the sādhana. The first, in the macrocosmic context, takes place prior to the core practices. The second, in the microcosmic context, is part of the yoga of taking death on the path that leads to the dharmakāya. The first meditation on emptiness is parallel to the periodic destructions of the world, while the second corresponds to deaths during the life cycle of human beings. Hence, both are liminal points at which the yogis visualize away their environment and bodies respectively, just before they create in their minds the celestial mansion of the maṇḍala and the deities dwelling there. In other words, this is a type of ritual death; the meditators erase their old world so that a new reality can arise.

Therefore, from the perspective of the practice, to meditate here on sheer nothingness would seem to be the most appropriate, but this is not permissible from the Madhyamaka point of view. For the vast majority of Tibetan writers, the Mantra Vehicle is part of the Mahāyāna, and the emptiness meditated upon during the sādhana is no different from the emptiness of the Madhyamaka school.[263] On the other hand, most Tibetan authors agree that the meditation on emptiness here is not entirely identical to the meditation on

262. Tib. *byang chub sems*, Skt. *bodhicitta*.

263. Not everyone agrees. For example, according to David Jackson, Sa skya Paṇḍita maintained that there is a separate Madhyamaka theory of tantra. See Jackson 1985, 28. On the other hand, Sa skya scholars nowadays do not accept such a difference.

emptiness of the Pāramitā Vehicle, but the extent to which these two meditations differ is subject to much debate.

Most tantric meditations on emptiness are accompanied by the recitation of one of the following mantras: *oṃ svabhāva śuddhāḥ sarva dharmāḥ svabhāva śuddho 'haṃ* or *oṃ śūnyatā jñāna vajra svabhāva ātmako 'haṃ*. However, the meditation on emptiness in the macrocosmic context is accompanied by one of the best-known verses of the *Guhyasamāja Tantra*, found in its second chapter, devoted to the mind for enlightenment. Here, the Tathāgata, whose name is Vajra Body, Speech, and Mind of All Tathāgatas, dwells in absorption and utters the following verse:

> *abhāve bhāvanābhāvo bhāvanā naiva bhāvanā* |
> *iti bhāvo na bhāvaḥ syād bhāvanā nopalabhyate* ||[264]

This verse is obviously mantra-like, alliterating[265] the sounds *bha*, *va*, and *na*. Moreover, it puns on the meanings derived from the root *bhū*. *Bhāva* can mean "being," "existing," "that which exists," "an entity," "an existing thing," and "all earthly objects." Thus *bhāva* indicates both a thing and a state of existence. In the first sense, it can be translated as an entity or a thing; in the second sense, as a state of existence, *bhāva* can mean existing and *abhāva* not existing. *Bhāvanā*, usually translated as meditation, is a noun in the causative form, and carries the meanings of "causing to be," "bringing into existence," "creating," and "producing."

The pun on the meaning of the nature of existence (*bhū*, *bhāva*) and of meditation (*bhāvanā*) in the sense of "causing to be" is germane at this point in the practice. The verse is recited immediately after yogis visualize away ordinary appearances, right before they begin to visualize the new reality of the maṇḍala. Here, they may reflect on the disappearance of their ordinary world and whether that world is "caused to be" by the mind—or they may ask themselves whether the maṇḍalic world exists, whether it is more real or less real than their ordinary world.

The meaning of the Sanskrit mantra is fluid and enigmatic, and the more one reflects on it, the more implications one finds. It is precisely this fluidity that serves as the basis for reflections during the meditation and, as I have shown elsewhere,[266] allows for a variety of interpretations throughout history. Still, this mantra is somewhat different from other mantras recited during this

264. On different readings of this verse, see Bentor 2009b, note 3.

265. Skt. *anuprāsa*.

266. See Bentor 2009b.

tantric practice, insofar as it has overt philosophical content—that is, it resembles verses from Buddhist philosophical treatises.

The pun on *bhū* and *bhāvanā* is lost when the Sanskrit verse is translated into other languages. The etymology of the Tibetan verb for "to meditate" (*sgom pa*) is not "to cause to be" but rather "to habituate." Still, in certain contexts the meaning of the Sanskrit word does carry through. Needless to say, an adequate translation into English is quite impossible. Moreover, a translation from Tibetan will necessarily be different from a translation from Sanskrit. I have chosen the following possibility for my translation of this verse in *Ocean of Attainments*: "In the absence of being, there is no meditation, and meditation cannot be meditated upon. Therefore a state of being that is nonbeing leaves no object for meditation."[267]

This verse appears, with small variations, in the *Concise Sādhana*, where Nāgārjuna introduces it with "You should meditate on the three worlds as devoid of intrinsic nature[268] in ultimate truth," and concludes "Uttering this verse, meditate on the nature of the animate and inanimate worlds as empty, and bless them through this yoga as the ground of wisdom."[269] Thus Nāgārjuna instructs the yogis to meditate on everything as empty, that is to say, ultimately devoid of intrinsic nature, or the ground of wisdom—a key term here. In writings on Madhyamaka, Nāgārjuna emphasizes that emptiness is that which makes change possible;[270] in the *Concise Sādhana*, emptiness is more explicitly understood as the ground or potential for all phenomena.

Hence, that into which yogis dissolve their entire ordinary world is the ground or potential for the arising of their special maṇḍalic world. In other words, the elimination of all appearances of the world and its inhabitants—to whatever extent the case may be—lays the ground for the special appearances of the maṇḍala during the creation stage. While in Madhyamaka terms this is called "emptiness," in *Formulating the Sādhana* Nāgabuddhi instructs the yogis to recite this verse in accordance with the destruction of the three realms at the end of the eon by the burning seven suns that turn everything "into the nature of space."[271] Yet the empty eon at the periodical end of the

267. Mkhas grub rje, *Bskyed rim dngos grub rgya mtsho*, 33a5–6.

268. Tib. *dngos po med par*, Skt. *niḥsvabhāva*.

269. Tib. *ye shes kyi sa*, Skt. *jñānabhūmi*. Nāgārjuna, *Mdor byas, Piṇḍīkrama Sādhana*, Tōh 1796, 2b3–5; L 16cd–18.

270. *Dbu ma rtsa ba, Mūlamadhyamakakārikā*, chap. 24, Tōh 3824, and *Rtsod pa bzlog pa, Vigrahavyāvartanīkārikā*, Tōh 3828, v. 70.

271. Nāgabuddhi, *Rnam gzhag rim pa, Vyavastholi*, chap. 1, Tōh 1809, 121b4–5, Tanaka 2016, 80–81.

world is understood not as a mere empty space but as possessing the potential to recreate the new world. In his commentary on *Formulating the Sādhana*, Tsongkhapa glosses the "meditation on the nature of space" as a "meditation on emptiness in correspondence with the destroyed world."[272] In another work, Tsongkhapa explains the meaning of "ground":

> As the space formed when the previous world is emptied serves as a support [or ground] for the evolution of the subsequent world, so the wisdom of great bliss serves as a support for the evolution of the celestial mansion, and therefore it is called the ground of wisdom.[273]

Still, the empty space that the meditation on emptiness corresponds to here, the state of the world during twenty intermediate eons, is described in the *Abhidharmakośa* as mere space.[274] This interpretation created discomfort among Tibetan scholars, and led to disagreements in which each side criticized the other for "negating too much" or "negating too little."

Gorampa's Critique

It is well known that Gorampa Sönam Sengé,[275] reputed for his philosophical writings on emptiness, criticized Tsongkhapa's interpretation of Madhyamaka.[276] Let us look at his work on the creation stage of the Guhyasamāja in the context of the meditation on emptiness. The question that concerns Gorampa is: What, if anything, remains after ordinary appearances are dissolved into emptiness? In other words, do any of the ordinary appearances eliminated during the meditation on emptiness reemerge later on? Gorampa takes to task some Tibetan scholars who purportedly fail to dissolve *all* phenomena into emptiness before creating the pure world of the maṇḍala in their minds. Addressing them, he says:

272. Tsong kha pa, *Rnam gzhag rim pa'i rnam bshad*, 58b1–2.

273. Tsong kha pa, *Bung ba'i re skong*, 11a6–b1. See also Mkhas grub rje, *Bskyed rim dngos grub rgya mtsho*, 43b3–5.

274. Tib. *nam mkha' tsam*, Skt. *ākāśamātra*. See Vasubandhu, *Mdzod 'grel, Kośabhāṣya*, chap. 3, v. 90cd, Tōh 4090, 156b4–157a4; Pradhan 1975, 179; Pruden 1988–1990, 477–478.

275. Bsod nams seng ge (1429–1489).

276. See Cabezón, in his introduction to the translation of Go rams pa's *Lta ba'i shan 'byed*, with Geshe Lobsang Dargyay 2007, 52–57, under the title *Freedom from Extremes*. Go rams pa's *Lta ba'i shan 'byed* was translated once more by Khenpo Jamyang Tenzin and Pauline Westwood, 2014.

> Some Tibetans who explain the Mantra Vehicle through their own fabrications, without transmitted instruction, say about the meaning of the meditation on emptiness for accumulating wisdom[277] that [meditators] must shed true existence with respect to appearances but should not remove the illusion-like appearances that do not truly exist. This is so because to remove them would be to depreciate conventional existence, a nihilistic view. Furthermore, since a nihilistic view causes sentient beings to be born in hell, it is unsuitable for accumulating wisdom.[278]

What Gorampa means here is that "some Tibetans" negate too little, or do not sufficiently eliminate "ordinary appearances," while meditating on emptiness during the creation stage. And because they eliminate only the true existence of appearances, but not the illusion-like appearances that do not truly exist, they fail in an essential precondition for the arising of the pure maṇḍala: the removal of *all* appearances. The reason that "some Tibetans" do not eliminate illusion-like appearances, according to Gorampa, is their conviction that this would constitute nihilistic emptiness and a depreciation of conventional existence.

Gorampa then presents arguments to refute the position of his opponents through a *reductio ad absurdum*. If "some Tibetans" fail to eliminate all appearances during their meditation on emptiness, removing only the true existence of appearances but not the appearances themselves, these appearances will resurface as soon as the meditation on emptiness is over:

> When you are a yogi sitting inside a small room meditating on a huge maṇḍala wheel of the celestial mansion and its deities, is this "small room" outside the celestial mansion or inside it? Is the cushion you have spread [for yourself] now found above the seat of the lotus, the lunar disk, and so on, or is it below it? Do the clothes you are wearing cover the many faces and arms you

277. Like other Sa skya authors, Go rams pa refers to the meditation on emptiness during the sādhana as "accumulation of wisdom."

278. Go rams pa, *Gsang ba 'dus pa'i sgrub thabs kun tu bzang po'i nyi 'od kyi don 'grel lam bzang gsal ba'i snang ba*, 18b2–5.

> meditate on or tightly enfold them? Please think this over carefully and then tell us.[279]

Here, Gorampa ridicules the notion that those aspects of ordinary reality that were not sufficiently eliminated during the meditation on emptiness might reappear during the visualization of the pure realm of the maṇḍala. Nor does he accept that appearances become cognitively blocked and temporarily imperceptible during the meditation on emptiness, only to reemerge when it is over.

Gorampa goes on to demonstrate that this position contradicts not only the experience of meditating on the creation stage, as indicated in the preceding citation, but also the authority of scriptures and the position of the opponents themselves, who maintain that the entire world and its inhabitants dissolve into clear-light-emptiness.

> Thus you contradict your own position, because (1) you yourself say that eliminating appearances in this way constitutes a nihilistic view that depreciates conventional existence and causes sentient beings to be born in hell, rather than serving as an appropriate means for meditation on the ground of wisdom [i.e., meditation on emptiness] and so forth; and (2) because it follows that meditation on the ground of wisdom and so forth can be a cause for destroying these appearances. What is the difference here?[280]

At the same time, Gorampa rejects the idea that all appearances are dissolved into nothingness during the meditation on emptiness in the creation stage, since this would imply either that they later reemerge without a cause or that present appearances are nonexistent, having all been annihilated.[281]

Gorampa thus avoids the following alternatives: (1) that during the meditation on emptiness all appearances are merely imperceptible at a cognitive level for a while, and (2) that they are obliterated into nothingness. Gorampa maintains, moreover, that the opponents themselves remove all appearances

279. Go rams pa, *Gsang ba 'dus pa'i sgrub thabs kun tu bzang po*, 19a3–5. Other Sa skya scholars such as A myes zhabs [writing in 1636]—emphasize that if ordinary appearances are not removed during the meditation on emptiness, then in arising from within the continuum of emptiness, the appearance of the deity will not dawn. See A myes zhabs, *Gsang 'dus dkyil 'khor sgrub thabs rnam bshad*, 63a5–6.

280. Go rams pa, *Gsang ba 'dus pa'i sgrub thabs kun tu bzang po*, 19b2–3.

281. Go rams pa, *Gsang ba 'dus pa'i sgrub thabs kun tu bzang po*, 18b5–19b1.

by dissolving them into clear-light-emptiness, and yet fault their proponents for doing so.

Gorampa must have had Tsongkhapa in mind when he repudiated "some Tibetans," but if we still have doubts as to the identity of Gorampa's unnamed opponents, Amyé Shap eradicates them when, paraphrasing the words of Gorampa cited above, he explicitly states that this is the position of the Riwo Gendenpa[282]—that is to say, the early Gelukpas.[283]

We still need to examine, however, whether Tsongkhapa did in fact claim that meditators should not eliminate illusion-like appearances during the creation stage, as Gorampa says of his opponent. This would not seem to be the case, since Tsongkhapa, too, instructs meditators to dissolve all appearances in the context of the creation stage:

> The Pāramitā Vehicle does not specify that while meditating on emptiness one must definitely dissolve appearances, but the Mantra Vehicle specifies that one must definitely do so.[284]

And:

> At the level of awareness which understands that in ultimate truth all phenomena do not exist at all, *all appearances cease.*[285]

According to Tsongkhapa, then, all appearances, including conventional ones, cease at this point in the creation-stage meditation on emptiness. My purpose here is not to defend Tsongkhapa against Gorampa's attacks, but to understand what is at stake in these discussions. As we recall, Gorampa states that the very persons who criticize their opponents for dissolving all appearances into clear-light-emptiness do so themselves. Hence, although Tsongkhapa instructs yogis to dissolve all appearances, this does not preclude him from being Gorampa's "some Tibetans."

Indeed, Tsongkhapa and Gorampa both stress that all appearances must be dissolved during this meditation on emptiness. Likewise, both maintain that it is not sufficient merely to dispel all appearances; one must meditate on emptiness in accordance with the view of the Madhyamaka. Gorampa stresses

282. Tib. *Ri bo dge ldan pa.*

283. A myes zhabs, *Gsang 'dus dkyil 'khor sgrub thabs rnam bshad,* 62a4.

284. Tsong kha pa, *Bskyed rim zin bris,* 15b1–2.

285. Tsong kha pa, *Bskyed rim zin bris,* 15a6; emphasis mine.

that yogis should meditate on the emptiness of essence and of cause and fruit, through the reasoning that phenomena are devoid of one and many.[286] Tsongkhapa similarly maintains that:

> While meditating on the meaning of the mantra *śūnyatā*, one should recollect the view of the Madhyamaka, and visualize all phenomena in the world and its inhabitants dissolving into clear light. Both are necessary, for it is meaningless to visualize the latter without meditating on the former.[287]

Consequently, both scholars share the opinion that during the creation stage, the yogi must both dissolve all appearances and meditate on emptiness as taught by the Madhyamaka school. As we have seen, the dissolution of all appearances makes sense in the context of the creation stage, while meditation on emptiness in accordance with the Madhyamaka's philosophical position is regarded as the foundation of the meditation. Thus both Gorampa and Tsongkhapa must tread a fine line between the two ways to meditate on emptiness in this context, in fact instructing yogis to meditate on each of the two. This is another case in which the line is ambiguous, and each side criticizes the other for falling into one or another of the extremes rather than straddling both.

But we have not reached the end of Gorampa's argument yet. Next, he speaks of "early Tibetans" (who were criticized by "some Tibetans" mentioned before):

> ["Some Tibetans" say,] without understanding this crucial point, "early Tibetans" think that through the practice of the so-called forceful[288] meditation on emptiness—a mere recitation of the mantra—all appearances at once become imperceptible. This is a serious misunderstanding, since it would imply that emptiness causes the destruction of appearances in the same way that a hammer causes the destruction of a pot.[289]

The issue, Gorampa points out, is that "some Tibetans" do not go far enough in their negation, and failing to realize this, attack "early Tibetans" for negating

286. Go rams pa, *Gsang ba 'dus pa'i sgrub thabs kun tu bzang po*, 24a5–b6.

287. Tsong kha pa, *'Dod 'jo*, 55a3–4.

288. Tib. *btsan thabs*, Skt. **haṭha*.

289. Go rams pa, *Gsang ba 'dus pa'i sgrub thabs kun tu bzang po*, 18b4–5.

too much. Furthermore, "some Tibetans" criticize "early Tibetans" for meditating on emptiness in an unusual way—through the mere recitation of a mantra that makes all appearance instantaneously imperceptible.[290]

Clearly Gorampa finds fault with "some Tibetans," not only for their views vis-à-vis the meditation on emptiness in the context of the creation stage, but also for their criticisms of the "early Tibetans." But is Gorampa's description of their writings consistent with judgments Tsongkhapa or his disciples actually express concerning the "early Tibetans"?

Tsongkhapa does indeed reproach those who meditate on nihilistic emptiness in the context of the Mantra Vehicle's meditation:

> It is absurd to suppose that merely by applying one's mind to their cessation, all appearances become imperceptible, and thereby one abides in absorption in the three doors of liberation.[291]

And also:

> Numerous other tantras and authentic treatises explain that emptiness in the context of the creation stage is precisely the same as in the Madhyamaka. Therefore the claim of many persons of inferior intellect that the emptiness meditated on here is merely a fanciful nihilistic emptiness is a colossal tale told by those who are ignorant of the system.[292]

Khedrup Jé is even harsher in his criticism.[293] The reader is advised to read the relevant passages in the translation below and to find their echo in Gorampa's words cited above.[294] Just as Gorampa describes "some Tibetans" who find fault with the "early Tibetans," Khedrup Jé is critical of the position that reciting the mantra of emptiness can turn the world and its inhabitants into nothing whatsoever.

290. Our concern here is not so much with the analogy of the hammer that destroys phenomena, found in writings on the Madhyamaka, as with the unique idea of a mantra with the power to make all appearance instantaneously imperceptible. For the analogy of the hammer, see Candrakīrti, *Dbu ma la 'jug ma*, *Madhyamakāvatāra*, chap. 6, v. 34, Tōh 3861; and its *Bhāṣya*; and La Vallée Poussin 1911, 311.

291. Tsong kha pa, *Rnam gzhag rim pa'i rnam bshad*, 9a4.

292. Tsong kha pa, *'Dod 'jo*, 55b5–6.

293. Mkhas grub rje, *Bskyed rim dngos grub rgya mtsho*, 32a2–33a1.

294. See also Bentor 2015b.

But who were those "early Tibetans"? Having noted that "some Tibetans" are criticized not only for their view of the meditation on emptiness but also for their censure of some "early Tibetans," we may reasonably suppose that these "early Tibetans" are members of the Sakya school. Indeed, we find the method of forcefully meditating on emptiness through the mere recitation of a mantra in the writings of the early Sakya Masters. In his commentary on Saroruha's[295] *Hevajra Sādhana*,[296] Künga Nyingpo[297] explains that after accumulating merit, "to accumulate wisdom, one meditates forcefully on emptiness." And this means:

> One meditates on all phenomena, oneself, and so forth, as imperceptible, as nothing whatsoever, empty.[298]

Similarly, his son Sönam Tsemo[299] explains in his own commentary on this sādhana, the main Hevajra sādhana of the early Sakyapas, that:

> To accumulate wisdom, one meditates forcefully on emptiness. That is to say, by reciting the mantra while reflecting on its meaning, one meditates on oneself and everything else as empty.
>
> Generally speaking, meditation on emptiness by deconstruction leads to the understanding that [all things] are devoid of inherent nature because they are free of one and many and so forth, and this understanding is then stabilized with the mantra. "Meditating forcefully" means merely reciting the mantra.
>
> Furthermore, there are two meditations: The meditation on appearances as lacking an inherent nature,[300] and the meditation on the absence of appearances.[301] Here, one meditates on the absence of appearances.[302]

295. In the colophon of the Derge, he is called Slob dpon Padma; in the colophon of the Sanskrit edition, his name is given as Ācārya Saroruha; in the title of Bsod nams rtse mo's work, he is called Mtsho skyes.

296. *Dgyes pa rdo rje'i sgrub thabs*, *Hevajra Sādhana*, Tōh 1218; Sanskrit editions in *Dhīḥ* 2003, 133–144; and Gerloff 2017, 97–116.

297. Kun dga' snying po (1092–1158).

298. Kun dga' snying po, [*Mtsho skyes kyi*] *Mngon rtogs tshig gi bum pa*, 344b2–3.

299. Bsod nams rtse mo (1142–1182).

300. Tib. *snang la rang bzhin med par bsgom pa*.

301. Tib. *snang med du bsgom pa*.

302. Bsod nams rtse mo, *Kyai rdo rje'i sgrub thabs mtsho skyes kyi ṭīkā*, 10a1–3.

In this treatise, Sönam Tsemo explicitly sets aside the meditation on all appearances as devoid of inherent existence and instructs the yogis to meditate merely on the absence of appearances. At the same time, both Künga Nyingpo and Sönam Tsemo consider this meditation to be a means for accumulating wisdom in order to purify the stain of conceptualization—primarily the labeling of self and person—and attaining the rūpakāya from the dharmakāya, the essence of which is emptiness.[303] Hence, for these lamas, the meditation on emptiness cannot be said to consist solely of a meditation on the absence of appearances.

Nevertheless, according to the early Sakya masters, the meditation on emptiness during this phase of the creation stage relies on the forceful method, with an emphasis not on the emptiness of the inherent existence of all phenomena, but rather on the absence of appearances. This is the exact position of the "early Tibetans" criticized by "some Tibetans" according to Gorampa.

In later eras, Sakya scholars interpreted the position of the early Sakya masters as describing a meditation on emptiness according to the view of the Madhyamaka school. For example, Ngorchen Kunga Sangpo, in his own commentary on *Hevajra Sādhana*, cites the above passage from Sönam Tsemo[304] and then states that this method is indeed consistent with the Madhyamaka system. Ngorchen Kunga Sangpo continues:

> Mantrins who have maintained—without first examining through the "wisdom of individual analysis"—that the mind abiding merely in nonapprehension is [the mind of] accumulating wisdom [i.e., the mind meditating on emptiness] do not understand how to attain the body of the deity free of the duality of profundity and manifestation. Therefore, no matter how stable their visualization is during the creation stage, they cannot go beyond saṃsāra. For this reason, having trained in the tantras and their commentaries, one should be knowledgeable in the scriptural tradition of the Madhyamaka.[305]

For Ngorchen Kunga Sangpo, then, the meditation on emptiness while accumulating wisdom cannot be accomplished without an examination through wisdom in accordance with the method of the Madhyamaka. In

303. Kun dga' snying po, [*Mtsho skyes kyi*] *Mngon rtogs tshig gi bum pa*, 7b1–8a3; Bsod nams rtse mo, *Kyai rdo rje'i sgrub thabs mtsho skyes kyi ṭīkā*, 10a3–b3.

304. *Kyai rdo rje'i sgrub thabs mtsho skyes kyi ṭīkā*, 10a2–3.

305. Ngor chen, *Zla zer*, 75a5–6.

this respect, he is similar in his position to Tsongkhapa, Khedrup Jé, and Gorampa.[306]

In accordance with Gorampa[307] on this point, more than two hundred years later, Amyé Shap too maintains that Sönam Tsemo's position is valid:

> When yogis examine the mode of existence of things that appear in the context of the Pāramitā Vehicle, they do not find these phenomena. Similarly, in the context of the Vajra Vehicle, yogis meditate on emptiness by reciting the mantra *oṃ śūnyatā jñāna vajra svabhāva ātmako 'haṃ* while reflecting on its meaning, without any perceptible appearances whatsoever. Since our precious teacher Sönam Tsemo considered this the supreme method, he taught that of the two methods, (1) meditation on appearances devoid of inherent nature and (2) meditation on the absence of appearances, the method to be used here is the meditation on the absence of appearances.[308]

As we have seen, Sönam Tsemo names two possible meditations on emptiness here: meditating forcefully on the absence of appearances through the recitation of the mantra and meditating on the emptiness of inherent nature through reasoning. He then instructs the yogis of the creation stage to meditate on the first. Ngorchen Kunga Sangpo classifies these two methods according to the faculties of the meditators: the first type is for meditators "endowed with supreme intellect who thoroughly understand the view of emptiness," while the latter is "for beginners who have not yet realized emptiness, or meditators who have realized it, but still need to habituate to it."[309] Gorampa follows Kunga Sangpo explicitly.[310]

This is how later Sakya masters preserved the meditation on emptiness recommended by the early Sakya masters while providing an alternative method in accordance with the teachings of the Madhyamaka. Later scholars of other schools, including Dakpo Tashi Namgyal[311] and Kongtrul Yönten Gyatso,

306. Regarding the sequence of these masters, Kun dga' bzang po wrote his commentary on *Hevajra Sādhana* in 1419, the year Tsong kha pa passed away, while Tsong kha pa wrote his *Rnam gzhag rim pa'i rnam bshad* in 1404 and the *'Dod 'jo* in 1415. See Tshe tan zhabs drung, 211–213, and Jinpa 2019, 387 and 390.

307. Go rams pa, *Gsang ba 'dus pa'i sgrub thabs kun tu bzang po*, 24b4–6.

308. A myes zhabs, *Gsang'dus dkyil 'khor 'khor sgrub thabs rnam*, 69b5–70a2.

309. Ngor chen, *Zla zer*, 71b3–4.

310. Go rams pa, *Gsang ba 'dus pa'i sgrub thabs kun tu bzang po*, 24b3–25a1.

311. Dwags po Bkra shis rnam rgyal (1513–1587).

likewise refer to these two methods of meditating on emptiness: forceful meditation and meditation based on examination.[312]

The point here is that there were in fact Sakya lamas who instructed yogis to meditate forcefully on emptiness, just as Gorampa claims, and that these were criticized by members of the rising Geluk sect. Thus it is likely that Gorampa has in mind certain objections—like those of Khedrup Jé—to the position of Künga Nyingpo and Sönam Tsemo when he takes issue with "some Tibetans" who criticize "early Tibetans" for maintaining that "by merely reciting the mantra all appearances become instantaneously imperceptible."[313]

As we saw, it was in their commentaries on the *Hevajra Sādhana* by Saroruha that Künga Nyingpo and Sönam Tsemo instructed yogis to meditate through the forceful method on the absence of appearances. In his *Ocean of Attainments*, after explaining why the position of "some people" contradicts both reason and their own premises, Khedrup Jé argues that their position contradicts the scriptures as well. He first offers a few examples already provided by Tsongkhapa,[314] then, for no apparent reason, supplies a further example of his own, the position of Saroruha in his *Hevajra Sādhana*:

> Likewise, in his *Hevajra Sādhana*, the Mahāsiddha Saroruha teaches that after reciting the mantra that begins with *oṃ śūnyatā*, you "should meditate on the meaning of this mantra as: myself and the three realms are devoid of essence."[315]

To the casual reader, this may seem to be simply one more in a string of examples, but Sakya masters, including Ngorchen Kunga Sangpo and Gorampa, understood that Khedrup Jé was taking aim here at members of their own school. The case of Khedrup Jé is notable, not only because of his quick temper and sharp tongue, but because he had left the Sakyapa to join the disciples of Tsongkhapa and was writing against his former school.

312. Dwags po Bkra shis rnam rgyal, *Gsang sngags rdo rje theg pa'i spyi don mdor bsdus pa legs bshad nor bu'i 'od zer*, 93b5–94a1; an English translation in Roberts 2011, 512. Kong sprul yon tan rgya mtsho, *Shes bya kun khyab*, vol. 3, p. 188; an English translation in Guarisco and McLeod 2008, 91.

313. Go rams pa, *Gsang ba 'dus pa'i sgrub thabs kun tu bzang po*, 18b2–5.

314. Tsong kha pa, *Rnam gzhag rim pa'i rnam bshad*, 8b6–9b5.

315. Tib. *ngo bo nyid dang bral bar*, Skt. *nirābhāsa*. Mkhas grub rje, *Bskyed rim dngos grub rgya mtsho*, 33b5–6. The Saroruha passages is from *Dgyes pa rdo rje'i sgrub thabs*, *Hevajra Sādhana*, Tōh 1218, 2b5; Sanskrit (which is slightly different): *Dhīḥ* 2003, 134; and Gerloff 2017, 99.

To conclude, we have followed Gorampa's analysis of "what remains in śūnyatā" in the first major meditation on emptiness in the sādhana, and his criticisms of "some Tibetans" for negating too little or failing to dissolve all phenomena into emptiness. These "some Tibetans," according to him, unaware of their own misapprehension, criticize certain "early Tibetans" for negating too much. We may now identify the "some Tibetans" Gorampa had in mind as Tsongkhapa and his disciple Khedrup Jé. Furthermore, we have shown that the "early Tibetans" reproached by Khedrup Jé are the early Sakya forefathers, Künga Nyingpo and Sönam Tsemo. And we have also understood the sources of their respective views and the gist of their arguments.

We may never uncover the original character of the creation stage, but we find more and more evidence for a historical process spanning several centuries that gradually brings it in line with Madhyamaka views. One major source of tension between scholars who maintain that one should meditate on the emptiness of inherent existence and those who advocate meditation on the absence of appearances is that meditating on nothing whatsoever makes very good sense in the context of the first phase of the creation stage. While meditation on nihilistic emptiness in the creation stage faced no objections in the early days of the second millennium, in subsequent generations, when Madhyamaka became a predominating view in Tibet, the later Sakyapa and the Gelukpa gave yogis the seemingly paradoxical instruction to meditate on both the absence of appearances and the emptiness of inherent existence.

Khedrup Jé's criticism of nihilistic meditation was valid in his day, and the Sakya teachers shared his opinion. The Gelukpa, however, never taught meditation on nihilistic emptiness in the context of the creation stage, since it had gone out of favor by their time (a process to which their perceived founder no doubt contributed). Consequently, Gelukpas' criticism of earlier teachers who meditated on nihilistic emptiness in this context flared into sectarian debate. These are more than "mere" dogmatic arguments. Not only do they shed light on the rise to prominence of the Madhyamaka view of emptiness in tantric meditation and the tensions created by this process, but they illuminate facets of the meditation on emptiness that received less emphasis in Madhyamaka treatises.

Straddling Emptiness and Nothingness

How do yogis meditate on emptiness in correspondence with the empty eon? As we have seen, the empty space during the periodical destruction of the world is characterized by a total absence, and as such does not concur with the Madhyamaka view of emptiness. Meditation on the empty eon will be meditation on the mere absence of appearances, a nihilistic meditation that negates too much. But this is exactly what authoritative scriptures such as *Formulating the Sādhana* instruct the yogis to do. Khedrup Jé explains how to meditate at this point of the sādhana on emptiness rather than on nothingness:

> In the case of the Mantra Vehicle, when you engage in this mode of meditation on emptiness, even though dualistic appearances have not been eliminated insofar as the level of appearances[316] is concerned, at the level of apprehension,[317] coarse dualistic appearances are eliminated. Therefore, even if you do not retain the visualization of the animate and inanimate realms in dissolution, that is fine. But when you purposely direct your concentration to the process of dissolution in order to eliminate the dualistic appearances at the level of your mind, Ārya Nāgārjuna and his disciples explain that in this context the animate and inanimate realms are dissolved into clear light... The purpose of practicing in this way is to facilitate the elimination of coarse dualistic appearances on the level of apprehension and so forth. Hence, you imagine that the animate and inanimate realms do not arise in your own mind, but at the same time you do not meditate on them as turning into nothing at all.[318]

Prāsaṅgika and Yogācāra Meditations on the Verse of Emptiness

To return to that verse recited during the meditation on emptiness at this point in the sādhana as found in the second chapter of the *Guhyasamāja Tantra*:

> *abhāve bhāvanābhāvo bhāvanā naiva bhāvanā* |
> *iti bhāvo na bhāvaḥ syād bhāvanā nopalabhyate* ||

Candrakīrti interprets it by means of the tantric hermeneutical method called "the four ways,"[319] which consists of the literal, shared, hidden, and ultimate levels of interpretation.[320] Even though Candrakīrti does not explicitly say so,

316. Tib. *snang ngor.*

317. Tib. *nges ngor.*

318. Mkhas grub rje, *Bskyed rim dngos grub rgya mtsho*, 41a5–b3.

319. Tib. *tshul bzhi.*

320. The literal: Tib *tshig gi don* or *yi ge'i don*, Skt. *akṣarārtha*; the shared: Tib. *spyi'i don*, Skt. *samastāṅga*; the hidden: Tib. *sbas pa*, Skt. *garbhin*; and the ultimate: Tib. *mthar thug pa*, Skt. *kolika*.

the literal level of interpretation here is clearly based on Nāgārjuna's *tetralemma*.[321] Still, we should not rush to the conclusion that since this work is written by "a Candrakīrti," a Madhyamaka explanation is what we must expect here. In his literal level of interpretation of this verse, Candrakīrti explains (I summarize and interpret):

1. [If there is no being or things], there can be no meditation (*bhāvanā* = causing to be), because if there is no being or things, there cannot be causing to be.
2. [If there is being or things], then meditation [causing to be] is not a meditation, because even without meditation [causing to be], there are existing things.
3. [If there are both being and no being or things and no things], that which is both a thing and a no-thing would not exist, therefore, that thing [that is both] would not be a thing.
4. [If there are neither being nor no being and neither things nor no-things], then, there cannot be meditation [causing to be]. Therefore no meditation can be perceived.

So far, this is the literal level of interpretation; but if we look at all four levels of interpretation, what we find here is not the usual tantric hermeneutic by means of "the four ways,"[322] but rather the fourfold meditation common in Yogācāra writings:[323]

The first level is "apprehending things to the extent they exist"—here, according to the four possibilities of Nāgārjuna. The second stage is "apprehending Mind Only" or "mental-events-only" by realizing that external things are creations of the mind.[324] In the third stage, Candrakīrti maintains that given the absence of things, neither is there Mind Only, and the two truths are indivisible. On the ultimate level, for those who realize the stage

321. See Bentor 2009b, 92.

322. In the usual "four ways," the shared level of interpretation is shared by both creation or creation and completion stages, both sūtra and tantra, and so on; the hidden level often refers to practices with the consort, the subtle body, and so forth; and the ultimate level of interpretation applies to the completion stage alone.

323. Candrakīrti, *Sgron gsal, Pradīpoddyotanaṭīkā*, Tōh 1785, 24a2–b4; Chakravarti 1984, 31–32.

324. Tib. *sems kyi rang bzhin*, Skt. *cittamaya*.

of union[325]—and here Candrakīrti does use tantric terminology—there is no more clinging to meditator, meditation, and object of meditation.

The Yogācāra methods offer more dynamic processes particularly applicable to meditative transformations, including the creation stage. During the sādhana, at first yogis visualize away their ordinary world and reflect on the extent to which it exists. In the second stage, they create their enlightened realm in their minds—with themselves as deities and with their environment as the celestial mansion of the maṇḍala—and they meditate on Mind Only. In the third stage, they realize that this creation, much like their ordinary world, is not real; by understanding that the true nature of all phenomena is not mental-event only, they understand that neither is there Mind Only. Finally, after dissolving their visualization into emptiness, they realize the suchness of all things and the nonduality of emptiness and appearances.

Nevertheless, in comparison to the Sanskrit, the Tibetan translation of Candrakīrti's explanations of "the four methods" of meditation here is a step toward the Madhyamaka view. While the Sanskrit may be translated as "When there are not any animate and inanimate things, there is no meditation," the Tibetan is "When there is no *essence*[326] to all the animate and inanimate things, there is no meditation." Since in the Sanskrit explanation there is no equivalent to the word "essence" found in the Tibetan, in theoretical terms the difference between these two versions is significant.[327]

When we examine Tibetan commentaries on Candrakīrti's treatise, we find that Butön more or less reproduces Candrakīrti's explanation of the fourfold meditation without commenting on it.[328] Apparently, Butön was not troubled by questions such as the philosophical school of this meditation.[329] This is in spite of the fact that Butön actually knew Sanskrit, and could see that the meaning of our verse in its Tibetan rendering was different from the meaning of the Sanskrit version. Butön was an important teacher in the lineage that eventually led to Tsongkhapa; Tsongkhapa had great reverence for Butön, although, as we have seen, he did not always agree with him.

Unlike Butön, for Tsongkhapa, the Ārya School of the Guhyasamāja cannot but hold the philosophical positions of the Madhyamaka School. Hence,

325. The stage of union (Tib. *zung 'jug gi rim pa*, Skt. *yuganaddhakrama*) of the completion stage is the fifth of the five stages in Nāgārjuna's *Pañcakrama*.

326. Tib. *ngo bo nyid*.

327. See Bentor 2009b, 93–94.

328. Bu ston, *Mdor byas 'grel chen*, 13b6–14b3.

329. As we will see, in his explanation of another step in the sādhana, the dissolution into the moon, Bu ston explicitly advocates Mind Only. See Bu ston, *Mdor byas 'grel chen*, 34a5–6.

in his commentary, Tsongkhapa glosses "being" as "an inherently existing being," "non-being" as "absence of own essence," and "meditation" as "meditation on suchness."[330] Tsongkhapa does not delve into the subject of the fourfold meditation and the problems that this poses for Madhyamaka, claiming that only the literal and shared levels of interpretations are relevant to the creation stage,[331] while the term Mind Only appears in the hidden level of interpretation alone.[332]

Still, Tsongkhapa does address the question of the nature of the external world that appears in Candrakīrti's explanation of the shared level of interpretation.[333] Tsongkhapa explains the meaning of the term "external appearance" or "external aspect"[334] found in the *Illuminating Lamp*, by specifying that it refers to external objects that "exist by their own essence"[335] and by adding that things have no existence "apart from being merely imputed by the mind."[336] On the other hand, in *Ocean of Attainments*, Khedrup Jé summarizes Tsongkhapa's explanation without a reference to the external appearances or aspects that appear in the *Illuminating Lamp*.[337] Additionally, Tsongkhapa glosses the phrase "created by the mind" or "of the nature of the mind"[338] in the *Illuminating Lamp* as "of the nature of being merely imputed by the mind."[339] Thus, rather than taking the explanation of the *Illuminating Lamp* at its (Yogācāra) face value, Tsongkhapa gives it a Prāsaṅgika Madhyamaka spin.

In another of his commentaries, Tsongkhapa elaborates on the subject of external objects and Mind Only:

330. Tsong kha pa, *Sgron gsal mchan*, 90b2–93b6.

331. Tsong kha pa, *Rnam gzhag rim pa'i rnam bshad*, 9a2.

332. The hidden and ultimate levels pertain to practices with the consort, to the subtle body, and to the completion stage alone.

333. See Candrakīrti, *Sgron gsal, Pradīpoddyotanaṭīkā*, Tōh 1785, 24a5; Chakravarti 1984, 31.

334. Tib. *phyi rol gyi rnam pa*, Skt. *bāhyākāra*.

335. Tib. *rang gi ngo bo nyid kyis grub pa*.

336. Tib. *sems kyis btags pa tsam las*; Tsong kha pa, *Sgron gsal mchan*, 91b3–4

337. Mkhas grub rje, *Bskyed rim dngos grub rgya mtsho*, 40a1–2. Likewise, when Tsong kha pa refers to the literal and shared levels of interpretation of our verse, he mentions neither the status of external objects nor Mind Only. See Tsong kha pa, *Rnam gzhag rim pa'i rnam bshad*, 9a2–3.

338. Tib. *sems kyi rang bzhin*, Skt. *cittamaya*.

339. Tib. *sems kyis btags pa tsam gyi rang bzhin*; Tsong kha pa, *Sgron gsal mchan*, 91b6. The Candrakīrti passage is in *Sgron gsal, Pradīpoddyotanaṭīkā*, Tōh 1785, 24a6; Chakravarti 1984, 31.

> When [the *Illuminating Lamp*] explains the verse on the shared level of interpretation, there appears something like a refutation of external objects and an establishment [of them] as Mind Only; and there are similar occurrences also in other cases. It seems that [some people], unable to examine this very thoroughly, did not understand that the position of Ārya Nāgārjuna and his disciples in general, and the position of the commentator [Candrakīrti] in particular, which accept external objects as conventional designations. Therefore they say that the system of the *Illuminating Lamp* does not accept external objects. However, since I have already extensively explained elsewhere why this is unacceptable and how to eradicate the extreme views of eternalism and nihilism, I will not elaborate here.[340]

Tsongkhapa cannot accept that the author of the *Illuminating Lamp* rejects external objects. For him, there is a crucial difference between the position that external objects exist as conventional designations and saying that external objects do not exist *at all*. According to Tsongkhapa, the Ārya school of the Guhyasamāja maintains that external objects exist as conventional designations; this causes him to offer an alternative gloss to the line of the *Illuminating Lamp*, in its Tibetan translation, that refers to external objects—namely that although appearing, they have no inherent existence, but rather are mere mental imputations.

For Tsongkhapa and Khedrup Jé, then, there is no doubt that Candrakīrti and Nāgārjuna, who wrote on the tantric practice of the sādhana, do not accept the theory of Mind Only, but rather hold the view of the Prāsaṅgika Madhyamaka School.

The Goal of the Meditation on Emptiness

Another question must be asked: To what extent do yogis practicing the creation stage need to meditate on the emptiness of intrinsic existence prior to their engagement in the sādhana? Is realization of emptiness the fruit of the meditation on the sādhana, or is it a prerequisite for it? The meditation on emptiness in the macrocosmic context takes place before the core practices of the sādhana begin. Can it be the fruit of the practice, or is it the path itself?

340. Tsong kha pa, *Mtha' gcod*, 72b6–73a2. This is a commentary on a number of difficult points in Candrakīrti's *Sgron gsal*, *Pradīpoddyotanaṭīkā*.

Or else is it one of the seemingly paradoxical aspects of taking the fruit as the path? There is no single, simple answer to these questions.

For Geluk and Kagyü scholars, the main authority for the purpose of meditation on emptiness, in the present context, is Dīpaṅkaraśrījñāna—called Atiśa in our texts.[341] In his commentary on a sādhana of Cakrasaṃvara according to Lūyīpāda, Dīpaṅkaraśrījñāna lists six purposes for meditating on emptiness here:

> (1) to gain the ability to realize emptiness; (2) to restore your recollection of emptiness; (3) to stabilize your concentration; (4) to complete the accumulation of wisdom; (5) to shed conceptualization of your ordinary body, speech, and mind; and (6) to realize that the maṇḍala of the celestial mansion and its deities in their entirety are emanations of emptiness.[342]

In his own commentary on Lūyīpāda's sādhana, Tsongkhapa concludes with regard to the first three purposes that those who have not realized emptiness will newly realize it, those who have realized it already will recollect their realization, and those who have realized emptiness and settled in their realization will stabilize their realization by reciting the mantras.[343] Thus meditators on the creation stage do not need to have realized emptiness already, as they can attain such a realization for the first time by means of the Mantra Vehicle, while those who have gained this realization before can deepen their level of realization.

The fourth purpose of the meditation on emptiness is to complete the accumulation of wisdom after merit has been accumulated during the preliminaries. Regarding the fifth purpose—shedding ordinary perception of one's existence, in accordance with Tsongkhapa[344]—Khedrup Jé explains this in relation to the question of how to avoid meditation on mere absence:

341. For the Dge lugs see for example Tsong kha pa, *'Dod 'jo*, 52a2–5; and Mkhas grub rje, *Bskyed rim dngos grub rgya mtsho*, 41b3–5. For the Bka' brgyud, see for example Dwags po Bkra shis rnam rgyal, *Gsang sngags*, 94a4–b1; an English translation in Roberts 2011, 513; and Kong sprul Blo yon tan rgya mtsho, *Shes bya kun khyab*, vol. 3, 188; an English translation in Guarisco and McLeod 2008, 91–92.

342. Dīpaṅkaraśrījñāna, Mar me mdzad ye shes, *Mngon par rtogs pa rnam par 'byed pa*, *Abhisamayavibhaṅga*, Tōh 1490, 189b1–2. This is a commentary on Lūyīpāda, *Bcom ldan mngon par rtogs pa*, *Bhagavadabhisamaya*, Tōh 1427, 186b. For a study of this sādhana, see Gray 2011.

343. Tsong kha pa, *'Dod 'jo*, 52a2–5. See also his *Bung ba'i re skong*, 11b3–4.

344. Tsong kha pa, *'Dod 'jo*, 52b1–2.

> You must prevent the ordinary appearance from arising in your cognition. Still, you cannot stop ordinary appearances by meditating on them as mere nothingness. Rather, when you withdraw the cognition that engages with the conventional world of ordinary appearances and set your mind on emptiness—the ultimate truth—ordinary appearances cease to arise within the sphere of your cognition. This is one of the reasons for meditating on emptiness. You should understand the distinction between preventing ordinary appearances from arising within the sphere of cognition and actually ceasing their existence.[345]

The Empty Visualization

The sixth purpose of the meditation on emptiness listed by Dīpaṅkaraśrījñāna—the realization that the celestial mansion and its deities are emanations of emptiness—is of paramount importance for the practice of the sādhana. The meditation on emptiness here is combined with the subsequent visualization of the maṇḍala; the yogis must realize that emptiness and appearances are united indivisibly, in the sense that, while the maṇḍala appears, it is empty of intrinsic nature. Once again following Tsongkhapa,[346] Khedrup Jé explains:

> In all subsequent meditations on the circle of deities, the appearance aspect will arise as a manifestation of emptiness. For example, when you abide in a prolonged equipoise on the nature of things and then rise from it into a post-meditative state, then, through the power of your meditative equipoise, the diversity of phenomena will appear to your pure, postmeditative, worldly wisdom, subjective mind as illusion-like—appearing yet devoid of intrinsic nature. Likewise, here, too, first you meditate on emptiness and immediately afterward visualize the circle of deities. So long as the impact of your equipoise on emptiness remains undiminished in your cognition, everything will arise as an illusion-like circle of deities—which, although they appear, are devoid of intrinsic nature. It is for this reason that you should meditate on emptiness now.[347]

345. Mkhas grub rje, *Bskyed rim dngos grub rgya mtsho*, 42a2–3.

346. Tsong kha pa, *'Dod 'jo*, 52b2–4.

347. Mkhas grub rje, *Bskyed rim dngos grub rgya mtsho*, 42a4–6.

When yogis visualize the maṇḍala after meditating first on emptiness, the celestial mansion and deities arise as an illusory roleplay. This is because the meditation on emptiness purifies the subsequent visualization, enabling it to arise as illusion-like.

The second meditation on emptiness during the sādhana is the meditation on emptiness in the microcosmic context, included in its core practices as part of the yoga of taking death on the path that leads to the dharmakāya. But first, still within the macrocosmic context, the celestial mansion is visualized.

5. Correspondences between the Meditation, Cosmos, and Person

The Meaning of the Correspondences between the Meditation, Cosmos, and Person

Nāgabuddhi's *Formulating the Sādhana* had a tremendous impact on Tibetan authors who wrote about the Ārya tradition of the Guhyasamāja. As early as the eleventh century, the Tibetan scholar and translator Gö Khukpa Lhetsé devoted a considerable part of the introduction to his extensive treatise on the Guhyasamāja's practice to the correlation of steps of both the creation and completion stages with cosmogonic and personal events.[348] Gö uses the terms "ground of purification" and "its purifier" to describe these correlations.[349] For example, the destruction of the world is a ground of purification that is purified by the meditation on emptiness, and the creation of the world is a ground of purification that is purified by the visualization of the celestial mansion of the maṇḍala. Likewise, death, during which the bodily constituents dissolve, is the ground that is purified by the dissolution of the specially visualized deities. In this part of his introduction, he emphasizes not the meditative steps but rather their grounds of purification, as described in detail in *Formulating the Sādhana*, the *Abhidharmakośabhāṣya*, and the *Vinaya*.[350]

The underlying notion is that the meditation on the sādhana can actually affect both the cosmos and the person; this is the meaning of the terminology

348. 'Gos Khug pa lhas btsas, *Gsang 'dus stong thun*, 7a2–14a4.

349. Tib. *sbyang gzhi* and *sbyong byed*.

350. Nāgabuddhi, *Rnam gzhag rim pa*, *Vyavastholi*, chap. 1, Tōh 1809, 121b4–5; Tanaka 2016, 80–81. Vasubandhu, *Mdzod 'grel*, chap. 3, vv. 45–46, Tōh 4090, 144a5–b3; Pradhan 1975, 158; Pruden 1988–1990, 451–452 for a description of the evolution of circles of wind, water, and gold; chap. 3, vv. 90 and 98, 155b3–157a4 and 162a5–163a3; Pradhan 1975, 178–180 and 188–190; Pruden 1988–1990, 475–478 and 487–489 for a description of the evolution of beings in the world and so forth. *'Dul ba rnam par 'byed pa* or *Lung rnam 'byed*, *Vinayavibhaṅga*, Tōh 3, 48b1–51b5.

of purification used here. By means of the sādhana, the meditators purify their impure reality, the ground of purification. In other words, through their meditation, yogis can destroy their ordinary environment in order to create the pure world of the celestial mansion of the maṇḍala, where they will be enlightened. The correlation described by Gö between the ground of purification and the purifier is concerned with the details of the practice. For instance, the changing of the color of the principal deity from white to blue during the sādhana has as its ground of purification the transformation of the pure and radiating bodies of the first beings in the eon to ordinary physical bodies after eating coarse food.[351] Sakya scholars, including Rendawa Shönu Lodrö, closely follow the explanations of Gö Khukpa Lhetsé in this matter.[352]

One of Tsongkhapa's earlier works on the subject of tantra was his commentary on *Formulating the Sādhana*,[353] composed in 1404,[354] even before his famous *Great Treatise on the Stages of the Mantric Path*.[355] The correspondences between the person, cosmos, and sādhana drawn in *Formulating the Sādhana* create a unified system, which is consistent with Tsongkhapa's general mission to create a harmonized structure. In his commentary on *Formulating the Sādhana*, Tsongkhapa expands on Nāgabuddhi's patterns as well as on the *Vajrasattva Sādhana*. While *Formulating the Sādhana* relates steps of the practice to birth, intermediate state, and death, the *Vajrasattva Sādhana* links the three parts of the sādhana to the attainment of the three bodies of the Buddha. By meditating on emptiness, yogis attain the dharmakāya;[356] by visualizing the principal deity, they attain the saṃbhogakāya; and by placing the deities on their bodies and so forth, they attain the nirmāṇakāya.[357] Integrating both approaches, Butön Rinchen Drup links three steps of the sādhana to death, the intermediate state, and rebirth on the one hand, and to the attainment of the three bodies of the Buddha on the other.[358]

351. 'Gos Khug pa lhas btsas, *Gsang 'dus stong thun*, 9a6–b1.

352. Red mda' ba, *Yid kyi mun sel*, 6b6–8b6.

353. Tsong kha pa, *Rnam gzhag rim pa'i rnam bshad*.

354. See Tshe tan zhabs drung 1982, 211; Jinpa 2019, 387.

355. Tsong kha pa, *Sngags rim chen mo*, composed in 1405.

356. Candrakīrti, *Rdo rje sems dpa'i sgrub thabs*, *Vajrasattva Sādhana*, Tōh 1814, 199a2–3; Luo and Tomabechi 2009, 14.8 and 47.4–5.

357. According to Candrakīrti, *Rdo rje sems dpa'i sgrub thabs*, *Vajrasattva Sādhana*, Tōh 1814, 199b2–3; Luo and Tomabechi 2009, 16.8 and 49.5–7.

358. Bu ston, *Mdor byas 'grel chen*, 51a4–b2. Bu ston accepts the authenticity of Candrakīrti's *Vajrasattva Sādhana*.

In accordance with his tendency toward coherent and comprehensive systems, Tsongkhapa, following Butön, stresses the unique correspondences between the grounds, paths, and fruits: (1) the grounds of purification are ordinary birth, death, and intermediate state; (2) the purifiers are the tantric practices of the creation and completion; and (3) the fruit of purification are the three bodies of the Buddha—the dharmakāya, saṃbhogakāya, and nirmāṇakāya respectively. These unique correspondences, according to Tsongkhapa, have a determining role in the transformation of ordinary human states into the three bodies of the Buddha that serve as the key for attaining enlightenment in this life through the practice of the highest tantric yoga.

Another scriptural source Tsongkhapa relies on in this matter is Āryadeva's *Compendium of Practices*, an important source on the completion stage of the Guhyasamāja according to the Ārya tradition composed in the very beginning of the ninth century.[359] According to this treatise:

> For ordinary ignorant beings, the so-called intermediate being[360]—the cause of saṃsāra—will take place. But for those who have obtained the transmitted instruction of all tathāgatas through the lineage of the gurus, the so-called self-blessing stage will take place... In the same way [the yogis] whose nature is the vajra body emanate in bodies... endowed with the excellent qualities of all buddhas.[361]

For Āryadeva, then, instead of the intermediate state that will naturally occur to ordinary people after they have died, qualified yogis who engage in the tantric practice can attain the "self-blessing stage,"[362] the third of the five stages as it appears in Nāgārjuna's *Five Stages*. From this stage, they will ultimately arise in the vajra body of the Buddha. In his *Fulfilling the Bee's Hopes*, Tsongkhapa elaborates on this:

359. See Tomabechi 2008, 175, note 23.

360. Tib. *bar do*, Skt. *antarābhava*.

361. Āryadeva, *Spyod pa bsdus pa'i sgron ma*, *Caryāmelāpakapradīpa*, chap. 6, Tōh 1803, 85b2–4; Sanskrit, Tibetan, and English translation in Wedemeyer 2007, B: 42a; Sanskrit and Tibetan in Pandey 2000, 57 and 269; an English translation in Kilty 2013, 130.

362. Tib. *bdag la byin gyis brlab*, Skt. *svādhiṣṭhāna*. This is the title of the third chapter of the *Rim pa lnga pa*, *Pañcakrama*, Tōh 1802; Sanskrit and Tibetan in Mimaki and Tomabechi 1994; Sanskrit and French translation in Tomabechi 2006.

> How does the saṃbhogakāya of the meditator on the creation stage purify the intermediate being? Instead of the intermediate being that occurs naturally for an ordinary person, the yogi meditating on the creation stage arises as the First Lord through the five manifest awakenings.[363]

Tsongkhapa continues to explain that this meditation ripens the yogi's mental continuum for the third of the five stages, the self-blessing stage or the illusory body. This in turn will ripen the yogi's mental continuum to attain the saṃbhogakāya of the Buddha at the culmination of the fifth stage, when the yogi attains the fruit of purification.[364] Thus there are two purifiers for the intermediate state. The first is the meditation on the First Lord during the creation stage, and the second the meditation on the illusory body during the completion stage. Yogis must first meditate on the purifier of the creation stage, which will ripen their mental continuum for the purifier of the completion stage. Then, the meditation on the purifier of the completion stage ripens them for the fruit of purification.

A similar, yet extended, explanation is found in the *Oral Instruction of Mañjuśrī*,[365] likewise dedicated to the completion stage of the Guhyasamāja cycle. This work was written by Jñānapāda, "the founder" of the Guhyasamāja school named for him.[366] In this treatise we find an explication how the three Buddha's bodies are attained.[367] In his commentary, Vaidyapāda explains that

363. Tib. *mngon byang*, Skt. *abhisambodhi*. Tsong kha pa, *Bung ba'i re skong*, 19b4–5.

364. Tib. *sbyangs pa'i 'bras bu*.

365. Jñānapāda, *Zhal lung*, *Dvikramatattvabhāvanā*, Tōh 1853, 15a5–b1; a Tibetan edition and an English translation in Dalton 2019, vv. 351–357.

366. See "Jñānapāda School" above.

367. "No doubt you will attain the three kāyas." Jñānapāda, *Zhal lung*, *Dvikramatattvabhāvanā*, Tōh 1853, 15b1; a Tibetan edition and an English translation in Dalton 2019, v. 357c. Yogis first endeavor in their meditation until their minds enter the realm (Tib. *dbying*) and they realize space-like clarity and supreme joy. Then, when they attain the form of a five-year-old child that possesses supernatural powers, they experience an unparalleled perfecr bliss. Finally, when they propel themselves to another rebirth, they truly realize the nirmāṇakāya. The phrase "the form of a five-year-old child endowed with supernatural powers" (Tib. *rdzu 'phrul shugs ldan pa, lo lnga lon pa'i byis pa'i gzugs*) recalls the explanation of the intermediate being as described by Vasubandhu's *Abhidharmakośa* and its autocommentary: its size is that of a five- or six-year-old child (Tib. *byis pa lo lnga'am drug lon pa lta bu*, Skt. *pañcaṣaḍvarṣasya dāraka*; *Mdzod 'grel*, *Kośabhāṣya*, chap. 3, v. 13a–b, Tōh 4090); and endowed with supernatural powers (Tib. *las kyi rdzu 'phrul shugs dang ldan*, Skt. *karmarddhivegavān*; *Kośa*, *Mdzod*, chap. 3, v. 14b, Tōh 4089).

the three stages seen by this-worldly people, who do not know the nature of the mind, as death, intermediate state, and rebirth are for the yogi three bodies of the Buddha. Therefore the three stages seen by this-worldly people as death, intermediate state, and rebirth are for the yogi the three bodies of the Buddha.[368] Hence, while the *Compendium of Practices* mentions only how, instead of the intermediate state that naturally occurs to ordinary beings, the capable yogi will arise in the self-blessing stage, the *Oral Instruction of Mañjuśrī* expands this notion to the three bodies of the Buddha that will arise in place of the three ordinary cyclic events of a person.

On this basis, Tsongkhapa presents his design that encompasses all three bodies of the Buddha. Instead of the ordinary death that naturally occurs, yogis of the highest tantra will attain the dharmakāya; likewise, instead of ordinary rebirth, they will attain the nirmāṇakāya that intentionally takes on a coarse body for the sake of the disciples. Once more, each ground of purification has two purifiers, one in the creation stage and the other in the completion stage, that must be practiced in sequence.[369] The fruit of purification, as we saw, cannot be attained during the creation stage, but only at the culmination of the completion stage. The goal of the creation stage is not to transform the yogi's birth, death, and intermediate state into the actual bodies of the Buddha, but rather to ripen them for the "three bodies of the completion stage."[370]

According to Tsongkhapa, three individual steps during the creation stage

368. According to Vaidyapāda, when the yogis realize space-like clarity and supreme joy, they experience the dharmakāya, while this-worldly people who do not know the nature of the mind designate this "death." Then, when yogis experience an unparalleled perfect bliss in the form of a five-year-old child endowed with supernatural powers, they attain the saṃbhogakāya, but this-worldly people designate this "intermediate state." Finally, when yogis attain the nirmāṇakāya, this-worldly people designate this "rebirth." Vaidyapāda, *Mdzes pa'i me tog, Sukusuma*, Tōh 1866, 132b2–4.

369. At times, the two purifiers are called the Buddha's body on the path. For example, the First Lord is called the saṃbhogakāya of the path of the creation stage, while the illusory body is the saṃbhogakāya of the completion stage. Moreover, the purifiers of the completion stage are divided into five different purifiers in sequence, one for each of the five stages of the completion stage. For example, death has five purifiers during the completion stage: (1) the metaphorical clear light during body isolation and speech isolation, (2) mind isolation, (3) the metaphorical clear light during the illusory body, (4) the actual clear light during the fourth stage, and (5) the actual clear light during the fifth stage. This brings about the attainment of the dharmakāya of the Buddha, the fruit of the purification. See Tsong kha pa, *Bung ba'i re skong*, 18a1–3.

370. The three bodies of the completion stage on the path are the analogical and actual clear light, the pure and impure illusory bodies, and the coarse nirmāṇakāya of the path. See Tsong kha pa, *Rnam gzhag rim pa'i rnam bshad*, 51b4–6.

ripen the yogi's continuum for the completion stage: The meditation on emptiness serves to purify the yogi's future death, and its eventual fruit will be the dharmakāya. The visualization of the First Lord serves to purify the yogi's future intermediate state, and its fruit will be the saṃbhogakāya. The transformation into Vajrasattva serves to purify the yogi's future rebirth, and its fruit will ultimately be the nirmāṇakāya. As we will see, not all Tibetan scholars agree on this point.

Having drawn these correlations, Tsongkhapa warns against authors who delight in collating similar phenomena and draw connections between every step of the sādhana and cosmogonic and personal events.[371] For Tsongkhapa, real correspondences are unique features of the Ārya tradition of the Guhyasamāja that are capable of bringing about the fruit of awakening within one lifetime, even during this age of decline. Moreover, he maintains that applying a correspondence to a certain step of the creation stage does not necessarily mean that the corresponding object is its ground of purification.

Correspondences with Macrocosmic Events

Formulating the Sādhana correlates the visualization of the celestial mansion of the maṇḍala to the periodical creation of the physical world.[372] While commenting briefly on the meditation, it describes in detail the cosmological events during the evolution of the world on the basis of the *Abhidharmakośa* and its autocommentary.[373] On this authority, numerous Tibetan scholars acknowledge a similarity between the meditation on the celestial mansion and the periodic creation of the world. The meditation begins with a visualization of the maṇḍalas of the four physical elements, a visualization that corresponds to the formation of the cylindrical wind, water, and the ground of gold that evolve when the new physical world is formed. The visualization of the actual celestial mansion that follows it parallels the formation of the mountains, continents, and so on during the evolution of the world.

Tibetan scholars disagree, though, on the nature of the affinity between these two events. Some see them as a ground-to-be-purified and the purifying practice in the sense that the practice can achieve an actual transforming effect on the macrocosmic world. To give a few examples, according to

371. Tsong kha pa, *Rnam gzhag rim pa'i rnam bshad*, 46a1–3.

372. Nāgabuddhi, *Rnam gzhag rim pa*, *Vyavastholi*, chap. 1, Tōh 1809, 122a2–4; Tanaka 2016, 82–83.

373. Vasubandhu, *Mdzod 'grel*, *Kośabhāṣya*, chap. 3, vv. 45–49a, Tōh 4090, 144a4–b6; Pradhan 1975, 157–158; Pruden 1988–1990, 451–452. See also Jinpa 2017, 283–306.

Gö Khukpa Lhetsé, one of the earlier Tibetans to write on Guhyasamāja sādhana:[374] "The ground of purification of the generation of the celestial mansion is the evolution through shared karma of [the world with] Mount Meru, the seven golden mountains, the four continents, the celestial mansion of the gods and people, the trees..." In his *General Survey of Tantric Systems*, Rinchen Sangpo[375] relates the physical world as the ground of purification to the meditation on the celestial mansion as its purifier.[376] Likewise, the Third Karmapa, Rangjung Dorjé,[377] instructs the meditator to visualize the celestial mansion in accordance with the evolution of the external world, though the nature of this accord is not spelled out.[378] Rendawa, who follows Gö, specifically notes that the evolution of the world with Mount Meru and the four continents is the ground of purification of the meditation on the celestial mansion.[379] Tsongkhapa, in his commentary on *Formulating the Sādhana*, also points out these similarities and provides detailed descriptions of the evolution of the world, based both on the *Abhidharmakośa* and the *Yogācārabhūmi*.[380] Still, for Tsongkhapa, the visualization of the celestial mansion cannot be the purifier of the evolution of the world.[381]

Khedrup Jé, on his part, minimizes the import of correspondences between the sādhana and macrocosmic events, and omits any description of the evolution of the physical world. His reservations are as follows:

> The visualization of the celestial mansion is a meditation that corresponds to the evolution of the mountains, continents, and so forth during the evolution of the world. When you apply the correspondences in this way, the generation of the celestial mansion—the

374. 'Gos Khug pa lhas btsas, *Gsang 'dus stong thun*, 7a6–b1.

375. Rin chen bzang po (958–1055).

376. Rin chen bzang po, *Rgyud sde spyi'i rnam gzhag*, 18b1–3. Some may be familiar with this title as one of the works of Mkhas grub rje, however, this work is written by Rin chen bzang po.

377. Rang byung rdo rje (1284–1339).

378. Rang byung rdo rje, *Gsang ba 'dus pa'i sgrub pa'i thabs phyi nang gzhan gsum gsal ba*, 4a6–b1.

379. Red mda' ba, *Yid kyi mun sel*, 6b6–7a2.

380. These descriptions are found in Asaṅga, *Sa'i dngos gzhi, Maulībhūmi*, Tōh 4035, 18b5–19a2; a Sanskrit edition in Bhattacharya 1957, 36–38; an English translation in Kajiyama 2000, 190–192.

381. Tsong kha pa, *Rnam gzhag rim pa'i rnam bshad*, 11a2–b6. See also his *Bung ba'i re skong*, 11b5–12b1.

> purifier—corresponds in a merely general way to the ground of purification, which is the evolution of the mountains, continents, and so forth. You need not relate the mountains, continents, and so forth to each part of the celestial mansion, such as the portals and so forth.
>
> What does it mean to purify the impure world by meditating on the celestial mansion? It is not that, through your meditation on the celestial mansion, you can transform this present impure world into a pure celestial mansion. Rather, you can purify your own capacity to partake in the impure world in the future [meaning that you yourself will not experience the impure world]. The purpose of this meditative purification is to ripen your mental continuum for the completion stage, in which you will develop the capacity to partake in the celestial mansion of wisdom.[382]

Here, Khedrup Jé claims that meditating on the sādhana does not enable yogis to bring about a true transformation in their outer world. Their achievements can affect only themselves, for no matter how much they meditate the world will remain impure. However, they can purify themselves and transform their own abilities. Thus, by meditating on the celestial mansion of the maṇḍala here, yogis can transform the way they will partake in the impure world in the future. Another reason that yogis cannot actually transform their environment is related to Khedrup Jé's [and other Geluk scholars'] position on the restricted power of the mind, the foundation of the creation stage, discussed above.

Nor does Tsongkhapa maintain that yogis actually purify their environment. For him, when yogis meditate on the celestial mansion, their goal is not to abolish the ordinary appearances of the world as they appear to their sense consciousness but to shed that which appears to the mental consciousness as the ordinary world. As we will soon see, Tsongkhapa strongly rejects the position that the meditation on the first deities residing in the maṇḍala can purify the first people of the eon.[383]

Following the visualization of the celestial mansion, yogis meditate on the first deities that dwell there, called "specially visualized deities."[384] *Formulating*

382. Mkhas grub rje, *Bskyed rim dngos grub rgya mtsho*, 49b5–50a1.

383. Tsong kha pa, *Sngags rim chen mo*, 463.

384. Tib. *lhag par mos pa*, Skt. *adhimokṣa*.

the Sādhana explains this meditation[385] and elsewhere[386] describes how the first beings of the eon,[387] who were endowed with extraordinary qualities, became ordinary people[388] due to their ignorance.[389] On this basis, Tibetan scholars of all schools who write on this subject maintain that the meditation on these deities is similar to the evolution of the inhabitants of the world after the formation of their habitat. Again, the nature of this similarity is the subject of much debate. Gö Khukpa Lhetsé regards the first beings in Jambudvīpa at the beginning of the eon as the ground of purification of the meditation on the specially visualized deities.[390] Additional Tibetan scholars, including Butön[391] and Rendawa,[392] follow Gö in this matter.

The affinity between these two groups of beings goes further. As *Formulating the Sādhana*[393] specifies, the first beings in Jambudvīpa are reborn

385. Nāgabuddhi, *Rnam gzhag rim pa, Vyavastholi*, chap. 1, Tōh 1809, 121a7–b3; Tanaka 2016, 79–80. This is found in the short synopsis of the practice at the opening of the treatise, in which Nāgabuddhi instructs the yogis that, after visualizing the celestial mansion, they should place there all the deities beginning with Akṣobhya "through special visualization." According to both Nāgārjuna (*Mdo bsre, Sādhanasūtramelāpaka*, Tōh 1797, 12a3) and Nāgabuddhi (*Rnam gzhag rim pa, Vyavastholi*, chap. 1, Tōh 1809, 122a4–5; Tanaka 2016, 83), the scriptural source for visualizing the specially visualized deities is chap. 11, v. 5cd, of the *Guhyasamāja Tantra*, where the deities are referred to as "three vajras."

386. Nāgabuddhi, *Rnam gzhag rim pa, Vyavastholi*, chap. 1, Tōh 1809, 123a1–4; Tanaka 2016, 87–88. These two instructions, however, do not appear one after the other, as we would expect.

387. Tib. *bskal pa dang po pa'i mi rnams*, Skt. *prāthamikakalpikā manuṣyāḥ*.

388. Tib. *tha mal ba'i mi*, Skt. *prākṛtamanuṣya*.

389. In doing so, *Formulating the Sādhana* follows especially the *Abhidharmakośa*, the *Vinayavibhaṅga*, and the *Saṃvarodaya Tantra*. See Vasubandhu, *Mdzod 'grel, Kośabhāṣya*, chap. 3, v. 98, Tōh 4090, 162a5–163a3; Pradhan 1975, 186–187; Pruden 1988–1990, 487. See also the *'Dul ba rnam par 'byed pa* or *Lung rnam 'byed, Vinayavibhaṅga*, Tōh 3, 48b1–51b5. See also the *Sdom 'byung, Saṃvarodaya Tantra*, Tōh 373, 266a4–5; Sanskrit and Tibetan editions, along with an English translation in Tsuda 1974, chap. 2, vv. 11–12ab.

390. 'Gos Khug pa lhas btsas, *Gsang 'dus stong thun*, 7b3–9a6.

391. Bu ston, *Mdor byas 'grel chen*, 27b1–4. Bu ston explains here that the withdrawal of the specially visualized deities into one's body aims to purify the people of the first kalpa whose constituents became ordinary. Still, it should be noted that with regard to the meditation on the specially visualized deities, Bu ston states that it is "*like* the birth of a person of the first kalpa." Bu ston, *Mdor byas 'grel chen*, 26a5.

392. Red mda' ba, *Yid kyi mun sel*, 7a5–6.

393. Nāgabuddhi, *Rnam gzhag rim pa, Vyavastholi*, chap. 1, Tōh 1809, 122a7–b1; Tanaka 2016, 85.

through a miraculous birth,[394] since they instantaneously appear with all their limbs and faculties intact, without going through wombs or eggs. Likewise, the special visualized deities are visualized instantaneously, and not through the stages of seed syllables, emblems, and so forth. For these reasons, Tibetan authors maintain that the visualization of the first deities dwelling in the celestial mansion should be associated with the evolution of the first inhabitants of Jambudvīpa after its creation.

Tsongkhapa and Khedrup Jé agree that there is a certain similarity here, but they vehemently object to the position that the first beings in the world are the ground of purification for the meditation on the specially visualized deities.[395] As we have seen, Tsongkhapa stresses that applying correspondences is not merely a matter of collating similar phenomena in order to draw analogies between the meditation on the mantric path on the one hand and the destruction and evolution of the world and its inhabitants on the other.[396] In what seems to be a response to positions such as that of Gö, Butön, and Rendawa, Tsongkhapa says:

> Tibetans who were learned in the Guhyasamāja explained that the evolution of the world and its beings during the first eon is the ground of purification for meditation on the path in the present. But I would not say so, since such a statement fails to distinguish between objects of correspondence and grounds of purification.[397]

Tsongkhapa then cites Dharmakīrti, who in his *Pramāṇasiddhi* says that it is possible to prevent faults that are about to arise and thus avoid the karma that would have arisen from them. "But how could one destroy what has already been done?"[398] Tsongkhapa continues:

> Thus, while it is possible to block what is about to come by blocking the potential of its cause, you cannot bring about the blocking of a fruit that has already appeared.

394. Tib. *rdzus te skyes pa*, Skt. *upapāduka*.

395. Mkhas grub rje, *Bskyed rim dngos grub rgya mtsho*, 70b5–6 and 81a2–3.

396. Tsong kha pa, *Rnam gzhag rim pa'i rnam bshad*, 46a1–3.

397. Tsong kha pa, *Rnam gzhag rim pa'i rnam bshad*, 46a4–6. See also Mkhas grub rje, *Bskyed rim dngos grub rgya mtsho*, 81a1–2.

398. Dharmakīrti, *Tshad ma rnam 'grel, Pramāṇavārttika, Pramāṇasiddhi*, Tōh 4210, 118a5–6; Sanskrit and Tibetan editions in Miyasaka 1971–1972, vv. 278cd–279ab; an English translation in Jackson 1992, 472, vv. 278–279ab.

Tsongkhapa further remarks:

> The position that meditation on the path at present can purify the birth, death, and intermediate state of beings who lived and died during the first eon, together with their environment, is just like the notion of using this year's fire to burn the ashes of last year's firewood. Hence, this is futile advice.[399]

Thus, for Tsongkhapa, in a coherent, systematic explanation of the creation stage, there is no place for retroactive purification of the "Buddhist original sin." For him, the yogis cannot even undo their own pasts, let alone the pasts of other beings.[400] The purpose of the sādhana is the transformation of the yogi's own birth, death, and intermediate state, not those of others. Moreover, the practice is intended to affect the yogi's birth, death, and intermediate state in the future, not those that have already occurred in the past. Khedrup Jé echoes this position in his *Ocean of Attainments*.[401] He stresses that yogis meditating in the present day are of a different mental continuum than the people of the first eon; therefore, there is no reason whatsoever to take them as purifiers and grounds of purification.[402]

Nevertheless, says Tsongkhapa, while the meditation on the sādhana cannot affect the long-gone people of the first eon, it is appropriate to recognize the similarity between the appearance of these beings, miraculously born soon after the evolution of their habitat, and the instantaneous visualization of the first deities who dwell in the celestial mansion that has just been visualized. One may acknowledge such an affinity as long as the distinctions between corresponding objects and grounds of purification are maintained. In Tsongkhapa's own words:

> The samsāric evolution of the physical world and its inhabitants during the first eon are corresponding objects, but the yogis meditating on the path at present do not purify them. Therefore, by

399. Tsong kha pa, *Rnam gzhag rim pa'i rnam bshad*, 45b5–6.

400. Tsong kha pa, *Rnam gzhag rim pa'i rnam bshad*, 48b4–49a2; Mkhas grub rje, *Bskyed rim dngos grub rgya mtsho*, 81a6–b3.

401. Mkhas grub rje, *Bskyed rim dngos grub rgya mtsho*, 81a2–3.

402. Mkhas grub rje, *Bskyed rim dngos grub rgya mtsho*, 73a1–3.

> meditating on the path, yogis purify their future saṃsāric events [death, intermediate state, and rebirth].[403]

There is another important reason that Tsongkhapa and Khedrup Jé preserve the connection between the present meditation on the specially visualized deities and the sentient beings of the past. In order to transform their future death, intermediate state, and birth into the three bodies of the Buddha, yogis must meditate on a path that accords with these three events. The meditation on the dissolution of the specially visualized deities into clear light is the first step on this path and will serve toward the transformation of the yogi's future death into the dharmakāya. In order to dissolve the specially visualized deities, they must first be generated.

This meditation toward a particular soteriological end has to accord with a ground of purification, in this case, the yogi's ordinary death—the death of a person born from a womb in Jambudvīpa and endowed with the six constituents.[404] In place of this ordinary death, the dharmakāya of a buddha will eventually arise. Though the first people of the eon were miraculously born and endowed with remarkable qualities, they soon turned into ordinary human beings and died ordinary deaths. Hence, their death is no different from the yogi's future death.

In this way, Tsongkhapa and Khedrup Jé preserve the authoritative explanation of *Formulating the Sādhana*. This explanation, as we have seen, elaborates on the meditation on the specially visualized deities, but does not interpret the birth of the first people of the eon as the ground of purification of the meditation on the specially visualized deities. Furthermore, it understands the dissolution of these deities into clear light as the purifier of the yogi's death.

To conclude, the generation of the specially visualized deities is not intended to purify a ground of purification. It is simply a meditation that corresponds to the evolution of the people of the first eon; it takes place after the visualization of the celestial mansion, which corresponds to the periodical evolution of the physical world. By contrast, the dissolution of the specially visualized deities into clear light is not merely a meditation in correspondence, but a meditation that is intended to eventually purify the practitioner's future death and takes it as its ground of purification. The death of the first people of the eon was no

403. Tsong kha pa, *Rnam gzhag rim pa'i rnam bshad*, 49a1–2. Mkhas grub rje follows this in his *Bskyed rim dngos grub rgya mtsho*, 73a1–3.

404. These are earth, water, fire, wind, channels, and drops, or else bone, marrow, and semen received from the father, and flesh, skin, and blood received from the mother.

different than the future death of a person who meditates on the path in the present day, making the correlation possible. To cite Tsongkhapa:

> In order to meditate on the three bodies that are similar to the three phenomena of the ground [death, intermediate state, and rebirth], yogis must first create a support [for these bodies]. While this [support] must correspond to the evolution of the world, the evolution of the deities who reside there, their dissolution into clear light and so on, must correspond to the evolution of the sentient beings of the first eon, their death, and so forth.[405]

And:

> The purpose of generating the specially visualized deities in this way is to create a support that will realize the dharmakāya.[406]

This discussion leads us to the sādhana's correspondences to microcosmic events, death, intermediate state, and rebirth on the ground of purification.

Correspondences with Microcosmic Events

On the basis of *Formulating the Sādhana*, Tibetan scholars mostly agree that the creation and completion stages of the Guhyasamāja serve to purify the yogis' death, intermediate state, and rebirth. Usually they agree that the meditation on emptiness prior to the visualization of the deity leads to the purification of death, but they provide divergent accounts of the steps involved in purifying the intermediate state and rebirth. They also vary with regard to which step of the sādhana affects which of these events.

The difficulty arises because *Formulating the Sādhana* refers to the meditation that corresponds to the intermediate state, birth, and death only in vague terms.[407] Much of the difference in opinion among Tibetan scholars results from this ambiguity. Furthermore, as we have seen above, while in *Formulating the Sādhana* the meditation is on the single deity, Vajradhara, Nāgārjuna's

405. Tsong kha pa, *Rnam gzhag rim pa'i rnam bshad*, 48b5–6.

406. Tsong kha pa, *Slob tshul*, 14a2–3.

407. For more details, see Bentor 2015c.

Concise Sādhana instructs the yogis to visualize themselves as two deities: initially as the First Lord and later as Vajrasattva.[408]

Gö Khukpa Lhetsé, as well as Rendawa, who follows him, draw their system of correspondences on the basis of *Formulating the Sādhana*, and therefore do not include the First Lord in their scheme. They maintain that meditation on the single deity Vajradhara serves to purify both the intermediate state and rebirth.[409] Butön, in his commentary on the *Concise Sādhana*, supplies a different explanation: that the meditation on the First Lord facilitates the purification of the intermediate being, while the meditation on Vajrasattva serves the purification of rebirth.[410] In this way, as we saw above, Butön creates an elegant correlation between the three grounds of purification, namely, death, the intermediate state, and rebirth, and the three major parts of the sādhana.

Candrakīrti's *Vajrasattva Sādhana*—whose authenticity is not accepted by members of the Sakya school such as Rendawa—has no instructions specifically regarding the First Lord, but it divides the meditation into three distinct parts and links them respectively to the attainment of the three bodies of the Buddha. On this basis, as noted already, Butön links the three parts of the sādhana not only to death, the intermediate state, and rebirth, but also to the attainment of the three bodies of the Buddha.[411]

Tsongkhapa follows his lead, explaining that there are three stages of purification.[412] The meditation on emptiness serves to purify the yogi's future death, and its fruit is the dharmakāya. The visualization of the First Lord serves to purify the yogi's future intermediate state, and its fruit is the saṃbhogakāya. The transformation into Vajrasattva serves to purify the yogi's future rebirth, and its fruit is the nirmāṇakāya.

Rendawa seems to have been familiar with the views of Butön. According to Rendawa's biography, he studied the Guhyasamāja according to the Ārya tradition with Butön, though Rendawa was only sixteen years old when Butön

408. Nāgārjuna, *Mdor byas, Piṇḍīkrama Sādhana*, Tōh 1796, 3b7–4a3, L 51–54. As we saw, in his *Mdo bsre, Sādhanasūtramelāpaka*, Tōh 1797, at first the nature of Vajradhara's body is wisdom; later, he transforms into a visible body.

409. 'Gos Khug pa lhas btsas, *Gsang 'dus stong thun*, 10b1–2 and 12b3–13a5; Red mda' ba, *Yid kyi mun sel*, 6b6–8b6.

410. Bu ston, *Mdor byas 'grel chen*, 36a7–37a2 and 38b3–39b4.

411. Bu ston, *Mdor byas 'grel chen*, 51a4–b2.

412. Tsong kha pa, *Bung ba'i re skong*, 15b2–21b5.

passed away.[413] Nonetheless, he chooses to follow Gö Khukpa Lhetsé rather than Butön in this matter. On the other hand, the Sakya scholar Rongtön Sheja Kunrik,[414] who often followed Rendawa, in this context rejects the position of Rendawa on the very grounds offered by Butön.[415] We see that although these Tibetan lamas belonged to the same lineage of teachings on the Guhyasamāja sādhana, and some were direct disciples of the others, they differed about textual interpretations and decisions.

413. See Roloff 2009, 99 and 213. It was through Red mda' ba that Tsong kha pa received teachings on Bu ston's commentary on the *Mdor byas*. See Tsong kha pa, *Gsan yig*, 5a1–2, and *Mtha' gcod*, 40b4.

414. Rong ston Shes bya kun rig (1367–1449).

415. Rong ston, *Gsang 'dus rnam bshad*, 6a3–7a4.

6. Meditation on the Celestial Mansion

Here begins the actual creation of the "creation stage." After the entire world and its inhabitants—the yogi's ordinary environment—are dissolved into emptiness, the ground of wisdom and the potential for all, the meditators begin to create the enlightened world of the maṇḍala.

Meditation on the Enclosures, the Source of Phenomena, and the Lotus

The Fire and Vajra Enclosures

Just before the meditation on emptiness, yogis visualize the wheel of protection, which was dissolved into emptiness together with the entire world and its inhabitants. Tsongkhapa's *Guhyasamāja Sādhana* instructs the yogi to recommence the visualization with a meditation on the protection wheel. This wheel can be seen in two-dimensional depictions of the maṇḍala as the two outer rings. The outermost perimeter is a ring of fire in the five colors of the maṇḍala—white, blue, green, red, and yellow—called also "fire mountain"[416] or a "garland of light."[417] In two-dimensional depictions, a circle of vajras[418] can be seen within the fire ring. In three-dimensional maṇḍalas visualized during the sādhana, these are not rings or circles, but rather spheres or enclosures that envelop and protect the entire maṇḍala. For this reason, Tsongkhapa's *Guhyasamāja Sādhana* instructs the meditators to visualize a vajra enclosure, including a vajra ground,[419] vajra fence,[420] vajra tent,[421] and vajra canopy.[422]

416. Tib. *me ri.*

417. Tib. *'od phreng,* Skt. *raśmimālā.*

418. Tib. *rdor phreng,* Skt. *vajrāvalī.*

419. Tib. *rdo rje sa gzhi,* Skt. *vajrabhūmi.*

420. Tib. *rdo rje'i rwa ba,* Skt. *prākāra.*

421. Tib. *rdo rje'i gur,* Skt. *vajrapañjara.*

422. Tib. *bla re,* Skt. *vitāna.*

The first point of dispute in this section arises because none of the main sādhanas of the Ārya tradition—neither the *Concise Sādhana*, the *Sādhana Incorporating the Scripture*, nor the *Vajrasattva Sādhana*—mention any visualization of protection by fire and vajras here. Moreover, another meditation on protection seems redundant here, since the meditation on emptiness in the previous stage is regarded as protection in ultimate truth,[423] and the meditation on the protection wheel before [the meditation on emptiness] is called "protection in relative truth." Indeed, neither Ngorchen Kunga Sangpo nor Butön mention any meditation on protection at this point, while Amyé Shap objects to the visualization of the entire protective enclosure here.[424] The reason Tsongkhapa and Khedrup Jé maintain that it is inappropriate not to meditate on the vajra enclosure here is because the enclosure appears in maṇḍala drawings and three-dimensional depictions, as well as in works on the maṇḍala such as Nāgabodhi's *Maṇḍala Ritual*.[425]

Meditation on the Source of Phenomena

Next, Tsongkhapa's *Guhyasamāja Sādhana* instructs to meditate on the "source of phenomena,"[426] which, as its name indicates, is the ground of all things. The source of phenomena is visualized as a triangular pyramid, standing on a point with its wide side pointing upward, empty inside, obviously indicating birth. In two-dimensional depictions of the maṇḍala, however, it is said to be drawn as a circle [or two concentric circles] within the vajra ring.[427] Its color is either white,[428] signifying natural purity,[429] or white outside and red inside, which, along with its shape of the bhaga, signify the wisdom of great

423. Tib. *don dam pa'i srung ba*. See, for example, Candrakīrti, *Rdo rje sems dpa'i sgrub thabs*, *Vajrasattva Sādhana*, Tōh 1814, 197b5; Luo and Tomabechi 2009, 9.8 and 41.12.

424. This step is not included in Ngor chen, *Gsang 'dus dkyil 'khor gyi sgrub thabs dngos grub rgya mtsho*; Bu ston, *Mdor byas 'grel chen*, 15a1; and A myes zhab, *Gsang 'dus dkyil 'khor sgrub thabs rnam bshad*, 87a1–4.

425. *Dkyil chog nyi shu pa*, *Maṇḍalaviṃśatividhi*, chap. 4, v. 17, Tōh 1810, 134a3–4; Tanaka 2004, 31. This passage is referred to by Tsong kha pa in his *Bskyed rim zin bris*, 16a3; see also *Sngags rim chen mo*, 502–503; and Mkhas grub rje, *Bskyed rim dngos grub rgya mtsho*, 43b5–44a3.

426. Tib. *chos 'byung*, Skt. *dharmodaya*.

427. Doboom Tulku 1996, 57 and 65.

428. Tsong kha pa, *Gsang mngon*, 29a1, and Abhayākaragupta, *Dkyil chog rdo rje 'phreng ba*, *Vajrāvalī Maṇḍalavidhi*, Tōh 3140, 38a5; Mori 2009, §13.2.2, 236–237.

429. Tsong kha pa, *Bung ba'i re skong*, 12b5.

bliss that arises when the white and red elements meet in the lotus of the consort.[430] This great bliss gives birth to the wisdom that realizes the three doors of liberation, signified by the three corners of the source of phenomena. The triangular bhaga signifies the subject—the wisdom born of great bliss—and its hollow interior signifies its object—emptiness.[431] The bhaga also alludes to the word *evaṃ* at the opening line of the *Guhyasamāja Tantra*, in which, we are told, the Blessed One dwells in the bhaga of the Vajra Queen, the place that gave birth to the teachings of the tantra. The word *evaṃ* consists of the letter *e*, whose shape in Indian scripts is triangular, and *vaṃ*, which indicates the indivisible unity of emptiness and the wisdom of great bliss.

The entire maṇḍala, with its celestial mansion and deities, that will be visualized in the sādhana is contained within the source of phenomena. Hence, when the yogi meditates on the source of phenomena, the yogi's world and its inhabitants will arise as a miraculous display of the indivisible unity of wisdom of great bliss and emptiness. Thus the scriptures and their commentaries stress the symbolism of the source of phenomena as the origin for everything, the womb of the mother of all—not of ordinary things, but as a spiritual birth into the path to enlightenment taught in the *Guhyasamāja Tantra*. The great bliss, signified by the triangle and the white and red colors, gives birth to the wisdom out of which everything emanates.

It would be surprising, then, to find a lama who would not wish to include the meditation on the source of phenomena in their sādhanas. Still, Khedrup Jé and Amyé Shap both mention early lamas who do not instruct the yogi to meditate on the source of phenomena.[432] This is because, apart from saying "in the midst of the space realm," the *Concise Sādhana* and the *Vajrasattva Sādhana* do not teach an explicit meditation on the source of phenomena.

Meditation on the Lotus

Within the source of phenomena, the meditators visualize a variegated lotus[433] with sixty-four petals. In maṇḍala drawings, within the rings of vajras and the source of phenomena (the latter is usually not visible), there is a ring of

430. Mkhas grub rje, *Bskyed rim dngos grub rgya mtsho*, 46a6–b1.

431. See Dge 'dun rgya mtsho, *Gsang bskyed*, 21b5–6.

432. Mkhas grub rje, *Bskyed rim dngos grub rgya mtsho*, 44b1; A myes zhabs, *Gsang 'dus dkyil 'khor sgrub thabs rnam bshad*, 87a2. According to A myes zhabs, the early lamas who do not instruct on the source of phenomena include 'Gos and Rngog, who were learned in the tradition of the Guhyasamāja.

433. Tib. *pad rwa* or *padma rwa ba*, Skt. *padmadala*.

variegated lotus, signifying that the maṇḍala within it is unstained by the faults of saṃsāra.[434] Butön sides with those who meditate on the lotus, since it appears in maṇḍala paintings, but Ngorchen Kunga Sangpo does not include it in his own sādhana.[435] Khedrup Jé shows that without the lotus ring, the measurements of the maṇḍala would not agree with Nāgabodhi's authoritative treatise on the maṇḍala.[436]

Meditation on the Four Disks

Within the lotus, the four disks of the physical elements, wind, fire, water, and earth, are visualized from their respective seed syllables *yaṃ*, *raṃ*, *baṃ*, and *laṃ*. They stand vertical, in the colors of the elements—blue, red, white, and yellow respectively. The wind disk is bow-shaped with its straight side facing to the east, the fire disk is triangular with its point facing to the east, the water disk is round, and the earth disk is square. The seed syllables of the elements are flanked by two *hūṃs*, standing horizontally with their heads facing west. When the *yaṃ*, *raṃ*, *baṃ*, and *laṃ* transform into the four disks, the *hūṃs* transform into vajras. Next, the four disks merge together and transform into a crossed vajra, which is why the disks themselves are not seen in maṇḍala depictions.

The meditation on the disks of the four physical elements corresponds to the evolution of the disks of wind, water, and earth during the periodic evolution of the world.[437] A light wind descends from the first dhyāna, gradually increases, and ultimately creates the wind disk. Then a continuous rain with drops the size of chariot wheels falls on the wind disk, accumulates over a long period of time, and forms the water. Finally, a wind churns the water disk and creates the golden ground just as film is formed over boiling milk.

434. See, for example, Paṇ chen Bsod nams grags pa, *Gsang 'dus bskyed rim rnam gzhag*, 27a5.

435. Bu ston, *Mdor byas 'grel chen*, 15a3–5; Ngor chen, *Gsang 'dus dkyil 'khor gyi sgrub thabs dngos grub rgya mtsho*, 4b4.

436. Mkhas grub rje, *Bskyed rim dngos grub rgya mtsho*, 46b5–47b2. See Nāgabodhi, *Dkyil chog nyi shu pa*, *Maṇḍalaviṃśatividhi*, Tōh 1810; Tanaka 2004.

437. See Nāgabuddhi, *Rnam gzhag rim pa*, *Vyavastholi*, chap. 1, Tōh 1809, 121b5–122a1; Tanaka 2016, 82; and Tsong kha pa, *Bung ba'i re skong*, 11b6–12b1. These follow Vasubandhu's *Mdzod 'grel*, *Kośabhāṣya*, chap. 3, vv. 45–49a, Tōh 4090, 144a4–b6; Pradhan 1975, 157–158; Pruden 1988–1990, 451–452; and Asaṅga, *Sa'i dngos gzhi*, *Maulībhūmi*, Tōh 4035, 18b5–19a2; Bhattacharya 1957, 36–38.

Though during the evolution of the world there is no fire disk, according to Nāgabuddhi the fire abides in a latent form within the other three disks.[438]

In his sādhana, Tsongkhapa instructs the meditators to visualize the four disks in the nature of the four mothers, Locanā, Māmakī, Pāṇḍarā, and Tārā, which gives rise to another disagreement.[439] Both the *Concise Sādhana* and the *Vajrasattva Sādhana* mention the meditation on the four disks that arise from their respective seed syllables, but these two basic sādhanas do not refer to their nature as that of the four mothers.[440] Yet famous verses of the *Guhyasamāja Tantra* declare that the five aggregates are proclaimed as the five buddhas, while the earth is called Locanā, the water Māmakī, the fire Pāṇḍarā, and the wind Tārā.[441] Furthermore, both the *Vajrasattva Sādhana* and the *Sādhana Incorporating the Scripture* cite another verse from the *Guhyasamāja Tantra* as the scriptural source for this meditation,[442] and Candrakīrti's *Illuminating Lamp* explicitly refers to the four mothers in its interpretation of this verse.[443] Khedrup Jé says on this:

> Hence, those who do not understand this profound, definitive interpretation forego the explicit explanation of glorious Candrakīrti with respect to meditating on the four disks in the nature of the four mothers, and instead meditate on the various emblems, such as the banner, the blazing fire, the vase, and the jewel, something taught neither by Nāgārjuna and his disciples nor in the *Root* and *Explanatory Tantras*.[444]

The meditation on emblems beginning with a banner can be traced to

438. Nāgabuddhi, *Rnam gzhag rim pa*, chap. 1, Tōh 1809, 121b7–122a1; Tanaka 2016, 82.

439. Tsong kha pa, *Gsang mngon*, 29b1.

440. Nāgārjuna, *Mdor byas*, *Piṇḍīkrama Sādhana*, Tōh 1796, 2b5–7; L 19b–22; Candrakīrti, *Rdo rje sems dpa'i sgrub thabs*, *Vajrasattva Sādhana*, Tōh 1814, 197b5–6; Luo and Tomabechi 2009, 9.10–11.1 and 41.15–42.1.

441. *Gsang 'dus*, chap. 17, Tōh 442; Zhol 44a6–7; Stog 74b4–5; Fremantle 1971, vv. 50–51; and Matsunaga 1978, vv. 50–51. See the section "The Nature of the Transformation of the Ordinary Body into a Buddha's Body" above.

442. *Gsang 'dus*, chap. 11, Tōh 442; Zhol 15a2–3; Stog 25b3; Dunh 27b5; Fremantle 1971, v. 3ab; and Matsunaga 1978, v. 3ab. See Candrakīrti, *Rdo rje sems dpa'i sgrub thabs*, *Vajrasattva Sādhana*, Tōh 1814, 197b7; Luo and Tomabechi 2009, 10.3–4 and 42.4–5, and Nāgārjuna, *Mdo bsre*, *Sādhanasūtramelāpaka*, Tōh 1797, 11b7.

443. Candrakīrti, *Sgron gsal*, *Pradīpoddyotanaṭīkā*, chap. 11, v. 3, Tōh 1785, 77b1–2; Chakravarti 1984, 96.

444. Mkhas grub rje, *Bskyed rim dngos grub rgya mtsho*, 49a1–2.

Ratnākaraśānti's commentary on the *Concise Sādhana*,[445] a tradition that was continued in the Sakya school, including Ngorchen Kunga Sangpo.[446] This point of contention—whether the four disks of the elements are visualized as the four mothers or as marked with various emblems—may seem insignificant to the modern reader, but it gradually became a distinctive hallmark of each of these Tibetan schools.

The Merging of the Four Disks into the Crossed Vajra

The subsequent meditation on the merging of the four disks of the physical elements into the crossed vajra bears a number of parallels to the completion stage of the path. Tsongkhapa draws correlations between this fusion and the dissolution of the inner winds into the indestructible drop that brings about the realization of clear light during the completion stage.[447] Tsongkhapa raises an objection to explanations such as the following provided by Ngorchen Kunga Sangpo:

> Then visualize that the fire is lighted by the wind, the water is boiled by the fire, the earth dissolved by the water, and everything merges together into one taste and transforms into a crossed vajra.[448]

Khedrup Jé repeats Tsongkhapa's objection:

> Those who say that the wind ignites the fire, the fire boils the water, the water dissolves the earth, and thereby the four disks merge together and so forth offer pointless elaborations that strongly

445. Ratnākaraśānti, *Rin chen phreng ba, Piṇḍīkṛta Sādhana Vṛtti Ratnāvalī*, Tōh 1826, 28a3–b5. According to Ratnākaraśānti, the wind disk is marked with a banner, the fire disk with a blazing garland, the water disk with emanating waves like an ocean of milk, and the earth disk with an eight-spoke wheel.

446. Ngor chen, *Gsang 'dus dkyil 'khor gyi sgrub thabs dngos grub rgya mtsho*, 4b4. The four emblems that mark the four disks here are a banner, a blazing fire, a vase full of water, and a three-pronged vajra. Note that Mkhas grub rje includes a vase and not a water disk with emanating waves, as does Kun dga' bzang po, which may indicate that Mkhas grub rje has in mind a tradition closer to that of the Sa skya than to that of Ratnākaraśānti.

447. Tsong kha pa, *Bung ba'i re skong*, 13a1–5.

448. Ngor chen, *Gsang 'dus dkyil 'khor gyi sgrub thabs dngos grub rgya mtsho*, 5a1. See also Bu Ston, *Mdor byas 'grel chen*, 15b2–3, and A myes zhabs, *Gsang 'dus dkyil 'khor sgrub thabs rnam bshad*, 87b1. For Tsong kha pa's objection, see Tsong kha pa, *Bskyed rim zin bris*, 16b2–3.

> contradict the stages of the inner dissolution. Therefore those who do not understand the meaning of the tantras should not provide elucidations![449]

A meditation similar to the one described by Ngorchen Kunga Sangpo is found in the blessing of the inner offering at the beginning of the sādhana.[450] There, the wind that stirs, the fire that ignites, and so forth blend the inner offerings into a fully purified and crystal-clear substance whose taste is one. The *Later Tantra of the Guhyasamāja* relates this to the joining of the yogi's vajra with the consort's lotus.[451] Tsongkhapa regards the link between the merging of the four disks and the blessing of the inner offerings as lacking any scriptural authority in the Ārya tradition; Khedrup Jé calls it a pointless elaboration.

As is the case throughout *Ocean of Attainments*, some of the arguments about the celestial mansion are inherited from the Tengyur, while others arose among Tibetan scholars. The details of the disagreements, as well as their previous occurrences among Indian and Tibetan scholars, can be found in the translation and notes below.

The Celestial Mansion and the Relationship between Its Two- and Three-Dimensional Depictions[452]

The nave of the crossed vajra, created through the merging of the four disks of the physical elements, forms the foundation on which the celestial mansion rests. As can be seen in plates 1 and 3, the height of the crossed vajra is more than half the height of the entire structure, hence disciples who approach the palace are dwarfed by its size and must look up toward the level where the deities reside.[453] Straight ahead of them, the disciples are fenced out with the immense five prongs of the crossed vajra, which block the staircases that lead to the gates of the mansion (see plate 3).

The nave of the crossed vajra is in the color of the principal deity of the maṇḍala. Hence, in the Guhyasamāja maṇḍala, the foundation on which the

449. Mkhas grub rje, *Bskyed rim dngos grub rgya mtsho*, 49a2–3.

450. Tsong kha pa, *Gsang mngon*, 9b6–10a2.

451. *Rgyud phyi ma, Uttara Tantra*, Tōh 443, 153b7; Matsunaga 1978, vv. 128–131.

452. This description is based on the three-dimensional Guhyasamāja maṇḍala in Gyümé Monastery (Rgyud med dgon) in Hunsur, India, and on the two-dimensional drawings in Don 'grub rdo rje [Rong tha] 1999, following p. 71.

453. According to Mkhas grub rje, authoritative scriptures do not specify an exact height for the nave of the crossed vajra. See his *Bskyed rim dngos grub rgya mtsho*, 56a1–2.

celestial mansion rests is blue, the color of Akṣobhya. The crossed vajra has twenty prongs in variegated colors, five in each of the four directions, each emerging from a mouth of the sea monster. The upper prongs are always blue, and the central prong is in the colors of the tathāgata in each direction: white in the east, yellow in the south, red in the west, and green in the north. The right and left prongs in each direction are in the color of the neighboring tathāgata; thus, in the eastern direction, the right prong is yellow, the color of Ratnasaṃbhava, and the left is green, the color of Amoghavajra. The lower prong is in the color of the tathāgata in the opposite direction, such that in the east the lower prong is red, the color of Amitābha. The staircase is in the color of the tathāgata in that direction, white in the east, the color of Vairocana. At the top of the stairway, the disciples are met with the mouth and teeth of the sea monster, out of which the blue prong emerges.

In front of the maṇḍala gates are monumental ornamented portals of the same height as the maṇḍala palace (see plate 5 and diagram 1). These portals are seen in two-dimensional depictions of the maṇḍala as well. However, as in ancient maps, two-dimensional representations combine two angles of viewing the maṇḍala, aerial and sideway perspectives, concurrently (see plate 2 and diagram 1). Thus, while parts of the celestial mansion are shown as if seen from above, numerous details are shown as seen from the horizontal vantage point of one who approaches the palace. As a consequence, in two-dimensional representations, the prongs, depicted from an aerial view, and the portals, shown from a horizontal perspective, cover the same area of the painting. But since the portals partially hide the prongs, the portals are seen as if encompassed by the curving prongs, and only the tips of the central prongs are seen as they reach the lotus ring. One of the points of dispute addressed in this chapter of *Ocean of Attainments* is how to properly portray these two elements of the mansion, one depicted from a vertical perspective and the other from a horizontal perspective, in two-dimensional drawings.

The portals rest on four columns, two on each side, in the color associated with the particular direction; these columns in turn rest on golden vases (see plates 4 and 5). They are comprised of eleven ornamented layers, which lend them a monumental appearance. Since the sequence of layers in a Guhyasamāja maṇḍala is distinct from that of Cakrasaṃvara and Vajrabhairava, knowledgeable disciples can immediately recognize which celestial mansion they are approaching. In the case of the Guhyasamāja, in an ascending order the layers are gold, precious "drip-like" ornament, jewels, "hoof-like" ornament, dark layer, multicolored layer, dark layer, drip-like ornament, jewels,

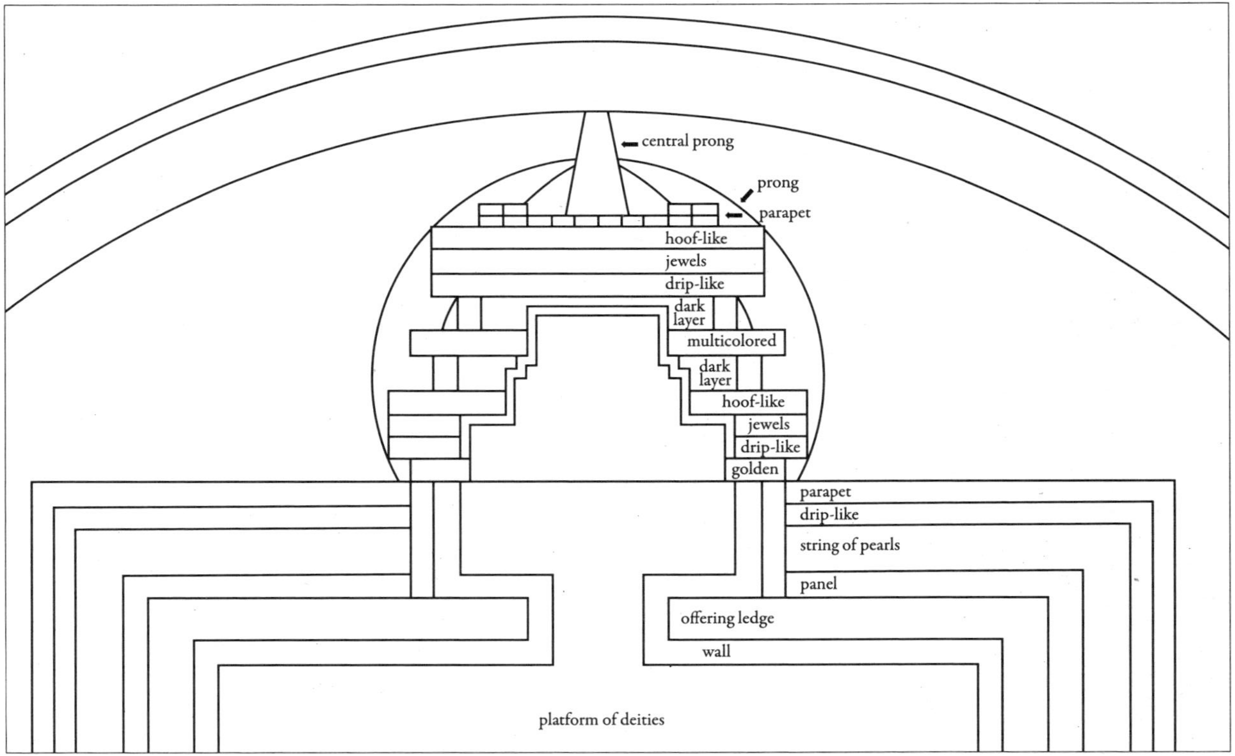

Diagram 1. A sideview of the maṇḍala's wall and portal.

hoof-like ornament, and railings.[454] The so-called dark layers are not dark, but simply unornamented posts larger than the other layers. Though the posts themselves are plain, the space to the right and left of the posts is filled with animals such as lions and peacocks. Strands of pearls and jewels cover the upper portion of the gate's opening (see plate 5).

The Tibetan name of the portal, *rta babs*, may indicate a ramp for dismounting a horse, evoking the architecture of a royal palace. Khedrup Jé, however, does not accept the position that there seems to be a horse at the entryway of the portal. Another discussion related to the portal is whether there is a space between the portal and the gate in either three-dimensional maṇḍalas or maṇḍala drawings.

The ornaments above the portals contribute to their majestic appearance (see plate 5). At the center there is a Dharma wheel with ten spokes and a rim mounted on a lotus and lunar seats. To the right and left of the wheel are a buck and a doe facing it, their eyes directed at its tip. They are flanked by two monkeys holding parasols with suspending tassels, topped by a crescent moon, jewels, and a vajra. At the corners of both the tenth and eleventh layer of the portals are pennants. In two-dimensional drawings of the maṇḍala, the buck and the doe are seen between the curving prongs of the vajras, and the central prong of the crossed vajra is visible from between the spokes of the wheel (see plate 2).

To the right and left of each portal are two wish-fulfilling trees growing out of "vases of excellence,"[455] adorned with the seven royal treasures of a universal monarch[456] (see plate 4). In two-dimensional drawings, the trees appear to have been placed on the roof next to the pennants.[457] Floating in the space behind the trees are the tathāgatas of the four directions. At the level of the roof, four goddesses emerge from clouds with flowers in their hands (see plates 6 and 7). In two-dimensional drawings, the tathāgatas and goddesses are depicted further away from the wish-fulfilling trees and pennants.

The wall of the celestial mansion is in fact transparent (see plates 6 and 7), although it consists of five colored layers: from the outer layer inward, white,

454. Tib. *gser, rin chen shar bu, rin po che, rmig pa, mun pa, varaṇḍa, mun pa, rin chen shar bu, rin po che, rta rmig*, and *mda' yab*; Skt. *suvarṇa, bakūlī, ratna, khura, andhakāra, varaṇḍa, andhakāra, bakūlī, ratna, khura*, and *kramaśīrṣa*. See Abhayākaragupta, *Dkyil chog rdo rje 'phreng ba, Vajrāvalī Maṇḍalavidhi*, Tōh 3140, 23b1–2; Mori 2009, §12.2.5, 162–163. For the case of Cakrasaṃvara and Vajrabhairava, see the translation and notes below.

455. Tib. *bum pa bzang po*, Skt. *bhadraghaṭa*.

456. See Mvy. 3621–3628.

457. Tib. *ba dan*, Skt. *patāka*.

yellow, red, green, and blue. These are the colors of the five tathāgatas, but here they remain the same in every direction. In two-dimensional drawings, the wall can be seen as five black lines around the ground of the mansion or the main lines.[458] Sixteen offering goddesses stand on the red ledges in front of the walls, partly blocking the view of the interior mansion (see plates 4 and 7). There are four goddesses on each side, two to the right and left of each gate, wearing various ornaments and garments, standing in various postures, and holding various offerings in their hands. In two-dimensional drawings, the red offering ledge with the sixteen deities encompasses the five layers of the wall. The offering ledge comes to an end upon reaching the gates.

The higher, nontransparent portion of the wall consists of five layers (see plate 6). The lowest panel among them has a red surface decorated with geometrical shapes: triangles, squares, and circles. The literal meaning of the Tibetan name of this panel is "brick,"[459] and it can be seen on the entrance gates to monasteries as well.[460] In two-dimensional drawings, this is the third square section of the celestial mansion, red in color. The argument in this context is against those, including Sönam Tsemo and Pakpa Lodrö Gyaltsen,[461] who maintain that the surface of the panel is yellow.[462] The tradition of the yellow color of this panel is said to have been transmitted from Śraddha.[463]

Above this panel is a layer called "clear appearance,"[464] since it allows external light to illuminate the interior of the palace (see plate 6). This layer consists of four bands[465] with apertures flanked by small capitals. In front of these bands are round and vertical strands of pearls, decorated with various ornaments, which shield the openings. The literal meanings of the Sanskrit and Tibetan terms are "strands" and "semi-strands."[466] The "strands" are semicircular necklaces of pearls hung on their two sides, and the "semi-strands" are

458. Tib. *rtsa thig*, Skt. *mūlasūtra*.

459. Tib. *pha gu*, Skt. *khura*.

460. An example can be found on the main entrance gate to Gyümé Monastery in Hunsur.

461. 'Phags pa Blo gros rgyal mtshan (1235–1280).

462. Bsod nams rtse mo, *Kye rdo rje'i dkyil 'khor du slob ma smin par byed pa'i cho ga dbang gi chu bu chen mo*, work 20, 57b5–6; 'Phags pa Blo gros rgyal mtshan, *Gsang ba 'dus pa 'jam pa'i rdo rje lha bcu dgu'i sgrub thabs*, work 110, 220b4.

463. See Ngor chen, *Zla zer*, 105a6.

464. Tib. *gsal snang*.

465. Tib. *ska rags*, Skt. *mekhalā*.

466. Tib. *drwa ba drwa phyed*, Skt. *hāradhahāra*.

vertical strands of pearls that descend as far as the curved strands. In maṇḍala drawings, the bands and apertures are not depicted; only the round and vertical strands of pearls are seen in black color on a blue background, the fourth square section of the celestial mansion.

Above the strands of pearls are "drip-like ornaments."[467] In two-dimensional drawings, this is the fifth square section of the celestial mansion, white in color with a visible "drip-like" or drop-like pattern. In three-dimensional maṇḍalas, the white drip-like layer is suspended from the red eaves just above it. The upper layer of the wall is the white railings or parapet[468] in the form of half-lotus petals. The literal meaning of the Tibetan term is "arrow-shelter." On the lower roof above the walls are victory banners[469] and pennants.[470] To represent their swinging motion in the wind, the victory banners and pennants whorl three times (see plate 5).

The Inner Mansion

The inner mansion (see plate 8 and diagram 2) at the center houses the thirty-two deities seated on their thrones upon the deities' platform.[471] It should be pointed out that in two-dimensional drawings, the deities' platform is shown from an aerial perspective as if seen from above, while the architectural elements surrounding the platform, including the walls, the offering ledge, the portals, and so forth, are shown as in a side view. Thus in maṇḍala drawings, the deities' platform is the square area within the main lines (see diagram 3),[472] which is the border between the wall and the deities' platform. The diagonal lines[473] divide the deities' platform into the four colors of the tathāgatas: white in the east, yellow in the south, red in the west, and green in the north. Maṇḍala drawings, as well as the three-dimensional maṇḍalas in Gyümé Monastery, do not depict the deities that rest on the platform, but only their emblems.

In the outermost square are the ten fierce deities who guard the perimeter: four at the gates, four at the intermediate directions, and two above and

467. Tib. *shar bu*, Skt. *bakulī* or *vakulī*.

468. Tib. *mda' yab*, Skt. *kramaśīrṣa*.

469. Tib. *rgyal mtshan*, Skt. *dhvaja*.

470. Tib. *ba dan*, Skt. *patāka*.

471. Tib. *lha snam* or *lha yi snam bu*, Skt. *devatāpaṭṭikā*.

472. Tib. *rtsa thig*, Skt. *mūlasūtra*.

473. Tib. *zur thig*, Skt. *koṇasūtra*.

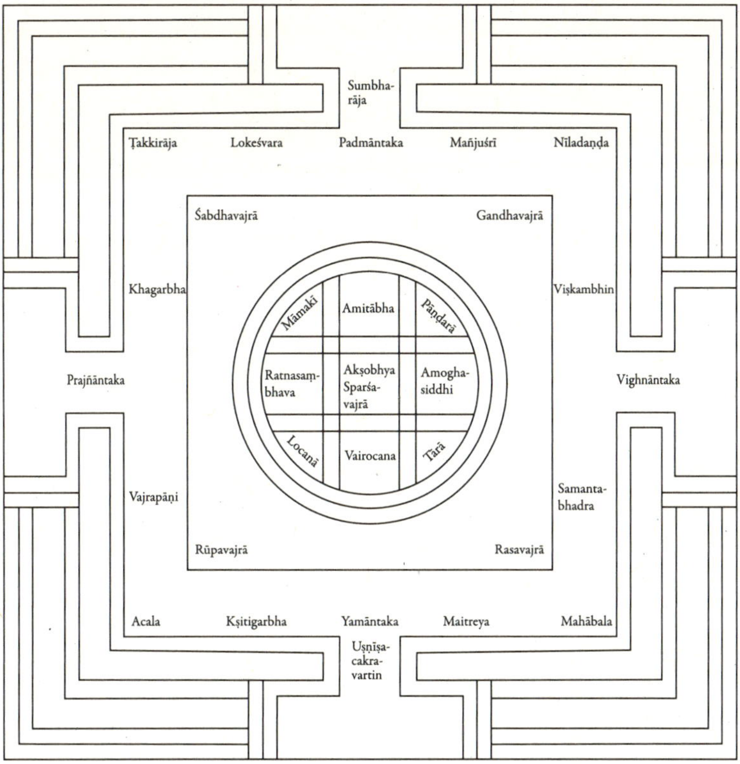

Diagram 2. Locations of the deities in the celestial palace.

below the platform (see diagram 2). In some of the two-dimensional drawings, Uṣṇīṣacakravartin, the fierce deity above, is placed east of Yamāntaka, the fierce deity in the east; Sumbharāja, the fierce deity below, is placed west of Padmāntaka, the fierce deity in the west. In three-dimensional maṇḍalas, Uṣṇīṣacakravartin is placed above Akṣobhya, the principal deity of the maṇḍala, but below the peaked roof, slightly to the east and facing the west; Sumbharāja is placed upon the nave of the crossed vajra a short distance away, behind and below the principal deity.

The eight bodhisattvas are in the same square to the right and left of each of the gates within the mansion. Four of the vajra ladies are in the corners of the next square, the second square within the inner palace, while Sparśavajrā, the Vajra Lady of Tangibles, who is the consort of Akṣobhya, dwells with him on the central seat. There are also eight vases filled with nectar in this square, two in each of the four directions (see plate 2).

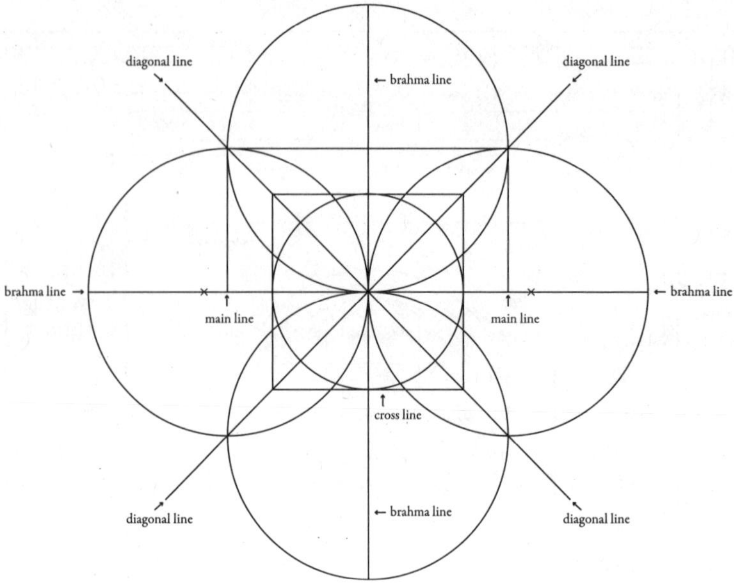

Diagram 3. The main lines of the maṇḍala.

Up to this point we have been describing the exterior of the inner mansion with its twenty-two deities. Now we will turn to its interior, the innermost part of the mansion, the abode of the five tathāgatas and their consorts. The innermost mansion is surrounded by a circular garland of vajras; in between the vajras are eight columns (see plate 8). In two-dimensional drawings, two rings are depicted: the outer light garland[474] and the inner vajra garland.[475] However, the light garland is not found in three-dimensional maṇḍalas, since it is not an actual part of the mansion. It is drawn in order to represent the light radiating into the innermost mansion from above.

The area within the circular vajra garland is divided into nine quadrants:[476] the seats of the five tathāgatas and the four mothers (see diagram 2). In two-dimensional maṇḍalas, two straight lines are drawn between each of the deities' domains. The color of the central quadrant is blue, and in three dimensions the central seat is slightly raised above the surrounding seats and Sumbharāja abides below it.

The thirty-two deities of the maṇḍala abide on thirty-one seats, since

474. Tib. *'od 'phreng*, Skt. *raśmimālā*.

475. Tib. *rdo rje phreng ba*, Skt. *vajrāvalī*.

476. Tib. *re'u mig*, Skt. *koṣṭha*.

Akṣobhya and his consort share a single seat. All these seats have a variegated lotus at their base, but their upper parts differ. Akṣobhya, his consort, and the ten fierce deities abide on solar disks. The deities in the east have lunar seats and in the south jewel seats, with the exception of Māmakī, who has a vajra seat. In the west, the deities are seated on lotus flowers, and in the north on crossed vajras.

The celestial mansion is topped with a square lower roof (see plate 9) surrounded by railings and a sea monster at each of the four corners (see plates 5, 6, and 7). The upper roof covering the nine quadrants is higher in order to accommodate Uṣṇīṣacakravartin, the fierce deity above the principal deity (see plate 8). Its top is decorated with a finial of vajras, jewels, and precious gems (see plate 5). The roofs cannot be seen in two-dimensional drawings.

The square celestial mansion is surrounded by a series of rings that give the entire structure its round shape, as the name "maṇḍala" indicates (see plate 10). In three-dimensional meditations, these rings are in fact complete enclosures, but since depicting three-dimensional mansions in this way would block them from view, these are shown as mere rings in three dimensions as well. The outer ring is another "garland of light,"[477] consisting of a blazing five-colored flame. Within it is the vajra ring, which becomes a complete vajra enclosure in three-dimensional meditations. The third ring is a variegated lotus,[478] indicating that the entire celestial mansion and the deities within are untainted by the impurities of saṃsāra.

477. Tib. *'od 'phreng*, Skt. *raśmimālā*.

478. Tib. *pad rwa* or *padma rwa ba*, Skt. *padmadala*.

Plate 1. A wooden model of the Guhyasamāja maṇḍala, Gyümé Monastery.

Plate 2. The Guhyasamāja maṇḍala in colors from Rongtha.

Plate 3. The prong and stairway in the western direction, Gyümé Monastery.

Plate 4. A corner side view of the Guhyasamāja maṇḍala, Gyümé Monastery.

Plate 5. The western side of the Guhyasamāja maṇḍala, Gyümé Monastery.

Plate 6. A closeup of part of the western side of the Guhyasamāja maṇḍala, Gyümé Monastery.

Plate 7. A closer view of the upper part of the wall of the Guhyasamāja maṇḍala, Gyümé Monastery.

Plate 8. The wooden model of the Guhyasamāja maṇḍala, with its roof removed, Gyümé Monastery.

Plate 9. The roof of wooden model taken off and inverted, Gyümé Monastery.

Plate 10. The three outer rings of the Guhyasamāja maṇḍala in the southern direction, Gyümé Monastery.

7. Generation of the Specially Visualized Deities and Their Deeds

Meditation on the Specially Visualized Deities

The meditation on the celestial mansion is followed by a meditation on the specially visualized deities, the first deities who dwell in the maṇḍala of the Guhyasamāja. The unusual name for these deities, translated here as "specially visualized deities," is based on the way they are visualized. In his sādhana, Tsongkhapa states: "Merely through a special visualization, the thirty-two deities appear fully formed upon their seats instantly and simultaneously."[479] This is based on Nāgārjuna's *Concise Sādhana*, which instructs the yogi: "Meditate on the deities in the maṇḍala [through] special visualization."[480] The word "through" appears in brackets because it appears in Sanskrit, but not in the Tibetan, although some preposition is certainly needed. The Sanskrit word here is *adhimuktyā* in the instrumental case, while the Tibetan is *lhag par mos [pa]*. Both the Sanskrit and Tibetan terms carry multiple meanings, and Khedrup Jé plays on them in his explanation (below). "Visualization" is only one possible English translation among many, including "intention," "aspiration," "conviction," "faith," and "devotion." Khedrup Jé explains how to visualize these deities:

> The thirty-two deities do not appear gradually out of their seed syllables, emblems, and so forth, but rather, at the very moment your mind intends (*mos pa*) for all the deities to be placed inside the maṇḍala, you should visualize (*mos pa*) them at once fully formed, with heads, arms, and so forth, as in a miraculous birth.[481]

According to Tsongkhapa, while the specially visualized deities arise

479. Tsong kha pa, *Gsang mngon*, 31a4–5.

480. Nāgārjuna, *Mdor byas*, *Piṇḍīkrama Sādhana*, Toh 1796, 3a7; L 36ab.

481. Mkhas grub rje, *Bskyed rim dngos grub rgya mtsho*, 69a2–3.

instantaneously, the yogis then must develop the clarity of their visualization in stages: "Generate the thirty-two deities instantly and simultaneously, merely through a special visualization, and develop the clarity of your visualization gradually."[482]

The reason these deities appear instantly is because they evolve in a parallel manner to the first people of the eon, who were miraculously born with all their faculties unimpaired. As we have seen,[483] the generation of the specially visualized deities does not have its own ground of purification. Only the meditation on their dissolution later on is capable of leading to the transformation of the yogi's future death. But in order to be able to dissolve the specially visualized deities, the yogis must first create them. Though this meditation is an integral part of the sādhana, we have not yet reached the core of the practice, endowed as it is with soteriological import. While the core practices of the sādhana serve for the future attainment of the three bodies of the Buddha, the purpose of the meditation on the specially visualized deities is to create a "person"[484] that will realize the dharmakāya.[485]

The sādhana arranged by Tsongkhapa describes each of the thirty-two specially visualized deities, beginning with the yogi as Vajradhara and his consort Sparśavajrā, the four other tathāgatas, the four mothers, the four vajra ladies, the six bodhisattvas, and the ten fierce deities. It details the colors, crowns, and emblems of each deity, as well as the facial expressions, ornaments, and garments of the female deities and the fierce deities.[486]

Note that according to Tsongkhapa, the principal deity of this maṇḍala is not Akṣobhya but Vajradhara. In fact, Akṣobhya is not included in this maṇḍala, although some of the deities, including Sparśavajrā and the four surrounding tathāgatas, are crowned by Akṣobhya. Not surprisingly, the question who is the principal deity of the specially visualized deities is a matter of dispute, one that is not easily resolvable due to conflicting scriptural authorities. On this occasion, Khedrup Jé "reminds" us that each vajra word of the tantra can teach several different meanings.[487] Khedrup Jé alludes here to differ-

482. Tsong kha pa, *Rnal 'byor dag rim*, 10b3. Mkhas grub Nor bzang rgya mtsho expands on this in his *Gsang ba 'dus pa'i bskyed rim gyi don gsal bar byed pa'i sgron me*, 51a4–5.

483. In the section "Correspondences with Macrocosmic Events" above.

484. Tib. *rten*.

485. Tsong kha pa, *Slob tshul*, 12b4–5, and *Rnam gzhag rim pa'i rnam bshad*, 48b5–6; Mkhas grub rje, *Bskyed rim dngos grub rgya mtsho*, 73a5–6.

486. Tsong kha pa, *Gsang mngon*, 31a4–37b3.

487. Mkhas grub rje, *Bskyed rim dngos grub rgya mtsho*, 70b1–2.

ent suggestions about the exact lines in the *Guhyasamāja Tantra* that serve as the scriptural authority for the meditation on the specially visualized deities.

According to Nāgabuddhi's introduction, Bhavyakīrti, and Ratnākaraśānti, the principal deity of the specially visualized deities is Akṣobhya,[488] while according to Nāgārjuna's *Concise Sādhana* he is Vajrasattva,[489] and in Nāgārjuna's *Sādhana Incorporating the Scripture,* Candrakīrti's *Vajrasattva Sādhana,* and the first chapter of *Formulating the Sādhana,* the principal deity is Vajradhara.[490] Since the works of the Ārya tradition of the Guhyasamāja have a greater authority in Tsongkhapa's eyes, he maintains that the principal deity is Vajradhara.[491]

The Deeds of the Specially Visualized Deities

After the specially visualized deities have been placed on their respective thrones in the celestial mansion, the yogis visualize them performing deeds of enlightenment—initiating all sentient beings and bringing them to the stage of buddhahood. In doing so, these deities fulfill the general Mahāyāna goal of acting out of great compassion for the sake of all sentient beings, leading them to complete awakening. They achieve this goal through the tantric means of drawing sentient beings into the maṇḍala, initiating them with the bodhicitta of the principal deity of the maṇḍala and his consort, and leading them to attain bliss. Next having become Vajrasattvas, they proceed to their individual buddhafield—another central notion of Mahāyāna.

None of the four main sādhanas of the Ārya tradition of the Guhyasamāja

488. Nāgabuddhi, at the opening of his *Rnam gzhag rim pa, Vyavastholi,* chap. 1, Tōh 1809, 121b2. Bhavyakīrti, *Sgron ma rab gsal, Prakāśikā,* Tōh 1793, 7b6. Ratnākaraśānti, *Rin chen phreng ba, Ratnāvalī,* Tōh 1826, 31a4.

489. Nāgārjuna, *Mdor byas, Piṇḍīkrama Sādhana,* Tōh 1796, 3a4; L 30d.

490. Nāgārjuna, *Mdo bsre, Sādhanasūtramelāpaka,* Tōh 1797, 12a3; Candrakīrti, *Rdo rje sems dpa'i sgrub thabs, Vajrasattva Sādhana,* Tōh 1814, 198a4; Luo and Tomabechi 2009, 11.6 and 43.13. Nāgabuddhi, *Rnam gzhag rim pa, Vyavastholi,* chap. 1, Tōh 1809, 121b2–3; Tanaka 2016, 80.

491. Tsong kha pa, *Rnam gzhag rim pa'i rnam bshad,* 5b2–3.

instruct the yogis to meditate on the deeds of the specially visualized deities.[492] Tsongkhapa identifies the scriptural authority in the Ārya tradition for this practice in the *Guhyasamāja Tantra*:

> Then the Blessed One, the Tathāgata Bodhicittavajra, dwelt in absorption in the samādhi called "vajra overpowering of all tathāgatas."[493] As soon as the Blessed One, the lord of all tathāgatas, dwelt in absorption, the entire realm of space abided in the vajra nature of all tathāgatas. Then, as many as there were sentient beings residing in the entire realm of space, through the blessing of Vajrasattva all of them attained the bliss and mental rapture of all tathāgatas.[494]

We will return to this passage, as well as to the terms "past event"[495] and the "practice that follows,"[496] below.[497] This meditation does not serve to purify a ground of purification, but rather it enacts a "past event," a deed of the Tathāgata Bodhicittavajra, who conferred blessings on all sentient beings at the beginning of the *Guhyasamāja Tantra*. In the "practice that follows" the past event, yogis take the fruit of the practice, the deed of the tathāgata on the path.

492. That is, the *Concise Sādhana*, the *Sādhana Incorporating the Scripture*, the *Vajrasattva Sādhana*, and *Formulating the Sādhana*. But in another context, Jñānapāda instructs yogis to visualize all sentient beings entering the maṇḍala. See his *Kun bzang sgrub thabs*, *Samantabhadra Sādhana*, v. 37, Tōh 1855, 30b2. Various Tibetan manuals, including Bu ston, *Mdor byas 'grel chen*, 27a4–6; Rang byung rdo rje, *Gsang ba 'dus pa'i sgrub pa'i thabs phyi nang gzhan gsum gsal ba*, 5a4–6; Ngor chen, *Gsang 'dus dkyil 'khor gyi sgrub thabs dngos grub rgya mtsho*, 9a1; and Tsong kha pa, *Gsang mngon*, 37b3–6, do instruct the yogi to visualize the deities acting for the sake of sentient beings at this point.

493. Tib. *de bzhin gshegs pa thams cad zil gyis gnon pa rdo rje zhes bya ba'i ting nge 'dzin*, Skt. *sarvatathāgatābhibhavanavajra samādhi*.

494. *Gsang 'dus*, chap. 1, Tōh 442; Zhol 3a5–b1; Stog 4a6–7 [the rest is missing]; Fremantle 1971, 178; and Matsunaga 1978, 5. See also Bentor 2006, 2009a. In explaining the shared level of interpretation (*spyi don*), Tsong kha pa says that the samādhi called "vajra overpowering of all tathāgatas" teaches the specially visualized deities and their deeds. See his *Sgron gsal mchan*, 62a3–b1.

495. Tib. *sngon byung*, Skt. *bhūtapūrva*.

496. Tib. *rjes 'jug*.

497. See the section "The Samādhis in the First Chapter of the *Guhyasamāja Tantra* and Enacting Past Events" below.

Withdrawing the Specially Visualized Deities into the Body

Tsongkhapa describes in his sādhana how hook-like light-rays that emanate from the blue *hūṃ* at the yogi's heart draw the thirty-two deities and place them at certain points on the yogi's body, where they become inseparable in nature from the bodily constituents, the aggregates, and so forth.[498] The *Vajrasattva Sādhana* specifies that the five buddhas are in the nature of the aggregates, the goddesses in the nature of the sensory spheres, the bodhisattvas in the nature of the sense bases, and the fierce kings in the nature of the limbs of the body.[499]

Though the *Vajrasattva Sādhana* explains that these deities are placed on the maṇḍala of one's body[500] and according to the *Concise Sādhana* on the wheel of the body,[501] Khedrup Jé stresses that neither the placing of the specially visualized deities on the body nor their withdrawal into the body are the practice of the body maṇḍala.[502] Other early Tibetan scholars, however, do use the term "body maṇḍala" in this context. According to Butön: "[The meditators] should visualize their bodies as body maṇḍalas made of the tiniest particles of all tathāgatas."[503] Both Ngorchen Kunga Sangpo and Tsongkhapa use very similar wordings in this context.[504] We will return to this disagreement in the section about the meditation on the body maṇḍala below.

According to Gö Khukpa Lhetsé, Butön, Rendawa, and Rongtön Sheja Kunrik among others, the meditation on the specially visualized deities' withdrawing into the body and then dissolving into clear light is a purifier; its

498. Tsong kha pa, *Gsang mngon*, 37b6–38b3.

499. Candrakīrti, *Rdo rje sems dpa'i sgrub thabs, Vajrasattva Sādhana*, Tōh 1814, 198b3–4; Luo and Tomabechi 2009, 12.13–13.3 and 45.3–7. See the section "The Nature of the Transformation of the Ordinary Body into a Buddha's Body" below.

500. Tib. *rang gi lus kyi dkyil 'khor*, Skt. *svakāyamaṇḍala*; Candrakīrti, *Rdo rje sems dpa'i sgrub thabs, Vajrasattva Sādhana*, Tōh 1814, 198b3; Luo and Tomabechi 2009, 12.13–13.1 and 45.4.

501. Tib. *lus kyi 'khor lo*, Skt. *kāyacakra*; Nāgārjuna, *Mdor byas, Piṇḍīkrama Sādhana*, Tōh 1796, 3a7, L 37a.

502. See the section "Meditation on the Body Maṇḍala" below. See also Bentor 2015a.

503. Bu ston, *Mdor byas 'grel chen*, 228a3.

504. Ngor chen, *Gsang 'dus dkyil 'khor gyi sgrub thabs dngos grub rgya mtsho*, 9a2–3; Tsong kha pa, *Rnal 'byor dag rim*, 13a2–3.

ground of purification is the death of the first people of the eon.[505] On the other hand, Tsongkhapa does not understand the withdrawal of the specially visualized deities into the body as the purifier of a certain ground of purification.[506] He rather sees this meditation, just like the deeds of the specially visualized deities, as a step in taking-in-the-path, a "past event" described in the *Guhyasamāja Tantra*, as the fruit of the practice.[507]

Is the "Withdrawal of the Specially Visualized Deities into the Body" Part of the Core Practice?

As explained above, the core of the practice consists of meditations aimed at the transformation into the three Buddha's bodies by serving to eventually purify the yogi's death, intermediate state, and rebirth. But Tibetan scholars disagree about the exact point in the sādhana at which this transformation begins. As we have just seen, Tsongkhapa does not ascribe a soteriological role to the withdrawal of the specially visualized deities into the body. Unlike other Tibetan scholars, he sees no reason or possibility to purify the Buddhist "original sin" of the people of the first eon who lost their remarkable qualities and became ordinary. Therefore he does not include this meditation in the core of the practice but regards it as the last step of the preliminary meditations within the First Yoga.[508] For him, the central practice of the yoga that takes the three Buddha's bodies on the path begins only afterward.

The demarcation of the core practices is not clear. Both the *Concise Sādhana* and *Vajrasattva Sādhana* divide the core practice into four yogas: yoga, subsequent yoga, higher yoga, and great yoga.[509] These sādhanas note where each of the four yogas ends, but not where the first of these yogas begins. Moreover,

505. 'Gos Khug pa lhas btsas, *Gsang 'dus stong thun*, 10a1 and 10a6–b1; Bu ston, *Mdor byas 'grel chen*, 27b1–4 (Bu ston does distinguish between the withdrawal of the specially visualized deities into the body and their dissolution into clear light); Red mda' ba, *Yid kyi mun sel*, 7a5–6; Rong ston, *Gsang 'dus rnam bshad*, 6a2–3.

506. Tsong kha pa clearly delineates between the withdrawal of the specially visualized deities into the body and their dissolution into clear light, as we will soon see.

507. For the scriptural authority for the meditation on withdrawing the specially visualized deities into the body, see the section "The Samādhis in the First Chapter of the *Guhyasamāja Tantra* and Enacting Past Events" below.

508. After concluding his explanation of the *de nyid* of withdrawing the maṇḍala of the specially visualized deities into the body, Tsong kha pa says: "These first eleven *de nyid*-s are preliminaries to the main part of the yoga." Tsong kha pa, *Rnal 'byor dag rim*, 13a3.

509. Tib. *rnal 'byor, shin tu rnal 'byor, rnal 'byor che*, and *rjes su rnal 'byor*, Skt. *yoga, atiyoga, mahāyoga*, and *anuyoga*.

the name of the first stage among the four yogas, called "yoga," is used not only in this specific sense, but also as a general term for "practice," thus enabling various interpretations. Tsongkhapa differs from other Tibetan scholars, including Butön and Ngorchen Kunga Sangpo, who do include the withdrawal of the specially visualized deities into the body within the step called yoga.[510]

The onset of the core practices may also be delineated at the point that the five manifest awakenings begin.[511] Here, too, Tsongkhapa differs. While Butön includes the withdrawal of the specially visualized deities in the first manifest awakening, the manifest awakening from suchness,[512] Tsongkhapa does not. For him, the manifest awakening from suchness is a soteriological practice whereby, through the meditation on clear-light-emptiness, death is taken on the path to the dharmakāya. Thus it is unrelated to the withdrawal of the specially visualized deities into the body.

510. See Bu ston, *Mdor byas 'grel chen*, 27b1, and Ngor chen, *Gsang 'dus dkyil 'khor gyi sgrub thabs dngos grub rgya mtsho*, 9a1–3.

511. Tib. *mngon par byang chub pa*, or *mngon byang*, Skt. *abhisambodhi*.

512. Tib. *de bzhin nyid las byang chub pa*. Bu ston, *Mdor byas 'grel chen*, 27a7–b1.

8. The Core of the Practice

(1) The Yoga of Taking Death, Intermediate State, and Rebirth as the Path That Leads to the Three Buddha's Bodies

For Tsongkhapa, the core of the practice includes the three meditations that take the three Buddha's bodies on the path in order to eventually achieve the soteriological goal of transforming the yogis' death, intermediate state, and rebirth into the dharmakāya, saṃbhogakāya, and nirmāṇakāya.

(2) Dissolution of the Specially Visualized Deities into Clear Light: The Yoga of Taking Death on the Path That Leads to the Dharmakāya

Tsongkhapa maintains that the dissolution of the specially visualized deities into clear light serves to purify the future ordinary death of the yogis, its grounds of purification. The ultimate fruit of this practice is the *dharmakāya*. As we have seen, however, this fruit cannot be reached by means of the creation stage alone, but only at the culmination of the entire tantric path. In their meditation here, the yogis habituate to the dawning of the clear light of death while aspiring to eventually transform the ordinary experience of death into the realization of the ultimate clear light.

In the previous step, the withdrawal of the specially visualized deities into the body, the deities became indivisible in nature from various bodily constituents of the yogi. Therefore, in this step of the meditation, when the deities gradually dissolve into clear light, the yogi's ordinary body dissolves as well. In other words, the yogis undergo a type of ritual death and will be reborn in the new, meditative body of the "First Lord" of the creation stage.

The order of the dissolution into clear light is also of great significance. The deities do not dissolve in keeping with their tathāgata families; rather, they dissolve according to the stages of dissolution of the twenty-five coarse elements during ordinary death. The twenty-five coarse elements are the five aggregates,[513] the four physical elements,[514] the six faculties,[515] the five sense objects,[516] and the five wisdoms of the ground time.[517] The meditation's correspondence to the sequence of the dissolution during the yogi's future death stresses the potential of the practice to affect its ground of purification.

In their book *Death, Intermediate State, and Rebirth in Tibetan Buddhism*, Lati Rinbochay and Jeffrey Hopkins explain in detail the stages of the dissolution of the twenty-five coarse elements together with the deities.[518] These dissolutions are also described in the translation below. To summarize in brief: first the five aggregates—forms, feelings, perceptions, conditioning, and consciousness—dissolve in stages. As the form aggregate dissolves, so too does the mirror-like wisdom[519] of the ground time, the earth element, the eye faculty, and the forms within one's continuum,[520] along with the sinews and the right and left shoulders. The deities that dissolve at that time are Vairocana, Locanā, Kṣitigarbha, Rūpavajrā, Maitreya, Yamāntaka, and Acala.[521]

Though this list may seem arbitrary, it is primarily based on famous verses[522] of the *Guhyasamāja Tantra* that link aspects of the person with the buddhas of the maṇḍala:[523] "The five aggregates are proclaimed as the five buddhas, the vajra sense bases as the supreme maṇḍala of bodhisattvas." Āryadeva's *Compendium of Practices*[524] cites these verses of the *Guhyasamāja Tantra* in order to point out that elements of the body are equivalent to the buddhas of the maṇḍala. The scriptural authority for the entire sequence of dissolutions is

513. Tib. *phung po*, Skt. *skandha*.

514. Tib. *khams*, Skt. *dhātu*.

515. Tib. *dbang po*, Skt. *indriya*.

516. Tib. *yul*, Skt. *viṣaya*.

517. Tib. *ye shes*, Skt. *jñāna*.

518. Lati Rinbochay and Hopkins 1979. This book is a translation of a treatise by Dbyangs can dga' ba'i blo gros (1740–1827), *Gzhi sku gsum gyi rnam gzhag rab gsal sgron me*, 2b1–6b8.

519. Tib. *me long lta bu'i ye shes*, Skt. *ādarśajñāna*.

520. Tib. *gzugs kyi yul*, Skt. *rūpaviṣaya*.

521. See Nāgārjuna, *Mdor byas, Piṇḍīkrama Sādhana*, Tōh 1796, 3b1–2; L 39; and Tsong kha pa, *Bskyed rim zin bris*, 21a6.

522. See the section "The Nature of the Transformation of the Ordinary Body into a Buddha's Body" above.

523. *Gsang 'dus*, chap. 17, Tōh 442; Zhol 44a6–7; Stog 74b4–5; Fremantle 1971, v. 50; and Matsunaga 1978, v. 50.

524. Āryadeva, *Spyod bsdus, Caryāmelāpakapradīpa*, chap. 2, Tōh 1803.

the *Vajra Garland Tantra*,[525] cited in both the *Concise Sādhana* and in *Formulating the Sādhana*.[526] The *Vajra Garland Tantra* specifies that in each of the first five cycles, two fierce deities dissolve as well. According to these scriptural authorities, Vairocana dissolves with the form aggregate, Locanā with the earth element, and Kṣitigarbha with the eye faculty. The mirror-like wisdom of the ground time, as well as forms, external or internal, are identified with Vairocana and Rūpavajrā.

Formulating the Sādhana details the external signs that accompany the dissolution of each of the twenty-five coarse elements; these appear with small variations in the translation below.[527] For example, when the form aggregate dissolves, the limbs become attenuated, and the body declines and loses its strength. When, subsequently, the mirror-like wisdom of the ground time dissolves, vision becomes blurred and cloudy, and so forth.

The dissolution of the consciousness aggregate and its accompanying stages are less clear. According to the *Concise Sādhana*, the natural appearance[528] enters the aggregate of consciousness, and consciousness enters into clear light.[529] Tsongkhapa explains that the natural appearance consists of the eighty inherent activities of the conceptual mind and the three total appearances free of conceptualization.[530] Butön interprets the line "the natural appearance enters into the aggregate of consciousness" to mean that the mental faculties, along with the hundred-and-sixty inherent activities of the conceptual mind, dissolve into the three total appearances: "appearance"[531] dissolves

525. *Rgyud rdo rje phreng ba*, *Vajramālā Tantra*, chap. 68, Tōh 445, 275a7–b6.

526. Nāgārjuna, *Mdor byas*, *Piṇḍīkrama Sādhana*, Tōh 1796, 3b1–4, L 39–44ab; Nāgabuddhi, *Rnam gzhag rim pa*, *Vyavastholi*, chap. 4, Tōh 1809, 129b6–130a2, Tanaka 2016, 130. The Sanskrit in the editions of the *Mdor byas* (L 39; T 38), and the *Rnam gzhag rim pa*, chap. 4 (Tanaka 2016, 130), has in addition here the bodhisattva Maitreya.

527. Nāgabuddhi, *Rnam gzhag rim pa*, *Vyavastholi*, chap. 4, Tōh 1809, 130a2–b6; Tanaka 2016, 131–136.

528. Tib. *rang bzhin gyis snang ba*, Skt. *prakṛtyābhāsa*. Nāgabuddhi also has *prakṛtyābhāsa*, but the Tibetan is *rang bzhin gyi snang ba*. See his *Rnam gzhag rim pa*, *Vyavastholi*, chap. 4, Tōh 1809, 130a5; Tanaka 2016, 130. According to Tsong kha pa's explanation just below, "nature" and "appearance" should not be linked by any proposition, rather the term is a coordinative compound (*dvandva*), meaning instristic natures and appearances.

529. Nāgārjuna, *Mdor byas*, *Piṇḍīkrama Sādhana*, Tōh 1796, 3b3–4; L 43–44ab.

530. Tsong kha pa, *Rnam gzhag rim pa'i rnam bshad*, 81a1–2; and *Mtha' gcod*, 101a4–b1.

531. Tib. *snang ba*, Skt. *āloka*.

into "enhanced appearance,"[532] "enhanced appearance" into "approaching attainment,"[533] and "approaching attainment" into clear light.[534]

The internal signs that accompany the eight dissolutions are divided into two groups of four. First are the four appearances that resemble a mirage, smoke, fireflies, and a butter-lamp respectively.[535] In other words, they begin with signs of fire or light, proceed to mere flickers of light, and end with a feeble source of light. Then, when the corporal elements of the body dissolve, the sensation transforms significantly: four experiences arise that are like the clear autumn sky, devoid of any additional coarse, dualistic appearance. Still, the first three experiences are suffused respectively in moonlight, sunlight, and the darkness of night. Then the fourth internal sign is untainted by any condition or any coarse dualistic appearances whatsoever.

Khedrup Jé explains how to meditate on the dissolution of the specially visualized deities into clear light:

> Visualizing yourself as Vajradhara, meditate on Kṣitigarbha embraced by Rūpavajrā[536] at the centers of your two eyeballs, and then maintain the conviction that the two deities are the essence of your eye faculty and the entire sensory sphere of the forms of your body. Then, do not merely think, "Kṣitigarbha and his consort have dissolved into clear light," but rather discern how your eye faculty and your sensory sphere of forms, which arose in the appearance of Kṣitigarbha with his consort, enter into the dharmakāya of indivisible bliss and emptiness. In this way, too, you should understand the other dissolutions. Such a habituation will become a special ripener for a swift entry of the winds—the wind that circulates through the eye and so forth—into the central channel of the subtle body, and for a smooth arising of the clear light during the completion stage.[537]

532. Tib. *mched* or *snang ba mched pa*, Skt. *ālokābhāsa*.

533. Tib. *thob* or *snang ba thob pa*, Skt. *ālokopalabdha*.

534. Bu ston, *Mdor byas 'grel chen*, 30b6–31a1. Bu ston's explanation here is similar to that of Mkhas grub rje.

535. See the *Rgyud phyi ma, Uttara Tantra*, Tōh 443, 154b4; Matsunaga 1978, vv. 150cd–151ab. The four signs: mirage, Tib. *smig rgyu 'dra ba*, Skt. *marīcikākāra*; smoke, Tib. *du ba lta bu*, Skt. *dhūmrākāra*; fireflies, Tib. *mkha' snang 'dra ba*, Skt. *khadyotākāra*; and butter-lamp, Tib. *mar me ltar 'bar*, Skt. *dīpavajjvala*.

536. Tib. Gzugs rdo rje ma, Eng. Vajra Lady of Forms.

537. Mkhas grub rje, *Bskyed rim dngos grub rgya mtsho*, 95a3–6.

Khedrup Jé also guides the yogi to meditate on the dissolution of the specially visualized deities into clear light as a preparatory practice for the future realization of the clear light:

> Even as a novice in the yoga who has not yet attained the capacity to practice the completion stage, you should practice the sādhana during the four sessions, and when the moment of your death approaches, you will have habituated the transmitted instruction on the withdrawal of the specially visualized deities into clear light. For you must first develop a good intellectual understanding of deity yoga and the stages of dissolution explained above. Then you may withdraw the specially visualized deities into your body and maintain a stable meditation with the resolve: My such-and-such aggregate is such-and-such a deity. Then you should focus single-pointedly on visualizing the appearances of the respective deities on the respective locations on your body, as explained in the case of the body maṇḍala below. And when the signs of the dissolution of the form aggregates, the eye faculty and so forth, explained earlier, begin to arise, you will recognize them, reflecting: "This is a sign of dissolution."
>
> After your form aggregate, which is indivisible from Vairocana; your eye faculty, which is indivisible from Kṣitigarbha; and so forth dissolve into the clear light of indivisible bliss and emptiness, you should cultivate a stable meditation on the successive dissolutions into the continuing state of the clear-light-wisdom of indivisible great bliss and emptiness, empty of intrinsic existence. Then, maintaining a stable divine identity as Vajradhara, visualize this body turning into a sphere of light, and this light gathering from above and below into your heart as steam evaporates on a mirror and dissolving completely into the continuing state of wisdom of indivisible bliss and emptiness. So long as your mindfulness is not impaired, you will be mindful of this wisdom. This is the supreme transmitted instruction on the transfer of consciousness at death.
>
> Currently in Tibet, there is a well-known transmitted instruction on the transfer of consciousness regarded as impressive. To receive it, one must propitiate the lamas with offerings of nothing but gold. But for all its grand names, it cannot rival [this consciousness transfer of ours].[538]

538. Mkhas grub rje, *Bskyed rim dngos grub rgya mtsho*, 94b2–95a2.

While most of the opponents Khedrup Jé attacks in *Ocean of Attainments* are Tibetan lamas who wrote on the Guhyasamāja sādhana, this criticism may be aimed at the great transference of the Drigung school.[539]

So far, the meditation on the dissolutions of the twenty-five coarse elements has been taken as part and parcel of the creation stage, but this point is debated. For example, in Āryadeva's *Compendium of Practices*, the dissolutions of the twenty-five coarse elements are included in the meditation on body isolation of the completion stage,[540] and in Nāgabuddhi's *Formulating the Sādhana*, they are part of the meditation on the ultimate truth maṇḍala.[541] On the other hand, as we have just seen, the *Concise Sādhana* certainly includes this meditation in the creation stage.

One of the reasons for the disagreement on the question of where this meditation belongs is the position of Indian and Tibetan scholars that while the creation stage purifies birth, the completion stage purifies death. For example, Gö Khukpa Lhetsé maintains: "Birth is the conventional truth and death is the ultimate truth. These two are the grounds of purification of the creation and completion stage respectively."[542] Sakya scholars, including Drakpa Gyaltsen, Rendawa, and Rongtön Sheja Kunrik, follow Gö in this matter.[543] If this is the case, a meditation on the dissolution of the twenty-five coarse elements in correspondence with death should not be included in the creation stage.

However, Tsongkhapa strongly disagrees with the position that the creation and completion stages do not share grounds of purification.[544] As we have seen,[545] for Tsongkhapa both the creation and completion stages jointly purify all three cyclic events in the life of a person—birth, death, and the intermediate stage.[546]

539. Tib. *'Bri gung 'pho ba chen mo*. See Kapstein 1998.

540. Āryadeva, *Spyod bsdus*, *Caryāmelāpakapradīpa*, chap. 2, Tōh 1803.

541. Nāgabuddhi, *Rnam gzhag rim pa*, *Vyavastholi*, chap. 4, Tōh 1809, 129b5–130a2; Tanaka 2016, 129–131.

542. 'Gos Khug pa lhas btsas, *Gsang 'dus stong thun*, 16a5. See also 14a4–5.

543. Grags pa rgyal mtshan, *Rgyud kyi mngon rtogs*, 68a2–4; Red mda' ba, *Yid kyi mun sel*, 6b3–6; Rong ston, *Gsang 'dus rnam bshad*, 5a2–4.

544. Tsong kha pa, *Sngags rim chen mo*, chap. 11, 454–455; and Mkhas grub rje, *Bskyed rim dngos grub rgya mtsho*, 82b6–83a6.

545. See the section "The Meaning of the Correspondences between the Meditation, Cosmos, and Person."

546. Another factor involved here is the demarcation between the creation and completion stage, which is unclear, and specifically the question of whether the stage of body isolation pertains to the creation or completion stage.

Meditation on Emptiness in the Microcosmic Context

An important meditation on emptiness takes place at the culmination of the dissolution of the specially visualized deities into clear light, as yogis recite the mantra of emptiness: *oṃ śūnyatā jñāna vajra svabhāva ātmako 'haṃ*. At this point in the sādhana, the entire visualization of the maṇḍala and its deities dissolves into clear-light-emptiness. The tantric meditation on clear light is united here with the meditation on emptiness of the Pāramitā Vehicle.

For Tsongkhapa, the same emptiness is meditated upon in both the Pāramitā and Mantra Vehicles, but the ways of meditating on emptiness in these two vehicles are different.[547] At the same time, as we have noted,[548] this meditation is not only on emptiness but also on the divine identification with the dharmakāya. Khedrup Jé also stresses that the subjective mind that meditates on emptiness in the Mantra Vehicle is different from the mind meditating on emptiness in the Pāramitā Vehicle:

> At the stage of buddhahood, emptiness and wisdom are actually paired like water poured into water, but at this stage you should meditate by imagining the essence of the wisdom of your mind and objective pure emptiness in one taste, unobstructed by even the slightest dualistic appearance. Furthermore, you should know that there is no distinction between the emptiness meditated upon in the Pāramitā Vehicle and the emptiness meditated upon in the creation and completion stages, but there are a great many special differences between these two vehicles in terms of the method for maintaining the object perceived in the meditation, the subjective mind that meditates, and so forth.[549]

Hence, during the meditation on emptiness in the microcosmic context, the emphasis is on maintaining the divine identity of the deity and on the subjective mind, not only on the objective emptiness, though the two are nondual.

Elsewhere in his *Great Treatise on the Stages of the Mantric Path*, Tsongkhapa lists six purposes of the meditation on emptiness during the creation

547. See the section "Meditation on Emptiness in the Creation Stage" above.

548. See the section "Divine Identity or Pride" above.

549. Mkhas grub rje, *Bskyed rim dngos grub rgya mtsho*, 41a3–5.

stage:[550] (1) Without meditating on emptiness during the creation stage, it would be impossible for the yogis of the creation stage to ripen their mental continuum for its realization during the completion stage. (2) Many tantras, including the *Guhyasamāja Tantra*, instruct the yogis to meditate on emptiness and on the ultimate truth of the absence of intrinsic nature before they visualize the appearance aspect of the maṇḍala and its deities. (3) During the creation stage, yogis must take the three Buddha's bodies on the path, and in order to take the dharmakāya on the path they must meditate on emptiness. (4) One of the goals of the creation stage is to purify the yogis' ordinary birth, death, and intermediate state, and in order to purify their ordinary deaths, they need to meditate on emptiness. (5) Without meditating on emptiness first, the appearance aspect will not arise as illusion-like. (6) Among the special tantric vows yogis of the creation stage must maintain are vows to continuously reflect on emptiness.[551]

Sakya scholars express similar ideas about the purpose of meditating on emptiness here. Even Kúnga Nyingpo and Sönam Tsemo, who maintain that yogis must meditate on the absence of appearances before they visualize the celestial mansion of the maṇḍala, list some of the same purposes: (1) This meditation serves to purify the stains of conceptualization, such as labeling of person and self. (2) Without making the ordinary empty, it is not possible to generate oneself as a deity. (3) Without uniting the two accumulations of merit and wisdom-emptiness, liberation is not possible. (4) In order for the rūpakāya to arise from the dharmakāya, yogis must meditate on emptiness, the essence of the dharmakāya.[552]

In conclusion, much of what was said above about meditation on emptiness in the macrocosmic context is similarly applicable to the microcosmic context. This is also a liminal point of the practice in which yogis visualize away their own ordinary identity just before visualizing themselves as the deity. Once more entering a type of ritual death, the yogis shed all ordinary appearances and clinging, and take on a new identity as the deity by maintaining its divine pride.

To reiterate, the ground of purification of this meditation are the twenty-five

550. Tsong kha pa, *Sngags rim chen mo*, 489–490. See also Mkhas grub rje, *Bskyed rim dngos grub rgya mtsho*, 41a1–3. This list is different from the six points made by Dīpaṅkaraśrījñāna mentioned in the section "The Goal of the Meditation on Emptiness" above.

551. See also Tsong kha pa's explanation in his *Dngos grub snye ma*, 46a2–48a4; an English translation in Sparham 2005, 104–109.

552. Kun dga' snying po, [*Mtsho skyes kyi*] *Mngon rtogs tshig gi bum pa*, 344b2–345a3; Bsod nams rtse mo, *Kyai rdo rje'i sgrub thabs mtsho skyes kyi ṭīkā*, 10a3–b3.

coarse constituents that dissolve during the death of a person born from a womb. The purifier is the realization of clear light actualized by the meditators on the creation stage, which can eventually bring about the actual clear light of the meditators on the completion stage and the stage of union. Ultimately, instead of undergoing ordinary death, the meditators will arise as the dharmakāya. Thus a yogi practicing the creation stage meditates on a *path* that corresponds to the arising of the clear light of death at the time of the *ground*. However, the dawning of the clear light of death is not a direct realization of the actual clear light, because if it were, all beings would be liberated without any effort by their death.[553]

In this way, the fruit of dharmakāya is taken on the path here. Death, during which the bodily constituents of the aggregates and so on dissolve and all the coarse conceptual proliferations are pacified, corresponds to the dharmakāya. Yet in order to attain the Buddha's bodies, the path has to accord with both the rūpakāya and dharmakāya. Hence, having realized emptiness and developed the identity of the dharmakāya, yogis must now maintain the identity of the rūpakāya and take it on the path. The following steps of the sādhana are aimed at attaining the two aspects of the rūpakāya, the saṃbhogakāya and nirmāṇakāya.

(3) The Yoga of Taking the Intermediate State on the Path That Leads to the Saṃbhogakāya

The yoga of taking the intermediate state on the path that leads to the saṃbhogakāya is the meditation on the deity called "the First Lord." This yoga serves to purify the yogi's future intermediate state and eventually transform it into the saṃbhogakāya of the Buddha. In other words, instead of the intermediate being that would naturally arise to an ordinary human being, the yogi will ultimately attain the saṃbhogakāya. But during the creation stage, the yogi arises as the First Lord, so called because it is the first deity visualized during the core practices. In the following step of the meditation, the first deity will transform into Vajrasattva's nirmāṇakāya in correspondence with the intermediate being who is born. The First Lord is the "body" of yogis who have discarded their ordinary bodily constituents in the previous step of the practice by dissolving them into clear light. During this ritual interim, wherein yogis do not take the ordinary intermediate state that leads to rebirth in saṃsāra yet are not reborn in the special body of the deity, during their practice they abide as the First Lords.

553. See Mkhas grub rje, *Bskyed rim dngos grub rgya mtsho*, 99a6–b3.

Before turning to the meditation, Khedrup Jé describes the intermediate being—the ground of purification of the practice.[554] According to the Mantra Vehicle, the intermediate being evolves in a reverse order to the stages of death. When, during the clear light of death, the wind[555] on which the mind rides begins to waver slightly, the mind goes through the three stages of approaching attainment, enhanced appearance, and appearance, each lasting for only a short while. Śāstras, such as the *Yogācārabhūmi*, describe the intermediate being as arising from death in a process of simultaneous cessation and origination, like the pointer moving on a scale when the weight is shifted.[556]

The Moon and Mind Only

The First Lord is visualized within the continuum of clear-light-emptiness into which the deities dissolved in the previous step of the sādhana. However, its visualization is not a straightforward process of gradual creation, but rather a mixture of evolution, mingling, and dissolution. Soon after the yogis visualize the deity's seats and seed syllables,[557] they dissolve them into a moon orb, and then the entire physical world and all sentient beings also dissolve into the moon orb.

The total dissolution of the animate and inanimate worlds seems somewhat

554. The scriptural authorities for the description of the intermediate state here are Vasubandhu, *Mdzod, Abhidharmakośa*, and *Mdzod 'grel, Kośabhāṣya*, Tōh 4089–4090; Asaṅga, *Sa'i dngos gzhi, Maulībhūmi*, Tōh 4035; Asaṅga, *Chos mngon pa kun las btus pa, Abhidharmasamuccaya*, Tōh 4049; *Mngal gnas, Nandagarbhāvakrānti Nirdeśa*, Tōh 57, and *Mngal 'jug, Āyuṣman Nandagarbhāvakrānti Nirdeśa*, Tōh 58; and Nāgabuddhi, *Rnam gzhag rim pa, Vyavastholi*, chap. 1, Tōh 1809, 123a4–b1. For overviews of the intermediate being, see Wayman 1974; Cuevas 1996 and 2003; Blezer 1997, 6–38; and Kritzer 2000. Note that our sources do not follow the literature of the *Bar do thos grol*, the so-called "Tibetan Book of the Dead."

555. Tib. *srog 'dzin rlung*, Skt. *prāṇa*. See the *Rgyud rdo rje phreng ba, Vajramālā Tantra*, chap. 32, Tōh 445, 243a7–b1.

556. Asaṅga, *Sa'i dngos gzhi, Maulībhūmi*, Tōh 4035, 10a2–3; Bhattacharya 1957, 19.1–2. The first disagreements Mkhas grub rje raises in describing the intermediate being are "inherited disputes" on the shape of the intermediate being and its lifespan. Another argument is against Bu ston, who maintains that the newly evolved being cannot be called an intermediate being until all three minds of approaching attainment, enhanced appearance, and appearance have evolved. See Bu ston, *Mdor byas 'grel chen*, 32b4–33b1. Without referring to Bu ston by his name, Tsong kha pa objects to this position. See his *Rnam gzhag rim pa'i rnam bshad*, 28a3–b5; Mkhas grub rje follows him; see his *Bskyed rim dngos grub rgya mtsho*, 100a4–b2.

557. First, a solar disk, lunar disk, and lotus arise from the seed syllables *oṃ āḥ hūṃ* respectively, and the three syllables are stacked up on the lotus. See Tsong kha pa, *Gsang mngon*, 39a4–b2.

redundant once, during the previous meditation on emptiness, all the yogis' visualizations, along with the yogis themselves, have already dissolved into clear light. But while the previous dissolution was into clear-light-emptiness out of which the yogi is born as a deity, here everything dissolves into the moon. Several Indian commentaries explain the meditation on the moon orb here as a meditation on Mind Only. In other words, all the deities during the core practice will arise as emanations of the yogis' minds.

This is not surprising; as we have mentioned already, the Mind Only approach is the most suitable of the Buddhist approaches to explain the creation stage. For example, in the sūtric visualization described in the *Samādhi of Direct Encounter*, the term "Mind Only" is used to explain how disciples see the visions of buddhas and their buddhafields.[558] There, the disciples think that the entire world is Mind Only, because however they imagine things, that is how they appear. Furthermore, as mentioned above, when Vajrayāna Buddhism evolved in India, the predominant philosophical systems were the Yogācāra school and Yogācāra-Madhyamaka synthesis, not the Madhyamaka.

We find the explanation that the moon in this context is Mind Only in commentaries on the *Concise Sādhana*. These commentaries belong to the Ārya tradition of the Guhyasamāja and are ostensibly in accordance with Prāsaṅgika Madhyamaka. Nāgārjuna himself, the author of the *Concise Sādhana*, does not mention the term "Mind Only" in his sādhana; he explains: "Visualize the completely perfect moon orb as bodhicitta, and in it the entire moving and unmovable worlds."[559] Thus Nāgārjuna glosses the moon orb as bodhicitta, the seed of rebirth, both physical and meditative. But in commenting on this verse, Muniśrībhadra instructs the yogi to meditate on the complete moon orb as Mind Only, in the nature of the radiant light of wisdom.[560] Likewise, Bhavyakīrti, in his own commentary on the *Concise Sādhana*, advises the yogi to meditate on the moon of Mind Only.[561] Similarly, the Candrakīrti who composed the *Vajrasattva Sādhana* explains that yogis should meditate on the complete moon orb, not as bodhicitta but as Mind Only.[562]

Butön is not troubled by the occurrence of concepts of Mind Only in works of the Ārya tradition of the Guhyasamāja. In his own commentary on the

558. *Pratyutpannabuddhasaṃmukhāvasthitasamādhi*, Harrison 1990, 42, 3L.

559. Nāgārjuna, *Mdor byas*, *Piṇḍīkrama Sādhana*, Tōh 1796, 3b6–7, L 49cd–50ab.

560. Muniśrībhadra, *Rim pa lnga'i don mdor bshad pa*, *Pañcakramārthaṭippaṇi*, Tōh 1813, 156a4–5; Jiang and Tomabechi 1996, 17.1.

561. Bhavyakīrti, *Rim pa lnga'i dka' 'grel*, *Pañcakramapañjikā*, Tōh 1838, 2b3.

562. Candrakīrti, *Rdo rje sems dpa'i sgrub thabs*, *Vajrasattva Sādhana*, Tōh 1814, 199a5; Luo and Tomabechi 2009, 15.7–8 and 47.16–17.

Concise Sādhana, he glosses the line cited above, "visualize the completely perfect moon orb as bodhicitta," as "visualize its essence as Mind Only." Regarding the phrase "and in it the entire moving and unmovable worlds," Butön explains: "the purpose here is that you will realize that all phenomena is Mind Only, and that the two truths are indivisible." Butön then explains the mantra recited here, *oṃ dharma dhātu svabhāva ātmako 'haṃ*, to mean: "everything moving and unmoving, subsumed as one's Mind Only, endowed with the nature of dharmadhātu, free of arising, destroying, and remaining, that am I."[563]

Conversely, Tsongkhapa glosses "Mind Only," *sems tsam* in Tibetan, as *rlung sems tsam*, meaning "mere wind-and-mind."[564] For him, the root of all phenomena is not Mind Only, but mere wind-and-mind.[565] He applies the notion of mere wind-and-mind to the ground of purification of the meditation—the intermediate being, who has left behind the coarse physical body of its former life, and is made of mere wind-and-mind. During the practice of the creation stage, Tsongkhapa instructs the yogi to meditate not on Mind Only but on mere wind-and-mind. The purifier that now appears as a moon orb is mere wind-and-mind; furthermore, the First Lord, the deity visualized from the moon, has a subtle wisdom body arising from pure wind-and-mind.

Likewise, Tsongkhapa glosses the mantra *oṃ dharma dhātu svabhāva ātmako 'haṃ* recited here not as referring to Mind Only, as did Butön, but as: "The root of all the phenomena, animate and inanimate, mere wind-and-mind, appearing as moon, that am I."[566] Elsewhere, Tsongkhapa glosses this mantra as "All the animate and inanimate do not exist but through the moon; the moon itself is mere wind-and-mind, and that am I." He then continues:

> This is the ground of the intermediate being, the cause from which it evolves, mere wind-and-mind. While the Pāramitā Vehicle explains that the root of all phenomena is mind, this system of the Mantra Vehicle teaches that the wind that serves as the mind's mound is the root of all the animate and inanimate worlds. These are extremely sublime key points of the path; therefore, you should thoroughly understand this.[567]

563. Bu ston, *Mdor byas 'grel chen*, 34a4–b1; an English translation in Yoshimizu 1987, 27.

564. Tsong kha pa, *Gsang mngon*, 39b1–2.

565. See also Tsong kha pa, *Rim lnga gsal sgron*, chap. 7, 233b6–235a2; an English translation in Kilty 2013, 389–391.

566. Tsong kha pa, *Gsang mngon*, 39b1–2.

567. Tsong kha pa, *Bskyed rim zin bris*, 24a5–b2; see also his *Bung ba'i re skong*, 19b3.

Tsongkhapa calls this meditation "abiding in absorption on wisdom alone,"[568] a term found in two of the Indian sādhanas, cited from the *Sarvabuddha-samāyoga Tantra*.[569]

Neither Tsongkhapa nor Khedrup Jé refer to the term "Mind Only" in the works of the Ārya tradition of the Guhyasamāja such as those cited above. However, Khedrup Jé seems to refer to a position like Butön's, which understands everything as Mind Only:

> Some lamas say the purpose here is that you will realize that all phenomena are Mind Only, and that the two truths are indivisible. They do not understand that the author of the *Illuminating Lamp* accepts external things as conventional designations, which is also the view of Ārya Nāgārjuna. Both the animate and inanimate realms that are dissolved and the wind and mind into which they dissolve—that arise as the appearance of the moon—are but conventional truth, as is anything that accords with the conventional designations of the Mantra and Pāramitā Vehicles. Thus the point here is not to indicate that the two truths are indivisible. For these reasons, their argument is insubstantial.[570]

For Tsongkhapa and his followers, the Ārya tradition of the Guhyasamāja has to be the tradition of the Madhyamaka school, even if certain views that do not follow the Madhyamaka may have found their way into the scriptures of the Ārya tradition of the Guhyasamāja. There can be no doubt that Tsongkhapa encountered the notion of Mind Only in the commentaries on the *Concise Sādhana*, which he cites in his own works. Yet he deliberately chose to overlook them for the sake of a perfect harmonious system whereby the Ārya tradition of the Guhyasamāja fully concords with the views of the Madhyamaka school. In doing so, Tsongkhapa diverged decisively from Indian works as well as from Tibetan scholars such as Butön, who made no attempt to present a unified philosophical approach to the Vajrayāna and the Madhyamaka.[571]

568. Tib. *ye shes tsam la snyoms 'jug pa*, Skt. *jñānamātrasamāpatti*.

569. *Sangs rgyas mnyam sbyor*, Tōh 366, 185a5. The two sādhanas are Candrakīrti's *Rdo rje sems dpa'i sgrub thabs*, *Vajrasattva Sādhana* (Tōh 1814, 199a6–7; Luo and Tomabechi 2009, 15.12 and 48.4–5) and Nāgārjuna's *Mdo bsre*, *Sādhanasūtramelāpaka* (Tōh 1797, 12b3). See also Muniśrībhadra's *Rim pa lnga'i don mdor bshad pa*, *Pañcakramārthaṭippaṇi*, Tōh 1813, 156a6; Jiang and Tomabechi 1996, 17.

570. Mkhas grub rje, *Bskyed rim dngos grub rgya mtsho*, 104a2–4.

571. See for example Bu ston, *Mdor byas 'grel chen*, 34a4–b1.

Moreover, the solution he finds for understanding these commentaries on the *Concise Sādhana* in Madhyamaka terms is quite remarkable, as taking Mind Only (*sems tsam*) to mean mere wind-and-mind (*rlung sems tsam*) is in complete agreement with all the other parts of the puzzle. The mere wind-and-mind that is the root of the animate and inanimate worlds has the following correspondences: On the level of the ground of purification, it corresponds to the intermediate being made of mere wind-and-mind. On the level of the creation stage, the First Lord has a subtle wisdom body arising from pure wind-and-mind. During the completion stage, it corresponds to the pure and impure illusory bodies made of mere wind-and-mind. We may recall that this meditation on the First Lord will serve for the ripening of the mental continuum of the meditator on the illusory bodies during the completion stage. Finally, at the level of the fruit, the mere wind-and-mind will give rise to the saṃbhogakāya.

Let us look at another example, this time from Nāgārjuna's *Five Stages*: "By the mind ignorant beings are bound in saṃsāra, and by that very mind yogis reach the abode of the sugatas."[572] This line echoes the theory of Mind Only; however, Tsongkhapa explains:

> This teaches that sentient beings are born through the power of the wind-and-mind of the clear light of death, and that for yogis skillful in means, this very wind-and-mind that circles in saṃsāra arises as the illusory body and becomes awakened. Commentaries on the *Five Stages* explain the meaning of this verse differently.[573]

Fully aware that his interpretation does not accord with the traditional commentaries on the *Five Stages*, Tsongkhapa glosses "mind" in Nāgārjuna's *Five Stages* as wind-and-mind, arguing that such wind-and-mind arises as the illusory body. Tsongkhapa justifies his reading on the basis of the passage in Āryadeva's *Compendium of Practices* cited above.[574]

By glossing "mind" as wind-and-mind in a work by Nāgārjuna, Tsongkhapa not only eliminates any indication of theories of Mind Only from this

572. Nāgārjuna, *Rim lnga, Pañcakrama*, chap. 3, v. 16, Tōh 1802, 52b3; Tomabechi 2006, 157.

573. Tsong kha pa, *Rim lnga gsal sgron*, chap. 7, 232b4–6; an English translation in Kilty 2013, 387–388.

574. Āryadeva, *Spyod bsdus, Caryāmelāpakapradīpa*, chap. 6, Tōh 1803, 85b2–4; Sanskrit, Tibetan, and English translation in Wedemeyer 2007, B: 42a; Sanskrit and Tibetan in Pandey 2000, 57 and 269. See the section "The Meaning of the Correspondences between the Meditation, Cosmos, and Person" above.

context—he also links the mere wind-and-mind that is the cause of the intermediate being at the ground of purification to the mere wind-and-mind that gives rise to the rūpakāya when buddhahood is attained. Thus, while in the original verse the mind is the foundation of both saṃsāra and enlightenment, according to Tsongkhapa the ground of everything is the mere wind-and-mind, as he states in his *Lamp to Illuminate the Five Stages*:

> The root of everything animate and inanimate is none other than mere wind-and-mind, and such mere wind-and-mind is then generated into the single body of the stage of union [at the culmination of the tantric path].[575]

In this way, Tsongkhapa links mere wind-and-mind at the level of the ground, paths, and fruit.[576]

In conclusion, we should note that the notion of mere wind-and-mind is shared by Tibetan scholars belonging to various schools, including the Kagyü[577] and Sakya.[578] However, Tsongkhapa's interpretation of this term is unique. In this ingenious move, Tsongkhapa removes the philosophical school

575. Tsong kha pa, *Rim lnga gsal sgron*, chap. 9, 307a2–3; an English translation in Kilty 2013, 505.

576. Another dispute in the present context is about the way the moon orb should be visualized. As we have seen, the visualization begins with the arising of a solar disk, lunar disk, and lotus, and the three syllables *oṃ āḥ hūṃ* are stacked on the lotus. According to Red mda' ba, the lotus and the three syllables dissolve into the lunar disk from above, and the solar disk dissolves into the lunar disk from below; after they merge together, a moon arises. See his *Yid kyi mun sel*, 7b3–4 and 107b1–2. Here, Red mda' ba follows 'Gos khug pa las btsas, who explains that the moon is formed by entering it from above and below. See his *Gsang 'dus stong thun*, 12b5. Ngor chen also adopts 'Gos khug pa las btsas's reading. See his *Gsang 'dus dkyil 'khor gyi sgrub thabs dngos grub rgya mtsho*, 9b2–3. Tsong kha pa and Mkhas grub rje object to the position that the moon that is the root of all animate and inanimate realms is no different from the first lunar disk. They maintain that the first lunar disk must also transform into the moon of "manifest awakening from the moon." See Tsong kha pa, *Sgron gsal mchan*, 237b1–3; *Bskyed rim zin bris*, 24a3–4; *Slob tshul*, 15a5–b1; and Mkhas grub rje, *Bskyed rim dngos grub rgya mtsho*, 105b1–2.

577. See Dkon mchog yan lag, *Bstan bcos zab mo nang don gyi gting thun rab gsal nyi ma'i snying po*, 93b1; Dwags po Bkra shis rnam rgyal, *Gsang sngags rdo rje theg pa'i spyi don mdor bsdus pa legs bshad nor bu'i 'od zer*, 139b4; an English translation in Roberts 2011, 568; and Kong sprul Yon tan rgya mtsho, *Shes bya kun khyab*, vol. 3, p. 225; an English translation in Guarisco and McLeod 2008, 144.

578. See Red mda' ba, *Yid kyi mun sel*, 13a2–5 and 30b2, and Stag tshang Lo tsā ba, *Zhabs lugs rdzogs rim snying gi thig le*, p. 134.

of Mind Only from this context while building a system that is able to accommodate not only the purifiers and their grounds of purifications of the tantric sādhana, but its Madhyamaka theoretical basis. Hence, the comprehensive system Tsongkhapa designed is not limited to the Vajrayāna, but encompasses both sūtra and tantra.

Awakening in This Body

Khedrup Jé refers to the topic of enlightenment in this very body in a puzzling paragraph at the opening of *Ocean of Attainments*, where he raises questions but provides no complete answers:

> It is not possible that the present body produced by previous karma and afflictive emotions would transform into a buddha's body. How is a buddha's body attained after the present body is forsaken? If the present body is abandoned and a buddha's body is obtained by taking a new birth, then the premise that one is awakened in this life would be vitiated. On the other hand, if the present body is abandoned and a buddha's body adorned with the major and minor marks of a buddha is attained without taking a new birth, then the buddha's body arises without an accordant cause,[579] and this is unacceptable. Therefore you need to engage in these practices after having fully understood through which accordant cause the buddha's body is attained, through the power of which antidote the present impure body is discarded, how the saṃbhogakāya is attained after discarding it, and so on.[580]

Here, Khedrup Jé advises the yogi to develop a thorough understanding of the accordant cause that leads to the Buddha's body as well as of the antidote that serves to discard the present impure body and thereby leads to the achievement of the saṃbhogakāya. He does not supply the answers in *Ocean of Attainments*, since these are found not in the creation stage but the completion stage. In speaking about the accordant cause that leads to the Buddha's body, Khedrup Jé alludes to the wind in the term "mere wind-and-mind." The notion of mere wind-and-mind enabled the early Geluk scholars to solve the paradox of attaining awakening in this life, as advocated by the Vajrayāna, despite the fact that the present body produced by previous karma and afflictive emotions cannot transform into a buddha's body.

579. Tib. *rigs 'dra'i rgyu*.

580. Mkhas grub rje, *Bskyed rim dngos grub rgya mtsho*, 4a1–3.

As we have seen,[581] while the *Guhyasamāja Tantra* itself preserves a certain ambiguity regarding the extent to which the aggregates and buddhas are to be regarded as identical, the commentaries take their identity for granted; this identity serves as the rationale for the practice. On the other hand, the ordinary body, saturated with desire, hatred, and ignorance, is seen as a cause of saṃsāra. Since the physical body of Buddha Śākyamuni could not have been purified during his life, under the bodhi tree he reached "nirvāṇa with remainder,"[582] and only upon his death, when his impure aggregates ceased to exist, did he attain "nirvāṇa without remainder."[583]

The Geluk tradition does not accept the notion of *tathāgatagarbha* in which sentient beings are pure by nature and therefore do not require any fundamental purification. Therefore Tsongkhapa and Khedrup Jé maintain that the ordinary human body must change before buddhahood can be attained. According to Tsongkhapa:

> Since yogis who are awakened in one lifetime are awakened after changing their bodies, they meditate on the path first in human bodies; however, eventually, when the fruit is attained, their bodies change.[584]

The canonical authorities Tsongkhapa invokes for his position are Āryadeva's *Compendium of Practices* and Candrakīrti's *Illuminating Lamp*, both of which state that when yogis are awakened in the present lives, their bodies must change[585] before they can attain the vajra body.[586] But as Khedrup Jé says in the citation above, changing a body would vitiate the premise that the yogi is awakened in a single lifetime.

581. See the section "The Nature of the Transformation of the Ordinary Body into a Buddha's Body" above.

582. Tib. *phung po lhag ma dang bcas pa'i mya ngan las 'das pa*, Skt. *sopadhiśeṣanirvāṇa*.

583. Tib. *phung po lhag ma med pa'i mya ngan las 'das pa*, Skt. *nirupadhiśeṣanirvāṇa*.

584. Tsong kha pa, *Rnam gzhag rim pa'i rnam bshad*, 20a3–4.

585. Tib. *brje ba*, Skt. *parivarta*.

586. Āryadeva's *Spyod bsdus*, *Caryāmelāpakapradīpa* reads: Tib. *phyung po'i khog pa brjes te rdo rje'i lus su gyur nas*, Skt. *kalevaraṃ parivartya vajrakāyo*. See chap. 9, Tōh 1803, 100a2–3. Sanskrit, Tibetan, and English translation in Wedemeyer 2007, B: 63b; Sanskrit and Tibetan in Pandey 2000, 88 and 332. In the same text one also reads: Tib. *'dir rang gi gzugs yongs su brjes par 'gyur ro*, Skt. *atra svarūpaparivarto bhavati*. See chap. 11, Tōh 1803, 104b1–2. Sanskrit, Tibetan, and English translation in Wedemeyer 2007, B: 71a; Sanskrit and Tibetan in Pandey 2000, 98 and 353. Candrakīrti reads: Tib. *tshe 'di nyid la rang gi ngo bo brje ba*, Skt. *iha iva janmani svarūpaparivartana*. See his *Sgron gsal*, *Pradīpoddyotanaṭīkā*, Tōh 1785, 68b4; Chakravarti 1984, 86.

The answer to this conundrum is based on the unique perspective of human physiology offered by the higher tantras, one in which the relation between mind and body is quite different than in early Buddhism. An intermediate being formed of wind-and-mind means that the mind of the intermediate being rides on its subtle body made of wind[587] and these two cannot be separated. Moreover, the wind has certain subtle corporeal aspects that separate from the old aggregates of the dying person when the intermediate being is formed. In other words, not each and every physical aspect of the ordinary body is discarded at death; certain subtle aspects are carried to the intermediate state.

Likewise, the First Lord during the creation stage is formed of mere wind-and-mind, as is the illusory body[588] during the completion stage. While both are formed of mere wind-and-mind, the intermediate being leads to saṃsāra alone, whereas the illusory body can bring the yogi to awakening. The illusory body is especially emphasized in the so-called father tantras, such as the *Guhyasamāja Tantra*, our concern here. The illusory body of a yogi skillful in the completion stage can leave the yogi's coarse body, just as the intermediate being separates itself from the dead body.[589] The mere wind-and-mind of both the illusory body and the intermediate beings are not a completely new entity, but rather appear as a result of accordant causes and conditions and carry certain corporeal features.

The corporeal aspect is not lost in buddhahood as well. From early Buddhism on, buddhahood has been described in terms of the two or more bodies or *kāyas* of the Buddha, thus affirming a certain corporeality in the awakened state. Similar to the term "corpus," *kāya* carries meanings that include "a collection" as well as "a *physical* entity." Specifically in the rūpakāya, certain corporeal elements are present, such as the major and minor marks of the Buddha, the saṃbhogakāya, or the seven features of union.[590]

Tsongkhapa emphasizes that at the end of the completion stage, there must be an accordant cause for the rūpakāya,[591] and Khedrup Jé follows him. "An accordant cause" is a cause that is of the same type as the result; in order for the

587. Tib. *rlung*, Skt. *prāṇa*. The term *prāṇa* is used in general and specific meanings. The general meaning is wind (Tib. *rlung*), while as one of the ten winds, for example, the "life-sustaining wind," it is translated into Tibetan as *srog 'dzin* or *srog 'dzin rlung*.

588. Tib. *sgyu lus*, Skt. *māyādeha*.

589. Tsong kha pa, *Rim lnga gsal sgron*, chap. 7, 238b6–239a1; an English translation in Kilty 2013, 396.

590. Tib. *kha sbyor yan lag bdun*. These seven features encompass the characteristics of all three bodies: resources, union, great bliss, absence of intrinsic nature, uninterrupted continuum, compassion, and unceasing.

591. Tsong kha pa, *Rim lnga gsal sgron*, chap. 2, 63a1–2; an English translation in Kilty 2013, 118.

cause of the rūpakāya to be an accordant cause, it must have certain corporeal features. The illusory body is the main bodily aspect during the completion stage that is similar in type to the rūpakāya and will give rise to it. According to Tsongkhapa, the illusory body is the unique and substantial cause[592] of the resultant rūpakāya endowed with major and minor marks of the Buddha.[593] The substantial cause for the mind of the illusory body is the preceding mind of clear light that arises for advanced yogis during the phase of mind-isolation[594] in the completion stage, while the substantial cause for its body is the wind on which the mind of mind-isolation is mounted.[595]

The illusory body is the key to resolving the paradox of attaining buddhahood in this life—after discarding the impure old body, but without undergoing death and rebirth. It is in the illusory body that yogis reach the moment of their awakening. Unlike the coarse contaminated body, the subtle illusory body formed of mere-wind-and-mind can be purified just prior to the attainment of enlightenment. At the culmination of the completion stage, the mind of innate great bliss, which directly realizes clear-light-emptiness, results in the dharmakāya; the illusory bodies purified by the actual clear light results in the rūpakāya. For Tsongkhapa, these are the two exclusive causes of a buddha's body.[596]

Thus yogis change their bodies not by dying and taking on a new life but by discarding their coarse ordinary bodies while retaining the subtle corporeal elements of the wind upon which the subtle mind rides.

The Five Manifest Awakenings

With the dissolution into the moon orb, the first of the four yogas, called simply "yoga," ends, and subsequent yoga begins.[597] Another classification of the steps of the sādhana used by our Tibetan sources is the five manifest awakenings,

592. Tib. *nyer len.*

593. Tsong kha pa, *Rim lnga gsal sgron*, chap. 2, 63b2–3, and chap. 8, 271a4; an English translation in Kilty 2013, 119 and 444.

594. Tib. *sems dben*, Skt. *cittaviveka.*

595. Tsong kha pa, *Rim lnga gsal sgron*, chap. 7, 238b5–6; an English translation in Kilty 2013, 396.

596. Tsong kha pa, *Rim lnga gsal sgron*, chap. 8, 287b2–4; an English translation in Kilty 2013, 470.

597. As we saw above, both the *Concise Sādhana* and *Vajrasattva Sādhana* divide the core practice into four yogas: yoga, subsequent yoga, higher yoga, and great yoga (Skt. *yoga, anuyoga, atiyoga*, and *mahāyoga*).

though this term is not explicitly found in the basic Indian sādhanas of the Guhyasamāja.[598] There are a number of variations in the list of the five manifest awakenings.[599] Their order here is considered characteristic of the Ārya school:[600] (1) the manifest awakening from suchness,[601] (2) from the moon,[602] (3) from the seed syllable,[603] (4) from the emblem,[604] and (5) from the complete body.[605] The first awakening from suchness took place in the previous step of the meditation, the dissolution into clear light. It is within the continuum of clear-light-emptiness that the First Lord is visualized. The second awakening, the manifest awakening from the moon, is the meditation on the moon orb. The three latter manifest awakenings are within subsequent yoga.

With the beginning of subsequent yoga and the manifest awakening from the seed syllables, a process of increasing manifestation of the First Lord commences. First, the three seed syllables, a white *oṃ*, red *āḥ*, and blue *hūṃ*, appear from the moon orb.[606] Then, in the manifest awakening from the emblem, as both Tsongkhapa and Ngorchen Kunga Sangpo describe, the five Tathāgata families, together with numerous deities invited from the ten directions, dissolve into the three seed syllables and impregnate them with awakening, thereby transforming them into a white five-pronged vajra.[607]

However, the *Concise Sādhana*, the basic manual of the Guhyasamāja sādhana, does not explain the meditation here on the basis of the complete series of manifest awakenings: "Visualize the three syllables at the center of the moon, and then the First Lord, who resembles a white jasmine moon arising from the three syllables."[608] Thus there is no mention of the emblem of vajra here. In his commentary on the *Concise Sādhana*, Butön relies on the *Illuminating Lamp*, which describes a great five-pronged vajra that arises from the

598. See Tsong kha pa, *Rnal 'byor dag rim*, 13b3–14a5.

599. See, for example, English 2002, 149–154.

600. See Tsong kha pa, *Bskyed rim zin bris*, 20b2–4, and his *Sngags rim chen mo*, 504.

601. Tib. *de bzhin nyid las byang chub pa*.

602. Tib. *zla ba las byang chub pa*.

603. Tib. *sa bon las byang chub pa*.

604. Tib. *phyag mtshan las byang chub pa*.

605. Tib. *sku rdzogs pa las byang chub pa*.

606. Tsong kha pa, *Gsang mngon*, 39b2–3.

607. Tsong kha pa, *Gsang mngon*, 39b3–5; Ngor chen, *Gsang 'dus dkyil 'khor gyi sgrub thabs dngos grub rgya mtsho*, 9b5.

608. Nāgārjuna, *Mdor byas*, *Piṇḍīkrama Sādhana*, Tōh 1796, 4a1, L 51cd–52abc.

three syllables upon the moon.[609] Both Tsongkhapa and Khedrup Jé agree that although this is not clear in the *Concise Sādhana*, yogis should meditate on a vajra during the manifest awakening from the emblem.[610]

Then, in the fifth manifest awakening from the complete body, the yogis visualize the vajra transforming into themselves as the First Lord. The point of disagreement in this context is whether, as with the other deities of the Guhyasamāja maṇḍala, the First Lord also has three faces and six arms. This is because Muniśrībhadra explains in his commentary on the *Concise Sādhana* that the First Lord has just one face and two arms,[611] and both Butön and Ngorchen Kunga Sangpo follow this.[612] On the basis of *Formulating the Sādhana*, Tsongkhapa and Khedrup Jé maintain that all deities of the Guhyasamāja have three faces that signify the conventional illusory body, the ultimate mind of clear light, and their indivisibility.[613] Khedrup Jé concludes:

> Those who say that it is inappropriate for the First Lord—the main signifier of the body of union, the saṃbhogakāya—to have three faces do not understand the meaning of the tantra.[614]

Disagreements about the Meditation on the First Lord

Another major argument is against the Tibetan scholars who based their system of correspondence on *Formulating the Sādhana*, which does not mention the First Lord, but rather refers to a single deity, Vajradhara, throughout the core practices.[615] When there is no other purifier, this single deity must then

609. Bu ston, *Mdor byas 'grel chen*, 35a7–b1. The *Illuminating Lamp* passage is found in Candrakīrti, *Sgron gsal, Pradīpoddyotanaṭīkā*, Tōh 1785, 78b2; Chakravarti 1984, 96.

610. Tsong kha pa, *Slob tshul*, 15b3–4; Mkhas grub rje, *Bskyed rim dngos grub rgya mtsho*, 107a3–4.

611. Muniśrībhadra, *Rim pa lnga'i don mdor bshad pa, Pañcakramārthaṭippaṇi*, Tōh 1813, 156b1–2, Jiang and Tomabechi 1996, 17. Note that this work is translated into Tibetan by Bu ston himself.

612. Bu ston, *Mdor byas 'grel chen*, 35b4–6; Ngor chen, *Gsang 'dus dkyil 'khor gyi sgrub thabs dngos grub rgya mtsho*, 9b6.

613. Tsong kha pa, *Rnam gzhag rim pa'i rnam bshad*, 68a5–69a2; Mkhas grub rje, *Bskyed rim dngos grub rgya mtsho*, 107a6–b1. See Nāgabuddhi, *Rnam gzhag rim pa, Vyavastholi*, chap. 3, Tōh 1809, 127b4–128a4; Tanaka 2016, 114–115.

614. Mkhas grub rje, *Bskyed rim dngos grub rgya mtsho*, 107b2–3.

615. See the section "Dissimilarities among Guhyasamāja Sādhanas of the Ārya School" above.

purify both the intermediate state and rebirth. Hence, Gö Khukpa Lhetsé and Rendawa maintain that the first steps of the visualization of the deity purify the intermediate being, while the latter purify rebirth.[616] Butön and Tsongkhapa do not agree.[617] Tsongkhapa says:

> Such an explanation by diverting the words of the master [Nāgabuddhi] into another point is most inappropriate.[618]

Khedrup Jé concurs.[619] Tsongkhapa then concludes:

> Therefore, if you are mistaken in recognizing the individual correspondences of birth, death, and the intermediate state during the creation stage, you will certainly be mistaken in understanding the crucial points that are taught over and over in the tantra and commentaries—the system according to which after the mind-isolation and the clear light [respectively], the saṃbhogakāya arises as the illusory body and as the body of union, and then transforms into the nirmāṇakāya. Therefore this is extremely important.[620]

616. According to 'Gos Khug pa lhas btsas, the intermediate being is the ground of purification of the meditation on the three seed syllables *oṃ āḥ hūṃ* upon the lotus, while "the grounds of purification of the five manifest awakenings are five among the eight phases in the womb." See his *Gsang 'dus stong thun*, 12b4–5 and 10b2–3. According to Red mda' ba, the three syllables upon the lotus correspond to the body, speech, and mind of the intermediate being. Then the meditation on the three syllables upon the moon, which is the manifest awakening from the seed syllable, corresponds to the fetus during the first three phases in the womb. Subsequently, the meditation on the manifest awakenings from the emblem and from the complete body correspond to the two last phases in the womb. See his *Yid kyi mun sel*, 7b2–8a1. Rebirth is called here the phases of the fetus in the womb. According to our texts, rebirth begins at conception and ends when the new being appears outside the womb; this sequence of events is often referred to as "the five [or eight] phases in the womb."

617. According to Bu ston, Nāgabuddhi, in his *Rnam gzhag rim pa*, clearly explains that the *yoga* and *anuyoga* are the purifiers of the intermediate state. See Bu ston, *Mdor byas 'grel chen*, 36a7.

618. Tsong kha pa, *Rnam gzhag rim pa'i rnam bshad*, 26a2–4. Note that Tsong kha pa uses the name "First Lord" here to refer to the single deity, although Nāgabuddhi's *Rnam gzhag rim pa*, *Vyavastholi*, does not use this term.

619. Mkhas grub rje, *Bskyed rim dngos grub rgya mtsho*, 101b5–6.

620. Tsong kha pa, *Rnam gzhag rim pa'i rnam bshad*, 27b1–2. See also Mkhas grub rje, *Bskyed rim dngos grub rgya mtsho*, 102b2.

This is also related to the discussion of the illusory body above.[621] Khedrup Jé elaborates on this:

> Thus it is explicitly taught here that the saṃbhogakāya of the fruit, the illusory body of the path, and the intermediate being of the ground time all correspond with each other. Therefore those who maintain that the First Lord is the saṃbhogakāya and needs to transform into the nirmāṇakāya, but do not say that the First Lord corresponds to the intermediate being but rather to birth in the womb, contradict themselves, and their view falls very far afield from the position of Ārya Nāgārjuna and his disciples.[622]

The meditation on the First Lord during the creation stage serves to ripen the yogi's continuum to attain the illusory bodies during the completion stage. The ultimate fruit of these two meditations is the saṃbhogakāya of the Buddha.

Another point of dispute in relation to the meditation on the First Lord is the shapes the fetus takes in the womb, which, according to Gö Khukpa Lhetsé and Rendawa, are purified through the manifest awakenings. While, as we saw, Tsongkhapa and Khedrup Jé regard the five awakenings as purifiers of the intermediate state, not of rebirth and the phases of the fetus in the womb, Gö Khukpa Lhetsé draws detailed relations between the meditation on the manifest awakenings and the five phases in the womb as purifier and grounds of purification respectively.

According to Gö Khukpa Lhetsé and Rendawa, in his commentary on the *Illuminating Lamp*, the meditation on the three syllables upon the moon orb, which is the manifest awakening from the seed syllables *oṃ*, *āḥ*, and *hūṃ*, corresponds to the fetus during the first three phases in the womb.[623] Then, the grounds of purification of the manifest awakening from the emblem and from the complete body purify the fourth and fifth phases in the womb. Moreover, during the first three phases, the fetus intrinsically[624] has the respective shape of each of the seed syllables; likewise, during the fourth phase, it takes the

621. See the section "Awakening in this Body."

622. Mkhas grub rje, *Bskyed rim dngos grub rgya mtsho*, 102a5–6. Mkhas grub rje uses here the term "First Lord," which is part of his terminology.

623. 'Gos Khug pa lhas btsas, *Gsang 'dus stong thun*, 11b2–5; Red mda' ba, *Yid kyi mun sel*, 7b4–8a1.

624. Tib. *rang chos su* ['Gos], *rang bzhin gyi* [Red mda' ba].

shape of the tathāgata's emblem. Interestingly, in his *Replies to Druppa Pal*,[625] Rendawa seems to express a reservation regarding the fetus being in the shape of the emblem during the fourth phase in the womb, saying that he has not seen a clear explanation for this.

In order to establish his position that the visualization of the deity purifies both the intermediate state and rebirth, Rendawa takes a passage of *Formulating the Sādhana* describing the stages of rebirth to refer to an earlier point in this text that relates the intermediate being to the meditation on yoga and subsequent yoga.[626] This is a well-known hermeneutical method, and Rendawa justifies it by citing Dharmakīrti on this point.[627] He then concludes:

> Such a way of relating passages is not an explanation displeasing to the ear.[628]

Tsongkhapa objects to both of Rendawa's positions—that the meditation on this deity here also purifies rebirth, and that the fetus has the shapes of the seed syllables that purify it. In wording that seems to echo or be echoed by Rendawa, Tsongkhapa says:

> This is not pleasing to the ear. While ignoring the special correspondences applied by eminent teachers such as Glorious Nāgabuddhi between the intermediate being and the saṃbhogakāya, they establish their arguments with great insistence by relying on false proofs of shapes such as *oṃ*, which are refuted by "the non-observation of the suitable to appear."[629]

The term "the non-observation of the suitable to appear" means that what is there must be observable, and if one does not see it, it is not there. Tsongkhapa is saying here that not only does the position of the opponent contest *Formulating the Sādhana*, it also contradicts empirical evidence. Had the

625. Red mda' ba, *Bsgrub pa dpal bas zhus lan*, Kathmandu, 48a6–b2; TBRC, 303b.

626. Nāgabuddhi, *Rnam gzhag rim pa*, *Vyavastholi*, chap. 1, Tōh 1809, 124a4–5 and 123b1–2; Tanaka 2016, 94 and 90. For details see Bentor 2015c.

627. The citation is in Dharmakīrti's commentary on the *Mngon par rtogs pa'i rgyan*, *Abhisamayālaṅkāra*: *Mngon par rtogs pa'i rgyan zhes bya ba'i 'grel pa rtogs par dka' ba'i snang ba'i 'grel bshad*, *Abhisamayālaṅkāravṛtti Duravabodhālokaṭīkā*, Tōh 3794, 248b3.

628. Red mda' ba, *Bsgrub pa dpal bas zhus lan*, Kathmandu, 47b3; TBRC, 303a.

629. Tib. *snang rung ma dmigs pa*, Skt. *dṛśyānupalabdhi*. Tsong kha pa, *Rnam gzhag rim pa'i rnam bshad*, 27b6–28a.

fetus taken the shapes of the three seed syllables or the emblem in its different phases, we would have been able to observe those shapes, but since we do not see them, they must not be there. Therefore the fetus does not have these shapes in the womb.

Khedrup Jé summarizes his position:

> After first explaining the characteristics of the intermediate being, *Formulating the Sādhana* goes on to teach the visualization of the deity by means of the yoga and subsequent yoga in correspondence with the intermediate being. Thus this text clearly indicates that you should meditate on the First Lord in correspondence with the intermediate being. After that, *Formulating the Sādhana* describes how the intermediate being takes rebirth in the womb, and then explains the need to meditate on transforming into the nirmāṇakāya and so forth in correspondence with taking birth by means of the remaining yogas.[630] Thus it is with great clarity that *Formulating the Sādhana* applies the transformation into the nirmāṇakāya to rebirth in the womb.[631]

The final disagreement we will mention in this section is about awakening in the intermediate state. The notion of attaining nirvāṇa in the intermediate state is discussed in earlier texts, including the *Abhidharmakośa*.[632] Tsongkhapa and Khedrup Jé emphasize that this is not the case here:

> Therefore, if you maintain that "those who awaken in the intermediate state" actually attain the intermediate state, and awaken as intermediate beings by meditating on the path, you have not developed a proper understanding of the way awakening is attained in the unexcelled mantra. Therefore you must reach a thorough understanding of how awakening is attained: In place of the intermediate state, you should attain the illusory body and purify it by dissolving it into clear light. In doing so, you will attain the actual clear light and the pure illusory body that arises from it, and arrive at the union that still requires practice. The mental continuum of the

630. These are the "immense yoga," Tib. *shin tu rnal 'byor*, Skt. *atiyoga*, and the "great yoga," Tib. *rnal 'byor chen po*, Skt. *mahāyoga*.

631. Mkhas grub rje, *Bskyed rim dngos grub rgya mtsho*, 101b5–6.

632. See Vasubandhu, *Mdzod 'grel*, *Kośabhāṣya*, chap. 3, v. 12d, Tōh 4090, 117a5–118b5; Pradhan 1975, 122–123; Pruden 1988–1990, 386–388.

> union that still requires practice—sustained without a moment's disruption—transforms into the union of no more practice that unifies the saṃbhogakāya and the dharmakāya, the mind of great bliss. Through this transformation, you will awaken. Though I have described this only in brief, take pains to understand it.[633]

This may or may not refer to Rendawa's discourse on yogis who actualized the clear light of death and then attained the mental natural body of the intermediate being.[634] The greater significance of this topic, however, is for the meditation on the illusory body during the completion stage.

(4) The Yoga of Taking Rebirth on the Path That Leads to the Nirmāṇakāya

Which Rebirth Is Purified?

The yoga of taking rebirth on the path that leads to the nirmāṇakāya is the meditation that begins with the transformation of the First Lord into the nirmāṇakāya of Vajrasattva. For Tsongkhapa, this yoga serves to purify the yogi's future rebirth and to ultimately attain the nirmāṇakāya of the Buddha. Instead of the rebirth that would naturally arise for an ordinary human being, the yogi meditating on the creation stage provisionally arises as Vajrasattva's nirmāṇakāya of the creation stage. On the level of the ground of purification, the yoga of taking birth as the nirmāṇakāya corresponds to the intermediate being, who is propelled by the karma produced from latent habituations since time without beginning to take rebirth, and therefore enters into a womb. The goal of this yoga is to put an end to this process of continuous rebirths.

The *Sādhana Incorporating the Scripture* explains: "The body whose nature is wisdom cannot act for the sake of sentient beings. Therefore" it transforms into the nirmāṇakāya.[635] Likewise, *Formulating the Sādhana* draws correspondences between the saṃbhogakāyas—who cannot be seen by ordinary people and therefore take nirmāṇakāyas in order to act for the sake of their ordinary disciples—and the intermediate beings who become an object for the corporeal eye by entering the womb. *Formulating the Sādhana* also alludes to

633. Mkhas grub rje, *Bskyed rim dngos grub rgya mtsho*, 82b1–3. See Tsong kha pa, *Rim lnga gsal sgron*, chap. 7, 264b4–265a6; an English translation in Kilty 2013, 431–432.

634. See Red mda' ba, *Bsgrub pa dpal bas zhus lan*, Kathmandu, 48b5–6; TBRC, 304a.

635. Nāgārjuna, *Mdo bsre, Sādhanasūtramelāpaka*, Tōh 1797, 12b4–5.

the periodic event in the life of the buddhas, who, as the saṃbhogakāya bodhisattva bound for just one rebirth residing in Tuṣita, cannot act for the sake of impure sentient beings in the Desire Realm, being invisible to them, and therefore enter into a womb to take a coarse nirmāṇakāya.[636]

However, immediately after *Formulating the Sādhana* explains the evolution of beings in the world and the meditation that corresponds to it, this work portrays at length the four modes of birth—birth from an egg, birth from the womb, birth from warmth and moisture, and miraculous birth. Then it goes on to clarify why, for their last rebirths, the bodhisattvas chose to be born in the continent of Jambudvīpa and teach the Dharma there.[637] After some discussion, *Formulating the Sādhana* concludes: "'All the buddhas who appear in the past, present, and future enter existence in the nature of human beings, and as such attain the siddhi of the omniscient stage.' Therefore the stages of birth into human existence are taught here."[638]

As we will see, Tsongkhapa finds the authority for his position in this latter passage of *Formulating the Sādhana*. However, the vast majority of Tibetan scholars elaborate on meditations for the purification of each of the four modes of birth. Such explanations are also found in treatises composed in the Indian subcontinent, as in Ratnarakṣita's commentary on the *Saṃvarodaya Tantra*.[639] Butön follows both explanations of *Formulating the Sādhana*. On the one hand, he declares: "Here I will explain in accordance with the human beings in Jambudvīpa... since the bodhisattva in his final saṃsāric existence awakens in a human body in Jambudvīpa."[640] On the other hand, he presents the four modes of birth and ascribes four practices for purifying them.[641]

Tibetan lamas of all schools delineated four kinds of meditation for

636. Nāgabuddhi, *Rnam gzhag rim pa*, *Vyavastholi*, chap. 1, Tōh 1809, 123b1–3 and 124b5; Tanaka 2016, 91 and 96–97.

637. Nāgabuddhi, *Rnam gzhag rim pa*, *Vyavastholi*, chap. 1, Tōh 1809, 122a5–b1; Tanaka 2016, 83–85.

638. Nāgabuddhi, *Rnam gzhag rim pa*, *Vyavastholi*, Tōh 1809, 122b7–123a1; Tanaka 2016, 87. Our text cites here the *Thun mong ma yin pa'i gsang ba*, Āsādhāraṇaguhya.

639. *Padma can*, *Padminī*, Tōh 1420, 11a3–5.

640. Bu ston, *Mdor byas 'grel chen*, 25a3–b1.

641. Bu ston, *Mdor byas 'grel chen*, 24b3–25a1.

purifying these four modes of birth.[642] These authors include Drakpa Gyaltsen,[643] Serdingpa,[644] the Third Karmapa Rangjung Dorjé,[645] Barawa Gyaltsen Palsang,[646] Rongtön Sheja Kunrik,[647] Jikmé Lingpa,[648] Jamyang Khyentsé Wangpo,[649] and Kongtrul Yönten Gyatso.[650] There are no two identical descriptions among them.

Tsongkhapa and Khedrup Jé object to each and every system that identifies specific steps in the sādhana as purifiers of the four modes of birth.[651] This is because the path of the unexcelled mantra is intended only for human beings endowed with characteristics essential for the practice of the sādhana, who will attain awakening within several lifetimes as human beings. Moreover, yogis who engage in the path of the unexcelled mantra from the very beginning of their practice can be enlightened within one lifetime; why would they need to purify their future birth from an egg? Khedrup Jé concludes:

> A similarity between birth from an egg and a meditation does not necessarily turn them into a ground of purification and its purifier...
>
> Furthermore, those who produce numerous systems of the creation stage in this way merely demonstrate their delight in their own elaborations, but have surely not developed even a coarse understanding of the essential points of the two stages. The goal of yogis who meditate on the creation stage is to ripen their continuum for the meditation of the completion stage. The methods

642. See Bentor 2006, 193–194.

643. Grags pa rgyal mtshan (1147–1216). To give an example, Grags pa rgyal mtshan maintains that instantaneous visualization of the deity purifies miraculous birth; generation through the five manifest awakenings—which include solar and lunar disks—purifies birth from warmth and moisture, since the sun warms and the moon moistens; the visualization of the fruitional deity from a heap of drops purifies birth from egg; and sending forth the deities from the womb of the mother purifies birth from womb. See his *Rgyud kyi mngon rtogs*, 69a3–5.

644. Gser sdings pa (born in the twelfth century).

645. Rang byung rdo rje (1284–1339).

646. 'Ba' ra ba Rgyal mtshan dpal bzang (1310–1391).

647. Rong ston Shes bya kun rig (1367–1449).

648. 'Jigs med gling pa (1729/1730–1798).

649. 'Jam dbyangs Mkhyen brtse dbang po (1820–1892).

650. Kong sprul Yon tan rgya mtsho (1813–1899).

651. Tsong kha pa, *Rnam gzhag rim pa'i rnam bshad*, 13b1–20a4; and his *'Dod 'jo*, 63b2–66b2. Mkhas grub rje, *Bskyed rim dngos grub rgya mtsho*, 75b3 and 73b6–75a3.

> of creation and completion taught in the tantra pertain to disciples who devote themselves exclusively to the unexcelled mantra, and who primarily practice the path of awakening in this life. Not a few tantras and mahāsiddhas teach that the person practicing such a path must certainly be a human being born from a womb in Jambudvīpa, endowed with the six constituents, as will presently be explained.[652]

Khedrup Jé also explains why *Formulating the Sādhana* refers to the four modes of birth:

> Here, in order for you to understand this, *Formulating the Sādhana* teaches the four modes of birth viable for inhabitants of the world; from among these four modes of birth, it then teaches how to generate the deities... in accordance with the stages of saṃsāric rebirth of the people of Jambudvīpa. But if you misunderstand this and maintain that the four different rituals of generating deities were taught for purifying the four modes of birth, you miss the point.[653]

Rebirth as Human Beings

Rebirth begins at the moment of conception, when the intermediate being dies; its consciousness enters into the midst of the semen and blood and lasts until the fetus is born outside the womb. Before elucidating the yoga of taking rebirth, Khedrup Jé describes various features of embryology on the basis of both nontantric and tantric scriptural authorities.[654] These include: the

652. Mkhas grub rje, *Bskyed rim dngos grub rgya mtsho*, 75a3–6.

653. Mkhas grub rje, *Bskyed rim dngos grub rgya mtsho*, 75b5–6. See also Tsong kha pa, *Rnam gzhag rim pa'i rnam bshad*, 13b6–14a1.

654. Moreover, Mkhas grub rje follows Tsong kha pa, who relied on writings on this subject by Tibetan scholars from approximately the eleventh to twelfth centuries, including 'Gos Khug pa lhas btsas (*Gsang 'dus stong thun*, 10b3–13b3) and Glo gros 'byung gnas (*Bstan rim chen mo*, 292–296), as well as Bu ston (*Mdor byas 'grel chen*, 37a2–38b3). The nontantric scriptures include the third chapter of Vasubandhu's *Mdzod, Abhidharmakośa*; Asaṅga, *Sa'i dngos gzhi, Maulībhūmi*, Tōh 4035; the *Mngal gnas* and *Mngal 'jug, Nandagarbhāvakrānti Nirdeśa*; as well as *'Dul ba phran tshegs kyi gzhi, Vinayakṣudrakavastu*; see Kritzer 2014. The tantric sources include the *Sdom 'byung, Saṃvarodaya Tantra*; the *Lha mo bzhis zhus pa, Caturdevīparipṛcchā*; the *Rgyud rdo rje phreng ba, Vajramālā Tantra*; and Nāgabuddhi's *Rnam gzhag rim pa, Vyavastholi, Formulating the Sādhana*. The latter source itself cites various sources just mentioned.

three conditions for conception; the three unfavorable conditions that would obstruct pregnancy; how the intermediate being enters the womb; how the seventy-two channels of the patents' subtle body are activated and the inner fire[655] ignited; how, when the intermediate being dies, the three appearances arise from the clear light at the death of the intermediate being in reverse order; how the channels and cakras of the subtle body of the child evolve; the length of pregnancy; the future gender; and how the child exits the womb at the end of thirty-eight weeks.

In the description of conception, we encounter another term associated with the Yogācāra philosophical school. The *Yogācārabhūmi*, which Tsongkhapa follows in his description of conception, states that the two drops of semen and blood mingle in the mother's womb, and the consciousness-base-of-all[656] endowed with all seeds[657] penetrates the mixture.[658] In both his commentary on *Formulating the Sādhana* and the *Great Treatise on the Stages of the Path to Enlightenment*, Tsongkhapa adds that those who do not accept the consciousness-base-of-all maintain that it is the mental consciousness[659] which enters into new life.[660] Apparently following this advice, Khedrup Jé does not argue here, but simply says that the consciousness[661] enters into the midst of the semen and blood.[662]

Correspondence to the Grounds of Purification

Yet another controversy rages around the relations of the sādhana to its grounds of purification—in this context, rebirth. It is crucial for Tsongkhapa that the steps of the practice here correspond to the stages of rebirth. He finds two faults in the position of his opponents. Firstly, their sādhanas do not allude to rebirth, the ground of purification. Secondly, their meditation does

655. Tib. *gtum mo*.

656. Tib. *kun gzhi rnam par shes pa*, Skt. *ālayavijñāna*.

657. Tib. *sa bon thams cad pa*, Skt. *sarvabījaka*.

658. Asaṅga, *Sa'i dngos gzhi*, *Maulībhūmi*, Tōh 4035, 12a3–5; Bhattacharya 1957, 24.1–5. See also Schmithausen 1987, 127–128 and Kritzer 2000, 255. See Tsong kha pa, *Rnam gzhag rim pa'i rnam bshad*, 35b3–5 and *Lam rim chen mo*, 247; an English translation of the later in Cutler 2000, 312.

659. Tib. *yid kyi shes pa*.

660. Tsong kha pa, *Rnam gzhag rim pa'i rnam bshad*, 35b5, and Tsong kha pa, *Lam rim chen mo*, 247; an English translation in Cutler 2000, 312.

661. Tib. *rnam shes*.

662. Mkhas grub rje, *Bskyed rim dngos grub rgya mtsho*, 108b3.

not correspond to the intermediate being who enters the womb. Yet Tsongkhapa must employ certain hermeneutical methods in order to establish this correspondence.

The argument about the second point centers on the interpretation of a line from the basic sādhana, the *Concise Sādhana*, on the transformation of the First Lord into Vajrasattva through the entry of/into Akṣobhya (*akṣobhyānupraveśena*).[663] A straightforward understanding of this phrase is as "the entry *of* Akṣobhya" and not "the entry *into* Akṣobhya"; the latter is the interpretation espoused by Butön and Tsongkhapa. The dispute is whether it is Akṣobhya who enters into the First Lord or the First Lord who enters into Akṣobhya. The significance of this dispute is that only if the First Lord enters into Akṣobhya does the First Lord correspond to the intermediate being who enters into the red and white bodhicittas, the semen and blood, of the father and mother and takes on a new life in the womb.

The Tibetan translations of this line read *mi bskyod pa ni rjes zhugs pas*[664] and *mi bskyod pas ni rjes zhugs pas*.[665] While the first version could be considered somewhat ambiguous, in the second case it is clear that it is Akṣobhya who enters. None of the Tibetan translations of this work available to me read *mi bskyod pa la*, "enter into Akṣobhya."[666] Some of the commentators on the *Concise Sādhana* also understood Akṣobhya as the one doing the entering. In his commentary on this passage, *Kṛṣṇasamayavajra has *mi bskyod pa yi rjes zhugs pas*, "through the entry of Akṣobhya."[667] However, Butön does not agree:

> This position does not conform with the ground of purification,

663. Nāgārjuna, *Mdor byas*, *Piṇḍīkrama Sādhana*, Tōh 1796, 4a2; L 53a.

664. Nāgārjuna, *Mdor byas*, *Piṇḍīkrama Sādhana*, Tōh 1796, 4a2; Cone 4a2; and Peking 4788 5a5. I would like to thank Roger Wright, now Rhonwen Sayer, for informing me about this additional version of the *Piṇḍīkrama Sādhana* in the Peking, and for providing me with a copy.

665. Nāgārjuna, *Mdor byas*, *Piṇḍīkrama Sādhana*, Golden Tengyur 5a6; Narthang 5a6; and Peking 2661, 4b2.

666. Paṇ chen Bsod nams grags pa explains that the Tibetan translation here is mistaken, and the actual import of this line of the *Piṇḍīkrama Sādhana* is *mi bskyod pa la rjes zhugs pa*, that is to say, "entry into Akṣobhya." See his *Gsang 'dus bskyed rim rnam gzhag*, 52b5–6.

667. Nag po dam tshig rdo rje, *Rim pa lnga'i dka' 'grel*, *Pañcakramapañjikā*, Tōh 1841, 160b4–6. Similarly, in his commentary on the *Sgron gsal*, Bhavyakīrti describes how Akṣobhya emanates from the yogi's heart, purifies the afflictive emotion of hatred in all the realms of sentient beings, returns, and enters into oneself. See his *Rab tu sgron gsal*, *Prakāśikā*, Tōh 1793, 9a6–b1 and 121b5.

> because the intermediate being does not produce its own body by its own semen.[668]

For the meditation to serve to purify the yogi's rebirth, the First Lord, who corresponds to the intermediate being, has to enter Akṣobhya, who corresponds to the drop of semen and blood in which the intermediate being takes birth. Tsongkhapa follows Butön in this matter:

> The First Lord is like the intermediate being... Akṣobhya is like the drop in which the intermediate being takes birth. The entry of the First Lord into Akṣobhya is similar to the entry of the intermediate being into the drop in the vulva. The transformation into the nirmāṇakāya following this entry is like taking birth following the entry of the intermediate being.[669]

The description of this step of meditation in Tsongkhapa's *Guhyasamāja Sādhana* is brief: "I enter and become Vajrasattva's nirmāṇakāya."[670] Akhu Ching Sherab Gyatso[671] describes how to visualize this: The yogis, visualizing themselves as the First Lord sitting on the throne, must now elevate themselves in space, and Akṣobhya takes the First Lord's place on the throne.[672] The yogis as the First Lord then descend and enter Akṣobhya through his crown.[673]

Who are the Tibetans who maintain that Akṣobhya enters into the yogi visualized as the First Lord, thus following the tradition of *Kṛṣṇasamayavajra? The *Blue Annals* tell us that Gö Khukpa Lhetsé was among the disciples of *Kṛṣṇasamayavajra.[674] Indeed, according to Panchen Sönam Drakpa, these Tibetans are followers of the tradition of Gö Khukpa Lhetsé.[675] Additionally, the meditation prescribed by Ngorchen Kunga Sangpo in his sādhana is exactly what Butön and Tsongkhapa disapprove of:

668. Bu ston, *Mdor byas 'grel chen*, 39a4–5.

669. Tsong kha pa, *Sgron gsal mchan*, 63b1–2.

670. Tsong kha pa, *Gsang mngon*, 40a4–5.

671. A khu ching Shes rab rgya mtsho (1803–1875).

672. See also Tsong kha pa, *Bskyed rim zin bris*, 25a6–b1.

673. A khu ching, *Mi bskyod mgon po'i zhal lung*, 75a3–4; an English translation in Jinpa 1999, 138.

674. See Roerich 1949, 360.

675. Bsod nams grags pa, *Gsang 'dus bskyed rim rnam gzhag*, 52b1–2.

> The Akṣobhyas merge together and *enter into me*; thereby I become Vajrasattva's nirmāṇakāya.[676]

Let us compare the sādhana of Ngorchen Kunga Sangpo to that of Tsongkhapa. According to Ngorchen:

> I visualize Akṣobhya emanating from the heart of the First Lord and [multiplying to] pervade the entire space realm. The Akṣobhyas purify the obscuration of hatred of sentient beings possessing hatred. Then they merge together and *enter into me*. Thereby I become Vajrasattva's nirmāṇakāya.[677]

According to Tsongkhapa:

> The father-mother tathāgatas from[678] their natural abode are absorbed in union for the sake of guiding sentient beings. Akṣobhya[s] formed from their bodhicittas pervade the entire space realm and bless all sentient beings, who then attain pure bliss and mental rapture. Then, all the Akṣobhyas merge together inside the celestial mansion, and I [the First Lord] enter [into that] and become Vajrasattva's nirmāṇakāya.[679]

In both cases, the Akṣobhyas pervade the entire space realm, act for the benefit of sentient beings, and merge together; ultimately, the meditator becomes Vajrasattva's nirmāṇakāya. However, in the sādhana of Ngorchen Kunga Sangpo, there are no father-mother tathāgatas in union, no bodhicitta, and no bliss—in other words, there are no connotations of rebirth in this sādhana. Furthermore, while according to Tsongkhapa the "I," the meditator, enters into the Akṣobhyas in correspondence with the intermediate being who enters into the drop of semen and blood, according to Ngorchen Kunga Sangpo, the

676. Ngor chen, *Gsang 'dus dkyil 'khor gyi sgrub thabs dngos grub rgya mtsho*, 10a1–2. Though this sādhana was written in 1423, after the death of both Red mda' ba in 1412 and Tsong kha pa in 1419, most likely it preserves a tradition of earlier Sa skya lamas, as A myes zhabs tells us. See his *Gsang ba 'dus pa'i dkyil 'khor 'khor lo sgrub pa'i thabs rnam par bshad pa nges don phrin las rgya mtsho'i 'byung gnas*, 124a5–6.

677. Ngor chen, *Gsang 'dus dkyil 'khor gyi sgrub thabs dngos grub rgya mtsho*, 10a1–3.

678. Or in their natural abode according to his *Sgron gsal mchan*, 63b3, which has *na* for the *nas* found in the *Gsang mngon*, 40a1.

679. Tsong kha pa, *Gsang mngon*, 40a1–6.

Akṣobhyas enter into the meditator, and this cannot correspond to rebirth. Moreover, if Akṣobhya emanates from the heart of the yogi visualized as the First Lord, as Ngorchen Kunga Sangpo has it in his sādhana, insofar as these correspondences are concerned, this would entail that the intermediate being would produce its new body by its own semen, as Butön said in the citation above. Tsongkhapa and Khedrup Jé follow Butön in this matter. Khedrup Jé says:

> Some early and later Tibetan lamas maintain this as well, but it is extremely inappropriate because: (1) it is the intermediate being that enters into the midst of the commingled coarse constituents of the semen and blood, and not the semen and blood that enter the intermediate being; (2) the semen and blood are the semen and blood of the parents, and the intermediate being does not enter the semen and blood produced from its own body; (3) if this were so, the instruction of *Formulating the Sādhana* to visualize the deities here according to the samādhi of vajra overpowering taught in the *Guhyasamāja Tantra* would be irrelevant.[680]

The third point refers to the scriptural authority of the meditation here. Tsongkhapa establishes his method of the visualization by relying on *Formulating the Sādhana*,[681] which explains that conception takes place through the samādhi of the vajra overpowering of all tathāgatas, taught in the *Guhyasamāja Tantra*:

> Then, the Blessed One, the Tathāgata Bodhicittavajra, dwelt in absorption in the samādhi called "vajra overpowering of all tathāgatas."[682] As soon as the Blessed One, the Lord of all tathāgatas, dwelt in absorption, the entire realm of space abided in the vajra nature of all tathāgatas. Then, as many as there were sentient beings residing in the entire realm of space, through the blessing of

680. Mkhas grub rje, *Bskyed rim dngos grub rgya mtsho*, 111a6–b2.

681. Nāgabuddhi, *Rnam gzhag rim pa*, *Vyavastholi*, Tōh 1809, 124a2–3; Tanaka 2016, 93.

682. Tib. *de bzhin gshegs pa thams cad zil gyis gnon pa rdo rje zhes bya ba'i ting nge 'dzin*, Skt. *sarvatathāgatābhibhavanavajra samādhi*. For more on this samādhi, see the section "The Samādhis in the First Chapter of the *Guhyasamāja Tantra* and Enacting Past Events" below.

> Vajrasattva all of them attained the bliss and mental rapture of all tathāgatas.[683]

Following Butön, Tsongkhapa applies one of the hidden levels of interpretation of this passage to conception.[684] On the basis of *Formulating the Sādhana*, the tathāgata dwelling in absorption with his queen corresponds to both the ground and the path.[685] At the level of the ground of purification, it corresponds to the parents absorbed in union, while at the level of the practice on the path, it corresponds to "the father-mother tathāgatas who were absorbed in union for the sake of guiding sentient beings."[686] The *entire realm of space* mentioned in the *Guhyasamāja Tantra* appears in both Tsongkhapa and Ngorchen's sādhanas, where it is pervaded by Akṣobhyas, but only Tsongkhapa relates the Akṣobhyas to bodhicittas. The attainment of *pure bliss and mental rapture*, not found in Ngorchen's text, occurs in both the *Guhyasamāja Tantra* and Tsongkhapa's *Guhyasamāja Sādhana*; both the *Illuminating Lamp* and *Formulating the Sādhana* describe how the parents experience bliss while conceiving a child.[687] Both Butön and Tsongkhapa arrived at their positions

683. *Gsang 'dus*, chap. 1, Tōh 442; Zhol 3a5–b1; Stog 4a6–7 [the rest is missing]; Dunh 3a1–4; Fremantle 1971, 178; and Matsunaga 1978, 5.

684. Tsong kha pa, *Sgron gsal mchan*, 61a6–63b6; and his *Rnam gzhag rim pa'i rnam bshad*, 36a4–6. See Bu ston, *Mdor byas 'grel chen*, 39a5. In his *Sgron gsal*, Candrakīrti explains this passage by means of three among the four levels of interpretation (Tib. *tshul bzhi*): the shared (Tib. *spyi don*, Skt. *samastāṅga*), the hidden (Tib. *sbas don*, Skt. *garbhī*), and the ultimate (Tib. *mthar thug tu*, Skt. *kolikavyākhyā*) levels of interpretation. Tsong kha pa applies the shared level of interpretation to the specially visualized deities and their deeds, one of the hidden level to the emanation of the Supreme King of Maṇḍalas arising from the union with the consort below, and the ultimate level to the completion stage. See his *Sgron gsal*, *Pradīpoddyotanaṭikā*, Tōh 1785, 14b5–15a6; Chakravarti 1984, 20.

685. Nāgabuddhi, *Rnam gzhag rim pa*, *Vyavastholi*, Tōh 1809, 124a4, Tanaka 2016, 94.

686. Tsong kha pa, *Gsang mngon*, 41a1–2.

687. Candrakīrti, *Sgron gsal*, *Pradīpoddyotanaṭikā*, Tōh 1785, 15a3–5; Chakravarti 1984, 20. Nāgabuddhi, *Rnam gzhag rim pa*, Tōh 1809, 124a2–3; Tanaka 2016, 93. Both works describe how when the parents join the two organs, the seventy-two thousand channels of the subtle body are aroused and the parents are satisfied by bliss. Furthermore, the empty interior of the seventy-two thousand channels corresponds to *the entire space realm* in the *Guhyasamāja Tantra*.

on the basis of these works.[688] For more about the passage of the tantra just cited, see below.[689]

As we have seen,[690] both *Formulating the Sādhana* and the *Sādhana Incorporating the Scripture* do not mention the First Lord. Hence, the entry of/into Akṣobhya is not found there. Instead, the transformation into a visible form of the deity takes place only with the subsequent step of the meditation.[691] Moreover, the transformation into Vajrasattva's nirmāṇakāya, our concern here, is the subject of Ngorchen Kunga Sangpo's work[692] on the difference in the practice of the "higher yoga" between Nāgārjuna's *Concise Sādhana* and the *Sādhana Incorporating the Scripture.*

In answering one of Druppa Pal's questions, Rendawa describes the practice here without the entry of/into Akṣobhya in accordance with the *Sādhana Incorporating the Scripture* and *Formulating the Sādhana*:

> Invoking Akṣobhya from his natural abode and thereby transforming into the nirmāṇakāya is inappropriate. As the saṃbhogakāya does not appear to ordinary beings, and therefore transforms into the nirmāṇakāya and acts for the sake of others, just so the yogis first generate themselves as the saṃbhogakāya and then transform into the nirmāṇakāya...[693]

Here, Rendawa describes the visualization through the four manifest awakenings without mentioning Akṣobhya or the entry of one deity into another, then continues:

688. Bu ston, *Mdor byas 'grel chen*, 38b5–39b3. Furthermore, Tsong kha pa adds to the three levels of interpretation found in the *Illuminating Lamp* the "missing" literal level of interpretation, in which he delineates how the lines of the *Guhyasamāja Tantra* cited above are applied to lines of the sādhana and how these lines correspond to conception at the ground of purification. See Tsong kha pa, *Sgron gsal mchan*, 63b1–6; see also his *Rnam gzhag rim pa'i rnam bshad*, 43a1–3.

689. The section "The Samādhis in the First Chapter of the *Guhyasamāja Tantra* and Enacting Past Events" below.

690. See the section "Dissimilarities among Guhyasamāja Sādhanas of the Ārya School" above.

691. Nāgabuddhi, *Rnam gzhag rim pa*, *Vyavastholi*, Tōh 1809, 124b5–6; Tanaka 2016, 97. Nāgārjuna, *Mdo bsre*, *Sādhanasūtramelāpaka*, Tōh 1797, 12a7–13a2.

692. Ngor chen, *Shin tu rnal 'byor gyi khyad par sgrub thabs kyi yan lag tu bris pa*.

693. Red mda' ba, *Bsgrub pa dpal bas zhus lan*, Kathmandu, 47b3–4; TBRC, 303b–304a. Reading *bkug nas sprul skur sgyur ba* for *skyo ba kun sprul skur 'gyur ba* in the Kathmandu version.

> Therefore the yogis visualize themselves as both the saṃbhogakāya and the nirmāṇakāya in their respective forms. You should know this in all the deity yogas of the Vajra Vehicle; otherwise, you are mistaken about the crucial points of the path. Therefore invoking Akṣobhya from his natural abode and then transforming him into a nirmāṇakāya, and citing the samādhi of vajra overpowering for proving this, are irrelevant.[694]

It is perhaps in reply to this claim that Khedrup Jé finds fault with the position of the Tibetan lamas cited above:

> If this were so, the instruction of *Formulating the Sādhana* to visualize the deities here according to the samādhi of vajra overpowering taught in the *Guhyasamāja Tantra* would be irrelevant.[695]

Where Does Akṣobhya Come From?

Rendawa disagrees not only with the entry of/into Akṣobhya but also with the invocation of Akṣobhya from his natural abode. Why does this question matter?

While Akṣobhya does not appear in Rendawa's aforementioned explanation of the visualization, Rendawa objects to the methods of others.[696] In Ngorchen's sādhana, cited above, Akṣobhya emanates from the heart of the meditator visualized as the First Lord.[697] According to Tsongkhapa's *Guhyasamāja Sādhana*, on the other hand, Akṣobhya is formed from the bodhicittas of the father-mother tathāgatas who are absorbed in union from their natural abode.[698] Rendawa disagrees:

694. Red mda' ba, *Bsgrub pa dpal bas zhus lan*, Kathmandu, 49a2–3; TBRC, 304a.

695. Mkhas grub rje, *Bskyed rim dngos grub rgya mtsho*, 111b1–2.

696. In this he appears to be following the *Sādhana Incorporating the Scripture* and *Formulating the Sādhana*.

697. Ngor chen follows the method of Nāgārjuna's *Mdor byas*.

698. Mkhas grub rje provides three interpretations for the meaning of "natural abode," in the context of the invitation of the field for accumulating merit. (1) The abode where awakening initially took place; (2) the nature of all phenomena, dharmakāya, emptiness; (3) 'Og min, Akaniṣṭha. See his *Bskyed rim dngos grub rgya mtsho*, 18a4–6. In order to make the visualization easier, later Dge lugs lamas locate the natural abode within the inner mansion of the maṇḍala. See, for example, A khu ching, *Mi bskyod mgon po'i zhal lung*, 74b5–6; an English translation in Jinpa 1999, 137.

> If by invoking Akṣobhya from his natural abode, the yogi transforms into the nirmāṇakāya, then the meditations on issuing forth the Supreme King of Maṇḍalas and so forth[699] will be the enlightened activities of someone else who has been already awakened, and therefore will not be steps toward perfecting the yogi's own accumulations.[700]

According to Rendawa, if the transformation of the saṃbhogakāya into the nirmāṇakāya is achieved through the participation of an awakened Akṣobhya, from this point of the meditation onward, the identity of the yogi will be that of Akṣobhya who has already attained buddhahood. Hence, all the coming steps of the sādhana will not be the yogi's own deeds.

Khedrup Jé objects to such an opinion in what seems to be a response to Rendawa's words:

> Some later lamas say that it is inappropriate for the yogi to enter into Akṣobhya, formed from the bodhicitta of the father-mother victorious ones—who from their own natural abodes are absorbed in union—and transform into the nirmāṇakāya. The reason is that in such a case, during the Supreme King of Maṇḍalas, meditations on emanating, performing the deeds and so forth would be the enlightened activities of someone who had already awakened in the past, rather than steps to perfect the yogi's own accumulations. Such a position would be extremely unreasonable.[701]

Khedrup Jé then provides arguments why he thinks this position is flawed, as we see in the translation below. I will present here only the last of Khedrup Jé's arguments, one that emphasizes the correspondence to conception during the ground of purification:

> Although the semen and blood of the father and mother that arrive in the secret place of their body initially belong to the parents, once the consciousness of the intermediate being enters there, mingles, develops, and emerges out of the womb as a person, whatever this person may do is not the activity of the parents but of their

699. Tib. *dkyil 'khor rgyal mchog*, Skt. *maṇḍalarājāgrī*; this part of the sādhana is described below.

700. Red mda' ba, *Bsgrub pa dpal bas zhus lan*, Kathmandu, 48b4–5; TBRC, 304a.

701. Mkhas grub rje, *Bskyed rim dngos grub rgya mtsho*, 114b3–5.

> offspring. Likewise, you should first meditate on Akṣobhya, invoking him from his natural abode, and then enter and mingle with him. From then on, while you abide in the identity of Vajrasattva, any deed you perform is your own doing; hence, your claim that someone else carries out these activities is invalid.[702]

It is clear that Khedrup Jé is responding here to Rendawa's *Replies to Druppa Pal*, and there are several other such clear cases.

Nowhere does the *Guhyasamāja Sādhana* mention that the jñānasattva enters into the samayasattva. Sakya opponents, including Ngorchen and Rendawa, who suggest a different method for the transformation of the First Lord into Vajrasattva's *nirmāṇakāya*, certainly do not refer to this step of the meditation in terms of the jñānasattva entering into the samayasattva. Yet the meditation on Akṣobhyas entering the First Lord, rather than the other way around, does bear similarity to the method of the two sattvas, in which a real deity arriving from divine quarters, such as the natural abode, enters the yogi visualized as the deity. In rejecting the entry of Akṣobhyas into the First Lord, Tsongkhapa and Khedrup Jé deny also the possibility of associating this step of the *sādhana* with the meditation on the jñānasattva that occurs in other tantric cycles.

While this is a point of controversy,[703] for Geluk scholars, the meditation that serves to purify rebirth consists not only of the transformation of the First Lord to Vajrasattva's nirmāṇakāya but also of the three subsequent steps of the sādhana: the meditation on the body maṇḍala; the blessing of the body, speech, and mind; and the meditation on the triple sattvas, including the sealing with the lord of the tathāgata family. These steps serve to bless the yogi born into new spiritual life in correspondence with the fetus before it emerges out of the womb on the ground of purification.

(5) Meditation on the Body Maṇḍala

While there is certainly a verse in the eighth chapter of the *Guhyasamāja Tantra* devoted to the body maṇḍala,[704] meditation on the body maṇḍala in the context of the Guhyasamāja may be best accounted for as a later development

702. Mkhas grub rje, *Bskyed rim dngos grub rgya mtsho*, 115a3–5.

703. See "Completion of the Four Yogas" in the section "The Samādhis in the First Chapter of the *Guhyasamāja Tantra* and Enacting Past Events" below.

704. *Gsang 'dus*, *Guhyasamāja Tantra*, chap. 8, v. 9, Tōh 442; Zhol 11b7; Stog 39b6; Dunh 20b5–21a1; Fremantle 1971 v. 9; and Matsunaga 1978, v. 9.

borrowed from other tantric cycles. Additionally, while the explanatory tantra of the *Guhyasamāja Tantra* entitled *Vajra Garland* is an important scriptural source for the meditation on the body maṇḍala of the Guhyasamāja, the relevant chapters are found at the very end of this tantra and so could be a later addition.[705] Regardless, many of the examples about the meditation on the body maṇḍala in *Ocean of Attainments* are taken from the Cakrasaṃvara and Hevajra cycles, not the Guhyasamāja.

The meditation on the body maṇḍala consists of two stages. First, the yogis meditate on their bodies as the celestial mansion, then visualize the thirty-two deities on individual parts of their bodies that have become the palaces for these deities. In the first stage, the four sides of the body—the front, back, right, and left sides—become the four sides of the maṇḍala. The four orifice-pathways—the mouth, nose, anus, and urethra—become the four gates. The eight limbs—the shins, thighs, forearms, and upper arms—become the eight pillars of the pavilion. The mental components of the yogi's body are also transformed. The eye consciousness becomes the mirrors, the nose consciousness the garlands of flowers, and so forth.

During the second meditation, yogis visualize the transformation of the essence of the various elements of the body into the thirty-two deities of the maṇḍala.[706] In this way, they visualize the five aggregates, the four physical elements, the five senses and their five objects, the mind-heart, joints, and channels with sinews, and the ten limbs transforming one by one into the five tathāgatas, the four mothers, the five vajra ladies, the eight bodhisattvas, and the ten fierce deities.

The meditation on the body as the celestial mansion is taken to correspond to the *path* and *fruit*, but not to the *ground*, whereas the meditation on the *deities* of the body maṇḍala does correspond to the gradual development of the bodily constituents of the fetus on the *ground* of purification. According to the *Concise Sādhana*, in terms of the four yogas, "higher yoga" consists of the meditation on the body maṇḍala, while "great yoga" begins with the following step of blessing of body, speech, and mind and includes the meditation on the triple sattvas as well.[707]

705. *Rgyud rdo rje phreng ba*, *Vajramālā*, Tōh 445, chapters 64 and 68.

706. On differences of opinion on this matter, see below.

707. Nāgārjuna, *Mdor byas*, *Piṇḍīkrama Sādhana*, Tōh 1796; *atiyoga* is found in L 53–68, *mahāyoga* in L 69–93; the meditation on the triple sattvas is in L 91–92.

A True Transformation?

The simplest meditation on the body maṇḍala is *nyāsa*, or "emplacement," common to both Buddhist and Hindu tantric practices. By touching various points on the body while reciting the corresponding mantras of the deities, the yogi renders the body divine.[708] Nonetheless, disagreements concerning the "degree" of divination achieved by the practices of *nyāsa* and the body maṇḍala are found in both Buddhist and Hindu treatises.

According to certain Indian sādhanas of Cakrasaṃvara, the entire path can be completed through meditation on the body maṇḍala alone.[709] This fact enhances the perceived capacity of the meditation on the body maṇḍala to achieve an actual deification. In the context of the meditation on the body maṇḍala of the Guhyasamāja, this is not quite the case. Nevertheless, the tension we saw above between the different approaches to the identification of deities with bodily constituents is especially high in the present context.[710] If this identification is taken at face value, then, when the Guhyasamāja deities are placed on the body maṇḍala, the yogis' bodies are deified; hence, transformative powers are indeed ascribed even to this step of the creation stage.

There are additional examples that demonstrate the sense that actual transformations are indeed taking place through the meditation on the body maṇḍala. According to the *Vajra Garland Tantra*, an explanatory tantra of the Guhyasamāja cycle: "The body has become the celestial mansion, the perfect support of all buddhas."[711] Khedrup Jé glosses this: "meaning that you should meditate on your body, which has become the celestial mansion."[712] Thus the body maṇḍala is given a specific subordinate role to transform the ordinary impure body into a pure divine mansion. Likewise, in one of the authoritative works on the body maṇḍala, Lūyīpāda explains that when yogis set deities

708. As shown by Gavin Flood, scriptures of the *Pāñcarātra Āgama* such as the *Jayākhyasaṃhita* maintain that through the meditation on *nyāsa*, the yogis become equal to the gods, endowed with supernatural powers, fearless and victorious over death. See Flood 2006, 113, and his translation, 188–193.

709. Vajraghaṇṭa, *'Khor lo sdom pa'i lus dkyil gyi mngon rtogs*, Tōh 1434; see Mkhas grub rje, *Bskyed rim dngos grub rgya mtsho*, 131a2–6.

710. See the section "The Nature of the Transformation of the Ordinary Body into a Buddha's Body" above.

711. Tib. *lus ni gzhal yas khang du 'gyur*; *Rgyud rdo rje phreng ba*, *Vajramālā Tantra*, chap. 68, Tōh 445, 275a2.

712. Mkhas grub rje, *Bskyed rim dngos grub rgya mtsho*, 119a1–2.

on the psycho-physical constituents of their bodies, these constituents are purified.[713]

On the other hand, early Geluk scholars, including Khedrup Jé, maintain that the actual fruit of the sādhana is achieved only during later stages on the path. Strictly speaking, the meditation on the body maṇḍala is simply a step in the practice of taking rebirth on the path to the nirmāṇakāya; as such, its effect is limited to the eventual purification of the yogis' future rebirths. Specifically, the role of this step of meditation is to render the subtle body serviceable during the completion stage.

Thus we find a wide range of positions with regard to this meditation, from a mere visualization to an actual metamorphosis that transforms the psycho-physical elements of the yogi's body into the celestial mansion of the body maṇḍala and the deities within.

The degree to which the yogi's body transforms becomes yet more ambiguous when we ask: Whose body is transformed here? Is it the yogi's body or the body of the deity visualized by the yogi? The manuals appear to speak about the yogi's body. For example, in Tsongkhapa's *Guhyasamāja Sādhana*, we find: "The front, back, right, and left sides of *my body* become the four sides of the maṇḍala."[714] However, the term "my body" is not as straightforward as it may seem, because we know that at this stage of the sādhana, yogis visualize themselves as Vajrasattva's nirmāṇakāya. If "my body" is in fact the visualized body of Vajrasattva's nirmāṇakāya, the "body" here is not as corporeal as it would seem.

Moreover, the parts of the body meditated upon as the celestial mansion are not only physical but also mental. In other words, the body parts are not only thighs, forearms, belly, and tongue, but the consciousness of the senses, the mental consciousness, and the mind. As we will see, when Khedrup Jé explains how to meditate on the body as a celestial mansion, he speaks about "moments of the mental continuum."[715]

Let us consider a query raised by Tsongkhapa that demonstrates the blurring of the term "transformation" during the meditation on the body maṇḍala:

> Query: Having completed earlier the transformation of the body

713. Lūyīpāda, *Bcom ldan 'das mngon par rtogs pa*, *Bhagavadabhisamaya*, Tōh 1427, 186b. For a study of this sādhana, see Gray 2011. Tib. *de dag ni phung po dang khams dang skye mched rnams kyi lha'i rnam par dag pa'o*, Skt. *evaṃ skandhadhatvāyataneṣu devatāviśuddhiḥ*.

714. Tsong kha pa, *Gsang mngon*, 40a6; following the *Rgyud rdo rje phreng ba*, *Vajramālā Tantra*, chap. 68, Tōh 445, 275a2.

715. Mkhas grub rje, *Bskyed rim dngos grub rgya mtsho*, 126b3–4.

> into the celestial mansion of the maṇḍala,[716] it is inappropriate to later meditate on the body as a deity, because one person does not have two bodies.[717]

How, once the parts of the body have been transformed into portals, railings, and additional components of the celestial mansion, can the same parts be transformed in the second stage of the meditation into the deities residing in the celestial mansion? Tsongkhapa replies:

> If that is so, since you have already meditated on the form aggregate as Vairocana, it would follow that it would be inappropriate to meditate on [the nature] of the form of the body as the Rūpavajrā[718] and so forth...[719] Therefore it is not that the extent of the actual state can be distinguished from the state being meditated upon by a conceptual mind. For in the Mantra Vehicle there are many occasions in which, even after you have already meditated on yourself as a buddha, still you meditate on the purification of the two obscurations.[720]

Likewise, Khedrup Jé explains:

> You should understand that even after generating the eye organ as the wheel upon the portal, the continuum of the ordinary eye organ still remains intact; therefore, it is not inappropriate to generate the eye organ once again as Kṣitigarbha. Otherwise, if you meditated on yourself today as Vajradhara, it would not be suitable to meditate on yourself as Vairocana tomorrow. Hence, do not habituate yourself merely to recite the sādhana, but rather direct your meditation inward. You should meditate after making the appropriate distinctions between the true mode of being and the mode of mental apprehension.[721]

716. Reading *rten* for *brten pa*.

717. Tsong kha pa, *Bskyed rim zin bris*, 30a1.

718. Tib. Gzugs rdo rje ma, Eng. Vajra Lady of Forms.

719. Here Tsong kha pa adds: "the meditation on the sense organs, the eye and so forth, as bodhisattvas, the meditation on the physical elements, the earth and so forth as the four mothers, Locanā and so forth, will also be inappropriate."

720. Tsong kha pa, *Bskyed rim zin bris*, 30a2–4.

721. Mkhas grub rje, *Bskyed rim dngos grub rgya mtsho*, 130b5–131a1.

The meditation on the body maṇḍala became the focus of disagreements between early and later Geluk scholars, as well as between Geluk and Sakya scholars. We will begin by addressing discussions of the meditation on the body as the celestial mansion of the maṇḍala, then continue to disagreements regarding the visualization of deities on individual parts of the body.

Meditation on the Body as the Celestial Mansion

According to Tsongkhapa's *Guhyasamāja Sādhana*: "The front, back, right, and left sides of my body become the four sides of the maṇḍala... In this way, all the parts of the body become the respective parts of the celestial mansion."[722]

In his *Wish-Granting Cow*, Tsongkhapa makes three points:

> It is not that you visualize a second celestial mansion within the celestial mansion that you have generated before.

And:

> When it is time to meditate on the body maṇḍala, you do this on the basis of the celestial mansion that you have visualized earlier, but without dissolving the former celestial mansion.[723]

Also:

> The very mental continuum that earlier generated the celestial mansion from now on proceeds without dissolving the celestial mansion. Hence, when you begin to meditate on the body as the celestial mansion, a subsequent similar [mental continuum] arises

722. Tsong kha pa, *Gsang mngon*, 40a6–b2; following the *Rgyud rdo rje phreng ba*, *Vajramālā Tantra*, chap. 68, Tōh 445, 275a2–6.

723. Tsong kha pa, *'Dod 'jo*, 121a6.

> on the basis of your earlier similar [mental continuum] and each part of the body.[724]

In his own commentary on the Cakrasaṃvara body maṇḍala, Ngorchen Kunga Sangpo cites this passage only to object to this method, but we will not go into this here.[725]

Earlier in Tsongkhapa's *Guhyasamāja Sādhana*, yogis visualized a celestial mansion with themselves as the principal deity of the maṇḍala surrounded by other deities. Then all the deities dissolved, and the yogis were eventually transformed into Vajrasattva's nirmāṇakāya. According to Tsongkhapa, the celestial mansion of the body maṇḍala is not another celestial mansion within the one visualized before. Nor has the former celestial mansion been dissolved and a new one generated. Rather, the mental continuum that engaged in the visualization of the celestial mansion earlier is now joined with the respective parts of the body, and arises as a subsequent mental continuum of the celestial mansion of the body maṇḍala.

Hence, the outer and body maṇḍalas are not two separate entities; the visualization of the first is the basis for the latter. In other words, the former visualization of the outer maṇḍala is no less important than the body of the yogi/deity for the creation of the celestial mansion of the body maṇḍala. Once more, although the explanation mentions "each part of the body," it remains ambiguous whether this refers to the yogi's body or the visualized body of the deity.

Early and later Geluk scholars do not agree on the question of which of the two, the outer maṇḍala or the body, is the substantial cause[726] of the body maṇḍala. We will now examine this difference of opinion.

724. Tsong kha pa, *'Dod 'jo*, 122b5–6. Mkhas grub rje follows this method: "Do not dissolve the celestial mansion you previously meditated on, nor generate another celestial mansion within the previous celestial mansion... When it is time to generate your body as the celestial mansion of the maṇḍala, do not dissolve the mental continuum of the celestial mansion on which you formerly meditated, but rather visualize the subsequent moments of the mental continuum of the earlier celestial mansion, arising through the transformation of the respective parts of your body." See his *Bskyed rim dngos grub rgya mtsho*, 126b3–4.

725. Ngor chen, *Dril bu pa'i lus dkyil gyi bshad pa*, 375b1–2.

726. Tib. *nyer len*.

Disagreements among Geluk Scholars

According to Tsongkhapa:

> The way to meditate on the body as the celestial mansion is to meditate on a maṇḍala that is similar in type to the outer maṇḍala and that arises through the simultaneous gathering of the parts of the outer maṇḍala—the four sides and so forth—and the parts of the yogi's body—the front and the back of his body and so forth—as the substantial cause and the cooperative conditions.[727]

This explanation is not as straightforward as we might wish it to be. Though Tsongkhapa clearly distinguishes between the substantial cause and the cooperative conditions[728] for the body maṇḍala, he does not explicitly state what is the substantial cause. We may surmise that the outer maṇḍala, mentioned first, is the substantial cause, while the parts of the yogi's body, mentioned subsequently, are the cooperative conditions. If so, the visualization of the outer maṇḍala plays a greater part than the yogi's body in creating the body maṇḍala; moreover, the transformation of the body is not particularly corporeal in nature.

Geluk scholars active in the fifteenth to sixteenth centuries adopted this understanding of the relation between the substantial cause and cooperative conditions during the meditation on the body as the celestial mansion. According to the Second Dalai Lama, Gendun Gyatso,[729] the substantial cause is the visualization of the former celestial mansion, while the individual parts of the body are the cooperative conditions:

> On the basis of a previous, similar moment in which the former celestial mansion acted as the substantial cause and the individual parts of the body acted as the cooperative conditions, subsequent moments of mental continuum similar to the former celestial mansion are made into the basis of forming the individual parts of the body [maṇḍala]. In this way, you visualize that [the body maṇḍala] is formed in actuality.[730]

727. Tsong kha pa, *Bung ba'i re skong*, 21b3–4.

728. Tib. *lhan gcig byed rkyen*.

729. Dge 'dun rgya mtsho (1476–1542).

730. Dge 'dun rgya mtsho, *Gsang ba 'dus pa'i rim pa dang po'i lam la slob pa'i tshul*, 30a1.

Panchen Sönam Drakpa explains this meditation through the example of dyeing a cloth. When a blue dye is applied to a white cloth and the cloth turns blue, the cloth is the substantial cause of the product, while the dye is the contributing condition. Sönam Drakpa explains:

> As, for example, when you make the earlier moment of a woolen cloth the substantial cause, and the earlier moment of the lac dye the cooperative condition, these will turn into a subsequent colored woolen cloth of a similar type. Likewise, when you make an element similar in type to the earlier moment of the outer maṇḍala the substantial cause, and the propelling of the thought "the individual parts of the body become the respective parts of the celestial mansion" the cooperative condition, these will become the celestial mansion of the body maṇḍala, which is a subsequent element similar to the body.[731]

Note that in this explanation, both the substantial cause and the cooperative condition are mental. The substantial cause arises from the visualization of the outer maṇḍala, and the cooperative conditions are not the individual parts of the body that turn into the respective parts of the body maṇḍala, but rather the propelling of the thought to that effect.

However, when we look at the writing of some Geluk scholars from the seventeenth to nineteenth centuries, we discover that the substantial cause and the cooperative conditions have been reversed. For example, Changkya Ngawang Chöden[732] explains:

> By making the parts of your body the substantial cause and the parts of the outer maṇḍala the cooperative conditions, visualize the celestial mansion of the body maṇḍala.[733]

Similar explanations are provided by Jamyang Zhepé Dorjé[734] and Drakpa Shedrup.[735]

731. Bsod nams grags pa, *Gsang 'dus bskyed rim rnam gzhag*, 53b5–54a1.

732. Lcang skya Ngag dbang chos ldan (1642–1714).

733. Lcang skya Ngag dbang chos ldan, *Gsang chen myur lam*, 21a2.

734. 'Jam dbyangs bzhad pa'i rdo rje (1648–1721/22).

735. Grags pa bshad sgrub (1675–1748). See 'Jam dbyangs bzhad pa'i rdo rje, *Gsang 'dus bskyed rim khrid kyi zin bris*, 34a1–2; and Grags pa bshad sgrub, *Gsang 'dus bskyed rim gnad don kun gsal*, p. 52.

In the case of the first group of scholars, when the substantial cause is the visualization of the outer maṇḍala, the nature of the subsequent product—the celestial mansion of the body maṇḍala—is mental. By contrast, in the second case, in which the substantial cause is the yogi's body, the result is more material in nature, though not necessarily physical. It seems that these later Geluk scholars felt that for the meditation on the body maṇḍala to have a greater impact, their actual bodies would have to be the substantial cause. Such is the explanation of Akhu Ching Sherab Gyatso:

> Taking the body as the substantial cause has greater significance, because such a meditation leaves imprints for emanating the celestial mansion from the parts of the two illusory bodies and from Vajradhara's body during the path and resultant stages, respectively.[736]

Even if Akhu Ching would have liked to see a more substantial transformation of his impure body into the divine palace of the maṇḍala, he still reminds us that the only effect the meditation on the body maṇḍala can have within the creation stage is to ripen toward the illusory body during the completion stage and the Buddha's body at the resultant stage. In support of his position, Akhu Ching cites the scriptures we have seen already, the *Vajra Garland Explanatory Tantra* and Tsongkhapa's *Guhyasamāja Sādhana*, which indeed convey the sense of an actual bodily transformation.[737] Akhu Ching also resorts to reasoning:

> The definition of a substantial cause is this: "That which primarily brings into being as its continuum that substance." So nowhere is it said that cooperative conditions can become that effect.[738]

Clearly, Akhu Ching is eager to see an actual effect on the yogi's body. Still, he is hesitant to reach a conclusion that would explicitly contradict the position of earlier masters, whom he names. He says:

736. A khu ching, *Mi bskyod mgon po'i zhal lung*, 76a1–5; an English translation in Jinpa 1999, 140.

737. *Rgyud rdo rje phreng ba, Vajramālā Tantra*, chap. 68, Tōh 445, 275a2: "The body turns into the celestial mansion"; Tsong kha pa, *Gsang mngon*, 41a2: "All the parts of the body turn into the respective parts of the celestial mansion."

738. A khu ching, *Mi bskyod mgon po'i zhal lung*, 76a6–b1; an English translation in Jinpa 1999, 141. For the sake of consistency in the terminology I have replaced "material cause" with "substantial cause."

> In any case, it is difficult to reach a definite, conclusive position on this.[739]

Moreover, Akhu Ching is well aware of the limitations of logical reasoning with regard to yogic experiences:

> It is, however, vital to ensure that one does not fall into excessive analysis, for experiential realizations based on imaginative meditations both on the path and resultant stages are infinite.[740]

It is palpable that the methods of formal debate that developed in the Geluk school had an effect on the analysis of the later scholars. Still, Akhu Ching certainly allows the meditation to have its own operational logic. For the sake of achieving actual results, the meditators have to convince themselves that their visualizations have genuine effects. There is a clear tension here between the limitations of mere mental imaginations and the wish of the meditators to see real bodily as well as spiritual transformations.

Meditation on the Respective Parts of the Body as the Deities of the Maṇḍala

In the second step of the meditation on the body maṇḍala, yogis meditate on the transformation of the mental and physical components of their bodies into the deities residing in the body maṇḍala. This is the meditation that relates to *nyāsa*, or "emplacement," and to the special link between the ordinary, impure psycho-physical constituents of the body and their purified aspects in the forms of the thirty-two deities of the Guhyasamāja maṇḍala.[741] The yogis visualize that each of the five aggregates, respectively, becomes the corresponding tathāgata, each of the four physical constituents the equivalent mother, each of the six senses a bodhisattva, and so on.

739. A khu ching, *Mi bskyod mgon po'i zhal lung*, 76b1; an English translation in Jinpa 1999, 141.

740. A khu ching, *Mi bskyod mgon po'i zhal lung*, 76b1–2; an English translation in Jinpa 1999, 141, with minor changes.

741. See the section "The Nature of the Transformation of the Ordinary Body into a Buddha's Body" above.

Disagreements between Tsongkhapa and Khedrup Jé on This Meditation

In the first step of this meditation, the form aggregate transforms into Vairocana, whose seed syllable is *oṃ*. Tsongkhapa instructs in his sādhana:

> [In the area] from the crown of my head to my hairline, the essence of the form aggregate, white *oṃ*, transforms into white Vairocana.[742]

The relation between the white seed syllable *oṃ* and the essence of the form aggregate is somewhat unclear here. Tsongkhapa explains this further in one of his explanatory works on the sādhana:

> In the area from the crown of the head to the hairline, visualize the seed syllable, the essence of the form aggregate that abides in the appearance of a white *oṃ*, transforming into Vairocana, complete with faces and arms. Then imagine that Vairocana turns into indivisible essence with the form aggregate.[743]

This meditation begins with the visualization of the area from the crown to the hairline as the seed syllable white *oṃ*, which is the essence of the form aggregate. Then, the seed syllable transforms into Vairocana, and finally the yogi meditates on the indivisibility of Vairocana and the form aggregate.

But according to Khedrup Jé:

> It is perfectly sufficient to visualize the deities from their respective seed syllables—for example, visualizing your eye organ completely transformed into the syllable *thlīṃ*, and the *thlīṃ* into Kṣitigarbha. But it is not sufficient to generate *thlīṃ* in your own mind without a basis for it, then generate Kṣitigarbha from it, and after that merely to imagine that Kṣitigarbha is indivisible from your own eye organ.[744]

Khedrup Jé offers his alternative suggestion because, for him, a significant transformation of all the psycho-physical constituents of one's body into the seed syllables of the deities is crucial. He explains:

742. Tsong kha pa, *Gsang mngon*, 41a2–3.

743. Tsong kha pa, *Slob tshul*, 16b5–17a1. See also his *Bung ba'i re skong*, 21b6–22a1.

744. Mkhas grub rje, *Bskyed rim dngos grub rgya mtsho*, 125b5–126a1.

> "Meditation on the body maṇḍala" does not signify merely meditating on deities at various locations on the body. It means that having made the respective parts of the body into bases for generating the individual deities, you meditate on these deities.[745]

Hence, for Khedrup Jé, merely visualizing that the essence of the psycho-physical constituent abides in the appearance of the seed syllable, as instructed by Tsongkhapa, is insufficient as an initial step for transforming elements of the impure body into pure deities within the visualization of the creation stage. Therefore he requires a complete transformation of each psycho-physical constituent into the respective seed syllable *within the visualization* before the seed syllable transforms into a deity.

The discrepancy between the instructions provided by Tsongkhapa and Khedrup Jé did not remain unnoticed by later members of the Geluk tradition. Norsang Gyatso presents first Tsongkhapa's method and then Khedrup Jé's instructions; he does not discuss why they differ, but rather leaves it for the reader "to examine what are their intentions":

> Here is the method of visualizing the psycho-physical constituents as the deities: Taking Kṣitigarbha, for example, the All-knowing Lord [Tsongkhapa] instructs the yogi to imagine the eye faculty as the essence of *thlīṃ*; the *thlīṃ* transforms into Kṣitigarbha, who is then placed on the eye; and finally, the yogi imagines Kṣitigarbha indivisible in essence from the eye faculty. According to Khedrup Jé, however, the yogi meditates on the eye faculty transforming into *thlīṃ*, and the *thlīṃ* transforms into Kṣitigarbha.[746]

Likewise, Drakpa Shedrup points out the difference between the instructions of the two masters. He opts for the method of Tsongkhapa because other scholars prefer it as well, but leaves us wondering why:

> In the area from the crown to the hairline, visualize the essence of the form aggregate, white *oṃ*, that then transforms into Vairocana as described in the sādhana. Khedrup Jé explains, on the other hand, that the form aggregate transforms into *oṃ*, and from the *oṃ* the yogi visualizes Vairocana and so forth. But many other scholars

745. Mkhas grub rje, *Bskyed rim dngos grub rgya mtsho*, 124b5–6.

746. Nor bzang rgya mtsho, *Gsang ba 'dus pa'i bskyed rim gyi don gsal bar byed pa'i sgron me*, 107b3–5.

> explain that according to the words of the sādhana, the yogi should visualize the essence of the form aggregate itself in the appearance of *oṃ*; hence, this is the way to meditate.[747]

Still, most Geluk scholars take no notice of the dissimilarity between these two forefathers of their tradition; some follow Tsongkhapa, while others follow Khedrup Jé in this matter.[748]

In the present context of the deities residing in the maṇḍala, some later Geluk scholars distinguish between the substantial causes of the deities that are the psycho-physical constituents of the body and the cooperative conditions—the seed syllables of the deities. According to Changkya Ngawang Chöden:

> Visualize Vairocana from your form aggregate as the actual substantial cause, and the syllable *oṃ*, on which you meditate as indivisible in essence from this form aggregate, as the cooperative condition. Then cultivate stable divine identification and clear appearance, and seal with bliss and emptiness.[749]

Jamyang Zhepé Dorjé provides a similar explanation while emphasizing that the basis for the meditation here is not just the yogi's body, but rather the yogi's body visualized as Vajrasattva's nirmāṇakāya:

> Generate the respective deities who are endowed with bodily nature from the respective parts of your body, visualized as Vajrasattva's nirmāṇakāya—the actual substantial causes—and the seed syllables on which you meditate as indivisible in essence from respective parts of the body—the cooperative conditions.[750]

At the same time, Jamyang Zhepé Dorjé mentions that the deities are endowed with bodily nature.[751]

747. Grags pa bshad sgrub, *Gsang 'dus bskyed rim gnad don kun gsal*, 53.

748. To this latter group who follow Mkhas grub rje belongs the Second Dalai Lama, Dge 'dun rgya mtsho, who was a disciple of Mkhas grub Nor bzang rgya mtsho, who followed Tsong kha pa. See Dge 'dun rgya mtsho, *Gsang ba 'dus pa'i rim pa dang po'i lam la slob pa'i tshul*, 30b2–3.

749. Lcang skya Ngag dbang chos ldan, *Gsang chen myur lam*, 21a4–6.

750. 'Jam dbyangs bzhad pa'i rdo rje, *Gsang 'dus bskyed rim khrid kyi zin bris*, 34a2–6.

751. Tib. *lus kyi rang bzhin can gyi lha*.

Even great Tibetan scholars were confused by the conflicting position, as Akhu Ching Sherab Gyatso recounts:

> In following the positions presented in the manuals of Changkya Rinpoche and the previous all-knowing incarnation,[752] the Teacher explained that you should visualize yourself as Vajradhara's nirmāṇakāya; and in the area between the crown and the hairline of your head, visualize the form aggregate of your body as the substantial cause and the syllable *oṃ*, indivisible in essence from it [form aggregate], as the cooperative condition. But in another instance of teaching, the Teacher said that the *oṃ*, indivisible from the body aggregate, is the substantial cause, while the cooperative condition is the mind that visualizes this.[753]

To conclude, Geluk scholars after Tsongkhapa were certainly willing to challenge, or improve upon, their founder's explanations of the working of his *Guhyasamāja Sādhana*. Their modifications seem to have resulted from the internal contradictions in the notion of transforming the body by means of creative visualization. Their aim was to find a way to reconcile between, on the one hand, the limitations placed by general Buddhist theoretical considerations on the transformative power of the mind, and, on the other hand, the point of view of meditators who seek a more substantial transformation than visualization alone can provide.

Is the Body Maṇḍala Uncontrived?

The discussion of whether the body maṇḍala is uncontrived is certainly related to the question of to what extent the transformation into the body maṇḍala is real. However, the debates on this question are no doubt rooted in Vajraghaṇṭa's verses on the body maṇḍala. As we will soon see, these verses became the basis for major tension between Geluk and Sakya scholars.

Vajraghaṇṭa, an important Indian authority on the body maṇḍala, has several enigmatic verses understood by all the Tibetan commentators with whom I have consulted to refer to the body maṇḍala. These verses describe it as unconstructed or naturally present, in contrast to painted and colored powder maṇḍalas that are constructed or contrived. According to Vajraghaṇṭa:

752. Tib. *kun mkhyen*.

753. A khu ching, *Mi bskyod mgon po'i zhal lung*, 76b6–77a2; an English translation in Jinpa 1999, 142.

> [The external maṇḍala] is explained as prepared in stages, depicted in paintings, or drawn by way of strings and colored powder, [while] sentient beings are naturally present nondual maṇḍalas. The nature of the two constructed ones is intended to accord with the disciple.[754]

While some earlier Tibetan scholars explained the naturally present body maṇḍala in terms of *tathāgatagarbha* theory, Geluk and Sakya scholars, including Tsongkhapa, Khedrup Jé, and Ngorchen Kunga Sangpo, offered a different interpretation. According to Ngorchen's commentary on Vajraghaṇṭa:

> The constructed maṇḍalas are painted and colored powder maṇḍalas. They are designated as constructed because the artists and ritual masters respectively need to produce them anew. On the other hand, the [coarse] body of the yogi, along with the channels and elements [of the subtle body], are present, and therefore it is unnecessary to reproduce them.[755]

The same position is expressed by Tsongkhapa in his *Great Treatise on the Stages of the Mantric Path* and *Wish-Granting Cow*.[756] We know that Ngorchen was aware of these works by Tsongkhapa, since he criticizes other passages from them.[757] Khedrup Jé follows the position of Tsongkhapa and Ngorchen on this matter in his *Ocean of Attainments*.

Though these three scholars agree on the meaning of Vajraghaṇṭa's verse on constructed versus naturally present maṇḍalas, they differ in their position on the roles of these maṇḍalas in the mantric path. Several Tibetan scholars explain that painted, colored powder, and body maṇḍalas are meant for disciples endowed with different capacities. Among them are Sönam Tsemo, Rangjung Dorjé, Butön, and Kongtrul Yönten Gyatso.[758]

754. Vajraghaṇṭa, *'Khor lo sdom pa'i dbang, Cakrasaṃvaraṣeka*, Tōh 1431, 219b5–6. For a discussion of the numerous problems in establishing the Sanskrit and Tibetan texts of these verses, see Bentor 2017a, 232–236.

755. Ngor chen kun dga' bzang po, *Dril bu pa'i lus dkyil gyi bshad pa*, 371a4–5.

756. Tsong kha pa, *Sngags rim chen mo*, 304; and *'Dod 'jo*, 137b2–3.

757. See Bentor 2017a, 237–243.

758. See Bsod nams rtse mo, *De'i dbang gi bya ba mdor bsdus*, 119a2–4; Rang byung rdo rje, *Lus kyi dkyil 'khor gyi 'thad pa lung sbyor*, 2a4–b6; Bu ston, *Lus dkyil dbang chog*, 5b5–7; and Kong sprul Yon tan rgya mtsho, *Shes bya kun khyab*, 1982, vol. 2, 652; an English translation of this work in Guarisco and McLeod 2005, 211.

For Tsongkhapa, on the other hand, the distinctions made between the three maṇḍalas are not significant during the initial initiation into the maṇḍala at the start of the practice, but rather during the completion stage.[759] Khedrup Jé also takes this position and explains that by habituating to the meditation on the body maṇḍala during the creation stage, the channels, winds, and drops in the subtle body become serviceable.[760] Then, during the completion stage, the yogis meditate by penetrating the vital points of their subtle bodies as causes for the supreme siddhi of awakening. Painted and colored powder maṇḍalas are inferior to body maṇḍalas, since they can serve to accumulate merit, confer initiations, and so forth at the level of relative truth, but not for the arising of the wisdom of ultimate truth, as does the body maṇḍala.

According to Tsongkhapa, since body maṇḍalas are generated from elements of the body that are not newly constructed but have existed since rebirth, a body maṇḍala requires an actual rather than a visualized body to serve as its basis.[761] For example, when yogis practice with action consorts, the deities placed on the consort's body serve to create her body as a body maṇḍala. However, when she is a wisdom consort, her body is merely contrived by the yogi's mind and cannot be a basis for a body maṇḍala.

We can see that the explanation about body maṇḍalas being uncontrived or unconstructed on the basis of Vajraghaṇṭa's verses adds to the confusion with regard to the nature of the transformation into body maṇḍalas—in other words, whether the transformation is corporeal to some extent or only mental, and specifically whether it is the yogi's body or the yogi's body visualized as the deity that is transformed.

Khedrup Jé's final remarks at the end of the chapter on the body maṇḍala attest to this. He explains that when yogis meditate on themselves as Vajrasattva's nirmāṇakāya, they have three faces and six meditative eyes; nevertheless, they need not place Kṣitigarbhas on their right and left faces:

> Since *you have* two eyes, you must generate two Kṣitigarbhas... If you were to generate Kṣitigarbhas from eyes of the right and left faces which you *do not in reality possess*, then the bases for generation

759. Tsong kha pa, *Sngags rim chen mo*, 307; *'Dod 'jo*, 137a6–b4; and *Dril dbang*, 3b2–4.

760. Mkhas grub rje, *Bskyed rim dngos grub rgya mtsho*, 125b1–3.

761. See Tsong kha pa, *Bskyed rim zin bris*, 30a4–5 and Mkhas grub rje, *Bskyed rim dngos grub rgya mtsho*, 126a2–4.

> would be contrived and thus unsuitable for generating the uncontrived deities of the maṇḍala.[762]

The requirement for the body maṇḍala to have an uncontrived basis leads Khedrup Jé to disregard the visualized limbs of the deity.

Khedrup Jé then raises another difficulty: a case in which yogis must visualize on their limbs a number of deities larger than the number of their actual limbs. For example, in the *Abhidhānottara Tantra* yogis are instructed to generate twelve Mamos from the twelve arms they possess as the deity.[763] According to Khedrup Jé:

> Simply generating the Mamos from the twelve arms is not the proper way to generate the body maṇḍala; rather, you must first visualize your own two arms completely transformed into the twelve arms of Heruka, and then generate the twelve Mamos from these twelve arms whose essence is indivisible from the emblems they hold.[764]

Another example:

> Consequently, the celestial mansion, upon which you meditated earlier, arose in your mind solely by means of mental contrivance; later on, when you begin to meditate on the body maṇḍala, the subsequent moments of the mental continuum of the celestial mansion will not be contrived by the mind, but will be visualized from bases of generation that actually exist. This is the method for generating the body maṇḍala that accords with the tantras, the writings of mahāsiddhas, and the treatises of Indian scholars.[765]

Here, the outer celestial mansion in which the yogi (as the deity) resides is visualized by the yogi and is therefore mentally contrived. This celestial mansion, as we saw, serves as one of the bases (whether substantial or cooperative) for the body maṇḍala. This is because the body maṇḍala is created on the basis of both the earlier mental moment that visualized the outer celestial mansion and the

762. Mkhas grub rje, *Bskyed rim dngos grub rgya mtsho*, 130a1–3. Emphasis mine.

763. *Mngon par brjod pa'i rgyud bla ma*, *Abhidhānottara Tantra*, chap. 9, Tōh 369, 268a6–b1; a Sanskrit edition and an English translation in Kalff 1979, 286, lines 44a3–4 and 160–161.

764. Mkhas grub rje, *Bskyed rim dngos grub rgya mtsho*, 130b1.

765. Mkhas grub rje, *Bskyed rim dngos grub rgya mtsho*, 126b4–5.

respective part of the body. The body maṇḍala arises as a subsequent mental moment of these two elements. Hence, while the earlier mental moment is contrived, when it joins with the respective part of the body that actually exists in relative truth, it also exists to the same extent.

Perhaps the reason Khedrup Jé did not agree with Tsongkhapa, but rather stressed that each part of the body must first be completely transformed, has something to do with the explanation that body maṇḍalas are uncontrived or unconstructed on the basis of Vajraghaṇṭa's verses. Tsongkhapa, followed by Ngorchen Kunga Sangpo, presented this explanation before Khedrup Jé; however, since this question is part of the first phase of Khedrup Jé's ongoing debates with the Sakya scholars, Khedrup Jé emphasized this point. This brings us to his famous disputes with the Sakya scholars.

Disagreements with Sakya Scholars

The debates on the body maṇḍala in the *Ocean of Attainments* are what made this work famous among Tibetan scholars. While only a very few Tibetans can specify the exact topics debated here, these arguments have become part of the intersectarian tension between Sakyas and Geluks. David Jackson addresses the oral tradition of the Sakya school on this issue in the following words:

> mKhas grub rje's polemical writings concerning the Hevajra body-*maṇḍala* stirred up the emotions of monks in gTsang to such an extent that the religious scholars at Sa skya were temporarily forbidden to travel until the outstanding tantric expert Ngor chen Kun dga' bzang po (1382–1456) had written his two replies in 1426.[766]

And:

> A few years before founding Ngor, while in his early forties, Ngorchen was forced to assume much responsibility for the Sakya School. In 1425, when Thekchen Chöje passed away, that school and the Sakya Khön family lost their most eminent representative, who had been honored as the Ming emperor's preceptor. The same year, when the learned tantric expert within Tsongkhapa's new Geluk Order, Khedrupje, wrote his anti-Sakya tantric polemics, it fell to Ngorchen to reply.[767]

766. Jackson 2007, 354–355.

767. Jackson 2010, 178.

In the autobiography of Lowo Khenchen Sönam Lhuṇdrup,[768] we read that when Ngorchen was invited to Lowo,[769] he replied that he could not leave Central Tibet "because of a work by Khedrup Jé that says that the body maṇḍala of Hevajra is not an authentic teaching."[770] In a later biography of Ngorchen, written by Ngaripa Sanggyé Puntsok,[771] we find that Ngorchen could not travel because of a dispute in which it was claimed that "the body maṇḍala of the Sakyapa was not explained in the tantra and treatises."[772]

On this basis, we might conclude that Khedrup Jé's *Ocean of Attainments* was written as an anti-Sakya attack that challenged the authenticity of the body maṇḍala of Hevajra as practiced by this school. This polemical writing provoked such a commotion in Sakya that Ngorchen Kunga Sangpo could not travel until he responded to the criticism of Khedrup Jé. Moreover, though he had no part in this dispute, Ngorchen was chosen to counter the opinion of Khedrup Jé. This indeed seems to be the common oral tradition among members of the Sakya school.

These polemical writings are considered to be found in the chapter on the body maṇḍala in the work translated here. However, recent research has shown the difficulty in establishing a time frame for these events and uncovering their exact circumstances.[773] There is no doubt that Khedrup Jé criticized Ngorchen Kunga Sangpo, as well as other contemporary Sakya scholars such as Rongtön Sheja Kunrik and Rendawa, as we have seen.[774] But the debates between Sakya scholars who either went on to become Ngorpas and Gelukpas or remained Sakyapas began before Khedrup Jé came into the picture. As we have pointed out already,[775] while both Tsongkhapa and Ngorchen Kunga Sangpo strove to create a harmonious system, their choices could not always be the same, thereby giving rise to disputes between them. One such attack by Ngorchen on later lamas who wrote "many inadequate explanations" was

768. Glo bo mkhan chen Bsod nams lhun grub (1456–1532).

769. Glo bo.

770. Kramer 2008, 116–117 (Tibetan) and 146 (English translation). See also Heimbel 2017a, 239–240.

771. Mnga' ris pa Sangs rgyas phun tshogs (1649–1705).

772. For a Tibetan edition of the text and an English translation see Heimbel 2017a, 230.

773. Davidson 1991, 221; Heimbel 2017a, 229–241, 276, and 282–284; Heimbel 2017b; and Bentor 2017b.

774. For Mkhas grub rje's criticism of Rong ston see van der Kuijp 1985b, 87–88. See also notes to the translations below.

775. See the section "Tsongkhapa, Khedrup Jé, and Polemical Literature" above.

cited above,[776] where we saw that Tsongkhapa was most likely included among these "later lamas."

Khedrup Jé's admiration for Tsongkhapa's wisdom and research shines through in his *Ocean of Attainments*. It is not surprising, then, that after Tsongkhapa's death in 1419, Khedrup Jé took it upon himself to respond to Ngorchen's criticism. Ngorchen Kunga Sangpo's commentary on the body maṇḍala of Cakrasaṃvara[777] is a polemical work that is highly critical of Tsongkhapa while citing his works verbatim.[778]

Hence, we ought to bear in mind that Khedrup Jé's *Ocean of Attainments*, written sometime in the early 1420s, did not initiate the debate as such. Moreover, the bulk of the criticism in the chapter on the body maṇḍala is not about the body maṇḍala of Hevajra, and the two replies Ngorchen wrote in 1426 do not refer to most of the topics discussed in this chapter. Nevertheless, Ngorchen knew that the sarcasm in this chapter was directed at him.

The first topic in Khedrup Jé's chapter on the body maṇḍala is *tathāgatagarbha*. Before describing the arguments, we must consider the implications of maṇḍalas naturally present in sentient beings in the context of the creation stage. If the yogis' bodies are identified with maṇḍalas of awakened beings even before they begin their practice, their bodies are already deified. What is the use, then, of meditating on deities within the body in order to attain buddhahood? This notion affects the practice of visualization as well, since in meditating on the body maṇḍala as already present there, the yogis work with something that is actual and even constantly actualized in their body. It also questions the role of visualization as the foundation of the creation stage.

Khedrup Jé opens his chapter on the body maṇḍala by criticizing "some Tibetan lamas" who interpret the aforementioned verse of Vajraghaṇṭa[779] on the body maṇḍala in terms of *sugata* essence or *tathāgatagarbha*. As is usually the case, this argument was not originally made by Khedrup Jé, but rather by

776. See the section "The Guhyasamāja Sādhanas of the Ārya School" above.

777. Ngor chen, *Dril bu pa'i lus dkyil gyi bshad pa*, work 184.

778. Ngor chen quotes Tsong kha pa, *Sngags rim chen mo* and *'Dod 'jo*. For more details, see Bentor 2017a, 237–243. In this work, Ngor chen uses the common Sa skya method of argument, consisting of three steps: refuting the position of others (Tib. *dgag*), establishing one's own system (Tib. *bzhag*), and dispelling remaining objections (Tib. *spang*).

779. Vajraghaṇṭa, *'Khor lo sdom pa'i dbang gi bya ba mdor bsdus pa*, *Cakrasaṃvaraṣekaprakriyopadeśa*, Tōh 1431, 219b5–6; a Sanskrit edition in Finot 1934, 62.

Tsongkhapa in his *Great Treatise on the Stages of the Mantric Path*, written in 1405, and the *Wish-Granting Cow*, written in 1415.[780]

Moreover, Ngorchen Kunga Sangpo also speaks against "other lamas" who maintain that dharmadhātu, or suchness, abides constantly and stably in all sentient beings, and that this is the ultimate truth maṇḍala of Cakrasaṃvara.[781] This is not surprising, since, in general, the Sakyapas were not proponents of the *tathāgatagarbha* theory.

More surprising is the fact that although Vajraghaṇṭa says explicitly that "sentient beings are naturally present nondual maṇḍalas," all three scholars criticize "some Tibetan lamas" who maintained this on the same grounds and presented the same alternative interpretation, which is neither the literal meaning of the line nor an obvious option. It is clear, then, that these scholars did not develop their interpretations independently, but were familiar with each other's works. While they engaged in vigorous dispute, they selectively incorporated each other's views in their own writings. We see, then, that the early fifteenth century saw considerable polemic among Tibetan scholars, as well as not a small degree of constructive dialogue.

All three masters reject the literal reading of this line for the same reason: If one were to understand Vajraghaṇṭa as saying that sentient beings are naturally present maṇḍalas, it would contradict the following line in the same work, in which Vajraghaṇṭa explains that the purpose of the initiation is to turn disciples who do not know the nature of the maṇḍala into suitable vessels for the practice of Cakrasaṃvara.[782] While all three masters express the same objection, Khedrup Jé has the sharpest tongue:

> If one is a buddha, but does not recognize this, then how could a buddha who *does not even know* who he or she is *know* all phenomena? Therefore a stupid buddha who *does not know* any of the objects of knowledge would be most astonishing![783]

This is rather unpleasant on the part of Khedrup Jé, but it is not possible that his vitriol is being directed at Ngorchen, since Ngorchen agrees with the Gandenpas that there are no actual maṇḍalas in the continuum of all sentient beings.

780. Tsong kha pa, *Sngags rim chen mo*, 303–304; and *'Dod 'jo*, 122a3–b1 and 137a3–b4. On the date of the *'Dod 'jo* see Jinpa 2019, 390.

781. Ngor chen, *Dril bu pa'i lus dkyil gyi bshad pa*, 370a1–4.

782. See Bentor 2017a and 2017b.

783. Mkhas grub rje, *Bskyed rim dngos grub rgya mtsho*, 116b6.

About ten years after *Ocean of Attainments* was completed, while residing in Ganden[784] after his bitter dispute with the Sakya masters,[785] Khedrup Jé composed his own commentary on the Cakrasaṃvara initiation practice according to Vajraghaṇṭa. In this work, Khedrup Jé identifies the opponent Tsongkhapa had apparently not wished to disclose. Such uncharacteristic behavior was perhaps the result of his acrimony with the Sakyas. Khedrup Jé says:

> In his commentary on the sādhana by Vajraghaṇṭa, the master Sönam Tsemo teaches that the yogis visualize their bodies as existing from the very beginning as maṇḍalas.[786]

Indeed, in the opening of his own commentary on Vajraghaṇṭa's treatise, Sönam Tsemo argues that although people are not ordinarily aware of this, maṇḍalas are present naturally in their bodies, and the purpose of the initiation is to make the disciples aware of this presence.[787]

And here we come to the first crucial point. In his *Ocean of Attainments*, Khedrup Jé ridicules the very uneasy position in which Ngorchen finds himself. On the one hand, he agrees with Tsongkhapa, while on the other, he belongs to the tradition attacked by Tsongkhapa. Ngorchen agrees with Tsongkhapa on the issue of *tathāgatagarbha*, although he belongs to the same school as Sönam Tsemo. Thus, in the following passage, Khedrup Jé criticizes unnamed Tibetans who accept the position of Sönam Tsemo regarding

784. Dga' ldan.

785. While the *Bskyed rim dngos grub rgya mtsho* was written in Dpal 'khor chos sde (also called Dpal 'khor sde chen), the *Bde dril bskyed rim* was written in Dga' ldan. There are no dates in the colophons; however, from 1432 until his death in 1438, Mkhas grub rje was the abbot of Dga' ldan. If he completed his commentary on Vajraghaṇṭa in Dga' ldan, it was after he had to leave Dpal 'khor chos sde, and about ten years after he wrote the *Bskyed rim dngos grub rgya mtsho*.

786. Mkhas grub rje, *Bde dril bskyed rim*, 8a6–9b1. See also his *Dge bshes kon ting gu[g] shri ba la phul ba*, 158a5.

787. Bsod nams rtse mo, *De'i dbang gi bya ba mdor bsdus*, 118a1–4. It should be emphasized that when Tsong kha pa first criticized "some lamas," a criticism which we now know refers to Bsod nams rtse mo, in his *Great Treatise on the Stages of the Path of Mantra*—written in 1405, when Dga' ldan Monastery had not yet been built—he most likely regarded himself as a Sakyapa, just like Ngor chen. Hence, both Ngor chen and Tsong kha pa critique a view held by one of the forefathers of the Sa skya school, thus writing against the tradition of their predecessors.

maṇḍalas naturally present in the bodies of sentient beings, but reject the theory of *tathāgatagarbha*:

> Those who accept this [the tradition of Sönam Tsemo] and at the same time say that they cannot tolerate the position that in the continuum of sentient beings there is an "essence body"[788] endowed with all the qualities of permanence, stability, freedom, and the fruit, [must] wail loudly: "We are unable to analyze anything through any method that follows reasoning, yet nevertheless everything we say is driven by desire, driven by hatred, driven by ignorance."[789]

In *Ocean of Attainments*, Khedrup Jé takes several full pages to describe the errors of "some Tibetan lamas" who adhered to the tathāgatagarbha theory and why their premises lead them to absurd consequences.[790]

In addition to this offensive on the position of Sönam Tsemo, in this chapter on the body maṇḍala Khedrup Jé continues to subtly allude to other works by Ngorchen that do not agree with Sönam Tsemo.[791] Throughout several pages,[792] he refutes the reasoning of Rendawa viciously: "Since your mind is unable to fully fathom the meaning of the tantra, you surely have qualms of this kind."[793] And: "O child who has never studied the subject of contradiction and relationship, it is beyond your ability to interpret the meaning of the sūtra and tantra."[794] And: "How will you ever realize the profound vital points of the completion stage?"[795] We may ask, though, whether Rendawa's status in the Sakya headquarters in the 1420s was really high enough to inspire such turmoil. Khedrup Jé concludes his presentation of the opponents in the chapter on the body maṇḍala with extremely harsh words:

> Therefore it would be of great advantage for those deprived of the

788. Tib. *ngo bo nyid sku*, Skt. *svābhāvikakāya*.

789. Mkhas grub rje, *Bskyed rim dngos grub rgya mtsho*, 118a5–b1.

790. Mkhas grub rje, *Bskyed rim dngos grub rgya mtsho*, 116b1–118b1.

791. In the following paragraph of the *Bskyed rim dngos grub rgya mtsho*, Mkhas grub rje alludes to Ngor chen, *Lta ba ngan sel*, 334b1–3.

792. Mkhas grub rje, *Bskyed rim dngos grub rgya mtsho*, 119a2–123b2.

793. Mkhas grub rje, *Bskyed rim dngos grub rgya mtsho*, 122a4–5.

794. Mkhas grub rje, *Bskyed rim dngos grub rgya mtsho*, 122b3.

795. Mkhas grub rje, *Bskyed rim dngos grub rgya mtsho*, 123a3–4.

> transmitted instruction of the lamas, who have not studied the tantras and the works of the Great Charioteers much, and who lack the capacity to analyze the scriptures using pure reason, to rest a while in their investigation of the two stages of the path of Vajradhara; thus too their followers, who strive to outdo each other in the boldness of their attempted explanations of the teachings, and those who are content merely to watch the mouths of these followers; and it is also of great benefit to the teachings of the Victorious One.[796]

It is no wonder, then, that the Sakyapas were unhappy. But did this ignite the crisis among the Sakyapas? As we saw, the two refutations Ngorchen wrote in 1426 do not engage with the cycle of Cakrasaṃvara or the theory of *tathāgatagarbha*, but rather with the *Hevajra Tantra* and the Lamdré[797] tradition. Jackson, cited above, mentioned that "Mkhas grub rje's polemical writings concerning the Hevajra body-*maṇḍala* had stirred up the emotions of monks in gTsang."[798] Van der Kuijp noted that Khedrup Jé and Ngorchen Kunga Sangpo "had a tremendous fall-out over the interpretation of the *lus-dkyil* of Hevajra."[799] He also described Ngorchen's reply as "a polemical work dealing with the *maṇḍala* of Hevajra, conceived as a reply to and criticism of Mkhas grub rje's aside on the same in his *Bskyed-rim-dngos-grub-rgya-mtsho*."[800]

While the body maṇḍala of Hevajra is indeed not the immediate concern of Khedrup Jé's chapter on the body maṇḍala, toward the end of the same chapter he launches an attack that seems enigmatic to the casual reader, though apparently it was quite comprehensible to Sakya masters of his time:

> In many [works on] the body maṇḍala of the mother tantra, Tibetans write that: "The crown of the head is the crossed vajra, the soles of the feet the vajra ground, the ribs the vajra fence, the skin the vajra tent and canopy, the bodily hair the net of the arrows, and the nails the blazing fire mountain."[801]

In these lines on the mother tantra, Khedrup Jé disapproves of certain

796. Mkhas grub rje, *Bskyed rim dngos grub rgya mtsho*, 124b2–4.

797. Tib. *Lam 'bras*.

798. Jackson 2007, 354–355. See also Jackson 2010, 178.

799. van der Kuijp 1985a, 51.

800. van der Kuijp 1985c, 88.

801. Mkhas grub rje, *Bskyed rim dngos grub rgya mtsho*, 126b6–127a1. My translation of this passage is tentative.

correlations made by "Tibetans" between parts of the body and elements of the celestial mansion of the maṇḍala. It is precisely in response to these highly perplexing comments that Ngorchen wrote his refutation in two versions, *Abolishing Wrong Statements* and *Dispelling Wrong Views*, in 1426.[802] Both of these texts open with a direct quotation of the passages by Khedrup Jé that correlate parts of the body with elements of the maṇḍala cited above, and continue with a point-for-point refutation of his positions.[803]

We find the same correlations between the body of the yogi and the maṇḍala in the *Sādhana of the Hevajra Body Maṇḍala* by Pakpa Lodrö Gyaltsen.[804] In Sakya works on the Hevajra body maṇḍala, these correlations are standard. Ngorchen also makes the same analogies in his own 1410 work on the body maṇḍala of Hevajra according to the tradition of Pakpa.[805]

Were these terse and apparently obscure statements in Khedrup Jé's *Ocean of Attainments* understood by adherents of the Sakya tradition to invalidate their understanding of the body maṇḍala of Hevajra? These correlations were criticized already in Tsongkhapa's commentary, written in 1415.[806] How, then, are we to explain the timing of the Sakya crisis, which took place in the mid-1420s, and the anger against Khedrup Jé?

In an attempt to address these questions, let us look at Butön's commentary on the *Yoginīsañcaryā Tantra*.[807] Butön cites the correlations between the body and the yogi and the maṇḍala above without identifying his opponents, then cites additional correlations found in Kṛṣṇa's *Saṃvaravyākhyā* that are different but equally obscure.[808] What is important for our purposes is his conclusion:

> Other than this, I have not seen any other [explanation] in the cycle of Cakrasaṃvara.[809]

802. Ngor chen, *Smra ba ngan 'joms*, 270a1–287b6, and *Lta ba ngan sel*, 287b6–310a3.

803. Ngor chen Kun dga' bzang po, *Smra ba ngan 'joms*, 271b1–272a1, and *Lta ba ngan sel*, 288b3–289a3.

804. 'Phags pa Blo gros rgyal mtshan, *Kyai rdo rje lus dkyil gyi sgrub thabs*, 263b6–264a2.

805. Ngor chen, *Kye rdo rje'i lus kyi dkyil 'khor gyi sgrub pa'i thabs rnal 'byor snying po*, 298. I would like to thank Jörg Heimbel for drawing my attention to this matter and for providing me with a copy of this work.

806. Tsong kha pa, *'Dod 'jo*, 124a2–4.

807. *Kun spyod, Yoginīsañcaryā Tantra*, Tōh 375.

808. See Kṛṣṇa, *Sdom pa bshad pa, Saṃvaravyākhyā*, Tōh 1460, 7a4.

809. Bu ston Rin chen grub, *Kun spyod rgyud 'grel*, 39a1–4.

Tsongkhapa reproduces this in his own commentary,[810] and so does Khedrup Jé. However, and this is crucial, while Tsongkhapa cites Butön's conclusion faithfully, according to Khedrup Jé, Butön says:

> No other Indian treatise explains it in this way.[811]

Notably, in *Ocean of Attainments*, Khedrup Jé seldom distorts the position of his opponent in such a way. In this instance, he is clearly led by his passion. Partly following Tsongkhapa, Khedrup Jé comments:

> No authentic tantra or Indian treatise ever explains this, and there is nothing in what they explain from which anyone could derive such a meaning. Still, they fancy in their minds that there are no distinctions whatsoever between the body maṇḍala and merely placing the deities on the body. Numerous foolish talks that have received the title "supreme transmitted instructions" have appeared in manuals on the practice of the body maṇḍala written by Tibetans. I will not go into detail refuting or accepting them here.[812]

We may recall that according to Ngaripa Sanggyé Puntsok, Ngorchen could not travel because of a dispute in which it was claimed that "the body maṇḍala of the Sakyapa was not explained in the tantra and treatises." In his reply, Ngorchen defends the transmitted instruction of the Sakyapas criticized by Khedrup Jé:

> And even if it were not taught explicitly, those who understand the meaning have explained that it is necessary to meditate after completing what is missing according to the transmitted instructions of the lineage of the lamas. Although there is much variation in the instructions of the different lineages of lamas with regard to the means of completing what has been missing, the venerable Sakya lamas, endowed with Dharma eyes, hold this position that has arisen from the transmitted instruction and accords with the position of the master Jitāri.[813]

810. Tsong kha pa, *'Dod 'jo*, 124a2–4.

811. Mkhas grub rje, *Bskyed rim dngos grub rgya mtsho*, 127a2–3.

812. Mkhas grub rje, *Bskyed rim dngos grub rgya mtsho*, 127a4–5.

813. Ngor chen, *Smra ba ngan 'joms*, 273a1–3.

Ngorchen then cites the *Caturmudrā Sādhana*,[814] a work by Jitāri belonging to the cycle of Hevajra that describes the correlation between the body and the celestial mansion of the maṇḍala in a similar way to Pakpa Lodrö Gyaltsen. According to Ngorchen, Pakpa completed the correlations between parts of the body and elements of the maṇḍala that were missing in the tradition of Cakrasaṃvara by relying on this work on Hevajra by Jitāri. In his *Dispelling Wrong Views*, Ngorchen repeats this assertion, then asks:

> What contradiction is there in completing what is missing in the case of Cakrasaṃvara in accordance with the work on Hevajra by the master Jitāri?[815]

Ngorchen is aware of the fact that Butön criticized a Sakya founder:

> In his commentary on the *Yoginīsañcaryā* and in his commentary on *Sādhana of Kṛṣṇa*,[816] All-Knowing Butön employs similar language; however, he says "other than merely 'the tent is a string of bones,' I have not seen another [such explanation] in any cycle of Cakrasaṃvara." But he says nothing like "no other Indian treatise explains it in this way." This is an obvious lie; therefore, what need is there for proof?[817]

In this passage, Ngorchen does not write against Butön, but rather objects to Khedrup Jé's misrepresentation of Butön's last lines, using the loaded term "lie." Khedrup Jé certainly raises graver charges than does Butön, as the former denies any Indian scriptural authority for the specific correlations between the yogi's body and the protection wheel of the maṇḍala. However, this choice to understand charges against specific correlations as a total refutation of the authenticity of the Sakya tradition of the Hevajra body maṇḍala—as the Sakya oral tradition upholds—could only have taken place in the context of high tensions.

Khedrup Jé was quite aware of the charges that had been lodged against

814. Jitāri, *Phyag rgya bzhi yi sgrub thabs*, *Caturmudrā Sādhana*, Narthang Tengyur, *phu*, 143b5–144a2; and Peking Tengyur, 4690, *phu*, 144b7–147a4.

815. Ngor chen, *Lta ba ngan sel*, 290a3–4.

816. Bu ston, *Kun spyod rgyud 'grel* and *Nag po pa'i sgrub thabs*.

817. Ngor chen, *Smra ba ngan 'joms*, 272a3–4. In his *Lta ba ngan sel*, 289b1, the other version of his reply to Mkhas grub rje, Ngor chen repeats his words and concludes: "Do not speak such obvious lies!"

him. In his reply to another Sakya master known as Konting Gushri,[818] Khedrup Jé protested against those who claimed that he refuted the Lamdré teachings, whose foundation is the Hevajra cycle:

> Those who say that I refuted the Lamdré should examine carefully: Where did I refute the Lamdré? When did I refute it? How did I refute it? In the presence of whom did I refute it? In what writing of mine did I refute it? They should search for the source that would not ultimately vanish like a rainbow in the sky.[819]

I will conclude this discussion by noting that it is easy to see how the claim that Khedrup Jé questioned the validity of the *Hevajra Tantra* or Lamdré tradition of the Sakyapas gained traction. I, for my part, have found no evidence to support the contention that Khedrup Jé refuted the authenticity of the entire Sakya Hevajra cycle.

(6) Blessing the Body, Speech, and Mind

The process of rendering the yogi divine is composed of a series of practices that may have been independent or semi-independent meditations capable of achieving the goal, that became subordinated to the complete sādhana. While the meditation on the body maṇḍala, which, as we have seen, relies on the traditions of the mother tantra, may have been adapted from that cycle, the blessing of the body, speech, and mind is a step of the sādhana that is closely linked to the *Guhyasamāja Tantra* itself and even to its name. Though called in short *Guhyasamāja*, its complete name could be translated as "the union of the concealed secrets of the body, speech, and mind of all tathāgatas."[820] In its instructions on blessing the body, speech, and mind, Guhyasamāja sādhanas incorporate quite a few verses from the *Guhyasamāja Tantra* on the attainment of the Buddha's body, speech, and mind.[821] According to Tsongkhapa,

818. Kon ting Gu shri, identified by Jörg Heimbel as Nam mkha' bzang po from Sa skya's Nyi lde bla brang. See Heimbel 2017a, 129, and n. 328.

819. Mkhas grub rje, *Dge bshes kon ting gu*[*g*] *shri ba la phul ba*, 153a4–5.

820. Tib. *De bzhin gshegs pa thams cad kyi sku gsung thugs kyi gsang chen gsang ba 'dus pa*, Skt. *Sarvatathāgatakāyavākcittarahasyaguhyasamāja*.

821. The verse of invitation is found in chap. 11, v. 4; the verses for request in chap. 12, Fremantle 1971, vv. 71–76; Matsunaga 1978, vv. 70–75; the verses of stabilization are in chap. 7, vv. 28–30; and the mantra for holding divine pride is at the beginning of chap. 6. The scriptural authority for blessing the body, speech, and mind collectively is found in chap. 2, Zhol 5b7; Stog 9a1–2; Fremantle 1971, 190; Matsunaga 1978, 9.

the goal of the blessing is to purify the grounds of purification of the fetus in the womb, and to transform them into the Buddha's body, speech, and mind.

The buddhas of the body, speech, and mind, also known as vajra body, vajra speech, and vajra mind, are Vairocana, Amitābha, and Akṣobhya respectively, together with their consorts Locanā, Pāṇḍarā, and Māmakī. The yogis request to be blessed with vajra body, speech, and mind—that is to say, to turn the ordinary nature of their bodies, speech, and minds into the nature of the Buddha's body, speech, and mind. The request is granted through the entry of Vairocana, Amitābha, and Akṣobhya, along with their consorts, into the yogis' heads, throats, and hearts, saturating the yogis with bliss. The yogis stabilize their experience by meditating on the transformation of their own bodies into the body of the Buddha and so forth. Then they maintain the divine identity of these three tathāgatas. During the union with the consort in a following step of the sādhana, the yogis will develop the divine identity of Ratnasaṃbhava and Amoghasiddhi as well. In this way, they will become the five tathāgatas of the maṇḍala.[822] After attaining mastery of the body, speech, and mind separately, the yogis meditate on the blessing of their body, speech, and mind collectively.

In following the *Sādhana Incorporating the Scripture* and the *Vajrasattva Sādhana*, Tsongkhapa's *Guhyasamāja Sādhana* describes the dissolution of the three tathāgatas into the yogis as the entry of the jñānasattva.[823] In sādhanas of other tantric cycles, for example the Vajrabhairava, one of the culminating points of the entire practice is the invitation of the jñānasattvas and their dissolution into the samayasattvas. Since this step is not included in the sādhana of the Guhyasamāja, some Tibetan scholars explain this "lacuna" by applying the role of the entry of the jñānasattva to the blessings of the body, speech, and mind. Thus Panchen Losang Chökyi Gyaltsen describes the blessing of the three doors as an alternative to the entry of the jñānasattva, while Norsang Gyatso calls the blessing of the body, speech, and mind "the best entry of the jñānasattva."[824]

Disagreements about this step of the sādhana are related to the identification

822. See the section "Becoming the Five Tathāgatas of the Guhyasamāja Maṇḍala" above.

823. See Nāgārjuna, *Mdo bsre, Sādhanasūtramelāpaka,* Tōh 1797, 13a2–3; and Candrakīrti, *Rdo rje sems dpa'i sgrub thabs, Vajrasattva Sādhana,* Tōh 1814, 200b2–3; Luo and Tomabechi 2009, 19.7 and 52.4.

824. Paṇ chen Blo bzang chos kyi rgyal mtshan, *Bskyed rim dngos grub rgya mtsho'i snying po,* 59b5–6; Nor bzang rgya mtsho, *Gsang ba 'dus pa'i bskyed rim gyi don gsal bar byed pa'i sgron me,* 118b4.

of its ground of purification.[825] Tsongkhapa regards the blessing of the three doors as a part of the meditation on Vajrasattva's nirmāṇakāya that purifies rebirth; specifically, it serves to purify the body, speech, and mind of the fetus. For him, phases of human life that follow birth out of the womb cannot serve as grounds for purification. On the other hand, according to Butön, Rongtön, and Amyé Shap, the grounds of purification of the blessings are the phases following birth outside the womb when a body incapable of action becomes capable of action, a mouth that cannot speak learns how to speak, and a mind that cannot make distinctions learns how to differentiate.[826]

(7) Meditation on the Triple Sattvas

The deity created through the creation stage has to embody all three sattvas. So far, the yogis have visualized themselves as the samayasattvas; now they meditate on the subtle jñānasattvas that abide at their hearts. At the heart of the jñānasattvas they place the samādhisattva, the syllable *hūṃ*, and meditate on themselves as Vajradhara, who embodies these triple sattvas.

As noted, sādhanas such as that of Vajrabhairava prescribe the invitation of the jñānasattva to dissolve into the samayasattva. In other words, the jñānasattva, the actual deity, merges with the visualization and is sealed in it to create a nondual entity in a process in which, in a sense, the simulacrum is transformed into actual reality. The meditation according to *Guhyasamāja Sādhanas*, by contrast, is an exercise in increasing levels of subtlety. The *Concise Sādhana* describes the jñānasattva as subtle[827] and the samādhisattva is the syllable *hūṃ*.[828]

The samayasattva is the meditator visualized as and maintaining the divine pride of Vajrasattva's nirmāṇakāya. The term samayasattva (*dam tshig sems dpa'*) is translated at times as "pledge being" or "commitment being" in the sense of the being that the yogi pledges to become, similar to *iṣṭadevatā* (*yi dam*). In our texts, however, the word *samaya* is understood in a different way. On the scriptural authority of Abhayākaragupta, Tsongkhapa explains that *samaya* is derived from the root *sam-i*, which means "coming together" or

825. See "Completion of the Four Yogas" in the section "The Samādhis in the First Chapter of the *Guhyasamāja Tantra* and Enacting Past Events" below.

826. Bu ston, *Mdor byas 'grel chen*, 45a7–b2; Rong ston, *Gsang 'dus rnam bshad*, 6b2; and A mye zhabs, *Gsang 'dus dkyil 'khor sgrub thabs rnam bshad*, 137a6–b1.

827. Tib. *phra mo*, Skt. *sūkṣmaṃ*.

828. Nāgārjuna, *Mdor byas, Piṇḍīkrama Sādhana*, Tōh 1796, 5b1–2; L 92ab.

"joining."[829] This refers to the jñānasattva who joins and unites with the samayasattva that generally occurs in sādhanas, with the *Guhyasamāja Sādhanas* being an exception.[830]

Regarding the specific context of the *Guhyasamāja Sādhana*, we find an explanation in the *Vajrasattva Sādhana*: "It is called 'samayasattva' because it is generated through the samādhi of vajra origination from samaya[831] as taught in the first chapter of the *Guhyasamāja Tantra*."[832] As we will see,[833] Vajrasattva's nirmāṇakāya, which is the samayasattva, is generated through the samādhi of vajra origination from samaya.

The meaning of the term *jñānasattva*, "wisdom being," is clearer; its nature is wisdom. As for the *samādhisattva*—"concentration being"—in his *Great Treatise on the Stages of the Mantric Path*, Tsongkhapa asks: How can a seed syllable or a letter mean a sentient being?[834] In reply, he once more cites Abhayākaragupta, who gives the example of the embryo in its first phase in the womb and concludes that just as the newly formed embryo, who lacks any form with face and hands, is called a sentient being, here too the conventional designation "sentient being" is used.[835]

The subtlety of the triple sattvas is also evident in reference to this practice's ground of purification. According to Khedrup Jé, the meditation on the samayasattva corresponds to the temporal coarse body of the being in the womb,

829. Tsong kha pa, *Sngags rim chen mo*, 516; and *Slob tshul*, 20a1–3. See Abhayākaragupta, *Man ngag snye ma*, *Āmnāyamañjarī*, Tōh 1198, 122a4–5.

830. The *Man ngag snye ma* is a commentary on the *Saṃpuṭa Tantra*.

831. Tib. *dam tshig 'byung ba rdo rje*, Skt. *samayodbhavavajra*.

832. *Gsang 'dus*, *Guhyasamāja Tantra*, chap. 1, Tōh 442; Zhol 3b2; Stog missing; Dunh 3a4–b1; Fremantle 1971, 178; Matsunaga, 1978, 5. See Candrakīrti, *Rdo rje sems dpa'i sgrub thabs*, *Vajrasattva Sādhana*, Tōh 1814, 201b1; Luo and Tomabechi 2009, 22.7–8 and 55.12–14.

833. See "Completion of the Four Yogas" in the section "The Samādhis in the First Chapter of the *Guhyasamāja Tantra* and Enacting Past Events" below.

834. Tib. *sems can*, Skt. *sattva*. Tsong kha pa, *Sngags rim chen mo*, 516.

835. Abhayākaragupta, *Man ngag snye ma*, *Āmnāyamañjarī*, Tōh 1198, 122a5–6.

and the jñānasattva and the samādhisattva correspond to its innate subtle body, though there are disputes on their exact identification.[836]

As for the fruit of this practice, it is in the context of the meditation on the triple sattvas that Akhu Ching Sherab Gyatso chooses to emphasize the superiority of mantra over sūtra in reference to their capacity to activate the most subtle levels of the body, speech, and mind: "Although Sūtra paths can purify body, speech, and mind both at the gross and subtle levels, they cannot do so at the very subtle level."[837] Akhu Ching then continues in saying that on the mantra path, by contrast, the yogi can achieve the most subtle mind. Since the nature of this mind is innate bliss, the yogi can attain the actual clear light that experiences emptiness directly and dissolves the subtle winds.

Still, the most subtle body and mind are not activated during the creation stage itself. The meditation of the triple sattvas during the creation stage affects the level of the ground, and ripens conditions toward the path of the completion stage, but it cannot achieve the subtle and most subtle levels.

There are two points of contention pertaining to the triple sattvas. One is how to reconcile the instruction to meditate on a jñānasattva who is similar to the samayasattva, given that the samayasattva is blue with three faces and six arms, while the jñānasattva is red with one face and two arms. Khedrup Jé strongly attacks his teacher Rendawa, who maintains that it is not appropriate to meditate on the jñānasattva as red in color with one face and two arms, as Tsongkhapa instructs in his *Guhyasamāja Sādhana*.[838]

836. Mkhas grub rje, *Bskyed rim dngos grub rgya mtsho*, 116a5–6. Dge lugs scholars do not agree on this point. For some early Dge lugs scholars, including Nor bzang rgya mtsho and Dge 'dun rgya mtsho, the jñānasattva corresponds to the very subtle mind and the samādhisattva to the very subtle wind; see Nor bzang rgya mtsho, *Gsang ba 'dus pa'i bskyed rim gyi don gsal bar byed pa'i sgron me*, 125a3–125b3, and Dge 'dun rgya mtsho, *Gsang ba 'dus pa'i rim pa dang po'i lam la slob pa'i tshul*, 35b2–4. But some latter Dge lugs scholars reverse this. For Paṇ chen Blo bzang chos kyi rgyal mtshan, the jñānasattva corresponds to the subtle innate body made of the very subtle wind-and-mind and the samādhisattva to the very subtle mind; see his *Bskyed rim dngos grub rgya mtsho'i snying po*, 60b1–2. Lcang skya Ngag dbang chos ldan states that some scholars reverse these two; see his *Gsang chen myur lam*, 24a8–b1. According to Grags pa bshad sgrub, the jñānasattva corresponds to the subtle innate body, while the samādhisattva corresponds to the subtle innate indivisible wind and mind; see his *Gsang 'dus bskyed rim gnad don kun gsal*, 57. A khu ching maintains that the jñānasattva corresponds to the very subtle wind and the samādhisattva to the very subtle mind; see his *Mi bskyod mgon po'i zhal lung*, 83a1–2; an English translation in Jinpa 1999, 154.

837. A khu ching, *Mi bskyod mgon po'i zhal lung*, 82b3–4; an English translation in Jinpa 1999, 153.

838. Mkhas grub rje, *Bskyed rim dngos grub rgya mtsho*, 137a4; Red mda' ba, *Bsgrub pa dpal bas zhus lan*, Kathmandu, 51a2–3; TBRC, 306a; Tsong kha pa, *Gsang mngon*, 49b3–4.

This disagreement results from discrepancies in the Indian sources. Scholars such as Bhavyakīrti and Ratnākaraśānti explain that the jñānasattva is similar to the samayasattva,[839] while Candrakīrti's *Vajrasattva Sādhana* instructs: "Visualize the jñānasattva with two arms, red in color."[840] As we have seen,[841] Rendawa maintains that "the *Vajrasattva Sādhana* was not written by Glorious Candrakīrti,"[842] whereas Tsongkhapa and Khedrup Jé accept this work as authentic. According to Rendawa, "all the tantras explain that jñānasattva is similar to the samayasattva," but Khedrup Jé finds this statement "astonishing," and provides counterexamples.[843] Khedrup Jé concludes that it is appropriate to meditate on the jñānasattva as red in color, basing this assertion on the scriptural authority of the *Vajrasattva Sādhana* and the commentaries on the *Concise Sādhana* written by Bhavyakīrti and Abhayākaragupta.[844]

The second argument we will mention concerns an invocation related to the jñānasattva, which results from different readings of a line from the *Sādhana Incorporating the Scripture* that is written in a peculiar syntax. According to the Derge, the *jñānasattva is invoked* with a seed syllable,[845] but in the Peking and the Narthang, there is *invocation by means of* the seed syllable of the jñānasattva.[846] Khedrup Jé brings yet another version in which a deity is invoked *from* the seed syllable *of* the *jñānasattva*,[847] while both Ngorchen Kunga Sangpo and Rendawa speak of invocation of the jñānasattva.[848] Khedrup Jé's wording indicates that his criticism of "some people" is addressing Ngorchen. According to Khedrup Jé, this line of the *Sādhana Incorporating*

839. Bhavyakīrti, *Rab tu sgron gsal, Prakāśikā*, chap. 10, Tōh 1793, 25b4; Ratnākaraśānti, *Rin chen phreng ba, Ratnāvalī*, Tōh 1826, 46b2–3.

840. Candrakīrti, *Rdo rje sems dpa'i sgrub thabs, Vajrasattva Sādhana*, Tōh 1814, 201b1–2; Luo and Tomabechi 2009, 22.9–10 and 55.16–17.

841. In the section "The Guhyasamāja Sādhanas of the Ārya School" above.

842. Red mda' ba, *Bsgrub pa dpal bas zhus lan*, Kathmandu, 51a4–5; TBRC, 306b.

843. Mkhas grub rje, *Bskyed rim dngos grub rgya mtsho*, 137a4.

844. Mkhas grub rje, *Bskyed rim dngos grub rgya mtsho*, 137b7–138a1; Bhavyakīrti, *Rim pa lnga'i dka' 'grel, Pañcakramapañjikā*, Tōh 1838, 2b7; Abhayākaragupta, *Rdzogs pa'i rnal 'byor gyi phreng ba, Niṣpannayogāvali*, Tōh 3141, 99b5; Sanskrit and Tibetan editions with an English translation of the latter text in Lokesh Chandra and Nirmala Sharma 2015, 36–37.

845. Nāgārjuna, *Mdo bsre, Sādhanasūtramelāpaka*, Tōh 1797, 13b1.

846. Nāgārjuna, *Mdo bsre, Sādhanasūtramelāpaka*, Peking, 15a3; Narthang, 15a2.

847. Mkhas grub rje, *Bskyed rim dngos grub rgya mtsho*, 138a1–2.

848. Ngor chen, *Gsang 'dus dkyil 'khor gyi sgrub thabs dngos grub rgya mtsho*, 12a5–b1; Red mda' ba, *Bsgrub dpal bas zhus lan*, Kathmandu, 51a3–4; TBRC, 306a–b.

the Scripture is concerned not with the invitation of the jñānasattva, but with the meditation on the lord of the Tathāgata family in the next step.

(8) Sealing with the Lord of the Tathāgata Family

This is the final step of the core practices; it concludes a long process of visualizations that build toward the awakening of the yogis themselves. First, the yogis conceive of themselves as the specially visualized deities that dissolve into emptiness for the sake of eventually attaining the dharmakāya. Then they meditate on the First Lord in order to attain the saṃbhogakāya, and finally on Vajrasattva's nirmāṇakāya that will eventually turn into the nirmāṇakāya. Now that the yogis have become the Buddha's three bodies "of the creation stage," they, as the triple sattvas, can "seal" their visualization by placing Vajradhara and his consort Vajradhātvīśvarī on their head-crowns.

According to Panchen Losang Chökyi Gyaltsen, all the deities surrounding the principal deity have already been sealed during the meditation on the specially visualized deities, since their generation did not require the completion of the meditation on the triple sattvas.[849]

(9) The Yoga with the Consort[850]

Can Women Attain Enlightenment through Vajrayāna Practices?

Modern scholars who wish to demonstrate the significance of women in Vajrayāna must read the writings of our author, Khedrup Jé, on the subject. Manuals of Vajrayāna practices, including Tsongkhapa's *Guhyasamāja Sādhana*, are explicit about the participation of women in the practice. Thus the question arises: Do women achieve their own spiritual goals by means of these practices, or are they merely instrumental in the progress of men? The position of Tsongkhapa and Khedrup Jé is that just like men, women can attain enlightenment by means of Vajrayāna practices. This position is also found in Indian treatises from approximately the ninth to tenth centuries. According to Candrakīrti's *Illuminating Lamp*:

849. Paṇ chen Blo bzang chos kyi rgyal mtshan, *Bskyed rim dngos grub rgya mtsho'i snying po*, 43b2–3. See also Dge 'dun rgya mtsho, *Gsang bskyed*, 31b3–4.

850. See Bentor 2015d.

> It is not only men who attain awakening born from passion, but women as well attain this.[851]

Similar positions are also found in works belonging to the tradition of Cakrasaṃvara. In his commentary on the *Vajraḍāka Tantra*, Bhavabhadra explains:

> The *yoginīs* will bestow siddhis of ultimate truth-wisdom on the male practitioners... And the male practitioners will bestow the ultimate truth pristine wisdom on the *yoginīs* as well... Thus, by means of this path, both men and women will attain [awakening] without difficulty.[852]

Here we find equal participation of women in the practice as well as in its goal. These statements are not directed at male practitioners alone and do not privilege men in any way. On the basis of works such as those of Candrakīrti and Bhavabhadra, Tsongkhapa explains in his own commentary on the *Illuminating Lamp*:

> Just as in relying on his consort, the male practitioner attains enlightenment by meditating on the generation of the wisdoms of the four empty states, also in relying on the male practitioner, the consort meditates on the clear light arising from the generation of the four empty states, and is thereby awakened in this life.[853]

If read in ignorance of their authors' names, one might have thought that some of these passages, hundreds of years old, were written by twenty-first-century advocates of equality for women. This contrasts with the opinions expressed by various scholars, such as Bernard Faure: "[F]emale figures of Tantric Buddhism... are relegated to a passive role," and "this female *mudrā*... is a symbol of *prajñā* (wisdom), and as such she is utterly passive and inferior in status."[854] Another example is David Snellgrove:

> The reverse situation is scarcely suggested, namely that a woman

851. Candrakīrti, *Sgron gsal, Pradīpoddyotanaṭikā*, chap. 13, Tōh 1785, 103b6; Chakravarti 1984, 127.

852. Bhavabhadra, *Rdo rje mkha' 'gro'i rnam par bshad pa, Vajraḍākavivṛti*, Toh 1415, 5b6–7.

853. Tsong kha pa, *Sgron gsal mchan*, 299b2–3.

854. Faure 2003, 124–126.

> requires a male partner in order to experience the Four Joys... The whole theory and practice is given for the benefit of males.[855]

Yet this is what Tsongkhapa says about the four joys and about the complete symmetry of male and female practitioners:

> As in relying on the mother, the four joys are generated in the mental continuum of the father, so also in relying on the father, the four joys arise in the mental continuum of the mother.[856]

And:

> The equivalent of a male practitioner who generates the four joys by relying on an actual consort is a female practitioner who generates the four joys by relying on her male companion. Also similar are the ways of generating the four joys descending and stabilizing below, of generating the four empty states in the forward and reverse orders, and of meditating by uniting bliss and emptiness during the fourth joy and the fourth empty in the forward order, and so on.[857]

Moreover, Tsongkhapa emphasizes that women also attain enlightenment in this lifetime:

> How does a human being endowed with a female body awaken in this life? As for example, by relying on the mother, the father induces the four joys and the four empty states, then generates the pure and impure illusory bodies from the [wind and] mind of clear light of the four empty states, and subsequently actualizes the union of no more learning in this lifetime, just so the mother, by relying on the father, also induces the four joys and the four empty states, then generates the pure and impure illusory bodies from the wind and mind of the clear light of the four empty states, and subsequently actualizes the union of no more practice in this lifetime.[858]

855. Snellgrove 1987, 287.

856. Tsong kha pa, *Mtha' gcod rin chen myu gu*, 124a6.

857. Tsong kha pa, *Mtha' gcod rin chen myu gu*, 124a4–6.

858. Tsong kha pa, *Bung ba'i re skong*, 23b3–5.

Furthermore, Tsongkhapa asserts that a jewel-like disciple—the best type of disciple, according to the *Illuminating Lamp*[859]—might very well be female:

> A jewel-like disciple, who attains the supreme accomplishment in this life, is not necessarily only a man; this disciple can be a woman as well.[860]

It is not my aim to argue that the writings of Candrakīrti or Tsongkhapa on this point reflect the actual social situations of their times. My point here is that even though quite a few books and articles have been written on women in Buddhism in recent decades, these passages have been widely neglected. I find it quite instructive to read what some Indian and Tibetan writers think about the position of women in Vajrayāna practice, in particular on the question of women's potential to reach enlightenment.

There is no doubt that the Indian and Tibetan authors cited above were aware that the manuals are not written from the perspectives of women. I find it significant that they still take pains to emphasize the symmetry between male and female Vajrayāna practitioners, as well as the potential of women to attain enlightenment. For example, Tsongkhapa, who is more explicit on this matter, does not attempt to refute the fact that the sādhanas are written through a male lens; rather, he aims to explain it:

> Though it seems that the majority of the tantras and the Indian sādhanas teach mostly from the point of view of a man, it is not impossible [to attain enlightenment, the stage of Vajradhara,] in a body of a woman.[861]

This being the case, why are the scriptures written from a male point of view and not from the perspective of a woman practitioner? In response, Tsongkhapa says that since the practice of a male practitioner is the same as that of a female practitioner, "the method of training on the path for women is not taught in detail separately."[862]

859. Candrakīrti, *Sgron gsal, Pradīpoddyotanaṭīkā*, Tōh 1785, 3a7–b3; Chakravarti 1984, 4.

860. Tsong kha pa, *Mtha' gcod*, 123a6. See also his *Bung ba'i re skong*, 23b3.

861. Tsong kha pa, *Rnam gzhag rim pa'i rnam bshad*, 19a3. Tsong kha pa relies here on the *Gsang 'dus, Guhyasamāja Tantra* and Candrakīrti's commentary on it, which he cites. See *Gsang 'dus, Guhyasamāja Tantra*, chap. 13, Tōh 442; Zhol 20b4; Stog 35a3; Fremantle 1971, v. 27; and Matsunaga 1978, v. 25; and Candrakīrti, *Sgron gsal, Pradīpoddyotanaṭīkā*, Tōh 1785, 103b6–7; Chakravarti 1984, 127.

862. Tsong kha pa, *Mtha' gcod*, 123b5–6.

We may well remain skeptical whether the sādhanas indeed address both male and female practitioners equally. However, it is clear that it was important for Tsongkhapa that the practice would enable both men and women to attain enlightenment. He stresses women's potential to reach the goal of the path in several of his works on Vajrayāna practices. Such an approach was not Tsongkhapa's own invention—important Indian authors on Vajrayāna held very similar positions.

In closing, I would like to call attention to certain problems in the methodology of scholars who aim to demonstrate the equal potential of women in Vajrayāna to reach awakening. Some of them apply various feminist theories to explain why scholars were predisposed to fail to recognize the true role of women, and speak about male dominance, colonialist judgments, and so on. However, had they relied on the positions of Candrakīrti, Bhavabhadra, and Tsongkhapa instead of trying to explain things away, we probably would have been even more inclined to agree with their conclusions about the potential of women to attain enlightenment.

By That Very Passion They Are Released

The yoga with the consort is based on a notion expressed in a well-known verse of the *Hevajra Tantra*: "By passion sentient beings are bound and by that very passion they are released."[863] Tsongkhapa and Khedrup Jé maintain that the teachings of the Mantra Vehicle are meant for human beings with passionate bodies[864] who dwell in the Desire Realm.[865] They cite in this regard an explanatory tantra of the Guhyasamāja, the *Compendium of Vajra Wisdom Tantra*: "Unless the mantrin and his consort unite, and their vajra and lotus are joined, they will be unable to identify the three types of awareness.[866] Those unable to join their *bhaga*s and *liṅga*s will not attain the samādhi of great bliss."[867]

We find a similar statement in commentaries on the *Guhyasamāja Tantra*. The *Illuminating Lamp* asks: "For whose sake was this *Tantra* taught?" And

863. *Brtag gnyis*, Tōh 418, 16a4–5; Snellgrove 1959, II.ii.51.

864. Tib. *'dod pa'i rten can gyi mi.*

865. Tib. *'dod pa'i khams*, Skt. *kāmadhātu*. Tsong kha pa, *Rnam gzhag rim pa'i rnam bshad*, 17a5–b1; Mkhas grub rje, *Bskyed rim dngos grub rgya mtsho*, 76a1–77b4.

866. The white appearance, the red-enhanced appearance, and the black appearance of approaching attainment.

867. *Ye shes rdo rje kun las btus pa*, *Vajrajñānasamuccaya Tantra*, Tōh 447, 283b1–2.

it replies: "For the sake of passionate people."[868] Likewise, the *Guhyasamāja Tantra* begins with the following line: "The Blessed One, the Tathāgata Mahāvairocanavajra was absorbed in the samādhi called 'the method of great passion of all tathāgatas.'"[869] The *Illuminating Lamp* explains: "The *Guhyasamāja Tantra* teaches this samādhi to instruct those sentient beings in the desire realm who are attached to objects about liberation through the five attributes of passion."[870]

Here we encounter the term "past event,"[871] which will be discussed below.[872] The past event takes place in the *Guhyasamāja Tantra*; in this context, it is the samādhi called "the method of great passion."[873] In practicing the sādhana, yogis enact this past event in what is called "the practice that follows"[874] the past event. The *Sādhana Incorporating the Scripture* elaborates on this notion: "In the first chapter of the *Guhyasamāja Tantra*, the Blessed One was absorbed in the samādhi called 'the method of great passion' to demonstrate that the stage of enlightenment arises through passion. Likewise, during the creation stage, meditators should practice the First Yoga,[875] displaying liberation by means of passion for sentient beings engaged in passion."[876] Thus this sādhana relates the practice of great passion specifically to the First Yoga of the creation stage.

Both the *Vajrasattva Sādhana* and the *Compendium of Practices* describe how Buddha Śākyamuni performed three kinds of deeds: In a body free of passion, he descended from Tuṣita, displayed awakening in Bodhgaya, and so forth for disciples on the ground of hearers who adhere to the lower path. For those on the path of the Mahāyāna who aspire to the vast path, he elucidated

868. Candrakīrti, *Sgron gsal, Pradīpoddyotanaṭīkā*, Tōh 1785, 2a5–b1; Chakravarti 1984, 2. See Campbell 2009, 295; and also Tsong kha pa, *Rnam gzhag rim pa'i rnam bshad*, 18a4–5.

869. Tib. *de bzhin gshegs pa thams cad kyi 'dod chag chen po'i tshul zhes bya ba'i ting nge 'dzin*, Skt. *sarvatathāgatamahārāganayaṃ* [*vajraṃ*] *samādhi*; or "the vajra-great-passion of all tathāgatas." *Gsang 'dus, Guhyasamāja Tantra*, chap. 1, Tōh 442; Zhol 2b2; Stog 3b3; Fremantle 1971, 176; and Matsunaga 1978, 4.

870. Candrakīrti, *Sgron gsal, Pradīpoddyotanaṭīkā*, Tōh 1785, 12b7–13a1; Chakravarti 1984, 18. See also Tsong kha pa, *Sgron gsal mchan*, 53b3–54b2.

871. Tib. *sngon byung*.

872. See the section "The Samādhis in the First Chapter of the Guhyasamāja Tantra and Enacting Past Events."

873. Tsong kha pa, *Sgron gsal mchan*, 53b5–54b2.

874. Tib. *rjes 'jug*.

875. This is the first among the three samādhis that comprise the creation stage.

876. Nāgārjuna, *Mdo bsre, Sādhanasūtramelāpaka*, Tōh 1797, 13b2–4.

all modes of the perfection of wisdom. Again, for those earnestly intent on the profound path, he taught practices with passion by absorbing in the samādhi called "the method of great passion," taught in the first chapter of the *Guhyasamāja Tantra*.[877]

The *Vajrasattva Sādhana* then concludes: "Just so, after engaging in the First Yoga, the practicing yogi should abide in the samādhi called 'enjoying all desires,' taught in the seventeenth chapter of the *Guhyasamāja Tantra*, for displaying liberation through passion to sentient beings engaging in passion."[878] Thus, just as the tathāgata was absorbed in union with his consort in the past event, so the yogi does the same in the practice that follows.

In commenting on the samādhi known as "the method of great passion," Tsongkhapa explains that buddhahood, difficult to attain by means of other paths even if one endeavors for many eons, is attained here in one lifetime by means of sublime bliss. He adds that in terms of the view of emptiness, *the objective aspect*, there is no difference between the unexcelled tantra, the three lower tantras, and the Mahāyāna. But the key to swiftness on the path of the unexcelled tantra is *the subjective aspect* of the innate great bliss, through which yogis meditate on the meaning of suchness.[879]

The Rarity of Meeting the Required Conditions

Having explained this, Tsongkhapa and Khedrup Jé emphasize how rare it would be to encounter both yogi and consort who meet the manifold requirements specified in the tantras.[880] The yogi must be endowed with extremely sharp faculties and have achieved mastery of deity yoga. When he practices yoga with the consort, he must block the melting constituents from emitting outside by meditating on the syllable *phaṭ* on the tip of his vajra. He should then fully experience the four joys of the creation stage and join bliss with emptiness until all objects appear as a display of bliss and emptiness. The

877. Candrakīrti, *Rdo rje sems dpa'i sgrub thabs*, *Vajrasattva Sādhana*, Tōh 1814, 201b6–202a1; Luo and Tomabechi 2009, 23.11–24.2 and 57.5-12; Āryadeva, *Spyod bsdus*, *Caryāmelāpakapradīpa*, chap. 9, Tōh 1803, 94b4–6; Sanskrit, Tibetan, and English translation in Wedemeyer 2007, B: 54b–55a; Sanskrit and Tibetan in Pandey 2000, 78 and 310–311.

878. Candrakīrti, *Rdo rje sems dpa'i sgrub thabs*, *Vajrasattva Sādhana*, Tōh 1814, 202a1–2; Luo and Tomabechi 2009, 24.2–4 and 57.12–16.

879. Tsong kha pa, *Sgron gsal mchan*, 54a2–3.

880. Tsong kha pa, *Rim lnga gsal sgron*, chap. 2, 67b6–68a1; an English translation in Kilty 2013, 125.

goal is to attain bliss endowed with the realization of emptiness. Khedrup Jé concludes:

> This being so, it goes without saying that nowadays it would be rare indeed to encounter both such a yogi and an actual consort endowed with all the required characteristics... When all the essential characteristics explained in the tantras and reliable works of the mahāsiddhas are fulfilled, the yogi may then rely on an actual consort. But how are we to find a yogi and consort endowed with such perfect characteristics?... Therefore those who are not endowed with such essential characteristics should rely on a wisdom mudrā—a visualized consort—in their practice of generating the joys and the wisdom of bliss and emptiness.[881]

Khedrup Jé encourages the yogi to practice with a wisdom consort:

> Hence, even without resorting to an actual consort, by relying on a wisdom consort you should be able to induce bliss that is similar to that of union with an actual consort.[882]

It should be noted that the basic sādhana, the *Concise Sādhana*, mentions only an actual consort—of a low caste,[883] though endowed with exceptional qualities—while the other three sādhanas offer a choice between an actual or a wisdom consort.[884] Having considered the instructions in these sādhanas, Tsongkhapa concludes that the yogi should emanate a consort from his heart, and so he instructs in his *Guhyasamāja Sādhana*.[885] Furthermore, on the basis of the use of the verb "imagine" or "conceptualize"[886] in the *Guhyasamāja Tantra*, Tsongkhapa deduces that the visualization of the yogi with his consort is

881. Mkhas grub rje, *Bskyed rim dngos grub rgya mtsho*, 143b2–144a3.

882. Mkhas grub rje, *Bskyed rim dngos grub rgya mtsho*, 143a6.

883. Tib. *sme sha can*, Skt. *rajaka*.

884. Nāgārjuna, *Mdor byas*, *Piṇḍīkrama Sādhana*, Tōh 1796, 5b2–3; L 94. See also Nāgārjuna, *Mdo bsre*, *Sādhanasūtramelāpaka*, Tōh 1797, 13b4–5; Candrakīrti, *Rdo rje sems dpa'i sgrub thabs*, *Vajrasattva Sādhana*, Tōh 1814, 202a4–5; Luo and Tomabechi 2009, 24.9–10 and 58.4–5; and Nāgabuddhi, *Rnam gzhag rim pa*, *Vyavastholi*, chap. 3, Tōh 1809, 126a6; Tanaka 2016, 105.

885. Tsong kha pa, *Rnam gzhag rim pa'i rnam bshad*, 61a1–3; and his *Gsang mngon*, 50a2–3.

886. Tib. *brtag par bya*, Skt. *vikalpayed*. This verb is used with regard to the seed syllable on the vajra and lotus.

merely imputed through conceptualization,[887] and not real or actual.[888] Thus the early Geluk scholars make every effort to discourage performing the practice with an actual consort, even threatening yogis with hell:

> Those who lack yoga but engage in yogic practice and unite with a consort, and those who lack wisdom but pretend to possess it, will surely go to hell.[889]

It should be noted here that for Tsongkhapa the distinction between the Mantra and Pāramitā Vehicles is not that the former is meant for disciples who have not abandoned desire, while the latter is for those free from desire.[890] For Tsongkhapa, the difference between the two vehicles is whether or not the disciple can practice deity yoga. However, in order to be awakened in that very life in the Desire Realm, the yogis must belong to the uppermost category of practitioners of the unexcelled tantra, the jewel-like persons,[891] be able to apply passion on the path, devote themselves exclusively to the practice, and embark from the onset of their meditation on the path of the unexcelled tantra.[892] Hence, there are a number of requirements for yogis meditating on the tantric path that are difficult to fulfill.

We may note in closing that an interesting distinction is made in this context between tantra and mantra. According to the *Illuminating Lamp*, the *sādhaka*, or yogi, should be well-trained in tantra and mantra.[893] Tsongkhapa explains that "tantra" refers to tantras that teach the sixty-four arts of love, and "mantra" refers to meditations on the deity, recitations, and so forth.[894] Both Tsongkhapa and Khedrup Jé list the eight types of arts of love

887. Tib. *rnam par rtog pas btags pa tsam nyid.* According to Mkhas grub rje, the consort must first appear as the daughter of a low-caste person. But then she dissolves into emptiness and arises as Sparśavajrā (Tib. Reg bya rdo rje ma). See his *Bskyed rim dngos grub rgya mtsho*, 144a5.

888. *Gsang 'dus, Guhyasamāja Tantra*, chap. 7, Tōh 442; Zhol 10b5–6; Stog 17b7; Fremantle 1971, v. 19cd; and Matsunaga 1978, v. 19cd. See Tsong kha pa, *Sgron gsal mchan*, 173b3–6.

889. Mkhas grub rje, *Bskyed rim dngos grub rgya mtsho*, 144a1–2; quoting *Heruka mngon 'byung, Herukābhyudaya*, chap. 7, Tōh 374, 6b2–3.

890. Tsong kha pa, *Sngags rim chen mo*, 18–19; an English translation in Hopkins 1977, 111–113.

891. Tib. *rin po che lta bu'i gang zag.*

892. Mkhas grub rje, *Bskyed rim dngos grub rgya mtsho*, 76b3–4.

893. Candrakīrti, *Sgron gsal, Pradīpoddyotanaṭīkā*, Tōh 1785, 136a5–6; Chakravarti 1984, 162. See also Mkhas grub rje, *Bskyed rim dngos grub rgya mtsho*, 141b3–4.

894. Tsong kha pa, *Sgron gsal mchan*, 336a6.

that, when multiplied by eight, become sixty-four, and cite the *Vajraḍāka Tantra.*[895]

The Purpose of the Union with the Consort

The main goal of union with the consort during the tantric path is to attain the wisdom of great bliss—a mind that can realize emptiness and meditate on the union of bliss and emptiness. In this practice, the bodhicitta descends to the tip of the yogi's jewel but is not emitted. Tsongkhapa stresses that if the bodhicitta emerges outside, the ground for great bliss is destroyed.[896] But the realization of the union of bliss and emptiness for the sake of the yogi's own awakening is not the primary purpose of the union at this stage of the sādhana. The goal here is to emanate the maṇḍala of the Guhyasamāja, called the Supreme King of Maṇḍalas,[897] for the sake of others. In order to engender this maṇḍala, the yogi and his consort as the principal deity and his queen must be absorbed in union, and the bodhicitta must be drawn forth to the lotus of the mother.

At the same time, another purpose of the yoga with the consort here is to experience the four joys of the creation stage and to join bliss with emptiness so that all visualized appearance will arise as a display of bliss and emptiness. Khedrup Jé calls this "the main factor that makes the creation stage a ripener for the completion stage" and "a sublime essence of the path of the creation stage."[898] Still, as we saw, for inducing such a bliss, the yogi is advised to rely on a wisdom consort.

The union with the consort is the final step in the First Yoga, but it is not included in the core of the practice. The First Yoga consists of three parts: the core practices, the preparatory practices that precede the core, and the yoga with the consort that follows it. The union with the consort is a transitional

895. Tsong kha pa, *Sgron gsal mchan*, 508b2–3; Mkhas grub rje, *Bskyed rim dngos grub rgya mtsho*, 141b6–142a2. See the *Rdo rje mkha' 'gro rgyud, Vajraḍāka Tantra*, chap. 49, Tōh 370, 109a4–6; and Bhavabhadra's commentary on it, *Rdo rje mkha' 'gro'i rnam par bshad pa, Vajraḍākavivṛti*, chap. 49, Tōh 1415, 195a4–5 and 197b4–5. The list of the eight types of love is very similar to that of Āryadeva and the *Kāmasūtra*. See Āryadeva, *Spyod bsdus, Caryāmelāpakapradīpa*, Tōh 1803, 102a5–7; Sanskrit, Tibetan, and English translation in Wedemeyer 2007, B: 67a–b; Sanskrit and Tibetan in Pandey 2000, 93–94 and 341–342; the *Kāmasūtra* (Doniger and Kakar 2003, 28–74) and Gedün Chöpel (Hopkins 1992, 65–66).

896. Tsong kha pa, *Sgron gsal mchan*, 173b2–3.

897. Tib. *dkyil 'khor rgyal mchog*, Skt. *maṇḍalarājāgrī*.

898. Mkhas grub rje, *Bskyed rim dngos grub rgya mtsho*, 142b5–143a2.

step leading from the core practices, whose goal is soteriological, to the deeds for the sake of others that follow them at the end of the sādhana. As we saw, the purpose of the sādhana's core is to ripen for the transformation of the yogi's birth, death, and intermediate state into the three bodies of the Buddha. According to Tsongkhapa, this goal is completed when the yogi seals the visualization with the lord of the tathāgata family following the meditation on the triple sattvas that concludes the third transformation, that of rebirth into the nirmāṇakāya.[899] This is because other than the purification of the yogi's birth, death, and intermediate state, there is no saṃsāric element that serves as a ground of purification for the practice.

From now on, the yogis meditate on the sādhana as though they are endowed with the three bodies of the Buddha and everything they do is enlightened activity for the sake of all sentient beings. According to Butön and Tsongkhapa, the union with the consort that serves as a bridge between the first and the second samādhis is not applied to any saṃsāric event as its ground of purification, but rather to the deeds of buddhahood for the sake of the disciples in correspondence with the fruit.[900] This yoga reenacts the "past event" in the first chapter of the *Guhyasamāja Tantra*, when the tathāgata was absorbed in the samādhi of great passion and thereafter emanated the maṇḍala. During the sādhana, the fruit of the union with the consort is the Supreme King of Maṇḍalas in the next step of the practice. In this sense, the following steps of the sādhana are similar to those that precede the core practices, such as the deeds of the specially visualized deities.

(10) The Samādhis in the First Chapter of the Guhyasamāja Tantra *and Enacting Past Events*

Some general observations on the relationship between the *Guhyasamāja Tantra* and its practices have been presented above.[901] In what follows, we will focus on a series of samādhis in which the teacher of the *Guhyasamāja Tantra* abides in order to demonstrate the teachings. We will look at the hermeneutical methods used to locate the scriptural authority for various steps of

899. See the section "Sealing with the Lord of the Tathāgata Family" above.

900. Bu ston, *Mdor byas 'grel chen*, 49b4; Tsong kha pa, *Rnam gzhag rim pa'i rnam bshad*, 55a4–b5. See also Mkhas grub rje, *Bskyed rim dngos grub rgya mtsho*, 87a5–b6.

901. See the section "The Relationship between the *Guhyasamāja Tantra* and Its Sādhanas" above.

the sādhana in samādhis displayed in the first chapter of the *Guhyasamāja Tantra*.[902]

Tsongkhapa distinguishes two types of steps in his *Guhyasamāja Sādhana*: (1) steps that are purifiers of the grounds of purification—birth, death, and the intermediate state—and (2) steps that enact the enlightened deeds of a tathāgata in the first chapter of the *Guhyasamāja Tantra*. The first type has a substantial role in leading to a true transformation of the practitioners into enlightened beings, while the latter has a secondary effect. Regarding the second type, by enacting the "past events," yogis follow the example of the life of the Teacher of the *Guhyasamāja Tantra* and apply the fruit of their practice during their path by performing the deeds of enlightened beings. The terms used here are "past events"[903] and the "practices that follow them"[904]—the enactment of these deeds during the sādhana.

At the beginning of the *Guhyasamāja Tantra*, the Tathāgata is absorbed in union with the Vajra Queen and performs various "deeds" to demonstrate his teachings to the great assembly that surrounds him. As Vairocanavajra, he is absorbed in union in the samādhi called "the method of great passion of all tathāgatas" and makes the entire array of tathāgatas enter into his own body. These tathāgatas emerge as the four female buddhas[905] and the five vajra ladies of the sense objects.[906] Note that the female enlightened beings are present at the very beginning of the *Guhyasamāja Tantra*.

Next, in the first chapter of the *Guhyasamāja Tantra*, the Tathāgata in his appearance as Akṣobhya brings about the maṇḍala. Buddha Bodhicittavajra takes his seat at its center, and the five tathāgatas dwell in his heart. As soon as Bodhicittavajra dwells in absorption, the entire realm of space abides as having the vajra nature of all tathāgatas, and all sentient beings attain the bliss and mental rapture of all tathāgatas. Then Bodhicittavajra once more abides in absorption and empowers the personification of the great *vidyā* through the empowerment of the mantra of all tathāgatas; immediately, all tathāgatas see him as having three faces.

902. See Bentor 2009a.

903. Tib. *sngon byung*. This and the following term appear in the *Ye shes rdo rje kun las bsdus pa*, *Jñānavajrasamuccaya*, Tōh 450, 23b1 (not to be confused with the *Ye shes rdo rje kun las btus pa*, *Vajrajñānasamuccaya*, Tōh 447).

904. Tib. *rjes 'jug*.

905. Tib. Sangs rgyas spyan, Māmakī, Gos dkar mo, and Dam tshig sgrol ma, Skt. Locanā, Māmakī, Pāṇḍaravāsinī, and Samaya Tārā.

906. Tib. *gzugs*, *sgra*, *dri*, *ro*, *reg*, Skt. *rūpa*, *śabdha*, *gandha*, *rasa*, *sparśa*, Eng. forms, sounds, smells, tastes, and objects of touch.

This series of events and others are emulated and enacted by the yogis during the sādhana. But since the relationship between the *Guhyasamāja Tantra* and its practices is indeed far from obvious, Indian and Tibetan scholars link these past events to the meditation in different ways. At times, the hermeneutical methods, called the "seven ornaments,"[907] offered by the cycle of the Ārya tradition of the Guhyasamāja, especially in Candrakīrti's *Illuminating Lamp* and in one of the explanatory tantras,[908] are used to bridge the gap by explaining how specific passages in the *Guhyasamāja Tantra* are related to certain steps of the practice.

Often, a single passage of the *Guhyasamāja Tantra* is interpreted through more than one "ornament" to explain multiple steps of the sādhana. Usually, the interpretable meaning[909] is applied to the creation stage and the definitive meaning[910] to the completion stage. In more elaborate cases, as we will see, the four levels of interpretations—the literal, shared, hidden, and ultimate levels—are used to explain the practice. The shared level of interpretation is usually applied to the creation stage and the ultimate to the completion stage.

The Relationship between the Past Events and the Sādhana

Tsongkhapa relates the famous opening line of the *Guhyasamāja Tantra*, "The Blessed One was dwelling in the *bhaga* of the Vajra Queen," to the meditation on the source of phenomena.[911] Like the *bhaga* of the queen, the source of phenomena that encompasses the celestial mansion of the maṇḍala has the shape of a triangular pyramid, and thus denotes birth into a new state through the practice of the sādhana. When the yogis attain the goal of the tantric path, they too will become enlightened beings abiding in the *bhaga* of the Vajra Queen.

The first deed of the Blessed One, now called Great Vairocana-Vajra, is to absorb himself in union in the samādhi called "the method of great passion

907. Tib. *rgyan bdun*, Skt. *saptālaṃkāra*.

908. *Ye shes rdo rje kun las btus pa*, *Vajrajñānasamuccaya*, Tōh 447, 285b2–7.

909. Tib. *drang don*, Skt. *neyārtha*.

910. Tib. *nges don*, Skt. *nītārtha*.

911. Tib. *chos 'byung*, Skt. *dharmodaya*. Tsong kha pa, *Sgron gsal mchan*, 33a5–b3; and Mkhas grub rje, *Bskyed rim dngos grub rgya mtsho*, 44a6–45a6.

of all tathāgatas."[912] We have already discussed this topic in the section on the yoga with the consort above.

The next event in the first chapter is taken to be the past event of the emanation of the first maṇḍala. According to the *Guhyasamāja Tantra*:

> Then, the Tathāgata Akṣobhya blessed the immaculate square maṇḍala of Mahāsamaya in the *bhaga* of the Vajra Queen, the essence of the body, speech, and mind of all tathāgatas.[913]

In his *Illuminating Lamp*, Candrakīrti glosses "blessed" as "emanated," "in the *bhaga*" as "in the abode of wisdom," and "the maṇḍala of Mahāsamaya" as "the maṇḍala of Great Vajradhara."[914] In other words, the Tathāgata Akṣobhya emanated the maṇḍala of Great Vajradhara in the abode of wisdom.

Butön explains how this past event is related to the practice that follows it:

> This teaches that in the past event Akṣobhya emanated the celestial mansion of the maṇḍala at the center of the source of phenomena; and in the practice that follows, yogis should visualize the ground of wisdom,[915] the vajra ground, and the celestial mansion with the deity's seats.[916]

This past event, then, is the scriptural authority for the first stages in the core of the practice: the meditation on emptiness in the macrocosmic context, the visualization of the source of phenomena, the lotus, and the four disks and their merging into the crossed vajras, as well as the visualization of the celestial mansion with the seats of the deities.

Next, the *Guhyasamāja Tantra* describes this maṇḍala in a verse:

> Its essence is clarity,

912. Tib. *de bzhin gshegs pa thams cad kyi 'dod chag chen po'i tshul zhes bya ba'i ting nge 'dzin*, Skt. *sarvatathāgatamahārāgavajraṃ* [*nayaṃ*] *samādhi*. *Gsang 'dus*, chap. 1, Tōh 442; Zhol 2b2; Stog 3b3; Dunh, 1a3; Fremantle 1971, 176; and Matsunaga 1978, 4. The Derge edition and some of the Sanskrit manuscripts have "the vajra of great passion of all tathāgatas." See Tsong kha pa, *Sgron gsal mchan*, 53b3–54b2.

913. *Gsang 'dus*, chap. 1, Tōh 442; Zhol 2b7–3a1; Stog 4a1–2; Fremantle 1971, 178; and Matsunaga 1978, 5.

914. Candrakīrti, *Sgron gsal*, *Pradīpoddyotanaṭīkā*, Tōh 1785, 13b6; Chakravarti 1984, 19.

915. Tib. *ye shes kyi sa*, Skt. *jñānabhūmi*.

916. Bu ston, *Sgron gsal bshad sbyar*, 66a2–3.

replete with myriad forms,
suffused with clouds of buddhas,
pervaded with lambent light-rays
and endowed with disks, a clear one and so forth;
this is the abode of all tathāgatas.[917]

The *Illuminating Lamp* explains that "its essence is clarity" means that the deities inside the celestial mansion can be seen from outside, just as images appear within a crystal; "suffused with clouds of buddhas" refers to the deities dwelling in the maṇḍala; and the "disks" are the seats of the deities, the "clear one" is a lunar seat, and so forth.[918]

Both the *Vajrasattva Sādhana* and the *Sādhana Incorporating the Scripture* cite this verse as the scriptural authority for the visualization of the maṇḍala.[919] Butön understands the entire verse to describe only the celestial mansion without the deities residing there.[920] But Tsongkhapa maintains that the line "suffused with clouds of buddhas" indicates that not only the celestial mansion but also the deities are referred to here.[921]

The event that follows is regarded to be the past event anticipating the visualization of the lord of the specially visualized deities. The *Guhyasamāja Tantra* states:

Then the Blessed One, the Lord of the vajra body, speech, and mind

917. *Gsang 'dus*, chap. 1, Tōh 442; Zhol 3a1–2; Stog 4a2–3; Dunh 1b3–4; Fremantle 1971, v. 1; and Matsunaga 1978, v. 1.

918. Candrakīrti, *Sgron gsal, Pradīpoddyotanaṭīkā*, Tōh 1785, 14a1–2; Chakravarti 1984, 19.

919. Candrakīrti, *Rdo rje sems dpa'i sgrub thabs, Vajrasattva Sādhana*, Tōh 1814, 198b2–3; Luo and Tomabechi 2009, 12.8–13 and 44.13–45.2; Nāgārjuna, *Mdo bsre, Sādhanasūtramelāpaka*, Tōh 1797, 12a4–5. Mkhas grub rje deliberates whether there is a contradiction in the context of citing this verse in both works, but concludes that there is none. See his *Bskyed rim dngos grub rgya mtsho*, 69b3–70a4.

920. Bu ston, *Sgron gsal bshad sbyar*, 66a3. According to Bu ston, the deities take their seats in the maṇḍala only in the following event.

921. Tsong kha pa, *Sgron gsal mchan*, 58a3–b4. According to Tsongkhapa, this verse is a scriptural authority for the maṇḍalas of both the specially visualized deities and the Supreme King of Maṇḍalas, since their characteristics are similar. See his *Sgron gsal mchan*, 58a4 and 59a2. See also Mkhas grub rje, *Bskyed rim dngos grub rgya mtsho*, 70a4–5.

> of all tathāgatas, took his seat at the center of the great maṇḍala[922] of all the tathāgatas.[923]

The *Illuminating Lamp* explains that the Lord here is Great Vajradhara,[924] and in the practice that follows, according to Tsongkhapa's *Guhyasamāja Sādhana*, Vajradhara is the principal deity of the specially visualized deities.[925] Butön adds that the practice that follows this event is the instantaneous generation of the thirty-two specially visualized deities.[926]

The next step corresponds to the gathering of the specially visualized deities into the body. According to the *Guhyasamāja Tantra*:

> Then the Tathāgata Akṣobhya, the Tathāgata Ratnaketu, the Tathāgata Amitāyus, the Tathāgata Amoghasiddhi, and the Tathāgata Vairocana[927] entered[928] the heart of the Tathāgata Bodhicittavajra.[929]

Butön and Tsongkhapa maintain that Bodhicittavajra here is Vajradhara.[930] Note that previously it was Akṣobhya who blessed or emanated the maṇḍala; now Akṣobhya is included among the five tathāgatas who enter the principal deity of the maṇḍala. Butön explains this by saying that since the principal deity has changed, the former principal deity, Akṣobhya, has joined the deities that surround him. Tsongkhapa disagrees, explaining that the five tathāgatas

922. While the Sanskrit editions of the tantra have here *maṇḍala* or *mahāmaṇḍala* and the Tibetan translations in the Zhol and Stog editions have *dkyil 'khor chen po*, both the Derge and Peking edition of Candrakīrti's *Sgron gsal*, *Vajrasattva Sādhana*, have *dam tshig chen po'i dkyil 'khor* here; the Sanskrit is *mahāsamayamaṇḍala*, meaning "the maṇḍala of mahāsamaya."

923. *Gsang 'dus*, chap. 1, Tōh 442; Zhol 3a2–3; Stog 4a3–4; Fremantle 1971, 178; and Matsunaga 1978, 5.

924. Tib. Rdo rje 'chang chen po, Skt. Mahāvajradhara. Candrakīrti, *Sgron gsal*, *Pradīpoddyotanaṭīkā*, Tōh 1785, 14a2–3; Chakravarti 1984, 19. This is the explanation in the interpretable meaning.

925. Tsong kha pa, *Gsang mngon*, 31a4.

926. Bu ston, *Sgron gsal bshad sbyar*, 66a4.

927. Tib. Mi bskyod pa, Rin chen dpal, Tshe dpag tu med pa, Gdon mi zab bar grub pa, and Rnam par sang mdzad.

928. The Sanskrit edition has "abided in."

929. *Gsang 'dus*, chap. 1, Tōh 442; Zhol 3a3–5; Stog 4a4–6; Fremantle 1971, 178; and Matsunaga 1978, 5.

930. Bu ston, *Sgron gsal bshad sbyar*, 66b1–3. Tsong kha pa, *Sgron gsal mchan*, 59a4–6.

in the past event represent the entire families of the five tathāgatas—comprised of the thirty-one specially visualized deities—that enter the yogi as the principal deity in the practice that follows this past event.[931]

Both scholars agree that this line of the *Guhyasamāja Tantra* is the scriptural authority for the meditation on gathering the specially visualized deities into the body. In this step of the sādhana, each of the deities enter a specific location on the yogi's body and become inseparable with the bodily constituents: the five buddhas with the aggregates, the four mothers with the four physical elements, the vajra ladies with the sensory spheres, the bodhisattvas with the sense bases, and the fierce deities with the limbs of the body.[932]

The following step in the practice is the deeds of the specially visualized deities. Next, the *Guhyasamāja Tantra* teaches:

> Then, the Blessed One, the Tathāgata Bodhicittavajra, dwelt in absorption in the samādhi called "vajra overpowering of all tathāgatas."[933] As soon as the Blessed One, the lord of all tathāgatas, dwelt in absorption, the entire realm of space abided in the vajra nature of all tathāgatas. Then, as many as there were sentient beings residing in the entire realm of space, through the blessing of Vajrasattva all of them attained the bliss and mental rapture of all tathāgatas.[934]

The hermeneutical methods employed by the *Illuminating Lamp* to explain the previous passages are the interpretable meaning and the definitive meaning. Only the interpretable meanings have been presented above, since they alone apply to the creation stage.[935] In explaining the present passage, the *Illuminating Lamp* employs the hermeneutical method called the "four ways,"[936] using three of the four:[937] the shared, the hidden, and the ultimate levels of interpretations. The shared level of interpretation is applied here to the deeds

931. Tsong kha pa, *Sgron gsal mchan*, 61b6–62a3.

932. See Tsong kha pa, *Gsang mngon*, 37b6–38b3.

933. Tib. *de bzhin gshegs pa thams cad zil gyis gnon pa rdo rje zhes bya ba'i ting nge 'dzin*, Skt. *sarvatathāgatābhibhavanavajra samādhi*.

934. *Gsang 'dus*, chap. 1, Tōh 442; Zhol 3a5–b1; Stog 4a6–7 [the rest is missing]; Fremantle 1971, 178; and Matsunaga 1978, 5.

935. The definitive meaning is applied to the completion stage.

936. Tib. *tshul bzhi*.

937. The way of interpretation not employed here is the literal meaning.

of the specially visualized deities during the creation stage, the hidden to the experience of great bliss, and the ultimate to the completion stage.

On the shared level of interpretation, the *Illuminating Lamp* glosses the line "the entire realm of space abided in the vajra nature of all tathāgatas" in the *Guhyasamāja Tantra* as "came to be residents in the maṇḍala of Great Vajradhara."[938] In other words, everyone in the entire space realm entered the maṇḍala of Vajradhara so that he would initiate them. The line "through the blessing of Vajrasattva all [sentient beings] attained the bliss and mental rapture of all tathāgatas" is interpreted thus: "attained Vajrasattva-hood and thereby attained bliss and mental rapture." The *Illuminating Lamp* concludes its explanation of this past event by saying: "In this way, [the yogis] generate Great Vajradhara through special visualization."[939]

This explains the practice as described in the sādhanas. Before being gathered into the body, the specially visualized deities perform their enlightened deeds of initiating all sentient beings. In Tsongkhapa's *Guhyasamāja Sādhana*, the yogis emanate light rays from their hearts that draw all sentient beings into the maṇḍala, and in the maṇḍala they are initiated.[940] In this way, all sentient beings attain the bliss and mental rapture of all the tathāgatas; becoming Vajrasattva, they proceed to their own buddha field. This step of the practice is not found in any of the four main Indian Guhyasamāja sādhanas, but various Tibetan scholars, including Rangjung Dorjé, Butön, Ngorchen Kunga Sangpo, and Tsongkhapa, instruct yogis to meditate on these deeds.[941]

The scriptural authority for this step is the past event in the *Guhyasamāja Tantra* cited above. According to Khedrup Jé, yogis emulate here

> the deeds of the Teacher, Vajradhara, who, at the beginning of the tantra taught by him,[942] emanated a maṇḍala and conferred initiation on all sentient beings. In following the exemplary life of the Teacher in the past event, disciples apply the fruit of the practice on the path.[943]

938. Candrakīrti, *Sgron gsal, Pradīpoddyotanaṭīkā*, Tōh 1785, 14b7; Chakravarti 1984, 20.

939. Tib. *lhag par mos pas*, Skt. *adhimokṣeṇa*. Candrakīrti, *Sgron gsal, Pradīpoddyotana*, Tōh 1785, 15a7–b1; Chakravarti 1984, 20.

940. Tsong kha pa, *Gsang mngon*, 37b3–6.

941. Rang byung rdo rje, *Gsang ba 'dus pa'i sgrub pa'i thabs phyi nang gzhan gsum gsal ba*, 5a4–6. Bu ston, *Mdor byas 'grel chen*, 27a4–7. Ngor chen, *Gsang 'dus dkyil 'khor gyi sgrub thabs dngos grub rgya mtsho*, 8b5–9a1. Tsong kha pa, *Sgron gsal mchan*, 62a6.

942. That is, the *Guhyasamāja Tantra*.

943. Mkhas grub rje, *Bskyed rim dngos grub rgya mtsho*, 89a2–3; see also 90b1.

Thus, during their meditation on the sādhana, yogis take their own future enlightened activities on the path. As enlightened beings motivated by great compassion, they will engage in enlightened activities, such as acting for the sake of sentient beings, according to the teachings of the Mahāyāna.

When the *Illuminating Lamp* explains the same past event employing the hidden level of interpretation, it applies it to the experience of bliss. Here is the event in the tantra once more:

> Then, the Blessed One, the Tathāgata Bodhicittavajra, dwelt in absorption in the samādhi called "vajra overpowering of all tathāgatas." As soon as the Blessed One, the lord of all tathāgatas, dwelt in absorption, the entire realm of space abided in the vajra nature of all tathāgatas. Then, as many as there were sentient beings residing in the entire realm of space, through the blessing of Vajrasattva all of them attained the bliss and mental rapture of all tathāgatas.

The *Illuminating Lamp* explains it thus (the lines of the *Guhyasamāja Tantra* commented upon here are in italics):

> *As soon as the Blessed One, the lord of all tathāgatas, dwelt in absorption, the entire realm of space*, that is to say, the empty interior of the seventy-two thousand channels, *abided in the vajra essence of all tathāgatas*, that is to say, partook in the nature of wisdom of skillful methods. *Then, through the blessing of Vajrasattva,* that is to say, through the arising of skillful wisdom, *all sentient beings*, that is to say, the psycho-physical constituents, the aggregates, and so forth, *in the entire space realm, as many as were there, attained the bliss and mental rapture of all tathāgatas*, that is to say, when they joined their organs, they were melted by the fire of great passion and experienced the bliss of supreme joy. This is the hidden level of interpretation.[944]

In the hidden level of interpretation, the space realm is not external, but found within the channels of the subtle body; "all sentient beings" means the aggregates, sensory spheres, and sense bases within the body. When the father-mother abide in union, they experience the bliss of supreme joy. Tsongkhapa adds that Vajrasattva blesses with the jasmine-like drop of bodhicitta

944. Candrakīrti, *Sgron gsal, Pradīpoddyotanaṭīkā*, Tōh 1785, 15a2–5; Chakravarti 1984, 20.

that pervades the seventy-two thousand hollow channels within the bodies of the father-mother.[945] When they join their organs, it is the bodhicitta that is melted by the fire of great passion. It descends within the channels and blesses their aggregates, sensory spheres, and sense bases, leading the father-mother to experience bliss or *attain the bliss and mental rapture of all tathāgatas*. The father-mother are then overwhelmed with bliss or *overpowered* by it. Therefore the samādhi is called "vajra overpowering of all tathāgatas."

The *Illuminating Lamp* is not explicit about to which step in the sādhana or in "the practice that follows" the past event in the *Guhyasamāja Tantra* is related. Still, we may assume that it refers to the union with the consort. Butön indeed applies the past event to the union with the consort in the sādhana, as well as to the secret offerings.[946] Tsongkhapa elaborates on this by differentiating between the hidden level of interpretation that is applied to the path and the hidden level of interpretation that is applied to the ground.[947] When applied to the path, this passage teaches that by absorbing themselves in union, the yogi and the consort generate the wisdom of bliss and emptiness.[948]

The ground of purification in this case is the moment of conception in which the intermediate being takes birth in the mingled drop of the parents' semen and blood. In the future life of the yogi, this moment will eventually be replaced with a divine conception as a deity. We may recall that the yogis practice the sādhana in order to purify their future death, birth, and intermediate state. The step during the creation stage that serves to transform the future moment of conception is the transformation of the First Lord into Vajrasattva's nirmāṇakāya. Tsongkhapa finds the scriptural authority for this in *Formulating the Sādhana*, which mentions the samādhi called "vajra overpowering of all tathāgatas" in the context of its explanation of conception on the ground of purification.[949]

Tsongkhapa elaborates even further on this past event by adding another hermeneutical method to explain it: the literal level of interpretation,[950] which

945. Tsong kha pa, *Sgron gsal mchan*, 63a1–6. See also Mkhas grub rje, *Bskyed rim dngos grub rgya mtsho*, 112b1–113a5.

946. Bu ston, *Sgron gsal bshad sbyar*, 69b7–70a5.

947. Tsong kha pa, *Sgron gsal mchan*, 63a6–b1; Mkhas grub rje, *Bskyed rim dngos grub rgya mtsho*, 112a5–6.

948. Tib. *bde stong gi ye shes*.

949. Tsong kha pa, *Rnam gzhag rim pa'i rnam bshad*, 35b5–36a2. See Nāgabuddhi, *Rnam gzhag rim pa*, *Vyavastholi*, chap. 1, Tōh 1809, 124a2–3; Tanaka 2016, 93.

950. Tib. *tshig gi don* or *yi ge'i don*, Skt. *akṣarārtha*.

is not found in the *Illuminating Lamp*.[951] His goal is to support his position concerning one of the points in which he differs from other lamas.[952] By supplying his own literal level of interpretation, he is able to illustrate that the transformation of the First Lord into Vajrasattva's nirmāṇakāya corresponds to conception and that the First Lord who enters into Akṣobhya in his *Guhyasamāja Sādhana*[953] corresponds to the intermediate being, as discussed above.

Finally, when explained in the ultimate level of interpretation, this past event refers to the yogis meditating on the completion stage who visualize the illusory body dissolving into clear light, thereby realizing the actual clear light and purifying their mental proliferations of dualistic appearances.[954]

Completion of the Four Yogas

The *Guhyasamāja Tantra* continues:

> Then the Blessed One, the Tathāgata, Bodhicittavajra, was absorbed in the samādhi called the "vajra origination from samaya of the vajra body, speech, and mind of all tathāgatas,"[955] and blessed this personification[956] of the great *vidyā*[957] with the blessing of the mantra of all tathāgatas. As soon as the Blessed One, the Tathāgata Bodhicittavajra, gave his blessing, all tathāgatas perceived him as having three faces.[958]

951. Tsong kha pa, *Sgron gsal mchan*, 63b2–6; Mkhas grub rje, *Bskyed rim dngos grub rgya mtsho*, 113a5–b5. Bu ston aptly notes that in *Rnam gzhag rim pa, Vyavastholi*, Nāgabuddhi applies this event to the transformation into the nirmāṇakāya during the atiyoga. See his *Sgron gsal bshad sbyar*, 70a5.

952. See the section "The Yoga of Taking Rebirth on the Path That Leads to the Nirmāṇakāya" above.

953. Tsong kha pa, *Gsang mngon*, 40a1–6.

954. See Candrakīrti, *Sgron gsal, Pradīpoddyotanaṭīkā*, Tōh 1785, 15a5–7; Chakravarti 1984, 20; Tsong kha pa, *Sgron gsal mchan*, 63a6–64a4; Mkhas grub rje, *Bskyed rim dngos grub rgya mtsho*, 112a4–5.

955. Tib. *dam tshig 'byung ba rdo rje'i zhes bya ba'i ting nge 'dzin*, Skt. *samayodbhavavajra samādhi*.

956. Tib. *skyes bu gzugs*, Skt. *puruṣamūrti*.

957. Tib. *rig pa chen po*, Skt. *mahāvidyā*.

958. *Gsang 'dus*, chap. 1, Tōh 442; Zhol 3b1–3, Stog missing; Dunh 3a4–b1; Fremantle 1971, 178; and Matsunaga 1978, 5–6.

In explaining this passage in the interpretable meaning, the *Illuminating Lamp* says that these lines teach the visualization of the totally pure and impure bodies of the deities.[959] Tsongkhapa adds that the visualization of the deities briefly taught above[960] is now taught once more.[961] The yogis visualize the deities by generating "a personification of the great *vidyā*" through the five manifest awakenings and bless it with the mantras of all tathāgatas—in other words, they place the mantras on the visualized deity.[962]

According to the *Illuminating Lamp*, these lines of the *Guhyasamāja Tantra* "indicate that by means of the method taught in the sādhana consisting of the four yogas, up to the end of the meditation on the triple sattvas, the meditator is blessed as the embodiment of great Vajradhara, the rūpakāya of all mantras."[963] Hence, these lines refer to the entire core of the practice of generating oneself as the deity Vajradhara, following the description in the sādhana, subsumed under the four yogas, yoga, subsequent yoga, higher yoga, and great yoga, up to and including the meditation on the triple sattvas, the samayasattva, jñānasattva, and samādhisattva.

As soon as the Tathāgata Bodhicittavajra blesses the personification, all tathāgatas perceive him as having three faces—in other words, they see him as the Guhyasamāja deity endowed with three faces. *Formulating the Sādhana* cites these lines in the context of rebirth from the womb, and specifically relates the past event in which all the tathāgatas see Bodhicittavajra to the moment a newborn child becomes an object of the corporeal eye on the ground of purification.[964] Tsongkhapa concludes: "Nāgabuddhi maintains that the passage in the *Guhyasamāja Tantra* teaches both the stage of samsaric rebirth [on the level of the ground] and the generation of the body of the deity that is similar to that [during the practice]."[965]

959. Candrakīrti, *Sgron gsal*, *Pradīpoddyotanaṭīkā*, Tōh 1785, 15b1; Chakravarti 1984, 20. According to Bu ston, the *totally pure body* is the body of wisdom, while the *impure body* is the body of mantra. See his *Sgron gsal bshad sbyar*, 70b3–4. The mantra body (Tib. *sngags kyi sku*, Skt. *mantramūrti*) and the wisdom body (Tib. *ye shes kyi sku*, Skt. *jñānamūrti*) are the bodies of the deity visualized during the creation stage and the completion stage respectively.

960. The maṇḍala emanated by Akṣobhya above that was described in a verse.

961. Tsong kha pa, *Sgron gsal mchan*, 64a4–65a3.

962. See also Bu ston, *Sgron gsal bshad sbyar*, 70b6–71a2.

963. Candrakīrti, *Sgron gsal*, *Pradīpoddyotanaṭīkā*, Tōh 1785, 15b4–5; Chakravarti 1984, 21.

964. Nāgabuddhi, *Rnam gzhag rim pa*, *Vyavastholi*, chap. 1, Tōh 1809, 124b4–6; Tanaka 2016, 96–97.

965. Tsong kha pa, *Rnam gzhag rim pa'i rnam bshad*, 42a2–3.

Formulating the Sādhana relates several events on the ground, path, and fruit of the practice. The event on the ground is the emergence of the fetus from the womb; the event on the fruit is the past event described in the *Guhyasamāja Tantra* in which Bodhicittavajra is perceived as having three faces; and the event on the path is the yogi's completion of the first part of the creation stage through the four yogas, in which he maintains divine pride.[966] Moreover, *Formulating the Sādhana* cites verses here on the identification of the ordinary body, consisting of the five aggregates and so forth, with the five buddhas and so forth, thus indicating a transformation from the ordinary body on the ground to the divine at the fruit.[967] In other words, instead of the ordinary rebirth that awaits ordinary people, the yogi who has completed the four yogas will be reborn as the deity.

Tsongkhapa further develops the correspondences between the intermediate being and rebirth on the ground, the saṃbhogakāya and nirmāṇakāya on the fruit, and the deities visualized during the creation stage on the path. He links the transformation of the fetus on the ground, the fetus that emerges from the womb and becomes an object of the corporeal eye, to the transformation of the saṃbhogakāya to the nirmāṇakāya on the fruit, which is effected in order to be seen by ordinary disciples who cannot perceive the saṃbhogakāya.[968] Likewise, the first deity generated on the path, the deity that corresponds to the intermediate being, is described in the *Sādhana Incorporating the Scripture*: "the personification of the great *vidyā*, the body whose nature is wisdom, cannot act for the sake of sentient beings..."[969] Therefore, during the sādhana, this deity is transformed into Vajrasattva's nirmāṇakāya.

We see a perfect interweaving of the ground, path, and fruit at the moment that the core practices of the sādhana are completed, when instead of ordinary rebirth in the future, the yogis arise as emanations of the deities. Khedrup Jé concludes: "Thus it is taught that the stage that replaces rebirth is identical to transformation-into-the-nirmāṇakāya."[970]

966. Nāgabuddhi has here: "the mantrin should develop divine pride with the resolve: 'This which has been achieved through the four yogas, that am I.'" See his *Rnam gzhag rim pa*, *Vyavastholi*, chap. 1, Tōh 1809, 124b7–125a1; Tanaka 2016, 97–98.

967. Nāgabuddhi quotes the *Lha mo bzhis zhus pa*, *Caturdevīparipṛcchā*, Tōh 446, 279b7–280a1. The Tibetan translation of this tantra is different from the passage in the *Rnam gzhag rim pa*.

968. Tsong kha pa, *Sgron gsal mchan*, 65b5–6.

969. Nāgārjuna, *Mdo bsre*, *Sādhanasūtramelāpaka*, Tōh 1797, 12b4–5.

970. Mkhas grub rje, *Bskyed rim dngos grub rgya mtsho*, 102a4.

Disputes

This last point is crucial for Tsongkhapa in his argument that all the steps of the sādhana—up to and including the meditation on the triple sattvas—serve to purify the yogi's death, birth, and intermediate state, which are taken on the path to the three bodies of the Buddha. Tsongkhapa points out:

> In this case, early scholars apply the stages of the practice up to the blessing of the three places to the period in the womb, and the meditation on the triple sattvas to the body emerging from the womb, the winds that abide in it, and the "short a."[971] Later lamas apply the placement of the body maṇḍala to the period in the womb, and the meditation on the blessing of the three places as well as on the triple sattvas to the newborn child.[972]

In another work, Tsongkhapa concludes:

> Therefore the early [scholars] who apply the meditation on the triple sattvas to the newborn one, as well as some later [lamas] who apply the meditation on both the blessing of the body, speech, and mind and on the triple sattvas to the newborn child, contradict both scriptures" [the *Guhyasamāja Tantra* and *Formulating the Sādhana*].[973]

We can identify one of the early scholars as Gö Khukpa Lhetsé, who claims exactly what the early scholars are said to have claimed:

> The ground of purification of the triple sattvas is the ordinary body emerging from the womb, the winds that abides in it, and the "short a" that abides in this body.[974]

One of the "later lamas" is Butön, who maintains that the blessing of the body, speech, and mind is applied not only to the newborn child but to

971. The "short a" in this context refers to the indestructible drop at the heart.

972. Tsong kha pa, *Rnam gzhag rim pa'i rnam bshad*, 43a6–b2.

973. Tsong kha pa, *Sgron gsal mchan*, 65b3–4. See also Mkhas grub rje, *Bskyed rim dngos grub rgya mtsho*, 115a5–b1.

974. 'Gos Khug pa lhas btsas, *Gsang 'dus stong thun*, 13b3–4.

his or her entire life.[975] Moreover, Butön does not completely agree with Candrakīrti's explanation of this past event. As we saw, in the *Illuminating Lamp*, Candrakīrti says that the past event:

> indicates that by means of the method taught in the sādhana consisting of the four yogas, up to the end of the meditation on the triple sattvas, the meditator is blessed as the embodiment of great Vajradhara, the rūpakāya of all mantras.[976]

Thus, according to the *Illuminating Lamp*, only when all four yogas are completed—including the meditation on the triple sattvas—does the yogi assume the rūpakāya of the creation stage. According to Butön:

> Even though the commentary [*Illuminating Lamp*] explains the transformation into the nirmāṇakāya as if it takes place at the end of the meditation on the triple sattvas, it was explained in this way due to convenience. But the meditation manuals do not present it in this way, for in the sādhanas of the two masters, the transformation into the nirmāṇakāya occurs during the "higher yoga."[977]

As we noticed before,[978] the four main sādhanas of the Ārya tradition of the *Guhyasamāja Tantra* do not prescribe identical practices, and one of the major points of difference relates to the "higher yoga," the third among the four yogas. Moreover, the four main sādhanas vary in their demarcation of the steps of the practice. Thus different scholars can choose from the four sādhanas the one that supports their position. Butön has chosen in this case the *Vajrasattva Sādhana*, which identifies our past event in the *Guhyasamāja Tantra* with the attainment of the nirmāṇakāya and the end of the "higher yoga," rather than with the completion of all four yogas.[979]

On the other hand, Tsongkhapa does accept Candrakīrti's position that through the stages of the four yogas, up to and including the meditation on

975. Bu ston, *Mdor byas 'grel chen*, 45b1–3.

976. Candrakīrti, *Sgron gsal*, *Pradīpoddyotanaṭīkā*, Tōh 1785, 15b4–5; Chakravarti 1984, 21.

977. Bu ston, *Sgron gsal bshad sbyar*, 71a6–7.

978. See the section "The Guhyasamāja Sādhanas of the Ārya School" above.

979. Bu ston, takes the line "by means of the method taught in the sādhana" in the *Sgron gsal* to refer to the *Mdor byas* and the *Rdo rje sems dpa'i sgrub thabs*. See Candrakīrti, *Rdo rje sems dpa'i sgrub thabs*, *Vajrasattva Sādhana*, Tōh 1814, 200a4–5; Luo and Tomabechi 2009, 18.6–9 and 50.18–51.3.

the triple sattvas, the yogis appear as Vajradhara with three faces.[980] Hence, for Tsongkhapa, the yogis must practice all four yogas before they assume nirmāṇakāya at the end of the "great yoga," the fourth yoga. For this reason, Tsongkhapa glosses "the sādhana" in the *Illuminating Lamp* as the *Concise Sādhana* that, unlike the *Vajrasattva Sādhana*, does not state that the nirmāṇakāya is assumed at the end of "higher yoga," but rather proceeds to the "great yoga."

The present dispute is unique in the sense that later generations of Geluk scholars tried to identify the opponents. We saw that as a rule, the names of the opponents are not spelled out; in this case, Tsongkhapa called them "early scholars" and "later lamas." Still, even though Norsang Gyatso "identified" "the early scholars" here, he was corrected by later generations who were further removed from the events. Norsang Gyatso attributed the position of the early scholars to Butön,[981] whereas Panchen Losang Chökyi Gyaltsen, who otherwise does not name names in his *Essence of the Ocean of Attainments*, identifies these opponents as followers of Gö Khukpa Lhetsé, and we have seen that such a position is indeed found in one of Gö's works.[982]

As is often the case, the dispute here addresses what might seem a very minor point. Still, much ink was spilled on this matter by Butön, Tsongkhapa, Khedrup Jé, and others, because it bears consequences for explanations regarding the meaning and purpose of the different steps of the creation stage.

The Supreme King of Maṇḍalas

Next, the *Guhyasamāja Tantra* describes the events that follow the perception of the three-faced Bodhicittavajra. All the tathāgatas sing praises, make offerings, prostrate themselves, and request that Bodhicittavajra explain the *Guhyasamāja Tantra*. After repeated requests:

> Then, the Blessed One, the Tathāgata, Vajra-body-speech-and-mind of all tathāgatas, being attentive to the request for teaching made by all tathāgatas, was absorbed in the samādhi called "vajra lamp of wisdom"[983] and induced the quintessential supreme [man-

980. Tsong kha pa, *Sgron gsal mchan*, 65a1–3.

981. Nor bzang rgya mtsho, *Gsang ba 'dus pa'i bskyed rim gyi don gsal bar byed pa'i sgron me*, 123a2–3.

982. Paṇ chen Blo bzang chos kyi rgyal mtshan, *Bskyed rim dngos grub rgya mtsho'i snying po*, 54a6. See Bentor and Dorjee 2019.

983. Tib. *ye shes sgron ma rdo rje*, Skt. *jñānapradīpavajra*.

> tra] of the tathāgata family of hatred, *vajradhṛk*, to issue forth from his own vajra body, speech, and mind. Once he was induced to issue forth,[984] the Blessed One, personification of the *vidyā* of the body, speech, and mind of all tathāgatas, in union with the great consort of Akṣobhya, appearing in black, white, and red colors, entered[985] the vajra body, speech, and mind of all tathāgatas.[986]

The *Illuminating Lamp* points out that this past event "indicates the maṇḍala emanated [immediately] after the First Yoga."[987] In other words, this refers to the Supreme King of Maṇḍalas emanated for the sake of leading other sentient beings to enlightenment in accordance with the bodhisattva ideal. The *Illuminating Lamp* continues to explain that having arisen from his samādhi, called the "vajra lamp of wisdom" of Akṣobhya, the Blessed One observes the realm of sentient beings bound by the five afflictive emotions. Knowing that "'I am the essence of awakening,' in order to purify the afflictive emotion of hatred of the disciples, he *induced the quintessential supreme [mantra] of the tathāgata family of hatred*, vajradhṛk, *to issue forth from his own vajra body, speech, and mind*... This is the first vajra being that issues forth."[988] (The lines of the *Guhyasamāja Tantra* commented upon here are in italics.)[989]

Tsongkhapa expands on this, maintaining that this explains how Akṣobhya, the first deity among the thirteen deities, issues forth or emanates, enters into the principal deity, and then takes his seat in the maṇḍala.[990] These thirteen deities are the deities who emanate at the end of the first chapter of the *Guhyasamāja Tantra*. After Akṣobhya purifies the disciples' afflictive emotion of hatred,[991] Vairocana purifies their afflictive emotions of delusion or ignorance,[992] and Lokeśvara (Amitābha) purifies their passion.[993] While the

984. According to the Sanskrit edition, "this was uttered."

985. According to the Sanskrit edition, "took his place."

986. *Gsang 'dus*, chap. 1, Tōh 442; Zhol 4a2–4; Stog 5b1–5; Fremantle 1971, 182; and Matsunaga 1978, 6.

987. Candrakīrti, *Sgron gsal*, *Pradīpoddyotanaṭīkā*, Tōh 1785, 18a5; Chakravarti 1984, 23.

988. According to the Sanskrit edition, "issuing forth from vajra being."

989. Candrakīrti, *Sgron gsal*, *Pradīpoddyotanaṭīkā*, Tōh 1785, 17b2–18a2; Chakravarti 1984, 23.

990. Tsong kha pa, *Sgron gsal mchan*, 73b2–3.

991. Tib. *zhe sdang*, Skt. *dveṣa*.

992. Tib. *gti mug*, Skt. *moha*.

993. Tib. *'dod chags*, Skt. *rāga*.

Guhyasamāja Tantra does not specify the afflictive emotions purified by each of the deities, the *Concise Sādhana* elaborates on this and Tsongkhapa's *Guhyasamāja Sādhana* follows it. In this way, during the Supreme King of Maṇḍalas, the yogis act for the sake of other sentient beings.

Conclusion

To conclude the section on the samādhis in the first chapter of the *Guhyasamāja Tantra*, we have examined how the *Illuminating Lamp* uses tantric hermeneutical methods to interpret the "past events" that appear in the *Guhyasamāja Tantra*, linking them to the sādhana in which yogis assume the three Buddha's bodies of the creation stage for their own sake and the sake of all sentient beings. The process of employing tantric hermeneutics to support specific practices did not stop at the Tibetan border. In Tibet, too, Candrakīrti's *Illuminating Lamp* would continue to be interpreted in light of the practices of different schools.

We observed the reasoning offered by Indian and Tibetan commentators in relating specific passages in the first chapter of the *Guhyasamāja Tantra* to certain steps of the sādhana, although the *Guhyasamāja Tantra* does not seem to describe this practice in a straightforward way. We saw that even though the practices that Butön and Tsongkhapa adhere to are very similar, and even though their commentaries are based on the same texts, in many cases their explanations are at variance. They differ not only with regard to the specific passages of the *Guhyasamāja Tantra* that they identify as the scriptural source for various steps of the sādhana, but also in their explanations of the meaning and purpose of these steps.

9. Concluding Practices: The Supreme Kings

According to both the *Sādhana Incorporating the Scripture* and the *Vajrasattva Sādhana*, the main part of the practice is comprised of three yogas: the First Yoga,[994] also called the Supreme King of Samādhis;[995] the Supreme King of Maṇḍalas;[996] and the Supreme King of Deeds.[997] The last step of the First Yoga, the union with the consort, is a transitional step leading from the First Yoga to the Supreme King of Maṇḍalas, in which the thirty-two deities conceived during the union with the consort emanate outside, perform their purificatory deeds, and take their seats in the maṇḍala, for this reason called the emanated maṇḍala.

Recall that according to the *Sādhana Incorporating the Scripture*, *Formulating the Sādhana*, and the *Vajrasattva Sādhana*, the First Yoga is practiced for the yogi's own sake, while the Supreme Kings are for the benefit of others.[998] Here is the explanation of the *Vajrasattva Sādhana*:

> Thus far you have practiced the Supreme King of Samādhis, which consists of excellent qualities for your own enlightenment, thus becoming an embodiment of the triple sattvas by means of the four yogas. Now you should engage in the display of the samādhi

994. Tib. *dang po sbyor ba*, Skt. *ādiyoga* [samādhi]. These terms are found also in Candrakīrti, *Sgron gsal*, *Pradīpoddyotanaṭīkā*, chap. 1, Tōh 1785, 18a5; Chakravarti 1984, 23.

995. Tib. *ting nge 'dzin rgyal po mchog*, Skt. *samādhirājāgrī*. See Candrakīrti, *Rdo rje sems dpa'i sgrub thabs*, *Vajrasattva Sādhana*, Tōh 1814, 201b5–6; Luo and Tomabechi 2009, 23.9–10 and 57.2–3.

996. Tib. *dkyil 'khor rgyal mchog*, Skt. *maṇḍalarājāgrī*. The Sanskrit term *maṇḍalarājāgrī* is found also in Candrakīrti, *Sgron gsal*, *Pradīpoddyotanaṭīkā*, Chakravarti 1984, 115.

997. Tib. *las kyi rgyal mchog*, Skt. *karmarājāgrīsamādhi*.

998. Nāgārjuna, *Mdo bsre*, *Sādhanasūtramelāpaka*, Tōh 1797, 14a3–4. Nāgabuddhi, *Rnam gzhag rim pa*, *Vyavastholi*, chap. 3, Tōh 1809, 126a6; Tanaka 2016, 105. Candrakīrti, *Rdo rje sems dpa'i sgrub thabs*, *Vajrasattva Sādhana*, Tōh 1814, 201b5–5; Luo and Tomabechi 2009, 23.9–11 and 57.1–5.

> called the Supreme King of Maṇḍalas for the purpose of enlightening others.[999]

Hence, while the First Yoga and more specifically the core practices subsumed in the four yogas—yoga, subsequent yoga, higher yoga, and great yoga—are soteriological practices for the yogi's own awakening, the Supreme Kings are practices for the sake of other beings according to the bodhisattva ideal. Here, the maṇḍala with its thirty-two deities is emanated outside; the deities engage in activities such as turning the wheel of the Dharma and purifying the disciples' mental afflictions, including clinging, hindrances, and so forth. These meditations correspond to the deeds of the Tathāgata at the level of the fruit and serve to ripen the meditators to the actual fruit.[1000] Hence, these steps of the meditation are not purifiers, but rather enactments of the deeds of the awakened ones that serve to ripen the actual fruit of the yogis.

In his commentary on *Formulating the Sādhana*, Tsongkhapa relates the steps of the sādhana during the Supreme Kings to various aspects of the deeds of the Buddha.[1001] The step of emanating the Supreme King of Maṇḍalas[1002] and performing general and specific deeds for the sake of sentient beings[1003] is similar to the Deed of the Body, in which the Buddha acts for the sake of others by emanating a body of the deity. The subtle meditation at the beginning of the Supreme King of Deeds is related to the Buddha's Deed of the Mind—abiding in an inward perfect peace.[1004] The mantra recitation for arousing the heart of the deities[1005] is similar to the Deed of Speech, the teaching of the Dharma. The dissolution of the principal father-mother of the Supreme King of Maṇḍalas[1006] is similar to the Buddha, who, after completing the deeds for the sake of his disciples, displayed nirvāṇa in that buddhafield. The four goddesses, who are the nature of the four qualities beyond measure, who arouse

999. Candrakīrti, *Rdo rje sems dpa'i sgrub thabs, Vajrasattva Sādhana*, Tōh 1814, 201b5–5; Luo and Tomabechi 2009, 23.9–11 and 57.1–5.

1000. Mkhas grub rje, *Bskyed rim dngos grub rgya mtsho*, 147a3–6.

1001. Tsong kha pa, *Rnam gzhag rim pa'i rnam bshad*, 55a5–b5; Mkhas grub rje, *Bskyed rim dngos grub rgya mtsho*, 87a6–b6. Mkhas grub rje's description is similar to that of Tsong kha pa, though not completely identical to it.

1002. Tsong kha pa, *Gsang mngon*, 52a4–59b3.

1003. Tsong kha pa, *Gsang mngon*, 59b3–67b1.

1004. See also Bu ston, *Mdor byas 'grel chen*, 51b3.

1005. Tsong kha pa, *Gsang mngon*, 67b3–68a6.

1006. Tsong kha pa, *Gsang mngon*, 68a6–b2.

the deities who have dissolved[1007] by singing a song, correspond to the Buddha, whose mind is aroused by the four qualities beyond measure after displaying the deed of nirvāṇa in one buddhafield. The arising of the deities in response,[1008] the offerings and praises made to them, and their acceptance of these offerings[1009] correspond to the Buddha, who arises in the aspect of the rūpakāya and becomes a receptacle for offerings wherever his disciples are.

In terms of the length of the practice, the core practices to which we have devoted most of the discussion are relatively short, while a large portion of the sādhana is devoted to the description of the Supreme King of Maṇḍalas, including the emanated deities, their attributes, the direction in which they dwell, their mantras, and so forth.

The Supreme King of Maṇḍalas

While the union with the consort is not included in the core practices that lead eventually to the yogi's awakening, it is still included in the First Yoga. The emanation of the maṇḍala with its deities as the outcome of the union with the consort is part of the second yoga of the creation stage, known as the Supreme King of Maṇḍalas. As we saw the four yogas—yoga, subsequent yoga, higher yoga, and great yoga—are practiced for the sake of the yogi's enlightenment, while the Supreme King of Maṇḍalas and the Supreme King of Deeds are for the sake of others.

According to Tsongkhapa, the meditation on the union with the consort is for the sake of both oneself and others.[1010] The taking of passion on the path in relation to the past event of the Teacher who was absorbed in the samādhi called "the method of great passion" is a meditation for one's own sake.[1011] However, the subsequent emanation of the Supreme King of Maṇḍalas serves for the sake of others as well.

The Indian works of the Ārya tradition do not agree on the exact point where the First Yoga ends and the Supreme King of Maṇḍalas begins. According to the *Vajrasattva Sādhana*, the Supreme King of Maṇḍalas begins with

1007. Tsong kha pa, *Gsang mngon*, 68b2–69a5.

1008. Tsong kha pa, *Gsang mngon*, 69a6–b1.

1009. Tsong kha pa, *Gsang mngon*, 69b6–74a2.

1010. Tsong kha pa, *Rnam gzhag rim pa'i rnam bshad*, 60b2–4.

1011. *Gsang 'dus, Guhyasamāja Tantra*, chap. 1, Tōh 442; Zhol 2b2; Stog 3b3; Fremantle 1971, 176; and Matsunaga 1978, 4.

the union with the consort;[1012] according to the *Sādhana Incorporating the Scripture*, it begins with the issuing-forth of Akṣobhya.[1013] For Tsongkhapa, however, the First Yoga consists of the steps up to and including the offerings made during the practice with the consort, and the Supreme King of Maṇḍalas begins with the generation of the celestial mansion for the thirty-two deities.[1014]

The "Seven Steps"

Tsongkhapa describes the visualization of the emanated maṇḍala and its deities in "seven steps":[1015] generation, sending forth, deeds, gathering, merging, initiation, and abiding on their seats.[1016]

1. The Step of Generation[1017]

When the yogi and his consort, visualized as Vajrasattva's nirmāṇakāya father-mother, absorb in union, the ensuing drop that remains in the lotus of the consort splits in two. One part is then generated into the celestial mansion with its thrones, while the other part becomes thirty-two drops, each set upon a throne.[1018] These thirty-two drops transform into the seed syllables of each of the deities; the seed syllables transform into the thirty-two emblems, vajra and so forth. These in turn transform into the respective thirty-two deities, with Akṣobhya and Sparśavajrā[1019] at the center. They are surrounded by the four remaining tathāgatas, the four mothers, the four remaining vajra ladies, the eight bodhisattvas, and the ten fierce protecting deities.

The *Concise Sādhana* devotes ninety-one verses to describe these deities, their attributes, the direction in which they reside, their mantras, and so on.[1020]

1012. Candrakīrti, *Rdo rje sems dpa'i sgrub thabs, Vajrasattva Sādhana*, Tōh 1814, 201b5; Luo and Tomabechi 2009, 23.9 and 57.1.

1013. Nāgārjuna, *Mdo bsre, Sādhanasūtramelāpaka*, Tōh 1797, 14a3–6.

1014. Tsong kha pa, *Rnal 'byor dag rim*, 20a4–b1. In Tsong kha pa's *Guhyasamāja Sādhana* the Supreme King of Maṇḍalas commences with the line "One part of the drop becomes *Bhrūṃ*." See his *Gsang mngon*, 52a6.

1015. Tib. *sgo bdun*.

1016. Tsong kha pa, *Bung ba'i re skong*, 26a1–5; and his *Rnal 'byor dag rim*, 20b1–6. See also his *Gsang mngon*, 59b3–67b1.

1017. Tib. *bskyed pa'i sgo*.

1018. Tsong kha pa, *Gsang mngon*, 52a5–b2.

1019. Tib. Reg bya Rdo rje ma, Eng. Vajra Lady of Tangibles.

1020. Nāgārjuna, *Mdor byas, Piṇḍīkrama Sādhana*, Tōh 1796, 6a2–9b2; L 107–197.

Likewise, *Formulating the Sādhana* dedicates its third chapter to the maṇḍala emanated here,[1021] and Tsongkhapa expands on it in his commentary on this work.[1022]

2. The Step of Sending Forth[1023]

The yogi draws each of the deities in turn from the lotus of the consort into his own heart through his vajra path. Then, while reciting the respective mantra of each deity, he sends them out in the ten directions. For Tsongkhapa, the scriptural authority for this meditation is the samādhi entitled "vajra lamp of wisdom" in the first chapter of the *Guhyasamāja Tantra*.[1024] The *Illuminating Lamp* recounts how, motivated by great compassion for all sentient beings, the yogi sends Akṣobhya forth to purify all sentient beings from the afflictive emotion of hatred, sends Vairocana forth to purify their ignorance, and so forth.[1025]

3. The Step of Performing the Deeds[1026]

Then, each of the thirty-two deities performs his or her respective general and specific deeds. The general deeds include turning the wheel of Dharma; the special deed of the tathāgatas is purifying the respective afflictive emotions of all sentient beings. The four mothers perform the four activities of pacifying, increasing, subjugating, and controlling. The five vajra ladies purify sentient beings clinging respectively to material forms, sounds, scents, tastes, and objects of touch. The eight bodhisattvas purify the five senses, minds, channels, sinews, and joints. The ten fierce deities overcome harmful beings in their respective quarters.

1021. Nāgabuddhi, *Rnam gzhag rim pa*, *Vyavastholi*, Tōh 1809, 126a5–129b3; Tanaka 2016, 106–128.

1022. See Tsong kha pa, *Rnam gzhag rim pa'i rnam bshad*, chap. 3, 60a1–77b1. This chapter is an explanation of the generation of the deities in the first step.

1023. Tib. *spro ba'i sgo*.

1024. In doing so, Tsong kha pa follows Nāgārjuna's *Mdo bsre*, *Sādhanasūtramelāpaka*, Tōh 1797, 14a4. For the samādhi entitled "vajra lamp of wisdom" (Tib. *ye shes sgron ma rdo rje*, Skt. *jñānapradīpavajra*), see the section "The Samādhis in the First Chapter of the *Guhyasamāja Tantra* and Enacting Past Events" above.

1025. Candrakīrti, *Sgron gsal*, *Pradīpoddyotanaṭīkā*, Tōh 1785, 17b6–18a2; Chakravarti 1984, 23.

1026. Tib. *mdzad pa'i sgo*.

4. The Step of Gathering Back[1027]

In order to perform their deeds, each deity has multiplied into countless deities that filled the ten directions. Now, the emanations of each of the thirty-two deities are gathered into a single body of the respective deity.[1028]

5. The Step of Merging[1029]

Each deity merges indivisibly with its own jñānasattva, which has been invited from its natural abode.

6. The Step of Conferring Initiation[1030]

The bodhicitta of the respective lord of the tathāgata family father-mother abiding in union confers initiation on each of the deities. This step derives its scriptural authority from the aforementioned past event in the *Guhyasamāja Tantra* in which the Blessed One was absorbed in the samādhi called "vajra lamp of wisdom" and emanated a maṇḍala. According to the *Illuminating Lamp*, this maṇḍala was emanated in order to initiate the tathāgatas who made the request;[1031] hence, in the practice that follows the past event, an initiation is conferred on all the deities.

7. The Step of Abiding on the Seat[1032]

In the last step, each deity takes his or her respective seat in the celestial mansion of the outer maṇḍala. With regard to Akṣobhya, he enters the heart of the yogi as peaceful Vajradhara, and thereby the yogi transforms into blue Dveṣavajra, while the lunar seat of Vajradhara becomes a solar seat for the new fierce principal deity of the maṇḍala.

1027. Tib. *bsdu ba'i sgo*.

1028. See also Nāgārjuna, *Mdo bsre, Sādhanasūtramelāpaka*, Tōh 1797, 14a5–6.

1029. Tib. *'dres pa'i sgo*.

1030. Tib. *dbang bskur ba'i sgo*.

1031. Candrakīrti, *Sgron gsal, Pradīpoddyotanaṭīkā*, Tōh 1785, 17b2–3; Chakravarti 1984, 23.

1032. Tib. *gnas pa'i sgo*.

The Celestial Mansion

Following the seven-step meditation on the deities, the yogis visualize the celestial mansion in a similar way. They draw the celestial mansion into their hearts, multiply it, and emanate it in the ten directions in order to purify the failings and flaws of the physical world. Then they gather them back into one and merge it with the jñānasattvas of the celestial mansion. Finally, this celestial mansion dissolves into the previous outer celestial mansion.[1033]

Examining Uncertainties

The three uncertainties examined here are inherited queries, to borrow Hugon's terminology,[1034] that are found in *Formulating the Sādhana* and are not issues first raised by Tibetan scholars. Tsongkhapa refers to them in his commentary on this treatise, and Khedrup Jé follows him.[1035]

Examining Uncertainties Concerning the Sealing of the Deities with the Four Seals

This query is raised in order to explain why, according to the *Sādhana Incorporating the Scripture*, the deities of the Supreme King of Maṇḍalas are sealed with the four seals,[1036] while according to *Formulating the Sādhana*, the *Guhyasamāja Tantra* does not teach the use of hand seals to generate the deities.[1037] According to Tsongkhapa, sealing with the four seals in this context does not refer to hand seals, but rather to the four stages of generating the deities of the Supreme King of Maṇḍalas: the dharma seal indicates the generation of the seed syllable; the insignia seal indicates the generation of the emblem; the

1033. Tsong kha pa, *Gsang mngon*, 67b1–3.

1034. See Hugon 2012.

1035. Tsong kha pa, *Rnam gzhag rim pa'i rnam bshad*, 65b5–75a5.

1036. Tib. *phyag rgya*, Skt. *mudrā*. Nāgārjuna, *Mdo bsre*, Sādhanasūtramelāpaka, Tōh 1797, 14a5.

1037. Nāgabuddhi, *Rnam gzhag rim pa*, *Vyavastholi*, chap. 3, Tōh 1809, 127b2–3; Tanaka 2016, 113.

great seal indicates the generation of the complete body; and the karma seal[1038] indicates the deeds of enlightened action performed by this body.[1039]

Examining Uncertainties Concerning the Appearance of the Deities

The purpose of raising this query is to explain why, while most deities in the lower tantras and several in the unexcelled tantra class have one face, all the deities in the Guhyasamāja maṇḍala have three faces. The answer is based on the explanation of the "vajra-joining-of-the-palms"[1040] in its definitive meaning.[1041] The fingers of the left hand are the five objects of the senses, while the fingers of the right hand are the five tathāgatas. When the palms are joined indivisibly, subject and object are integrated and the proliferation of dualistic appearances subsides. Hence, the faces of the Guhyasamāja deity are in fact one, but conceptualized as three. They stand for the two pairs of opposites and their nondual union as Vajradhara.

Khedrup Jé explains that such a union is a unique feature of this cycle, since the *Guhyasamāja Tantra* places particular emphasis on the illusory body, which is one of the facets united during the completion stage in order to create the stage of union.[1042] The other facet, the actual clear light—realized by the wisdom of great bliss that arises when all the winds have dissolved into the central channel of the subtle body—is explained extensively in the mother tantras. Khedrup Jé stresses that unless the illusory body is first dissolved into the clear light, the wisdom that dawns is the wisdom of ārya beings whose wisdom of great bliss realizes emptiness directly; it is not the stage of union of the completion stage. Since the *Guhyasamāja Tantra* specifically explains

1038. Tib. *las kyi phyag rgya*, Skt. *karmamudrā*.

1039. Tsong kha pa, *Rnam gzhag rim pa'i rnam bshad*, 66b6–67a2; and Mkhas grub rje, *Bskyed rim dngos grub rgya mtsho*, 153a6–b1. According to Nāgabuddhi, the four seals are the great seal, being endowed with body of the deity adorned with every quality of the Buddha; the samaya seal (*dam tshig gi phyag rgya*, *samayamudrā*); being endowed with the consort; the dharma seal, the syllables of the mantra; and the karma seal, acting for the sake of sentient beings and achieving their goals in the various forms of the deities. See Nāgabuddhi's *Rnam gzhag rim pa*, *Vyavastholi*, chap. 3, Tōh 1809, 127b3–4; Tanaka 2016, 114. See also Giebel 2001, 11.

1040. Tib. *rdo rje thal mo*, Skt. *vajrāñjali*.

1041. The answer is provided by Nāgabuddhi who cites the *Dgong pa lung ston*, *Sandhivyākaraṇa*, chap. 12, Tōh 444, 197b6–198a2 and 198b2–3. See his *Rnam gzhag rim pa*, *Vyavastholi*, chap. 3, Tōh 1809, 127b5–128a4; Tanaka 2016, 115–118.

1042. Mkhas grub rje, *Bskyed rim dngos grub rgya mtsho*, 155a2–b6.

the illusory body and its unification with the clear light, the path it teaches is greatly superior to the path expounded in any other tantra.

Examining Uncertainties Concerning the Number of Deities

This query is raised to explain why, according to the Ārya tradition, thirty-two deities dwell in the Guhyasamāja maṇḍala, while this number of deities is not found in the *Guhyasamāja Tantra* itself. Already, Candrakīrti's *Vajrasattva Sādhana* mentions different traditions for the number of deities residing in the maṇḍala: thirteen, nineteen, and twenty-five.[1043] According to Ngok Āryadeva,[1044] these are the traditions of Indrabodhi, Jñānapāda, and Paṇḍita Drinsumpa[1045] respectively.[1046] The first chapter of the *Guhyasamāja Tantra* describes a thirteen-deity maṇḍala, consisting of the five tathāgatas, the four mothers, and only four fierce deities. In his commentary on the *Vajrasattva Sādhana*, Tathāgatarakṣita calls the thirteen-deity maṇḍala "the heart maṇḍala of the Guhyasamāja."[1047] Such a maṇḍala can be found in Indrabhūti's (rather than Indrabodhi's) *Jñānasiddhi Sādhana*.[1048]

A nineteen-deity maṇḍala characterizes the system of the Jñānapāda school.[1049] This number of deities is found in the latter five chapters of the *Guhyasamāja Tantra*, but not in the first twelve chapters, considered the earlier section of this tantra.[1050] While Ngok Āryadeva maintains that a nineteen-deity model is in the tradition of Jñānapāda, Khedrup Jé, who believes that

1043. Candrakīrti, *Rdo rje sems dpa'i sgrub thabs*, *Vajrasattva Sādhana*, Tōh 1814, 196a3–4; Luo and Tomabechi 2009, 3.10–11 and 35.16–17.

1044. Rngog Āryadeva (twelfth century).

1045. Paṇḍi ta Mgrin gsum pa.

1046. Rngog Āryadeva, *Gsang ba 'dus pa'i 'grel pa sgron ma gsal bar byed pa'i ṭikka*, 179. He is followed on this point by Red mda' ba, *Yid kyi mun sel*, 97b6–98a2.

1047. Tathāgatarakṣita, *Rdo rje sems dpa'i sgrub pa'i thabs kyi bshad pa*, *Vajrasattvasādhana-vyākhyā*, Tōh 1835, 281a1–2.

1048. *Ye shes grub pa'i sgrub pa'i thabs*, *Jñānasiddhi Sādhana*, chap. 15, Tōh 2219, 53a3–b3; Sanskrit and Tibetan editions in Samdhong Rinpoche and Vrajvallabh Dwivedi with a team 1987, 167–168 and 214–215.

1049. Jñānapāda, *Kun bzang sgrub thabs*, *Samantabhadra Sādhana*, vv. 70–91, Tōh 1855, 32a2–33a2.

1050. Tanemura 2015, 327.

Jñānapāda lived after Candrakīrti, doubts that Candrakīrti could have had Jñānapāda in mind here.[1051]

According to both the *Illuminating Lamp* and *Formulating the Sādhana*, the number of deities in the emanated maṇḍala of the Ārya tradition is thirty-two, the same as the number of deities in the body maṇḍala taught in the *Vajra Garland Explanatory Tantra*.[1052] Both treatises say that this number was not taught explicitly in the *Guhyasamāja Tantra* in order to prevent the teaching from circulating without a master; nevertheless, the Blessed One himself taught this number in one of the explanatory tantras of the *Guhyasamāja*.

The Supreme King of Deeds

The Yoga Pertaining to the Actual Meditation Session

The Yoga of the Subtle Drop

While the practice of the sādhana up to this point has been considered coarse meditation, this yoga is subtle, because its object is the size of a mustard seed. Furthermore, whereas the practice of the Supreme King of Maṇḍalas, which consists of emanating the deities who act for the sake of other sentient beings, is considered to correspond to the deeds of the Buddha's body, the yoga of the subtle drop is said to correspond to the deed of the mind engaged in perfectly stable concentration. Tsongkhapa's *Guhyasamāja Sādhana* does not provide instruction on the yoga of the subtle drop, but in his *Great Treatise on the Stages of the Mantric Path*, he explains this meditation in detail.[1053]

The purpose of the yoga on a subtle object is to attain a mind steadily fixed on its object. First, yogis visualize a vajra the size of a mustard seed at the tip of the nose until they attain stable signs of seeing and touching. Signs of stable sight are attained when the vajra appears much clearer to the yogi's mind than

1051. Rngog Āryadeva, *Gsang ba 'dus pa'i 'grel pa sgron ma gsal bar byed pa'i ṭīkka*, 179. Mkhas grub rje, *Bskyed rim dngos grub rgya mtsho*, 156b1–2. According to current research Jñānapāda lived before Candrakīrti. According to Dalton and Szántó 2019, 264, Jñānapāda was active circa 770–820, and the Ārya school of the Guhyasamāja developed shortly after him. See Dalton and Szántó 2019, 264. See also Tomabechi 2008, 175.

1052. Candrakīrti, *Sgron gsal, Pradīpoddyotanaṭīkā*, Tōh 1785, 21b4–6; Chakravarti 1984, 27. Nāgabuddhi, *Rnam gzhag rim pa, Vyavastholi*, chap. 3, Tōh 1809, 128a5–7, Tanaka 2016, 119. *Rgyud rdo rje phreng ba, Vajramālā Tantra*, chap. 64, Tōh 445, 270a2–b4; this is cited in Nāgabuddhi, *Rnam gzhag rim pa, Vyavastholi*, chap. 3, Tōh 1809, 128a7–129a3; Tanaka 2016, 120–126.

1053. Tsong kha pa, *Sngags rim chen mo*, 473–481.

objects seen with the eyes, while the mind remains focused on the vajra until the end of the meditative session and the vajra remains unchanging. Signs of touch are attained when the yogis sense that they can touch the vajra with their hands.

Once the yogis achieve a mind stable on the subtle vajra, they should visualize a second vajra emanating from it, then a third, and so forth. Then, they will gather these vajras back in reverse order into the first vajra. Gradually, they increase the number of vajras until the vajras fill the sky, then they gather them back. Next, the yogis transform the vajra into their special deity, and practice emanating and gathering it back. At the end of the meditative session when all the emanations have been withdrawn, they should draw the subtle vajra into the heart of the jñānasattva at their hearts.

This yoga is considered to fulfill all the defining features of the union of mental quiescence[1054] and special insight,[1055] to the extent of rendering them unnecessary when the yogis practice the yoga on the subtle object. Attaining the signs of the object stability is regarded to amount to mental quiescence, while the emanation and regathering of the vajras and deities enable the yogis to gain special insight into things as they really are when they meditate on the principal deity dissolving into clear light, ultimate truth.

Once yogis have habituated to the meditation on the subtle vajra on the tip of the nose, they begin the meditation on a subtle object at the lower gate of the subtle body, the opening of the secret place. Visualizing themselves as Akṣobhya, the principal deity of the maṇḍala, in union with the consort, the yogis focus on the subtle drop at their secret place until they attain signs of seeing and touching. When they achieve stability, they draw the drop into the consort's lotus; within this drop, they visualize the complete maṇḍala of the celestial mansion and deities—with its own Akṣobhya as the principal deity. They meditate on this maṇḍala, called son-visualization, until they attain signs of seeing and touching.

Within this maṇḍala, the yogis should meditate again on Akṣobhya absorbed in union with his consort and on the drop originating from their union. Within this drop, they should visualize the complete maṇḍala as before, until they attain the signs of a stable mind on this maṇḍala, called grandson-visualization. The terminology of son- and grandson-visualization

1054. Tib. *zhi gnas*, Skt. *śamatha*.

1055. Tib. *lhag mthong*, Skt. *vipaśyanā*.

is found in the *Illuminating Lamp*, and the meditation on a subtle object is mentioned in the *Guhyasamāja Tantra*.[1056]

The yoga of the subtle object reminds us of the imagery of Vairocana's palace and the untold multitudes of buddhafields in each of the pores in Samantabhadra's body found in the *Gaṇḍavyūha Sūtra*.[1057] Alternately, it calls to mind a bodhisattva who can put Mount Meru, the king of mountains, into a mustard seed without enlarging the mustard seed and without shrinking Mount Meru, or a bodhisattva who can pour all the waters of the four great oceans into a single pore of his skin without causing discomfort to any of the aquatic creatures—images found in the *Vimalakīrtinirdeśa* and *Daśabhūmika* sūtras.[1058]

Indian and Tibetan scholars recognized these similarities and incorporated this imagery into their treatises on sādhanas, not only in the context of the yoga on a subtle object but elsewhere as well. For example, countless world-realms in the three times and ten directions contained within a single atom are described in the verses recited while tormas are presented to the guardians of the directions.[1059]

Akhu Ching explains how yogis visualize this: they begin with a single world, then multiply it by ten, one hundred, one thousand, and up to infinity, extending in the ten directions and the three times. Then, they visualize that such a universal system is contained within each atom of these worlds, and that, too, is contained within each atom of all the universes in the ten directions, yet all these universes dwell within one another without causing any obstruction. Likewise, the beings in every single world in this universe reside within the pores of each other's bodies. Akhu Ching recommends to use this method whenever offerings are made.[1060] As we can see, Tibetan scholars

1056. Candrakīrti, *Sgron gsal, Pradīpoddyotanaṭīkā*, chap. 3, v. 13, Tōh 1785, 29a6; Chakravarti 1984, 38. Here this verse is explained in the hidden level of interpretation. *Gsang 'dus*, chap. 3, Tōh 442; Zhol 7a5–6; Stog 11b.1–4, Fremantle 1971, vv. 12–14; and Matsunaga 1978, vv. 12–14. See also chap. 6, Zhol 9b3; Stog 15b4–6; Fremantle 1971, vv. 8–9; and Matsunaga 1978, vv. 8–9.

1057. Vaidya 1960; *Gaṇḍavyūha Sūtra*, 416, in Tōh 44, vol. *a*, 340a1–2. See Gómez 1977, 242, and 2010 [2011].

1058. *'Phags pa dri ma med par grags pas bstan pa, Vimalakīrtinirdeśa*, Gretil, chap. 5, §10–11; Tōh 176, 205b4–206a2; an English translation in Boin 1994, 141–144. *Sa bcu'i le'u, Daśabhūmika Sūtra*, chap. 10, passim, for example; Vaidya 1967, 61, lines 15–17; an English translation in Honda 1968, 270.

1059. Tsong kha pa, *Gsang mngon*, 12b5–13a5.

1060. A khu ching, *Mi bskyod mgon po'i zhal lung*, 42a2–b1; an English translation in Jinpa 1999, 74.

were cognizant of the affinity between the visions portrayed in the Mahāyāna sūtras and the tantric visualizations.

The Yoga of Recitation

There are two main types of mantra recitation during the creation stage: mental and voiced recitations. Mental recitation, called also vajra recitation, is silent, without any movement of the tongue and lips. In practicing the voiced recitation, the yogis take on the path the enlightened deeds of the speech of the Buddha, thus completing the triad of taking the deeds of the body, speech, and mind of the Buddha on the path. The deeds of the body were taken on the path during the practice of the Supreme King of Maṇḍalas, and the deeds of the mind during the yoga of the subtle drop.

Each deity in the Guhyasamāja maṇḍala has more than one mantra that is recited in the yoga of recitation. For example, the seed syllable[1061] of Akṣobhya is *hūṃ*; his name[1062] or essence[1063] mantra is *vajradhṛk*; and his heart mantra[1064] is *oṃ āḥ vajradhṛk hūṃ hūṃ*. Thus the heart mantras consist of the name mantra and the seed syllable interspersed with the three syllables *oṃ āḥ hūṃ*. The mantra *oṃ āḥ hūṃ* is the heart-essence of the suchness of all deities.[1065]

The four basic Indian sādhanas of the Ārya tradition are not clear about the specific mantras recited here. Butön, Tsongkhapa, and Khedrup Jé follow the system of Abhayākaragupta.[1066] In this system, the name-mantras of thirteen of the deities—the five tathāgatas,[1067] the four mothers,[1068] and four of

1061. Tib. *sa bon*, Skt. *bīja*.

1062. Tib. *mtshan sngags*.

1063. Tib. *nye snying*, Skt. *upahṛdayamantra*.

1064. Tib. *snying pa*, Skt. *hṛdayamantra*.

1065. Tsong kha pa, *Rnal 'byor dag rim*, 24b2–25a2, and Mkhas grub rje, *Bskyed rim dngos grub rgya mtsho*, 164b4.

1066. Bu ston, *Mdor byas 'grel chen*, 84b6. Mkhas grub rje, *Bskyed rim dngos grub rgya mtsho*, 164b3. See Abhayākaragupta, *Dkyil chog rdo rje phreng ba*, *Vajrāvalī Maṇḍalavidhi*, Tōh 3140, 18a1–7; Mori 2009, §10.8–9, 133–135. See also his *Rdzogs pa'i rnal 'byor gyi phreng ba*, *Niṣpannayogāvalī*, Tōh 3141, 99b5–7; Sanskrit and Tibetan editions, along with an English translation in Lokesh Chandra and Nirmala Sharma 2015, 36–37.

1067. The mantras of Akṣobhya, Vairocana, Ratnasaṃbhava [Ratnaketu], Amitābha [Lokeśvara], and Amoghasiddhi are respectively *vajradhṛk*, *jinajik*, *ratnadhṛk*, *ārolik*, and *prajñādhṛk*.

1068. The mantras of Locanā, Māmakī, Pāṇḍarā, and Tārā are respectively *moharati*, *dvṣarati*, *rāgarati*, and *vajrarati*.

the fierce deities[1069]—are taken from the first chapter of the *Guhyasamāja Tantra*. The name-mantras of the remaining deities, the five vajra ladies, the eight bodhisattvas, and the six remaining fierce deities are identical to their names. In Tsongkhapa's *Guhyasamāja Sādhana*, the heart mantras of the thirty-two deities are recited in the practice of voiced recitation.[1070]

Abhayākaragupta lists four methods of mantra recitation—samaya recitation, palanquin recitation, enraged recitation, and fierce recitation[1071]—while Ratnākaraśānti describes a fifth type of recitation in his *Hevajra Sādhana*,[1072] namely, heap recitation.[1073] The heart and essence mantras are recited in the samaya and fierce recitations, while the garland[1074] is recited in the palanquin, enraged, and fierce recitations.[1075] While reciting according to any of these methods, the yogis must maintain the divine identity of their deities and visualize both the mantras and the deities. In the samaya recitation, they visualize the deities emanating to act for the sake of sentient beings and then, together with their mantras, entering the yogi's mouth through the inhaled wind. In the palanquin recitation, the garland mantras circle through the yogi and his consort by entering the yogi's mouth, issuing from his vajra path into the lotus and ascending through the central channel of the consort, emerging from her mouth and entering through the yogi's mouth into his central channel. In the enraged recitation, the circular motion begins with the mouth of the consort and so forth. While reciting, the yogis visualize that all the deities

1069. The mantras of Yamāntaka, Prajñāntaka, Hayagrīva, and Vighnāntaka are respectively *yamāntakṛt*, *prajñakṛt*, *padmāntakṛt*, and *vighnāntakṛt*.

1070. Tsong kha pa, *Gsang mngon*, 67b5–68a6.

1071. Abhayākaragupta, *Man ngag snye ma*, *Āmnāyamañjarī*, chap. 12, Tōh 1198, 138b7–139a4.

1072. Ratnākaraśānti, *'Khrul pa spong ba'i sgrub pa'i thabs*, *Bhramahara Sādhana*, Tōh 1245, 194a7; a Sanskrit edition in Isaacson 2002, 173. The name "heap recitation" is found in Jālandhari, *Kye rdo rje'i sgrub thabs kyi mdor bshad pa dag pa rdo rje sgron ma*, *Hevajrasādhanavajrapradīpaṭippaṇīśuddha*, Tōh 1237, 92a2. See Tsong kha pa, *Sngags rim chen mo*, 523.

1073. See Tsong kha pa, *Rnal 'byor dag rim*, 24a5–6.

1074. Tib. *'phreng sngags*, Skt. *mālāmantra*, or root mantra, Tib. *rtsa sngags*, Skt. *mūlamantra*. The garland mantras of the four mothers and the nine fierce deities are taught in the fourteenth chapter of *Guhyasamāja Tantra*, while the garland mantras of the remaining deities are taught in other tantras. These mantras are not included in Tsong kha pa's *Guhyasamāja Sādhana*. See Bu ston, *Mdor byas 'grel chen*, 84b7–85a4; and Tsong kha pa, *Rnal 'byor dag rim*, 25a1.

1075. Tsong kha pa, *Rnal 'byor dag rim*, 24a3–5.

of the maṇḍala are reciting the mantra with them so that the recitations will multiply.[1076]

The Yoga Pertaining to the Periods between Meditative Sessions

In between the actual meditative sessions, yogis should engage in four yogas: the yoga of body enhancement, food yoga, the yoga of sleeping, and the yoga of rising. While the three latter yogas are carried out in conjunction with ordinary daily activities, the first yoga of body enhancement is practiced in order to revitalize the yogis' bodies, which have become weary from four sessions of intense practice, day and night. The yogis visualize nectar whose essence is the five tathāgatas pouring out from above and empowering them from head to toe, recovering their well-being and strength.[1077]

The remaining three yogas are ritual methods for carrying out necessary daily activities between meditative sessions. Yogis should consume their food and drink while visualizing themselves as Akṣobhya or Vajradhara and their victuals as inner fire offerings made to the deities dwelling in the *hūṃ* on their heart. The yogis bless their food as the tormas are blessed; they visualize their hands as the ladles used in outer fire offerings and their throats as blue five-pronged vajras with hollow middle prongs. They visualize wind, fire, earth, and water on their secret places, navels, hearts, and throats respectively. The wind ignites the fire that bakes the earth, and its heat boils the water. Consequently, when the food enters through the lotus of the throat and reaches the heart, the refined food satiates the deities. When the remaining food reaches the navel, the inner fire burns it into ashes that leave the body through the lower gate. In this way, food and drink is consumed not for the yogis' sake but as offerings dedicated to the deities.

While the yogas of body enhancement and intake of victuals appear in the Indian sādhanas by Nāgārjuna, the last two yogas do not.[1078] These are the yogas of sleep and rising up.[1079] When yogis fall asleep at night, they should dissolve all the deities on their bodies into clear light and remain focused on the clear light of sleep. When they wake up, they visualize that the four

1076. See Tsong kha pa, *Sngags rim chen mo*, 523.

1077. See Tsong kha pa, *Rnal 'byor dag rim*, 31b1–3.

1078. For the yoga of body enhancement, see Nāgārjuna, *Mdor byas*, *Piṇḍīkrama Sādhana*, Tōh 1796, 10b1–3, L 218–200; and for food yoga, see his *Mdor byas*, *Piṇḍīkrama Sādhana*, Tōh 1796, 10b3–7, L 221–209; and his *Mdo bsre*, *Sādhanasūtramelāpaka*, Tōh 1797, 14b7.

1079. See Tsong kha pa, *Rnal 'byor dag rim*, 31a5–b1.

goddesses invoke them with a song, whereby they rise in the body of the principal father-mother while in the continuum of clear light.

Offering Tormas

Another ritual performed between meditative sessions is the offering of tormas to the supra-worldly deities of the maṇḍala and to worldly deities, such as the guardians of the directions, in order to pacify obstructions and to attain siddhis. Yogis are advised to offer tormas after each of the four sessions, or at least at the completion of the last session. The scriptural source for offering the tormas is Abhayākaragupta's *Maṇḍala Vajra Garland*.[1080] While elaborate tormas may consist of porridge, pastry, milk, meat, beer, and so forth, simple tormas are made of grain and water alone, though beer is considered important. The tormas were blessed at the beginning of the practice as the inner offerings were blessed, hence, now the yogis hold them fully purified of the three spheres.[1081] Then they visualize the worldly deities dissolving into clear light and appearing as the deities of the Guhyasamāja, thus, their ordinary appearances and all attitudes toward them vanish. The yogis visualize the deities one by one, recite their mantras, and invite them to partake of the tormas either through the straw-like rays of their tongues or mentally. While making these offerings, the yogis should maintain the wisdom-mind experiencing the single taste of intrinsic emptiness and great bliss. Finally, they request that the worldly deities depart for their respective abodes.

1080. Abhayākaragupta, *Dkyil chog rdo rje 'phreng ba, Vajrāvalī Maṇḍalavidhi,* Tōh 3140, 88b5–89b7; Mori 2009, §48.1.1–4, 493–498.

1081. The offerer, the recipient, and the deed of offering.

10. The Preliminary Rituals

THE PRELIMINARY STAGES of the sādhana are not unique to the Ārya tradition of Guhyasamāja, but rather are common to a large number of mantric cycles. We may point out, in this regard, the process of creating a unified system of practice for a large number of tantric cycles. Each cycle borrows from the others to build a consistent format for the practice. Still, the identity of each cycle is preserved and emphasized. For example, explanatory works on the sādhana often describe three possibilities for any given course of action, then conclude that in that specific tradition the yogi should follow the third among them, since the other options usually belong to other tantric cycles. In this way, the cycle not only calls attention to certain methods of other systems but emphasizes the uniqueness of the undertaken tradition.

The preliminaries occupy more than one-third of this sādhana. On the whole, they consist of three parts: preparatory steps, establishing conducive conditions, and averting obstructive conditions. The preliminaries in part 1 of the translation below are divided into these three topics. But the two basic sādhanas of the Ārya tradition of Guhyasamāja, the *Concise Sādhana* and *Vajrasattva Sādhana*, expand mainly on the step of averting obstructive conditions by means of meditation on the protection wheel. The rituals for creating conducive conditions are based on the tradition of the Jñānapāda school.[1082]

The Preparatory Steps

The preparatory steps include guru yoga, instantaneous generation of the meditator into a deity, blessing the vajra and bell, blessing the inner and outer offerings, preparing the preliminary tormas, blessing the offerings for the

1082. Jñānapāda, *Kun bzang sgrub thabs*, *Samantabhadra Sādhana*, Tōh 1855.

self-generation, offering *maṇḍal,*[1083] taking refuge, developing the mind for enlightenment, and Vajrasattva meditation and mantra recitation.

Tsongkhapa's *Guhyasamāja Sādhana* begins with verses of supplication to the lineage masters, known as guru yoga. This is a practice of great importance in tantric Buddhism, to which Tsongkhapa devoted an entire separate work.[1084] It is followed by a request to the Indian and Tibetan lamas of the Guhyasamāja lineage to bestow ordinary siddhis and the supreme attainment of enlightenment. Next, right at the beginning of the sādhana, the practitioners dissolve themselves into emptiness; within the continuum of emptiness, they visualize themselves as Dveṣavajra.[1085] This is because, in the following step, they need to bless the vajra and bell as well as the offerings, a ritual which cannot be carried out by ordinary persons. Only those who are immersed in deity yoga can effectively perform the blessing with their transformative power. Note that, deity yoga, or the arising as an awakened being, which is the ultimate purpose of the sādhana, is employed at the very beginning of the practice.

Next is blessing the vajra and bell, a topic on which Khedrup Jé wrote extensively in his *Playful Fest for the Yogis*, while Panchen Losang Chökyi Gyaltsen provided a fascinating summary.[1086] In both of these works, however, the authors rely mostly on mother tantras.[1087] The following step of blessing the inner offerings does rely on the Ārya tradition of Guhyasamāja, specifically the *Later Tantra,*[1088] albeit in matters related to the completion stage and not the creation stage, our topic here.

With regard to the blessing of the inner offerings, the sādhanas of the Ārya tradition of the Guhyasamāja do not specify ritual methods for the inner offerings of the five meats and five nectars. Most scriptural authorities in this

1083. The *maṇḍal* in "offering *maṇḍal*" should not be confused with a maṇḍala of a deity (Tib. *dkyil 'khor*). In most Tibetan text the term *maṇḍal* is transliterated and not translated into Tibetan. This tradition is followed in the English translation here.

1084. Tsong kha pa, *Bla ma lnga bcu pa'i rnam bshad slob ma'i re ba kun skong*; translated into English by Sparham 1999.

1085. Tib. Zhe sdang rdo rje, Eng. Hatred Vajra.

1086. Mkhas grub rje, *Rnal 'byor rol pa'i dga' ston*. The explanation on the *vajra* and bell are found in 201a2–233a4. Paṇ chen Blo bzang chos kyi rgyal mtshan, *Bskyed rim dngos grub rgya mtsho'i snying po*, 3b3–8a3.

1087. Including the *Mkha' 'gro rgya mtsho'i rgyud*, *Ḍākārṇava Tantra*; the *Yang dag par sbyor ba'i rgyud*, *Sampuṭa Tantra*; the *Rdo rje mkha' 'gro rgyud*, *Vajraḍāka Tantra*; and the *Gur*, *Vajrapañjara Tantra*.

1088. *Rgyud phyi ma*, *Uttara Tantra*, Tōh 443, 153b5–154a1; Matsunaga 1978, vv. 128–133.

matter are found in cycles of mother tantras, such as Cakrasaṃvara, Hevajra, and Yamāri. After discussing a great diversity of ritual methods on the basis of mother tantras in his *Ocean of Attainments*, Khedrup Jé presents a method specific to the Guhyasamāja on the basis of the works of Tsongkhapa.[1089] Khedrup Jé objects to the position of Tibetan scholars who take the system of the great Indian synthesizer Abhayākaragupta in his *Cluster of Instructions* and *Maṇḍala Vajra Garland* as applicable to all three traditions of Guhyasamāja, Cakrasaṃvara, and Hevajra.[1090]

The five meats are of elephant or bull,[1091] horse, cow, dog, and human, while the five nectars are excrement, blood, semen, great meat, and urine.[1092] Both meats and nectars are purified into the five tathāgatas, Vairocana, Ratnasaṃbhava, Amitābha, Amoghasiddhi, and Akṣobhya respectively.[1093] While these five meats and five nectars as a whole are not found in the *Guhyasamāja Tantra*, several of these meats and nectars are listed in various contexts there.[1094] The *Illuminating Lamp* explains the line "the rituals of excrement, urine, and meat" in the sixteenth chapter of the *Guhyasamāja Tantra* by glossing *excrement and urine* as "the five nectars" and *meat* with "the five types of meat."[1095]

In commenting on these lines in his *Precious Sprout*, Tsongkhapa expands on this further and describes how the impure five meats and five nectars are transformed into pure nectars through a trifold ritual of purification, transformation, and blazing.[1096] Tsongkhapa relies here on the *Later Tantra* that

1089. Mkhas grub rje, *Bskyed rim dngos grub rgya mtsho*, 166b2–168a4.

1090. Mkhas grub rje, *Bskyed rim dngos grub rgya mtsho*, 168a4–b5. See Abhayākaragupta, *Man ngag snye ma*, *Āmnāyamañjarī*, Tōh 1198, *Snye ma* 34, 297a1; and his *Dkyil 'khor rdo rje phreng ba*, *Vajrāvalī Maṇḍalavidhi*, Tōh 3140, 89a1–2; Mori 2009, §48.1.2.

1091. Tib *glang po*, Skt. *hasti*.

1092. See *Rgyud rdo rje phreng ba*, *Vajramālā Tantra*, chap. 61, Tōh 445, 266a4–6.

1093. Tsong kha pa, *Sgron gsal mchan*, 156a3–4.

1094. The meats of elephants (or bulls), horses, dogs, and cows appear in *Gsang 'dus*, *Guhyasamāja Tantra*, chap. 6, Tōh 442; Zhol 10a1–2; Stog 16b1–2; Dunh 16b2; Fremantle 1971, v. 22; and Matsunaga 1978, v. 23. The meats of elephant (or bull), horse, and the great meat are found in chap. 16, Tōh 442; Zhol 38a7–b1; Stog 64b5–6; Dunh 71a1–2; Fremantle 1971, v. 49; and Matsunaga 1978, v. 37cd.

1095. Candrakīrti, *Sgron gsal*, *Pradīpoddyotanaṭikā*, Tōh 1785, 166b2–3; Chakravarti 1984, 194. See *Gsang 'dus*, *Guhyasamāja Tantra*, chap. 16, Tōh 442; Zhol 38a7–b1; Stog 64b5–6; Dunh 71a1–2; Fremantle 1971, v. 50; and Matsunaga 1978, v. 39ab.

1096. Tsong kha pa, *Mtha' gcod*, 136b4–138a3.

delineates how five nectars,[1097] but not five meats, are purified through a fourfold method of blazing, flaming, radiating, and taking a form (but not the trifold method on which Tsongkhapa instructs).[1098] Khedrup Jé follows Tsongkhapa's explanation, while noting that the scriptural authority for this is the *Later Tantra* that is "taken to explain the present context."[1099]

This is another example that demonstrates how a practice that has originated in the context of mother tantras was adapted by Indian and Tibetan treatises of the Guhyasamāja cycle; moreover, suitable scriptural authorities were found for it in the Guhyasamāja cycle.

It is also interesting to note that the presentation of the inner offerings at the end of the sādhana reenacts a moment during the creation of the world when the primordial gods churned the ocean by using Mount Meru as their churning stick whereby the nectar appeared. Likewise, in Tsongkhapa's *Guhyasamāja Sādhana*, the yogi visualizes the thumb of the left hand as *kṣuṃ* that transforms into the earth ground and the ring finger as *suṃ* that transforms into Mount Meru. Thereby, the nectar-essence is extracted from the center of the ocean resting on the earth.[1100] The scriptural authority Khedrup Jé mentions here is another mother tantra, the *Four Chapters Tantra*.[1101]

Geluk scholars do not agree on the precise manner of this visualization. Some maintain that the thumb is the earth arising from *kṣuṃ* and the ring finger is Mount Meru arising from *suṃ*,[1102] while others say that the thumb is Mount Meru arising from *suṃ* and the ring finger is the ocean resting on the

1097. The five meats are not mentioned in these verses, though "five powerful ones" are consumed there in addition to the five nectars, and these are taken to be the five meats. The phrase "likewise" (Tib. *de bzhin*, Skt. *tathā*) is taken to indicate that they are related to the five tathāgatas (Tib. *de bzhin gshegs pa*).

1098. The question appears in *Rgyud phyi ma*, *Uttara Tantra*, Tōh 443, 149a5; Zhol 49b4; Matsunaga 1978, v. 19cd. The reply is on 153b5–154a2; Zhol 53a1–3; Matsunaga 1978, vv. 128–133. Tsongkhapa cites here also Muniśrībhadra's commentary on the *Mdor byas*, *Piṇḍīkrama Sādhana*, that explains some of the lines of the *Later Tantra*. See Muniśrībhadra's *Rim pa lnga'i don mdor bshad pa*, *Pañcakramārthaṭippaṇi*, Tōh 1813, 167b6–168a4; Jiang and Tomabechi 1996, 35.

1099. Mkhas grub rje, *Bskyed rim dngos grub rgya mtsho*, 170a5–172a5; and 170a1.

1100. Tsong kha pa, *Gsang mngon*, 70a2–3.

1101. The *Gdan bzhi*, *Catuḥpīṭha Tantra*, Tōh 428, 198b1–2; a Sanskrit edition and an English translation in Szántó 2012, 2.3.131–132.

1102. These include Tsong kha pa, *Gsang mngon* 70a2–4; and Bsod nams grags pa, *Gsang 'dus bskyed rim rnam gzhag*, 72b1–4; Bsod nams grags pa points out that Mkhas grub rje instructs on the opposite method.

earth arising from *kṣuṃ*.[1103] While the reason for a preference of one of these over the other remains unclear, the awareness of there being two possibilities continues until today. Thus this matter remained significant.[1104]

Next is the blessing of the outer offerings. There is no doubt that these offerings of the various kinds of water, flowers, incense, light, perfume, food, and music are common to a large number of Buddhist traditions; moreover, they are patterned after the ritualized reception of respected guests according to ancient Indian customs. The yogis prepare and bless these offerings during the preparatory steps, but they present them to themselves only at the end of the sādhana, after having generated themselves as the deity.

With regard to the preliminary tormas, Tsongkhapa and Khedrup Jé say that although the two basic sādhanas of the Ārya tradition of the Guhyasamāja by Ārya Nāgārjuna and Candrakīrti[1105] do not explicitly teach the preliminary tormas, it is still appropriate to make them, as do some early Tibetan lamas, because Indian siddhas explained how to offer the preliminary tormas for Cakrasaṃvara, Hevajra, and Yamāntaka.[1106] In this case then, the methods of other tantric cycles are applied here for the offering of the preliminary tormas to the direction guardians.

The preliminary rituals conclude with the *maṇḍal* offerings and Vajrasattva meditation and mantra recitation.[1107]

Establishing Favorable Conditions

The second part of the preliminaries in Tsongkhapa's *Guhyasamāja Sādhana* is the establishment of favorable conditions for the practice by making offerings to the field of accumulating merit and the sevenfold worship. Nāgārjuna's

1103. Mkhas grub rje, *Bskyed rim dngos grub rgya mtsho*, 171b5; Paṇ chen Blo bzang chos kyi rgyal mtshan, *Bskyed rim dngos grub rgya mtsho'i snying po*, 72b3–4.

1104. In the nineteenth century, A khu ching noted that there are two methods here, one held by Mkhas grub rje and the other by Bsod nams grags pa, but that only the latter is found acceptable. See A khu ching, *Mi bskyod mgon po'i zhal lung*, 96a3–5; an English translation in Jinpa 1999, 180.

1105. That is, Nāgārjuna, *Mdor byed*, *Piṇḍīkrama Sādhana*, and Candrakīrti, *Rdo rje sems dpa'i sgrub thabs*, *Vajrasattva Sādhana*.

1106. Tsong kha pa, *Bskyed rim zin bris*, 5a1–3, and *Sngags rim chen mo*, 495; Mkhas grub rje, *Bskyed rim dngos grub rgya mtsho*, 14b5–15a1. The Indian siddhas include Saroruha and Lalitavajra. See Saroruha, *Dgyes pa rdo rje'i sgrub thabs*, *Hevajra Sādhana*, Tōh 1218, 1a4–5; *Dhīḥ* 2003, 133; and Gerloff 2017, 97; and Lalitavajra, *Rdo rje 'jigs byed kyi sgrub thabs*, *Vajrabhairava Sādhana*, Tōh 1998, 197a1.

1107. For more on the preliminary rituals, see Bentor 1996, 93–214.

Sādhana Incorporating the Scripture includes these practices under the second heading of this work, entitled "Concentrating on great compassion."[1108] Candrakīrti also instructs the aspirants to generate great compassion at the onset of the preparatory meditation.[1109] In this way, both wings of the bodhisattva path are at the foundation of the sādhana. This step emphasizes the accumulation of merit and bodhicitta—the intention to attain enlightenment for the benefit of all beings—whereas the coming steps are centered around the accumulation of wisdom or the understanding of emptiness. In this way, the Indian and Tibetan authors of the sādhanas stress the general Mahāyāna roots of tantric sādhanas.[1110]

This is also demonstrated in Tsongkhapa's *Guhyasamāja Sādhana*. Although the sevenfold worship[1111] does not appear in the sādhanas of the Ārya tradition of the Guhyasamāja, as we have seen, Tsongkhapa does include this practice in his own sādhana on the basis of Jñānapāda's sādhana of the Guhyasamāja.[1112] Tsongkhapa justifies this incorporation from another tradition by pointing out that this practice appears in the commentaries on the basic sādhanas of the Ārya tradition.[1113] Moreover, Tsongkhapa criticizes earlier Tibetan scholars of the Ārya tradition, such as Gö Khukpa Lhetsé, for not including the sevenfold worship in the sādhana. This case is another instance that provides us with an insight into the process of creating a consistent framework for the practice of various tantric cycles.

The offerings made here to the field of accumulating merit, including the lamas and the thirty-two deities of the Guhyasamāja maṇḍala, are performed

1108. Nāgārjuna, *Mdo bsre*, *Sādhanasūtramelāpaka*, Tōh 1797, 11a5–7 and 15a4. Tib. *snyin rje chen po la dmigs pa*. These practices do not appear in the basic sādhana by Nāgārjuna, the *Mdor byas*, *Piṇḍīkrama Sādhana*, Tōh 1796. Tsongkhapa follows this in his *Rnal 'byor dag rim*, 2b1–2.

1109. Candrakīrti, *Rdo rje sems dpa'i sgrub thabs*, *Vajrasattva Sādhana*, Tōh 1814, 196b2–3; Luo and Tomabechi 2009, 4.13–5.2 and 37.4–6.

1110. Regarding Tibetan authors, for example, A khu ching maintains that for any deed, including deity yoga, to become a cause for buddhahood, it is essential to have at least a contrived bodhicitta and a contrived conviction in the view of the absence of true existence of all phenomena. See A khu ching, *Mi bskyod mgon po'i zhal lung*, 26a6–b2; an English translation in Jinpa 1999, 46.

1111. Tib. *yan lag bdun*.

1112. See Tsong kha pa, *Bskyed rim zin bris*, 6a6–b1. The version Tsongkhapa has adopted for the sevenfold worship is taken as a whole from Jñānapāda, *Kun tu bzang po sgrub thabs*, *Samantabhadra Sādhana*, vv. 10–18, Tōh 1855, 29a6–b3; Tanaka 1996, 181–186.

1113. According to Tsongkhapa's *Slob tshul*, 3a3–4, commentaries on the *Vajrasattva Sādhana* include the sevenfold worship.

according to a specific tantric version that is somewhat different from the sevenfold practice of the sūtric tradition known as *Bhadracarīpraṇidhāna*.[1114] The sevenfold worship in the present context consists of offerings, prostrations, confession, rejoicing in virtuous deeds and dedicating the merit, taking refuge, generating the mind for enlightenment, and keeping the unshared vows. Thus the requests that the tathāgatas turn the wheel of Dharma and not pass to nirvāṇa are replaced with taking refuge and generating the mind for enlightenment. The reason for this is that while the sūtric sevenfold worship is offered to the nirmāṇakāya, the tantric sevenfold worship is offered to the saṃbhogakāya, who always teaches the Dharma and does not pass to nirvāṇa.[1115]

Furthermore, here the limbs of rejoicing in virtuous deeds and dedicating merit are combined into one limb, and the practice of keeping the unshared vows is added as the seventh limb. The keeping of the unshared vows is part of the worship for accumulating merit because no vow that was not taken before is newly taken here, nor are vows that have been broken restored. Rather, the unimpaired vows themselves are offered to the lama and the deities of the maṇḍala.[1116] There are eighteen vows altogether, belonging to the five tathāgata families.[1117] Once more, the verses recited during this meditation are found not in the *Guhyasamāja Tantra*, but in a number of other tantras, including the *Vajraśekhara* and the *Vajraḍāka*.[1118] Tsongkhapa devoted an entire work to these vows.[1119]

The Indian commentaries on the verses of the sevenfold worship in

1114. The *Bzang spyod smon lam*, *Samantabhadracarīpraṇidhāna*, found at the end of the *Gaṇḍavyūha Sūtra*, Tōh 44, and also separately as Tōh 1095.

1115. As explained by Mkhan zur Blo bzang bstan 'dzin, Teaching on the Guhyasamāja given at Jamyang Buddhist Centre, London, August 13, 2002.

1116. Tsong kha pa, *Bung ba'i re skong*, 8a2–3.

1117. Six vows of Vairocana, four of Akṣobhya, four of Ratnasaṃbhava, two of Amitābha, and two vows of Amoghasiddhi. According to other accounts, Amitābha has three vows, and altogether there are nineteen vows.

1118. *Rdo rje rtse mo*, *Vajraśekhara Tantra*, Tōh 480, 184a1–6; *Rdo rje mkha' 'gro*, *Vajraḍāka Tantra*, Tōh 370, 34b1–6.

1119. Tsong kha pa, *Dngos grub kyi snye ma*, translated into English by Sparham 2005. According to his *Bskyed rim zin bris* (10a1), among the many different translations of these verses into Tibetan, Tsongkhapa seems to prefer the version found in Rāhulaśrīmitra, Sgra gcan 'dzin dpal bshes gnyen, *Zung du 'jug pa gsal dbang gi bya ba*, *Yugalanaddhaprakāśasekaprakriyā*, Tōh 1818, 235a2–7, that was translated by Sa skya Paṇḍita and Śakyaśrībhadra.

Jñānapāda's *Samantabhadra Sādhana*[1120] interpret them in accordance with the Mind Only view. For example, these commentaries explain the verse recited while taking refuge to mean "I seek refuge in the sugatas who dwell in my mind," because there is nothing other than one's mind.[1121] As we have seen, Tsongkhapa tends to overlook mentions of the Mind Only theory in Indian works on the sādhana of the Guhyasamāja.[1122] In following Tsongkhapa's *Fulfilling the Bee's Hopes*, Khedrup Jé explains the line on taking refuge not in its literal meaning, but as "I seek refuge in the sugatas in whose mind dwells [wisdom] and compassion," and our translation follows this interpretation.[1123]

Khedrup Jé raises only one polemical issue within his explanation on the development of conducive conditions.[1124] The argument is related to different sources on the invitation of the field for accumulating merit together with the lama outside the Guhyasamāja cycle. In Tsongkhapa's *Guhyasamāja Sādhana*, the lama is invited as nondual with the maṇḍala of Akṣobhya; the argument is concerned with the system of Cakrasaṃvara as it appears in Tsongkhapa's *Wish-Granting Cow* and *Great Treatise on the Stages of the Mantric Path*.[1125] The criticism is against some lamas who object to *Kambala's instruction to visualize the lama as Vajrasattva on a lion throne in the cremation ground; especially against the claim that Vajradhara cannot dwell in a cremation ground.[1126] According to Tsongkhapa, those who maintain this position stray far from the principles of the Mantra Vehicle,[1127] and Khedrup Jé adds that

1120. Jñānapāda, *Kun tu bzang po sgrub thabs*, *Samantabhadra Sādhana*, vv. 10–18, Tōh 1855, 29a6–b3; Tanaka 1996, 181–186.

1121. Phalavajra explains that the sugatas are *rang gi rig pa ngo bo nyid* and *phyi rol ni ma yin no*. See his *Kun tu bzang po'i sgrub thabs kyi 'grel ba*, *Samantabhadra Sādhana Vṛtti*, Tōh 1867, 144b4. Thagana explicates that the sugatas dwell in the yogi's mind since there is nothing other than one's mind. See his *Kun bzang sgrub thabs 'grel ba*, *Samantabhadra Sādhana Vṛtti*, Tōh 1868, 193b2–3. The scholar Samantabhadra maintains that the nature of the sugatas is no different from one's mind. See his *Snying po snye ma*, *Sāramañjarī*, Tōh 1869, 7b1; Szántó, work in progress.

1122. For Tsongkhapa, the exclusive theoretical framework of the sādhana is Nāgārjuna's Madhyamaka. See the sections "The Guhyasamāja Sādhanas of the Ārya School" and "The Creation Stage and Deity Yoga" above.

1123. See Tsong kha pa, *Bung ba'i re skong*, 6a3–5, and also his *Bskyed rim zin bris*, 9a4–6.

1124. Mkhas grub rje, *Bskyed rim dngos grub rgya mtsho*, 17b3–18a3.

1125. Tsong kha pa, *'Dod 'jo*, 44a6–b2, and *Sngags rim chen mo*, 496. See also his *Bskyed rim zin bris*, 7a2–5.

1126. *Kambala, Lwa ba pa, *Bde mchog gi sgrub thabs gtsug nor*, *Cakrasamvara Sādhana Ratnacūḍāmaṇi*, Tōh 1443, 244b2–3.

1127. Tsong kha pa, *'Dod 'jo*, 48a4–5.

many errors will ensue, such as the idea that the cremation ground cannot be associated with purity.[1128] This is because the yogi should visualize the cremation ground arising as an aspect of the wisdom of Vajradhara, the principal deity of the maṇḍala. It should be added here that there are no cremation grounds at the surrounding perimeter of the Guhyasamāja maṇḍala, though they are found in the maṇḍalas of Cakrasaṃvara and Yamāntaka.

Averting Unfavorable Conditions

Before meditating on the main part of the sādhana, yogis meditate on the protection wheel in order to protect themselves and their environment for the duration of their practice. The goal is to eliminate impediments that may distract the aspirants from practicing the sādhana, trigger their wish to take part in mundane activities, confuse or afflict their minds, and so forth.[1129]

According to Tsongkhapa's *Guhyasamāja Sādhana*, based on the scriptural authority of the *Later Tantra*, the aspirants visualize a ten-spoked yellow wheel rapidly spinning clockwise, emanating garlands of clouds of blazing vajras in the ten directions, while visualizing themselves as white Vajradhara with his consort at the center of the hub. Then the yogi transforms into blue-black fierce Dveṣavajra surrounded by the ten fierce deities of the Guhyasamāja maṇḍala. Sumbharāja, the fierce deity in the nadir, emanates a second Sumbharāja who grips the heart of the obstructors with his hook, binds his lasso around their necks, fetches them, and hands them over to the ten fierce deities, who then encase them in triangular pits. With his vajra hammer, Sumbharāja then pounds the stakes on the obstructors' heads, immobilizing their bodies, speech, and minds. Then vajra fire spreads all around and burns the malicious beings that accompany the obstructors, who flee in every direction.[1130]

We may ask: Is this graphic description of defeating the obstructors as found in the sādhana and in Indian sources compatible with the declared purpose of the meditation on the protections wheel, which is to prevent the mind of the meditator from becoming distracted during the practice? This question has been often raised in recent years as part of the discourse about

1128. Mkhas grub rje, *Bskyed rim dngos grub rgya mtsho*, 18a1–3.

1129. See Mkhas grub rje, *Bskyed rim dngos grub rgya mtsho*, 31a4–b4, Nor bzang rgya mtsho, *Gsang ba 'dus pa'i bskyed rim gyi don gsal bar byed pa'i sgron me*, 25a5, and Dge 'dun rgya mtsho, *Gsang bskyed*, 16a2–3.

1130. Tsong kha pa, *Gsang mngon*, 21b1–28a5. See *Rgyud phyi ma, Uttara Tantra*, Tōh 443, 151b7–152a1; Matsunaga 1978, vv. 81–82.

violence in Buddhism. Obviously, Tibetan authors were aware of this disparity and attempted to solve it. For example, Panchen Sönam Drakpa stressed that the meditators must view the protections wheel, the fierce deities, the driving of the stakes, and so on as playful displays of emptiness.[1131] Likewise, Panchen Losang Chökyi Gyaltsen says: "The purpose of such a visualization is to purify ordinary appearances and attitudes to the obstructors and to benefit them."[1132] Akhu Ching Sherab Gyatso notes that by means of this meditation the obstructors can even be awakened, and that to "immobilize"[1133] the obstructors is to prevent them from moving from the clear light. Akhu Ching then concludes that there is no terrifying being with horns out there, only one's own karma and afflictive emotions and those of others, which appear in the form of malevolent influences and obstructors.[1134]

The meditation on the protection wheel has been the subject of numerous debates among Tibetan scholars. Their main concern, however, is not the violence involved in the meditation, but, as is usually the case, the efficacy of the practice. A related issue concerns discrepancies among the scriptural authorities for the practice: the *Guhyasamāja Tantra*,[1135] together with the *Later Tantra*,[1136] which is regarded at times as its final chapter, and the two basic sādhanas of the Ārya tradition, the *Concise Sādhana* and the *Vajrasattva Sādhana*.

A recurring debate, especially between Geluk and Sakya scholars, is whether the aspirants must visualize the protection wheel with ten spokes and whether it spins. As we have mentioned, the *Later Tantra* prescribes a meditation on a ten-spoked protection wheel spinning quickly with ten fierce deities, one on each spoke.[1137] Tsongkhapa and his disciples follow this

1131. Bsod nams grags pa, *Gsang 'dus bskyed rim rnam gzhag*, 16b1.

1132. Paṇ chen Blo bzang chos kyi rgyal mtshan, *Bskyed rim dngos grub rgya mtsho'i snying po*, 26b4–5.

1133. As found in Tsong kha pa, *Gsang mngon*, 28a3.

1134. A khu ching Shes rab rgya mtsho, *Mi bskyod mgon po'i zhal lung*, 58a2–4; an English translation in Jinpa 1999, 103. A khu ching presents here the position of A rig dge bshes Byams pa 'od zer (1728–1803).

1135. Especially chapters 13 and 14 cited in the translation below.

1136. *Rgyud phyi ma*, *Uttara Tantra*, Tōh 443, 148a6–157b7; Matsunaga 1978, 112–130.

1137. Another important authority for the meditation on a yellow ten-spoked wheel spinning clockwise is Abhayākaragupta's commentary on the Ārya tradition of the Guhyasamāja, the *Rim pa lnga pa'i dgongs 'grel zla ba'i 'od zer*, *Pañcakramamatiṭīkā Candraprabhā*, Tōh 1831, 183a6. See also his *Man ngag snye ma*, *Āmnāyamañjarī*, Tōh 1198, 127b7–128a2.

authority.[1138] However, Sakya scholars, including Rendawa, Ngorchen Kunga Sangpo, and Amyé Shap, do not accept this practice, which is not found in the *Concise Sādhana*. Instead, they instruct the yogis to visualize ten fierce deities, without a protection wheel, in the main and intermediate directions as well as in the zenith and nadir.[1139]

Why do these Sakya scholars object to the meditation on the protection wheel, and in particular to a wheel that spins quickly? According to Rendawa:

> If the wheel spins quickly while its motion is not apparent, the allocation [of the fierce deities] to the different directions will be uncertain. Thus it cannot be established that the fierce deities indeed protect the directions.[1140]

In response to objections such as the one raised by Rendawa, Tsongkhapa cites *Yaśobhadra's commentary on the *Later Tantra*, which explains: "While the wheel spins, the fierce deities do not move."[1141] How is this possible? In his *Cluster of Instructions*, Abhayākaragupta clarifies: "The seats of the fierce deities are upon the tips of the spokes, not quite touching them."[1142] Why does the wheel spin? "The wheel must spin so that the spokes of the wheel cut through the malicious ones."[1143] But if the spokes cut through the malicious ones, what prevents them from also cutting through the fierce deities who protect the meditator?

There are more than a dozen additional points of dispute related to the meditation on the protection wheel, such as Khedrup Jé's question of whether it is necessary to meditate on emptiness before visualizing the protection wheel—as Tsongkhapa instructs in his *Guhyasamāja Sādhana*—though this is not found in the basic meditation manual, the *Concise Sādhana*.[1144] This

1138. Tsong kha pa, *Gsang mngon*, 21b3–5; *Slob tshul*, 5b2–5; and *Bskyed rim zin bris*, 11b5; Mkhas grub rje, *Bskyed rim dngos grub rgya mtsho*, 22b1–5.

1139. Red mda' ba, *Bsgrub pa dpal bas zhus lan*, Kathmandu, 49a5–6; TBRC 304b. Ngor chen, *Gsang 'dus dkyil 'khor gyi sgrub thabs dngos grub rgya mtsho*, 3a4.3. A myes zhabs, *Gsang 'dus dkyil 'khor sgrub thabs rnam bshad*, 71a1–74b2.

1140. Red mda' ba, *Bsgrub pa dpal bas zhus lan*, Kathmandu, 49b5–6; TBRC, 305a.

1141. Tsong kha pa, *Slob tshul*, 6b1–2. See *Yaśobhadra/Nāropa, *Gsang ba thams cad kyi sgron ma'i rgya cher 'grel pa*, *Sarvauhyapradīpaṭīkā*, Tōh 1787, 219b5.

1142. Abhayākaragupta, *Man ngag snye ma*, *Āmnāyamañjarī*, Tōh 1198, 128b5–129b4.

1143. Mkhas grub rje, *Bskyed rim dngos grub rgya mtsho*, 23b3.

1144. Mkhas grub rje, *Bskyed rim dngos grub rgya mtsho*, 21b6–22a6. Tsong kha pa, *Gsang mngon*, 21b1.

query arises not only on account of the lack of scriptural authority, but because in the following step of meditation on emptiness everything, including the protection wheel, will then dissolve into emptiness.

Hence, this point is related to the diverse goals of the meditation on emptiness at different steps of the sādhana. For Tsongkhapa, the reason the protection wheel arises from the continuing state of emptiness—the dharmakāya—is to eliminate ordinary appearances and attitudes, while the meditation on emptiness in the following step is, as we saw above,[1145] a meditation on the ground of wisdom that will be applied in correspondence with the eon of the empty world.

In addition to the meditation on the spinning wheel with the ten fierce deities, following the method of the *Vajrasattva Sādhana*, Tsongkhapa instructs the meditators to visualize a protective enclosure formed of an iron vajra fence with a canopy above, surrounded by a concentric water fence, a fire fence, and a wind fence.[1146] Once more, Sakya scholars including Rendawa, Ngorchen Kunga Sangpo, and Amyé Shap do not accept this, since they do not acknowledge that the famous Candrakīrti who composed the *Illuminating Lamp* is also the author of the *Vajrasattva Sādhana*.[1147] This step of the practice concludes with the placing of the three syllables *oṃ āḥ hūṃ* on the crowns, throats, and hearts of the fierce deities. While there are various ways of classifying the protection rituals, in his *Fulfilling the Bee's Hopes*, Tsongkhapa states that the meditation on the enclosure is for protecting the place, whereas setting the three syllables on the three places of the fierce deities is for protecting oneself.[1148]

1145. See the section "Meditation on Emptiness in the Creation Stage."

1146. Tsong kha pa, *Gsang mngon*, 28a5–b2. See Candrakīrti, *Rdo rje sems dpa'i sgrub thabs*, *Vajrasattva Sādhana*, Tōh 1814, 197b1–2; Luo and Tomabechi 2009, 8.6–9 and 40.9–13.

1147. Red mda' ba, *Bsgrub pa dpal bas zhus lan*, Kathmandu, 50b6–51a1; TBRC, 306a. This step is not included in Ngor chen, *Guhyasamāja Sādhana*, *Gsang 'dus dkyil 'khor gyi sgrub thabs dngos grub rgya mtsho*. A myes zhabs, *Gsang 'dus dkyil 'khor sgrub thabs rnam bshad*, 83b2–4.

1148. Tsong kha pa, *Bung ba'i re skong*, 9b3–4.

11. The Aftermath

THESE STEPS of the sādhana take place during the Supreme King of Deeds, after the yoga of recitation. But since they close the actual practice, they are presented at the end of the introduction to the translation.

Dissolution of the Principal Deities into Clear Light

The principal deity of the maṇḍala dissolves into clear light together with his consort. In his *Guhyasamāja Sādhana*, Tsongkhapa describes this dissolution:

> The mother dissolves into the father, the father samayasattva dissolves into the jñānasattva, the jñānasattva into the samādhisattva [the syllable *hūṃ*], the vowel sign *ū* of the samādhisattva into the *ha*, the *ha* into its head, its head into the crescent moon of the *anusvāra*, the crescent moon into the drop, the drop into the *nāda*, and the *nāda* dissolves into clear light.[1149]

This meditation corresponds to the display of the Buddha's deed of passing into nirvāṇa when there are no longer disciples in his buddhafield.[1150] The main purpose of this meditation is to ripen the roots of merit for the manifestation of the innate wisdom during the completion stage, when the pure and impure illusory bodies dissolve into the actual and metaphorical clear light.[1151]

Khedrup Jé raises objections to those who maintain that the dissolution of the principal deities into clear light corresponds to the dissolution of the father-mother through the fire of great passion during saṃsāric rebirth. He reiterates that the meditations during the Supreme Kings do not correspond to the ground of purification, but to the fruit of the path alone.

1149. Tsong kha pa, *Gsang mngon*, 68a6–b2.

1150. Tsong kha pa, *Rnal 'byor dag rim*, 25a4–5, and Mkhas grub rje, *Bskyed rim dngos grub rgya mtsho*, 165a6.

1151. See Mkhas grub rje, *Bskyed rim dngos grub rgya mtsho*, 165a6–b2.

Arising in Response to the Invocation with a Song

Tsongkhapa's *Guhyasamāja Sādhana* has here:

> Unable to behold the principal deity, the four goddesses, who are the essence of the four qualities beyond measure, are in anguish. Wishing to see him, they invoke him with melodious songs.[1152]

This meditation corresponds to the event that follows the passing of the Buddha into nirvāṇa when no disciples remain to be guided by him. The four goddesses beyond measure then sing a song to invoke the Buddha to act for the sake of sentient beings in other realms of the world; in response, the Buddha arises.[1153] Likewise, the yogi, motivated by compassion, arises instantaneously from the clear light as the deity body consisting of the triple sattvas.[1154]

In practicing the sādhana, the meditators recite four verses of request to the principal deity to arise.[1155] These verses appear in the *Guhyasamāja Tantra*, where each of the four mothers or consorts address Mahāvajradhara in turn with "love songs" of praise.[1156] The principal deity then grants their wishes, while the yogis recite:

> Thus invoked through the power of prior aspiration and compassion, I arise from the clear light as the body of the deity, consisting of the triple sattvas and vividly seen by all the deities of the maṇḍala.[1157]

1152. Tsong kha pa, *Gsang mngon*, 68b2–3.

1153. See Tsong kha pa, *Rnal 'byor dag rim*, 25b6–26a1, and Mkhas grub rje, *Bskyed rim dngos grub rgya mtsho*, 165b3–6.

1154. See the section "Meditation on the Triple Sattvas" above.

1155. Tsong kha pa, *Gsang mngon*, 68b3–69a5.

1156. *Gsang 'dus*, chap. 17, Tōh 442; Zhol 47a7–b5; Stog 79b7–80b2; Dunh 88a1b4; Fremantle 1971, vv. 72–75; and Matsunaga 1978, vv. 72–75. These verses are found at the end of chapter seventeen, one of the concluding sections of this tantra, and are explained in Candrakīrti, *Sgron gsal, Pradīpoddyotanaṭīkā*, Tōh 1785, 195a6–196b4; Chakravarti 1984, 224–225. These verses are cited also by Nāgārjuna in his *Mdor byas, Piṇḍīkrama Sādhana*, Tōh 1796, 9b7–10a4, L 206–209.

1157. Tsong kha pa, *Gsang mngon*, 69a6–b1.

Praises, Offerings, and Tasting the Nectar

These ritual activities correspond to Buddha's deeds at the level of the fruit. When a nirmāṇakāya displays the deeds of the Buddha in other buddhafields, appearing there for the first time, all beings there welcome him with praises and offerings. In practicing the sādhana, the yogis arising as the principal deity of the maṇḍala are likewise received by praises and offerings.

While reciting the verses of praise, the yogis visualize that all the deities of the maṇḍala that surround the principal deity recite the praise to the yogis as the principal deity. These five verses of praise, found in the *Guhyasamāja Tantra* and explained in the *Illuminating Lamp*, eulogize the yogis for having been endowed with the excellent qualities of each of the five tathāgata families.[1158]

Four kinds of offerings, outer, inner, secret, and suchness offerings, are made to the yogis as the principal father-mother deities. The offerings made now have been prepared already during the preliminaries to the sādhana.[1159]

The *outer offerings* have been prepared through a fourfold process of clearing, purifying, generating, and blessing.[1160] After being blessed by various mantras, including the mantra of emptiness that purifies ordinary attitudes toward the offerings, they are endowed with three qualities: While they *appear* as offering substances, their *essence* is indivisible empty nature and great bliss, and their *function* is to serve as objects for the six senses that generate untainted great bliss.

For example, when the outer offering of visible objects is offered to the eyes of the yogis by the beautiful offering lady, the sensations aroused by the appearance of the offering as well as by the offering lady herself are transformed into a great bliss that is born in the yogis. When they are thus endowed with a mind of great bliss, all appearances of the three spheres—the

1158. Tsong kha pa, *Gsang mngon*, 69b1–6. The verses are in *Gsang 'dus, Guhyasamāja Tantra*, chap. 17, Tōh 442; Zhol 40b5–7; Stog 68b5–69a2; Fremantle 1971 vv. 1–5; and Matsunaga 1978, vv. 1–5. These verses are also found with variations in Nāgārjuna's *Mdor byas, Piṇḍīkrama Sādhana*, Tōh 1796, 10a4–7; L 211–215. Candrakīrti explains them in *Sgron gsal, Pradīpoddyotanaṭīkā*, Tōh 1785, 175a1–b3; Chakravarti 1984, 203. See also Tsong kha pa, *Sgron gsal mchan*, 462a4–463a6.

1159. See the section "The Preparatory Steps" above.

1160. See Mkhas grub rje, *Bskyed rim dngos grub rgya mtsho*, 14b5–16a6.

offerer, the offerings, and the recipient of the offerings—arise as a display of nondual bliss and emptiness.[1161]

The theoretical basis here is clearly the emptiness of the Madhyamaka and the bliss of the unexcelled tantras. According to the unexcelled tantra, yogis need not practice austerities while surrendering the five objects of the senses, but rather enjoy these objects while understanding their true nature. Since advanced yogis are no longer tainted by ordinary appearances and attitudes, the offerings arise to them as aspects of the wisdom of bliss and emptiness.

The *inner offerings* prepared during the preliminary rituals are offered now in an enactment of the churning of the ocean during the creation of the world.

For the *secret offerings*, the yogis visualize themselves as the principal deity of the maṇḍala absorbed in union with the consort, thereby experience great bliss. Since all the deities of the maṇḍala share a single continuum, at that moment all of them are satiated with great bliss.[1162]

The *offering of suchness* is made when the subjective mind that experiences great bliss indivisibly realizes the nature of objective emptiness.

Final Dissolution of the Visualization

Tsongkhapa's *Guhyasamāja Sādhana* has here:

> Hook-like light-rays emanating from the blue seed syllable *hūṃ* in my heart invite the deities of the maṇḍala from Vairocana to Sumbharāja and place them on sites of my body, the crown and so forth.[1163]

The deities of the maṇḍala are placed on the same sites on the yogi's body into which the specially visualized deities dissolved.[1164] The celestial mansion also dissolves into the body of the yogi as the principal deity, each part into the particular location on the body as in the meditation on the body maṇḍala. Only the yogi and his consort as the father-mother remain. They emanate light rays of bodhicitta that empower all sentient beings, purify their obscurations, and

1161. Mkhas grub rje, *Bskyed rim dngos grub rgya mtsho*, 166a5–b2. See also Āryadeva, *Spyod bsdus*, *Caryāmelāpakapradīpa*, chap. 10, Tōh 1803, 101b5–102a5; Sanskrit, Tibetan, and English translation in Wedemeyer 2007, B: 66b–67a; Sanskrit and Tibetan in Pandey 2000, 93 and 340–341.

1162. Mkhas grub rje, *Bskyed rim dngos grub rgya mtsho*, 172b2–3.

1163. Tsong kha pa, *Gsang mngon*, 73a1–3.

1164. See the section "Withdrawing the Specially Visualized Deities into the Body" above.

transform them into the *hūṃ* syllables, out of which they arise as Vajradharas. Ultimately, all these Vajradharas dissolve into the yogi as the principal deity.

The concluding line of the sādhana here is the mantra *oṃ yogaśuddhāḥ sarvadharmā yogaśuddho 'ham*;[1165] meaning that through this yoga, all phenomena have been rendered pure, and pure through yoga am I. The goal of the creation stage has been reached; by means of this yoga, everything in the world has been purified for the yogis, and the yogis themselves become pure.

The *Concise Sādhana* describes the dissolutions and explains the import of this purity as follows:

> The maṇḍala wheel enters into your own maṇḍala wheel, and the lord alone who is in a state of great bliss remains. The yogis who have practiced the four yogas in this way visualize the world and its inhabitants in the essence of *hūṃ* and imagine all beings arising from this *hūṃ* as Vajrasattvas. When they arise from their yoga, they perceive living beings and act accordingly.[1166]

When yogis arise from their sādhana practice, they should regard every aspect of the world as the celestial mansion, and every living being as a deity of the maṇḍala. Likewise, all sounds they hear should be taken as mantras of the Guhyasamāja, all scents as the Vajra Lady of Scents,[1167] and all tastes as the Vajra Lady of Tastes.[1168] In this way, yogis do not allow ordinary appearances and attitudes to arise to their minds, but instead regard everything as divine. This means that they have assumed all aspects of the fruit of the path in accordance with the tantric principle.

1165. See Tsong kha pa, *Gsang mngon*, 74a1.

1166. Nāgārjuna, *Mdor byas*, *Piṇḍīkrama Sādhana*, Tōh 1796, 10a7–b1; L 216cd–217.

1167. Tib. Dri rdo rje ma, Skt. Gandhavajrā.

1168. Tib. Ro rdo rje ma, Skt. Rasavajrā.

Ocean of Attainments

The Creation Stage of the Guhyasamāja,
the King of All Tantras

༄།།རྒྱུད་ཐམས་ཅད་ཀྱི་རྒྱལ་པོ་དཔལ་གསང་བ་
འདུས་པའི་བསྐྱེད་རིམ་དངོས་གྲུབ་རྒྱ་མཚོ།།

Khedrup Jé Gelek Palsangpo

Homage and Introduction

WITH GREAT DEVOTION I prostrate and take refuge in the lotus of the feet of the Venerable Teacher,[1169] endowed with great nonobjectifiable compassion, and to the feet of the most exalted Nāgārjuna, his disciples, and their lineage.[1170] May you take me under your care with great loving kindness in all my rebirths.

I bow down my head to Vajradhara,[1171] the supreme lord of all victorious ones, appearing as a spiritual teacher for the sake of his disciples, through display of manifestation moved by nonobjectifiable compassion, with incomparable kindness.

May the lord of the wheel, whose essence is nondual innate joy, pure and luminous, stainless like the sky, endowed with vajra body immaculate like a rainbow, protect me.

I prostrate to the protector, who for displaying the supreme path of skillful means, by abiding in the "samādhi on the method of great desire,"[1172] your mind, wisdom of great bliss emanates the celestial mansion with its deities.

I bow down with my head to Nāgārjuna and his disciples who attained the stage of Vajradhara, the elucidators of the meaning of the tantra, the ultimate discourse of the victorious ones, bound up with the six interpretive ends.[1173]

I will explain here the path ripening for the profound completion stage that transforms birth, death, and intermediate state into the three bodies of the

1169. Rje Tsong kha pa.

1170. This is the Ārya tradition of the *Guhyasamāja Tantra*, beginning with Nāgārjuna, who composed the basic sādhana of the practice.

1171. The revealer of the *Guhyasamāja Tantra*.

1172. This samādhi appears in the first chapter of the *Gsang 'dus*, *Guhyasamāja Tantra*, Tōh 442; Zhol 2b2; Stog 3b3; Dunh 1a3; Fremantle 1971, 176–177; and Matsunaga, 1978, 4. Tib. *de bzhin gshegs pa thams cad kyi 'dod chags chen po'i tshul*, Skt. *sarva tathāgata mahā raga naya*, for variant readings see the different editions of the text.

1173. The opening verses of Candrakīrti's *Sgron gsal*, *Pradīpoddyotana*, Tōh 1785, include this line as well.

Victorious One, [2a] by means of the transmitted instruction of the lama who is Lord Vajradhara, in accordance with the works on the meaning of the tantra written by the mahāsiddhas.

If you are a fortunate one, not content with a false path, but wishing to understand the meaning of the tantra, the profound path established through reasoning, according to the transmitted instructions of Ārya Nāgārjuna who attained the supreme attainment, listen with respect.

Wishing to draw all disciples out of saṃsāra and to set them in the supreme mansion of liberation, our teacher[1174] taught manifold and diverse entrance gates to the path, in accordance with the capacity of each one of them. Our teacher[1175] explained at length in his works all the following topics: how these teachings are clearly confined to the two paths, the Lesser Vehicle and the Great Vehicle; how the Great Vehicle or Mahāyāna as well is clearly confined to two Great Vehicles, the Mantra, and the Pāramitā Vehicles;[1176] what makes the Mantra Vehicle especially exalted of the two; how also the Mantra Vehicle is divided into the four classes of tantra; and what makes the higher classes among them especially exalted over the lower ones; how also the unexcelled tantric class is classified into father tantra and mother tantra; and how there is no distinction between them, both being tantras of nondual wisdom and method; the general system of the two stages of the unexcelled path together with their subcategories, and so on. Our teacher, undistinguished from Vajradhara, explained all these topics in detail, but since it would be too much, I will not write about this here. [2b]

[In Praise of the Guhyasamāja Tantra*]*

Among the several different entrance gates to the path, the vehicles, and the stages of the tantric classes that the Victorious One taught, the ultimate is the *Glorious Guhyasamāja*.[1177] This is because in explaining the name *Guhyasamāja Tantra* it was taught that all the essential [*secret*][1178] points of

1174. The Buddha.

1175. Tsong kha pa. See his *Sngags rim chen mo* and *Mtha' gcod.*

1176. These are the Tantra and Sūtra Vehicles, both belonging to the Mahāyāna. The Sūtra Vehicle is called here the Pāramitā Vehicle, Tib. *phar phyin gyi theg pa* or *pha rol tu phyin pa'i theg pa*, Skt. *pāramitāyāna*.

1177. Tib. *Gsang ba 'dus pa*, or *Gsang 'dus*, Tōh 442.

1178. Tib. *gsang ba*, Skt. *guhya*. Both Tsong kha pa's *Mtha' gcod*, 33b5, and his *Rim lnga gsal sgron*, 22a1, have *gsang ba'i gnad* for *gnad* in our text.

the Vajra Vehicle are *included*[1179] in it. Likewise the *Later Tantra* teaches: "Emaho! Extremely difficult to arrive at is this method for attaining awakening, the tantra called the *Guhyasamāja*, the highest of the higher tantras."[1180] Since the Guhyasamāja is *extremely difficult to arrive at* and has enormous importance,[1181] the yogis engaging in its creation and completion stages during the four sessions, and those who study, inquire,[1182] recite, make offerings to it, and meditate on the path of this tantra, and whoever sees, hears, memorizes, touches, has faith in it, up until who holds just a fragment of this tantra—all of them are regarded as being like Bodhivajra,[1183] that is, Vajradhara, and worthy of prostration.

The *Guhyasamāja Tantra* itself teaches as well: "Even the buddhas and bodhisattvas of the three times, and all those who have attained the stage of Vajradhara—when they encounter a master who unmistakenly teaches the path of the Guhyasamāja, they make offerings and prostration to this master, and utter words such as 'he is the father of all of us tathāgatas.'"[1184] It is taught that for this reason without relying on the path of the Guhyasamāja, it is impossible to be awakened.

The *Fifty Stanzas on the Guru* teaches: "The tathāgatas, abiding in the world realms in the ten directions, prostrate at the three times to the vajra master, from whom they received the supreme initiation."[1185] Thus it was taught that even after becoming buddhas, these very buddhas prostrate to the lama who had conferred initiation on them, when they were practicing the initial path.

1179. Tib. *'dus pa*, Skt. *samāja*.

1180. *Rgyud phyi ma*, *Uttara Tantra*, Tōh 443, 148b3–4; Matsunaga 1978, v. 4. D has *dga' ba* for *dka' ba*; and *rgyud kyi mchog gi mchog* for *rgyud kyi phyi ma'i phyi mar* in our text. Cited also in Tsong kha pa, *Mtha' gcod*, 33b5–6, and his *Rim lnga gsal sgron*, 22a1–2; English translation in Kilty 2013, 55. Paṇ chen Bsod nams grags pa, *Rgyud sde spyi'i rnam bzhag*, 40b2–41a5; English translation in Boord and Tsonawa 1996, 58–59, as well repeats this and some of the following citations.

1181. Here Mkhas grub rje paraphrases the *Rgyud phyi ma*, *Uttara Tantra*, Tōh 443, 157b1–4; Matsunaga 1978, vv. 210–213, in following Tsong kha pa, *Mtha' gcod*, 33b4–34a2, and his *Rim lnga gsal sgron*, 22a1–24a1.

1182. Or "copy," reading *'bri ba* for *'dri ba*.

1183. Tib. Byang chub rdo rje.

1184. A similar but not identical passage is found in *Guhyasamāja Tantra*, chap. 17, following v. 51, in Tōh 442; Zhol 44b1–5; Stog 75a2–b1; Dunh 82b3–83a3; Fremantle 1971, 390–391; and Matsunaga 1978, 104.

1185. Aśvaghoṣa, *Bla ma lnga bcu pa*, *Gurupañcāśikā*, Tōh 3721, 10a3–4, verse 2; Sanskrit edition in Lévi 1929, 259; and Szántó 2013, 443. See also Tsong kha pa's commentary on this work, *Bla ma lnga bcu pa'i rnam bshad*; Tibetan and English translation in Sparham 1999, 32–33 and 93.

[3a] Moreover, this was taught only with regard to a vajra master who teaches the path of the Guhyasamāja unmistakenly.

Furthermore, the *Oral Instruction of Mañjuśrī* as well praises the *Guhyasamāja*: "The tantra that *unites*[1186] all buddhas—the *secret*,[1187] the great secret, the utmost secret, is the unsurpassed great scripture."[1188] The *Oral Instruction of Mañjuśrī* also teaches that whether the essence of the teachings will remain or not depends on whether this tantra still exists: "It is explained that as long as the meaning of this tantra is transmitted into one's ear, so long the precious teachings of the Buddha remain, but when this transmission lineage is broken, the teachings of the Buddha will disappear. This all should know."[1189]

Also the *Secret Attainment* teaches: "There is no superior to the glorious Guhyasamāja, the jewel in the three worlds, supreme quintessence of all quintessences, unexcelled of the unexcelled of all tantras. How could those, who have not understood the Guhyasamāja with its instructions and explanations as well as its yoga of the completion stage, attain siddhis? It removes all doubts and clears the blurred perspective of ignorance. It is the jewel treasure-case of the Buddha. The simpletons who relinquish the glorious Guhyasamāja and are still hoping for siddhis by investigating through manifold conceptualizations are striking their fists at space or drinking mirage water."[1190] The *Illuminating Lamp* teaches that the Guhyasamāja is the root of all other tantras and the treasure-case of all sūtras, thus it is the pinnacle or the supreme of all tantras.[1191] [3b]

1186. Tib. *'dus pa*, Skt. *samāja*.

1187. Tib. *gsang ba*, Skt. *guhya*.

1188. Jñānapāda, *Rim pa gnyis pa'i de kho na nyid bsgom pa'i zhal lung*, *Dvikramatattvabhāvanā*, Tōh 1853, 15b6. D has *gsang las ches* for *gsang ba ches* in our text. These lines are cited in Tsong kha pa, *Mtha' gcod*, 34a4–b1, and in his *Rim lnga gsal sgron*, 22b1–2; for an English translation see Kilty 2013, 56.

1189. Jñānapāda, *Rim pa gnyis pa'i de kho na nyid bsgom pa'i zhal lung*, *Dvikramatattvabhāvanā*, Tōh 1853, 15b3–4. D has *yang* for *kyang*.

1190. Padmavajra, *Gsang ba grub pa*, *Guhyasiddhi*, chap. 1, Tōh 2217, 5a4–6; Sanskrit and Tibetan, Samdhong Rinpoche and Vrajvallabh Dwivedi 1987, 10–11, vv. 60–63 and 13–14, vv. 82–85. D has *'gyur* for *gyur*; *ni* for *kyang*; *bshad pa'i* for *bshad pa*; *gnas pa* for *gnas na*; *rdzogs pa'i rnal 'byor rim pa* for *rdzogs pa'i rim pa'i rnal 'byor*; *rdog pa* for *brdeg pa*; and *smig rgyu'i* for *smig skyu'i* in our text. These lines are also found in Tsong kha pa, *Mtha' gcod*, 34b2–5, and his *Rim lnga gsal sgron*, 22b5–23a2; for an English translation see Kilty 2013, 56–57. Cited as well in Bsod nams grags pa, *Rgyud sde spyi'i rnam bzhag*, 41a; English translation in Boord and Tsonawa 1996, 59.

1191. Candrakīrti, *Sgron gsal*, *Pradīpoddyotana*, Tōh 1785, 2a2–3; Chakravarti 1984, 1; English translation in Campbell 2009, 292. Our text follows also Tsong kha pa, *Sgron gsal mchan*, 5b2.

Not only in its own cycle but in other tantras as well is this tantra praised as supreme. Both the *Red* and *Black Yamāri* tantras teach: "The Guhyasamāja is the ultimate of tantras, such a tantra has never appeared, nor will it ever appear again."[1192] Also the great master Kṛṣṇācārya teaches: "With respect to the essence of the two stages of the path, the *Glorious Guhyasamāja* surpasses all tantras and is the primal of them all."[1193]

In this way, countless tantras and works of learned and accomplished masters teach that the Guhyasamāja is the supreme among all sūtras and tantras, and that without relying on its path it is impossible to reach the supreme siddhi of enlightenment.

[Why Is the Guhyasamāja Praised So?]

Such a way of teaching that this tantra is the foremost for both stages is not just mere words, rather the aim is that by means of gaining certitude a firm faith in this path will arise. Hence it is inappropriate to think, as do some vain ones without investigating, that it is a general practice that every tantra and every teaching contains high praises of itself, and so also the praises of this tantra are in this way.

[Classifications of the Unexcelled Tantras]

THEY ALSO SAY[1194] that there are teachings called nondual tantra superior over both the father and mother tantras. These are unknown to any Indian scholar, and are merely false proofs made up by SOME TIBETANS to establish

1192. *Gshin rje'i gshed dmar po'i rgyud*, *Raktayamāri Tantra*, Tōh 474, 213b3–4, and *Gshin rje gshed nag po'i rgyud*, *Kṛṣṇayamāri Tantra*, Tōh 467, 150b6. These lines are cited also in Tsong kha pa, *Mtha' gcod*, 34b1, and his *Rim lnga gsal sgron*, 22b4–5; for an English translation see Kilty 2013, 56.

1193. Kṛṣṇācārya, *Gsang ba'i de kho na nyid rab tu gsal ba*, *Guhyatattvaprakāśa*, Tōh 1450, 349b4. D has *dpal ldan 'dus pa'i lam gyi ni* for *dpal ldan 'dus rjes lam gyis ni*; *ngo bo las* for *ngo bo la*; and *yon* for *son* in our text. These lines are also cited in Tsong kha pa, *Mtha' gcod*, 24b3–4 and 34b4–5, and his *Rim lnga gsal sgron*, 12a3–4; an English translation in Kilty 2013, 38. In light of the very different readings, my translation of these lines is speculative.

1194. See Rin chen bzang po, *Rgyud sde spyi'i rnam bzhag*, 36b3–4; and Bsod nams rtse mo, *Rgyud sde spyi'i rnam gzhag*, work 1, 34b5–6; English translation in Verrill and Ngor Thartse Khenpo Sonam Gyatso 2012, 266. See Eimer 1989 for Bu ston's similar classification in his catalogues in his *Chos 'byung* and his *Rgyud 'bum gyi dkar chag*. See also Tsong kha pa, *Mtha' gcod*, 17a1–b6, and his *Rim lnga gsal sgron*, 3a3–5a4; English translation in Kilty 2013, 25–31. See also Mkhas grub rje, *Rgyud sde spyi'i rnam gzhag*; Lessing and Wayman 1968, 250–269.

that the tantra they are greatly fond of is a nondual tantra. These explanations are futile, and clinging to them should be abandoned.

[Awakening in This Life]

YOU should not be content in satisfying your mind with the mere words that yogis meditating on indivisible bliss and emptiness, on innate wisdom, and on the forward and reverse order of the four joys will be awakened in this life. Indeed the four joys and so on are very much indispensable, but for awakening in this life, [4a] it is necessary to attain in this life a saṃbhogakāya adorned with the major and minor marks of the Buddha and with the seven aspects of union.

It is not possible that the present body produced by previous karma and afflictive emotions would transform into a buddha body. How is a buddha body attained after the present body is forsaken? If the present body is abandoned and a buddha body is obtained by taking a new birth, then the premise that one is awakened in this life would be vitiated. On the other hand, if the present body is abandoned and a buddha body adorned with the major and minor marks of a buddha is attained without taking a new birth, then the buddha body arises without an accordant cause, and this is unacceptable. Therefore you need to engage in these practices after having fully understood through which accordant cause the buddha body is attained, through the power of which antidote the present impure body is discarded, how the saṃbhogakāya is attained after discarding it, and so on.

But if YOU SAY that without the least bit of a basis for attaining the body of the Victorious One adorned with the major and minor marks, just by habituating the mind to abide in bliss, clarity, and nonconceptuality, the dharmakāya of innate wisdom would manifest and you would be awakened; then you will need to accept a buddha endowed with the dharmakāya alone, without the saṃbhogakāya, without any major and minor marks, and so on, but with an ordinary body.

However, you should thoroughly comprehend through the kindness of the perfect guru, whom you have pleased, the method for attaining a body adorned with the major and minor marks in this life, after forsaking the impure body, as this is very extensively explained in the glorious *Guhyasamāja Tantra*, and is clearly analyzed in the transmitted instructions of Ārya Nāgārjuna and his disciples. Although other tantras do explain in detail the union of bliss and emptiness and so on, they are not completely clear and are not thorough about the method of attaining the body of wisdom adorned with the major and minor marks in this life after discarding the impure body. [4b]

Therefore you need to gain a conclusive understanding of the method that is difficult to realize by relying on other tantras. When you gain this, you will gain an unwavering faith that the glorious Guhyasamāja is the supreme among all scriptures, and that there is no path superior to this. If you do not understand that, and without seeing even a fraction of the methods for attaining a body adorned with the major and minor marks in this life on the basis of the unexcelled mantra,[1195] YOU SAY that you have a great faith in the unexcelled mantra, while YOU YOURSELF do not have any confidence, but rather blindly follow the words of others, it is obviously totally pointless.

Yet my glorious holy teacher[1196]—the essence of Vajradhara—explained how to practice on the path of the glorious Guhyasamāja. He wrote extensively on the ritual proceeding of the ripening initiation and on the sādhana of the creation stage, and he composed a *Commentary on Formulating the Sādhana*[1197] that clarifies the method of applying the creation stage in correspondence to its ground of purification. He also authored a guidance book that clearly teaches the method of practicing the completion stage, with detailed instruction, and so on.

But since he did not compose a work that analyzes in detail the reasons and so forth why each step of the sādhana should be practiced in a particular way, so that those with inferior minds will be made to understand, the arrogant ones who claim that they have superior intellect will lose all their doubts, the fortunate ones will develop their comprehension, and so that I too will not forget the teachings of my venerable lama, I will explain the reasons for each and every step of the sādhana, and the order of the visualizations, adorned with transmitted instruction.

The six main topics of the explanation are [5a] (1) characteristics of the yogis, (2) the reasons yogis should meditate on the creation stage before they meditate on the completion stage, (3) characteristics of the place of practice, (4) the practice—how the realization is attained, (5) the criteria for completing the creation stage by practicing in this way, and (6) how siddhis are attained upon the completion of the creation stage.

1195. Tib. *sngags bla med.*

1196. Rje Tsong kha pa.

1197. Tsong kha pa, *Rnam gzhag rim pa'i rnam bshad*, a commentary on Nāgabuddhi's *Rnam gzhag rim pa, Samāja Sādhana Vyavastholi*, Tōh 1809; Sanskrit and Tibetan in Tanaka 2016.

Characteristics of the Yogis

In the *Vajra Garland Tantra* Vajrapaṇi asks: "What qualities will be needed by a disciple who wishes to become a vessel for the yoga tantra?"[1198] In reply to the question "What pre-conditions are essential on entering the Vajra Vehicle?" the vajra teacher explains: "The most excellent and dedicated disciple is endowed with the attributes of faith, respect for the lama, the constant abiding in virtuous activities,[1199] the shedding of bad thoughts, the study of numerous scriptural transmissions, the renunciation of killing and harmfulness, the aspiration to release sentient beings, and perpetual effort."[1200]

[Cultivating the Shared Path]

The essential characteristics of disciples are not naturally present from the beginning, hence the need to cultivate and develop yourself. Herein are the stages for cultivation: first, you must rely on a spiritual teacher who will explain the freedoms and endowments, their crucial significance, the difficulties in attaining them, their transitory nature, and the wanderings through lower rebirths that follow death through the power of karma. It is not enough to understand these explanations at the intellectual level; you should meditate until the full experience has arisen in your mental continuum. Then, by means of the powers induced you should take refuge wholeheartedly, apply yourself in deep reflection to actions and their fruit, and practice the acceptance and rejection of virtue and vice in all their subtleties. Thereafter, you should ponder the general and specific failings of cyclic existence and develop an uncontrived attitude that diligently aspires to liberation. [5b]

1198. *Rgyud rdo rje phreng ba, Vajramālā Tantra*, chap. 1, Tōh 445, 211a1. D has *slob ma'i yon tan* for *slob ma yon tan* in our text. Cited also in Tsong kha pa's *Rim lnga gsal sgron*, 34b6; English translation in Kilty 2013, 76; and by Paṇ chen Bsod nams grags pa, *Rgyud sde spyi'i rnam bzhag*, 46a6–b1; English translation in Boord and Tsonawa 1996, 68.

1199. According to our text that has *lam* for *las*, the constant abiding in virtuous path.

1200. *Rgyud rdo rje phreng ba, Vajramālā Tantra*, chap. 65, Tōh 445, 271b5–6. Our text has *lam* for *las*; skips the line *gnyis med sgyu yang med pa dang* in D and has *gdon pa* for *'don pa* and *de la sogs pa'i yon tan ldan* for *de la sogs pa'i yang dag ldan* in D. Our text follows Tsong kha pa's *Rim lnga gsal sgron*, 35ab1–2; English translation in Kilty 2013, 76. The teacher here is Bcom ldan rdo rje.

[Joining the Mahāyāna]

After that, you should reflect deeply on how all sentient beings are afflicted with the sufferings of cyclic existence just as you yourself are, and recollect how all suffering creatures are none other than your own kind mother. In this way you should continue to cultivate the transmitted instructions for a long time. Beyond theoretical knowledge, you should strive for an uncontrived mind bound for enlightenment arising in your mental continuum with the wish to extract all beings from cyclic existence. Once the mind bound for enlightenment arises, you become a rider in the Mahāyāna, and any virtuous deed you may engage in, while being enveloped by the mind bound for enlightenment, will partake in the path of the Mahāyāna.

Unless the genuine experience of such a mind bound for enlightenment arises, you will not be able to abide in the Mahāyāna. If you are not enveloped by this mind, there is no reason to even think about being able to abide in the unordinary path of the mantra, no matter how much you may be sealed in the pure view of emptiness, and thereby strive to meditate on the maṇḍala wheel, recite mantras, meditate on the path of the subtle body, and so forth. Moreover it is exceedingly difficult to establish that you are on the path of the Mahāyāna, because noble disciples and solitary buddhas as well realize emptiness directly. Hence it is necessary to establish whether you are indeed on the path of great awakening on the basis of whether or not you are endowed with the conventional mind bound for enlightenment.

Therefore you must generate the mind bound for enlightenment by cultivating for a long time. However, if without cultivation, merely by repeating lines such as "my mind is set on awakening to buddhahood"[1201] at the beginning of an initiation and so forth, a mind bound for enlightenment could arise, then, by such a method, other paths as well, up to all the paths of the Buddha will arise in your continuum within a single day.

Therefore you must cultivate until a genuine experience arises, and when, through the power induced by it, a wish to engage in bodhisattva practices arises from the depth of the heart, [6a] you maintain the bodhisattva vows according to the prescribed ritual and practice the six perfections, thereby becoming a receptacle for initial entry into the Vajra Vehicle. Thus, if you wish to enter the Mantra Vehicle, you must begin with cultivation of the shared path through the supreme transmitted instructions.

1201. See for example, Advayavajra, *Lta ba ngan pa sel ba, Kudṛṣṭinirghāta,* Tōh 2229, 107a7; Mikkyō-seiten kenkyūkai 1988, 215.

[Entrance to the Mantra Path]

Should the teachings of the profound path of the unexcelled mantra be imparted on an unsuitable vessel, the disciple will be ruined in the present and future lives, and for the master the arising of the path in the continuum and the attainment of siddhis will be deferred for a long time, for the *Vajra Garland Tantra* teaches: "Just as the milk of a lioness should not be kept in a clay pot, so the great yoga tantras should not be conferred upon unsuitable vessels. If the personal instructions are explained to an unsuitable vessel, the disciple will die instantly, ruined in present and future lives, while the master's siddhis will decline."[1202]

Furthermore, the *Vajrapāṇi Initiation Tantra* also teaches that initiation should not be conferred on a disciple who has not perfected the mind bound for enlightenment.[1203] And the *Compendium of Practices* teaches that you must enter the mantra path gradually, as it is inappropriate to enter all at once, and likewise explains the method for a gradual entry as follows: First you must learn the thought of the Buddha Vehicle. When you become habituated to that, you must practice the creation stage, and once habituated to that, you must engage in the completion stage.[1204] The Buddha Vehicle here is the Great Vehicle of Pāramitās.[1205] Since there are a great many additional explanations, you should acquire a clear understanding of this method.

Once you have practiced in this way and thereby entered the mantra path, you must first receive initiation from a properly qualified teacher, who is certain to make you a suitable vessel for meditating on the path, for listening[1206] to the tantras and to the transmitted instructions, and so forth, in accordance with the teachings of the tantric scriptures. [6b] Indeed, you must enter the

1202. *Rgyud rdo rje phreng ba, Vajramālā Tantra*, chap. 65, Tōh 445, 272a3–4. Cited also in Tsong kha pa, *Sngags rim chen mo*, chap. 5, 161, and his *Rim lnga gsal sgron*, 35a3–5; English translation in Kilty 2013, 77.

1203. *Lag na rdo rje dbang bskur ba'i rgyud, Vajrapāṇyabhiṣeka Tantra*, Tōh 496, 148b3–6. See Tsong kha pa, *Sngags rim chen mo*, chap. 1, 51; English translation in Hopkins 1977, 165; and Tsong kha pa, *Rim lnga gsal sgron*, 35b2–36a1; English translation in Kilty 2013, 77–78.

1204. Āryadeva, *Spyod bsdus, Caryāmelāpakapradīpa*, chap. 1, Tōh 1803, 59b3–4; Sanskrit, Tibetan, and English translation in Wedemeyer 2007, A: 5a; Sanskrit and Tibetan in Pandey 2000, 5 and 163. This passage will be cited on [11b] below. Here Mkhas grub rje follows Tsong kha pa, *Sngags rim chen mo*, chap. 1, 53, and the *Rim lnga gsal sgron*, 36a3–6, English translation in Kilty 2013, 78, which paraphrase and cite the *Spyod bsdus*. See also Tsong kha pa, *Slob tshul*, 1b4.

1205. Tib. *pha rol tu phyin pa'i theg pa chen po*.

1206. Reading *nyan pa* for *mnyan pa* in our text.

mantric path by receiving an initiation from a properly qualified teacher, for the *Drop of the Great Seal* teaches: "Once initiation is conferred upon disciples shortly after they begin their practice, there is no doubt that they will turn into suitable vessels for explanations of the great secret. Without initiation there can be no siddhi, just as when sand is pressed, there is no butter. Those who explain tantras and instructions out of pride, without the conferral of initiation, will go to hell as soon as they die, masters and their disciples alike, even if they have attained siddhis. Therefore you should make every effort to request your lama for initiation."[1207]

The *Vajra Garland Tantra* likewise teaches: "Initiation is of primary importance, as all siddhis abide there. I will explain the meaning of this precisely, so first listen well. When disciples are perfectly initiated by the wise from the start, they become vessels for the yoga of the completion stage. If disciples have not been perfectly initiated, even when they understand the meaning of the tantra, master and disciple alike will go to the Great Unendurable Hell."[1208] Numerous tantras and works of mahāsiddhas, like the *Buddha Skull*, offer a similar teaching.[1209] Therefore in order for disciples to become suitable vessels, it is crucial to confer initiation upon them at the outset.

Regarding the initiation itself, you must first enter the maṇḍala, and then receive the four initiations one by one, beginning with the vase initiation. But the conferral of the three higher initiations to disciples who have neither entered the outer maṇḍala nor received the vase initiation should be utterly avoided, for the *Buddha Union Tantra* teaches: "Those who have not entered the maṇḍala, neglect their commitments, and do not know the essential secret [7a] even if they practice will achieve nothing."[1210] Likewise, the *Vajra Pavilion*

1207. *Phyag chen thig le, Mahāmudrātilaka Tantra*, Tōh 420, 66b4–5. D has *re zhig slob ma la* for *re shig gang tshe slob*; *dbang rnams lan cig bskur ba yis* for *lan cig dbang rnams kyis ni bskur*; *de tshe* for *de cha*; *dbang bskur med la gsal byed pa* for *dbang bskur med par 'chad byed pa*; and *bla ma la ni dbang don zhu* for *bla ma las ni dbang ned zhu*. This passage is cited in Tsong kha pa, *Sngags rim chen mo*, chap. 5, 157, and in his *Nā ro*, 4b4–6.

1208. *Rgyud rdo rje phreng ba, Vajramālā Tantra*, chap. 2, Tōh 445, 212a2–3. D has *sgrub pos rgyud kyi don shes kyang* for *sgrub po rgyud kyi don shas kyang*; *slob mar* for *slob ma*; and *mi bzad* for *mi zad*. This passage is cited in Tsong kha pa, *Sngags rim chen mo*, chap. 5, 157–158.

1209. *Sangs rgyas thod pa, Buddhakapāla Tantra*, Tōh 424. This and additional scriptures are cited in Tsong kha pa, *Sngags rim chen mo*, chap. 5, 158.

1210. *Sangs rgyas mnyam sbyor, Sarvabuddhasamayoga*, chap. 7, Tōh 366, 164b2–3. D has *dam tshig rnams ni spangs pa dag* for *dam tshig rnams kyang spangs pa dang*; *gsang ba yang dag* for *gsang ba'i de nyid*; and *ci yang* for *ci 'ang* in our text. This passage is cited in Tsong kha pa, *Sngags rim chen mo*, 159 and 432, and in his *Dngos grub snye ma*, 2a1–2; for an English translation see Sparham 2005, 28.

teaches: "A yogi who has not entered the maṇḍala, has not received initiation, has not seen consecration, and has not made fire offerings, will not achieve the supreme siddhi of enlightenment either in this or in other worlds."[1211] And the *Cakrasaṃvara Tantra* teaches: "Mantrins who wish to be yogis without seeing the maṇḍala strike at the air with their fists or drink a mirage of water."[1212] Thus countless tantras and works of mahāsiddhas teach that it is inappropriate to enter the Mantra Vehicle without first entering into the maṇḍala. The maṇḍala entered into by the disciple must be the very one that manifests the deity. It is inappropriate to discuss in this context other maṇḍalas such as the *bhaga* maṇḍala and so forth. Hence, conferring the higher initiation upon those who have not entered the maṇḍala or received the complete vase initiation is contradictory to all these scriptures.

Upon your initial request for initiation,[1213] the master will declare: "Do not reveal this supreme secret of all tathāgatas to those who have not entered the maṇḍala, lest you break your commitments." Thus you must keep your vow. Since many tantras and authoritative guides to maṇḍala rituals teach this, any departure from it will make you blameworthy of breaking the commitment. Therefore masters who have made the mantric commitments yet act in such a way, proclaiming the secret to those who are wholly unripe, commit a root downfall.

Furthermore, if it were appropriate[1214] to confer the secret initiation on disciples who have not received the vase initiation, [7b] an absurd state of affairs would ensue, for it would then also be appropriate to confer the wisdom initiation with a consort on disciples who have not received the secret initiation, the fourth initiation on those who have not received the wisdom initiation, the

1211. *Gur*, *Vajrapañjara Tantra*, chap. 8, Tōh 419, 45b2–3. D has: *rnal 'byor pa gang dbang bskur med / dkyil 'khor du ni ma zhugs dang* for *dkyil 'khor du ni ma zhugs dang / dbang bskur mad* [*med*] *pa'i rnal 'byor pa*; *gang zhig* for *gang gis* [twice]; *mthong dang* for *mthong zhing*; *ma byas pa* for *ma byas na*; *pha rol du* for *gzhan du yang*; and *de yi* for *de la* in our text. This passage is cited in Tsong kha pa, *Sngags rim chen mo*, chap. 5, 159, where he indicates that it is found in the eighth chapter of the tantra.

1212. *Bde mchog rtsa rgyud* = *Bde mchog nyung ngu*, Tōh 368, 216a2; Stog 6b1; English translation in Gray 2007, 176. D and Stog have *sngags pa* for *sngags pas*. D has *khu tshur gyis brdeg* and Stog has *khu tshur gyis rdeg* for *khu tshur brdeg pa* in our text. Cited also in Tsong kha pa, *'Dod 'jo*, 7a4, and his *Nā ro*, 5a3–4.

1213. Our text follows Tsong kha pa, *Sngags rim chen mo*, chap. 5, 159, which cites the *De bzhin gshegs pa thams cad kyi de kho na nyid bsdus pa'i mdo*, *Sarvatathāgatatattvasaṃgraha*, Tōh 479, 27a7–b1; Lokesh Chandra 1987, 22; for an English translation from the Chinese, see Giebel 2001, 75–76.

1214. Reading *rung na* for *rub na*.

vajra master initiation on those who have not received the five initiations of realization, and so forth.

Hence, even if the higher initiations are conferred upon disciples who have not yet entered into the maṇḍala and attained the complete vase initiation, they are ineffective. And instructing such a disciple in the completion stage would be like teaching it to someone who has never received initiation. This, for all masters and disciples, constitutes the supreme "means of attaining"[1215] the Unendurable Hell. Thus do not bring ruin on yourself and others out of a desire to gain little wealth and accumulate disciples.

Hence, if the disciple is still a novice cultivating the notions shared by all vehicles and endowed with negligible blessings while the master is unskilled in maṇḍala rituals, lacking in the proper practice of the sādhana, any simulated ritual performed by such a master should not be designated an initiation. To become a proper meditator on the creation stage, it is essential that the disciple has been made a suitable tantric vessel by receiving the initiations in the right order according to the tantric scriptures.

[The Stages of the Path][1216]

Having received initiation in this way, what are the stages of practicing the path?[1217]

[Maintaining the Vows and Commitments]

After being initiated, for every path you may practice, you should thoroughly understand the vows and commitments assumed in the course of the initiation. These vows and commitments should not be passed over as mere promises, but should be guarded as dearly as you guard your own life. [8a] Maintaining them as the basis for your practice, when you have meditated on the transmitted instructions of the two stages, the maṇḍala, and so forth, you will attain siddhis. Conversely, if you neglect your vows, you will never attain siddhis no matter how many eons you may strive.

1215. Tib. *sgrub thabs*, Skt. *sādhana*.

1216. The title of this section in our Tibetan text is "The Reasons Yogis Should Meditate on the Creation Stage before They Meditate on the Completion Stage." However, the actual discussion of this topic begins only below. For the sake of clarity, I have moved the original title down and added my own title, "The Stages of the Path," in brackets here.

1217. See Tsong kha pa, *Sngags rim chen mo,* chap. 12, 431–436; English translation in Yarnall 2013, 78–87.

This is so because the *Saṃvarodaya Tantra* teaches: "When yogis who persevere in the practice of the vows, as instructed during the initiation, and whose mental continua have become suitable vessels, meditate on the maṇḍala-wheel and so forth by means of the sublime and perfect transmitted teachings, they will attain and not by other means."[1218] The *Vajra Peak* also teaches: "Four kinds of persons in the world will not reach attainments even if they strive by every means for hundreds of eons. Those who have not cultivated the mind bound for enlightenment, those who have doubts, those who do not act according to the precepts, and those who lack faith will not achieve them."[1219] There are countless such teachings.

That is why the *Saṃvarodaya Tantra* teaches: "In wishing for the supreme siddhi of enlightenment, always guard your commitments, even if you lose your life, even if death is approaching."[1220] This is how you must persevere in guarding your vows, for if you do so, it will be as taught in the *Five Pledges*: "If you have not committed a downfall, you will reach enlightenment within sixteen lifetimes."[1221] Or as Vibhūticandra teaches: "Even if you have not med-

1218. *Sdom 'byung*, Tōh 373, 288a2–3; Sanskrit, Tibetan, and English translation in Tsuda 1974, chap. 18, vv. 36cd–37. Tsuda has *phyi nas man ngag ji bzhin du / dam tshig spyod pa la brtson pas* for *ji ltar nye bar bstan pa bzhin / phyi nas dam tshig spyod par brtson*; *rgyun gyis* for *rgyun las*; *bsgom pa'i rim* for *bsgom rim gyis*; *phun tshogs pas* for *phun tshogs kyis*; and *dngos grub 'gyur gyi* for *'grub par 'gyur ro* in our text. Our text does not seem to be a direct citation from the tantra itself, but from a different translation of this passage, such as the one that appears Tsong kha pa, *Sngags rim chen mo,* chap. 12, 431–436. The following quotations are likewise found in the *Sngags rim chen mo*, and some are also quoted in his *Dngos grub snye ma*, 52a2–62a5; for an English translation, see Sparham 2005, 115–131.

1219. *Rdo rje rtse mo*, *Vajraśekhara Tantra*, Tōh 480, 165a1–2. D has *brgya phrag stong du* for *brgya phrag dag tu*; *ci nas* for *ci ste*; *bzhi po* for *bzhi ni*; */ sems ni bskyed par ma gyur dang / dad med 'grub bar mi 'gyur nyid / the tshom 'dzin pa nyid dag dang / bka' bsgo ba ni mi byed pa'o /* for */ byang chub sems ni ma skyes dang / the tshom ldan pa nyid dang ni / bka' bzhin du ni mi spyod pa / dad pa med nyid 'grub mi 'gyur*. Again, our text follows Tsong kha pa, *Sngags rim chen mo*, chap. 11, 432, which seems to be another translation of the text.

1220. The *Sdom 'byung*, chap. 27, Tōh 373, 302a7; not in Tsuda 1974. D has *'chi bar mnyam par 'gro yang sla'i* for *'chi bar dus la bab kyang sla*. Once more our text follows Tsong kha pa, *Sngags rim chen mo,* chap. 11, 432, and his *Dngos grub snye ma*, 57b2–3; for an English translation see Sparham 2005, 123; as well as Tsong kha pa, *Bskyed rim zin bris*, 2b3–4, though our text twice does not have *bla* for *sla*. The first line here seems to have been mistakenly borrowed from the previous citation of this tantra.

1221. Padmasambhava, or Padmākara, *Dam tshig lnga pa*, *Samayapañca*, Tōh 1224, 28b2. This is also quoted in Tsong kha pa, *Sngags rim chen mo*, chap. 11, 433, and his *Dngos grub snye ma*, 53b3; for an English translation, see Sparham 2005, 116.

itated, if you are without downfall, you will reach enlightenment within sixteen lifetimes."[1222]

[Study, Reflection, and Meditation]

Those who abide thus in the pure commitments, before they meditate on the stages of the path, should gain, through the wisdom of study and reflection, a thorough understanding of the ways to meditate on the two stages, including all the aspects.[1223] Otherwise they will not know how to practice or where they err, [8b] since although they practice, their endeavor will either be fruitless or produce an undesired fruit.

Therefore, as the *Pearl Rosary* teaches: "Without understanding there is no learning, and without learning there is no reflection. Where both are lacking, there is no yoga, and where yoga is wanting, there is no attainment of siddhis."[1224] And as the *Clarifying the Meaning of Difficult Points in the Five Stages* teaches: "If you are endowed with wisdom perfected through study as well as through reflection, and apply them in meditation, you will attain the unexcelled siddhi. Taking this into account, the wise, who first strive to study and always make every effort, will duly attain siddhi. For how can someone who has doubts about the words realize their meaning?"[1225] And as the *Five*

1222. Vibhūticandra, *Sdom gsum 'od kyi 'phreng ba*, *Trisaṃvaraprabhāmālā*, Tōh 3727, 56b6. D has *nyid na'o* for *dag na 'grub* in our text. Tibetan edition and English translation of this text in Sobisch 2002, 21–175 passim; our verse is found on 172–173. These lines are quoted also in Tsong kha pa, *Sngags rim chen mo,* chap. 11, 433, and his *Dngos grub snye ma*, 53b3; for an English translation, see Sparham 2005, 116.

1223. See also Candrakīrti, *Rdo rje sems dpa'i sgrub thabs*, *Vajrasattva Sādhana*, Tōh 1814, 196a5; Luo and Tomabechi 2009, 4.1–2 and 36.6.

1224. Ratnākaraśānti, *Dgyes pa'i rdo rje'i dka' 'grel mu tig 'phreng ba*, *Hevajrapañjikāmuktikāvalī*, I.i, v. 6a, Tōh 1189, 221a5; Isaacson 2000, 124; and Tripathi and Negi 2001, 2; English translation in Isaacson 2000, 128. D has */ rtogs pa med na thos pa min / thos pa med na bsam du med / gnyis ka nyams pas rnal 'byor med / rnal 'byor med na 'grub mi 'gyur /* for */ blos gros med la thos med ma thos pa la'ang bsam pa med / gnyis bral rnal 'byor med cing rnal 'byor bral la'ang dngos grub med /*. Again, our text does not seem to be a direct citation from the commentary itself, but from a different translation of this passage, such as the one found in Tsong kha pa, *Sngags rim chen mo,* chap. 11, 434. This and the following quotations are translated in Yarnall 2013.

1225. *Vīryabhadra*, *Rim pa lnga pa'i dka' 'grel don gsal ba*, *Pañcakramapañjikā Prabhāsārtha*, Tōh 1830, 180a1–3. D has *sgom pa* for *bsgom pa*; *de la dngos grub* for *de las dngos grub*; *thog ma* for *thog mar*; *dngos grub legs par 'thob* for *dngos grub nges par thob*; *de yi* for *de yis*; and *ci ltar* for *ji ltar* in our text. The quotation in Tsong kha pa, *Sngags rim chen mo*, chap. 11, 434–35, is closer to D, except for *de las dngos grub* for *de la dngos grub*, and *thog mar* for *thog ma*.

Stages teaches: "The best disciples are those who have faith in their lama, are ever dedicated and devoted in their service, and who retain what they have studied."[1226] Thus you should clear every misconception regarding the essential points of the two stages through study and reflection.

[The Lama]

The meaning of the tantras is concealed in their profound vajra words so that you will have to rely on a master to help you understand them. Those who proudly engage in their own self-taught rationalism, their sharp intellect and so forth, but misconstrue the meaning of the tantras will ruin both themselves and others. Therefore put your trust in a genuine teacher who has mastered the meaning of the tantra, and after pleasing him, gain understanding of the essential points of the two stages through his oral instructions.

As is taught in the *Five Stages*, "The true meaning sealed in the glorious *Guhyasamāja Tantra* should be realized through the oral explanation of the lama following the explanatory tantras."[1227] [9a] Hence, you should understand that the essential points of the two stages sealed in the *Guhyasamāja Tantra* are made comprehensible through the orally transmitted instructions of a teacher who understands the scriptures and teaches them by clarifying the meaning of the *Guhyasamāja Tantra* by means of the explanatory tantras and in keeping with the intention of the mahāsiddhas.

But SOME who understand only the superficial meaning of the tantras take certain narrowed points[1228] that they transmit orally or write down on a tiny scroll and hide away, believing it to be transmitted instructions and deeming those who possess it superior teachers upon whom they assiduously rely. Believing them to be transmitted instructions even though they are wholly inconsistent with the pure tantras and Indian writings, these people hold

1226. Nāgārjuna, *Rim lnga, Pañcakrama*, chap. 1, v. 66abc, Tōh 1802, 48a2–3; Sanskrit and Tibetan in Mimaki and Tomabechi 1994, 12; Sanskrit and French translation in Tomabechi 2006, 122; English translation in Thurman 1995, 251. D, and Mimaki and Tomabechi 1994 have *slob ma'i dam pa yis* for *slob ma dam pa yin* in our text. Since the fourth line is omitted in our quotation, as in Tsong kha pa, *Sngags rim chen mo,* chap. 11, 435, the sentence is incomplete, hence *yin* for *yis*.

1227. Nāgārjuna, *Rim lnga, Pañcakrama*, chap. 1, v. 9, Tōh 1802, 45b3; Sanskrit and Tibetan in Mimaki and Tomabechi 1994, 2; Sanskrit and French translation in Tomabechi 2006, 106; English translation in Thurman 1995, 251. Our text and Mimaki and Tomabechi have *gnas* for *nas* in D. These lines are cited also in Tsong kha pa, *Sngags rim chen mo,* chap. 11, 435.

1228. This is a most tentative translation.

them superior to the explanation in the scriptures. Since this would cause all precious tantras to fade away until not even their names remain you should avoid it like poison.

If following the transmitted instructions of the lama helps you understand without difficulty the profound meanings of the tantra that previously you have not realized, then you should know it as the supreme transmitted instruction. Reliance on the transmitted instructions of a genuine lama is the means for apprehending entirely the most profound essence of the practice found in the precious tantric scriptures.[1229] To achieve this you must please the lama who is learned in the meaning of the tantra in every way possible and strive to study and reflect on this meaning. By studying and reflecting in this way and becoming learned in the method of the practice you may endeavor to engage in the two stages as skillfully as is humanly possible, having vigorously rid yourself of actions that are as pointless as winnowing chaff without grain.

The Reasons Yogis Should Meditate on the Creation Stage before They Meditate on the Completion Stage

In which sequence should the two stages be practiced?[1230] [9b] Some TIBETAN LAMAS[1231] say that the Victorious One taught the creation stage to disciples of inferior intelligence so that they would attain ordinary siddhis alone, but those who wish to attain the supreme siddhi of enlightenment should meditate on the completion stage from the very beginning.

But if the creation stage of the unexcelled mantra were not a cause for buddhahood, how could the deity yoga of the three lower classes of tantra be a cause for awakening?[1232] And since there is no completion stage in the three lower tantras, the three lower tantras would be in no way superior to the Pāramitā Vehicle as a cause for attaining buddhahood. A mantrin who affirmed such a position would be subject to ridicule.

For if the creation stage is not a cause for buddhahood, how can the vase

1229. Reading *rgyud sde* for *rgyud spa* in our text.

1230. Our text now follows Tsong kha pa, *Sngags rim chen mo*, chap. 11, 436–461; as well as his *Rim lnga gsal sgron*, 39a4–41b3; for an English translation see Kilty 2013, 84–87.

1231. Similar wording is found in Bsod nams rtse mo's commentary on the *Kye'i rdo rje rgyud, Hevajra Tantra*: Bsod nams rtse mo, *Kyai rdo rje'i rtsa rgyud brtag gnyis kyi rnam par bshad pa nyi ma'i 'od zer*, work, 6, 75a1–2. This tradition is attributed to the commentaries of the three bodhisattvas: Puṇḍarīka, Tōh 1347; Vajragarbha, Tōh 1180; and Vajrapāṇi, Tōh 1402. See also Tsong kha pa, *Sngags rim chen mo*, chap. 11, 455.

1232. See Tsong kha pa, *Sngags rim chen mo*, chap. 11, 446.

initiation be a cause for buddhahood? But since YOU YOURSELF[1233] agree that the five initiations of realization enact the capacity for attaining the five tathāgata families and remove obstacles to their attainment, and likewise [YOU agree] that the seven initiations of Kālacakra[1234] generate the capacity for attaining the seventh ground and so forth,[1235] YOU directly contradict YOUR own words and all the explanations in the tantric scriptures and are therefore not in an ideal state of mind.

If the entry of the jñānasattva into yourself visualized as the complete deity maṇḍala, the sealing of the jñānasattva in the samayasattva, making offerings, expressing praise, and so forth are not a cause for buddhahood, then making offerings to images and paintings and so forth cannot be a cause for buddhahood either. If proper meditation on the maṇḍala is not a cause for buddhahood, then how could the act of representing the maṇḍala either as a painting or a three-dimensional construction be a cause for buddhahood? [10a] If meditation on the deity, recitation of the profound dhāraṇīs and mantras, and so forth are not a cause for buddhahood, it would be ludicrous to expect that reading the scriptures and so forth without any meditation whatsoever might be a cause for buddhahood, for that would be tantamount to saying that no accumulation of merit of any kind is a cause for buddhahood.

Those who claim this do not even know the names of the tantras and sādhanas composed by mahāsiddhas like the sādhanas of Hevajra, of Cakrasaṃvara, and of Kālacakra. If such people were to start their meditation on the sādhana with the customary words: "I meditate in order to attain buddhahood for the sake of all sentient beings" that would be tantamount to saying: "my mother is a barren women." And if after visualizing the great generated maṇḍala before them and making offerings to it, they pronounce their aspirations with the words "through this virtue may I become Vajradhara," they might just as well have said: "through this virtue, may horns arise on the head of a rabbit." What, then, could better attest to their nature?

In the *Hevajra Tantra*, "Vajragarbha asked: The bliss experienced in the yoga of the completion stage is called great bliss. What is the use of the creation stage if it lacks such a meditation as that found in the completion stage?"[1236] Thus Vajragarbha asked, What does the creation stage offer that is not offered

1233. Reading *nyid* for *nyad* in our text.

1234. See Tsong kha pa, *Sngags rim chen mo*, chap. 11, 451.

1235. Reading *bdun gyis sa* for *bdun gyi sa* in our text.

1236. *Kye'i rdo rje mkha' 'gro ma dra ba'i sdom pa, Hevajra Tantra II*, Tōh 418, 15b2–3; Snellgrove 1959, II.ii.34. Snellgrove has *'di* for *nyid* and *rdzogs pa sgom pa* for *rdzogs pa bsgom pa* in our text. Our text inserts an additional line probably a result of a homoeoteleuton.

by the completion stage?[1237] In reply the Blessed One said: "O great bodhisattva! Through the power of your faith [in the completion stage], your faith [in the creation stage] has diminished.[1238] When there is no body, how can there be bliss? In such a case bliss cannot be spoken of. Beings are pervaded by bliss, pervaded by the pervader. Just as the scent of the flower rests in the flower, and in the absence of the flower it is not sensed, [10b] so in the absence of material form and so forth, there can be no experience of bliss."[1239]

For just as in the absence of a flower its scent would not arise, so the blissful mind that arises from the rūpakāya of the Buddha would not exist without it. Hence it is taught that as the completion stage alone is insufficient, the creation stage is necessary. Since numerous works explain that the creation stage produces the rūpakāya, the position that the creation stage is unnecessary contradicts infinite tantras and works of the learned and accomplished masters. Yet since there is so much to say about this, for the sake of brevity I will write no more at this point.

THOSE who claim this also say that in the final analysis the completion stage is a meditation on the definitive meaning.[1240] It seems that for them, meditation on the definitive meaning is equivalent to settling in no-thought-whatsoever. Hence, they maintain that apart from the nonmeditation of the Chinese Hwashang there is no cause for buddhahood. This view is utterly wrong and unacceptable, and scholars who know the meaning of the tantra should endeavor to refute it.

SOME[1241] misconstrue the expression "not a direct cause," in order to maintain that in terms of being a direct cause or not, the completion stage is superior and the creation stage inferior. This is an even poorer position than the previous one; for example, in the six-limbed yoga of the completion stage, the first five limbs are not a direct cause, and even the sixth limb of samādhi, apart from its final moment, is not a direct cause.

Therefore those who wish for the supreme siddhi of enlightenment must surely meditate on the creation stage. As the *Illuminating Lamp* teaches: "When you have practiced in such a way continuously during the four sessions,

1237. Reading *chog* for *mchog* in our text.

1238. In his *Sngags rim chen mo*, chap. 11, 445, Tsong kha pa glosses this verse with: *khyod rdzogs rim la dad pa'i shugs kyis bskyed rim las nyams so.*

1239. *Kye'i rdo rje mkha' 'gro ma dra ba'i sdom pa*, *Hevajra Tantra II*, Tōh 418, 15b3–4; Snellgrove 1959, II.ii.35–36.

1240. See Tsong kha pa, *Rim lnga gsal sgron*, 41b1–2; English translation in Kilty 2013; 87, and Tsong kha pa, *Sngags rim chen mo*, chap. 11, 445.

1241. Here Mkhas grub rje follows Tsong kha pa, *Sngags rim chen mo*, chap. 11, 458–459.

the roots of virtue will ripen, and thereby you will directly realize the vajra-like samādhi, [11a] and attain the siddhi of great seal in this lifetime."[1242] Thus, if after ripening your inner continuum through meditation on the creation stage during the four sessions, you meditate on the completion stage, you will attain the supreme siddhi. Hence in order to ripen for the meditation on the completion stage, you should meditate on the creation stage.

Therefore the *Hevajra Tantra* teaches: "By means of the yoga of the creation stage, practitioners should meditate on the proliferations of mental constructs. Once they have made the proliferations dream-like, they should use this very proliferation to de-proliferate."[1243] The *Five Stages* teaches: "The perfect buddhas imparted this method like the rungs of a ladder to those who abide in the creation stage and aspire to the completion stage."[1244] The *Compendium of Practices* teaches: "The perfect buddhas designed this method as the rungs of a ladder so that beginners may enter the ultimate truth."[1245] The mahāsiddha Ḍombhiheruka teaches: "Sumati![1246] First meditate on the creation stage, and keep your mind firm on all the hand gestures, pure mantras, rituals of invitation and visualization.[1247] And later,[1248] Sumati, by meditating

1242. Candrakīrti, *Sgron gsal, Pradīpoddyotana*, chap. 11, Tōh 1785, 80a4–5; the Sanskrit in Chakravarti 1984, 99, is mostly missing. D has *rtag pa* for *rtog pa*; *de dge ba'i rtsa ba* for *dge ba'i rtsa ba*; and *'thob par* for *thob par* in our text.

1243. *Kye'i rdo rje mkha' 'gro ma dra ba'i sdom pa, Hevajra Tantra II*, Tōh 418, 15a7; Snellgrove 1959, II.ii.29. D and Snellgrove have *spros pa nyid ni spros med byed* for *spros pa nyid kyang spros med bya* in our text, while the analogous section in Tsong kha pa, *Sngags rim chen mo*, chap. 12, 493, has *spros pa nyid kyis spros med bya*, which corresponds to the Sanskrit: *prapañcair niḥprapañcayet* [*niṣprapañcayet*] in Snellgrove. This reading was followed here.

1244. Nāgārjuna, *Rim lnga, Pañcakrama*, chap. 1, v. 2, Tōh 1802, 45a6–7; Sanskrit and Tibetan in Mimaki and Tomabechi 1994, 1; Sanskrit and French translation in Tomabechi 2006, 104; English translation in Thurman 1995, 250. These lines are cited by Tsong kha pa in a number of his works, including the *Sngags rim chen mo*, chap. 11, 459, the *Rim lnga gsal sgron*, 39a56; English translation in Kilty 2013, 84; and the *Nā ro*, 10a4.

1245. Āryadeva, *Spyod bsdus, Caryāmelāpakapradīpa*, chap. 1, Tōh 1803, 60b5; Sanskrit, Tibetan, and English translation in Wedemeyer 2007, A: 6b; Sanskrit and Tibetan in Pandey 2000, 7 and 167. Cited also in Tsong kha pa, *Sngags rim chen mo*, chap. 11, 459; and his *Rim lnga gsal sgron*, 40a1; for an English translation, see Kilty 2013, 85.

1246. Tib. Blo bzang.

1247. As noted, while our text has *cho ga*, D and the *Sngags rim chen mo* have *go cha*.

1248. Reading *phyi nas* for *phye nas* in our text.

on the completion stage with a mind delighted and continuously one with thatness, you will abandon cyclic existence, ever-intent on the innate."[1249]

Thus and so forth, countless tantras and works of mahāsiddhas teach that it is necessary to meditate first on the creation stage and then on the completion stage. Hence, instructing on the second stage without instructing on the first is contradictory to all the tantras and their commentaries. [11b]

[When Do You Begin Practicing the Completion Stage?]

Should you avoid meditating on the second stage until you have stabilized the first stage? Alternately, should you meditate in the early part of the session on the first stage and in the latter part on the second stage, or should you practice from the very beginning both stages together?

Ārya Nāgārjuna and his disciples hold the first possibility, for the *Compendium of Practices* teaches: "Having practiced the thought of the Buddha Vehicle, you practice the samādhi of single-mindedness on the New Vehicle.[1250] When you become habituated in single-mindedness on the New Vehicle, you may cultivate conceptual yoga.[1251] When you become habituated in conceptual yoga, you may abide in the beginner samādhi.[1252] Abiding in the beginner samādhi, you should practice the divisions of the hundred tathāgata families.[1253] Having learned the isolation of the body through the divisions of the hundred tathāgata families, you should abide in the samādhi of vajra body. Once situated in the isolation of the body, you may practice the isolation of

1249. Ḍombhiheruka, *Bdag med ma rnal 'byor ma'i sgrub thabs, Nairātmyāyoginī Sādhana*, Tōh 1306a, 215a4–5. D has *blo bzangs* for *blo bzang*; *sgom par* for *bsgom par*; *phan pa'i phyag rgya* for *lag pa'i phyag rgya*; *go cha* for *cho ga*; *bral mi bya* for *'bral mi bya*; *gcig gis* for *cig gi*; *bsgom pa* for *bsgom pas*; and *srid pa las byung* for *srid pa rnam spang* in our text. Cited also in Tsong kha pa, *Sngags rim chen mo*, chap. 11, 459.

1250. According to Tsong kha pa, "single-mindedness" is the creation of the deities through the five manifest awakenings. This does not mean meditation on a single deity, but rather that you are *singly mindful* of deities or *mindful* of yourself and the deity as *a single entity*. See his *Rim lnga gsal sgron*, 43a6–b1; English translation in Kilty 2013, 90.

1251. According to Tsong kha pa, "conceptual yoga" is a general name of the creation stage, but here it refers to the yoga of the subtle. See his *Rim lnga gsal sgron*, 43b3–4, English translation in Kilty 2013, 90.

1252. The "beginner concentration" is the yoga of the first stage. See Tsong kha pa, *Rim lnga gsal sgron*, 43b5, English translation in Kilty 2013, 90.

1253. These are explained in Āryadeva, *Spyod bsdus, Caryāmelāpakapradīpa*, chap. 2, Tōh 1803; see Wedemeyer 2007, Appendix III.

speech by means of the consonants and vowels. Having learned *prāṇāyāma*[1254] through the stage of vajra recitation, you will abide in the samādhi of vajra speech," and so forth.[1255]

Thus it is taught that when you have become habituated in the first stage you must practice the second, and likewise when you become habituated in each step of the completion stage, beginning with the isolation of the body, you must practice the stage that follows it. Hence there are many conclusive reasons for the requirement to practice the latter after becoming habituated in the former stage. Nevertheless, SOME EARLY TIBETAN LAMAS[1256] apparently taught that you should meditate in the early part of the session on the creation stage and in the latter part on the perfection. [12a]

[How Does the Creation Stage Serve as a Ripener for the Completion Stage?]

Your meditational deity blesses your continuum, purifies your abundant karmic obscurations, and generates an immense accumulation of merit in your inner continuum. This should bring about favorable conditions and eliminate adverse circumstances for the arising of the profound completion stage in your inner continuum.

But the following is the crucial point: It is the completion stage that purifies all seeds of appearance and attitude that proceed from ordinary birth, death, and the intermediate state, and actually transforms them into the three bodies. For only during the completion stage do the aspects of birth, death, and the intermediate state of the time of the ground arise in the inner continuum in actuality as they are. Prior to this, during the creation stage, aspects akin to birth, death, and the intermediate state of the time of the ground are perceived by the mind but no actual transformation occurs. Though birth, death,

1254. Tib. *srog dang rtsol ba*; how to control the energy currents in the body.

1255. Āryadeva, *Spyod bsdus, Caryāmelāpakapradīpa*, chap. 1, Tōh 1803, 59b4–7; Sanskrit, Tibetan, and English translation in Wedemeyer 2007, A: 5a–b; Sanskrit and Tibetan in Pandey 2000, 5–6 and 163–164. D has *dran pa gcig pa'i ting nge 'dzin la slob bo* for *dran pa gcig pa'i ting nge 'dzin gyis slob bo*; *las dang po pa* for *las dang ba pa*; *dbye ba la mkhas pas* for *dbye bas*; *rnam par dben pa* for *dben pa shes par gyur ba*; and *rtsol ba* for *rtsol ga shes pa* in our text. The beginning of our passage is cited in Tsong kha pa, *Sngags rim chen mo*, chap. 1, 53; English translation in Hopkins 1977, 168; and Tsong kha pa, *Rim lnga gsal sgron*, 43a1; English translation in Kilty 2013, 89.

1256. According to Tsong kha pa, these are followers of Myu gu lung pa ['Brog mi Shākya ye shes (993–1074/77)] and Mar pa. See his *Sngags rim chen mo*, chap. 11, 460. See also Bsod nams rtse mo, *Nyi ma'i 'od zer*, 75a6–b1.

and the intermediate state have not yet actually turned into the genuine three bodies of the buddhas, the aspects that resemble the three bodies in the mind of the meditator on the creation stage—those that correspond to the aspects of the completion stage as well—effectuate ripening for the completion stage by suppressing the manifestation of appearances and attitudes of ordinary birth, death, and the intermediate state.

Furthermore, constantly visualizing your aggregates, sensory spheres, and sense bases in the essence of the respective deities placed upon your transient body and on the respective points of the inner body, and visualizing their dissolution into clear light, will facilitate the gathering of all the body's winds from their respective points during the completion stage, and this will effectuate ripening for a far easier and quicker arising of the clear light, and so forth.

So long as you have not attained the union of the bliss and emptiness of the creation stage, the complete and authentic union of bliss and emptiness of the completion stage will not occur. And unless you are firmly habituated to the deity yoga of the creation stage, [12b] all the following practices will lack a basis: the arising of all appearances as the body of the deity from the hundred tathāgata families to one tathāgata family during the body isolation of the completion stage; their instant dawning to the yogi's mind in correspondence with the illusory body after the four empty states at the end of the mind isolation; and following that, the practice that relies on the wisdom consort,[1257] and so forth. For in that case all these meditations will be groundless, and without them, the subsequent steps of the completion stage will not take place. Therefore, if you wish the completion stage to arise as taught in the tantras, you must first engage thoroughly in the creation stage.

[How Much Should You Practice the Creation Stage before Meditating on the Completion Stage?][1258]

The twelfth chapter of the *Guhyasamāja Tantra*[1259] explains the creation stage in terms of the four stages of familiarization and achievement.[1260] The

1257. Reading *ye rgya* for *yi rgya* in our text.

1258. This section follows Tsong kha pa, *Mtha' gcod*, 49a3–50a5, and his *Rim lnga gsal sgron*, 41b4–43a1; English translation in Kilty 2013, 87–89.

1259. *Guhyasamāja Tantra*, Tōh 442; Zhol 19a5–7; Stog 32b4–33a1; Dunh 35b3–4; Fremantle 1971, vv. 61–66; and Matsunaga 1978, vv. 60–65.

1260. Tib. *bsnyed sgrub yang lag bzhi*. These are familiarization, approaching achievement, achievement, and great achievement; Tib. *bsnyen pa*, *nyer sgrub*, *sgrub pa*, and *sgrub pa chen po*; Skt. *sevā*, *upasādhana*, *sādhana*, and *mahāsādhana*.

Illuminating Lamp explains the meaning of these lines: the creation stage begins with the meditation on the ground of wisdom and continues up to the end of the Supreme King of Deeds.[1261] This chapter of the *Guhyasamāja Tantra* also teaches: "Or else, those who are firm in their yogic practice should meditate on the familiarization through the four vajras,"[1262] and the *Illuminating Lamp* explains that this refers to the condensed creation stage.[1263] The *Later Tantra* explains that the four vajras are: "The first, awakening from emptiness; the second, gathering the seed syllables; the third, completing the form; and the fourth, setting the syllables."[1264]

Nāropa clarifies the meaning of these lines: the explanation that the creation stage continues from the meditation on the ground of wisdom up to the Supreme King of Maṇḍalas refers to the extensive creation stage through the four vajras, while the condensed creation stage begins with the meditation on the ground of wisdom and ends with the setting of the syllables on the vajra and lotus of the father and mother.[1265] Since these are only the explicit words of the tantra, you must add to this the implicit explanation of the meditation on the subtle, the vajra recitation, and so forth. [13a]

The *Illuminating Lamp*, commenting on the eleventh chapter of the *Guhyasamāja Tantra*, explains the meditation on the single-mindedness of the six[1266] tathāgata families, beginning with the meditation on the ground of wisdom, and continues up to the triple sattvas, and adds that if you practice this in four

1261. Candrakīrti, *Sgron gsal, Pradīpoddyotanaṭīkā*, Tōh 1785, 94b1–2; Chakravarti 1984, 115; Sanskrit and English translation in Wayman 1977, 34–43.

1262. *Guhyasamāja Tantra*, Tōh 442; Zhol 19b1; Stog 33a1–2; Dunh 36a1; Fremantle 1971, v. 67ab; and Matsunaga 1978, v. 66ab.

1263. Candrakīrti, *Sgron gsal, Pradīpoddyotanaṭīkā*, Tōh 1785, 98a6–b2; Chakravarti 1984, 120. See also Tsong kha pa, *Sgron gsal mchan*, 285a5–b4. Reading *de* for *da* in our text. The term "abridged sādhana" is explained below [181a].

1264. *Rgyud phyi ma, Uttara Tantra*, Tōh 443, 154a4–5; Matsunaga 1978, v. 138. D, Stog, and Zhol have *bsdus pa yin* for *bsdus pa'o* and *gzugs ni* for *gzugs nyid*; Zhol has *dgad pa* for *dgod pa* in our text. This line is cited also in Candrakīrti, *Sgron gsal, Pradīpoddyotanaṭīkā*, Tōh 1785, 98b1–2; Chakravarti 1984, 120.

1265. *Yaśobhadra/Nāropa, *Gsang ba thams cad kyi sgron ma'i rgya cher 'grel pa, Sarvaguhyapradīpaṭīkā*, Tōh 1787, 225a2–3. In the Derge this work is attributed to *Yaśobhadra, Snyan grags bzang po. According to Tsong kha pa, some manuscripts point to Nāropa as the author, while others to *Yaśobhadra. See his *Rim lnga gsal sgron*, 31b6, English translation in Kilty 2013, 68.

1266. Reading *drug* for *drag* in our text.

sessions, it will ripen your continuum.[1267] This is identical to the condensed creation stage.[1268] The works of Ārya Nāgārjuna and his disciples did not teach any other condensed creation stage upon which you should meditate before the completion stage.[1269]

Therefore FOLLOWERS[1270] of Marpa's transmitted instructions who maintain that as preliminary to the five stages of the completion stage it is sufficient to meditate during the creation stage on the principal father-mother deity alone or else only on the solitary hero—and there are many such positions—contradict the works of Ārya Nāgārjuna and his disciples. The *Elucidating the Epitome of the Five Stages*—commenting on the root verses of the *Five Stages*—written by[1271] the venerable Marpa himself teaches:[1272] "Meditate on the mind bound for enlightenment, on the guru, on the yoga of your own deity, together with higher yoga, great yoga, subsequent yoga, on the stages of samādhi, and on familiarization, approaching attainment, great attainment, and the essence of attainment."[1273] And: "By cultivating well the creation stage, actualizing the appearances of the body of the deity and the supreme maṇḍala of the complete buddhas, you will reach the goal."[1274]

Thus [the holders of the transmitted instruction of Marpa's tradition] contradict the explanations that it is necessary to complete the practice of the creation stage by meditating on the entire maṇḍala of deities, subsumed under the four yogas, the three samādhis, or the four stages of familiarization and achievement. Moreover, since meditating on deity in such a wrong way is wanting of the purifiers of birth, death, and the intermediate state, it is futile

1267. Candrakīrti, *Sgron gsal*, *Pradīpoddyotanaṭīkā*, Tōh 1785, 80a4; Chakravarti 1984, 99; and Tsong kha pa, *Sgron gsal mchan*, 240a2–4.

1268. While Tsong kha pa's *Mtha' gcod*, 49b2, and *Rim lnga gsal sgron*, 42a4, have *sgrub thabs mdor bsdus 'di dang don gcig go*, our text has *bskyed rim mdor bsdus 'di dang gcig go*.

1269. Once more, our texts refer here to Tsong kha pa, *Mtha' gcod* and *Rim lnga gsal sgron*.

1270. See Tsong kha pa, *Mtha' gcod*, 49b6–50a1, and *Rim lnga gsal sgron*, 42a6–b2; English translation in Kilty 2013, 88–89.

1271. Reading *gis* for *gi* in our text.

1272. According to Derge edition of the Bstan 'gyur this work is by Nāropa, and was translated by the author and by Mar pa Chos kyi blo gros. According to our text as it appears in the old Zhol and old Bkra shis lhun po printing, this work was written by Mar pa. However, the Sku 'bum printing has Nāropa as the author.

1273. Tib. *bsnyen pa*, *nyer sgrub*, *sgrub pa che*, and *sgrub pa'i ngo bo*. Nāropa, *Rim pa lnga bsdus pa gsal ba*, *Pañcakramasaṅgrahaprakāśa*, Tōh 2333, 277b4–5. D has *rim pa ldan pa yis* for *rim pa ldan pa nyid*, and *sgrub pa'i ngo bo khyad par du* for *sgrub pa'i deb* in our text.

1274. Nāropa, *Rim pa lnga bsdus pa gsal ba*, *Pañcakramasaṅgrahaprakāśa*, Tōh 2333, 277a7b1. D has *rnams* for *rnam pa* in our text.

as a ripener of the completion stage. Therefore you should only meditate on the completion stage after ripening the inner continuum by way of the creation stage in which you meditate on the entire maṇḍala, at least according to the condensed practice of the sādhana as explained above. [13b]

Characteristics of the Place of Practice

The twelfth chapter of the *Guhyasamāja Tantra* teaches:[1275] "In areas of great isolation, abounding in flowers, fruit, and so forth, or in lonely mountains, all siddhis will be attained." This is the explicit interpretable meaning,[1276] while the explanatory tantra *Revelation of the Intention* teaches the definitive[1277] meaning:[1278] "Taking the aggregates as a place of great isolation," and so forth up to: "Isolation from being is pleasing. There you should practice the so-called 'vajra.'" In the context of the creation stage you should practice in a place endowed with characteristics as described in the interpretable and literal meaning. Thus, familiarize yourself with the particulars of the location where you should meditate on the creation stage, for in both of his Guhyasamāja sādhanas,[1279] Ārya Nāgārjuna described the site in this way.

The Practice—How the Realization Is Attained

There are two parts here: (1) the scriptures on which the explanation relies and (2) the practice based on these genuine scriptures.

The Scriptures on Which the Explanation Relies

To ensure that you rely on a master, Vajradhara[1280] concealed various portions of the creation stage in the *Guhyasamāja Tantra* and did not teach them

1275. *Guhyasamāja Tantra*, Tōh 442, Zhol 17a3–4, Stog 29a4–5, Dunh 31b2–3, Fremantle 1971, v. 3, Matsunaga 1978, v. 2. Zhol and Stog have *su* and Dunh has *sam* for *ni*, Zhol and Stog have *stsogs kyis brgyan* and Dunh has *stsogs brgyan* for *sogs pas brgyan*, Stog has *sgrub* for *bsgrub*.

1276. Tib. *drang ba'i don*, Skt. *neyārtha*.

1277. Tib. *nges pa'i don*, Skt. *nītārtha*.

1278. The *Dgong pa lung ston, Sandhivyākaraṇa*, Tōh 444, 200b7–201a2. D has *des* for *der* in our text.

1279. See the *Mdor byas, Piṇḍikrama Sādhana*, Tōh 1796, 2a1–2, L 6, T 6, and the *Mdo bsre, Sādhanasūtramelāpaka*, Tōh 1797, 11a3–4.

1280. Vajradhara, Rdo rje 'chang, is regarded as the teacher of the *Guhyasamāja Tantra*.

explicitly. Neither did he teach the various steps of the practice in a single section of the tantra, but rather scattered them randomly throughout the tantra from beginning to end. Therefore you should learn the meaning of the creation stage in its entirety with the four stages of familiarization and achievement and their ancillaries, through the transmitted instructions of a guru, who has followed explanatory tantras such as the *Later Tantra*,[1281] the *Vajra Garland Tantra*,[1282] and so forth.[1283]

Ārya Nāgārjuna,[1284] the teacher of the beneficial method of the creation stage that combines the *Guhyasamāja Tantra* with its explanatory tantras in this way, [14a] authored both the *Concise Sādhana*[1285] and the *Sādhana Incorporating the Scripture*.[1286] Master Nāgabuddhi[1287] wrote *Formulating the Sādhana*,[1288] which is mainly an explanation of the method of applying the purifier to the ground of purification in the creation stage, and briefly teaches the completion stage as well. The glorious Candrakīrti composed the *Vajrasattva Sādhana*,[1289] upon which both Tathāgatarakṣita and Līlavajra wrote commentaries.[1290] Paṇḍita Muniśrībhadra of Magadha, Atiśa, and others say that

1281. *Rgyud phyi ma*, *Uttara Tantra*, Tōh 443, one of the explanatory tantras of the *Guhyasamāja Tantra*, which at times is taken to be the eighteenth chapter of the *Guhyasamāja Tantra*.

1282. *Rgyud rdo rje phreng ba*, *Vajramālā Tantra*, Tōh 445.

1283. See Tsong kha pa, *Ye rdor*, 47a2–4, his commentary on the *Ye shes rdo rje kun las btus pa*, *Vajrajñānasamuccaya Tantra*, Tōh 447.

1284. In the following paragraphs, our text follows Tsong kha pa, *Mtha' gcod*, 35a6–38b2, and *Rim lnga gsal sgron*, 26b3–33b5; English translation in Kilty 2013, 62–71. Paṇ chen Bsod nams grags pa follows this. See his *Rgyud sde spyi'i rnam bzhag*, 41a5–44a1; English translation in Boord and Tsonawa 1996, 59–63.

1285. Nāgārjuna, *Mdor byas = Sgrub thabs mdor byas*, *Piṇḍikrama Sādhana*, Tōh 1796; La Vallée Poussin 1896; Ram Shankar Tripathi 2001.

1286. Nāgārjuna, *Mdo bsre*, *Sādhanasūtramelāpaka*, Tōh 1797.

1287. Our text has Klu byang, but according to its colophon in the Bstan 'gyur, the author is called Klu'i blo, corresponding to Nāgabuddhi in the Sanskrit manuscript.

1288. *Rnam gzhag rim pa*, *Samāja Sādhana Vyavastholi*, Tōh 1809; Sanskrit and Tibetan in Tanaka 2016.

1289. Candrakīrti, *Rdo rje sems dpa'i sgrub thabs*, *Vajrasattva Sādhana*, Tōh 1814; Sanskrit and Tibetan in Luo and Tomabechi 2009.

1290. Tathāgatarakṣita, *Rdo rje sems dpa'i sgrub pa'i thabs kyi bshad pa*, *Vajrasattva Sādhana Vyākhyā*, Tōh 1835. Līlavajra, *Rdo rje sems dpa'i sgrub thabs kyi 'grel pa*, *Vajrasattva Sādhana Nibandha*, Tōh 1815. Our text has Lalivajra for Līlavajra, but the two works by Tsong kha pa that Mkhas grub rje follows, the *Mtha' gcod*, 36a5, and *Rim lnga gsal sgron*, 30b2, have Lilavajra (for Līlavajra).

the *Vajrasattva Sādhana* was written by Candrakīrti and therefore should be accepted.[1291] But SOME LATER LAMAS[1292] have questioned the authorship of Candrakīrti and the notion that he had merely prosified the sādhana written by Ārya Nāgārjuna himself.

Their position is unfounded, because the *Vajrasattva Sādhana* contains many specific points not actually found in the *Concise Sādhana*. For example, it explains that if a yogi fails to find an external consort for the yoga with a consort, he should draw a wisdom consort from his heart. Furthermore, the *Vajrasattva Sādhana* also contains a variety of points not found in the *Sādhana Incorporating the Scripture* on how to apply the steps of the meditation to the scriptures that require explanation. Hence there is no foundation to the claim that anything of value in the *Vajrasattva Sādhana* is likewise present in Ārya Nāgārjuna's sādhana. Consequently, if YOU say is that there is no general presentation of the sādhana apart from the one written by Ārya Nāgārjuna, YOUR logic is flawed. Moreover, there is no indication whatsoever that it was not written by Candrakīrti.

Therefore the system of the creation stage should be understood on the basis of the four sādhanas of Ārya Nāgārjuna and his disciples taken together with the commentary entitled the *Illuminating Lamp*,[1293] since these scriptures adhere to the meaning of the *Guhyasamāja*. [14b]

The *Commentary on the Guhyasamāja*[1294] and the *Maṇḍala Rituals*[1295] both attributed to Ārya Nāgārjuna; the *Commentary on the Five Stages*,[1296] the *Illuminating the Meaning of the Five Stages*,[1297] and the *Instruction on the Stages*,[1298]

1291. See Muniśrībhadra, *Rim pa lnga'i don mdor bshad pa, Pañcakramārthaṭippaṇi*, Tōh 1813, 152b3; Jiang and Tomabechi 1996, 11. Note that this work is translated into Tibetan by Bu ston. Tsong kha pa mentions only Muniśrībhadra in this regard. See his *Rim lnga gsal sgron*, 30b2, English translation in Kilty 2013, 66.

1292. See Red mda' ba Gzhon nu blo gros, *Bsgrub pa dpal bas zhus lan*, Kathmandu, 51a4–5; TBRC, 306b.

1293. Candrakīrti, *Sgron gsal, Pradīpoddyotanaṭīkā*, Tōh 1785; Chakravarti 1984.

1294. Nāgārjuna, *Gsang ba 'dus pa'i rgyud kyi rgyud 'grel, Guhyasamāja Tantrasyatantraṭīkā*, Tōh 1784, 1b1–324a7.

1295. Nāgārjuna, *Gsang ba 'dus pa'i dkyil 'khor gyi cho ga, Guhyasamāja Maṇḍalavidhi*, Tōh 1798, 15b1–35a7.

1296. Nāgabodhi, *Nor bu'i phreng ba*, Tōh 1840, 14a6–157a7.

1297. Nāgabodhi, *Rim lnga don gsal, Pañcakramārthabhāskaraṇa*, Tōh 1833, 207b2–237a7.

1298. Nāgabuddhi/Nāgabodhi, *Rim pa khongs su bsdu ba, Kramāntarbhāvopadeśa Prakaraṇa*, Tōh 1812, 147a1–148b4. On the names Nāgabuddhi/Nāgabodhi, see van der Kuijp 2007 and Sinclair 2016.

attributed to Nāgabodhi;[1299] the *Ornaments on the Sādhana of the Guhyasamāja* and its commentary[1300] attributed to Candrakīrti, and so forth, are all false attributions and as such should not be trusted.

Accordingly, you should follow the authentic works of Ārya Nāgārjuna and his disciples, which explain the meaning of the *Guhyasamāja Tantra* and explanatory tantras. Their teachings are both explicit and implicit, and in the few instances where they remain unclear, you should learn how to practice by applying what is compatible with the mantra as a whole.

1299. Our text has Klu byang here.

1300. Candrakīrti, *Mngon rtogs rgyan, Samājābhisamayālaṅkāravṛtti,* Tōh 1817, 210b1–232b6.

Part 1. The First Yoga: Preliminary Stages

1. Preparatory Steps

The Practice Based on These Genuine Scriptures

There are four sections here: (1) the First Yoga,[1301] (2) the samādhi of the Supreme King of Maṇḍalas,[1302] (3) the samādhi of the Supreme King of Deeds,[1303] and (4) how to habituate your mind to the visualization during the creation stage.

The First Yoga

There are two sections here: (1) preliminary stages of the practice, and (2) explanation of the actual practice.

Preliminary Stages of the Practice

Again, there are three parts here: (1) the preparatory steps, (2) offerings to the field for accumulating merit, maintaining vows, and so forth, to establish favorable conditions, and (3) meditating on the protection wheel to avert unfavorable conditions.

The Preparatory Steps

Once more there are four parts here: (1) making the preliminary tormas, (2) the mode of sitting, (3) blessing the offerings, and (4) recitation of the hundred-syllable mantra of Vajrasattva.

1301. Tib. *dang po sbyor ba*, Skt. *ādiyoga*.

1302. Tib. *dkyil 'khor rgyal mchog gi ting nge 'dzin*, Skt. *maṇḍalarājāgrī samādhi*.

1303. Tib. *las rgyal mchog gi ting nge 'dzin*, Skt. *karmarājāgrī samādhi*.

Making the Preliminary Tormas

Even though no explanation on the preliminary tormas appears in the writings of Ārya Nāgārjuna and his disciples,[1304] the explanation of the practice of the preliminary tormas is especially clear in the context of Cakrasaṃvara. Hence the *Ḍākārṇava Tantra*[1305] teaches that you should make these offerings to the guardians of the field. Likewise at the beginning of his *Hevajra Sādhana*, the Mahāsiddha Saroruha[1306] teaches: "In a place that gratifies the mind, such as a cremation ground, make offerings and tormas."[1307] [15a] He then presents instructions on how to make offerings to the field for accumulating merit.

Who are the recipients of these tormas? In his commentary on this sādhana, the Mahāsiddha Jālandhari[1308] explains: "The yogis abiding in a place that gratifies the mind, such as a cremation ground, prepare the tormas and the offering substances and offer them as will be explained later."[1309] Thus the tormas for all the spirits, such as the directional guardians, as taught below, should be prepared at this time, and practitioners should offer them after they are cleared by abiding in yoga. Moreover, in the different sādhanas there are various instructions on how to offer the preliminary tormas, hence it is not inconsistent to make the preliminary tormas by applying the same pattern here too, and this appears in the manuals of Tibetan lamas as well.

How to prepare the tormas for the directional guardians? Clear, purify, and so forth the tormas to be offered later by means of deity yoga as was just explained. For this you need to visualize yourself as Dveṣavajra[1310] either through the "three rituals"[1311] or all at once, and then to bless the "inner offer-

1304. Such meditation is found neither at the beginning of Nāgārjuna's *Mdor byas* nor in Candrakīrti's *Rdo rje sems dpa'i sgrub thabs*.

1305. *Mkha' 'gro rgya mtsho*, Tōh 372.

1306. Tib. Mtsho skyes or Slob dpon Padma. According to the Sanskrit colophon the author is Ācārya Saroruha, while the Tibetan translation has Slob dpon Padma.

1307. Saroruha, *Dgyes pa rdo rje'i sgrub thabs, Hevajra Sādhana*, Tōh 1218, 1a4; *Dhīḥ* 2003, 133; Sanskrit, Tibetan, and English translation in Gerloff 2017, 97, 118, and 131. Part of this line is also cited below [79b4].

1308. Reading Jālandharipa for Jālendhāripa.

1309. Jālandhari, *Kye rdo rje'i sgrub thabs kyi mdor bshad pa dag pa rdo rje sgron ma, Hevajra Sādhana Vajrapradīpaṭippaṇīśuddha*, Tōh 1237, 74a3–4; Sanskrit, Tibetan, and English translation in Gerloff 2017, 167, 271, and 328. D has *gsangs* for *bsangs* in our text.

1310. Tib. Zhe sdang rdo rje, Eng. Hatred Vajra.

1311. Tib. *chog ga gsum*.

ings." With this you should clear and purify the preliminary tormas, and later on, offer these same tormas to the directional guardians and entrust them to assist you in your practice.

The Mode of Sitting

Be seated on a soft[1312] cushion, in the cross-legged meditation posture of the bodhisattva, facing east, as the *Concise Sādhana* teaches: "Sit on a soft cushion in the heroic cross-legged meditation posture";[1313] and as the *Vajrasattva Sādhana* teaches: "In a place agreeable to your mind, sit in the heroic cross-legged meditation posture facing east."[1314] [15b]

Blessing the Offerings

Now bless the offerings that you will make to yourself visualized as deity later on:

[Clearing:] As Virūpa[1315] teaches: "Then with the mantra of the three syllables, sprinkle mantrified pledge water on the offering substances."[1316] And as *Bhūvamati[1317] teaches: "Having been well-filled with *bi mu mā ra*,[1318] clear away all interferences."[1319] Thus you must clear away the interferences in the offering substances. As this is usually done with the individual action mantra,

1312. Reading *'jam pa* for *'ji pa*.

1313. Nāgārjuna, *Mdor byas, Piṇḍīkrama Sādhana*, Tōh 1796, 2a2; L 7ab; T 7ab. T has *mṛdvāsana* for śraddhāsana in L.

1314. Candrakīrti, *Rdo rje sems dpa'i sgrub thabs, Vajrasattva Sādhana*, Tōh 1814, 196b2; Luo and Tomabechi 2009, 4.12–13 and 37.3–4. D and Luo and Tomabechi have *mnyam par gnas* for *gnas* in our text.

1315. Reading Virūpa for Bhir ba pa in our text.

1316. Virūpa, *Dbu bcad ma'i sgrub thabs, Chinnamuṇḍa Sādhana*, Tōh 1555, 206a4. D has *yig gsum sngags kyis ni* for *yi ge gsum sngags kyis* in our text.

1317. Bhu ba blo ldan in our text, Dbus pa blo ldan in D.

1318. *Bi, mu, mā*, and *ra* are the first syllables of excrement, urine, great meat, and blood, Skt. *viṭ, mūtra, māṃsa*, and *rakta*; Tib. *dri chen, dri chu, sha chen*, and "*raktai*." See Tsong kha pa, *Sngags rim chen mo*, chap. 12, 528. D has *bi mu mā ra bde legs* for *bi mu ma ra 'di legs* in our text.

1319. *Bhūvamati, *'Khor lo bde mchog 'byung ba dkyil 'khor gyi cho ga, Cakrasamvarodaya Maṇḍalavidhi*, Tōh 1538, 135b3.

clear them here too by sprinkling them with the inner offerings that have already been empowered, while reciting the mantra of Vighnāntaka.[1320]

[Purifying:] Then, purify them either with *svabhāva*[1321] or *śūnyatā*,[1322] which are both suitable. Mindful of the meaning of this mantra, dissolve all offering substances in the clear light of indivisible bliss and emptiness, and thereby purify ordinary conceptualizations toward them.

[Generating:] Meditate on the appearance arising from the continuing state of wisdom of bliss and emptiness in the form of offering substances. Visualize skull cups arising from *āḥ*-s, and within them the first syllable of the respective name of each of the offering substance adorned with a dot.[1323] Visualize the syllables melting and transforming into the offering substances: their essence is indivisible empty nature and great bliss; their appearance is offering substances; and their function is to serve as objects for the six senses that generate untainted great bliss.

[Blessing:] You should bless the offerings beginning with flowers by reciting the name mantra of each offering interposed between *oṃ āḥ hūṃ*.[1324] The reason for pronouncing the three syllables is so the offerings will be blessed with the three vajras. Since *praticcha* and so forth is the mantra for making offerings, it should not be recited as part of the blessing.

The practice of clearing, purifying, and blessing the five offerings for enjoyment[1325] and the five offerings to the senses of the desire realm[1326] appears in the manuals of Tibetan lamas in this context. [16a]

The *Concise Sādhana* teaches: "The mantrins should no longer be tormented by austerities whereby they surrender the five sense-objects, [rather] by following the yoga tantra they will easily attain enlightenment."[1327] Thus the most distinctive characteristics of the mantra path are these: the five objects of the senses of the desire realm must be enjoyed while understanding their nature; they should not be tainted by ordinary appearances and attitudes; and

1320. Tib. Bgegs mthar byed. The mantra is *oṃ āḥ vighnāntakṛt hūṃ*, see Tsong kha pa, *Gsang mngon*, 14b2. Reading *vighnāntakṛt* for *vighnānatakṛt*.

1321. *Oṃ svabhāva śuddhāḥ sarvadharmāḥ svabhāva śuddho 'haṃ*.

1322. *Oṃ śūnyatā jñāna vajra svabhāva ātmako 'haṃ*. See Tsong kha pa, *Gsang mngon*, 14b2–3.

1323. The *anusvāra* written as a dot at the top of the syllable, making the vowel sound nasalized.

1324. *Oṃ puṣpe āḥ hūṃ*, and so forth. See Tsong kha pa, *Gsang mngon*, 14b4–5.

1325. Tib. *nyer spyod lnga*, Skt. *pañcopacāra*.

1326. Tib. *'dod yon lnga* or *'dod pa'i yon tan lnga*, Skt. *pañcakāmaguṇa*.

1327. Nāgārjuna, *Mdor byas, Piṇḍīkrama Sādhana*, Tōh 1796, 1a4–5, L 4; T 4.

everything pleasurable that arises should serve to enkindle great bliss. Therefore cultivate your mind by meditating on all the offerings for enjoyment and the offerings to the senses of the desire realm, each arising as an aspect of the wisdom of bliss and emptiness, and as you enjoy the offerings together with the deities, lamas, and so forth to whom you offer them, you and all the deities of the maṇḍala will experience the wisdom of bliss and emptiness.

You must understand what it means to enjoy the offering substances in this way, for the *Hevajra Tantra* teaches: "Make offerings of flowers and so forth, variously perfected from *hūṃ*."[1328] The commentary on the tantra entitled *Padmin* explains: "*Variously arising from hūṃ* means individual offerings of flowers and so forth arising from *hūṃ*."[1329] Thus it was taught that for generating the offering substances in the essence of Heruka's mind, you must generate them from *hūṃ*, for *hūṃ* signifies the innate wisdom of the mind of Heruka. If you do not understand this, and purify the offering substances into the emptiness of nothing whatsoever and then continue to meditate as though they will suddenly appear in space, you will generate nothing but great nonsense. [16b]

Recitation of the Hundred-Syllable Mantra of Vajrasattva[1330]

As the *Heart Ornament* teaches: "Clearly visualize Vajrasattva, the singular body of all the buddhas, abiding in the center of a white lotus and a lunar disk, embellished with a vajra and a bell, and recite the hundred-syllable mantra twenty-one times, in accordance with the ritual method. Since the supreme siddhas explained that the blessings prevent the amplification of failure and so forth, you should practice this mantra between meditation sessions. Reciting it a hundred thousand times, you will become the essence of purity."[1331] Many other tantras and Indian treatises explain that this mantra should be recited at the end of the main session, but it is not inappropriate to do so at this point as Tibetan lamas instruct in their meditation manuals.

1328. *Kye'i rdo rje mkha' 'gro ma dra ba'i sdom pa*, *Hevajra Tantra II*, Tōh 418, 14a1; Snellgrove 1959, II.i.5ab, which has *hūṃ ni* for *hūṃ las* in our text.

1329. Saroruha, *Kye'i rdo rje'i rgyud kyi dka' 'grel padma can*, *Hevajratantrapañjikā Padmin*, Tōh 1181, 156b5, which has *skyes pa* and not *rdzogs pa* here.

1330. See Tsong kha pa, *Gsang mngon*, 17b4–18a2.

1331. *Mañjuśrīkīrti, 'Jam dpal grags pa, *Snying po rgyan*, *Garbhālaṅkāra*, Tōh 2490, 238a5–7. D has *gyur pa* for *'gyur pas* in our text.

2. Establishing Favorable Conditions

Making Offerings to the Field for Accumulating Merit, Maintaining Vows, and So Forth to Establish[1332] *Favorable Conditions*[1333]

While in the case of Cakrasaṃvara and so forth, where Indian treatises do provide extensive instructions on the offerings made to the field for accumulating merit at this point in the practice, the *Concise Sādhana* and the *Sādhana Incorporating the Scripture* do not. However, the *Vajrasattva Sādhana* teaches: "Generate great compassion[1334] toward all sentient beings through the steps detailed below, and attain the stage of Vajrasattva for the sake of yourself and others."[1335] This line articulates the need to maintain common and uncommon vows and so forth through compassion.

The commentary on the *Concise Sādhana* written by Abhayākaragupta and the short commentary by Bhavyakīrti both explain how to make offerings to the field for accumulating merit: A light ray emanating from the white *hūṃ* that dwells on the lotus and solar disk at your heart invites the buddhas and so forth to reside in the space before you.[1336] [17a] Make offerings, prostrations, and so forth to them, and meditate successively on emptiness, signlessness,

1332. In the outline on [14b4] above, our text has *mthun rkyen bsgrub pa'i* for *mthun rkyan brten pa'i* here.

1333. See Tsong kha pa, *Gsang mngon*, 18a5–b2.

1334. This is the second point in Tsong kha pa, *Rnal 'byor dag rim*, 2b1–2, generating great compassion.

1335. Candrakīrti, *Rdo rje sems dpa'i sgrub thabs*, *Vajrasattva Sādhana*, Tōh 1814, 196b2–3, Luo and Tomabechi 2009, 4.13–5.2 and 37.4–7. D and Luo and Tomabechi have *bsgrub par* for *sgrub pa* in our text. In his *Slob tshul*, 3a2–4, Tsong kha pa points also to the commentary by Thub pa dpal and especially to commentaries on the *Rdo rje sems dpa'i sgrub thabs*, as the scriptural sources for engaging in the accumulation of merit here.

1336. The deities are invited from their natural place (*rang bzhin gyi gnas*) to the foreground. See below as well as Abhayākaragupta, *Rim pa lnga pa'i dgongs 'grel zla ba'i 'od zer*, *Pañcakramamatiṭīkā Candraprabhā*, Tōh 1831, 183a4–5, and Tsong kha pa, *Gsang mngon*, 18b1–2.

and wishlessness.[1337] Likewise, glorious Candrakīrti explains in his *Vajrasattva Sādhana*: "Having received the permission of a vajra teacher, offer *argha* water to the presence of your chosen deity."[1338] This line explicitly teaches that water for welcoming should be offered to the field for accumulating merit, but it implies other offerings as well.

It is inappropriate to maintain an ordinary identity while visualizing the light ray emanating from your heart, drawing the field for accumulating merit and returning back to your heart, and while visualizing the offering goddesses emanating from your heart and so forth. In the system of the Mantra Vehicle, yogis must free themselves of ordinary appearances and attitudes toward the three spheres of offerings: the recipient of the offerings, the offering substances themselves, and those who make the offering; and as in the Pāramitā Vehicle meditations, they should be thoroughly absorbed in the realization that the three spheres of offerings to the victorious ones do not truly exist.[1339] Here both of these are needed.

Thus you should visualize yourself as a deity, and the *hūṃ* set on your heart must be the seed syllable of the deity on which you meditate. For it is taught that when the *hūṃ* is white, you should visualize yourself as white Vajradhara, and in this case a lunar seat will be appropriate for the *hūṃ* rather than a solar seat. When you emanate deities from your body on other occasions in the sādhana, you should do so mainly while maintaining the divine identity either of Akṣobhya or Dveṣavajra as the case may be. In the present case too[1340] you should visualize yourself instantly as Akṣobhya Vajra, a variegated lotus with a solar disk on your heart surmounted by a blue *hūṃ*; a light ray emanating from this blue *hūṃ* draws the nondual lama-Akṣobhya-maṇḍala from the natural abode into the foreground [17b] and then dissolves back into your heart. Some texts say that the lotus on your heart should be red.

Both the *Abhidhānottara*[1341] and the *Saṃvarodaya*[1342] tantras explain that you should invite the lama together with the field for accumulating merit.

1337. Abhayākaragupta, *Rim pa lnga pa'i dgongs 'grel zla ba'i 'od zer, Pañcakramamatiṭīkā Candraprabhā*, Tōh 1831, 183a4–5. Bhavyakīrti, *Rim pa lnga'i dka' 'grel, Pañcakramapañjikā*, Tōh 1838, 1b2–3. See also Tsong kha pa, *Gsang mngon*, 18a5–b2.

1338. Candrakīrti, *Rdo rje sems dpa'i sgrub thabs, Vajrasattva Sādhana*, Tōh 1814, 196b2; Luo and Tomabechi 2009, 4.11–12 and 37.1–2. D and Luo and Tomabechi have *mdun du* for *drung du*; D has *arga* and Luo and Tomabechi have *argha* for *arghaṃ* in our text.

1339. For the Pāramitā Vehicle, see, for example, Conze 1975, 50.

1340. See Tsong kha pa, *Gsang mngon*, 18a5–b2.

1341. *Mngon par brjod pa'i rgyud bla ma*, Tōh 369.

1342. *Sdom 'byung*, Tōh 373.

The *Crown Jewel Sādhana* by *Kambala teaches how to visualize the lama: "Imagine the lama sitting on a lion throne in front of the lord of the cremation ground in an easterly direction."[1343] SOME LAMAS[1344] say that this is very inappropriate because it contradicts the *Abhidhānottara Tantra*, which explains that the lama is Bodhicittavajra[1345] of the sixth tathāgata family; and that it also contradicts Śrīdhara,[1346] who says that the lama appears as Vajradhara. Thus, THEY argue that the *Crown Jewel Sādhana* represents an enormous departure from the principles of the Mantra Vehicle, and therefore the author of the *Crown Jewel Sādhana* is certainly not *Kambala.

While this is arguable, THEIR position is highly improper in that it rejects the work of the mahāsiddha *Kambala, for the same sādhana also teaches: "Clearly envision the lama as Vajrasattva seated majestically on a throne, adorned with every ornament."[1347] In other words, this sādhana teaches that you should visualize the lama as Vajradhara. Therefore, citing [the *Abhidhānottara Tantra* and Śrīdhara] in order to refute the explanation about envisioning the lama as Vajradhara is altogether irrelevant.

Additionally, if THEY think that meditating on Vajradhara is incompatible with abiding in the cremation ground, THEY simply misunderstand the principles of the Mantra Vehicle to an even greater extent.[1348] This is so because the yogi should visualize the cremation ground at the surrounding perimeter of the maṇḍala, arising as an aspect of the wisdom of Vajradhara, the principal deity of the maṇḍala. [18a] Otherwise, many errors will ensue, as, for example, the idea that the cremation ground cannot be associated with purity.

Among those who dwell in the cremation ground the *Abhidhānottara Tantra* speaks of supreme heroes and yoginīs: "A supreme gathering of the

1343. *Kambala, Lwa ba pa, *Bde mchog gi sgrub thabs gtsug nor, Cakrasamvara Sādhana Ratnacūḍāmaṇi*, Tōh 1443, 244b2–3.

1344. This argument is found in Tsong kha pa, *'Dod 'jo*, 48a1–b2, in the context of Cakrasaṃvara, but see also his *Bskyed rim zin bris*, 7a2–5, and his *Sngags rim chen mo*, chap. 12, 496.

1345. Tib. Byang chub kyi sems rdo rje, Eng. Vajra Mind for Enlightenment, the main tathāgata in the first chapter of the *Guhyasamāja Tantra*.

1346. Śrīdhara, *Gshin rje gshed dmar po'i sgrub thabs, Raktayamāri Sādhana*, Tōh 2023, 88b1.

1347. *Kambala, Lwa ba pa, *Bde mchog gi sgrub thabs gtsug nor, Cakrasaṃvara Sādhana Ratnacūḍāmaṇi*, Tōh 1443, 244b2–3. D has *'gying bag tu* for *'gying bag can* and *bzhugs pa snang bar gyur pa gsal bar* for *bzhugs pa gsal bar* in our text. See Tsong kha pa, *'Dod 'jo*, 48a2, where he has *ma nges bzhin du bkag pas shin tu mi rigs te* for *ma nges bzhin du grub chen gyi gzhung bkag pas shin tu 'ang mi rigs te*.

1348. See Tsong kha pa, *'Dod 'jo*, 48a4–5.

heroes and various paramount yoginīs."[1349] Likewise the *Saṃvarodaya Tantra* teaches: "At the center of the cremation ground you should visualize an assembly of masters who have perfected their great siddhis and supernatural powers."[1350] Therefore there is nothing whatsoever that is inappropriate in this method.

There are three methods for visualizing the lama: (1) as no different from the principal deity of the maṇḍala or Vajradhara, (2) as lord of the tathāgata family of the principal deity, and (3) as abiding in the cremation ground.[1351] Since all three methods are referred to by authentic scholars and siddhas, any one of them is fine, but in the present case you should visualize the lama as no different from the principal deity.

What is the "natural abode" from which the deities are drawn?[1352] The *Abhidhānottara Tantra* teaches: "Invoke those who have already attained."[1353] Hence you should invite the wisdom maṇḍala of the saṃbhogakāyas that reside where awakening initially took place. According to a second explanation, "natural" in "natural abode" means the dharmakāya, indivisible from the *nature* of all phenomena, which is emptiness. Since the deities arise from the continuing state of the dharmakāya in the form of the rūpakāya, they are invited from their natural abode. In the third instance, being invited from the No-Higher Heaven[1354] means being invited from a specific place.[1355] *Kambala, the *Cluster of Instructions*, and so forth explain that after drawing the deities, the light ray dissolves back into the heart.[1356]

1349. *Mngon par brjod pa'i rgyud bla ma*, chap. 9, Tōh 369, 271b4; Sanskrit and English translation in Kalff 1979, 183 and 293. The sentence, as cited here, is incomplete.

1350. *Sdom 'byung*, Tōh 373, 286b3; Sanskrit, Tibetan, and English translation in Tsuda 1974, chap. 17, v. 45cde. Tsuda has *dngos grub rdzu 'phrul yang dag par / thob pa'i slob dpon gyi ni tshogs / dur khrod dbus su blta bar bya* for *grub chen rdzu 'phrul yang dag thob slob dpon / tshogs ni dur khrod dbus su blta bar bya.*

1351. See also Tsong kha pa, *Sngags rim chen mo*, chap. 12, 496.

1352. See Tsong kha pa, *Gsang mngon*, 18b1–2; and *'Dod 'jo*, 48b2–5; and *Bung ba'i re skong*, 4b6–5a2.

1353. *Mngon brjod rgyud bla ma*, chap. 4, Tōh 369, 254a2. D has *sngon grub pa rnams* for *sngon grub pa ni* in our text. This line could also be translated as "those who are already in existence."

1354. Tib. 'Og min, Skt. Akaniṣṭha.

1355. Reading *no* for *na* in our text.

1356. *Kambala, Lwa ba pa, *Bde mchog gi sgrub thabs gtsug nor, Cakrasaṃvara Sādhana Ratnacūḍāmaṇi*, Tōh 1443. Abhayākaragupta, *Man ngag snye ma, Āmnāyamañjarī*, Tōh 1198. See Tsong kha pa, *'Dod 'jo*, 48b3–4, and *Gsang mngon*, 18b2.

The Sevenfold Worship[1357]

Although there are many different sequences in the stages of prostrations, offerings, and so forth to the field for accumulating merit, [18b] here the offerings come first, as shown in the commentaries on the sādhana.[1358]

[Offerings]

Visualize the goddesses who hold the articles for each offering emanating from the *hūṃ* on the heart and filling the entire space. As the articles are offered, recite the mantras and make the specific hand gestures. The mantras of offering are taught in the *Vajra Garland Tantra*: "Then make befitting offerings according to the ritual method. To the Blessed One make offerings of music, songs, and so forth, while reciting the respective mantra according to the sequence. The mantra of offering [flowers] is: *oṃ sarva tathāgata puṣpe pūjā megha samudra spharaṇa samaya śriye āḥ hūṃ*. While offering each substance, pronounce its respective name 'form'[1359] and so forth as before."[1360] The meaning of *sarva tathāgata* is "all tathāgatas," *puṣpe* is "flower," *pūjā* is "offerings," *megha samudra* is "ocean of clouds," *spharaṇa* is "diffusing," *samaya śriye* is "accept as pledge," and *āḥ* and *hūṃ* are the seed syllables of speech and mind. Follow the same pattern for the other offerings, the five offerings for enjoyment and the five offerings to the senses of the desire realm.[1361]

Thus the mantra for making the offerings is *oṃ sarva tathāgata puṣpe pūjā megha samudra spharaṇa samaya śriye āḥ hūṃ*, and so forth.[1362] While reciting *oṃ*, visualize the goddesses emanating, and when reciting *hūṃ*, complete the hand gesture, snap your fingers, and make the gesture of vajra gathering.

1357. See also Tsong kha pa, *Bskyed rim zin bris*, 7b5–10b6, and *Bung ba'i re skong*, 5a6–8a3.

1358. In the sūtric way of the sevenfold worship, such as the *Bhadracarī(caryā)-praṇidhāṇa*, *Bzang spyod smon lam*, prostration is followed by the offerings.

1359. First offered are flowers, incense, light, fragrance, food, and music. The name of the flower offering, *puṣpe*, is replaced with *dhūpe*, *āloke*, *gandhe*, *naividyā*, *śapta*, and so forth. Then come the five offerings to the senses, forms, sounds, scents, tastes, and objects of touch with their respective names *rūpa*, *śabda*, *gandha*, *rasa*, and *sparśa*.

1360. *Rgyud rdo rje phreng ba*, *Vajramālā Tantra*, chap. 54, Tōh 445, 257a7–b2. D has *go rims* for *go rim*; *hūṃ gi sngags ni rjes su brjod* for *hūṃ mchod pa'i sngags ni rjes su mchod*; and *gzugs la sogs pa snga ma bzhin* for *gzung la sogs snga ma bzhin* in our text.

1361. See Tsong kha pa, *Gsang mngon*, 18b2–4.

1362. The phrase "and so forth" indicates that this explanation refers not only to offering flowers but to the other offerings too.

At that moment visualize the goddesses being drawn into the seed syllable in your heart. When you bless the offering recite the mantra *oṃ puṣpe āḥ hūṃ*, and so forth, as the *Vajrasattva Offering Ritual* teaches: "Then offer the flowers while reciting *oṃ puṣpe āḥ hūṃ* or the three syllables."[1363] [19a]

[Prostrations[1364]]

Having made offerings in this way, prostrate yourself to all the residents of the maṇḍala, while reciting these verses of the *Later Tantra*:

> I prostrate to all the immense ones equal to the mind-for-enlightenment: forms, feelings, perceptions, the conditioned, and consciousnesses, the six sensory spheres, the six faculties, earth, water, fire, wind, and space.
>
> I prostrate to the immense ones equal to the mind-for-enlightenment endowed with qualities of[1365] ignorance, fault,[1366] desire, and vajra, born out of union with the consort, perpetually joined, who experience[1367] diversity through joy.
>
> I prostrate to the immense ones equal to the mind-for-enlightenment, gathering, joy, appearance, unchanging, the nature of the cause and the fruit, phenomena that pertains to the mind, delusion, anger, desire, obscurations, and vajra.[1368]

1363. Kṛṣṇa, *Rdo rje sems dpa' mchod pa'i cho ga, Vajrasattva Pūjāvidhi*, Tōh 1820, 259b56. D has *vajra puṣpe* for *puṣpe*; *yi ge 'bru gsum* for *yi ge gsum*; and *me tog byin gyis brlab par bya'o*, for *me tog gyis mchod par bya'o*.

1364. See Tsong kha pa, *Gsang mngon*, 18b4–19a4.

1365. The commentary below reads the *chos dang bcas* together with *'dod chags*, even though the *rdo rje* appears in between them; Skt. *rāgasavajradharmān*.

1366. Tib. *nyes pa*, the Sanskrit has *dveṣa* here, but the correspondence in the commentary below is made with the tathāgata family of Rin chen, and therefore explains it as pride.

1367. The *Rgyud phyi ma, Uttara Tantra*, Tōh 443, 157a5, and Tsong kha pa, *Gsang mngon*, 19a2, and *Bskyed rim zin bris*, 8b2, have *myos pa* [being intoxicated] for *myong ba* [experiencing] in our text.

1368. *Rgyud phyi ma, Uttara Tantra*, Tōh 443, 157a3–6; Matsunaga 1978, vv. 205–207. D and Zhol have *dga' bas myos pa'i* for *dga' ba mnyong ba'i*; and D has *spro* for *sdud* and *gtogs chos* for *thogs chos* in our text. These lines also appear in Tsong kha pa, *Gsang mngon*, 18b4–19a4. Both the tantra and the sādhana have *myos pa'i* for *myong ba* in our text.

Here is the meaning of these lines: To whom are you prostrating and how? *To* all *those who are equal* in their perfection of renunciation and realization to Bodhicittavajra[1369]—Vajradhara, the wisdom of nondual profundity and manifestation that arises in the form of the *immense* deities of the maṇḍala.

Who are they?

(1) The five purified aggregates: *forms, feelings, perceptions, the conditioned, and consciousnesses* are the five tathāgata families.[1370]

(2) The *six* [purified] *sensory spheres* who, according to the tradition of Jñānapāda,[1371] are the six vajra ladies,[1372] the sixth one being Dharmadhātuvajrā,[1373] although here they are the five vajra ladies[1374] and Samantabhadra.

(3) The *six* [purified] *faculties* are the six bodhisattvas: the purified eyes are Kṣitigarbha, the purified ears are Vajrapāṇi, the purified nose is Khagarbha, the purified tongue is Lokeśvara, [19b] the purified body is Sarvanīvaraṇaviṣkambhin, and the purified mind is Maitreya. Does this contradict the explanation that Maitreya is the purified nerves and sinews and Samantabhadra is the purified joints?[1375] Each deity has several purified aspects, and two among them are applied respectively in these two cases, hence there is no contradiction.

(4) The purified *earth, water, fire,* and *wind* are respectively Locanā, Māmakī, Pāṇḍarā, and Tārā; the purified *space* is Mañjuśrī.

(5) *Ignorance* is Yamāntaka,[1376] the fierce deity of the tathāgata family of ignorance [Vairocana]. The general name *fault* is applied in this case specifically to pride,[1377] thus this is Prajñāntaka, the fierce deity of the tathāgata family of Ratnasaṃbhava that purifies pride. The one *endowed with the*

1369. Tib. Byang chub kyi sems rdo rje, Eng. Vajra-Mind-for-Enlightenment, the main tathāgata in the first chapter of the *Guhyasamāja Tantra*.

1370. These are Akṣobhya, Vairocana, Ratnasaṃbhava, Amitābha, and Amoghasiddhi.

1371. Ye shes zhabs called also Buddhajñānapāda, Sangs rgyas ye shes zhabs, see the section "Jñānapāda" in the *Introductory Essay*. See also Tsong kha pa, *Slob tshul*, 3a5–6.

1372. Tib. Rdo rje ma, Skt. Vajrā.

1373. Tib. Chos dbyings rdo rje ma.

1374. These are Rūpavajrā, Śabdavajrā, Gandhavajrā, Rasavajrā, and Sparśavajrā.

1375. See the meditation on the body maṇḍala below. See also Tsong kha pa, *Bskyed rim zin bris*, 8a3.

1376. These are the four fierce deities set in the four directions of the maṇḍala.

1377. See Tsong kha pa, *Slob tshul*, 3b2–3, and *Bskyed rim zin bris*, 8a6.

nature of desire[1378] is Hayagrīva, the fierce deity of the tathāgata family of Amitābha, who purifies desire. *Vajra* is Amoghasiddhi, as the *Illuminating Lamp* explains the term *vajrarati* in its interpretable meaning: "*Rati* is fondness; fondness toward whom? Toward her lord Vajra, who is Amoghasiddhi." Therefore *Vajra* here is Vighnāntaka, the fierce deity of the tathāgata family of Amoghasiddhi.

Many meanings can be applied to *consort*,[1379] but it was explained that here these are the five mothers, Locanā and so forth, who while holding the vases confer the initiations called the five initiations for realization.[1380] Since the deities of the maṇḍala are *perpetually joined* with the innate bliss that arises out of *union* with the consort, that is, the seal, all appearances in their *diversity* arise as a display of *the state of experiencing the joy* of bliss and emptiness, and therefore they are *equal to the mind-for-enlightenment.*

Gathering is Ṭakkirāja,[1381] *joy* is Nīladaṇḍa, *appearance* is Mahābala, [20a] *likewise, unchanging* is Acala. *The cause and fruit* refer to the qualities of the path, progression from a lower stage upward in stages: *the nature of the cause* is Sumbharāja, who [resides below, in the maṇḍala], and *the nature of the fruit* is Uṣṇīṣacakravartin, [who abides above, and therefore] is signified by the attainment of the fruit. The two latter fierce deities are the essence of purified consciousness, and therefore are *the phenomena that pertains to the mind.*

Regarding the classification of the tathāgata families of the remaining six fierce deities: *Delusion* is Acala, who belongs to the tathāgata family of Vairocana. *Anger* refers to the two fierce deities abiding above and below,[1382] who belong to the tathāgata family of Akṣobhya. *Desire* is Nīladaṇḍa of the Amitābha tathāgata family. *Obscurations* are *faults*, as explained earlier,[1383] with reference to Ṭakkirāja of the tathāgata family of Ratnasaṃbhava. And

1378. As noted above, our text takes *chos dang bcas* together with *'dod chags*, even though the *rdo rje* appears in between them; Skt. *rāgasavajradharmān*.

1379. According to Tsong kha pa, *Slob tshul*, 3b3, *rig pa* here means *rig ma*.

1380. Tib. *rig pa*.

1381. These are the six remaining fierce deities of the Guhyasamāja maṇḍala.

1382. These are once more Uṣṇīṣacakravartin and Sumbharāja.

1383. See [19b2–3] above and Tsong kha pa, *Bskyed rim zin bris*, 8a6.

vajra is Mahābala of the tathāgata family of Amoghasiddhi. This accords with the explanation of Nāropa in his commentary on the *Later Tantra*.[1384]

Since the steps of the sevenfold worship, from confession to the maintenance of shared vows—the two bodhicitta vows endowed with the essence of the resolve and its fulfillment—are not found in the works of Ārya Nāgārjuna and his disciples, you should meditate on these steps with the verses that are found in *Mañjuvajra Sādhana* of the *Guhyasamāja*.[1385] I will explain the meaning of these verses in brief.[1386] [20b]

[Confession]

> All the turbidity I have accumulated through my conceptualizations in this beginningless[1387] river of existence, I confess in the presence of the greatly compassionate ones, in accordance with the ritual method.

By taking this stanza as the basis of exposition,[1388] the step of confession will be explained:

> The FEATURE of turbidity is abundance, so all of it must be taken into account. Hence *all the turbidity*, whose NATURE is transgression, that *I have accumulated* INDUCED by *my conceptualizations* since *beginningless* TIME in this PLACE *the river of existence*, *I confess in the presence of the* SPHERE of the *greatly compassionate ones*, the lamas and the deities residing in the maṇḍala, through the METHOD that *accords with the ritual* taught by the Victorious One, complete with

1384. *Yaśobhadra/Nāropa, *Gsang ba thams cad kyi sgron ma'i rgya cher 'grel pa*, *Sarvaguhyapradīpaṭīkā*, Tōh 1787, 233a7–b2. See also Tsong kha pa, *Bskyed rim zin bris*, 7b6, where he says that these verses of prostration are found in the *Rgyud phyi ma*, *Uttara Tantra*, Tōh 443, and that Nāropa explained that these are verses recited during the prostration to the thirty-two deities.

1385. *Gsang 'dus 'Jam rdor gyis sgrub thabs*; this is the *Kun bzang sgrub thabs* or *Sgrub thabs kun bzang*, *Samantabhadra Sādhana*, by Jñānapāda, Tōh 1855, 29a6–b3; Tanaka 1996, 181–186. These verses appear in Tsong kha pa, *Gsang mngon*, 19a5–20a4, as well.

1386. While in the Tibetan text all the following verses appear first and then each verse is explained, here each verse is followed by its explanation.

1387. D and our text have *thog med* for *thogs med* in Tsong kha pa, *Gsang mngon*, 19a4.

1388. The verse recited for confession is explained through six key points: feature, nature, inducement, time, place, sphere of addressees, and method.

> the four antidotal powers[1389] and devoid of conceptualization of the three spheres [of confession][1390] as truly existing.

[Rejoicing and Dedication]

> I truly rejoice in all the virtuous deeds of the perfect buddhas, the bodhisattvas, the sublime beings, and others, and wholly dedicate them for the attainment of enlightenment.

The meaning of this is: *I rejoice* with *true* joy *in all the virtues attained by*[1391] *the perfect buddhas and the bodhisattvas, the sublime* disciples and solitary buddhas, and all *others* who are not *sublime beings*, but ordinary beings; [21a] and I *wholly dedicate* all the virtues accumulated in the three times *for the attainment of enlightenment.*

[Taking Refuge]

Refuge in the Buddha

> At all times do I seek refuge in the sugatas in whose mind dwells [wisdom][1392] and the method of true and boundless compassion, attained through the play of the untainted moon-like mind.

At all times do I seek refuge in the sugatas. What sort of sugatas? Sugatas distinguished by way of all the perfected qualities of method and wisdom simultaneously and continuously *dwell in their mind.* These are the perfected *method of true and boundless compassion* and nondual wisdom *attained through* a continual increase—*like* the waxing *moon*—of *the play of mind* or its expression or its manifestation, *untainted* by dualistic appearances.

1389. The power of support, the power of applying the antidote, the power of repentance, and the power of refraining forever from wrongdoing.

1390. The person who makes the confession, the lamas and the deities residing in the maṇḍala before whom the confession is made, and the nonvirtuous deeds that are confessed.

1391. Reading *kyis* for *kyi.*

1392. This line can also be translated also as: "I seek refuge in the sugatas who dwells in my mind." See the section "Establishing Favorable Conditions" in the introduction.

REFUGE IN THE DHARMA

> At all times do I seek refuge in the true Dharma, the foundation of endowments of the sublime beings, wholly free of all conceptualizations, whose essence is the single taste of all phenomena.

At all times do I seek refuge in the true Dharma. The Dharma is the truth of the path,[1393] the wisdom arising from meditative equipoise, the *foundation of endowments*—the excellent qualities of abandonment and realization *of the sublime beings, free* in its ground *of all conceptualization* of dualistic appearances. The Dharma is also the truth of cessation,[1394] understanding that within their natural state *all* diverse *phenomena* and their subjects share a *single taste,* the *essence* of suchness.

REFUGE IN THE SAṄGHA

> At all times do I seek refuge in the assembly of masters of rigorous practice, truly freed from bondage, endowed with excellence born of supreme compassion, who abide on the [bodhisattva] levels of Joy and higher still.

I *seek refuge* in the *saṅgha*, the *assembly* of bodhisattvas who are *masters* or superior to ordinary bodhisattvas in their *rigorous practice* of the Mahāyāna because they *abide on the bodhisattva levels of Joy and higher still,* and are *endowed with the excellence* of mind-for-enlightenment *born of* the mother *of supreme compassion*, and *truly free* of *bondage* at their respective levels.

[Generating the Mind for Enlightenment]

> I shall generate the mind for sublime enlightenment, adorned with earnest aspiration, that totally eliminates the habitual tendencies of all obscurations, by means of pure resolve and ripening.

I shall generate, that is, focus on, *the mind for sublime enlightenment,* the object of attainment, *adorned with earnest aspiration* for the sake of others, both the wishing *resolve* and motivated by it, the engaging mind-for-enlightenment

1393. The fourth among the four truths of the noble ones.

1394. The third among the four truths of the noble ones.

that totally eliminates the habitual tendencies of all obscurations, that result from *ripening* of previous karma, through the *pure* practice. [21b]

[Pledging Reliance on the Path]

> I shall truly abide on the singular path of the sugatas and their spiritual offspring, in the perfections of generosity and so forth, and in the excellent qualities of the ten virtues, with a mind whose essence is all the fully enlightened buddhas.

I shall truly abide on the singular path of the sugatas and their spiritual offspring, the six *perfections, generosity and so forth*, the main pillar of the path of the Mahāyāna, and in the *excellent* ethical conduct of *the ten* paths of *virtuous* actions. This method is superior to the Pāramitā Vehicle, because even while on the path, one strives *with a mind* that takes the fruit as the path—imagining the practice of the six perfections as the *essence of all fully enlightened buddhas*.

This is the explanation of the commentaries on the *Samantabhadra Sādhana*.[1395]

[Maintaining the Unshared Vows]

Meditate with "All the buddhas and bodhisattvas! Turn your thoughts to me!" and so forth up to "I will establish sentient beings in nirvāṇa."[1396] The

1395. As noted, the verses recited during the stages from confession to relying on the path are found in the *Kun bzang sgrub thabs*, *Samantabhadra Sādhana*, by Jñānapāda, Tōh 1855, 29a6–b3; Tanaka 1996, 181–186. These verses are explained in the commentaries on this work: Phalavajra, *Kun tu bzang po'i sgrub pa'i thabs kyi 'grel pa*, *Samantabhadra Sādhana Vṛtti*, Tōh 1867, 144a1–146a2; and Thagana, *Kun bzang sgrub thabs 'grel ba*, *Samantabhadra Sādhana Vṛtti*, Tōh 1868, 192b7–195a5.

1396. See Tsong kha pa, *Gsang mngon*, 20a4–21a5. These verses are found in a number of Indian works including the *Vajraśekhara Tantra* (chap. 2, Tōh 480, 184a1–6); the *Sarvadurgatipariśodhana* (Skorupski 1983, 146); the *Sampuṭodbhava* (chap. 3.4); the *Vajraḍāka Tantra* (chap. 12; Sugiki 2017); and Abhayākaragupta's *Vajrāvalī* (Mori 2009, §20.6). Tsong kha pa dedicated a whole treatise to this subject (*Dngos grub kyi snye ma*, see especially folios 11b–22a; English translation in Sparham 2005, 45–62).

distinctive feature here is that the vows have already been taken in the past,[1397] and are therefore different from vows maintained as prerequisites for receiving initiation through the pure ritual method of the initiation. Here vows that were not taken previously are not pledged and vows that have been broken are not restored.[1398]

1397. New vows are not taken here. The purpose is rather to reinforce and enhance the vows that have already been taken, and these are offered to the lama and the deities of the maṇḍala, as an offering of practice for the accumulation of merit. This practice is still part of the sevenfold worship.

1398. See also Tsong kha pa, *Bung ba'i re skong*, 8a2–3.

3. Averting Unfavorable Conditions

Meditating on the Protection Wheel to Avert Unfavorable Conditions

[Meditation on Emptiness prior to the Visualization of the Protection Wheel]

The *Concise Sādhana* teaches: "Abide in the samādhi of Dveṣavajra."[1399] But prior to this there is no explicit explanation whatsoever in this text about meditation on the protection wheel. Abhayākaragupta explains that at the beginning of the visualization of the protection wheel, you meditate on the essence, cause, and fruit of phenomena as empty, and from the continuing state of emptiness you visualize a quickly spinning yellow wheel with the fierce deities set upon its spoke.[1400]

SOME LATER LAMAS[1401] say that the tradition of Jñanapāda teaches you to meditate on emptiness before visualizing the protection wheel, [22a] but such is not the intention of Ārya Nāgārjuna and his disciples. This is so because the meditation on the protection wheel after everything has been dissolved into emptiness is a different system in which meditators visualize the celestial mansion within the protection wheel. But in this instance it is not so, because while reciting "In the absence of being, there is no meditation,"[1402]

1399. Nāgārjuna, *Mdor byas, Piṇḍīkrama Sādhana*, Tōh 1796, D 2a2; L 7c; T 7c.

1400. See Tsong kha pa, *Sgron gsal mchan*, 370a2, where he says that whereas Nāgārjuna and his disciples do not clearly maintain that one must meditate on the yellow ten-spoked wheel, Abhayākaragupta explains that meditating on the wheel is very good. Abhayākaragupta teaches that one should meditate on a yellow protection wheel with ten spokes, after meditating on emptiness in both his commentary on Nāgārjuna's *Mdor byas, Piṇḍīkrama Sādhana*, and *Rim lnga, Pañcakrama*, entitled *Rim pa lnga pa'i dgongs 'grel zla ba'i 'od zer, Pañcakramamatiṭīkā Candraprabhā*, Tōh 1831, 183a6, and in his *Man ngag snye ma, Āmnāyamañjarī*, Tōh 1198, 127b4–7.

1401. See Red mda' ba, *Bsgrub pa dpal bas zhus lan*, Kathmandu, 49a5–b2; TBRC, 304b.

1402. This verse will be discussed in chap. 4 below.

you dissolve the protection wheel in clear light, and meditate on the ground of wisdom. Therefore, THEY SAY,[1403] if you meditate on emptiness before visualizing the protection wheel, you end up meditating twice on the ground of wisdom. Moreover, THEY SAY[1404] that this system does not even teach the protection wheel and that if the wheel spins quickly, the allocation of the deities to the different directions will be uncertain, thus it cannot be established that the fierce deities do, indeed, guard the directions.[1405]

These positions are very unreasonable. The "meditation on the ground of wisdom" is explained as a meditation on emptiness that is applied in correspondence with the eon[1406] of the empty world on the ground of purification. Such is not the purpose of the meditation here, which is rather to dispel ordinary appearances and attitudes prior to the visualization of the protection wheel, so that the protection wheel and its fierce deities will arise from the continuing state of the dharmakāya. How then could it be a meditation on the ground of wisdom?

Were it not so, the absurd consequence of YOUR proposition would be that all meditations on emptiness, including the meditation on emptiness for cleansing and purifying the offerings at the beginning of the sādhana, and the meditation on emptiness for dissolving the specially visualized deities into clear light below, would be meditations on the ground of wisdom, and therefore it would be necessary to meditate many times on the ground of wisdom. Thus, since before every meditation beginning with the meditation on a single deity in the kriyā and caryā tantras there is a meditation on emptiness, it is extremely unreasonable to assert that it is inappropriate to meditate on emptiness before the protection wheel here.

[Meditation on the Protection Wheel, the Residence of the Protecting Deities]

Although neither the works of Ārya Nāgārjuna and his disciples nor the *Guhyasamāja Tantra* include any explicit teachings with regard to the

1403. See Red mda' ba, *Bsgrub pa dpal bas zhus lan*, Kathmandu, 49b1–2; TBRC, 304b.

1404. See Ngor chen, *Gsang 'dus dkyil 'khor gyi sgrub thabs dngos grub rgya mtsho*, work 106, 3b3–6, who teaches that one should visualize the ten fierce deities, but without the protection wheel. Bu ston offers two methods of meditation on protection with and without the wheel. See his *Mdor byas 'grel chen*, 9a2–6.

1405. See Red mda' ba, *Bsgrub pa dpal bas zhus lan*, Kathmandu, 49b1–2; TBRC, 304b.

1406. Skt. *kalpa*.

meditation on the wheel, [22b] the explanatory tantras give clear instructions.[1407] The *Later Tantra* teaches: "At the center, the yogis should visualize a wheel with ten spokes that is yellow all around, with ten fierce deities issuing from ten embodiments of wisdom, one on each spoke. They envision the wheel as a blocking vajra, perfect and most splendid, that radiates a multitude of vajra flames. While the wheel is spinning, [the deities] do not seem to be in motion."[1408] This indicates that the wheel is yellow and spinning.

Ārya Nāgārjuna and his disciples cite the *Later Tantra* on other occasions too. The *Illuminating Lamp* likewise explains the meaning of the *Guhyasamāja Tantra* by citing this very *Later Tantra* with regard to many points of the creation stages, such as the generation of the four vajras, and in numerous presentations of the completion stage with its six limbs of yoga. Thus it is a great oversight to say that the Ārya tradition does not regard the *Later Tantra* as a major authority.

There is nothing wrong with maintaining that while the wheel is spinning, the fierce deities cannot identify the directions to guard, for the *Later Tantra* teaches: "While the wheel is spinning, [the deities] do not seem to be in motion."[1409] This means that while *the wheel is spinning*, the fierce deities *do not move* in different directions, that is to say, they remain in their places and do not spin. Hence, although the wheel spins, the fierce deities do not have to spin. Therefore those who find fault with the spinning of the wheel find fault with the tantra.

Thus the explanation in the *Commentary on the Vajrasattva Sādhana* about meditating on the wheel as well as the explanation of Abhayākaragupta are sound.[1410] However the position of many EARLY TIBETANS and of LATER

1407. See Tsong kha pa, *Bskyed rim zin bris*, 11a6–b4.

1408. *Rgyud phyi ma, Uttara Tantra*, Tōh 443, 151b7–152a1; Matsunaga 1978, vv. 81–82. D and Zhol have *bsgom* for *bsgoms* and *'bar ba'i* for *'bar bas*; D has *'gog pa'i rdo rjes* for *'gog pa'i rdo rje*; and Zhol has *mdzes pa* for *mdzes pas* and *'phro bas* for *spros bas* in our text. Tsong kha pa, *Sgron gsal mchan*, 370a2–4, has the same readings as the Zhol, except for *'phros bas*. The varying readings make my translation most tentative. See also Tsong kha pa, *Bung ba'i re skong*, 8a4–5.

1409. *Rgyud phyi ma, Uttara Tantra*, Tōh 443, 152a1; Matsunaga 1978, v. 82d.

1410. Līlavajra, *Rdo rje sems dpa'i sgrub thabs kyi 'grel pa, Vajrasattva Sādhana Nibandha*, Tōh 1815, 205b6–206a2. Abhayākaragupta, *Rim pa lnga pa'i dgongs 'grel zla ba'i 'od zer, Pañcakramamatiṭīkā Candraprabhā*, Tōh 1831, 183a6; and *Man ngag snye ma, Āmnāyamañjarī*, Tōh 1198, 127b7–128a2.

TIBETAN SCHOLARS[1411] who maintain that it is appropriate not to meditate on the wheel is incorrect.

Therefore first meditate on emptiness by reflecting on the meaning of the mantra *oṃ svabhāva śuddhāḥ sarva dharmāḥ svabhāva śuddho 'haṃ.*[1412] Then from the continuing state of emptiness *paṃ* appears and transforms into a variegated lotus, and an *āḥ* arises and turns into a solar disk. Upon it is a *bhrūṃ* that becomes a yellow ten-spoked wheel spinning swiftly clockwise. [23a] Since the *Later Tantra* teaches "cloud-like vajra flames radiate,"[1413] at this point you should meditate on "a series of cloud-like vajra flames radiating in the ten directions."[1414]

[What Is the Shape of the Protection Wheel on Which You Meditate?]

The *Guhyasamāja Tantra* and other Indian scriptures do not explain this very clearly.[1415] But when the *Cluster of Instructions* teaches: "within the center of the hub of the ten-spoked yellow wheel,"[1416] it provides an indication regarding the shape of the wheel. Generally, saying *within* does not in itself establish that the hub is hollow, for as a *Purification*[1417] *Tantra* teaches: "Vajrasattva and so forth abide in all of them within the spokes."[1418] However, this is not so in the present case because the *Cluster of Instructions* teaches: "I abide within the space at the center of the hub of the ten-spoked yellow wheel spinning clockwise,"[1419] and so forth. Thus it is taught that you visualize yourself as a

1411. See the positions of Bu ston, Red mda' ba, and Ngor chen in notes 1403 and 1404 above.

1412. See Tsong kha pa, *Gsang mngon*, 21b1–3.

1413. *Rgyud phyi ma, Uttara Tantra*, Tōh 443, 152a1; Zhol 51b4; Matsunaga 1978, v. 82c. Zhol has *'phro bas* for *spros pas* in our text and in D.

1414. See Tsong kha pa, *Gsang mngon*, 21b3–4.

1415. The following lines are based on Tsong kha pa, *'Dod 'jo*, 37b3–6.

1416. Abhayākaragupta, *Man ngag snye ma, Āmnāyamañjarī*, Tōh 1198, 130a6; cited also in Tsong kha pa, *Sngags rim chen mo*, chap. 12, 501–502; for an English translation see Yarnall 2003, 564.

1417. Reading *sbyong rgyud* for *spyod rgyud*.

1418. *Ngan song thams cad yongs su sbyong ba gzi brjid, Sarvadurgatipariśodhana*, Tōh 483, [version A], 62b2; Skorupski 1983, 314. D has *thams cad du* for *thams cad na* and *rdo rje sems sogs sems dpa' mchog* for *bzhugs pa'i rdo rje sems dpa' sogs* in our text. Our text follows Tsong kha pa, *'Dod 'jo*, 37b4. See also his *Sngags rim chen mo*, chap. 12, 502.

1419. Abhayākaragupta, *Man ngag snye ma, Āmnāyamañjarī*, chap. 12, Tōh 1198, 127b7. D has *g.yas skor* for *g.yas bskor* in our text. This line is cited also in Tsong kha pa, *Sngags rim chen mo*, chap. 12, 501–502; for an English translation see Yarnall 2003, 564.

deity within the space of the empty hub, hollow all around. Therefore you understand that the fierce deities that reside at the zenith and the nadir are visualized at the upper and lower points within the hollow interior of the hub. Thus the hub of the wheel with its upper and lower spokes resembles a convergence of double-edged spikes; and the principal deity is visualized within the bulge at the center, while the fierce deities that reside at the zenith and nadir are visualized within the upper and lower points.

It is stated clearly that the other eight fierce deities on the horizontal plane are set upon the tips of the spokes in the eight directions, and it is explained in many other sources as well that you should set the fierce deities upon the spokes. Thus there is no hollow space below the fierce deities, as no authentic tantra or Indian scripture explains that each spoke of the wheel is like a room or a tent, and that the fierce deities are visualized within them. If the fierce deities are within the spokes and do not spin while the wheel does, [23b] then the spokes of the wheel must cut through the fierce deities. But if the fierce deities should also spin, it would be impossible to ascertain which direction each of them takes. If the fierce deities were placed between the spokes and the hub, this would contradict YOUR OWN[1420] position that the spokes are the abode of the fierce deities, and all authentic teachings of the explanatory tantras and Indian scriptures about placing the fierce deities on the spokes. Hence, such a practice belongs to the tradition of the Old School of the Mantra Vehicle.

Therefore, while the wheel spins, the fierce deities do not spin.[1421] This means that the fierce deities are not quite touching the wheel, and the wheel must spin so that the spokes of the wheel cut through the malicious ones.

[How to Meditate on the Deities of the Protection Wheel][1422]

[The Principal Deity]

The *Sādhana Incorporating the Scripture* teaches: "The third chapter of the *Guhyasamāja Tantra* teaches: 'Abiding in the midst of the space realm,' and so forth up until 'visualize an image at the center.'"[1423] This concise explanation

1420. See Kun dga' snying po, *Rdo rje gur las gsungs pa'i khro bcu'i srung 'khor*, work 45, 1b5–2a3.

1421. See Tsong kha pa, *Gsang mngon*, 21b4–5.

1422. See also Tsong kha pa, *Bskyed rim zin bris*, 11b6–12a1.

1423. *Guhyasamāja Tantra*, Tōh 442; Zhol 6b6–7; Stog 10b5–7; Dunh 9b2–3; Fremantle 1971, vv. 1a and 3ab; and Matsunaga 1978, vv. 1a and 3ab. Zhol has *nam mkha'i khams* as our text.

indicates that at first you should visualize the 'image of Bodhicittavajra.'[1424] The fifteenth chapter of the *Guhyasamāja Tantra* teaches: 'Equal in light to Vairocana, Vajrasattva, the Great King, the Buddha, the holder of the three vajras.'[1425] This indicates that you should visualize yourself as great Vajradhara white in color."[1426] Likewise, the *Vajrasattva Sādhana* teaches: "Visualize yourself in the form of great white Vajradhara."[1427] Thus it is established that you need to generate yourself as white Vajradhara at the center of the wheel.

Which form does white Vajradhara have? The master Abhayākaragupta explains that you should visualize him with three faces and six arms.[1428] In this regard, SOME LATER[1429] LAMAS[1430] say that although Abhayākaragupta explains it in this way, [24a] the commentary of Muniśrībhadra explains: "By meditating on the door of liberation of emptiness, the yogis remove their ordinary identity, and instantly turn into the form of great white Vajradhara, with two arms and one face abiding on a seat of a lotus and a lunar disk."[1431] Therefore, THEY SAY, it is appropriate to visualize Vajradhara with one face and two arms. Claiming that the work of Muniśrībhadra refutes Abhayākaragupta is ridiculous, and this position does not reflect the meaning of the tantra in a reliable way.

You should meditate according to the following explanation. The *Sādhana*

1424. Tib. Byang chub kyi sems rdo rje. This is the tathāgata that appears in the first chapter of the *Guhyasamāja Tantra* in the section that is regarded as the "past event" enacted by the creation stage.

1425. *Guhyasamāja Tantra*, Tōh 442; Zhol 31b4–5; Stog 53a2; Dunh 57b1; Fremantle 1971, v. 35bcd; and Matsunaga 1978, v. 35bcd. Zhol has *sangs rgyas sku gsum rdo rje 'dzin* for *sangs rgyas rdo rje gsum 'dzin 'gyur* in our text; Fremantle has here *buddhas trikāyavajradhṛk*; and Matsunaga has *sambuddhakāyavajradhṛk*.

1426. Nāgārjuna, *Mdo bsre, Sādhanasūtramelāpaka*, Tōh 1797, 11a5–b1. D has *nam mkha'* for *nam mkha'i*; *mdor bsdus te gsungs pa de la* for *mdor bsdus par gsungs pa 'dis*; *bya ba ste* for *bya ste*; and *bdag nyid ji lta ba bzhin* for *ji lta ba bzhin du* in our text. While our text provides only the beginning and end of the citation of the third chapter, the *Mdo bsre* has the entire passage. See also Tsong kha pa, *Bung ba'i re skong*, 8a6.

1427. Candrakīrti: *Rdo rje sems dpa'i sgrub thabs, Vajrasattva Sādhana*, Tōh 1814, 196b4; Luo and Tomabechi 2009, 5.7 and 37.14–15. D and Luo and Tomabechi have *dkar por* for *dkar pos* in our text.

1428. Abhayākaragupta, *Rim pa lnga pa'i dgongs 'grel zla ba'i 'od zer, Pañcakramamatiṭīkā Candraprabhā*, Tōh 1831, 183a7. Also noted in Tsong kha pa, *Bung ba'i re skong*, 8b1.

1429. Reading *phyis kyi* for *phyis kyis* in our text.

1430. See Bu ston, *Mdor byas 'grel chen*, 9a6–b4.

1431. Thub pa dpal, *Rim pa lnga'i don mdor bshad pa, Pañcakramārthaṭippaṇi*, Tōh 1813, 152a4–5; Jiang and Tomabechi 1996, 10.

Incorporating the Scripture teaches: "Then through the entry of/into[1432] Akṣobhya in the manner of the samādhi entitled 'vajra lamp of wisdom'[1433] taught in the first chapter of the *Guhyasamāja Tantra*,[1434] you are transformed into Dveṣavajra."[1435] Thus, when Akṣobhya enters into yourself, visualized as white Vajradhara at the center of the protection wheel in the manner of the samādhi "vajra lamp of wisdom" taught in the *Guhyasamāja Tantra*, you are transformed into Dveṣavajra. This is also the method taught in the *Vajrasattva Sādhana*.[1436]

Now, this is how the manner of samādhi "vajra lamp of wisdom" is taught in the *Guhyasamāja Tantra*: "Then the Blessed One, the tathāgata, Bodhicittavajra, was absorbed in the samādhi called the 'vajra origination from samaya of the vajra body, speech, and mind of all tathāgatas,' and blessed this personification[1437] of the great vidyā[1438] with the blessing of the mantra of all tathāgatas. As soon as the Blessed One, the Tathāgata Bodhicittavajra blessed, all tathāgatas perceived him as having three faces."[1439] [24b]

That being so,[1440] all tathāgatas beginning with Akṣobhya sang praises, made offerings and prostrations to the tathāgata, whom they perceived as having three faces, and requested him to teach the Guhyasamāja. Then Vajradhara said: "This is excellent! And yet if it is bewildering to all the tathāgatas, how

1432. The question whether Akṣobhya enters into you or you enter into Akṣobhya is a highly polemical issue.

1433. Tib. *ye shes sgron ma rdo rje*, Skt. *jñānapradīpavajra*.

1434. *Guhyasamāja Tantra*, Tōh 442; Zhol 4a2–4; Stog 5b1–5; Dunh 4a5–b4; Fremantle 1971, 182–183; and Matsunaga 1978, 6.

1435. Nāgārjuna, *Mdo bsre*, *Sādhanasūtramelāpaka*, Tōh 1797, 11b1. D and P have *ye shes sgron ma* for *ye shes sgron ma rdo rje*; D has *mi bskyod pa bskyed pas* and P has *mi bskyod pa bskyed pas rjes su zhugs pas* for *mi bskyod pa bskyed pa rjes su zhugs pas* in our text. These different readings are significant for the different positions regarding the meditation here. See Tsong kha pa, *Gsang mngon*, 22a5–24a5.

1436. Candrakīrti: *Rdo rje sems dpa'i sgrub thabs*, *Vajrasattva Sādhana*, Tōh 1814, 196b5–197a1; Luo and Tomabechi 2009, 5.12–6.4 and 38.4–13.

1437. Tib. *skyes bu gzugs*, Skt. *puruṣamūrti*.

1438. Tib. *rig pa chen po*, Skt. *mahāvidyā*.

1439. *Guhyasamāja Tantra*, Tōh 442; Zhol 3b1–3; Stog missing; Dunh 3a4–b1; Fremantle 1971, 178–179; and Matsunaga 1978, 5–6. Our text begins here with the *samādhi vajra* origination from *samaya*. The Zhol mistakenly reads *byang chub kyi sems rdo rje'i* for *byang chub kyi sems rdo rje*, and *byin gyi brlabs* for *byin gyis brlabs* in our text.

1440. The following is a mixture of paraphrasing and citing the first chapter of the *Guhyasamāja Tantra*, Tōh 442; Zhol 3b3–4a3; Stog 5a1–b3 [beginning missing]; Dunh 3b1–4b2; Fremantle 1971, 178–183; and Matsunaga 1978, 6.

much more so will it be to the other bodhisattvas!" Thereupon the tathāgatas surrounding the Teacher were astonished and asked the Blessed One to bless all tathāgatas and teach them. Since such a blessing in response to a request is initiation, their request was: May you confer initiation upon us and teach us the Guhyasamāja. This indicates that it is inappropriate to teach the tantra without conferring initiation upon those who engage in the practice that follows.[1441] How was their request fulfilled? The *Illuminating Lamp* teaches: "In order to initiate them the Blessed One emanated the wisdom maṇḍala."[1442] Thus it is stated that by emanating the wisdom maṇḍala the Blessed One conferred initiation.

[How to Transform Yourself, Visualized as Vajradhara, into Dveṣavajra]

In the "past event"[1443] the Blessed One was absorbed in the samādhi called "vajra lamp of wisdom," and induced Akṣobhya to issue forth and then dissolve back into the Blessed One. This is taught in the *Guhyasamāja Tantra*: "Then, the Blessed One, the Tathāgata, Vajra-body-speech-and-mind-of-all-tathāgatas, being attentive to the request for teaching made by all tathāgatas, was absorbed in the samādhi called 'vajra lamp of wisdom' and induced the quintessential supreme mantra of the tathāgata family of hatred, *vajradhṛk*, to issue forth from his own vajra body, speech, and mind. [25a] Once he was induced to issue forth, the Blessed One, personification of the *vidyā* of the body, speech, and mind of all tathāgatas, in union with the great consort of Akṣobhya, appearing in black, white, and red colors, entered the vajra body, speech, and mind of all tathāgatas."[1444]

Thus Akṣobhya issues forth and dissolves into Vajradhara, who was earlier perceived by all tathāgatas as having three faces. But[1445] how in that interim, before Akṣobhya dissolved into him, could Vajradhara have acquired one face and two arms? Ārya Nāgārjuna and his disciples taught that the way Akṣobhya dissolves into Vajradhara here must accord with the *Guhyasamāja Tantra*,

1441. Tib. *rjes 'jug*, the practice that follows the "past event" in the *Guhyasamāja Tantra*. See the section "The Samādhis in the First Chapter of the *Guhyasamāja Tantra* and Enacting Past Events" in the introduction.

1442. Candrakīrti, *Sgron gsal, Pradīpoddyotanaṭīkā*, Tōh 1785, 17b3; Chakravarti 1984, 23.

1443. Tib. *sngon byung*.

1444. *Guhyasamāja Tantra*, Tōh 442; Zhol 4a2–4; Stog 5b1–5; Dunh 4a5–b4; Fremantle 1971, 182–183; and Matsunaga 1978, 6. Reading *rig pa'i skyes bu* for *rigs pa skyes bu* in our text.

1445. Reading *gyi* for *gyis* in our text.

which teaches that Akṣobhya issues forth through the samādhi of "vajra lamp of wisdom."[1446] Therefore THOSE WHO SAY that Vajradhara has one face and two arms should have known this, but since THEY did not examine even the letters of the tantra, they err. And this is why the explanation of the Paṇḍita Muniśrībhadra[1447] is likewise inappropriate.

[The Consort of the Principal Deity]

Hence, Vajradhara is white and has three faces and six arms. Furthermore, he is accompanied by the mother, for the *Illuminating Lamp* teaches: "*Induced to issue forth* here means that while abiding in absorption the Blessed One brought Akṣobhya forth."[1448] Thus the method for bringing Akṣobhya forth is to abide in absorption with the mother and to draw him out of her womb.[1449] It is appropriate[1450] for the mother to be Vajradhātvīśvarī,[1451] as Muniśrībhadra explains.[1452] When Akṣobhya enters,[1453] the father must transform into Dveṣavajra while the mother transforms into Sparśavajrā.[1454] The *Illuminating Lamp* explains the line of the *Guhyasamāja Tantra* cited above,[1455] [25b] "'similar to the blazing light of the Buddha,' means similar in color to the

1446. See Nāgārjuna's *Mdo bsre, Sādhanasūtramelāpaka*, Tōh 1797, 11b1, and Candrakīrti's *Rdo rje sems dpa'i sgrub thabs, Vajrasattva Sādhana*, Tōh 1814, 196b5–197a1, Luo and Tomabechi 2009, 5.12–6.4 and 38.4–13; both cited above [24a].

1447. See above [24a].

1448. Candrakīrti, *Sgron gsal, Pradīpoddyotanaṭīkā*, Tōh 1785, 18a1–2; Chakravarti 1984, 23.

1449. See also Tsong kha pa, *Sgron gsal mchan*, 72b4; and his *Bung ba'i re skong*, 8b4–5.

1450. Reading *'thad pa* for *'thang pa*.

1451. Tib. Rdo rje dbyings kyi dbang phyug ma, Eng., She Who Rules the Vajra Realm.

1452. *Rim pa lnga'i don mdor bshad pa, Pañcakramārthaṭippaṇi*, Tōh 1813, 152a5; Jiang and Tomabechi 1996, 10. See also Tsong kha pa, *Bung ba'i re skong*, 8b1. Muniśrībhadra explains that the consort is Rdo rje dbyings kyi dbang phyug ma, Vajradhātvīśvarī.

1453. Tsong kha pa, *Gsang mngon*, 23a5–6.

1454. Tib. Reg bya Rdo rje ma, Eng., Vajra Lady of Tangibles.

1455. *Guhyasamāja Tantra*, chap. 3, Tōh 442; Zhol 6b7; Stog 10b5–6; Dunh 9b2; Fremantle 1971, v. 1d ; and Matsunaga 1978, v. 1d. The first line of this verse was cited on [23b] above

lord of the tathāgata family."[1456] Thus, in this case the colors of the father and mother must be identical.[1457]

[Vajradhara and the First Lord]

The fifteenth chapter of the *Guhyasamāja Tantra* teaches: "Equal in light to Vairocana, Vajrasattva, the Great King."[1458] The *Vajrasattva Sādhana* applies this line to the generation of the First Lord;[1459] the *Sādhana Incorporating the Scripture* applies it to the generation of Vajradhara, the principal deity of the protection wheel;[1460] while the *Illuminating Lamp* applies it to the effect of engaging in *caryā*.[1461] However, as the *Revelation of the Intention Tantra* teaches: "Each word has multiple meanings."[1462] Thus, since each vajra word of the tantra teaches many different meanings, you should not think that these works are contradictory.[1463]

Since here Vajradhara and the First Lord are similar in their colors, faces, and arms, the intention of Ārya Nāgārjuna and his disciples was that the line from chapter fifteen is equally applicable to both of them. It is necessary to explain the line *the Buddha, the holder of the three vajras*[1464] to mean that yourself visualized as Vajradhara blesses your body, speech, and mind with the three syllables, the essence of the three vajras.

1456. Candrakīrti, *Sgron gsal, Pradīpoddyotanaṭīkā*, chap. 3, Tōh 1785, 27a1; Chakravarti 1984, 35.

1457. When white Vajradhara transforms into blue Dveṣavajra, white Vajradhātvīśvarī transforms into blue Sparśavajrā.

1458. *Guhyasamāja Tantra*, Tōh 442; Zhol 31b4–5; Stog 53a2–3; Dunh 57b1; Fremantle 1971, v. 35bc; and Matsunaga 1978, v. 35bc. These lines were cited on [23b] above. Now this line is cited from the translation of Candrakīrti, *Rdo rje sems dpa'i sgrub thabs, Vajrasattva Sādhana*, Tōh 1814, and here the sequence of these lines is different.

1459. Candrakīrti, *Rdo rje sems dpa'i sgrub thabs, Vajrasattva Sādhana*, Tōh 1814, 199a7–b1; Luo and Tomabechi 2009, 15.14–16.3 and 48.7–12.

1460. Nāgārjuna, *Mdo bsre, Sādhanasūtramelāpaka*, Tōh 1797, 11a7–b1.

1461. Tib. *spyod pa*, Eng. "practice." Candrakīrti, *Sgron gsal, Pradīpoddyotanaṭīkā*, Tōh 1785, chap. 15, 141b5; Chakravarti 1984, 167.

1462. *Dgongs pa lung bstan [ston] pa'i rgyud, Sandhivyākaraṇa Tantra*, Tōh 444, 187a5.

1463. Here Mkhas grub rje follows Tsong kha pa, *Mtha' gcod*, 133a1–3.

1464. The following line in the verse from chapter fifteen of the *Guhyasamāja Tantra*, just cited. Tōh 442; Zhol 31b4–5; Stog 53a2–3; Dunh 57b1; Fremantle 1971, v. 35d; and Matsunaga 1978, v. 35d. As was noted above, the Zhol has *sangs rgyas sku gsum rdo rje 'dzin* for *sangs rgyas rdo rje gsum 'dzin 'gyur* in our text; Fremantle has here *buddhas trikāyavajradhṛk*; and Matsunaga has *sambuddhakāyavajradhṛk*.

[The Principal Deity as Triple Sattvas]

Visualizing yourself as Vajradhara you must also be endowed with the triple sattvas, for the *Later Tantra* teaches: "Meditate on the vajra holder,[1465] the personification[1466] of the *vidyā*,[1467] endowed with the four resources. Meditate on him as trifold, through the divisions into body, speech, and mind."[1468] The *Later Tantra* continues, as cited above:[1469] "A wheel yellow all around," and so forth.[1470] Nāropa explained *the vajra holder, the personification of the vidyā* as Vajradhara, meditated upon at the center of the protection wheel. And he is *endowed with the four resources* means endowed with the three vajras of body, speech, and mind, as well as with the jñānasattva, in total, four.[1471]

The fourteenth chapter of the *Guhyasamāja Tantra* teaches: [26a] "Being meditatively absorbed in lustrous Vajrasattva emanating sparkling and radiant light, visualize an image at the end[1472] of the triple vajra body, and

1465. Tib. *rdo rje can*, Skt. *vajrin*.

1466. Tib. *skyes bu*, Skt. *puruṣa*.

1467. Tib. *rig pa*.

1468. *Rgyud phyi ma*, *Uttara Tantra*, Tōh 443, 151b6–7; Matsunaga 1978, v. 80. See also Tsong kha pa, *Sgron gsal mchan*, 370a2–3, and his *Bung ba'i re skong*, 8b1–2.

1469. See above [22b1].

1470. *Rgyud phyi ma*, *Uttara Tantra*, Tōh 443, 151b7–152a1; Matsunaga 1978, vv. 81–82.

1471. *Yaśobhadra/Nāropa, Snyan grags bzang po, *Gsang ba thams cad kyi sgron ma'i rgya cher 'grel pa*, *Sarvaguhyapradīpaṭīkā*, Tōh 1787, 219b2–3. See also Tsong kha pa, *Sgron gsal mchan*, 370a4–5 and his *Bskyed rim zin bris*, 11b4.

1472. Tib. has *mthar* for the Skt. *paryantaṃ*. The difference in meaning between *paryantaṃ* and *mthar* results in various Tibetan interpretations, as can be seen below. Candrakīrti glosses this with *bdag nyid can* (*ātmaka*), which could be translated as "consists of" or "composed of" or "contains," hence it takes the phrase *rdo rje sku ni gsum gyi mthar gzugs brnyan*, *trivajrakāyaparyantaṃ bimbaṃ*, to mean an image that consists of or embodies the three Vajra Bodies. See his *Sgron gsal*, *Pradīpoddyotanaṭīkā*, Tōh 1785, 133a6; Chakravarti 1984, 158. Whereas most Tibetan authors indeed took the term triple vajra body as a *bahuvrīhi*, they also understood *mthar* in its literal meaning "end," Tsong kha pa prefers the translation of Pa tshab, which has: *rdo rje gsum sku'i mthar thug pa* for *rdo rje sku ni gsum gyi mthar*. Tsong kha pa glosses *mthar thug pa* with "abiding at the lower end," meaning Sumbharāja, the fierce deity abiding below the maṇḍala. See his *Sgron gsal mchan*, 370b1.

engage in the practice."[1473] The two first lines here teach the visualization of Dveṣavajra, and the two last lines, *at the end of the triple vajra body* and so forth, mean that *at the end*, that is to say, below the body of Vajradhara triple *sattvas*, *you should visualize the image* of Sumbha,[1474] who *engages in the practice* of summoning the obstructing forces and so forth.[1475]

Therefore,[1476] at the center of the protection wheel, visualize yourself as white Vajradhara possessing three faces and six arms and embracing the white mother, Vajradhātvīśvarī, who is also endowed with three faces and six arms. The three places of the father are blessed with triple vajra, meaning that he assumes triple sattvas.

[The Surrounding Deities]

Then[1477] with the light of the samādhisattva at your heart, invite Akṣobhya surrounded by the ten fierce deities from their natural abode. They enter through the crown of the head or the mouth of the father, pass through his vajra path, and emerge at the lotus of the mother as eleven melted drops, and then become eleven long *hūṃs*, which transform into Akṣobhya and the ten fierce deities. Thus visualized,[1478] Akṣobhya is drawn to your heart and issues forth again with *vajradhṛk*, emanating in the ten directions to perform general and specific deeds. Gathering back, Akṣobhya then mingles with the jñānasattva, and enters you. Thereupon your former lunar seat transforms into the solar seat where

1473. *Guhyasamāja Tantra*, Tōh 442; Zhol 29b6–7; Stog 49b4–5; Dunh 54b2; Fremantle 1971, v. 61; and Matsunaga 1978, v. 61. Zhol has *ri gsum rnam thar* for *ni gsum gyi mthar*; Zhol and Stog have *bsams nas* for *bsams la*; and Dunh has *bzang po'i* for *bzang ba'i*; *gsum gyi sku'i mthar* for *sku ni gsum gyi mthar*; and *gzer bar* for *gzungs brnyan* in our text. In commenting on this verse, Candrakīrti has *ni gsum gyi mthar* as well. See his *Sgron gsal*, *Pradīpoddyotanaṭīkā*, Tōh 1785, 133a7. According to Tsong kha pa, *Sgron gsal mchan*, 370b1, Patsab has: *rdo rje gsum sku'i mthar thug pa* for *rdo rje sku ni gsum gyi mthar*. Tibetan edition and an English translation of the Dunhuang version in Cantwell and Mayer 2008, 175.

1474. Tib. Gnod mdzes.

1475. See Tsong kha pa, *Sgron gsal mchan*, 370b1–2. Candrakīrti glosses *gzugs brnyan*, *bimbaṃ*, with *gnod mdzes kyi gzugs*, *sumbharūpaṃ*. See his *Sgron gsal*, Tōh 1785, 133a6–b1; Chakravarti 1984, 158. Tsong kha pa explains that this is the form of Sumbharāja, the fierce deity abiding below the maṇḍala, who emanates a second Sumbharāja abiding in front of you. The Dunhuang ms. IOL Tib J 438 has *gzer bar for gzugs brnyan* (*bimbaṃ*) in our text. See Cantwell and Mayer 2008, 175.

1476. This follows Tsong kha pa, *Gsang mngon*, 21b5–22b3.

1477. See Tsong kha pa, *Gsang mngon*, 22b3–23b5.

1478. Reading *bskyed pa* for *bskyod pa* in our text.

you become Dveṣavajra, triple sattvas, and your consort turns into Sparśavajrā. Then, visualize each fierce deity issuing forth through his respective mantra for issuing[1479] and rest on the lotus and solar seat within the wheel, not quite touching the ten spokes: the eight spokes and the upper and lower spokes.[1480] [26b]

SOME[1481] say that you need to visualize ten *hūṃ*s on the seats of the ten spokes and then the ten fierce deities emerging from them. THEY say that it is inappropriate to draw the ten fierce deities out of the mother's womb, since the works of Ārya Nāgārjuna and his disciples do not explain it should be done in such a way. However, this is not the case, for the *Concise Sādhana* teaches: "The mantrin should emanate the ten fierce deities."[1482] The term *emanate* here means that the fierce deities who were generated in the womb of the mother, and then drawn into your heart, now issue forth, but it does not mean that they are simply generated through the transformation of the *hūṃ*s.

For this reason, the *Sādhana Incorporating the Scripture* explains: "The thirteenth chapter of the *Guhyasamāja Tantra* teaches: 'The fierce deities born from the abode of hatred, who are always intent on killing, will attain by means of killing for yogis endowed with supreme qualities.'[1483] Therefore the ten fierce kings arise from long syllables *hūṃ*s.'"[1484] The *Illuminating Lamp* explains the line *emanating sparkling and radiant light*, and so forth, cited above by saying: "When through the method taught in the sādhana, the yogis endowed with the yoga of Bodhicittavajra send Akṣobhya forth and make him

1479. Tsong kha pa, *Gsang mngon*, 24a5–26b2. Black Yamāntaka emerges with the mantra *yamāntakṛt*, White Prajñāntaka with *prajñāntakṛt*, Red Hayagrīva or Padmāntaka with *padmāntakṛt*, Black Vighnānataka with *vighnānatakṛt*, Black Acala with *acala*, Blue Ṭakkirāja with *ṭakkirāja*, Blue Nīladaṇḍa with *nīladaṇḍa*, Blue Mahābala with *mahābala*, Blue Uṣṇīṣacakravartin with *uṣṇīṣacakravartin*, and Blue Sumbharāja with *sumbharājā*.

1480. See Tsong kha pa, *Bskyed rim zin bris*, 12a5–6.

1481. See Red mda' ba, *Bsgrub pa dpal bas zhus lan*, Kathmandu, 49b3–4; TBRC, 304b–305a. According to Bu ston this system is followed by *Kṛṣṇasamayavajra, Nag po dam tshig rdo rje, and "Tibetan lamas" (*bod kyi bla ma dag*). See *Kṛṣṇasamayavajra, *Rim pa lnga'i dka' 'grel, Pañcakramapañjikā*, Tōh 1841, 158b2. Bu ston, however, rejects this system. See his *Mdor byas 'grel chen*, 10a5–6.

1482. Nāgārjuna, *Mdor byas, Piṇḍīkrama Sādhana*, Tōh 1796, 2a3; L 8a; T 8a.

1483. *Guhyasamāja Tantra*, Tōh 442; Zhol 20b5; Stog 35a4–5; Dunh 38b1; Fremantle 1971, v. 29; and Matsunaga 1978, v. 27. D and Zhol have *sgrub pa* for *grub pa* in our text. See Cantwell and Mayer 2008, 170. Note that our text refers to the interpretable level of interpretation, while Cantwell and Mayer refer to the definitive level of interpretation, and that in Candrakīrti's *Sgron gsal, Pradīpoddyotanaṭīkā*, Tōh 1785, follows the interpretable meaning.

1484. Nāgārjuna, *Mdo bsre, Sādhanasūtramelāpaka*, Tōh 1797, 11b2. D has *sgrub pa* for *grub pa* in our text.

enter themselves, they should visualize [themselves as Vajradhara] who *emanates sparkling and radiant light* [now] as [Dveṣavajra] who somewhat bares his fangs at the center of a luminous red maṇḍala; then they emanate the ten fierce deities and set them in the various directions."[1485]

Thus, because both Nāgārjuna and Candrakīrti explicitly taught that you should draw out the fierce deities and place them on the spokes, THOSE who maintain that Nāgārjuna and Candrakīrti did not explain this have not examined the scriptures. Hence, it is appropriate to draw the fierce deities out of the mother's womb, as explained in the commentaries of Abhayākaragupta,[1486] the *Intense Illuminating Lamp*,[1487] the *Jewel Rosary*,[1488] and the *Vajrasattva Sādhana*.[1489]

With regard to the line in the *Guhyasamāja Tantra* cited above, "The fierce deities born from the abode of hatred,"[1490] [27a] the commentary explains that they emerge out of the *hūṃs*.[1491] And again, as the *Concise Sādhana* teaches: "The fierce deities arise from *hūṃs* that rest upon solar disks. They are terrifying with their dazzling lights radiating and their left legs stretched forth."[1492] The *Sādhana Incorporating the Scripture* and the *Vajrasattva Sādhana* likewise explain that they are generated from *hūṃs*.[1493] But since neither Ārya Nāgārjuna and his disciples nor the *Root* and *Explanatory* tantras explain

1485. The line from the *Guhyasamāja Tantra*, chap. 14, Tōh 442; Zhol 29b6–7; Stog 49b4–5; Dunh 54b2; Fremantle 1971, v. 61; and Matsunaga 1978, v. 61, cited above [26a]. This line is explained in Candrakīrti's *Sgron gsal, Pradīpoddyotanaṭīkā*, Tōh 1785, 1335a–b1; Chakravarti 1984, 158. D has *byung ba'i* for *'byung ba'i*; *dbyung zhing* for *dbyung cing*; *chud par* for *tshud par*; *bsgoms la* for *bsgom la*; and *gzhag nas* for *bzhag nas* in our text. Reading *cung zad* for *cung thad* in our text. See also Tsong kha pa, *Sgron gsal mchan*, 369b3–370a2, and his *Bung ba'i re skong*, 8b2.

1486. Abhayākaragupta, *Rim pa lnga pa'i dgongs 'grel zla ba'i 'od zer, Pañcakramamatiṭīkā Candraprabhā*, Tōh 1831, 183b1.

1487. Bhavyakīrti, *Rab tu sgron gsal, Prakāśikā*, Tōh 1793, 84b1.

1488. Ratnākaraśānti, *Rin chen phreng ba, Ratnāvalī*, a commentary on the *Mdor byas*, Tōh 1826, 21a5–7.

1489. The three previous scriptures are already mentioned by Bu ston, *Mdor byas 'grel chen*, 10a6.

1490. *Guhyasamāja Tantra*, chap. 13, Tōh 442; Zhol 20b5; Stog 35a4–5; Dunh 38b1; Fremantle 1971, v. 29; and Matsunaga 1978, v. 27.

1491. Nāgārjuna, *Mdo bsre, Sādhanasūtramelāpaka*, Tōh 1797, 11b2, cited above.

1492. Nāgārjuna, *Mdor byas, Piṇḍīkrama Sādhana*, Tōh 1796, 2a2–3, L 8; T 8.

1493. Nāgārjuna, *Mdo bsre, Sādhanasūtramelāpaka*, Tōh 1797, 11b2. Candrakīrti, *Rdo rje sems dpa'i sgrub thabs, Vajrasattva Sādhana*, Tōh 1814, 197a1; Luo and Tomabechi 2009, 6.5 and 38.14.

through which emblem they are generated, SOME LAMAS[1494] say that there is no reason whatsoever to generate the fierce deities through meditation on "the three rituals."[1495]

After the fierce deities issue forth, you should set them in their places so they will fulfill their task of overcoming the malevolent influences in the ten directions, Indra and so forth. You should set them on their seats as soon as they issue forth, since can they perform their tasks only when in place. To command the fierce deities, you must transform into Dveṣavajra[1496] with the entry of Akṣobhya, since Akṣobhya belongs to the tathāgata family of hatred.

The fierce deity at the zenith faces west and is situated above the principal deity but slightly aslant to the east from the vertical line that goes up through the principal deity. The fierce deity in the nadir faces east and is situated behind the principal deity but slightly aslant to the west from the vertical line that goes down through the principal deity. The distance between the principal deity and the fierce deities in the east and west is slightly longer than the distance between the principal deity and the fierce deities in the zenith and nadir. Therefore, when the fierce deities at the zenith and nadir or their signs are drawn in painted or colored powder maṇḍalas, their locations are respectively east of the fierce deity in the east and west of the fierce deity in the west.

[Driving the Stakes]

Then the stakes are driven into the obstructers, [27b] as the *Concise Sādhana* teaches: "In order to destroy all obstructions, the mantrin should command Sumbharāja, and drive in the stakes.[1497] *Oṃ Sumbha Nisumbha hūṃ gṛhṇa gṛhṇa hūṃ gṛhṇāpaya gṛhṇāpaya hūṃ ānaya ho bhagavan vidyā-rājā hūṃ phaṭ.*[1498] By means of the deity endowed with a fierce form, the wise one

1494. This position supports the system of Tsong kha pa's *Gsang mngon*, which does not teach that the *hūṃ*s turn into the emblems of each of the fierce deities, and these turn into the fierce deities, as Bu ston has it. See his *Mdor byas 'grel chen*, 10a6–7. In Tsong kha pa, *Gsang mngon*, 23a1, the *hūṃ*s transform immediately into the fierce deities.

1495. Tib. *cho ga gsum*.

1496. See Tsong kha pa, *Bung ba'i re skong*, 8b2–3.

1497. Note that in Tsong kha pa's *Gsang mngon* it is not the yogi as Dveṣavajra who drives the stakes but rather Sumbharāja who does so. Hence this line is understood as "order Sumbharāja to drive the stakes."

1498. See also Tsong kha pa, *Gsang mngon*, 27a5–6, and the *Guhyasamāja Tantra*, chap. 14, Tōh 442; following v. 25 in Fremantle 1971 and Matsunaga 1978; Zhol 28a6–7; Stog 48a3–4; Dunh 52b3–4; as well as the commentary in Candrakīrti's *Sgron gsal, Pradīpoddyotanaṭīkā*, Tōh 1785, 128a4–6; Chakravarti 1984, 153.

should summon the chief of the obstructers and then, following the ritual method, drive the stakes."[1499] Accordingly, after commanding Sumbharāja, you should summon the obstructions. The *Vajrasattva Sādhana* teaches how this is done: "Then visualize a second emanation of Sumbharāja arriving from the Sumbharāja that abides below. He sits before you in the form of Sumbharāja,[1500] and receives the command—the 'mantra of four *hūṃ*s,'[1501] taught in the fourteenth chapter of the *Guhyasamāja Tantra*."[1502] Hence look at Sumbharāja at the nadir, whereupon he will emanate a second Sumbharāja who will then arrive before you and ask for your order. You will then command him with the mantra of four *hūṃ*s: "Quickly catch and fetch the obstructers."[1503]

As for the meaning of the mantra *oṃ Sumbha Nisumbha* and so forth, the three letters *a*, *u*, and *m* of the *oṃ* signify the three vajras beginning with the vajra body. By combining the first two letters, *o* is formed, and by ornamenting it with the letter *m*, it turns into the single syllable *oṃ*. This signifies the indivisible nature of the three vajras. When you recite this syllable, while understanding the meaning it signifies, you gain merit, and therefore it is called "the jewel holding mantra." As the *Vajra Peak* teaches: "What is *oṃ*? It is described as the bestower of all excellence, riches, glory, prosperity, good fortune, [28a] affirmation, and auspiciousness, and hence it is called 'the jewel-holding mantra.'"[1504] This should be known also in every instance in which the mantra appears below.

Regarding the rest of the mantra,[1505] *Sumbha* is the great subduer, *Nisumbha* is the great subduer of all; with these two names call Sumbharāja. *Hūṃ* urges him; *gṛhṇa gṛhṇa* is catch, catch! that is, Catch the fleeing harmful ones!;

1499. Nāgārjuna, *Mdor byas, Piṇḍīkrama Sādhana*, Tōh 1796, 2a3–5; L 9cd–10; T 9cd–10. D has *dbang po* for *bdag po* and *blo dang ldan pas* for *blo dang ldan pa'i* in our text. For editions of verses 10–13 of the *Mdor byas*, on the basis of the Tibetan versions in D and P as well as on Ratnākaraśānti's commentary *Mdor bsdus pa'i sgrub thabs kyi 'grel ba rin chen phreng ba*, see, Mayer 2004, 157–159. See also Bu ston, *Mdor byas 'grel chen*, 12a1.

1500. This is redundant, the Sanskrit here is different, "like a servant."

1501. This is the mantra *oṃ Sumbha Nisumbha* and so forth.

1502. Candrakīrti, *Rdo rje sems dpa'i sgrub thabs, Vajrasattva Sādhana*, Tōh 1814, 197a3–4; Luo and Tomabechi 2009, 6.12–13 and 39.6–8.

1503. See Tsong kha pa, *Gsang mngon*, 27a3–5.

1504. *Rdo rje rtse mo, Vajraśekhara Tantra*, Tōh 480, 156a2–3.

1505. See Candrakīrti's *Sgron gsal, Pradīpoddyotanaṭīkā*, chap. 14, Tōh 1785, 128a4–6; Chakravarti 1984, 153. See also Tsong kha pa's *Sgron gsal mchan*, 358a1–5, and his *Bung ba'i re skong*, 8b5–9a2.

gṛhṇāpaya gṛhṇāpaya is: Exhort him to catch, exhort him to catch! Exhort your retinue to catch them!; *hūṃ* urges; *ānaya ho bhagavan*: Fetch, O Blessed One! The *Illuminating Lamp* explains this: Bound by the vajra lasso, their hearts pierced by the vajra hook, they are then fetched. Calling him *vidyārāja*, king of knowledge motivates Sumbharāja, *hūṃ phaṭ*, urges him to kill.[1506]

As for the implements of Sumbharāja,[1507] the *Intense Illuminating Lamp* explains that the first two arms hold a vajra and a bell, the middle arms hold a lasso and a hook, and the lower two arms hold a sword and a vajra hammer.[1508] SOME LAMAS[1509] maintain that he has one face and two arms, the right one holding a vajra hammer and the left a noose with a hook; and SOME LAMAS maintain that he has two arms holding a hook and a noose. Still, none of these positions seem reliable or appropriate.

The *Guhyasamāja Tantra* teaches: "Trodden under the feet of Vajrasattva, the lord of all tathāgatas, bound by vajra hook and vajra lasso is the best way to fetch the maiden."[1510] As explained,[1511] the vajra—the emblem of Sumbharāja—turns into a vajra hook, and fetches that which is to be acquired. Accordingly, visualize that[1512] while the other emblems Sumbharāja holds in his six arms remain as they are, the vajra in his first right hand turns into a vajra hook. [28b] With this hook he pierces[1513] the heart of the main obstructers, the ten guardians of the directions, and with his lasso he binds them around their necks, fetches them, and hands them over to the ten fierce deities.

Then, SOME LAMAS say,[1514] you should visualize the ten fierce deities treading over the obstructers and SOME say you should visualize the obstructers

1506. Candrakīrti, *Sgron gsal, Pradīpoddyotanaṭīkā*, Tōh 1785, 128a5–6; Chakravarti 1984, 153. D has *bcings la* for *chings*, *khug*[?] for *phug*, and *khug shig* for *khug cig* in our text.

1507. This passage follows Bu ston, *Mdor byas 'grel chen*, 11a7–b2.

1508. Bhavyakīrti, *Rab tu sgron gsal, Prakāśikā*, Tōh 1793, 84a7.

1509. See Rang byung rdo rje, *Gsang ba 'dus pa'i sgrub pa'i thabs phyi nang gzhan gsum gsal ba*, 3b3–4.

1510. *Guhyasamāja Tantra*, chap. 14, Tōh 442; Zhol 28a7–b1; Stog 48a5; Dunh 52b4–5; Fremantle 1971, v. 27; and Matsunaga 1978, v. 27. See also Tsong kha pa, *Bung ba' re skong*, 9a2.

1511. This refers to the explanation of this verse in Candrakīrti's *Sgron gsal, Pradīpoddyotana-ṭīkā*, Tōh 1785, 128a6–7; Chakravarti 1984, 153.

1512. See Tsong kha pa, *Gsang mngon*, 27a6–b2, and also Bu ston, *Mdor byas 'grel chen*, 11b2–3.

1513. Our text has *phug* for *bzung* in Tsong kha pa's *Gsang mngon*.

1514. See Rang byung rdo rje, *Gsang ba 'dus pa'i sgrub pa'i thabs phyi nang gzhan gsum gsal ba*, 3b5.

in front of the ten fierce deities, but you should meditate as explained by *Kṛṣṇasamayavajra:[1515] Beyond the ten fierce deities, visualize ten long *hūṃ*s and then emerging from them are ten triangular pits that encase the obstructers. Visualize eight obstructers in the cardinal and intermediate directions and the obstructer at the zenith east of the one in the east and the obstructer at the nadir west of the one in the west.

Then, the *Concise Sādhana* goes on to teach how to drive the stakes: "The mantrin should meditate on the Great King, Vajra Deathless[1516] as Vajra Stake,[1517] the color of the petals of a blue *utpala* lotus, emitting light abounding with garlands of flames. The lower part of his body, from the navel down, is shaped like a spike, and the upper part is in the form of a fierce deity with three faces and six arms. When he looks down at the host of obstructers while reciting the mantra and driving the vajra stake into the host of obstructers, they become immobilized."[1518]

SOME LAMAS maintain that this passage means that you meditate on the ten guardians of the directions, each with a *hūṃ* on his head, and these *hūṃ*s transform into vajra stakes. However, the *Vajrasattva Sādhana* teaches: "Then visualize a second Amṛtakuṇḍalin[1519] emanating at the northern gate. Standing there he transforms into ten stake-forms that take their position on the heads of the ten chief obstructers."[1520] Then the *Vajrasattva Sādhana* cites a verse from the thirteenth chapter of the *Guhyasamāja Tantra*:[1521] "Meditate on the mightily fierce Vajra Deathless as Vajra Stake. Drive this stake[1522] that

1515. See his *Rim pa lnga'i dka' 'grel, Pañcakramapañjikā*, Tōh 1841, 158b1–7. See also Tsong kha pa, *Bung ba'i re skong*, 9a2–3, the *Slob tshul*, 7b5–6, and *Bskyed rim zin bris*, 13b1.

1516. Tib. Rdo rje bdud rtsi, Skt. Vajrāmṛta.

1517. Tib. Rdo rje phur bu, Skt. Vajrakīla.

1518. Nāgārjuna, *Mdor byas, Piṇḍīkrama Sādhana*, Tōh 1796, 2a5–b2; L 11–13; T 11–13. D has *utpala sngon po* for *utpala sngon po'i*; *'bar phreng* for *'bar 'phreng*; *'od ldan pa* for *'od ldan pas*; *rdo rje phur bu des* for *rdo rje phur bus nges*; and *bgegs kyi lus* for *bgegs kyi tshogs* in our text. T. has *nikhanet* instead of *nikhaned*. For parallel lines from Dunhuang, see Mayer 2004, 157–159.

1519. Tib. Bdud rtsi 'khyil ba.

1520. Candrakīrti, *Rdo rje sems dpa'i sgrub thabs, Vajrasattva Sādhana*, Tōh 1814, 197a5–6, Luo and Tomabechi 2009, 7.6–8 and 39.13–16. D and Luo and Tomabechi have *phur pa'i rnam pa bcu* for *phur bu'i rnam pa bcur* in our text.

1521. *Guhyasamāja Tantra*, chap. 13, Tōh 442, Zhol 22b2; Stog 38a4–5; Dunh 41b4–5; Fremantle 1971, v. 75; Matsunaga 1978, v. 79. Both the Sanskrit and Tibetan in the *Rdo rje sems dpa'i sgrub thabs* are somewhat different from that found in the *Guhyasamāja Tantra* itself.

1522. This phrase is found only in the Sanskrit.

emanates sparkling and radiant light into the heads of the obstructers in the ten directions."[1523]

Hence, [29a] visualize Amṛtakuṇḍalin who abides in the north emanating a second Amṛtakuṇḍalin, who transforms into stakes, each of which has the form of a fierce Amṛtakuṇḍalin in its upper part, and a single-pointed spear below the navel, for in this regard, the *Guhyasamāja Tantra* teaches: "Drive these blazing spark-like stakes into the circle of obstructers in the ten directions."[1524] Accordingly, you should visualize[1525] Amṛtakuṇḍalin transforming into ten blazing-spark-like stakes that pierce the heads of the directional guardians and their attendants.

EARLY LAMAS[1526] maintain that you yourself should then recite the mantra *oṃ gha gha* and so forth commanding Sumbharāja, but this is not the case because in interpreting the meaning of this mantra, the *Illuminating Lamp* explains that the yogis call upon Vajra Stake by uttering "*vajrakīla*" and so forth,[1527] but it does not say that they invoke Sumbharāja. If they were commanding Sumbharāja it would be appropriate to call upon Sumbharāja. Therefore, as the *Vajrasattva Sādhana* teaches: "Then, visualize Sumbharāja arising, and pounding his vajra hammer as he recites the mantra,"[1528] visualize Sumbharāja reciting the mantra and pounding the stakes. Thus Sumbharāja commands the stakes by means of the mantra [*oṃ gha gha* and so forth].[1529]

Does this not contradict the following line of the *Sādhana Incorporating the Scripture*: "With the mantra *oṃ gha gha* and so forth command Sumbharāja

1523. Candrakīrti, *Rdo rje sems dpa'i sgrub thabs, Vajrasattva Sādhana*, Tōh 1814, 197a7–b1; Luo and Tomabechi 2009, 8.1–4 and 40.3–8. This verse is cited also in Nāgārjuna's *Mdo bsre, Sādhanasūtramelāpaka*, Tōh 1797, 11b3–4.

1524. Whereas above Mkhas grub rje cited this verse as it appears in the *Vajrasattva Sādhana*, here he cites the *Guhyasamāja Tantra* itself: chap. 13, Tōh 442; Zhol 22b2; Stog 38a4–5; Dunh 41b4–5; Fremantle 1971, v. 75cd; and Matsunaga 1978, v. 79cd. The Sanskrit is somewhat different. See Candrakīrti's *Sgron gsal, Pradīpoddyotanaṭīkā*, Tōh 1785, 111a6–b1; Chakravarti 1984, 135. For the edition and translation of the Dunhuang version, see Cantwell and Mayer 2008, 173.

1525. See Tsong kha pa, *Gsang mngon*, 27b5–6.

1526. Ngor chen explains that you should address Sumbharāja with this mantra. See his *Gsang 'dus dkyil 'khor gyi sgrub thabs dngos grub rgya mtsho*, work 106, 4a2.

1527. Candrakīrti, *Sgron gsal, Pradīpoddyotanaṭīkā*, Tōh 1785, 132b6–133a1; Chakravarti 1984, 158. Here Mkhas grub rje follows the glossing of Tsong kha pa, *Sgron gsal mchan*, 369a2.

1528. Candrakīrti, *Rdo rje sems dpa'i sgrub thabs, Vajrasattva Sādhana*, Tōh 1814 197a6; Luo and Tomabechi 2009, 7.8–9 and 39.17–18.

1529. This follows Tsong kha pa, *Rnal 'byor dag rim*, 8a1–5, and *Slob tshul*, 8a6–b3.

and drive the stake"?[1530] The meaning of this line is that when you command Sumbharāja in your mind, "exhort the stake," Sumbharāja arises, and with *oṃ gha gha* and so forth drives the stakes. Furthermore, the *Sādhana Incorporating the Scripture* explains that the mantra of the stakes of fierce Amṛtakuṇḍalin[1531] is the mantra for exhorting the stakes—whose nature is Amṛtakuṇḍalin.[1532]

The mantra is *oṃ gha gha ghātaya ghātaya sarva duṣṭāṃ phaṭ phaṭ kīlaya kīlaya sarva pāpāṃ phaṭ phaṭ hūṃ hūṃ hūṃ vajra kīla*[1533] *vajradhara ājñāpayati sarva vighnānāṃ kāya vāk citta [vajra] kīlaya hūṃ hūṃ hūṃ phaṭ phaṭ.*[1534] Regarding its meaning:[1535] *oṃ* has been already explained; [29b] *gha gha* is *ghātaka*[1536] calling out "Killer!"; *ghātaya ghātaya sarvaduṣṭāṃ* means calling out "vanquish all the malevolent ones!"; *phaṭ phaṭ* is the seed syllable that urges him; *kīlaya kīlaya* means drive the stakes, and make them immobile; *sarvapāpāṃ* are all those who have evil intentions; this term has two usages, "evil" and "those who have evil intentions," and the meaning here is the latter; *phaṭ* means splitting; *hūṃ hūṃ hūṃ* invoke the suchness of the body, speech, and mind respectively; *vajrakīla*[1537] is the invocation of Vajra Stake; *vajradhara ājñāpayati*[1538] means obey the command of Vajradhara—here the yogi having assumed the divine identity of Vajradhara makes the invocation; *kāya vāk citta vajra[ṃ]* is the vajra body, speech, and mind of the obstructers; *hūṃ hūṃ phaṭ phaṭ* is the exhortation once again.

Given that in the *Guhyasamāja Tantra* and the *Illuminating Lamp* mantras occur in all sorts of patterns, what would be the appropriate name for this

1530. Nāgārjuna, *Mdo bsre, Sādhanasūtramelāpaka*, Tōh 1797, 11b4–5. D has *zhes bya ba* for *ces bya ba* and *bka' bsgo* for *bsgo*.

1531. Tib. here Bdud rtsi thabs sbyor. See the Mvy. 4330.

1532. Nāgārjuna, *Mdo bsre, Sādhanasūtramelāpaka*, Tōh 1797, 11b4. D has *thab* for *thabs* and *phur bu rnams kyis oṃ gha gha zhes bya ba la sogs pa'i sngags kyis* for *phur bu rnams kyi* in our text. See Tsong kha pa, *Rnal 'byor dag rim*, 8a5–6, and *Slob tshul*, 8b2–3.

1533. Reading *vajrakīla* for *vajrakīlaya*.

1534. This mantra is found in the *Guhyasamāja Tantra*, chap. 14, following v. 58. See also Nāgārjuna, *Mdor byas, Piṇḍikrama Sādhana*, following v. 13, Tōh 1796, 2b2; and Candrakīrti, *Rdo rje sems dpa'i sgrub thabs, Vajrasattva Sādhana*, Tōh 1814, 197a6–7; Luo and Tomabechi 2009, 7.9–11 and 39.18–40.3.

1535. This follows Candrakīrti's *Sgron gsal, Pradīpoddyotanaṭīkā*, Tōh 1785, 132b6–133a2; Chakravarti 1984, 158; and Tsong kha pa's *Sgron gsal mchan*, 368b5–369a3. See also Tsong kha pa, *Bung ba'i re skong*, 9a3–6; *Slob tshul*, 7b6–8a4; and *Bskyed rim zin bris*, 13b4–6, with some small differences.

1536. Reading *ghātaka* for *ghataka* as in Chakravarti 1984, 158.

1537. Reading *vajrakīla* for *vajrakīlaya*.

1538. Reading *ājñāpayati* for *ajñāpayati*.

mantra?[1539] The *Illuminating Lamp*[1540] explains that all the mantras recited are included within four classes as taught in the *Vajra Crown*[1541] and the *Explanatory Tantra Vajra Garland*.[1542] A mantra that has *oṃ* at the beginning and no *svāhā* at the end is called "tail-less"; a mantra of the opposite kind is called "headless"; when a mantra has both *oṃ* at the beginning and *svāhā* at the end, it is called "snake"; and a mantra with neither of these is called "abbreviated." In the present case the mantra is called "tail-less."[1543] You should be aware of this in other contexts as well.

Then as the *Concise Sādhana* teaches: "Visualize a vajra fire spreading all around,[1544] setting fire to the malicious ones who flee hither and thither."[1545] [30a] Visualize:[1546] "Once again vajra fire ablaze with lights emanates from the fierce deities and their stakes. Spreading in the ten directions, it burns the malicious ones who accompany the obstructers, and they flee hither and thither." A single Sumbharāja recites the mantra ten times and pounds each of the stakes, not a Sumbharāja multiplied by ten. At this point the second Sumbharāja is gathered into the Sumbharāja below.[1547]

1539. This follows Tsong kha pa, *Slob tshul*, 7a5–b1; and *Bskyed rim zin bris*, 13a4–5. See also Bu ston, *Mdor byas 'grel chen*, 12a6.

1540. The names of these different mantras are found in Candrakīrti, *Sgron gsal, Pradīpoddyotanaṭikā*, chap. 14, Tōh 1785, *sprul, sarpa*, 118a; *btus pa, uddhāra*, 126b; *mgo med, kabandha*, 127a; *mtha' med, niranta*, 128a; Chakravarti 1984, 143, 151, 151, 153.

1541. Tib. *Rdo rje gtsug tor, Vajroṣṇīṣa Tantra*, cited in Candrakīrti, *Sgron gsal, Caryāmelāpakapradīpa*, chap. 14, Tōh 1785, 118a4 and 124a5; Chakravarti 1984, 151. For brief citations from this tantra, see Banarsi Lal 2001, vol. 2, 65–67. See also Bu ston, *Mdor byas 'grel chen*, 11a2.

1542. *Rgyud rdo rje phreng ba, Vajramālā Tantra*, chap. 23, Tōh 445, 236a6–b1.

1543. See Candrakīrti, *Sgron gsal, Pradīpoddyotanaṭikā*, chap. 14, Tōh 1785, 132b6; Chakravarti 1984, 158.

1544. As was just noted, while our text has *bsdigs bcas pas* here, this is not found in the Bstan 'gyur text. Furthermore, the Sanskrit here is *samantāt*. Tsong kha pa (*Slob tshul*, 9b1–4) explains that the translation by Rin chen bzang po has *rdo rje me ni sngags bcas bas*, but in later translations the word *sngags* does not appear, nor does it appear in the commentary. So the reading *bsdigs* may have developed from *sngags*. At this point, according to the reading of the Bstan 'gyur text, the yogis visualize vajra fire spreading all around.

1545. Nāgārjuna, *Mdor byas, Piṇḍīkrama Sādhana*, Tōh 1796, 2b3; L 15; T 14. D has *me yis kun du ni* for *me ni bsdigs bcas pas*; *'phro bas* for *'phro ba*; *tshig pa* for *tshig pas*; and *'bros par* for *bros par* in our text. Read *palāpitāṃś* for *pralāpitāṃś*.

1546. See Tsong kha pa, *Gsang mngon*, 28a4–5.

1547. See Tsong kha pa, *Gsang mngon*, 28a4.

[Meditating on the Vajra Enclosure]

Then the *Concise Sādhana* teaches: "Drive the stakes in the ten directions and bring the malicious ones that are at the zenith and nadir under your power as well."[1548] The *Vajrasattva Sādhana* explains how to bring the malicious ones in the ten directions including the zenith and the nadir under your power: "Then, while reciting the mantra of Ṭakkirāja,[1549] *Ṭakki hūṃ jaḥ*, visualize four concentric fences, beyond the fierce deities, made of iron, water, fire, and wind.[1550] Then, with *hūṃ*,[1551] visualize a stūpa-like vajra tent abiding on the iron fence. While reciting the three syllables, visualize a protective covering, and with *hūṃ*[1552] visualize the ground in the nature of crossed vajra."[1553]

Accordingly, while reciting *Ṭakki hūṃ jaḥ* four times, visualize the four fences one encircling the other:[1554] "Beyond the fierce deities there is an iron vajra fence." Here, too, the spaces between the larger vajras are filled with smaller and smaller vajras down to the tiniest ones, leaving no space between them at all, so that it is utterly impossible to fit any more in.[1555] "Beyond it, visualize a water wall," spraying water droplets surrounded by light-rays. "Beyond that, visualize a fire wall," radiating light-rays ablaze in five colors swirling clockwise. "Beyond that, visualize a wind wall," moving in the same pattern as the fire wall, swirling vigorously with fierce howls. [30b]

Upon the iron fence visualize a stūpa-like vajra tent arising from *hūṃ*. The *Sādhana Incorporating the Scripture* teaches here: "With *hūṃ mdzad*

1548. Nāgārjuna, *Mdor byas, Piṇḍīkrama Sādhana*, Tōh 1796, 2b3; L 16ab; T 15ab. D has *phus bus* for *phur bu* in our text.

1549. Tib. 'Dod pa'i rgyal po.

1550. In Tsong kha pa, *Gsang mngon*, 28a5–b2, the mantra is recited four times and with each recitation another circular fence arises beyond the previous one. These fences are made of iron, water, fire, and wind, respectively.

1551. As noted, according to both the Bstan 'gyur and the Sanskrit the vajra tent is visualized upon *hūṃ*. In Tsong kha pa, *Gsang mngon*, 28b2, the vajra tent is visualized arising from *hūṃ*.

1552. Once more in Tsong kha pa, *Gsang mngon*, 28b2–3, the vajra ground arises from *hūṃ*.

1553. Candrakīrti, *Rdo rje sems dpa'i sgrub thabs, Vajrasattva Sādhana*, Tōh 1814, 197b1–2; Luo and Tomabechi 2009, 8.6–9 and 40.9–13. D has *hūṃ gi* for hūṃ gis twice; *sngags 'di* for *sngags ni 'di*; and D and Luo and Tomabechi have *rlung rnams kyi* for *rlung gyi* and *de la* for *da la* in our text.

1554. See Tsong kha pa, *Gsang mngon*, 28a5–b2.

1555. See also Tsong kha pa, *Sngags rim chen mo*, chap. 12, 501; and *Bung ba'i re skong*, 9a6–b2.

visualize a vajra net."[1556] Thinking that *hūṃkāra*[1557] is the equivalent term of *hūṃ mdzad*, SOME LAMAS explain that the light emanates from the syllable *hūṃkāra* and transforms into a tent of vajra net. However, *kāra* is used both for *mdzad* and syllable, and in this context it should be translated as "syllable," as it is wrong to translate it as *mdzad*. Therefore *hūṃkāra* here must be the syllable *hūṃ*.

"Under this tent, and upon the fence visualize a vajra canopy"[1558] arising from *hūṃ*, leaving no space between the fence, the tent, and the canopy. Even though the *Maṇḍala Vajra Garland* explains that the fence vajras can be either five-pronged or three-pronged,[1559] here they must be five-pronged. Likewise, although many other sources explain that the fence is made of crossed vajras, the *Vajrasattva Sādhana* calls it "an iron fence,"[1560] and since it is a vajra fence, it must be a fence of blue vajras.

There are different methods of visualizing the shape of the enclosure. While in the traditions of Cakrasaṃvara and so forth it is said to be square, here it is fine to visualize it round.[1561] With regard to the height of the protection wheel,[1562] in many sādhanas, such as the *Crown Jewel Sādhana* of Cakrasaṃvara by the mahāsiddha *Kambala, the protection wheel extends from the abode of Brahmā above to the golden ground below,[1563] while the *Maṇḍala Vajra Garland* explains that it extends from No-Higher Heaven above to the wind disk below.[1564] As for its width,[1565] in his *Commentary on the Root Tantra of Cakrasaṃvara* and so forth, *Kambala explains that it is as

1556. Nāgārjuna, *Mdo bsre*, *Sādhanasūtramelāpaka*, Tōh 1797, 11b5.

1557. Reading *kāra* for *kara* in our text.

1558. See Tsong kha pa, *Gsang mngon*, 28b1.

1559. Abhayākaragupta, *Dkyil chog rdo rje phreng ba*, *Vajrāvalī Maṇḍalavidhi*, Tōh 3140, 24b6; Mori 2009, §12.2.7, 167 and 169. See also Tsong kha pa, *Sngags rim chen mo*, chap. 12, 501.

1560. Candrakīrti, *Rdo rje sems dpa'i sgrub thabs*, *Vajrasattva Sādhana*, Tōh 1814, 197b1; Luo and Tomabechi 2009, 8.8 and 40.12.

1561. See also Tsong kha pa, *Bung ba'i re skong*, 9b2–3.

1562. See also Tsong kha pa, *Sngags rim chen mo*, chap. 12, 501; *Bung ba'i re skong*, 9b2–3; and *Slob tshul*, 10a1.

1563. Lwa ba pa, *Bde mchog gi sgrub thabs gtsug nor*, *Cakrasaṃvara Sādhana Ratnacūḍāmaṇi*, Tōh 1443, 246b5; but see Tsong kha pa, *'Dod 'jo*, 41b3–6.

1564. Abhayākaragupta, *Dkyil chog rdo rje phreng ba*, *Vajrāvalī Maṇḍalavidhi*, Tōh 3140, 38a6–7; Mori 2009, §13.2.2, 236–237. See Tsong kha pa, *'Dod 'jo*, 41b5–6.

1565. See also Tsong kha pa, *Sngags rim chen mo*, chap. 12, 501; *Bung ba'i re skong*, 9b3; and *Slob tshul*, 10a2.

wide as one wishes it to be,[1566] while the *Ritual of Cakrasaṃvara Maṇḍala* by Kṛṣṇācārya teaches that it extends "to the iron mountains and is surrounded by a garland of vajras."[1567] The treatises of the *Guhyasamāja* do not explain its measurements in height and width. [31a]

Then you should visualize: "Arising from *hūṃ* on the level below is a ground" of crossed "vajras. Arising beyond it, in all the cardinal and intermediate directions, is a lattice of arrows, radiating blazing fire of wisdom."[1568] Since some scholars[1569] maintain that these arrows have heads made of five-spoked vajras, visualize them in the form of five-spoked vajras that crisscross swiftly with lightning-like flashes in the cardinal and intermediate directions, zenith, and nadir.

SOME LAMAS[1570] explain the meditation on the vajra enclosure as protecting the environment of the meditator, while blessing the three doors with the three syllables protects the yogis themselves, for as the *Sādhana Incorporating the Scripture* and the *Vajrasattva Sādhana* both teach: "With the three syllables, visualize a protective covering."[1571] Accordingly, by blessing the three places on the bodies of all the deities while uttering the three syllables, visualize your body, speech, and mind in the nature of the three vajras; in this way you put on the protective covering.

[The Purpose of Meditating on the Protection Wheel]

What is the purpose of meditating on the protection wheel in this way, before meditating on the main part of the *Sādhana*? The thirteenth chapter of the

1566. Lwa ba pa, *Bde mchog gi sgrub thabs gtsug nor, Cakrasaṃvara Sādhana Ratnacūḍāmaṇi*, Tōh 1443, 246a4; but see Tsong kha pa, *'Dod 'jo*, 41b6.

1567. Spyod pa nag po pa, *Bcom ldan 'das bde mchog 'khor lo'i dkyil 'khor gyi cho ga, Bhagavacchrīcakrasamvara Maṇḍalavidhi*, Tōh 1446, 281b2. See Tsong kha pa, *'Dod 'jo*, 41b6.

1568. See Tsong kha pa, *Gsang mngon*, 28b1–2.

1569. See Prajñārakṣita, *Mngon par rtogs pa'i dka' 'grel, Abhisamayapañjikā*, Tōh 1465, 36a3–4. See also Tsong kha pa, *Sngags rim chen mo*, chap. 12, 501.

1570. Bu ston, *Mdor byas 'grel chen*, 9a2, divides the protection into three subsections: protection of oneself, protections of the place, and protection of the yoga. Several Sakya scholars follow him, among them Ngor chen, *Gsang 'dus dkyil 'khor gyi sgrub thabs dngos grub rgya mtsho*, work 106, 3a3–4b2.

1571. Nāgārjuna, *Mdo bsre, Sādhanasūtramelāpaka*, Tōh 1797, 11b5. Candrakīrti, *Rdo rje sems dpa'i sgrub thabs, Vajrasattva Sādhana*, Tōh 1814, 197b2, Luo and Tomabechi 2009, 8.8–9 and 40.12–13. D and Luo and Tomabechi have *go cha la* for *go cha*.

Guhyasamāja Tantra teaches:[1572] "Wherever you practice your resolve born of concentration, so long as you abide by the yoga of concentration, you will be blessed by the buddhas." The *Illuminating Lamp* explains it thus: "*Concentration* and so forth is the ritual of protection as an element of virtuous activity for the beginner." Then, "*abide by the yoga of concentration* means while practicing the yoga of Vajrasattva and so forth; *by the buddhas* means by one's own deity; and *blessed* means becoming one."[1573]

The name of this samādhi, "vajra pacifying impediments to sentient beings,"[1574] taught in the *Guhyasamāja Tantra* in conjunction with the driving in of the stakes during meditation on the protection wheel is explained in the *Illuminating Lamp*: "*Sentient beings* are the yogis and so forth. [31b] *Impediments to sentient beings* are the obstructers who lead them astray by turning them away, confusing their minds, and so forth. *Pacifying* the impediments means banishing them."[1575]

Accordingly,[1576] you should know that as you meditate on the main part of the *sādhana in four sessions*, you will be *blessed by the deity* owing to your meditation on the protection wheel, *becoming one* with it or *equal to the deity in capability*, that is to say, you will be endowed with great capability. Neither will the *obstructers confuse your mind* and distract you from practicing the sādhana, nor will you wish to participate in social activities and so forth, nor will your body and mind be afflicted, impaired, and so forth. Rather you will perfect your practice of deity yoga. In this way *beginners*—those who are practicing

1572. *Guhyasamāja Tantra*, Tōh 442; Zhol 22b2; Stog 38a3–4; Dunh 41b4; Fremantle 1971, v. 74; and Matsunaga 1978, v. 78. The Zhol has *gnas na* for *gnas nas* in our text. Cited also in Candrakīrti, *Rdo rje sems dpa'i sgrub thabs*, *Vajrasattva Sādhana*, Tōh 1814, 197b3; Luo and Tomabechi 2009, 9.1–2 and 40.17–41.1–3; and in Nāgārjuna, *Mdo bsre*, *Sādhanasūtramelāpaka*, Tōh 1797, 11b3–4, though the translations into Tibetan in both are different.

1573. Candrakīrti, *Sgron gsal*, *Pradīpoddyotanaṭikā*, Tōh 1785, 111a4–6; Chakravarti 1984, 135.

1574. Tib. *'gro ba 'dul ba zhi ba rdo rje*, Skt. *jagadvinayaśāntivajra*. This name is found in the *Guhyasamāja Tantra*, shortly after the verse just cited. See Tōh 442; Zhol 22b2; Stog 38a5; Dunh 41b5; Fremantle 1971, after v. 75; and Matsunaga 1978, after v. 79. Dunh has here *skye 'gro 'dul ba'i snying po rdo rje*.

1575. Candrakīrti, *Sgron gsal*, *Pradīpoddyotanaṭikā*, Tōh 1785, 111a1; Chakravarti 1984, 135. D has *khrid pa* for *'khrid pa* in our text.

1576. This paragraph is based on Candrakīrti, *Sgron gsal*, *Pradīpoddyotanaṭikā*, Tōh 1785, 111a1–2; Chakravarti 1984, 135; that comments on chap. 13, Fremantle 1971, v. 74; and Matsunaga 1978, v. 78. See also Tsong kha pa, *Sgron gsal mchan*, 318a1–5.

the creation stage—will engage in this *virtuous ancillary*—beneficial for the meditation on the main part of the deity yoga.

Here ends the explanation about meditating on the protection wheel in order to avert unfavorable conditions.

Part 2. The First Yoga: The Actual Meditation

4. Meditating on the Ground of Wisdom

Explanation of the Actual Meditation—the First Yoga

There are four sections here: (1) the yoga of taking death as the dharmakāya—the specially visualized deities, (2) the yoga of taking the intermediate being as the saṃbhogakāya—visualizing the First Lord, (3) the yoga of taking birth as the nirmāṇakāya—transforming into Vajrasattva's nirmāṇakāya together with (a) the setting of the body maṇḍala; (b) the blessing of the three doors; (c) the meditation on the triple sattvas; and (4) seeking and absorbing in union with the consort to demonstrate that these three bodies are attained through the *dharma* of passion.

The Yoga of Taking Death as the Dharmakāya—The Specially Visualized Deities

The first topic has three parts: (1) visualization of the celestial mansion—the place where you will be awakened, (2) visualization of the deities—the indwellers of the maṇḍala who will be awakened there, and (3) dissolution of the specially visualized deities into clear light[1577]—the method of awakening. [32a]

Visualization of the Celestial Mansion—The Place Where You Will Be Awakened

The first topic consists of two further parts: (1) meditation on the ground of wisdom in correspondence with the empty eon that follows the destruction of the previous world and (2) visualization of the vajra ground and meditating on the celestial mansion in correspondence with the evolution of the subsequent world.

1577. Below this title appears as "dissolution of the specially visualized deities into the ultimate maṇḍala."

Meditation on the Ground of Wisdom in Correspondence with the Empty Eon That Follows the Destruction of the Previous World

Again, the first topic is composed of the following: (1) refutation of the claim that it is not necessary to meditate on emptiness during the creation stage, (2) the method of meditating on the ground of wisdom, and (3) the purpose of meditating on emptiness at this point of the sādhana.

Refutation of the Claim That It Is Not Necessary to Meditate on Emptiness During the Creation Stage

SOME PEOPLE[1578] of inferior mental capacity, who are not very learned and lack proper spiritual companions, have such qualms as these: THEY THINK that during the creation stage, you should meditate on the appearance aspect alone—the circle of deities—while the meditation on the emptiness aspect—the suchness of phenomena—should take place during the completion stage. THEY SAY[1579] that the meditation on emptiness that precedes the meditation on the celestial mansion during the creation stage is not based on understanding the view of the Middle Way but has another objective. In order for the appearance of the pure celestial mansion and its deities to arise, the ordinary appearance of the animate and inanimate realms must not arise, and that is why meditators visualize the present appearance of the animate and inanimate realms only as nothing whatsoever, like space, by reciting the mantra *śūnyatā*[1580] or the verse beginning with "in the absence of being, there is no meditation."[1581]

But this is a misconception that makes every effort to meditate on the creation stage a fruitless labor. I will proceed to explain this. Such statements (1) contradict reason, (2) contradict YOUR own premises, and (3) contradict scriptures.

1. How do these statements contradict reasoning? Firstly, regarding YOUR

1578. This point is raised as a qualm in Tsong kha pa, *Sngags rim chen mo*, chap. 12, 489–90 and 443.

1579. See Sa chen Kun dga' snying po, *Mngon rtogs tshig gi bum pa*, work no. 54, 7b2–3, and Bsod nams rtse mo, *Kyai rdo rje'i sgrub thabs mtsho skyes kyi ṭīkā*, work 6, 10a1–3. See also Go rams pa, *Gsang ba 'dus pa'i sgrub thabs kun tu bzang po'i nyi 'od kyi don 'grel*, work 78, 18b2–19b4. This issue is discussed in Bentor 2015b.

1580. *Oṃ śūnyatā jñāna vajra svabhāva ātmako 'haṃ*.

1581. These recitations accompany the meditation on emptiness; see below [39a]–[40a] and Tsong kha pa, *Gsang mngon*, 28b4.

position that yogis should meditate on the animate and inanimate realms as totally nonexistent: since these realms are perceptible, meditating on them as though they are totally nonexistent involves an extremely nihilistic view. [32b] Since the arising of a nihilistic view is in itself a cause for rebirth in the worst of hells, you should strive to block that view rather than to meditate on it.

If YOU meditate thus with a nihilistic view while reciting the mantra śūnyatā, does this mean you actually visualize it annihilating the animate and inanimate realms or does it mean that you simply recite the mantra and verse as though they signify that animate and inanimate realms are nonexistent? No matter what YOU maintain: in the first case, that the meditation on the mantra and verse cause the destruction of the entire animate and inanimate realms—this is even worse than meditating on the god Īśvara as the creator of all the worlds. In the second case, the literal and shared levels of interpretation of the verse[1582] "In the absence of being, there is no meditation" would signify that the animate and inanimate realms do not exist at all. However, the literal and shared levels of interpretation of the verse do in fact refute the position that the animate and inanimate realms do not exist at all. Therefore such a misconception is out of place, being far afield from the meaning of the mantra śūnyatā, as will be explained below.

2. How do these positions contradict YOUR own premises? It is one thing to meditate on the animate and inanimate realms as entirely nonexistent, and another to meditate in order to block appearances and one's attitude to them as being ordinary. This is so because meditating on the animate and inanimate realms as entirely nonexistent is itself a very ordinary attitude that should be blocked, being an extremely nihilistic view that depreciates the existence of the animate and inanimate realms altogether.

Furthermore, YOU agree that the earlier offerings to the field of accumulation were intended for the accumulation of merit, whereas here the purpose of the meditation is to accumulate wisdom. If this were an accumulation of wisdom, it would indeed contradict nonapprehension in relation to suchness. Furthermore, if the purpose of meditating on the animate and inanimate realms as entirely nonexistent is to accumulate wisdom, then the nonexistence of the animate and inanimate realms would be identical to the suchness of phenomena. [33a] Understand that those who say there are no past and future

1582. Mkhas grub rje refers here to the explanation of this verse, in the literal and shared levels of interpretation, in Candrakīrti, *Sgron gsal, Pradīpoddyotanaṭīkā*, Tōh 1785, 24a2–6; Chakravarti 1984, 31.

lives and that the nonexistence of present appearances is the true condition are even more dimwitted than the Heretical Materialistic School.[1583]

3. How do these positions contradict the scriptures?[1584] A large number of scriptures teach that generally, mantrins in the creation stage should meditate on emptiness, and that in this case specifically, they should use wisdom to discern all phenomena as being devoid of true existence and meditate on the profound and well-established view of the Middle Way, for the first chapter of the *Saṃpuṭa Tantra* teaches: "You should first cleanse the stains of embodied beings by meditating on emptiness. Make the 'sphere of form' empty,[1585] so too sound,"[1586] and so forth. Thus, at the beginning of the meditation on the sādhana, the mantrin should establish that the eighteen sensory spheres are empty and meditate on this. The third chapter of the *Four Chapters Tantra* teaches this as well,[1587] and so too the fourth chapter of the *Saṃpuṭa Tantra*: "Then, abiding in a meditation hut,[1588] you should view all phenomena as devoid of self, and recite in your mind: since external and internal things are posited by the mind and do not exist except in the mind, all phenomena are primordially nonarising and therefore intrinsically pure."[1589] Thus this is taught clearly.

1583. Tib. Rgyang 'phen, Skt. Āyata, Lokāyata, or Cārvāka.

1584. Mkhas grub rje follows here Tsong kha pa, *Rnam gzhag rim pa'i rnam bshad*, first 9b1–4, and then 8b6–9b1.

1585. As noted, our text is different here.

1586. *Yang dag par sbyor ba*, Tōh 381, 74a3; Sanskrit and Tibetan in Elder 1978, 44 and 122–23; and Skorupski 1996, 217; English translation in Elder 1978, 163. These lines are cited also by Bsod nams rtse mo, *Kyai rdo rje'i sgrub thabs mtsho skyes kyi ṭīkā*, work 9, 10a6; and Grags pa rgyal mtshan, *Rgyud kyi mngon rtogs*, work 1, 39a6. D and the two Tibetan editions have *dang por* for *dang po*; *bsams pas ni* for *rnam bsams la* in our text [the Skt. is *vicintya*]; and *gzugs kyi khams ni stong pa yi* for *gzugs khams zhes bya stong pa ste*. D has *sgra la de nyid kyis ni bya* and Elder and Skorupski have *sgra la yang ni de yis bya* for *de bzhin du ni sgra yang bya* in our text. Mkhas grub rje follows here, for the most part, the reading in Tsong kha pa, *Rnam gzhag rim pa'i rnam bshad*, 9b1–2. The only difference is that while the *Rnam gzhag rim pa'i rnam bshad* has *stong nyid rnams bsam pas* our text has *stong nyid rnam bsams la*. For Abhayākāragupta's commentary on this line, see his *Man ngag snye ma*, *Āmnāyamañjarī*, Tōh 1198, 11a. (The translation here is of our text, not the text of the Bstan 'gyur nor of the Sanskrit text.)

1587. *Gdan bzhi*, *Catuḥpīṭha Tantra*, Tōh 428, 188a4; English translation in Szántó 2012, 244.

1588. Tsong kha pa *Rnam gzhag rim pa'i rnam bshad*, 9b3, has *bsam gtan gyi khyad par* for *bsam gtan gyi khang par* in our text.

1589. In his *Rnam gzhag rim pa'i rnam bshad*, 9b3, Tsong kha pa specifies that he cites the fourth chapter in the third *brtag pa* of the *Saṃpuṭa*, Tōh 381.

Furthermore, Ārya Nāgārjuna teaches in his *Concise Sādhana*: "You should meditate on the three worlds [and being][1590] as devoid of being[1591] in ultimate truth. In the absence of being, there is no meditation and meditation cannot be meditated upon. Therefore a state of being that is nonbeing leaves no object for meditation. Uttering this verse, meditate on the nature of the animate and inanimate worlds as empty and bless them through this yoga as the ground of wisdom."[1592] [33b]

Hence, while meditating on the meaning of the verse,[1593] you should envision the animate and inanimate realms as ultimately devoid of being, but not as entirely nonexistent. The *Illuminating Lamp* explains this verse in both literal and shared levels of interpretation: at the literal level of interpretation, it explains the essence, cause, and fruit of phenomena as empty of existence by its own characteristics; and at the shared level of interpretation, it expounds the

1590. This phrase is not found in the Sanskrit editions.

1591. Tib. *dngos po med par*, Skt. *niḥsvabhāva*.

1592. Nāgārjuna, *Mdor byas, Piṇḍīkrama Sādhana*, Tōh 1796, 2b3–5; L 16cd–18; T 15cd–17. D has *dngos po med la bsgom pa'i dngos* for *dngos po med pas sgom pa med*; *bsgom pa min* for *sgom pa min*; *'di yis rgyu mi rgyu'i* for *'di yi brgyu mi'i brgyu'i*; and *bdag nyid can rnams* for *bdag nyid che rnams*. The four lines of L 17 and T 16 are found in the *Guhyasamāja Tantra*, Tōh 442, chap. 2, Zhol 6a2; Stog 9a5–6; Dunh 8b4; Fremantle 1971, v. 3; and Matsunaga 1978, v. 3; and also in Tsong kha pa, *Gsang mngon*, 28b4. The Sanskrit is somewhat different: *abhāve bhāvanābhāvo bhāvanā naiva bhāvanā, iti bhāvo na bhāvaḥ syād bhāvanā nopalabhyate*. The editions of the *Guhyasamāja Tantra* in Fremantle and Matsunaga, Nāgārjuna's *Mdor byas*, and T. have *abhāve bhāvanābhāvo* for *abhāvabhāvanā bhāvo* in L. My translation is only one suggestion among several possible ones. For a detailed discussion of this verse, see Bentor 2009b. For the interpretation of this verse in the literal and shared level of interpretations in Candrakīrti's *Sgron gsal, Pradīpoddyotanaṭīkā* (Tōh 1785, 24a2–6; Chakravarti 1984, 31), see the section "Meditation on the Four-Line Verse Beginning with 'In the Absence of Being'" below. The Sanskrit verse is in fact a mantra which puns on the meanings derived from the root *bhū*. Among these meanings are "being," "existing," "a thing," "a state of existence," as well as "causing to be," "creating," and "meditating." The Sanskrit word for "meditation," *bhavānā*, is related to the word meaning to bring into existence, since by meditating practitioners create their world. This pun is lost when the Sanskrit verse is translated into other languages. The corresponding word in Tibetan, *sgom pa*, is related to habituation, and therefore the Tibetan translation here conveys a somewhat different notion. For some other translations of this verse, see Bhattacharyya 1931, 11; Bagchi 1965; Tucci 1934–1935, 353–53; Snellgrove 1959, part 1, 77; Fremantle 1971, 34; Filippani-Ronconi 1972, 190; Eastman 1980, 18–19; Gäng 1988, 123.

1593. The four lines of Nāgārjuna's *Mdor byas*; L. 17; T. 16 that are found in the *Guhyasamāja Tantra*, chap. 2, Tōh 442, Zhol 6a2; Stog 9a5–6; Dunh 8b4; Fremantle 1971, v. 3; and Matsunaga 1978, v. 3.

three doors of liberation.[1594] Out of the four levels of interpretation only these two are applicable here. It would be altogether absurd to equate the meditation on animate and inanimate realms as entirely nonexistent with the meditation on the three doors of liberation.

The *Samantabhadra Sādhana* likewise teaches: "Having perceived by means of compassion that everyone in this world is caught up in a web of conceptions, the mantrin should meditate on the perfect mind for awakening—beyond compare, in accordance with the ritual method."[1595] Thus you should meditate first on [emptiness], the ultimate mind for awakening.[1596]

[How Should You Meditate on This?]

The *Samantabhadra Sādhana* continues: "Since they lack essence, all things are empty; since they lack intrinsic causes, they are signless; and since they are devoid of conceptual thoughts, they are free of wishes."[1597] After the three doors of liberation, in the *Samantabhadra Sādhana* comes the mantra of emptiness.[1598] The mantra denotes the three doors of liberation, which is the meaning of the meditation here.

Likewise, in his *Hevajra Sādhana* the Mahāsiddha Saroruha teaches that after reciting the mantra that begins with *oṃ śūnyatā*, you "should meditate on the meaning of this mantra as: myself and the three realms are devoid of

1594. Candrakīrti explains this verse in the four levels of interpretation (*tshul bzhi*): the literal, shared, hidden, and ultimate. See his *Sgron gsal, Pradīpoddyotanaṭikā*, Tōh 1785, 23b7–24b4; Chakravarti 1984, 31–32. For four levels of interpretation see Steinkellner 1978; Broido 1983 and 1988; Thurman 1988; and Arénes 1998 and 2002. However, here Mkhas grub rje follows Tsong kha pa, *Rnam gzhag rim pa'i rnam bshad*, 9a2–4.

1595. Jñānapāda, *Kun du bzang po'i sgrub pa'i thabs, Samantabhadra Sādhana*, Tōh 1855, 29b3–4; Sanskrit and Tibetan in Tanaka 1996, 186. D and Tanaka have *cho gas de ltar* for *cho ga 'di ltar* in our text, and Tanaka has *snying rje* for *snying rjes*. Mkhas grub rje's text is similar to that of Tsong kha pa, *Sngags rim chen mo*, chap. 12, 497; for an English translation, see Yarnall 2013, 202.

1596. In this paragraph, Mkhas grub rje follows Tsong kha pa, *Sngags rim chen mo*, chap. 12, 497–498.

1597. Jñānapāda, *Kun du bzang po'i sgrub pa'i thabs, Samantabhadra Sādhana*, Tōh 1855, 29b4; Sanskrit and Tibetan in Tanaka 1996, 187. D and Tanaka have *rang bzhin* for *de bzhin* and *bral bas* for *bral pa'i* in our text. Tsong kha pa, *Sngags rim chen mo*, chap. 12, 497, has here *de bzhin rgyu dang bral bas*; English translation in Yarnall 2013, 204.

1598. *Oṃ śūnyatā jñāna vajra svabhāva ātmako 'haṃ.*

essence."[1599] And the glorious Candrakīrti in his *Vajrasattva Sādhana* teaches: "Then, with the verse of the mind for awakening that is taught in the second chapter of the *Guhyasamāja Tantra*,[1600] you should dissolve the wheel of protection together with the three realms in suchness."[1601] [34a] It would be utterly absurd to dissolve them in suchness by meditating on nonexistence rather than on suchness.[1602]

[The Fundamentals of the Visualization]

There are countless similar instructions in the scriptures about meditating on the absence of true existence, on emptiness, on the absence of essential nature, on the three doors of liberation, and so forth.[1603] In particular, throughout the creation stage, whenever you meditate on the appearance aspect—the circle of deities, or on the ancillaries—you must indeed meditate on emptiness.

You must practice the illusion-like union of appearance and emptiness whereby the objective aspect of the mind that realizes emptiness arises as the appearance of the deities. This method was taught by the great master of the maṇḍala Buddhajñāna in a very extensive way that clarifies misconceptions. It will generate joy in the wise who are endowed with probing minds, even if they understand this only partially, as I will explain forthwith.

Buddhajñāna teaches in his *Samantabhadra Sādhana*: "There is no saṃsāric suffering whatsoever apart from what arises from the stream of ordinary conceptual thoughts. The mind obstructing this [conceptualization] will realize

1599. Saroruha, *Dgyes pa rdo rje'i sgrub thabs*, *Hevajra Sādhana*, Tōh 1218, 2b5; *Dhīḥ* 2003, 134; Sanskrit, Tibetan, and English translation in Gerloff 2017, 99, 119 and 134. D has *bdag khams gsum po* for *bdag dang khams gsum po dag* in our text. Note that the Sanskrit equivalent of *ngo bo nyid* is *nirābhāsa*. While the Sanskrit colophon attributes this work to Ācārya Saroruha, the Tibetan version has here Slob dpon Padma.

1600. The verse mentioned above, [32a4] etc.

1601. Candrakīrti, *Rdo rje sems dpa'i sgrub thabs*, *Vajrasattva Sādhana*, Tōh 1814, 197b3–4; Luo and Tomabechi 2009, 9.4–5 and 41.5–7. D and Luo and Tomabechi have *srung ba* for *bsrung ba*.

1602. The early Sa skya scholars Sa chen Kun dga' snying po and Bsod nams rtse mo express similar ideas about the purpose of meditating on emptiness here. See their *[Mtsho skyes kyi] Mngon rtogs tshig gi bum pa*, 344b2–345a3, and *Kyai rdo rje'i sgrub thabs mtsho skyes kyi ṭīkā*, 10a3–b3, respectively.

1603. In the coming lines Mkhas grub rje follows Tsong kha pa's *Sngags rim chen mo*, chap. 12, 493–494.

directly.[1604] Conceptual thoughts will not appear to [the mind] endowed with a vast and profound nature."[1605]

What misconceptions does this clarify?[1606] In his commentary, Master Thagana raises the following qualm: All methods of meditation on deity yoga as explained at length above must be practiced *solely* for the sake of liberation from saṃsāra. But the root of saṃsāra is self-grasping, so no matter how much you meditate on the creation stage, you can never vitiate the root of saṃsāra even slightly. This is so because the meditation has no way to counter the self-grasping mode of apprehension at the root of saṃsāra. And therefore, you cannot achieve liberation from saṃsāra no matter how much you meditate on the creation stage.[1607] [34b]

One possible answer to this qualm is that the aim of the meditation on the creation stage is only the ordinary shared siddhis, not the supreme siddhi of enlightenment, and that is why however much you meditate on the creation stage, you will not be liberated from saṃsāra. Another plausible answer is that while there is no way to counter the self-grasping mode of apprehension—the root of saṃsāra—in the course of meditation, it is nevertheless considered possible to achieve liberation from saṃsāra by meditating on the creation stage.

Thagana does not provide any of these answers since their entailments are uncertain. Rather, he explains in reply that there is a way to directly counter the self-grasping mode of apprehension at the root of saṃsāra in the meditation on the creation stage itself and thus the argument that the creation stage does not vitiate self-grasping—the root of saṃsāra—is unsubstantiated.[1608] In a transitional clause to his comments on these lines by Buddhajñāna,[1609] Master Vaidyapāda explains: "Elucidating this passage in brief, it was taught that

1604. The Sanskrit of this line may also be translated as: "and its antidote is the mind that is realized directly."

1605. Jñānapāda, *Kun du bzang po'i sgrub pa'i thabs, Samantabhadra Sādhana*, Tōh 1855, 35b6–7. D has *rnam par 'gal bar* for *rnam pa 'gal bar* and *mngon sum du ni* for *mngon sum nyid du* in our text. Cited also in Tsong kha pa, *Sngags rim chen mo*, chap. 12, 490. As Szántó, work in progress, points out, this verse is quoted in the *Abhayapaddhati*, which has been preserved in Sanskrit. For the Sanskrit and English, see Luo 2010, 5.

1606. Mkhas grub rje follows here Tsong kha pa's *Sngags rim chen mo*, chap. 12, 490.

1607. Thagana, *Kun bzang sgrub thabs 'grel ba, Samantabhadra Sādhana Vṛtti*, Tōh 1868, 229b1–2.

1608. Thagana, *Kun bzang sgrub thabs 'grel ba, Samantabhadra Sādhana Vṛtti*, Tōh 1868, 229b3.

1609. Vaidyapāda says this in between his explanations on Jñānapāda's *Yan lag bzhi pa'i sgrub thabs kun tu bzang mo, Caturaṅga Sādhana Samantabhadrī*, Tōh 1856, 42a7. See the following note.

the inconceivable nature of the maṇḍala circle, as explained above, is an antidote to saṃsāric suffering."[1610]

[Explaining the Lines of Buddhajñāna]

The term *ordinary conceptual thoughts* in the line *apart from what arises from the stream of ordinary conceptual thoughts* does not signify clinging to the impure environment, body, and resources, but refers in this context to conceptual thoughts that grasp to I and mine, for in his *Commentary on the Samantabhadra Sādhana*, Thagana explains: "*Ordinary conceptual thoughts* are conceptual thoughts of I and mine."[1611] And because Ratnākaraśānti in his *Commentary on the Maṇḍala Ritual of the Guhyasamāja* also says: "Since *ordinary conceptual thoughts* here are explained as a mental discourse with aspects of I and mine, grasped and grasper, they are labeled the *suffering* that is the nature of saṃsāra; [35a] and thus they are the main cause of the suffering that is the nature of saṃsāra."[1612] In this regard, since self-grasping is the main cause of saṃsāric suffering, this is clearly the meaning of the verse *apart from that there is no saṃsāric suffering whatsoever.* Here ends the explanation of the lines *there is no saṃsāric suffering whatsoever apart from what arises from the stream of ordinary conceptual thoughts.*

As for the meaning of the words *the mind obstructing this will realize directly,* all commentaries explain *the mind obstructing* self-grasping is the mind endowed with the aspect of the maṇḍala circle. It obstructs in as much as it is *an obstructing aspect,*[1613] that is to say, by running directly counter to this mode of apprehension. Yogis meditating on the creation stage experience this

1610. Vaidyapāda, *Yan lag bzhi pa'i sgrub thabs kun tu bzang mo'i rnam par bshad pa, Caturaṅga Sādhana Samantabhadrīṭīkā*, Tōh 1872, 176b4. D has *gnyen po yin par gsungs pa* for *gnyen por gsungs pa* in our text, which follows that of Tsong kha pa, *Sngags rim chen mo*, chap. 12, 490. Mkhas grub rje continues to follow here Tsong kha pa's *Sngags rim chen mo*, chap. 12, 490–491.

1611. Thagana, *Kun bzang sgrub thabs 'grel ba, Samantabhadra Sādhana Vṛtti*, Tōh 1868, 229b2–3, cited also Tsong kha pa, *Sngags rim chen mo*, chap. 12, 490–491.

1612. Ratnākaraśānti, *Gsang ba 'dus pa'i dkyil 'khor gyi cho ga'i 'grel pa, Guhyasamāja Maṇḍalavidhiṭīkā*, Tōh 1871, 127a5–7. According to its colophon it is also called *Bzhi brgya lnga bcu pa'i 'grel ba*. D has *rnam pa can gyi yid gyis* for *rnam pa can gyi yid gyi* in our text, which follows Tsong kha pa's *Sngags rim chen mo*, chap. 12, 491.

1613. While Jñānapāda's *Sgrub thabs kun bzang* and its commentaries have *rnam par 'gal bar*, Tsong kha pa's *Sngags rim chen mo* and our text have *rnam pa 'gal bar*. Thus Tsong kha pa and Mkhas grub rje take the verbal prefix *rnam par* here as a noun *rnam pa* and understand the phrase *obstructing* as *having an obstructing aspect*.

mind endowed with an aspect of the maṇḍala circle, and therefore they *will realize directly*. The reason this *obstructing aspect* runs directly counter the self-grasping mode of apprehension is that *being endowed with a vast and profound nature it does not give rise to conceptual thoughts*. When the mind *endowed with* aspects of the *vast and profound* maṇḍala circle arises, *conceptual thoughts* that grasp at I and mine *do not appear*, that is to say, they are not perceived.

[How Is the Visualization of the Maṇḍala an Antidote to Self-Grasping?]

On this point SOME SAY[1614] that just because self-grasping is not perceived when the aspect of the maṇḍala appears to the mind meditating on the creation stage, it should not be concluded that the visualization of the maṇḍala is an antidote to self-grasping. Otherwise, it would follow that even the meditative absorption of infinite space could be an antidote to self-grasping. [35b] In reply Ratnākaraśānti says: This is not the case "since the mind endowed with the aspect of the maṇḍala engages in dispelling all false conceptualizations, but not because these two minds simply do not appear simultaneously."[1615]

And says Ratnākaraśānti: "The meditative absorptions of infinite space and so forth do not engage in the aspect of selflessness. Because they do not turn away from the view of the self, they do not avert the suffering caused by it. Furthermore, aging, dying and so forth, which continue from one birth to another, are the truth of suffering. The cause of suffering—the view of the self and so forth—is the truth of the origin of suffering. The antidote to this—the maṇḍala circle—is the truth of the path. The 'complete transformation of the basis'[1616] of the essence of the mental continuum, in order to fully annihi-

1614. These objections are raised in Ratnākaraśānti, *Gsang ba 'dus pa'i dkyil 'khor gyi cho ga'i 'grel pa, Guhyasamāja Maṇḍalavidhiṭīkā*, Tōh 1871, 127a4–5, and then answered by him, see below.

1615. That is to say, not because when the maṇḍala appears false conceptualizations cannot appear. Ratnākaraśānti, *Gsang ba 'dus pa'i dkyil 'khor gyi cho ga'i 'grel pa, Guhyasamāja Maṇḍalavidhiṭīkā*, Tōh 1871, 127a7–b1. This and the following citation are found also in Tsong kha pa, *Sngags rim chen mo*, chap. 12, 491.

1616. Ratnākaraśānti, who is classified as belonging to the Yogācāra-Madhyamaka School, here uses the Yogācāra term, complete transformation of the basis. Tib. *gnas yongs su gyur ba*, Skt. *āśrayaparāvṛtti*.

late the rise of suffering, is the truth of cessation of suffering; and this is the ultimate truth."[1617]

Thus Ratnākaraśānti clearly distinguishes between two methods of meditation: (1) The meditative absorption of infinite space does not turn the mind away from selflessness, hence this meditation does not prevent self-grasping. Therefore, even if yogis meditate on infinite space, they will not be liberated from saṃsāric suffering. (2) The mind endowed with the aspect of the maṇḍala circle engages in selflessness and blocks the object grasped at as a self. Therefore this mind is able to counteract self-grasping.

The wisdom-realizing-selflessness can obstruct self-grasping by countering its mode of apprehension, since self-grasping is a mistaken apprehension while wisdom-realizing-emptiness is not. Furthermore, establishing whether or not an apprehension is erroneous depends on whether or not there is supportive-valid-cognition proving that what has been apprehended is actually so. As the master logician Dharmakīrti said: "Of the [two], the one that is supported by valid cognition invalidates the other."[1618] [36a]

These points of contention create uncertainties even for the learned and knowledgeable. Lacking a view of selflessness that directly counteracts self-grasping—the root of saṃsāra—you will lose[1619] the essence of the path that liberates from saṃsāra. The wise must understand these points and such ways of responding to them in the context of both the creation and completion stages.

Thus, while focusing on one and the same object, there are two minds that directly oppose each other in terms of their mode of apprehension, one that is supported by valid cognition and the other that is not; and on this basis they

1617. Ratnākaraśānti, *Gsang ba 'dus pa'i dkyil 'khor gyi cho ga'i 'grel pa, Guhyasamāja Maṇḍalavidhiṭīkā*, Tōh 1871, 127b3–5. D and Tsong kha pa's *Sngags rim chen mo*, chap. 12, 491, have *de'i rgyu can* for *des na da'i rgyu can*; *de'i gnyen por gyur ba dkyil 'khor kyi 'khor lo ni* for *de'i gnyen por gyur ba'i dkyil 'khor lor gyur pa ni*; and *'di ni 'dir don dam pa'o* for *'dir don dam pa'o* in our text. D has *dga' ba* for *rga ba*, and *la sogs pa'i* for *la sogs pa ni* in the *Sngags rim chen mo* and our text.

1618. Dharmakīrti, *Tshad ma rnam 'grel, Pramāṇavārttika, Parārthānumāna*, Tōh 4210, 143a5–6; Miyasaka 1971–1972, v. 99cd; Sanskrit and English translation in Tillemans 2000, 138–39. The "other" is the one that is not supported by a valid cognition. In this context, the mind that understands selflessness will invalidate the self-grasping mind. In the original verse, as Tillemans 2000, 138–39, explains, this refers to "the treatise's assertion and the counter-thesis put forth by the proponent." This line is also cited in Tsong kha pa, *Sngags rim chen mo*, chap. 12, 492. Mkhas grub rje still follows the *Sngags rim chen mo* quite closely.

1619. Reading *stor* for *ster* in our text.

exist as the object to be undermined and that which undermines it.[1620] If one becomes habituated to the antidote without parting from the factors that help cultivate its habituation, then gradually, as habituation increases, the opposing forces desist. Ultimately through this process, ordinary thoughts or self-grasping can be eradicated.

This is so because the *Samantabhadra Sādhana* teaches: "When an opposing event occurs even once, it will be enhanced and as the practice of visualizing [the maṇḍala circle] intensifies it will halt the opposite [ordinary conceptual thought] entirely."[1621] Such is the meaning of the following verse from the *Treatise on Valid Cognition*: "Since all [flaws] susceptible to decrease and increase are accompanied by their antidotes, by instilling such antidotes through habituation, the negativities in some [minds] may be extinguished."[1622]

Here Ratnākaraśānti establishes "the irreversibility of the transformation" by citing the following verse from the *Treatise on Valid Cognition*:[1623] "[The mind] naturally cognizes the correct object without being obstructed [by contradictory conditions]."[1624] And Phalavajra establishes that the root of saṃsāra is self-grasping, by citing [the following verse from the *Treatise on Valid Cognition*]: "So long as there is [an apprehension of] the self, there is a notion of

1620. In this sentence Mkhas grub rje elaborates on Tsong kha pa's *Sngags rim chen mo*, chap. 12, 492.

1621. Jñānapāda, *Kun bzang sgrub thabs*, Tōh 1855, 35b7–36a7. D, which is quite different here, has *lan cig gyur ba'ang de bgrod rgyas gyur ba* for *lan gcig 'gyur ba'ang de drod rgyas 'gyur bar* in our text, but Tsong kha pa's *Sngags rim chen mo*, chap. 12, 492, has here *lan cig 'gyur ba'ang de bgrod rgyas 'gyur bar*. D has *mthong ba'i bslabs pa rnam par 'phel ba yis* for *mthong dang bslab pa rnam par 'phel ba dag*, while here the *Sngags rim chen mo*, chap. 12, 492 also has *mthong dang bslabs pa rnam par 'phel ba dag*, and at the end of the fourth line, both D and the *Sngags rim chen mo* have *byed* for *'gyur* in our text. Since this verse is quite difficult, it is not surprising that there are quite a few variant readings here. Therefore my translation is partly based on the commentaries by Thagana and Phalavajra and on Tsong kha pa's explanation in the *Sngags rim chen mo*, chap. 12, 492.

1622. Dharmakīrti, *Tshad ma rnam 'grel, Pramāṇavārttika, Svārthānumāna*, Tōh 4210, 103a2; Sanskrit and Tibetan editions in Miyasaka 1971–1972, v. 220; English translation in Yaita 1988, 435–436, and Dunne 2004, 369.

1623. Dharmakīrti, *Tshad ma rnam 'grel, Pramāṇavārttika, Pramāṇasiddhi*, Tōh 4210, 115b3–4; Sanskrit and Tibetan in Miyasaka 1971–1972, v. 210c; English translation in Yaita 1988, 436, and Dunne 2004, 369–370.

1624. In commenting on the line of Jñānapāda's *Kun bzang sgrub thabs, Samantabhadra Sādhana*, in his *Gsang ba 'dus pa'i dkyil 'khor gyi cho ga'i 'grel pa, Guhyasamāja Maṇḍalavidhiṭīkā*, Tōh 1871, 127b2, Ratnākaraśānti cites the entire following verse of Dharmakīrti's *Tshad ma rnam 'grel, Pramāṇavārttika*.

another,"[1625] and so forth.[1626] Thagana and Phalavajra as well present the philosophical view of the *Samantabhadra Sādhana* with many citations from the *Treatise on Valid Cognition*. [36b]

Furthermore, numerous learned scholars of the Mantra Vehicle often establish their point in this context by citing the *Treatise on Valid Cognition* as their authority. Therefore, O YOU who claim that the treatises of the two master logicians[1627] do not pertain to the inner field of learning of Buddhist teaching in general, and that they are irrelevant particularly in the context of the Mantra Vehicle, do not refute the Eye of the World [Dharmakīrti] through your nescient reasoning.[1628]

[Emptiness and Appearances—the Yoga of Nondual Profundity and Manifestations]

Therefore, as Phalavajra explains, dissolving the mind endowed with the aspect of the maṇḍala circle in the suchness of selflessness is "common to all three samādhis" during the sādhana, beginning with the First Yoga.[1629] Hence, in certain instances during the creation stage, such as the purification into the ground of wisdom, the dissolution of the specially visualized deities into clear light and so forth, you visualize the dissolution of dualistic appearances, and so meditate mainly on suchness. But apart from these instances, for the most part you meditate on the appearance aspect, the circle of deities. Here you still need to develop a powerful understanding with regard to all the circles of deities, namely, that phenomena are empty of intrinsic existence, and then to practice seeing their arising as illusion-like. You should meditate on all appearances in the following way: while taking the deities as your focus in visualization, the objective aspect of your mind—which understands the meaning of appearances without intrinsic existence—rises as a maṇḍala with a celestial

1625. Dharmakīrti, *Tshad ma rnam 'grel, Pramāṇavārttika, Pramāṇasiddhi*, Tōh 4210, 116a1; Sanskrit and Tibetan in Miyasaka 1971–1972, v. 219c; Sanskrit and German translation in Vetter 1984, 119.

1626. Phalavajra, in his commentary on Jñānapāda's *Kun bzang sgrub thabs*, cites this and the previous lines. See his *Kun tu bzang po'i sgrub pa'i thabs kyi 'grel pa, Samantabhadra Sādhana Vṛtti*, Tōh 1867, 185b3–4.

1627. Dignāga and Dharmakīrti.

1628. In this context in his *Sngags rim chen mo*, chap. 12, 493, Tsong kha pa attacks with stronger words than Mkhas grub rje.

1629. See Phalavajra's commentary on Jñānapāda's *Kun bzang sgrub thabs*, entitled *Kun tu bzang po'i sgrub pa'i thabs kyi 'grel pa, Samantabhadra Sādhana Vṛtti*, Tōh 1867, 185a6.

mansion and deities. In this way you become habituated in the yoga of nondual profundity and manifestation.

When you practice in this way, all meditations on the circle of deities during the creation stage become a path that runs directly counter to the self-grasping mode of apprehension—the root of saṃsāra—and this becomes a cause for liberation from all saṃsāric sufferings. It is therefore imperative to gain an understanding of this essential point, the enormity of which is unfathomable.

Were not this meditation an antidote to self-grasping, it would be quite impossible to establish that the meditation on impure appearances as lacking true existence and illusion-like [37a] is an antidote to counteract grasping at true existence. The mind that establishes impure appearances as devoid of true existence and meditates on them as illusion-like is wisdom in isolation. On the other hand, the mind that visualizes the maṇḍala circle and meditates on its appearance as devoid of intrinsic existence arises in the nature of the two accumulations: (1) based on the visualization of the maṇḍala circle, in the nature of merit accumulation, and (2) based on its arising in a mode that apprehends the absence of intrinsic existence, in the nature of wisdom accumulation.

The accumulation of merit here is attained through the exclusive method of the Mantra Vehicle and is consequently far superior to the accumulation of merit of the Pāramitā Vehicle. Furthermore, the greater the accumulation of merit, the greater the accumulation of wisdom becomes. Hence, in terms of its effectiveness as an antidote to grasping at true existence, the mind that takes the circle of deities for its focus and apprehends the absence of its intrinsic existence is a hundred times superior to a mind that takes a sprout for its focus and apprehends there an absence of intrinsic existence. Therefore you should use this human opportunity in a beneficial way by striving hard on a path such as this, whereby a single mind arises in the unique nature of the two accumulations, endowed with the full power to eradicate saṃsāra.

Having recognized the full force of this meaning, the *Hevajra Tantra* likewise teaches: "By means of the yoga of the creation stage, practitioners should meditate on the proliferations of mental constructs. Once they have made the proliferations dream-like, they should use this very proliferation to deproliferate."[1630] And the *Vajra Pavilion* teaches: "For example, the moon in

1630. *Kye'i rdo rje mkha' 'gro ma dra ba'i sdom pa'i rgyud kyi rgyal po*, *Hevajra Tantra II*, Tōh 418, 15a7; Snellgrove 1959, II.ii.29. Cited already above [11a]. D, T, and Snellgrove have *spros pa nyid ni spros med byed* for *spros pa nyid kyang spros med bya* in our text, while the analogous section in Tsong kha pa's *Sngags rim chen mo*, chap. 12, 493, has *spros pa nyid kyis spros med bya*, which corresponds to the Sanskrit *prapañcair niḥprapañcayet* in Snellgrove. Mkhas grub rje again follows the *Sngags rim chen mo*, chap. 12, 493, from the point where he leaves it above [36b].

the water, O friends, is neither true nor false. [37b] Just so, the nature of this maṇḍala circle is both transparent and manifesting."[1631]

In this way, too, the Indian mahāsiddhas explain the yoga of nondual profundity and manifestation—in which the understanding mind focuses on emptiness while its objective aspect arises as deities—taking this very explanation by Jñānapāda as their source.[1632] As the Mahāsiddha Śrīdhara says in his *Sādhana of Black Yamāri*: "There is no other valid alternative. Eminent ones like Jñānapāda clarify this precisely."[1633] Hence, the position that during practices of the Mantra Vehicle any meditation on emptiness must take place during the completion stage would be the pointless utterance of SOMEONE whose mind is not in the least familiar with the system of the Mantra Vehicle.

[The Yoga of the Illusion-Like Is Not the Yoga of the Illusory Body]

In particular, Ārya Nāgārjuna and his disciples make clear that the yoga of the illusion-like—wherein the body of the deity appears like the moon in water or a rainbow in the sky, yet is devoid of intrinsic existence—occurs during the creation stage; nevertheless, this yoga should not be considered the practice of the illusory body of self-blessing during the completion stage. Therefore THOSE[1634] who maintain that this yoga of the illusion-like body of the deity is the illusory body of self-blessing are all but obscured by the force of karma and deprived of the good fortune to realize the profound meaning of the illusory body.

For the *Compendium of Practices* teaches: "Those meditators who engage in the system of the sūtras or dwell in the creation stage recite and visualize in similitudes, likening all phenomena to illusions or dreams or reflected images. However, through these analogies they do not understand the transmitted

1631. *Gur, Vajrapañjara Tantra*, chap. 14, Tōh 419, 59b1–2. D has *ji ltar chu nang zla ba ste* for *dper na chu nang zla ba ni*; *bden min brdzun pa min pa ltar* for *grogs dag bden min brdzun pa'ang min*; *de ltar dkyil 'khor 'khor lo yi* for *de bzhin dkyil 'khor 'khor lo 'dir*; and *lus kyi rang bzhin rnyog pa med* for *dwangs shing gsal ba'i rang bzhin no*. Mkhas grub rje's text is very similar to that of Tsong kha pa's *Sngags rim chen mo*, chap. 12, 493.

1632. In Jñānapāda, *Kun bzang sgrub thabs, Samantabhadra Sādhana*, Tōh 1855, 35b6–36a1.

1633. Śrīdhara, *Gshin rje gshed nag po'i sgrub thabs, Kṛṣṇayamāri Sādhana*, Tōh 1923, 6b5. Cited also in Tsong kha pa's *Sngags rim chen mo*, chap. 12, 494.

1634. See Tsong kha pa, *Sngags rim chen mo*, chap. 12, 493–494 and *Rim lnga gsal sgron*, 235a3–239b2; English translation in Kilty 2013, 391–397.

instruction on self-transformation—how the body of the deity, whose nature is mind, is achieved through wisdom alone."[1635]

Furthermore, it is taught that the illusion-like yoga of the deity's body—which appears yet is devoid of intrinsic existence—is indispensable for the kriyā and caryā tantras. [38a] Hence, had that yoga been the illusory body of self-blessing, then the ultimate completion stage of the unexcelled tantra would be found in the kriyā and caryā tantras. This is because the first among the six deities on which you must meditate in kriyā tantra[1636] is called the suchness of yourself and the deity;[1637] and this is explained as emptiness—the real nature of yourself visualized as a deity.

Moreover, Ārya Nāgārjuna and his disciples maintain that the methods for the correct realization of emptiness and for meditation on it are found in the Vehicles of Disciples and the Solitary Buddhas as well, and, as goes without saying, in the Pāramitā Vehicle of Mahāyāna.[1638] Likewise, in the lower tantras, too, as noted, there are meditations on the meaning of the deity body that appears yet is devoid of intrinsic existence. Moreover, the *Concentration Continuation* teaches: "Blocking your vital energy and exertion, as you forsake sleep, you should imagine [the sounds of the syllables] abiding in fire, quiescent, untainted by words yet endowed with the syllables of the mantra."[1639] As

1635. Āryadeva, *Spyod bsdus, Caryāmelāpakapradīpa*, chap. 6, Tōh 1803, chap. 6, 84b6–7; Sanskrit, Tibetan, and English translation in Wedemeyer 2007, B: 41a; Sanskrit and Tibetan in Pandey 2000, 56 and 366. D, Wedemeyer, and Pandey all have *gang mdo sde la sogs pa'i* for *gang mdo sde'i sgom pa po* for *bsgom pa po*; *lta bu zhes dper* for *lta bu'o zhes dpar*; *byin gyis brlab pa'i* for *byin gyis rlob pa'i*; and *shes par ni* for *shes par* in our text; D and Pandey have *man ngag shes* for *man ngag ye shes* in our text. Cited also in Tsong kha pa, *Rim lnga gsal sgron*, 236b4–5; English translation in Kilty 2013, 393.

1636. For the six deities of the kriyā tantra, see Tsong kha pa, *Sngags rim chen mo*, chap. 2, 77–79; English translation in Hopkins 1981, 104–109; and Mkhas grub rje, *Rgyud sde spyi'i rnam gzhag*; Tibetan and English translation in Lessing and Wayman 1968, 158–161.

1637. Reading *gi* for *gis* in our text.

1638. See Tsong kha pa, *Sngags rim chen mo*, chap. 1, 11; English translation in Hopkins 1977, 99.

1639. *Bsam gtan gyi phyi ma rim par phye ba, Dhyānottarapaṭalakrama*, Tōh 808, 224b1. This is the fourth among the four main bya ba'i rgyud, kriyā tantras. D has *nang nas* for *nang gnas*; *yan lag ldan* for *yang dag ldan*; and *rtsol ba'ang* for *rtsol ba* in our text. This passage is cited in Tsong kha pa, *Sngags rim chen mo*, chap. 2, 98, in the section on kriyā tantras; for an English translation, see Hopkins 1981, 156. The text of the *Sngags rim chen mo* is identical to that of the Stog, except for having *rtsol ba for rtsol ba'ang*.

extensively taught,[1640] during the concentration entitled "abiding in fire,"[1641] meditate on fire in conjunction with wind yoga,[1642] which is a meditation on *prāṇāyāma*.[1643]

Through this meditation perfect bliss and warmth arise,[1644] bringing bliss, clarity, and nonconceptuality to the mind abiding in nonconceptuality. Nevertheless, although remarkable, this does not mean that the experience of the unexcelled tantra is also found in kriyā and caryā tantras. The wisdom of bliss and emptiness, whereby the bliss of melting and emptiness are unified, certainly occurs at some point in the creation stage of the unexcelled tantra. However, in none of these cases can the meaning of the completion stage of the unexcelled tantra be found. You must understand and thoroughly discern the differences between these stages.

The glorious Ārya Nāgārjuna makes clear that at all points in the creation stage you should practice the illusion-like appearances pervaded by emptiness, as he teaches in the *Five Stages*: [38b] "Yogis should continuously carry out all activities: applying mantras and mudrās, visualizing the maṇḍalas, fire offerings, tormas, and so forth, as illusion. Every sort of activity: pacifying, increasing, overpowering and subjugating, summoning, and so forth, should be like Indra's bow [rainbow]. Yogis should enjoy sensual pleasure, singing, music, and so forth and other forms of play, like the moon that is reflected in water. They should regard the encounter of the eyes and other senses, with forms, sounds, scents, tastes, and the objects of touch, as illusion-like. But why

1640. See Tsong kha pa, *Sngags rim chen mo*, chap. 2, 82; English translation in Hopkins 1981, 113; and chap. 2, 100; Hopkins 1981, 158. Whereas in the highest yoga the practitioners meditate on wind yoga only after they have stabilized their meditation on deity yoga, in kriyā tantra they should practice wind yoga and meditate on the deity simultaneously.

1641. The practice of the kriyā tantra includes mantra repetitions followed by three concentrations without mantra repetition. The concentration of "abiding in fire" is the first of these three.

1642. Tib. *rlung sbyor*.

1643. Tib. *srog rtsol*.

1644. This is an internal sign for completing the concentration of abiding in fire, which arises by visualizing the fire and practicing wind yoga. See Tsong kha pa, *Sngags rim chen mo*, chap. 2, 100; English translation in Hopkins 1981, 158; Lessing and Wayman 1968, 196–197.

explain so much when the Vajrayāna teaches that in actuality whatever the yogi focuses on should be conceived of as only illusion?"[1645]

[Tantric Vows and the View of Emptiness]

It is taught that disciples of the Pāramitā Vehicle endowed with sharp faculties must first attain a thorough understanding of the suchness of phenomena and arrive at a true realization; only then will they generate the mind for awakening. Therefore, as long as they have not attained a thorough understanding of emptiness, they will not generate the mind for awakening. Within the Mahāyāna, disciples who devote themselves to the Mantra Vehicle are endowed with faculties sharper even than those of disciples of the Pāramitā Vehicle. If, after empowerment of the unexcelled tantra, they do not seek the view of selflessness of phenomena, or having found it, do not practice it continuously, they will meet with the eleventh[1646] of the fourteen root downfalls that [Aśvaghoṣa] taught: "The eleventh is the conceptualization of phenomena without names and so forth."[1647] Hence the claim that YOU need not med-

1645. *Pañcakrama*, *Rim lnga*, chap. 3, vv. 29–33, Tōh 1802, 53a2–5; Sanskrit and Tibetan in Mimaki and Tomabechi 1994, 35–36; Sanskrit and French translation in Tomabechi 2006, 160–161. Mimaki and Tomabechi 1994 has *sbyin sreg gtor ma la sogs kun* for *sbyin sreg gtor ma'i bya ba kun*; *sgeg dang nye bar longs spyod dang* for *sgeg sogs nye bar spyod pa*; *chu zla dag dang mtshungs par bya* for *chu zla bzhin du rab tu bya*; *mig la sogs pa 'jug 'gyur ba* for *mig la sogs pa rab 'jug pa*; and in the last verse, *rdo rje theg pa de nyid du / 'dir ni mang du bshad ci dgos / rnal 'byor pas ni gang gang dmigs / de de sgyu ma bzhin du brtag /* for *'dir na mang du bshad ci dgos / rdo rje theg par rnal 'byor pas / de nyid gang gang dmigs bya ba / de de sgyu ma kho nar gsungs /*. Mkhas grub rje's text is very similar to that of Tsong kha pa's *Sngags rim chen mo*, chap. 12, 489.

1646. Tsong kha pa's *Sngags rim chen mo*, chap. 12, 490, which Mkhas grub rje follows here, has *rtsa ltug bcu bzhi pa las* for *rtsa ltug bcu gcig pa las* in our text.

1647. See Aśvaghoṣa, *Rdo rje theg pa rtsa ba'i ltung ba bsdus pa*, *Vajrayānamūlāpattisaṃgraha*, Tōh 2478, 179b2; Lévi 1929, 266, v. 7cd, though unfortunately part of the line is missing. Still, the wording in translation of this work is different from that in our text because it is the commentary that is cited here, see *Mañjuśrīkīrti, *Rdo rje theg pa'i rtsa ba'i ltung ba'i rgya cher bshad pa*, *Vajrayānamūlāpattiṭīkā*, Tōh 2488, 216b1. For Tsong kha pa's explanation, see his *Dngos grub snye ma*, 46a2–48a4; English translation in Sparham 2005, 104–107. Our text follows Tsong kha pa's *Sngags rim chen po*, chap. 12, 490. Nameless phenomena are explained as empty of own-being. In his *Dngos grub snye ma*, Tsong kha pa explains that the ninth downfall occurs through a denial of the teaching on emptiness, while the eleventh downfall, mentioned here, occurs when a yogi who has attained the view of emptiness—the selflessness of phenomena—fails to practice it continuously. See his *Dngos grub snye ma*, 47a6–b1; English translation in Sparham 2005, 106.

itate on emptiness during the creation stage is out of place here and creates bondage to mistaken thinking.

The Method of Meditating on the Ground of Wisdom[1648]

[39a] I have already explained in a general way how to meditate on the union of the circle of deities and emptiness during other phases of the creation stage, and I will repeat this again below. But now I will explain how to meditate on emptiness in the context of the meditation on the ground of wisdom.[1649]

[Meditation on the Four-Line Verse Beginning with "In the Absence of Being"]

Ārya Nāgārjuna and his disciples maintain[1650] that you should recite the verse on the mind of awakening, as taught by Great Vajradhara in the second chapter of the *Guhyasamāja Tantra*, and meditate on its meaning.[1651] [The *Illuminating Lamp* explains this verse in] the four levels of interpretation,[1652] two of them, the hidden and ultimate levels of interpretation, are not applicable in this context.[1653] The meditation here is on the literal and shared levels of interpretation, so it is necessary to explain these two.

First, at the literal level of interpretation, the meaning of the four-line verse beginning with *in the absence of being, there is no meditation*,[1654] is this: If, while using reason to examine *being* in the animate and inanimate realms, you fail to find anything, and take this to mean that *there are no* animate and inanimate

1648. This explanation partly follows Tsong kha pa's *Rnam gzhag rim pa'i rnam bshad*, 8b6–9b1, and the *Sgron gsal mchan*, 90b2–93b6.

1649. Tib. *ye shes kyi sa*, Skt. *jñānabhūmi*.

1650. See [33a5–6] above, Nāgārjuna teaches this in his *Mdor byas*, *Piṇḍikrama Sādhana*, Tōh 1796, 2b4; L 17; T 16; Candrakīrti in his *Rdo rje sems dpa'i sgrub thabs*, *Vajrasattva Sādhana*, Tōh 1814, 197b4; Luo and Tomabechi 2009, 9.6–7 and 41.8–11.

1651. This is the four-line verse, which begins with "In the absence of being, there is no meditation," found in the *Guhyasamāja Tantra*, chap. 2, Tōh 442, Zhol 6a2; Stog 9a5–6; Dunh 8b4; Fremantle 1971, v. 3; and Matsunaga 1978, v. 3.

1652. Tib. *tshul bzhi*, the literal, shared, hidden, and ultimate levels of interpretation. See above [33b].

1653. Candrakīrti, *Sgron gsal*, *Pradīpoddyotanaṭīkā*, Tōh 1785, 23b7–24b4; Chakravarti 1984, 31–32.

1654. The complete verse is found on [33a] above.

realms, your meditation will be devoid of meditation on suchness.[1655] In other words, this *is not a meditation*, for inasmuch as the meditator, the object of the meditation, and so forth are wholly nonexistent, there can be no meditation on suchness.

The yogi, observing that in the absence of intrinsic existence neither action nor actor are possible—and thus holding that there is some degree of intrinsic existence that can *be meditated upon*—does *not meditate* on suchness.[1656] This is so because it would be senseless for action and actor to have intrinsic existence, as the *Root of Wisdom* teaches: "If the path had intrinsic existence, meditation would be impossible."[1657]

Therefore there is no common basis for *a state* wholly *devoid of being* and the intrinsic existence of *being*,[1658] nor is there a third possibility that is neither of the two; [39b] *leaving* us with *no* intrinsically existing meditator, meditation, or *object for meditation*.[1659] This explanation at the literal level clarifies the wording of the tantra to an extent conveyed by the power of the words themselves.[1660]

Second, the shared level of interpretation:[1661] It is possible to classify embodied beings in many segments, including directions such as upper and lower; to classify their sense cognitions into time segment [earlier, later, and during], and to classify uncompounded phenomena in relation to other objects and times. If these segments and wholes exist in reality, then in reality they are either singular or plural. If singular in reality, they should in reality be entirely identical and without any differences, but if plural in reality, then their segments and wholes should be completely separated with no connection

1655. This is an explanation of the first line, *dngos po med pas sgom pa med*: "In the absence of being, there is no meditation." The explanation here partly follows Tsong kha pa's *Sgron gsal mchan*, 90b2–91a4, which comments on Candrakīrti's *Sgron gsal, Pradīpoddyotanaṭīkā*, Tōh 1785, 24a2–3, but is not identical to it.

1656. This is an explanation of the second line, *bsgom par bya ba bsgom pa min*: "Meditation cannot be meditated upon."

1657. Nāgārjuna, *Rtsa she*, Mūlamadhyamakakārikā, chap. 24, v. 24ab, Tōh 3824, 15b2; Sanskrit and English translation in Siderits and Katsura 2013, 280–281; English translation in Garfield 1995, 309. These lines are also cited by Tsong kha pa in his *Sgron gsal mchan*, 90b5.

1658. This is an explanation of the third line, *de ltar dngos po dngos med pas*: "therefore, a state of being that is nonbeing."

1659. This is an explanation of the fourth line, *sgom pa dmigs su med pa'o*: "leaves no object for meditation."

1660. This is the literal level of interpretation.

1661. This partly follows Tsong kha pa's *Sgron gsal mchan*, 91a4–b6, which comments on the *Sgron gsal*, Tōh 1785, 24a2–6, Chakravarti 1984, 31.

between them. By means of this reasoning, you should eliminate real existence from all phenomena.[1662]

Now, if you maintain that emptiness notwithstanding, compounded and uncompounded phenomena are empty of real existence, but that this very emptiness—the *absence* of real existing *being*[1663]—really exists, you will *not meditate* on suchness either.[1664] This is so because clinging to emptiness as existing in reality is "an unremedied view,"[1665] for the *Illuminating Lamp* explains: "After eliminating all phenomena by sorting them into upper and lower and so forth, *there is no meditation* even on the view: 'compounded and uncompounded phenomena are empty,' because such a view clings to emptiness."[1666] This explains the door of liberation of *emptiness.*

Meditating on the object *to be meditated upon* with the view that cause and effect exist in reality even to the slightest extent is likewise *not a meditation* on suchness,[1667] because by means of the reasoning that refutes arising from the four extremes,[1668] [40a] we understand that neither the creation nor the creator exist in realty. This explains [the door of liberation of] *signlessness. Therefore* a fruitional *state of being* that is wished-for *does not* exist in reality but only as a mere mental imputation.[1669] This is so because no wish, wisher, and so forth really exist in any way, and this is the explanation of the door of liberation of

1662. This is an explanation of the first half of the first line: "In the absence of being."

1663. In his *Sgron gsal mchan*, 91a6, Tsong kha pa has: *de rnams bden pas stong pa'i stong pa* for *bden pa'i dngos po med pa'i stong nyid* in Mkhas grub rje's work. Tsong kha pa's words here may be translated as: "the emptiness, of which they [all phenomena] are truly empty, truly exists."

1664. This is an explanation of the second half of the first line: "there is no meditation."

1665. This alludes to Nāgārjuna's line: "The victorious ones taught that it is through emptiness that all points of view are remedied. But those who adhere to emptiness as a view remain unremedied." *Rtsa she, Mūlamadhyamakakārikā*, chap. 13, v. 8, Tōh 3824, 8a6–7; Sanskrit and English translation in Siderits and Katsura 2013, 145; English translation in Garfield 1995, 212.

1666. Candrakīrti, *Sgron gsal, Pradīpoddyotanaṭīkā*, Tōh 1785, 24a3–4; Chakravarti 1984, 31.

1667. This is an explanation of the second line: *bsgom par bya ba bsgom pa min*, "meditation cannot be meditated upon," here in the shared level of interpretation.

1668. The four extremes of intrinsic existence are arising from itself, from another, from both, and without cause. See Siderits and Katsura 2013, 18.

1669. This is an explanation of the third line: *de ltar dngos po dngos med pas*, "therefore, a state of being that is nonbeing," here in the shared level of interpretation.

wishlessness that *leaves no* intrinsically existing non-merely-imputed *object for meditation.*[1670]

Such explanations are classified as "the shared level of interpretation" because this view of emptiness is shared by the Mantra and Pāramitā Vehicles. Moreover, within the Mantra Vehicle itself this view of emptiness is shared by the four classes of tantra, and the creation and completion stages of the unexcelled mantra.

Therefore you should first thoroughly understand this meaning of meditation on emptiness, and nourish your certainty in the present context with all your might. Since the animate and inanimate realms *lack* any real essence, you should meditate on the meaning of emptiness, signlessness, and wishlessness, which *leave no object for meditation*, no meditation, and no meditator. In the present context Vaidyapāda and Phalavajra also teach that you should establish emptiness by reasoning about the absence of singularity and plurality and then by meditating on it.[1671]

[Meditation on the Mantra **oṃ śūnyatā jñāna vajra svabhāva ātmako 'haṃ***]*

Numerous other tantras and works of mahāsiddhas teach that while meditating on emptiness in the present context, you should recite and reflect on the meaning of the mantra śūnyatā.[1672] If you comprehend the meaning of this mantra, a special understanding will arise in your mind about the meditations on emptiness throughout the creation stage, including the meditation on emptiness prior to the generation of the celestial mansion, and the meditation on emptiness during the dissolution of the specially visualized deities into clear light later on in the sādhana. [40b] This mantra (*oṃ śūnyatā*) is taught also in

1670. This is an explanation of the fourth line: *bsgom pa dmigs su med pa'o*, "leaves no object for meditation."

1671. Vaidyapāda, *Yan lag bzhi pa'i sgrub thabs kun tu bzang mo'i rnam par bshad pa, Caturaṅga Sādhana Samantabhadriṭīkā*, Tōh 1872, 138a1–b6. See also Tsongkhapa's *Sngags rim chen mo*, chap. 12, 498. Phalavajra, *Kun tu bzang po'i sgrub pa'i thabs kyi 'grel pa, Samantabhadra Sādhana Vṛtti*, Tōh 1867, 146b4–5.

1672. This is in contrast to the meditation on the verse that begins with "in the absence of being" in the context of the meditation on the ground of wisdom. A meditation on the meaning of the mantra śūnyatā will occur during the dissolution of the specially visualized deities into clear light later on in the sādhana.

the *Guhyasamāja Tantra* itself for meditating on emptiness when the specially visualized deities dissolve into clear light.[1673]

Here is the meaning of the mantra *oṃ śūnyatā jñāna vajra svabhāva ātmako 'haṃ*:[1674] *Oṃ* has already been explained, *śūnya* is empty, *tā* is -ness, *jñāna* is wisdom, *vajra* is *dorje*. The word "vajra" has many usages: it can mean incurable, indivisible, overcoming [opposing forces] and so forth, but here it means indivisible. *Oṃ śūnyatā jñāna vajra* thus means: objective emptiness and subjective wisdom are indivisible, like water poured into water, unobstructed by even the slightest dualistic appearance. *Svabhāva* is own nature; pure by nature is explained as being free of distinctions between the times of the cause and the fruit.[1675] *Ātmaka* is consisting, *ahaṃ* is I, *-ko haṃ* bridges over when the *a* [of *ahaṃ*] is latent. When *-ko haṃ* is separated, it turns into *-ka ahaṃ*. You should understand this in all similar cases. To summarize the meaning of the mantra: the indivisible nature of emptiness—pure by nature—and wisdom—its subject, that am I.

[How to Meditate on Emptiness Here?]

Therefore the method of meditation on emptiness in the present context is considerably different from the method of meditation on emptiness in the Pāramitā Vehicle. In the Pāramitā Vehicle you must first analyze through reason, and when you have reached an understanding of emptiness, you meditate on this understanding, without laxity, excitement, and so forth. While here in the creation stage, if you are endowed with intelligence, you analyze thoroughly using your reason, and if endowed with lesser intelligence, you determine that no phenomena truly exist to any extent on the basis of the teachings of lamas. You cultivate a sound understanding of this over a period of time, and then you meditate not only mainly on emptiness but as explained in relation to the meaning of the mantra, [41a] maintaining as you certainly must a divine identity with the resolve: The nature of the

1673. In Tsong kha pa, *Gsang mngon*, at this point of the practice, meditators do not recite this mantra, but rather the verse from the second chapter of the *Guhyasamāja Tantra* beginning with "In the absence of being." But later in the practice, during the meditation on the dissolution of the specially visualized deities, yogis do recite this mantra while meditating on emptiness. The mantra appears in the *Guhyasamāja Tantra*, Tōh 442, at the beginning of chap. 3, Zhol 6b6; Stog 10b4–5; Dunh 9b1–2; Fremantle 1971 before v. 1; and Matsunaga 1978 before v. 1.

1674. Here Mkhas grub rje follows Tsong kha pa's *Sgron gsal mchan*, 98b3–6.

1675. Tsong kha pa's *Sgron gsal mchan*, 98b4, followed here has *dus gnyis kar* for *dus gnyis ka'i tshe* in our text.

dharmakāya—which is indivisible objective emptiness and subjective wisdom of great bliss—that am I.

So that the practice of taking the aspect of the rūpakāya on the path will be complete in all characteristics, you must take the aspect of the dharmakāya on the path. There are several reasons for this: (1) because from now on you have to cultivate a path that accords in aspect with the rūpakāya and maintain divine identity with the rūpakāya, you will need to do so with regard to the dharmakāya as well; there is no difference here; (2) because it is very clear from the meaning of the mantra that you must do so; (3) because otherwise, since the practice of taking the aspect of the dharmakāya on the path during the creation stage will not be complete, the ripening for the completion stage will not be complete; and (4) the practice of taking the aspect of the rūpakāya on the path will not be complete in all characteristics. I will explain this in the coming section with supporting scriptural sources.

At the stage of buddhahood, emptiness and wisdom are actually paired like water poured into water, but at this stage you should meditate by imagining the essence of the wisdom of your mind and objective pure emptiness in one taste, unobstructed by even the slightest dualistic appearance. Furthermore, you should know that there is no distinction between the emptiness meditated upon in the Pāramitā Vehicle and the emptiness meditated upon in the creation and completion stages, but there are a great many special differences between these two vehicles in terms of the method for maintaining the object perceived in the meditation, the subjective mind that meditates, and so forth.

In the case of the Mantra Vehicle, when you engage in this mode of meditation on emptiness, even though dualistic appearances have not been eliminated insofar as the level of appearances[1676] is concerned, at the level of apprehension,[1677] coarse dualistic appearances are eliminated. Therefore, even if you do not retain the visualization of the animate and inanimate realms in dissolution, that is fine. But when you purposely direct your concentration to the process of dissolution in order to eliminate the dualistic appearances at the level of your mind, Ārya Nāgārjuna and his disciples explain that in this context the animate and inanimate realms are dissolved into clear light. [41b] Hence, visualize the animate and inanimate realms turning into a mass of

1676. Tib. *snang ngor*.

1677. Tib. *nges ngor*.

light in the manner of "centripetal dissolution" and "twin dissolutions,"[1678] and everything will gradually fade away and disappear.[1679] Then in this state recollect the view of emptiness, maintain divine identity with the dharmakāya, and meditate in this way for as long as possible. This is the transmitted instruction of the holy lama, and it is very crucial.

The purpose of practicing in this way is to facilitate the elimination of coarse dualistic appearances on the level of apprehension and so forth. Hence you imagine that the animate and inanimate realms do not arise in your own mind, but at the same time you do not meditate on them as turning into nothing at all. Thus this visualization is different in every respect from the meditation [of SOME PEOPLE of inferior intelligence][1680] on the animate and inanimate realms turning into nothing at all. Therefore, if you fear that your meditation will turn into a reflection on nihilistic emptiness, your intellect is extremely coarse. The distinction between *not arising in your mind* and *nothing at all* is enormous and your fear is totally unreasonable.

The Purpose of Meditating on Emptiness at This Point of the Sādhana

[For What Purpose Do You Meditate on Emptiness before You Visualize the Celestial Mansion?]

In his commentary on Lūyīpāda's *Cakrasaṃvara Sādhana*,[1681] Atiśa said: "Recite three times the two forms of the mantra[1682] so that you will: (1) gain the ability to realize emptiness, (2) restore your recollection of emptiness, (3) stabilize your concentration, (4) complete the accumulation of wisdom, (5) shed conceptualization of your ordinary body, speech, and mind, and (6) realize that the maṇḍala of the celestial mansion and its deities in their entirety are

1678. Tib. *ril 'dzin* and *rjes gzhig*, Skt. *piṇḍagrāha* and *anubheda*. Nāgārjuna explains *ril 'dzin* as a withdrawal from the head and the feet to the heart, and *rjes gzhig* as dissolution of both the animate and inanimate worlds into clear light.

See his *Rim lnga, Pañcakrama*, chap. 4, vv. 25–28, Tōh 1802, 55a1–2; Sanskrit and Tibetan in Mimaki and Tomabechi 1994, 45–46; Sanskrit and French translation in Tomabechi 2006, 171.

1679. Reading *mi snang bar* for *mi sdang bar* in our text.

1680. See the beginning of this discussion on [32a] above.

1681. Lūyīpāda, *Bcom ldan 'das mngon par rtogs pa, Bhagavadabhisamaya*, Tōh 1427; Sakurai 1998 and *Dhīḥ* 2008.

1682. The mantras: *oṃ śūnyatā jñāna vajra svabhāva ātmako 'ham* and *oṃ svabhāva śuddhāḥ sarvadharmāḥ svabhāva śuddho 'ham*. Both are listed by Lūyīpāda in his *Bcom ldan 'das mngon par rtogs pa, Bhagavadabhisamaya*, Tōh 1427, 187a4–5; Sakurai 1998, 4.

emanations of emptiness."[1683] The short commentary by the great translator Rinchen Sangpo explains: The first purpose pertains to practitioners with dull faculties who will become capable of realizing emptiness through the power of the mantra. The second purpose pertains to practitioners with middling faculties who will become capable of restoring their forgotten recollection of emptiness.[1684] And the remaining four purposes pertain to practitioners with sharp faculties.[1685] [42a]

Regarding the fifth purpose listed by Atiśa, for transforming the grounds of the meditation into special supreme appearance—such as transforming the body, resources, environment, and so forth that are the grounds for the meditation on the deities, the celestial mansion, and so forth—their appearance as being ordinary must cease.[1686] This is so because your cognition cannot take in at the same time the double appearance of a single object [one pure and the other ordinary].[1687] Therefore you must prevent the ordinary appearance from arising in your cognition. Still, you cannot stop ordinary appearances by meditating on them as mere nothingness. Rather, when you withdraw the cognition that engages with the conventional world of ordinary appearances and set your mind on emptiness—the ultimate truth—ordinary appearances cease to arise within the sphere of your cognition. This is one of the reasons for meditating on emptiness. You should understand the distinction between preventing ordinary appearances from arising within the sphere of cognition and actually ceasing their existence.

1683. Dīpaṅkaraśrījñāna, *Mngon par rtogs pa rnam par 'byed pa, Abhisamayavibhaṅga*, Tōh 1490, 189b1–2. D has *lus ngag yid gsum spong ba* for *lus ngag yid gsum gyi rtog pa spong ba* and *stong pa nyid kyi rnam 'phrul du* for *stong pa'i rnam 'phrul du* in our text which follows Tsong kha pa's commentary on Lūyīpāda's sādhana, *'Dod 'jo*, 52a2–5. See also his *Bung ba'i re skong*, 11b3–4.

1684. While our text has *brjod pa*, other prints as well as the works of Tsong kha pa mentioned above have *brjed* for *brjod* in our text. Yet Kano's edition of Rin chen bzang po's commentary has *brjed pa*, which could be translated as "will be able to restore their recollection of reciting [and meditating on] emptiness."

1685. Rin chen bzang po, *Mngon par rtogs pa'i dka' ba'i gnas bshad pa*, 4a6–7, edited by Kano 2014, 16. Kano has *gso ba* for *gso nus pa*, and omits *dang po ni, gnyis pa ni 'bring pos*, but has *'bring gis* later on. According to Rin chen bzang po, the first two purposes are for practitioners possessing dull faculties, the second two purposes for practitioners possessing sharp faculties, and the last two for middling faculties. But Mkhas grub rje follows Tsong kha pa's works, the *'Dod 'jo* and the *Bung ba'i re skong*, mentioned in a previous note.

1686. This follows Tsong kha pa, *'Dod 'jo*, 52b1–2.

1687. Tsong kha pa's *'Dod 'jo*, 52b2 has *de gnyis* for *snang ba de* in our text. And Nor bzang rgya mtsho, *Gsang ba 'dus pa'i bskyed rim gyi don gsal bar byed pa'i sgron me*, 38a3–4, has *dag pa'i snang ba dang tha mal gyi snang ba gnyis* for *snang ba de* in our text.

One of the main reasons for meditating on emptiness here, as taught by the sixth purpose listed by Atiśa, is that in all subsequent meditations on the circle of deities, the appearance aspect will arise as a manifestation of emptiness.[1688] For example, when you abide in a prolonged equipoise on the nature of things and then rise from it into a post-meditative state, then, through the power of your meditative equipoise, the diversity of phenomena will appear to your pure, post-meditative, worldly-wisdom subjective mind as illusion-like—appearing yet devoid of intrinsic nature. Likewise, here, too, first you meditate on emptiness, and immediately afterward you visualize the circle of deities. So long as the impact of your equipoise on emptiness remains undiminished in your cognition, everything will arise as an illusion-like circle of deities—which, although they appear, are devoid of intrinsic nature. It is for this reason that you should meditate on emptiness now.

This is also the point made in the *Hevajra Sādhana Eliminating Bewilderment.*[1689] The absence of appearances you experience when you have dissolved yourself in emptiness is described in this sādhana as nonconceptual wisdom; and the subsequent appearance of the protection wheel that you visualize instantaneously is explained as pure worldly wisdom.[1690] [42b]

[Further Crucial Points on the Meditation on Emptiness]

There is yet another important reason for the meditation on emptiness. The maṇḍala wheels of the rūpakāyas of the Buddha with celestial mansions and deities, such as maṇḍalas of the saṃbhogakāyas of the Buddha, are the wisdom of the dharmakāya that arise in the appearance of the rūpakāyas—propelled[1691] by prior aspirations and the cultivation of the mind-for-enlightenment for the sake of the disciples. Yet just like the present ordinary body and mind, the Buddha's body and wisdom are not distinct in nature.

Therefore, here in the Mantra Vehicle you should take the fruit in the path by meditating on yourself, beginning in the present moment, in the state of the Buddha. For this reason, the Mantra Vehicle is called the fruit-vehicle. Therefore, in this context as well, when you meditate on emptiness, you should

1688. See Tsong kha pa, *'Dod 'jo*, 52b2–4.

1689. Ratnākaraśānti, *'Khrul pa spong zhes bya ba'i sgrub pa'i thabs*, *Bhramaharahevajra Sādhana*, Toh 1245, 190a4; Isaacson 2002, 159. Ratnākaraśānti has here a longer expression: *dam pa'i byang chub kyi sems 'jig rten las 'das pa stong pa nyid kyi ye shes spros dang bral zhing rnam par rtog pa dang bral.*

1690. Tib. *dag pa 'jigs rten pa'i ye she*, Skt. *śuddhalaukikajñana.*

1691. Reading *'phen pa* for *phan pa* in our text.

maintain a divine identity of the dharmakāya—indivisible emptiness and wisdom. Then, from within the continuing state of the dharmakāya, you should arise in the appearance of the maṇḍala of the rūpakāya—with its celestial mansion and deities—through the power of recollecting your wishing prayer to act for the sake of the disciples. You do so by visualizing the objective aspect of the wisdom of the dharmakāya arising as the maṇḍala of the celestial mansion and its deities.

The mahāsiddha Saroruha teaches this as well: In meditating on emptiness "you should visualize yourself and the three realms as devoid of essence. Then, by recollecting your previous wishing prayer, from a *Raṃ*[1692] a solar disk will arise in space, at its center there is...,"[1693] and so forth. And Ḍombiheruka teaches: "The yogis should recollect their wishing prayers, made prior to the meditation on emptiness of intrinsic nature."[1694] The master Vajraghaṇṭa also explains it in this way.[1695]

Without understanding this, your meditation on the path that corresponds in its aspect to the rūpakāya, your practice of taking the fruit in the path and so forth, will not be complete in all essential characteristics. [43a] It is very important that throughout your meditation on the sādhana, the celestial mansion and its deities should not be distinct in nature, like the celestial gods and their environment at present; and also that you should be free of the attitude that the principal and surrounding deities—just like the ordinary principal with its surrounding deities in the present—have a separate mental continuum and possess a different nature. If you do not meditate on the singular wisdom of the dharmakāya whose objective aspect arises as the maṇḍala of the celestial mansion and its deities, there will be no basis for it to arise.

Many of the sādhanas of Cakrasaṃvara, Hevajra, and so forth, as well as

1692. D has *Raṃ* for *ri* in our text.

1693. Saroruha, *Dgyes pa rdo rje'i sgrub thabs*, *Hevajra Sādhana*, Tōh 1218, 2b5–6; *Dhīḥ* 2003, 134; Sanskrit, Tibetan, and English translation in Gerloff 2017, 99, 119 and 134. Part of this phrase was cited on [33b5] above. D has *bdag khams gsum po* for *bdag dang khams gsum po dag* in our text. Again, note that the Sanskrit equivalent of *ngo bo nyid* is *nirābhāsa*. This passage is referred to also in Tsong kha pa, *Sngags rim chen mo*, chap. 12, 500.

1694. Ḍombiheruka, *Bdag med ma rnal 'byor ma'i sgrub thabs*, *Nairātmyāyoginī Sādhana*, Tōh 1306a, 213a4. D has *bsgoms* for *bsgom* in our text. These lines are cited also in Tsong kha pa, *Sngags rim chen mo*, chap. 12, 500, which has *sgom* for *bsgom* in our text.

1695. In his *Sngags rim chen mo*, chap. 12, 500, Tsong kha pa specifies that Vajraghaṇṭa explained this in his *Kyai rdor kyi sgrub thabs*, also called *Dpa' bo gcig pa'i sgrub pa'i thabs*, *Ekavīra Sādhana*, Tōh 1226, 30a4.

Ratnākaraśānti's *Sādhana of Black Yamāri*,[1696] the *Cluster of Instructions*,[1697] and so forth, teach that the accumulation of merit consists of making offerings to the assembly-field, the keeping of vows and so forth, while the accumulation of wisdom is the meditation on emptiness here. These works are written mainly from the point of view that takes the gathering-of-the-two-accumulations at the beginning of the sādhana as a yoga that is the cause for generating the principal deity in accordance with the cause of birth at the ground stage. In this case, the offerings to the field for accumulating merit are applied in correspondence with the karma of past lives, and the meditation on emptiness, with the previous death.

But here in the context of the Guhyasamāja, by meditating on the generation of the four elements and the celestial mansion in correspondence with the evolution of the world, the world is purified [in one's mind], while the meditation on the ground of wisdom corresponds to the destruction of the former world, prior to the new evolution. This is so because as *Formulating the Sādhana* teaches: "When our world is destroyed [seven suns in succession], burn up the three realms and turn them into the nature of space. In accordance with this, the meditator on the creation stage should recite and meditate on the verse that begins with 'in the absence of being.'"[1698]

The absence of the world's appearance when the previous world has been destroyed [43b] and the absence of the world's appearance to the subjective mind that meditates on emptiness here are applied in correspondence.[1699] This does not mean, however, that you should meditate on the world turning into nothing at all here as happens when the world is destroyed. Additionally, as the *Vajrasattva Sādhana* teaches: "This is the ultimate protection."[1700] Many

1696. Ratnākaraśānti, *Gshin rje'i dgra nag po'i sgrub pa'i thabs ku mu da kha bye ba*, *Kṛṣṇayamāri Sādhana Protphullakumudā*, Tōh 1935, 59a3.

1697. Abhayākaragupta, *Man ngag snye ma*, Tōh 1198, passim. These two works are referred to also in the *Sngags rim chen mo*, chap. 12, 497 and 500.

1698. Nāgabuddhi, *Rnam gzhag rim pa*, *Vyavastholi*, chap. 1, Tōh 1809, 121b4–5; Tanaka 2016, 80–81. D and Tanaka have *khams gsum pa* for *khams gsum po thams cad*; *sgom pa pos* for *bsgom pas kyang*; *dngos po med la* for *dngos po med pa*; and *bsam par bya'o* for *bsgom par bya'o* in our text.

1699. See Tsong kha pa, *Bung ba'i re skong*, 11a4–6.

1700. Candrakīrti, *Rdo rje sems dpa'i sgrub thabs*, *Vajrasattva Sādhana*, Tōh 1814, 197b5; Luo and Tomabechi 2009, 9.8 and 41.12. D and Luo and Tomabechi have *srung ba* for *bsrung ba* in our text.

other scriptures explain it in this way;[1701] thus, the meditation on emptiness is most excellent for averting obstructions as well.

Why is the meditation on emptiness in this way called meditation on the ground of wisdom? As Abhayākaragupta explained: "*Wisdom* is great bliss,"[1702] and the *ground* is the *foundation*, the source of phenomena. When you are absorbed in meditative equipoise on the meaning of the indivisible unity of *wisdom* of great bliss and emptiness, the cessation of all appearances of the animate and inanimate realms in your mind is called *ground*. For just as during the evolution of the world, space is the *foundation* out of which the maṇḍalas of the elements, beginning with the wind maṇḍala, are successively formed, so in close correspondence, the meditation on emptiness constitutes the *foundation* for the celestial mansion in the sādhana. The Sanskrit equivalent of "ground" [*sa* in Tibetan] is *bhūmi*, whose etymology means *ground*, because it is *foundation*.

The explanation of the meditation on the ground of wisdom is complete.

1701. See Tsong kha pa, *Sngags rim chen mo*, chap. 12, 500, which cites Kamalarakṣita on this point.

1702. This is a paraphrase of Abhayākaragupta's commentary on Nāgārjuna's *Mdor byas* and *Rim pa lnga pa*, entitled *Rim pa lnga pa'i dgongs 'grel zla ba'i 'od zer, Pañcakramamatiṭīkā Candraprabhā*, Tōh 1831, 193a1–194a6.

5. Meditation on the Celestial Mansion

Visualization of the Vajra Ground and Meditation on the Celestial Mansion in Correspondence with the Evolution of the Subsequent World

There are two sections here: (1) generating the vajra ground, and (2) meditating on the celestial mansion.

Generating the Vajra Ground

[Visualizing the Protection Wheel]

The works of Ārya Nāgārjuna and his disciples, such as the *Concise Sādhana*, do not make amply clear that at this point, upon arising from emptiness, you should visualize the protection wheel. On this account, the vast majority of EARLY TIBETAN LAMAS[1703] generate the four elements from the continuing state while rising from emptiness without visualizing the protection wheel. [44a]

To do so is inappropriate for the following reasons. The purpose of meditating on the protection wheel during the preliminaries is to safeguard against obstructions during the practice of the main part of the sādhana. There are two types of protection: the conventional protection is the meditation on the protection wheel and the ultimate protection is the meditation on the ground of wisdom. Therefore, although you have dissolved the appearance of the protection wheel [the conventional protection] during the meditation on the ground of wisdom [the ultimate protection], this is not flawed in as much as you were not maintaining the purpose of protection.

1703. Ngor chen Kun dga' bzang po, *Gsang 'dus dkyil 'khor gyi sgrub thabs dngos grub rgya mtsho*, work 106, 4b4–5a2, teaches that after the meditation on emptiness you should visualize the source of phenomena and the four wheels of the physical elements. Likewise, Rang byung rdo rje does not instruct the yogi to visualize the protection wheel following the meditation on emptiness in his *Gsang ba 'dus pa'i sgrub pa'i thabs phyi nang gzhan gsum gsal ba*, 4a6.

But if, during the meditation on the main part of the sādhana, having risen from emptiness a yogi does not visualize the protection wheel, that yogi will not achieve the purpose of averting obstructions. And likewise, if a yogi does not meditate on the vajra fence during the meditation on the celestial mansion, it would be senseless for it to appear in painted maṇḍalas, and unnecessary to draw it with the fire mountain. Since this position contradicts many authoritative works and even YOU do not appear to accept it, the method is inconsistent.

Therefore you must instantly visualize the form of the protection wheel with the vajra fence and fire mountain within the continuing state of the dharmakāya. In the Ārya tradition the celestial mansion is not generated within the hub of the ten-spoked protection wheel, and therefore you do not need to visualize the ten-spoked wheel and the fierce deities. Three commentaries on Lūyīpāda's *Cakrasaṃvara Sādhana* teach: "When the visualization of the Blessed One is fully completed, the variegated vajra fence enclosing the samaya wheel is also completed."[1704] These scriptures explain that with the generation of the principal deity and the celestial mansion, you should simultaneously visualize the complete vajra fence as well. In the Ārya tradition the method is similar.

[Meditation on the "Source of Phenomena"][1705]

The *Concise Sādhana* teaches: "Abiding in the midst of the space realm,"[1706] and the *Vajrasattva Sādhana* teaches: [44b] "In the midst of the space element."[1707] Apart from these lines, the generation of the "source of phenomena" is not

1704. See Prajñārakṣita, *Mngon par rtogs pa'i dka' 'grel, Abhisamayapañjikā*, Tōh 1465, 36b2–3. D has *rdzogs pa* for *yongs su rdzogs pa*; *de'i tshe* for *de nyid kyi tshe*; *ra ba* for *phreng ba yang*; and *rdzogs pas so* for *rdzogs pa'i phyir ro* in our text. See also Tathāgatavajra, *Lū yi pa'i mngon par rtogs pa'i 'grel pa'i ṭī kā khyad par gsal byed, Lūyipādābhisamayavṛittiṭīkāviśeṣadyota*, Tōh 1510, 287b7–288a1. D has *gang gi tshe kho na* for *gang gi tshe*; *bcom ldan 'das kyi dkyil 'khor bskyed pa'i* for *bcom ldan 'das yongs su rdzogs pa*; *tshe kho nar* for *tshe*; *bcad pa'i* for *gcod pa'i*; and *bskyed pa'i phyir ro* for *rdzogs pas so* in our text. Our text follows Tsong kha pa, *'Dod 'jo*, 55a6–b1.

1705. Tib. *chos 'byung*, Skt. *dharmodaya*.

1706. Nāgārjuna, *Mdor byas, Piṇḍīkrama Sādhana*, Tōh 1796, 2b5; L 19a; T 18a. L and T have *ākāśadhātumadhyastham*.

1707. Candrakīrti, *Rdo rje sems dpa'i sgrub thabs, Vajrasattva Sādhana*, Tōh 1814, 197b5; Luo and Tomabechi 2009, 9.9 and 41.13.

explicitly taught. Taking this into account, EARLY LAMAS[1708] explain this to mean in the midst of space, the nature of which is the *dharma* realm, but do not provide additional instructions about meditating on the source of phenomena. It would be unacceptable since on this matter both the *Vajrasattva Sādhana* and the *Sādhana Incorporating the Scripture* cite the eleventh chapter of the *Guhyasamāja Tantra*: "In the midst of the space vajra, visualize..."[1709] The line "in the midst of space" is similarly taught in the third chapter of the *Guhyasamāja Tantra*: "Abiding in the midst of the space element."[1710] These passages explain where the celestial mansion must be visualized.[1711] In commenting on this line of the third chapter, the *Illuminating Lamp* clarifies: "*Abiding in the midst of the space element* means abiding at the source of phenomena."[1712]

Qualm: The scriptures explain this because the space element—the nature of which is emptiness—is synonymous with the source of phenomena; this, however, does not refer to the meditation on the source of phenomena that is triangular in shape.

Reply: Indeed, such a notion would occur to people who do not know how to apply the explanatory tantras to the *Guhyasamāja Tantra*. However, in the *Later Tantra*, where the bodhisattvas ask some fifty-three questions in order to understand the meaning concealed in the *Guhyasamāja Tantra*, they implore the tathāgata: "We implore you, O lord, to explain the tantra entitled *Guhyasamāja* taught by the preceptor of truth, since we wish to understand

1708. A myes zhabs points out that the early lamas who do not explain the source of phenomena include 'Gos and Rngog, who were learned in the tradition of the *Gsang ba 'dus pa*. See his *Gsang 'dus rnam bshad*, 87b2.

1709. *Guhyasamāja Tantra*, Tōh 442; Zhol 15a2–3 Stog 25b3; Dunh 27b5; Fremantle 1971, v. 3a; and Matsunaga 1978, v. 3a. Zhol has *rdo rje'i dbus gnas par* for *rdo rje dbus su bsam* in our text; Fremantle and Matsunaga have *khavajramadhyagataṃ cintet*. Candrakīrti, *Rdo rje sems dpa'i sgrub thabs*, *Vajrasattva Sādhana*, Tōh 1814, 197b7, Luo and Tomabechi 2009, 10.3 and 42.5. D and Luo and Tomabechi have *nam mkha'i khams kyi dbus gnas bsam* for *nam mkha' rdo rje dbus su bsam* in our text. Nāgārjuna, *Mdo bsre*, *Sādhanasūtramelāpaka*, Tōh 1797, 11b7. D has *bsgom* for *bsam* in our text.

1710. *Guhyasamāja Tantra*, Tōh 442; Zhol 6b6 and 7a6; Stog 10b5; Dunh 9b2; Fremantle 1971, v. 1; and Matsunaga 1978, v. 1. The Zhol has here *nam mkha'i dbyings kyi dbus gnas par*, while our text has: *nam mkha'i khams kyi dbus gnas par*. Fremantle and Matsunaga have *ākāśadhātumadhyasthaṃ*. The eleventh chapter of the *Guhyasamāja Tantra* is considered to be an explanation of the third chapter.

1711. Reading *ston* for *sten* in our text.

1712. Candrakīrti, *Sgron gsal*, *Pradīpoddyotanaṭīkā*, Tōh 1785, 26b6; Chakravarti 1984, 35.

its concealed meaning, and we seek the benefit of sentient beings."[1713] In that explanatory tantra,[1714] when the bodhisattvas, beginning with Maitreya, inquire about the meaning of the term "space element" in the line of the *Guhyasamāja Tantra* teaching on the visualization of the celestial mansion in the midst of the space element, the bodhisattvas ask: "How should we meditate on the 'source of phenomena?'"[1715] [45a] In reply the tathāgatas explain: "You should meditate on a triangle, because of the division into body, speech, and mind."[1716] These lines make it clear that you should meditate on a celestial mansion within this kind of a triangular shape as the source of phenomena.

Therefore the source of phenomena is an upright triangle with its tapering side pointing downward and the other two corners pointing upward.[1717] It is shaped as the birth-giving-place of the consort, and it is hollow inside. The source of phenomena standing on a point signifies that during the beginning stage, the accumulation of good qualities is minute, while the upper part that grows wider signifies that when you are ascending through the stages of the path, to "engaging through belief"[1718] and upward, the good qualities increase progressively.[1719] Likewise Ratnākaraśānti explains that the triangular shape signifies the three doors of liberation.[1720] Since the *Later Tantra* teaches "because of the division into body, speech, and mind,"[1721] it is explained that the triangle also signifies the three vajras, vajra body, vajra speech, and vajra mind.

When the *Illuminating Lamp* explains the line *abided in the* bhaga *of the*

1713. *Rgyud phyi ma, Uttara Tantra,* Tōh 443, 148b4–5; Matsunaga 1978, vv. 4c and 5. D and Zhol have *yang dag gsung bas* for *yang dag gsungs pas* and D has *gang bshad pa* for *gang gsungs pa* in our text.

1714. *Rgyud phyi ma, Uttara Tantra,* Tōh 443, is regarded as one of the explanatory tantras of the *Guhyasamāja Root Tantra.* It opens with a series of questions the bodhisattvas asked the tathāgata, which are then answered.

1715. *Rgyud phyi ma, Uttara Tantra,* Tōh 443, 149a3; Matsunaga 1978, v. 15c.

1716. *Rgyud phyi ma, Uttara Tantra,* Tōh 443, 151b7, Matsunaga 1978, v. 80cd. See also Tsong kha pa, *Bung ba'i re skong,* 12b6–13a1.

1717. See Tsong kha pa, *Sngags rim chen mo,* chap. 12, 504.

1718. Tib. *mos spyod* or *mos pas spyod pa'i sa,* Skt. *adhimukticaryābhūmi.*

1719. See Tsong kha pa's *Bung ba'i re skong,* 12b4–13a1, and *Slob tshul,* 11a2.

1720. See Tsong kha pa, *'Jam rdor sgrub thabs,* 4b3–5a1. Note that in his *Rnam bshad chu rgyun log smra'i dri ma 'khrud byed,* 53a4–b6, Mus srad pa Byams pa Rdo rje rgyal mtshan criticizes Mkhas grub rje for stating so in our text. See also Tsong kha pa, *Mtha' gcod,* 69b4.

1721. *Rgyud phyi ma, Uttara Tantra,* Tōh 443, 151b7; Matsunaga 1978, v. 80cd, cited above.

Vajra Queen at the opening of the *Guhyasamāja Tantra*[1722] in its literal and shared levels of interpretation, it clearly denotes that the source of phenomena which encompasses the celestial mansion—where Vajradhara, the teacher of the *Guhyasamāja Tantra*, resides—has the shape of the *bhaga* of the queen.[1723] Therefore you should understand clearly the importance of meditating on the source of phenomena with its triangular shape of the birth-giving-place during the meditation on the maṇḍala in the practice that follows the events in the *Guhyasamāja Tantra*.[1724]

In this regard, as the explanatory tantra of the Guhyasamāja, the *Tantra Requested by Indra* explains the meaning of *evaṃ* as: "The syllable *e* is wisdom, the syllable *va* is lord of amorous delight, and the drop [*ṃ*] is the indestructible[1725] reality. From these [all] syllables are born. The knower of suchness, who understands these two syllables [*evaṃ*] that are the dharma seal, [45b] will become a [buddha] who turns the wheel of Dharma for all sentient beings. The person who constantly recites these two syllables without understanding their meaning will be excluded from the Buddha's teachings like an ascetic who has forsaken his possessions.[1726] Since the all-knower abides in the two syllables *evaṃ*, which are illusory, *evaṃ* is uttered at the opening of sacred teachings.[1727] Therefore, O Śakra, the lord of gods, if you wish your state to endure, bear in mind that the two syllables are illusory, and let them be your guru of the sacred teachings."[1728] Several other tantras[1729] teach that the two syllables *e* and *vaṃ* subsume all the essential points that are expressed in the unexcelled

1722. *Guhyasamāja Tantra*, Tōh 442; Zhol 1b2–3; Stog 1b3–2a2; Dunh missing; Fremantle 1971, 174–175; and Matsunaga 1978, 4. The Zhol has *bzhugs* for *zhugs* in our text; "abided in," Skt. *vijahāra*.

1723. Candrakīrti, *Sgron gsal, Pradīpoddyotanaṭīkā*, Tōh 1785, 8b3–10a7; Chakravarti 1984, 12–13.

1724. See Tsong kha pa's *Sgron gsal mchan*, 33a5–b3.

1725. The Skt. here is *anāhata*, meaning unstruck.

1726. According to the Sanskrit and the Tibetan translation of Pa tshab as included and explained in Tsong kha pa's *Sgron gsal mchan*, 37b1–2, the last line could be translated as "like a rich person who has forsaken his wealth or the enjoyment of his wealth."

1727. This line is cited in Tsong kha pa's *Rim lnga gsal sgron*, 61a2–3, Kilty 2013, 115.

1728. *Lha'i dbang pos zhus pa, Devendraparipṛcchā*, cited in Candrakīrti's *Sgron gsal*, Tōh 1785, 10a1–3; Chakravarti 1984, 13; Sanskrit and English translation in Wayman 1977, 181–82; Sanskrit, Tibetan, and English translation in Issacson and Sferra 2014, 166, 206, 258–259. This tantra was not translated into Tibetan, but parts of it are cited in the *Sgron gsal* and other works; see Wayman 1977, 85, and Issacson and Sferra 2014, 166. D has *skor byed* for *bskor byed* in our text.

1729. See Tsong kha pa, *Sgron gsal mchan*, 38a4–b2.

tantras. Therefore, if you thoroughly understand the meaning of *evaṃ*, you will realize in full the meaning of the tantra.

Hence, numerous meanings are signified by the syllables *e* and *vaṃ*, and there are *e* and *vaṃ* of the ground, path, and fruit.[1730] But in the present case you should know that the syllable *e* signifies profound emptiness, and the syllable *vaṃ* signifies wisdom of great bliss that is indivisibly united with emptiness. And you should likewise understand that the wisdom that unites bliss and emptiness—the *evaṃ* of the path—is the main cause of Vajradhara. Furthermore, the three corners of the source of phenomena signify the meaning of the syllable *e*—intrinsic emptiness of the three doors of liberation—while its form as the *bhaga* of the consort signifies the meaning of *vaṃ*—wisdom [born] of great bliss.

Meditating on the maṇḍala of the celestial mansion and its deities as comprised within the source of phenomena signifies that all the good qualities of the perfections of the place, body, retinue, and resources of Vajradhara are attained through the meditation on the wisdom of bliss and emptiness. In brief, [46a] all the good qualities on the path and the fruit are miraculous emanations created by the wisdom of bliss and emptiness.[1731] Hence you should meditate on the source of phenomena in order to understand that all the good qualities of the Mantra Vehicle are comprised within it.

As the *Secret Attainment* teaches: "I resort to you, source of bliss of all beings, embodiment of supreme joy, pure, arising from the wisdom body, tranquil abode of all buddhas, divine syllable of the source of phenomena, the well-shaped *e*, adorned with *vaṃ* at its center, abode of all bliss, jeweled receptacle of the buddhas."[1732] The same scripture also teaches: "The tranquil syllable of the 'source of phenomena' is entirely an emanation of wisdom's own nature, the excellent complete wisdom, pure and free of mental elaborations, supreme and pure, worshipped by all the buddhas, inexpressible and

1730. See Tsong kha pa, *Rim lnga sgal sgron*, 44a4–46a1, and Mkhas grub rje, *Rgyud sde spyi'i rnam*, in Lessing and Wayman 1968, 332–337.

1731. See also Tsong kha pa, *Bung ba'i re skong*, 12b4–13a1.

1732. Padmavajra, *Gsang ba grub pa*, *Guhyasiddhi*, chap. 2, vv. 20cd–22, Tōh 2217, 6a7–b2; Sanskrit and Tibetan in Samdhong Rinpoche and Vrajvallabh Dwivedi 1987, 13–14 and 19. D and the Sarnath edition have *mchog tu dga' ba* for *mchog tu dka' ba*; *lus las byung* for *lus la 'byung*; *blo yis* for *sangs rgyas*; *bzang ba* for *bzang po*; and *gnas gyur bas* for *'byung gnas su* in our text, which follows, for the most part, Tsong kha pa's *'Dod 'jo*, 192b2–4.

all-pervading abode, everything is its emanation."[1733] If you meditate on the maṇḍala, make offerings, and so forth while understanding these essential points, you are much superior to someone who meditates, makes offerings, and so forth without understanding them. Hence you should understand this definitive meaning of meditating on the maṇḍala as being comprised within the source of phenomena.

Regarding the color of the source of phenomena: a large number of scriptures, including the *Maṇḍala Vajra Garland*, explain its color[1734] as white, signifying natural purity.[1735] Some scriptures explain that the color is white outside and red inside—in these cases you should know that the white and red colors of the source of phenomena in the shape of the *bhaga* signify the wisdom of great bliss that arises when the white and red elements meet in the lotus of the consort; [46b] its three corners signify the wisdom of bliss and emptiness that realizes the three doors of liberation. Both of these positions with regard to the color of the source of phenomena are acceptable.

[The Lotus and the Outline of the Celestial Mansion]

Within the source of phenomena meditated upon in this way, visualize the vajra ground at the center. SOME TIBETAN LAMAS,[1736] who hold that the works of Ārya Nāgārjuna and his disciples do not actually explain the visualization of the lotus, leave out the instructions on visualizing it. This is incongruous, because if you do not meditate on the lotus seat of the crossed vajra, it would be utterly senseless to draw a lotus in maṇḍala depictions. Hence the consequence of YOUR position is that it is wrong to paint the lotus.

Should the lotus appear in maṇḍala depictions? When Master Abhayākaragupta clarifies the meaning of the line from the *Guhyasamāja*

1733. Padmavajra, *Gsang ba grub pa*, *Guhyasiddhi*, chap. 2, vv. 17d–19, Tōh 2217, 6a6–7; Sanskrit and Tibetan in Samdhong Rinpoche and Vrajvallabh Dwivedi 1987, 13 and 18. D and the Sarnath edition have *bzang po'i* for *lha rdzas*; *rnam par 'phrul* for *rnam par sprul*; *phyag byas pa'i* for *phyag byas pa*; and *khyab par gnas* for *khyab pa'i gnas* in our text, which again with some exceptions follows Tsong kha pa's *'Dod 'jo*, 192b5–193a1. The beginning of the first verse is not found in our text.

1734. Reading *kha dog* for *kha deg* in our text.

1735. Abhayākaragupta, *Dkyil chog rdo rje phreng ba*, *Vajrāvalī*, Tōh 3140, 38a5; Mori 2009, §13.2.2, 236–37.

1736. Ngor chen Kun dga' bzang po, *Gsang 'dus dkyil 'khor gyi sgrub thabs dngos grub rgya mtsho*, work 106, 4b4, does not mention visualization of a lotus within the source of phenomena. This argument, though, is found already in Abhayākaragupta's *Dkyil chog rdo rje phreng ba*, *Vajrāvalī*, Tōh 3140, just before the lines from it cited immediately below.

Tantra[1737] and the *Concise Sādhana*,[1738] *abiding in the midst of the space realm*, he says that the space realm is the source of phenomena and at its center there is a lotus, as he explains in the *Maṇḍala Vajra Garland*: "Here the wisdom ground and the sky element are the source of phenomena. At its center visualize a lotus and four maṇḍalas of wind, fire, water, and earth resting upon it. Imagine that these four maṇḍalas merge together and become a crossed vajra. Upon it, visualize a lunar disk, and upon that, arising from a *bhrūṃ*, the celestial mansion. Since this is the meaning here,[1739] it would be a great mistake to say that the crossed vajra does not rest upon a lotus."[1740]

This must have been the intention of Ārya Nāgārjuna and his disciples as well. Consider the following:[1741] Generally the authoritative works give two methods for the measuring cord used in the drawing of the maṇḍala, sixty-four small units and ninety-six small units. As the *Saṃvarodaya Tantra* teaches: "The marking lines of the maṇḍala are sixty-four in number,"[1742] and therefore the measuring cord is sixty-four small units long; whereas Master Nāgabodhi teaches in his *Twenty Maṇḍala Rituals*: [47a] "The measuring cord is twice the size of the maṇḍala, neither thick nor thin,"[1743] thus, the measuring cord is ninety-six small units long. These are the only two alternatives, and no great authoritative scholar has ever attributed any other length to the measuring cord. Great experts of both systems maintain that the measuring cord is twice the size of the maṇḍala.

The sixty-four small units of the measuring cord refer to the length of the

1737. *Guhyasamāja Tantra*, chap. 11, Tōh 442; Zhol 15a2–3; Stog 25b3; Dunh 27b5; Fremantle 1971, v. 3a; and Matsunaga 1978, v. 3a. See above [44a–b].

1738. Nāgārjuna, *Mdor byas, Piṇḍīkrama Sādhana*, Tōh 1796, 2b5; L 19a; T 18a. Skt. *ākāśadhātumadhyastham*.

1739. This refers to the meaning of the lines of Nāgārjuna's *Mdor byas, Piṇḍīkrama Sādhana*, Tōh 1796, 2b4–7; L 18cd, 19a and d and 23; T 17cd, 18a and d and 22; cited in Abhayākaragupta's *Dkyil chog rdo rje phreng ba, Vajrāvalī*, Tōh 3140, just before.

1740. Reading *'dir* for *'dor* in our text. Abhayākaragupta, *Dkyil chog rdo rje phreng ba, Vajrāvalī*, Tōh 3140, 25b5–6; Mori 2009, §12.3.3, 173. Mori has *ye shes sa* for *ye shes kyi sa*; *khang ngo* for *khang*; and *rdo rje'o* for *rdo rje'e* in our text.

1741. See also Tsong kha pa, *Sngags rim chen mo*, chap. 6, 219–225. Mkhas grub rje will return to the lotus in a few paragraphs.

1742. *Sdom 'byung*, Tōh 373, 286a1; Sanskrit, Tibetan, and English translation in Tsuda 1974, chap. 17, v. 29ab. D and Tsuda have *thig skud* for *thig gi* in our text.

1743. Nāgabodhi, *Dkyil chog nyi shu pa, Maṇḍalaviṃśatividhi*, chap. 8, v. 2, Tōh 1810, 136b3; Tanaka 2001, 317. D has *gnyis* for *nyis* in our text.

main part of the maṇḍala from one main line to the other.[1744] Therefore, in this case, the distance from one tip of the prong of the crossed vajra to the other is doubled.[1745] The length of ninety-six small units refers to the maṇḍala with its inhabitants, while the distance from one parapet to the other is twice as long [i.e., it has one hundred and ninety-two small units].

A measuring cord of sixty-four small units entails two gate units, one for the height of the portal, and one for the Dharma wheel together with the tip of the prong of the crossed vajra. And a measuring cord of ninety-six small units entails four gate units, three gate units for the height of the portal, and one gate unit for the Dharma wheel together with the tip of the prong of the crossed vajra. The lotus ring is two small units long, the vajra ring two small units, and the fire mountain, one gate unit. Since there is no cremation ground,[1746] no authoritative scripture explains additional measurements. This being the case, when the measuring cord is of ninety-six small units, from one parapet[1747] of the maṇḍala to the other, there are twelve gate units, and from the parapet to the end of the fire mountain there are six gate units on each side. Thus twenty-four gate units equal ninety-six small units.[1748] Master Nāgabodhi explains: "The portal, which is three times the gate in size, rests on columns that stand on vases."[1749] Thus it follows that the portal is three gate units in height, and the measuring cord is twice the length of the maṇḍala.

If there is no lotus ring, there will be twelve gate units from one parapet to the other, [47b] while from the parapet to the fire mountain in each direction there will be no more than five and a half gate units. Hence the measuring cord from the fire mountain in the east to the end of the fire mountain in the west will be short one gate unit from being twice the length of the maṇḍala. This directly contradicts the explanation given by Master Nāgabodhi: "The measuring cord is twice the size of the maṇḍala."[1750] Therefore, unless you dare to argue with Nāgabodhi, you will have to accept the lotus unequivocally.[1751]

1744. Tib. *rtsa thig*, Skt. *mūlasūtra*. The main line is the square line around the celestial mansion. For illustrations see diagram 3 and Mori 2009, 642.

1745. This is the crossed vajra upon which the celestial mansion rests. Its length is one hundred twenty-eight units.

1746. There are no cremation grounds in the Guhyasamāja maṇḍala.

1747. Tib. *mda' yab*, Skt. *kramaśīrṣa*.

1748. This means that there are four small units, *cha chung*, in one gate unit.

1749. Nāgabodhi, *Dkyil chog nyi shu pa*, *Maṇḍalaviṃśatividhi*, chap. 4, v. 15ab, Tōh 1810, 134a2; Tanaka 2004, 31.

1750. The same line was cited at the end of above [46b].

1751. Reading *gdon* for *gden* in our text.

[The Four Maṇḍalas of the Physical Elements and the Crossed Vajra]

Then, to create the crossed vajra at the navel of the lotus, first visualize the maṇḍalas of the four physical elements. The *Concise Sādhana* teaches this: "Meditate on a wind maṇḍala that arises from the seed syllable *yaṃ* adorned with two vajras, each arising from a *hūṃ*. Upon the wind maṇḍala, visualize a fire maṇḍala that arises from the seed syllable *raṃ* adorned with two vajras, each arising from a *hūṃ*. Upon that maṇḍala, visualize a water maṇḍala that arises from the seed syllable *baṃ* adorned with two vajras, each arising from a *hūṃ*. And upon that, visualize an earth maṇḍala that arises from the seed syllable *laṃ* adorned with two vajras, each arising from a *hūṃ*."[1752] The *Vajrasattva Sādhana* explains this in exactly the same way.[1753] Therefore you should visualize the maṇḍalas of the physical elements accordingly. The four syllables, *yaṃ* and so forth, are the seed syllables of the four physical elements; and the *hūṃ*s are the seed syllables[1754] of the vajras on either side of each maṇḍala, supporting them at the edges.

You must visualize these four maṇḍalas in the nature of the four mothers, Locanā and so forth,[1755] for this visualization of the maṇḍalas of the four physical elements is taught in the eleventh chapter of the *Guhyasamāja Tantra*: "In the midst of the space vajra, visualize a maṇḍala born from all-vajra."[1756] [48a] Both the *Sādhana Incorporating the Scripture* and the *Vajrasattva Sādhana* explain this while pointing to these lines of the *Guhyasamāja Tantra*.[1757] Commenting on this, the *Illuminating Lamp* elucidates: "*Visualize a maṇḍala, born of all-vajra*, comprised and abiding *in the midst of the space vajra*. *All-vajras* are

1752. Nāgārjuna, *Mdor byas*, *Piṇḍīkrama Sādhana*, Tōh 1796, 2b5–7; L 19b–22; T 18b–21. D has *rnam par bsam* for *bsam par bya* twice.

1753. Candrakīrti, *Rdo rje sems dpa'i sgrub thabs*, *Vajrasattva Sādhana*, Tōh 1814, 197b5–6; Luo and Tomabechi 2009, 9.9–10.1 and 41.13–42.1.

1754. Reading *gi sa bon* for *gis bon* in our text.

1755. Tib. Spyan ma, Māmakī, Gos dkar mo, and Sgrol ma; Skt. Locanā, Māmakī, Pāṇḍarā, and Tārā.

1756. *Guhyasamāja Tantra*, Tōh 442; Zhol 15a2–3; Stog 25b3; Dunh 27b5; Fremantle 1971, v. 3ab; and Matsunaga 1978, v. 3ab. Zhol has *nam mkha' rdo rje'i dbus gnas par / dkyil 'khor rdo rje kun skyes bsam* for *dkyil 'khor rdo rje kun las skyes / nam mkha' rdo rje'i dbus su bsam* in our text. The sequence of lines here corresponds to the sequence as it appears in Nāgārjuna's *Mdo bsre* and Candrakīrti's *Rdo rje sems dpa'i sgrub thabs*. See below.

1757. Nāgārjuna, *Mdo bsre*, *Sādhanasūtramelāpaka*, Tōh 1797, 11b7. Candrakīrti, *Rdo rje sems dpa'i sgrub thabs*, *Vajrasattva Sādhana*, Tōh 1814, 197b6–7; Luo and Tomabechi 2009, 10.1–2 and 42.1–2.

the four mothers, Locanā and so forth. Meditate on the maṇḍalas of these mothers arising successively."[1758]

Then the *Concise Sādhana* teaches: "The four maṇḍalas merged together form the maṇḍala of the vajra foundation."[1759] And the *Vajrasattva Sādhana* teaches: "Visualize the four maṇḍalas merging together and transforming into a single earth maṇḍala."[1760] The *earth maṇḍala* and the *vajra foundation* form the crossed vajra, as in the line of Ārya Nāgabodhi: "The portal endowed with vajra finials,"[1761] explained as the crossed vajra in maṇḍala paintings.[1762]

The visualization of the crossed vajra from the four maṇḍalas merged together as one in this way is explained in the *Sādhana Incorporating the Scripture* by pointing to the eighth chapter of the *Guhyasamāja Tantra*: "The peaceful vajra holders should visualize them merging at their will."[1763] What this signifies according to the *Illuminating Lamp* is the gathering of maṇḍala deities into one's body at the end of the meditation session on the sādhana.[1764] Still, because various dissimilar meanings can be derived with regard to each

1758. Candrakīrti, *Sgron gsal, Pradīpoddyotanaṭīkā*, Tōh 1785, 77b1–2; Chakravarti 1984, 96. D has *rdo rje kun las skyes pa* for *rdo rje kun las bskyed pa* in our text. Reading *dkyil 'khor* for *dkyil 'khar* in our text.

1759. Nāgārjuna, *Mdor byas, Piṇḍīkrama Sādhana*, Tōh 1796, 2b7; L 23ab; T 22ab. D has *bsdu* for *bsdus*, and *rdo rje sa yi dkyil 'khor* for *rdo rje'i sa gzhi'i dkyil 'khor* in our text, which follows Tsong kha pa, *Rnam gzhag rim pa'i rnam bshad*, 11a2–3. The Sanskrit is somewhat different.

1760. Candrakīrti, *Rdo rje sems dpa'i sgrub thabs, Vajrasattva Sādhana*, Tōh 1814, 197b6–7; Luo and Tomabechi 2009, 10.1–2 and 42.1–2. D and Luo and Tomabechi have *'bab pa zhig* for *'ba' zhig* in our text.

1761. Nāgabodhi, *Dkyil chog nyi shu pa, Maṇḍalaviṃśatividhi*, chap. 4, v. 17c, Tōh 1810, 134a3; Tanaka 2004, 31.

1762. In maṇḍala paintings the finials of the crossed vajra are seen as though resting upon the portals. However, these two-dimensional paintings represent the maṇḍala as seen from above. In three-dimension depictions the crossed vajra is at the bottom while the portals are high above.

1763. Nāgārjuna, *Mdo bsre, Sādhanasūtramelāpaka*, Tōh 1797, 11b7. The *Mdo bsre* does not mention the eighth chapter of the *Guhyasamāja Tantra* here. However, the line it cites at the end of this section, "should also merge them," is found in the eighth chapter, v. 11b. See *Guhyasamāja Tantra*, Tōh 442; Zhol 12a1; Stog 20a1–2; Dunh 21a2; Fremantle 1971, v. 11ab; and Matsunaga 1978, v. 11cd. My translation is based on the commentary on this verse in Candrakīrti's *Sgron gsal, Pradīpoddyotanaṭīkā*, Tōh 1785, 60a4–5; Chakravarti 1984, 76; and on Tsong kha pa's *Sgron gsal mchan*, 192a3–5. As it appears in our text this line may be understood as "Should one desire the peaceful vajra holder, *vajradhṛk*, one should visualize the mergings."

1764. This is partly, but not wholly, based on Tsong kha pa's *Sgron gsal mchan*, 192a3–5.

vajra word of the tantras, Nāgārjuna and his disciples provide diverse interpretations, but you must not suppose that these are contradictory.

The *Sādhana Incorporating the Scripture* connects the visualization of the crossed vajra to the eighth chapter of the *Guhyasamāja Tantra*, [which the *Illuminating Lamp* interprets by citing] the *Revelation of the Intention*, in the context of the definitive interpretation of the flower offering and so forth.[1765] [48b] The definitive interpretation of the lines *the peaceful vajra holders should visualize them merging at their will* can be gleaned from the explanation of the *Illuminating Lamp*, which also cites the explanatory tantra *Revelation of the Intention*: "Yoke the mothers Locanā and so forth, with the physical elements, earth,[1766] and so forth respectively. Having set [the physical elements] at the stage of no-being,[1767] you then yoke[1768] them to the bodies of the deities."[1769]

In fact, this is the explanation of the offering of the four flowers in the definitive meaning.[1770] But the definitive meaning of the lines just cited from the same chapter of the *Guhyasamāja Tantra*, "The peaceful vajra holders

1765. While Nāgārjuna's *Mdo bsre, Sādhanasūtramelāpaka*, Tōh 1797, itself does not mention the *Dgongs pa lung ston, Sandhivyākaraṇa*, Tōh 444, Tsong kha pa explains this. See *Dgongs pa lung ston, Sandhivyākaraṇa*, Tōh 444, 181b7–182a7. Candrakīrti's *Sgron gsal, Pradīpoddyotanaṭīkā*, Tōh 1785, 60b5–61a1; Chakravarti 1984, 76–77; has just *lung* here, but Tsong kha pa identifies it as the *Dgongs pa lung ston* in his *Sgron gsal mchan* 193b1. The *Guhyasamāja Tantra* citation is Tōh 442; Zhol 12a1–2; Stog 20a3–4; Dunh 21a3–4; Fremantle 1971, vv. 13–14; and Matsunaga 1978, vv. 14–15.

1766. Literarily the "mighty one," Tib. *dbang chen*, Skt. *māhendra*.

1767. Or in Madhyamaka terminology, devoid of own nature. Tib. *dngos med*, Skt. *niḥsvabhāva*.

1768. As was noted above, our text—which follows Candrakīrti, *Sgron gsal, Pradīpoddyotanaṭīkā*, Tōh 1785—has *sbyor ba* for *sbyor bas*.

1769. Candrakīrti, *Sgron gsal, Pradīpoddyotanaṭīkā*, Tōh 1785, 60b5–6; Chakravarti 1984, 76. D has *go rims* for *go rim*. Our text cites the version of the *Sgron gsal*, which is cited in Tsong kha pa's *Sgron gsal mchan*, 193b1–194a4. These lines are understood to refer to the yoga of the inner winds during the completing stage, which then lead to the realization of clear light, and finally to the arising in the body of union. The citation is *Dgongs pa lung ston, Sandhivyākaraṇa*, Tōh 444, 182a7. This is only the end of the first and the beginning of the second verse. D has *go rims* for *go rim*; *sa la* for *dbang chen*; *bkod pas* for *'god pas*; and *sbyor bas* for *sbyor ba*.

1770. This refers to Candrakīrti's explanation of the following verse in chap. 8, v. 14/15 of the *Guhyasamāja Tantra*, Tōh 442; Zhol 12a2; Stog 20a3–4; Dunh 21a4; Fremantle 1971, v. 14; and Matsunaga 1978, v. 15. See his *Sgron gsal, Pradīpoddyotanaṭīkā*, Tōh 1785, 60b5–61a1; Chakravarti 1984, 76–77. Tsong kha pa comments on this in his *Sgron gsal mchan*, 193b1–194a4.

should visualize them merging at their will,"[1771] has a similar meaning. Thus this interpretation of the lines on the four flowers explains our verse as well.[1772] This is because there is no other explanation in the *Revelation of the Intention* that clearly elucidates these two lines.

Therefore the meaning here is: the earth-wind of one's body is Locanā, the water-wind is Māmakī, the fire-wind is Pāṇḍarā, and the wind-wind is Tārā. The clear light reality of ultimate truth, the stage of no-being, will manifest only when you have practiced entering, abiding, and dissolving, according to the transmitted instructions of the profound vajra recitation, by gathering and merging all these together—the four physical elements, and the separately circulating winds of the four mothers—into the indestructible drop. This is the definitive interpretation of the four maṇḍalas merging into one from which the crossed vajra is generated.

This wisdom of clear light is differentiated into five wisdoms, and therefore the crossed vajra is explained as the pure five wisdoms. The five wisdoms also occur as the five wisdoms during the path. This actual clear light is the basis for the body of union, which is the maṇḍala of wisdom together with its deities. Thus, in order to signify this definitive interpretation, you should now meditate on the crossed vajra as the support of the celestial mansion. [49a] This indeed is the intention of the passage in the *Illuminating Lamp*, where the maṇḍalas of the four physical elements are yoked together with the four mothers.[1773]

Hence THOSE[1774] who do not understand this profound, definitive interpretation forego the explicit explanation of glorious Candrakīrti with respect to meditating on the four maṇḍalas in the essence of the four mothers, and

1771. *Guhyasamāja Tantra*, chap. 8, Tōh 442; Zhol 12a1; Stog 20a1–2; Dunh 21a2; Fremantle 1971, v. 11ab; and Matsunaga 1978, v. 11cd.

1772. In other words, the explanation in the definitive level of interpretation of the verse of the *Guhyasamāja Tantra*, chap. 8, Tōh 442; Fremantle 1971, v. 14; Matsunaga 1978, v. 15; is also the explanation in the definitive level of interpretation of the *Guhyasamāja Tantra*, chap. 8, Tōh 442; Fremantle 1971, v. 11ab; Matsunaga 1978, v. 11cd.

1773. Candrakīrti, *Sgron gsal*, *Pradīpoddyotanaṭīkā*, Tōh 1785, 60b4–61a1; Chakravarti 1984, 76; which quotes the passage of the *Dgongs pa lung ston* cited above.

1774. Ngor chen Kun dga' bzang po, *Gsang 'dus dkyil 'khor gyi sgrub thabs dngos grub rgya mtsho*, work 106, 4b5–5a1, teaches that one should visualize respectively a banner, a blazing fire, a vase, and a vajra on the four wheels of the physical elements. Bu ston, *Mdor byas 'grel chen*, 15b2, says that lamas (*bla ma dag*) maintain this on the basis of Ratnākaraśānti's explanation in his commentary on the *Mdor byas*. See Ratnākaraśānti, *Rin chen phreng ba*, *Ratnāvalī*, Tōh 1826, 28a3–b5.

instead meditate on the various emblems, such as the banner,[1775] the blazing fire, the vase, and the jewel, which are neither taught by Nāgārjuna and his disciples nor the *Guhyasamāja* root and explanatory tantras. Likewise, THOSE[1776] who say that the wind ignites the fire, the fire boils the water, the water dissolves the earth, and thereby the four maṇḍalas merge together, and so forth, offer pointless elaborations that strongly contradict the stages of the inner dissolution. Therefore THOSE who do not understand the meaning of the tantras should not provide elucidations!

[Qualm:] If the meditation on the maṇḍalas of the physical elements here corresponds to the evolution of the maṇḍalas of wind, water, and earth during the evolution of the world, and since there is no fire maṇḍala in the ground of purification, why do you meditate on a fire maṇḍala here?

[Reply:] Though there is no separate evolution of the fire maṇḍala in the ground of purification, through the churning of the water element by the wind, the surface of the water gradually thickens like scum, ripens completely, and turns into gold and so forth. Here there is fire at work to ripen and so forth, hence the fire element abides and, imperceptibly, pervades the other maṇḍalas so that a ground of purification wherein to apply the meditation on the fire maṇḍala is not lacking. Therefore *Formulating the Sādhana* teaches: "Indeed, within the [wind, water, and gold maṇḍalas] the fire maṇḍala too abides."[1777]

[The Visualization of the Celestial Mansion from the Syllable Bhrūṃ]

After meditating on the crossed vajra in this way, visualize at its nave[1778] a white syllable *bhrūṃ* [49b] emanating rays of a multitude of[1779] buddhas, as the eleventh chapter of the *Guhyasamāja Tantra* teaches: "In the midst of the space vajra, visualize a maṇḍala born from all-vajra and in it imagine the

1775. Reading *dan* for *don*.

1776. Ngor chen, *Gsang 'dus dkyil 'khor gyi sgrub thabs dngos grub rgya mtsho*, work 106, 5a1, teaches that one should visualize the wind igniting the fire, the fire boiling the water, the water dissolving the earth, and then all of them merging together as one taste that turns into the crossed vajra.

1777. Nāgabuddhi, *Rnam gzhag rim pa*, *Vyavastholi*, chap. 1, Tōh 1809, 121b7–122a1; Tanaka 2016, 82. D and Tanaka have *de dag gi* for *de rnams kyi*.

1778. Reading *bya* for *ba*.

1779. Literally "clouds," Tib. *sprin*, Skt. *megha*.

syllable *bhrūṃ*, emanating a multitude of[1780] vajras."[1781] There are various explanations on how to generate the celestial mansion: in our case from *bhrūṃ*, in certain other cases, including the Hevajra cycle—from a wheel, some people say—from the transformation of the body of Vairocana and so forth. Yet the meaning of all these explanations is similar, since the wheel is the emblem of Vairocana and *bhrūṃ* is the seed syllable of Vairocana.

The meaning signifies here that the ground of purification is the physical world in which sentient beings reside; and this physical world is—from among the five aggregates—the form aggregate [whose pure aspect is Vairocana]. Likewise, the purifier is the celestial mansion, the abode in which the deities dwell, and therefore, you should generate the celestial mansion from the seed syllable, or the emblem or the body of Vairocana, considered to be the pure form aggregate—from among the five pure aggregates—and meditate on the celestial mansion in the essence of Vairocana.

The *Vajrasattva Sādhana* likewise relates the meditation on *bhrūṃ* to the verse from the *Guhyasamāja Tantra* just cited,[1782] while the *Sādhana Incorporating the Scripture* relates this meditation on the celestial mansion arising through the transformation of the *bhrūṃ* to the following verse of the eleventh chapter of the *Guhyasamāja Tantra*: "With the syllable *bhrūṃ* meditate on the abode."[1783] This abode is the celestial mansion.

The visualization of the celestial mansion is a meditation that corresponds to the evolution of the mountains, continents, and so forth during the evolution of the world. When you apply the correspondences in this way, the generation of the celestial mansion—the purifier—corresponds in a merely general way to the ground of purification, which is the evolution of the mountains, continents, and so forth. You need not relate the mountains, continents, and so forth to each part of the celestial mansion, such as the portals and so forth. [50a]

1780. Once more, literally "clouds."

1781. *Guhyasamāja Tantra*, Tōh 442; Zhol 15a2–3; Stog 25b3; Dunh 27b5; Fremantle 1971, v. 3; and Matsunaga 1978, v. 3. Zhol has *rdo rje kun skyes bsam* for *rdo rje kun las skyes* and *rdo rje'i sprin* for *rdo rje sprin* in our text. The first two lines of this verse were cited above [47b6–48a1], but here the sequence corresponds to that of the *Guhyasamāja Tantra*.

1782. Candrakīrti, *Rdo rje sems dpa'i sgrub thabs*, *Vajrasattva Sādhana*, Tōh 1814, 197b7; Luo and Tomabechi 2009, 10.3–4 and 42.4–7. This is a different translation of the verse.

1783. Nāgārjuna, *Mdo bsre*, *Sādhanasūtramelāpaka*, Tōh 1797, 12a1. D has *gyis* for *gyi* in our text, and Zhol also has *gyis*. Mkhas grub rje below [70a6] also has this verse with *gyis* for the *gyi* here. The *Guhyasamāja Tantra* passage is Tōh 442; Zhol 15a3–4; Stog 25b5; Dunh missing; Fremantle 1971, v. 5c; and Matsunaga 1978, v. 5c. Zhol has *bsgoms* for *bsgom* in our text. The Sanskrit here is different.

What does it mean to purify the impure world by meditating on the celestial mansion? It is not that, through your meditation on the celestial mansion, you can transform this present impure world into a pure celestial mansion. Rather, you can purify your own capacity to partake in the impure world in the future [meaning that you yourself will not experience the impure world]. The purpose of this meditative purification is to ripen your mental continuum for the completion stage, in which you will develop the capacity to partake in the celestial mansion of wisdom.

Meditating on the Celestial Mansion[1784]

Visualize the square celestial mansion with four gates, arising instantaneously from the seed syllable *bhrūṃ*, replete with all essential characteristics. There are two sections here: (1) measurements for drawing and meditating on the celestial mansion of the maṇḍala and (2) the essentials for drawing and meditating on it.

Measurements for Drawing and Meditating on the Celestial Mansion

Two methods are used for drawing the celestial mansion: one pertains to the deities and the other to the patrons of the ritual. With regard to the deities, as taught in the sixteenth chapter of the *Guhyasamāja Tantra*, the measurements of the three maṇḍalas of the tathāgata families of mind,[1785] body,[1786] and speech,[1787] are twelve, sixteen, and twenty cubits respectively. Similarly, the *Vajra Pavilion* teaches: "Three cubits for the vajra holder,[1788] four cubits for the

1784. We would like to thank Geshe Blo bzang rab 'byor of Rgyud smad Monastery in Hunsur, without whose help we could not have translated this chapter. For the Sanskrit equivalents of the Tibetan terms in this chapter, see Tanaka 2004 [Nāgabodhi, *Dkyil chog nyi shu pa*, *Maṇḍalaviṃśatividhi*, Tōh 1810]; Mori 2009 [Abhayākaragupta, *Dkyil chog rdo rje phreng ba*, *Vajrāvalī*, Tōh 3140]; La Vallée Poussin 1896 [Nāgārjuna, *Mdor byas*, *Piṇḍīkrama*, Tōh 1796]; Bahulkar 2006 and Klein-Schwind 2008 [Dīpaṃkarabhadra, *Dkyil 'khor gyi cho ga*, *Maṇḍalavidhi*].

1785. This is found in the *Guhyasamāja Tantra*, chap. 4, Tōh 442; Zhol 7b6; Stog 12b1; Dunh 11b3; Fremantle 1971, v. 9ab; and Matsunaga 1978, v. 9ab.

1786. *Guhyasamāja Tantra*, chap. 16, Tōh 442; Zhol 36b3; Stog 61b3; Dunh 67a3–4; Fremantle 1971, v. 2; and Matsunaga 1978, v. 2.

1787. *Guhyasamāja Tantra*, chap. 16, Tōh 442; Zhol 36b6; Stog 62a2; Dunh 67b3; Fremantle 1971, v. 8; and Matsunaga 1978, v. 9.

1788. Tib. Mi bskyod pa, Skt. Akṣobhya.

maṇḍala of the Buddha,[1789] five cubits for Vairocana, six cubits for the Lord of the Dance,[1790] and seven cubits for the King of Horses."[1791] Thus definite measurements are explained for each of the maṇḍalas of the [five] tathāgata families.

In the case of the patrons, the *Maṇḍala Vajra Garland* cites a tantra:[1792] "A universal emperor should draw a maṇḍala reaching a *yojana* on all sides. When the wise ones consider the minds of the disciples, [50b] there is no fault whatever in any dimension they may choose. When the treatises teach that it is beneficial to draw the entire maṇḍala in the palm of your hand any way you wish, what is there to say about drawing the maṇḍala on the ground and so forth?"[1793] Thus it is taught that as far as disciples are concerned, there are no specific measurements.[1794]

Likewise Nāgabodhi teaches: "Adapting to the disciple's capacity, the vajra teacher[1795] should draw maṇḍalas anywhere from a single cubit to a thousand cubits in dimension."[1796] The *Saṃvarodaya Tantra* teaches: "Beginning from half a cubit [up to one hundred cubits]."[1797] And Dīpaṅkarabhadra similarly teaches: "In accordance with the mental capacity of each being, measurements and so forth are specified; but what is the point of fixed measurements and so forth, with respect to attainments that come through wisdom and method?"[1798] Therefore the dimensions are taught in order to accommodate

1789. Tib. Rin chen 'byung ldan, Skt. Ratnasaṃbhava.

1790. Tib. 'Od dpag med, Skt. Amitābha.

1791. Tib. Don yod grub pa, Skt. Amoghasiddhi. *Gur*, *Vajrapañjara Tantra*, chap. 2, Tōh 419, 31b6. D and Stog have *snang byed la ni khru lnga nyid* for *khru lnga ba ni snang byed pa'o*; *padma gar dbang drug pa ste* for *gar dbang phyug gi khru drug dang*; and *lcags kyi rgyal po de bzhin bdun* for *rta yi rgyal po'i khru bdun pa* in our text.

1792. Abhayākaragupta notes that these are the words of the Blessed One.

1793. Abhayākaragupta, *Dkyil chog rdo rje phreng ba*, *Vajrāvalī*, Tōh 3140, 35a3–5; Mori 2009, §12.6.10, 221–222. D and Mori have *phyi rol dkyil 'khor bri bar bya* for *dkyil 'khor rab tu bri ba bya* and *mthil du bri bya nas* for *mthil du bris byas nas* in our text.

1794. Reading *che chung* for *cha chung* in our text.

1795. Tib. *sngags pa*, Skt. *vajrin*.

1796. Nāgabodhi, *Dkyil chog nyi shu pa*, *Maṇḍalaviṃśatividhi*, chap. 4, v. 19, Tōh 1810, 134a4–5; Tanaka 2004, 31.

1797. *Sdom 'byung*, *Saṃvarodaya Tantra*, Tōh 373, 286a1; Sanskrit, Tibetan, and English translation in Tsuda 1974, chap. 17, v. 23a. D and Tsuda have *la sogs nas brtsam nas* for *sogs nas yang dag brtsam* in our text.

1798. Dīpaṅkarabhadra, *Gsang ba 'dus pa'i dkyil 'khor gyi cho ga* = *Dkyil chog bzhi rgya lnga bcu pa*, *Guhyasamāja Maṇḍalavidhi*, Tōh 1865, 78b5–6; Bahulkar 2006, 135, vv. 239cd–240ab; Klein-Schwind 2008, v. 239cdef. D has *mdzad* for *bshad*; *tshad sogs* for *tshang sogs*; and *nges pas* for *nges pa* in our text.

those who prefer specific numbers, but you should understand that in actuality there are no specific measurements for drawing maṇḍalas.

The eighth chapter of the *Guhyasamāja Tantra* explains these measurements for the meditation: "Visualize a wheel maṇḍala extending a hundred *yojanas*,"[1799] and "a very beautiful square *caitya* extending ten million *yojanas*, made of the four kinds of jewels, clear and immaculate in nature."[1800] Thus it was taught that the maṇḍalas to be visualized might extend to a hundred or even ten million *yojanas*. In commenting on this line, the *Illuminating Lamp* explains that the maṇḍala is called *caitya* here, since it is similar to a *caitya*.[1801] SOME EXPLAIN[1802] that *made of the four kinds of jewels* means the four elements in the nature of the four pure mothers. But these are the sayings of arrogant people who dispense their explanations with no understanding of Candrakīrti's instructions about meditating on the four maṇḍalas in the nature of the four mothers, [51a] and generating the celestial mansion from *bhrūṃ*.

The Essentials for Drawing and Meditating on the Celestial Mansion of the Maṇḍala

The *Concise Sādhana* teaches: "A square with four gates[1803] adorned with four portals,[1804] along four marking-lines, embellished with eight columns,[1805] ornamented with round and vertical strands of pearls,[1806] vajra gems, and crescent moons. The corners between the gate and the gateposts[1807] are decorated with vajras and jewels; great vajra columns [resting on] the vases, railings[1808] and

1799. *Guhyasamāja Tantra*, Tōh 442; Zhol 12a2; Stog 20a4; Dunh 21a4; Fremantle 1971, v. 15ab; and Matsunaga 1978, v. 16. The Zhol has *bsgom byas la* for *bsgom par bya* in our text.

1800. *Guhyasamāja Tantra*, Tōh 442; Zhol 12a2–3; Stog 20a4; Dunh 21a4; Fremantle 1971, v. 16abcd; and Matsunaga 1978, v. 18.

1801. Paraphrasing Candrakīrti's *Sgron gsal, Pradīpoddyotanaṭīkā*, chap. 8, Tōh 1785, v. 16, 61a5; Chakravarti 1984, 77. A *caitya* is both a stūpa and an object of veneration.

1802. See Red mda' ba, *Yid kyi mun sel*, 167a5–6.

1803. Tib. *sgo*, Skt. *dvāra*.

1804. Tib. *rta babs*, Skt. *toraṇa*, the four monumental entrances to the celestial mansion with eleven ornate layers that are shown projecting outward in two-dimensional representations of the maṇḍala.

1805. Tib. *ka ba*, Skt. *stambha*.

1806. Tib. *drwa ba drwa phyed*, Skt. *hārādhahāra*. The literal meaning of the Sanskrit and Tibetan terms is strings and half strings.

1807. Tib. *sgo khyud*, Skt. *niryūha*.

1808. Here the Tibetan is *bre*, but the Sanskrit is *kramaśīrṣa*, called also parapet.

eaves,[1809] embellished with pennants[1810] and bells, and ornamented with yak-tails[1811] and so forth."[1812]

To establish the meaning of these stanzas, there are two sections: (1) explanation of [the surroundings of the celestial mansion] between the light-garland and the portals, and (2) explanation of the actual celestial mansion along with the thrones.

[The Surroundings of the Celestial Mansion] between the Garland of Light and the Portals

The first section is again divided into two subsections: (1) explanation of the area between the garland of light and the crossed vajra and (2) explanation of the portals.

Explanation of the Area between the Garland of Light and the Crossed Vajra

[The Rings]

The outer ring is the "garland of light"[1813] consisting of a five-colored flame blazing out all around in the cardinal and intermediate directions. The malicious beings cannot bear to look at it. The vajra fence and vajra tent and so

1809. While our text has here *bya*, D has *phreng bar* and the Sanskrit is *pakṣiṇī*. The parallel line in Candrakīrti's *Sādhana* has *bya can*, and the Skt. is *pakṣiṇī*. See his *Rdo rje sems dpa'i sgrub thabs, Vajrasattva Sādhana*, Tōh 1814, 198a2; Luo and Tomabechi 2009, 10.6 and 43.2. Often the Tibetan parallel of *pakṣiṇī* is *bya 'dab*. However, according to Ratnākaraśānti's commentary, there are birds here: two peacocks in the east, two geese in the south, two ducks in the west, and in the north, two pheasants. See his *Rin chen phreng ba, Ratnāvalī*, Tōh 1826, 30a4–5.

1810. Tib. *ba dan*, Skt. *patāka*.

1811. Tib. *rnga yab*, Skt. *cāmara*.

1812. Nāgārjuna, *Mdor byas, Piṇḍīkrama Sādhana*, Tōh 1796, 2b7–3a2; L 24–26, T 23–25. D has *yang dag mdzes* for *nye bar mdzes*; *nor bu* for *nor du*; *zla phyed brgyan* for *zla phyed dang*; the line *grwa yi mtshams ni thams cad dang* is missing; and *rnga yab sogs kyis* for *rnga yab la sogs* in our text. D has *bre la phreng bar* for *bre la bya ni*. These lines are cited also in Candrakīrti's *Rdo rje sems dpa'i sgrub thabs, Vajrasattva Sādhana*, Tōh 1814, 198a1–2; Luo and Tomabechi 2009, 10.7–12 and 42.10–43.9; English translation in Wayman 1971, 560.

1813. Tib. *'od 'phreng*, Skt. *raśmimālā*. This, being the outermost circle or sphere of the maṇḍala, is made of multicolored lights or fires. See also Dīpaṅkarabhadra, *Gsang ba 'dus pa'i dkyil 'khor gyi cho ga = Dkyil chog bzhi rgya lnga bcu pa, Guhyasamāja Maṇḍalavidhi*, Tōh 1865, 73b1; Bahulkar 2006, 121, v. 104; Klein-Schwind 2008, v. 104.

forth have already been explained.[1814] The water-fence that used to be there has been dissolved in clear light now,[1815] so when you arise from the clear light, you need not meditate on the water fence anymore.

[The third ring within] the garland of light[1816] is the lotus,[1817] which is the base of crossed vajra,[1818] for as the *Maṇḍala Vajra Garland* explains: "The nave of the lotus is green, the corolla"[1819] between the nave and the petals "are yellow, and the petals are variegated in color."[1820] The distance from one end of the nave of the lotus to the other is equal to the length between one tip of the prong of the crossed vajra and the tip of the prong on the other side. [51b]

[The Crossed Vajra]

There are two kinds of crossed vajras: The first is three-pronged, with three prongs in each of the four directions—altogether twelve prongs—while the second is five-pronged, with five in each direction—altogether twenty prongs. In this context either of the two is suitable.

[The Colors of the Crossed Vajra]

The *Maṇḍala Vajra Garland* explains: "The nave of the crossed vajra is either black or the color of the principal deity of that maṇḍala."[1821] In the latter case, if

1814. Tib. *rdo rje'i rwa gur* or *rdo rje'i rwa ba dang gur*. These terms were explained in the discussion of the protection wheel above. In paintings the vajra fence, *rdo rje'i rwa*, Skt. *vajrāvalī*, is the second circle made of vajras, which serves for protection. Visualized three-dimensionally it is in fact a sphere. See also Dīpaṅkarabhadra, *Gsang ba 'dus pa'i dkyil 'khor gyi cho ga = Dkyil chog bzhi rgya lnga bcu pa, Guhyasamāja Maṇḍalavidhi*, Tōh 1865, 78b2; Bahulkar 2006, 135, v. 233; Klein-Schwind 2008, v. 233.

1815. During the meditation on the protection wheel, yogis meditate successively on four fences of iron, water, fire, and wind; see [30a] above. However, soon after this they dissolve the physical world and the beings dwelling there into emptiness, see [32a] above.

1816. The lotus circle is actually inside both the garland of light and the vajra-fence.

1817. Here our text just has *padma*, the third circle of lotus petals, also called Tib. *pad rwa* or *padma rwa ba*, Skt. *padmadala*.

1818. Tib. *sna tshogs rdo rje*, Skt. *viśvavajra*.

1819. Tib. *ge sar*, Skt. *keśara*.

1820. This is a paraphrase of Abhayākaragupta, *Dkyil chog rdo rje phreng ba, Vajrāvalī*, Tōh 3140, 38a5; Mori 2009, §13.2.2, 236–237.

1821. Abhayākaragupta, *Dkyil chog rdo rje phreng ba, Vajrāvalī*, Tōh 3140, 38a2; Mori 2009, §13.2.2, 235–237. D and Mori have *nag po'o* for *nag po 'am* and *kha cig tu gtso bo'i de bzhin gshegs pa'i mdog go* for *yang na dkyil 'khor de'i gtso bo'i kha dog tu bya ba* in our text.

the color of the lord of the tathāgata family of the principal deity accords with the color of the principal deity, that is fine. However, in cases like Mañjuvajra Guhyasamāja,[1822] where the lord of the family is dark Akṣobhya but the color of the principal deity is yellow, the lord of the family prevails over the principal deity, so the nave of the crossed vajra must be black. In the present context the nave is black like the principal deity.

The prongs set in the different directions should be colored as explained in the *Maṇḍala Vajra Garland*: "The colors of the central prongs [in each of the four directions] are those of the tathāgatas of that direction. The other [surrounding] prongs should be in the colors of the tathāgatas in their respective quarters. When the crossed vajra is five-pronged, the colors should accord with the tathāgatas at the center and the four directions. Hence the prongs should be appropriate in color."[1823] This means that when the vajra has twelve-prongs, the central prong in the east is white, while the right and left prongs facing inward are green and yellow respectively. When the vajra has twenty prongs, the upper prong that accords with the color of Akṣobhya in the center is blue, while the lower prong is red, the color of Amitābha—the Victorious One in the west. For the other directions follow this pattern in the appropriate manner.[1824]

The *Maṇḍala Vajra Garland* presents another position as well: "Elsewhere it is explained that all prongs in the same direction bear the same color as the tathāgata of that direction."[1825] [52a] Such an explanation is found in the *Crown Jewel Sādhana* and so forth,[1826] where, for example, all prongs in the east are white.[1827] According to another system, the color of the prong in each direction corresponds to that of the face of the deity turned in that direction,

1822. Tib. *Gsang 'dus 'jam rdor*.

1823. Abhayākaragupta, *Dkyil chog rdo rje phreng ba, Vajrāvalī*, Tōh 3140, 38a2–3; Mori 2009, §13.2.2, 235 and 237. D and Mori have *rang rang gi phyogs rnams* for *rang gi phyogs* and *glo* for *blo* in our text.

1824. In the east the upper prong is blue, the lower red, the right is green, and the left is yellow; in the south the upper prong is blue, the lower is green, the right is white, and the left red; in the west the upper prong is blue, the lower is white, the right is yellow, and the left is green; and in the north the upper prong is blue, the lower is yellow, the right is red, and the left is white. See also Tsong kha pa, *Bskyed rim zin bris*, 16b4–17a1.

1825. Abhayākaragupta, *Dkyil chog rdo rje phreng ba, Vajrāvalī*, Tōh 3140, 38a3–4; Mori 2009, §13.2.2, 235–237. D and Mori have *rang rang gi phyogs* for *rang gi phyogs* and *kha dog kyang kha cig tu'o* for *mdog go zhes kha cig tu'o* in our text.

1826. Reading *sogs na yod de* for *sogs na yod do* in our text.

1827. *Kambala, Lwa ba pa, *Bde mchog gi sgrub thabs gtsug nor, Cakrasaṃvara Sādhana Ratnacūḍāmaṇi*, Tōh 1443, 247a2.

for example, the prongs should be in the colors of the four faces of the principal deity Cakrasaṃvara.

[The Dimensions of the Crossed Vajra][1828]

The nave of the crossed vajra is square, and its dimensions are as the *Maṇḍala Vajra Garland* specifies: "The nave of the crossed vajra is twelve 'gate units' in dimension."[1829] Thus the width of the nave is twelve gate units in each direction.

[The Length of the Prongs Protruding from the Nave]

When the measuring cord[1830] is ninety-six small units in length,[1831] and the height of the portal is three gate units, the prongs protrude four gate units; and when the measuring cord is sixty-four small units in length, and the height of the portal is one gate unit, the prong protrudes two large units.[1832] These are the two definitive systems explained in the *Maṇḍala Vajra Garland*.

Therefore, when the size of the portal is three gate units, each prong protrudes sixteen small units.[1833] The length and width of the prongs in the four directions and the center are equal, yet the prongs in the four directions do not reach the tip of the middle prong, but touch it two small units before the tip, because two units are needed for the curve.[1834] Therefore, when the width[1835] and depth[1836] of the entryway are the same size as the gate,[1837] the lines of the

1828. See Tsong kha pa, *Sngags rim chen mo*, chap. 6, 231.

1829. Tib. *sgo tshad*, Skt. *dvārapramāṇa*. A "gate unit" is the width of the gateway or portal. Abhayākaragupta, *Dkyil chog rdo rje phreng ba, Vajrāvalī*, Tōh 3140, 25b6; Mori 2009, §12.3.4, 174 and 176.

1830. Tib. *thig skud*, Skt. *sūtra*.

1831. Tib. *cha phran*.

1832. Tib. *cha chen*, Skt. *mahābhāga*.

1833. Tib. *cha chung*, Skt. *mātrika*. A small unit is a quarter of the gate unit.

1834. See Tsong kha pa's *'Dod 'jo*, 83a2, and *Sngags rim chen mo*, chap. 6, 231–232.

1835. Tib. *'gram*, Skt. *kapola* or *kapolaka*. The width of the entrance way is equal to the line at the back side of the entrance way called *kapola*, which literally means cheek or forehead. See the following note.

1836. Tib. *logs*, Skt. *pakṣa* or *pakṣaka*. The depth of the entrance way is equal to the line on the side of the entrance way. The literal meaning of the Tibetan *logs* and the Sanskrit *pakṣa* or *pakṣaka* is side, i.e., the side of the entrance way. For illustrations of these lines within the entrance way or the porch, see Tanaka 2004, 34 and Mori 2009, 640.

1837. This refers to the Guhyasamāja maṇḍala.

right and left prongs protrude beyond the tips of the column, but when the width and depth of the entryway are not the same size as the gate,[1838] and the portal is three gate units, the right and left prongs are exactly sixteen small units long when measured with a cord curving from the tip of the line of the suspending banners[1839] along the inner line of the prong. But THOSE who nowadays measure the length of the right and left prongs by way of the longer side of the curve arrive at a number greater than sixteen small units.

The *Maṇḍala Vajra Garland* explains: [52b] "The prongs of the crossed vajra that emerge from a sea monster's mouth peek out a little over the sides of the portals beyond the layer of the suspending banners. Their width at the center is three small units and their length is sixteen small units."[1840] Thus, when the height of the portal is three gate units and the width and depth of the entryway are not the same size as the gate, it is inappropriate for the outer line at the root of the prong, which is sixteen small units long, to extend beyond the outer line of the suspending banners. Likewise, when the width and depth of the entryway are the same size as the gate, it is inappropriate for the border of the curving outer lines of the prongs to extend beyond the outer line of the tip of the column. Therefore a line curving from the border extending beyond the outer line of the prongs contradicts the instructions given in the *Maṇḍala Vajra Garland*.

Similarly, when the height of the portal is one gate unit, each of the prongs is eight small units long, but the prongs in the different directions must curve. When these prongs are measured with a cord along their inner line, they curve at the point the cord reaches a length of eight small units and their tips touch the central prong two small units before its tip. Such measurements are in keeping with the instructions given in the *Ḍākārṇava Tantra*: "The point that emerges from the tip of the column is the great radiant crossed vajra."[1841] Hence, the system of others with regard to the border of the curving prongs surely contradicts the instruction of this tantra.

If having accepted the two systems, the one with portals three gate units high and prongs sixteen small units long, and the other with portals one gate

1838. This refers to the maṇḍala of Cakrasaṃvara and Bhairava.

1839. Tib. *dar dpyangs*, Skt. *añcala*. See Mori 2009, 640, for the location of this line.

1840. Abhayākaragupta, *Dkyil chog rdo rje phreng ba*, *Vajrāvalī*, Tōh 3140, 24b6–25a1; Mori 2009, §12.2.7, 168–169. D and Mori have *gzhogs* for *phyogs* in our text. This refers to two-dimensional depictions where the vajra prongs are seen around the portals. Cited also in Tsong kha pa, *Sngags rim chen mo*, chap. 6, 231.

1841. *Mkha' 'gro rgya mtsho*, chap. 10, Tōh 372, 162b1. D has *'thon* for *thon* and *chen po'o* for *chen po* in our text. Cited also in Tsong kha pa, *Sngags rim chen mo*, chap. 6, 232.

unit high, and prongs eight small units long, YOU nevertheless maintain that the curving point of the prongs extend beyond the lines of the suspending banners and the columns, YOU obviously contradict YOUR own position, because then there will be more than twenty small units when measured along the inner line of the prongs from the junction which YOU claim is the curving point. [53a]

If YOU maintain YOUR position regarding the curving point, but still assert that while the curving prongs do not touch the central prong more than two small units before the tip, they are sixteen small units long—and you insist that this is the position of YOUR LAMA, YOU inevitably contradict the scriptural authorities of the tantras and the *Maṇḍala Vajra Garland*. While if YOU do so in order to compensate for the size of sixteen small units, you contradict what YOUR lama explains in his *Maṇḍala Ritual of the Vajra Realm*:[1842] "Draw a curve eight small units in length at the junction of the two at a distance of twenty-seven small units, from the line of twenty-two small units up to the line of the prong. In between the twenty-seventh and twenty-eighth units, the curve touches the prong above the sixth with eight and a half units, as before." This clearly explains that both the outer and inner lines of the prongs curve in touching the central prong. O fool, make haste to erase the explanation of YOUR LAMA by YOUR own hand.

THOSE who strive though lacking in intelligence are fools, imagining that if the face of the sea monster can be seen in its entirety it will look more beautiful. They babble all the while and deprecate the contradictions between their own positions and those of the tantras and Indian treatises. But if YOUR main concern is whether the painting looks beautiful or not, then when in YOUR three-dimensional maṇḍala the prongs do not touch each other in the four directions, they will resemble the pincers of a scorpion. And if YOU form such curving points in three-dimensional maṇḍalas, the prongs in the four directions will simply open out and separate. Obviously YOU have not given this the slightest thought.

[What Is the Width of the Prongs and Where Do They Touch the Nave?]

The prongs in the four directions are sixteen small units long, but what is their width at the thickest points? [53b] The *Maṇḍala Vajra Garland* explains:

1842. Tib. *Rdo rje dbyings kyi dkyil chog.*

"Their width at the center is three[1843] small units."[1844] Yet there is no explicit mention of the width of the central prong at its thickest point, which should be the same as that of the prongs in the four directions—one large unit, as the early lamas maintain. The width at the tip of the prong should be one small unit, [but] since it is taught that the height of the tip of the prong should be two small units above the Dharma wheel, [some] draw the prongs two small units wide. But in that case the prongs would not taper gradually, and their tips would form a square; likewise, if the width at the base of the prong is more than two small units, then the width in the middle of the central prong will be greater than a large unit, and that would be wrong. Even though there is no explicit mention of the width of the vajra prongs in the system where the portal is one gate unit high, it is considered equal to that in the system of four gate units for the portal.

[How Do the Prongs Join the Nave of the Vajra?]

When the prongs are four gate units long, they touch the nave at the point of four gate units from the right and the left.[1845] This is so because as cited earlier, the *Maṇḍala Vajra Garland* explains: "[The prongs of the crossed vajra that emerge from a sea monster's mouth peek out a little over] the sides of the portal,"[1846] and so forth [beyond the layer of the suspending banners]. Hence the bases of the prongs emerge from a sea monsters' mouth, above the layer of the suspending banners, while there are four gate units between the suspending banners on the two sides of the portal in the system of four gate units for the portal.

Although a three-pronged vajra does not have prongs above and below the central prong, a five-pronged vajra does have them. The point where the upper and lower prongs join the nave is at a distance of one large unit above and below the inner center of the central prongs.[1847] This is so because the distance between all the prongs—the right and left prongs as well as the upper and lower prongs—and the joining point at the nave must be equal.

In the system where the portal is one gate unit long, the point at which

1843. Reading *gsum* for *gsam* in our text.

1844. Abhayākaragupta, *Dkyil chog rdo rje phreng ba*, *Vajrāvalī*, Tōh 3140, 24b6–25a1; Mori 2009, §12.2.7, 168–169, cited above [52b].

1845. See Tsong kha pa's *'Dod 'jo*, 82b5–83a2.

1846. See the beginning of [52b] above. Abhayākaragupta, *Dkyil chog rdo rje phreng ba*, *Vajrāvalī*, Tōh 3140, 24b6–25a1; Mori 2009, §12.2.7, 168–169.

1847. Reading *rwa* for *ra* in out text.

the prongs meet the nave should be as specified in the *Maṇḍala Ritual* of *Jayabhadra [54a] quoted from the *Maṇḍala Vajra Garland*: "The distance between the mouth of one sea monster and the other on the opposite sides of the gate is three times that of the portal."[1848] Thus it is clear that the prongs in the different directions emerge at the point of eighteen small units to the right and the left of the nave, taking up two small units.[1849]

Explanation of the Portals[1850]

What is the distance from the gate[1851] to the portal,[1852] and what is the shape of the portals? Whatever the dimensions of the four walls, they should not extend beyond the nave of the crossed vajra. Likewise, whatever the height and length of the portals, the points where the columns that support them are set should not extend beyond the prongs of the crossed vajra.

[Is there a Dark Layer[1853] between the Portal and the Gate in Maṇḍala Drawings?][1854]

If there is a dark layer between the portal and the gate in maṇḍala drawings, then in the three-dimensional maṇḍalas and in meditations too there should be one small unit between the outer wall at the entryway[1855] and the edge of the nave of the crossed vajra. Hence the columns that support the portal should

1848. Or *Laṅkājayabhadra, Lang ka Rgyal ba bzang po, *Bde mchog gi dkyil 'khor bya ba'i thabs, Cakrasaṃvara Maṇḍalavidhi*, Tōh 1477, 93a2, has: *rta babs sgo yi sum 'gyur te, chu srin gdong byung rta babs dang*. See also Tsong kha pa, *'Dod 'jo*, 82b1, and *Sngags rim chen mo*, chap. 6, 232. The lines in our text accord with the *Vajrāvalī* rather than with *Jayabhadra's work. See Abhayākaragupta, *Dkyil chog rdo rje phreng ba, Vajrāvalī*, Tōh 3140, 27a7; Mori 2009, §12.4.1, 182.

1849. For Mus srad pa Byams pa Rdo rje rgyal mtshan's objection to this point see his *Dbang chu'i rtsod spong*, 31a2–3.

1850. See Tsong kha pa, *Sngags rim chen mo*, chap. 6, 233–235.

1851. Tib. *sgo*, Skt. *dvāra*.

1852. Tib. *rta babs*, Skt. *toraṇa*.

1853. Tib. *mun snam*, Skt. *andhakāra* or *andharī*. There are two systems for measuring the space between the portals and the gates, one that has a dark layer between them and one that does not.

1854. See Tsong kha pa, *Sngags rim chen mo*, chap. 6, 234–235.

1855. Tib. *sgo logs* or *logs*, Skt. *pakṣa* or *pakṣaka*.

be above[1856] the prongs of the crossed vajra at the edge of the nave. If there is no dark layer in the maṇḍala drawings, then the edge of the wall at the lower corner of the line of the side wall at the entryway will align with the end of the nave of the crossed vajra. In this case the columns that support the portals will be above the prongs of the crossed vajra at a distance of one small unit away from the edge of the nave of the crossed vajra.

Furthermore, when the width and depth of the entryway[1857] are the same size as the width of the gate, if YOU draw a dark layer between the portal and the gate in maṇḍala drawings, YOU contradict the explanation of the Great Charioteers: "The distance from the main line[1858] to the line of the parapets[1859] is undoubtedly two gate units."[1860] Another consequence is that since the height of the column is only five small units, if YOU draw a dark layer between the portal and the gate, the lowest layer[1861] of the portal will not rest on the column. For these reasons there is no dark layer in maṇḍala drawings.

[Yet another reason the dark layer should not appear in maṇḍala drawings is as follows:] Even in the case of a portal one gate unit in height,[1862] the prongs of the crossed vajra in the four directions should emerge at the point that is at a distance of six small units to the right and left from the *brahma* line.[1863] [54b] But if you draw a dark layer between the gate and the portal, the prongs of the crossed vajras would not emerge from the line of the column, and this contradicts the [*Ḍākārṇava*] *Tantra* that teaches: "The point that emerges from the tip of the column is the great radiant crossed vajra."[1864]

1856. Reading *steng* for *stang* in our text.

1857. As explained in notes 1833–34, the width and depth of the entryway are equal to the lines at the back and the side of the entryway called *'gram, kapola* and *logs, pakṣa.*

1858. Tib. *rtsa thig,* Skt. *mūlasūtra.* For illustrations see Mori 2009, 642, and diagram 3.

1859. Tib. *mda' yab,* Skt. *kramaśīrṣa.* These are wall structures surrounding the roof and the four portals.

1860. Tib. *sgo tshad,* Skt. *dvārapramāṇa.* The width of the gateway, which is also used as a unit of measurement for drawing the celestial mansion.

1861. Tib. *snam bu,* Skt. *paṭṭikā.* The layers of the portal, eleven in number.

1862. The portal can be either one or three gate units high.

1863. Tib. *tshangs thig,* Skt. *brahmasūtra.* The *brahma* lines are the two lines drawn first across the center that divide the maṇḍala circle into four quarters. The first *brahma* line is the vertical line from "east" to "west" [the viewer faces east]. The second *brahma* line is the horizontal line from "north" to "south."

1864. *Mkha' 'gro rgya mtsho,* chap. 10, Tōh 372, cited above [52b].

[Is there a Dark Layer between the Gate and the Portal in Visualized Maṇḍalas?]

For meditational purposes the reason for omitting the dark layer is no longer valid because in that case there would be space for it between the gate and the portal. Hence, in meditations as in three-dimensional maṇḍalas there is indeed a dark layer between the gate and the portal, whether the width and depth of the entryway[1865] are the same[1866] size as the width of the gate or not, regardless of which tradition you choose to follow concerning the height of the portal.[1867] This dark layer signifies the empty space between the gate and the portal, not the space between the columns.

In the *Maṇḍala Vajra Garland*, the size of the dark layer is one small unit in maṇḍala drawings, meditations, and three-dimensional maṇḍalas alike. The *Maṇḍala Vajra Garland* explains: "The position that the columns of the portals emerge from the lines of the walls and are seven small units long each is incongruous because the columns that support the portals stand on a square platform[1868] some small distance from the celestial mansion. Since they stand on the same level, they [the columns] appear to be joined to the platforms, and thus it is appropriate to draw them skirting the platforms."[1869]

Thus, in order to refute the position that the lines of the columns that support the portals emerge from the lines of the walls, [the *Maṇḍala Vajra Garland*] argues that the columns stand some small distance from the celestial mansion. Hence it is maintained that in every case the portals stand some small distance from the celestial mansion. Smṛtijñānakīrti in his *Secret Drawing Ritual* also refutes the position that the portal and the celestial mansion are joined when the height of the portal is one gate unit: "Do not combine the

1865. The *'gram, kapola* and the *logs, pakṣa.*

1866. Reading *mnyam* for *minyam* in our text.

1867. There are two systems for measuring the height of the portal, one gate unit and three gate units.

1868. Tib. *stegs bu*, Skt. *vedī* or *vedikā*. Below [55b] Mkhas grub rje explains that this term refers also to the offering ledge, Tib. *'dod snam, 'dod yon gyi snam bu*, Skt. *vedī* or *vedikā*, the protruding ledge for the offering goddesses.

1869. Abhayākaragupta, *Dkyil chog rdo rje phreng ba, Vajrāvalī*, Tōh 3140, 25a1–2; Mori 2009, §12.2.7, 168 and 169. D and Mori have *'thon* for *thon* and *mnyam po* for *mnyam pa* in our text. Cited in Tsong kha pa, *Sngags rim chen mo*, chap. 6, 234.

portal with the edge of the gate. Rather leave a space of three small units away from the inner roof of the portal."[1870] [55a]

Moreover, authoritative treatises do not teach that the portal is joined to the gate, which would be unreasonable. Hence it is absolutely wrong to join the portals with the gates in three-dimensional celestial mansions. Śraddhākaravarman too says: "Leave three units from the inner roof[1871] of the portal."[1872] In other words, the portal should be three units away from the inner roof of the gate.

[More Disputes about the Portals]

Some people maintain that it is as if there were a horse[1873] at the side wall of the entryway to the portal and that the celestial mansion is like a stūpa with five pinnacles.[1874] This is a mere fabrication based on a false transmission [of Buddhaguhya's line]: "The outer shape [of the celestial mansion] should be like a stūpa, in the shape of a castle."[1875]

Therefore they are inconsistent with many works of the Great Charioteers who explain that the height of the columns that hold up the portals is five small units. Their argument cannot withstand reasoning that relies on scriptures, and they lack even the slightest proof based on incontestable scriptures and reasoning. Those who rely on these words demonstrate but their own stupidity. Otherwise, since the celestial mansion is indicated here through terms such as "castle-like," it arguably has the form of polygonal tower, a hilltop fort, and so forth.

1870. Smṛtijñānakīrti, *Gsang ldan gyi thig chog*, Tōh 2585, 150b15–6. D has *dag la* for *dag las*; *sgo yi* for *sgo'i*; and *twa ra ṇa* for *rta ra dang* in our text. The citation of this passage in Tsong kha pa, *Sngags rim chen mo*, chap. 6, 234, has *dag la* for *dag las* as well, but the rest follows the Derge.

1871. Tib. *ya phubs*.

1872. Śraddhākaravarman, *Dkyil 'khor gyi thig gdab pa'i mdor bsdus pa, Saṅkṣiptamaṇḍalasūtra*, Tōh 2505, 206b3. See also his autocommentary: *Dkyil 'khor gyi thig gdab pa'i mdor bsdus pa'i 'grel pa, Saṅkṣiptamaṇḍalasūtravṛtti*, Tōh 2506, 211a4.

1873. The Tibetan name of the portal, *rta babs*, indicates a ramp for dismounting a horse, possibly reminiscent of the architecture of an Indian royal palace. See also Bu ston, *Mdor byas 'grel chen*, 18a1.

1874. There are two different statements here. The second statement is refuted already in the Bstan 'gyur. See Padmasambhava, or Padmākara, *Gzhal yas khang gsal bar byed pa'i mngon rtogs mun sel sgron ma*, Tōh 3706, 6a4. See also Bu ston, *Mdor byas 'grel chen*, 18a3.

1875. Buddhaguhya, *Dkyil 'khor gyi chos mdor bsdus pa, Dharmamaṇḍalasūtra*, Tōh 3705, 2b4; English translation in Lo Bue 1987, 796.

OTHERS[1876] maintain that Buddhaguhya explains: "Since at each of the four outer corners of the gatehouse there are four columns, supporting the ends of eight beams that form the base of the portal, the columns should be built accordingly from top to bottom."[1877] Therefore four columns should be placed at the four corners at the side wall of the entryway,[1878] and the portals are set above the gates. It appears that this treatise is falsely attributed to Buddhaguhya, because the height of the columns that support the portals is only five small units, hence the portals erected on the columns near the wall will not reach the top of the gates. [55b] Moreover even if the portals reached the gate, it would follow that the height of the celestial mansion would only be five small units.

If YOU maintain that the height of the celestial mansion is only five small units, then the heads of the deities in the thirteen deity maṇḍalas of both Red and Black Yamāri,[1879] who sit on a lotus and solar seats upon the inner crossed vajra, would not fit under the roof. This is so because the deities must rise to a height of one gate unit [four small units]; and because the inner sides of the right and left prongs of the twenty-pronged crossed vajra must emerge at a distance of one third of a small unit from the nave, while the upper and lower prongs as well as the right and left prongs must meet the central prong at an equal distance from the nave. Hence, the height of the nave must be at least five and a third small units, while the height of the wall is only five small units.

In YOUR system it is not possible to explain that the dark layer between the gate and the portal in maṇḍala drawings is the empty space found in instructions for meditation purposes. Thus YOUR system is greatly mistaken. This is so because the meaning of the word *platform*[1880] in the recent citation of the *Maṇḍala Vajra Garland*[1881] is "offering ledge";[1882] and it is situated not far

1876. See Bu ston, *Mdor byas 'grel chen*, 18a1–3.

1877. This refers to the top of the column, Tib. *ka gzhu*, and the base of the column, Tib. *ka gdan*. Buddhaguhya, *Dkyil 'khor gyi chos mdor bsdus pa*, *Dharmamaṇḍalasūtra*, Tōh 3705, 2b4; English translation in Lo Bue 1987, 796–797.

1878. Tib. *sgo logs*, Skt. *pakṣa*.

1879. Tib. Gshin rje gshed.

1880. The Sanskrit term *vedī* is translated into Tibetan in this line of the *Dkyil chog rdo rje phreng ba* as *stegs bu*. This red platform on which the offering goddesses stand can be seen in plates 4 and 7.

1881. Abhayākaragupta, *Dkyil chog rdo rje phreng ba*, *Vajrāvalī*, Tōh 3140, 25a1–2; Mori 2009, §12.2.7, 168 and 169.

1882. Here Mkhas grub rje uses here the Tibetan term *'dod snam*, short for *'dod yon gyi snam bu*, for the Sanskrit term *vedī*; the protruding ledge for the offering goddesses. See the section "The Ledge for the Offering Goddesses" below [61b].

from the columns supporting the portal. The offering ledge and the columns supporting the portal are on the same level as the underlying ground, so when seen from a distance they appear to be joined.

Therefore [the *Maṇḍala Vajra Garland*] explains that it is appropriate to draw the line of the column as arising from the line of the offering ledge. It is maintained that although the offering ledge rests upon the nave of the crossed vajra and the columns arise from the nave, it is inappropriate to set them on different levels. When the crossed vajra has three prongs, the nave may be lower, and in such a case the offering ledge and the columns will be at the same level. But when the crossed vajra has five prongs, the nave of the vajra must be higher, hence there will be a small difference in height between the offering ledge and the columns that support the portals. [56a] Nevertheless, when seen from afar the difference in level is not apparent, so it is appropriate that they would appear to be joined. Authoritative scriptures do not specify an exact height for the nave of the crossed vajra, hence it is appropriate to draw the three-pronged and five-pronged crossed vajras in keeping with aesthetic considerations.

[The Columns Supporting the Portal][1883]

*Jayabhadra as quoted from the *Maṇḍala Vajra Garland* teaches: "The columns supporting the portals that rest upon the vases on the platform should rise straight up."[1884] Thus the total height of the columns—including the vases they rest on and the square platforms on which the vases rest—is five small units in height.

As to the number of columns,[1885] EARLY TIBETAN SCHOLARS maintain that each of the portals in the four directions rests on four columns. But SOME OTHER SCHOLARS say that this is not right, because according to the *Vajrodaya*: "There are four portals and eight columns."[1886] Likewise, the

1883. See Tsong kha pa, *Sngags rim chen mo*, chap. 6, 232, 235.

1884. *Jayabhadra, or *Laṅkājayabhadra, *Bde mchog gi dkyil 'khor bya ba'i thabs, Cakrasaṃvara Maṇḍalavidhi*, Tōh 1477, 93a2, is cited in Abhayākaragupta, *Dkyil chog rdo rje phreng ba, Vajrāvalī*, Tōh 3140, 27a7; Mori 2009, §12.4.1, 182. Our text cites the version of the *Vajrāvalī*, while *Jayabhadra's texts as it appears in the Derge is: *'dod yon bum pa las byung ba'i rta babs kyi ni ka ba'o*. Still, while both the *Vajrāvalī* and *Jayabhadra have *bum pa las [']byung pa'i*, our text has *bum pa la gnas pa'i*. As above [53b–54a], these lines are likely cited from the *Vajrāvalī* and not from *Jayabhadra's work.

1885. See Tsong kha pa, *Sngags rim chen mo*, chap. 6, 232.

1886. Ānandagarbha, *Rdo rje 'byung ba, Vajrodaya*, Tōh 2516, 37a4. See also Tsong kha pa, *'Dod 'jo*, 85a3–4.

Cluster of Instructions explains: "The eight columns supporting the portal are the eightfold noble path."[1887] This does not contradict the *Entirely Secret Tantra*, which explains that there are four columns supporting each portal: "The portals and their columns are the four proper abandonments."[1888] Commenting on this verse, Ratnākaraśānti says: "The portals and their pairs of columns are the four proper abandonments."[1889] Thus he clarifies that each portal rests on a pair of columns. So THEY SAY.[1890]

However, in the *Cluster of Instructions* we find: "Nāgabodhi taught that the purified aspects of the gate-posts[1891] are the four bases of miraculous powers."[1892] Thus, in his *Maṇḍala Rituals*, Nāgabodhi counts each pair of gate-posts in each direction of the maṇḍala as one [56b] and on this basis explains that the four pure bases of miraculous powers are the four gate posts. Similarly, here too, although there are four columns supporting each portal, two on each side, the two columns on the right are counted as one and the two columns on the left are counted as one. Accordingly, the eight pure liberations[1893] and the eightfold noble path are associated with the eight columns supporting the portals. Additionally, in taking into account that there are columns supporting the portal in each of the four directions, their purified aspects are explained as the four proper abandonments.[1894] All these are similar ways of classifying the number of columns, hence they are not contradictory. Yet, since it would be very difficult to balance the portal on only two columns and would not be pleasing to look at, it is better to set each portal on four columns.

1887. Abhayākaragupta, *Man ngag snye ma, Āmnāyamañjarī*, chap. 18, Tōh 1198, 168b1. D has *brgyad rnam par dag pas sgo'i ka ba brgyad rnams so* for *brgyad pa ni rta babs kyi ka ba brgyad do* in our text.

1888. Tib. *yang dag spong ba*, Skt. *samyakprahāṇa*. *Thams cad gsang ba rgyud, Sarvarahasya Tantra*, Tōh 481, 6b5; English translation in Wayman 1984, 548.

1889. Ratnākaraśānti, *Thams cad gsang ba'i bshad sbyar gsang ba'i sgron ma, Sarvarahasyani bandharahasyapradīpa*, Tōh 2623, 146a3.

1890. In his *'Dod 'jo*, 85a5, Tsong kha pa has *zhes gsung mod kyang* for *zhes zer mod kyang* in our text.

1891. Tib. *sgo khyud*, Skt. *niryūha*.

1892. Abhayākaragupta, *Man ngag snye ma, Āmnāyamañjarī*, chap. 18, Tōh 1198, 168a7–b1. Nāgabodhi has here: *rdzu 'phrul rkang pa sgo khyud ni, bzhi ste de yang rnam pa bzhi*. See his *Dkyil chog nyi shu pa, Maṇḍalaviṃśatividhi*, chap. 12, v. 40, Tōh 1810, 140b6–7; Tanaka 2000, 36.

1893. Tib. *rnam thar brgyad*, Skt. *vimokṣāṣṭaka* or *aṣṭamovimokṣa*.

1894. Tib. *yang dag spong ba*, Skt. *samyakprahāṇa*.

[THE WIDTH OF A PORTAL]

*Jayabhadra taught that, in the system where the portal is one gate unit, "The distance between the mouth of one sea monster and the other on the opposite side of the gate is three times that of the portal."[1895] Thus it is explained that the width of the portal is three gate units, but this does not refer to the width of the layer[1896] at the upper side of the portal, because when the portal is one gate unit, the width of its lower layer[1897] is fourteen small units. Rather [*Jayabhadra] refers to the width at the base of the portal, and since there is no wall at the base [of the portal, the line *three times the length of the portal*] must apply to the distance between the columns at the base of the portal; thus, there are three gate units between the columns of each portal.

When the portal is three gate units and the width and depth[1898] of the entryway are the same size as the gate,[1899] there are sixteen small units between the inner sides of the columns; such is the width of the portal at its base. When the width and depth of the entryway are not the same size as the gate,[1900] there are fourteen small units between the inner sides of the columns; [57a] and that is the width of the portal at its base. In this case although there are sixteen small units between the mouths of the sea monsters[1901] on each side of the portal, there is a space of one small unit for each of the suspending banners[1902] to the left and right of the columns.[1903] The suspending banners are ornaments hung from the roof of the portal to the right and left of the columns. Hence their space is not included in the width of the base of the portal.

If there is a beam between the lower layer of the portal and its supporting column, the banners or the column's ornaments are suspended from the edge of the beam, and if there is no beam they hang down from the edge of the "precious

1895. This was cited above [53b–54a]. *Jayabhadra, or *Laṅkājayabhadra, *Bde mchog gi dkyil 'khor bya ba'i thabs, Cakrasaṃvara Maṇḍalavidhi*, Tōh 1477, 93a, as cited in Abhayākaragupta, *Dkyil chog rdo rje phreng ba, Vajrāvalī*, Tōh 3140, 27a7; Mori 2009, §12.4.1, 182.

1896. Tib. *snam bu*, Skt. *paṭṭikā*.

1897. Tib. *snam bu 'og ma*.

1898. As explained above, the width and depth of the entryway are equal to the lines located behind and beside the entryway, called *'gram* and *logs* in Tibetan and *kapola* and *pakṣa* in Sanskrit. For illustrations, see Tanaka 2004, 34, and Mori 2009, 640.

1899. This, in the case of the Guhyasamāja maṇḍala.

1900. This refers to the maṇḍalas of Cakrasaṃvara and Bhairava.

1901. Tib. *chu srin*, Skt. *makara*.

1902. Tib. *dar dpyangs*, Skt. *añcala*. See Mori 2009, 640, for the location of this line according to the system of Abhayākaragupta's *Dkyil chog rdo rje phreng ba, Vajrāvalī*.

1903. Hence the distance between the columns is still fourteen small units.

drip-like" ornament.[1904] Some texts explain that on the layer of banners[1905] there is a lion on an elephant suspending garlands[1906] of jewels from his mouth.[1907] This does not mean that one should depict the banners hanging from the mouth of the elephant[1908] but rather that these should be depicted on the banners.[1909]

[The Layers of the Portal][1910]

The eleven layers of the portals in ascending order are gold, precious "drip-like" ornament, jewels, "hoof-like" ornament, dark layer, multi-colored layer, dark layer, "drip-like" ornament, jewels, "hoof-like" ornament, and parapets.[1911] The height of the fifth and seventh layers [the two dark layers] is one and a half small units, while the height of each of the other nine layers is one small unit. Thus there are two layers of the same height and nine layers of the same height.

Or alternatively, the eleven layers in ascending order are[1912] "drip-like" ornament, jewels, "hoof-like" ornament, gold, sea monster,[1913] gold, "hoof-like" ornament, jewels, "hoof-like" ornament, gold, and parapets. When the portal is three gate units, the height of the third, seventh, and ninth layers is one small unit, that of the fourth, sixth, and tenth layers is half a small unit, and the remaining five layers are one and a half small units. [57b] Thus there are five layers of the same height and a pair of three layers of the same height.

It is taught that the sides of the "hoof-like" ornaments and multi-colored

1904. Tib. *rin chen shar bu*, Skt. *bakulī* or *vakulī*. See "line p" in Mori 2009, 640.

1905. Tib. *dar dpyangs kyi snam bu*, Skt. *añcalapaṭṭikā*.

1906. Tib. *do shal*, Skt. *hāra*.

1907. This sentence is a citation of Abhayākaragupta, *Dkyil chog rdo rje phreng ba*, *Vajrāvalī*, Tōh 3140, 27b2; Mori 2009, §12.4.1, 182–183.

1908. Tsong kha pa, *Sngags rim chen mo*, chap. 6, 235, has lion here instead of elephant.

1909. See Bu ston, *Mdor byas 'grel chen*, 18b1–3.

1910. See Tsong kha pa, *Sngags rim chen mo*, chap. 6, 235–236.

1911. Tib. *gser*, *rin chen shar bu*, *rin po che*, *rmig pa*, *mun pa*, *varaṇḍa*, *mun pa*, *rin chen shar bu*, *rin po che*, *rta rmig*, and *mda' yab*; Skt. *suvarṇa*, *bakūlī*, *ratna*, *khura*, *andhakāra*, *varaṇḍa*, *andhakāra*, *bakūlī*, *ratna*, *khura*, and *kramaśīrṣa*. See Abhayākaragupta, *Dkyil chog rdo rje phreng ba*, *Vajrāvalī*, Tōh 3140, 23b1–2; Mori 2009, §12.2.5, 162–163. For illustrations, see diagram 1 and Mori 2009, 640–641.

1912. This is in the case of Bhairava. See Abhayākaragupta, *Dkyil chog rdo rje phreng ba*, *Vajrāvalī*, Tōh 3140, 23b3; Mori 2009, §12.2.5, 162–163.

1913. Tib. *chu srin*, Skt. *makara*.

layers should be elegantly decorated with victory banners,[1914] pennants,[1915] lions, eight-legged lions,[1916] peacocks,[1917] as well as male and female kinnaras.[1918] Thus depictions of these animals should be placed as far as possible at the level of the dark layers [above the "hoof-like" ornaments and multi-colored layers]. The translation of the *Maṇḍala Vajra Garland* by Pang Lotsāwa[1919] has eight-legged tigers instead of lions.[1920]

The explanation adorn[1921] "the portal with splendid canopies,[1922] necklaces, and strings of pearls"[1923] means that they should be depicted as covering the opening of the portal.[1924] The meaning of the garlands and so forth is taught as: "the strings of pearls above that emerge out of the mouths of sea monsters and so forth should be drawn as beautifully as possible."[1925] A space of half a small unit is apportioned within the opening of the portal for ornaments such as jewels and so forth.

[The Top of the Portal][1926]

Some Indians[1927] maintain that only a buck and a doe are found on the eleventh level of the portal but no parapets. However, the *Maṇḍala Vajra Garland* refutes this by citing Nāgabodhi: "The portal, three times the gate in

1914. Tib. *rgyal mtshan*, Skt. *dhvaja*.

1915. Tib. *ba dan*, Skt. *patāka*.

1916. Tib. *seng ge rkang pa bgyad pa*, Skt. *śārdūla*.

1917. Tib. *rma bya*, Skt. *mayūra*.

1918. Tib. *mi'am ci* and *mi'am ci mo*. This is a citation of Abhayākaragupta, *Dkyil chog rdo rje phreng ba*, *Vajrāvalī*, Tōh 3140, 28a2; Mori 2009, §12.4.3, 184–185, that adds *nang pa*, *haṃsa*.

1919. Dpang lo tsā ba (1276–1342).

1920. As noted above, the Skt. in Abhayākaragupta, *Vajrāvalī*, is *śārdūla* and not *śarabha*.

1921. This is a citation of Abhayākaragupta, *Dkyil chog rdo rje phreng ba*, *Vajrāvalī*, Tōh 3140, 28a1–2; Mori 2009, §12.4.3, 184–185.

1922. Tib. *bla re*, Skt. *vitāna*.

1923. Tib. *do shal dang do shal phyed pa*, Skt. *hārārdhahāra*.

1924. Tib. *kyog po'i nang*, Skt. *vakrābhyantara*. See Abhayākaragupta, *Dkyil chog rdo rje phreng ba*, *Vajrāvalī*, Tōh 3140, 38a1; Mori 2009, §13.2.2, 235–236.

1925. This is a citation of Abhayākaragupta, *Dkyil chog rdo rje phreng ba*, *Vajrāvalī*, Tōh 3140, 24a3; Mori 2009, §12.2.6, 164 and 166.

1926. See Tsong kha pa, *Sngags rim chen mo*, chap. 6, 236–237.

1927. This objection is found in Abhayākaragupta, *Dkyil chog rdo rje phreng ba*, *Vajrāvalī*, Tōh 3140, 24a6; Mori 2009, §12.2.6, 165–166. See also Tsong kha pa, *Sngags rim chen mo*, chap. 6, 236.

size, which rests on columns that stand on vases, has 'directional'[1928] parapets and resounding bells."[1929] The *Maṇḍala Vajra Garland* then explains: "Here there are two sections of parapet behind the tails of the buck and doe that face each other and flank the seat [of the Dharma wheel]."[1930] The term *directional* signifies the two higher sections of parapet. Therefore the buck and doe do not rest on the lower parapet, but at the level of the higher parapet.[1931] Since there are sections of parapet behind the tails of both the buck and doe there are four parapets altogether on each portal.

Above the two sets of parapets at the right and left outer corners of the portals there are two monkeys holding parasols. [58a] For it is taught that there are two white parasols,[1932] the size of two small units, with overhanging tassels, topped by a crescent moon, jewels, and a vajra, and these parasols have jeweled handles three small units in height.[1933] Additional systems are taught as well. Place victory banners and pennants the size of one small unit upon the external parts of the two parapets. At the center of the eleventh layer of the portal there is a golden wheel with ten spokes and a rim mounted on a lotus with lunar seats, two small units in size. To the right and left of the seat of the wheel are the buck and doe, one small unit in height. The buck and doe face the Dharma wheel at a distance of half a small unit; their necks are raised

1928. Our text, which follows Abhayākaragupta, *Dkyil chog rdo rje phreng ba, Vajrāvalī*, has *phyogs can*, as does the Tibetan translation of Nāgabodhi's text. The Tibetan translation of Nāgabodhi's work has *bya 'dab*. The Sanskrit is *pakṣiṇī*. Below Mkhas grub rje interprets *phyogs can* to mean the parapets on either side.

1929. Abhayākaragupta, *Dkyil chog rdo rje phreng ba, Vajrāvalī*, Tōh 3140, 24a6–7; Mori 2009, §12.2.6, 165–166. The line of Nāgabodhi is from his *Dkyil chog nyi shu pa, Maṇḍalaviṃśatividhi*, chap. 4, v. 15, Tōh 1810, 134a2–3; Tanaka 2004, 31. The Tibetan translation of Nāgabodhi's work has *gnas pa* for *gnas pa'i*; *rta babs sgo yi sum 'gyur te* for *sgo las sum 'gyur rta babs ni*; *mda' yab dang ni bya 'dab dang ldan* for *phyogs can mda' yab dag dang ldan*; and *ldan zhing dril bu nges par 'khrol* for *dril bu'i sgra ni yang dag sgrogs* in our text. Note that our text cites the line of Nāgabodhi's text as it appears in Abhayākaragupta, *Dkyil chog rdo rje phreng ba, Vajrāvalī*.

1930. Abhayākaragupta, *Dkyil chog rdo rje phreng ba, Vajrāvalī*, Tōh 3140, 24a7–b1; Mori 2009, §12.2.6, 165–166.

1931. The second level of the parapet is found only on the right and left sides. At the center of this level are the Dharma wheel flanked by the buck and the doe. See also Abhayākaragupta, *Dkyil chog rdo rje phreng ba, Vajrāvalī*, Tōh 3140, 24b1 and 26b1–2; Mori 2009, §12.2.6, 165–167 and §12.3.5, 177–178.

1932. In the Sanskrit the equivalents of *g.yog* [*g.yogs*] and *gdugs* are written together in the locative case: *paṭale cchatre śvete*. See Mori 2009, §12.3.5, 177–178.

1933. See Abhayākaragupta, *Dkyil chog rdo rje phreng ba, Vajrāvalī*, Tōh 3140, 26b1–2; Mori 2009, §12.3.5, 177–178.

one small unit, their heads are up tilted and their eyes look at the tip of the wheel.[1934] In two-dimensional drawings of the maṇḍala the central prong of the crossed vajra should appear between the spokes of the wheel, as explained in the *Maṇḍala Vajra Garland*.[1935]

[To the Right and Left of the Portal][1936]

To the right and left of the portal nearby are two wish-fulfilling trees growing out of "vases of excellence,"[1937] adorned with the seven royal treasures,[1938] the elephant, and so forth.[1939] According to Bhavyakīrti, the wheel is yellow with eight spokes; the elephant is white with six tusks; the horse is green; the queen is sixteen years old and dark blue in color; the jewel is yellow with six sides; the master of the house is red and holds an inexhaustible treasury; the general is black, furnished with armor, and holding a spear and sword.[1940] A sūtra explains that the jewel is blue and has eight sides. Floating in space are siddhas and embodied goddesses who emerge from the clouds holding flowers.[1941]

1934. Our text follows Abhayākaragupta, *Dkyil chog rdo rje phreng ba, Vajrāvalī*, Tōh 3140, 24a4–5; Mori 2009, §12.2.6, 165–167.

1935. See the citation of Abhayākaragupta, *Dkyil chog rdo rje phreng ba, Vajrāvalī*, Tōh 3140, above [52b].

1936. See Tsong kha pa, *Sngags rim chen mo*, chap. 6, 237.

1937. Tib. *bum pa bzang po*, Skt. *bhadraghaṭa*.

1938. These are the seven royal treasures of a universal monarch listed immediately below. See the Mvy. 3621–3628.

1939. Our text follows Abhayākaragupta, *Dkyil chog rdo rje phreng ba, Vajrāvalī*, Tōh 3140, 28a2–3; Mori 2009, §12.4.3, 184–185, and Tsong kha pa, *'Dod 'jo*, 85b2–5.

1940. Bhavyakīrti, *Rab tu sgron gsal, Prakāśikā*, Tōh 1793, 16b4–6.

1941. *Chos yang dag par sdud pa'i mdo, Dharmasaṃgīti Sūtra*, Tōh 238, 21a5. Our text follows Abhayākaragupta, *Dkyil chog rdo rje phreng ba, Vajrāvalī*, Tōh 3140, 28a3; Mori 2009, §12.4.3, 184–185.

Explaining the Actual Celestial Mansion Along with the Thrones

[The Walls][1942]

[58b] There are two systems for creating the fivefold wall:[1943] depositing the five lines horizontally from outermost to innermost or stacking them vertically one on top of the other. But the latter system is inappropriate because the former system is the one used in drawings and can likewise be applied to meditations;[1944] and when the lines are stacked vertically, the width of the wall is only a fifth of a small unit in size and thus much too narrow; likewise, it would be difficult to set the panel[1945] on top of the wall and so forth. Thus the width of the base of the wall is a twentieth of a gate unit.[1946] The *Maṇḍala Rituals of the Guhyasamāja* explains this: "The lines of the maṇḍala should not touch each other but have the space of a grain[1947] between them."[1948] Hence it is taught that each line should be a twentieth of a gate unit in width [a fifth of a small unit].

In this regard SOME LATER TIBETANS[1949] maintain that since the width of all five lines of the wall is only one small unit, if each line is a twentieth of a gate unit in width [a fifth of a small unit], there will be no space between the lines of the wall, hence this contradicts the position [of the *Maṇḍala Rituals of the Guhyasamāja*] that there should be the space of one grain between the lines. So say THOSE who are mentally incapable of understanding even this much,

1942. Tib. *rtsig pa*, Skt. *bhitti*.

1943. Our text follows Abhayākaragupta, *Dkyil chog rdo rje phreng ba*, *Vajrāvalī*, Tōh 3140, 37b3; Mori 2009, §13.2.1, 234–235, as well as Tsong kha pa, *Sngags rim chen mo*, chap. 6, 237–238, and *'Dod 'jo*, 86a5–6.

1944. According to Abhayākaragupta, *Dkyil chog rdo rje phreng ba*, *Vajrāvalī*, this is the method in the meditation on the maṇḍala.

1945. Tib. *pha gu*. For a discussion of the panel see below [61b].

1946. Since one gate unit is four small units.

1947. Tib. *nas*, Skt. *yava*.

1948. Dīpaṅkarabhadra, *Gsang ba 'dus pa'i dkyil 'khor gyi cho ga = Dkyil chog bzhi rgya lnga bcu pa*, *Guhyasamāja Maṇḍalavidhi*, Tōh 1865, 79a4; Bahulkar 2006, 136, v. 249; Klein-Schwind 2008, v. 249. The same verse appears in the *Sdom 'byung*, *Saṃvarodaya Tantra*, Tōh 373, cited below, but there are certain differences between the two Tibetan translations. See note 1950.

1949. See Ngor chen, *Zla zer*, 104b6–105a5. Our text follows Tsong kha pa, *'Dod 'jo*, 86b1–6.

but do not hesitate to criticize those siddhas of supreme attainment whose fame in India was like the sun. THOSE TIBETANS are indeed outrageous.

For if this were so, it would contradict the *Saṃvarodaya Tantra* that teaches: "The lines should be drawn leaving a space of just one grain between them."[1950] This, because in the system of the *Saṃvarodaya Tantra* the width of the wall is one small unit,[1951] and when a small unit is divided into five it becomes a twentieth of a gate unit. Hence, THEY should say without hesitation: There are contradictions even within the tantras spoken by Vajradhara. These explanations of the *Saṃvarodaya Tantra* and *Maṇḍala Rituals of the Guhyasamāja* follow the system of one cubit for the main line. [59a] In one cubit[1952] there are twenty-four fingers,[1953] and in a span of a finger[1954] there are seven grains. Thus, roughly calculated, the width at the base of each layer of the wall is one grain.

Regarding the meaning of the phrase [of the *Maṇḍala Rituals of the Guhyasamāja*] "The lines should not touch each other but have the space of a grain between them," Dārikapa explains: "You should not blend the lines but leave the space of a grain between them."[1955] This means that the colored powders of the maṇḍala should not be blended; it does not mean that they should have a space between them that prevents them from touching each other. In his commentary on the *Maṇḍala Rituals of the Guhyasamāja*, Ratnākaraśānti explains the verse "The lines should not touch each other but have the space of a grain between them" as "[This refers to] the size of the lower levels [of the wall], but you should draw the walls as elegantly as possible at their upper levels."[1956] This explanation relates to two-dimensional colored maṇḍalas, but

1950. *Sdom 'byung*, Tōh 373, 286a2–3; Sanskrit, Tibetan, and English translation in Tsuda 1974, chap. 17, v. 32ab. D and Tsuda have *phan tshun bar du nas re tsam, shong ba'i tshang du bri ba ste* for *ri mo phan tshun dag gi bar, nas tsam du ni gdab pa bya* in our text.

1951. In his *'Dod 'jo*, 86b3, Tsong kha pa has a fourth of a gate unit which equals a small unit.

1952. Tib. *khru*, Skt. *hasta*. For this and the following measurements, see Vasubandhu, *Mdzod 'grel*, *Kośabhāṣya*, chap. 3, v. 87, Tōh 4090, 155a2–6; Pradhan 1975, 176–177; Pruden 1988–1990, 474.

1953. Tib. *sor mo*, Skt. *aṅguli*.

1954. Tib. *sor tshig*, Skt. *aṅguliparvan*. According to Vasubandhu, three *sor tshig*, *aṅguliparvans* make one *sor mo*, *aṅguli*. See his *Mdzod 'grel*, *Kośabhāṣya*, chap. 3, following v. 86, Tōh 4090, 155a5; Pradhan 1975, 176; Pruden 1988–1990, 474.

1955. Dārika, *'Khor lo sdom pa'i dkyil 'khor gyi cho ga de kho na nyid la 'jug pa*, *Cakrasaṃvara Maṇḍalavidhi Tattvāvatāra*, Tōh 1430, 210a3.

1956. Ratnākaraśānti, *Gsang ba 'dus pa'i dkyil 'khor gyi cho ga'i 'grel pa*, *Guhyasamāja Maṇḍalavidhiṭīkā*, Tōh 1871, 98a3–4.

in the case of three-dimensional depictions and for meditation purposes there is no difference in width between the lower and upper levels of the wall.

[The Colors of the Five Lines of the Walls]

The sequence of colors of the five lines of the walls should accord with the colors of the five tathāgatas in the different directions of the maṇḍala, if this is clearly specified.[1957] The *Maṇḍala Vajra Garland* explains that if this is not clearly specified, the colors should accord with those of the lords of the tathāgata family in each direction.[1958] The colors of the lines of the wall, outer to inner, should follow the colors of the tathāgatas of the maṇḍala as you circle clockwise beginning from the east and ending at the center. This explanation has priority, but certainly the colors are not necessarily restricted in this way. In the present context the colors of the lines starting from the outside are respectively white, yellow, red, green, and blue according to the sequence of the colors of the five tathāgatas in the four cardinal directions and the center. Master Nāgabodhi teaches: "The lines, white, yellow, red, green, and blue, should be equal, one twentieth of a gate unit each."[1959] Thus the colors of the five lines of the wall are not defined by the colors of the directions.[1960]

[How Far Does the Wall Reach at the Entryway?][1961]

When the width[1962] and depth[1963] of the entryway are the same size as the gate, the wall reaches the edge of the nave of the crossed vajra. Although the fronts of the five lines of the wall are equal, [59b] when the width and depth of the entryway are not the same size as the gate, there is one small unit between the front of the lower line of the wall and the edge of the nave of the crossed vajra. When the five lines of the wall before the lower part of the side wall of the entryway are unequal in length, it is more elegant to extend them slightly forward.

1957. See Tsong kha pa's *'Dod 'jo*, 86b6–87a4.

1958. Abhayākaragupta, *Dkyil chog rdo rje phreng ba*, *Vajrāvalī*, Tōh 3140, 37b1–3; Mori 2009, §13.2.1, 234–235.

1959. Nāgabodhi, *Dkyil chog nyi shu pa*, *Maṇḍalaviṃśatividhi*, chap. 10, v. 2, Tōh 1810, 137a6–7; Tanaka 2000, 358.

1960. See Tsong kha pa's *'Dod 'jo*, 87a2.

1961. See Tsong kha pa, *Sngags rim chen mo*, chap. 6, 238.

1962. Tib. *'gram*, Skt. *kapola* or *kapolaka*.

1963. Tib. *logs*, Skt. *pakṣa* or *pakṣaka*.

[The Beams over the Entryway]

SOME SAY[1964] that the measurement of one small unit for the width of the wall as measured from the inner edge of the side wall of the entryway to the other inner edge and from the outer edge of the wall to the other outer edge refers to maṇḍala drawings. But while meditating, the beam of the side wall of the entryway is eight small units above, hence there is a space of two small units between the gate and the portal. The reason for this is that in maṇḍala drawings the beams that support the inner roof[1965] are in front of the side wall of the entryway, whereas if the wall is built in this location in a three-dimensional maṇḍala, the beam will not reach the top of the columns. This is so because the *Maṇḍala Vajra Garland*,[1966] the *Commentary on the Saṃvarodaya Tantra*,[1967] and the *Maṇḍala Rituals* by Vibhūti[1968] explain that the line eight small units long that runs from the inner edge of the side wall of the entryway to the other edge denotes the beam over the entryway. THEY say that if one claims that it is appropriate to place the beam not in front of the side wall at the entryway but alongside the two inner lines of that side wall, then the wall of the inner roof will not be ten small units, hence the wall would dangle in space, and this would be unacceptable. So THEY SAY.

This is not correct, because if while maintaining that it is certain that the beam is eight small units long and the front wall is ten small units, YOU argue that it is not correct to let the wall float in space without a beam, then if a beam were placed from the front edge of the side wall of the entryway to the other front edge, it would not reach the other side because the beam is only eight small units long; [60a] likewise, if a beam were placed from one inner edge of the side wall of the entryway to the other inner edge, the wall would float in space, because the wall is ten small units long, while the beam [which is only eight small units long] would be one small unit short on either side; then YOUR system has the same fault you blame us for! This is so because in YOUR system[1969] as well the wall is ten small units long while the beam is only

1964. See Tsong kha pa's *'Dod 'jo*, 87a4–5.

1965. Tib. *ya phubs*, Skt. *skandha*. See Abhayākaragupta, *Dkyil chog rdo rje phreng ba*, *Vajrāvalī*, Tōh 3140, 22a7; Mori 2009, §12.2.3, 158–159.

1966. Abhayākaragupta, *Dkyil chog rdo rje phreng ba*, *Vajrāvalī*, Tōh 3140, 22a6–7; Mori 2009, §12.2.1, 155–156.

1967. Ratnarakṣita, *Padma can*, *Padminī*, Tōh 1420, 57a4 and 58b6.

1968. See also Tathāgatavajra, *Bde mchog gi dkyil 'khor gyi cho ga*, *Sambara Maṇḍalavidhi*, Tōh 1511, 319a.

1969. See Tsong kha pa's *'Dod 'jo*, 87b5–88a2.

eight small units. Yet YOU maintain that there is no part of the wall that is not supported by the beam.

The basis for YOUR misunderstanding is the statement that the beam is eight small units long. The point here is that since at their meeting points with the upper side walls of the entryway, the five lines of the walls are not equal, the beam, one small unit wide, should be made to slant. This being the case, the length of the inner side of the beam is eight small units, but its outer side is slightly less than ten small units. For example, the *Maṇḍala Vajra Garland* explains that the line from one outer edge of the side wall of the entryway to its other edge is ten small units long; and this area is painted in the five colors [that is, the wall].[1970] But of the five colors only the outer one is ten small units long, and the four inner lines are not necessarily ten small units long. Likewise, the length of eight small units refers to the inner side of the beam, while the length of its outer side is not necessarily fixed. The *Commentary on the Saṃvarodaya Tantra* also teaches: "You should know that the beam, which is ten small units long, rests upon the [wall], eight small units long."[1971] Thus here, too, the beam is ten small units long.

[Embellished with Eight Columns]

Although the two pairs of columns below the beam over the side wall of the entryway do not appear as lines in the maṇḍala paintings, they are in fact visualized, since the *Maṇḍala Vajra Garland* teaches: "While the two columns below the beam are not drawn in maṇḍala paintings, they should be conceived of in meditations on the maṇḍala, for it is taught: '[the celestial mansion is] square with four gates embellished with eight columns.' Whereas in this context the discussion is not about the eight inner columns of the maṇḍala, [60b] which are not found in Cakrasaṃvara maṇḍalas and so forth, the verse *embellished with eight columns* is a characteristic shared by all maṇḍalas."[1972]

In this regard SOME TIBETANS[1973] say that the statement "a characteristic shared by all maṇḍalas" was written by a scholar[1974] at a moment of scattered

1970. Abhayākaragupta, *Dkyil chog rdo rje phreng ba*, *Vajrāvalī*, Tōh 3140, 22a7; Mori 2009, §12.2.1, 155–156.

1971. Ratnarakṣita, *Padma can*, *Padminī*, Tōh 1420, 57a4.

1972. Abhayākaragupta, *Dkyil chog rdo rje phreng ba*, *Vajrāvalī*, Tōh 3140, 23a3; Mori 2009, §12.2.4, 160–161.

1973. This is found in Tsong kha pa, *'Dod 'jo*, 88a5.

1974. This refers to Abhayākaragupta who says so in *Dkyil chog rdo rje phreng ba*, *Vajrāvalī*, Tōh 3140, just cited.

attention, because there are explanations about square maṇḍalas with one gate, round maṇḍalas with four gates, and so forth. Likewise, the *Ḍākārṇava Tantra* specifies that the three wheels have columns and the *Abhidhānottara Tantra* specifies a Cakrasaṃvara maṇḍala with nine inner quadrants,[1975] hence some maṇḍalas of Cakrasaṃvara do require inner columns.[1976]

It seems that THEY do not understand the intention of *Maṇḍala Vajra Garland* and therefore do not understand why it is appropriate. This is so because the explanation of the *Maṇḍala Vajra Garland* cited above *a characteristic shared by all maṇḍalas*, refers only to the line *embellished with eight columns.*[1977] Not a single word indicates that the *characteristic square with four gates* is shared by all maṇḍalas. The maṇḍalas said to share this characteristic are not maṇḍalas in general, but only square maṇḍalas with four gates. Thus it is entirely clear that all maṇḍalas that share the characteristic of eight columns are square maṇḍalas with four gates. Since square maṇḍalas with one gate and more are specified in the tantras as well, there is nothing problematical about this. Were this not so, it would mean that the author of the *Maṇḍala Vajra Garland* forgot his own explanation about the fourth round maṇḍala of the power of speech that pertains to dharmadhātu in the same work.

[Objection:] Even though it is certain that square maṇḍalas with four gates are embellished with eight columns, this does not necessarily refer to the eight columns beneath the beams of the side walls of the entryways, but rather to the eight columns of the inner maṇḍala.

[Reply:] The statement that [the eight beams] are not found in Cakrasaṃvara maṇḍalas [61a] does not mean that no Cakrasaṃvara maṇḍala has eight inner columns.[1978] Rather the statement points to maṇḍalas such as the sixty-two deity Cakrasaṃvara maṇḍala.

Although there are three sets of eight columns in the three wheels of Cakrasaṃvara maṇḍala, these columns are not specific[1979] to the commitment maṇḍala of the ground which is *square with four gates*. The property

1975. Tib. *re'u mig*, Skt. *koṣṭha*.

1976. *Mkha' 'gro rgya mtsho*, Tōh 372, 162a7. *Mngon brjod rgyud bla ma*, Tōh 369, 282b7 (chap. 13) and 319a5–7 (chap. 32).

1977. Abhayākaragupta, *Dkyil chog rdo rje phreng ba*, *Vajrāvalī*, Tōh 3140, 23a3–4; Mori 2009, §12.2.4, 160–161.

1978. This refers to the line of Abhayākaragupta, *Dkyil chog rdo rje phreng ba*, *Vajrāvalī*, Tōh 3140, 23a3–4; Mori 2009, §12.2.4, 160–161, cited above.

1979. Reading *sgos* for *dgos* in our text here and in the following lines as in Tsong kha pa, *'Dod 'jo*, 88b6.

square with four gates is shared here, but the property *embellished with eight columns* is not shared. The eight columns are specific to square maṇḍalas with four gates, for this is the point of our debate. In other square Cakrasaṃvara maṇḍalas with four gates there are eight columns specific to that and there are also eight columns that support the roof of the three wheels, but this is in no way problematical. Therefore it is all right if the roof of a specific maṇḍala that is square with four gates is not supported by eight inner columns; however, we do not maintain that these eight columns are necessarily absent from every Cakrasaṃvara maṇḍala.

The area that is *embellished with eight columns* is a square maṇḍala, but the celestial mansion does not include the portals. Therefore it is INAPPROPRIATE to specify that the columns in question here are the eight COLUMNS drawn to the right and left of the gate, for these are the columns of the portal. Thus, since the other possibilities have been refuted, the columns that are referred to in the verse *embellished with eight columns* must certainly mean the columns beneath the beam of the side walls of the entryway.

The *Maṇḍala Vajra Garland* refutes the position that since the beam over the entryway and so forth must be supported by two columns, the gateposts and the back and side walls of the entryway rise one on top of the other.[1980] This is so because it would not be possible for the back wall of the entryway to float in space and consequently the side wall of the entryway could not stand vertically if there were no beam for the side wall. [61b] The intention of the *Maṇḍala Vajra Garland* is to signify that in the absence of a beam, there need not be a column to support that beam.

[The Offering Ledges, Panels, Strands of Pearls, "Drip-like" Ornaments, Eaves, and Parapets]

[THE LEDGE FOR THE OFFERING GODDESSES[1981]]

The offering ledge outside the walls surrounds the lower edge of the walls.[1982] But the *Vajraḍāka Tantra* specifies that the ledge stops before the gates, as explained in many other scriptures as well. Hence some works teach: "The four

1980. Abhayākaragupta, *Dkyil chog rdo rje phreng ba*, *Vajrāvalī*, Tōh 3140, 23a4; Mori 2009, §12.2.4, 159–161.

1981. Tib. *'dod snam*, Skt. *vedī* or *vedikā*. The protruding ledge for the offering goddesses, called also *stegs bu kha khyer* or *kha 'khyer*. In two-dimensional drawings this protruding ledge, red in color, is the second square section of the celestial mansion outside the walls.

1982. Our text continues to follow Tsong kha pa, *'Dod 'jo*, 89a6–b1, and Tsong kha pa, *Sngags rim chen mo*, chap. 6, 243–244.

kinds of mindfulness should be known as the four platforms."[1983] The terms "platform,"[1984] "stand,"[1985] "bearer,"[1986] and "offering ledge"[1987] are synonyms.[1988] The colors of the offering ledge[1989] according to the *Maṇḍala Vajra Garland* may be crystal, gold, ruby, or those of other precious stones.[1990] The sixteen[1991] offering goddesses in various colors standing on the ledge wear ornaments and garments of various colors, take various postures, and hold various offering substances in their hands.

The *Maṇḍala Vajra Garland* explains that the offering ledges are the same height as the base on which the columns supporting the portal rest.[1992] Accordingly it may be understood that the prongs of the crossed vajra are clearly visible.

1983. See, for example, Durjayacandra, *Dkyil 'khor gyi cho ga'i sgrub thabs bzang po yongs su gzung ba, Suparigraha Maṇḍalavidhi Sādhana*, Tōh 1240, 147a7. D has *dran pa nye bar gzhag pa bzhi* for *dran pa nyer gzhag bzhi po ni* and *brjod pa nyid* for *shes pa bya* in our text.

1984. Tib. *kha khyer* or *kha 'khyer*, Skt. *vedī* or *vedikā*.

1985. Tib. *stegs bu*, Skt. *vedī* or *vedikā*.

1986. Tib. *gzungs*, Skt. *dhāraṇī*.

1987. Tib. *'dod snam*, Skt. *vedī* or *vedikā*.

1988. Except for *gzungs*, all these Tibetan terms are used to translate *vedī* or *vedikā*.

1989. See Tsong kha pa, *'Dod 'jo*, 89b4–5.

1990. Abhayākaragupta, *Dkyil chog rdo rje phreng ba, Vajrāvalī*, Tōh 3140, 37b4; Mori 2009, §13.2.1, 234–235.

1991. There are four offering goddesses in each direction, two on each side of the entryway.

1992. Abhayākaragupta, *Dkyil chog rdo rje phreng ba, Vajrāvalī*, Tōh 3140, 25a1–2; Mori 2009, §12.2.7, 168 and 169.

[The Panels][1993]

Early Tibetan lamas[1994] maintain that the surface of the panel is yellow. But according to the instruction of the *Maṇḍala Vajra Garland*, the surface of the five lines of the wall is red, and on it are "layers of jewels: jeweled triangles, drops, squares, and circles."[1995]

[The Strands of Pearls][1996]

Suspended over the panel are round strands and vertical strands of pearls dropping from the mouths of the sea monsters in front of the four golden bands.[1997] Since as explained[1998] there are apertures[1999] in these bands, there should be

1993. Tib. *pha gu*, Skt. *khura*. The lower square border at the top of the celestial mansion over the open walls. In two-dimensional drawings this is the third square section of the celestial mansion, red in color and decorated with colored geometrical forms. In classical western architecture the superstructure over the columns, called the entablature, commonly consists of three elements: architrave, frieze, and the cornice on top. Thus the panel or architrave is the lowest element of the entablature. In the celestial mansion the entablature consists of six elements or layers, as specified above. See also Tsong kha pa, *Sngags rim chen mo*, chap. 6, 241.

1994. Tsong kha pa (*'Dod 'jo*, 90a1–2) calls them *gong ma rnams* and Ngor chen (*Zla zer*, 105b1–2) refers to them as those who follow the instruction transmitted from Śraddha, but also mentions that so does Bsod nams rtse mo, *Zla zer*, 106a1. Indeed, Bsod nams rtse mo explains that the panel is yellow. See his *Kye rdo rje'i dkyil 'khor du slob ma smin par byed pa'i cho ga dbang gi chu bu chen mo*, work 20, 57b5–6. See also 'Phags pa, *Gsang ba 'dus pa 'jam pa'i rdo rje lha bcu dgu'i sgrub thabs*, work 110, 220b4.

1995. Abhayākaragupta, *Dkyil chog rdo rje phreng ba*, *Vajrāvalī*, Tōh 3140, 27b2–3; Mori 2009, §12.4.1, 182–183. See also Tsong kha pa, *Gsang mngon*, 29b3–4.

1996. Tib. *drwa ba drwa phyed*, Skt. *hārādhahāra*. The square border above the panel or architrave. In two-dimensional drawings this is the fourth square section of the celestial mansion, blue in color with visible strands of pearls. The literal meaning of the Sanskrit and Tibetan terms is strands and semi-strands. See also Tsong kha pa, *Sngags rim chen mo*, chap. 6, 241–242.

1997. Tib. *ska rags*, Skt. *mekhalā*. Our text follows here Tsong kha pa, *'Dod 'jo*, 90a2–6, who in turns follows Abhayākaragupta, *Dkyil chog rdo rje phreng ba*, *Vajrāvalī*, Tōh 3140, 27b3–4; Mori 2009, §12.4.2, 183–184. See also Tsong kha pa, *Gsang mngon*, 29b4–5.

1998. According to Tsong kha pa's *Sngags rim chen mo*, chap. 6, 241, this is taught by Tibetan lamas.

1999. Literarily our text has a black basis, Tib. *gzhi nag po*. The bands, Tib. *ska rags*, are also called transparencies (lit. clear appearance, Tib. *gsal snang*) since they admit light into the mansion.

small capitals[2000] made of precious substances there supporting them at the same height as in maṇḍala drawings.

The round strands are made of pearls strung on red threads [62a] and precious gems on golden threads suspended on either side, and above and below them. The text explains that the vertical strands are garlands of jewels suspended on either side of the round strands of pearls, although they are slightly shorter.[2001] That is why the text explains that the round strands curve, [while the vertical strands do not].

There are three methods taught[2002] for suspending objects from the lower tip of the vertical strands: tying large gems with golden threads to them, or as some works specify, yak-tails with jeweled handles,[2003] or else yak-tails on bells.[2004] Hence, alternate as suitable these three methods [of suspending objects] from the lower tip of each vertical strand. Certain works[2005] teach that crescent moons on lotuses topped by suns adorned with half vajras should be hung with the strands. Other texts specify that they should be hung with jewels, and still others, vajras resting on lotuses; in the latter case the vajras should be whole, not half vajras.

2000. Tib. *bre phul*, Skt. *āsāra*. The term *āsāra* also refers to the first layer of the portal, the golden layer, Tib. *gser*, Skt. *suvarṇa*. See Abhayākaragupta, *Dkyil chog rdo rje phreng ba*, *Vajrāvalī*, Tōh 3140, 24a2; Mori 2009, §12.2.5, 162–163, and the illustration in Tanaka 2004, 35.

2001. Abhayākaragupta, *Dkyil chog rdo rje phreng ba*, *Vajrāvalī*, Tōh 3140, 27b3–5; Mori 2009, §12.4.2, 183–184.

2002. All these cases are mentioned in Abhayākaragupta, *Dkyil chog rdo rje phreng ba*, *Vajrāvalī*, Tōh 3140, 27b3–4; Mori 2009, §12.4.2, 183–184. See also Tsong kha pa, *Sngags rim chen mo*, chap. 6, 242.

2003. Tib. *rin po che'i yu ba can gyi rnga yab*, Skt. *ratnadaṇḍacāmara*.

2004. Tib. *dril bu'i mthar rnga yab*, Skt. *gaṇṭāntacāmara*.

2005. Once more all these cases are mentioned in Abhayākaragupta, *Dkyil chog rdo rje phreng ba*, *Vajrāvalī*, Tōh 3140, 27b3–4; Mori 2009, §12.4.2, 183–184.

[The "Drip-Like" Layer][2006]

As explained, either jewels or "drip-like" ornaments may be drawn on the drip-like layer. In the first instance, the jewels resemble those on the panels,[2007] and in the second, Nāgabodhi teaches in his *Maṇḍala Rituals* translated by Chel[2008] they are "rain gutter,[2009] parapets,[2010] and so forth."[2011] This accords with the translation of drip-like ornament as rain gutter. In maṇḍala drawings, the drip-like layer appears above the layer of the pearl strands, but [three-dimensionally] it is actually suspended from the ends of the rafters[2012] of the eaves overhanging the outer side of that layer.

[The Eaves][2013]

Tibetan lamas maintain that the eaves are positioned on the outer edge of the ROOF of the celestial mansion itself and are thus lined up with the ledge for the offering goddesses. Since it is difficult to measure the gateposts[2014] and the back wall of the entryway directly,[2015] it is explained that in three-dimensional maṇḍalas the architectural elements should be inconspicuous and set up as elegantly as possible.

2006. Tib. *shar bu'i snam bu*, Skt. *bakulīpaṭṭī*. The square border at the top of the celestial mansion above the strands of pearls. In two-dimensional drawings this is the fifth square section of the celestial mansion, white in color with visible "drip-like ornaments." Our text continues to follow Tsong kha pa, *'Dod 'jo*, 90a6–b3. See also *Sngags rim chen mo*, chap. 6, 242.

2007. Tib. *pha gu*, Skt. *khura*.

2008. Dpyal lo tsā ba dpal chos kyi bzang po, died 1216. He is mentioned in the colophons of Abhayākaragupta's *Man ngag snye ma*, Tōh 1198 and also Tōh 2033, 2034, 2094, and more.

2009. Zhang, Yisun 1993, *Bod Rgya tshig mdzod chen mo* dictionary has *chu 'gro sa'i wa kha*.

2010. See the citation above [51a] of Nāgārjuna's *Mdor byas*, *Piṇḍīkrama Sādhana*, Tōh 1796, 3a1, L 26, T 225, where the Derge has *bre la phreng ba* and Ratnākaraśānti's commentary, Tōh 1826, 30a4, has *bre yi phreng ba* and the Sanskrit of the *Piṇḍīkrama* is *kramaśīrṣa*. In his *Sngags rim chen mo*, chap. 6, 243, Tsong kha pa says that *bre phreng* is used to translate *kramaśīrṣa*.

2011. Klu'i byang chub, *Dkyil chog nyi shu pa*, *Maṇḍalaviṃśatividhi*, Tōh 1810. The version in the Derge is translated by Tilakakalaśa and Pa tshab Nyi ma grags.

2012. Tib. *lcam*.

2013. Tib. *bya 'dab*, Skt. *pakṣiṇī*.

2014. Tib. *sgo khyud*, Skt. *niryūha*.

2015. Tib. *'gram*, Skt. *kapola* or *kapolaka*.

[The Parapets][2016]

It is taught that the celestial mansion will have an elegant appearance if the parapets are placed at a distance of eight small units from the main line,[2017] [62b] whereas if they are less than seven small units away from the main line, the drip-like ornaments will have a clumsy appearance, since they will then seem to have their heads cut off.[2018] Therefore the parapet should be placed just above the layer of the drip-like ornaments. The Sanskrit equivalent of the term parapets is *kramaśīrṣa*, which literally means a row of heads.[2019] It is taught that in maṇḍala drawings the parapets only extend as far as the line of the suspending banners,[2020] but in visualization they extend above the side wall[2021] of the entryway.[2022] Therefore the lower layers of the drip-like ornaments, the strands of pearls, and the panels extend precisely to these points.

[Victory Banners and So Forth]

The *Maṇḍala Vajra Garland* teaches that the parapets are shaped like half lotus petals and upon them are placed victory banners[2023] and pennants.[2024] Furthermore, at the sides, "on the parapets shaped like half lotus petals," are "eight victory banners or pennants on golden or jeweled vases."[2025] Some say that [the victory banners and pennants] are placed on the layer of the parapets, but this means that they should not be on the parapets themselves or

2016. Tib. *mda' yab*, Skt. *kramaśīrṣa*. The upper layer at the top of the celestial mansion. In two-dimensional drawings this is the sixth square section of the celestial mansion in white with notches or crenelations. Our text continues to follow Tsong kha pa, *'Dod 'jo*, 90b3–91a2.

2017. Tib. *rtsa thig*, Skt. *mūlasūtra*.

2018. See Abhayākaragupta, *Dkyil chog rdo rje phreng ba*, *Vajrāvalī*, Tōh 3140, 23a1; Mori 2009, §12.2.3, 158–159.

2019. This is to denote that the parapet wall has notches or crenelations. In other words, the wall and the spaces within it alternate.

2020. Tib. *dar dpyangs*, Skt. *añcala*. See Mori 2009, 640, for the location of this line.

2021. Tib. *sgo logs* or *logs*, Skt. *pakṣa* or *pakṣaka*.

2022. See Abhayākaragupta, *Dkyil chog rdo rje phreng ba*, *Vajrāvalī*, Tōh 3140, 23a2; Mori 2009, §12.2.4, 159–161.

2023. Tib. *rgyal mtshan*, Skt. *dhvaja*.

2024. Tib. *ba dan*, Skt. *patāka*. Abhayākaragupta, *Dkyil chog rdo rje phreng ba*, *Vajrāvalī*, Tōh 3140, 27b6; Mori 2009, §12.4.3, 184–185. See also Tsong kha pa, *Gsang mngon*, 29b6.

2025. Abhayākaragupta, *Dkyil chog rdo rje phreng ba*, *Vajrāvalī*, Tōh 3140, 27b6; Mori 2009, §12.4.3, 184–185. D and Mori have *rgyal mtshan dang* for *rgyal mtshan nam* in our text.

else that they should be on the two higher sections of parapet. However, it is clearly taught [that they should be on] *the parapets shaped like half lotus petals*, hence the victory banners and pennants should be placed on the parapets upon vases at the center between the two higher sections of parapet.

The victory banners[2026] "are tied to poles studded with jewels and their tips are adorned with crescent moons, jewels, and vajras. They are decorated with triple tasseled cloths to which ringing bells are attached. Their tips are ornamented with the king of deer, the king of swans, a *garuḍa*, a fish, and a sea monster. Because they swing in the wind, they whorl three times and are thus majestic in appearance. The small bells that ring with the sound *silsil* are decorated with yak tails." The tips of the tassel are decorated with [four] pairs of inimical animals.[2027] [63a] The pennants[2028] are similar to the victory banners, only they are not decorated with pairs of inimical animals.[2029] There are altogether four [victory banners and] pennants located at each of the four directions.

[According to the *Maṇḍala Vajra Garland*:] "Between the gates and the gate-posts are crescent moons with jewels suitably colored red, yellow, green, or black upon them, and adorned above with half or whole vajras."[2030] The crescent moons, jewels, and vajras are one small unit high. The *Maṇḍala Vajra Garland* explains that the crescent moons, jewels, and vajras are placed at the outer edge of the gate and the gate posts, but then the *Maṇḍala Vajra Garland* cites a scripture that teaches: "The masters should draw a sequence of moons, suns, jewels, and vajras, adorned with vajras or only jewels, at the inner and outer corners of the gateway ledges."[2031] Accordingly, they should be situated at the inner and outer corners of the offering ledge and the walls as well.

2026. The following is a citation of Abhayākaragupta, *Dkyil chog rdo rje phreng ba*, *Vajrāvalī*, Tōh 3140, 27b7–28a1; Mori 2009, §12.4.3, 184–185.

2027. These are also called *mi mthun g.yul rgyal*: half lion half *garuḍa*, half conch shell half sea-monster, and half fish half otter. See Dagyab 1995/2015, 111.

2028. Tib. *ba dan*, Skt. *patāka*.

2029. See Abhayākaragupta, *Dkyil chog rdo rje phreng ba*, *Vajrāvalī*, Tōh 3140, 28a1; Mori 2009, §12.4.3, 184–185.

2030. See Abhayākaragupta, *Dkyil chog rdo rje phreng ba*, *Vajrāvalī*, Tōh 3140, 27a4–5; Mori 2009, §12.4.1, 181–182.

2031. Tib. *stegs bu*, Skt. *vedī*. Abhayākaragupta, *Dkyil chog rdo rje phreng ba*, *Vajrāvalī*, Tōh 3140, 27a4–6; Mori 2009, §12.4.1, 181–182. D and Mori have *gcig po ni* for *gcig bu nyid* in our text. Our text follows the citation in Tsong kha pa, *Sngags rim chen mo*, chap. 6, 244.

[The Interior of the Celestial Mansion][2032]

[The Eight Bodhisattvas, the Ten Fierce Deities, and the Vajra Ladies]

First, I will explain a little about the method of drawings the lines. To create the outer area of the deity platform[2033] for the eight bodhisattvas and the fierce deities,[2034] measure one gate unit in from the meeting point of the *brahma* line[2035] and the main line,[2036] and there draw four lines in the four directions between the diagonal lines.[2037] As the *Maṇḍala Vajra Garland* teaches: "Inside the square of the main lines leave one gate unit for the deity platform,[2038] and draw the cross line[2039] between the two diagonal lines."[2040]

[The Prose Description of the Inner Mansion]

The *Maṇḍala Vajra Garland* teaches in its prose description of the line drawings that "To place the four vajra ladies within the platform [of the bodhisattvas and the fierce deities], draw the first circular line around the inner mansion at a distance of one gate unit from that platform by holding the thread on the nave of the *brahma* line at the *brahma* or Īśāna line.[2041] Then draw the second circular line within the previous line at a distance of one small unit from the ring of the 'vajra garland.'"[2042] [The *Maṇḍala Vajra Garland*] teaches this in the context of the maṇḍala of Mañjuvajra [Guhyasamāja].[2043] [63b]

2032. See Tsong kha pa, *Sngags rim chen mo*, chap. 6, 225–227.

2033. Tib. *lha snam* or *lha yi snam bu*, Skt. *devatāpaṭṭikā*.

2034. See diagram 2.

2035. Tib. *tshangs thig*, Skt. *brahmasūtra*.

2036. Tib. *rtsa thig*, Skt. *mūlasūtra*.

2037. Reading *zur thig* for *thur thig* in our text.

2038. Tib. *lha snam* or *lha yi snam bu*, Skt. *devatāpaṭṭikā*.

2039. Tib. *ngos thig*, Skt. *tiryaksūtra*.

2040. Tib. *zur thig*, Skt. *koṇasūtra*. Abhayākaragupta, *Dkyil chog rdo rje phreng ba*, *Vajrāvalī*, Tōh 3140, 28a4; Mori 2009, §12.5.1.1, 186–187. D and Mori have *sgo'i tshad du lha snam* for *sgo'i lha snam* in our text.

2041. This is the line at the northeastern direction.

2042. Tib. *rdo rje phreng ba*, Skt. *vajrāvalī*. This ring is at the core of the celestial mansion and not the outer ring called the "vajra garland" at the beginning of this chapter. Abhayākaragupta, *Dkyil chog rdo rje phreng ba*, *Vajrāvalī*, Tōh 3140, 28a4; Mori 2009, §12.5.1.1, 186–187.

2043. Tib. Gsang 'dus 'jam rdor.

Then [this treatise] describes the distinctive features of the Ārya tradition: "Here specifically there is a third circular line[2044] within the second circular line at a distance of one small unit from the ring of the 'vajra garland.' Inside the first ring[2045] is the 'light garland'[2046] and there are no circular lines beyond it."[2047] Accordingly draw the first circular line at a distance of one gate unit in from the cross line of the first platform of the bodhisattvas and the fierce deities. Draw the second circular line inside the first at a distance of one small unit from [the outer line of] the light garland, and within that, a third circular line at a distance of one small unit from [the outer line of] the vajra garland.

[The Verse Description of the Inner Mansion]

In the verse description of line drawings, the *Maṇḍala Vajra Garland* teaches: "Draw [two] circular lines [to create a ring] seven and eight small units respectively from the *brahma* line. Then draw two [straight] lines at a distance of two and three small units from the *brahma* line, from one end of the [vajra] ring to the other in each direction. At a distance of one small unit beyond the outer circle [of the light garland] draw another circle. The diagonal lines should be three small units from the outer circle."[2048] Accordingly, the cross line is drawn as [described] above at a distance of one gate unit from the main line, and the first circle is drawn at a distance of three small units inside that cross line.

But are these two instructions not contradictory?[2049] As [the *Maṇḍala Vajra Garland* explains in citing] the master Nāgabodhi: "[The first line] should be the length of a quadrant[2050] from the *brahma* line. The second line, half a quadrant long, the third, a quadrant and a half long, and an additional line, half a quadrant long. The vajra garland should be luminous and adorned

2044. In order to create two rings, three circular lines must be drawn.

2045. The ring of the "light garland" is situated between the first and second circles.

2046. Tib. *'od phreng*, Skt. *raśmimālā*. This ring too is at core of the celestial mansion.

2047. Abhayākaragupta, *Dkyil chog rdo rje phreng ba*, *Vajrāvalī*, Tōh 3140, 28b5–6; Mori 2009, §12.5.2, 189. Cited also in Tsong kha pa, *Sngags rim chen mo*, chap. 6, 225.

2048. Abhayākaragupta, *Dkyil chog rdo rje phreng ba*, *Vajrāvalī*, Tōh 3140, 36a2–3; Mori 2009, §12.7.4, 227. Cited also in Tsong kha pa, *Sngags rim chen mo*, chap. 6, 225.

2049. Tsong kha pa, *Sngags rim chen mo*, chap. 6, 226.

2050. Tib. *stegs bu*, Skt. *vedi*. This refers to the square area allocated for each of the seats in the inner mansion.

with lights in the five colors."[2051] According to this citation, it is the prose explanation that should be followed. But Nāgabodhi also teaches that [64a] "The radius of the innermost circle should be half the distance from the main line to the center."[2052] According to this second citation, it is the explanation in verse that should be followed. [However] there is no contradiction here, for either one of these two systems can be followed.

When the outer circle of the light garland is drawn in colored sand, it should be nine small units from the center, but in meditation, the border between the interior and exterior of the inner mansion is the outer circle of the vajra garland, not the outer circle of the light garland. This is so because the light garland is created by the light that radiates out of the vajra [above] and not from the base of the maṇḍala.[2053] Therefore in drawings the light garland is at a distance of eight small units from the center. But this does not contradict the fact that the size of the innermost mansion is half that of the main line from the center.[2054]

To create the nine quadrants,[2055] draw four straight lines in the four directions at a distance of two small units from the center where the two brahma lines meet. Then draw four additional straight lines at a distance of one small unit beyond them.

2051. Abhayākaragupta, *Dkyil chog rdo rje phreng ba*, *Vajrāvalī*, Tōh 3140, 28b7; Mori 2009, §12.5.2, 189–190. D and Mori have *kyi* for *kyis*. Our text follows the readings of Tsong kha pa, *Sngags rim chen mo*, chap. 6, 226. Only the last two lines are found in Nāgabodhi, *Dkyil chog nyi shu pa*, *Maṇḍalaviṃśatividhi*, chap. 4, v. 12cd, Tōh 1810, 134a1; Tanaka 2004, 31.

2052. Our text follows the citation of Nāgabodhi in Abhayākaragupta's *Dkyil chog rdo rje phreng ba*, *Vajrāvalī*, Tōh 3140, 28b6–7; Mori 2009, §12.5.2, 189. However, the text of Nāgabodhi is different. In D the sequence of the lines is reversed and D has *phyed kyis ni* for *phyed kyis so* and *nang gi dkyil 'khor tshad yin te* for *dbus kyi 'khor lo yi ni tshad* in our text. See Nāgabodhi, *Dkyil chog nyi shu pa*, *Maṇḍalaviṃśatividhi*, chap. 4, v. 12ab, Tōh 1810, 133b7–134a1. The Sanskrit of Nāgabodhi as found in Tanaka 2004, 31 is also different from the Sanskrit in Mori 2009, §12.5.2, 189.

2053. While the ring of the light garland appears in two-dimensional drawings, it is not actually there, hence its size is not taken into account. It is drawn in order to represent the light that enters the inner mansion from above.

2054. As Nāgabodhi just explained.

2055. Tib. *re'u mig*, Skt. *koṣṭha*.

[Are There Gates in the Inner Mansion?]

The *Vajra Garland Explanatory Tantra* teaches: "The three circular lines are endowed with four gates,[2056] embellished with three vajra garlands."[2057] Thus it may seem as though the verse indicates a four-gated maṇḍala in which there is an inner mansion with four gates as well. However, in their teachings Ārya Nāgārjuna and his disciples do not refer to doors inside the mansion. Another translation of the *Vajra Garland Explanatory Tantra* has: "At its center, the four-gated [maṇḍala] is surrounded by vajra garlands with three prongs."[2058] SOME LAMAS[2059] say that it is necessary to examine whether the same meaning appears in the Sanskrit version of the *Vajra Garland Explanatory Tantra* or whether the text says "at the center of the four-gated [maṇḍala]." If the latter is the case, there is no need to speak of four gates within [the inner mansion]. [64b]

On this point SOME LATER TIBETANS explain that one should draw an [additional] square connecting the four corners and the diagonal lines along the rim of the vajra garland, and only beyond that square draw the cross lines for the platform of the deities. [Such an additional square] contradicts all the tantras and works of Indian scholars and there is no proof [that it should be drawn], hence it is inappropriate. Moreover, the *Vajra Garland Explanatory Tantra* teaches: "Draw the lines of the foremost mansion, perfect in all respects, there to manifest the abode of all the victorious ones."[2060] Thus the *Tantra* explains that the *foremost mansion* consists of nine quadrants, the dwelling place of the five victorious ones. Then [the *Vajra Garland Explanatory Tantra* explains:] "Beyond [the foremost mansion] place the [four] vajra ladies in the intermediate directions."[2061] Thus it is taught that the four vajra ladies are placed at the intermediate directions beyond the [nine quadrants of the] inner mansion. But this does not mean that between the seats of the five victorious ones and the four vajra ladies there is another empty platform upon which there are no deities. The *Concise Sādhana* teaches: "After placing the male and

2056. The "four-gated [maṇḍala]" is the usual term used to describe the entire celestial mansion.

2057. *Rgyud rdo rje phreng ba*, *Vajramālā Tantra*, chap. 54, v. 28, Tōh 445, 254b7. D has *sgo bzhi pa* for *sgo bzhi la* in our text, as does Stog 225b5.

2058. See Bu ston, *Sgron gsal bshad sbyar*, 96b2.

2059. See Tsong kha pa, *Sgron gsal mchan*, chap. 4, 115a3–5.

2060. *Rgyud rdo rje phreng ba*, *Vajramālā Tantra*, chap. 54, v. 28, Tōh 445, 255a1. D has *de las dbang po'i pho brang ni* for *de la dang po pho brang rim* in our text, as does Stog 225b5.

2061. *Rgyud rdo rje phreng ba*, *Vajramālā Tantra*, chap. 54, v. 34, Tōh 445, 255a4–5.

female tathāgatas in the first chamber[2062] of deities, the yogi should issue the vajra ladies forth to the second chamber of deities."[2063]

Thus, if we drew the lines as YOU have suggested, the seats of the vajra ladies would be in the third chamber of deities. Nāgabodhi teaches: "Beyond the inner maṇḍala [the master] should draw four lines."[2064] He does not say that one should add another line between the inner maṇḍala and the main line, while according to YOU one should draw eight lines[2065] [beyond the inner maṇḍala].

With regard to the vajra garland [around] the nine quadrants, the *Glorious Foremost Commentary*[2066] explains: "As all the buddhas turned the wheel of Dharma unhindered in the mode of Vajrayāna, the circular lines of vajra garlands circle above the eight columns."[2067] Based on this explanation, SOME TIBETAN LAMAS[2068] say that if the vajra [garland] were a beam circling above [but not below], [65a] there would be no dividing line on the ground between the inner [nine quadrants] and outer [square of the four vajra ladies]. Thus in three-dimensional maṇḍalas and for meditation purposes there should be a raised wall consisting of a garland of three pronged vajras that surrounds the nine quadrants. THEY say that the wall reaches just below the knees of the deities, but it is more appropriate for the wall of the vajra garland to reach one small unit higher than the seats of the deities.

The *Maṇḍala Vajra Garland* teaches that the central quadrant of the nine is the space for either the emblem or the seat of the principal deity.[2069] Hence, [the principal deity] resides on the central quadrant surrounded by vajras at its base. The rest of the interior mansion is divided by pairs of parallel lines into eight quadrants, each one small unit wide. In three-dimensional

2062. Tib. *rim pa*, Skt. *puṭa*.

2063. Nāgārjuna, *Mdor byas*, *Piṇḍīkrama Sādhana*, Tōh 1796, 7b2–3, L 146, T 144.

2064. Nāgabodhi, *Dkyil chog nyi shu pa*, *Maṇḍalaviṃśatividhi*, chap. 4, v. 13ab, Tōh 1810, 134a1; Tanaka 2004, 31.

2065. Four lines for the cross line and four lines for the additional square.

2066. Our text has *Dpal mchog 'grel pa* as does Tsong kha pa, *Sngags rim chen mo*, chap. 6, 244. But these lines are found in Tōh 1884. See the following note. The *Dpal mchog 'grel pa* is likely Ānandagarbha, *Dpal mchog dang po'i 'grel pa*, *Paramādivivaraṇa*, Tōh 2511. See, specifically, 4b3 and 23b1.

2067. Ratnavajra, *Mi bskyod rdo rje'i sgrub pa'i thabs*, *Akṣobhyavajra Sādhana*, Tōh 1884, 148a4–5. D has *rdo rje'i tshul* for *rdo rje theg pa'i tshul* and *bskor bar* for *rab tu bskor bas* in our text. Our text follows Tsong kha pa's *Sngags rim chen mo*, chap. 6, 244.

2068. See Ngor chen, *Zla zer*, 107b6–108a6.

2069. See Tsong kha pa, *Sngags rim chen mo*, chap. 6, 245.

maṇḍalas and for meditation purposes these [parallel lines] are drawn to signify the eight columns that emerge from in between the vajras. They do not indicate beams, for as Nāgabodhi teaches: "Within, draw eight elegant columns adorned by vajras; the nine quadrants are separated by vajra columns at intervals."[2070] The *Cluster of Instructions* teaches: "Upon [these columns] are four beams signifying the four types of specific-perfect discernment,[2071] for they are capable of bearing burdens for the sake of others."[2072] Hence, the four beams above the columns intersect with the round vajra beams.

[The Height of the Interior and Exterior Areas of the Inner Mansion]

Now I will examine this. Is there a difference in the height of the roof and the grounds of the interior and exterior areas of the inner mansion? There is no clear explanation anywhere; however, there must be a difference in height between these areas, because in maṇḍala drawings there is a dividing line. On the other hand, in both three-dimensional maṇḍalas and for meditation purposes there is no color difference between the inner and outer platform of the deities. For example, in the eastern direction both areas are white, the color of Vairocana and so forth, [65b] and there is no dividing line or anything else that separates them. Hence it follows that there is no division between the inner and outer platforms of the deities.

What then should be the difference in height [that would delineate the border between the inner and outer platforms]? It is difficult to establish this with any certainty; however, it seems that if the difference in height were one large unit or more, there would be a problem, since such a large discrepancy would make it hard to set the roof. One possibility would be to follow[2073] the system of Cakrasaṃvara, in which there is a difference in height. In this case the body wheel is raised two small units above the ground of the samaya wheel.[2074] However, the Guhyasamāja maṇḍala is slightly different from the [Cakrasaṃvara

2070. Nāgabodhi, *Dkyil chog nyi shu pa, Maṇḍalaviṃśatividhi*, chap. 4, vv. 13cd–14ab, Tōh 1810, 134a1–2; Tanaka 2004, 31. This is cited also in Abhayākaragupta, *Dkyil chog rdo rje phreng ba, Vajrāvalī*, Tōh 3140, 29a1; Mori 2009, §12.5.2, 189–190.

2071. Tib. *so so yang dag par rig pa*, Skt. *pratisamvid*.

2072. Abhayākaragupta, *Man ngag snye ma, Āmnāyamañjarī*, chap. 18, Tōh 1198, 168b3–4. D has *khur khur bar* for *khur 'khur bar* and *nus pa nyid kyi phyir ro* for *nus pa'i phyir ro* in our text, which follows Tsong kha pa, *Sngags rim chen mo*, chap. 6, 245.

2073. Reading *'gres* for *'gros* in our text.

2074. In Cakrasaṃvara maṇḍala the ground consists of the samaya wheel, and the body wheel is found on top of it.

maṇḍala], so I think it would be better if the difference in height were one fourth of a small unit. Based on this, you must consider the difference in height between the innermost mansion [and its surrounding areas] as well.

[Where Is Sumbharāja Placed?]

Where are the upper and lower fierce deities [Uṣṇīṣacakravartin and] Sumbharāja placed in the celestial mansion? In maṇḍala drawings, Sumbharāja is placed west of the fierce deity of the west,[2075] but where is he placed in three-dimensional maṇḍalas and meditation? Can Sumbharāja dwell below the nave of the crossed vajra? He cannot be accommodated in the space between the nave of the crossed vajra and the variegated lotus, hence he will have to dwell below the nave of the variegated lotus. Likewise, in drawings the upper fierce deity, [Uṣṇīṣacakravartin], is placed east of the fierce deity of the east.[2076] But in three-dimensional maṇḍalas and in meditation, Uṣṇīṣacakravartin cannot fit below the roof of the celestial mansion so he would have to be placed above it.

In that case, if the upper and lower fierce deities dwelled beyond the roof of the maṇḍala and below the variegated lotus they would not be included within the maṇḍala. Therefore the number of deities placed within the maṇḍala would be less than thirty-two, and the efforts of Nāgabodhi and Candrakīrti to include all thirty-two deities in the maṇḍala would be in vain. [66a]

How then can we place the upper and lower fierce deities inside the maṇḍala? We need to examine whether Sumbharāja can be placed in the space between the principal deity and the nave of the crossed vajra. If Sumbharāja is placed below the nave, the problem stated earlier will not be solved, thus this solution is unacceptable. For this reason, Sumbharāja is placed upon the nave of the crossed vajra while the central quadrant is raised one gate unit above the inner platform of the deities [the remaining eight quadrants] and is encircled by a vajra wall. Sumbharāja is placed within the round enclave formed in this way below the central quadrant of the innermost mansion and upon the nave of the crossed vajra a short distance away, behind and below the principal deity. This is the explanation given by my holy lama, otherwise there would be no space for the fierce deity at the nadir. Based on this, you should consider the difference in height between the inner maṇḍala [and its surrounding areas].

2075. This is west of Hayagrīva [or Padmāntaka].

2076. This is east of Yamāntaka.

[The Maṇḍala Roof]

Where in the maṇḍala roof does the upper fierce deity, Uṣṇīṣacakravartin, abide? First, you must know how to construct the roof of the celestial mansion, so I will explain. The *Maṇḍala Vajra Garland* describes in great detail the lines of the maṇḍala, but not the way the roof is constructed. Other authentic Indian works do not explain this clearly either. Hence it is said: It would seem that understanding this subject presents some difficulties.

However, SOME TIBETAN LAMAS[2077] say that, according to the *Kosala*, "At the level of each gate there are two columns; one end of these column rests on the vajra line and the other [reaches] the nave of the maṇḍala."[2078] Thus it is taught[2079] that [in maṇḍala drawings] the height of the column from the base of the wall to the point where the tip reaches the center of the maṇḍala [is four large units]. [66b] Accordingly, the height of the roof of the outer maṇḍala is half of the width of the maṇḍala. The height of the fivefold wall is three large units and one small unit,[2080] and the space of the strands of pearls are two small units. Therefore that [i.e., the strands of pearls] should be at the level of the inner beam. The drip-like ornaments are suspended toward the outside of the strands of pearls, hence they are not counted when measuring the height of the inner roof. Since the parapet is above the structure,[2081] its height is likewise not counted in the measurements of the lower roof. So THEY say.

In response, our lama,[2082] Vajradhara, whose utterances arise out of perfect valid knowledge, teaches that the citation from the *Kosala* does not specify that the columns are four large units in height. However, a composition said to be by Buddhaguhya explains: "Inside there are eight columns that support the edges of four large beams; twenty-eight rafters cover the [nine] quadrants

2077. Our text follows now Tsong kha pa, *Sngags rim chen mo*, chap. 6, 245–246. See Ngor chen, *Zla zer*, 103b2–104a2, and Mus srad pa, *Rnam bshad chu rgyun log smra'i dri ma 'khrud byed*, 68b5.

2078. See Śākyamitra, *Ko sa la'i rgyan, Kosalālaṅkāra*, Tōh 2503, 91a1–2.

2079. Reading *bstan pas* for *brten pas* in our text, as in Tsong kha pa, *Sngags rim chen mo*, chap 6, 246.

2080. Tsong kha pa adds in his *Sngags rim chen mo*, chap 6, 246, that the panels are one small unit.

2081. Tib. *pu shu*.

2082. See Tsong kha pa, *'Dod 'jo*, 97b2–5.

[formed by] the four large beams;[2083] and the roof-laths[2084] should be fitted accordingly."[2085] Most Tibetan lamas agree on this, so it is accepted to do so.

[The Roof of the Outer Maṇḍala][2086]

Construct a square of columns one small unit in width and fourteen small units in height. As for the location of these columns, begin at the junctures of the *brahma* lines with the main lines in the four directions and proceed toward the center on each side for a distance of one large unit; then leave five small units to the right and left and there set the columns. Small capitals upon the columns support straight beams one small unit in height. Arrange as you can the rafters over four golden bands upon the beams. The edges of the rafters that emerge a little outside [the roof] form the faces of sea monsters, from the mouths of which are suspended round and vertical strands of pearls. Upon the rafters are laths[2087] covered with eaves. The tips of the wood laths extend from the roof a little further than the rafters and that is where the drip-like ornaments are hung. From the back side of the eaves [67a] rise the railings-like parapets.

[The Roof of the Inner Mansion]

I will describe the construction of the roof of the inner mansion separately, because as we have seen, there is a specific reason and purpose for placing the ground of the central quadrant slightly higher than one large unit above [the eight outer quadrants] that form the main platform of the deities. As mentioned, there are eight columns within the ring of the vajra garland: two white columns in the east adorned with wheels, two yellow columns in the south adorned with jewels, two red columns in the west adorned with lotuses, and two green columns in the north adorned with swords. The length and width of these columns have already been indicated. The small capitals set on these eight columns support a circular beam. Within the circular beam are four

2083. Reading *gdung chen* for *rin chen* in our text, as in the Derge.

2084. Tib. *gral ma*.

2085. Buddhaguhya, *Dharmamaṇḍalasūtra*, *Dkyil 'khor gyi chos mdor bsdus pa*, Tōh 3705, 2b6–7; English translation in Lo Bue 1987, 797. Cited also by Tsong kha pa, *Sngags rim chen mo*, chap. 6, 246.

2086. See Tsong kha pa, *Sngags rim chen mo*, chap 6, 246.

2087. Tib. *gral ma*.

straight beams in a checkered pattern.[2088] The edges of these beams rest on the capitals of the columns. There are no rafters and laths in the roof of the inner mansion, but beneath the beams there is a canopy.[2089]

Small columns are evenly placed around the open space[2090] within the outer roof. The small capitals upon them support a circular beam all around which rest the tips of the rafters. In order to support the central round beam the columns are beveled.[2091] Two beams that run north–south are affixed to the circular beam at their northern and southern ends; the ends should be separated by more than one large unit. Below the beams that run north–south there are four central beams slightly more than one large unit apart. The edges of the rafters rest on these beams and the tips of the eaves should extend slightly beyond them. [67b] Constructing the roof of a three-dimensional celestial mansion in this way will provide it with bright light within.

A treatise said to be written by Buddhaguhya teaches: "The outer shape of the celestial mansion should be like a stūpa, in the shape of a castle, a royal palace, or a pavilion on a mountain top."[2092] Thus it is explained that the celestial mansion can either be shaped on the outside like a stūpa, or a castle, or a royal palace with a peaked roof, or a round tent taller in the center, whichever of these possibilities is found most suitable. I will not go into extensive disputations here with those who take this position.[2093]

[The Finial]

Whatever form you choose for the roof, decorate on top with a finial of vajras, jewels, and precious gems, for the *Kosala* teaches: "*Vajra* is a jeweled vajra, *jewels* are wish-fulfilling jewels, and *precious gems* are rubies and so forth. Thus you should create a small chamber ornamented with these on top."[2094] Hence the finial should be embellished with a stack of ornaments: at the top place a five-pronged vajra made of precious substances; below it nine facets of wish-fulfilling jewels, and below that [the finial] is decorated with precious

2088. Tib. *mig mangs ris*.

2089. Tib. *nam rgyan*.

2090. Tib. *kha gdang*.

2091. Tib. *seg kha*; spelled also *gsegs ka* or *bsegs kha*.

2092. Buddhaguhya, *Dkyil 'khor gyi chos mdor bsdus pa*, *Dharmamaṇḍalasūtra*, Tōh 3705, 2b4; English translation in Lo Bue 1987, 796. The first line was cited above [55a]. Cited by Tsong kha pa, *Sngags rim chen mo*, chap. 6, 246.

2093. See Tsong kha pa, *Sngags rim chen mo*, chap. 6, 246.

2094. Śākyamitra, *Ko sa la'i rgyan*, *Kosalālaṅkāra*, Tōh 2503, 25a1–2.

gems, such as rubies. The total height of the finial should be one large unit. Thus, in both three-dimensional maṇḍalas and maṇḍalas for meditation, [Uṣṇīṣacakravartin,] the upper fierce deity, will have ample space facing west and slightly to the east over the principal deity, and below the peaked roof.

[The Colors Within]

Nāgabodhi elucidates the colors within: "Know that the quadrants are white in the east, yellow in the south, red in the west, green in the north, and a brilliant *indranīla* at the center."[2095] These are the colors of the grounds and ceilings of the quadrants. The *Maṇḍala Vajra Garland* explains the colors of the maṇḍala ground in this way: [68a] "The ground of the inner maṇḍala within the main line is divided into the four directions by the two diagonal lines. The color of each direction is the same as that of the tathāgata of that direction. The same holds true in the maṇḍala for meditational purposes where the ceiling and columns are likewise the colors of the four directions. The quadrants are adorned with the emblems of the tathāgatas, and the ground is the color of the principal deity in the center."[2096] Thus the east is white, the south yellow, the west red, the north green, and the center blue.[2097]

The colors of the interior side of the walls follow the colors of the fivefold wall and not the colors of their directions. SOME LAMAS EXPLAIN that the color of the interior sides of the walls is blue. However, the luminosity of each tathāgata of the four directions strikes them, and therefore the interior walls appear whitish-blue, yellowish-blue, reddish-blue, and greenish-blue respectively.

[The Mantric Path][2098]

According to the Mantra Vehicle, in order to render the disciples into suitable vessels for practicing mantra, they must first be initiated into a maṇḍala with all its characteristics. Then they become yogis of the creation

2095. Nāgabodhi, *Dkyil chog nyi shu pa, Maṇḍalaviṃśatividhi*, chap. 10, vv. 3–4ab, Tōh 1810, 137a6–7; Tanaka 2000, 358.

2096. Abhayākaragupta, *Dkyil chog rdo rje phreng ba, Vajrāvalī*, Tōh 3140, 38b3–4; Mori 2009, §13.2.4, 238–239. D has *phyogs bzhi'i thig rnams de bzhin no* for *phyogs bzhi'i thog rnams kyang de bzhin no*, and *rang rang gi* for *rang gi* in our text; Mori has *thog* for *thig* (the Sanskrit is *paṭala*) and the rest is as in D.

2097. See Tsong kha pa, *Gsang mngon*, 31a1.

2098. See Tsong kha pa, *Sngags rim chen mo*, chap. 6, 246–247.

and completion stages who must tread the mantric path by meditating on the yoga of the maṇḍala with its celestial mansion and the deities dwelling therein. Ultimately, they are awakened in the form of the maṇḍala wheel with its mansion and deities. Hence, it is deemed extremely important for mantric practitioners to understand the system of the maṇḍala. However, nowadays it would seem that mantric practitioners who understand this deeply and without fail are exceptionally rare. Therefore I have provided a short analysis according to the flawless teachings of the lama. Nevertheless, you must deepen your understanding by listening carefully to the masters.

[The Seats of the Deities]

All the deities have identical lower seats of variegated lotuses, thirty-one seats in all.[2099] The [upper] seats are not identical: with regard to the peaceful deities, in the east, Vairocana and the others have lunar seats; in the south, Māmakī has a vajra seat, and the other deities have jewel seats; in the west, all the deities have red lotus seats; [68b] and in the north, all the deities have crossed vajras; the principal deity and the ten fierce deities occupy solar seats. The *Concise Sādhana* explains this implicitly or explicitly in the context of the Supreme King of Maṇḍalas.[2100] The source reference will be given below.

The *Vajra Garland Explanatory Tantra* elucidates: "The deities occupying seven seats of variegated lotuses and lunar seats and two other solar seats are surrounded by the hateful and loving[2101] retinue."[2102] Thus Amitābha and Māmakī dwell on solar seats, while the other seven deities occupy lunar seats. The *Vajra Garland Explanatory Tantra* continues: "Vajrapāṇi dwells on an immaculate solar seat and the others on lunar seats; [all the deities] dwell on variegated lotuses."[2103] In other words, Vajrapāṇi dwells on a solar seat while the other seven bodhisattvas occupy lunar seats. Either of the two systems is acceptable, so do not fear that they are contradictory.

The *Vajrasattva Sādhana* explains in the context of the meditation on the lord of the specially visualized deities: "Visualize [Vajradhara] abiding in the

2099. The principal deity and his consort share a single seat. Our text here and below follows the lines in Tsong kha pa, *Gsang mngon*, 31a1–4.

2100. Nāgārjuna, *Mdor byas*, *Piṇḍīkrama Sādhana*, Tōh 1796, 6a2–9b3, L 107–198c, T 105–195c.

2101. Preferring *dga'* as in the Derge over *rgal* in our text.

2102. *Rgyud rdo rje phreng ba*, *Vajramālā Tantra*, chap. 54, v. 32abc, Tōh 445, 255a3–4. D has *'khor dga'* for *'khor rgal* and *dga' bar bcas* for *dga' mar bshad* in our text.

2103. *Rgyud rdo rje phreng ba*, *Vajramālā Tantra*, chap. 54, v. 36, Tōh 445, 255a6. D has *lha mo* for *lhag ma* in our text.

center of the maṇḍala in the heroic cross-legged posture upon a lotus and a solar seat."[2104] Thus the seat of the principal deity is a solar seat, which is incompatible with the practice of visualizing him on a lunar seat above the lotus.

[The Vases]

The *Maṇḍala Vajra Garland* explains that you should draw eight vases, four small units high, in the "second square"[2105] of the deities beyond the inner circle at a distance of four small units to the right and left of the *brahma* line.[2106] There are two ways to color the eight vases; either in gold or in accordance with the color of the tathāgata of that direction. The vases are filled with nectar imbued with the nature of bodhicitta.

Here we end our account of the celestial mansion along with the thrones.

2104. Candrakīrti, *Rdo rje sems dpa'i sgrub thabs, Vajrasattva Sādhana,* Tōh 1814, 198a3; Luo and Tomabechi 2009, 11.5 and 43.2–3.

2105. Tib. *rim pa gnyis pa,* Skt. *dvitīyapura.* This is a square where four of the vajra ladies dwell, just beyond the ring of the vajra garland that surrounds the inner nine quadrants.

2106. Abhayākaragupta, *Dkyil chog rdo rje phreng ba, Vajrāvalī,* Tōh 3140, 39b4–5; Mori 2009, §13.3.1. 242 and 243.

6. Meditation on the Specially Visualized Deities

Visualization of the Deities—The Indwellers of the Maṇḍala Who Will Be Awakened There[2107]

There are four topics here: [69a] (1) placing the specially visualized deities,[2108] (2) the "deeds" of the specially visualized deities, (3) gathering the specially visualized deities into the body, and (4) dissolution of the specially visualized deities into the ultimate maṇḍala.

Placing the Specially Visualized Deities

The first section includes three subsections: (1) how to visualize the deities and in correspondence with whom, (2) the reason for visualizing the deities in correspondence with the people of the first eon, and (3) the meaning of purifying the ground of purification by means of the creation stage.

How to Visualize the Deities and in Correspondence with Whom

[Why the Deities Here Are Called Specially Visualized Deities]

The *Concise Sādhana* teaches: "You should meditate on the specially visualized [deities][2109] in the maṇḍala according to the ritual method."[2110] And

2107. Above [31b6], our text has *brten pa* for *rten* here in the same heading in the outline.

2108. Tib. *lhag mos kyi lha.*

2109. Tib. *lhag par mos*, the Skt. is different: *adhimuktyā.*

2110. Nāgārjuna, *Mdor byas*, *Piṇḍīkrama Sādhana*, Tōh 1796, 3a7; L 36ab; T 35ab. D has *dkyil 'khor pa* for *dkyil 'khor la* in our text. The Sanskrit has *adhimuktyā* in the instrumental case for *lhag mos* in Tibetan, and *māṇḍaleyān* for *dkyil 'khor pa*. Hence this verse could be translated as: "Thus meditate on the indwellers of the maṇḍala, with special visualization [or intense aspiration], according to the ritual method." However, our author understands this verse differently.

the *Sādhana Incorporating the Scripture* teaches: "With a mind endowed with special intent/visualization (*lhag par mos pa can*)."[2111] The thirty-two deities do not appear gradually out of their seed syllables, emblems, and so forth, but rather, at the very moment your mind intends (*mos pa*) for all the deities to be placed inside the maṇḍala, you should visualize (*mos pa*) them at once fully-formed, with heads, arms, and so forth, as in a miraculous birth.

[How and Where to Visualize the Deities]

The *Concise Sādhana* explains:

> Meditate on yourself with a consort at the center of the maṇḍala, having three faces and six arms and an appearance equal in splendor to the blue *indranīla* gem.
>
> Visualize Vairocana, Ratnasaṃbhava, Amitābha, and Karmarāṭ,[2112] in the cardinal directions, one after the other starting from the east, all of them likewise endowed with three faces and six arms.
>
> Place the mothers Moharati and so forth[2113] endowed with three faces and six arms in the intermediate directions starting from the direction of fire.[2114]
>
> Similarly, place Rūpavajrā and so forth[2115] at the four outer intermediate directions, while Sparśavajrā[2116] abides with Vajrasattva.[2117]
>
> You should place the bodhisattvas Maitreya and Kṣitigarbha on the eastern platform,[2118] Vajrapāṇi and Khagarbha on the southern platform, Lokeśa and Mañjughoṣa on the western platform, [69b]

2111. Tib. *lhag par mos pa can kyi sems kyis*. In this paragraph there is a play on the word *mos pa*. Nāgārjuna, *Mdo bsre*, *Sādhanasūtramelāpaka*, Tōh 1797, 12a3.

2112. Tib. Rnam snang mdzad, Rin chen, 'Od dpag med, and Las kyi rgyal.

2113. These are the mothers Locanā, Māmakī, Pāṇḍaravāsinī, and Tārā. Tib. Spyan ma, Māmakī, Gos dkar mo, and Sgrol ma. On the problematic use of the name Moharati, Gti mug dga' ma, see in the chapter of the body maṇḍala below.

2114. This means the southeast.

2115. These are Rūpavajrā, Śabdhavajrā, Gandhavajrā, and Rasavajrā. Tib. Gzugs rdo rje, Sgra rdo rje ma, Dri rdo rje ma, and Ro rdo rje ma.

2116. Tib. Reg bya rdo rje, Eng., Vajra Lady of Tangibles.

2117. That is, together with the principal deity at the center of the maṇḍala.

2118. Tib. *snam bu*, Skt. *paṭṭikā*.

> Sarvanīvaraṇaviṣkambhin and Samantabhadra on the northern platform.[2119]
>
> Visualize the fierce deity Yamāntaka at the eastern gate, Aparājita at the southern gate, Hayagrīva at the western gate, and Amṛtakuṇḍalin at the northern gate.[2120]
>
> Meditate on Acala, Ṭakkirāja,[2121] Nīladaṇḍa, and Mahābala respectively in the intermediate directions beginning in the southeast.[2122]
>
> Likewise meditate on the fierce and mighty Sumbharāja below and on Uṣṇīṣacakravartin above.[2123]

The color of their bodies, their emblems, and so forth are explained in the section on the Supreme King of Maṇḍalas.

[Where Is It Taught in the Guhyasamāja Tantra *That You Should Place the Specially Visualized Deities inside the Celestial Mansion?]*[2124]

The *Vajrasattva Sādhana* teaches: "The first chapter of the *Guhyasamāja Tantra* points to the scriptural authority for this: "Its essence is clarity, replete with myriad forms, suffused with clouds of buddhas, pervaded with lambent

2119. Tib. Byams pa and Sa yi snying po at the east, Phyag na rdo rje and Mkha' snying po at the south, 'Jig rten dbang phyung and 'Jam pa'i dbyangs at the west, Sgrib pa thams cad rnam sel and Kun tu bzang po at the north.

2120. Tib. Gshin rje gshed at the eastern gate, Gzhan gyis mi thub at the southern gate, Rta mgrin at the western gate, and Bdud rtsi 'khyil pa at the northern gate.

2121. Or Ṭarkvirāja.

2122. Tib. Mi g.yo, 'Dod pa'i rgyal po, Dbyug sngon, and Stobs po che, respectively, in the intermediate directions beginning with the southeast.

2123. Tib. Gnod mdzes rgyal po and Gtsug tor 'khor lo bsgyur ba. Nāgārjuna, *Mdor byas, Piṇḍīkrama Sādhana*, Tōh 1796, 3a2–7; L 27–35; T 26–34. D has *rnam pa can* for *lta bu la*; *dang* for *dpal*; *shar la sogs pa'i phyogs su bsam* for *me yi mtshams nas brtsams nas su / rim pa bzhin du nges par dgod*; again *rnam pa can* for *lta bu la*; *rim pa ji bzhin* for *rim bzhin du ni*; *kyang ni* for *dang ni*; *gzhan gyis me thub* for *gzhan gyis mi thub*; *de yi* for *de'i*; and *gtsug tor 'khor los sgyur rgyal* for *gtsug tor 'khor lo bsgyur ba* in our text.

2124. The following discussion follows Tsong kha pa's *Sgron gsal mchan*, 58b4–59a1.

light-rays, and endowed with disks—a clear one and so forth—this is the abode of all tathāgatas."[2125]

Whereas the *Vajrasattva Sādhana* cites this verse following the instructions about placing the thirty-two deities inside the celestial mansion, the *Sādhana Incorporating the Scripture* only cites it following the instructions about meditating on yourself as the principal of the specially visualized deities, and subsequently explains: "This verse shows that you should meditate on [the specially visualized deities in the context of] the samādhi of placing the surrounding deities inside the maṇḍala."[2126]

The *Illuminating Lamp* explicates the verse in this way: "*Its essence is clarity* means that even those who abide outside the celestial mansion can see the deities inside the maṇḍala as forms appearing within a crystal. The meaning of *replete with myriad forms*[2127] is endowed with distinguished properties of variegated colors such as *indranīla*. *Suffused with clouds of buddhas*[2128] [70a] means pervaded by the emanated deities of the maṇḍala. *Pervaded with lambent light-rays*[2129] refers to the multitude of blazing and flickering[2130] light-rays of the fierce deities in the ten directions. As for *endowed with disks, a clear one and so forth*, the clear one refers to the seat of the lunar disk and so forth[2131]

2125. Candrakīrti, *Rdo rje sems dpa'i sgrub thabs*, *Vajrasattva Sādhana*, Tōh 1814, 198b2–3; Luo and Tomabechi 2009, 12.8–13 and 44.13–45.2. D and Luo and Tomabechi have *gzugs ldan par* for *gzugs ldan pa*. The passage from the *Guhyasamāja Tantra* is: chap. 1, Tōh 442; Zhol 3a1–2; Stog 4a2–3; Dunh 1b3–4; Fremantle 1971, v. 1; and Matsunaga 1978, v. 1. Zhol has *sna tshogs gzugs kyis kun tu rgyas* for *kun nas sna tshogs gzugs ldan pa*; *sangs rgyas sprin kyis kun tu khyab* for *sangs rgyas sprin dang yang dag ldan*; and *'od zer 'phro ba mang po 'khrug* for *'od zer 'bar zhing 'khrug pa po* in our text.

2126. Nāgārjuna, *Mdo bsre*, *Sādhanasūtramelāpaka*, Tōh 1797, 12a4–5. D has *ting nge 'dzin kyis dbang du byas te lhag par mos pa la dmigs par stan pa yin no* for *ting nge 'dzin du mos par bya ste* in our text. Our text follows Tsong kha pa's *Sgron gsal mchan*, 58b4–5.

2127. While above [69b] the verse is cited from Candrakīrti's *Rdo rje sems dpa'i sgrub thabs* that has *kun nas sna tshogs gzugs ldan par*, Candrakīrti's *Sgron gsal* has *sna tshogs gzugs kyis kun du rgyas*.

2128. Again, while the citation above is *sangs rgyas sprin dang yang dag ldan*, here we have *sangs rgyas sprin kyis kun tu khyab*.

2129. Here Candrakīrti's *Rdo rje sems dpa'i sgrub thabs* has *'od zer 'bar zhing 'khrug pa po*, while Candrakīrti's *Sgron gsal* has *'od zer 'phro ba mang po 'khrug*.

2130. The Sanskrit is somewhat different here.

2131. In his *Sgron gsal mchan*, 58b2–3, Tsong kha pa explains that this refers to the seat of the peaceful deities, while the fierce ones have a solar seat.

with which the celestial mansion is endowed. The abode of all tathāgatas means the abode of all tathāgatas as the supporting maṇḍala."[2132]

Is there is contradiction here? The answer is no, since the explanation of the *Commentary on the Vajrasattva Sādhana* seems to be the same as that of the *Illuminating Lamp.*[2133] *With clouds of buddhas* means suffused with peaceful deities, and *emanating light-rays* indicates the fierce deities. Hence both the celestial mansion and the deities residing inside it are indicated here, and this is the meaning of the lines in the *Illuminating Lamp* as well. The *Vajrasattva Sādhana* and the *Sādhana Incorporating the Scripture* as well cite this verse as the scriptural authority for both celestial mansion and deities; they do not cite it as the scriptural authority for the deities alone.[2134]

Since the characteristics of the deities and the celestial mansion of the maṇḍala of the specially visualized deities and the Supreme King of Maṇḍalas are similar,[2135] it is appropriate in both cases to cite the verse *suffused with clouds of buddhas* [as scriptural authorities]. Thus there is no contradiction between these two sādhanas and the *Illuminating Lamp.*[2136] The two sādhanas apply this verse to the specially visualized deities, and the *Illuminating Lamp*[2137] explains this same verse as meaning *pervaded by the emanated deities.*[2138]

2132. Candrakīrti, *Sgron gsal, Pradīpoddyotanaṭīkā,* Tōh 1785, 13b6–14a2; Chakravarti 1984, 19.

2133. The commentary by Līlavajra, *Rdo rje sems dpa'i sgrub thabs kyi 'grel pa, Vajrasattva Sādhana Nibandha,* Tōh 1815, 206b2, is very similar to Candrakīrti's *Sgron gsal.* The commentary by Tathāgatarakṣita, *Rdo rje sems dpa'i sgrub pa'i thabs kyi bshad pa, Vajrasattva Sādhana Vyākhyā,* Tōh 1835, 282b3–5, is also similar. These three works interpret the line on lambent light-rays as the fierce deities in the ten directions, but none of them explain the meaning of clouds of buddhas as the peaceful deities. All three explain this line as referring to the emanated deities of the maṇḍala. Our text mainly follows Tsong kha pa's *Sgron gsal mchan,* 58b6.

2134. See also Tsong kha pa, *Rnam gzhag rim pa'i rnam bshad,* 65b1–2.

2135. Here Mkhas grub rje follows Tsong kha pa, *Sgron gsal mchan,* 58a4 and 59a2.

2136. That is, Candrakīrti's *Rdo rje sems dpa'i sgrub thabs, Vajrasattva Sādhana,* Tōh 1814 and Nāgārjuna's *Mdo bsre, Sādhanasūtramelāpaka,* Tōh 1797.

2137. See above [70a1].

2138. Candrakīrti's *Sgron gsal,* Tōḥ 1785, 14a1; Chakravarti 1984, 19, explains the line *suffused with clouds of buddhas* as meaning *pervaded with the emanated deities of the maṇḍala,* by applying it not to the specially visualized deities, but to the Supreme King of Maṇḍalas. This is because the latter is also called the emanated maṇḍala, since it emanates from the drop on the lotus of the mother.

[*The Principal Deity of the Specially Visualized Deities*]

The eleventh chapter of the *Guhyasamāja Tantra* teaches: "With the syllable *bhrūṃ* meditate on the abode and visualize the arising of the three vajras."[2139] The *Illuminating Lamp* explains this as meaning: "First meditate on the celestial mansion, and then meditate on the three signs of the solar disk and so forth as part of the five manifest awakenings."[2140] [70b] Both the *Sādhana Incorporating the Scripture* and *Formulating the Sādhana* cite this line as the scriptural source for the generation of the specially visualized deities, and specifically explain that *visualize the arising of the three vajras* means generate Vajradhara.[2141] As several different meanings can be taught in every vajra word of the tantra, you should not assume there is a contradiction here, but rather retain your understanding according to the explanation above.[2142]

Thus Ārya Nāgārjuna and his disciples interpret the teaching of the *Guhyasamāja Tantra* on Akṣobhya emanating the assembly maṇḍala and Vajradhara, the lord of the body, speech, and mind of all tathāgatas, taking his place at the center of the maṇḍala of the great samaya—as indicating the

2139. *Guhyasamāja Tantra*, Tōh 442; Zhol 15a3–4; Stog 25b5; Dunh missing; Fremantle 1971, v. 5cd; and Matsunaga 1978, v. 5cd, partly cited above [49b].

2140. This is based on Tsong kha pa's explanation. Candrakīrti, *Sgron gsal*, Tōh 1785, 77b5; Chakravarti 1984, 97. D has here: *de bzhin du gzhi dkyil 'khor bsams la mtshan ma gsum bsgom par ba'i gzhan du ni ma yin no*. In his *Sgron gsal mchan*, 234a5, Tsong kha pa explains that the three signs are the [seats of] the sun, the moon, and the lotus. And in his *Rnam gzhag rim pa'i rnam bshad*, 12b4, Tsong kha pa says that Candrakīrti's *Sgron gsal*, Tōh 1785, explains this line as: "You should first meditate on the celestial mansion, and afterward meditate on the three signs, the solar disk, and so forth as part of the manifest awakening from the moon."

2141. Nāgārjuna, *Mdo bsre*, *Sādhanasūtramelāpaka*, Tōh 1797, 12a3. D has *gnas ni bskyed pa sngon 'gro bas / rdo rje gsum bskyed bsgom par bya* for *yi ge Bhrūṃ gyis gnas gnas bsgoms te / rdo rje gsum 'byung bsgom par bya* in our text. Tsong kha pa's *Sgron gsal mchan*, 234a6, has just *rdo rje gsum 'byung bsgom par bya*. In his *Rnam gzhag rim pa'i rnam bshad*, 12b3, Tsong kha pa has the version of the *Guhyasamāja Tantra*. Nāgabuddhi, *Rnam gzhag rim pa*, *Vyavastholi*, chap. 1, Tōh 1809, 122a4–5; Tanaka 2016, 83. D and Tanaka have *gnas ni bsgom pa sngon 'gro bas* for *yi ge bhruṃ gyis gnas bsgoms te* and *bskyed* for *'byung* in our text.

2142. This follows Tsong kha pa, *Rnam gzhag rim pa'i rnam bshad*, 12b4–5, and *Sgron gsal mchan*, 234a5–b1. In *Sgron gsal mchan*, Tsong kha pa points out that Nāgārjuna's *Mdo bsre*, *Sādhanasūtramelāpaka*, Tōh 1797, 13a3–4, applies these verses from the eleventh chapter of the *Guhyasamāja Tantra* to the blessing of the body, speech, and mind.

specially visualized deities.[2143] In the *Concise Sādhana* the principal deity of the specially visualized deities is Vajrasattva,[2144] while in the *Sādhana Incorporating the Scripture* and *Vajrasattva Sādhana* the principal deity is Vajradhara.[2145] Thus the principal deity of the specially visualized deities is not Akṣobhya but Vajradhara, who belongs to the sixth tathāgata family, and his divine identity should thus be maintained.[2146] Furthermore, whenever the *Guhyasamāja Tantra* explains the six types of single-pointed mindfulness of the six tathāgata families or whenever it explains the different types of the five manifest awakenings of the individual families, the principal deity of the Supreme King of Maṇḍalas may belong to any tathāgata family, but the principal deity of the specially visualized deities is certainly Vajradhara, who belongs to the sixth family.

Thus generating the specially visualized deities as in miraculous birth is a meditation that corresponds to the evolution of the inhabitants of the world—following the evolution of the inanimate world.

2143. This refers to the passage of the *Guhyasamāja Tantra* that precedes the first verse of the first chapter cited above, Tōh 442; Zhol 2b6–3a1; Stog 4a1–2; Dunh 1b2; Fremantle 1971, 176–177; and Matsunaga 1978, 5. Our text relies here not only on the *Guhyasamāja Tantra*, but also on its interpretation in Candrakīrti's *Sgron gsal*, Tōh 1785, 13b4–6; Chakravarti 1984, 19; and on Tsong kha pa's *Sgron gsal mchan*, 57b1–58a4.

2144. Nāgārjuna, *Mdor byas*, *Piṇḍīkrama Sādhana*, Tōh 1796, 3a4; L 30d, T 29d.

2145. Nāgārjuna, *Mdo bsre*, *Sādhanasūtramelāpaka*, Tōh 1797, 12a3. Candrakīrti, *Rdo rje sems dpa'i sgrub thabs*, *Vajrasattva Sādhana*, Tōh 1814, 198a4; Luo and Tomabechi 2009, 11.6 and 43.13.

2146. See Bu ston, *Mdor byas 'grel chen*, 26a6–b1, and Tsong kha pa, *Rnam gzhag rim pa'i rnam bshad*, 5b1–6a3.

[How the Inhabitants of the World Evolve, in Brief][2147]

A god passes away in the Heaven of Clear Light[2148] and is born as Great Brahmā. Then the realms Priests of Brahmā,[2149] the Retinue of Brahmā,[2150] and [71a] the six classes of the gods of the desire realm[2151] evolve in succession from the upper to the lower heavens. Then, the peoples of the northern, eastern, western, and southern continents[2152] evolve in turn followed by hungry ghosts,[2153] animals, and denizens of hell. When one sentient being is born in the Hell of Ceaseless Torment,[2154] the evolution of the inhabitants of the world is complete. The nature of things is such that the realm that is destroyed last is the first one formed.

It is certain that all these beings will be reborn through one of the four modes of birth. *Formulating the Sādhana* explains this in detail: "These are the four modes of birth: Birth from an egg, birth from a womb, birth from heat and moisture, and miraculous birth,"[2155] and so forth[2156] up to: "What is miraculous birth? It is the instantaneous birth of sentient beings with all major and minor limbs intact, and all faculties sound and unimpaired. Who are these beings? They are gods, denizens of hell, intermediate beings, people of the first eon,

2147. See Vasubandhu, *Mdzod 'grel, Kośabhāṣya*, chap. 3, vv. 90cd, Tōh 4090, 156b4–157a4; Pradhan 1975, 179; Pruden 1988–1990, 477–478; *'Dul ba rnam par 'byed pa, Vinayavibhaṅga*, Tōh 3, 48a1–51b5; and Asaṅga, *Sa'i dngos gzhi, Maulībhūmi*, Tōh 4035, 20b4–21a5; Bhattacharya, 1957, 41.17–42.1; English translation in Kajiyama 2000, 196. See also the *Aggañña Sutta, Dīgha Nikāya* 27; *Mahāvastu*, 1, 338–348; English translation in Jones 1949, 285–294. See also the commentary of Dge 'dun grub, *Mdzod ṭig thar lam gsal byed*, 115b6–116a5; English translation in Patt 1993, 687, and Jinpa 2017, 302–306.

2148. Tib. *'od gsal*, Skt. *ābhāsvara*.

2149. Tib. *tshangs pa'i mdun*, Skt. *brahmapurohita*.

2150. Tib. *tshangs ris*, Skt. *brahmakāyika*.

2151. Tib. *'dod lha*, Skt. *kāmadeva*.

2152. Tib. *sgra mi snyan, ba glang spyod, lus 'phags po*, and *'dzam bu gling*, Skt. *uttarakuru, godānīya, videha* or *pūrvavideha*, and *jambudvīpa*.

2153. Tib. *yi dwags*, Skt. *preta*.

2154. Tib. *mnar med*, Skt. *avīci*, the lowest hot hell.

2155. Nāgabuddhi, *Rnam gzhag rim pa, Vyavastholi*, chap. 1, Tōh 1809, 122a5; Tanaka 2016, 83–84.

2156. Here Nāgabuddhi's *Rnam gzhag rim pa* explains the types of beings born in the first three modes of birth.

and so forth."[2157] Although such a range of sentient beings is included within the four modes of birth during the evolution of the world's inhabitants, the creation stage is not applied in correspondence to other modes of birth or other beings but only to humans. And among humans the correspondences are not applied to the inhabitants of the three other continents, but only to those in Jambudvīpa.

[How Did the People of the First Eon Appear in Jambudvīpa?][2158]

Having passed away in the God Realm of Clear Light,[2159] they were miraculously born in Jambudvīpa. *Formulating the Sādhana* teaches: "They are adorned with all the good qualities of the Buddha."[2160] [71b] The *Abhidharmakośa*[2161] and the *Monastic Guidelines*[2162] likewise explain that they are ornamented with the qualities of the Buddha.[2163] Thus (1) they are endowed with features that are similar to the major and minor marks of a

2157. Nāgabuddhi, *Rnam gzhag rim pa, Vyavastholi*, chap. 1, Tōh 1809, 122a7–b1; Tanaka 2016, 85. D and Tanaka have: *ma rdzogs pa med pa* for *ma rdzogs pa med par*; *cig car* for *cig char*; and *de dag kyang gang zhe na* for *de gang zhe na* in our text.

2158. See Vasubandhu, *Mdzod 'grel, Kośabhāṣya*, chap. 3, vv. 90cd, Tōh 4090, 156b4–157a4; Pradhan 1975, 179; Pruden 1988–1990, 477–478; *'Dul ba rnam par 'byed pa, Vinayavibhaṅga*, Tōh 3, 48a1–51b5; Nāgabuddhi, *Rnam gzhag rim pa, Vyavastholi*, chap. 1, Tōh 1809, 123a1–4 and 123b4–6. See Asaṅga, *Sa'i dngos gzhi, Maulībhūmi*, Tōh 4035, 20b6–21a5; Bhattacharya, V. 1957, 42.1–18; English translation in Kajiyama 2000, 196–197. See also the commentary of Dge 'dun grub, *Mdzod ṭig thar lam gsal byed*, 115a6–116b1; English translation in Patt 1993, 694–697. See also the *Aggañña Sutta* in the *Dīgha Nikāya*, 27.

2159. Tib. *'od gsal*, Skt. *ābhāsvara*.

2160. Nāgabuddhi, *Rnam gzhag rim pa, Vyavastholi*, chap. 1, Tōh 1809, 123a1; Tanaka 2016, 87.

2161. Vasubandhu, *Mdzod 'grel, Kośabhāṣya*, chap. 3, v. 98, Tōh 4090, 162a5–6; Pradhan 1975, 186–187; Pruden 1988–1990, 487.

2162. *'Dul ba rnam par 'byed pa, Vinayavibhaṅga*, Tōh 3, 48b4–5.

2163. In his *Rnam gzhag rim pa'i rnam bshad*, 20b3–21a3, Tsong kha pa compares the lists of the special qualities of the first beings in these three texts: Nāgabuddhi, *Rnam gzhag rim pa, Vyavastholi*, Vasubandhu, *Mdzod 'grel, Kośabhāṣya*, and the *'Dul ba rnam par 'byed pa*; and finds scriptural authority there for all but the first of these qualities: being adorned with all the good qualities of the Buddha. According to Tsong kha pa, since the first beings are endowed with features similar to the major and minor marks, they are described here as being adorned with all the good qualities of the Buddha. Still, he stresses that this phrase does not appear in either Vasubandhu, *Mdzod 'grel, Kośabhāṣya*, or the *'Dul ba rnam par 'byed pa, Vinayavibhaṅga*.

buddha, like the universal monarchs,[2164] (2) their faculties are unimpaired, (3) they travel through space by means of miraculous powers born of their own karma, (4) since there is no distinction between day and night, their bodies shine with a light of their own, (5) their life spans may be infinite, (6) and being free of dependence on material food, they live on delight.[2165]

At that time, the surface of the great earth is covered with a nutritive essence, formed much like the skin on boiled milk when it cools, and endowed with a splendid color, smell, and taste; its color is like that of fresh butter, its taste is like unrefined honey. When a strong imprinted craving for food is awakened in one person of the first eon, that person[2166] dips a fingertip in it, tastes it, and develops a desire for it. Upon seeing this, the others do the same. Since they eat material food, their bodies become coarse and heavy, the light of their bodies no longer shines, and they are unable to travel in space as before. When darkness approaches in the absence of their bodily light, the sun and moon appear in the world through the power of karma, and temporal junctures like asterisms, days and nights, and months come into being.[2167] Those who eat little of this food grow beautiful, and those eating more of it develop ugly complexions. Therefore the former say to the latter: "I am beautiful and you are ugly." Due to their nonvirtuous spite, the nutritive essence of the earth disappears.

When they foregather and lament, earth-cream appears, its color yellow like the *dong kha* flower and its taste as before. They soon repeat their previous behavior till once again they begin to despise each other, and as a result the earth-cream [72a] disappears.[2168] When they lament all over again, a splendid thicket of sprouts appears, similar in color to the orange *ka dam pa* flower and with the same taste as before. When they repeat their previous behavior again here and begin to despise one another, the sprouts disappear.[2169]

Afterward, although no field has been plowed or planted anywhere, *salu*

2164. Tib. *'khor los bsgyur rgyal*, Skt. *cakravartin*.

2165. This is based in part on Nāgabuddhi, *Rnam gzhag rim pa*, *Vyavastholi*, chap. 1, Tōh 1809, 123a1–2; Tanaka 2016, 87–88. Their seventh quality is being miraculously born, as mentioned above.

2166. No gender exists yet.

2167. The *'Dul ba rnam par 'byed pa*, *Vinayavibhaṅga*, Tōh 3, 49b1–3, enumerates additional temporal units here.

2168. *'Dul ba rnam par 'byed pa*, *Vinayavibhaṅga*, Tōh 3, 49b6–50a6, retells these events once more.

2169. *'Dul ba rnam par 'byed pa*, *Vinayavibhaṅga*, Tōh 3, 50a6–b5, retells these events once more.

rice[2170] appears, devoid of husks and chaff, and with roots four fingers long. The rice they reap in the morning grows back in the morning, and the rice they reap in the evening grows back by evening, ready to be eaten, with no sign that it was ever reaped. Since this food is much coarser, when they eat the rice, its crude wastes turn into feces and urine. Through the power of karma, the doors of their evacuation protrude as male and female organs respectively, and thus the different appearances of men and women develop.

Being unclad, when they look at each other, their previous imprints are stirred with thoughts of mutual desire. In passionate response some engage in sexual activity, and seeing this, others cast dirt at them and so forth,[2171] saying: "You are bad." Then they build houses so that others will not see them doing what is unseemly. Thus the first house was built on account of desire.

At dawn they gather the *salu* rice for their morning meal, and at dusk for their evening meal. But one lazy being gathers rice for the morning and evening meals at the same time. Then others start gathering rice for two and three or more days at a time. Seeing that, still others gather rice for a month or more at a time, the harvested rice stalks no longer sprout, and the rice develops husks and chaff.

Due to the events explained here according to the *Monastic Guidelines*,[2172] beings with the exceptional bodies described earlier gradually come to have ordinary bodies in their lifetime. After that, people steal rice from each other and so forth, [72b] and because of this, they all gather together and appoint as their leader one good-natured person who is called the King Esteemed by Many.[2173] Among his descendants are the Śākyas who then rule the land.

Hence, the specially visualized deities in the meditation take on the appearance of male and female, in accordance with the people of the first eon who were miraculously born and gradually developed male and female organs.[2174]

[The Lord of Consciousness]

Here *Formulating the Sādhana* teaches: "The lord of consciousness, the Great Vajradhara, progenitor of sentient beings, emanated the realm of sentient

2170. Skt. śāli.

2171. *'Dul ba rnam par 'byed pa*, *Vinayavibhaṅga*, Tōh 3, 51a2, here enumerates other objects that are cast at them.

2172. *'Dul ba rnam par 'byed pa*, *Vinayavibhaṅga*, Tōh 3.

2173. Tib. *mang pos bkur ba'i rgyal po*, Skt. *rājamahāsaṃmata*.

2174. See Tsong kha pa, *Rnam gzhag rim pa'i rnam bshad*, 21b2–3, and Nāgabuddhi, *Rnam gzhag rim pa*, *Vyavastholi*, chap. 1, Tōh 1809, 123b4–6; Tanaka 2016; 91–92.

beings after generating the world."[2175] That which is the consciousness of[2176] the emanator of the impure realm of sentient beings, and that which is its lord as well, is the mind of sentient beings. By accumulating shared karma, it generates the world, and by accumulating unshared karma, it generates the sentient beings who dwell there. Since it governs this generation, it is called "lord" or "maker." As *Engaging in the Middle Way* teaches: "Every school of non-Buddhists speaks in its own treatises about persons and so forth. The Victorious One, who did not regard them as creators, taught that mind alone is the creator in and of the world."[2177]

Great Vajradhara is the progenitor of the circle of deities who are pure sentient beings, because it is taught that the celestial mansion and its deities all emanate as parts of his own body. Although the mind of the intermediate state during the time of the ground is called "the lord of consciousness, the mind vajra" in *Formulating the Sādhana*, it does not necessarily follow that the lord of consciousness and Vajradhara are synonymous.[2178] [73a] The explanation that Vajradhara generates the saṃsāric sentient beings is a mistake that ought not be made.

The Reason for Visualizing the Deities in Correspondence with the People of the First Eon[2179]

[Qualm:] What is the cause and what is the purpose of meditating on the specially visualized deities in accordance with people of the first eon?

[Reply:] The way people of the first eon are born is taken as an analogous event here, applied in correspondence with the generation of the specially visualized deities. However, the birth of people of the first eon is not taken as the

2175. Nāgabuddhi, *Rnam gzhag rim pa*, *Vyavastholi*, chap. 1, Tōh 1809, 122a4; Tanaka 2016, 83. D and Tanaka have *sems can skyed par* for *sems can bskyed par* and *'jig rten bskyed kyi* for *'jig rten bskyed pa'i* in our text. See also Tsong kha pa, *Rnam gzhag rim pa'i rnam bshad*, 12b6–13a6.

2176. Tsong kha pa, *Rnam gzhag rim pa'i rnam bshad*, 12b6, has *ni* for *yi* here, which can be translated as "The emanator of the impure realm of sentient beings is consciousness," and so forth.

2177. Candrakīrti, *Dbu ma la 'jug pa*, *Madhyamakāvatāra*, chap. 6, v. 86, Tōh 3861, 208a6–7; Li 2015, 15; French translation in La Vallée Poussin 1911, 240.

2178. Nāgabuddhi, *Rnam gzhag rim pa*, *Vyavastholi*, chap. 1, Tōh 1809, 123b7; Tanaka 2016, 93. Tib. *rnam par shes pa'i bdag po thugs rdo rje*, Skt. *vijñānādhipatiś cittavajra*. However, in the context of the evolution of the people in the world, the lord of consciousness is called Great Vajradhara, the progenitor of the world and sentient beings, as cited just above.

2179. See Tsong kha pa, *Bung ba'i re skong*, 22b2–24b5.

ground of purification for the meditation here. This is so because there is no purpose whatsoever in taking them as such, and there is no relation whatsoever between the birth of those sentient beings who passed away innumerable eons ago and the yogis who are now purifying themselves by meditating on the path, and who are of a different mental continuum.

[Qualm:] What is the purpose, then, of taking the people of the first eon as the corresponding object?

[Reply:] For transforming your ordinary birth, death, and intermediate state into the three bodies, you should meditate during the First Yoga on a path that accords with the birth, death, and intermediate being of the time of the ground. Therefore the dissolution of the specially visualized deities into clear light is a meditation that corresponds to the death in stages of a person of Jambudvīpa, endowed with the six constituents.[2180] The visualization of the First Lord through the five manifest awakenings corresponds to the evolution, subsequent to that death, of an intermediate being who would be born as a person in Jambudvīpa. And the transformation of the First Lord into Vajrasattva's nirmāṇakāya is a meditation that corresponds to the birth of that intermediate state in a womb of a woman in Jambudvīpa. The first meditation among these three, the meditation in correspondence with death, requires a prior support that bears resemblance to a person approaching death. To this end you must generate the specially visualized deities.

[Qualm:] Is it not sufficient to generate the specially visualized deities in correspondence with a person now alive who is approaching death? What is the purpose of applying this meditation in correspondence with the people of the first eon? [73b]

[Reply:] The generation of the celestial mansion is a meditation corresponding to the evolution of the world, so it is reasonable that the generation of the first deities inside the celestial mansion should be a meditation corresponding to the evolution of the first inhabitants of the world after its creation. As explained above, the first deities to be generated inside the celestial mansion are the specially visualized deities, and the first humans to evolve in Jambudvīpa are the people of the first eon. Since the two are similar, they are applied in correspondence.[2181]

[Qualm:] The meditation on the dissolution of the specially visualized deities in correspondence with the stages of death must accord with the stages of death of the person [whose birth is taken as an analogous event for generating

2180. These are earth, water, fire, wind, channels, and drops, or else bone, marrow, and semen received from the father, and flesh, skin, and blood received from the mother.

2181. See Tsong kha pa, *Rnam gzhag rim pa'i rnam bshad*, 21b2–22a1.

the deities]. Therefore the meditation must accord with the stages of death of humans of the first eon and thus it will not be suitable for the purification of the yogi's death at a future time.

[Reply:] The dissolution of coarse and subtle elements during the stages of death is in no way different for a person of the first eon who gradually became an ordinary human being with the six constituents and a living person who possesses the six constituents. Therefore there is no contradiction in accepting a common basis for these two meditations: the meditation corresponding to the stages of death-dissolution of a person of the first eon who gradually became ordinary; and the meditation corresponding to the stages of the death-dissolution of a living yogi endowed with the six constituents.

[Qualm:] Why is every correspondence to birth, death, and the intermediate state throughout the sādhana, beginning with the generation of the specially visualized deities, applied solely in relation to the people of Jambudvīpa?

[Reply:] Concerning this, there are two sections: refuting the system of others and establishing our own position.

Refuting the System of Others[2182]

[Are There Four Different Rituals to Purify the Four Modes of Birth?]

Some Tibetan lamas[2183] say that the Blessed One taught four ritual methods of generating deities for the purification of the four modes of birth:

(1) In birth from an egg, the womb produces an egg, and the egg gives birth to swans, cranes, and so forth. [74a] To purify this birth, it is taught that you should generate the deities from a small[2184] seed embraced by sun and moon. This is so because the *Abhidhānottara Tantra* teaches: "The yogi

2182. Our text follows here Tsong kha pa, *Rnam gzhag rim pa'i rnam bshad*, 19b3–5, and *'Dod 'jo*, 63b2–66b2. This topic is discussed in Bentor 2006.

2183. See Ratnarakṣita's commentary on the *Sdom 'byung*, the *Padma can*, *Padminī*, chap. 2, Tōh 1420, 11a2; Rin chen bzang po, *Rgyud sde spyi'i rnam bzhag*, 19a2–3; Gser sdings pa, *Rim lnga don bzhi ma*, 164; Grags pa rgyal mtshan, *Rgyud kyi mngon rtogs*, work 1, 69a3–5; 'Ba' ra ba, *Bskyed rim zab don 'gal du skyon med*, 29b4–5; Bu ston, *Mdor byas 'grel chen*, 24b3–25a1; Rong ston Shes bya kun rig, *Gsang 'dus rnam bshad*, 8b4–9a1, and his *Gsang sngags kyi spyi don slob dpon grags 'od kyi zhus lan*, 320.

2184. Whereas Bu ston, *Mdor byas 'grel chen*, 24b4, has *chud pa*, "a seed enclosed," our text has *sa bon chung ba*, "a small seed."

should meditate on the egg-born one without a yoga of song, soundlessly yet not-soundlessly."[2185]

(2) Birth from a womb is how horses, bulls,[2186] people, and so forth are born. To purify this birth, you should generate the deity from a seed that has entered into the womb of the father-mother deities and dissolved there, just as you arouse "the one who has dissolved" with a song, for the *Abhidhānottara Tantra* teaches: "Meditators should visualize the womb-born one with the yoga of song."[2187]

(3) Birth from heat and moisture is birth from external heat and moisture, as in the case of worms, moths, and so forth. To purify this birth, you should generate the deity from a seed—signifying the consciousness of the intermediate being—on an open lotus with a sun ray—signifying heat—and a lunar disk—signifying moisture—or alternately, generate the deity from a seed on a lotus and a solar disk encapsulating moisture and heat, for the *Lotus Commentary on the Saṃvarodaya Tantra* teaches: "Arising from merely a lunar disk and a seed is [for] birth from heat and moisture."[2188]

(4) In a miraculous birth one is born instantly with all major and minor limbs and faculties intact. To purify this birth, generate the deity instantaneously, as the master Vajraghaṇṭa teaches: "Meditate without a seed, as in a miraculous birth."[2189]

Therefore these LAMAS SAY that in the present context you should generate the specially visualized deities instantaneously to purify the miraculous birth of the people in Jambudvīpa.

2185. *Mngon par brjod pa'i rgyud bla ma*, chap. 9, Tōh 369, 270b3; Sanskrit and English translation in Kalff 1979, 291, line 48b1 and 175–176. D has *sgra nyams* for *sgra min* in our text. Bu ston, *Mdor byas 'grel chen*, 25b4, has as well *sgra min*. These may be two different translations of the Sanskrit śabdāśbda. Sugiki 2018, 14–15, points out that according to chapter fifteenth of the *Ḍākārṇava Tantra*, the four layers (*puṭa*) of Heruka maṇḍala correspond to fourfold concepts, including the four modes of birth. See *Mkha' 'gro rgya mtsho'i rgyud*, *Ḍākārṇava Tantra*, Tōh 372, 169a4–179b5.

2186. Or elephants, Tib. *glang po*.

2187. *Mngon par brjod pa'i rgyud bla ma*, chap. 9, Tōh 369, 270b2–3. D has *ni* for *kyis* in our text. Bu ston, *Mdor byas 'grel chen*, 25b4, has *kyis* as well.

2188. Ratnarakṣita, *Padma can*, *Padminī*, Tōh 1420, 11a4. D as well as Bu ston, *Mdor byas 'grel chen*, 24b5, have *tsam las skyes pa ni skye gnas* for *tsam las skyes pa'i skye gnas* in our text.

2189. Vajraghaṇṭa, *Bde mchog lhan cig skyes pa'i sgrub thabs*, *Sahajaśamvara Sādhana*, Tōh 1436, 233a6. D has *sems can rdzus te skyes pa bzhin / gang zhig skad cig sbyor ba yis / sa bon med par rnam par bsgom / rang nyid rdo rje mkha' 'gror gyur /* for *sems can rdzus te skyes pa bzhin / sa bon med par rnam par bsgom /* in our text.

[Our Replies]

This position is highly inappropriate because:[2190]

(1) In explaining the stages of birth at the ground of purification, the second chapter of the *Saṃvarodaya Tantra* teaches: "People who do not apprehend the samādhi on the illusion-like" and so forth up to: [74b] "The saṃsāric being sees[2191] its parents embracing and so forth.[2192] Then, its consciousness, mounted on the wind as though riding a swift horse, arrives directly, in an instant through a joy most intense, and enters by way of the mouth. As soon as the seventy-two thousand channels are aroused, the *āli* and *kāli* melt, whereby paramount joy is attained. Its consciousness then abides in the form of a drop in the midst of semen and blood."[2193] In this way the *Saṃvarodaya Tantra* teaches the stages of birth for *a human being born from a womb*. And in the thirteenth chapter,[2194] which explains the creation stage that purifies this mode of birth, there is no mention of arousing "the one who has dissolved" with song; conversely, you should generate the deity through the five manifest awakenings. Thus your explanation for the generation ritual, which you maintain is meant to purify birth from an egg, contradicts the *Saṃvarodaya Tantra*.

(2) If it were necessary to arouse "the one who has dissolved" with song to purify birth from the womb, this would contradict scriptures like *Formulating the Sādhana*, which clarify that the generation of Vajrasattva's nirmāṇakāya later on is intended to purify human birth from a womb.[2195] Moreover, this contradicts your own standpoint as well, since YOU too accept the teaching of *Formulating the Sādhana*, and in that context there is no mention of arousing "the one who has dissolved" with song.

(3) If the sādhanas of Cakrasaṃvara by Lūyīpāda and others were merely

2190. See Tsong kha pa's *'Dod 'jo*, 63a3–66b2.

2191. The Sanskrit is different here. See Tsuda 1974, 74.

2192. Nāgabuddhi, *Rnam gzhag rim pa*, *Vyavastholi*, chap. 1, Tōh 1809, 123b7; Tanaka 2016, 92–93, which paraphrases this passage elaborates here: The parents experience mutual desire, and therefore bless the vajra, hug, kiss and so forth, and join their two organs.

2193. *Sdom 'byung*, Tōh 373, 266a4–7; Sanskrit, Tibetan, and English translation in Tsuda 1974, chap. 2, vv. 11ab and 14–17ab. A prose version of these verses is found in Nāgabuddhi, *Rnam gzhag rim pa*, *Vyavastholi*, chap. 1, Tōh 1809, 123a2–3 and 123b7–124a1; Tanaka 2016, 88 and 93. These people are subject to death, intermediate state, and rebirth. After a short portrayal of the intermediate state, the *Sdom 'byung*, *Saṃvarodaya Tantra*, describes their rebirth.

2194. The *Sdom 'byung*, *Saṃvarodaya Tantra*, Tōh 373, 266a5; Sanskrit, Tibetan, and English translation in Tsuda 1974, chap. 13, vv. 13–14.

2195. Nāgabuddhi, *Rnam gzhag rim pa*, *Vyavastholi*, chap. 1, Tōh 1809, 123b2–3; Tanaka 2016, 89.

generation rituals for purifying birth from an egg, this would contradict the explanation[2196] that the entry of the space-*nāda*[2197]—in between the sun and moon, or in between the white and red moon, or amid the white moon on which red radiance is formed—corresponds to the consciousness of the intermediate being who sees its future parents lying together, and then enters between the semen and blood of the father and mother; and this would contradict the *Abhidharma* and the *Yogācārabhūmi*, which do not explain birth from an egg in this way.

(4) The position that the instantaneous generation of the specially visualized deities here is intended to purify the miraculous birth of the first people of the eon has already been refuted above. [75a]

(5) In particular, in support of an instantaneous generation of the deity to purify miraculous birth, YOU cite the line of the master Vajraghaṇṭa: "Meditate without a seed, as in a miraculous birth,"[2198] but this is improper. During the practice there are two bodies: the mantra body,[2199] the body of the deity you visualize during the creation stage, and the wisdom body,[2200] the body of the deity you generate during the completion stage. In this passage the master Vajraghaṇṭa refers to the moment in the completion stage when the wisdom-body arises instantaneously—in consonance with a miraculous birth—from clear light as an illusory body fully-formed with heads, arms, and so forth. Therefore those who are learned in the system of the mantra and understand it according to the Tantric scripture will laugh when they see that this line by Vajraghaṇṭa is cited as a scriptural source for the method of meditating on the creation stage.

Furthermore, those who produce numerous systems of the creation stage in this way merely demonstrate their delight in their own elaborations, but they have surely not developed even a coarse understanding of the essential points of the two stages. The goal of yogis who meditate on the creation stage is to ripen their continuum for the meditation of the completion stage. The methods of creation and completion taught in the tantra pertain to disciples who devote themselves exclusively to the unexcelled mantra, and who primarily practice the path of awakening in this life. Not a few tantras and mahāsiddhas

2196. According to Tsong kha pa's *'Dod 'jo*, 64b4–65a3, this refers to the explanation in the *Sdom 'byung*, Tōh 373, 266a5–7; Sanskrit, Tibetan, and English translation in Tsuda 1974, chap. 2, vv. 13–16.

2197. In his *Padma, Padminī*, Tōh 1420, 12b1, which is a commentary on the *Sdom 'byung*, Ratnarakṣita glosses the intermediate being with space.

2198. Vajraghaṇṭa, *Bde mchog lhan cig skyes pa'i sgrub thabs, Sahajaśamvara Sādhana*, Tōh 1436, 233a6; cited above [74a].

2199. Tib. *sngags kyi sku*, Skt. *mantramūrti*.

2200. Tib. *ye shes kyi sku*, Skt. *jñānamūrti*.

teach that the person practicing such a path must certainly be a human being born from a womb in Jambudvīpa, endowed with the six constituents, as will presently be explained.

Hence, if YOU explain that the creation stage purifies the four modes of birth, beginning with birth from an egg, it follows that in the completion stage as well there must be four methods of meditation that correspond to the birth, death, and intermediate state of these four beings, born through the four modes of birth. [75b] Likewise it follows that a yogi who meditates from the start on the uncommon path toward awakening in *one lifetime*—by means of the path of the unexcelled mantra—must still undergo the four modes of birth, birth from an egg and so forth.

How to repudiate the contradiction with traditions, such as that of Lūyīpāda, who in his works on Cakrasaṃvara explains that the generation ritual in the line of the *Abhidhānottara Tantra*[2201] "without arousing 'the one has dissolved' with song" refers to a birth from an egg?[2202] Here in the *Guhyasamāja* there is no causal vajra holder in the appearance of the father-mother deities in union who resemble the father who plants the seed in the womb and the mother who retains this seed in the womb. Seeing these as mere similarities, the *Commentary on the Abhidhānottara Tantra* teaches that the sun and the moon or the white and red moons are *like* an egg,[2203] the seed in their midst is *like* a chick, and the transformation of this seed into the body of the deity is *like* a chick that breaks the shell of the egg and hatches out.[2204]

However, the similarity between birth from an egg and the meditation does not necessarily turn them into a ground of purification and its purifier. As was just explained, you purify birth from a womb by meditating in correspondence with birth from a womb in which the *nāda*—signifying the intermediate being—enters in the midst of the sun and moon or in the midst of the white and red moons—which signify the semen and blood of the father and

2201. According to the *Mngon par brjod pa'i rgyud bla ma*, *Abhidhānottara Tantra*, Tōh 369, the meditation on the egg-born is without song, while the meditation on the womb-born is with song. See above [74a].

2202. See Tsong kha pa, *'Dod 'jo*, 65b5–66a1. Tsong kha pa has here "without arousing with song," thus omitting "the one who has dissolved."

2203. While our text has the "sun and the moon or the moon," Tsong kha pa, *'Dod 'jo*, 65b5–66a12, has the sun and the moon or the [white and red] moons.

2204. Śūraṅgavajra, *Rtsa ba'i rgyud kyi snying po 'dus pa nges par brjod pa'i rgyud bla ma rtsa ba rtsa ba'i 'grel ba*, *Mūlatantrahṛdayasaṅgrahābhidhānottaratantramūlamūlavṛtti*, Tōh 1414, 158b3.

mother. There is no contradiction here, since similarity in one aspect does not necessarily entail dissimilarity in any other aspects.

Here, in order for you to understand this, *Formulating the Sādhana* teaches the four modes of birth viable for inhabitants of the world; from among these four modes of birth, it then teaches how to generate the specially visualized deities and the deities of the four yogas in accordance with the stages of saṃsāric rebirth of the people of Jambudvīpa.[2205] But if you misunderstand this and maintain that the four different rituals of generating deities were taught for purifying the four modes of birth, YOU miss the point.[2206] Furthermore, many of the instructions appearing in *Formulating the Sādhana*—such as the explanation that generating the deity corresponds only to the people of Jambudvīpa, as well as questions about the reasons for this and responses to them—would surely be irrelevant. [76a]

Establishing Our Own Position

[Why Does the Meditation Correspond with the Stages of Saṃsāric Rebirth of Human Beings in Jambudvīpa?]

It is crucial to understand the meaning of the teachings in *Formulating the Sādhana* concerning these two points: in general, the reason for meditating on the specially visualized deities in correspondence with the stages of saṃsāric rebirth of human beings; and in particular, the reason for meditating in correspondence with the stages of saṃsāric rebirth of human beings in Jambudvīpa. In this regard *Formulating the Sādhana* teaches: "All the buddhas who appear in the past, present, and future do so in the nature of human beings, and as such, attain the siddhi of the omniscient stage. This is why the stages of birth into human existence are taught here."[2207]

THERE ARE THOSE[2208] who dispute the point that all buddhas of the three times awaken in a human body, since some awaken in a body of No-Higher Heaven.[2209] THEY maintain that even if one were to allow that to be established,

2205. Nāgabuddhi, *Rnam gzhag rim pa*, *Vyavastholi*, chap. 1, Tōh 1809, 122a5–b1; Tanaka 2016, 83–85.

2206. See also Tsong kha pa, *Rnam gzhag rim pa'i rnam bshad*, 13b6–14a1.

2207. Nāgabuddhi, *Rnam gzhag rim pa*, *Vyavastholi*, chap. 1, Tōh 1809, 122b7–123a1; Tanaka 2016, 87.

2208. See Tsong kha pa, *Rnam gzhag rim pa'i rnam bshad*, 17a2–5. Tsongkhapa raises this issue as *gal te... zhe na*, and not as *kha cig 'di nyam du* in our text.

2209. Tib. *'og min*, Skt. *akaniṣṭha*.

it still cannot be accepted as a proof. This is so because although bodhisattvas such as Śvetaketu[2210] have displayed awakening in a body of Jambudvīpa, yogis meditating on the specially visualized deities and on the deities of the four yogas during the sādhana are by no means required to do so in correspondence with the stages of the saṃsāric birth of human beings in Jambudvīpa.

[Awakening in the Same Lifetime in which the Yogi Begins to Practice the Unexcelled Mantra]

In reply we say,[2211] while it is not established that all the buddhas of the three times are awakened in human bodies, there is nothing wrong in our position. This is so because the explanation of *Formulating the Sādhana* refers not to buddhas in general, but specifically to buddhas of the three times, awakening in the same lifetime during which they set forth from the onset of their practice on the non-shared path of the unexcelled mantra, and having attained enlightenment as human beings in Jambudvīpa. [76b] Thus, since we speak about awakening in this lifetime by relying on the unexcelled mantra, it is established that the meditator on the creation stage of the deity is indeed required to do so in correspondence with the stages of the saṃsāric birth of human beings in Jambudvīpa.

What is the proof that all buddhas of the three times who achieve buddhahood in the same lifetime in which they set forth from the onset of their practice on the non-shared path of the unexcelled mantra are awakened perforce in human bodies? A person who is awakened in this way has to be a human being with a passionate body, since the teachings of the unexcelled mantra are meant for the foremost disciples who devote themselves exclusively to the practice and embark from the onset of their meditation on the path of the unexcelled mantra; these disciples are able to take the desire for joining the two organs on the path.

According to the teachings of the unexcelled mantra, the dissolution of the white and red constituents engenders wisdom of great bliss; still, only those with passionate bodies crave sexual union. From among the beings in the desire realm, the gods join the two organs when the male and female are in union, but though their organs are in union, they merely emit a tiny amount

2210. Tib. Dam pa Tog dkar po, the name of Buddha Śākyamuni in his previous life, when he resided in Tuṣita Heaven, Tib. *dga' ldan*.

2211. See Tsong kha pa, *Rnam gzhag rim pa'i rnam bshad*, 17a5–b1, and *Bung ba'i re skong*, 23a1–b3.

of air.[2212] Because the gods of the desire realm lack the white and red constituents, as well as the channels and wheels of the subtle body that serve as their vessel, they lack any basis for engendering the wisdom of great bliss contingent on the white and red constituents, and thus a basis for meditating on the completion stage by penetrating the vital points of the body.[2213]

The unexcelled mantra gives special prominence to those yogis who take the desire for joining the two organs on the path. The *Compendium of Vajra Wisdom Tantra* teaches: "Unless [the yogi and his consort] activate their vajra and lotus by mantra and mudrā, and then join them, [77a] they will be unable to identify the three types of awareness.[2214] Those unable to join their *bhagas* and *liṅgas* will not attain the samādhi of great bliss."[2215] And: "Those who truly identify the natural appearance through the bliss arising from conjoining the vajra and lotus will abide at the stage of great bliss."[2216] Likewise, the *Sādhana Incorporating the Scripture* teaches: "In the first chapter of the *Guhyasamāja Tantra*, the Blessed One was absorbed in the samādhi called 'the method of great passion'[2217] to demonstrate that the stage of enlightenment arises through passion. Accordingly, during the creation stage, meditators should practice the First Yoga,[2218] displaying liberation by means of passion for sentient beings

2212. See Tsong kha pa, *Rnam gzhag rim pa'i rnam bshad*, 17b3, who cites Vasubandhu, *Mdzod 'grel, Kośabhāṣya*, chap. 3, v. 69b-c, Tōh 4090, 150b6; Pradhan 1975, 169; Pruden 1988–1990, 465.

2213. Reading *dang / lus*, as in the other versions of this work, for *dag brnyas* in our text.

2214. The white appearance, the red enhanced appearance, and the black appearance of approaching attainment.

2215. *Ye shes rdo rje kun las btus pa, Vajrajñānasamuccaya Tantra*, Tōh 447, 283b1–2. D has *phyag rgya mngon par 'dus byas* for *phyag rgyas sngon du mngon par 'du byas*; *gang gis bha ga* for *bha ga*; and *sbyor bar mi nus pa* for *sbyor mi nus pa*. Our text follows the reading in Tsong kha pa, *Rnam gzhag rim pa'i rnam bshad*, 17b6–18a1.

2216. *Ye shes rdo rje kun las btus pa, Vajrajñānasamuccaya Tantra*, Tōh 447, 283b3–4. D has *mnyams par sbyor ba'i* for *mnye bar sbyor ba'i* and *rab tu gnas par* for *gnas par* in our text.

2217. *Guhyasamāja Tantra*, Tōh 442; Zhol 2b2; Stog 3b3; Dunh 1a3; Fremantle 1971, 176–177; and Matsunaga 1978, 4. The full name of this concentration is "the method of great passion of all tathāgatas," *de bzhin gshegs pa thams cad kyi 'dod chag chen po'i tshul zhes bya ba'i ting nge 'dzin, sarvatathāgatamahārāgavajraṃ [nayaṃ] nāmasamādhi*. D and some of the Sanskrit mss. have "the vajra of great passion of all tathāgatas."

2218. Tib. *dang po sbyor ba*, Skt. *ādiyoga*, this is the first among the three samādhis that comprise the creation stage.

engaged in passion."[2219] The *Illuminating Lamp* explains this as follows: "The *Guhyasamāja Tantra* teaches this samādhi to instruct those sentient beings who are attached to objects in the desire realm, about liberation through the five attributes of passion."[2220] The same scripture asks: "For whose sake was this *Tantra* taught?" And it replies: "For the sake of passionate people."[2221]

Only animals, hungry ghosts, gods in the two lower classes of the desire realm, and humans join the two organs.[2222] Other beings cannot do this. Among those who can, beings of the lower realms do not qualify to meditate on the pure path of the Mantra Vehicle. The gods of the desire realm cannot unite the white and red constituents, which is the basis for engendering great bliss. As the *Primary Ground*[2223] teaches: "Since in animals, hungry ghosts, and humans bodily bliss and[2224] suffering are mixed together, [77b] they engage in sexual union. When men and women unite with each other, semen is emitted. The gods who belong to the desire realm engage as well in sexual union, but no semen is emitted. Rather, at that time, a tiny amount of air is emitted through their sexual organs."[2225] The same scripture teaches: "The bodies of the gods are immaculate and odorless, both within and without, free from impurities like sweat, bad smells, bones, tendons, veins, kidneys, hearts, and so forth."[2226] This indicates that they lack the channels and

2219. Nāgārjuna, *Mdo bsre, Sādhanasūtramelāpaka*, Tōh 1797, 13b2–4. D has *'di ltar* for *ji ltar*; *bstan pa'i phyir* for *bstan par bya ba'i phyir* twice; *tshul rdo rje* for *tshul*; *zhugs* for *'jug*, and *bskyed* for *skye* in our text, and omits the *kyang* before *dang po sbyor ba*.

2220. Candrakīrti, *Sgron gsal, Pradīpoddyotanaṭīkā*, Tōh 1785, 12b7–13a1; Chakravarti 1984, 18. D has *de ni* for *da ni* in our text. See also Tsong kha pa, *Sgron gsal mchan*, 53b3–54b2.

2221. Candrakīrti, *Sgron gsal, Pradīpoddyotanaṭīkā*, Tōh 1785, 2a5–b1; Chakravarti 1984, 2. See Campbell 2009, 295, and also Tsong kha pa, *Rnam gzhag rim pa'i rnam bshad*, 17b1–18a5.

2222. See Tsong kha pa, *Rnam gzhag rim pa'i rnam bshad*, 18a5–b6.

2223. Asaṅga, Tib. *Sa'i dngos gzhi*, Skt. *Maulībhūmi*. This name is used in our text for the first part of the *Rnal 'byor spyod pa'i sa, Yogācārabhūmi*, Tōh 4035.

2224. D has *'am* for *dang* in our text as well as in Tsong kha pa, *Rnam gzhag rim pa'i rnam bshad*.

2225. Asaṅga, *Sa'i dngos gzhi, Maulībhūmi*, Tōh 4035, 51b6–7; Bhattacharya 1957, 100.12–16. D has *yi dags* for *yi dwags*; *'am* for *dang*; *'dres par* for *'dres mar*; and *de dag ni* for *de dag la ni* in our text. Cited also in Tsong kha pa, *Rnam gzhag rim pa'i rnam bshad*, 18b1–2. See also Vasubandhu, *Mdzod 'grel, Kośabhāṣya*, chap. 3, v. 69.b–d, Tōh 4090, 150b4–7; Pradhan 1975, 169; Pruden 1988–1990, 465.

2226. Asaṅga, *Sa'i dngos gzhi, Maulībhūmi*, Tōh 4035, 46b7–47a1; Bhattacharya 1957, 91.17–18. D has *mi rnams kyi mi gtsang ba'i rdzas 'di lta ste* for *mi gtsang ba'i rdzas* in our text.

wheels in which yogis meditating on the completion stage can penetrate the vital points.

[Qualm:] This being so, why is it that only the people of Jambudvīpa are taken into account here though there are people in the other three continents as well?

[Reply:] The reason is that the people of Jambudvīpa abide on the ground of karma, while those of the other three continents abide on the ground of resources.[2227] What is the meaning of the phrases "the ground of resources" and "the people of Jambudvīpa abide on the ground of karma"? Since the people of the three other continents are endowed with a multitude of resources, they abide on the ground of resources. However, they do not abide on the ground of karma, since ordinary people born in the other three continents are not different in terms of their intellectual faculties, being unable to analyze through the great wisdom of discernment or investigate with precise wisdom. Furthermore, they are not very dissimilar during their present lives when it comes to lifespans, resources, faith, wisdom, compassion, and so forth on account of the karma they accumulated in previous lives. This is so because the karma of people in all three continents is by and large of a similar type; [78a] and also because the fruit of actions performed in one life cannot accumulate for ripening in the same life.

Such is not the case for the people of Jambudvīpa. In Jambudvīpa the fruit of previous karma creates a particularly great diversity in lifespan, quantity of resources, profusion of diseases, and so forth. Moreover, the karmic fruit of previous wrongdoing creates great misery in the same lifetime, with intense suffering due to very coarse afflictive emotions like deceit, hypocrisy, haughtiness, desire and so forth, and disease and so forth. Yet, due to previous virtuous actions, certain people, like those of the Middle Country,[2228] are able to grasp meaning in its entirety as soon as a syllable is uttered, because their faculties of faith and so forth are exceedingly sharp, and because of their cleverness and courage. This is not the case in the other three continents, so that when the bodhisattva displays the twelve "deeds" in the land of human beings after passing away in Tuṣita, he does so by being born in the Middle Country of Jambudvīpa, and not in the three other continents. Furthermore, in Jambudvīpa there are many who have known the experience of observing the ripened fruit of the virtuous and nonvirtuous actions they performed in their own lifetimes, whereas nothing of this sort occurs in the other three continents. Therefore the people of Jambudvīpa are called "abiding on the ground of karma."

2227. See also Bu ston, *Mdor byas 'grel chen*, 25a3–b4.

2228. Tib. *yul dbus*, Skt. *madhyadeśa*. The land where Buddhist teachings flourish.

The *Saṃvarodaya Tantra* teaches this as well: "The people of the three continents—Pūrvavideha in the east, Aparagodānīya in the west, and Uttarakuru in the north[2229]—are sustained by great resources. Lacking discursive and inquiring minds and their intellects being weak, they are ignorant and wanting in discrimination."[2230] While: [78b] "Those who are fortunate enough to have been born in Jambudvīpa are renowned as 'those on the ground of karma.' This is so because, due to their good and bad actions, they are either superior, middling, or inferior, for the ripening of karma accumulated in former lives is seen there in everyone. Yet they are afflicted by arrogance, avarice, viciousness, deceit, hypocrisy, pride, desire, hatred, ignorance, and so forth, as well as old age and disease."[2231] And: "The foremost people of Jambudvīpa who are born in the Middle Country are endowed with dull, middling, or sharp faculties according to the virtues of their former lives."[2232]

Likewise *Formulating the Sādhana* teaches: "The vajra master said: The people of Pūrvavideha in the east, Aparagodānīya in the west, and Uttarakuru in the north are endowed with great resources. However, their intellects are weak, they are ignorant, and therefore lack discursive and inquiring minds. The people of Jambūdvīpa abide on the ground of karma, since due to their good and bad actions, they are superior, middling, or inferior, for the ripening fruit of their karma there is visible in each of them. Furthermore, since the people of Jambudvīpa are bent on deceit, hypocrisy, haughtiness, jealousy, and viciousness, they are afflicted with epidemics, diseases, and so forth. Nevertheless, they are able to understand as soon as the first syllable is uttered,

2229. Tib. Lus 'phags, Ba glang spyod, and Sgra mi snyan.

2230. *Sdom 'byung*, Tōh 373, 266a1; Sanskrit, Tibetan, and English translation in Tsuda 1974, chap. 2, vv. 5cd–6. Tsuda has *longs spyod chen pos* for *longs spyod chen po'i* and *blun rmongs bye brag mi phyed cing / rtog med rnam par spyod med pa'o* for *rnam rtog med cing rnam spyod med / blun rmongs bye brag mi phyed pa'o* in our text.

2231. *Sdom 'byung*, Tōh 373, 266a1–3; Sanskrit, Tibetan, and English translation in Tsuda 1974, chap. 2, vv. 7–8. Tsuda has *'dzam bu gling du* for *'dzam bu gling rnams*; *skyes pa* for *skyes pa'i*; *legs byas nyes par byas pa'i las* for *legs byas dang ni nyes byas las*; *tha ma rnams* for *tha ma yi*; *sngon gyi* for *snga ma'i*; *skye bo rnams la snang bar 'gyur* for *skye bo kun la mthong bar 'gyur*; *rgyags pa* for *rgyags dang*, *sems rnams* for *sems dang*; *g.yo sgyu* for *g.yo rgyu*; *gti mug la sogs kyis* for *gti mug sogs rnams dang*; and *rims dang nad la sogs pas gzir* for *rga dang nad kyis rab tu gzir* in our text.

2232. *Sdom 'byung*, Tōh 373, 266a3; Sanskrit, Tibetan, and English translation in Tsuda 1974, chap. 2, v. 9. Tsuda has *gtso bo mchog* for *mchog gtso bo*; *yul dbus su ni skyes pa ste* for *yul gyi dbus su skyes pa de*; and *sngon gyi dge ba la ltos nas / dbang po rno 'bring rtul por 'gyur* for *dbang po rtul 'bring rnon po rnams / skye ba snga ma'i dge ba ltos* in our text.

since they have sharp faculties and are skillful. That is why bodhisattvas are born among the people of Jambudvīpa and teach the Dharma there."[2233]

In his commentary on the fourteenth chapter of the *Vajra Sky Traveler Tantra*, Bhavabhadra also teaches: "Thus the yoginīs reside in the regions and provinces of Jambudvīpa, for this continent abides on the ground of karma, and therefore karma bears fruit, while in the other continents, the fruit of karma accumulated during one's lifetime will not ripen in that lifetime [79a] but in later lives. Since karma does not bear fruit in the other continents, the yoginīs do not journey there."[2234] Thus Bhavabhadra explains that since in the other three continents the fruit of karma from one life does not ripen in that lifetime, the yoginīs of the twenty-four sites do not journey to the other continents.

Although it might be preferable to elucidate the citations from the *Saṃvarodaya Tantra* in *Formulating the Sādhana* according to the interpretation of the *Illuminating Lamp*, which expounds the four modes of awakening through practices free of desire,[2235] I will refrain from so doing for fear of verbosity. But you should attain knowledge of this through the writings of the venerable lama Tsongkhapa.[2236]

To summarize the point of these scriptures: In Jambudvīpa the fruit of previous karma creates widespread differences with respect to sharpness of faculties, wisdom, faith, and so forth, hence it is reasonable to find differences between those who have the good fortune to practice the mantra path and those who do not. However, in the other three continents such differences would not be reasonable. In Jambudvīpa the fruit of karma accumulated through a lifetime ripens in that same lifetime, while in the other three continents it does not. Thus only in Jambudvīpa can human beings attain complete awakening as a fruit of their meditation on the path of the unexcelled mantra in the same lifetime.

2233. Nāgabuddhi, *Rnam gzhag rim pa*, *Vyavastholi*, chap. 1, Tōh 1809, 122b3–6; Tanaka 2016, 86–87. D and Tanaka have *mi rnams* for *mi rnams la*; *de lta mod* for *de lta mong*; *de na* for *des na*; omit the *yang* after *'di lta ste*; have *sgyu* for *rgyu*; *dregs pa* for *drags pa*; *bsam pas* for *sems dang*; and *sku 'khrungs* for *'khrungs*; D has *mi spyod* for *mi dpyod* and *gnas kyis* for *gnas kyi*, and Tanaka has *de ni* for *des na* and *skye ba'i* for *skye bo'i* in our text.

2234. *Rgyud kyi rdo rje mkha' 'gro'i rnam par bshad pa*, *Vajraḍākavivṛti*, Tōh 1415, 88a2–4. This is Bhavabhadra's commentary on the *Rdo rje mkha' 'gro*, *Vajraḍāka*, Tōh 370. D as well as Tsong kha pa, *Rnam gzhag rim pa'i rnam bshad*, 15a6, have *sa* for *sa ba* in our text.

2235. See Candrakīrti, *Sgron gsal*, *Pradīpoddyotanaṭīkā*, Tōh 1785, 2b3–4; Chakravarti 1984, 2.

2236. See Tsong kha pa, *Rnam gzhag rim pa'i rnam bshad*, 16a6–17a1.

[The Five Types of Disciples Who Practice the Unexcelled Mantra]

Among human beings in Jambudvīpa, who might be capable of meditating on some path of the unexcelled mantra such as the *Guhyasamāja*? The *Illuminating Lamp* elaborates upon five types of disciples: the four vessels for group teachings[2237] are persons who are like the blue lotus, white lotus, lotus, and sandalwood[2238] and the vessels for individual teachings[2239] are the jewel-like persons.[2240] However, the foremost disciples who devote themselves exclusively to meditation on the path of awakening in this life are the jewel-like persons.[2241]

[Women Attaining Enlightenment through the Unexcelled Mantra]

Furthermore, both men and women can engage in the mere practice of the path either in the Pāramitā Vehicle or the lower or higher tantras. [79b] However, the path of awakening in this life within the systems of the Pāramitā Vehicle and the three lower tantras is appropriate only for men, not women. Nonetheless, women too can awaken in this life by relying on the path of the extraordinary unexcelled mantra,[2242] for as the thirteenth chapter of the *Guhyasamāja Tantra* teaches: "The great vidyās, Locanā and so forth, always heed the meaning of sensual objects. As they resort to desire at will, they attain [the stage of Vajradhara] by enjoying sensual pleasures."[2243] And the *Illuminating Lamp* comments on this: "In order to explain that women as well as men can attain awakening, born from desire,[2244] the *[Guhyasamāja] Tantra*

2237. Tib. *tshogs bshad*, Skt. *satravyākhyāna*.

2238. Tib. *utpala*, *pad dkar*, *padma*, and *tsan dan*; Skt. *utpala*, *puṇḍarīka*, *padma*, and *candana*.

2239. Tib. *slob bshad*, Skt. *śiṣyavyākhyāna*.

2240. Tib. *rin po che*, Skt. *ratna*.

2241. Candrakīrti, *Sgron gsal*, *Pradīpoddyotanaṭīkā*, Tōh 1785, 3a7–b3; Chakravarti 1984, 4. See also Tsong kha pa, *Rnam gzhag rim pa'i rnam bshad*, 19a1–2; Mkhas grub rje in Lessing and Wayman 1968, 218–221; Wayman 1977, 117; and Thurman 1988, 142–143.

2242. See Tsong kha pa, *Mtha' gcod*, 123a4–125b6, and *Bung ba'i re skong*, 23b1–24a4.

2243. *Guhyasamāja Tantra*, Tōh 442; Zhol 20b4; Stog 35a3; Dunh 38a5; Fremantle 1971, v. 27; and Matsunaga 1978, v. 25. The phrase in square brackets is not found in the *Guhyasamāja Tantra*, but in Candrakīrti, *Sgron gsal*, *Pradīpoddyotanaṭīkā*, Tōh 1785.

2244. The previous verse of the *Guhyasamāja Tantra* speaks about the [male] Vajra Lords, Rdo rje bdag po, who by meditating on the meaning of desire, attain awakening born from desire. The present verse refers to the great female *vidyās*, and the following verse, to the neuter.

teaches: *The great vidyās* and so forth."[2245] The *Illuminating Lamp* continues: "*the great vidyā* is a well-trained consort, and *Locanā and so forth* are the four types of women, Padminī and so forth."[2246]

Furthermore, the mahāsiddha Saroruha teaches in his *Hevajra Sādhana*: "The yogi wishing to achieve Hevajra dwells with a consort in a place that gratifies the mind, such as a cremation ground."[2247] Accordingly, yogis endowed with all the essential characteristics designated in the tantras should, even during the creation stage, practice together with consorts. Similarly, women endowed with the complete essential characteristics for practicing the path abide together with male companions,[2248] and likewise practice the two stages. Except for special cases, females[2249] practice in exactly the same way as male yogis. Therefore neither the tantras nor the Indian treatises elaborate on a separate practice for women on the path.[2250] [80a]

Just as the four joys are generated in the mental continuum of the father by way of reliance on the mother, so, too, are they generated in the mental continuum of the mother by way of reliance on the father.[2251] And just as the male practitioner generates the wisdom of the four empty states by way of reliance on the consort, so, too, the consort generates the wisdom of the four empty states by way of reliance on the male[2252] and eventually attains the illusory body. Having abandoned her female body in this lifetime, she attains a body adorned with the major and minor marks and awakens. It is vitally important to become proficient in these essential points.

There is no suggestion at all in the Pāramitā Vehicle and the three lower

2245. Candrakīrti, *Sgron gsal, Pradīpoddyotanaṭīkā*, Tōh 1785, 103b6–7; Chakravarti 1984, 127. D has *sgrub par* twice for *bsgrub par* in our text.

2246. Candrakīrti, *Sgron gsal, Pradīpoddyotanaṭīkā*, Tōh 1785, 103b7; Chakravarti 1984, 127. D has *spyan la sogs pa ni padma spyan la sogs pa'o* for *spyan la sogs zhes pa ni padma can la sogs pa'o* in our text. The Sanskrit has *padmam* for *padma can* in our text. The line "are the four types of women" here is based on Tsong kha pa's *Sgron gsal mchan*, 299a4–5. In it Tsong kha pa explains that it is possible to attain awakening in this life in a female body as well. See also his *Rnam gzhag rim pa'i rnam bshad*, 19a3–6.

2247. *Dgyes pa rdo rje'i sgrub thabs, Hevajra Sādhana*, Tōh 1218, 1a4; *Dhīḥ* 2003, 133; Sanskrit, Tibetan, and English translation in Gerloff 2017, 97, 118, and 131. D has *dpal dkyes* for *dgyes pa'i*, and it omits the *tu*. Partly cited above [14b6–15a1]. While the Sanskrit colophon attributes this work to Ācārya Saroruha, the Tibetan version has here Slob dpon Padma.

2248. Tib. *thabs*, Skt. *upāya*, literally "method."

2249. Tib. *shes rab ma*, Skt. *prajñā*, literally "wisdom."

2250. See Tsong kha pa, *Mtha' gcod*, 123b3–6.

2251. See Tsong kha pa, *Mtha' gcod*, 124a6.

2252. See Tsong kha pa, *Sgron gsal mchan*, 299b2–3.

tantras about how to replace the female body and attain a body adorned with the major and minor marks without passing away from this life, and since this is not made perfectly clear in other unexcelled tantras either, you must learn it with lamas who know the fundamental meaning of the tantra, and who follow the essential points of the Guhyasamāja as clearly explicated by Ārya Nāgārjuna and his disciples.

To conclude, all who awaken in a passionate body reside in Jambudvīpa, therefore, all who awaken in this life through the mantric path have passionate bodies, and therefore reside in Jambudvīpa. For this reason, it is likewise established who are the beings at the time of the creation of the world with whom the meditation on the specially visualized deities corresponds. You should meditate in correspondence with the stages of saṃsāric evolution for human beings in Jambudvīpa.[2253]

2253. See Tsong kha pa, *Rnam gzhag rim pa'i rnam bshad*, 19b2–3, which has human beings in Jambudvīpa for beings in Jambudvīpa in our text.

7. The Significance of Purification by Means of the Creation Stage

The Meaning of Purifying the Ground of Purification by Means of the Creation Stage

There are two topics here: (1) removing uncertainty as it pertains to the explanation of correspondence with the stages of saṃsāric evolution, and (2) why the other parts of the sādhana are not applied in correspondence with the stages of saṃsāric evolution.

Removing Uncertainty as It Pertains to the Explanation of Correspondence with the Stages of Saṃsāric Evolution

There are two topics here: (1) points of uncertainty that may arise in those endowed with an inquiring mind and (2) our response to these points of uncertainty.

Points of Uncertainty that May Arise in Those Endowed with an Inquiring Mind[2254]

[The Purpose of Drawing Correspondences and the Difference between a Ground of Purification and a Corresponding Object]

[80b] Although it is conceivable that there are similarities and correspondences between stages of the saṃsāric evolution of the world and its inhabitants—as previously explained—and the stages of meditating on the celestial mansion and the deities dwelling therein, what is the point of understanding such similarities? If mantrins failed to understand these similarities, still, by meditating on the sādhana they could attain their purpose unobstructed. If

2254. See Tsong kha pa, *Rnam gzhag rim pa'i rnam bshad*, 45a6–53a4.

the lack of understanding were to obstruct them, then since there is no such thing as perfect similarity and nothing without a partial similarity,[2255] this would lead to the utterly absurd result of having to meditate on the sādhana on the strength of knowing every single entity with which it shares a partial similarity.

Conversely, if you maintain that although it is unnecessary to understand the similarities the meditation shares with every single entity, still by understanding the correspondences as previously explained and by meditating in correspondence with them, you will turn away the appearances of your ordinary body and environment, and generate the special appearances of the celestial mansion and the deities dwelling therein; and it is for this purpose that you must understand the similarities. This too is unnecessary, since it has been established that even without understanding the modes of correspondence, by habituating the meditation on your body and environment in the aspects of the deities and the celestial mansion, you will block the ordinary appearances of your environment and body and experience the arising of special appearances.

If, however, the purpose of applying correspondences is to identify the individual grounds of purification and their purifiers—such as "this and that saṃsāric world and its sentient beings are purified by this and that yoga of the celestial mansion and its deities"—then how, pray, could the no-longer existing world and inhabitants of the first eon be purified by meditating now on a corresponding path?

Our Response to These Points of Uncertainty

Applying correspondences is not just a matter of collating similar phenomena in order to merely recognize that there is a similarity whereby the two following elements essentially correspond: the meditation on the mantric path on the one hand and the destruction and evolution of the habitat and the inhabitants of the world on the other. [81a] Therefore the first point of YOUR criticism, which leads to utterly absurd results, becomes invalid. Furthermore, we do not maintain that in order for the special appearance of their bodies and environment to arise, mantrins must first seek an understanding of the correspondences with the evolution and destruction of the world and its inhabitants. Thus the second point of YOUR criticism is also invalid.

Other EARLY AND LATER TIBETANS who were learned in the Guhyasamāja[2256] explained that the evolution of the world and its beings during the

2255. Our text repeats this last phrase.

2256. See 'Gos Khug pa lhas btsas, *Gsang 'dus stong thun*, 7b3–10b1.

first eon is the ground of purification for meditation on the path in the present. However, our holy lama Tsongkhapa[2257] maintains that if YOU hold such a position because you fail to distinguish between the ground of purification and a corresponding object,[2258] it will be as though YOU are trying to burn the ashes of last year's firewood with this year's fire, and consequently he does not accept such a method.

[The Three Bodies of the Ground, Path, and Fruit]

Why is this so? The position of Ārya Nāgārjuna and his disciples is that by and large, the uncommon fruit attained during the age of decline through the mantric path within the meditator's lifetime is the stage of the three bodies that bear certain similarities to the three phenomena at the ground—birth, death, and the intermediate state. Although the ultimate stage of the three bodies is the three bodies of the union of no more practice, there are three bodies in the path that correspond with them.

Death at the ground level corresponds in aspect to the dharmakāya because the aggregates and so forth dissolve, and all the coarse mental proliferations subside. The intermediate being corresponds in aspect to the saṃbhogakāya, because both are made of wind and mind alone, and thus possess an extremely subtle body like a rainbow body. When the intermediate being takes birth by entering the semen and blood of the father and mother, it turns into an object for the physical eye of ordinary people and becomes capable of acting like them. This corresponds to the saṃbhogakāya, which displays a nirmāṇakāya by taking on coarse bodily constituents for the sake of disciples and acting for their benefit by means of manifesting to ordinary people. [81b]

Consequently, for the yogi meditating on the three paths that are similar to birth, death, and intermediate state, the three bodies of the path will arise instead of the birth, death, and intermediate states that take place naturally for ordinary people. These are the three bodies of the completion stage: (1) the dharmakāya of the path, the manifestation of the clear light, ultimate truth; (2) the saṃbhogakāya of the path that arises from the dharmakāya of the path as an illusory body made of wind and mind alone; (3) and the nirmāṇakāya of the path—taken by that saṃbhogakāya—who acts for the sake of others by intentionally taking a body of coarse elements for the benefit of the disciples.

2257. See his *Rnam gzhag rim pa'i rnam bshad*, 46a4 and 45b5–6.

2258. Tsong kha pa, *Rnam gzhag rim pa'i rnam bshad*, 46a4, has here: *chos mthun kyi yul dang sbyang gzhi gnyis ma phyed pa* for *sbyang gzhi dang chos mthun gnyis ma phyed pa* in our text.

Each of the three bodies has an actual body and a similitude; and the three actual bodies are the three bodies of the supreme attainment in this life and in the intermediate state. You must understand the distinctions between the different categories of the three bodies.

This is a homogenous continuum[2259] arising from habituation to the three bodies on the path of the completion stage, which transform into the three ultimate bodies. In order to ripen for these three bodies of the completion stage, during the creation stage the yogi should meditate on: (1) the dissolution of the specially visualized deities into clear light that corresponds to death at the ground; (2) the First Lord who corresponds to the intermediate state; and (3) Vajrasattva's nirmāṇakāya that corresponds to birth.[2260]

These three bodies, unlike the bodies explained in other treatises, are the supreme special qualities of the system of the Guhyasamāja. Thus, while people lacking skillful means undergo birth, death, and the intermediate state, the cause of saṃsāra, yogis use their powerful skillful means to transform birth, death, and the intermediate state into the three bodies of the path[2261] that bear a similarity to them, as the *Compendium of Practices* teaches: "For ordinary ignorant beings, the so-called intermediate being—the cause of saṃsāra—will take place. But for those who have obtained the transmitted instruction of all tathāgatas through the lineage of the lamas, the so-called self-blessed stage will take place—just as a cloth painting or a wall painting appears within a mirror. [82a] In the same way [the yogis] whose nature is the vajra body emanate in bodies endowed with the excellence of all aspects, adorned with the thirty-two marks of a great being and so forth, so beautiful to behold, one cannot gaze enough, in short, with all the excellent qualities of the buddhas."[2262] Thus instead of the intermediate state that occurs for ordinary people, it is the illusory body adorned with the major and minor marks that arises here.

The same scripture teaches: "Therefore, regarding those who realize suchness, but who, due to incomplete conditions, have not yet completed

2259. Tib. *rigs 'dra'i rgyun*.

2260. For a few lines our text did not follow Tsong kha pa's *Rnam gzhag rim pa'i rnam bshad*, beginning at folio 46b6, but from this point on it will.

2261. This word is not found in Tsong kha pa's *Rnam gzhag rim pa'i rnam bshad*. Mkhas grub rje here emphasizes the correspondence with the three bodies of the path. Tsong kha pa refers to the latter in *Rnam gzhag rim pa'i rnam bshad*, 47b5–48a3.

2262. Āryadeva, *Spyod bsdus, Caryāmelāpakapradīpa*, chap. 6, Tōh 1803, 85b2–4; Sanskrit, Tibetan, and English translation in Wedemeyer 2007, B: 42a; Sanskrit and Tibetan in Pandey 2000, 57 and 269. D, Wedemeyer, and Pandey have *rdo rje sems dpa'i* for *rdo rje'i* and *sangs rgyas thams cad kyi yon tan* for *sangs rgyas kyi yon tan thams cad* in our text.

the practice of *caryā*[2263] as previously explained—when they abandon all views and die, if they fully realize that death is the ultimate truth and birth is the conventional truth—they may, on rare occasions, generate the firm resolution: 'I shall dissolve myself into clear light, discard my ordinary body, and arise through the self-blessed stage.' If concentration on this resolution is maintained, it will continue into another life, and they will thereby become omniscient."[2264]

Thus, if yogis whose time to transmigrate arrives before they can engage in the practice of *caryā* in this life transform their deaths into the dharmakāya of the path and, while still dissolved in the clear light of death, are about to arise, then through the impetus of the thought "I shall arise as the body of the father-mother desire deity," they will arise not in the ordinary intermediate state that occurs naturally but rather as the illusory body made of wind and mind alone. Based on this explanation it should be understood that yogis who are awakened *in this life* generate the dharmakāya of the path that corresponds to the aspect of death, and from this they arise in the illusory body that corresponds to the aspect of the intermediate state. [82b]

Therefore, if YOU[2265] maintain that "those who awaken in the intermediate state" actually attain the intermediate state and awaken as intermediate beings by meditating on the path, YOU have not developed a proper understanding of the way awakening is attained in the unexcelled mantra. Therefore you must reach a thorough understanding of how awakening is attained: In place of the intermediate state, you should attain the illusory body and purify it by dissolving it into clear light. In doing so, you will attain the actual clear light and the pure illusory body that arises from it and arrive at the union that still requires practice. The mental continuum of the union that still requires practice—sustained without a moment's disruption—transforms into the union of no more practice of the saṃbhogakāya and the dharmakāya, the mind of great bliss. Through this transformation you will awaken. Though I have described this only in brief, take pains to understand it.

2263. Tib. *spyod pa.*

2264. Āryadeva, *Spyod bsdus, Caryāmelāpakapradīpa*, chap. 11, Tōh 1803, 106a6–b1; Tibetan and English translation Wedemeyer 2007, 330, 656, no Sanskrit; reconstructed Sanskrit and Tibetan in Pandey 2000, 103 and 363. D, Wedemeyer, and Pandey have *lta ba thams cad* for *lta ba* and *mngon par rtogs nas* for *rtogs nas* in our text. See Bu ston, *Rgyud sde spyi'i rnam par gzhag pa rgyud sde rin po che'i mdzes rgyan*, 14a3–b1; English translation in Hopkins 2008b, 235–236.

2265. See Mar pa lo tsā ba Chos kyi blo gros, *Zab lam snying po Nāro'i chos drug gsang ba bdud rtsi'i chu rgyan*, 578. See also Tsong kha pa, *Rim lnga gsal sgron*, 264b4–265a6, Kilty 2013, 431–432.

Hence, you purify by taking birth, death, and the intermediate state as the ground of purification and meditate on the path that shares correspondences with them. Accordingly, the aim is making it understood that you must engage in the particular methods of meditation that correspond to the particular grounds of purification, so that the meditative states will take the place of the grounds. It is for this reason that correspondences are drawn between individual stages of the creation stage and states of birth and death in cyclic existence and not merely to collate similarities. Nevertheless, although the specially visualized deities are generated in correspondence with people of the first eon, those people are not the ground of purification in this meditation, for the reasons explained above.

The twelfth chapter of the *Cluster of Instructions* applies the generation of the specially visualized deities in correspondence with the intermediate state,[2266] but this entails many errors since it contradicts the position of Ārya Nāgabuddhi, who explains that the generation of the specially visualized deities corresponds to the evolution of beings after the evolution of the world. It also contradicts the fact that the visualization of the First Lord is the one that is applied in correspondence with the intermediate state, and so forth, and is thus inappropriate.[2267]

[Do the Creation and Completion Stages Share a Ground of Purification?]

Most of THE EARLY AND LATER LAMAS of the Guhyasamāja in Tibet[2268] [83a] offer unanimously the explanation that the creation stage purifies birth, while the completion stage purifies death, and consequently, they specify different grounds of purification for the creation and completion. They base their claim on the line of the *Compendium of Practices*: "The so-called

2266. Abhayākaragupta, *Man ngag snye ma, Āmnāyamañjarī*, chap. 12, Tōh 1198, 118b5.

2267. See Tsong kha pa, *Rnam gzhag rim pa'i rnam bshad*, 22a1–3.

2268. See 'Gos Khug pa lhas btsas, *Gsang 'dus stong thun*, 14b6–15b5; Bu ston, *Mdor byas 'grel chen*, 1b4; Grags pa rgyal mtshan's *Rgyud kyi mngon rtogs*, work 1, 68a2–4; Red mda' ba, *Yid kyi mun sel*, 6b4–5; and Ngor chen Kun dga' bzang po, *Zla zer*, work 55, 18b3–6. A similar argument is made in Tsong kha pa, *Sngags rim chen mo*, chap. 11, 454; see also Mkhas grub rje, *Rgyud sde spyi'i rnam gzhag* in Lessing and Wayman 1968, 330–333.

birth is conventional truth, and that which is named death is ultimate truth. A yogi who finds these two stages through the grace of the lama becomes a buddha."[2269]

If this is the case, can the creation stage in and of itself entirely purify birth? If so, the creation stage in and of itself should lead to the supreme siddhi of awakening. If not, it follows that to purify birth entirely, the purifying agency of the completion stage is needed as well. Likewise, if the completion stage can purify death entirely in and of itself, then it should lead to supreme siddhi of awakening, and therefore the creation stage would be futile as a cause for supreme siddhi of awakening. However, if the completion stage cannot purify death in and of itself, it follows that the creation stage is also necessary to purify death, and therefore the assertion that the two stages have separate grounds of purification is vitiated.

What is the meaning then of the verse from the *Compendium of Practices* cited above? When mantrins meditating on the completion stage but unable to practice *caryā* in this lifetime pass away, and reach the supreme attainment in the intermediate state, their *death*s will dawn as the *ultimate truth*–clear light, and their *rebirth*s will dawn as the *conventional truth*–illusory body, and as such they will arise rather than as the intermediate beings that ordinarily arise after death.[2270] Thus *the two stages* referred to in the verse are [not the creation and completion stages, but] the stages of clear light and the illusory body that arise instead of naturally occurring death and the intermediate state.[2271] *Finding them* means: having attained clear light and the illusory body [and not ordinary death and rebirth that neither require the grace of the lama nor lead to buddhahood], *the yogis will become buddhas.*

Hence, such a serious error—taking *the two stages* to mean the creation stage and the completion stage—results from YOUR as yet exceedingly limited understanding of the profound points of the completion stage. Know therefore that the creation and completion stages do indeed have a common

2269. Āryadeva, *Spyod bsdus, Caryāmelāpakapradīpa*, chap. 11, Tōh 1803, 106b3; Tibetan and English translation in Wedemeyer 2007, 331, 656, no Sanskrit; reconstructed Sanskrit and Tibetan in Pandey 2000, 103 and 364. D, Wedemeyer, and Pandey have *gang zhig skye ba kun rdzob bden zhes bya* for *skye ba zhes bya kun rdzob bden pa ste* and *rim gnyis de dag* for *rim gnyis 'di dag.* These lines are cited also in Tsong kha pa, *Rnam gzhag rim pa'i rnam bshad*, 49a2–4, and *Sngags rim chen mo*, chap. 11, 454.

2270. See Hopkins 2008b, 235.

2271. The literal translation of this line is: Thus *the two stages* referred to in the verse are the stages of death and the intermediate stage following death *arising as clear light and the illusory body* and not allowing them to become the naturally occurring death and the intermediate state.

ground of purification, but separate paths of ripening and liberation as purifiers.[2272] [83b]

[Why Must the Meditation Correspond to Birth and the Intermediate State of a Human Being in Jambudvīpa as Well?]

Once it is established that the meditator—on the two stages of the path in correspondence with birth, death, and the intermediate state—is a human being in Jambudvīpa, as explained above, the stages of birth, death, and the intermediate state to which this meditation corresponds must be those of a human being in Jambudvīpa. This is so because meditation in correspondence is no mere collation of similarities. Rather, it aims at bringing about a transformation into the three bodies by means of a path that corresponds to the meditator's own birth, death, and intermediate state.[2273]

Qualm: We acknowledge that death should correspond to the death of a human being in Jambudvīpa, but why is it necessary to maintain that birth and the intermediate state should also be those of a human being in Jambudvīpa? After all, is it not certain that a human being who dies in Jambudvīpa can be reborn only as a human being in Jambudvīpa?

Response: Since the meditation on the path of the creation and completion stages of the highest mantra takes the fruit in the path, it is not enough for the meditation to correspond solely to the grounds of purification. It must also correspond to the three bodies of the fruit. Therefore the main path of the creation stage should bear the following characteristics. Initially, the way of meditation must correspond to the grounds of purification; in the final stages, with the fruit; and in the middle, with the completion stage. Hence, the meditation in correspondence with birth here must correspond not only with birth on the ground of purification but also with the course of birth as a supreme nirmāṇakāya of the fruit.

Since the meditation must correspond with both ends, while only a human being born in Jambudvīpa can display awakening in the supreme nirmāṇakāya, it follows that the meditation during the creation stage must likewise correspond to the birth of a human being in Jambudvīpa. This is also why the meditation in correspondence with the intermediate being must conform with the intermediate being that will be born as a human being in Jambudvīpa, [84a] for that intermediate being is destined to be born there.

2272. See also Tsong kha pa, *Rim lnga gsal sgron*, 264bff; Kilty 2013, 431ff.

2273. This and the following two paragraphs follow the *Rnam gzhag rim pa'i rnam bshad*, 48a2–b3.

What Is the Meaning of Purifying the Three Grounds of Purification Through the Purifier—the Creation Stage?

Regarding purifications in general, as the *Five Stages* teaches: "The mantrin absorbed in the illusion-like samādhi must purify by means of the true end."[2274] There are instances in which it is taught that the remedy purifies, but in this case the purification occurs by clearing impurities, as the *Concise Sādhana* teaches: "The wise should carefully observe the three worlds that are deluded as a result of faulty imprints for conceptualization and purify them with yoga tantra."[2275]

Three methods of purification are explained in the Tantra and Sūtra Vehicles:[2276]

(1) The purification of impurities in the mental continuum through the path is not carried out by blocking the streaming of accordant[2277] mental moments by means of a remedy. Rather the purification is achieved when the subsequent mental moment arises free of impurities from an earlier and impure mental moment through the power of the remedy.

(2) When self-grasping is purified by means of a remedy, no accordant subsequent mental moment free of impurities is induced to arise; nor is a mental moment that corresponds to the preceding one induced to arise in its stead. Rather, self-grasping is purified by making it impossible for any accordant subsequent mental moments ever to arise again.

(3) There are occasions when the clearing of impurities that obstruct the actualization of the true nature of things by means of a remedy is referred to as the purification of the true nature of things.

In the case of the creation stage, the purification does not occur as a result of:

(1) generating an accordant subsequent mental continuum of birth, death, and the intermediate state free of impurities, since a genuine birth, death, and intermediate state free of impurities would be impossible;

(2) clearing impurities that obstruct birth, death, and the intermediate state from becoming manifest, [84b] because they are already manifest in every sentient being and have been so since beginningless time.

2274. Nāgārjuna, *Rim lnga, Pañcakrama*, chap. 1, v. 5cd, Tōh 1802, 45b1; Sanskrit and Tibetan in Mimaki and Tomabechi 1994, 1; Sanskrit and French translation in Tomabechi 2006, 105. D and Mimaki and Tomabechi 1994 have *ting 'dzin gnas* for *ting nge 'dzin* in our text. The Sanskrit is *stho*.

2275. Nāgārjuna, *Mdor byas, Piṇḍīkrama Sādhana*, Tōh 1796, 1a4; L 3; T 3.

2276. See Tsong kha pa, *Rnam gzhag rim pa'i rnam bshad*, 50a5–b3.

2277. Or homogenous. Tib. *rigs 'dra*.

(3) This, too, is distinct from the purification of self-grasping, since it [the purification of self-grasping] does not require the cultivation of a path that corresponds with self-grasping; nor is it necessary to generate something different with shared characteristics in place of the discontinued self-grasping mind.

Thus you should understand the meaning of purifying the three grounds of purification, birth, death, and the intermediate state, through the two stages of creation and completion—the purifiers—as follows: By means of the path that corresponds to the three grounds of purification, these three are actually prevented from arising, and in their place, the three bodies of the path and of the fruit that corresponds to them are induced to arise.

Why the Other Parts of the Sādhana Are Not Applied in Correspondence with the Stages of Saṃsāric Evolution[2278]

Qualm: Why do we not apply the meditation on the protection wheel and the union with the consort, along with the subsequent steps of the *sādhana* in correspondences with the ground of purification?

The response is in two parts: (1) refuting the system of others, and (2) establishing our own position.

Refuting the System of Others

[Applying the Meditation on the Protection Wheel and So Forth in Correspondences with the Ground of Purification]

The followers of the system of Gö[2279] explain that according to Lama Tsunmochen[2280] the protection wheel and the outer Iron Mountains are applied in correspondence. This is inappropriate because there are no grounds of purification apart from the world and its beings. *Formulating the Sādhana* clearly explains how the generation of the celestial mansion is applied in correspondence with the evolution of the world while the meditation on the

2278. See Tsong kha pa, *Rnam gzhag rim pa'i rnam bshad*, 53a4–56a3.

2279. See 'Gos Khug pa lhas btsas, *Gsang 'dus stong thun*, 7a1–2.

2280. Tib. Btsun mo can. Tsong kha pa's *Rnam gzhag rim pa'i rnam bshad*, 53a4, has only Bla ma Btsun mo can here, without mentioning 'Gos Khug pa lhas btsas. According to Tsong kha pa, *Rim lnga gsal sgron*; 34a6; Kilty 2013, 75; and *Blue Annals*, Roerich 1979, 360, Btsun mo can was one of the main teachers from whom 'Gos Khug pa lhas btsas heard the exposition of the *Gsang ba 'dus pa*.

ground of wisdom just before it is applied in correspondence with emptying the previous world.[2281] Another reason the position of Gö is inappropriate is that it would entail the evolution of the Iron Mountains in the subsequent world prior to the emptying of the four continents and Mount Meru in the previous world and only then would the four continents and Mount Meru of the subsequent world evolve, which is not the case.[2282]

Since the specially visualized deities are applied in correspondence with the first people of the eon, SOME LATER LAMAS[2283] [85a] say that the gathering of accumulations during the preparations[2284] is similar to the accumulation of karma by sentient beings many lifetimes ago, in order to be reborn as human beings during the first eon.[2285] The meditation on emptiness that follows is similar to the death of these beings who have accumulated the karma. The subsequent visualization of the First Lord—the principal deity of the protection wheel—is similar to the rising of these beings in the intermediate stage. The transformation of the First Lord into Dveṣavajra is similar to the rebirth of these beings.

THEY SAY that since the *Four Chapters Tantra* teaches that the fence, lattice, and pegs of the protection wheel are generosity, morality, and patience,[2286] the accumulation of virtue by means of these three is similar to the accumulation of karma in order to be born during the first eon. The meditation on the ground of wisdom that follows this is similar to the death of these beings who have accumulated karma and the subsequent meditation on the specially visualized deities is similar to their rebirth as human beings in the first eon.

These positions simultaneously contradict (1) YOUR own premises and (2)

2281. Nāgabuddhi, *Rnam gzhag rim pa, Vyavastholi*, chap. 1, Tōh 1809, 122a1–4; Tanaka 2016, 82–83.

2282. The meditation on the protection wheel is followed by the meditation on the ground of wisdom that is applied in correspondence to the emptying of the previous world. If the Iron Mountains were the ground of purification of the protection wheel, then the sequence of cosmogonical events would be as described here.

2283. See Bu ston, *Mdor byas 'grel chen*, 25b4–26a4, and Tsong kha pa, *Rnam gzhag rim pa'i rnam bshad*, 53a6–b4.

2284. Bu ston, *Mdor byas 'grel chen*, 25b5, has *dang po sbyor ba* for *sbyor ba* in our text, the "First Yoga."

2285. Reading *myong 'gyur* for *myong gyur* in our text.

2286. *Gdan bzhi, Catuḥpīṭha Tantra*, Tōh 428, 213b6–214a1. See also Szántó 2012, 412. This passage is cited by Bu ston, *Mdor byas 'grel chen*, 26a1–3.

authoritative scriptures and are flawed because they (3) give rise to infinite regress[2287] and (4) indicate your misunderstanding of meanings.

(1) How do these positions contradict YOUR OWN premises? YOU[2288] refute the position of *Kṛṣṇasamayavajra,[2289] who maintains that the First Lord emanates Akṣobhya from his own heart, then draws Akṣobhya back into himself [the First Lord], and thereby the First Lord transforms into Vajrasattva's nirmāṇakāya. YOU maintain that *Kṛṣṇasamayavajra's position does not correspond to the ground of purification because the intermediate being does not produce its own body by means of its own semen. However, when YOU present YOUR own system, YOU say that the meditator as the First Lord of the protection wheel—who is equivalent to the intermediate being—generates Akṣobhya from the semen of father-mother absorbed in union, and draws him [Akṣobhya] into oneself—the meditator as the First Lord—thereby transforming the First Lord into Dveṣavajra, which is equivalent to taking birth. This position is inconsistent with YOUR OWN WORDS, and YOU should clearly accept total defeat.[2290] [85b]

(2) How does YOUR position contradict the authoritative scriptures? Immediately after his explication of the manner in which the world is destroyed and emptied, Master Nāgabuddhi states: "In accordance with this, the meditator on the creation stage should recite and meditate on the verse that begins with 'in the absence of being.'"[2291] Thus Nāgabuddhi clearly advocates meditation on the ground of wisdom in correspondence with the dissolved world. Hence, applying the meditation on the ground of wisdom in correspondence with the death of sentient beings in the past who will be reborn in the next life as human beings in the first eon plainly contradicts the *Formulating the Sādhana*. And if you apply the field of accumulating merit, the protection wheel, and so forth to the ground of purification, the sādhana will then be incomplete with respect

2287. Tib. *thug pa med pa*, Skt. *anavasthā*.

2288. Bu ston, *Mdor byas 'grel chen*, 39a3–5. See also out text [111a4–b1 and 114b5–115a3] below.

2289. Nag po dam tshig rdo rje, *Pañcakramapañjikā*, *Rim pa lnga'i dka' 'grel*, Tōh 1841, 160b4.

2290. Tib. *'khor gsum*. This means: You are totally defeated, since you have committed the three serious errors in logic. For explanations of this debating term see, for example, Perdue 1992, 58; Onoda 1992, 47–48; and Dreyfus 2003, 217 and 381, n46.

2291. Nāgabuddhi, *Rnam gzhag rim pa*, *Vyavastholi*, chap. 1, Tōh 1809, 121b5; Tanaka 2016, 81. D and Tanaka have *sgom pa pos* for *bsgom pas*; *med la* for *med pas*; and *bsam par bya'o* for *bsgom par bya'o* in our text. See the meditation on emptiness, above.

to purifying the ground of purification, because the *Concise Sādhana* does not prescribe offerings to the field of accumulating merit.

(3) Giving rise to infinite regress. The consequence of your position is utterly absurd, since it entails applying correspondences also to the births, deaths, and intermediate states of sentient beings who have accumulated karma to be reborn as the beings who have accumulated karma many lifetimes ago in order to be reborn as human beings of the first eon; and it would then be necessary to apply the correspondences to earlier and earlier rebirths as well. If YOU applied the correspondences to the intermediate state that follows the death of the sentient being who has accumulated karma many lifetimes ago in order to be reborn as a person of the first eon, but not apply the correspondence to the intermediate being that follows the death of a sentient being who has accumulated karma that would be experienced in the next life after rebirth, that would be inconsistent. Thereafter YOU must also clarify to which type of intermediate being you should apply in correspondence with the meditation—beginning at the ground of wisdom and leading up to the visualization of the celestial mansion.

(4) Misunderstanding this point. THOSE who do not understand that the aim of applying the meditation here in correspondence with birth, death, and the intermediate state on the ground of purification [86a] is the purification of the meditator's own birth, death, and intermediate being—and who maintain that the grounds of purification are the birth, death, and intermediate state of earlier and earlier rebirths of those who will be reborn as the first people of the eon—are obviously unable to focus their minds on the object of concentration no matter what they do while meditating on the sādhana.[2292]

[Applying the Meditation on the Consort and So Forth in Correspondences with the Ground of Purification]

Furthermore, TIBETAN LAMAS SAY[2293] that (1) this meditation, starting with the transformation of the First Lord into Vajrasattva's nirmāṇakāya and up to the triple sattvas, corresponds to taking birth in the womb, emerging out of it, and completing the life stages of body, speech, and mind; (2) seeking the consort corresponds to taking a wife from one's clan; (3) the union of the vajra and

2292. See Tsong kha pa, *Rnam gzhag rim pa'i rnam bshad*, 53b4–54a6.

2293. See 'Gos Khug pa lhas btsas, *Gsang 'dus stong thun*, 13b3–14a2; Bu ston, *Mdor byas 'grel chen*, 51b7–52a5; Red mda' ba, *Yid kyi mun sel*, 8a3–b1; and Tsong kha pa, *Rnam gzhag rim pa'i rnam bshad*, 54a6–b5. But see also Tsong kha pa, *Sngags rim chen mo*, chap. 12, 509–510.

lotus corresponds to the arousing of the parents' organs at the ground time; (4) engaging in the act of passion and making offerings [of bodhicitta] correspond to the husband and wife coupling and thereby being satisfied with joy; (5) engendering of the Supreme King of Maṇḍalas corresponds to the birth of sons and daughters to these parents; (6) making offerings and so forth corresponds to raising these sons and daughters to adulthood by providing food, clothing, and so forth with the intention of nurturing them; (7) the meditation on the subtle drop corresponds to those sons and grandsons among them who, in order to purify their minds and develop perfect wisdom, learn topics of knowledge and attain their own purposes and those of others; (8) yogis who have practiced the creation stage, who please the deities with ritual services and fire offerings, and who attain the siddhis, correspond to those sons and grandsons among them who by pleasing the king and so forth perfectly fulfill their wishes.[2294] SO THEY SAY.

These are merely the mental fabrications of those who do not understand the meaning of the creation stage, none of which was ever taught by Ārya Nāgārjuna and his disciples. [86b] For the aim of purifying the ground of purification through the creation stage is the awakening of the yogis themselves; to achieve this, it is sufficient that they purify the stages of their own saṃsāric birth by meditating in correspondence with them. If in order to attain enlightenment the yogis must purify all their sons, grandsons, and so forth by meditating in correspondence with the stages of their descendants' saṃsāric rebirth, the consequences will be utterly absurd: (1) they will be unable to awaken until all their future relations do; (2) their relations will awaken without having actually meditated on the path; (3) no matter how much they purify themselves, in order to attain the stage of the three bodies, their path will include many grounds of purification belonging to the mental continuum of other people rather than their own birth, death, and intermediate state; and (4) they will have to meditate in correspondence with the stages of the saṃsāric rebirth of their own sons, grandsons, and great-grandsons and their sons, grandsons, great-grandsons, and so forth.

Establishing Our Own Position

The *Illuminating Lamp* explains: "Through the line *absorbed* and so forth the *Guhyasamāja Tantra* teaches the ritual of protection as an element of virtuous

2294. In Tsong kha pa, *Rnam gzhag rim pa'i rnam bshad*, 54a6–b5, while the first seven points are attributed to "Tibetan lamas," the eighth point, with certain variations, is ascribed to "some," Tib. *'ga zhig*.

activity for the beginner."[2295] Hence the preliminary offerings to the field of accumulating merit and the meditation on the protection wheel are preparatory and ancillary to the main part of the sādhana. Neither these nor the concluding steps and activities amid the meditative session should be applied to the ground of purification,[2296] for otherwise, it would be necessary to clarify why *Formulating the Sādhana* does not explain how they are to be applied to the ground of purification.

Here are the reasons for not teaching the method of applying the later steps of the sādhana to the ground of purification, beginning from the union with the consort: The main part of the sādhana is generally understood to have four determinants: (1) the place where the yogi awakens; [87a] (2) the being who is to awaken there; (3) the essence into which the yogi awakens; and (4) the "deeds" of the awakened being.[2297]

The place where the yogi awakens is the celestial mansion arising from the ground of wisdom on the vajra ground. The being awakened there is the specially visualized deity. The essence into which the yogi awakens consists of the three bodies of the path: (a) the dharmakāya, or the clear light into which the specially visualized deities dissolve; (b) the saṃbhogakāya generated as the First Lord; (c) and the nirmāṇakāya formed through the transformation of the First Lord into blue Vajrasattva.

These stages of the meditation fulfill the purpose of purifying the environment, as well as purifying birth, death, and the intermediate state, and transforming them into the three bodies. Other than the impure environment as well as birth, death, and the intermediate state there are no additional grounds to be purified. That is why there are no explanations about applying the stages of the meditation starting from the seeking of the consort in correspondence with the ground of purification. The explanation given in the *Illuminating Lamp*, that generating the deity by seeking the consort and absorbing in union

2295. Candrakīrti, *Sgron gsal, Pradīpoddyotanaṭīkā*, chap. 13, Tōh 1785, 111a4–5; Chakravarti 1984, 135. In his *Sgron gsal mchan*, 318a1–2, Tsong kha pa explains that *beginner* means a meditator on the creation stage, *part of* etc. means part of the main part of the sādhana, and *the ritual of protection* is the ritual of the protection wheel. For these lines see *Gsang 'dus, Guhyasamāja Tantra*, cited above [31a], chap. 13, Tōh 442; Zhol 22b2; Stog 38a3–4; Dunh 41b4; Fremantle 1971, v. 74; and Matsunaga 1978, v. 78.

2296. See Tsong kha pa, *Rnam gzhag rim pa'i rnam bshad*, 54a4–6.

2297. See Tsong kha pa, *Rnam gzhag rim pa'i rnam bshad*, 54b4–55a2.

with her is a stage of saṃsāric rebirth,[2298] merely indicates an analogy to the process by which a mother and father beget a son, and does not imply a correspondence with the process of saṃsāric rebirth as the ground of purification.

Therefore the steps of the sādhana beginning with the seeking of the consort are applied in correspondence with the stage of the fruit of buddhahood and not with saṃsāric processes, for the *Sādhana Incorporating the Scripture* teaches: "Just as in the *Guhyasamāja Tantra* the Teacher was absorbed in the samādhi called 'the method of great passion,' likewise during the creation stage mantrins should practice the First Yoga."[2299] Thus the absorption in union with the consort is applied in correspondence with the stage of the fruit, hence, the *Vajrasattva Sādhana* also teaches that this practice should be applied to the "deeds" of the fruitional time.[2300]

Furthermore, according to the *Vajrasattva Sādhana* and the *Compendium of Practices*, the Teacher displayed three modes of practice: (1) practice without passion through the nirmāṇakāya that has descended from Tuṣita Heaven; [87b] (2) the practice of the grounds and the perfections; and (3) the practice of passion. For the sake of disciples who cultivate by means of the latter practice, the Teacher emanated the *dhāraṇī maṇḍala*[2301] and the thirteen deities for empowering them. Likewise, yogis first meditate on actualizing the stage of the three bodies by taking their own aspiration in the path, and then, through the yoga of seeking the consorts and abiding in union with them, they emanate the deities of the maṇḍala and perform deeds for the sake of others—in

2298. Candrakīrti, *Sgron gsal, Pradīpoddyotanaṭīkā*, chap. 8, Tōh 1785, 60a3; Chakravarti 1984, 76. D has *srid pa bskyed pa'i rim pa* for *srid pa skye ba'i rim pa* in our text, which carries a somewhat different meaning. See also Tsong kha pa, *Rnam gzhag rim pa'i rnam bshad*, 55a2–4.

2299. Nāgārjuna, *Mdo bsre, Sādhanasūtramelāpaka*, Tōh 1797, 13b3. D is somewhat different: *le'u dang po las* for *ston pas*; after *tshul* they add: *rdo rje / zhes bya ba'i ting nge 'dzin*; they have *zhugs par mdzad pa* for *zhugs* pa; and *bskyed* for *skye*. This passage is cited above as well [77a].

2300. Candrakīrti, *Rdo rje sems dpa'i sgrub thabs, Vajrasattva Sādhana*, Tōh 1814, 202a1–2; Luo and Tomabechi 2009, 24.2–3 and 57.12–14.

2301. Tib. *gzungs dkyil*, Skt. *dhāraṇīmaṇḍala*, this is the maṇḍala emanated at the beginning of the first chapter of the *Guhyasamāja Tantra*. See Tōh 1785, 13b4 [though it has *gzugs* for *gzungs*]; Chakravarti 1984, 19; and Tsong kha pa, *Sgron gsal mchan*, 57b1.

correspondence with the Teacher who performs deeds for the sake of others through the practice of desire.[2302]

The meditation on the two subtle objects of concentration[2303] in order to stabilize the mind corresponds to the Buddha's deed of mind—abiding in perfect inner absorption.[2304] The mantra recitation for stirring the heart of the deities is similar to the Buddha's deed of speech—the teaching of the Dharma. The meditation, recitation, and so forth of the principal deity father-mother[2305] and their dissolution at the conclusion of the sādhana[2306] are similar to the Buddha's deed of revealing nirvāṇa in that buddhafield after he completed his deeds for the sake of direct disciples. Arousing the deities who have dissolved through the songs of the four mothers in the nature of the four qualities beyond measure,[2307] the rising of the deities in response,[2308] presenting offerings and praises to the deities, and the acceptance of the offerings by the deities[2309]—these correspond to the Buddha, who, after he has revealed nirvāṇa in a particular buddhafield, once his mind is stirred by the four qualities beyond measure, arises in the appearance of the rūpakāya and becomes a receptacle for offerings of the world wherever direct disciples of the Buddha's body are found.[2310] For this reason, in *Formulating the Sādhana*, these later steps of the sādhana beginning with the union with the consort are applied to the deeds of the Buddha, and not to the stages of saṃsāric rebirth.

Thus[2311] [88a] with regard to the following positions[2312]—(a) that it is

2302. Candrakīrti, *Rdo rje sems dpa'i sgrub thabs*, *Vajrasattva Sādhana*, Tōh 1814, 201b6–202a1; Luo and Tomabechi 2009, 23.11–24.2 and 57.5–12. This passage is cited again below [140b]. Āryadeva, *Spyod bsdus, Caryāmelāpakapradīpa*, chap. 9, Tōh 1803, 94b4–6; Sanskrit, Tibetan, and English translation in Wedemeyer 2007, B: 54b–55a; Sanskrit and Tibetan in Pandey 2000, 78 and 310–311. See Tsong kha pa, *Rnam gzhag rim pa'i rnam bshad*, 55a4–b2. Here Tsong kha pa points out that these Deeds of the Teacher are the Deeds of his Body.

2303. See our text below [159a3–5].

2304. Tib. *nang du yang dag 'jog pa*, Skt. *pratisaṃlayana*.

2305. Tsong kha pa, *Rnam gzhag rim pa'i rnam bshad*, 55b4, adds here: "of the Supreme King of Maṇḍalas."

2306. See Tsong kha pa, *Gsang mngon*, 52b4–68b2.

2307. See Tsong kha pa, *Gsang mngon*, 68b2–69a5.

2308. See Tsong kha pa, *Gsang mngon*, 69a6–b1.

2309. See Tsong kha pa, *Gsang mngon*, 69b6–74a2.

2310. See Tsong kha pa, *Rnam gzhag rim pa'i rnam bshad*, 55b2–5.

2311. See Tsong kha pa, *Rnam gzhag rim pa'i rnam bshad*, 55b5–56a2.

2312. See above [86a].

necessary, as previously claimed, to apply the creation stage in correspondence with the sons, grandsons, and so forth at the time of the ground; (b) that, as SOME maintain,[2313] the dissolution of the deities and their arousal through song toward the end of the sādhana are applied in correspondence with the death of the sons and grandsons upon the completion of their lifespan and with the relatives who grieve and mourn their death, and that [the arising once again of the principal deity and the offerings made to him] are applied in correspondence with their sons and grandsons, who, out of attachment to their relatives and owing to their karma, are reborn and enjoy objects of desire and so forth—you must understand that these explanations are pointless and only make the fool happy, for as previously explained, they are inappropriate.

2313. See Red mda' ba, *Yid kyi mun sel*, 8b1–2.

8. The Deeds of the Specially Visualized Deities and Their Gathering into the Body

The "Deeds" of the Specially Visualized Deities

The *Guhyasamāja Sādhana* teaches: Visualize a light-ray, emanating from the seed syllable *hūṃ* on your heart, drawing all sentient beings from the ten directions. They enter the maṇḍala in the entry-mode of Vajrasattva. The bodhicitta, emanated through the absorption in union of the father-mother, initiates them, and they attain the bliss and mental rapture of all tathāgatas. Becoming Vajrasattva, they proceed to their own buddhafield.[2314]

Taking into account that the *Concise Sādhana*, *Sādhana Incorporating the Scripture*, *Formulating the Sādhana*, and *Vajrasattva Sādhana* do not explain this meditation clearly and explicitly, the *Intense Illuminating Lamp*,[2315] *Kṛṣṇasamayavajra,[2316] and others do not accept the deeds of the specially visualized deities. But these deeds are clearly understood from the *Guhyasamāja Tantra* and the *Illuminating Lamp*. According to the *Guhyasamāja Tantra*, during the samādhi of vajra overpowering:[2317] "As soon as the Blessed One, the lord of all tathāgatas,[2318] dwelt in absorption, the entire realm of space came to abide in the vajra nature of all tathāgatas."[2319] [88b] The *Illuminating Lamp* explains this as "*Came to abide in the vajra nature of all tathāgatas*

2314. Tsong kha pa, *Gsang mngon*, 37b3–6.

2315. Bhavyakīrti, *Rab tu Sgron gsal, Prakāśikā*, Tōh 1793.

2316. Nag po dam tshig rdo rje, *Rim pa lnga'i dka' 'grel, Pañcakramapañjikā*, Tōh 1841.

2317. Tib. *de bzhin gshegs pa thams cad zil gyis gnon pa rdo rje zhes bya bya'i ting nge 'dzin*, Skt. *sarvatathāgatābhibhavanavajranāmasamādhi*.

2318. Tib. *Byang chub kyi sems rdo rje*, Skt. *Bodhicittavajra*.

2319. *Guhyasamāja Tantra*, chap. 1, Tōh 442; Zhol 3a5–b1; Stog 4a6–7 [the rest is missing]; Dunh 3a1–4; Fremantle 1971, 178–179; and Matsunaga 1978, 5.

means they came to be indwellers of the maṇḍala of the tathāgata."[2320] Therefore the *Guhyasamāja Tantra* and its commentary teach the meditation on the specially visualized deities.

Immediately afterward the *Guhyasamāja Tantra* teaches: "Then as many as there were sentient beings residing in the entire realm of space, through the blessing of Vajrasattva all of them attained the bliss and mental rapture of tathāgatas."[2321] The *Illuminating Lamp* explains: "What did those who have come to be indwellers of the maṇḍala of Great Vajradhara do? The [*Guhyasamāja*] *Tantra* speaks of *sentient beings* and so forth,[2322] which means that *all sentient beings* entered *through* the entry-mode of glorious *Vajrasattva* and attained Vajrasattva-hood,[2323] thereby *attained bliss and mental rapture*. This is the shared level of interpretation."[2324] Thus both the *Guhyasamāja Tantra* and the *Illuminating Lamp* teach the deeds of the specially visualized deities.

This explanation of the *Illuminating Lamp* falls under the category of the shared level of interpretation because its significance is shared by the creation and completion stages alike. How do we know that this explanation refers to the specially visualized deities[2325] of the creation stage? Because after completing the explanation of the passage, the *Illuminating Lamp* teaches: "In this way, generate Great Vajradhara through special visualization."[2326]

There are primarily four modes of entering into a maṇḍala: (1) through the gate as disciples entering the maṇḍala to receive initiation; (2) directly from above as the jñānasattva enters to bless the samayasattva; (3) from below visualizing the maṇḍala raised through mantra[2327] and mudrā in order to enter the

2320. Candrakīrti, *Sgron gsal, Pradīpoddyotanaṭīkā*, Tōh 1785, 14b7; Chakravarti 1984, 20. D has *rdo rje 'chang chen po* for *de bzhin gshegs pa* in our text. Chakravarti has *mahāvajra* and in the following line *mahāvajradhāra* for *rdo rje 'chang chen po* in D. Read *āveśena* for *āvegena* in Chakravarti; Tib. has *'jug pa*.

2321. *Guhyasamāja Tantra*, Tōh 442; Zhol 3b1; Stog missing; Dunh 3a3–4; Fremantle 1971, 178–179; and Matsunaga 1978, 5.

2322. This refers to the aforementioned lines.

2323. Tib. *rdo rje sems dpa' nyid*, Skt. *vajrasattvatvaṃ*.

2324. Candrakīrti, *Sgron gsal, Pradīpoddyotanaṭīkā*, Tōh 1785, 14b7–15a1; Chakravarti 1984, 20.

2325. Reading *lhag mos kyi* for *lhag mos kyis* here.

2326. Tib. *lhag par mos pas*, Skt. *adhimokṣeṇa*. The meaning of this term is discussed above [69a]. Candrakīrti, *Sgron gsal, Pradīpoddyotanaṭīkā*, Tōh 1785, 15a7–b1; Chakravarti 1984, 20.

2327. Tib. *rdo rje zhugs*, Skt. *vajrāvega*. According to Abhayākaragupta's *Dkyil chog rdo rje phreng ba, Vajrāvalī*, Tōh 3140, 37a7–b1; Mori 2009, §13.1.3, 233, the mantra recited here is *oṃ vajra vegā krama hūṃ*.

maṇḍala and open the doors without stepping over the colored powder, i.e., the entry through the power of the vajra; [89a] (4) from the four directions of the maṇḍala through the unhindered vajra-like entryway of Vajrasattva. In the present context, this fourth mode is the mode of entry.

Meditating on the initiation conferred to beings through the samādhi of "vajra overpowering" in this way corresponds to the "deeds" of the Teacher, Vajradhara, who, at the beginning of the [*Guhyasamāja*] *Tantra* taught by him, emanated a maṇḍala and conferred initiation on all sentient beings. In following the exemplary life of the Teacher in the "past event,"[2328] disciples apply the fruit of the practice in the path, but they do not apply this meditation to the ground of purification of samsaric processes.

Gathering the Specially Visualized Deities into the Body

The *Concise Sādhana* teaches: "Further, by means of the yoga of union, visualize these buddhas entering your body one by one abiding on the body wheels."[2329] And the *Vajrasattva Sādhana* teaches that "Having visualized the thirty-two deities emanating as the outer maṇḍala, you should then place them on the maṇḍala of your body: the five buddhas in the nature of the aggregates, the knowledge-goddesses in the nature of the sensory spheres, the bodhisattvas in the nature of the sense bases, and the fierce kings in the nature of the limbs of the body."[2330] Accordingly, you should place the deities abiding in the outer maṇḍala upon the maṇḍala of your body. The line *the maṇḍala of your body* means your body, and it is there that you should set the deities. This instruction does not indicate that gathering the deities into your body is the meditation on the body maṇḍala. The reason for this will be explained in the context of the body maṇḍala below. [89b]

2328. Tib. *sngon byung*, Skt. *bhūtapūrva*.

2329. Nāgārjuna, *Mdor byas*, *Piṇḍīkrama Sādhana*, Tōh 1796, 3a7; L 36cd–37ab; T 35cd–36ab. D has *'khor lo* for *'khor lor* and *rdzogs* for *rtogs* in our text.

2330. Candrakīrti, *Rdo rje sems dpa'i sgrub thabs*, *Vajrasattva Sādhana*, Tōh 1814, 198b3–4; Luo and Tomabechi 2009, 12.13–3 and 45.3–7. D and Luo and Tomabechi have *rnam par dgod par* for *dgod par*. Luo and Tomabechi have *phung po'i rang bzhin gyis* for *phung po'i rang bzhin gyi*; *skye mched kyi rang bzhin gyis* for *skye mched kyi rang bzhin gyi*; and *yan lag gi rang bzhin gyis* for *yan lag gi rang bzhin gyis* in our text. The Sanskrit is *svabhāvena*.

[Where Does the Guhyasamāja Tantra *Explain the Gathering of the Specially Visualized Deities into Your Body?]*

The *Sādhana Incorporating the Scripture* teaches that the verse of the *Guhyasamāja Tantra* "The semen issued from union,[2331] according to the ritual method,"[2332] and so forth, is applied to the next step in which the specially visualized deities enter into clear light, and not to the present step of gathering the deities into the body.[2333] Likewise the *Vajrasattva Sādhana* cites the following verses from the seventeenth chapter of the *Guhyasamāja Tantra* as the scriptural source for visualizing the deities that have already been gathered into your body in the nature of your aggregates and so forth, but not for gathering them into your body: "Taken together the five aggregates are proclaimed the five buddhas, the vajra sense-bases, i.e., the supreme maṇḍala of bodhisattvas;[2334] the earth is called Locanā; the water element, Māmakī; the fire, Pāṇḍarā; and the wind, Tārā."[2335]

What then is the scriptural source for gathering the deities? The *Sādhana Incorporating the Scripture* and *Vajrasattva Sādhana* cite the first chapter of the *Guhyasamāja Tantra*, "Endowed with disks—a clear one and so forth,"[2336] which appears above[2337] as the scriptural source for the generation of the celes-

2331. Tib. *dam tshig*, Skt. *samaya*. According to Candrakīrti, *Sgron gsal, Pradīpoddyotanaṭīkā*, Tōh 1785, 54b6; Chakravarti 1984, 69; in the present context, this is the union of wisdom and means in the context of rebirth.

2332. *Guhyasamāja Tantra*, chap. 7, Tōh 442; Zhol 11a6; Stog 18b6–7; Dunh 19b2; Fremantle 1971, v. 33; and Matsunaga 1978, v. 33.

2333. Nāgārjuna, *Mdo bsre, Sādhanasūtramelāpaka*, Tōh 1797, 12a5. The entire verse appears on [90b] below.

2334. Our text skips the prose passage found in the *Guhyasamāja Tantra* here.

2335. Candrakīrti, *Rdo rje sems dpa'i sgrub thabs, Vajrasattva Sādhana*, Tōh 1814, 198b4–5; Luo and Tomabechi 2009, 13.4–7 and 45.8–16. See *Gsang 'dus, Guhyasamāja Tantra*, Tōh 442; Zhol 44a6–7; Stog 74b4–5; Dunh 82a5–b1; Fremantle 1971, vv. 50–51; and Matsunaga 1978, vv. 50–51. The Zhol has *mdor na phung po lnga rnams ni* for *phung po lnga ni mdor bsdus na*; *rab tu bsgrags* for *rab tu grags*; *skye mched nyid dag kyang* for *skye mched nyid kyang ni*; *spyan zhes bya ba yin* for *spyan ma zhes su grags*; *chu yi khams ni mā ma kī* for *chu khams mā ma kī ru dran*; and *dkar dang sgrol ma zhes bya ba / me dang rlung du rab tu bsgrags* for *me ni gos dkar mo zhes bya / rlung ni sgrol mar rab tu grags* in our text.

2336. *Guhyasamāja Tantra*, chap. 1, Tōh 442; Zhol 3a1–2; Stog 4a2–3; Dunh 1b3–4; Fremantle 1971, v. 1; and Matsunaga 1978, v. 1. The Zhol has *la stsogs* for *la sogs* in our text.

2337. See our text above [69b].

tial mansion and the specially visualized deities residing therein.[2338] This passage is immediately followed[2339] by the lines on the gathering of the specially visualized deities: "Then the Tathāgata Akṣobhya, the Tathāgata Ratnaketu, the Tathāgata Amitāyus, the Tathāgata Amoghasiddhi, and the Tathāgata Vairocana[2340] entered[2341] the heart of the Tathāgata Bodhicittavajra."[2342]

The *Illuminating Lamp* comments on this: "*Entered the heart of Bodhicittavajra* means that the maṇḍala[2343] of the deities, comprised within the five tathāgata families, entered[2344] the body of Bodhicittavajra once more. This is the interpretable meaning."[2345] [90a] Since the interpretable meaning is applied to the creation stage, any application of these lines to cases other than the specially visualized deities is irrelevant here. Akṣobhya in this instance is the very Tathāgata Akṣobhya who was present in the assembly surrounding Vajradhara in the "past event,"[2346] whereas the line *comprised within the five tathāgata families* refers to the deities that are included in the tathāgata family of Akṣobhya up to the two fierce deities[2347] in the practice that follows the "past event," according to the teachings of the *Illuminating Lamp.*[2348]

The *Illuminating Lamp* explains how you should gather the deities into your body: "A hook-like ray of light emanating from the seed syllable at your

2338. Nāgārjuna, *Mdo bsre, Sādhanasūtramelāpaka*, Tōh 1797, 12a1–5. Candrakīrti, *Rdo rje sems dpa'i sgrub thabs, Vajrasattva Sādhana*, Tōh 1814, 198b2; Luo and Tomabechi 2009, 12.9–11 and 44.15–45.1.

2339. In fact, there is one line in between, and Bu ston, *Sgron gsal bshad sbyar*, 66a4–5, for example, regards it, and not the verse "endowed with disks, clear and so on," as the scriptural authority for generating the specially visualized deities.

2340. Tib. Mi bskyod pa, Rin chen dpal, Tshe dpag tu med pa, Gdon mi zab bar grub pa, and Rnam par sang mdzad. Note that in the Derge these names have been standardized.

2341. The Sanskrit has "abided in."

2342. *Guhyasamāja Tantra*, Tōh 442; Zhol 3a3–5; Stog 4a4–6; Dunh 1b5 [the beginning only]; Fremantle 1971, 178–179; and Matsunaga 1978, 5.

2343. While the Sanskrit is *cakra*, the Tibetan is *dkyil 'khor.*

2344. The Sanskrit here means "took their abode."

2345. Candrakīrti, *Sgron gsal, Pradīpoddyotanaṭīkā*, Tōh 1785, 14a3–4; Chakravarti 1984, 19.

2346. Tib. *rjes 'jug.*

2347. While in the passage of the *Guhyasamāja Root Tantra* cited above five buddhas entered into the heart of Bodhicittavajra, in Tsong kha pa, *Gsang mngon*, only four buddhas are withdrawn into the body—Akṣobhya is not among them. In the sādhana, thirty-one deities enter into the principal deity, some of which belong to the tathāgata family of Akṣobhya.

2348. See Tsong kha pa's *Sgron gsal mchan*, 62a3.

heart[2349] draws them, and infuses them into your body with the nature of the aggregates, the sensory spheres, and so forth."[2350] As cited above, after drawing the deities, set them upon your own body in the same locations where they are set in the body maṇḍala, and visualize them becoming inseparable from the respective components of your body, such as the five aggregates, four elements, and the eyes and so forth.

Regarding the meaning of *the yoga of union* in the verse from the *Concise Sādhana* above, *Kṛṣṇasamayavajra explains that it refers to the father-mother absorbed in union,[2351] and the *Jewel Rosary* explains that it points to the four unions,[2352] but these are irrelevant conjectural designations.[2353]

The meaning can be understood on the basis of the following scriptural sources. The thirteenth chapter of the *Guhyasamāja Tantra* explains how you should gather the deities into your body at the end of the meditative session: "While reciting, send forth the vajras; having completed this, gather them."[2354] The *Illuminating Lamp* comments on this: "In order to demonstrate the yoga of union, the *Guhyasamāja Tantra* teaches *while reciting send forth the vajras* and so forth. The *vajra*s are the bodies of emanated deities, and *reciting* means arising from their seats. After they have arisen from their places, you should *send them forth*, and set them on yourself in the nature of the aggregates and so forth."[2355] [90b] Thus *union* here means fusing the deities with your own aggregates and so forth as indivisible essences.

Hence gathering the specially visualized deities into the body corresponds to the exemplary life of the Teacher in the "past event." The practice that follows this takes the fruit in the path and is not applied to the ground of purification for your own sake. Still, it has the special purpose of laying the ground for the entry of the specially visualized deities into clear light.

2349. See Tsong kha pa, *Gsang mngon*, 37b5.

2350. Candrakīrti, *Sgron gsal, Pradīpoddyotanaṭīkā*, Tōh 1785, 13a4; Chakravarti 1984, 18.

2351. Nag po dam tshig rdo rje, *Rim pa lnga'i dka' 'grel, Pañcakramapañjikā*, Tōh 1841, 159b7–160a1.

2352. Ratnākaraśānti, *Rin chen phreng ba, Ratnāvalī*, Tōh 1826, 32a6–b1.

2353. This follows Bu ston, *Mdor byas 'grel chen*, 28a1–2.

2354. *Guhyasamāja Tantra*, Tōh 442; Zhol 20a6; Stog 34b1–2; Dunh 37b3–4; Fremantle 1971, v. 15; and Matsunaga 1978, v. 13. The Zhol has *rab tu bsdu bar bya* for *bsdu ba rab tu bya*. See also Tsong kha pa's *Sgron gsal mchan*, 295b4–5.

2355. Candrakīrti, *Sgron gsal, Pradīpoddyotanaṭīkā*, Tōh 1785, 102a7–b1; Chakravarti 1984, 125. D has *rdo rje sprul pa'i* for *rdo rje ste sprul pa'i* in our text.

9. The Yoga of Taking Death as the Dharmakāya

Dissolution of the Specially Visualized Deities into the Ultimate Maṇḍala

The *Concise Sādhana* teaches: "Yogis should bring the deities into suchness by way of the wheel[2356] of ultimate truth. When they slay the assembly of tathāgatas, they will achieve the supreme siddhi."[2357] According to the *Sādhana Incorporating the Scripture*, the scriptural authority for this meditation is this verse of the *Guhyasamāja Root Tantra*: "Those who desire the fruit should drink the semen issued[2358] from union, according to the ritual method. When they slay the assembly of tathāgatas, they will achieve the supreme siddhi."[2359] But the *Illuminating Lamp* applies this verse of the *Guhyasamāja Root Tantra* to awakening in the intermediate state.[2360]

The *Concise Sādhana* refers to the following verse of the *Vajra Garland Tantra* as the scriptural source for the entry of the specially visualized deities into clear light: "These are arranged as the *Vajra Garland Tantra* makes

2356. The Bstan 'gyur has "vajra" for "wheel" here.

2357. Tib. *dngos grub rab mchog*, Skt. *sutarāṃ siddhi*. Nāgārjuna, *Mdor byas*, *Piṇḍīkrama Sādhana*, Tōh 1796, 3a7–b1; L 37cd–38ab; T 36cd–37ab. D has *rdo rje* for *'khor lo*; *bya bas* for *byas bas*; and *thob par* for *'grub par* in our text. T has *siddhim* for *vidhim* in L. Note that in his Corrections, La Vallée Poussin (1986, xv) "corrects" *Mārayet tv āgataṃ* to *Sārayet tathāgataṃ*. T reproduces the text of La Vallée Poussin but in a note has also *tathāgataṃ* and *tāgataṃ* for *tvāgataṃ*.

2358. The Tibetan has *phung* for *kṣaret* in the Sanskrit.

2359. Nāgārjuna, *Mdo bsre*, *Sādhanasūtramelāpaka*, Tōh 1797, 12a5–6. D has *bsad nas* for *bsad na* [but the *Guhyasamāja Tantra* has *bsad na* as our text] and *thob par* for *'grub par* in our text [the *Guhyasamāja Tantra* also has *'thob par* here]. *Gsang 'dus*, *Guhyasamāja Tantra*, chap. 7, Tōh 442; Zhol 11a6; Stog 18b6–7; Dunh 19b2; Fremantle 1971, v. 33; and Matsunaga 1978, v. 33.

2360. See Tsong kha pa, *Sgron gsal mchan*, 180a1–4.

clear."[2361] But in the seventh chapter of the *Illuminating Lamp* the verses of the *Vajra Garland Tantra* "included in the form aggregate"[2362] and so forth are applied to awakening in the intermediate state,[2363] while in the eleventh chapter of the *Illuminating Lamp* the verses of the *Vajra Garland Tantra* are applied to the entry of the illusory body into clear light in this life,[2364] and *Formulating the Sādhana* applies them both to the stages of death at the ground and to the completion stage on the path.[2365] Nevertheless, as explained earlier,[2366] each vajra word of the tantra imparts many different meanings; [91a] moreover all these cases are but the entry of the aggregates and so forth into clear light according to the stages of death at the ground. Thus, given that these verses are suitable in all of these cases, Nāgārjuna and his disciples cite them for each one.

[*The Meaning of the Lines of the* **Guhyasamāja Root Tantra** *in Terms of the Entry of the Specially Visualized Deities into Clear Light*][2367]

The *Guhyasamāja Root Tantra* teaches: "The semen issued from union[2368] according to the ritual method."[2369] *Union* here is the union of method and wisdom, the father and mother, at the ground time; *semen* is the seed that arises when the father and mother absorb in union; and *issue* is the coming forth. When the consciousness of the intermediate state enters into this seed, the embryo gradually develops through the phases in the womb, "the

2361. Nāgārjuna, *Mdor byas, Piṇḍīkrama Sādhana*, Tōh 1796, 3b1; L 38cd; T 37cd. D has *'di don* for *'di ni* in our text, the Sanskrit is *asyārtha*.

2362. These are the lines of the *Rgyud rdo rje phreng ba, Vajramālā Tantra*, chap. 68, Tōh 445, 275a7–b1, that are cited in a different form in Nāgārjuna, *Mdor byas, Piṇḍīkrama Sādhana*, Tōh 1796, 3b1–2; L 39; T 38.

2363. Candrakīrti, *Sgron gsal, Pradīpoddyotanaṭīkā*, Tōh 1785, 54b7–55a1; Chakravarti 1984, 70.

2364. Candrakīrti, *Sgron gsal, Pradīpoddyotanaṭīkā*, Tōh 1785, 80b5–6; Chakravarti 1984, 100. See also Tsong kha pa, *Sgron gsal mchan*, 241b5.

2365. Nāgabuddhi, *Rnam gzhag rim pa, Vyavastholi*, chap. 4, Tōh 1809, 129b3–4; Tanaka 2016, 128–129. See also Tsong kha pa, *Rnam gzhag rim pa'i rnam bshad*, 77b2–5.

2366. See above [25b3] and [90b6].

2367. In Candrakīrti, *Sgron gsal, Pradīpoddyotanaṭīkā*, Tōh 1785, 54b5–7; Chakravarti 1984, 69–70, and in Tsong kha pa, *Sgron gsal mchan*, 179a1–6. See also Tsong kha pa's *Bskyed rim zin bris*, 20b4–21a3.

2368. Tib. *dam tshig*, Skt. *samaya*.

2369. *Guhyasamāja Tantra*, chap. 7, Tōh 442; Zhol 11a6; Stog 18b6–7; Dunh 19b2; Fremantle 1971, v. 33a; and Matsunaga 1978, v. 33a, cited above [89b].

liquid-cream-like fetus"[2370] and so forth,[2371] attains the stages of a child, youth, and adult, with all the aggregates, sensory spheres, and sense bases complete, and experiences the five sensual pleasures. Thus the *Illuminating Lamp* teaches that this line refers to meditators born from a womb.[2372]

What should the meditators do after they have attained their own complete aggregates and so forth from their father and mother?[2373] The *Guhyasamāja Root Tantra* teaches: "Those who desire the fruit should drink according to the ritual method."[2374] *They should drink* means they should dissolve into clear light. What should they dissolve? Their own aggregates, sensory spheres, and sense bases, which have become indivisible from the deities of the maṇḍala. How? *According to the ritual method* taught in the *Vajra Garland Tantra*: "That which is included in the form aggregate"[2375] and so forth. For what purpose? Because they *desire the fruit* of attaining the body of union of Vajradhara purified by clear light in the future.

Then *Guhyasamāja Root Tantra* teaches: "When they slay the assembly of tathāgatas, they will achieve the supreme siddhi."[2376] Thus they *slay the assembly* of the five aggregates, taught by the designation tathāgatas.[2377] During the completion stage, the meditators slay them by dissolving the moving winds into the central channel of the subtle body as in the death process. But here during the creation stage the meditators slay them by visualizing their dissolution according to the death process [91b] and by concentrating on this visualization, *they will achieve the supreme siddhi.*

You should understand it in this way because the explanation on awakening

2370. Tib. *mer mer po*, Skt. *kalala*.

2371. See the stages of development of the fetus below [110a].

2372. This explanation is found in Candrakīrti, *Sgron gsal, Pradīpoddyotanaṭīkā*, Tōh 1785, 54b5–6; Chakravarti 1984, 69. See also Tsong kha pa, *Sgron gsal mchan*, 179a6.

2373. See Candrakīrti, *Sgron gsal, Pradīpoddyotanaṭīkā*, Tōh 1785, 54b7–55a1; Chakravarti 1984, 70; and Tsong kha pa, *Sgron gsal mchan*, 179a6–b2.

2374. *Guhyasamāja Tantra*, chap. 7, Tōh 442; Zhol 11a6; Stog 18b6–7; Dunh 19b2; Fremantle 1971, v. 33ab; and Matsunaga 1978, v. 33ab.

2375. *Rgyud rdo rje phreng ba, Vajramālā Tantra*, chap. 68, Tōh 445, 275a7–b1. These lines are cited in a different form in Nāgārjuna, *Mdor byas, Piṇḍīkrama Sādhana*, Tōh 1796, 3b1–2; L 39; T 38.

2376. *Guhyasamāja Tantra*, chap. 7, Tōh 442; Zhol 11a6; Stog 18b6–7; Dunh 19b2; Fremantle 1971, v. 33cd; and Matsunaga 1978, v. 33cd.

2377. This alludes to the line "The five aggregates are proclaimed as the five buddhas" in the *Guhyasamāja Tantra*, chap. 17, Tōh 442; Zhol 44a6–7; Stog 82b5; Dunh 148.4; Fremantle 1971, v 50; and Matsunaga 1978, v. 50. See Candrakīrti, *Sgron gsal, Pradīpoddyotanaṭīkā*, Tōh 1785, 55a2–5; Chakravarti 1984, 70; and Tsong kha pa, *Sgron gsal mchan*, 179a3–b1.

in this life—as in this context—is often equally applied to awakening in the intermediate state. Therefore, in the introduction to this verse, the *Illuminating Lamp* elucidates: "Here, in what follows, the *Guhyasamāja Root Tantra* teaches this verse in order to explain the method of entering into the highest limit by means of the maṇḍala of ultimate truth, equally[2378] for all yogis."[2379]

[The Stages Through Which the Specially Visualized Deities Enter into Clear Light]

These are explained in the *Vajra Garland Explanatory Tantra*:

1. Included in the form aggregate are the mirror-like wisdom, the earth element, the eye faculty, and form as the fifth aspect,[2380] together with the two fierce deities;[2381]
2. The aggregate of feeling, the wisdom of equanimity, the water element, the ear faculty, and sound as the fifth aspect, together with the two fierce deities;
3. The aggregate of perceptions, the wisdom of discernment, the element of fire, the nose faculty, and scent as the fifth aspect, together with the two fierce deities;
4. The aggregate of conditioning, the wisdom of purposive acts, the air-wind element, the tongue faculty, and taste as the fifth aspect, together with the two fierce deities;
5. The natural appearances together with the fierce deities above and below enter the aggregate of consciousness, and consciousness too enters into

2378. Tib. *thun mong ba*, Skt. *sādhāraṇa*. This is the reason for the assertion, just above, that the explanation on awakening in this life is often equally applied to awakening in the intermediate state.

2379. Candrakīrti, *Sgron gsal*, *Pradīpoddyotanaṭīkā*, Tōh 1785, 54b4–5; Chakravarti 1984, 69, just before the explanation of v. 33 of the *Guhyasamāja Tantra*. See also Tsong kha pa, *Rnam gzhag rim pa'i rnam bshad*, 78b2–3.

2380. The Sanskrit has here *rūpaṃ ca pañcamaṃ*. This form is repeated below.

2381. The Sanskrit of Nāgārjuna's *Mdor byas*, *Piṇḍīkrama Sādhana*, Tōh 1796; L 39; T 38, adds here Maitreya, Byams pa. Nāgabuddhi's *Rnam gzhag rim pa*, *Vyavastholi*, chap. 4, Tōh 1809, 129b6; Tanaka 2016, 130, which cites this passage as well, has here *khro bo byams par yang dag ldan* for *khro bo gnyis dang yang dag ldan* in the *Mdor byas* and in our text; the Sanskrit according to Tanaka is *maitreyasaṃyutaṃ*.

clear light. This is explained as "accompanied by nirvāṇa," all-empty, and *dharmakāya*.[2382]

Now I will explain their meaning. In order to transform death into the dharmakāya, you must generate the four wisdoms of the four empty states, whereby your aggregates and so forth dissolve as in the process of death at the ground. This meditation on the specially visualized deities entering clear light during the creation stage serves to ripen the cultivation of the wisdoms of the empties through a similar process of dissolving the winds during the completion stage. [92a] Therefore here too the deities set upon your body—which have become indivisible entities with your aggregates and so forth—do not dissolve into clear light all at once.

Nor is it certain that the members of the five tathāgata families dissolve according to their own families, for it is taught that Khagarbha and Amitābha,[2383] and likewise Lokeśvara and Amoghasiddhi,[2384] dissolve simultaneously and so forth. Therefore, in the meditation here, the deities—united indivisibly with your aggregates and so forth—dissolve into clear light according to the stages of dissolution for the twenty-five coarse elements during death at the ground time. The twenty-five coarse elements are the five aggregates, the four physical elements, the six sensory spheres, the five sense bases, and the five wisdoms of the ground time.[2385]

[The Five Dissolutions]

(1) When persons who are born from a womb and are endowed with the six constituents die in stages,[2386] the form aggregate is the first to dissolve,[2387]

2382. The *Rgyud rdo rje phreng ba*, *Vajramālā Tantra*, Tōh 445. Our text follows the readings in Nāgārjuna's *Mdor byas*, *Piṇḍīkrama Sādhana*, Tōh 1796, 3b1–4; L 39–44ab; T 38–43ab, and in the Nāgabuddhi's *Rnam gzhag rim pa*, *Vyavastholi*, chap. 4, Tōh 1809, 129b6–130a2; Tanaka 2016, 129–131.

2383. Tib. Nam snying and 'Od dpag med.

2384. Tib. 'Jig rten dbang phyug and Don grub.

2385. Tib. *phung po lnga*, *khams bzhi*, *skye mched drug*, *yul lnga*, and *ye shes lnga*; the five *skandhas*, four *dhātus*, six *āyatanas*, five *viṣayas*, and five *jñānas*.

2386. See Tsong kha pa's *Mtha' gcod*, 99a6–102a3, and *Bung ba'i re skong*, 15b4–17a2, and also his *Rnam gzhag rim pa'i rnam bshad*, 82b1–6, which in turn are based on Nāgabuddhi, *Rnam gzhag rim pa*, *Vyavastholi*, chap. 4, Tōh 1809, 129b4–130b5; Tanaka 2016, 129–135.

2387. See Nāgabuddhi, *Rnam gzhag rim pa*, *Vyavastholi*, chap. 4, Tōh 1809, 130a2–5; Tanaka 2016, 131–132.

whereupon all the limbs become attenuated, and the body declines and loses its strength. The mirror-like wisdom of the ground time is explained in the *Compendium of Practices* as the simultaneous appearance of many objects, much as reflected images appear in a mirror.[2388] When the mirror-like wisdom dissolves, vision becomes blurred and cloudy. When the earth element dissolves, the entire body becomes very dry. Then, when the eye faculty dissolves, dying persons are no longer able to open and close their eyes. When the forms within one's continuum[2389] dissolve simultaneously, the complexion of the body fades, and it diminishes in strength. The forms within one's continuum are not outer forms but one's own bodily forms included within one's continuum.

Accordingly, you should first visualize the deities uniting indivisibly with your body: Vairocana, Locanā, Kṣitigarbha, and Rūpavajrā dissolving into clear light.[2390] Furthermore, the line *together with the two fierce deities*[2391] [92b] means that you need to visualize Yamāntaka and Acala dissolving as well.[2392] The reason for this is that they belong to the form aggregate, and thus, when the form aggregate dissolves, they too dissolve. Although Maitreya is not mentioned here explicitly,[2393] the implication is that he dissolves at that time.

(2) After the dissolution of the form aggregate during death at the ground, the aggregate of feeling dissolves.[2394] At that time the dying person does not experience feelings of sensory consciousness that depend on the combination of wind, bile, phlegm, and so forth. The wisdom of equanimity at the ground is

2388. Āryadeva's *Spyod bsdus, Caryāmelāpakapradīpa*, chap. 2, Tōh 1803, 65a7–b1; Sanskrit, Tibetan, and English translation in Wedemeyer 2007, A: 13a; Sanskrit and Tibetan in Pandey 2000, 16 and 186. These lines are paraphrased also in Bu ston, *Mdor byas 'grel chen*, 29a4–5; Tsong kha pa, *Mtha' gcod*, 99b5, *Bung ba'i re skong*, 17a5–b3, and his *Rnam gzhag rim pa'i rnam bshad*, 80b1. See also Dbyangs can dga' ba'i blo gros, *Gzhi sku gsum gyi rnam gzhag*, 2b1–2; English translation in Lati Rinbochay and Hopkins 1979, 35.

2389. Tib. *yul gzugs*. Nāgabuddhi has *gzugs kyi yul* in his *Rnam gzhag rim pa, Vyavastholi*, chap. 4, Tōh 1809, 130a4. The Sanskrit, according to Tanaka 2016, 131, is *rūpaviṣaya*.

2390. Tib. Rnam snang, Spyan ma, Sa'i snying po, and Gzugs rdo rje ma.

2391. In the *Rgyud rdo rje phreng ba, Vajramālā Tantra*, Tōh 445, cited on [91b] above.

2392. Tib. Gshin rje gshed and Mi g.yo.

2393. According to Tsong kha pa, *Gsang mngon*, 38b4, Maitreya also dissolves here. As was noted above, according to the Sanskrit of Nāgārjuna's *Mdor byas, Piṇḍīkrama Sādhana*, Tōh 1796; L 39; T 38, and Nāgabuddhi's *Rnam gzhag rim pa, Vyavastholi*, chap. 4, Tōh 1809, 129b6; Tanaka 2016, 130, Maitreya also dissolves here.

2394. See Nāgabuddhi, *Rnam gzhag rim pa, Vyavastholi*, chap. 4, Tōh 1809, 130a5–b1; Tanaka 2016, 132–133.

explained in the *Compendium of Practices*[2395] as understanding sentient beings with no legs and those with two legs as the same phenomenal aspect in being "mind only."[2396] When the wisdom of equanimity dissolves, mental consciousness is no longer mindful of the three feelings.[2397] When the water element dissolves, the body's saliva, sweat, urine, blood, semen, and so forth nearly dry up. When at the same time the ear faculty dissolves, the outer and inner sounds are no longer heard. When the sound within one's continuum[2398] dissolves, the humming sound inside the ear no longer arises.

Accordingly, you should visualize the deities united indivisibly with your body: Ratnasaṃbhava, Māmakī, Vajrapāṇi, Śabdhavajrā, and the two fierce deities, Prajñāntaka and Ṭakkirāja,[2399] who belong to the tathāgata family of Ratnasaṃbhava and are included in the series of dissolutions of the aggregate of feelings, all dissolve into clear light.[2400]

(3) During death at the ground following that, the aggregate of perception dissolves.[2401] The *Compendium of Practices* explains that since perception is the discernment of the category of sentient beings as two-legged, four legged, and so forth, when perception dissolves, the distinctions between these sentient beings no longer appear.[2402] The wisdom of discernment at the time of

2395. This is based on Tsong kha pa's *Mtha' gcod*, 100a5, and *Rnam gzhag rim pa'i rnam bshad*, 80b3–4, which paraphrase Āryadeva's *Spyod bsdus, Caryāmelāpakapradīpa*, chap. 2, Tōh 1803, 65b1–2; Sanskrit, Tibetan, and English translation in Wedemeyer 2007, A: 13a; Sanskrit and Tibetan in Pandey 2000, 16 and 186.

2396. Tib. *sems tsam*, Skt. *cittamātra*.

2397. According to Tsong kha pa's *Mtha' gcod*, 100a5–6, the dying person is no longer mindful of the three feelings of mental consciousness. Dbyangs can dga' ba'i blo gros, *Gzhi sku gsum gyi rnam gzhag*, 3a1, explains that the dying person is no longer mindful of pleasure, pain, and neutral feelings that accompany mental consciousness.

2398. Tib. *yul sgra*.

2399. Or Ṭarkvirāja. Tib. Shes rab mthar byed and 'Dod rgyal.

2400. Tib. Rin 'byung, Māmakī, Phyag rdor, Sgra rdo rje ma, and also the two fierce ones Shes rab mthar byed and 'Dod rgyal. See Tsong kha pa, *Gsang mngon*, 38b5–6, which has Gzhan gyis mi thub pa, Aparājita, instead of Shes rab mthar byed here.

2401. See Nāgabuddhi, *Rnam gzhag rim pa, Vyavastholi*, chap. 4, Tōh 1809, 130b1–3, Tanaka 2016, 133–134.

2402. This is based on Tsong kha pa's *Mtha' gcod*, 100b1, and *Rnam gzhag rim pa'i rnam bshad*, 83a6–b1, which paraphrase Āryadeva's *Spyod bsdus, Caryāmelāpakapradīpa*, chap. 6, Tōh 1803, 61b7–62a1; Sanskrit, Tibetan, and English translation in Wedemeyer 2007, A: 8a, C: 45a–b; Sanskrit and Tibetan in Pandey 2000, 20 and 173. Nāgabuddhi's *Rnam gzhag rim pa, Vyavastholi*, chap. 4, Tōh 1809, 130b1; Tanaka 2016, 133; and Tsong kha pa's *Rnam gzhag rim pa'i rnam bshad*, 83b1, have *dran par mi 'gyur* for *mi snang bar 'gyur* in our text (the dying person no longer recognizes these sentient beings).

the ground is explained as discernment of names.[2403] Hence when it dissolves, dying persons no longer remember names.[2404] [93a] When the fire of the body dissolves, the ability to digest food diminishes. When the nose faculty dissolves simultaneously, the inhalation of air through the nose lessens, while exhalation becomes forceful and long. When scent within the body dissolves, dying persons can no longer smell their bodies.

Accordingly, you should visualize the deities indivisibly united with your body: Amitābha, Pāṇḍaravāsinī, Khagarbha, Gandhavajrā, Hayagrīva, and Nīladaṇḍa dissolving into clear light.[2405] Why is it that both Avalokiteśvara and Mañjuśrī, who belong to the tathāgata family of Amitābha, are missing here, while Khagarbha, who belongs to the tathāgata family of Ratnasaṃbhava, is added?[2406] In the main category here are the aggregates from form up to consciousness, and since the earlier they are, the coarser they are, and the later they are, the more subtle they are, they dissolve in the order of their coarseness [from coarse to subtler]. Therefore, as each of the aggregates dissolve, the elements, faculties, objects of the senses, and limbs that dissolve simultaneously are taken as one category. Therefore the nose faculty does not dissolve when the aggregate of feelings dissolve[2407] but rather when the aggregate of perception dissolves.[2408] Thus, although Khagarbha belongs to the tathāgata family of Ratnasaṃbhava, in terms of the stages of dissolution, it is taught that Khagarbha is included in the series of dissolution of Amitābha. The others follow the same pattern as well.

(4) When during death at the ground following that, the aggregate of conditioning[2409] dissolves, the person dying is no longer able to move, act,

2403. This is based on Tsong kha pa's *Mtha' gcod*, 100b2, and *Rnam gzhag rim pa'i rnam bshad*, 80b5, which paraphrase Āryadeva's *Spyod bsdus*, *Caryāmelāpakapradīpa*, chap. 6, Tōh 1803, 65b2–3; Sanskrit, Tibetan, and English translation in Wedemeyer 2007, A: 13b; Sanskrit and Tibetan in Pandey 2000, 16 and 187.

2404. According to Nāgabuddhi, *Rnam gzhag rim pa*, *Vyavastholi*, chap. 4, Tōh 1809, 130b1–2, Tanaka 2016, 133, the dying persons no longer remember also the names of their relatives and so forth.

2405. Tib. 'Od dpag med, Gos dkar mo, Nam mkha'i snying po, Dri rdo rje ma, Rta mgrin, and Dbyug sngon can. See Tsong kha pa, *Gsang mngon*, 38b6–39a1.

2406. See Tsong kha pa, *Mtha' gcod*, 100b3–6, and *Rnam gzhag rim pa'i rnam bshad*, 83b2–5.

2407. The aggregate of feelings dissolves in the second dissolution together with Rin 'byung, while the nose faculty dissolves in the third dissolution together with 'Od dpag med.

2408. The nose faculty dissolves together with the aggregate of perception in the third dissolution together with 'Od dpag med.

2409. Tib. *'du byed*, Skt. *saṃskāra*.

and so forth.[2410] The wisdom of purposeful acts at the ground is explained as knowing how to accomplish one's own purposes.[2411] When that dissolves, the person dying is no longer mindful of any external activity and purpose typical of ordinary people. When at that time the air-wind element dissolves, the ten winds[2412]—the "life-sustaining wind"[2413] and so forth—shift from their respective places. It is taught that at this point the tactile faculty and the "definitely moving wind"[2414] that perform the tactual activities must dissolve. [93b] Therefore just as when the four faculties—the eye and so forth—dissolve, the four objects of the senses—forms and so forth—dissolve, so here too the objects of touch must dissolve. When at that time the tongue faculty dissolves, the tongue becomes swollen and short, and its root turns blue. When the taste within one's continuum[2415] dissolves, the person dying no longer experiences any of the six tastes.

In accordance with these dissolutions, you should meditate on the deities uniting indivisibly with your body: Amoghasiddhi, Tārā, Lokeśvara, Rasavajrā, Samantabhadra, Vighnāntaka, and Mahābala dissolve into clear light.[2416] Additionally,[2417] just as with the dissolution of the tactile faculty, the objects of touch dissolve, so with the dissolution of Ṣarvanīvaraṇaviṣkambhin,[2418] Sparśavajrā[2419] must dissolve simultaneously. Therefore, when you gather the deities into your body, visualize Sparśavajrā

2410. See Nāgabuddhi, *Rnam gzhag rim pa*, *Vyavastholi*, chap. 4, Tōh 1809, 130b3–4; Tanaka 2016, 134–135.

2411. This is based on Tsong kha pa, *Mtha' gcod*, 100b6–101a1, and *Rnam gzhag rim pa'i rnam bshad*, 80b6, which paraphrase Āryadeva's *Spyod bsdus*, *Caryāmelāpakapradīpa*, Tōh 1803, 65b3; Sanskrit, Tibetan, and English translation in Wedemeyer 2007, A: 13b; Sanskrit and Tibetan in Pandey 2000, 16 and 187.

2412. For the ten winds, the five main winds, and five ancillary winds, see, for example, Āryadeva, *Spyod bsdus*, *Caryāmelāpakapradīpa*, chap. 2, Tōh 1803, 64b4; Sanskrit, Tibetan, and English translation in Wedemeyer 2007, A: 12a; Sanskrit and Tibetan in Pandey 2000, 25 and 183; and also Tsong kha pa, *Rnam gzhag rim pa'i rnam bshad*, 83b6–84a1.

2413. Tib. *srog 'dzin*, Skt. *prāṇa*.

2414. Tib. *nges par brgyu ba'i rlung*, one of the ancillary winds.

2415. Tib. *yul ro*.

2416. Tib. Don grub, Sgrol ma, 'Jig rten dbang phyug, Rdo rde rje ma, Kun bzang, Bgegs mthar byed, and Stobs po che. See Tsong kha pa, *Gsang mngon*, 39a1–2.

2417. This following paragraph is not found in Tsong kha pa's *Mtha' gcod*, unlike the rest of the description here.

2418. Tib. Sgrib pa thams cad rnam sel.

2419. Tib. Reg bya Rdo rje ma, Eng., Vajra Lady of Tangibles.

embracing you and entering into your body,[2420] and then embracing Sarvanīvaraṇaviṣkambhin[2421] at your vajra gate,[2422] and meditate on her as the essence of all the elements of touch in your body.

(5) The *Vajra Garland Tantra* teaches: "The natural appearance together with the fierce deities above and below enter the aggregate of consciousness, and consciousness too enters into clear light. This was explained as 'accompanied by nirvāṇa,' all-empty, and dharmakāya."[2423] *The fierce deities above and below* means the two fierce deities set on the crown of the head and the soles of the feet,[2424] *greatly*[2425] means perfectly,[2426] and *together*[2427] means having, but the latter does not indicate Sparśavajrā.[2428] *Natural appearance* means the eighty intrinsic conceptual minds[2429] and the three total appearances free of conceptualization.[2430] *They enter the aggregate of consciousness, and consciousness too enters into clear light* means that following the earlier dissolutions during death at the ground, the eighty intrinsic conceptual minds dissolve into "appearance,"[2431] "appearance" dissolves into "enhanced

2420. Reg bya Rdo rje ma is not only the consort of the yogi as the principal deity but also the consort of Sgrib sel. See Tsong kha pa, *Gsang mngon*, 44b3.

2421. Tib. Sgrib pa thams cad rnam sel.

2422. Reg bya rdo rje ma is set at the vajra gate, Tsong kha pa, *Gsang mngon*, 44b1–5.

2423. See the citation from the *Rgyud rdo rje phreng ba, Vajramālā Tantra*, Tōh 445, above [91b]; and Nāgārjuna, *Mdor byas, Piṇḍīkrama Sādhana*, Tōh 1796, 3b3; L 43; T 42. This passage is based on Tsong kha pa, *Rnam gzhag rim pa'i rnam bshad*, 81a1–4.

2424. These are Uṣṇīṣacakravartin and Sumbharāja, Tib. Gtsug tor 'khor los bsgyur ba and Gnod mdzes rgyal po respectively; see Tsong kha pa, *Gsang mngon*, 39a2–3.

2425. This refers to Tib. *shin tu*, Skt. *saṃ*, in *shin tu bcas, saṃyuktaṃ*.

2426. Tib. *yang dag par*.

2427. Tib. *bcas pa*, Skt. *yuktaṃ*.

2428. In his *Mdor byas 'grel chen*, 30b3–4, Bu ston explains that Reg bya rdo rje ma, Sparśavajrā, dissolves in fifth cycle, by interpreting the phrase *shin tu bcas* as together with Reg bya rdo rje ma. See also Tsong kha pa, *Mtha' gcod*, 101a3–4, and *Rnam gzhag rim pa'i rnam bshad*, 81a1.

2429. Tib. *rtog pa rang bzhin brgyad cu*. Āryadeva, *Spyod bsdus, Caryāmelāpakapradīpa*, chap. 4, Tōh 1803, 78b3–4; Sanskrit, Tibetan, and English translation in Wedemeyer 2007, A: 31b; Sanskrit and Tibetan in Pandey 2000, 44 and 242. D, Pandey, and Wedemeyer have *rang bzhin rnam pa brgyad [b]cu*.

2430. Tib. *rtog med kun tu snang pa gsum*. As noted in the section "Dissolution of the Specially Visualized Deities into Clear Light" above, while the Tibetan has "a genitive" here (*rang bzhin gyi ni snang ba nyid*), this term is a coordinative compound (*dvandva*) meaning, instrisic natures and appearances.

2431. Tib. *snang ba*, Skt. *āloka*.

appearance,"[2432] "enhanced appearance" into "approaching attainment,"[2433] and then "approaching attainment" dissolves into clear light. This clear light is the experience of the clear light of death, also synonymous with all-empty and dharmakāya. [94a] Such is the meaning of the line *This was explained as "accompanied by nirvāṇa," all-empty, and dharmakāya*.

You must be skilled in the usages of quite a few terms, such as the three bodies, the five wisdoms, nirvāṇa, and the realization of ultimate truth not only in the contexts of the path and the fruit but also with regard to the time of the ground and the ways in which the terms birth, death, and intermediate state are used not only with reference to the time of the ground but also in relation to the two stages on the path—the creation and completion stages. Therefore you should visualize the deities indivisibly united with your body: Uṣṇīṣacakravartin, Sumbharāja, and Mañjuśrī[2434] dissolving into clear light, in correspondence with the way consciousness and the empty states dissolve during death at the ground.[2435]

[Further Explanations on the Dissolutions]

Since the dissolutions of the three empty states here are dissolutions of mental faculties, why is it not taught that the sensory sphere of mental objects[2436] and the sense bases of mental objects[2437] dissolve at the same time? It is not taught at this point because the compounded aspects of the sensory sphere of mental objects and the sense bases of mental objects have been included in the previous dissolutions, and the uncompounded aspects cannot dissolve into clear light here.[2438]

Why is it not taught that wisdom dissolves simultaneously with consciousness as before? According to the *Compendium of Practices*, the wisdom of the dharma realm at the ground is consciousness purifying karma and afflictive

2432. Tib. *mched* or *snang ba mched pa*, Skt. *ālokābhāsa*.

2433. Tib. *thob* or *snang ba thob pa*, Skt. *ālokopalabdha*.

2434. Tib. Gtsug tor 'khor los bsgyur ba, Gnod mdzes rgyal po, and 'Jam dpal.

2435. See Tsong kha pa, *Gsang mngon*, 39a2–3.

2436. The last among the eighteen sensory spheres.

2437. The last among the twelve medias of perception.

2438. See Tsong kha pa, *Mtha' gcod*, 101b2–3, and *Rnam gzhag rim pa'i rnam bshad*, 81a4–6.

emotions.[2439] Being a type of consciousness, it is not taught separately and has been dissolved already together with consciousness.

It is taught that the ways of entering clear light during death at the ground and during the completion stage are largely similar. Hence you should understand that the stage of death whereby the clear light of death gradually manifests at the time of the ground to an ordinary person born from a womb and endowed with the six constituents is similar to the manifestation of the clear light to a meditator on the completion stage achieved through the power of yoga. [94b] This is the special token of Ārya Nāgārjuna and his disciples, a convention known only in their system of teaching. Due to this, when meditators attain the illusory saṃbhogakāya, they attain it in the same way that the intermediate being is attained.[2440]

Since the verses from the scriptures cited above were taught in the context of the dissolution of the specially visualized deities into clear light, you should understand the essential points of this profound transmitted instruction as follows: Even as a novice in the yoga who has not yet attained the capacity to practice the completion stage, you should practice the sādhana during the four sessions, and when the moment of your death approaches, you will have habituated the transmitted instruction on the dissolution of the specially visualized deities into clear light. For you must first develop a good intellectual understanding of deity yoga and the stages of dissolution explained above. Then you may gather the specially visualized deities into your body and maintain a stable meditation with the resolve: My such-and-such aggregate is such-and-such a deity. Then you should focus one-pointedly on visualizing the appearances of the respective deities on the respective locations on your body, as explained in the case of the body maṇḍala below. And when the signs of the dissolution of the form aggregates, the eye faculty, and so forth, explained earlier, begin to arise, you will recognize them, reflecting: "This is a sign of dissolution."

After your form aggregate, which is indivisible from Vairocana, your eye faculty, which is indivisible from Kṣitigarbha, and so forth dissolve into the clear light of indivisible bliss and emptiness, you should cultivate a stable meditation on the successive dissolutions into the continuing state of clear light realized by the wisdom of indivisible great bliss and emptiness—empty of intrinsic existence. Then, maintaining a stable divine identity as Vajradhara,

2439. This is based on Tsong kha pa's *Mtha' gcod*, 101b3–5, and *Rnam gzhag rim pa'i rnam bshad*, 81a6–b1, which cites Āryadeva's *Spyod bsdus*, *Caryāmelāpakapradīpa*, Tōh 1803, 65b3–4; Sanskrit, Tibetan, and English translation in Wedemeyer 2007, A: 13b; Sanskrit and Tibetan in Pandey 2000, 16–17 and 187.

2440. See Tsong kha pa, *Mtha' gcod*, 101b4–102a2.

visualize this deity's body turning into a sphere of light, and this light [95a] withdrawn from above and below into your heart—as steam evaporates on a mirror—and dissolved completely into the continuing state of wisdom of indivisible bliss and emptiness. Be mindful of this wisdom as long as you maintain your mindfulness. This is the supreme transmitted instruction on the transfer of consciousness at death. Currently in Tibet, there is a well-known transmitted instruction on the transfer of consciousness regarded as impressive. To receive it, one must propitiate the lamas with offerings of nothing but gold. But for all its grand names, it cannot rival [this consciousness transfer of ours].[2441]

Here then is an example for the dissolution of the specially visualized deities into clear light: Visualizing yourself as Vajradhara, meditate on Kṣitigarbha embraced by Rūpavajrā[2442] at the centers of your two eyeballs, and then maintain the conviction that the two deities are the essence of your eye faculty and the entire sensory sphere of the forms in your body. Then, do not merely think "Kṣitigarbha and his consort have dissolved into clear light," but observe how your eye faculty and your sensory sphere of forms, which arose in the appearance of Kṣitigarbha with his consort, enter into the dharmakāya of indivisible bliss and emptiness. In this way, too, you should understand the other dissolutions. Habituation in this way will become a special and smooth ripener for a swift entry of the winds—the wind that circulates through the eye and so forth—into the central channel of the subtle body, and for the arising of the clear light during the completion stage.

[Meditation on the Emptiness Mantra]

Following the meditation on the dissolutions, you should meditate on the meaning of the mantra as the *Concise Sādhana* teaches: "In order to stabilize, you should recite the mantra *oṃ śūnyatā jñāna vajra svabhāva ātmako 'haṃ*."[2443] [95b] EARLY LAMAS[2444] explain that *to stabilize* in this instance means to stabilize the ultimate truth maṇḍala, but it seems that they do not understand the purpose of the mantra. Know, therefore, that the purpose of the mantra is to stabilize your divine identity as the dharmakāya when you dissolve yourself in clear light.[2445]

2441. This seems to refer to the 'Bri gung 'pho ba chen mo. See Kapstein 1998.

2442. Tib. Gzugs rdo rje ma, Eng., Vajra Lady of Forms.

2443. Nāgārjuna, *Mdor byas*, *Piṇḍīkrama Sādhana*, Tōh 1796, 3b4; L 44cd; T 43cd.

2444. See Bu ston, *Mdor byas 'grel chen*, 31a5–6.

2445. See Tsong kha pa, *Sgron gsal mchan*, 98b5–6.

How to meditate on the meaning of the mantra? There are two ways to explain the meaning of this mantra: The first way is to translate the Sanskrit words. But since the translation of individual words does not necessarily elucidate the meaning of the mantra, a second way would be to explain what the mantra signifies through signs conveyed by the Buddha that are undisclosed to others. The first way has already been followed in the context of meditating on the ground of wisdom. *Śūnyatā* is translated as emptiness, *jñāna* as wisdom, and so forth. Grammarians who only examine the meaning of the mantra to this extent may be thorough in their own ways, but they can only understand it in a limited way.

As for the second meaning,[2446] as the *Revelation of the Intention* teaches: "Recite *oṃ* as the first, *śūnyatā* as the second, *jñāna* as the third, *vajra* as the fourth, *svabhāvātmako* as the fifth, and *ahaṃ* as the sixth. In this way the six sugatas were taught to the supreme beings."[2447] The profound meaning of the transmitted instruction on the vajra recitation is explained by pointing out that the six segments of the mantra signify successively the five main winds of the subtle body, which are the winds of the five lords, and the indestructible drop at the heart. And similarly, pointing out that dividing this mantra into three parts forms three pairs, signifies the arising, entering, and abiding of the winds. [96a] This is how the supreme essential points of the vajra recitation are taught, and there are other similar explanations. No matter how much the grammarians probe the meaning of this mantra, how can they possibly understand it even in part? It is not in the domain of the lower tantras, nor even in that of meditators on the creation stage.

Therefore, when SOME TIBETAN LAMAS[2448] explain the meaning of the mantra taught in the *Concise Sādhana*,[2449] citing the scripture of the *Revelation of the Intention*,[2450] their explanation is entirely irrelevant. How can THEY

2446. See Tsong kha pa, *Sgron gsal mchan*, 139b5–140a5.

2447. See Nāgabuddhi, *Rnam gzhag rim pa*, *Vyavastholi*, chap. 4, Tōh 1809, 130b6–131a1; Tanaka 2016, 136, which attributes these lines to an explanatory tantra. Tsong kha pa specifies in his *Rnam gzhag rim pa'i rnam bshad*, 87a2, that this tantra is the *Dgongs pa lung ston*, *Sandhivyākaraṇa Tantra*, Tōh 444; see chap. 3, 170a4–5. Note that this mantra appears in the third chapter of the *Guhyasamāja Tantra*. The version of the *Dgongs pa lung ston* is slightly different from that of the *Rnam gzhag rim pa* and from our text. D has *oṃ ni gcig dang yang dag ldan* for *oṃ ni dang po gcig dang ldan*; *jñāna zhes ni sum pa yin* for *jñāna zhes ni sum pa nyid*; and *vajra zhes bya bzhi pa'o* for *vajra zhes pa bzhi pa'o* in our text.

2448. See Bu ston, *Mdor byas 'grel chen*, 32a3–7.

2449. Nāgārjuna, *Mdor byas*, *Piṇḍīkrama Sādhana*, Tōh 1796, is an instruction on the creation stage, not on the vajra recitation during the completion stage.

2450. The *Dgongs pa lung ston*, *Sandhivyākaraṇa Tantra*, chap. 3, Tōh 444, 170a.

say that the meaning of the mantra on which practitioners of the creation stage meditate is the vajra recitation on which only practitioners of the completion stage should meditate? Furthermore, it seems that they do not even begin to understand the meaning of each element when the mantra is divided into three and six segments.[2451] But since it would be too verbose, I will refrain from writing my refutations and affirmations here.

Therefore in this case you should meditate on the meaning of the mantra as explained above. And after reciting the mantra, you should remain in the divine identity of the dharmakāya with the resolve "The invisible nature of emptiness pure by nature and the wisdom that is its subject, that am I."[2452]

Following that, the *Concise Sādhana* teaches: "This is the ultimate maṇḍala, without appearance, without marks, called the ultimate truth, the abode of all tathāgatas."[2453] Thus this, which is designated the ultimate truth, free of mental proliferations of dualistic appearance, which merges into one taste with the emptiness—devoid of existence by its own characteristics—that appears to the subjective mind, is the source of all tathāgatas. The actual clear light of the meditators on the completion stage is the source of all deities of the meditators on the stage of union. [96b] Whereas here the ultimate truth dharmakāya of the meditators on the creation stage, the clear light into which the specially visualized deities have been dissolved, is the source of all the deities, beginning from the saṃbhogakāya, the First Lord, and up to the Supreme King of Maṇḍalas.[2454] Here the explanation about the specially visualized deities is completed.

2451. Bu ston, in his *Mdor byas 'grel chen*, 33a5–6, explains that the three pairs of syllables are the vajra body, vajra speech, and vajra mind. In his *Rnam gzhag rim pa'i rnam bshad*, 87b4–5, Tsong kha pa does not agree with such a position held by "some people," Tib. *kha cig*.

2452. See Tsong kha pa, *Sgron gsal mchan*, 98b3–6.

2453. Nāgārjuna, *Mdor byas, Piṇḍīkrama Sādhana*, Tōh 1796, 3b4–5; L 45; T 44.

2454. For an English translation of the last passage, see Tenzin Dorjee and Russell 1995, 163, note 60.

10. The Yoga of Taking the Intermediate State as the Saṃbhogakāya

The Yoga of Taking the Intermediate Being as the Saṃbhogakāya—Visualizing the First Lord

There are two parts here: (1) the intermediate being, the ground of purification, and (2) how to visualize the First Lord in correspondence with this ground of purification.

The Intermediate Being, the Ground of Purification

There are three sections here: (1) the essential characteristics of the intermediate being and its duration, (2) explanation of the specific intermediate being that displays awakening in Jambudvīpa after rebirth, and (3) explaining the three minds—the mind that passes into the intermediate being, the mind at the death of intermediate being, and the mind at rebirth into new life.

The Essential Characteristics of the Intermediate Being and Its Duration[2455]

Why is it called intermediate being or the intermediate state?[2456] It is called an "intermediate state" because that is the state which occurs between death in the previous life and rebirth in the subsequent life. It has other synonyms as well: Since it searches for scent and its body grows by scenting, it is called "scent eater." Since its mind proceeds in its search of a birthplace, free of factors like semen and blood,[2457] and evolves instantaneously, it is called "mind-engendered." Since it is actually approaching the state of birth, it is called "verging-on-existence." Because its mode of being seeks a birthplace, it is called "birth-seeking."

As for the body-size[2458] of the intermediate being, the autocommentary on the *Abhidharmakośa* teaches: "Its height is that of a five- or six-year-old child, yet its faculties are clear."[2459] This refers to an intermediate being who will be born as a human. Moreover, its subtle body has cast off coarse elements like flesh and blood; and as the *Abhidharmakośa* explains: "All its faculties are complete, it is unimpeded and endowed with miraculous powers due to

2455. See Tsong kha pa, *Rnam gzhag rim pa'i rnam bshad*, 22a3–24b6; Vasubandhu, *Mdzod 'grel, Kośabhāṣya*, chap. 3, vv. 10–17, Tōh 4090, 116a4–122b5; Pradhan 1975, 119–129; Pruden 1988–1990, 383–399; the commentary of Dge 'dun grub, *Mdzod ṭig thar lam gsal byed*, 88a3–91b4; English translation in Patt 1993, 600–611; and Dbyangs can dga' ba'i blo gros, *Gzhi sku gsum gyi rnam gzhag*, 6b8–10b5; English translation in Lati Rinbochay and Hopkins 1979, 49–57. For more about the intermediate being, see Wayman 1974; Cuevas 1996 and 2003; and Blezer 1997.

2456. This paragraph follows Tsong kha pa, *Rnam gzhag rim pa'i rnam bshad*, 23a4–b1, which in turn is based on—but not identical to—Asaṅga, *Sa'i dngos gzhi, Maulībhūmi*, Tōh 4035, 10b2–4; Bhattacharya 1957, 20.9–13; see Wayman 1974, 233. See also Vasubandhu, *Mdzod 'grel, Kośabhāṣya*, chap. 3, v. 40c–41a, Tōh 4090, 140b3–141a1; Pradhan 1975, 153; Pruden 1988–1990, 441–442; as well as Patt 1993, 638.

2457. This and the following clauses are not found in Asaṅga, *Sa'i dngos gzhi, Maulībhūmi*, Tōh 4035, but rather in Vasubandhu's *Mdzod 'grel, Kośabhāṣya*, chap. 3, vv. 40c–41a, Tōh 4090, 140b4–5; Pradhan 1975, 130; Pruden 1988–1990, 441–42.

2458. Reading *tshad* for *chad* in our text.

2459. Vasubandhu, *Mdzod 'grel, Kośabhāṣya*, chap. 3, following v. 13ab, Tōh 4090, 119a3; Pradhan 1975, 124; Pruden 1988–1990, 390. Tsong kha pa, *Rnam gzhag rim pa'i rnam bshad*, 23b2, cites the last line here in order to explain the line in Nāgabuddhi's *Rnam gzhag rim pa, Vyavastholi*, chap. 1, Tōh 1809, 124a5; Tanaka 2016, 89, which is equivalent to it but the Tibetan translation of Vasubandhu's work has *rno ba* (sharp) for *gsal ba* (clear). The Sanskrit of the *Kośa* here is *paṭu*.

karma."[2460] It is complete in its faculties, with nothing omitted, and since it cannot be obstructed even by a vajra and so forth, [97a] it is unimpeded. It is endowed with miraculous powers due to karma that even the Buddha cannot block.

"Birth state" is the first moment in which, after dying, the intermediate being takes rebirth in a worldly realm. "Death state" is the last moment at the end of that life. The so-called "preceding state" is the entire lifespan between the two.[2461] The intermediate being has the facial and bodily appearances of the "preceding state" wherein it will take birth. Therefore the *Abhidharmakośa* teaches: "It has the shape of the future 'preceding state.'"[2462] Ārya Asaṅga likewise explains: "Its facial and bodily appearances are those of its future rebirth."[2463] SOME TIBETANS say that it takes the shape of the body it had in the previous life; and SOME SAY that during the first half life it takes the shape it had in its previous life,[2464] and during the second half it takes the shape of its subsequent life,[2465] and so forth. Such statements represent the talk of fools, and are thus of no account.

The *Abhidharmakośa* explains that the intermediate being is destined for

2460. Vasubandhu, *Mdzod, Abhidharmakośa*, chap. 3, v. 14b–d, Tōh 4089, and *Mdzod 'grel, Kośabhāṣya*, Tōh 4090, 120a1–3; Pradhan 1975, 125; Pruden 1988–1990, 392.

2461. For the "preceding state," see Vasubandhu, *Mdzod 'grel, Kośabhāṣya*, chap. 3, v. 13ab, Tōh 4090, 119a1–3; Pradhan 1975, 123; Pruden 1988–1990, 390. In his *Rnam gzhag rim pa'i rnam bshad*, 25a2, Tsong kha pa explains that the "preceding state" is preceding in regard to the death-state of the following life, but it is not preceding in regard to the intermediate state. These four stages of life appear also in Vasubandhu's *Mdzod 'grel, Kośabhāṣya*, chap. 3, before vv. 37d–38b, Tōh 4090, 139b2; Pradhan 1975, 151; Pruden 1988–1990, 438: (1) *srid pa bar ma, antarābhava*, (2) *skye ba'i srid pa, upapattibhava*, (3) *dus snga ma'i srid pa, pūrvakālabhava*, and (4) *'chi ba'i srid pa, maraṇabhava*. See also the Mvy. 7679–7682, where the "preceding state" is called as *sngon logs kyi srid pa*.

2462. Vasubandhu, *Mdzod*, Tōh 4089, and *Mdzod 'grel, Kośabhāṣya*, chap. 3, v. 13ab, Tōh 4090, 118b7; Pradhan 1975, 123; Pruden 1988–1990, 390. This work explains here that since both the intermediate being and its future "preceding state" are projected by the same karma, they take the same form.

2463. Asaṅga, *Chos mngon pa kun las btus pa, Abhidharmasamuccaya*, Tōh 4049, 78a5; Pradhan 1950, 43; French translation in Walpola 1971, 68; English translation in Boin-Webb 2001, 94. A similar but not identical passage appears as well in Asaṅga, *Sa'i dngos gzhi, Maulībhūmi*, Tōh 4035, 10a5; Bhattacharya 1957, 19.8.

2464. See Mar pa, *Zab lam snying po Nāro'i chos drug gsang ba bdud rtsi'i chu rgyan*, work 48, p. 578.

2465. See Sgam po pa Bsod nams rin chen, *Dmar khrid gsang chen*, 24b1.

a place of rebirth and cannot avoid being born there,[2466] while Ārya Asaṅga explains that, "its future birth can still change."[2467] Both systems maintain that after its death, an intermediate being may be reborn once more in the intermediate state, and therefore it is not certain that every intermediate being will indeed take birth in the world.

Ārya Asaṅga teaches that the intermediate beings destined for the lower realms resemble a black mat or night darkness while the intermediate beings destined for the fortunate realms resemble a white cloth or a moonlit night.[2468] The *Sūtra on Entering the Womb* teaches that the colors of intermediate beings destined for hell, animals, and hungry ghosts resemble in turn that of a burned log, smoke, and water, whereas the intermediate beings destined to be humans and gods of the desire realm are golden in color, and the intermediate beings destined for the form realm are white.[2469] [97b]

No intermediate being is destined for rebirth in the formless realm,[2470] but beings who die in the formless realm go through the intermediate state before being reborn in one of the other two realms. The *Primary Ground*[2471] explains that the intermediate beings destined for birth as gods, humans, and in the

2466. Vasubandhu, *Mdzod, Abhidharmakośa*, chap. 3, v. 14d, Tōh 4089, and *Mdzod 'grel, Kośabhāṣya*, Tōh 4090, 120a3; Pradhan 1975, 125; Pruden 1988–1990, 392.

2467. Asaṅga, *Chos mngon pa kun las btus pa, Abhidharmasamuccaya*, Tōh 4049, 78a5; Pradhan 1950, 43; French translation in Walpola 1971, 68; English translation in Boin-Webb 2001, 93.

2468. Based on Asaṅga, *Sa'i dngos gzhi, Maulībhūmi*, Tōh 4035, 10a3–4; Bhattacharya 1957, 19.3–5; and Asaṅga's *Chos mngon pa kun las btus pa, Abhidharmasamuccaya*, Tōh 4049, 78a3–4; Pradhan 1950, 42; French translation in Walpola 1971, 68; English translation in Boin-Webb 2001, 93, but note that the translation here is inadequate. Our passage appears in Tsong kha pa, *Rnam gzhag rim pa'i rnam bshad*, 25a4–5.

2469. *Mngal gnas, Nandagarbhāvakrānti Nirdeśa*, Tōh 57, 211a5–7; English translation in Kritzer 2014, 40. See also *'Dul ba phran tshegs kyi gzhi, Vinayakṣudrakavastu*, Tōh 6, 125a5–7. For the different versions of the *Sūtra on Entering the Womb*, the *Mngal gnas, Nandagarbhāvakrānti Nirdeśa*, Tōh 57 and the *Mngal 'jug, Āyuṣman Nandagarbhāvakrānti Nirdeśa*, Tōh 58, see Kritzer 1998 and 2014. At times these two sūtras are called, respectively, the *Longer Sūtra on Entering the Womb* and the *Shorter Sūtra on Entering the Womb*. This passage is cited in Tsong kha pa, *Rnam gzhag rim pa'i rnam bshad*, 25a5–6.

2470. See also Asaṅga, *Sa'i dngos gzhi, Maulībhūmi*, Tōh 4035, 10b4; Bhattacharya 1957, 20.14.

2471. Tib. *Sa'i dngos gzhi*, Skt. *Maulībhūmi*, by Asaṅga. As already noted, this name is used in our text for the first part of the *Rnal 'byor spyod pa'i sa, Yogācārabhūmi*, Tōh 4035.

lower realms proceed upward, straight ahead, and upside down respectively.[2472] The intermediate beings see beings of their own type and their future places of birth.[2473]

As for the life span of the intermediate being,[2474] the *Primary Ground* clearly teaches: "The life span of an intermediate being is up to seven days, yet it is uncertain when it will find conditions for rebirth in a worldly realm. If it cannot find the conditions for rebirth by the seventh day, it dies and takes birth once more in the intermediate state. It can remain in this way for up to seven weeks, but after that it will most assuredly find conditions for rebirth."[2475] Therefore the position that there are intermediate beings who remain for more than three years is a great error that contradicts all the scriptures and their commentaries. Do not rely on the words of fools.

The *Primary Ground* teaches that the intermediate being can discern "this is my previous body," but it does not develop a wish for it, since its mind prevents this, and a wish for an object arises instead.[2476]

Explanation of the Specific Intermediate Being That Displays Awakening in Jambudvīpa after Rebirth[2477]

Formulating the Sādhana teaches: "The bodhisattva, who had but one birth remaining, was in the fullness of youth, and was adorned with all the major

2472. Asaṅga, *Sa'i dngos gzhi, Maulībhūmi*, Tōh 4035, 10a6–7; Bhattacharya 1957, 20.2–3. See also Tsong kha pa, *Rnam gzhag rim pa'i rnam bshad*, 25a6. See also Vasubandhu, *Mdzod 'grel, Kośabhāṣya*, chap. 3, introducing v. 15d, Tōh 4090, 121b5; Pradhan 1975, 127; Pruden 1988–1990, 397; and the *Mngal gnas, Nandagarbhāvakrānti Nirdeśa*, Tōh 57, 211b1.

2473. See Asaṅga, *Sa'i dngos gzhi, Maulībhūmi*, Tōh 4035, 10a6–7; Bhattacharya 1957, 19.9–20.1; see also Vasubandhu, *Mdzod 'grel, Kośabhāṣya*, chap. 3, v. 14ab, Tōh 4090, 119b5–6; Pradhan 1975, 1214–1215; Pruden 1988–1990, 392; and the *Mngal gnas, Nandagarbhāvakrānti Nirdeśa*, Tōh 57, 211b2; see also Tsong kha pa, *Rnam gzhag rim pa'i rnam bshad*, 24b3, [where Tsong kha pa says that the intermediate beings see the places where both themselves and the beings of their own type will be reborn] and 25b2–3.

2474. See Tsong kha pa, *Rnam gzhag rim pa'i rnam bshad*, 22b4–23a4.

2475. Asaṅga, *Sa'i dngos gzhi, Maulībhūmi*, Tōh 4035, 10a7–b1; Bhattacharya 1957, 20.4–6; English translation in Wayman 1974, 233–234. D has *de ltar thogs na yang* for *re ltar thogs na, yang zhag bdun du gnas so / skye ba'i rkyen ma rnyed na zhag bdun phrag bdun gyi bar du yang gnas so* for *yang zhag bdun phrag bdun gyi bar du yang gnas so* in our text.

2476. This is a very loose paraphrase of Asaṅga, *Sa'i dngos gzhi, Maulībhūmi*, Tōh 4035, 10a4–5; Bhattacharya 1957, 20.4–6. See also Tsong kha pa, *Rnam gzhag rim pa'i rnam bshad*, 24b5.

2477. See Tsong kha pa, *Rnam gzhag rim pa'i rnam bshad*, 23b2–24a4.

and minor marks. As such he abided in the intermediate state and entered his mother's womb, whereby the light emitted from him illuminated a billion worlds."[2478] The autocommentary on the *Abhidharmakośa* explains: "The intermediate being of the bodhisattva was like a youth in his prime [98a] adorned with the major and minor marks. As such, abiding in the intermediate state, he entered his mother's womb, whereby a billion worlds with their four continents were illuminated."[2479] These two explanations are similar and therefore it is established[2480] that the intermediate being of the bodhisattva who transmigrates from Tuṣita and enters into his mother's womb is a youth adorned with the major and minor marks, whose light illuminates a billion worlds together with their four continents.

Though *Formulating the Sādhana* does not explain how his intermediate being takes birth in a womb, the autocommentary of the *Abhidharmakośa* teaches: "In her dream his mother saw a young white elephant entering her womb,"[2481] and *Dharmasubhūti[2482] explains that "a white elephant with six tusks entered the womb of the Buddha's mother."[2483] In order to avoid a contradiction with the intermediate being of the bodhisattva whose body is endowed with major and minor marks, the *Abhidharmakośa* explains that "this was only an omen, as for example king Kṛkin's" dream signs, "since for many lives the bodhisattva was held back from animal rebirth."[2484] Thus the *Abhidharmakośa* explains that there is no reason to take these words of *Dharmasubhūti as definitive because they are not found in any of the three divisions of the Buddhist canon.[2485] If nevertheless you take them as definitive, you should be aware that this verse describes the dream of the Buddha's mother.

2478. Nāgabuddhi, *Rnam gzhag rim pa*, *Vyavastholi*, chap. 1, Tōh 1809, 123a5–6; Tanaka 2016, 89. D and Tanaka have *srid pa bar ma na* for *srid pa bar mar*, and *'jug pa'o* for *'jug go* in our text.

2479. Vasubandhu, *Mdzod 'grel*, *Kośabhāṣya*, chap. 3, following v. 13ab, Tōh 4090, 119a3–4; Pradhan 1975, 124; Pruden 1988–1990, 390. While the Sanskrit is *bodhisattvasya*—[the intermediate being] of the bodhisattva—the Tibetan has *byang chub sems dpa' ni*.

2480. In Tsong kha pa, *Rnam gzhag rim pa'i rnam bshad*, 23b2–24a1.

2481. Vasubandhu, *Mdzod 'grel*, *Kośabhāṣya*, chap. 3, following v. 13ab, Tōh 4090, 119a3–4; Pradhan 1975, 124; Pruden 1988–1990, 390.

2482. Tib. Chos ldan rab 'byor. The Sanskrit is different.

2483. Vasubandhu, *Mdzod 'grel*, *Kośabhāṣya*, chap. 3, following v. 13ab, Tōh 4090, 119a6–7; Pradhan 1975, 124; Pruden 1988–1990, 391.

2484. These signs are listed in Vasubandhu, *Mdzod 'grel*, *Kośabhāṣya*, chap. 3, following v. 13ab, Tōh 4090, 119a5, Pradhan 1975, 124, Pruden 1988–1990, 390–391.

2485. Vasubandhu, *Mdzod 'grel*, *Kośabhāṣya*, chap. 3, following v. 13ab, Tōh 4090, 119a6–b2; Pradhan 1975, 124; Pruden 1988–1990, 390–391.

Explaining the Three Minds—the Mind That Passes into the Intermediate Being, the Mind at the Death of the Intermediate Being, and the Mind at Rebirth into New Life

There are two parts here: (1) establishing our own position, and (2) refuting the position of others.

Establishing Our Own Position

The stages of the dissolution of the elements and so forth during the death of a person born from a womb and endowed with the six constituents is taught in the *Stages of Self-Blessing* by Āryadeva: "The earth element dissolves into water, the water dissolves into fire, the fire into the subtle element, the wind dissolves into the mind, the mind [98b] dissolves into mental events, the mental events into ignorance,[2486] and ignorance into clear light."[2487] The meaning of such dissolutions is that as the capability of the earlier one subsides, the capability of the latter becomes more apparent.[2488] This occurs as if the earlier capability transmutes into the latter, and it is therefore designated as "dissolution." When earth dissolves into water, there is an appearance resembling a mirage;[2489] when water dissolves into fire, there is an appearance resembling smoke; when fire dissolves into wind, there is an appearance resembling fireflies. When among numerous subtle and coarse winds, the wind that is the mount of the eighty intrinsic conceptual minds[2490] begins to dissolve into appearance, there arises an experience that is like a burning butter-lamp.

During the mind of "appearance" itself there arises an experience like the clear autumn sky suffused in moonlight devoid of any additional coarse

2486. Reading *ma rig pa* for *rig pa* in our text, as on [98b6] below. D 112b5, and Pandey 1997, 173 and 183, have *ma rig pa* as well.

2487. Āryadeva, *Bdag byin gyis brlab pa'i rim pa rnam par dbye ba, Svādhiṣṭhānakrama-prabheda*, vv. 20–21, Tōh 1805, 112b5; Sanskrit and Tibetan in Pandey 1997, 173 and 183; English translation Wedemeyer 1999, 386. Cited also in Tsong kha pa, *Rim lnga gsal sgron*, 213a2–3; English translation in Kilty 2013, 355. These lines appear in Abhayākaragupta, *Man ngag snye ma, Āmnāyamañjarī*, Tōh 1198, as well, 193a1–2.

2488. See Tsong kha pa, *Ye rdor ṭīkā*, 16b1–2.

2489. For this and the following signs, see the *Rgyud phyi ma, Uttara Tantra*, Tōh 443, 154b4; Matsunaga 1978, vv. 150cd–151ab.

2490. Tib. *rang bzhin brgyad cu'i rtog pa*. These eighty minds are listed in Āryadeva's *Spyod bsdus, Caryāmelāpakapradīpa*, chap. 4, Tōh 1803, 78a3–b4; Sanskrit, Tibetan, and English translation in Wedemeyer 2007, A: 31a–b; Sanskrit and Tibetan in Pandey 2000, 43–44 and 239–241, who has Tib. *rang bzhin rnam pa brgyad cu'i sems nyid*, Skt. *aśītividhaṃ cittam*.

dualistic appearance. And when the wind that is its mount dissolves and the mind of "enhanced appearance" arises, an experience like that sky of the clear autumn suffused in sunlight appears. And when the wind that is its mount dissolves and the mind transforms into "approaching attainment": In the early part of the approaching attainment, an experience like the clear autumn sky suffused in the dark of night with no other appearance arises in the mind; during the latter part of approaching attainment, that awareness subsides as well, and one loses consciousness. When the wind that is its mount dissolves, after waking up from that unconscious state, there arises a very lucid emptiness, a clarity like that of the autumn sky untainted by any condition or any coarse dualistic appearances whatsoever. This is what is called the clear light of death. The mind, mental events, and ignorance taught in the *Stages of Self-Blessing* above are synonyms for appearance, enhanced appearance, and approaching attainment respectively.[2491] [99a]

Likewise, during death at the time of the ground when the four empty states arise through the stages of the dissolution of the winds, the heart is the ultimate site of the dissolution of these winds. The *Vajra Garland Tantra* teaches: "During transference between lives the 'life-sustaining wind'[2492] of the afflicted mind first has a form like a fish."[2493] This verse explains the evolution of the life-sustaining wind at the beginning of transference between lives. The same scripture also teaches where it resides: "The life-sustaining wind resides in the heart."[2494] This shows that at the beginning the life-sustaining wind evolves in the heart, and at the end it dissolves where it was initially formed. The *Compendium of Practices* teaches this as well: "After they reach the indestructible drop, they become insubstantial."[2495] Thus it is taught that after all the winds dissolve into the indestructible drop, the insubstantial—that is to say, the clear light—arises.

With regard to the indestructible drop, the *Compendium of Practices* teaches: "The indestructible drop is in the center of the heart, luminous, like

2491. This is explained in Āryadeva's *Spyod bsdus*, *Caryāmelāpakapradīpa*, chap. 4, Tōh 1803, 77a6–7; Sanskrit, Tibetan, and English translation in Wedemeyer 2007, A: 29b–30a; Sanskrit and Tibetan in Pandey 2000, 42 and 236.

2492. Tib. *srog ['dzin] rlung*, Skt. *prāṇa*.

2493. *Rgyud rdo rje phreng ba*, *Vajramālā Tantra*, chap. 32, Tōh 445, 243a7–b1. D has *nyid* for *yid*, and adds *skad cig gcig la yang dag 'gro*, after the first line. See also Tsong kha pa, *Rim lnga gsal sgron*, 73b4; English translation in Kilty 2013, 132.

2494. *Rgyud rdo rje phreng ba*, *Vajramālā Tantra*, chap. 68, Tōh 445, 276b1.

2495. Āryadeva, *Spyod bsdus*, *Caryāmelāpakapradīpa*, chap. 3, Tōh 1803, 69a3; Sanskrit, Tibetan, and English translation in Wedemeyer 2007, A: 18b; Sanskrit and Tibetan in Pandey 2000, 25 and 203. D, Pandey, and Wedemeyer have *thob na* for *thob nas* in our text.

a pure butter lamp; it is the unchanging syllable[2496] *A*, supreme and subtle, foremost in excellence."[2497] Thus the indestructible drop resides in the heart. The *Vajra Garland Tantra* explains: "When the eight channels coming out of the heart are further divided, they become the 72,000 channels."[2498] Hence the channels too evolve first from the heart. For this reason, the *Primary Ground* explains that the place where the semen and blood mix and into which the intermediate being enters develops into the heart of the fetus.[2499] Then the body is formed above and below, and lastly, with death, consciousness leaves the body from the heart. This is in accordance with the *Vajra Garland Tantra*, an explanatory tantra of the *Guhyasamāja* and the explanations of Ārya Nāgārjuna and his disciples.[2500]

Therefore, for yogis who meditate on a *path* that concurs with the arising in stages of the clear light of death at the time of the *ground*, [99b] all the winds enter, dwell, and dissolve[2501] in the heart. Hence, you should strive to fully understand the transmitted instructions concerning the generation of the clear light of the *path* in correspondence with the clear light of death. To explain that the clear light of death in this life at the ground and the clear light of death during the death of the intermediate being as ultimate truth is merely to label them as such, because at that point there is a similarity between the experience that resembles a cloudless sky when all mental proliferations are pacified, and the direct realization of the ultimate truth. However, this is not a direct realization of the ultimate truth, because if it were, it would follow that all beings would be liberated without any effort.

In rising from this actualization of the clear light of death, the minds of appearance, enhanced appearance, and approaching attainment arise in reverse order, that is, by reversing the process explained above. Hence, as the

2496. Tib. *mi 'gyur*, Skt. *akṣara*.

2497. Āryadeva, *Spyod bsdus*, *Caryāmelāpakapradīpa*, chap. 3, Tōh 1803, 72a3; Sanskrit, Tibetan, and English translation in Wedemeyer 2007, A: 23a; Sanskrit and Tibetan in Pandey 2000, 31 and 217. D, Pandey, and Wedemeyer have *snying gi* for *snying kha'i*, and *'bar* for *gsal*, in our text. See also Tsong kha pa, *Rim lnga gsal sgron*, 126b6; Kilty 2013, 222.

2498. *Rgyud rdo rje phreng ba*, *Vajramālā Tantra*, chap. 30, Tōh 445, 242a5–7.

2499. Asaṅga, *Sa'i dngos gzhi*, *Maulībhūmi*, Tōh 4035, 12b4–5; Bhattacharya 1957, 24.18–25.1. In following Tsong kha pa's *Rnam gzhag rim pa'i rnam bshad*, 37b5–6, which relies on this passage of the *Rnal 'byor spyod pa'i sa*, *Yogācārabhūmi*, Mkhas grub rje, in our text below [108a5–6], also notes that the place where consciousness first enters would be the heart of the child, and at death, consciousness would depart from that very place. See also Schmithausen 1987, 303, n. 242, and Wayman 1974, 238, n. 26.

2500. See Tsong kha pa, *Rim lnga gsal sgron*, 73b1–74b3; English translation in Kilty 2013, 132–133.

2501. Tib. *zhugs gnas thim gsum*.

wind begins[2502] to waver slightly during the experience of death clear light, approaching attainment arises and the intermediate being begins to form. The arising of approaching attainment and the evolution of the intermediate state are simultaneous, because as taught in accordance with all the sūtras and tantras, the higher and lower abhidharmas,[2503] and the *Treatise on the Grounds*,[2504] the cessation of the death state and the evolution of the intermediate state are simultaneous, like the shifting balance of a weighted scale; likewise, since all its faculties and limbs evolve simultaneously, the intermediate being is miraculously born.

Therefore, at the very moment the intermediate being evolves, its mind is approaching attainment, which arises in reverse order from death. During this moment the mind is approaching attainment, while the body is that of the intermediate being. Thereupon the mind of enhanced appearance is immediately born and after that, the mind of appearance and then the eighty intrinsic conceptual minds are born, and the intermediate being swiftly seeks a birthplace, scent for its nourishment, and so forth. [100a]

When the intermediate being dies, and one is born in a womb, the winds that naturally circulate during the intermediate state dissolve, and appearance arises, and when that dissolves, enhanced appearance arises, and when that dissolves, approaching attainment arises, and when that dissolves in turn, clear light arises; all these are produced for only a short while.[2505] The mind of approaching attainment, which arises in the reverse order from the clear light at the death of the intermediate being, is called the birth state, and this is the mind that first takes birth in the womb. Thereupon the mind of enhanced appearance is born, and out of it, the mind of appearance and out of that the eighty intrinsic conceptual minds. From the wind that is the mount of appearances, the wind with the special capability of supporting consciousness is born. From that arises a fire element that has the special capability of supporting consciousness. And from that, the water element with a special capability of the same kind is born, and from that, the earth element with

2502. Reading *rtsom* for *rnam* in our text.

2503. *Mngon pa gong 'og* are the Mahāyāna Abhidharma of Asaṅga and the non-Mahāyāna Abhidharma of Vasubandhu. See Asaṅga, *Chos mngon pa kun las btus pa*, *Abhidharmasamuccaya*, Tōh 4049, 78a6; Pradhan 1950, 43; French translation in Walpola 1971, 68; English translation in Boin-Webb 2001, 94.

2504. Tib. *Sa sde*. This is often a general name of the five works of the *Yogācārabhūmi*, but here it probably refers to Asaṅga, *Sa'i dngos gzhi*, *Maulībhūmi*, Tōh 4035, 10a2–3; Bhattacharya 1957, 19.1–2, which was cited above.

2505. See also Dbyangs can dga' ba'i blo gros, *Gzhi sku gsum gyi rnam gzhag*, 11b4; English translation in Lati Rinbochay and Hopkins 1979, 60.

a special capability of the same kind is born. From these four elements the aggregates and so forth develop, and the fetus is completed in the womb.

Refuting the Position of Others

SOME LAMAS[2506] refute the following explanation of the *Cluster of Instructions*:[2507] The intermediate being evolves with the dawn of approaching attainment that arises from the state of the all-empty, which is the clear light of death. The enhanced appearance is the mind of the intermediate state that wishes to take birth in the desire realm, and appearance is the mind that takes birth. THEY SAY that it is not appropriate for the intermediate being to evolve during approaching attainment, because all three minds are necessary for the evolution of the intermediate being. They find their scriptural support in the *Vajra Garland Tantra*: "The three types of consciousness [approaching attainment, enhanced appearance, and appearance] attained here [in the intermediate state], endowed with the characteristics of all three appearances, are the root intrinsic to every sentient being in the world."[2508] [100b] Thus, THEY SAY, since arising from clear light and the birth of the intermediate state take place like the shifting balance of a weighted scale, the emerging mind that wishes to begin to arise from clear light has two aspects: the unclear mind that is approaching attainment, and the clear mind that is enhanced appearance. The clear mind that is born as the intermediate being is appearance.

This is inappropriate. Are the two minds arising from the clear light of death, the clear and unclear minds, (1) the death state, or (2) the intermediate state, or (3) a category that does not belong to either of these two states? In the first case, the death state is the all-empty, and therefore it would contradict the argument that it is approaching attainment or enhanced appearance. The second case contradicts the argument that the minds of approaching attainment and enhanced appearance precede the intermediate being. In the third case, if another category—clear and unclear minds that do not belong to either of the two states—intervened between the death state and the birth of intermediate state, that would obviously contradict YOUR position that the end of the

2506. See Bu ston, *Mdor byas 'grel chen*, 32b4–33b1; and Tsong kha pa, *Rnam gzhag rim pa'i rnam bshad*, 28a3–b5.

2507. Abhayākaragupta, *Man ngag snye ma, Āmnāyamañjarī*, Tōh 1198, 193a3–4, has: *'dir 'od gsal ba ni thams cad stong pa ste 'chi ba'o, stong pa chen po ni snang ba thob pa ste dri za'i sems can gyi ngo bo can sems so, thabs ni snang ba mched pa ste, 'dod pa nye bar len pa'i sems so, shes rab ni snang ba ste skye ba bzung ba'i sems so.*

2508. *Rgyud rdo rje phreng ba, Vajramālā Tantra*, chap. 59, Tōh 445, 264a5. D has *gang 'di* for *gang 'dir* in our text.

death state and the birth of the intermediate state occur simultaneously, like the shifting balance of a scale. If two such mental stages between the death state and the intermediate state occurred, that would contradict the explanation given in the *Primary Ground* that there is no interruption between the death state and the intermediate state: "The intermediate being emerges without interruption from that direction [of death] in a simultaneous occurrence of cessation and birth, like the pointer[2509] moving on a scale when the weight is shifted."[2510]

The meaning of the passage from the *Vajra Garland Tantra* above is that the minds of the three appearances are the root of the eighty intrinsic conceptual minds in the mental continuum of all sentient beings. However, there is no indication in that passage that the minds of the three appearances arise before the first stage in the evolution of sentient beings. Therefore the citation of this scripture is irrelevant. [101a]

How to Visualize the First Lord in Correspondence with This Ground of Purification

There are two sections here: (1) refuting the imputation of others, and (2) establishing our own position.

Refuting the Imputation of Others[2511]

[Describing the Instructions in Formulating the Sādhana and Other Scriptures]

Immediately after completing its description of the characteristics of the intermediate being, *Formulating the Sādhana* explains: "This indicates that the meditators on the creation stage visualize the body of the deity through the stages of 'yoga' and 'subsequent yoga.'"[2512] The *Concise Sādhana* clarifies that

2509. Tib. *thor to*, Skt. *prāntana.*

2510. Asaṅga, *Sa'i dngos gzhi*, *Maulībhūmi*, Tōh 4035, 10a2–3; Bhattacharya 1957, 19.1–2. D has *mthon dman* for *mtho dman* in our text, which follows Tsong kha pa, *Rnam gzhag rim pa'i rnam bshad*, 29a2–3.

2511. See Tsong kha pa, *Rnam gzhag rim pa'i rnam bshad*, 26a2–28a4.

2512. Tib. *rnal 'byor* and *rjes su rnal 'byor*, Skt. *yoga* and *anuyoga*. Nāgabuddhi, *Rnam gzhag rim pa*, *Vyavastholi*, chap. 1, Tōh 1809, 123b1–2; Tanaka 2016, 90. D and Tanaka have *sgom pa* for *bsgom pa*.

among the five manifest awakenings[2513] during the generation of the First Lord, the manifest awakenings from suchness and from the moon are included within the yoga, while the three other manifest awakenings—the manifest awakenings from the seed syllables, from the emblem, and from the complete body—are included within the subsequent yoga.

Formulating the Sādhana teaches that thereupon the consciousness of the intermediate being, formed after the death of a person of the first eon, arrives posthaste, of its own accord, riding the horse-of-wind, and enters through the gate of Vairocana and into the womb.[2514] This scripture points out that the *Guhyasamāja Tantra* explains this by means of "the samādhi of vajra overpowering,"[2515] and adds that this is taught in the *Wisdom Sūtra* as well.[2516] Then the being that has entered the womb gradually develops and manifests the five embryonic phases: "After that, it gradually develops, first in the form of 'the liquid-cream-like' embryo"[2517] and so forth up until "the five phases have become manifest."[2518]

Then *Formulating the Sādhana* immediately continues: "After that, hair and nails"[2519] and so forth, up to "after that, by the end of a ten month period,

2513. Tib. *mngon par byang chub pa*, or *mngon byang*, Skt. *abhisambodhi*. Though this term is not found in Nāgārjuna's *Mdor byas, Piṇḍīkrama Sādhana*, Tōh 1796, according to the Ārya school the sequence of the five manifest awakenings is: (1) the manifest awakening from suchness, Tib. *de bzhin nyid las byang chub pa*, (2) the manifest awakening from the moon, Tib. *zla ba las byang chub pa*, (3) the manifest awakening from the seed syllable, Tib. *sa bon las byang chub pa*, (4) the manifest awakening from the emblem, Tib. *phyag mtshan las byang chub pa*, (5) the manifest awakening from the complete body, Tib. *sku rdzogs pa las byang chub pa*.

2514. Nāgabuddhi, *Rnam gzhag rim pa, Vyavastholi*, chap. 1, Tōh 1809, 123b4–124a2; Tanaka 2016, 93.

2515. Tib. *de bzhin gshegs pa thams cad zil gyis gnon pa rdo rje zhes bya ba'i ting nge 'dzin*, Skt. *sarvatathāgatābhibhavanavajranāmasamādhi*, in the *Guhyasamāja Tantra*, Tōh 442; Zhol 3a5–b1; Stog 4a6–7 [the rest is missing]; Dunh 3a1–4; Fremantle 1971, 178; and Matsunaga 1978, 5. See also our text above [88a] and below [112a].

2516. Tib. *Shes rab kyi mdo*, Skt. *Prajñāsūtra*. This is a reference to *Sdom 'byung, Saṃvarodaya Tantra*, Tōh 373, 266a6–7; Sanskrit, Tibetan, and English translation in Tsuda 1974, chap. 2, vv. 15–16, which explains here how the intermediate being enters the mingled semen and blood.

2517. Tib. *mer mer po*, Skt. *kalala*. The five phases in the womb are explained below [110a].

2518. Nāgabuddhi, *Rnam gzhag rim pa, Vyavastholi*, chap. 1, Tōh 1809, 124a4–5, Tanaka 2016, 94.

2519. Nāgabuddhi, *Rnam gzhag rim pa, Vyavastholi*, Tōh 1809, 124a5–6; Tanaka 2016, 94, adds "facial hair." The following passage through to "that am I" is entirely a quotation from the *Rnam gzhags rim pa*.

the being is delivered out of the mother's womb in the way indicated by 'the samādhi of vajra origination from samaya'[2520] taught in the *Guhyasamāja Tantra*.[2521] Thereby, the scent-eater, the being that hovers nearby, turns into an object of the corporeal eye, as the *Guhyasamāja Tantra* teaches: [101b] 'All tathāgatas clearly[2522] perceived the Blessed One, the Tathāgata, Bodhicitta-vajra as having three faces.'[2523] Here in the great yoga tantra called *Request of the Four Mothers*, the Blessed One explains: 'The water element is the father'[2524] and so forth[2525] up to '[the five aggregates] are taught as the essential nature [of the five buddhas].'[2526] This passage shows that the mantrin should maintain a divine identity with the resolve: 'What has been achieved through the four yogas, that am I.'"[2527] This is explained in great detail, and *Formulating the Sādhana* shows how it is taught in the *Guhyasamāja Tantra* as well.

2520. Tib. *dam tshig 'byung ba rdo rje'i zhes bya ba'i ting nge 'dzin*, Skt. *samayodbhavavajra-nāmasamādhi*.

2521. *Guhyasamāja Tantra*, Tōh 442; Zhol 3b2; Stog missing; Dunh 3a5; Fremantle 1971, 178–179; and Matsunaga 1978, 5.

2522. This word is not in the Zhol.

2523. *Guhyasamāja Tantra*, Tōh 442; Zhol 3b2–3; Stog missing; Dunh 3b1; Fremantle 1971, 178–179; and Matsunaga 1978, 5.

2524. D has "father" (*pha*) for "earth" (*sa*) in our text. The *Lha mo bzhis zhus pa*, *Caturdevīparipṛcchā*, Tōh 446, has *pha* as well.

2525. Our text skips here Nāgabuddhi's explanations that (while the water element is called the father) the fire element is called the mother. The skin, flesh, and blood are called the mother and the bones, marrow, and semen are called the father. See his *Rnam gzhag rim pa*, *Vyavastholi*, Tōh 1809, 124b6; Tanaka 2016, 97.

2526. *Lha mo bzhis zhus pa*, *Caturdevīparipṛcchā*, Tōh 446, 279b7–280a1. The Tibetan translation in the Derge differs from the one in Nāgabuddhi's *Rnam gzhag rim pa*, from which Mkhas grub rje cites.

2527. Nāgabuddhi, *Rnam gzhag rim pa*, *Vyavastholi*, chap. 1, Tōh 1809, 124a5–6 and 124b4–125a1; Tanaka 2016, 94 and 96–97. D and Tanaka have *tha mar* for *mthar*; *'byung ba'i rdo rje* for *'byung ba rdo rje*; *la* after *ting nge 'dzin*; *'khor gyi* for *'khor ba'i*; adds *'dir* before *gsung*; has *pha* for *sa*; *bcom ldan 'das kyis* for *bcom ldan 'das kyi*; and *lha mo bzhis zhus pa'i rnal 'byor* for *lha mo bzhis zhus pa zhes bya ba rnal 'byor*. This passage appears below as well [115b].

[The Dispute]

Some Tibetan lamas[2528] are uncomfortable with the fact that this passage of *Formulating the Sādhana* teaches the visualization of the First Lord in correspondence with the intermediate being. Therefore, after citing *Formulating the Sādhana*: "This indicates that the meditators on the creation stage visualize the body of the deity through the stages of yoga and subsequent yoga" up to "the five phases in the womb have become manifest";[2529] they explain that the visualization of the First Lord is applied to the phases in the womb.[2530]

This explanation, which shifts the words of the master in another direction, is highly inappropriate. After first explaining the characteristics of the intermediate being, *Formulating the Sādhana* goes on to teach the visualization of the deity by means of the yoga and subsequent yoga in correspondence with the intermediate being. Thus this text clearly indicates that you should meditate on the First Lord in correspondence with the intermediate being. After that *Formulating the Sādhana* describes how the intermediate being takes rebirth in the womb, and then explains the need to meditate on transforming into the nirmāṇakāya and so forth in correspondence with taking birth by means of the remaining yogas.[2531] Thus it is with great clarity that *Formulating the Sādhana* applies the transformation into the nirmāṇakāya to rebirth in the womb. [102a]

The *Sādhana Incorporating the Scripture* likewise teaches: "The meditation on oneself as Great Vajradhara is the subsequent yoga. Then, the body—its nature being wisdom, which is taught[2532] in the first chapter of the

2528. See Red mda' ba, *Bsgrub pa dpal bas zhus lan*, Kathmandu, 47a5–b5; TBRC, 302b–303a. Here Mkhas grub rje follows Tsong kha pa, *Rnam gzhag rim pa'i rnam bshad*, 26a2–27b2.

2529. Nāgabuddhi, *Rnam gzhag rim pa*, *Vyavastholi*, chap. 1, Tōh 1809, 123b1–2 to 124a5; Tanaka 2016, 90 to 94. D and Tanaka have *sgom par* for *bsgom par* and *bstan te* for *bstan to*. Nāgabuddhi lists the five stages at 124a4–5; Tanaka 2016, 94.

2530. 'Gos Khug pa lhas btsas, *Gsang 'dus stong thun*, 11b2, as well maintains that the ground of purification of the visualization of the First Lord through the five manifest awakenings are stages in the womb.

2531. These are the "higher yoga," Tib. *shin tu rnal 'byor*, Skt. *atiyoga*, and the "great yoga," Tib. *rnal 'byor chen po*, Skt. *mahāyoga*, see our text below [179b4–180a6].

2532. This word is omitted in Nāgārjuna's *Mdo bsre*, *Sādhanasūtramelāpaka*, Tōh 1797.

Guhyasamāja Tantra,[2533] as the great[2534] personification[2535] of the *vidyā*[2536]—cannot act for the sake of sentient beings, hence..."[2537] The *Sādhana Incorporating the Scripture* explains this as the reason for the transformation of the First Lord into the nirmāṇakāya here. And *Formulating the Sādhana* teaches that because the saṃbhogakāya cannot act for the sake of other human beings, in order to take birth as the nirmāṇakāya the First Lord transforms into the nirmāṇakāya, as the intermediate being takes birth in the womb of the mother.[2538] The teachings of both scriptures here are similar in meaning.

Similarly, the first chapter of the *Illuminating Lamp* explains: "With *then the tathāgatas Akṣobhya* and so forth, the *Guhyasamāja Tantra* teaches that in order to act for the sake of sentient beings, the tathāgatas enact the deed of holding a nirmāṇakāya by taking the aggregates and so forth."[2539] Thus it is taught that the stage which replaces[2540] rebirth is identical to transformation-into-the-nirmāṇakāya. The *Five Stages* also teaches: "The conventional truth is illusion, as is the *saṃbhogakāya*, and this illusion is the scent-eater being."[2541] Thus it is explicitly taught here that the saṃbhogakāya of the fruit, the illusory body of the path, and the intermediate being of the ground time all correspond with each other. Therefore those who maintain that the First Lord is the saṃbhogakāya and needs to transform into the nirmāṇakāya, but do

2533. *Guhyasamāja Tantra*, Tōh 442; Zhol 3b2; Stog missing; Dunh 3a5; Fremantle 1971, 178–179; and Matsunaga 1978, 5.

2534. This word is omitted in Nāgārjuna's *Mdo bsre*, *Sādhanasūtramelāpaka*, Tōh 1797. The Zhol print of the *Guhyasamāja Tantra*, Tōh 442; Zhol. 3b2, has *rig pa chen po'i* [*mahāvidyā*] *skyes bu'i gzugs* [*puruṣamūrti*] for *rigs pa'i skyes bu chen po'i gzugs can* here.

2535. Tib. *skyes bu chen po'i gzugs can*.

2536. Tib. *rig pa*.

2537. Nāgārjuna, *Mdo bsre*, *Sādhanasūtramelāpaka*, Tōh 1797, 12b4–5. D has *rdo rje 'chang chen por* for *rdo rje 'chang chen po'i*; *bzhin* for *bzhin du*; *rig pa'i* for *rigs pa'i*; and omits *chen po* after *skyes bu* and *du bstan pa'i* before *ye shes*.

2538. Nāgabuddhi, *Rnam gzhag rim pa*, *Vyavastholi*, chap. 1, Tōh 1809, 123b2–3; Tanaka 2016, 91.

2539. Candrakīrti, *Sgron gsal*, *Pradīpoddyotanaṭīkā*, Tōh 1785, 14b4–5; Chakravarti 1984, 20. D has *phung po la sogs par* for *phung po la sogs* in our text. See *Gsang 'dus*, *Guhyasamāja Tantra*, Tōh 442; Zhol 3a3–5; Stog 4a4–6; Dunh 1b4–5; Fremantle 1971, 178–179; and Matsunaga 1978, 5.

2540. Reading *dod* for the unclear syllable.

2541. Nāgārjuna, *Rim lnga*, *Pañcakrama*, chap. 3, vv. 26cd–27a, Tōh 1802, 53a1; Sanskrit and Tibetan in Mimaki and Tomabechi 1994, 35; Sanskrit and French translation in Tomabechi 2006, 160. D and Mimaki and Tomabechi 1994 have *bden pa'i* for *bden pa*, and *sems can gyur* for *sems can nyid*.

not say that the First Lord corresponds to the intermediate being but rather to birth in the womb, contradict themselves, and their view falls very far afield from the position of Ārya Nāgārjuna and his disciples. [102b]

If YOU fail to grasp the crucial points of applying the correspondences of birth, death, and the intermediate state during the creation stage in this way, you will not understand how during the completion stage, after the stages of mind-isolation[2542] and the clear light, you arise in the impure and pure illusory body, hold the nirmāṇakāya, and so forth. These crucial points are taught over and over in *Formulating the Sādhana*, in the *Guhyasamāja Tantra* and its commentaries, and in the works of Ārya Nāgārjuna and his disciples, and unless you understand them, you will miss the vital essence of the path.

[Additional Disputes]

SOME EARLY LAMAS say[2543] that the solar disk, the lunar disk, the lotus, and the three syllables on the lotus correspond respectively to the father, mother, and the intermediate being, as well as to all three falling into a swoon of bliss. During the womb-phases of "the liquid-cream-like,"[2544] "the oblong,"[2545] and "the viscous,"[2546] the embryo is intrinsically endowed with a tathāgata family, and thus, naturally takes the shapes of the seed syllables *oṃ*, *āḥ*, and *hūṃ* respectively. These three phases correspond to the three syllables that arise from the moon. "The solidified" fetus[2547] corresponds to the emblem of vajra, and the fetus "with the limbs slightly protruding"[2548] corresponds to the complete body of the First Lord. Thus these five phases in the womb are the ground of purification of the First Lord.

2542. Reading *sems* for *sams*.

2543. This is based on Tsong kha pa, *Rnam gzhag rim pa'i rnam bshad*, 27b2–4. See 'Gos Khug pa lhas btsas, *Gsang 'dus stong thun*, 12b4–5.

2544. Tib. *mer mer po*. Nāgabuddhi's *Rnam gzhag rim pa*, *Vyavastholi*, chap. 1, Tōh 1809, 124a4–5, also has *mer mer po*; the Sanskrit in Tanaka 2016, 94, is *kalala*. This work is the source for the Tibetan and Sanskrit in the following notes as well.

2545. Tib. *nar nar po*. Nāgabuddhi has Tib. *ltar ltar po*, Skt. *arbuda*. Tsong kha pa's *Rnam gzhag rim pa'i rnam bshad* has *ltar ltar po* as well, 27b3.

2546. Tib. *ltar ltar po*. Nāgabuddhi has Tib. *gor gor po*, Skt. *peśin*. Tsong kha pa's *Rnam gzhag rim pa'i rnam bshad* has *gor gor po* as well, 27b4.

2547. Tib. *'khrang 'gyur*. Nāgabuddhi has Tib. *mkhrang gyur*, Skt. *ghana*.

2548. Tib. *rkang lag 'gyus pa*. This is the same in Nāgabuddhi's *Rnam gzhag rim pa*, Tōh 1809; the Sanskrit is *praśakha*.

Moreover, SOME EARLY LAMAS[2549] say that the expanded vajra of the father corresponds to the solar disk, the passion of the male and female to the lunar disk, the expanded lotus of the mother to the lotus, the three syllables on it to the body, speech, and mind of the intermediate being, and their mingling to the mingling of the intermediate being with the semen and blood, which results in the attainment of the ground of wisdom. THEY EXPLAIN that during the first three phases in the womb,[2550] the fetus takes the shape of the three seed syllables, and during the two middle phases[2551] the embryo is endowed with Buddha essence,[2552] and thus, its shape is that of the emblem while the fifth phase in the womb is similar to the previous one. While ignoring the special correspondences that Ārya Nāgārjuna and his disciples apply between the intermediate being and the saṃbhogakāya, [103a] THEY establish their view with great insistence, on the basis of false proofs, such as the shape of the seed syllables and emblems, that one can refute by "non-observation-of-that-which-should appear."[2553]

Thus this is most inappropriate because: (1) there is no proof whatsoever for such correspondences; and (2) if since the embryo is intrinsically endowed[2554] with tathāgata family and sugata essence, it naturally takes the shape of the seed syllables and emblems, it would follow that at all times all sentient beings naturally take the shape of the seed syllables and emblems; and (3) when the intermediate being dies, the first mind born in the birth-state mingles with the semen and blood of the parents, but the intermediate being cannot mingle[2555] with the semen and blood; and (4) if the solar disk and lotus are applied in correspondence with the expanded vajra and lotus of the father and mother, and the mingling of these and the three syllables into the moon orb is applied in correspondence with the mingling of the semen, blood, and

2549. This is based on Tsong kha pa, *Rnam gzhag rim pa'i rnam bshad*, 27b4–28a2. See Red mda' ba, *Yid kyi mun sel*, 7b2–4, and *Bsgrub pa dpal bas zhus lan*, Kathmandu, 47b5–48a1; TBRC, 303a.

2550. Tsong kha pa's *Rnam gzhag rim pa'i rnam bshad*, 27b5, and Bu ston's *Mdor byas 'grel chen*, 36a5–7 have two phases here.

2551. According to the sources mentioned in the previous note, these are the third and fourth phases in the womb.

2552. Tib. *sangs rgyas kyi snying po can*.

2553. *Snang rung ma dmigs pa, dṛśyānupalabdhi*, "the nonobservation of the suitable to appear," see Tillemans 1999, 151–169. You should observe what is there, for example; a pot on the table, if you do not see it, it is not there.

2554. Reading *yod pa* for *yad pa*.

2555. Reading *'dres pa* for *'das pa*.

the intermediate being, it would follow that the intermediate being[2556] enters between the vajra and lotus of the father and mother, mingled as one during the ground time, and that the secret places of the father and mother are no different from the semen and blood.

Furthermore, SOME LATER LAMAS[2557] explain that the lunar disk, solar disk, and lotus correspond to the three appearances in reverse order; the three syllables from which they are generated correspond to the wind on which the mind rides; the three syllables on the lotus to the body, speech, and mind of the intermediate being; their mingling to the intermediate being taking birth; and the moon orb, perfected by the emanation and gathering, to the aggregates of the intermediate being, perfected by its consciousness riding on the mount of the wind. However, this position is likewise inadmissible, since it seems to apply correspondences according to the premise that the three appearances of the reverse order serve as a prior cause for the birth of the intermediate being, and this would be erroneous, as previously established.

Moreover, all three positions fall totally outside the above description of the explanatory method in the works of Ārya Nāgārjuna and his disciples explained above, [103b] and therefore, scholars should not be satisfied with them.

Establishing Our Own Position

I will explain the method of applying the correspondence to the ground of purification.[2558] The intermediate being is endowed with an extremely subtle body. Having abandoned the coarse body of the elements, the intermediate being is comprised of mere wind-and-mind that arises from the clear light of death in the reverse order and therefore it is called "endowed with a mind-engendered body" and "endowed with a wisdom body."

Regarding the visualization of the deity in correspondence with the intermediate being:[2559] *The manifest awakening from suchness* is similar to the clear light of death, and in arising from it, first *the manifest awakening from the*

2556. Reading *bar do* for *bar da*.

2557. See Bu ston, *Mdor byas 'grel chen*, 34a6–7 and Tsong kha pa, *Rnam gzhag rim pa'i rnam bshad*, 28a3–5.

2558. From here until [104a2] our text follows Tsong kha pa's *Rnam gzhag rim pa'i rnam bshad*, 30a2–b1.

2559. As detailed in note 2513 above, the meditation here consists of five manifest awakenings. The first, the awakening from suchness, is shared with the gathering of the specially visualized deities into clear light, and the actual generation of the First Lord begins with the awakening from the moon.

moon is displayed[2560] as a cause for generating the deity. The purpose is to enable you to understand the need for maintaining a divine identity of the deity's body generated from consciousness riding on the wind that merely appears in the form of the completely perfect moon; this body of the deity is the saṃbhogakāya, an extremely subtle wisdom body that corresponds to the intermediate being.

Here the lunar disk, solar disk, and lotus[2561] that arise while in emptiness correspond to the three appearances that arise in reverse order from the clear light of death at the time of the ground. Both sets of three syllables, those that serve as the seed syllables for generating these three [the lunar disk, solar disk, and lotus] and those set on top of one another after the lunar disk, solar disk, and lotus have been visualized, correspond to the winds serving as the mounts of the three types of consciousness in the reverse order. Each of the three types of consciousness has two winds—engendering winds and coexisting winds—and thus there are two sets of winds here.

Their mingling[2562] signifies the indivisibility of the wind and mind at the time of the ground. [104a] The meditation on such mingling and on the arising as the completely perfect moon, as well as on the light emanating from this moon, which gathers the entire animate and inanimate realms and dissolves them into the moon,[2563] is taught in the *Vajra Garland Tantra:* "The stages of birth, abiding, being destroyed, and the intermediate state—however much the people of the world impute them—are [but] emanations of the wind of mind."[2564] This signifies that consciousness mounted on the wind is the root of all phenomena in the animate and inanimate realms.[2565]

2560. Reading *ston* for *stong* here.

2561. The manifest awakening from the moon begins with visualization of a lunar disk, a solar disk, and a lotus. See Tsong kha pa, *Gsang mngon*, 39a4–6.

2562. Following the visualization of the lunar and solar disks, the lotus, and the three seed syllables, all these mingle and become a moon orb. See Tsong kha pa, *Gsang mngon*, 39a6–b1.

2563. See Tsong kha pa, *Gsang mngon*, 39a6–b2.

2564. *Rgyud rdo rje phreng ba, Vajramālā Tantra*, chap. 59, Tōh 445, 265b1–2. D has *brtags pa* for *btags pa* in our text.

2565. See Tsong kha pa, *Rnam gzhag rim pa'i rnam bshad*, 30a2–b1, and *Rim lnga gsal sgron*, 233b6–235a2; English translation in Kilty 2013, 390–391. This refers to the line of Tsong kha pa, *Gsang mngon*, 39b2: "The root of all the phenomena of the animate and inanimate realms, the mere wind-and-mind appearing as the moon, that am I."

[ANOTHER DISPUTE]

SOME LAMAS[2566] say the purpose here is so you will realize that all phenomena are Mind Only, and that the two truths are indivisible. They do not understand that the author of the *Illuminating Lamp* accepts external things as conventional designations, which is also the view of Ārya Nāgārjuna. Both the animate and inanimate realms that are dissolved and the wind and mind into which they dissolve—that arises as the appearance of the moon—are but conventional truth, as is anything that accords with the conventional designations of the Mantra and Pāramitā Vehicles. Thus the point here is not to indicate that the two truths are indivisible. For these reasons, both of YOUR arguments are insubstantial.

[OUR EXPLANATION CONTINUED]

In the next step in the sādhana,[2567] consciousness mounted on the wind arises in the appearance of the moon, and from it, like bubbles on the water, the three seed syllables arise. This corresponds to the speech of the intermediate being formed from mere wind-and-mind. The generation of the five-pronged white vajra from the transformation of these seed syllables corresponds to the mind of the intermediate being. The generation of oneself from that as the body of the First Lord corresponds to the body of the intermediate being. The light rays emanating from the seed syllables, inviting the five tathāgata families together with a circle of numerous deities, and their dissolution into the syllables and so forth correspond to the deeds of the intermediate beings.[2568] It is sufficient to apply the correspondences merely in a coarse way [104b] since there are no special subtle correlations here like those between on the one hand the body, speech, and mind of the intermediate being, which evolve simultaneously, and on the other hand the seed syllables, emblem, and complete body visualized here one after another. This is similar to the case of applying the visualization of the celestial mansion to the evolution of the world.[2569]

2566. See Bu ston, *Mdor byas 'grel chen*, 34a4–6.

2567. See Tsong kha pa, *Gsang mngon*, 39b2–5. Here are the last three manifest awakenings: the awakenings from the seed syllables, from the emblem, and from the complete body.

2568. See Tsong kha pa, *Rnam gzhag rim pa'i rnam bshad*, 30b1–4.

2569. Though the visualization of the celestial mansion is applied in correspondence to the evolution of the world, this is done in a general way without relating the visualization of specific parts of the palace, such as its portals and walls to particular components of the world, such as its mountains and continents. See [49b] above.

[Correspondences to the Saṃbhogakāya of the Fruit and the Completion Stage]

This visualization of the First Lord—according to the works of Ārya Nāgārjuna and his disciples cited above—must correspond not only to the intermediate being at the ground of purification but also to the saṃbhogakāya of the fruit. This is how the visualization at this point corresponds to the saṃbhogakāya: Although at the stage of buddhahood, there is nothing apart from innate clear light and all-empty with no appearance, increase, and approaching attainment, nevertheless, the three appearances and the winds on which they mount are the cause of the innate clear light, and they therefore correspond to the lunar disk, the solar disk, the lotus, and the three seed syllables upon the lotus. Their mingling and arising in the appearance of the moon correspond to the fruitional clear light indivisible from the wind upon which it rides that emerge from the three appearances during the path.

The seed syllables that arise from the moon, the emanated light rays that invite the five tathāgata families together with a circle of numerous deities, their dissolution, the vajra, and the complete body all signify the actual clear light, which is the wisdom of indivisible bliss and emptiness, which mounts on the wind that arises as the appearance of the body, speech, mind, and deeds of the Victorious One at the time of the fruit. Further, the vajra with its five prongs signifies the mind with its five wisdoms, and that vajra marked by the three syllables signifies the invisibility of the three vajras of body, speech, and mind.

When you visualize yourself as the First Lord, you engage in the visualization for a long time, while maintaining a firm divine identity with the resolve: "This Vajradhara, who is merely pure-wind-and-mind arising as the extremely subtle wisdom body, that am I." [105a] This meditation is very important for the ripening of the profound completion stage in which you meditate on the illusory body, and therefore it is wrong to belittle it.

Thus, in perfect accord with the nectar of the words of the venerable lama Tsongkhapa himself, who is inseparable from Vajradhara, I, without any failing, have explained to the fortunate ones how to apply the visualization of the First Lord in correspondence with both the ground and the fruit.

[The Instruction of the Concise Sādhana*]*

The *Concise Sādhana* also teaches the visualization of the First Lord in this way.

> After entering into clear light, mantrins display the arising too.

> They visualize the form of the deity, by means of the yoga of the mantra-body. They meditate on a solar disk, abiding in the midst of the space realm with a lunar disk upon it. There, great mantrins visualize an eight-petal red lotus, and upon it, they meditate on the three syllables. As the mantra, the lotus, and the solar disk enter into the lunar disk, they visualize[2570] the completely perfect moon orb as bodhicitta, and in it, the totality of the moving and immovable worlds.[2571]

The significance of the line *by means of the yoga of the mantra-body* is: The mantra body is that which arises in the mind of the meditator on the creation stage as the body of the First Lord through the five manifest awakenings; the wisdom body is that which arises in the meditator on the completion stage as the illusory body or the body of union from the mere wind-and-mind of the four empty states.[2572] Regarding the line *abiding in the midst of the space realm*, the *Illuminating Lamp* explains again and again that abiding in the midst of the space realm means abiding in clear light.[2573] [105b] In this instance therefore it means: within the manifest awakening from suchness that is abiding in clear light.

Having reflected on the meaning of the subsequent line of the *Concise Sādhana* cited above: *as the mantra, the lotus, and the solar disk enter into the lunar disk*, EARLY LAMAS maintain[2574] that the lunar disk in between—into which the lotus and the three syllables enter from above and the solar disk from below—is the moon of *manifest-awakening-from-the-moon*. But this is not true, since the eleventh chapter of the *Illuminating Lamp* teaches: "With the mantra *oṃ śūnyatā* and so forth everything is made 'being-less.'[2575]

2570. Tib. *rnam par brtag*, Skt. *vibhāvayet*.

2571. Nāgārjuna, *Mdor byas*, *Piṇḍīkrama Sādhana*, Tōh 1796, 3b5–7; L 46–50ab; T 45–49ab. D has *bstan par* for *brtag par*; *lha yi* for *lha'i*; *dmigs par 'gyur* for *dmigs par bya*; *de yi steng du yang* for *kyang ni de steng du*; *der ni* for *dar yang*; *ni de nas bsam* for *yang bsgom par bya*; *nyi ma* for *gnyis ka*; *rdzogs 'gyur* for *rdzogs pa*; and *rgyu dang mi rgyu* for *brgyu dang mi brgyu* in our text.

2572. See Tsong kha pa, *Sgron gsal mchan*, 3b2–5.

2573. Candrakīrti, *Sgron gsal*, *Pradīpoddyotanaṭīkā*, Tōh 1785, 28a5–30a3; Chakravarti 1984, 38–39.

2574. This follows Tsong kha pa, *Sgron gsal mchan*, 237b1–5. See also his *Bskyed rim zin bris*, 24a3–4, and *Slob tshul*, 15a5–b1. For the opponents, see 'Gos Khug pa lhas btsas, *Gsang 'dus stong thun*, 12b5; Red mda' ba, *Yid kyi mun sel*, 107b1–2; and Ngor chen, *Gsang 'dus dkyil 'khor gyi sgrub thabs dngos grub rgya mtsho*, work 106, 9b2–3.

2575. Tib. *dngos po med pa*, Skt. *nirābhāsī*.

With the three syllables, *oṃ* and so forth, the lunar disk, the solar disk, and the lotus arise; visualize the three syllables on the navel of the lotus and all of these transforming completely into a clear disk, which is a lunar disk."[2576] This teaches that the moon is generated through the transformation of the lunar disk, the solar disk, the lotus, and the three syllables. The *Vajrasattva Sādhana* teaches this in a similar way.[2577] The *Sādhana Incorporating the Scripture* teaches: "Visualize all of these dissolving and transforming into something like a lunar disk."[2578]

Hence what the *Concise Sādhana* signifies here is that the solar disk and the lotus should also enter the lunar disk located between them and all should intermingle and transform completely in order to form the subsequent moon orb.[2579] The phrase *the moving and immovable* and so forth in the citation from the *Concise Sādhana* above means that the animate and inanimate realms in their entirety dissolve into the moon.

Next the *Concise Sādhana* teaches: "For the sake of firm concentration, meditators recite the mantra: *oṃ dharma dhātu svabhāva ātmako 'haṃ*."[2580] The meaning of the line *for the sake of firm concentration* is for the sake of a firm divine identity. Regarding the meaning of the mantra: *Oṃ* has already been explained; *dharma* is phenomena; *dhātu* is realm or space, and means the root of the ultimate end; [106a] *svabhāva* is nature, which signifies that the wind and mind are the root of all phenomena in the animate and inanimate realms; and *ātmako 'haṃ* indicates maintaining a divine identity with the resolve, "This very wind and mind arising in the aspect of a moon, that am I."

The *Illuminating Lamp* explains the definitive meaning of this mantra, by citing the explanatory tantra *Revelation of the Intention*:[2581] "*Oṃ* should be

2576. Candrakīrti, *Sgron gsal, Pradīpoddyotanaṭīkā*, Tōh 1785, commentary on v. 10, 79a1–3; Chakravarti 1984, 98. Candrakīrti glosses "clear disk" here (*gsal ba'i dkyil 'khor, svacchamaṇḍala*) in the *Guhyasamāja Tantra*, as the lunar disk, and this is taken as the *awakening from the moon*. See *Guhyasamāja Tantra*, chap. 11, Tōh 442; Zhol 15a6; Stog 26a2; Dunh missing; Fremantle 1971, v. 10b; and Matsunaga 1978, v. 10b.

2577. Candrakīrti, *Rdo rje sems dpa'i sgrub thabs, Vajrasattva Sādhana*, Tōh 1814, 199a5; Luo and Tomabechi 2009, 15.7–8 and 47.15–16.

2578. Nāgārjuna, *Mdo bsre, Sādhanasūtramelāpaka*, Tōh 1797, 12b1. D has *bsdus te* for *bsdus nas* in our text.

2579. Nāgārjuna, *Mdor byas, Piṇḍīkrama Sādhana*, Tōh 1796, 3b6–7; L 49; T 48.

2580. Nāgārjuna, *Mdor byas, Piṇḍīkrama Sādhana*, Tōh 1796, 3b7; L 50cd; T 49cd.

2581. See also our text above [95b4–5]; as pointed out in note 2447, Candrakīrti's *Sgron gsal, Pradīpoddyotanaṭīkā*, Tōh 1785, 28b6; Chakravarti 1984, 37, has just "explanatory tantra" here without specifying which one. In his *Sgron gsal mchan*, 105b2, Tsong kha pa comments that this explanatory tantra is the *Dgongs pa lung ston, Sandhivyākaraṇa Tantra*, Tōh 444.

known as the first, *dharma* the second, *dhātu* as the third, the fourth is known as *svabhāva*, *ātmaka* is the fifth, and *ahaṃ* is maintained as the sixth. After reciting this mantra, you should meditate while you are absorbed in it."[2582] Why is this the definitive meaning?[2583] The first five segments of the mantra indicate the five light rays of the winds upon which the actual clear light is mounted, and *ahaṃ* indicates the actual clear light itself. *Reciting this mantra* means bringing about the actual clear light that rides the five winds; *after* [that] means during the completion stage; those being *absorbed in it* are the yogis meditating on the bodies of the deities who arise from the clear light as the illusory body in the appearance of the father-mother desire deity or as the body of[2584] union.

Now, during the creation stage, after meditating on this mantra as explained in its interpretable meaning,[2585] you should meditate on the First Lord through the five manifest awakenings. The mantra has been explained here in its definitive meaning because the meditation on the First Lord at this point serves to ripen your arising in the illusory body from clear light when you will meditate on the completion stage. Although apparently earlier virtuous teachers[2586] presented various ways of interpreting this mantra in its definitive meaning, their explanations appear to be unreliable. Their misunderstanding of the completion stage seems to render their presentations pointless. [106b] This completes the explanation of *the manifest awakening from the moon*.

Thirdly, *manifest awakening from the seed syllable*. The *Concise Sādhana* teaches: "After engaging in the yoga in this way, yogis should undertake the subsequent yoga."[2587] Among the five manifest awakenings, the first two are taught as yoga and the following three as subsequent yoga. Their meanings will be explained below. The *Concise Sādhana* explicitly teaches the *manifest awakening from the seed syllable* with: "Yogis should visualize the three syllables

2582. Candrakīrti, *Sgron gsal, Pradīpoddyotanaṭīkā*, Tōh 1785, 28b5–7; Chakravarti 1984, 37. D has *ahaṃ* for *āhaṃ* in our text.

2583. Tsong kha pa's *Sgron gsal mchan*, which our text follows here, adds that this meaning is the definitive meaning, 105b1–3.

2584. Reading *gi* for *gis* in our text.

2585. The ṃantra is explained in Candrakīrti, *Sgron gsal, Pradīpoddyotanaṭīkā*, Tōh 1785, in its interpretable meaning on 27b5–28a1; Chakravarti 1984, 36, and definitive meaning on 28a1–b7; Chakravarti 1984, 36.

2586. See Red mda' ba, *Yid kyi mun sel*, 107b2–108b6.

2587. Nāgārjuna, *Mdor byas, Piṇḍīkrama Sādhana*, Tōh 1796, 3b7–4a1; L 51ab; T 50ab. D has *dmigs nas su* for *dmigs nas ni*.

once more at the center of the moon."[2588] Meditate that from the former moon, white *oṃ*, red *āḥ*, and blue *hūṃ* appear, like bubbles on the water.[2589]

Regarding *the manifest awakening from the emblem*, the *Concise Sādhana* teaches: "Thereupon, that which resembles a white jasmine moon arises from the three syllables."[2590] Even though this scripture does not explain more than this, the *Sādhana Incorporating the Scripture* teaches: "Set the three seed syllables upon the lunar disk; from that divine identity of being the vajra arises."[2591] Hence this sādhana points to the emblem of vajra as well as to maintaining its divine identity. The *Jewel Rosary* explains how to maintain divine identity: Maintain divine identity with the mantra *vajra ātmako 'haṃ*.[2592]

Then, through the transformation of the vajra marked with the three seed syllables, you are engendered as the First Lord.[2593] This is the *manifest awakening from the complete body*, and the *Concise Sādhana* explains here: "Visualize the First Lord."[2594]

[*The Instruction in the* Guhyasamāja Tantra *and Other Scriptures*]

The method of engendering the First Lord through the five manifest awakenings in this way is likewise taught in the eleventh chapter of the *Guhyasamāja Tantra*: "The Vajra Wisdom[2595] should meditate on the great seal for the sake of

2588. Nāgārjuna, *Mdor byas, Piṇḍīkrama Sādhana*, Tōh 1796, 4a1; L 51cd; T 50cd.

2589. See Tsong kha pa, *Gsang mngon*, 39b2–3.

2590. Nāgārjuna, *Mdor byas, Piṇḍīkrama Sādhana*, Tōh 1796, 4a1; L 52ab; T 51ab.

2591. Nāgārjuna, *Mdo bsre, Sādhanasūtramelāpaka*, Tōh 1797, 12b4.

2592. Ratnākaraśānti, *Rin chen phreng ba, Ratnāvalī*, Tōh 1826, 37b7–38a1. Tsong kha pa, *Gsang mngon*, 39b5, glosses *vajra ātmako 'haṃ*, as "the nature of vajra am I."

2593. See Tsong kha pa, *Gsang mngon*, 39b4–5.

2594. Nāgārjuna, *Mdor byas, Piṇḍīkrama Sādhana*, Tōh 1796, 4a1; L 52c; T 51c.

2595. I take Vajra Wisdom as the subject of the sentence in following Candrakīrti's *Sgron gsal, Pradīpoddyotanaṭīkā*, that glosses *ye shes rdo rje* with *sgrub pa po*. Otherwise, this verse *as it appears in our text* could be translated as: "Meditate on the great seal by means of the supreme vajra syllables of the mantra. For attaining all awakenings [you should meditate] through vajra wisdom."

attaining [through][2596] all awakenings, by means of the supreme vajra syllables of the mantra."[2597] [107a] This verse, cited in both the *Sādhana Incorporating the Scripture* and the *Vajrasattva Sādhana*, means: The three seed syllables of the vajra body, speech, and mind are the three vajra *syllables*. Since they are the source of all mantras, they are *the supreme mantra*.[2598] Gö renders this line as: "The supreme mantra of the three vajra syllables."[2599] By means of this mantra, *meditate on the great seal*—the body of the deity.[2600] Is there an additional significance here? The phrase *all awakenings* refers to the five manifest awakenings, hence *attaining* here must be by means of all five manifest awakenings.

The *Illuminating Lamp* explains: "A great five-pronged vajra arises from the three syllables that are set upon the moon disk." And: "suchness, moon, seed syllables, emblem, and body arise in succession."[2601] Therefore you should certainly generate the First Lord through the five manifest awakenings. Do not assume that since the *Concise Sādhana* does not teach this specifically, you do not need to generate the First Lord through the emblem.

2596. This addition is based on the interpretation of the verse below, though it is not necessarily the most obvious choice. Neither the *Guhyasamāja Tantra* (nor Nāgārjuna's *Mdor byas, Piṇḍīkrama Sādhana,* for this matter) mention the five manifest awakenings in this context. Moreover, the straightforward meaning of the term all awakenings (*byang chub thams cad, sarvabodhi*) refers to the goal of the practice rather than to its method—the five manifest awakenings, as this verse is interpreted in our text. The purpose of the explanation in our text is to identify a scriptural source for the visualization of the First Lord through *the five manifest awakenings*.

2597. *Guhyasamāja Tantra*, Tōh 442; Zhol 15a1; Stog 25a7–b1; Dunh 27b3; Fremantle 1971 v. 1; and Matsunaga 1978, v. 1. The Zhol has *rdo rje gsum yig sngags kyi mchog* for *sngags kyi yi ge rdo rje mchog*, and *phyag rgya chen po* for *phyag rgya chen por* in our text. These variations are discussed below. See also the interpretation of Candrakīrti's *Sgron gsal, Pradīpoddyotanaṭīkā*, Tōh 1785, of this verse, 77a2–3; Chakravarti 1984, 96.

2598. Nāgārjuna, *Mdo bsre, Sādhanasūtramelāpaka*, Tōh 1797, 12b3. D has *rdo rje mchog gsum yi ge sngags* for *sngags kyi yi ge rdo rje mchog* in our text. Candrakīrti, *Rdo rje sems dpa'i sgrub thabs, Vajrasattva Sādhana*, Tōh 1814, 199b1; Luo and Tomabechi 2009, 16.5–6 and 48.15–49.2. D and Luo and Tomabechi have *rdo rje gsum yig sngags mchog gis* for *sngags kyi yi ge rdo rje mchog*; *bsgom pa ni* for *rnam bsgom pa*; *bya ba ste* for *thob bya'i phyir*; *mnyam bskyed pa'i* for *dag gis bya*; and the order of the last two lines is reversed. See also Candrakīrti, *Sgron gsal, Pradīpoddyotanaṭīkā*, Tōh 1785, 77a2–4; Chakravarti 1984, 96.

2599. While the Zhol has *rdo rje gsum yig sngags kyi mchog*, according to Mkhas grub rje here the translation of 'Gos Khug pa lhas btsas is *rdo rje yig gsum sngags kyi mchog*.

2600. Mkhas grub rje follows here Tsong kha pa's *Sgron gsal mchan*, 232b1–3.

2601. Candrakīrti, *Sgron gsal, Pradīpoddyotanaṭīkā*, Tōh 1785, 78b2; Chakravarti 1984, 96.

[Faces and Arms of the First Lord]

Nāgārjuna[2602] and his disciples teach specifically that the First Lord is white, and the *Intense Illuminating Lamp*[2603] and the *Jewel Rosary*[2604] explain that he has three faces and six arms, yet SOME TIBETAN LAMAS[2605] say that it is inappropriate to maintain that the First Lord has three faces and six arms, since the commentary by Muniśrībhadra[2606] explains that he has one face and two arms.

This is unreasonable because (1) it was established in the context of the protection wheel above that white Vajradhara has three faces and six arms, and here it is similarly established;[2607] [107b] and because (2) in response to the question why all the deities of the Guhyasamāja have three faces, *Formulating the Sādhana* cites the interpretation in the definitive meaning of "vajra joining of palms" taught in the *Revelation of the Intention Tantra* that the body of ultimate union is signified by the conventional illusory body, the ultimate mind of clear light, and their indivisibility, while the deity that signifies them has three faces.[2608] THOSE WHO SAY that it is inappropriate for the First Lord—the main signifier of the body of union, the saṃbhogakāya—to have three faces do not understand the meaning of the tantra.

2602. Reading *yab* for *mab* in our text.

2603. Bhavyakīrti, *Rab tu sgron gsal, Prakāśikā*, Tōh 1793.

2604. Ratnākaraśānti, *Rin chen phreng ba, Ratnāvalī*, Tōh 1826, 38a2.

2605. See Bu ston, *Mdor byas 'grel chen*, 35b4–6.

2606. Muniśrībhadra, Thub pa dpal, *Rim pa lnga'i don mdor bshad pa, Pañcakramārthaṭippaṇi*, Tōh 1813, 156b1–2; Sanskrit edition in Jiang and Tomabechi 1996, 17. Note that this work is translated into Tibetan by Bu ston.

2607. See Mkhas grub rje, [23b6–24a2].

2608. Nāgabuddhi, *Rnam gzhag rim pa, Vyavastholi*, chap. 3, Tōh 1809, 127b4–128a4; Tanaka 2016, 115–118. See also our text below [153b1–156a3]. The *Revelation of the Intention Tantra, Dgong pa lung ston, Sandhivyākaraṇa*, passage is Tōh 444, chap. 12, 197b6–198a2 and 198b2–3. See also Tsong kha pa, *Rnam gzhag rim pa'i rnam bshad*, 67a6 and 68a5–69a2.

11. The Yoga of Taking Birth as the Nirmāṇakāya

The Yoga of Taking Birth as the Nirmāṇakāya—Transforming into Vajrasattva's Nirmāṇakāya

This yoga also includes setting the body maṇḍala, blessing the three doors, and meditating on the triple sattvas.

There are four sections here: (1) the ground of purification—taking birth in a womb, (2) the meditation that corresponds to it, (3) a separate explanation of how to meditate on the body maṇḍala, and (4) the blessing of the body, speech, and mind and the meditation on the triple sattvas.

The Ground of Purification—Taking Birth in a Womb[2609]

This is how a human being takes birth in a womb:[2610] Three conditions must be present for conception in a womb, (1) the mother is healthy, fit, and still fertile, (2) the male and female desire each other and join together, and (3) the scent-eater intermediate being hovers nearby and wishes to enter. As the *Sūtra on Entering the Womb* teaches: "When the father and mother desire each other and join together, and the mother is fit and still fertile, and the scent-eater is present nearby, wishing to enter, O Nanda[2611]— 'scent-eater' is an appellation of a being in the intermediate state."[2612]

2609. See Tsong kha pa, *Rnam gzhag rim pa'i rnam bshad*, 33b6–41b4. See also Jinpa 2017, 339–368.

2610. Birth takes place after the intermediate being enters in the midst of the semen and blood and dies there, and not when the fetus emerges out of the womb.

2611. Tib. *Dga' bo*.

2612. As noted above, there are two versions of this *Sūtra*, the *Mngal gnas*, *Nandagarbhāvakrāntinirdeśa*, Tōh 57, and the *Mngal 'jug*, *Āyuṣman Nandagarbhāvakrānti Nirdeśa*, Tōh 58. However, the version cited here is from the *'Dul ba phran tshegs kyi gzhi*, *Vinayakṣudrakavastu*, Tōh 6, 125a3–4; English translations of this and the following passages from these scriptures are found in Kritzer 2014, 39–108. For the different versions of these accounts, see Kritzer 1998 and 2014. This passage is cited also in Tsong kha pa, *Rnam gzhag rim pa'i rnam bshad*, 34a2–3.

Furthermore, [108a] the *Sūtra on Entering the Womb* teaches that three flaws must not be present: (1) flaws in the mother's womb, such as obstructions of wind, bile, and phlegm, or a barley-grain-like center in the womb, or an ant-waisted-like womb and so forth; (2) flaws in pregnancy fluids, as when the semen and blood fail to appear simultaneously at the entrance of the womb, or else appear in a decayed state;[2613] (3) flaws of karma—if the parents have not accumulated karma that would result in their obtaining a child, or the child has not accumulated karma that would result in being parented by them. When any of these three flaws occur, no embryo will form in the womb.[2614]

Once the parents lie down together and engage in churning their organs, the "descending wind"[2615] shifts upward, thereby igniting the ordinary inner heat[2616] at the threefold junction[2617] of the bodies of both. Melted by its heat,[2618] the white and red constituents descend through the empty space within the seventy-two thousand channels of the parents,[2619] and satisfy the five aggregates and the faculties of the parents with bliss, and again everything becomes mingled in the secret lotus of the mother. Finally, very thick clear drops of semen and blood issue from the father and mother respectively, and the consciousness of the intermediate being enters in the midst of their commingled substances. The place where consciousness first enters will become the heart of the fetus. When the consciousness ultimately departs from whence it entered, death occurs. Hence, in a gradual death, consciousness is surely transferred from the heart.

The scent-eater hovering nearby sees the father and mother lying together, and since it clings to desire, [108b] it enters. The *Primary Ground* explains: Seeing its parents lying together, it becomes aroused with an attraction to one of them and a wish to separate from the other. If it is to be born as a male, it is attracted to the mother and wishes to separate from the father, and if it is to be born a female, the opposite occurs. Thus it sees only the one to whom it is attracted, whether male or female, and does not see the other.

2613. Reading *rul ba* for *dul ba*.

2614. This is a summary of the scriptures on this subject. See *'Dul ba phran tshegs kyi gzhi, Vinayakṣudrakavastu*, Tōh 6, 125b6–126a7; the *Mngal gnas, Nandagarbhāvakrānti Nirdeśa*, Tōh 57, 211b5–212a6; and the *Mngal 'jug, Āyuṣman Nandagarbhāvakrānti Nirdeśa*, Tōh 58, 237a7–b4. Our text follows Tsong kha pa, *Rnam gzhag rim pa'i rnam bshad*, 34a4–6.

2615. Tib. *thur sel*, Skt. *apāna*.

2616. Tib. *gtum mo*, Skt. *caṇḍālī*.

2617. Tib. *sum mdo*, Skt. *śṛṅgāṭaka*.

2618. Reading *drod* for *dod*.

2619. Reading *pha ma* for *la ma*.

When it imagines being embraced by him or her, the only parts of the male or female body that appear to it are the sexual organs, male or female, as the case may be. Consequently, anger is engendered in it, and due to this anger, the intermediate being dies, and its consciousness immediately enters in the midst of the commingled semen and blood.[2620]

[How Does the Intermediate Being Enter the Womb?]

It is not certain that consciousness first enters only by way of the mother's secret gate. *Formulating the Sādhana* teaches that it enters through the gate of Vairocana: "When it sees the two organs in union, it is overwhelmed with desire, and therefore abandons the intermediate state. Mounting the wind as on horseback, the lord of consciousness, the vajra mind, arrives posthaste and in an instant or fraction of an instant enters like the jñānasattva through the gate of Vairocana."[2621]

Some early Tibetan lamas say that since it is taught that excrement stands for Vairocana, the gate of Vairocana is the lower gate and for this reason they maintain that the intermediate being enters through the lower gate.[2622] However, this is highly inappropriate, because the same scripture teaches *like the jñānasattva*, which means that the intermediate being enters through the gate of Vairocana as the jñānasattva enters the samayasattva, and the jñānasattva does not enter through the lower gate of the samayasattva. Therefore the gate of Vairocana is the gate at the crown of the head, the place of the body upon which the vajra body Vairocana is set,[2623] [109a] and that is what is meant by the line: the intermediate being enters the body like the jñānasattva enters the samayasattva.

The *Saṃvarodaya Tantra* teaches that it also enters through the mouth: "First[2624] seeing the father and mother in union, the intermediate being enters

2620. This is paraphrasing Asaṅga, *Sa'i dngos gzhi*, *Maulībhūmi*, Tōh 4035, 11b5–12a2; Bhattacharya 1957, 23.5–12, which appears in Tsong kha pa's *Rnam gzhag rim pa'i rnam bshad*, 35a6–b2, with some small differences.

2621. Nāgabuddhi, *Rnam gzhag rim pa*, *Vyavastholi*, chap. 1, Tōh 1809, 123b7–124a1; Tanaka 2016, 92–93. D and Tanaka have *spang te* for *'ong ste*; *zhon nas* for *zhon te*; and *sgo nas zhugs* for *sgor zhugs*. According to our text below [108b], the gate of Vairocana is the crown of the head, the place upon which the Vairocana is set in the body maṇḍala.

2622. This is based on Tsong kha pa, *Rnam gzhag rim pa'i rnam bshad*, 34b4.

2623. This refers to the body maṇḍala and to the blessing of the body.

2624. This word is found neither in Tsuda 1974 nor in the Derge.

through the path of the mouth by the power of very intense joy."[2625] You may wonder whether the mouth is that of the father or the mother, but the *Vajra Garland Tantra* teaches that it is the mouth of the father: "The consciousness riding the wind of previous karma, if it travels at all, moves toward the father's mouth, and then falls under the power of desire. When fire and sun arise in the menses channel of the secret place, it [consciousness] is overwhelmed with powerful desire that intensifies greatly, and driven by the wind of karma[2626] it enters through the mouth of the father to the point where the vajra and lotus meet. Then it turns into the seed from which sentient beings evolve."[2627]

That is why even though its consciousness enters the mother's womb when the intermediate being dies, initially it enters through the father's mouth or the crown of his head, and emerges from his secret place, and only then enters the mother's lotus and is reborn in the midst of the commingled semen and blood. It is in correspondences with this process that the ritual methods are taught.[2628] On the several occasions during the sādhana when the deity is made to emerge from the womb, the syllables signifying all invited buddhas or the intermediate being—that are set in space and so forth—initially enter through the crown of the head or the mouth of the father, and the deity is

2625. *Sdom 'byung*, Tōh 373, 266a6; Sanskrit, Tibetan, and English translation in Tsuda 1974, chap. 2, Tib. vv. 14ab and 15cd, Skt. v. 14. Tsuda has *pha ma'i kun tu sbyor sogs ni / srid pa'i skye bos mthong gyur nas /* for *dang po pha ma'i kun sbyor las / srid pa'i skye po can du mthong /* in our text, and *shin tu dga' dang bcas stobs kyis / kha yi lam nas 'jug par 'gyur /* for *shin tu nges bar kun dga'i stobs / kha'i lam la rab tu 'jug*. Note also that the wording in the citation of the verse above [74a6–b1] is different. However, the citation here is almost identical to that of Tsong kha pa, *Rnam gzhag rim pa'i rnam bshad*, 34b5–6.

2626. See Alakakalaśa's commentary on this tantra, *Rdo rje phreng ba'i rgya cher 'grel pa zab mo'i don gyi 'grel pa, Vajramālāṭīkāgambhīrārthadīpikā*, Tōh 1795, 131a3.

2627. *Rgyud rdo rje phreng ba, Vajramālā Tantra*, chap. 17, Tōh 445, 230a2–3. Cited in Tsong kha pa, *Rnam gzhag rim pa'i rnam bshad*, 34b6–35a2, where the chapter number is specified. Our text is almost identical to that of the *Rnam gzhag rim pa'i rnam bshad*, the only difference is *chags pa mchog tu 'dod par* for *chags pas mchog tu 'dod par*. D has *sngon la* for *sngon las*; *brgya lam gang tshe 'khrul gyur na* for *brgya la gang tshe 'gro 'gyur na*; *pha yi mkha' la mtshungs par gnas* for *pha yi kha la mchungs par ldan*. Tsong kha pa's *Rnam gzhag rim pa'i rnam bshad* has *chags pa mchog tu 'dod par 'gyur* for *chags pas mchog tu 'dod par 'gyur*, and D has *'jug pa pha yi kha yi rlung* for *'jug pa rtsa yi kha yi rlung*. The Bkra shis lhun po version has *me dang nyi ma* as D for *ma dang nyi ma* in the Zhol. Cited also in Bu ston, *Mdor byas 'grel chen*, 38b1–3, which is also similar to the reading of the *Rnam gzhag rim pa'i rnam bshad*, but Bu ston has *sngon las rlung gis* for *sngon las rlung gi*; *'gro gyur na* for *'gro 'gyur na*; *mtshungs par ldan* for *mchungs par ldan*; and *me dang nyi ma 'tshar ba na* for *me dang nyi ma 'char ba na*. Considering these variant readings, the translation offered here is very tentative.

2628. See the explanation of how the First Lord transforms into Vajrasattva's nirmāṇakāya below.

then generated from the drop that emerges through the vajra path into the lotus of the mother.

The autocommentary on the *Abhidharmakośa* explains that the intermediate being enters through the door of the mother's womb: "Intermediate beings do not enter by piercing the mother's belly, [109b] but through the door of the birthplace. For this reason, when twins are born, the one who emerges later is called the elder brother and the one who emerges earlier is called the younger brother."[2629] Thus it is necessary to maintain that there are three modes of entering into the womb. However, since the intermediate being cannot be obstructed, it has no real need for an opening like a door to enter.[2630] The autocommentary on the *Abhidharmakośa* explains that insects are known to emerge out of a split ball of iron.[2631]

[A Boy or a Girl?]

Moreover, if the sentient being is to be male, he will dwell in the womb inclining toward the mother's right side and facing her back. If it is to be a female, she will incline toward the mother's left side facing forward. This, due to the mode of aroused desire and the wish to embrace when it first sees its mother and father lying together.[2632]

It is taught that one can ascertain whether it will be a boy or a girl and so forth[2633] from the way the father's wind moves when his final drop of semen is emitted while he and the mother lie together, for the *Saṃvarodaya Tantra* teaches: "The wise can determine [the child's gender] instantly at the very moment the seed descends: If the wind moves to the right, it will always be a

2629. Vasubandhu, *Mdzod 'grel, Kośabhāṣya*, chap. 3, following v. 13ab, Tōh 4090, 119a3; Pradhan 1975, 124, English translation in Pruden 1988–1990, 391. Cited in Tsong kha pa, *Rnam gzhag rim pa'i rnam bshad*, 35a2–3.

2630. Vasubandhu, *Mdzod, Abhidharmakośakārikā*, chap. 3, v. 14c, Tōh 4089; and *Mdzod 'grel, Kośabhāṣya*, Tōh 4090, 120a2; Pradhan 1975, 125; English translation in Pruden 1988–1990, 391.

2631. This is a paraphrase of Vasubandhu, *Mdzod 'grel, Kośabhāṣya*, chap. 3, following v. 14c, Tōh 4090, 120a2–3; Pradhan 1975, 125; English translation in Pruden 1988–1990, 392. Our text is almost identical to Tsong kha pa, *Rnam gzhag rim pa'i rnam bshad*, 35a4–5, except for *thu lum* for *tho lum*.

2632. Vasubandhu, *Mdzod 'grel, Kośabhāṣya*, chap. 3, following v. 15ab, Tōh 4090, 120b7–121a3; Pradhan 1975, 126; English translation in Pruden 1988–1990, 395. See also Nāgabuddhi, *Rnam gzhag rim pa, Vyavastholi*, chap. 1, Tōh 1809, 124b3–4; Tanaka 2016, 96; and Tsong kha pa, *Rnam gzhag rim pa'i rnam bshad*, 41a1–4.

2633. Such as a neuter. Tib. *ma ning*, Skt. *napuṃsaka*.

male. If the wind moves to the left, it will certainly be a female. If the wind moves between the two, it will always be a neuter."[2634]

This ends the discussion concerning entry into the womb.

[How the Embryo Develops][2635]

The consciousness of the intermediate being, which first mingles with the semen and blood in the mother's secret place, subsequently moves to the place of origins in the mother's womb and develops there. [110a] The *Sūtra on Entering the Womb* teaches that the place of origins is located between the lower part of the mother's stomach and the upper part of her intestines.[2636]

There are five phases in the womb. *Formulating the Sādhana* teaches that these five phases are "the liquid-cream-like," "the viscous," "the globular," "the solidified," and "with the limbs slightly protruding."[2637] Both the *Sūtra*

2634. *Sdom 'byung*, Tōh 373, 266b5–6; Sanskrit, Tibetan, and English translation in Tsuda 1974, chap. 2, vv. 26–27. Tsuda has *mkhas pas sa bon lhung ba'i rim / dus kyi skad cig yang dag mtshon / g.yas nas rlung ni rgyu ba gang / thams cad du ni skyes bur 'gyur /* for *sa bon lhung dus yud tsam la / rim pa mtshon bya lags pa'i blo / g.yas par brgyu ba'i rlung dag las / thams cad tshe na skyes par 'gyur /* and *g.yon nas rlung ni rgyu ba gang / nges par bud med rnams su 'gyur / gnyis ka'i dbus rgyu'i sa bon gang / rtag tu ma ning 'gyur ba'o /* for *gal te g.yon par rlung brgyu na / nges par bud med dag tu 'gyur / gnyis ka'i dbus brgyu'i rlung dag las / rtag tu ma nang dag tu 'gyur /*. Again, this passage is not cited from the *Sdom 'byung*, *Saṃvarodaya Tantra*, as we know it. See also the chapter on entering the womb in the *'Dul ba phran tshegs kyi gzhi*, *Vinayakṣudrakavastu*, Tōh 6, 135b2–4.

2635. See Kritzer 2014.

2636. Once more, this refers to the chapter on entering the womb in the *'Dul ba phran tshegs kyi gzhi*, *Vinayakṣudrakavastu*, Tōh 6, 135b2; English translation in Kritzer 2014, 69, rather than to the *Mngal gnas*, Tōh 57, *Nandagarbhāvakrānti Nirdeśa*, or to the *Mngal 'jug*, *Āyuṣman Nandagarbhāvakrānti Nirdeśa*, Tōh 58. Cited also in Tsong kha pa, *Rnam gzhag rim pa'i rnam bshad*, 37b2.

2637. Nāgabuddhi, *Rnam gzhag rim pa*, *Vyavastholi*, chap. 1, Tōh 1809, 124a4–5; Tanaka 2016, 94. Tib. *mer mer po*, *ltar ltar po* or *ldar ldar po*, *gor gor po*, *mkhrang gyur* or *'khrang gyur*, and *rkang lag 'gyus pa*, Skt. *kalala*, *arbuda*, *peśin*, *ghana*, and *praśakha*, see above [102b]. There are variations in the names of these stages among the different sources. For example, in the *Kośa* the Tibetan terms are *nur nur po*, *mer mer po*, *nar nar po*, *mkhrang 'gyur*, and *rkang lag 'gyus pa*.

on Entering the Womb[2638] and the commentary on the *Abhidharmakośa*[2639] explain that the first phase is "the oval,"[2640] and the second is "the liquid-cream-like," while the *Primary Ground* explains the stages in a reverse order.[2641] Still it seems that apart from a mere difference in the order of the names given, the general meaning is similar, and thus, no contradiction.

The liquid-cream-like is covered on the outside with something like cream, while inside it is highly liquified. When that is ripened by the wind,[2642] it turns into the viscous fetus, which is like cream both outside and in, thick as yogurt but not yet flesh-like. When that is ripened by the wind, it turns into the globular, spheric fetus,[2643] which becomes fleshy but cannot withstand pressure. When that in turn is ripened by the wind, it becomes the solidified fetus, which can withstand pressure, whereupon that is ripened by the wind, and becomes the fetus with its limbs slightly protruding—five protrusions marking the two thighs, the two shoulders, and the head. Then, stage by stage, the hair on the head, the nails, bodily hair, and the sense organs—the eyes and so forth—appear in their various shapes and the gender marks. The sūtra cited in the commentary on the *Abhidharmakośa* teaches: "The hair on the head, bodily hair, nails, and so forth, the sense organs in their various shapes, and the markings come into being."[2644] [110b] Yaśomitra explains that *markings* are the bases of the sense organs—the eyes and so forth.[2645]

2638. Only in the version of entering into the womb in the *Vinaya*, *'Dul ba phran tshegs kyi gzhi*, *Vinayakṣudrakavastu*, Tōh 6, 127a4–7 and 129a3–7, the *nur nur po* is first and the *mer mer po* second. In the *Mngal gnas*, *Nandagarbhāvakrānti Nirdeśa*, Tōh 57, 214a7–b3, and in the *Mngal 'jug*, *Āyuṣman Nandagarbhāvakrānti Nirdeśa*, Tōh 58, 239b3–5, the order is reversed. But see the *Sdom 'byung*, *Saṃvarodaya Tantra*, Tōh 373, 266a7–b2; Tsuda 1974, chap. 2, vv. 17–20; and also Tsong kha pa, *Rnam gzhag rim pa'i rnam bshad*, 37b6–38a1.

2639. Vasubandhu, *Mdzod 'grel*, *Kośabhāṣya*, chap. 3, following v. 19a–c, Tōh 4090, 123a5–6; Pradhan 1975, 130; English translation in Pruden 1988–1990, 400.

2640. Tib. *nur nur po*.

2641. That is to say, first *mer mer po* and then *nur nur po*. Asaṅga, *Sa'i dngos gzhi*, *Maulībhūmi*, Tōh 4035, 14a5. Bhattacharya 1957, 28.1–2, has *mer mer po*, *nur nur po*, *ltar ltar po*, *mkhrang gyur*, and *rkang lag 'gyus pa*.

2642. The *Mngal gnas*, *Nandagarbhāvakrānti Nirdeśa*, Tōh 57, and the *Mngal 'jug*, *Āyuṣman Nandagarbhāvakrānti Nirdeśa*, Tōh 58, specify the names of this and the following winds.

2643. Tib. *rlor rlor po*.

2644. Vasubandhu, *Mdzod 'grel*, *Kośabhāṣya*, chap. 3, following v. 19a–c, Tōh 4090, 123a5; Pradhan 1975, 130; English translation in Pruden 1988–1990, 400. D has *sogs pa* for *sogs dang*, and *skye bar 'gyur* for *'byung bar 'gyur* in our text.

2645. Yaśomitra, Grags pa bshes gnyen, *Chos mngon pa'i mdzod kyi 'grel bshad*, *Abhidharmakośaṭīkā*, Tōh 4092, 272a2–3.

The *Saṃvarodaya Tantra* teaches: "First the embryo has the shape of the oval; the liquid-cream-like comes second; third, the viscous; and fourth, the globular.[2646] Urged on by the winds, it assumes a fish-like form. After a lapse of five months, the five limbs evolve from the seed. The hair of the head and body, the nails, and the gender markings appear in the seventh month. The sense organs in their particular shapes develop in the eighth month. In the ninth month the fetus is perfectly complete. In the tenth month it is endowed with a mind."[2647]

Hence, it is taught that after the body has been completed in the ninth month, it will develop the intention to emerge outside in the tenth month. According to the *Sūtra on Entering the Womb* it will be born at the end of the thirty-eighth week.[2648] The *Primary Ground* teaches that it will be born four days after that.[2649] It seems that all agree that the fetus remains in the womb for nine whole months and the beginning of the tenth.

This ends the discussion on development in the womb.

[How the Fetus Is Born from the Womb]

The *Sūtra on Entering the Womb* explains that when it has completed its development in this way by the thirty-eighth week, a wind born of prior karma and called "limbs"[2650] rises up and turns the being abiding in the womb completely around. With arms clenched tightly, it then heads from the womb

2646. Tib. *nur nur po, mer mer po, ltar ltar po,* and *gor gor po*; Skt. *kalala, arbuda, peśin,* and *ghana.*

2647. *Sdom 'byung,* Tōh 373, 266a7–b2; Sanskrit, Tibetan, and English translation in Tsuda 1974, chap. 2, vv. 17–20. Tsuda has *dang po'i rnam pa nur nur po* for *dang por nur nur po rnam pa*; *mer mer po ni* for *mer mer po na*; *ltar ltar por* for *ltar ltar po*; *de bzhin bzhi pa gor gor po* for *bzhi pa gor gor po nyid do*; *bskul tsam gyis* for *bskul bas na*; *sha* for *nya* (Skt. *māṃsa*); *zla ba bdun na skra dang spu / sen mo rtags ni skye bar 'gyur* for *skra spu sen mo rnams dang rtags / zla ba bdun gyis skye bar 'gyur*; *zla ba brgyad na dbang po dang / lus kyi yang lang 'byung bar 'gyur* for *dbang po rnams dang gzugs rnams ni / zla ba brgyad la skye bar 'gyur*; *zla ba dgu na* for *zla ba dgu yis*; and *zla ba bcu na* for *zla ba bcu yis.*

2648. *Mngal gnas, Nandagarbhāvakrānti Nirdeśa,* Tōh 57, 219b3–5; and *Mngal 'jug, Āyuṣman Nandagarbhāvakrānti Nirdeśa,* Tōh 58, 244a6–b3; *'Dul ba phran tshegs kyi gzhi, Vinayakṣudrakavastu,* Tōh 6, 136b3–4. See also Tsong kha pa, *Rnam gzhag rim pa'i rnam bshad,* 38b3–4.

2649. Asaṅga, *Sa'i dngos gzhi, Maulībhūmi,* Tōh 4035, 14a2; Bhattacharya 1957, 27.5–6.

2650. Our text has *yan lag* as does *'Dul ba phran tshegs kyi gzhi, Vinayakṣudrakavastu,* Tōh 6, 136b3, while the *Mngal gnas, Nandagarbhāvakrānti Nirdeśa,* Tōh 57, 219b4, has *yan lag sdud pa,* "assembling the limbs." See also Kritzer 2014, 72, n. 386.

toward the door of the source of phenomena. Then a wind called "facing downward,"[2651] born of prior karma, rises up and pushes this being into the path of the urinary tract of the mother, with its feet pointing upward and its head down. Furthermore, the *Sūtra on Entering the Womb* teaches that, in the thirty-sixth week, the fetus no longer likes its dwelling place in the womb and wishes to leave it. [111a] By the thirty-seventh week, it has the notion that its dwelling place in the womb has become filthy and malodorous. Then, when the thirty-eighth week has elapsed, it is propelled by the wind toward the gate of the womb and emerges outside.[2652]

While the former body of the scent-eating intermediate being, fashioned of mere very subtle wind and mind, is indiscernible to the corporeal eye of ordinary people, once it enters the semen and blood commingled in the womb, where it matures and then emerges outside, it becomes an object of perception by the corporeal eye of ordinary people. *Formulating the Sādhana* explains that this mode of birth is explained through the stages of the samādhi of the vajra origination from samaya in the *Guhyasamāja Tantra*.[2653] The meaning of this will soon be explained.

Here ends the discussion of the ground of purification, that is, taking birth in the womb.

The Meditation That Corresponds to This: Which Stage of the Purifier Corresponds to Which Stage in the Ground of Purification

There are two parts here: (1) how the First Lord transforms into Vajrasattva's nirmāṇakāya and (2) how the visualization of placing the deities on the transformed body and so forth is applied to the ground of purification.

How the First Lord Transforms into Vajrasattva's Nirmāṇakāya

There are two sections here: (1) refuting the position of others and (2) establishing our own system.

2651. Tib. *kha thur du lta ba*, Skt. *avāṅmukha*.

2652. *Mngal gnas*, *Nandagarbhāvakrānti Nirdeśa*, Tōh 57, 219b2–5; *Mngal 'jug*, *Āyuṣman Nandagarbhāvakrānti Nirdeśa*, Tōh 58, 244a4–b3; *'Dul ba phran tshegs kyi gzhi*, *Vinayakṣudrakavastu*, Tōh 6, 136b3–4.

2653. Nāgabuddhi, *Rnam gzhag rim pa*, *Vyavastholi*, chap. 1, Tōh 1809, 124b4–5; Tanaka 2016, 96. Tib. *dam tshig 'byung ba rdo rje*, Skt. *samayodbhavavajra*. See the *Gsang 'dus*, *Guhyasamāja Tantra*, Tōh 442; Zhol 3b1–3; Stog missing; Dunh 3a4–b1; Fremantle 1971, 178–179; and Matsunaga 1978, 5–6.

Refuting the Position of Others[2654]

The transformation of the First Lord into the nirmāṇakāya is not mentioned in the *Sādhana Incorporating the Scripture*. The *Concise Sādhana* teaches only: "Transform through entry of/into[2655] Akṣobhya."[2656] The *Intense Illuminating Lamp*,[2657] the *Jewel Rosary*,[2658] and Samayavajra[2659] maintain[2660] that Akṣobhya emanates from the heart, performs actions for the sake of sentient beings, gathers back and dissolves into you, whereby you transform into Akṣobhya.[2661] SOME EARLY AND LATER TIBETAN LAMAS[2662] maintain this as well, but it is extremely inappropriate because: [111b] (1) it is the intermediate being that enters into the midst of the commingled coarse constituents of the semen and blood, and not the semen and blood that enter the intermediate being; (2) the semen and blood are the semen and blood of the parents, and the intermediate being does not enter the semen and blood produced from its own body; (3) in that case, the instruction of *Formulating the Sādhana* to visualize the deities here according to the samādhi of vajra overpowering[2663] taught in the *Guhyasamāja Tantra* would be irrelevant; (4) moreover it would contradict *Formulating the Sādhana*, which teaches that Akṣobhya, into which the First

2654. Based on Tsong kha pa, *Rnam gzhag rim pa'i rnam bshad*, 42b5–43b1.

2655. This is the point of controversy here. Is it Akṣobhya who enters into the First Lord or is it the First Lord who enters Akṣobhya? D 4a2 and P 4788, 5a5, have *mi bskyod pa ni rjes zhugs pas*, while G 5a6, N 5a6, and P2661, 4b2, have *mi bskyod pas ni rjes zhugs pas*, for *mi bskyod pa rjes su zhugs pas bsgyur* in our text. L 53a and T 52a have *akṣobhyānupraveśena*.

2656. Nāgārjuna, *Mdor byas*, *Piṇḍīkrama Sādhana*, Tōh 1796, 4a2; L 53a; T 52a.

2657. Bhavyakīrti, *Rab tu sgron gsal*, *Prakāśikā*, Tōh 1793, 121b5.

2658. Ratnākaraśānti, *Rin chen phreng ba*, *Ratnāvalī*, Tōh 1826, 38a4–7.

2659. Or *Kṛṣṇasamayavajra, [Nag po] Dam tshig rdo rje, *Rim pa lnga'i dka' 'grel*, *Pañcakramapañjikā*, Tōh 1841, 160b4–6.

2660. See also Bu ston, *Mdor byas 'grel chen*, 39a3–5.

2661. Tsong kha pa, *Rnam gzhag rim pa'i rnam bshad*, 42b6, which Mkhas grub rje follows here, has "transform into the nirmāṇakāya" instead of "transform into Akṣobhya." The wording of the *Rnam gzhag rim pa'i rnam bshad* is very similar to that of Bu ston, *Mdor byas 'grel chen*, 39a3–4.

2662. Bsod nams grags pa, *Gsang 'dus bskyed rim rnam gzhag*, 52b1–2, identifies these lamas as the followers of the tradition of 'Gos. See also Ngor chen, *Gsang 'dus dkyil 'khor gyi sgrub thabs dngos grub rgya mtsho*, work 106, 10a1–3. Thus the "early lamas" here are the followers of 'Gos and the later are Ngor chen and so forth.

2663. Tib. *zil gyis gnon pa rdo rje*, Skt. *abhibhavanavajra*, in the first chapter of the *Guhyasamāja Tantra*, Tōh 442; Zhol 3a5–b1; Stog 4a6–7 [the rest is missing]; Dunh 3a1–4; Fremantle 1971, 178–179; and Matsunaga 1978, 5. See [112a] below.

Lord is to be transformed, should be applied in correspondence to the liquid-cream-like fetus, first to evolve among the five phases in the womb when the semen and blood of the parents commingle in the womb.

Establishing Our Own System

[How Is the First Lord Transformed into the Nirmāṇakāya?]

When applying the transformation of the First Lord into the nirmāṇakāya to the ground of purification,[2664] *Formulating the Sādhana*[2665] refers to the method[2666] of the samādhi of vajra overpowering all tathāgatas[2667] taught in the first chapter of the *Guhyasamāja Tantra*, as well as to the *Prajñāsūtra*,[2668] which teaches that when the seventy-two thousand channels are aroused, both male and female are satiated with bliss of paramount joy. Thus *Formulating the Sādhana* teaches that both the samādhi of vajra overpowering taught in the *Guhyasamāja Tantra* and the scripture belonging to the mother tantra, the *Saṃvarodaya Tantra*, describe the emergence of the drop in which the intermediate being takes rebirth. Moreover, it is necessary to apply the explanations of these scriptures not only to the ground of purification but also to the transformation into the nirmāṇakāya. For if *Formulating the Sādhana* explained only the ground of purification but not how to generate the deities in correspondence with it, it would follow that this scripture does not teach any of the most necessary matters.

How does the samādhi of vajra overpowering explain this? [112a] The *Guhya-samāja Tantra* teaches: "Then the Blessed One, the Tathāgata Bodhicittavajra, dwelt in absorption in the samādhi called vajra overpowering all tathāgatas.[2669]

2664. Our text closely follows here Tsong kha pa, *Sgron gsal mchan*, 62b1–4.

2665. Paraphrasing here Nāgabuddhi, *Rnam gzhag rim pa*, *Vyavastholi*, chap. 1, Tōh 1809, 124a2–3; Tanaka 2016, 93. See also Tsong kha pa, *Rnam gzhag rim pa'i rnam bshad*, 36a6–37a4.

2666. D has *rigs pa* for *rim pa* in our text. The Sanskrit is *nyāya*. Our text follows Tsong kha pa, *Sgron gsal mchan*, 62b1.

2667. This is the complete name of this samādhi, Tib. *de bzhin gshegs pa thams cad zil gyis gnon pa rdo rje*, Skt. *sarvatathāgatābhibhavanavajra*.

2668. Tib. *Shes rab kyi mdo*; this is the *Sdom 'byung*, *Saṃvarodaya Tantra*, Tōh 373, 266a7; Sanskrit, Tibetan, and English translation in Tsuda 1974, chap. 2, v. 16, cited already on [74b] above. This will be discussed below.

2669. Tib. *de bzhin gshegs pa thams cad zil gyis gnon pa rdo rje*, Skt. *sarvatathāgatābhi-bhavanavajra*.

As soon as the Blessed One, the lord of all tathāgatas, dwelt in absorption, the entire realm of space abided in the vajra nature of all tathāgatas. Then, as many as there were sentient beings residing in the entire realm of space, through the blessing of Vajrasattva all of them attained the bliss and mental rapture of all tathāgatas."[2670]

The *Illuminating Lamp* explains these lines at four levels of interpretation:[2671] According to the shared level of interpretation,[2672] this passage explains the specially visualized deities and their deeds, which are described above.[2673] According to the ultimate interpretation,[2674] the lines show that *what is to be overpowered* are the five aggregates—indicated by the term tathāgatas—of the meditator on the illusory body, and *the method used for overpowering* is the purification of the mental proliferations of dualistic appearances by dissolving them in clear light, whereby the three empty states[2675] dissolve in turn, and then the all-empty [the fourth type]—the actual clear light—is realized.

[The Hidden Levels of Interpretation]

There are two hidden levels of interpretation:[2676] When these lines are explained in conjunction with the hidden desire on the *path*, they teach that by absorbing in union the male and female practitioners generate wisdom of bliss and emptiness. And when these lines are explained in conjunction with the hidden desire on the *ground*, they show that the ground of purification for the transformation of the First Lord into nirmāṇakāya is the mingled drop of semen and blood from the parents where the intermediate being takes birth.

2670. *Guhyasamāja Tantra*, chap. 1, Tōh 442; Zhol 3a5–b1; Stog 4a6–7 [the rest is missing]; Dunh 3a1–4; Fremantle 1971, 178–179; and Matsunaga 1978, 5.

2671. Tib. *tshul bzhi*. Candrakīrti, *Sgron gsal, Pradīpoddyotanaṭikā*, Tōh 1785, 14b5–15a6; Chakravarti 1984, 20. This is based on Tsong kha pa, *Sgron gsal mchan*, 62b1–64a4.

2672. Tib. *spyi don*, Skt. *samastāṅga*.

2673. Above [88b2–4].

2674. Tib. *mthar thug tu*, Skt. *kolikavyākhyā*. See Candrakīrti, *Sgron gsal, Pradīpoddyotanaṭikā*, Tōh 1785, 15a5–7; Chakravarti 1984, 20; and Tsong kha pa, *Sgron gsal mchan*, 63a6–64a4.

2675. These three empty states are the empty, the very empty, and the greatly empty states. Tib. *stong pa, shin tu stong pa, stong pa chen po*, and *thams cad stong pa*; Skt. *śūnya, atiśūnya, mahāśūnya*, and *sarvaśūnya*.

2676. Tib. *sbas don*, Skt. *garbhī*. See Candrakīrti, *Sgron gsal, Pradīpoddyotanaṭikā*, Tōh 1785, 15a2–5; Chakravarti 1984, 20. This paragraph is based on Tsong kha pa, *Sgron gsal mchan*, 62b2–4, and his *Rnam gzhag rim pa'i rnam bshad*, 36a4–6.

At the literal level of interpretation,[2677] these lines explain the purifier—that is, they teach how the meditator on the creation stage actually transforms the First Lord into the nirmāṇakāya. [112b]

First, here is the way the ground of purification is explained.[2678] On the level of the *ground*, when the parents lie down together and the fire of great desire dissolves the white and red constituents, these melted constituents fill the hollow of the all-empty space within the seventy-two thousand channels and descend. This elucidates the line of the *Guhyasamāja Tantra* cited above:[2679] "As soon as the Blessed One dwelt in absorption, the entire realm of space abided in the vajra nature of all tathāgatas." The meaning of *abided in the vajra nature of all tathāgatas* is that the melted constituents are the essence of the five aggregates of those who lie together, and this *nature* is called vajra because that which descends cannot be reversed by anything at all.

Next the *Guhyasamāja Tantra* teaches: "Then as many as there were sentient beings residing in the entire realm of space, through the blessing of Vajrasattva all of them attained the bliss and mental rapture of all tathāgatas."[2680] This means: Through the descent of the melting constituents within the hollow channels that are the *realm of space*, *as many* aggregates, sensory spheres, and sense bases of the father and mother *as there were*—which are the basis of designation[2681] of *sentient beings*—were blessed *through the blessing of Vajrasattva*, who is the wisdom of skillful methods. He blessed them with the melted constituents that are like jasmine,[2682] and thereby the father and mother *attain the bliss and mental rapture of all tathāgatas*, that is, the five aggregates of the father and mother overwhelmed with bliss.[2683]

[Regarding the name of the samādhi, *vajra overpowering all tathāgatas* in the *Guhyasamāja Tantra*,] what is *overpowered* here are the five aggregates of the parents designated tathāgatas. The agency of *overpowering* are the constituents melting within the channels. The method of *overpowering*

2677. Tib. *yig don*, Skt. *akṣarārtha*. This level of interpretation is not found in Candrakīrti's *Sgron gsal*, *Pradīpoddyotanaṭīkā*, Tōh 1785, but only in Tsong kha pa, *Sgron gsal mchan*, 62b4.

2678. Mostly following Tsong kha pa, *Sgron gsal mchan*, 62b4–63a6. Below Mkhas grub rje will follow the next passage in the *Sgron gsal mchan*, 63a6–b6.

2679. See above [112a].

2680. See above [112a].

2681. Tib. *tha snyad gdags pa'i gzhi*.

2682. Reading *kun da* for *kun de*.

2683. See Candrakīrti, *Sgron gsal*, *Pradīpoddyotanaṭīkā*, Tōh 1785, 15a4–5; Chakravarti 1984, 20; and Tsong kha pa, *Sgron gsal mchan*, 63a3–6.

is overwhelming of the five aggregates with bliss. The mind of Vajradhara who abides single-pointedly in the resolution, "I will explain this" [113a] is the samādhi of *vajra overpowering.*

The *Illuminating Lamp* explains it this way: "The Blessed One dwelt in absorption in the samādhi by the name vajra overpowering of all tathāgatas. *All tathāgatas* who are the nature of the aggregates and so forth are overpowered, that is to say, unified, by the aspect of relative bodhicitta. The samādhi is vajra-like because it is indestructible." Then "*As soon as the Blessed One, the lord of all tathāgatas, dwelt in absorption, the entire realm of space,* that is to say, the empty interior of the seventy-two thousand channels, *abided in the vajra nature of all tathāgatas,* that is to say, partook in the nature of wisdom of skillful methods. *Then, through the blessing of Vajrasattva,* that is to say, through the arising of skillful wisdom, *all sentient beings,* that is to say, the psycho-physical constituents, the aggregates, and so forth,[2684] *as many as there were in the entire realm of space, attained the bliss and mental rapture of all tathāgatas,* that is, when they join their organs, they are melted by the fire of great passion and experience the bliss of supreme joy. This is the hidden level of interpretation."[2685]

[The Literal Level of Interpretation]

Now I will explain the literal level of interpretation and how it is applied to the creation stage.[2686] The line in [Tsongkhapa's] sādhana:[2687] "The father-mother Buddha are absorbed in union in[2688] their natural abode, for the sake of guiding sentient beings,"[2689] is equivalent in meaning to the line of the *Guhyasamāja Tantra*: *dwelt in absorption in the samādhi called vajra overpowering*

2684. Reading *skandha* for *sthāṇva* in Chakravarti 1984, 20; Tib. has *phung po.*

2685. Candrakīrti, *Sgron gsal, Pradīpoddyotanaṭīkā,* Tōh 1785, 15a2–5; Chakravarti 1984, 20; Tsong kha pa, *Sgron gsal mchan,* 62b4–63a6. D has *rtsa phran* for *rtsa*; *rdo rje sems dpa' byin gyi rlabs kyis* for *rdo rje sems dpa'i byin gyis brlabs kyis*; and *ting nge 'dzin gang gi* for *ting nge 'dzin gang gis* in our text.

2686. Following Tsong kha pa, *Sgron gsal mchan,* 63b2–4; and his *Rnam gzhag rim pa'i rnam bshad,* 43a1–3.

2687. Here the text of Tsong kha pa, *Gsang mngon,* is related to the lines of the *Guhyasamāja Tantra,* cited above on [112a].

2688. Tsong kha pa, *Gsang mngon,* 40a1, has *nas* for *na* here, but his *Sgron gsal mchan* has *na.*

2689. Tsong kha pa, *Gsang mngon,* 40a1–2. This sādhana has *de bzhin gshegs pa* for *sangs rgyas* in our text.

all tathāgatas, and is similar to the parents lying together at the time of the ground. The line in [Tsongkhapa's] sādhana[2690] "Then Akṣobhya[s], the nature of the Vajra tathāgata family formed from their drops while absorbing in union [113b] pervade the entire realm of space" is equivalent in meaning to the line of the *Guhyasamāja Tantra*: *As soon as the Blessed One, the lord of all tathāgatas, dwelt in absorption, the entire realm of space abided in the vajra nature of all tathāgatas.*

Regarding the time of the ground, the line[2691] "the entire realm of space" corresponds to the empty interior of the seventy-two thousand channels of the parents. The line in [Tsongkhapa's] sādhana "Akṣobhya[s] who pervade"[2692] corresponds to the hollow[2693] channels filled with the melting constituents. "These Akṣobhyas bless all sentient beings, who thereby attain pure bliss and mental rapture"[2694] is equivalent in meaning to the line of the *Guhyasamāja Tantra*: *Then, as many as there were sentient beings residing in the entire realm of space, through the blessing of Vajrasattva all of them attained the bliss and mental rapture of all tathāgatas.* And at the time of the ground this corresponds to the aggregates and so forth of the parents who are blessed by the melted constituents and are overwhelmed with bliss. The line in [Tsongkhapa's] sādhana "All the Akṣobhyas merge together inside the celestial mansion"[2695] corresponds to the semen and blood of the parents commingling in the secret lotus. The First Lord who "enters there"[2696] corresponds to the intermediate being who dies as it enters in the midst of the semen and blood of the birthplace.

[The Phases in the Womb]

As was taught, pregnancy, from the entry of consciousness into the parents' semen and blood in the womb to the completion of nine months of development, occurs in five stages. These are further divided into the five stages of the semen and the five stages of the blood, and both are applied to the five tathāgata families.[2697] *Formulating the Sādhana* teaches: "Further, through

2690. Paraphrasing Tsong kha pa, *Gsang mngon*, 40a2–3.

2691. This line is found in both the *Guhyasamāja Tantra* and Tsong kha pa, *Gsang mngon*.

2692. Again, paraphrasing Tsong kha pa, *Gsang mngon*, 40a2–3.

2693. Reading *sbubs* for *sgrubs*.

2694. Paraphrasing Tsong kha pa, *Gsang mngon*, 40a3.

2695. See Tsong kha pa, *Gsang mngon*, 40a4.

2696. This refers to Tsong kha pa, *Gsang mngon*, 40a4, which has: "and I enter [there]."

2697. See Tsong kha pa, *Rnam gzhag rim pa'i rnam bshad*, 38b5–39b4.

the blessing of the five tathāgatas, [114a] the five phases arise, beginning with the phase of the seed. Here, the liquid-cream-like embryo is blessed by Akṣobhya, the viscous embryo by Ratnasaṃbhava, the globular by Amitābha, the solidified fetus by Amoghasiddhi, and the fetus with the limbs slightly protruding by Vairocana. Next I will explain the five phases of the blood: 'The fluid'[2698] is blessed by Akṣobhya, 'the red'[2699] by Amitābha, 'the glob'[2700] by Ratnasaṃbhava, 'the solidified'[2701] by Amoghasiddhi, and 'the commingled'[2702] by Vairocana."[2703] The *Saṃvarodaya Tantra* also teaches a somewhat different method for applying these stages to the five tathāgata families.[2704]

What is the purpose of applying the five phases in the womb to the five tathāgatas families here?[2705] These two scriptures do not explain that the five phases are the respective grounds of purification for the five tathāgatas. Their aim is to clarify that as the being who has taken birth in the womb is completed through the five phases of development, so in the sādhana, the deities placed on the nirmāṇakāya are comprised of the five tathāgata families, and this nirmāṇakāya, into which the First Lord has transformed, must be applied in correspondence to the phases in the womb. Another aim is to elucidate that since the first of the five phases in the womb, the stage of the liquid-cream-like embryo, is applied to Akṣobhya, when during the meditation, the First Lord, like the intermediate being, first enters, it is into Akṣobhya that he has to enter.

Furthermore, among the five phases in the womb, the stage of the liquid-cream-like embryo, formed as soon as the parents' semen and blood mingle, is

2698. Tib. *zhu ba*, Skt. *dravam*.

2699. Tib. *dmar po*, Skt. *rakta*.

2700. As can be seen in note 2703, our text has *gong bu ni* for *gor gor po* in the Bstan 'gyur; the Sanskrit is *peśin*. In his *Rnam gzhag rim pa'i rnam bshad*, 39a1–2, Tsong kha pa explains that the two are the same.

2701. Tib. *mkhrang gyur* or *'khrang 'gyur*, Skt. *ghana*.

2702. Tib. *yang dag par 'gres pa*, Skt. *sammiśra*.

2703. Nāgabuddhi, *Rnam gzhag rim pa*, *Vyavastholi*, chap. 1, Tōh 1809, 124a6–b1; Tanaka 2016, 94–95. D has *ltar ltar po* and Tanaka has *lhar lhar po* for *ldar ldar po* in our text; D and Tanaka have *'od dpag med kyi'o* for *'od dpag tu med pa'i'o*; *mkhrang gyur* for *'khrang 'gyur*; *don yod grub pa'i'o* for *don yod grub pa yi'o*; *mi bskyod pa'o* for *mi bskyod pa'i'o*; and *gor gor po* for *gong bu ni* in our text.

2704. *Sdom 'byung*, Tōh 373, 266b2–3; Sanskrit, Tibetan, and English translation in Tsuda 1974, chap. 2, vv. 21–22. Cited in Tsong kha pa, *Rnam gzhag rim pa'i rnam bshad*, 39a4–6.

2705. See Tsong kha pa, *Rnam gzhag rim pa'i rnam bshad*, 39b1–3, and also Bu ston, *Mdor byas 'grel chen*, 39b5–7.

mostly comprised—among the five elements—of water, [114b] while in terms of the purity of the element, among the five tathāgata families Akṣobhya should be classified with the element of water. Therefore, in [Tsongkhapa's] sādhana Akṣobhya is formed from the bodhicittas of the father-mother Buddha and mingles into one, then there the First Lord enters.

[Correspondences to the Ground of Purification]

Why is the term *nirmāṇakāya* used for the deity formed when the First Lord enters Akṣobhya? So that the meditation will correspond to the fruitional saṃbhogakāya—not an object perceived by the eyes of ordinary people—who, for the sake of the disciples, displays the nirmāṇakāya that takes on coarse elements. In this way, the First Lord, who is similar to the saṃbhogakāya, transforms [by entering] into Akṣobhya, analogous to the taking on of coarse elements, and hence the term *nirmāṇakāya* is used in the context of Akṣobhya.

SOME LATER LAMAS[2706] say that it is inappropriate for the yogi to enter into Akṣobhya, formed from the bodhicitta of the father-mother victorious ones—who from their own natural abode are absorbed in union—and transform into the nirmāṇakāya.[2707] The reason is that in such a case, during the Supreme King of Maṇḍalas, meditations on emanating, performing the deeds and so forth would be the enlightened activities of someone who had already awakened in the past, rather than steps to perfect the yogi's own accumulations.

Such a position would be extremely unreasonable because (1) during the Supreme King of Maṇḍalas you should visualize the deities emanating, performing their specific deeds, merging with their respective jñānasattvas in their natural abodes, then visualize Akṣobhya reappearing and dissolving into yourself while the other deities abide in their respective abodes within the maṇḍala, and following this, you should recite mantras and so forth.[2708] This is clearly explained by Ārya Nāgārjuna and his disciples, and you too maintain it. If so, the mantra recitation and so forth become the enlightened speech activities of someone who has already awakened in the past, [115a] they could not be steps that lead to the yogi's own attainments. Such an argument would be fully compatible with your position. (2) Several authoritative books written by mahāsiddhas teach various ritual methods for generating the deities

2706. See Red mda' ba, *Bsgrub pa dpal bas zhus lan*, Kathmandu, 48b4–5; TBRC, 303b–304a.

2707. See Tsong kha pa, *Gsang mngon*, 40a1–6.

2708. See Tsong kha pa, *Gsang mngon*, 52a5–68a6.

whereby a light emanates from the seed syllable and emblems, inviting the countless buddhas and bodhisattvas of the ten directions, they dissolve there, and then, as a result of a complete transformation, you are generated as a deity. Thus it follows that the plentiful systems that teach this in the four classes of tantra would be inappropriate. (3) In the case of Cakrasaṃvara and Hevajra too, the generation of the samayasattva, the entry of the jñānasattva into it, and everything that follows, including the meditations and recitations, would be enlightened activities of someone else who has been already awakened, not steps to perfect the yogi's own accumulations.

Therefore, although the semen and blood of the father and mother that arrive in the secret place of their body initially belong to the parents, once the consciousness of the intermediate being enters there, mingles, develops, and emerges out of the womb as a person, whatever this person may do is not the activity of the parents but of their offspring. Likewise, you should first meditate on Akṣobhya, invoking him from his natural abode, and then enter and mingle with him. From then on, while you abide in the identity of Vajrasattva, any deed you perform is your own doing; hence, YOUR claim that someone else carries out these activities is invalid.

How the Visualization of Placing the Deities on the Transformed Body[2709] *and So Forth Is Applied to the Ground of Purification*[2710]

EARLY SCHOLARS[2711] applied the meditation up to the blessing of the body, speech, and mind to the period in the womb. They applied the visualizations of the triple sattvas respectively to the body emerging from the womb, the

2709. This is Vajrasattva's nirmāṇakāya that is undergoing a process of transformation from the First Lord, a process that will be completed when the triple sattvas are set.

2710. See Tsong kha pa, *Rnam gzhag rim pa'i rnam bshad*, 43a6–44a1.

2711. Nor bzang rgya mtsho, *Gsang ba 'dus pa'i bskyed rim gyi don gsal bar byed pa'i sgron me*, 123a2–3, attributes this position to Bu ston. However, this is not the position of Bu ston himself, but a position Bu ston attributes to "Tibetan lamas"; his own method is different. See his *Mdor byas 'grel chen*, 48b5–6. This position is, however, held by 'Gos Khug pa lhas btsas, *Gsang 'dus stong thun*, 13b3–4, as pointed out by Paṇ chen Blo bzang chos kyi rgyal mtshan, *Bskyed rim dngos grub rgya mtsho'i snying po*, 54a6. See also see Red mda' ba, *Yid kyi mun sel*, 8a2–3.

wind that abides in it, and to the "short *A*."[2712] LATER LAMAS[2713] apply the meditation on the body maṇḍala to the period in the womb, and both the blessing of the three places and the triple sattvas to the newly born child. [115b] Neither EARLY nor LATER SYSTEM is appropriate.

The *Guhyasamāja Tantra* teaches: "Then the Blessed One, the Tathāgata, Bodhicittavajra, was absorbed in the samādhi called 'vajra origination from samaya of the vajra body, speech, and mind of all tathāgatas,' and blessed this personification[2714] of the great vidyā[2715] with the blessing of the mantra of all tathāgatas. As soon as the Blessed One, the Tathāgata Bodhicittavajra, blessed, all tathāgatas perceived him as having three faces."[2716]

Formulating the Sādhana explains that these lines of the *Guhyasamāja Tantra* elucidate how to set the deities on the body transforming into the nirmāṇakāya: "After this, by the end of a ten-month period, the being is delivered out of the mother's womb in the way indicated by the samādhi of vajra origination from samaya, taught in the *Guhyasamāja Tantra*. Thereby, the scent-eater, the being that hovers nearby, turns into an object of the corporeal eye, as the *Guhyasamāja Tantra* teaches: *All tathāgatas* clearly *perceived* the Blessed One, the Tathāgata Bodhicittavajra, *as having three faces*."[2717] In this way *Formulating the Sādhana* relates the two events "as soon as he was delivered from the womb" and "perceived him as having three faces." This establishes that the line cited above *blessed the personification of the great vidyā with the mantra* must be applied to an event before emergence from the womb.

2712. Reading *rlung dang a thung* for *rlung a thung*, as in Tsong kha pa's *Rnam gzhag rim pa'i rnam bshad*, 43b1. A similar passage appears in 'Gos Khug pa lhas btsas, *Gsang 'dus stong thun*, 13b3–4, and, as just noted, Bu ston, in his *Mdor byas 'grel chen*, 48a5–6, attributes it to "Tibetan lamas."

2713. Nor bzang rgya mtsho, *Gsang ba 'dus pa'i bskyed rim gyi don gsal bar byed pa'i sgron me*, 123a2–3, attributes this position to Red mda' ba, but as Paṇ chen Blo bzang chos kyi rgyal mtshan specifies in his *Bskyed rim dngos grub rgya mtsho'i snying po*, 54a6, this is the system of Bu ston. See Bu ston, *Mdor byas 'grel chen*, 45a6–b3.

2714. Tib. *skyes bu gzugs*, Skt. *puruṣamūrti*.

2715. Tib. *rig pa chen po*, Skt. *mahāvidyā*.

2716. *Guhyasamāja Tantra*, Tōh 442; Zhol 3b1–3; Stog missing; Dunh 3a4–b1; Fremantle 1971, 178–179; and Matsunaga 1978, 5–6. The Zhol has mistakenly *byang chub kyi sems rdo rje'i* for *byang chub kyi sems rdo rje*, and *byin gyi brlabs* for *byin gyis brlabs* in our text.

2717. Nāgabuddhi, *Rnam gzhag rim pa*, *Vyavastholi*, chap. 1, Tōh 1809, 124b4–6; Tanaka 2016, 96–97. See above [101a–b]. D and Tanaka have *tha mar* for *mthar*; *'byung ba'i* for *'byung ba*; *rdo rje'i* for *rdo rje*; *ting nge 'dzin la* for *ting nge 'dzin*; and *'khor gyi* for *'khor ba'i* in our text. See *Gsang 'dus*, *Guhyasamāja Tantra*, Tōh 442; Zhol 3b1–3; Stog missing; Dunh 3a4–b1; Fremantle 1971, 178–179; and Matsunaga 1978, 5–6.

The *Illuminating Lamp* explains the meaning of the line *the blessing of the mantra* in the *Guhyasamāja Tantra*: "This indicates the following: [116a] By means of the method taught in the sādhana consisting of the four yogas, up to the end of the meditation on the triple sattvas, the meditator is blessed as the embodiment of great Vajradhara, the rūpakāya of all mantras."[2718] This clearly shows that you should generate a body blessed by all mantras by means of the steps taught in the sādhana up to the triple sattvas. Hence, all the steps up to the triple sattvas should be applied to the birth process until the fetus turns toward the door of the womb.[2719]

Even though there is no speech in the womb, the tongue, the basis of speech, exists there, so there is nothing inconsistent in applying the correspondence to the blessing of speech.[2720] This being so, in correspondence with the gradual ripening of the aggregates, sensory spheres, sense bases, and the major and minor limbs in the womb, you should set the deities successively on the body of the First Lord transformed into nirmāṇakāya. The *body* of the nirmāṇakāya is blessed in correspondence with the complete evolution of the parts of the body of the being in the womb; *speech* is blessed in correspondence with the evolution of the eight bases of speech[2721] and the wind of breath that circulates through the mouth; the *mind* is blessed in correspondence with the evolution of perfect mental engagement through which the mind consciousness moves toward its objects.

The correspondences of the triple sattvas depend on detailed knowledge of the special essential points of the completion stage. Roughly speaking, in a general way, the samayasattva, meditated upon as the body of Vajrasattva's nirmāṇakāya, corresponds to the temporal coarse body of the being in the womb, while the jñānasattva and the samādhisattva correspond to its innate subtle body.

2718. Candrakīrti, *Sgron gsal, Pradīpoddyotanaṭīkā*, Tōh 1785, 15b4–5; Chakravarti 1984, 21. The Sanskrit is somewhat different. D has *sgrub pa'i thabs* for *bsgrub pa'i thabs* and *bar gyi* for *bar gyis* in our text, which follows Tsong kha pa, *Rnam gzhag rim pa'i rnam bshad*, 43b3. See *Gsang 'dus, Guhyasamāja Tantra*, Tōh 442; Zhol 3b2; Stog missing; Dunh 3a4–b1; Fremantle 1971, 178–179; and Matsunaga 1978, 5.

2719. See Tsong kha pa's *Sgron gsal mchan*, 65a1–3, and his *Rnam gzhag rim pa'i rnam bshad*, 43b3–5.

2720. See Tsong kha pa's *Sgron gsal mchan*, 65b4, and his *Rnam gzhag rim pa'i rnam bshad*, 43b5.

2721. These are the chest, throat, palate, tongue, nose, teeth, crown, and lips. Tib. *khog pa, mgrin pa, rkan, lce, sna, so, spyi bo*, and *mchu*.

12. How to Meditate on the Body Maṇḍala

A Separate Explanation of How to Meditate on the Body Maṇḍala

[116b] There are two parts here: (1) refuting the systems of others and (2) establishing our own system.

Refuting the Systems of Others[2722]

Some Tibetan lamas[2723] claim the master Vajraghaṇṭa taught that[2724] "sentient beings are naturally present nondual maṇḍalas," and that "the body maṇḍala is an unconstructed maṇḍala," and therefore, although the bodies of all beings have existed from the very beginning as maṇḍalas, they lack any awareness of this and in order to become aware, they meditate by visualizing something that already exists. Such a position is utterly wrong and entirely unsubstantiated, for if so, it would follow that there is no truth-of-suffering, according to which the bodies of beings are born through karma and afflictive emotions, or that the maṇḍala of Vajradhara is formed through

2722. See Bentor 2017a and 2017b.

2723. In his *Bde dril bskyed rim*, 8b6, Mkhas grub rje indicates that such a position is maintained by Bsod nams rtse mo in his commentary on the practice according to Dril bu pa. See Bsod nams rtse mo, *'Khor lo Bde mchog dril bu pa'i gzhung gi dbang gi bya ba mdor bsdus*, 7a1–3. The following deliberation follows Tsong kha pa's commentary on this work by Dril bu pa, the *Dril dbang*, 1b4–4a1; his *'Dod 'jo*, 122a3–b1 and 137a3–b4; and his *Sngags rim chen mo*, chap. 7, 303–305.

2724. The first line is found in Vajraghaṇṭa, *'Khor lo sdom pa'i dbang gi bya ba mdor bsdus pa*, Tōh 1431, 219b5–6; Finot 1934, 62. The second is a paraphrase of this and the following verse; see Finot 1934, 62. Abhayākaragupta cites this verse in at least two of his works, the *Man ngag snye ma*, *Āmnāyamañjarī*, chap. 23, Tōh 1198, 214a2, and the *'Jigs pa med pa'i gzhung 'grel*, *Abhayapaddhati*, Tōh 1654, 199b2; Sanskrit and Tibetan in Chog Dorje 2009, 47 and 181–82. I would like to thank Professor Harunaga Isaacson for pointing out the citation in the Abhayākaragupta and for sending me its Sanskrit version. Elsewhere I have discussed certain Tibetan interpretations of the opening verses of this work by Vajraghaṇṭa in more detail; see Bentor 2017a.

karma and afflictive emotions. Moreover, that would imply a common basis for real Vajradhara and saṃsāric beings. And furthermore, sentient beings experiencing saṃsāric suffering would necessarily be Vajradharas. No part of the body and mind would then be omitted from the meditation of the maṇḍala, and all parts of the body and mind would be true aspects of the maṇḍala.

If this were so, it would be necessary to maintain that obscuration is tantamount to wisdom, and so forth. If all sentient beings were true buddhas, this would contradict the fact that the vessel-world is not a true celestial mansion of self-appearing wisdom; and therefore, it would not be possible for saṃsāra to be an object of knowledge. If one is a buddha, but does not recognize this, then how could a buddha who *does not know* even who he or she is *know* all phenomena? Therefore such a stupid buddha who *does not know* any of the objects of knowledge would be most astonishing!

Furthermore, [117a] if this is what YOU maintain, YOU must agree that one who is a buddha and recognizes this would not need to meditate on the path ever again. Hence, once having understood the body maṇḍala, the yogi would not need to meditate on any path at all. Therefore, if YOU say this, and at the same time maintain that it is necessary to tread the grounds and paths in stages by meditating on the path, YOU are out of your mind. What could be more astonishing than YOUR assertion that one who has attained the eleventh ground of Universal Light,[2725] taught as the highest achievable ground in the path of the Pāramitā Vehicle, is still at a much lower stage than the stage of Vajradhara in the Mantra Vehicle, when at the same time YOU assert that all sentient beings exist from the very beginning as true maṇḍalas of Vajradhara?!

Do the respective parts of the maṇḍala—which have existed from the start in a nonapparent and nonmanifested manner on the respective parts of the body and mind of sentient beings—become manifest by means of meditation on the path? The position that all parts of the fruit truly exist in the cause from the very beginning in a nonapparent manner is the whole tradition of the Saṃkhya School. Furthermore, if the bodies of all sentient beings actually existed as maṇḍalas from the start, then every act of killing a sentient being would constitute the heinous[2726] sin of killing a tathāgata. And it would likewise follow that someone who performs the ten nonvirtuous actions would be a buddha. How can I describe the infinite consequences of such a position?

THERE ARE SOME STUPID PEOPLE WHO SAY that the aim of every

2725. Tib. *kun tu 'od*, Skt. *samantaprabhā*.

2726. Literally "immediate," refers to a heinous action that brings about an immediate retribution in the lowest hell.

meditation on the creation stage is to understand what the meditator has not recognized—namely, that the external world has ever been a celestial mansion of the maṇḍala while the sentient beings dwelling in the world have ever been deities. [117b] This can be refuted by way of the following reasoning: Those who hold such a position necessarily maintain that it would be impossible for the impure animate and inanimate realms that are the ground of purification to come into being. And thus, any system based on a ground of purification and a purifier would be unreasonable. If all sentient beings were nothing but Vajradhara, there could be no possible distinction between those who are competent to practice the mantra path and those who are not. For those who do not experience the possibility of afflictive emotions and obstructions to omniscience, it is pointless to meditate on the two stages of the path, and so forth. Therefore, YOU WHO SAY SO and claim YOU are accomplished in the mantra path, tell me, who would be unaccomplished?!

Furthermore, SOME MAINTAIN[2727] that when yogis meditate on themselves as a deity, they actually become that deity. But since they are not a deity, yet meditate as though they were, their cognition is false, and thus, cannot serve as a suitable basis for effecting buddhahood. Such a position can also be refuted with the above-stated reasoning. Moreover, when yogis meditate during the sādhana practice in accordance with the deeds of the specially visualized deities, initiating all sentient beings, purifying all their wrong-doings and obscurations, placing them on the stage of Vajrasattva and so forth—are these sentient beings in truth as the yogis visualize them, or not?

If they are, this means that sentient beings have all become Vajradhara. Consequently, unenlightened sentient beings cannot exist, and neither can sentient beings who have not attained initiation nor sentient beings who have not completed the purification of their wrong-doing and obscurations. And if the sentient beings are not as the yogis visualize them, then the yogis meditate in contradiction to reality. Thus the cognition of the yogis will be false, and false cognition is unsuitable as a basis for effecting buddhahood. What would YOU say to this?

Furthermore, it would be necessary to maintain that upon the consecration of the paintings and images of the Buddha, and so forth, [118a] they actually become buddhas. When offerings are made by visualizing the entire realm of space filled with flowers and so forth—if these offerings existed as visualized,

2727. See Puṇḍarīka, *Dri ma med pa'i 'od*, *Vimalaprabhā*, Tōh 1347, 228b–230a; Jagannatha Upadhyaya 1986, vol. 3, 67.31–69.5. See also Grags pa bshad sgrub, *Rdo rje 'jigs byed bskyed rim*, 151–153.

they would be perceived,[2728] yet, they are imperceptible,[2729] and therefore the argument is refuted.[2730] If they do not exist as visualized, the cognition that perceives them as such is false, and thus it is unsuitable as a basis for effecting buddhahood.

There are numerous other such arguments. During initiations, as soon as the water initiation of Akṣobhya has been conferred, the disciples become Akṣobhya, so why must they later be purified of pride and other afflictive emotions through the initiations of Ratnasaṃbhava and the other tathāgatas? If, while meditating on yourself as Vajradhara, experience confirms that your body is in no way adorned with the major and minor marks of the Buddha and your mind is thoroughly unable to realize all phenomena, yet at the same time you claim to be a buddha, then you belie reality. And if you hold no "pride in conceit,"[2731] and are cognizant that you possess no buddha qualities,[2732] yet at the same time claim you are a buddha, this will surely engender a major transgression of monastic vows. Hence, you must not behave unrestrainedly under the influence of erroneous views.

THOSE who accept these views yet say they cannot tolerate the position that there is an "essence body"[2733] in the continuum of sentient beings endowed with all the qualities of permanence, stability, freedom, and the fruit [must perforce] wail aloud: "We are unable to analyze anything by way of reason when whatever we say is driven by desire, hatred, and ignorance."[118b]

SOME SAY:[2734] Although this has been discussed at length, taking into account that the suchness of the bodies of sentient beings and the suchness of the deities of the maṇḍala are not distinct in nature, we maintain that all sentient beings exist primordially as maṇḍalas, but we do not agree that they exist as the actual maṇḍalas of the buddhas. SO THEY SAY. If this were so, it would be likewise unreasonable to differentiate between constructed [colored

2728. Tib. *snang du rung*, Skt. *dṛśya*, suitable to appear, see the following note.

2729. Tib. *mi dmigs pa*, Skt. *anupalabdhi*. This is a reference to the term *snang rung ma dmigs pa*, *dṛśyānupalabdhi*, nonobservation of the suitable to appear, see a note in our text above [103a].

2730. Reading *khegs* for *khags* in our text.

2731. Tib. *mngon pa'i nga rgyal*. One of the seven prides, wherein one thinks one has attained something not attained.

2732. This refers to the ten powers of the Buddha, the four fearlessnesses, the four perfect understandings, and so forth.

2733. Tib. *ngo bo nyid sku*, Skt. *svābhāvikakāya*.

2734. See Tsong kha pa, *Sngags rim chen mo*, chap. 7, 304, and the response of Mus srad pa Byams pa rdo rje rgyal mtshan in his *Dbang chu'i rtsod spong*, 48a6–50b5.

powder and painted cloth] maṇḍalas and those that are unconstructed [body maṇḍalas], since the suchness of colored powder and painted cloth maṇḍalas on the one hand and the suchness of the [body maṇḍalas] deities on the other are not distinct in nature.

Furthermore,[2735] if the meditation on the body maṇḍala were merely a visualization of one's body existing primordially as a maṇḍala, this would contradict the explanation that during the practice of Guhyasamāja all deities of the body maṇḍala are generated from seed syllables, and therefore YOUR position would be extremely displeasing to the ear of scholars.

Moreover, SOME EARLIER LAMAS[2736] explained that when you meditate on the deities to be placed on the body, you should visualize each deity in its respective form, but when you meditate on the celestial mansion, you should merely visualize individual parts of your own body in the nature of, or as substitutes for, individual parts of the celestial mansion without meditating on their respective forms as such. For example, you would meditate on the eight major joints of your body in the nature of, or as substitutes for, the eight pillars of the celestial mansion, without visualizing their forms. This is inappropriate, since if it were sufficient to meditate on the nature of the celestial mansion or on a substitute for it, without visualizing the form of the celestial mansion itself, then it would also be sufficient to meditate on the deities in this way. The reason for this is that (1) these two meditations are similar in every respect and (2) authoritative sources teach that you should meditate on the celestial mansion in the same mode that you meditate on the deities in their respective forms. It is taught, for example, that you should meditate on the torso—being one-span-long square—in the form of a maṇḍala with four corners and four doors. As Ārya Nāgabuddhi taught: "The body maṇḍala of the yogi that appears as a celestial mansion is formed by first drawing the Brahmā line, and then dividing the area into squares and so forth."[2737] [119a] And the *Vajra Garland Explanatory Tantra* teaches this as well: "The body has become the celestial mansion, which is the perfect support for all buddhas."[2738]

2735. See Tsong kha pa, *'Dod 'jo*, 122a6–b1.

2736. In his *Bde dril bskyed rim*, 8b4, Mkhas grub rje points out that this is the tradition of the Zhwa lu pa. Tsong kha pa as well objects to such a position. See his *Sngags rim chen mo*, chap. 7, 303–305; *Slob tshul*, 16b1–3; and *Bskyed rim zin bris*, 28a6–b1; as well as his *'Dod 'jo*, 121a6–b2, in the context of mother tantras.

2737. Nāgabuddhi, *Rnam gzhag rim pa*, *Vyavastholi*, chap. 2, Tōh 1809, 125a2; Tanaka 2016, 98. D and Tanaka have *yis* for *yi*.

2738. *Rgyud rdo rje phreng ba*, *Vajramālā Tantra*, chap. 68, Tōh 445, 275a2. D has *'gyur* for *gyur*; *brten* for *bsten*; and *kun gyis* for *kun gyi* in our text.

And: "Meditate on them as the celestial mansion,"[2739] meaning that you should meditate on your body, which has become the celestial mansion.

[Some Additional Arguments of Other Opponents]

SOME LAMAS of the Tibetan *Guhyasamāja Tantra*[2740] say that it is not appropriate to place the thirty-two deities, visualized according to their iconographies, on the yogi's body—transformed into Vajrasattva—since the *Concise Sādhana* clearly states that you should place only the seed syllables of these deities there: "Then, those who know the divisions of the aggregates and so forth should place the deities from Vairocana up to Sumbharāja on their bodies by actually setting the seed syllables of these deities on their bodies."[2741] From this we understand that Ārya Nāgārjuna and his disciples intend that you should meditate on the deities by placing their respective seed syllables on the appropriate locations of your body rather than by meditating on the forms of the deities.

THEY ALSO SAY[2742] that it is inappropriate to place the five vajra ladies[2743] upon the father, because should you place the five vajra ladies—who are the five purified sense objects[2744]—on the five organs of the mother, and the seed syllables of the bodhisattvas[2745]—who are the five purified senses[2746]—on the five organs of the father, then when the father and mother join in union, the deities placed on the sense bases[2747] would also join in union. Because of this,

2739. *Rgyud rdo rje phreng ba*, *Vajramālā Tantra*, chap. 68, Tōh 445, 275a6.

2740. See Red mda' ba, *Bsgrub pa dpal bas zhus lan*, Kathmandu, 49b6–50a3; TBRC, 305a. In his *Sgron gsal mchan*, 191b1, Tsong kha pa likewise objects to the opinion that during the body maṇḍala the yogi meditates on the seed syllables in the nature of the deities without generating the deities themselves.

2741. Nāgārjuna, *Mdor byas*, *Piṇḍīkrama Sādhana*, Tōh 1796, 4a3; L 55; T 54. D has *sa bon gyis* for *sa bon gyi*, and *dgod pas* for *dgod pa* in our text. The readings in our text are the same as in Red mda' ba, *Bsgrub pa dpal bas zhus lan*, Kathmandu, 50a1; TBRC, 305a, cited here.

2742. See Red mda' ba, *Bsgrub pa dpal bas zhus lan*, Kathmandu, 50a3–5; TBRC, 305a–b. See also Tsong kha pa's *Rnam gzhag rim pa'i rnam bshad*, 58b3–5.

2743. Tib. Rdo rje ma-s. These are Tib. Gzugs rdo rje ma, Sgra rdo rje ma, Dri rdo rje ma, Ro rdo rje ma, and Reg bya rdo rje ma; Skt. Rūpavajrā, Śabdavajrā, Gandhavajrā, Rasavajrā, and Sparśavajrā.

2744. Tib. *yul lnga*: material forms, sounds, smells, tastes, and objects of touch.

2745. These are Tib. Sa snying, Phyag rdor, Nam snying, 'Jig rten dbang phyug, Sgrib sel, Skt. Kṣitigarbha, Vajrapāṇi, Khagarbha, Lokeśvara, Vikṣambhin.

2746. Tib. *dbang po lnga*, Skt. *pañcendriya*.

2747. Tib. *skye mched*, Skt. *āyatana*.

the *Concise Sādhana* does not instruct you to place the five vajra ladies on the body of the father, nor does the *Vajra Garland Explanatory Tantra* offer instructions about placing the five vajra ladies in the context of the body maṇḍala.

THEY SAY that were this not so, and you placed the five bodhisattvas joined in union with the vajra ladies on the father, you would also have to place the vajra ladies embraced by the bodhisattvas on the mother.[2748] Similarly, [119b] following the same reasoning, you would also have to place the ten fierce male deities embraced by the ten fierce female deities on the limbs of the father, and the ten fierce female deities embraced by the ten fierce male deities on the limbs of the mother.

THEY SAY[2749] that the instructions in *Formulating the Sādhana* on placing the ladies of the five sense objects refer to the body maṇḍalas of both the father and mother. THEY ALSO SAY[2750] that it is inappropriate to place the four mothers, Locanā and so forth, on the navel, heart, throat, and crown of the head,[2751] for the *Concise Sādhana* teaches: "The mantrin places Locanā, Māmakī, Pāṇḍaravāsinī, and likewise Tārā on the earth, and so forth,"[2752] meaning that the four mothers are placed in the positions of the four physical elements. Therefore, THEY SAY, it is appropriate to place Locanā on the genitals, the location of the earth-wind; Tārā on the navel, the location of the wind-wind; Māmakī on the heart, the location of the water-wind; and Pāṇḍaravāsinī on the throat, the location of the fire-wind.

So THEY SAY,[2753] but these are simply wrong assertions.

2748. Rūpavajrā embraced by Kṣitigarbha and so forth.

2749. See Red mda' ba, *Bsgrub pa dpal bas zhus lan*, Kathmandu, 50a5–6; TBRC, 305b.

2750. See Red mda' ba, *Bsgrub pa dpal bas zhus lan*, Kathmandu, 50a6–b3; TBRC, 305b–306a.

2751. In Tsong kha pa, *Gsang mngon*, 42a2–b3, Spyan ma is at the navel, Māmakī at the heart, Gos dkar mo at the throat, and Sgrol ma at the crown of the head.

2752. Nāgārjuna, *Mdor byas*, *Piṇḍīkrama Sādhana*, Tōh 1796, 5b4; L 96cd–97ab; T 95cd–96ab.

2753. A similar position is attributed by Bu ston, *Mdor byas 'grel chen*, 42a4, to Tibetan lamas.

[Our Response to These Arguments]

[The Five Vajra Ladies]

In the context of placing the deities on the body of the mother,[2754] the *Concise Sādhana* teaches: "Upon the mother visualize the vajra ladies, beginning with Rūpavajrā, absorbed in union with the bodhisattvas, Kṣitigarbha and so forth."[2755] This clearly indicates that the five vajra ladies embraced by the five bodhisattvas should be placed on the body of the mother, and hence, it is established that the five bodhisattvas embraced by the five vajra ladies should be placed on the body of the father as well.

Your statement about *Formulating the Sādhana* and the explanation there that placing the five vajra ladies refers to the body maṇḍalas of both the father and mother clearly contradicts the scripture itself, for in a transitional passage[2756] on placing the deities, *Formulating the Sādhana* teaches: [120a] "That being so, now I will explain the causes and fruits of placing the deities in the nature of the aggregates, the sensory spheres, and the sense bases of your own body maṇḍala."[2757] Hence, the deities should be placed on your own body as the father. If it were taught here that the deities should be placed on the body of the mother, it would be appropriate to explain that the fierce female deities are placed there as well, which is not the case.[2758]

Then too, the explanation about placing Maitreya on the nerves and sinews is immediately followed by the explanation about placing the five vajra ladies on the body of the yogi,[2759] which is followed in turn by the explanation on placing the ten fierce deities on the limbs.[2760] Hence the explanation that refers the mother is irrelevant here.

2754. See below [144b].

2755. Nāgārjuna, *Mdor byas, Piṇḍīkrama Sādhana*, Tōh 1796, 5b4–5; L 97cd–98ab; T 96cd–97ab. This is in the context of the meditation on the consort, not the body maṇḍala.

2756. This passage is found after the description of the body as a celestial mansion, introducing the placing of the deities dwelling there.

2757. Nāgabuddhi, *Rnam gzhag rim pa, Vyavastholi*, chap. 2, Tōh 1809, 125a3–4; Tanaka 2016, 99. D and Tanaka have *rang bzhin gyis* for *rang bzhin gyi*.

2758. While the ten fierce male deities are placed on the body of the father, on the body of the mother or the consort are placed ten fierce female deities. See below [144b].

2759. See Nāgabuddhi, *Rnam gzhag rim pa, Vyavastholi*, chap. 2, Tōh 1809, 125b6–7; Tanaka 2016, 102–103.

2760. See Nāgabuddhi, *Rnam gzhag rim pa, Vyavastholi*, chap. 2, Tōh 1809, 126a2–4; Tanaka 2016, 104–105.

YOU state that if the five bodhisattvas placed on the sensory organs are embraced by the five vajra ladies, it follows that the ten fierce male deities placed on the limbs should be embraced by the ten fierce female deities. This shows that YOU do not understand the system of the body maṇḍala. This is so because the five sensory organs and the five objects subsumed in the mental continuum exist separately in the body and are the ground of purification or the bases for generating the deities. Likewise, the five bodhisattvas and the five vajra ladies are generated from faculties and sensory objects that are separate. However, no two separate right arms exist as a basis for generating Yamāntaka and Vetālī.[2761]

Otherwise, according to YOUR position, it would be reasonable to maintain that while the five tathāgatas should be placed on the body of the father, the four mothers should not be placed there. And while the four mothers should be placed on the body of the consort, the five tathāgatas should not be placed there. This is comparable to the position YOU maintain that when the five bodhisattvas are placed on the body of the father, it is inappropriate to place the five vajra ladies on his body; and when the five vajra ladies are placed on the body of the mother, it is inappropriate to place the five bodhisattvas on her body. If we said such a thing, what would YOU answer?!

Furthermore, [120b] in the *Concise Sādhana*, when the deities are placed on the body of the mother, she is described mainly as an action consort [a real

2761. Mkhas grub rje argues here that indeed the five bodhisattvas placed on the sensory organs are embraced by the five vajra ladies. However, it is not possible to conclude on this basis that the ten fierce male deities placed on the limbs should be embraced by the ten fierce female deities. The five bodhisattvas are the purified aspects of the five sensory organs and the five vajra ladies are the purified aspects of the five sense objects. When sensations occur the five sensory organs and their five objects are united. For example, when the eye meets a form, or the nose meets a scent the sense and its object are united. Importantly not only the senses but their objects as well are "subsumed in the mental continuum" of the yogis; that is to say, they belong to the ordinary saṃsāric existence of the yogis and thus must be purified before the yogis can be awakened. For this reason, the senses and their objects are the ground of purification, and their purifiers are the five bodhisattvas and the five vajra ladies. Just as the sensory organs and their objects are united during a sensation, the five bodhisattvas and the five vajra ladies embrace each other.

The limbs of the body, too, are grounds of purification of the creation stage and are purified by the ten fierce male deities. But unlike the sensory organs paired with their objects, the limbs are not paired. For example, a hand holding a hammer is not necessarily united with it. Therefore there is no reason for the ten fierce male deities to embrace the ten fierce female deities.

The visualization of Yamāntaka arising on the right arm of the yogi's body is described in Tsong kha pa, *Gsang mngon*, 45a4; and the visualization of Vetālī on the right arm of the consort is described on 51b2.

consort].[2762] If in that context you do not generate the five sensory organs of the action consort as the five bodhisattvas, then because your sensory organs are generated as the five bodhisattvas, the sensory organs of the consort will therefore be generated as the five bodhisattvas and likewise the five sensory objects subsumed in the mental continuum of the consort will be generated as the five vajra ladies. Hence, it would be ludicrous to purify and bless the five sensory objects that are subsumed in your mental continuum.

In establishing that there are thirty-two deities in the *emanated maṇḍala*, both *Formulating the Sādhana* and the *Illuminating Lamp* cite the explanation in the *Vajra Garland Explanatory Tantra* that there are thirty-two deities in the *body maṇḍala*.[2763] The verse cited is: "The bodies of the victorious one abides successively in the body of the vajra master."[2764] These lines indicate that the body of the vajra master is the base upon which the thirty-two deities are placed. And thus, the view that the deities are placed on the bodies of both the father and the mother is idle talk.[2765] Moreover, if the number of deities in the *emanated maṇḍala* is determined on the basis of the number of deities in the *body maṇḍalas* of both the father and mother, then, according to YOUR view, it would be necessary to maintain[2766] that there are many more than thirty-two deities on the *emanated maṇḍala*, because the fierce female deities and fierce male deities on the body would be counted separately.

So why do the *Vajra Garland Explanatory Tantra* and *Concise Sādhana* provide no clear explanation about placing the five vajra ladies on the body maṇḍala of the father? It is assumed that you will easily understand that since there are five faculties, there must be five sensory objects for them to perceive; or else that you will be able to understand on your own the explanation that while gathering the specially visualized deities into your body, you should visualize the five vajra ladies drawn into the doors of each of your faculties [121a] and become indivisibly united with the five sensory objects within your mental continuum.

2762. Tib. *las kyi phyag rgya*, Skt. *karmamudrā*.

2763. Nāgabuddhi, *Rnam gzhag rim pa*, *Vyavastholi*, chap. 3, Tōh 1809, 128a7; Tanaka 2016, 120. Candrakīrti, *Sgron gsal*, *Pradīpoddyotanaṭīkā*, Tōh 1785, 22b1; Chakravarti 1984, 27.

2764. *Rgyud rdo rje phreng ba*, *Vajramālā Tantra*, chap. 64, Tōh 445, 270a2. D has *sku la ni* for *lus 'di la* in our text. Cited in Nāgabuddhi, *Rnam gzhag rim pa*, *Vyavastholi*, chap. 3, Tōh 1809, 128a7; Tanaka 2016, 120.

2765. Here Mkhas grub rje responds to the argument he presented above [119b1], in following Tsong kha pa's *Bskyed rim zin bris*, 29a4–5.

2766. Reading *'dod* for *'god* in our text.

[THE DEITIES THEMSELVES SHOULD BE PLACED ON THE BODY, AND NOT JUST THEIR SEED SYLLABLES]

The instruction to place only the seed syllables of the deities on the body and not the deities themselves contradicts the *Concise Sādhana*, which gives explicit instructions to meditate on the deities: "Having placed *thlīṃ* on their eyes, mantrins should meditate on Kṣitigarbha, and having placed *oṃ* on their ears, they should meditate on Vajrapāṇi."[2767] *Formulating the Sādhana* likewise teaches: "Having placed the five tathāgatas on them, the five aggregates become a cause for enlightenment,"[2768] and also: "The blessed one explained the causes and the fruits of placing the bodhisattvas on the sense bases of the eye and so forth."[2769] Thus these scriptures and others explain that you should place the deities themselves on the body.

The *Sādhana Incorporating the Scripture* specifies the principle of these placements on the body maṇḍala in particular: "The eighth chapter of the *Guhyasamāja Tantra* teaches: 'Those who know the ritual method should place the five tathāgata families and the descendants of the victorious ones on areas of the body: up to the mid-point between the two breasts, on the mid-point atop the crown, down to the feet, on the navel, on the waist, and on the secret place.'"[2770]

The *Illuminating Lamp* comments on this: "Once you have practiced yoga and subsequent yoga[2771] according to the stages in the sādhana,[2772] the *Guhyasamāja Tantra* teaches how you and your consort become the five tathāgatas: *Those who know the ritual method* and so forth, *up to the mid-point between*

2767. Nāgārjuna, *Mdor byas, Piṇḍīkrama Sādhana*, Tōh 1796, 4a6; L 62; T 61.

2768. Nāgabuddhi, *Rnam gzhag rim pa, Vyavastholi*, chap. 2, Tōh 1809, 125a5; Tanaka 2016, 99. D and Tanaka have *dgod pa* for *bkod pa* in our text.

2769. Nāgabuddhi, *Rnam gzhag rim pa, Vyavastholi*, chap. 2, Tōh 1809, 125b1–2; Tanaka 2016, 101.

2770. Nāgārjuna, *Mdo bsre, Sādhanasūtramelāpaka*, Tōh 1797, 12b5–6. D has *nu ma'i bar nas klad pa'i rgya bar du* for *nu ma'i dbus bar spyi gtsug mtha' yi bar* and *cho ga shes pas rkang mthil bar du dgod* for *cho ga shes pas yang na rkang pa'i bar* in our text. Nor bzang rgya mtsho notes the first variation as well. See his *Gsang ba 'dus pa'i bskyed rim gyi don gsal bar byed pa'i sgron me*, 108a5–b1. For the lines of the tantra, see *Gsang 'dus, Guhyasamāja Tantra*, chap. 8, Tōh 442; Zhol 11b7; Stog 19b7; Dunh 20b5–21a1; Fremantle 1971 v. 9; and Matsunaga 1978, v. 9. The text of the Zhol is identical to our text. The Sanskrit is somewhat different.

2771. Tib. *rjes su rnal 'byor*, Skt. *anuyoga*. Thus here begins the practice of *shin tu rnal 'byor* or *shin tu sbyor ba, atiyoga*. See Tsong kha pa, *Sgron gsal mchan*, 190b2–4.

2772. In his *Sgron gsal mchan*, 190b2, Tsong kha pa explains that this sādhana is Nāgārjuna's *Mdor byas, Piṇḍīkrama Sādhana*, Tōh 1796.

the two breasts and so forth.[2773] *The mid-point between the two breasts* means the location of the heart, where you should place the tathāgata family of Akṣobhya [born from][2774] the seed syllable *hūṃ* and *up to* means till there. *Atop of the crown* means up to the hairline,[2775] where you should place Vairocana born from the seed syllable *oṃ*. *Those who know the ritual method* [121b] are those who know the creation stage. *Midway* here is a point between the heart and the crown. Where is that? The region of the throat, the maṇḍala of the mouth.[2776] That is where you should place Amitābha who rises from the syllable *āḥ*. *Down to* tip of *the feet* means from the root of the thighs to the feet. The word *and*[2777] here is a concise way of indicating *on the two feet*. There you should place Amoghasiddhi born from the seed syllable *hā*. As concerns *the navel, waist, and the secret place*—the seventh is missing—that is where you should place Ratnasaṃbhava born from the seed syllable *svā*. *The victorious ones* are the tathāgatas Vairocana and so forth. *Their descendants* belong to their tathāgata families.[2778] You should place all of them in the nature of the lords of the five tathāgata families, according to the ritual method taught in the sādhana."[2779]

These lines clearly explain both the actual generation of the deities born from their respective seed syllables and the method for placing the five tathāgatas and all the deities belonging to their families on your own body

2773. Note that while the *Guhyasamāja Tantra* mentions six places on the body (omitting the throat), Candrakīrti's *Sgron gsal, Pradīpoddyotanaṭīkā*, interprets these as the five locations where the five tathāgata are placed.

2774. This is in accordance with the Sanskrit and with the corresponding cases of the other tathāgatas below.

2775. Following Candrakīrti's *Sgron gsal, Pradīpoddyotanaṭīkā*, Tōh 1785, 59b6; Chakravarti 1984, 75, our text specifies that the hairline is the end of the hair or the border of the area where hair grows on the crown of the head.

2776. As noted, the *Guhyasamāja Tantra* does not mention the throat or the mouth, the locations associated with speech and Amitābha.

2777. In fact, the word *dang* is not found in the Tibetan translation of this line of the *Guhyasamāja Tantra* (Zhol, Stog, Dunhuang, and Derge). Tsong kha pa, *Sgron gsal mchan*, 191a2, comments on this as well.

2778. Our text as well as Candrakīrti's *Sgron gsal, Pradīpoddyotanaṭīkā*, add here "The *victorious ones* and their *descendants*, called *victorious* and *descendants* are the Tathāgatas Vairocana and so forth and those who belong to their Tathāgata families."

2779. Candrakīrti, *Sgron gsal, Pradīpoddyotanaṭīkā*, Tōh 1785, 59b4–60a3; Chakravarti 1984, 75–76. D has *ji srid kyi bar du* for *ji srid pa'i bar du*; *shes pas so* for *shes pa'o*; *bar zhes byi ba* for *bar shes bya ba*; *brla* for *brla'i*; *bol* for *bar ro*; *yi ge svā* for *svā*, and *dged pa* for *dgod pa* in our text.

and that of your consort.[2780] From this we learn that anyone who claims Ārya Nāgārjuna and his disciples did not explain how to place the deities themselves on the body has never delved into the *Illuminating Lamp*.

Therefore the meaning of the verse of the *Concise Sādhana* cited above, "Then, those who know the divisions of the aggregates and so forth, should place the deities from Vairocana up to Sumbharāja on their bodies by actually placing the seed syllables of these deities on their bodies,"[2781] is that *those who know the divisions of the aggregates and so forth*, should not place the seed syllables alone, but rather should first generate the aggregates[2782] and so forth as the seed syllable of the respective deity, and then place the deities born from the seed syllables on the respective locations of the body. SAYING that the teaching in the *Concise Sādhana* that you should place the seed syllables on the body [122a] means that you should not place the deities there would be the equivalent of stating that because there is a cause, there is no fruit. Such a statement would be very crude.

The passage in the *Guhyasamāja Tantra* just cited[2783] explains that you should place Vairocana from the hairline to the crown, Amitābha from the throat to the hairline, and Akṣobhya from the heart to the nether part of the throat. Applying the same pattern, it seems permissible to place Ratnasaṃbhava from the heart to the navel, and Amoghasiddhi from the bottom of the navel to the roots of the thighs. According to the above passage of the *Illuminating Lamp*, understood literally however, it appears that Ratnasaṃbhava is placed so as to cover the three locations, navel, waist, and the secret place, while Amoghasiddhi covers the roots of the thighs down to the toes. Either of the two possibilities is appropriate.[2784]

2780. Here Mkhas grub rje responds to the position he presented above [119a2–4] in following Tsong kha pa's *Sgron gsal mchan*, 191a4–b1, and his *Bskyed rim zin bris*, 29a2–4.

2781. Nāgārjuna, *Mdor byas*, *Piṇḍīkrama Sādhana*, Tōh 1796, 4a3; L 55; T 54; cited on [119a2–3]. As was noted there, our text has *gyi* for *gyis* and *dgod pa* for *dgod pas* in D.

2782. Reading *phung* for *lung* in our text.

2783. *Guhyasamāja Tantra*, chap. 8, Tōh 442; Zhol 11b7; Stog 19b7, Dunh 20b5–21a1; Fremantle 1971, v. 9; and Matsunaga 1978, v. 9. This passage was cited above [121a]. As we saw, the *Guhyasamāja Tantra* itself does not mention the throat nor Amitābha.

2784. Here Mkhas grub rje follows Tsong kha pa's *Sgron gsal mchan*, 191a4–b1, with some variations, and his *Bskyed rim zin bris*, 30a6–b1. A discussion of this topic is found as well in Bu ston, *Mdor byas 'grel chen*, 41a4–b4.

[The Four Mothers]

You[2785] maintain that if, as explained, the four mothers, Locanā and so forth, are placed on the four physical elements, earth and so forth, then they should be placed on the secret place and so forth.[2786] Since YOUR mind is unable to fully fathom the meaning of the tantra, you surely[2787] have qualms of this kind. The division of wind into the five basic winds is as follows: The secret place is the abode of the earth-wind, the "descending wind";[2788] the navel is the location of the wind-wind, the "uniform wind";[2789] the heart is the location of the water-wind, the "life-sustaining wind";[2790] the throat is the location of the fire-wind, the "ascending wind";[2791] and the entire body is the location of the space-wind, the "pervading wind."[2792]

In the present context it is explained that the four mothers, Locanā and so forth, are placed on the four physical elements, earth and so forth. In general, there are several instances in which the winds of the four elements are applied to the four mothers, Locanā and so forth, but here the four elements of earth and so forth are the body's aspects of solidity, [122b] fluidity, warmth, and motility; and these are generated as the four mothers.

Here is the method for placing the mothers on the elements: Take all five basic winds as a single element of wind, and make them into the ground for generating Tārā. But[2793] it would be unsuitable to generate Locanā from the earth-wind and so forth, because the descending wind lacks the features of solidity. Hence, a position such as YOURS results from a failure to differentiate between the earth and the earth-wind. Otherwise, would you maintain that the pervading wind is space? If YOU maintain that the descending wind has the characteristics of solidity, YOU would then have to acknowledge that there is no contradiction between earth, water, fire, and wind. O child who has

2785. Here Mkhas grub rje responds to the argument he presented above [119b2–4], in following Tsong kha pa, *Bskyed rim zin bris*, 30b3–6. See Red mda' ba, *Bsgrub pa dpal bas zhus lan*, Kathmandu, 50a6–b3; TBRC, 305b–306a.

2786. These are the secret place, or the genitals as well as the navel, the heart, and the throat.

2787. Reading *bden* for *bde na* in our text.

2788. Tib. *thur sel*, Skt. *apāna*.

2789. Tib. *mnyam gnas*, Skt. *samāna*.

2790. Tib. *srog 'dzin*, Skt. *prāṇa*.

2791. Tib. *gyen rgyu*, Skt. *udāna*.

2792. Tib. *khyab byed*, Skt. *vyāna*.

2793. Reading *kyi* for *kya* in our text.

never studied the subject of contradiction and relationship, it is beyond your ability to interpret the meaning of the sūtra and tantra.

How do we know that the aspect of solidity is taken as earth and so forth in this case? Because the *Vajrasattva Sādhana* of glorious Candrakīrti clearly explains so in the context of placing the four mothers, Locanā and so forth, on the body: "Place the one called Moharati[2794] who is Locanā [with][2795] the nature of the earth element" and so forth,[2796] up to "and place the one called Vajrarati who is Tārā [with] the nature of the air/wind element. Then visualize them as solidity, fluidity, warmth, and motility."[2797] The *Vajra Garland Explanatory Tantra* likewise teaches this most clearly: "The Blessed Mother Locanā abides in the earth element, which is the flesh and so forth of this [body of the vajra master]. The Blessed Mother Māmakī abides in the water element, which is blood and so forth. The Blessed Mother Pāṇḍarā abides in the fire element, which is warmth and so forth. The Blessed Mother Tārā abides in the air/wind element, which is motility and so forth."[2798] [123a] What intelligent person[2799] would claim that flesh is the earth-wind and blood is the fire-wind?[2800]

For this reason, in the context of the dissolution of the twenty-five *coarse* elements, it is explained that earth, water, fire, wind, and so forth dissolve in the following way: The aspects of the body's solidity, fluidity, warmth, and motility are taken respectively as the physical elements, and then these physical

2794. Since D and Luo and Tomabechi have *zhes bya bas* for *zhes bya ba* in our text, the reading of the Bstan 'gyur could be translated as: "With [the mantra] *moharati* place Locanā with the nature of the earth element," and so forth. But Mkhas grub rje does not accept this; see below [123b5].

2795. This instrumental, too, is found in the Bstan 'gyur, but not in our text.

2796. Candrakīrti, *Rdo rje sems dpa'i sgrub thabs*, *Vajrasattva Sādhana*, Tōh 1814, 199b5–6; Luo and Tomabechi 2009, 17.4–6 and 49.15–17. D has *moharāti* and Luo and Tomabechi has *moharati* for *mohārati*; Luo and Tomabechi has *zhes bya bas* for *zhes bya ba* and *rang bzhin gyis so* for *rang bzhin zhes bya'o* in our text. The *Vajrasattva Sādhana* adds here: place Dveṣarati, who is Māmakī, with the nature of the water element, and place Rāgarati, who is Gos dkar mo, Pāṇḍarā, with the nature of the fire element.

2797. Candrakīrti, *Rdo rje sems dpa'i sgrub thabs*, *Vajrasattva Sādhana*, Tōh 1814, 199b6; Luo and Tomabechi 2009, 17.6–7 and 49.17–18.

2798. *Rgyud rdo rje phreng ba*, *Vajramālā Tantra*, chap. 64, Tōh 445, 270a3–4. D has *mi bskyod* for *bskyod* in our text. These lines are cited in Nāgabuddhi, *Rnam gzhag rim pa*, *Vyavastholi*, chap. 3, Tōh 1809, 128b2–3; Tanaka 2016, 121. While the Derge edition of the *Rgyud rdo rje phreng ba*, *Vajramālā Tantra*, Tōh 445, has *yang 'di'i*, the *Rnam gzhag rim pa* has *'di yi*.

2799. Reading *shes* for *shas* in our text.

2800. Reading *me* for *ma* in our text.

elements are taken in terms of the dissolution of their capacity to serve as a support for consciousness. This is because it is taught that along with these dissolutions, the four mothers on the body, Locanā and so forth, dissolve as well. On the other hand, the dissolutions of the *subtle* elements—when earth dissolves into water, the experience resembling a mirage dawns, and so forth—are taught in terms of the dissolution of the coarse features, from among the several subtle and coarse aspects of the winds of the four elements.

If YOU are not aware of these distinctions, and if you do not know the difference between the dissolutions of coarse and subtle aspects, how will YOU ever realize the profound vital points of the completion stage? With regard to the so-called "dissolution of the subtle aspects," earth, water, and fire are coarse, while the air/wind element is subtler, yet there are several grades of subtlety and coarseness within the subdivisions of the wind itself.

The winds of the physical elements, the earth-wind and so forth, are defined through several aspects, such as the correspondence between the individual color, function, and so forth of the five basic winds and the four elements, their locations, and so forth. But the earth-wind is not defined as such because it is both earth and wind. The earth is taken as yellow, the water as white, and the wind as green on the basis of their correlation with the colors of the three maṇḍalas comprising the underlying ground of the world[2801] and not because of their correlation to any color of the earth, water, and wind on the surface of the earth. [123b] The location of the earth element on the body can be either the secret place or the navel without any contradiction. How otherwise would YOU explain the instruction in the *Saṃpuṭa Tantra*[2802] to place Locanā at the navel, the abode of the earth, and Tārā at the crown of the head, the abode of the wind?

2801. According to the Buddhist cosmology described in Vasubandhu's *Mdzod, Abhidharmakośa*, Tōh 4089, our world rests on three maṇḍalas or disks of gold, water, and wind. See the *Mdzod, Abhidharmakośa* and its autocommentary *Mdzod 'grel, Kośabhāṣya*, chap. 3, vv. 45–46, Tōh 4090, 144a5–b3; Pradhan 1975, 157–158; English translation in Pruden 1988–1990, 451–52.

2802. *Yang dag par sbyor ba'i rgyud, Saṃpuṭa Tantra*, Tōh 381, *brtag pa* 4, *rab byed* 2, 98b1. Red mda' ba, *Bsgrub pa dpal zhus lan*, Kathmandu, 50a6–b3; TBRC, 305b–306a, cites the *Saṃpuṭa Tantra* on this point, but maintain that this is not the intention of Nāgārjuna in the *Mdor byas*: "The mantrin places Locanā, Māmakī, and likewise Pāṇḍaravāsinī and Tārā on the earth, and so forth." See Nāgārjuna, *Mdor byas, Piṇḍīkrama Sādhana*, Tōh 1796, 5b4; L 96cd–97ab; T 95cd–96ab.

[THE MANTRAS FOR GENERATING THE FOUR MOTHERS]

Furthermore, SOME SAY that it is inappropriate to maintain that Locanā is generated from [her name mantra] Moharati,[2803] Māmakī from [her name mantra] Dveṣarati, and so forth for the following reasons: (1) this contradicts the explanation of the *Concise Sādhana* that you should place the seed syllable of each deity on the respective part of the body; (2) according to this reasoning it also would be necessary to generate the other deities from their respective name mantras; and (3) since the other deities are generated from their seed syllables, there is no reason whatsoever to generate the four mothers from their name mantra.

How to explain the teachings of the *Vajrasattva Sādhana*: "Place the one called Moharati who is Locanā [with] the nature of the earth element"[2804] and so forth. The answer is that the *Concise Sādhana* teaches: "The mantrin should make [the four female buddhas] Moharati and so forth enter the four elements beginning with earth."[2805] In order to clarify that *Moharati and so forth* in this line are among the names of Locanā and the other mothers, the *Vajrasattva Sādhana* explains: *Moharati is Locanā*[2806] and she is *the nature of the earth element*.[2807] In Tibetan Moharati is called Timuk Gama.[2808]

The correct version of the *Vajrasattva Sādhana* has: "Place the one called Moharati who is Locanā, the nature of the earth element."[2809] Hence it is not correct to cite this line with the instrumental case to mean: "With [the mantra] Moharati, place Locanā and so forth." The meaning of the line in the *Concise Sādhana* "The mantrin should make [the four female buddhas]

2803. Reading *moharati* for *mohārati* in our text.

2804. Candrakīrti, *Rdo rje sems dpa'i sgrub thabs*, *Vajrasattva Sādhana*, Tōh 1814, 199b5; Luo and Tomabechi 2009, 17.4 and 49.15. D and Luo and Tomabechi have *zhes bya bas* our text has *zhes bya ba*. These lines were cited above [122b4]. As noted there, the text of Mkhas grub rje differs from that of Candrakīrti's *Rdo rje sems dpa'i sgrub thabs*.

2805. Nāgārjuna, *Mdor byas*, *Piṇḍīkrama Sādhana*, Tōh 1796, 4a6; L 61ab; T 60ab. While the Sanskrit is *moharatyādikair*, the Tibetan translation does not have instrumental *gti mug dga' sogs*. The Sanskrit could be understood as: "The mantrin should cause [them] to enter into the earth and so forth with Moharati, and so forth."

2806. Here Mkhas grub rje agrees with Bu ston, *Mdor byas 'grel chen*, 26b3–4.

2807. Once more this is different from the text of Candrakīrti's *Rdo rje sems dpa'i sgrub thabs*, Tōh 1814.

2808. Tib. Gti mug dga' ma.

2809. Mkhas grub rje has *mo ha ra ti zhes bya ba* for *mo ha ra ti zhes bya bas* and *rang bzhin zhes bya'o* for *rang bzhin gyis so* in Candrakīrti, *Rdo rje sems dpa'i sgrub thabs*, *Vajrasattva Sādhana*, Tōh 1814, 199b5; Luo and Tomabechi 2009, 49.15.

Moharati and so forth enter the four elements beginning with earth" is [124a] you should place Moharati and so forth. With what? With the mantra of her seed syllable.[2810] However, do not conclude that this mantra should be the name mantra.

[On Which Organs are the Bodhisattvas and the Vajra Ladies Placed?]

Furthermore, the *Jewel Rosary* that comments on the *Concise Sādhana* maintains that you should place Kṣitigarbha on the right eye and Rūpavajrā[2811] on the left eye, and so forth.[2812] This is mere prattle that explicitly contradicts the *Vajra Garland Explanatory Tantra*: "On both eye organs place the Tathāgata Kṣitigarbha, and on both ear organs place the Sugata Vajrapāṇi."[2813]

[Does the *Guhyasamāja Tantra* Teach Meditation on the Body as the Celestial Mansion?]

Some unwitting Tibetans say that although the Cakrasaṃvara tradition teaches that you should meditate on the body as the celestial mansion, it is inappropriate to meditate on the body as the celestial mansion in the Guhyasamāja tradition, because no such meditation is taught in the *Concise Sādhana*, the *Sādhana Incorporating the Scripture*, the *Vajrasattva Sādhana*, the *Illuminating Lamp*, and so forth. So they say; however, *Formulating the Sādhana* teaches: "I will begin by explaining the body maṇḍala. The body maṇḍala of the yogi that appears as a celestial mansion is formed by first drawing the Brahmā line and then dividing the area into squares. As the *Later Tantra* teaches: 'It is explained that there are three kinds of maṇḍalas:

2810. In Tsong kha pa, *Gsang mngon*, 42a2–b4, Locanā is generated from the seed syllable *laṃ*, Māmakī from *maṃ*, Pāṇḍarā from *paṃ*, and Tārā from *taṃ*.

2811. Tib. Gzugs rdo rje ma, Eng. Vajra Lady of Forms.

2812. Ratnākaraśānti, *Rin chen phreng ba*, *Ratnāvalī*, Tōh 1826, 48a4–5. In Tsong kha pa, *Gsang mngon*, 42b4–43a1, Kṣitigarbha is placed on the eye organ and Rūpavajrā at the door to the eye.

2813. *Rgyud rdo rje phreng ba*, *Vajramālā Tantra*, chap. 64, Tōh 445, 270a4–5. D has *de mig dbang* for *de yi mig dbang* and *bde gshegs* for *bder gshegs* in our text. These lines are cited in Nāgabuddhi, *Rnam gzhag rim pa*, *Vyavastholi*, chap. 3, Tōh 1809, 128b3; Tanaka 2016, 121–122.

the *bhaga* maṇḍala, the bodhicitta maṇḍala, and the body maṇḍala.'"[2814] With such prattle, heedless of the relevant passages in the scriptures, THEY demonstrate their own stupidity.

[Qualm:][2815] Is it sufficient, on account of these lines, to merely visualize your own body in the nature of the square celestial mansion, without being required to meditate meticulously on each and every part of your body as respective parts of the celestial mansion? [124b]

[Reply:] Well, the *Vajra Garland Explanatory Tantra* teaches: "The body has become the celestial mansion" and so forth, up to: "The five wisdoms are perfectly proclaimed as the five pure lines. The five aggregates are the five pure colors of the maṇḍala.[2816] Meditate on them as a celestial mansion. You should understand this as the First Yoga."[2817] Tell me, what maṇḍala other than the Guhyasamāja could this passage refer to in the context of the meditation during the First Yoga!?

[CONCLUSION]

Therefore it would be of great advantage for those deprived of the transmitted instruction of the lamas, who have not studied the tantras and the works of the Great Charioteers much, and who lack the capacity to analyze the scriptures using pure reason, to rest a while in their investigation of the two stages of the path of Vajradhara; thus too their followers who strive to outdo each other in the boldness of their attempted explanations of the teachings, and those who are content merely to watch the mouths of these followers; and it is also of great benefit to the teachings of the Victorious One.

2814. Nāgabuddhi, *Rnam gzhag rim pa*, *Vyavastholi*, chap. 2, Tōh 1809, 125a2–3; Tanaka 2016, 98. Partly cited above [118b]. D and Tanaka as well as Bu ston have *yis* for *yi* in our text. See *Rgyud phyi ma*, *Uttara Tantra*, Tōh 443, 152b4; Matsunaga 1978, v. 100. D and Zhol have *grags* for *bya*; *lus kyi dkyil 'khor zhes bshad pa* for *dkyil 'khor lus su gsungs pa ste*; and *gsum po dkyil 'khor yin par gsungs* for *dkyil 'khor rnam pa gsum du brtag* in our text. The passage in Nāgabuddhi's *Rnam gzhag rim pa* that cites the *Rgyud phyi ma* here is similar to our text, but D and Tanaka have *brtags* for *brtag* and *zhes* for *ces* in our text.

2815. See Tsong kha pa, *'Dod 'jo*, 121b1. In his *Bde dril bskyed rim*, 8b4, Mkhas grub rje identifies the opponents here as the Zha lu pa-s.

2816. See Tsong kha pa, *Gsang mngon*, 40b5–6.

2817. *Rgyud rdo rje phreng ba*, *Vajramālā Tantra*, chap. 68, Tōh 445, 275a2 and 5–6. D has *'gyur* for *gyur*; *re khā* for *re ga*; *phung po lnga ni rnam dag lnga* for *phung po lnga ni yang dag par*; *dbye* for *byed*; and *dang po sbyor bar* for *dang po'i sbyor bar*. For the first line see also [119a] above.

Establishing Our Own System

There are two sections here: (1) general explanation about the method for generating one's body as maṇḍala with its celestial mansion and deities, and (2) the specific explanation—which deity is generated from which seed syllable at which location on the body.

General Explanation about the Method for Generating One's Body as Maṇḍala with Its Celestial Mansion and Deities

"Meditation on the body maṇḍala" does not signify merely meditating on deities at various locations on the body. It means that having made the respective[2818] parts of the body into bases for generating the individual deities, you meditate on these deities. Were this not the case, the lower tantras would likewise contain diverse explanations on the body maṇḍala.

[The Difference Between the Body Maṇḍala and Outer Maṇḍalas]

The bases for generating the celestial mansion and deities of outer maṇḍalas, such as the colored powders and painted maṇḍalas, are their seed syllables, emblems, and so forth. These bases are constructed anew by artists and painters [125a] and the celestial mansion and deities are then generated from them. For this reason, outer maṇḍalas are called "constructed maṇḍalas." Conversely the bases for generating body maṇḍalas are the individual parts of the body, which are not newly constructed but have been there all along, perfectly present since birth from one's parents. Because body maṇḍalas are generated from such bases, they are called "unconstructed maṇḍalas."[2819]

Thus, since the bases for generating the body maṇḍala are intrinsic and have existed ever since the body was formed, [Vajraghaṇṭa] teaches: "Sentient beings are naturally present nondual maṇḍalas."[2820] This would be like calling the basis-for-creating-a-maṇḍala itself "a maṇḍala," before the celestial mansion had been drawn with colored powders and so forth. Once the celestial mansion has been created, when the yogi meditates on the deities, there is no distinction between the outer maṇḍala and the body maṇḍala, since both

2818. Reading *de dang de* for *da dang de* in our text.

2819. See Tsong kha pa's *Dril dbang*, 3a2–5.

2820. See [116b1] above. See also Tsong kha pa's *Sngags rim chen mo*, chap. 7, 303–305; and *Dril dbang*, 3a2–3.

are contrived and imputed by the mind. Therefore the *Vajraḍāka Tantra*,[2821] the *Vasantatilaka*,[2822] and other scriptures call the entire creation stage a contrived yoga.

Qualm:[2823] If there is no difference between the bases[2824] for generating these two maṇḍalas other than their being either constructed or unconstructed, when the master Vajraghaṇṭa teaches: "The nature of the two constructed ones is meant to accord with the disciple. These maṇḍalas should not be produced for those who are well-skilled; since they will be liberated by seeing the true meaning,"[2825] which of these two maṇḍalas, the body maṇḍala or the constructed outer maṇḍala, does he hold to be superior?

Reply: Since they differ in their bases for generation, the one being constructed, the other not, they must also be different in terms of which is superior and which inferior.[2826] [125b] This is so because the completion stage is the main cause of the supreme siddhi [awakening], specifically when you meditate by penetrating the vital points of your body. To this end, you should now [during the creation stage] bless all the parts of your body by generating them as deities. As you habituate this over and over, the channels, winds, and drops in your body will become serviceable. The meditation of the creation stage is a special ripener for the realization of the completion stage so that it will easily arise when you meditate by penetrating the vital points in your body. However, when you bless colored powders, painted maṇḍalas, and so forth by generating them as deities, they are similar to the body maṇḍala in their capacity to achieve purposes such as accumulating merit, conferring initiations, and so forth [relative truth]. Nonetheless, you cannot generate wisdom [ultimate

2821. *Rdo rje mkha' 'gro ma rgyud*, *Vajraḍāka*, chap. 50, Tōh 370, 124b6. These lines are also cited in this contest in Tsong kha pa's *Sngags rim chen mo*, chap. 7, 307, and also chap. 11, 444.

2822. Kṛṣṇācārya, *Dpyid kyi thig le*, *Vasantatilaka*, Tōh 1448, 298b5–299a6.

2823. See Tsong kha pa's *Dril dbang*, 3b2–4 and his *'Dod 'jo*, 137a6–b4.

2824. Reading *gzhi* for *bzhi* in our text.

2825. Vajraghaṇṭa, *'Khor lo sdom pa'i dbang gi bya ba mdor bsdus pa*, *Cakrasaṃvaraṣekaprakriyopadeśa*, Tōh 1431, 219b6; Finot 1934, 62. D has *nyid* for *gnyis* in our text. See also Abhayākaragupta, *Man ngag snye ma*, *Āmnāyamañjarī*, chap. 23, Tōh 1198, 214a2–3, and his *'Jigs pa med pa'i gzhung 'grel*, *Abhayapaddhati*, Tōh 1654, 199b2–3; Sanskrit and Tibetan in Chog Dorje 2009, 47 and 82. For more details, see Bentor 2017a. I would like to thank Professor Harunaga Isaacson for pointing out the citation in the Abhayākaragupta and for sending me its Sanskrit version.

2826. See also Mkhas grub rje, *Dge bshes kon ting gu*[*g*] *shri ba la phul ba*, 158a5–6.

truth] using meditation to penetrate the vital points through the use of colored powders and painted maṇḍalas.[2827]

The line by Vajraghaṇṭa, the two constructed maṇḍalas *should not be produced for those who are well-skilled*,[2828] means that producing these maṇḍalas is not regarded as the principal method for skillful persons.[2829] The reasons for this are: (1) *Since they* [those who are well-skilled] *will be liberated by seeing the true meaning.* That is, having penetrated the vital points in the body, the well-skilled *will be liberated by seeing the true meaning.* (2) Their method, the meditation on the unconstructed maṇḍala is the supreme ripener. Therefore, in the creation stage too, you must make the respective aspects of your body, such as the aggregates, sensory spheres, sense bases, and so forth into bases for generating the deities, and then completely transform these bases, and generate them as the respective deities.

[How Are the Deities Generated from Their Seed Syllables?][2830]

It is perfectly sufficient to visualize the deities from their respective seed syllables, for example, visualizing your eye organ completely transformed into the syllable *thlīṃ*, and the *thlīṃ* into Kṣitigarbha. [126a] But it is not sufficient to generate *thlīṃ* in your own mind without a basis for it, then generate Kṣitigarbha from it, and after that merely to imagine that Kṣitigarbha is indivisible from your own eye organ. When you gathered the specially visualized deities into your body during a previous step in the practice,[2831] you placed the deities on your body and then simply visualized them as indivisible in essence from your aggregates, sensory spheres, sense bases, but this was not a meditation on the body maṇḍala as such.

Therefore, during the absorption in union with the consort below,[2832] when you place the deities on the body of your consort, if the consort is an action consort, and if the seed syllables arise from the transformation of the respective aggregates and so forth of her body, and you generate the deities

2827. See Tsong kha pa, *Dril dbang*, 3b2–4; *Sngags rim chen mo*, chap. 7, 307; and *'Dod 'jo*, 137a6–b4.

2828. Vajraghaṇṭa, *'Khor lo sdom pa'i dbang gi bya ba mdor bsdus pa, Cakrasaṃvaraṣekaprakriyopadeśa*, Tōh 1431, 219b6, cited above [125a].

2829. Tsong kha pa, *Sngags rim chen mo*, chap. 7, 307, has *thabs snga ma* for *thabs bcos ma*, and *gzung* for *gsung* in our text.

2830. On this point Mkhas grub rje differs from Tsong kha pa. See Bentor 2015a.

2831. See above [89a–90b].

2832. See below [139bff].

from them, this will result in the body maṇḍala of the consort. But if she is a wisdom consort, her body, which is the basis of generation, will be merely contrived by the mind, as she does not have an actual body. Therefore, no matter which method you use to place the deities on her body, it will not be a body maṇḍala.[2833]

[Generating the Body as the Celestial Mansion]

When this is the method for generating the deities of the body maṇḍala, then what is the method for generating the body as the celestial mansion?[2834] Previously you generated the outer maṇḍala and at the center of its celestial mansion you meditated on yourself as the First Lord who was then transformed into the Vajrasattva's nirmāṇakāya. When you proceed to meditate on the body of yourself as Vajrasattva's nirmāṇakāya as the celestial mansion, you do not meditate on it in the space left after the former maṇḍala has been dissolved, nor do you meditate on a second celestial mansion generated from the body of Vajrasattva's nirmāṇakāya at the abode of the principal deity within the former celestial mansion. Rather, as the *Sādhana Incorporating the Scripture* teaches,[2835] you should generate the celestial mansion from the seed syllable *bhrūṃ* and visualize yourself as Vajrasattva's nirmāṇakāya at the center of the celestial mansion. Next you should place all thirty-two deities on the body of yourself as Vajrasattva's nirmāṇakāya, [126b] and then abide in the celestial mansion as explained above.

The line *the celestial mansion explained above* must refer to the outer maṇḍala, because in that context it is not taught that you should generate the body as the celestial mansion of the maṇḍala. This, then, proves that you do not dissolve the celestial mansion you previously meditated on, nor do you generate another celestial mansion within the previous celestial mansion. As explained earlier, the *Vajra Garland Tantra* and *Formulating the Sādhana* both teach that you should meditate on your body in the form of the celestial mansion.[2836]

This, then, is how you should meditate:[2837] When it is time to generate

2833. This follows Tsong kha pa, *Bskyed rim zin bris*, 30a4–5.

2834. See Tsong kha pa's *'Dod 'jo*, 121a2–6.

2835. Nāgārjuna, *Mdo bsre*, *Sādhanasūtramelāpaka*, Tōh 1797; the meditation on the celestial mansion through the seed syllable *Bhrūṃ* is found at 12a1, the line "to abide in the celestial mansion explained above" is found at 14a2–3.

2836. See above [124b].

2837. See Mkhas grub rje, *Bde dril bskyed rim*, 9a3–6.

your body as the celestial mansion of the maṇḍala, do not dissolve the mental continuum of the celestial mansion on which you formerly meditated, but rather, visualize the subsequent moments of the mental continuum of the earlier celestial mansion, arising through the transformation of the respective parts of your body. Consequently, although the celestial mansion that arose in your mind, upon which you meditated earlier, was generated solely by means of mental contrivance, later on when you begin to meditate on the body maṇḍala, the subsequent moments of the mental continuum of the celestial mansion will not be contrived by the mind but will be visualized from bases of generation that actually exist.

This is the method for generating the body maṇḍala that accords with the tantras, the writings of mahāsiddhas, and the treatises of Indian scholars. I will refrain from elaborating on the special unshared methods of the body maṇḍalas of Cakrasaṃvara and so forth because they are not relevant here and also in order to avoid verbosity. However, you are advised to learn them through the great explanation of the writings of Lūyīpāda written by our Precious Master Tsongkhapa.[2838]

[The Debate in the Context of Mother Tantras]

In many [works on] the body maṇḍala of the mother tantra, TIBETANS write that:[2839] "The crown of the head is the crossed vajra; the soles of the feet, the vajra ground; the ribs, the vajra fence; the skin, the vajra tent and canopy; [127a] the bodily hair, the net of arrows; and the nails, the blazing fire mountain." They also say: "The four channels of the heart are the four gates; the eyes, the wall with five lines; the nose, the jeweled bricks; the teeth, the hanging jeweled nets and nets with half-loops; the tongue and lips, the offering ledge," and so forth.

In this regard, the All-Knowing Butön Rinpoché says: "The *Saṃvaravyākhyā* teaches: 'When the body is generated in due order, the vajra stakes arise simultaneously, bound very tightly with a thread leaving no gaps. The string of bones becomes the tent.' *No other Indian treatise explains this in such*

2838. Tsong kha pa, *'Dod 'jo*, 121a2–6.

2839. Mkhas grub rje here follows Tsong kha pa, *'Dod 'jo*, 124a2–4. For these lines see Bsod nams rtse mo, *'Khor lo bde mchog dril bu pa'i gzhung gi mngon par rtogs pa*, 2a3–4. Bsod nams rtse mo has *gur* for *gur dang bla re* in our text. Ngor chen cites the following two paragraphs in his *Kyai rdo rje'i lus kyi dkyil 'khor la rtsod pa spong ba smra ba ngan 'joms*, work 49, 271b2–272a1; and in his *Kyai rdo rje'i lus kyi dkyil 'khor la rtsod pa spong ba lta ba ngan sel*, work 50, 288b3–289a3. Ngor chen then replies to the arguments in both of these works. Mkhas grub rje repeats this argument and responds to Ngor chen in his *Gnam lcags 'khor lo*, 2a6–8a1. For a further discussion of their debate, see Bentor 2017b.

a way."[2840] This is correct,[2841] since it accords with the method of visualizing the body as a celestial mansion. Furthermore, SOME TIBETANS maintain that even though there are only nine deities in the outer maṇḍala, there are one hundred fifty-seven or more deities in the body maṇḍala.[2842] THEY ALSO SAY that not a single deity is shared by the body maṇḍala and the outer maṇḍala, and so forth.[2843]

No authentic tantra or Indian treatise ever explains this, and there is nothing in what they explain from which anyone could derive such a meaning.[2844] Still THEY fancy in their minds that there are no distinctions whatsoever between the body maṇḍala and merely placing the deities on the body.[2845] Numerous foolish talks that have received the title "supreme transmitted instructions" have appeared in manuals on the practice of the body maṇḍala written by TIBETANS. I will not go into detail refuting or accepting them here.

The Specific Explanation—Which Deity Is Generated from Which Seed Syllable at Which Location on the Body

Firstly, which part of the body is generated as which part of the celestial mansion? The meditation accords with the *Vajra Garland Explanatory Tantra*:

> The body has become the celestial mansion, [which is] the perfect

2840. Bu ston, *Kun spyod rgyud 'grel*, 39a2–4. See Kṛṣṇa, *Sdom pa bshad pa*, *Saṃvaravyākhyā*, Tōh 1460, 7a4. D has *go rims* for *go rim*, *skyes ni* for *skyes nas* in our text. My translation here is most tentative.

2841. Reading *mad pa* for *med pa*, as in the Bkra shis lhun po edition.

2842. For such a position, see also Bla ma dam pa Bsod nams rgyal mtshan, *Lam 'bras bu dang bcas pa'i gdam ngag gi rnam par bshad pa man ngag gi mdzod*, 19b3–21a2; English translation in Stearns 2011, 82–85. Ngor chen replies to this in both his *Smra ba ngan 'joms*, work 49, 273b3–275a2; and *Lta ba ngan sel*, work 50, 291a3–294b4. Mkhas grub rje then responds in both his *Dge bshes kon ting gu[g] shri ba la phul ba*, 157a1–4, and his *Gnam lcags 'khor lo*, 8a1–17a2.

2843. Ngor chen refutes this criticism in both the *Smra ba ngan 'joms*, work 49, 275a2–277a3, and *Lta ba ngan sel*, work 50, 295a1–297a4. Mkhas grub rje disputes with him again in his *Gnam lcags 'khor lo*, 17a2–22a2.

2844. Ngor chen then responds to this in his *Smra ba ngan 'joms*, work 49, 277b6–286b4, and *Lta ba ngan sel*, work 50, 299a6–309a6, and Mkhas grub rje rebuts him in his *Gnam lcags 'khor lo*, 23a3–47a1.

2845. Ngor chen responds to this again in his *Smra ba ngan 'joms*, work 49, 277a3–b6, and *Lta ba ngan sel*, work 50, 298b3–299a6, and Mkhas grub rje rejoins in his *Gnam lcags 'khor lo*, 22a2–23a7.

support for all buddhas. The four cornered maṇḍala is described through the division of the four sides of the body: front, back, right, and left sides.[2846] [127b] The four gates of the maṇḍala are explained through the division into upper and lower gates.[2847] The configurations of "nose-tips"[2848] are expressed as the four portals. The jeweled nets are explained as intestines, the sinews as the nets with half loops, part [of the bodhicitta] as the half-moons, and the vase as belly. The shins, thighs, forearms, and upper arms are explained as the eight pillars. Auditory consciousness is explained as banners, olfactory consciousness as garlands of flowers, gustatory consciousness as jeweled bricks, tactile consciousness as brocade pendants, and mental consciousness as two deer. The eyes are explained as the sign of the Dharma wheel, the ears as vajras all around, the nose as banners, and the tongue as bells. The pure body is explained as the tail fans and the mind as the central lotus. The winds on which conceptual thoughts are mounted are the perfect supports. The five wisdoms are perfectly proclaimed as the five pure lines [representing the five walls of the maṇḍala].[2849] The five aggregates are the five pure colors of the maṇḍala. Meditate on them as the celestial mansion."[2850]

In these verses, *the part* is one-sixteenth of the white bodhicitta.[2851] *The ears* are explained *as vajras all around*, meaning that you should meditate on the

2846. Note that the Bstan 'gyur is somewhat different here. Tsong kha pa's *Rnam gzhag rim pa'i rnam bshad*, 56b4, is identical to our text.

2847. These four gates of the body are the mouth, nose, anus, and urethra.

2848. Below, the "nose-tips" are explained as the secret place, navel, heart, and the tip of the nose.

2849. See Tsong kha pa, *Gsang mngon*, 40b1.

2850. *Rgyud rdo rje phreng ba*, *Vajramālā Tantra*, chap. 68, Tōh 445, 275a2–6. D has *'gyur* for *gyur*; *zur bzhi pa yi* for *zur bzhi pa ni*; *sna rtse bzhi yi* for *sna yi rtse mo'i*; *rta babs bzhi* for *rta babs bzhir*; *chu bar* for *rgyu mar*; *yang dag shes* for *yang dag bshad*; and *yang dag bshad* for *rnam par bshad*; the line *mig gi rnam shes me long sogs* is missing; *sgra yi rnam shes rol mo dang* for *sna ni ba dan du ni bshad*; *me tog phreng* for *me tog 'phreng*; *ras 'phan* for *dar 'phen*; *ri dags* for *ri dwags*; *yang dag brten* for *yang dag rten*; *re khā* for *re ga*; *phung po lnga ni rnam dag lnga* for *phung po lnga ni yang dag lnga*; and *dbye* for *byed*. For the first and last lines see [119a] and [124b] above.

2851. Mkhas grub rje follows here Bu ston, *Mdor byas 'grel chen*, 40a4, and Tsong kha pa's *Bskyed rim zin bris*, 28b4. A one-sixteenth of the white bodhicitta, that is to say of the moon, refers to the daily increase in the size of the moon during its waxing phase.

half-moons and vajras at the intermediate directions arising from the ear organ.

What are the four "nose-tips" on which you meditate as the four portals that arise from them? SOME EARLY LAMAS[2852] explain that the ultimate nose-tip is added to three nose-tips. But this is wrong since there is no basis whatsoever either etymologically or in terms of usage for the ultimate nose-tip on the body. The four nose-tips as explained in the *Vajra Garland Tantra* are as follows: "The three 'nose-tips' are the names for the 'noses' of the secret place, the heart and the face," while the fourth "nose-tip": "the hub of the channel-wheel [i.e., the *cakra*] arising on the sixty-four lotus petals in sequence is explained as a nose-tip."[2853] [128a] Therefore the four nose-tips are (1) the nose-tip of the sexual mark, the door of the secret opening; (2) the nose-tip of the heart, the hub of the heart cakra; (3) the familiar nose-tip of the face, on top of the door where the two nostrils meet; and (4) the nose-tip of the navel, the hub of the sixty-four channel wheels. The rest of the citation from the *Vajra Garland Tantra* is easy to understand.

[Qualm:] Why does the instruction on how to meditate on the body as the celestial mansion include the explanation about meditating on the consciousnesses of the senses and the mind as individual parts of the celestial mansion?

[Reply:] The etymological meaning of "body" is collection; and as the coarse and inert body is a composite of parts—from morsels of flesh down to tiny particles, the consciousnesses are collections of a multitude of moments. Since this is the basis of the etymology of "body," there is nothing wrong with such an instruction. Yet the basis of the etymology of "body" is not necessarily the basis for the usage of the word.[2854]

The method for generating the deities following the generation of the celestial mansion is taught in the *Concise Sādhana*:

> With the entrance of/into[2855] Akṣobhya, the mantrin meditates on

2852. Bu ston, *Mdor byas 'grel chen*, 40b1, calls them "some lamas," *bla ma kha cig*.

2853. *Rgyud rdo rje phreng ba*, *Vajramālā Tantra*, chap. 24, Tōh 445, 237a4 and 237a7. D has *rtsa yi* for *rtsa'i* and *snar ni bshad* for *sna rtser bshad* in our text. In this explanatory tantra this line is not a complete sentence, but could be translated as: "Characteristics of the three nose-tips called secret, heart, and face..." See Tsong kha pa, *Rim lnga gsal sgron*, 160b2–3; English translation in Kilty 2013, 272.

2854. Even though both body and mind share an etymological basis, the terms mind and body are not necessarily interchangeable.

2855. The reading here is the basis of a great controversy. See [111a–b] and Bentor 2015c.

themselves as Vajrasattva with three faces and six arms, radiating a splendor equal to that of sapphire.[2856] In Vajrasattva's right hands the mantrin visualizes a vajra, a wheel, and a lotus, and in his lefts, a bell, a jewel, and a sword.

Having done so, those who know the divisions of the aggregates[2857] and so forth should set the deities from Vairocana to Sumbharāja in sequence on their bodies by[2858] actually placing their seed syllables there.[2859] Those who know the mantra place white *oṃ* on their heads, the seed syllable of Vairocana, with the nature of the form aggregate. Then they meditate on the red *āḥ* of the Lord Amitābha, [128b] the nature of the aggregate of perception, on their mouths, and thereby attain the mastery of speech. On their hearts the mantrins place a splendid dark blue *hūṃ*, the syllable of Akṣobhya, the nature of the aggregate of consciousness. On their navels they set a yellow *svā*, syllable of the Lord Ratnasaṃbhava, the nature of the aggregate of feelings and endowed with the capacity to purify the feelings.[2860] On both feet the mantrins place the green-colored *hā*, the essence of the Lord of Action,[2861] who is the nature of the aggregate of conditioning.

Mantrins should make [the four female buddhas] Moharati and so forth enter the four elements beginning with earth in their respective aspects,[2862] solidity, fluidity, warmth, and motility.

Having placed *thlīṃ* upon their eyes, they meditate on Kṣitigarbha, and having placed *oṃ* upon their ears, they meditate on Vajrapāṇi.[2863] Having placed *oṃ* upon their noses, they meditate

2856. D has *'bar ba dang* for *lta bur ni* and *mnyams pa'i* for *'bar pa'i.*

2857. This refers to those who know which aggregate relates to which part of the body. These relationships are spelled out in the passage itself.

2858. As was noted there, our text has *gyi* for *gyis* here, and therefore Mkhas grub rje's interpretation is based on a different rendering from that of the texts of both the Bstan 'gyur and the Sanskrit work.

2859. This verse appeared above [119a2–3]. This is the practice summarized in one verse, while the rest of the passage provides the details.

2860. This line is explained below.

2861. Las kyi mgon po, Karmanātha, Amoghasiddhi.

2862. This line appeared above [123b]. As we saw there, for Mkhas grub rje Moharati is Locanā and not the mantra from which Locanā is generated.

2863. This verse appeared above [121a1–2].

> on Khagarbha, and having placed *āḥ*[2864] upon their tongues, they imagine Lokeśvara. Having visualized the syllable *hūṃ* set upon their minds, they meditate on Mañjughoṣa, and having meditated on the syllable *oṃ*[2865] over their whole body, they are mindful of Vikṣambhin. Having placed the syllable *maiṃ* at the channels,[2866] they imagine Maitreya, and having placed *saṃ* on all their joints, they visualize Samantabhadra.
>
> They meditate on Yamāntaka upon their right arms, on Aparājita upon their left, on Hayagrīva upon their mouths, and on Amṛtakuṇḍalin upon their vajra.[2867] They visualize Acala upon their right shoulder, and Ṭakkirāja[2868] upon their left, the very luminous Nīladaṇḍa upon their right knee, and Mahābala upon their left knee. They visualize Uṣṇīṣacakravartin on their head, and Sumbharāja set upon their feet.[2869] [129a]

This clarifies most of the details about placing the deities on parts of the body that have been generated into grounds of generation,[2870] from which part of the body to generate each of the deities and from which seed syllable to generate them. The line *endowed with the capacity to purify the feelings* indicates that feeling is the cause, and the syllable[2871] *svā* is the fruit. Hence, the teaching here is clearly that the syllable *svā* should be generated from the transformation of

2864. The Sanskrit here is *oṃ*.

2865. L has *hūṃ* here, T has *oṃ*, but a variant reading has *hūṃ* here.

2866. The Sanskrit has *śiraḥ* here. According Tsong kha pa, *Gsang mngon*, 45a1, the seed syllable *maiṃ* in the nature of the channels and the sinews is placed at the crown of the head.

2867. T has *vajre* for *vaktre* in L.

2868. T has Ṭakkirājakam for Ṭarkvirājakam in L.

2869. Nāgārjuna, *Mdor byas*, *Piṇḍīkrama Sādhana*, Tōh 1796, 4a2–b1; L 53–68; T 52–67. D has *'bar ba dang* for *lta bur ni*; *mnyams pa'i* for *'bar pa'i*; *rnam par bsam* for *bsam par bya*; *sa bon gyis* for *sa bon gyi*; *rnam snang mdzad kyi* for *rnam snang mdzad pa'i*; *ngo bo nyid kyis* for *ngo bo nyid kyi*; *mthing shun mdog* for *mthing shing mdog*; *rnam par dgod* for *rnam par bsgom*; *sna la rab bkod* for *sna la rnam dgod*; *hūṃ ni bsams nas su* for *hūṃ yig bsam nas ni*; *lus kun la* for *lus kun la'ang*; *bsgoms nas* for *bsgom nas*; *lag pa g.yas par* for *lag pa g.yas pa*; *shin rje gshed* for *shin rje gshad*; *g.yon par* for *g.yon pa*; *kha la bsam* for *kha la bsgom*; *mi g.yo mgon* for *mi g.yo pa*; *dbyug pa* for *dbyig pa*; and *gtsug tor 'khor los sgyur* for *gtsug tor 'khor lo sgyur*.

2870. In this brief line Mkhas grub rje states his position that differs from Tsong kha pa's. In the following lines he provides evidence in support of his opinion. For a discussion on this matter, see Bentor 2015a.

2871. Reading *yig* for *yi*.

the aggregate of feeling. Otherwise, it would be wholly irrelevant to say that these two are a cause and a fruit.[2872]

The *Concise Sādhana* cited above teaches that Maitreya is generated only from the channels of the body, but the *Vajra Garland Tantra* teaches: "The tathāgata Maitreya abides on all the channels and sinews of the body,"[2873] and the *Vajrasattva Sādhana* teaches: "Place *maiṃ*, the seed syllable of Maitreya, with[2874] the nature of sinews."[2875] Therefore you should generate Maitreya from both the channels and sinews of the body.[2876]

Although the *Concise Sādhana* does not explain the seed syllables of the ten fierce deities, they are all generated from *hūṃ*, as the *Vajrasattva Sādhana* teaches: "Place the ten fierce deities generated sequentially from long *hūṃ*s on the limbs beginning with the hands, with Yamāntaka on the right arm,"[2877] and so forth.

[What Are the Seed Syllables of the Four Mothers?]

The *Intense Illuminating Lamp*,[2878] the *Perfected Yoga Garland*[2879] and Kṛṣṇa's *Vajrasattva Offering Ritual*[2880] all explain that the seed syllables of the four

2872. Nāgabuddhi explains that the parts of the body and the deities are respectively the cause and its fruit. See his *Rnam gzhag rim pa*, *Vyavastholi*, chap. 2, Tōh 1809, 125a4, 125b2, and 126a2; Tanaka 2016, 99, 101, and 104.

2873. *Rgyud rdo rje phreng ba*, *Vajramālā Tantra*, chap. 64, Tōh 445, 270a7. This line is cited in Nāgabuddhi, *Rnam gzhag rim pa*, *Vyavastholi*, chap. 3, Tōh 1809, 128b5 (where part of this verse is omitted); Tanaka 2016, 123. The Sanskrit equivalent of *rtsa rgyus* in the *Rnam gzhag rim pa* is *snāyuḥ*, but in Tsong kha pa, *Gsang mngon*, 45a1, *rtsa rgyus* turns into *rtsa dang rgyus*.

2874. Note that the Sanskrit equivalent of *rang bzhin la* in the Tibetan translation is *svabhāvena*.

2875. Candrakīrti, *Rdo rje sems dpa'i sgrub thabs*, *Vajrasattva Sādhana*, Tōh 1814, 200a1; Luo and Tomabechi 2009, 17.12 and 50.8.

2876. As in Tsong kha pa, *Gsang mngon*, 45a1.

2877. Candrakīrti, *Rdo rje sems dpa'i sgrub thabs*, *Vajrasattva Sādhana*, Tōh 1814, 200a2–3; Luo and Tomabechi 2009, 17.14–18.1 and 50.11–13. D has *hūṃ ring por* for *hūṃ ring po las* in our text.

2878. Bhavyakīrti, *Rab tu Sgron gsal*, *Prakāśikā*, Tōh 1793, 9b4–5.

2879. Abhayākaragupta, *Rnal 'byor rdzogs phreng*, *Niṣpannayogāvalī*, Tōh 3141, 97a4 and 99b6; Sanskrit, Tibetan, and English translation in Lokesh Chandra and Nirmala Sharma 2015, 25 and 37.

2880. Kṛṣṇa, *Rdo rje sems dpa' mchod pa'i cho ga*, *Vajrasattva Pūjāvidhi*, Tōh 1820, 259b3.

mothers are *lāṃ*, *māṃ*, *pāṃ*, and *tāṃ*.[2881] Likewise, the *Ornament of Vajra Essence*,[2882] a tantra that partly accords with the *Guhyasamāja*, explains it in this way. This explanation appears in the tradition of Jñānapāda as well.[2883] EARLY TIBETAN LAMAS[2884] maintain that the seed syllables of the four mothers [129b] are the first syllable of the names of the mothers, Moharati[2885] and so forth, adorned with a drop of *anusvāra*. However, there seems to be no proof of this whatsoever.[2886]

[What Are the Seed Syllables of the Five Vajra Ladies?]

The seed syllables of the vajra ladies are not explicitly mentioned in the works of Ārya Nāgārjuna and his disciples. But as the *Intense Illuminating Lamp*, the *Perfected Yoga Garland*, and the *Jewel Rosary* explain, the vajra ladies are generated from *dzaḥ hūṃ baṃ hoḥ*.[2887] This appears in the *Ornament of Vajra Essence*[2888] as well as in the tradition of Jñānapāda,[2889] and is therefore correct. *Kṛṣṇasamayavajra and TIBETANS maintain that the seed syllables of the vajra ladies are the first syllables of their individual names adorned with a drop of *anusvāra*, that is, *ruṃ*, *śaṃ*, *gaṃ*, and *raṃ*.[2890] The *Vajrasattva Sādhana* does not in fact explain that the five vajra ladies are placed on the body of the father,

2881. This sentence follows Bu ston, *Mdor byas 'grel chen*, 41b5–6.

2882. *Rdo rje snying po rgyan gyi rgyud*, *Vajrahṛdayālaṅkāra Tantra*, Tōh 451, 38a7–b1. Bu ston, *Mdor byas 'grel chen*, 43a6–7, calls this tantra *Bshad rgyud rdo rje snying po rgyan*.

2883. See Jñānapāda, *Kun tu bzang po sgrub pa'i thabs*, *Samantabhadra Sādhana*, Tōh 1855, 30b5; Kano 2014, 67, v. 43.

2884. Bu ston, *Mdor byas 'grel chen*, 41b6, calls them "Tibetan lamas," Tib. *bod kyi bla ma dag*.

2885. Reading *moharati* for *mohārati* in our text.

2886. This last comment is not found in Bu ston.

2887. Bhavyakīrti, *Rab tu sgron gsal*, *Prakāśikā*, Tōh 1793, 12a3–4; Abhayākaragupta, *Rdzogs pa'i rnal 'byor gyi phreng ba*, *Niṣpannayogāvalī*, Tōh 3141, 97a4 and 99b6; Sanskrit, Tibetan, and English translation in Lokesh Chandra and Nirmala Sharma 2015, 36–37; and Ratnākaraśānti, *Ratnāvalī*, *Rin chen phreng ba*, Tōh 1826, 48a4–6. This list of scriptures is found as well in Bu ston, *Mdor byas 'grel chen*, 43a5–7, but Bu ston adds a commentary on Candrakīrti's *Rdo rje sems dpa'i sgrub thabs*, Tōh 1814. See Līlavajra, *Rdo rje sems dpa'i sgrub thabs kyi 'grel pa*, *Vajrasattva Sādhana Nibandha*, Tōh 1815, 207a3.

2888. *Rdo rje snying po rgyan gyi rgyud*, *Vajrahṛdayālaṅkāra Tantra*, Tōh 451, 38b2. See also Bu ston, *Mdor byas 'grel chen*, 43a6–7.

2889. See Jñānapāda, *Kun tu bzang po sgrub pa'i thabs*, *Samantabhadra Sādhana*, Tōh 1855, 30b5; Kano 2014, 67, v. 42.

2890. Bu ston accepts both these systems of seed syllables. See his *Mdor byas 'grel chen*, 43a7–b1.

but Līlavajra, in his commentary on this sādhana, explains this in the context of placing the body maṇḍala on the father: "Then, visualize the vajra ladies, Rūpavajrā[2891] and so forth, from the four seed syllables *dzaḥ hūṃ baṃ hoḥ*, and place[2892] their natures on respective locations of the body—forms and so forth."[2893]

[What Is the Relationship of the Number of Deities to the Number of Bodily Organs?]

When you meditate on yourself with three faces and six arms you have six meditative eyes. Nevertheless, there is no need to meditate on Kṣitigarbha on the eyes of your right face and left face, for it is enough to meditate on him on the eyes of your primary face. Likewise, it is sufficient to place Vajrapāṇi and Khagarbha upon the two ears and two nostrils of the main face, for as the *Vajra Garland Explanatory Tantra* makes clear: "On both eye organs abides the Tathāgata Kṣitigarbha, and on both ear organs the Sugata Vajrapāṇi."[2894] In like manner it is sufficient to place the fierce deities Yamāntaka and Aparājita on your primary arms alone.

What is the reason for this? [130a] There are two possibilities here. When the limbs, which are the grounds of purification or the bases for generating the deity, are[2895] manifold, you should generate manifold deities as well. For example, since you have two eyes, you must generate two Kṣitigarbhas. For the same reason you should generate as many Samantabhadras as you have joints,[2896] each Samantabhadra on its respective location on the body, as taught in the *Vajra Garland Explanatory Tantra*: "The Tathāgata Samantabhadra

2891. Tib. Gzugs rdo rje ma, Eng. Vajra Lady of Forms.

2892. Reading *dgod par* for *dged par* in our text.

2893. Līlavajra, *Rdo rje sems dpa'i sgrub thabs kyi 'grel pa*, *Vajrasattva Sādhana Nibandha*, Tōh 1815, 207a3–4. D has *rang bzhin lus la gnas pa'i* for *rang bzhin rnams lus kyi* and *rnams su dgod par* for *gnas pa dgod par* in our text.

2894. *Rgyud rdo rje phreng ba*, *Vajramālā Tantra*, chap. 64, Tōh 445, 270a4–5. Cited on [124a] above and in Nāgabuddhi's *Rnam gzhag rim pa*, *Vyavastholi*, chap. 3, Tōh 1809, 128b3; Tanaka 2016, 121–122.

2895. Reading *yod* for *yad* in our text.

2896. Kun tu bzang po, Samantabhadra, is placed on the joints of the body, see Tsong kha pa, *Gsang mngon*, 44b5–6.

abides on all the joints of the body."[2897] For example, if you were to generate Kṣitigarbhas from the eyes of the right and left faces that you do not in reality possess, then the bases for generation would be contrived and thus unsuitable for generating the uncontrived deities of the maṇḍala.

In the second possibility, the number of actual bodily limbs is not quite the same as the number of deities visualized. When the number of deities to be generated from the limbs is greater than the number of limbs you may need to generate deities not only on your primary limbs, but also on those that are visualized. For example, in the context of the body maṇḍala of Cakrasaṃvara, the ninth chapter of the *Abhidhānottara Tantra* explains that you should place twelve Mamos on the twelve arms of yourself visualized as Heruka.[2898]

How could you then meditate on a maṇḍala that is uncontrived? In the context of Cakrasaṃvara according to Lūyīpāda, Vajraghaṇṭa, and so forth, you generate the four mothers, Ḍākinī and so forth,[2899] from the four channels of the heart cakra, such as the triple-circled channel and so forth. Likewise, you generate the eight female gatekeepers from the eight channels at the cardinal and intermediate directions of the outer circle of the heart. However, the explanation of the *Abhidhānottara Tantra* is different; there you are instructed to generate twelve Mamos from the twelve arms of yourself as the deity.[2900] [130b] Yet, simply generating the Mamos from the twelve arms is not the proper way to generate the body maṇḍala; rather, you must first visualize your own two arms completely transformed into the twelve arms of Heruka, and then generate the twelve Mamos from these twelve arms whose essence is indivisible from the emblems they hold.

Conversely, in the case of Guhyasamāja, you have only two real arms, and only two fierce deities to generate from them. Therefore you need not generate the deities in numbers exceeding the arms you meditate on. Additionally, you should meditate on the two fierce deities within the palms of your two

2897. *Rgyud rdo rje phreng ba*, *Vajramālā Tantra*, chap. 64, Tōh 445, 270a6–7. Cited in Nāgabuddhi's *Rnam gzhag rim pa*, *Vyavastholi*, chap. 3, Tōh 1809, 128b5, (where part of this verse is omitted); Tanaka 2016, 122.

2898. *Mngon par brjod pa'i rgyud bla ma*, *Abhidhānottara Tantra*, chap. 9, Tōh 369, 268a6–b1; Sanskrit and English translation in Kalff 1979, 286, lines 44a3-4; and 160–161. See also Tsong kha pa, *'Dod 'jo*, 127b6.

2899. The four mothers in this context are Tib. Mkha' 'gro ma, Lāmā, Dum skye ma, and Gzungs can ma; Skt. Ḍākinī, Lāmā, Khaṇḍarohā, and Rūpiṇī. See Lūyīpāda, *Bcom ldan 'das mngon par rtogs pa*, *Bhagavadabhisamaya*, Tōh 1427, 188b1; Sakurai 1998, 6.

2900. *Mngon par brjod pa'i rgyud bla ma*, *Abhidhānottara Tantra*, chap. 9, Tōh 369, 268a6–b1; Sanskrit and English translation in Kalff 1979, 286, lines 44a3–4, and 160–161.

primary hands as reflected images arising in a mirror. The same pattern should be applied elsewhere.

[Further Remarks]

When you meditate on the body maṇḍala, no part of your body that has not been generated as the celestial mansion can be visualized as a deity. Likewise, when you complete the generation of the form aggregate as Vairocana, nothing not included within the form aggregate can be visualized as a deity. In other words, neither can the four elements be visualized as the mothers, nor can the sensory organs endowed with forms be visualized as the bodhisattvas. Nevertheless, although these parts of the body are not substantively distinct, there is nothing wrong here since your mind[2901] can differentiate them.

In this regard you should understand that even after generating the eye organ as the wheel upon the portal, the continuum of the ordinary eye organ still remains intact; therefore, it is not inappropriate to generate the eye organ once again as Kṣitigarbha. Otherwise, if you meditated on yourself today as Vajradhara, it would not be suitable to meditate on yourself as Vairocana tomorrow. Hence, do not habituate yourself merely to recite the sādhana, but rather direct your meditation inward. You should meditate after making the appropriate distinctions between the true mode of being and the mode of mental apprehension.[2902] [131a]

In conclusion, the body maṇḍala of the glorious *Guhyasamāja Tantra* is only applied in correspondence to the phases in the womb as its ground of purification. You should place it on the body of Vajrasattva's nirmāṇakāya after the First Lord has been transformed into him. You must generate the First Lord through the five manifest awakenings[2903] and the first manifest awakening among them—the manifest awakening from suchness[2904]—must be the dissolution of the specially visualized deities into clear light.[2905] The

2901. Reading *blos* for *bros* in our text.

2902. See Tsong kha pa, *Bskyed rim zin bris*, 30a1–4, and *'Dod 'jo*, 124a3–b1.

2903. Tib. *mngon par byang chub pa*, or *mngon byang*, Skt. *abhisambodhi*.

2904. Tib. *de bzhin nyid las byang chub pa*.

2905. See above [103b].

tantra as well as Ārya Nāgārjuna and his disciples conveyed this clearly and at great length in a harmonious manner.[2906]

Hence, you must understand that the claims that there are sādhanas in the system of the Guhyasamāja according to which you should meditate on the body maṇḍala alone, and that there are initiations into body maṇḍalas and so forth, undoubtedly come from Māra, and may deceive you and others too. In separate works dedicated to meditations on the body maṇḍala written by the mahāsiddhas of the Cakrasaṃvara tradition, such as Vajraghaṇṭa, the main points of the path—whereby birth, death, and the intermediate state are taken as the three bodies of the Buddha—can be completed in the meditation on the body maṇḍala alone. The tantra rightly teaches this as well. Nevertheless, it seems that numerous traditions of the body maṇḍala known in Tibet do not practice any of these systems but regard mere mental imputations as transmitted instructions and profound Dharma. Therefore do not let it be known that YOU are a cow following the words of a fool.

This brings to a close my exposition on the method of meditating on the body maṇḍala.

2906. Note that the five manifest awakenings as such do not appear in Nāgārjuna's basic sādhana, the *Mdor byas*, *Piṇḍīkrama Sādhana*, Tōh 1796, and neither the five manifest awakenings nor the First Lord appear in Nāgārjuna's *Mdo bsre*, *Sādhanasūtramelāpaka*, Tōh 1797.

13. Blessing the Three Doors and Meditating on the Triple Sattvas

The Blessing of the Body, Speech, and Mind and the Meditation on the Triple Sattvas

There are two sections here: (1) blessing the three doors and (2) meditating on the triple sattvas.

Blessing the Three Doors

You should bless each of the three doors [131b] as taught by Ārya Nāgārjuna and his disciples: Invite as instructed in the eleventh chapter of the *Guhyasamāja Tantra*.[2907] In making your request, recite the verses taught in the twelfth chapter, two for each door.[2908] Then stabilize with those taught in the seventh chapter, one verse for each door,[2909] and maintain divine identity with the mantras taught in the sixth chapter.[2910]

The *Sādhana Incorporating the Scripture* teaches the method of inviting the deities: "The eleventh chapter of the *Guhyasamāja Tantra* teaches: 'Visualize the syllable *hūṃ* abiding at the center of the vajra disk, *oṃ* at the

2907. *Guhyasamāja Tantra*, Tōh 442; Zhol 15a3; Stog 25b4–5; Dunh missing; Fremantle 1971, vv. 4–5b; and Matsunaga 1978, vv. 4–5ab. Matsunaga has the seed syllables as *oṃ*, *āḥ*, *hūṃ* respectively.

2908. *Guhyasamāja Tantra*, Tōh 442; Zhol 19b3–5; Stog 33a4–b3; Dunh 36a4–b3; Fremantle 1971, vv. 71–76; Matsunaga 1978, vv. 70–75; English translation in Wayman 1977, 35, vv. 70–75. The text of the Zhol, Stog, and Dunh is somewhat different from the text of Tsong kha pa's *Gsang mngon* that appears in each of the blessings of body, speech, and mind below.

2909. *Guhyasamāja Tantra*, Tōh 442; Zhol 11a3–5; Stog 18b1–3; Dunh 19a1–4; Fremantle 1971 vv. 28–30; and Matsunaga 1978, vv. 28–30; English translation in Fremantle 1990, 108.

2910. The mantras are found at the beginning of chapter 6 of the *Guhyasamāja Tantra*, Tōh 442; Zhol 9a3–5; Stog 14b5–15a1; Dunh 14b1–3; Fremantle 1971, 208–209; and Matsunaga 1978, 17; English translation in Wayman 1977, 25.

center of the clear disk, and *āḥ* at the center of the dharma disk.'"[2911] The *Illuminating Lamp* applies this verse to the meditation on the solar disk that arises from *hūṃ*, which follows the meditation on manifest awakening through suchness.[2912] But as I have already explained, each vajra word of the *Guhyasamāja Tantra* can express a wide variety of compatible meanings. In fact,[2913] the transmitted instruction of Ārya Nāgārjuna explicitly teaches the meditation on the solar disk that arises from the *hūṃ* on the heart, surmounted by another *hūṃ*, the visualization of the female buddhas emanating from this *hūṃ* who invite the buddhas, and so forth.

The following discussion is divided into four sections: (1) blessing the body, (2) blessing speech, (3) blessing the mind, and (4) maintaining a divine identity as Vajradhara, the indivisible three vajras.

Blessing the Body

The *Concise Sādhana* teaches: "The mantrin who has placed the deities on the aggregates and so forth and completed the practice of the body maṇḍala according to the ritual method should begin the great yoga."[2914] This passage describes the transition from the body maṇḍala to the blessings of the three doors. Next, the *Concise Sādhana* depicts the manner of inviting the buddhas who bless the body: [132a] "At the center of the crown, visualize a perfectly rounded lunar disk surmounted by a white syllable *oṃ* emanating five light rays. Imagine it[2915] then emanating the female Buddha [Locanā] united with the lord and [surrounded by] a multitude of Locanās, filling the entire space. Then meditate on the lord Vajra Body Vairocana, adorned with the thirty-two

2911. Nāgārjuna, *Mdo bsre*, *Sādhanasūtramelāpaka*, Tōh 1797, 13a3–4. D has *zhes rnam par bsam* for *ni rab tu bsam* in our text. See *Gsang 'dus*, *Guhyasamāja Tantra*, Tōh 442; Zhol 15a3; Stog 25b4–5; Dunh missing; Fremantle 1971 vv. 4–5ab; and Matsunaga 1978, vv. 4–5ab. The Zhol has *rab tu bsgom* for *rab tu bsam*; Matsunaga 1978 has the seed syllables as *oṃ*, *āḥ*, *hūṃ* respectively.

2912. Candrakīrti, *Sgron gsal*, *Pradīpoddyotanaṭīkā*, chap. 11, Tōh 1785, 77b3–4; Chakravarti 1984, 97. Mkhas grub rje follows here Tsong kha pa, *Sgron gsal mchan*, 234a1–b3.

2913. Although the *Guhyasamāja Tantra* does not specify this, the transmitted instruction of Ārya Nāgārjuna explicitly teaches that the female buddhas emanate and invite the male buddhas.

2914. Tib. *sbyor chen*, Skt. *mahāyoga*. Nāgārjuna, *Mdor byas*, *Piṇḍīkrama Sādhana*, Tōh 1796, 4b2–3; L 69; T 68.

2915. The *it* will be explained shortly.

major and eighty minor marks of a buddha, at the center of a multitude [of Vairocanas] filling the space. And before him I abide."[2916]

The meaning of the verse *imagine it emanating the female Buddha [Locanā] united with the lord* is: imagine that *it*—meaning *oṃ*—issues an assembly of Locanās who then invites an assembly of Vairocanas to fill the space, with the principal Vairocana and Locanā at their center abiding in union. Sitting before them make your request. You should know how to apply this pattern below as well.

Then the *Concise Sādhana* explains how to make the request while reciting the two verses taught in the twelfth chapter of the *Guhyasamāja Tantra*: "Then, the mantrin makes a request by reciting these two verses: May the holder of the buddha body, endowed with glory, on whom I meditate as indivisible from the three vajras, bless me now with vajra body. May the buddhas who reside in the ten directions, upon whom I meditate as indivisible from the three vajras, bless me now with vajra body."[2917] The first verse here is a request to the main Vairocana, and the second [132b] to the buddhas who accompany him.

This is the meaning of the above verses:[2918] Locanā who bestows great bliss is called *glory*, and he who is graced with her as his consort is called *endowed with glory*. *Holder* means he who holds the bodies of all the buddhas of the three times as his own essence. Thus *holder of the buddha body endowed with glory* addresses Vairocana. *Bless me* refers to the request of the mantrins who *meditate* on Vajradhara as *indivisible from the three vajras*, requesting him to *bless* them *now*, that is, this moment. How is the request made? "I ask you to bless me by turning my body into the essence of Vajra Body, Vairocana." Then once more invoke *the buddhas who reside in the ten directions* and who are his retinue; the rest of the second verse is the same as before.

The *Concise Sādhana* explains the way to meditate on the blessing granted through this request: "Visualize Vairocana united with Locanā blessing you

2916. Nāgārjuna, *Mdor byas*, *Piṇḍīkrama Sādhana*, Tōh 1796, 4b3–5; L 70–73ab; T 69–72ab. D has *de las* for *de nas*; *legs gnas pa* for *bzhugs bsam ste*; and *bsgom pa ni* for *bsgom pa na* in our text.

2917. Nāgārjuna, *Mdor byas*, *Piṇḍīkrama Sādhana*, Tōh 1796, 4b5–6; L 73cd–75; T 72cd–74. D has twice *bsgoms bas* for *bsgom pas* and twice *sku* for *skus* in our text. These verses are also found in the *Guhyasamāja Tantra*, chap. 12, Tōh 442; Zhol 19b3; Stog 33a4–6; Dunh 36a4–5; Fremantle 1971, vv. 71–72; and Matsunaga 1978, vv. 70–71; English translation in Wayman 1977, 35. While the *Mdor byas* has *byin gyis brlabs nas su*, Zhol has *byin gyis brlabs gnas byas te*. Matsunaga has *kāyalakṣitam* for the second occurrence of *kāyavajriṇaḥ*.

2918. See Candrakīrti, *Sgron gsal*, *Pradīpoddyotanaṭīkā*, chap. 12, Tōh 1785, 99b1–3; Chakravarti 1984, 121. See also Tsong kha pa's *Sgron gsal mchan*, 288b1–5; *Bskyed rim zin bris*, 31a5; and *Slob tshul*, 18a2–5.

by entering into you."[2919] Then you should meditate according to the *Vajrasattva Sādhana*: "As soon as you make this request, visualize the entire assembly of deities desiring each other, and thus experience the bliss of supreme joy. Then they enter into you in the nature of white light rays through the gate of Vairocana, in the manner of jñānasattvas. Attaining the ground of wisdom, your entire body will be filled and satisfied. Then stabilize with the verse taught in the seventh chapter of the *Guhyasamāja Tantra*."[2920]

The *Concise Sādhana* cites this verse from the seventh chapter of the *Guhyasamāja Tantra* on stabilizing the blessing: "Like the body of all buddhas [133a] complete with the five aggregates, may my body too be endowed with the nature of the Buddha body."[2921] This means:[2922] *Like the body of all buddhas*, that is, of the buddhas residing in the ten directions, who emanate *amplified with the five aggregates* that are related to Vairocana; *may my* body *too*, meaning the body of the mantrin, like that of Vairocana *be endowed with the nature of the bodies of* all *buddhas*. Gö's translation has "amplified [for *complete*] with the five aggregates."[2923]

Next maintain the divine identity of Vajra Body as the *Vajrasattva Sādhana* teaches: "Then maintain nondual divine identity, with the mantra taught in the sixth chapter of the *Guhyasamāja Tantra*: *oṃ sarva tathāgata kāya vajra*

2919. Nāgārjuna, *Mdor byas, Piṇḍīkrama Sādhana*, Tōh 1796, 4b6; L 76abc; T 75abc. D has *bsams nas* for *bsam nas*.

2920. Candrakīrti, *Rdo rje sems dpa'i sgrub thabs, Vajrasattva Sādhana*, Tōh 1814, 200b2–3; Luo and Tomabechi 2009, 19.6–9 and 52.2–6. D and Luo and Tomabechi omit *thams cad* after *lha'i tshogs* and add *nas* after *zhugs*, and they have *ye shes* for *ye shes kyi sa* in our text.

2921. Nāgārjuna, *Mdor byas, Piṇḍīkrama Sādhana*, Tōh 1796, 4b7; L 77; T 76. D has *rab gang ba* for *rab bkang bas*. See the *Gsang 'dus, Guhyasamāja Tantra*, chap. 7, Tōh 442; Zhol 11a3; Stog 18b1; Dunh 19a1–2; Fremantle 1971, v. 28; and Matsunaga 1978, v. 28. The Zhol has *rab tu rgyas*, has *ngo bo yis* for *ngo bo yi*, and the Zhol has *rang bzhin gyis*. The Zhol has *'drar gyur cig* for *'dra bar shog*. See also Candrakīrti's *Rdo rje sems dpa'i sgrub thabs, Vajrasattva Sādhana*, Tōh 1814, 200b3–4; Luo and Tomabechi 2009, 19.10–11 and 52.8–11. English translation in Fremantle 1971, 48; Yoshimizu 1987, 29; and Fremantle 1990, 108.

2922. See Candrakīrti's *Sgron gsal, Pradīpoddyotanaṭīkā*, chap. 7, Tōh 1785, 53b3–4; Chakravarti 1984, 68; and Tsong kha pa's *Sgron gsal mchan*, 176b1–4.

2923. As was just noted, the translation of this tantra by 'Gos has *rab tu rgyas* for *rab bkang bas* in our text and *rab gang ba* in the Bstan 'gyur.

svabhāva ātmako 'haṃ."[2924] Regarding the meaning of the mantra: *oṃ* has already been explained, *sarva* is all, *tathāgata* is thus-come-thus-gone, *kāya* is body,[2925] *vajra* is *dorje*, *svabhāva* is nature, *ātmako* is consisting, and *ahaṃ* is I. Hence the meaning of the mantra is: The indivisible nature of the body of all tathāgatas, that am I.

Blessing Speech

The *Concise Sādhana* teaches how to invite the buddhas to bestow the blessing: "On your tongue visualize a red *āḥ* on a lotus emanating Pāṇḍaravāsinīs in the sky, filling the realms of space. As before,[2926] visualize Vajra Speeches [Amitābhas] filling the space."[2927] From the *āḥ* at the center of your tongue visualize a red lotus with a red syllable *āḥ* at its center, and radiating from it, a multitude of Pāṇḍaravāsinīs, filling the space. [133b] They invite a multitude of Vajra Speech Amitābhas that fill the space, with the principal Amitābha and Pāṇḍaravāsinī at their center abiding in union. Sitting before them, make your request.[2928]

How is the request made? The *Concise Sādhana* teaches: "Then, the mantrin makes a request by reciting these two verses: May the path of Dharma Speech,[2929] endowed with glory, on which I meditate as indivisible from the three vajras, bless me now with vajra speech. May the buddhas who reside in the ten directions, on whom I meditate as indivisible from the three vajras,

2924. Candrakīrti, *Rdo rje sems dpa'i sgrub thabs*, *Vajrasattva Sādhana*, Tōh 1814, 200b4; Luo and Tomabechi 2009, 19.12–13 and 52.12–13. Luo and Tomabechi have *le'u bdun pa* for *le'u drug pa*. This mantra is found at the beginning of chap. 6 of the *Guhyasamāja Tantra*, Tōh 442; Zhol 9a3; Stog 14b6; Dunh 14b2; Fremantle 1971, 208–209; and Matsunaga 1978, 17; and in Nāgārjuna's *Mdor byas*, *Piṇḍīkrama Sādhana*, Tōh 1796, following L v. 77 and T v. 76. See also Wayman 1977, 25, and Yoshimizu 1987, 29.

2925. The Tibetan text has *sku 'am lus*, that is, "body, honorific or nonhonorific."

2926. As in the blessing of the body.

2927. Nāgārjuna, *Mdor byas*, *Piṇḍīkrama Sādhana*, Tōh 1796, 4b7–5a1; L 78–79ab; T 77–78ab. D has *ldan pas* for *ldan pa*; *rnam bsams* for *gnas bsams*; *gsung gi rdo rje'i sngags ni* for *sngar bzhin sngags pas gsung rdo rje*; and *nam mkha'i dbus na* for *rnam mkha' gang bar*.

2928. See Tsong kha pa, *Gsang mngon*, 47b5–48a2.

2929. The Sanskrit has Dharma or the path of speech.

bless me now with vajra speech."[2930] Amitābha is *endowed with glory* because he is graced with Pāṇḍarā as his consort. *Dharma* is Amitābha. He is the *path of speech* because he is the essence of the speech of all the buddhas. The rest is as before, except that *vajra body* is replaced with *vajra speech*.[2931]

The *Concise Sādhana* explains the meditation on the blessing granted through this request: "Partake in the blessing of speech by visualizing Pāṇḍarā united with her lord entering your tongue."[2932] Meditate as the *Vajrasattva Sādhana* teaches: "Having made such a request, visualize the assembled male and female buddhas joining their two organs and thereby melting in the fire of great passion—entering your mouth in the form of red light rays. In this way, you will attain mastery of speech. [134a] Stabilize the blessing with the following two verses."[2933]

The verse for stabilizing the blessing is taught in the *Guhyasamāja Tantra*: "As the speech of Vajra Dharma is perfect lingual discernment,[2934] so may my

2930. Nāgārjuna, *Mdor byas*, *Piṇḍīkrama Sādhana*, Tōh 1796, 5a1–3; L 79cd–81; T 78bcd–80. D has *dpal dang ldan* for *dpal ldan pa* and *rdo rje gsung du mdzad* for *rdo rje gsung gir mdzad* twice. These verses too are found in the *Guhyasamāja Tantra*, chap. 12, Tōh 442; Zhol 19b4; Stog 33a6–b1; Dunh 36a6–b1; Fremantle 1971, vv. 73–74; and Matsunaga 1978, vv. 72–73. In the last line Matsunaga has *tasya* for *me 'dya* and *vākpathodbhavam* for *vāgvajriṇaḥ*. See also Wayman 1977, 35, vv. 72–73.

2931. See Candrakīrti, *Sgron gsal*, *Pradīpoddyotanaṭīkā*, Tōh 1785, 99b3–4; Chakravarti 1984, 121.

2932. Nāgārjuna, *Mdor byas*, *Piṇḍīkrama Sādhana*, Tōh 1796, 5a3; L 82; T 81. D has *lhan cig nyid* for *lhan cig tu*; *bsams te* for *bsams nas*; and *gsung gi* for *gsung gis*.

2933. Candrakīrti, *Rdo rje sems dpa'i sgrub thabs*, *Vajrasattva Sādhana*, Tōh 1814, 200b7–201a1; Luo and Tomabechi 2009, 20.8–10 and 53.9–12. D and Luo and Tomabechi omit *lha'i* and have *brtan par* for *bstan par* in our text.

2934. Lingual discernment, the ability to teach the Dharma in every language, Tib. *nges tshig*, Skt. *nirukti*, is one of the four types of specific-perfect-discernment, Tib. *so so yang dag par rig pa*, Skt. *pratisamvid*: (1) discernment of phenomena, Tib. *chos*, Skt. *dharma*; (2) of meaning, Tib. *don*, Skt. *artha*; (3) of languages and etymologies or lingual discernment, Tib. *nges tshig*, Skt. *nirukti*; and (4) of eloquence, Tib. *spongs pa*, Skt. *pratibhāna*; see Mvy. 196–200.

speech be like that of the Dharma Holder."[2935] This means:[2936] *Vajra Dharma* is Amitābha. His *speech is perfect* because it is the fruit of attaining the four types of specific-perfect-discernment signified by *lingual discernment*; *so may my speech be like* means like the speech of Amitābha, that is, *like that of the Dharma Holder*, who is Amitābha. Next, the *Vajrasattva Sādhana* explains how to maintain divine identity of Vajra Speech: "Maintain nondual divine identity with the mantra: *oṃ sarva tathāgata vāk vajra svabhāva ātmako 'haṃ*."[2937] *Vāk* means "speech,"[2938] and the rest is as before.

Where do you visualize the lotus with the syllable *āḥ* at its center? The *Concise Sādhana* teaches: "On your tongue visualize a red *āḥ* on a lotus,"[2939] but the *Vajrasattva Sādhana* teaches: "On your throat place a red *āḥ* on a lotus."[2940] THOSE who maintain that the latter instruction does not accord with the position of Ārya Nāgārjuna and his disciples have clearly not scrutinized the famous works of this tradition. As Ārya Nāgārjuna himself explains in the *Sādhana Incorporating the Scripture*: "Place the three syllables upon the head, the throat, and the heart. [134b] Then a multitude of Locanās and so forth arising from these seed syllables invoke Vajra Body and so forth."[2941] Thus Ārya

2935. *Guhyasamāja Tantra*, chap. 7, Tōh 442; Zhol 11a3–4; Stog 18b2; Dunh 19a2–3; Fremantle 1971, v. 29; and Matsunaga 1978, v. 29. The Zhol has *gsung de nges tshig* for *nges pa'i tshig ni*; *de 'dra ste* for *de 'dra zhing*; and *'drar gyur cig* for *'dra bar shog*. Matsunaga has *sampadaḥ* for *sampadā*, and *tādṛśo vāco* for *tādṛśī vācā*. See also Nāgārjuna's *Mdor byas, Piṇḍīkrama Sādhana*, Tōh 1796, 5a3–4; L 83; T 82, and Candrakīrti's *Rdo rje sems dpa'i sgrub thabs, Vajrasattva Sādhana*, Tōh 1814, 201a1; Luo and Tomabechi 2009, 20.11–12 and 53.13–16. English translation in Fremantle 1971, 48; Yoshimizu 1987, 29–30; and Fremantle 1990, 108.

2936. See Candrakīrti, *Sgron gsal, Pradīpoddyotanaṭīkā*, Tōh 1785, 53b4–7; Chakravarti 1984, 68; and Tsong kha pa's *Sgron gsal mchan*, 176b4–177a2.

2937. Candrakīrti, *Rdo rje sems dpa'i sgrub thabs, Vajrasattva Sādhana*, Tōh 1814, 201a1–2; Luo and Tomabechi 2009, 21.1–2 and 53.17–54.2. This mantra is found at the beginning of chap. 6 of the *Guhyasamāja Tantra*, Tōh 442; Zhol 9a4; Stog 15a1; Dunh 14b3; Fremantle 1971, 208–209; and Matsunaga 1978, 17. See also Nāgārjuna's *Mdor byas, Piṇḍīkrama Sādhana*, Tōh 1796, following L v. 83 and T v. 82; and Wayman 1977, 25.

2938. The Tibetan text has *gsung ngam ngag*, that is, "speech, honorific or nonhonorific."

2939. Nāgārjuna's *Mdor byas, Piṇḍīkrama Sādhana*, Tōh 1796, 4b7–5a1; L 78ab; T 77ab. Above [133a] there was *lce yi* for *lce yis* here.

2940. Candrakīrti, *Rdo rje sems dpa'i sgrub thabs, Vajrasattva Sādhana*, Tōh 1814, 200b4–5; Luo and Tomabechi 2009, 20.2 and 52.15–16.

2941. Nāgārjuna, *Mdo bsre, Sādhanasūtramelāpaka*, Tōh 1797, 13a4. D has *spyan* for *spyan ma*.

Nāgārjuna too explains that you should place the syllable *āḥ* on the throat, and hence, no matter what you do, the meaning will be the same.[2942]

Blessing the Mind

The *Concise Sādhana* teaches how to invite the buddhas to bless the mind: "Visualize a shining reflected image of the sun[2943] upon your heart, surmounted by a *hūṃ* resembling dark blue azurite, endowed with the five rays of light. Imagine it[2944] drawing Māmakī surrounded by her assembly. As before, meditate on Vajra Mind Akṣobhya and make your request."[2945] Therefore visualize a solar disk appearing from the *hūṃ* on your heart, and upon it a dark *hūṃ* emanating light rays in the five colors, and radiating therefrom a multitude of Māmakīs. They invite a multitude of Vajra Mind Akṣobhyas to fill the space, with the principal Akṣobhya and Māmakī at their center abiding in union. Sitting before them, make your request.[2946]

[On Which Seat Does the Syllable Hūṃ *Abide?]*

The *Sādhana Incorporating the Scripture* cites the line of the *Guhyasamāja Tantra*: "Visualize *hūṃ* abiding at the center of a vajra disk."[2947] In his *Concise Sādhana* Ārya Nāgārjuna explains that the seat of the *hūṃ* is a solar disk,[2948] whereas the *Vajrasattva Sādhana* explains: "Then, visualize a dark *hūṃ* at the

2942. See Bu ston, *Mdor byas 'grel chen*, 46b2; and Tsong kha pa, *Rnal 'byor dag rim*, 17b2, and *Slob tshul*, 18b6–19a2.

2943. Note that the Sanskrit here is *śaśibimbaṃ*.

2944. This refers to the *hūṃ*. Once more D has *de las* for *de nas*.

2945. Nāgārjuna, *Mdor byas, Piṇḍīkrama Sādhana*, Tōh 1796, 5a4–5; L 84–85; T 83–84. D has *mthing shun* for *mthing shing* and *'od zer lngar* for *'od zer lnga*. The Sanskrit has *śaśi* for *nyi ma*, and Ratnākaraśānti has *zla ba* in his commentary. See his *Rin chen phreng ba, Ratnāvalī*, Tōh 1826, 44b6.

2946. See Tsong kha pa, *Gsang mngon*, 48b3–5.

2947. Nāgārjuna, *Mdo bsre, Sādhanasūtramelāpaka*, Tōh 1797, 13a3–4. See *Gsang 'dus, Guhyasamāja Tantra*, chap. 11, Tōh 442; Zhol 15a3; Stog 25b4; Dunh missing; Fremantle 1971, v. 4ab; and Matsunaga 1978, v. 4ab, which appeared above [131b2].

2948. Nāgārjuna, *Mdor byas, Piṇḍīkrama Sādhana*, Tōh 1796, 5a4; L 84ab; T 83ab.

center of the vajra on your heart."[2949] However, the *Illuminating Lamp* explains the line of the *Guhyasamāja Tantra*: "*Visualize* the syllable *hūṃ* abiding at the center of a vajra disk, that is to say a solar disk, for the intention here is that you meditate on a solar disk that emerges from the syllable *hūṃ*."[2950] Therefore YOU cannot say that Candrakīrti, the author of these two works,[2951] does not maintain that the *hūṃ* abides on a solar disk, and thus we accept both vajra and solar disks as appropriate. [135a] This instruction in the *Illuminating Lamp* to visualize the solar disk arising from *hūṃ* confirms that in both of the above blessings of body and speech, the lotus and lunar disk should emerge from the seed syllables *āḥ* and *oṃ* respectively.

[How Is the Request Made and the Blessing Granted?]

The *Concise Sādhana* teaches: "May the holder of vajra mind, endowed with glory, on whom I meditate as indivisible from the three vajras, bless me now with vajra mind. May the buddhas who reside in the ten directions, on whom I meditate as indivisible from the three vajras, bless me now with vajra mind."[2952] Akṣobhya is *endowed with glory* because he is graced with Māmakī as his consort. He is *vajra mind holder* because he holds as his essence a mind that by nature abides neither in saṃsāra nor in nirvāṇa, and which is unswayed by the proliferation of labels. The rest is as before, except that *vajra body* is replaced here with *vajra mind*.[2953]

2949. Candrakīrti, *Rdo rje sems dpa'i sgrub thabs*, *Vajrasattva Sādhana*, Tōh 1814, 201a2; Luo and Tomabechi 2009, 21.3 and 54.3–4. D and Luo and Tomabechi have *hūṃ kha dog nag po* for *hūṃ nag po*. According to Tsong kha pa's *Slob tshul*, 19a5–6, while Nāgārjuna's *Mdor byas*, *Piṇḍīkrama Sādhana*, instructs the yogi to generate a solar disk from *hūṃ*, the *Rdo rje sems dpa'i sgrub thabs*, *Vajrasattva Sādhana*, explains that the yogi should generate a vajra from *hūṃ*.

2950. Candrakīrti, *Sgron gsal*, *Pradīpoddyotanaṭīkā*, chap. 11, Tōh 1785, 77b3–4; Chakravarti 1984, 97.

2951. Candrakīrti's *Rdo rje sems dpa'i sgrub thabs*, *Vajrasattva Sādhana*, Tōh 1814, and the *Sgron gsal*, *Pradīpoddyotanaṭīkā*, Tōh 1785.

2952. Nāgārjuna, *Mdor byas*, *Piṇḍīkrama Sādhana*, Tōh 1796, 5a5–6; L 86–87; T 85–86. D has twice *bsgoms pas* for *bsgom pas*; *rdo rje thugs su* for *rdo rje'i thugs kyis*; and *rdo rje thugs su* for *rdo rje thugs kyis*. These verses are found in the *Guhyasamāja Tantra* as well, chap. 12, Tōh 442; Zhol 19b4–5; Stog 33b1–3; Dunh 36b1–3; Fremantle 1971, vv. 75–76; and Matsunaga 1978, vv. 74–75. Matsunaga has *cittasambhavāḥ* for the second occurrence of *cittavajriṇaḥ*. See also Wayman 1977, 35, vv. 74–75.

2953. See Candrakīrti, *Sgron gsal*, *Pradīpoddyotanaṭīkā*, Tōh 1785, 99b4–6; Chakravarti 1984, 121.

The *Concise Sādhana* teaches how to meditate on the blessing granted through this request: "Partake in the blessing of the mind by visualizing the entire assembly of Māmakīs together with Vajra Minds entering your heart."[2954] Meditate as the *Vajrasattva Sādhana* instructs: "As soon as you make the request, visualize the aforementioned assembled male and female buddhas—melted in the fire of great nondual passion—entering your heart in the form of black light rays. In this way you will attain mastery of mind. Stabilize the blessing with the following verse."[2955] [135b]

The verse for stabilizing the blessing is taught in the *Guhyasamāja Tantra*: "As the mind of the wholly excellent[2956] Lord of Secrets endowed with understanding, so may my mind be; may it resemble that of vajra holder."[2957] The meaning of this verse is explained in the *Illuminating Lamp*: "*The Lord of Secrets* is the ruler of the secret ones and foremost among those who teach thatness. He is *endowed with understanding*, because *understanding* is Sparśavajrā[2958] and being graced with her means being *endowed with understanding*."[2959] Both Māmakī and Sparśavajrā appear as the consort of Vajra Mind, but in this instance as the *Illuminating Lamp* teaches, she is Sparśavajrā. *Endowed with understanding* and endowed with wisdom are synonymous, for the consort is called *Wisdom*.[2960] As for *wholly excellent*, *wholly*

2954. Nāgārjuna, *Mdor byas*, *Piṇḍīkrama Sādhana*, Tōh 1796, 5a6; L 88; T 87. D has *thugs kyi* for *thugs kyis* and *brlab pa* for *brlab par*.

2955. Candrakīrti, *Rdo rje sems dpa'i sgrub thabs*, *Vajrasattva Sādhana*, Tōh 1814, 201a4–5; Luo and Tomabechi 2009, 21.10-11 and 54.15–18. D and Luo and Tomabechi have *bzhin du* for *ji lta ba bzhin du* and *brtan par* for *bstan par* in our text.

2956. Tib. *kun tu bzang po*, Skt. *samantabhadra*. This does not refer to the bodhisattva by this name.

2957. *Guhyasamāja Tantra*, chap. 7, Tōh 442; Zhol 11a4; Zhol 11a4; Stog 18b3; Dunh 19a3–4; Fremantle 1971, v. 30; and Matsunaga 1978, v. 30. The Zhol has *gsang ba'i bdag po blo ldan pa / kun tu bzang po'i thugs gang yin / rdo rje 'dzin pa lta bur ni / bdag gi sems kyang de 'drar gyur /* for *kun tu bzang po'i thugs gang yin / gsang ba'i dbang po blo ldan pa / bdag kyang de dang 'drar gyur te / rdo rje 'dzin dang mtshungs par shog /*. See also Nāgārjuna, *Mdor byas*, *Piṇḍīkrama Sādhana*, Tōh 1796, 5a6–7; L 89; T 88. D has *bdag po* for *dbang po*, and *'dra gyur cig* for *'drar gyur te*. See also Candrakīrti, *Rdo rje sems dpa'i sgrub thabs*, *Vajrasattva Sādhana*, Tōh 1814, 201a5; Luo and Tomabechi 2009, 21.12–13 and 55.1–4. English translation in Fremantle 1971, 48; Yoshimizu 1987, 29–30; and Fremantle 1990, 108.

2958. Tib. Reg bya Rdo rje ma, Eng. Vajra Lady of Tangibles.

2959. Candrakīrti, *Sgron gsal*, *Pradīpoddyotanaṭīkā*, Tōh 1785, 54a1; Chakravarti 1984, 69. D has *gtso bor gyur ces pa'i don to* for *gtso bor gyur pas na gsang ba'i bdag po'o*, and *reg rdo rje* for *reg bya rdo rje*.

2960. Tib. *shes rab ma*, Skt. *prajñā*.

means in every respect and *excellent* means immaculate. *May my mind resemble* means that it should be like the mind of Akṣobhya.

The *Vajrasattva Sādhana* teaches how to maintain a divine identity of Vajra Mind: "Maintain a nondual divine identity with the mantra *oṃ sarva tathāgata citta vajra svabhāva ātmako 'haṃ.*"[2961] *Citta* means "mind"[2962] and all the rest is as before.

Maintaining a Divine Identity as Vajradhara, the Indivisible Three Vajras

The *Concise Sādhana* teaches: "After blessing body, speech, and mind separately by assigning each to one of the three tathāgata families, the wise mantrin should once again take in the essence of all three with this mantra: *oṃ sarva tathāgata kāya vāk citta vajra svabhāva ātmako 'haṃ.*"[2963] [136a] *Taking in all three* means: maintaining divine identity as Vajradhara, the essence of all three vajras as one, or maintaining a divine identity as Vajradhara, the lord of all tathāgata families.[2964] You already know the meaning of the rest of the words and the mantra.[2965]

Where does the *Guhyasamāja Tantra* teach that blessing body, speech, and mind together signifies maintaining the divine identity of Vajradhara? The *Sādhana Incorporating the Scripture* does not apply this meditation to the *Guhyasamāja Tantra*, yet the *Vajrasattva Sādhana* explains that it is taught in the second chapter of the *Guhyasamāja Tantra*: "Generate mind as

2961. Candrakīrti, *Rdo rje sems dpa'i sgrub thabs*, *Vajrasattva Sādhana*, Tōh 1814, 201a5–6; Luo and Tomabechi 2009, 22.1–2 and 55.5–6. This mantra is found at the beginning of chap. 6 of the *Guhyasamāja Tantra*, Tōh 442; Zhol 9a3; Stog 14b5; Dunh 14b1; Fremantle 1971, 208; and Matsunaga 1978, 17. See also Nāgārjuna, *Mdor byas*, *Piṇḍīkrama Sādhana*, Tōh 1796, following L 89 and T 88, and Wayman 1977, 25.

2962. The Tibetan text has *sems sam thugs*. Both are honorific names for "mind."

2963. Nāgārjuna, *Mdor byas*, *Piṇḍīkrama Sādhana*, Tōh 1796, 5a7–b1; L 90; T 89. D has *vāk* for *bāk*.

2964. The terms translated here as *taking in*, *essence*, and *lord* are all derived from the Tibetan word *bdag*: *bdag nyid bya*, *bdag nyid*, and *bdag po*.

2965. In his *Slob tshul*, 19b2, Tsong kha pa explains that during the shared blessing of the body, speech, and mind, meditators should transfer their identification (*nga rgyal*) from Akṣobhya to Vajradhara.

body, body as mind, and mind as articulated speech."[2966] The word *as* here is better translated as *in the aspect of*.[2967] The *Illuminating Lamp* clarifies these lines with both definitive[2968] and interpretable[2969] levels of explanations. Here is the interpretable level of explanation: *Generate your mind in the aspect of body* means in the aspect of Vajra Body. *Generate your body in the aspect of mind* means in the aspect of Vajra Mind. *Generate your mind in the aspect of articulated speech* means in the aspect of Vajra Speech.[2970]

This explanation[2971] will also lessen any doubt about whether or not it is suitable to generate one's body as Vajra Body and speech as Vajra Speech. In order to dispel any doubt about whether the body and speech of the fruit attained will be inert as they are during the ground stage, the *Guhyasamāja Tantra* teaches *generate the mind in the aspect of Vajra Body*, as well as *in the aspect of Vajra Speech*. If any minor doubts remain concerning the suitability of generating the mind *in the aspect of* Vajra Mind or if more serious doubts remain concerning the suitability of generating the body *in the aspect of* Vajra Mind, [136b] it is taught that you should *generate the body in the aspect of mind*.

The *Illuminating Lamp* explains that the *Guhyasamāja Tantra* teaches blessings for body, speech, and mind separately using the word *generate* for each, whereas it teaches the blessings for body, speech, and mind not with *generate the mind in the aspect of body* and so forth for each one separately but by using *generate* with reference to all three.[2972]

2966. Candrakīrti, *Rdo rje sems dpa'i sgrub thabs*, *Vajrasattva Sādhana*, Tōh 1814, 201a7–b1; Luo and Tomabechi 2009, 22.5–7 and 55.10-12. See *Gsang 'dus*, *Guhyasamāja Tantra*, Tōh 442; Zhol 5b7; Stog 9a1–2; Dunh 8a5–8b1; Fremantle 1971, 190; and Matsunaga 1978, 9. Note that our text is almost identical with the text of the Zhol, while the text of the *Rdo rje sems dpa'i sgrub thabs* is somewhat different; see below. However, the Tibetan text of the *Rdo rje sems dpa'i sgrub thabs* seems to reflect the Sanskrit text better.

2967. This refers to Candrakīrti, *Rdo rje sems dpa'i sgrub thabs*, *Vajrasattva Sādhana*, Tōh 1814, which has *rnam pa*, while the Zhol edition of the *Guhyasamāja Tantra* as well as our text have *lta bu*. The Derge version of the *Guhyasamāja Tantra* has *rnam pa* and the Sanskrit equivalent here is *ākāra*. Mkhas grub rje follows here Tsong kha pa's *Sgron gsal mchan*, 87b4.

2968. Tib. *nges don*, Skt. *nītārtha*.

2969. Tib. *drang don*, Skt. *neyārtha*.

2970. Candrakīrti, *Sgron gsal*, *Pradīpoddyotanaṭikā*, Tōh 1785, 23a5–7; Chakravarti 1984, 30.

2971. See Tsong kha pa, *Sgron gsal mchan*, 87b6–88a3.

2972. See Tsong kha pa, *Sgron gsal mchan*, 88a3–b1.

Meditation on the Triple Sattvas

[The Samayasattva]

The *Concise Sādhana* teaches: "Having blessed yourself in this way, meditate on yourself as the samayasattva, abiding at the center of a lunar disk, endowed with the six signs."[2973] *The six signs* are the six hand emblems. Why are you—meditating on yourself as blue Vajradhara with six arms—called samayasattva here? The shared meaning of samayasattva is signified using a creative explanation of the actual meaning of a word by affixing extra letters to it. The word here is *samaya*, the Sanskrit equivalent of *dam tshig*.[2974] *Sam-eti*[2975] means coming together or joining, and *milati*[2976] means uniting. Thus you are called samaya because the jñānasattva joins and unites with you after you have cleared away ordinary pride and assumed the nature of the deities. As the *Cluster of Instructions* teaches: "[You are] called samaya because the essence of nondual wisdom that has assumed the nature of the deity, the jñānasattva, joins and unites with [you]."[2977]

The meaning of sattva, according to the *Cluster of Instructions* is: "It is called sattva because it acts for the benefit of sentient beings, [137a] and because it is a referent of the term *pure sentient being*."[2978] The specific etymological explanation for calling Vajrasattva's nirmāṇakāya samayasattva in this case, is offered in the *Vajrasattva Sādhana* as follows: "It is called samayasattva because it is

2973. Nāgārjuna, *Mdor byas*, *Piṇḍīkrama Sādhana*, Tōh 1796, 5b1; L 91; T 90. D has *byin gyis brlabs* for *byin brlabs nas*. This verse is also translated in Wayman 1977, 249–250.

2974. Mkhas grub rje partly follows here Tsong kha pa's explanation of the etymology of samayasattva in his *Sngags rim chen mo*, chap. 12, 516. Tsong kha pa on his part follows the explanation given by Abhayākaragupta, in the *Man ngag gi snye ma*; see below.

2975. Tsong kha pa, *Sngags rim chen mo*, chap. 12. The edition of New Delhi, 422a4, has *sameti* for *samati* in our text, while the edition of Mtsho sngon 1995, 516, has *las me ti* for *la sa me ti*.

2976. From Sanskrit √*mil*.

2977. Abhayākaragupta, *Man ngag snye ma*, *Āmnāyamañjarī*, Tōh 1198, 122a4–5. D has *mngon du byas pa'i* for *byas pa'i*; *'dir* after *phyir*; and *dam tshig go* for *dam tshig gi* in our text. Except for the last difference, which is obviously a mistake, our text is the same as that of Tsong kha pa, *Sngags rim chen mo*, the edition of New Delhi, 422a4–5.

2978. Abhayākaragupta, *Man ngag snye ma*, *Āmnāyamañjarī*, chap. 12, Tōh 1198, 122a5, immediately following the previous citation. Cited by Tsong kha pa in his *Sngags rim chen mo* as well.

generated through the samādhi of vajra origination from *samaya* as taught in the first chapter of the *Guhyasamāja Tantra*."[2979]

[The Jñānasattva]

About the meditation on the jñānasattva and on the samādhisattva, the *Concise Sādhana* teaches only this: "Meditate on the jñānasattva abiding at the center of [the samayasattva's] heart, and on its heart place the syllable *hūṃ*, which is called samādhisattva."[2980] On which kind of jñānasattva should you meditate? SOME SAY[2981] that it is inappropriate to meditate on a jñānasattva that is red in color, because all the tantras specify that you should meditate on a jñānasattva that is like you. This statement is astonishing. Well, for the time being, let us not argue about other tantras. First, look for a single word in the *Guhyasamāja Tantra* or its explanatory tantras that indicates that the jñānasattva must be exactly like yourself. If by *like yourself* YOU mean similar in color, then say so. But if what YOU require is likeness in every respect, you should place the body maṇḍala of thirty-two deities on the body of the jñānasattvas here.

In the few sources where it is taught that the jñānasattva is the same as you are yourself, [137b] the significance is that when the samayasattva belongs to the tathāgata family of Akṣobhya, the jñānasattva must also belong to it; likewise, when the samayasattva belongs to the tathāgata family of Vairocana, the jñānasattva must also belong to the tathāgata family of Vairocana, and so forth. This is so because as the *Illuminating Lamp* teaches: "The meaning of *by meditating on the lords of mantras* in the *Guhyasamāja Tantra* is: *meditating*

2979. Candrakīrti, *Rdo rje sems dpa'i sgrub thabs*, *Vajrasattva Sādhana*, Tōh 1814, 201b1; Luo and Tomabechi 2009, 22.7–8 and 55.12–14. D and Luo and Tomabechi have *tshul gyis* for *tshul las* and add *las* after *dam tshig* in our text. See the *Guhyasamāja Tantra*, Tōh 442; Zhol 3b2; Stog and Dunh missing; Fremantle 1971, 178; and Matsunaga 1978, 5. See our text [101a] above.

2980. Nāgārjuna, *Mdor byas*, *Piṇḍīkrama Sādhana*, Tōh 1796, 5b1–2; L 92; T 91. D has *snying ga'i dbus su phra mo* for *snying kha'i dbus na gnas pa yi*, that is to say, "meditate on the subtle jñānasattva." The Sanskrit is *saṃsthitaṃ sūkṣmaṃ*. While the Tibetan is *de ru dgod*, place there," the Sanskrit is *taddhṛdi nyaset*, "place on its heart."

2981. See Red mda' ba, *Bla ma bsgrub pa dpal bas zhus pa'i lan*, Kathmandu, 51a2–4; TBRC, 306a–b. Ratnākaraśānti's commentary on Nāgārjuna's *Mdor byas*, *Piṇḍīkrama Sādhana*, entitled *Rin chen phreng ba*, *Ratnāvalī*, Tōh 1826, 46b2–3, says: *de dang 'dra ba'i ye shes sems dpa' bsgoms*. Likewise, Karuṇaśrī, Thugs rje dpal, in his commentary on Candrakīrti's *Sgron gsal*, *Pradīpoddyotanaṭīkā*, entitled *Sgron ma gsal bar byed pa'i gsal byed dka' 'grel*, *Pradīpoddyotanoddyotapañjikā*, Tōh 1790, 124a4, has *rang snang*.

appropriately, according to the division into tathāgata families on the *lords of mantras*; *mantras* here are the samādhisattvas and[2982] the jñānasattvas."[2983]

Furthermore, if every deity belonging to the tathāgata family of Akṣobhya must be blue, then the color of the body of [yellow] Mañjuvajra[2984] must be blue as well.[2985] If YOU say that all the tantras determine that the jñānasattva must be similar to yourself only in the color of its body and emblems, how do YOU explain that the jñānasattva of dark blue Yamāntaka is a yellow Mañjuśrī holding a sword and a book and the jñānasattva of red Raktayamāri is white Daṇḍin marked with a fresh yellow human head; or that in certain meditations on Cakrasaṃvara the samayasattva is blue with four faces and twelve arms, while the jñānasattva at its navel is white with two arms, and so forth? While there is no regularity among these different cases, YOU should be careful in your speech.

Therefore, as Candrakīrti's *Vajrasattva Sādhana* teaches: "At the heart of the samayasattva, visualize a two-armed red jñānasattva absorbed in the yoga of union delighting the entire body."[2986] Thus a jñānasattva red in color is appropriate. Furthermore, the commentaries on the *Concise Sādhana* written by Bhavyakīrti and Abhayākaragupta [138a] teach that you should visualize the jñānasattva as red in color with one face and two arms holding a vajra

2982. Our text omits the phrase *dang bdag po*, which is found in D. This follows Tsong kha pa's *Sgron gsal mchan*, 273b5. Tsong kha pa explains here that during the First Yoga there are six lords of the families. Among them, when the lords are Rdo rje 'chang and Mi bskyod pa the samādhisattva is *hūṃ* and when the other four are the lords the samādhisattvas are *oṃ*, *sva*, *āḥ*, and *hā* respectively.

2983. Candrakīrti, *Sgron gsal*, *Pradīpoddyotanaṭīkā*, chap. 12, Tōh 1785, v. 63, 95a2; Chakravarti 1984, 115. As noted above, D adds *dang bdag po* after *ting nge 'dzin sems dpa'*; has *ci rigs par bsgoms pa* for *ci rigs par bsgom pa*; and *sngags kyi bdag por* for *sngags kyi bdag po*. Furthermore D begins the sentence with: *sngags ni yi ge oṃ la sogs pa ste*. This is a commentary on the line *sngags kyi bdag po bsgoms pa yis* in chap. 12 of the *Guhyasamāja Tantra*, Tōh 442; Zhol 19a6; Stog 32b5; Dunh 35b3; Fremantle 1971, v. 63; Matsunaga 1978, v. 62; Candrakīrti opens the list of mantras here with "the seed syllables *oṃ* and so forth."

2984. Tib. Gsang 'dus 'jam rdor, the principal deity of the Guhyasamāja according to the school of Jñānapāda.

2985. According to the main sādhana by Jñānapāda, the color of Gsang 'dus 'jam rdor is saffron-like. See his *Kun bzang sgrub thabs*, *Samantabhadra Sādhana*, Tōh 1855, 31a5; Kano 2014, 68, v. 52.

2986. Candrakīrti, *Rdo rje sems dpa'i sgrub thabs*, *Vajrasattva Sādhana*, Tōh 1814, 201b1–2; Luo and Tomabechi 2009, 22.9–10 and 55.16–17. D and Luo and Tomabechi have *tshim par* for *tshim par byed par* in our text.

and bell abiding on a lotus and lunar seat, embracing a consort that is similar to itself.[2987]

[Some Additional Debates]

The *Sādhana Incorporating the Scripture* teaches: "Invoke from[2988] the seed syllable of[2989] the jñānasattva upon the heart of the samayasattva."[2990] Having reflected on the meaning of this line, SOME PEOPLE[2991] maintain that after first meditating on yourself as the samayasattva, a light emanates from the *hūṃ* on your heart invoking a jñānasattva similar to yourself and places it on your heart. This is a mistaken interpretation of the *Sādhana Incorporating the Scripture*: first, because this line explains that [a sattva] is invoked from the seed syllable upon the heart of the jñānasattva, while YOU explain that it should be invoked from the seed syllable at the heart of the samayasattva; and second, because this line specifies *invoke from the seed syllable of the jñānasattva*, while YOU explain it as "invoke the jñānasattva from the seed syllable." Thus the meaning of the line from the *Sādhana Incorporating the Scripture* is: light emanating from the samādhisattva, which is the seed syllable at the heart of the jñānasattva, invokes, and so forth.[2992]

Moreover, THOSE who offer this explanation did not consult the tenth chapter of the *Guhyasamāja Tantra*,[2993] which teaches that you should make

2987. Bhavyakīrti, *Rim pa lnga'i dka' 'grel, Pañcakramapañjikā*, Tōh 1838, 2b7. Abhayākaragupta, *Rdzogs pa'i rnal 'byor gyi phreng ba, Niṣpannayogāvalī*, Tōh 3141, 99b5; Sanskrit, Tibetan, and English translation in Lokesh Chandra and Nirmala Sharma 2015, 36–37. This appears in Tsong kha pa, *Gsang mngon*, 49b3–4, as well.

2988. This difference between the Bstan 'gyur text and our text is a key to the discussion here. While D has *sa bon gyis* our text has *sa bon las*.

2989. Again the difference in reading is the key for the discussion here. D has *ye shes sems dpa'* for *ye shes sems dpa'i*.

2990. Nāgārjuna's *Mdo bsre, Sādhanasūtramelāpaka*, Tōh 1797, 13b1. D has *ye shes sems dpa'* for *ye shes sems dpa'i*. The version of D can be translated as: "Invoke the jñānasattva with the seed syllable at the heart of the samayasattva."

2991. See Ngor chen, *Gsang 'dus dkyil 'khor gyi sgrub thabs dngos grub rgya mtsho*, 12a5–b1, and Red mda' ba, *Bsgrub pa dpal bas zhus lan*, Kathmandu, 51a2–4; TBRC, 306a–b.

2992. Note that in fact Nāgārjuna's *Mdo bsre, Sādhanasūtramelāpaka*, Tōh 1797, 13b1–2, explains the meditation on the samādhisattva not in the line cited here, but in the following line.

2993. This refers to the *Guhyasamāja Tantra*, chap. 10, vv. 5–10, Tōh 442, and to the explanation of Candrakīrti in his *Sgron gsal, Pradīpoddyotanaṭīkā*, Tōh 1785, 73a5–74a5; Chakravarti 1984, 91–92.

all the wisdom deities into the triple sattvas and then invite them. Who do you think is invoking and placing the jñānasattva at the heart of *yeshepas* in their natural abode?!

What is the meaning of the name jñānasattva? Jñānasattva is a sattva whose nature is wisdom, [138b] as the *Guhyasamāja Tantra* teaches: "Visualize subtle maṇḍala dwellers at the center of your heart,"[2994] and the *Illuminating Lamp* explains this: "Visualize *subtle jñānasattvas*; they are *subtle* since their nature is wisdom."[2995] The meaning of the word *sattva* has been explained above.

Both the *Vajrasattva Sādhana* and the *Sādhana Incorporating the Scripture* explain the meaning of this by citing the twelfth chapter of the *Guhyasamāja Tantra*: "Visualize the samaya-[sattva] of the vajra body, speech, and mind, endowed with all supreme aspects; at its heart, the jñāna-[sattva], and on its head ornament, the supreme vajra holder. This most excellent samaya pleases all the buddhas."[2996]

[The Samādhisattva]

On what kind of a samādhisattva should you meditate at the heart of the jñānasattva? Meditate according to the *Vajrasattva Sādhana*: "Visualize the syllable *hūṃ* called samādhisattva on a solar disk at the heart of the

2994. *Guhyasamāja Tantra*, chap. 10, Tōh 442; Zhol 14b1; Stog 24a7; Dunh 26b1; Fremantle 1971, v. 10ab; and Matsunaga 1978, v. 10ab.

2995. Candrakīrti, *Sgron gsal, Pradīpoddyotanaṭīkā*, Tōh 1785, 74a2–4; Chakravarti 1984, 92. D has *sems dpa'* for *sems dbar* and *zhes bya ba'i bar du'o* for *zhes bya ba'i tha tshig go* (Skt. *yāvat*) in our text.

2996. Candrakīrti, *Rdo rje sems dpa'i sgrub thabs, Vajrasattva Sādhana*, Tōh 1814, 201b2–3; Luo and Tomabechi 2009, 22.12–23.2 and 56.1–8. D and Luo and Tomabechi have *rdo rje mchog 'dzin cod pan la'o* for *rdo rje 'dzin mchog cod pan la'o* in our text. Nāgārjuna, *Mdo bsre, Sādhanasūtramelāpaka*, Tōh 1797, 13a7–b1. D is quite different: *rnam pa mchog rnams kun ldan pa'i / snying gar ye shes dam tshig dang / dbu rgyan rdo rje 'dzin pa'i mchog / sangs rgyas thams cad mnyes 'gyur ba / 'di ni dam tshig mchog yin te / dngos grub thams cad 'grub pa'i mchog / dam tshig mchog gis rab tu bya /* for *rnam pa kun gyi mchog ldan pa'i / bdag nyid sku gsung thugs rdo rje'i / dam tshig thugs khar ye shes dang / rdo rje 'dzin mchog cod pan la'o / sangs rgyas rnams ni tshim byed pa'i / dam tshig 'di ni dam pa'o /* in our text. *Guhyasamāja Tantra*, Tōh 442; Zhol 18b4–5; Stog 31b5–6; Dunh 34b1–2; Fremantle 1971, vv. 47–48ab; and Matsunaga 1978, vv. 45–46ab. Our text follows the reading of Candrakīrti's *Rdo rje sems dpa'i sgrub thabs, Vajrasattva Sādhana*, Tōh 1814. The Zhol is quite different: *rnam pa'i mchog rnams kun ldan pa / sku gsung thugs ni rdo rje can / snying khar ye shes dam tshig dang / dbu rgyan rdo rje mchog 'dzin pa / sangs rgyas thams cad mnyes gyur pa / dam tshig mchog gis bya ba ni / dngos grub thams cad 'grub pa'i mchog / dam tshig mchog gis rab tu bya*. For an English translation see Wayman 1977, 32.

jñānasattva, an abundance of light, forever radiant as a great lamp, shining to dispel the darkness of ignorance."[2997] Why is it called a samādhisattva? When you meditate on this spot one-pointedly, which is supreme samādhi, innate wisdom is born, and thereby you become engaged in the yoga that leads to the ultimate liberation.

The tenth chapter of the *Guhyasamāja Tantra* explains: "[At the center of that] visualize a syllable made of the paramount letters."[2998] The *Illuminating Lamp* interprets this as follows: "*At the center of that*, that is, of the jñānasattva, on a lunar disk at its heart, [139a] *visualize* individual *akṣaras*[2999] whose nature is unchangeable and paramount in that they arise from the indestructible.[3000] This *syllable* is *hūṃ*."[3001] The *Guhyasamāja Tantra* continues: "Always meditate intently on a great five-pronged vajra."[3002] The *Illuminating Lamp* explains that "*intently* means that the yogi practices the ultimate liberation and this yoga is the meditation on the samādhisattva."[3003]

Both the *Sādhana Incorporating the Scripture* and the *Vajrasattva Sādhana* explain the meditation on the samādhisattva by pointing to the eleventh chapter of the *Guhyasamāja Tantra*: "Meditate on Akṣobhya Vajra abiding at the center of the maṇḍala of buddhas. Visualize the syllable *hūṃ* on the heart of

2997. Candrakīrti, *Rdo rje sems dpa'i sgrub thabs*, *Vajrasattva Sādhana*, Tōh 1814, 201b4; Luo and Tomabechi 2009, 23.3–5 and 56.10-12. D and Luo and Tomabechi omit the *nyi ma la* after *thugs khar* and the *chen po* after *phung po*. See also Tsong kha pa, *Gsang mngon*, 49b4–6.

2998. *Guhyasamāja Tantra*, chap. 10, Tōh 442; Zhol 14b1; Stog 24a7; Dunh 26b2; Fremantle 1971, v. 10cd; and Matsunaga 1978, v. 10cd. The first two lines of this verse are cited above [138b1].

2999. Tib. *yi ge*, Skt. *akṣara*, that is, "letters," but also "imperishable."

3000. Tib. *mi shigs pa*, Skt. *anāhata*, the indestructible drop or the unstruck sound, which refers to the cakra of the heart.

3001. Candrakīrti, *Sgron gsal*, *Pradīpoddyotanaṭīkā*, Tōh 1785, 74a4–5; Chakravarti 1984, 92. This passage immediately follows the previous one cited above. D has (mistakenly) *yi ga* for *yi ge*; *hūṃ ngo* for *hūṃ mo*; and *sbyor bas zhes pa* for *sbyor bas zhes bya ba*.

3002. *Guhyasamāja Tantra*, chap. 10, Tōh 442; Zhol 14b1; Stog 24b1; Dunh 26b2; Fremantle 1971, v. 11ab; and Matsunaga 1978, v. 11ab.

3003. Candrakīrti, *Sgron gsal*, *Pradīpoddyotanaṭīkā*, Tōh 1785, 74a5; Chakravarti 1984, 92.

Akṣobhya Vajra and set [your] mind [there] in the form of a drop."[3004] This chapter of the *Guhyasamāja Tantra* teaches two meditative absorptions[3005]—centripetal dissolution and twin dissolutions,[3006] the methods used by yogis to dissolve their aggregates and so forth into clear light during the completion stage.[3007] Furthermore, there are three types of centripetal dissolution, of the body, speech, and mind. The verse cited above explains the centripetal dissolution of the mind.

Hence, you should meditate in the following manner:[3008] Join indivisibly the minds of all sentient beings in the three realms with your own mind. Next, meditate on that indivisible mind as Akṣobhya, which is the samayasattva, then meditate on *hūṃ* on Akṣobhya's heart, which is the jñānasattva, and then place your mind in the form of a drop at the top of the syllable *hūṃ*, which is the samādhisattva. Although the *Illuminating Lamp* interprets the *Guhyasamāja Tantra* in this way,[3009] any word of the tantra explained at the definitive level of interpretation—which refers to the completion stage—can certainly be explained according to the interpretable level [referring to the creation stage]. [139b] Hence the *Sādhana Incorporating the Scripture* and the *Vajrasattva Sādhana* explain this verse at the interpretable level, and deem the interpretable level appropriate to be applied to the creation stage with reference to the meditation on the samādhisattva at the heart of the jñānasattva.

3004. Nāgārjuna, *Mdo bsre, Sādhanasūtramelāpaka*, Tōh 1797, 13b1–2. The *Mdo bsre* has here only the last two lines of this verse. Candrakīrti, *Rdo rje sems dpa'i sgrub thabs, Vajrasattva Sādhana*, Tōh 1814, 201b4–5; Luo and Tomabechi 2009, 23.6–7 and 56.14–17. D, Luo and Tomabechi have *dbus gnas pa* for *dbus gnas par*; *hūṃ yig snying gar bsgoms nas ni* for *snying khar yi ge hūṃ bsams nas*; and *gnas par bzhag* for *gyur par bzhag* in our text. *Guhyasamāja Tantra*, Tōh 442; Zhol 16b5–6; Stog 28b3–4; Dunh 30b4–5; Fremantle 1971, v. 42; Matsunaga 1978, vv. 41b–42a. The Zhol has Rdo rje mi bskyod, Vajrākṣobhya, for Mi bskyod rdo rje and *bsgoms* for *bsams* in our text. See Candrakīrti, *Sgron gsal, Pradīpoddyotanaṭīkā*, Tōh 1785, 85b6–7; Chakravarti 1984, 105.

3005. Tib. *bsam gtan*, Skt. *dhyāna*.

3006. Tib. *ril 'dzin* and *rjes gzhig*, Skt. *piṇḍagrāha* and *anubheda*. See Nāgārjuna's *Rim lnga, Pañcakrama*, chap. 4, vv. 25–28, Tōh 1802, 55a1–2; Tibetan and Sanskrit in Mimaki and Tomabechi 1994, 45–46; Sanskrit and French translation in Tomabechi 2006, 171.

3007. Mkhas grub rje follows here Tsong kha pa, *Mtha' gcod*, 116b5–117a3.

3008. See Candrakīrti, *Sgron gsal, Pradīpoddyotanaṭīkā*, Tōh 1785, 84b6–7; Chakravarti 1984, 105; and Tsong kha pa, *Sgron gsal mchan*, 252a6–254b1, and his *Mtha' gcod*, 117a2–3.

3009. See the previous note.

[Sealing with the Lord of the Tathāgata Family]

Having blessed the three doors and meditated on the triple sattvas you should visualize the lord of the tathāgata family upon the crown of the head. The *Concise Sādhana* does not explain this, while the *Sādhana Incorporating the Scripture* and *Vajrasattva Sādhana* explain only that you should "Visualize the lord of the tathāgata family on the head ornament."[3010] However, the twelfth chapter of the *Guhyasamāja Tantra* teaches: "On the head ornament, visualize the supreme vajra-holder. [This most excellent *samaya* pleases all the buddhas]."[3011] The *Illuminating Lamp* explains this: "Visualize the *vajra holder*, which is Great Vajradhara, abiding upon the *head ornament*, that is, the crown of the head. The dripping nectar that resembles a stream of lunar rays *pleases*, that is delights, those known as the *samaya*, *jñāna*, and *samādhi sattvas of all buddhas*."[3012] Karuṇaśrī explains that Vajradhara is white and has two arms, hence you should meditate on him holding vajra and bell, and embracing his consort.[3013]

3010. Nāgārjuna, *Mdo bsre*, *Sādhanasūtramelāpaka*, Tōh 1797, 13b1. D has *rang gi bdag po* for *rigs kyi bdag po*, and *bsgom* for *bsam*. Candrakīrti, *Rdo rje sems dpa'i sgrub thabs*, *Vajrasattva Sādhana*, Tōh 1814, 201b2; Luo and Tomabechi 2009, 22.10–11 and 55.17–18.

3011. *Guhyasamāja Tantra*, Tōh 442; Zhol 18b4–5; Stog 31b5; Dunh 34b1; Fremantle 1971, v. 47d; and Matsunaga 1978, v. 45d. See above [138b]. As was noted there, the Zhol has *dbu rgyan rdo rje mchog 'dzin pa* for *rdo rje 'dzin mchog cod pan la*.

3012. Candrakīrti, *Sgron gsal*, *Pradīpoddyotanaṭīkā*, Tōh 1785, 92a6–7; Chakravarti 1984, 112.

3013. Karuṇaśrī, Thugs rje dpal, *Sgron ma gsal bar byed pa'i gsal byed dka' 'grel*, *Pradīpoddyotanoddyotapañjikā*, Tōh 1790, 124a5. See Tsong kha pa, *Sgron gsal mchan*, 267b1, and *Gsang mngon*, 49b6–50a1.

14. The Yoga with the Consort

Seeking and Absorbing in Union with the Consort to Demonstrate that These Three Bodies Are Attained through the Dharma of Passion

There are two parts here: (1) seeking the consort and blessing and (2) the activities of passion and offerings.

Seeking the Consort and Blessing

[Introductory Remarks]

As explained earlier,[3014] the meditation on the specially visualized deities dissolving into clear light corresponds to the dharmakāya; the visualization of the First Lord corresponds to the saṃbhogakāya; and the meditation on the transformation of the First Lord into Akṣobhya[3015] corresponds to the nirmāṇakāya. In this way your meditation corresponds to the attainment of the three bodies for your own enlightenment. [140a] Thereafter, during the time of fruition, the three bodies you have attained for your own enlightenment perform enlightened activities by displaying three types of *caryā* practices:[3016] practices without passion for disciples who adhere to the lower path; practices of the grounds and perfections[3017] for those aspiring to the vast path; and practices with passion for those who are earnestly intent on

3014. Reading *sngar* for *star* in our text.

3015. Note that above the First Lord was transformed into Vajrasattva's nirmāṇakāya.

3016. This follows Tsong kha pa, *Sngags rim chen mo*, chap. 1, 6; English translation in Hopkins 1977, 91. Tsong kha pa refers there to Āryadeva's *Spyod bsdus, Caryāmelāpakapradīpa*, chap. 9, Tōh 1803, 94b4–6; Sanskrit, Tibetan, and English translation in Wedemeyer 2007, B: 54b–55a; Sanskrit and Tibetan in Pandey 2000, 78 and 310–311.

3017. Tib. *sa dang pha rol tu phyin pa*, Skt. *bhūmipāramitā*. These are Mahāyāna practices of the grounds or stages of the bodhisattva and the six perfections.

the profound path. The practices of seeking the consort and so forth are taught in reference to the meditation that accords with the latter.

In the "past event"[3018] the Teacher performed enlightened deeds such as absorbing in union with a consort, emanating hosts of maṇḍala residents, and placing all beings at the stage of the tathāgata. Correspondingly, here you meditate on seeking the consort, absorbing in union with her,[3019] and thereby you emanate the Supreme King of Maṇḍalas[3020] and perform the general and specific deeds.[3021]

Thus the *Sādhana Incorporating the Scripture* teaches: "Just as in the first chapter of the *Guhyasamāja Tantra*, the Blessed One was absorbed in the samādhi called 'the method of great passion' to demonstrate that the stage of enlightenment arises through passion,[3022] so too during the creation stage, yogis should practice the First Yoga, and display liberation by means of passion for the sake of sentient beings engaged in passion. Similarly in the seventeenth chapter of the *Guhyasamāja Tantra*:[3023] 'The Blessed One was absorbed in the samādhi called 'the glory of delight in all desires.' Therefore you should practice [this stage of the *sādhana*] through such steps as these.'"[3024] [140b]

3018. Tib. *sngon byung*, Skt. *bhūtapūrva*. This refers to the "samādhi of great passion" in the *Guhyasamāja Tantra*, chap. 1; see below.

3019. See Tsong kha pa, *Gsang mngon*, 50a2–52a4.

3020. See Tsong kha pa, *Gsang mngon*, 52a4–59b3. See the practice of the Supreme Maṇḍala King below.

3021. See Tsong kha pa, *Gsang mngon*, 59b3–67b1.

3022. *Guhyasamāja Tantra*, Tōh 442; Zhol 2b2; Stog 3b3; Dunh 1b3; Fremantle 1971, 176; Matsunaga 1978, 4. The full name of this samādhi is "the method of great passion of all tathāgatas" or "the vajra-great-passion of all tathāgatas," Tib. *de bzhin gshegs pa thams cad kyi 'dod chag chen po'i tshul zhes bya ba'i ting nge 'dzin*, Skt. *sarvatathāgatamahārāganayaṃ* [*vajraṃ*] *nāmasamādhi*. Nāgārjuna's *Mdo bsre, Sādhanasūtramelāpaka*, Tōh 1797, has *'dod chag chen po'i tshul rdo rje*, "the vajra method of great passion."

3023. *Guhyasamāja Tantra*, Tōh 442; Zhol 47b5; Stog 80b3; Dunh 88b4–5; Fremantle 1971, 404; Matsunaga 1978, 110. D of Nāgārjuna's *Mdo bsre, Sādhanasūtramelāpaka*, Tōh 1797, cited here has *'dod pa thams cad longs spyod pa*, while D of the *Guhyasamāja Tantra* has *de bzhin gshegs pa 'dod pa thams cad nye bar longs spyod pa'i dpal*, and Zhol and Stog of the *Guhyasamāja Tantra* have *'dod chags thams cad nye bar longs spyod pa'i rdo rje'i dpal*, our text has *'dod pa thams cad longs spyod pa'i dpal*. The Sanskrit in Matsunaga is *sarvakāmopabhogavajraśriya*.

3024. Nāgārjuna, *Mdo bsre, Sādhanasūtramelāpaka*, Tōh 1797, 13b2–4. D has *'di ltar* for *ji ltar*; *le'u dang po las* for *le'u dang por*; *tshul rdo rje* for *tshul*; *de bzhin du* for *bzhin du*; *bskyed* for *skye*; *dang po'i sbyor ba* for *dang po sbyor ba*; *rab tu bstan pa'i phyir* for *rab tu bstan par bya ba'i phyir*; repeats *rab tu* twice, and has *spyod pa'i / zhes bya ba'i* for *spyod pa'i dpal zhes bya ba'i* in our text.

The line in the first chapter of the *Guhyasamāja Tantra* just cited, "Just as the Blessed One was absorbed in the samādhi called 'the method of great passion'" and so forth, describes the past event. The Teacher was absorbed in union with the consort, and emanated the maṇḍala; then wishing to teach the *Guhyasamāja Tantra*, he conferred initiation on the tathāgatas of the maṇḍala, Vairocana, and so forth. The yogis who engage in the "practice that follows"[3025] this past event meditate in a corresponding manner. Likewise, the line of the seventeenth chapter of the *Guhyasamāja Tantra* just cited teaches that in the past event the Teacher was absorbed in union, emanated a maṇḍala, and performed the deeds. And here again you should meditate in a corresponding manner.

The *Vajrasattva Sādhana* likewise teaches: "Thus far you have practiced the Supreme King of Samādhis[3026] that consists of excellent qualities for your own enlightenment, thus becoming an embodiment of the triple sattvas by means of the four yogas. Now you should engage in the display of the samādhi called the Supreme King of Maṇḍalas,[3027] for the purpose of enlightening others. The Blessed One Śākyamuni performed the following deeds: Emanating in a body free of passion, he descended from the supreme abode of Tuṣita and so forth, until he reached the level of All Knowing. In this way he placed those who belong to the family of Hearers on the ground of Hearers. Again, for sentient beings on the Great Vehicle he elucidated all modes of the perfection of wisdom. Then to teach awakening born from passion to those who are earnestly intent on the profound,[3028] the Blessed One became absorbed in the samādhi

3025. Tib. *rjes 'jug*, the practice in the sādhana that enacts the past event.

3026. Tib. *ting nge 'dzin rgyal po mchog*, Skt. *samādhirājāgrī*, alias the First Yoga, Tib. *dang po sbyor ba*, Skt. *ādiyoga*[*samādhi*].

3027. Tib. *dkyil 'khor rgyal mchog*, Skt. *maṇḍalarājāgrī*.

3028. Here our text skips the lines of Candrakīrti's *Rdo rje sems dpa'i sgrub thabs*, *Vajrasattva Sādhana*, Tōh 1814, which mention the samādhis in the *Guhyasamāja Tantra* cited above.

called 'delight in all desires.'[3029] The following are the steps of the practice."[3030] Then the *Vajrasattva Sādhana* teaches union with the consort.

[The Consort You Should Seek for This Practice]

[141a] The *Concise Sādhana* teaches this in terms of an actual consort: "Having practiced the 'great yoga'[3031] in this way, the mantrin embodying the triple sattvas should engage in the practice of the consort[3032] through ritual yoga. He should find a girl of low caste[3033] endowed with a noble nature, adorned with beauty and youth, her color that of the blue *utpala* lotus, her eyes wide and perfect; and having been absorbed in samādhi, well-trained, and[3034] highly devoted to the yogi."[3035] The *Sādhana Incorporating the Scripture* teaches: "The fifteenth chapter of the *Guhyasamāja Tantra* has: a well trained daughter of a

3029. This is the samādhi taught in the *Guhyasamāja Tantra*, chap. 17, mentioned above [140a]. In the text of Candrakīrti, as we have it, the name of this samādhi is *'dod pa kun la[s] longs spyod pa* in Tibetan and *sarvakāmopabhoga* in Sanskrit. See his *Rdo rje sems dpa'i sgrub thabs, Vajrasattva Sādhana*, Tōh 1814, 202a2, Luo and Tomabechi 2009, 24.3 and 57.15. For the readings in the *Guhyasamāja Tantra*, see above.

3030. Candrakīrti, *Rdo rje sems dpa'i sgrub thabs, Vajrasattva Sādhana*, Tōh 1814, 201b5–202a3; Luo and Tomabechi 2009, 23.9–24.4 and 57.1–16. D has *thams cad mkhyen pa mdzad nas* while Luo and Tomabechi have *thams cad mkhyen par mdzad nas* for *thams cad mdzad nas*, and both have *mngon par sprul te* for *sprul te* in our text. Our text skips the lines after *bstan pa'i don du*, but returns to them below. D has *'dod pa kun las* for *'dod pa kun la* in our text and in Luo and Tomabechi. Both D and Luo and Tomabechi have *ting nge 'dzin 'di yis* for *ting nge 'dzin 'dis*; *bya* for *bya'o*; and *rim pa 'di* for *rim pa 'di ni* in our text. A similar passage is found in Nāgārjuna's *Mdo bsre, Sādhanasūtramelāpaka*, Tōh 1797, 13b2–4; see above [140a].

3031. Tib. *sbyor ba cher*, Skt. *mahāyoga*.

3032. D has here "should commence the 'great achievement,'" Tib. *sgrub pa chen po*, Skt. *mahāsādhanam*. However, the commentaries of Ratnākaraśānti, in his *Rin chen phreng ba, Ratnāvalī*, Tōh 1826, 47a2, and Bu ston, *Mdor byas 'grel chen*, 52a6, are similar to our text.

3033. I use the term "low-caste person" for *sme sha can* or *rme sha can* found in the Tibetan translations of this and the following passages. The Sanskrit term varies. According to La Vallée Poussin's edition of Nāgārjuna's *Piṇḍīkrama Sādhana*, the Sanskrit term is *rajaka*, while in Matsunaga's edition of the *Guhyasamāja Tantra*, chap. 15—that is cited below—it is *caṇḍāla*.

3034. Note that below [142a6–b1] our text provides a somewhat different interpretation.

3035. Nāgārjuna, *Mdor byas, Piṇḍīkrama Sādhana*, Tōh 1796, 5b2–3; L 93–95ab; T 92–94ab. D has *bdag nyid can* for *bdag nyid cen*; *sgrub pa chen po*, Skt. *mahāsādhanam*, for *phyag rgya bsgrub pa*; *brgyan pa ni* for *brgyan pa yi*; *sme sha can* for *rme sha can*; *bdag nyid che* for *bdag nyid che'i*; and *bslab* for *bslabs* in our text.

low-caste person."[3036] In this regard, the fifteenth chapter of the *Guhyasamāja Tantra* teaches: "In areas of great isolation, the *sādhaka* should always practice with a twelve-year-old girl belonging to a low caste and endowed with a noble nature."[3037] And: "The yogi should meditate by placing on his lap this excellent girl—fair-faced and made perfect with ornaments of all kinds."[3038] The meaning [of the practice] is as taught in these passages.

The *Vajra Garland Explanatory Tantra* teaches that a yogi belonging to the tathāgata family of Akṣobhya should seek as his consort a blue girl of a low-caste family—that is, an outcast or inferior family. A yogi belonging to the tathāgata family of Vairocana should have a white-colored daughter of a washer-man; a yogi belonging to the tathāgata family of Ratnasaṃbhava, the daughter of a garland maker; a yogi belonging to the tathāgata family of Amitābha, a daughter of a dancer; while a yogi belonging to the tathāgata family of karma,[3039] a daughter of a craftsman.[3040] The *Guhyasamāja Tantra* likewise explains the different kinds of consorts. [141b] In the present context the sādhana[3041] teaches that the consort should be a low-caste girl as the practice here relates to the tathāgata family of Akṣobhya.

What characteristics should this girl possess? The *Guhyasamāja Tantra* teaches: *endowed with a noble nature* and so forth.[3042] The *Illuminating Lamp* explains this: "*Endowed with a noble nature* means endowed with good qualities of faith and so forth."[3043] The meaning of *and so forth* should be understood as "endowed with the qualities of diligence, mindfulness, samādhi, and wisdom."[3044] The consort need not be *twelve years old*, because in

3036. Nāgārjuna, *Mdo bsre, Sādhanasūtramelāpaka*, Tōh 1797, 13b4. D adds after *gsungs pa'i*: *mtshan dang ldan pa'i*; meaning "endowed with the qualifications." But our text here ends with the word "or."

3037. *Guhyasamāja Tantra*, Tōh 442; Zhol 30b3; Stog 51a2–3; Dunh 55a3; Fremantle 1971, v. 2; and Matsunaga 1978, v. 2. Zhol has *sme sha can* for *rme sha can* in our text.

3038. *Guhyasamāja Tantra*, chap. 15, Tōh 442; Zhol 30b4; Stog 51a4; Dunh 55a4–5; Fremantle 1971, v. 4bcd; and Matsunaga 1978, v. 4bcd.

3039. Tib. Don grub, Skt. Amoghasiddhi.

3040. *Rgyud rdo rje phreng ba, Vajramālā Tantra*, chap. 44, Tōh 445, 249b3. This scripture has a somewhat different correlation between the five types of daughters and the five tathāgata families.

3041. This refers to Nāgārjuna's *Mdor byas, Piṇḍīkrama Sādhana*, Tōh 1796, cited above.

3042. See the *Guhyasamāja Tantra*, chap. 15, Tōh 442; Zhol 30b3; Stog 51a2–3; Dunh 55a3; Fremantle 1971, v. 2; and Matsunaga 1978, v. 2; cited above.

3043. Candrakīrti, *Sgron gsal, Pradīpoddyotanaṭikā*, Tōh 1785, 136a5; Chakravarti 1984, 162.

3044. This follows Tsong kha pa's *Sgron gsal mchan*, 376a4–5.

other contexts it is taught that she is sixteen or older; hence, the purpose here is to explain or specify what is generally indicated. Regarding the meaning of the two lines in the *Guhyasamāja Tantra* "In areas of great isolation, the *sādhaka* should always practice,"[3045] the *Illuminating Lamp* explains: "The *sādhaka* should train in *areas of* very *great isolation* where no one congregates; *sādhaka* here means an aspirant well-trained in tantra and mantra."[3046]

With regard to the term "tantra" mentioned here, the seventeenth chapter of the *Illuminating Lamp* teaches: "In order to explain the passionate practice, the glorious Lord of Great Bliss taught that one should embrace,[3047] kiss, suck,[3048] clap,[3049] bite, pinch, massage,[3050] swing, stretch, and elbow while ringing the consort's strings of pearls, bracelets, armlets, and anklets; throughout one should remain absorbed in union of the senses with their objects, the vajra with the lotus, and wisdom with method."[3051] The commentary on the *Vajraḍāka Tantra* teaches: "Embracing, kissing, clawing, [142a] biting, moving to and fro, making hissing sounds, the woman playing the role of the man, and the woman on top. Altogether there are eight actions, and these, when

3045. *Guhyasamāja Tantra*, chap. 15, Tōh 442; Zhol 30b3; Stog 51a2–3; Dunh 55a3; Fremantle 1971, v. 2; and Matsunaga 1978, v. 2.

3046. Candrakīrti, *Sgron gsal, Pradīpoddyotanaṭīkā*, Tōh 1785, 136a5–6; Chakravarti 1984, 162. D has *bral bas* for *bral ba'i* in our text. See above [141a3]. In his *Sgron gsal mchan*, 336a6, Tsong kha pa explains that "tantra" refer to tantras that teach the sixty-four arts of love, and "mantra" refers to meditations on the deity, recitations, and so forth.

3047. The list here is very similar to that of the *Kāmasūtra*; see Doniger and Kakar 2003, 28–74 and Hopkins 1992, 65–66.

3048. Tsong kha pa, *Sgron gsal mchan*, 508a6, explains that this refers to the lips and the tip of the lotus.

3049. This is missing from Bhavabhadra's *Rdo rje mkha' 'gro'i rnam par bshad pa, Vajraḍāka Vivṛti*, Tōh 1415, his commentary on the *Rdo rje mkha' 'gro rgyud, Vajraḍāka Tantra*, Tōh 370, cited below. The parallel passage in Āryadeva's *Spyod bsdus, Caryāmelāpakapradīpa*, Tōh 1803, has *kucagrahaṇa*, which is translated by Wedemeyer as "fondling the breast"; see Wedemeyer 2007, B: 67a–b.

3050. In his *Sgron gsal mchan*, 508a6, Tsong kha pa specifies that this refers to the breasts and the lower part.

3051. Candrakīrti, *Sgron gsal, Pradīpoddyotanaṭīkā*, Tōh 1785, 196b5–7; Chakravarti 1984, 225. D has *bstan par bya ba'i phyir* for *bstan pa'i phyir*; *sen mos* for *sen mo*; *thabs kyi* for *thabs kyis*; and *gdub kyi* for *gdub gyi* in our text. This passage appears as well in Āryadeva's *Spyod bsdus, Caryāmelāpakapradīpa*, chap. 10, Tōh 1803, 102a5–7; Sanskrit, Tibetan, and English translation in Wedemeyer 2007, B: 67a–b; Sanskrit and Tibetan in Pandey 2000, 93–94 and 341–342. See also Wayman 1977, 350–353.

multiplied by eight through a particular type of conceptualization, become sixty-four."[3052]

Accordingly, the *Illuminating Lamp* teaches that the *sādhaka* [*trained in tantra*][3053] should practice and habituate often as taught in the Śāstra of Love,[3054] the tantra that teaches the sixty-four arts of love at length. *Trained in mantra*[3055] are those *sādhaka*s who have been empowered, who have mastered all the common and uncommon pledges and vows, who have perfectly maintained them and made them the foundation[3056] of their practice—and who now habituate the yoga of meditation on deities, recitation of mantras, and so forth.

The *Guhyasamāja Tantra* teaches: "The yogi should meditate by placing on his lap this excellent girl—fair-faced and perfected with every ornament."[3057] The *Illuminating Lamp* explains: "*Excellent* means not attracted to other men,"[3058] which has the same meaning as the line of the *Concise Sādhana*: "highly devoted to the yogi."[3059] *Fair-faced* means according to the *Illuminating Lamp*: "she looks at the yogi,"[3060] and *vice versa*. With respect to *perfected with every ornament*, the *Illuminating Lamp* explains: "*Every ornament* means

3052. *Rdo rje mkha' 'gro rgyud*, *Vajraḍāka Tantra*, chap. 49, Tōh 370, 109a4–6, and Bhavabhadra's commentary on it, *Rdo rje mkha' 'gro'i rnam par bshad pa*, *Vajraḍāka Vivṛti*, chap. 49, Tōh 1415, 195a4–5 and 197b4–5, which has *srid* for *sred* and *brgyad po* for *brgyud* in our text. This passage appears also in Tsong kha pa, *Sgron gsal mchan*, 508b2–3, which has *srid kyi* for *sred kyi*, *rnam par rtog pa* for *rnam par mi rtog pa* and *brgyad* for *brgyud* in our text. The list here is very similar to that of the *Kāmasūtra*; see Doniger and Kakar 2003, 28–74 and Hopkins 1992, 65–66. Doniger and Kakar, 2003, 40, also discusses how the list of eight erotic techniques is multiplied to the sixty-four arts of love.

3053. See the explanation of Candrakīrti, *Sgron gsal*, *Pradīpoddyotanaṭīkā*, Tōh 1785, above [141b4].

3054. Tib. *Dga' ba'i bstan bcos*, Skt. *Kāmaśāstra*. Note that Gedün Chöpel (in Hopkins 1992, 38) mentions a work by Nāgārjuna called *Ratiśāstra*.

3055. See above [141b4].

3056. Reading *gzhi* for *bzhi* in our text.

3057. *Guhyasamāja Tantra*, chap. 15, v. 4, cited above [141a].

3058. Candrakīrti, *Sgron gsal*, *Pradīpoddyotanaṭīkā*, Tōh 1785, 136b4; Chakravarti 1984, 162. D has *gzhan rnams la ma chags pa* for *skyes pa gzhan la ma chags pa* in our text. The *Sgron gsal* has "not attracted to another," while Tsong kha pa's *Sgron gsal mchan*, 377a4, adds *skyes pa*, man. As usual, Mkhas grub rje follows Tsong kha pa.

3059. Nāgārjuna, *Mdor byas*, *Piṇḍīkrama Sādhana*, Tōh 1796, 5b3; L 95b; T 94b. Cited above [141a].

3060. Candrakīrti, *Sgron gsal*, *Pradīpoddyotanaṭīkā*, Tōh 1785, 136b4; Chakravarti 1984, 162.

skilled in the art of love, and *perfected* means that she is not deficient in any way."[3061] That is, she knows the sixty-four erotic techniques in the art of love, and is not deficient in any way.[3062]

Furthermore, the line *trained in tantra* above[3063] explains how to engage in the practice and this indicates a skillful knowledge of everything. Saying both "trained in tantra" and "trained in mantra" is not redundant since their causes and results are different. In the line from the *Concise Sādhana* "Having been absorbed in samādhi, she is well-trained,"[3064] *absorbed in samādhi* means trained in the mantra, and *well-trained* means trained in the tantra.[3065] [142b]

[The Yogi and the Exceptional Fulfillment of Essentials for This Practice]

Thus far the required qualifications of the consort have been explained. Yet, as is taught, not every yogi qualifies to practice with a consort. For practicing with an actual consort, the yogi must be perfected with manifold essential characteristics,[3066] such as having mastered deity yoga. Even during the creation stage when a yogi unites with an actual consort, the melting constituent descends to the tip of his vajra jewel. If this yogi is able to block the melting constituent by meditating only on the syllable *phaṭ*, without recourse to other yogic methods including wind yoga and so forth, he will certainly be able to block the melting constituent by visualizing the syllable *phaṭ* when he meditates on union with a wisdom consort. Therefore yogis should practice by focusing intensely on the syllable *phaṭ* right from the beginning of their meditation on the creation stage, as they fix their minds on the deity and cultivate clear appearance.[3067]

For a yogi who practices in this way with either one of these two consorts—an actual consort or a wisdom consort—when the melting constituent descends by means of the yoga of absorption in union, it will be blocked from being emitted outside the jewel through the meditation on the syllable *phaṭ*. The yogi will then be able to experience fully the four joys of the

3061. Candrakīrti, *Sgron gsal, Pradīpoddyotanaṭīkā*, Tōh 1785, 136b4–5; Chakravarti 1984, 162.

3062. This is based on Tsong kha pa's *Sgron gsal mchan*, 377a6.

3063. In the explanation of the *Sgron gsal*, Tōh 1785, above [141b3].

3064. Nāgārjuna, *Mdor byas, Piṇḍīkrama Sādhana*, Tōh 1796, 5b2–3; L 95a; T 94a. Cited above [141a].

3065. Reading *rgyud* for *brgyud*.

3066. Reading *zhig* for *zhag* in our text.

3067. Tib. *gsal snang*.

creation stage, and to join bliss with emptiness. The more the yogi habituates, the more the power of his practice will intensify, and the visualization of the maṇḍala wheel, recitations, and so forth will become enhanced. Additionally, all objects that appear will increasingly be enhanced into a display of bliss and emptiness. This is the sublime essence of the path of the creation stage, and hence the yogi must endeavor to habituate this fully. But so long as even the slightest indication of such an essence has not penetrated your ears, you should not suppose that the main thing is to practice the mere recitation of the words of the sādhana stages, [143a] and to count the number of recitations while letting your mind wander freely.

When your habituation becomes powerful enough, it will happen again and again that through the four joys of the creation stage, the four joys of the completion stage will be induced effortlessly while you meditate on the creation stage itself. This is also the main factor that makes the creation stage a ripener for the completion stage. Thus it is frequently recommended that the consort, among her other essential characteristics, must be skilled in the sixty-four arts of love, for each and every art of love has its own distinct way of inducing bliss. The more that bliss is enhanced, the more the mind will be enhanced in its realization of emptiness.

As for the meaning of joining bliss with emptiness: when bliss arises and you become concerned that the desire for bliss may happen, examine the nature of bliss with great care. Thus, while not allowing bliss to vanish entirely, let bliss be endowed with a mode of apprehending emptiness. The more realization of emptiness grows, the more fully you will be able to overcome your grasping at the self and thereby you will be endowed with the power to cut off the root of saṃsāra. Thus the main point at which the creation stage annihilates the root of saṃsāra begins here.

Hence, even without resorting to an actual consort, by relying on a wisdom consort you should be able to induce bliss that is similar to that of union with an actual consort. For this purpose, the consort you visualize must arise in your mind in the clear appearance of an actual consort.[3068] [143b] Therefore you must practice deity yoga assiduously until you attain a stable clear appearance of this kind. For indeed this is the only way those who meditate on the creation stage can take objects of desire and afflictive emotions in the path. Hence, if you did not attain a good understanding of this, it would be as though you had lost the foundation of the path of the creation stage.

This being so, it goes without saying that nowadays it would be rare indeed

3068. Reading *dngos kyi rig ma* for *dngos kya rig ma.*

to encounter both such a yogi and an actual consort[3069] endowed with all the required characteristics. So difficult it is to fathom a yogi of the creation stage who is able to block the bodhicitta by meditating on the syllable *phaṭ*. And if it is rare to find a yogi meditating on the creation stage who is able to block the constituents merely by meditating on the syllable *phaṭ*, how much rarer to find one meditating on the completion stage who must resort to many vigorous efforts like yogic exercises and wind yoga in order to block the constituents from emanating outside, disseminate them within, and so forth. Needless to say, this[3070] is as far from the meaning of the tantra as one shore of the ocean is from the other.

Therefore, when the yogi and his consort are endowed with the essential characteristics explained above, their acute faculties enable them to apprehend the view of emptiness through their critical reasoning. Both are skilled in the stages of the four joys, particularly in recognizing the exact moment innate wisdom arises. Furthermore, if the yogi is a meditator on the creation stage, he is able to hold the bodhicitta without emitting it through the power of the meditation on the syllable *phaṭ*. Or if the yogi is a meditator on the completion stage, he is able to hold the bodhicitta through the power of the winds, using his skill at the crucial point of taking the consort into the practice of wind yoga and so forth. When all the essential characteristics explained in the tantras and reliable works of the mahāsiddhas are fulfilled, the yogi may then rely on an actual consort.[3071] But how are we to find a yogi and consort endowed with such perfect characteristics? [144a]

If without so much as a rough understanding of the relevant terminology you put your faith in transmitted instructions that are false yet claim to be profound, and then put them unhesitatingly into practice, you will surely achieve an unendurable and exceedingly low rebirth, as explained in the *Rising of Heruka*: "Those who lack yoga but engage in yogic practice and unite with a consort, and those who lack wisdom but pretend to possess it will surely go to hell."[3072] Therefore those who are not endowed with such essential characteristics should rely on a wisdom mudrā—a visualized consort—in their practice of generating the joys and the wisdom of bliss and emptiness.

Therefore, the *Vajrasattva Sādhana* teaches: "Or emanate a wisdom consort

3069. Reading *bsten pa* for *bstan pa*.

3070. That is, finding a yogi practicing with an actual consort, both of whom are endowed with all the required characteristics.

3071. Reading *rig ma* for *rigs ma*.

3072. *Heruka mngon 'byung, Herukābhyudaya*, chap. 7, Tōh 374, 6b2–3; Stog 232b1–2. D and Stog have *'chos* for *chos* in our text.

from your heart[3073] and absorb in union with her. By emanating her through the mantra you act for the sake of sentient beings."[3074] To demonstrate this, the *Vajrasattva Sādhana* cites the *Entirely Secret Tantra*: "The great goddess, mother of the buddhas, dwelling in the heart, who engenders the yoga of the yogis [*yoginām̩ yoga*], is known as Vajradhātvīśvarī."[3075]

[The Practice]

First you must emanate a consort from your heart with the appearance of the daughter of a low-caste person. Do not emanate her with the appearance of Sparśavajrā,[3076] for the *Sādhana Incorporating the Scripture* is clear about how to emanate the daughter: "Emanate from your own heart a well-trained low-caste daughter endowed with the essential characteristics and place her before you."[3077] Likewise, *Formulating the Sādhana* teaches: "Mentally emanate a

3073. Reading *snying ga nas* for *snying gnas*. The Sanskrit here is *hṛdayāt*.

3074. Candrakīrti, *Rdo rje sems dpa'i sgrub thabs*, *Vajrasattva Sādhana*, Tōh 1814, 202a4–5; Luo and Tomabechi 2009, 24.9–10 and 58.4–5. D and Luo and Tomabechi have *snying gar* for *snying gnas*, and *sngags cig* for *sngags kyis*. Whereas until this point in the sādhana the practice has been for the sake of the yogis themselves, the following practice is intended to bring all sentient beings to their awakening.

3075. Tib. Rdo rje dbyings kyi dbang phyug ma, Eng. She Who Rules the Vajra Realm. *Thams cad gsang ba'i rgyud*, *Sarvarahasya Tantra*, Tōh 481, 3b3–4; Tibetan and English translation in Wayman 1984, v. 45. Wayman has *rnal 'byor pa yi rnal 'byor bskyed* for *rnal 'byor rnal 'byor 'bebs byed ma*; *sangs rgyas thams cad skyed mdzad yum* for *sangs rgyas rnams kyi sbyor bskyed ma*; and *bshad for grags* in our text that follows the citation of these lines in Candrakīrti's *Rdo rje sems dpa'i sgrub thabs*, *Vajrasattva Sādhana*, Tōh 1814, 202a6; Luo and Tomabechi 2009, 24.11–25.1 and 58.7–10. The Sanskrit is cited also in Candrakīrti's *Sgron gsal*, *Pradīpoddyotana*, in its commentary on chap. 5 of the *Guhyasamāja Tantra*; Fremantle 1971, vv. 7–8; Matsunaga 1978, vv. 6–7. See the *Sgron gsal*, Tōh 1785, 36a5–6; Chakravarti 1984, 48. D has *sangs rgyas kun gyi yum gyu'r ba* for *sangs rgyas thams cad skyed mdzad yum*. In the Sanskrit of Chakravarti here, Vajradhātreśvarī should be read Vajradhātvīśvarī; see Wayman 1977, 305–306, and Wayman 1984, 521. In his *Sgron gsal mchan*, 128b5, Tsong kha pa remarks that although this is not clear in the *Thams cad gsang ba'i rgyud*, the *Rdo rje sems dpa'i sgrub thabs* explains this. While the *Sgron gsal*, Tōh 1785, does not mention the source of its citation, Tsong kha pa identifies it. He also adds that Rdo rje dbyings kyi dbang mo is the consort of Rdo rje 'chang.

3076. Tib. Reg bya Rdo rje ma, Eng. Vajra Lady of Tangibles.

3077. Nāgārjuna, *Mdo bsre*, *Sādhanasūtramelāpaka*, Tōh 1797, 13b4–5. D has *lang* for *yang* in our text. Part of the first line here already appeared above [141a]. As previously noted, the *Mdo bsre* adds that this is taught in the *Guhyasamāja Tantra*, chap. 15.

daughter of your own tathāgata family, or take an actual daughter."[3078] Therefore first you should emanate a consort appearing like a daughter of your own tathāgata family, [144b] and then visualize her as Sparśavajrā, for the *Illuminating Lamp*, commenting on the seventh chapter of the *Guhyasamāja Tantra*, teaches: "Visualize her as a goddess in accordance with your own tathāgata family, such as Sparśavajrā or Locanā."[3079]

Having visualized the consort in this way, place the deities on her body in accordance with the *Concise Sādhana*:

> Visualize *oṃ* on the crown of her head, and place *āḥ* on her speech organs, *hūṃ* on her heart, *svā* on her navel, and *hā* on her feet.
>
> Place Locanā, Māmakī, Pāṇḍaravāsinī, and Tārā on the elements of earth and so forth.
>
> Visualize the five vajra ladies, Rūpavajrā[3080] and so forth, in union with the bodhisattvas Kṣitigarbha and so forth[3081] [on her sense organs].
>
> Place Vajravetālī on her right arm and Aparājitā on her left, Bhṛkuṭi on her mouth, Ekajaṭā[3082] on her secret place.[3083]
>
> Then place the [fierce] female deities [on her limbs], the Tathāgatī Viśvavajrī on her right shoulder, Viśvaratnā on her left shoulder, the Tathāgatī Viśvapadmā on her right knee, Viśvakarmā

3078. Nāgabuddhi, *Rnam gzhag rim pa*, *Vyavastholi*, chap. 3, Tōh 1809, 126a6; Tanaka 2016, 105. See also Tsong kha pa's *Rnam gzhag rim pa'i rnam bshad*, 60b6–61a1.

3079. See Candrakīrti, *Sgron gsal*, *Pradīpoddyotanaṭīkā*, Tōh 1785, 51b6–52a1; Chakravarti 1984, 67, but in fact, Mkhas grub rje refers to Tsong kha pa's commentary on this in his *Sgron gsal mchan*, 172b3–173a1.

3080. Tib. Rdo rje gzugs ma or Gzungs rdo rje ma, Eng. Vajra Lady of Forms. The remaining four vajra ladies are Sgra rdo rje ma, Dre rdo rje ma, Ro rdo rje ma, Reg bya rdo rje ma; Skt. Śabdhavajrā, Gandhavajrā, Rasavajrā, and Sparśavajrā.

3081. The remaining four bodhisattvas are Phyag rdor, Nam snying, 'Jig rten dbang phyug, and Sgrib sel; Skt. Vajrapāṇi, Khagarbha, Lokeśvara, and Sarvanīvaraṇaviṣkambhin.

3082. Some of the Sanskrit mss. have Ekajaṭī.

3083. These are Rdo rje ro langs ma, Gzhan gyis mi thub ma, Khro gnyer ma, and Ral pa gcig ma respectively. Reading Gzhan gyis mi thub ma for Gzhan gyi mi thub ma.

on her left knee,[3084] Gaganavajriṇī[3085] on the crown of her head, and Dharaṇīṃdharadevatī[3086] on her soles.[3087]

Meditate on all the [parts of her body] in the appearance of deities as [during the meditation on the body maṇḍala] earlier. As before, too, you should generate the fierce female deities from long *hūṃ*s;[3088] their colors, emblems, and so forth are the same as those of the ten fierce male deities. The imperative to place the five bodhisattvas beginning with Kṣitigarbha on her body is clearly taught in the line [just cited]: "Visualize the five vajra ladies, Rūpavajrā and so forth, in union with the bodhisattvas Kṣitigarbha and so forth."

According to Ratnākaraśānti's commentary, the *Jewel Rosary*, you should generate the Goddess of Compassion[3089] from *raṃ* and place her on the consort's heart; generate the Goddess of Loving Kindness[3090] from *maiṃ* and place her on the channels and sinews; generate the Vajra Lady of Dharma[3091] from *gaṃ* and place her on the joints. Then visualize these goddesses in union with the bodhisattvas, Mañjuśrī and so forth.[3092] [145a] These instructions are nonsensical[3093] and correspond with none of the authoritative books of the Ārya Cycle.[3094]

3084. These are Rdo rje ma, Sna tshogs rin chen, Sna tshogs Padma, and Sna tshogs las respectively.

3085. Tib. Rnam mkha'i rdo rje ma, Eng. Vajra Lady of Space.

3086. Tib. Sa yi sa 'dzin lha mo, Eng. the Earth Holding Goddess.

3087. Nāgārjuna, *Mdor byas, Piṇḍīkrama Sādhana*, Tōh 1796, 5b3–6; L 95cd–101; T 94b–100. D has *snyoms par 'jug pa* for *snyoms par 'jug par*; *gzhan gyis mi thub ma* for *gzhan gyi mi thub ma*; and *gnas par yang* for *gnas par ni*. T has *vinyastāṃ* for *vinyastā* and *devatīm* for *devatī* in L 100.

3088. As during the meditation on the body maṇḍala.

3089. Tib. Snying rje'i lha mo.

3090. Tib. Byams pa'i lha mo.

3091. Tib. Chos rdo rje ma. Ratnākaraśānti, *Rin chen phreng ba, Ratnāvalī*, Tōh 1826, 48a7, has Chos kyi dbyings kyi rdo rje ma.

3092. Ratnākaraśānti, *Rin chen phreng ba, Ratnāvalī*, Tōh 1826, 48a6–7. Ratnākaraśānti has here Mañjuśrī, Samantabhadra, and Maitreya.

3093. Here Mkhas grub rje follows Bu ston, *Mdor byas 'grel chen*, 53a5.

3094. In Tsong kha pa, *Gsang mngon*, 50b1–51b5, the three bodhisattvas Mañjuśrī, Samantabhadra, and Maitreya are not placed on the body of the consort. Only five and not eight bodhisattvas are placed on the consort, and therefore in total only twenty-nine deities and not thirty-two are placed on the body of the consort.

The Activities of Passion and Offerings

[Uniting the Vajra and Lotus]

First, the union of the vajra and lotus is taught in the following scriptures. The *Concise Sādhana* teaches: "After consecrating her in this way, the yogi should engage in the practice of the vajra and lotus. He should visualize [his vajra as] a five-pronged vajra born from the mantra *hūṃ*, and on its central prong meditate on *oṃ*. Likewise, he should visualize [her lotus as] an eight-petaled lotus arising from *āḥ*. [Both vajra and lotus are][3095] pervaded by five light-rays."[3096] The seventh chapter of the *Guhyasamāja Tantra* teaches: "By joining the two organs, he will attain the siddhi of buddhahood. He should visualize the seed syllables *hūṃ*, *oṃ*, *āḥ*, and *phaṭ*."[3097] Likewise, the *Vajrasattva Sādhana* teaches: "You should consecrate your vajra by visualizing your male organ with the syllable *hūṃ* as a five-pronged vajra, and place the syllable *oṃ* on its central prong. Then consecrate the lotus by placing *āḥ* at the 'source of phenomena' of your consort, and from it visualize a red eight-petaled lotus arising."[3098] This is how you should meditate.[3099]

Some Tibetans maintain that the lotus is white,[3100] and *Kṛṣṇasamayavajra[3101] maintains that the lotus is generated from the syllable *hrī* with anthers that are marked with *āḥ*s. These instructions contradict the *Vajrasattva*

3095. See below.

3096. Nāgārjuna, *Mdor byas*, *Piṇḍīkrama Sādhana*, Tōh 1796, 5b5–7; L 102–104a; T 101–102e. D has *de ltar 'dus byas* for *de ltar sbyar byas*; *dbus su* for *dbus la*; *a* for *āḥ*; *'od zer lnga yis* for *'od zer lnga yi*; and *rtse mo mnga' pa* for *rtse mo lnga pa*. T has *padyam* for *padmam* in L. A variant reading supplied in T for *athārabhet* in L is *samārabhet*, which better corresponds to *yang dag brtsam* in the Tibetan. The Sanskrit is somewhat different here.

3097. *Guhyasamāja Tantra*, Tōh 442; Zhol 10b5; Stog 17b6–7; Dunh 18a3–4; Fremantle 1971, vv. 18cd–19ab; and Matsunaga 1978, vv. 18cd–19ab. Matsunaga omits the syllable *āḥ*. See also Fremantle 1990, 108.

3098. Candrakīrti, *Rdo rje sems dpa'i sgrub thabs*, *Vajrasattva Sādhana*, Tōh 1814, 202b5–6; Luo and Tomabechi 2009, 26.10–12 and 60.4–7. D and Luo and Tomabechi have *rdo rje 'dus bya ba'o* for *rdo rje 'du bya ba'o*, skip the *la* after *chos 'byung*, and have *'dus byas pa'o* for *'du bya ba'o*.

3099. See Tsong kha pa, *Gsang mngon*, 51b5–52a2.

3100. Neither Bu ston, *Mdor byas 'grel chen*, 53b4, nor Ngor chen, *Gsang 'dus dkyil 'khor gyi sgrub thabs dngos grub rgya mtsho*, 13a2, mentions a white lotus.

3101. *Kṛṣṇasamayavajra, Nag po dam tshig rdo rje, *Rim pa lnga'i dka' 'grel*, *Pañcakramapañjikā*, Tōh 1841, 162a4.

Sādhana of glorious Candrakīrti [cited above].[3102] These are fabrications that obviously contradict the following scriptures as well. The *Illuminating Lamp* explains that you should generate the lotus from *āḥ*: "Consecrate the lotus of the consort from *āḥ*";[3103] the *Concise Sādhana* itself teaches: "Likewise [visualize an eight-petaled lotus] arising from *āḥ*,"[3104] and so forth. Regarding the line "He should visualize the syllable *phaṭ*,"[3105] the *Illuminating Lamp* explains: "He should make the bodhicitta descend with the syllable *phaṭ*."[3106] [145b] Both methods of absorption in union are explained by citing this line. The first is the meditation on a yellow syllable *phaṭ* at the opening of the secret place, head pointing inward [in order to block the drop from being emitted]. The second method is the uttering of the syllable *phaṭ* out loud when the drop is emitted.[3107]

The line of the *Concise Sādhana* "pervaded by five light rays"[3108] means that you should visualize your vajra and the lotus of your consort pervaded within by five light rays. The seventh chapter of the *Guhyasamāja Tantra* likewise teaches: "Meditate on the vajra and lotus pervaded by five light rays,"[3109] and the *Illuminating Lamp* explains this: "While absorbed in union, you should *meditate* on the *vajra and lotus* [*pervaded*, that is,] thoroughly suffused with *the five light rays*, white and so forth."[3110]

3102. Bu ston, *Mdor byas 'grel chen*, 53b4, also maintains that the opinion of *Kṛṣṇasamayavajra contradicts both Nāgārjuna's *Mdor byas* and the work of Candrakīrti.

3103. Candrakīrti, *Sgron gsal, Pradīpoddyotanaṭīkā*, Tōh 1785, 52a5; Chakravarti 1984, 67. D has *a* for *āḥ*. Tsong kha pa's *Sgron gsal mchan*, 173a5, has *a* as well. The *Sgron gsal* comments here on the *Guhyasamāja Tantra*, chap. 7, v. 19.

3104. Nāgārjuna, *Mdor byas, Piṇḍīkrama Sādhana*, Tōh 1796, 5b7; L 103cd; T 102cd.

3105. The line from the *Guhyasamāja Tantra*, chap. 7, v. 19ab, Tōh 442; Zhol 10b5, cited just above [145a3].

3106. Candrakīrti, *Sgron gsal, Pradīpoddyotanaṭīkā*, Tōh 1785, 52a6; Chakravarti 1984, 67.

3107. See Tsong kha pa, *Sgron gsal mchan*, 173b1–3.

3108. Nāgārjuna, *Mdor byas, Piṇḍīkrama Sādhana*, Tōh 1796, 5b7; L 104a; T 102e, cited above [145a].

3109. *Guhyasamāja Tantra*, Tōh 442; Zhol 10b5–6; Stog 17b7; Dunh 18a4; Fremantle 1971, v. 19cd; and Matsunaga 1978, v. 19cd. The Zhol has *'od zer rnam lngas* for *'od zer sna lngas* in our text. These lines of the tantra immediately follow the lines cited above.

3110. Candrakīrti, *Sgron gsal, Pradīpoddyotanaṭīkā*, Tōh 1785, 52a7; Chakravarti 1984, 67. In his *Sgron gsal mchan*, 173b6, Tsong kha pa adds that both the father and the mother visualize this.

[The Divine Identity of Passion]

After consecrating the vajra and lotus in this way, the *Concise Sādhana* teaches the practice of passion: "Following that, the yogi should engage in the practice. *Oṃ sarva tathāgata anurāgaṇa vajra svabhāva ātmako 'haṃ*. While maintaining the divine identity of Vajradhara, he should move with the song of *hūṃ*. When the bodhicitta is drawn forth, he should recite the mantra *phaṭ*."[3111] This shows that, while moving the vajra in the lotus, you should maintain the divine identity of Vajradhara and sing *hūṃ*, but it does not explicitly mention the deity whose divine identity the yogi should maintain while reciting the mantra *anurāgaṇa*. But the *Vajrasattva Sādhana* teaches: "Then, the yogi maintaining the divine identity of Ratnasaṃbhava, and having already aroused passion, engages in embracing, kissing, and so forth. With the mantra taught in the sixth chapter of the *Guhyasamāja Tantra*,[3112] he should maintain the divine identity of nonduality. This mantra is *oṃ sarva tathāgatānurāgaṇa vajra svabhāva ātmako 'haṃ*. Thus he engages in the divine identity of Ratnasaṃbhava."[3113] [146a]

Consequently, you should maintain the divine identity of passion by visualizing yourself as Ratnasaṃbhava, and immediately after that, change to the divine identity of Vajradhara and abide in union while singing *hūṃ*. Immediately after that, when the drop reaches inside your vajra jewel, change to the divine identity of Amoghasiddhi. While you visualize this and utter the syllable *phaṭ* aloud, the drop is drawn forth to the lotus of the mother.

3111. Nāgārjuna, *Mdor byas, Piṇḍīkrama Sādhana*, Tōh 1796, 5b7–6a1; L 104bcd–105; T 102def–103. D has *bskyod bya zhing* for *bskyod par bya* in our text.

3112. *Guhyasamāja Tantra*, Tōh 442; Zhol 9a5; Stog 15a2–3; Dunh 14b4–5; Fremantle 1971, 208; Matsunaga 1978, 17. At the beginning of chap. 6 of the *Guhyasamāja Tantra* the five tathāgatas pronounce five mantras: the mantra of Akṣobhya, *oṃ sarvatathāgatacitta-vajrasvabhāva ātmako 'haṃ*; the mantra of Vairocana, *oṃ sarvatathāgatakāyavajrasvabhāva ātmako 'haṃ*; the mantra of Amitāyus, *oṃ sarvatathāgatavāgvajrasvabhāva ātmako 'haṃ*; the mantra of Ratnaketu, *oṃ sarvatathāgatānurāgaṇavajrasvabhāva ātmako 'haṃ*; and the mantra of Amoghasiddhi, *oṃ sarvatathāgatapūjāvajrasvabhāva ātmako 'haṃ*. Candrakīrti's *Rdo rje sems dpa'i sgrub thabs, Vajrasattva Sādhana*, Tōh 1814, 203a4; Luo and Tomabechi 2009, 27.13 and 61.12–13, ends this part of the practice before moving on to the emanation of the maṇḍala for the sake of others by saying that here the practitioner has been blessed by being fully imbued with the five tathāgatas.

3113. Candrakīrti, *Rdo rje sems dpa'i sgrub thabs, Vajrasattva Sādhana*, Tōh 1814, 202b7–203a1; Luo and Tomabechi 2009, 27.2–5 and 60.14–61.1. D and Luo and Tomabechi have *gyi nga rgyal* for *gyis nga rgyal*.

[The Divine Identity of Offerings]

You should maintain the divine identity of offerings with the mantra, for the *Concise Sādhana* teaches: "After drawing forth, the mantrin should once more make offerings with the bodhicitta to the buddhas residing in the ten directions, and recite this mantra: *oṃ sarva tathāgata pūjā vajra svabhāva ātmako 'haṃ*."[3114] This explanation in itself does not indicate that you generate yourself as Amoghasiddhi, but as the *Vajrasattva Sādhana* teaches: "At this state of the bodhicitta, the yogi should aspire to the blessing of Amoghasiddhi, and maintain the divine identity of nonduality with the mantric[3115] stages of the offering taught in the sixth chapter of the *Guhyasamāja Tantra*."[3116] The *Sādhana Incorporating the Scripture* likewise clearly explains that you should maintain the divine identity of Ratnasaṃbhava and Amoghasiddhi during the passion and offering respectively.[3117]

In the "past event,"[3118] the *Guhyasamāja Tantra* teaches that Ratnasaṃbhava pronounced the mantra of maintaining the divine identity of passion, and Amoghasiddhi pronounced the mantra of offerings. Hence you should understand that in "the practice that follows," when you recite the respective mantras you must maintain the divine identity of these corresponding deities.

In the first mantra, *oṃ sarva tathāgata anurāgaṇa vajra svabhāva ātmako 'haṃ*, *anurāgaṇa* is passion, and the meaning of the rest is as explained before. [146b] Thus, in brief, the meaning of this mantra is "The indivisible nature of the passion of all tathāgatas, that am I." In the second mantra, *oṃ sarva tathāgata pūjā vajra svabhāva ātmako 'haṃ*, *pūjā* is offerings, and the meaning in brief is "The indivisible nature of the offerings to all tathāgatas, that am I." The *Revelation of the Intention Tantra* provides copious explanations of

3114. Nāgārjuna, *Mdor byas*, *Piṇḍīkrama Sādhana*, Tōh 1796, 6a1–2; L 106; T 104.

3115. The word "mantra" is not found in D nor in Luo and Tomabechi.

3116. Candrakīrti, *Rdo rje sems dpa'i sgrub thabs*, *Vajrasattva Sādhana*, Tōh 1814, 203a3–4; Luo and Tomabechi 2009, 27.9–10 and 61.7–9. D and Luo and Tomabechi have *byin gyis brlabs* for *byin gyis brlab pa*, and skip *sngags kyi* in our text. See the *Guhyasamāja Tantra*, Tōh 442; Zhol 9a6; Stog 15a4–5; Dunh 15a1; Fremantle 1971, 208; and Matsunaga 1978, 17.

3117. Nāgārjuna, *Mdo bsre*, *Sādhanasūtramelāpaka*, Tōh 1797, 14a1–3.

3118. This refers to the *Guhyasamāja Tantra*, Tōh 442, at the beginning of chap. 6 (mentioned twice above) in which Dkon mchog dpal, Ratnaketu, pronounces the mantra *oṃ sarva tathāgata anurāgaṇa vajra svabhāva ātmako 'haṃ*, and Grub pa rdo rje gdon mi za ba, Amoghasiddhi, the mantra *oṃ sarva tathāgata pūjā vajra svabhāva ātmako 'haṃ*. In his *Sgron gsal mchan*, 141a3–4, Tsong kha pa too explains that Ratnaketu during the "past event" corresponds to the meditator on the creation stage who during the "practice that follows" maintains the divine pride of Ratnaketu and recites his mantra.

the definitive meaning of these two mantras that are applied only to the completion stage.[3119] It would be inappropriate to write about this any further here.

Some[3120] maintain that as you utter the syllable *phaṭ*, you emit the drop into the lotus of the mother, and then draw it out of the lotus with the ring finger of your left hand, and offer it after reciting the mantras of the respective tathāgata of the maṇḍala. Some later lamas[3121] say this is fine since it accords with the practice of the lamas, but it is actually a great mistake that results from misunderstanding the main points of the mantra. If you emit it in this way, it will become an exceedingly great obstacle for the bodhicitta—the basis of bliss—to remain and increase in your body, and thus the basis for attaining great bliss will be lost.[3122]

Many further grave faults would then ensue: because during the creation stage you practice emitting the constituents, during the completion stage the blocking of the descending bodhicitta will take place naturally; there will be no reason whatsoever to meditate on the syllable *phaṭ* at the opening of your vajra jewel; and you will have to emit the semen at will, without fail, every day four times a day, during the four sessions of your practice of the elaborate creation stage, and so forth. Additionally, through the joy—born when the bodhicitta descends to the tip of the vajra jewel and is not emitted—you create visualized offerings to delight with great bliss all the deities that are placed on your body.[3123] To think that for this purpose the drop should be disseminated like the inner offerings and offered to the exterior deities would be intolerable nonsense.[3124] [147a] If for the purpose of emanating the Supreme King of Maṇḍalas from the drop, a mental emission would be insufficient and therefore you would have to emit the actual drop, then you would

3119. Bu ston, *Mdor byas 'grel chen*, 55a4–6, cites the *Dgongs pa lung ston, Sandhivyākaraṇa Tantra*, Tōh 444, in this matter.

3120. *Kṛṣṇasamayavajra explains this in his *Rim pa lnga'i dka' 'grel, Pañcakramapañjikā*, Tōh 1841, 162a6–b1. According to him, the best yogis will not lose their bodhicitta, but lesser practitioners may lose it and if this happens, they should draw the drop out of the lotus with the ring finger and the thumb of their left hands and offer it as our text describes.

3121. Bu ston, *Mdor byas 'grel chen*, 54b6–7, says that this is the explanation of *Kṛṣṇasamayavajra, and accords with the practice of lamas.

3122. See Tsong kha pa, *Sgron gsal mchan*, 173b3.

3123. Bu ston, *Mdor byas 'grel chen*, 55a1–2, explains that making offerings to all tathāgatas means making offerings to both the tathāgatas of the body maṇḍala and the tathāgatas of the ten directions.

3124. Reading *go ba'i* for *ga ba'i* in our text.

also have to emanate the actual deities, since their mental emanation would also be insufficient. These two cases are similar in every respect.

Therefore,[3125] you should mentally emit the drop, and imagine it proceeding into the lotus of the mother. You must visualize this drop as the source of all the deities, the five tathāgata families and so forth,[3126] for the *Sādhana Incorporating the Scripture* teaches: "Meditate on the most minute particle of the bodhicitta as the source of all tathāgatas and so forth."[3127]

With this the extensive explanation of the samādhi of the First Yoga is complete.

3125. Reading *des* for *das* in our text.

3126. Tsong kha pa, *Gsang mngon*, 52a4–5, has here: "The melted drop descents into the lotus of the mother. That very [drop] is the source of all the deities, the five tathāgata families and so forth."

3127. Nāgārjuna, *Mdo bsre*, *Sādhanasūtramelāpaka*, Tōh 1797, 14a2. D has *bsgoms* for *bsgom*.

Part 3. Concluding

15. The Supreme King of Maṇḍalas

Explaining the Samādhi of the Supreme King of Maṇḍalas[3128]

There are two sections here: (1) [the actual explanation] and (2) removing uncertainties concerning the Supreme King of Maṇḍalas.

[The Actual Explanation]

When you attained the three bodies for your own enlightenment as explained above, the nirmāṇakāya displayed the mode of absorbing in union with the consort by means of the practice of passion as just noted. Now you will emanate the maṇḍala wheel, turn the wheel of Dharma, purify the disciples' aggregates, the sensory spheres, and the sense bases, and then place them at the level of the tathāgata and so forth. By meditating in this way in correspondence with the deeds of passion during the fruit, you will take the fruit in the path. You will also ripen your continuum so that when you attain the union that still requires practice during the completion stage, you actually emanate the Supreme King of Maṇḍalas of the meditator on union, and act for the sake of fortunate disciples and so forth. To these ends, after my clarifications on seeking the consort and absorbing in union with her, I will now explain the Supreme King of Maṇḍalas together with the deeds of its enlightened beings. [147b]

The *Sādhana Incorporating the Scripture* explains that the Supreme King of Maṇḍalas begins by issuing forth Akṣobhya,[3129] while the *Illuminating Lamp* in the transitional point between the instructions on the issuing forth of Akṣobhya and Vairocana explains that "the issuing forth of the maṇḍala

3128. Tib. *dkyil 'khor rgyal mchog*, Skt. *maṇḍalarājāgrī*.

3129. This is not a direct citation, but a paraphrasing of Nāgārjuna's *Mdo bsre*, *Sādhana-sūtramelāpaka*, Tōh 1797, 14a3–6, which follows Tsong kha pa, with certain variations, in his *Sgron gsal mchan*, 73b3–74a2. See also his *Rnam gzhag rim pa'i rnam bshad*, 60b1–2, and his *Gsang mngon*, 59b3.

takes place only after the conclusion of the First Yoga."[3130] Hence according to the *Illuminating Lamp*, the issuing forth of Akṣobhya, the principal deity of the maṇḍala, is included in the First Yoga. Is there a discrepancy between these two explanations?

EARLY TEACHERS of the Guhyasamāja say that the explanation of the *Sādhana Incorporating the Scripture* is based on the premise that the First Yoga is practiced for the yogi's own enlightenment while the Supreme King of Maṇḍalas is practiced in order to lead others to enlightenment. The *Illuminating Lamp*, on the other hand, presumes that the First Yoga includes the issuing forth of the principal deity, whereas the Supreme King of Maṇḍalas includes the issuing forth of the surrounding deities. Therefore, THEY SAY, there is no discrepancy between the two. But this argumentation is wrong, because in order to resolve difficulties regarding the statement "these two ways of explanation do not accord and are therefore contradictory," they present detailed reasons for the incompatibility of the two explanatory methods, while on the same grounds they declare that there is no discrepancy.

We agree with the argumentation that there is no incompatibility whatsoever between these two explanations, but our argumentation for this is as follows: In relation to the First Yoga, the issuing forth of Akṣobhya is included in the Supreme King of Maṇḍalas, but in relation to the issuing forth of the thirty-one surrounding deities, the issuing forth of Akṣobhya takes place within the First Yoga, so there is no contradiction. The reason for this is that Akṣobhya must issue forth when the Vajrasattva's nirmāṇakāya father-mother are absorbed in union, while the remaining deities issue forth when Akṣobhya father-mother are absorbed in union, and therefore there is no contradiction.

[The "Seven Steps"][3131]

When you visualize the Supreme King of Maṇḍalas, you must generate each and every deity by means of the "seven steps" in the following way.[3132] Being absorbed in union, Vajrasattva's nirmāṇakāya father-mother [148a] delight all the deities of the body maṇḍala, and then the ensuing melted drop splits in two. One part is generated into the celestial mansion with its thrones, and the other part of the drop becomes thirty-two drops, each set upon a throne. These

3130. Candrakīrti, *Sgron gsal, Pradīpoddyotanaṭīkā*, chap. 1, Tōh 1785, 18a5; Chakravarti 1984, 23. Only the end of the sentence is a quotation. With significant variations, our text follows Tsong kha pa, *Sgron gsal mchan*, 73b3–74a2.

3131. Tib. *sgo bdun*. For the "seven steps" see Tsong kha pa, *Bung ba'i re skong*, 26a1–5, and his *Rnal 'byor dag rim*, 20b1–6.

3132. Tsong kha pa, *Gsang mngon*, 52a5–67b1.

thirty-two drops transform into the mantras of each of the deities interspersed with the three syllables *oṃ āḥ hūṃ*.[3133] The mantras transform into the thirty-two emblems, vajra and so forth,[3134] which are in turn transformed into the respective thirty-two deities,[3135] each and every one of which are endowed with a wholly perfect body. These stages of gradual visualization taken together comprise the first step called "the step of generation."[3136]

Following this comes the second step, "the step of sending forth":[3137] You should draw each of the deities abiding in the lotus of the consort into your own heart, and send them forth with their respective mantras so that they spread in the ten directions. Then the deities perform their respective general and specific deeds—this is the third step, "performing the deeds."[3138]

In the fourth, the "step of joining," unite the numerous emanations of each deity filling the ten directions into the bodies of the thirty-one deities respectively. In the fifth step, the "step of merging," you should merge each deity indivisibly with its own jñānasattva, which has been invited from its natural abode. In the sixth step, the "step of conferring initiation," the bodhicitta of the respective lord of the tathāgata family abiding in union with his consort confers initiation.[3139] In the seventh step, the "step of abiding on the seat," after returning, the deities abide on their individual seats within the outer maṇḍala.

[1. Explaining the First Step, the Step of Generation]

Early lamas say that the thirty-two parts of the drop become the thirty-two name mantras of each deity respectively. These mantras transform into thirty-two sets of *oṃ āḥ hūṃ*, that in turn are transformed into the thirty-two emblems and the thirty-two deities generated from them. So they say. This is inappropriate, because the *Request of the Four Goddesses* teaches: [148b] "The second part is explained by the ninth itself. The thirtieth and the tenth are the seed of the fifth. The second part is ornamented by the fifth and sixth.

3133. Tsong kha pa, *Gsang mngon*, 52a5–b4.

3134. Tsong kha pa, *Gsang mngon*, 52b4–53a2. Reading *sogs* for *segs* in our text.

3135. Tsong kha pa, *Gsang mngon*, 53a2–3.

3136. Tsong kha pa, *Gsang mngon*, 53a3–59b3.

3137. Tsong kha pa, *Gsang mngon*, 59b3–67b1.

3138. Tsong kha pa, *Gsang mngon*, 59b3–67b1.

3139. Tsong kha pa, *Gsang mngon*, 59b5–6.

That which arises is explained as the drop."[3140] This shows that the drop turns into the three seed syllables, but in no way demonstrates that the three seed syllables arise from the transformation of the mantras of each of the deities.

The *Concise Sādhana* teaches: "At the center of the lotus you should generate the deity issuing forth from the syllables of his mantra, blessed with the three vajras, and then again he becomes Hatred Vajra."[3141] This explains in brief the generation of the principal deity. The first two lines mean that the mantra of the respective deities interspersed with the three syllables is blessed by the three vajras. These lines do not indicate that the respective mantras that have become the three syllables are blessed by the three vajras.

The latter two lines are explained by the following verses of the *Concise Sādhana*: "Visualize Akṣobhya-vajra issuing forth from the mantra *vajradhṛk*," and so forth up to "Returning once again, Akṣobhya-vajra is seated in front of the vajra lord. Akṣobhya-vajra then enters into his [the vajra lord's] heart,[3142] whereby his [the vajra lord's] own previous form transforms into the stage of Hatred Vajra, the hero, radiating blue luminosity, abiding at the center of a solar disk, embellished with every ornament, and embraced by his consort, with three splendid faces, fierce, peaceful, and passionate. Abiding in the samādhi of Hatred Vajra, emanate the entire maṇḍala."[3143]

While the rest is easily understood, the line "Akṣobhya-vajra then enters into the vajra lord's heart" means that Akṣobhya issues forth, performs his deeds, merges with his jñānasattva, is initiated, [149a] and then appears once more, and abides in front of the principal deity. You need to maintain divine identity with the resolve "I am this Akṣobhya" and then to visualize yourself as

3140. *Lha mo bzhis zhus pa, Caturdevīparipṛcchā*, Tōh 446, 279b5–6. D as well as the Stog, 257a2–4, are quite different from our text. These lines are explained in Tsong kha pa's commentary on the *Lha mo bzhis zhus pa*, the *Bzhis zhus*, 37a3–6. They appear also in Candrakīrti's *Sgron gsal, Pradīpoddyotanaṭīkā*, Tōh 1785, 10a6–7; Chakravarti 1984, 14, and are interpreted by Tsong kha pa in his *Sgron gsal mchan*, 39a5–6. In his explanation Mkhas grub rje relies on these works by Tsong kha pa.

3141. Nāgārjuna, *Mdor byas, Piṇḍīkrama Sādhana, Mdor byas*, Tōh 1796, 6a2–3; L 107; T 105. D has *dbyung ba* for *byung ba* in our text. My translation of this verse follows the explanation in our text.

3142. My translation follows the explanation in our text below. For the argument for this, see above [102b–104a].

3143. Nāgārjuna, *Mdor byas, Piṇḍikrama Sādhana*, Tōh 1796, 6a3 and 6a5–7; L 108ab and 112c–115; T 10ab and 113. D has *sngags kyis dbyung ba* for *sngags las byung ba'i*; *mi bskyod rdo rje bsam pa yang* for *mi bskyod rdo rje can bsams pa'ang*; *snying ga* for *snying kha*; *bsgoms pa* for *bsgom pa*; twice *zhe sdang rdo rje* for *zhe sdang rdo rje'i*; *nīla* for *nila*; *dbus su* for *dbus na*; *zhal gsum gyis* for *zhal gsum gyi*; *mdzes* for *mdzad*; and *mdzad* for *bya* in our text.

Akṣobhya entering into the heart of the principal deity. Do not visualize each of your faces, arms, and so forth as Akṣobhya—who has issued forth through the mouth of the principal deity—merging with each face, arm, and so forth [of the principal deity] like water into water. Rather, visualize all parts of your body as Akṣobhya who has issued forth and instantaneously entered only the heart of the principal deity. This is a most important key point related to the completion stage.[3144]

The line from the *Concise Sādhana* cited above, "abiding at the center of a solar disk," indicates that you must visualize your previous lunar seat transforming or dissolving into a solar seat. The line[3145] "abiding in the samādhi of Hatred Vajra, emanate the entire maṇḍala" indicates that when you send forth the deities, you need not maintain the divine identity of each deity, but should send forth all remaining deities while maintaining[3146] the divine identity of Hatred Vajra.[3147]

Even though this is the case, when you initially generate the deities in the mother's lotus, you must maintain the divine identity of each deity with the resolve: "I am this and that deity." This is so because in the context of issuing forth Māmakī, the *Illuminating Lamp* teaches: "The Blessed One, Vajradhara indeed took the form of Māmakī,"[3148] and the *Guhyasamāja Tantra* as well teaches: "The Blessed One indeed took the form of a woman."[3149] In "the practice that follows"[3150] the "past event,"[3151] when the meditator maintains the divine identity of the principal deity, this deity should be Vajradhara.

[The Mantras, Emblems, and Forms]

What are the respective mantras—interspersed with the three syllables *oṃ āḥ hūṃ*—for generating each deity?[3152] The lines of the *Concise Sādhana*

3144. Reading *rim* for *ram* and *che* for *cha* in our text.

3145. Reading *ces* for *cas* in our text.

3146. Reading *gyis* for *gyi* in our text.

3147. See Tsong kha pa, *Rnal 'byor dag rim*, 22b2–3.

3148. Candrakīrti, *Sgron gsal, Pradīpoddyotanaṭīkā*, chap. 1, Tōh 1785, 19b6; Chakravarti 1984, 25.

3149. *Guhyasamāja Tantra*, chap. 1, Tōh 442; Zhol 4b6; Stog 7a1; Dunh folio missing; Fremantle 1971, 184; Matsunaga 1978, 7.

3150. Tib. *rjes 'jug*.

3151. Tib. *sngon byung*, Skt. *bhūtapūrva*.

3152. See Tsong kha pa, *Rnal 'byor dag rim*, 22a4–b2.

translated accurately by the Great Translator Rinchen Sangpo[3153] [149b] explains how to issue forth the five tathāgatas, the four mothers, and the four fierce deities through their respective name mantras: "Through the mantra *jinajik* the lord Vairocana issues forth,"[3154] and: "through the mantra *moharati* the goddess Locanā issues forth,"[3155] and so on, and also: "Aparājita issues forth with the mantra *prajñāntakṛt,*"[3156] and so on. Since these mantras are taught explicitly, by implication you should also know the mantras for issuing forth the other deities that are not taught explicitly, and send them forth with their respective name mantras.

Likewise, the *Concise Sādhana* teaches: "In the eastward direction the Vratin[3157] sends forth Maitreya and Kṣitigarbha through the seed syllables *maiṃ* and *thlīṃ*. He should place Vajrapāṇi and Khagarbha arising through the seed syllables *oṃ* successively on the southward panel."[3158] This shows explicitly that the mantras for generating the eight bodhisattvas are their respective seed syllables.[3159] Hence you should also know by implication the mantras for generating the remaining deities, which are not taught explicitly, and generate them from their respective seed syllables.

While this is the teaching found in the *Concise Sādhana*, the *Illuminating Lamp* prescribes generating the deities by means of their respective name mantras: "The vajra holders arising from their own mantras *vajradhṛk* and

3153. Tib. Lo chen Rin chen bzang po.

3154. Nāgārjuna, *Mdor byas, Piṇḍīkrama Sādhana*, Tōh 1796, 6a7; L 116ab; T 114ab. D has *sngags kyis dbyung ba* for *sngags las phyung ba'i* in our text. This and the following lines can likewise be understood to explain that the deities are born from the respective mantras and only then sent forth. But see the discussion below.

3155. Nāgārjuna, *Mdor byas, Piṇḍīkrama Sādhana*, Tōh 1796, 7a2; L 131cd; T 129cd. D has *sngags kyis dbyung* for *sngags las byung* in our text.

3156. Nāgārjuna, *Mdor byas, Piṇḍīkrama Sādhana*, Tōh 1796, 8a4; L 163a; T 161a. D has *sngags kyis ni* for *sngags kyis dbyung* in our text.

3157. Reading *zhugs* for *shugs* in our text.

3158. Nāgārjuna, *Mdor byas, Piṇḍīkrama Sādhana*, Tōh 1796, 7b6–7; L 154–155; T 152–153. D has *rim pa gsum pa shar gyi ni, snam bur brtul zhugs can gyis dbyung, maiṃ thlīṃ sa bon las byung ba, byams pa sa yi snying po gnyis* for *maiṃ thlīṃ sa bon las byung ba, byams pa sa yi snying po nyid, brtul shugs can gyis shar du dbyung* and *go rims* for *go rim* in our text. T has *tṛtīye* for *dvitīye* in L.

3159. Reading *kyi* for *kyis* in our text.

so forth."[3160] These two[3161] scriptures are not contradictory in their intention; either one is permissible. Therefore you may generate the deities either from the thirty-two seed syllables, *oṃ āḥ hūṃ hūṃ* and so forth, or from the thirty-two name mantras, *oṃ āḥ vajradhṛk hūṃ* and so forth.

The remaining passages in the *Concise Sādhana* that explain the deities' colors, emblems, and so forth are for the most part easy to understand and for the sake of brevity, I will refrain from citing them in their entirety here. [150a] Candrakīrti explains with regard to the "blue-red *utpala* lotus," the emblem of Māmakī,[3162] that its petals are blue while the root is red.[3163] Most editions of the *Concise Sādhana* say that the *utpala* lotus that Tārā holds as her emblem is white,[3164] but the commentary of *Kṛṣṇasamayavajra explains that it is blue,[3165] and Abhayākaragupta[3166] says it is a yellow-blue.[3167] Hence, while Indian manuscripts may offer several diverse explanations, it is appropriate[3168] to visualize the *utpala* lotus as blue with a little yellow, that is to say, green, as Abhayākaragupta explains. This is so because the line of the *Concise Sādhana* specifies that the emblem of Amoghasiddhi is a green lotus: "[In his left hands he holds a bell], a green lotus, and a jewel."[3169] For in this context Tārā belongs

3160. Candrakīrti, *Sgron gsal, Pradīpoddyotanaṭīkā*, chap. 12, Tōh 1785, 95a3–4; Chakravarti 1984, 115. See also *Sgron gsal mchan*, 274a6, where Tsong kha pa explains that there are two methods of generation in the womb: generating each deity from its own seed syllables, *oṃ* and so forth, and generating each deity from its name mantra *vajradhṛk* and so forth. He says that either method is fine. However, he says, in Nāgārjuna's *Mdor byas, Piṇḍīkrama Sādhana*, the mantras used for generating the deities are the seed syllables and the mantras used for issuing them forth are name mantras.

3161. Reading *gnyis* for *nyid* in our text.

3162. Nāgārjuna's *Mdor byas, Piṇḍīkrama Sādhana*, Tōh 1796, 7a55; L 137b; T 135b. D has *utpala sngo dmar*, and the Sanskrit is *nīlaraktotpala*. Tsong kha pa, *Gsang mngon*, 54b4, as well has *utpala sngo dmar*.

3163. Candrakīrti, *Sgron gsal, Pradīpoddyotanaṭīkā*, chap. 13, Tōh 1785, 115a6; Chakravarti 1984, 136, commenting on the *Guhyasamāja Tantra*, chap. 13, Tōh 442; Zhol 24a6–7; Stog 41a5; Dunh 45a4; Fremantle 1971, v. 125a; and Matsunaga 1978, v. 131a. Mkhas grub rje cites here Tsong kha pa's *Sgron gsal mchan*, 328a5.

3164. Nāgārjuna, *Mdor byas, Piṇḍīkrama Sādhana*, Tōh 1796, 7b2; L 144d; T 142d.

3165. *Kṛṣṇasamayavajra, Nag po dam tshig rdo rje, *Rim pa lnga'i dka' 'grel, Pañcakrama-pañjikā*, Tōh 1841, 163a7–b1.

3166. Reading Abhaya for Abhaba in our text.

3167. Abhayākaragupta, *Dkyil chog rdo rje phreng ba, Vajrāvalī*, Tōh 3140, 39a7; Mori 2009, §13.3.1, 241 and 243.

3168. Reading *legs* for *lags* in our text.

3169. Nāgārjuna, *Mdor byas, Piṇḍīkrama Sādhana*, Tōh 1796, 6b7; L 129b; T 127b.

to the tathāgata family of [green] Amoghasiddhi, just as the *utpala* lotus of Locanā [who belongs to the tathāgata family of white Vairocana] is white. Consequently, you should infer that the *utpala* lotus that Rasavajrā[3170] holds as her emblem is green.

Regarding the emblem of Yamāntaka, although some editions of the *Concise Sādhana* have "carrying a club, vajra, and wheel,"[3171] it is evident that this was translated from an inaccurate Indian manuscript,[3172] since the *Garland of Perfect Yoga* explains, "holding a vajra hammer, wheel, and vajra,"[3173] and the *Guhyasamāja Tantra* teaches, "In the eastern gate you should draw a hammer blazing with light."[3174] This accords as well with the *Twenty Maṇḍala Rituals* by Nāgabodhi and is therefore correct.[3175]

Hence SOME EXPLAIN the visualization in this way. However, according to Vajragarbha, this fierce deity "carries in his right hands a club, wheel, and vajra respectively."[3176] The context of the explanations in the *Guhyasamāja Tantra* and Nāgabodhi is the drawing of the emblems in colored-powder maṇḍalas. [150b] However, it is not certain that the emblems in colored-powder maṇḍalas are the same as in the meditation. For example, in colored-powder maṇḍalas, the emblem of Locanā is an eye.[3177]

The first two hands of Ṭakkirāja[3178] form the mudrā of *hūṃkāra*, whereby the two vajra fists are joined in back, the two little fingers embrace as in the "iron

3170. Tib. Ro rdo rje ma, Eng. Vajra Lady of Taste.

3171. Nāgārjuna, *Mdor byas*, *Piṇḍīkrama Sādhana*, Tōh 1796, 8a3; L 161a; T 159a. D as well as Tsong kha pa, *Gsang mngon*, 57b1, have *dbyug pa* for *dbyig pa* in our text, the Sanskrit is *daṇḍa*. D has *rnams* for *bsnams* in our text.

3172. In his commentary on Nāgārjuna's *Mdor byas*, *Piṇḍīkrama Sādhana*, Tōh 1796, Ratnākaraśānti has *tho ba*, hammer, as well. See his *Rin chen phreng ba*, *Ratnāvalī*, Tōh 1826, 62b4.

3173. Abhayākaragupta, *Rdzogs pa'i rnal 'byor gyi phreng ba*, *Niṣpannayogāvalī*, Tōh 3141, 98b6; Sanskrit, Tibetan, and English translation in Lokesh Chandra and Nirmala Sharma 2015, 33.

3174. *Guhyasamāja Tantra*, chap. 4, Tōh 442; Zhol 8a2; Stog 12b6; Dunh 12a2–3; Fremantle 1971, v. 16; and Matsunaga 1978, v. 16.

3175. Nāgabodhi, *Dkyil chog nyi shu pa*, *Maṇḍalaviṃśatividhi*, chap. 11, v. 9, Tōh 1810, 137b6; Tanaka 1999, 28.

3176. Vajragarbha, Rdo rje snying po, *Kye'i rdo rje bsdus pa'i don gyi rgya cher 'grel pa*, *Hevajrapiṇḍārthaṭīkā*, Tōh 1180, 35a4.

3177. According to Tsong kha pa, *Gsang mngon*, 54b3, Locanā holds a wheel, vajra, and white *utpala* lotus in her right arms and a bell, jewel, and sword in her left arms.

3178. Or Ṭarkvirāja, Tib. 'Dod rgyal.

fetters"[3179] mudrā, and the two index fingers are extended. Uṣṇīṣacakravartin makes the mudrā of *uṣṇīṣa*, as Abhayākaragupta taught: "Stretch the palms of your hands evenly facing upward, hold the nails of the thumbs over the nails of the ring fingers and make the two little fingers like needles, while the tips of your middle fingers hold tightly, and the forefingers form the shape of horns at their center. This was explained as the *uṣṇīṣa*-mudrā."[3180]

[2. The Step of Sending Forth][3181]

SOME EARLY LAMAS say that the mantras for sending forth are *jinajik oṃ*, *ratnadhṛk svā*, and so forth. This contradicts THEIR own position that the mantra for sending forth Akṣobhya is just his name mantra, *vajradhṛk*, not combined with a seed syllable. The *Guhyasamāja Root Tantra*, its *Commentary*, the *Concise Sādhana*, and *Formulating the Sādhana* all explain that the name mantra alone is the mantra for sending forth. Not one of these scriptures maintains that the name mantra should be combined with the seed syllable, and since this is not implied, doing so is not appropriate.

What motivates those who meditate on sending forth the deities through their name mantras in this way? In the case of sending Akṣobhya forth, the *Illuminating Lamp* teaches: "While observing the realm of sentient beings pervaded by the five afflictive emotions, the Blessed One[3182] discerned that awakening is perfect understanding of the nature of afflictive emotions and that 'I am the essence of that.' Then in order to purify the afflictive emotion of hatred among his disciples, [151a] he *brought forth from his vajra body, speech, and mind this supreme innermost essence of the tathāgata family of hatred*."[3183]

Thus you should develop all-encompassing compassion for all sentient

3179. Tib. *lcags sgrog*.

3180. Abhayākaragupta, *Rdzogs pa'i rnal 'byor gyi phreng ba*, *Niṣpannayogāvalī*, Tōh 3141, 99a5–6; Sanskrit, Tibetan, and English translation in Lokesh Chandra and Nirmala Sharma 2015, 33. This seems to be a paraphrase rather than a quote.

3181. See, Tsong kha pa, *Gsang mngon*, 59b3–67b1. While above [148a3] the term *spro ba'i sgo* was used, here we find *dbyung ba'i sgo*.

3182. The Blessed One, the tathāgata, vajra body, speech, and mind of all tathāgatas. Tib. *bcom ldan 'das de bzhin gshegs pa thams cad kyi sku gsung thugs rdo rje*, Skt. *bhagavān sarva tathāgata kāya vāk citta vajra*, in the *Guhyasamāja Tantra*, chap. 1, Tōh 442; Zhol 4a3; Stog 5b3; Dunh 4b1–2; Fremantle 1971, 182; and Matsunaga 1978, 6.

3183. Candrakīrti, *Sgron gsal*, *Pradīpoddyotanaṭīkā*, Tōh 1785, 17b6–18a1; Chakravarti 1984, 23. This is a citation from the *Guhyasamāja Tantra*, [referred to in the previous note] which adds "mantra" to "this supreme innermost essence of the tathāgata family of hatred." This mantra is *vajradhṛk*.

beings and reinforce your motivation with the resolve: "I will send forth Akṣobhya in order to purify the hatred of all sentient beings," and "I will send forth Vairocana to purify the ignorance of all sentient beings," and so forth. Then you should immediately draw the respective deity abiding in the womb of the mother through the path of your vajra into your heart, and while maintaining the divine identity of Dveṣavajra[3184] recite the name mantra of each deity and send it forth from your heart.

[3. The Step of Deeds][3185]

The deeds are of two kinds: shared and specific. The shared deeds include turning the wheel of Dharma by the tathāgatas who were sent forth. The deeds specific to each of the deities begin with "the purification of the hatred of sentient beings afflicted by hatred and placing them on the stage of Akṣobhya"[3186] up to the deed of Sumbharāja who "overcomes the poison of the inanimate and animate as well as the negative forces of nāgas and earth deities."[3187] Since these are easily understood and there are no conflicting positions, I will not enlarge on this subject.

[4. The Step of Joining]

Visualize the innumerable bodies of Akṣobhyas who have emanated to pervade the world realms joining together to become a single body of Akṣobhya and so forth.

[5. The Step of Merging]

The *Sādhana Incorporating the Scripture* teaches: "They [the deities of the maṇḍala] thoroughly purify sentient beings who delight in ignorance and so forth, merge together, and enter the wisdom wheel. When you summon them again place them on their respective seats and seal them with the four seals.

3184. Tib. Zhe sdang rdo rje.

3185. Tsong kha pa, *Gsang mngon*, 59b3–67b1.

3186. Tsong kha pa, *Gsang mngon*, 59b4–5.

3187. Tsong kha pa, *Gsang mngon*, 67a5.

[151b] This is the second samādhi called 'the supreme maṇḍala.'"[3188] Hence, the emanated deities are joined into a single deity and then merged with the jñānasattvas and finally placed on their respective seat. According to other scriptures, the jñānasattvas are invoked only after all the deities have been placed in the maṇḍala and merged with them but this is not the case.

[6. The Step of Conferring Initiation]

Some lamas explain that the tathāgatas ask [the lord of the family father-mother] to confer their initiation. In response the bodhicitta stream of the father-mother initiates them, and they become adorned with the lord of the tathāgata family as their respective head ornaments. This is most inappropriate, because it contradicts the lines of the *Concise Sādhana*: "Visualize [Ratnasaṃbhava] peaceful with three faces, yellow, black, and white, his hair tied in a topknot, wearing a crown, with Akṣobhya as head ornament," and so forth up to "Having issued forth from your heart, and completely purified those abiding in the state of pride, he takes his seat at the center of the jewel in the southern direction."[3189] Therefore these lines indicate that before performing the deeds, each of the deities already had a head ornament and this contradicts the position of some lamas who maintain that the tathāgatas are sealed only after their initiation.

It is also inappropriate because the fifteenth chapter of the *Guhyasamāja Tantra* teaches: "The vajra holders are gratified by the practice of Vajra-of-Beings."[3190] The *Illuminating Lamp* explains: "*Vajra-of-Beings* is Akṣobhya and *his practice* is being seated on the [initiate's] head. Thus *the vajra holders*—those who belong to the tathāgata family of Akṣobhya[3191]—*are gratified*, that is, initiated."[3192] The *Guhyasamāja Tantra* teaches also: "The meditation on

3188. Nāgārjuna, *Mdo bsre, Sādhanasūtramelāpaka*, Tōh 1797, 14a5–6. D has *'khor lor* for *'khor lo*; *bkug ste* for *bkug la*; *gnas ji lta ba bzhin du bkod nas* for *gnas ji lta ba bzhin du gnas par byas la*; *btab pa* for *gdab pa*; and *ting nge 'dzin gnyis pa* for *ting nge 'dzin te gnyis pa* in our text.

3189. Nāgārjuna, *Mdor byas, Piṇḍīkrama Sādhana*, Tōh 1796, 6b2–4; L 120a-c and 122; T 118a–c and 120. D has *zhi ba'i* for *zhi ba*; *gnag* for *nag*; *byung ste* for *phyung sta*; *gnas la* for *gnas na*; and *gsungs* for *gyur* in our text.

3190. *Guhyasamāja Tantra*, Tōh 442; Zhol 32a6–7; Stog 54a3–4; Dunh 58b2–3, 1; 27b3–4; Fremantle 1971, v. 55ab; and Matsunaga 1978, v. 55ab. The Zhol, Stog, and Dunh have *'gyur* for *bya* in our text, while D has *bya* as in our text, but the text of Dunh is different.

3191. Reading Mi bskyod pa for Mi bskyed pa in our text.

3192. Candrakīrti, *Sgron gsal, Pradīpoddyotanaṭīkā*, Tōh 1785, 144a2–3; Chakravarti 1984, 170.

Ratnaketu is intended for those who belong to the Jewel[3193] family"[3194] which the *Illuminating Lamp* interprets as: "they should be initiated with Ratnaketu as their head ornament."[3195] [152a] Thus the initiation is conferred by the bodhicitta of the respective lord of the tathāgata family abiding in union with his consort.[3196] Nowhere is it clarified that initiation is conferred after a request is made to the initiation deity.

Therefore, after the emanations have merged into one, the bodhicitta of the respective lord of the tathāgata family abiding in union with his consort confers initiation [on each deity], and then having returned, [this deity] takes its respective seat in the maṇḍala.

[7. The "Step of Abiding on the Seat"]

This is thus already understood.

Therefore, in this practice do not visualize that all the jñānasattvas enter the deities simultaneously only after they [the deities] have been placed on their seats, nor that initiation is conferred on all of them simultaneously as other scriptures maintain, but rather, that one by one, each deity merges with its respective jñānasattva, and the lord of their respective families confers initiation on each of them in turn. This accords with the position of the early lamas in the Ārya tradition of the Guhyasamāja, and is also the intention of Ārya Nāgārjuna and his disciples. However Bhavyakīrti[3197] and SOME LATER LAMAS maintain that after you invoke the jñānasattvas, who then merge with the respective deities, all the deities are simultaneously initiated and sealed. But that is not the meaning here.

Māmakī and Vajrapāṇi belong to the tathāgata families of both Akṣobhya and Ratnasambhava, and also to the Mañjuśrīvajra and the lotus families, hence either of the following is appropriate: as the *Illuminating Lamp*

3193. There is an extra syllable in this line.

3194. *Guhyasamāja Tantra*, Tōh 442; Zhol 32a7–32b1; Stog 54a5; Dunh 58b4; Fremantle 1971, v. 57ab; and Matsunaga 1978, v. 57ab. But our text cites the verse as it appears in Candrakīrti's *Sgron gsal, Pradīpoddyotanaṭīkā*, Tōh 1785.

3195. Candrakīrti, *Sgron gsal, Pradīpoddyotanaṭīkā*, Tōh 1785, 144a5–6; Chakravarti 1984, 170.

3196. Tsong kha pa, *Gsang mngon*, 59b5–6.

3197. Bhavyakīrti, *Rim pa lnga'i dka' 'grel, Pañcakramapañjikā*, Tōh 1838, 3a5–6.

explains, Māmakī is sealed with Ratnasambhava;[3198] or as the *Concise Sādhana* explains, she is sealed with Akṣobhya, and so forth.[3199] Do not consider these two explanations contradictory.

Here ends the presentation of the "seven steps."

Removing Uncertainties Concerning the Supreme King of Maṇḍalas

[152b] There are three sections here: (1) examining uncertainties concerning the sealing of the deities with the four seals, (2) examining uncertainties concerning the appearance of the deities, and (3) examining uncertainties concerning the number of deities.

Examining Uncertainties Concerning the Sealing of the Deities with the Four Seals[3200]

As noted, the passage of the *Sādhana Incorporating the Scripture* cited above teaches that all the deities of the Supreme King of Maṇḍalas must be sealed with the four seals:[3201] the samaya seal, the dharma seal, the karma seal, and the great seal.[3202] Here is the qualm and its resolution in *Formulating the Sādhana*: "Question: when there are no hand seals in the [*Guhyasamāja*] *Tantra*, how is the body of the deity—sealed with the four seals—generated? Reply: The body of the deity—the support adorned with every Buddha quality—is the great seal. The queen is the samaya seal. The syllables of the mantra are the dharma seal. Acting for the benefit of all sentient beings and accomplishing their purposes by means of various forms is the karma seal."[3203]

The question is whether the explanation about sealing the deities with these four seals when the deities of the Supreme King of Maṇḍalas are generated contradicts the fact that this [*Guhyasamāja*] *Tantra* does not stipulate using hand seals to generate the deities. Additionally, while [the *Sādhana Incorporating the Scripture*] explains that when the deities are generated they are

3198. Candrakīrti, *Sgron gsal, Pradīpoddyotanaṭīkā*, Tōh 1785, 144a5–6; Chakravarti 1984, 170.

3199. Nāgārjuna, *Mdor byas, Piṇḍīkrama Sādhana*, Tōh 1796, 7a4; L 136d; T 134d.

3200. See Tsong kha pa, *Rnam gzhag rim pa'i rnam bshad*, 65b5–67a2.

3201. Tib. *phyag rgya*, Skt. *mudrā*.

3202. Tib. *dam tshig gi phyag rgya*, *chos kyi phyag rgya*, *las kyi phyag rgya*, and *phyag rgya chen po*, Skt. *samayamudrā*, *dharmamudrā*, *karmamudrā*, and *mahāmudrā*.

3203. Nāgabuddhi, *Rnam gzhag rim pa, Vyavastholi*, chap. 3, Tōh 1809, 127b2–4; Tanaka 2016, 113–114. See also Tsong kha pa, *Rnam gzhag rim pa'i rnam bshad*, 65b5–67a2.

sealed with these four seals, the *Compendium of Truth of All Tathāgatas* and other tantras explain that it is necessary to make the three hand seals, the samaya seal, the karma seal, and the great seal.[3204]

The answer in *Formulating the Sādhana* is that nothing is amiss here. The samaya seal is the queen; the great seal is the body of the deity adorned with the major and minor signs; the dharma seal is the syllables of the mantra *hūṃ* and so forth; and the karma seal is the enlightened action of accomplishing the general and specific deeds performed by the various forms of the deities that emanate and act for the sake of all sentient beings.

[Qualm:][3205] If the samaya seal is the queen, [153a] the sealing of the five tathāgata families and the five bodhisattvas beginning with Kṣitigarbha with the four seals is unimpaired. But since the other deities do not have a queen, their sealing with the four seals will not be complete.[3206]

[Reply:] Here SOME LAMAS[3207] say that other tantras, such as yoga tantras, allude to the queen as the emblem,[3208] and here[3209] too, these tantras allude to the queens of the remaining deities as emblems. In this regard, our holy lama Tsongkhapa explains:[3210] The fourth chapter of the *Guhyasamāja Tantra* teaches: "[The wise] should place the seals with the prescribed ritual action."[3211] The *Illuminating Lamp* explains this: "There are three seals: the dharma seal, the insignia seal, and the great seal. The dharma seals are the syllables *hūṃ* and so forth, the insignia seals are the vajra and so forth, and the great seals are the wheel of the deities, Akṣobhya and so forth."[3212] Thus body, speech, and enlightened action are explained as the three other seals, and on this account

3204. *De kho na nyid bsdus pa, Sarvatathāgatatattvasaṃgraha*, Tōh 479, 30a3–33b7; Lokesh Chandra 1987, 76–77. See also Giebel 2001, 11. In our text this tantra is called *De nyid bsdus pa*, but Nāgabuddhi's *Rnam gzhag rim pa, Vyavastholi*, chap. 3, Tōh 1809, 127b4; Tanaka 2016, 114, refers to it as *De kho na nyid bsdus pa, Tattvasaṃgraha.*

3205. See Tsong kha pa, *Rnam gzhag rim pa'i rnam bshad*, 66a3–5.

3206. If the queen is the *samayamudrā*, the five tathāgatas and the five bodhisattvas will be sealed with all four seals, but the other deities will be sealed with only three seals.

3207. In Tsong kha pa's *Rnam gzhag rim pa'i rnam bshad*, 66b3, they are called "some scholars": *mkhas pa kha cig*.

3208. Reading *mtshan* for *mchen* in our text.

3209. Reading *'dir* for *'dar* in our text.

3210. See Tsong kha pa, *Rnam gzhag rim pa'i rnam bshad*, 66a6–b3.

3211. *Guhyasamāja Tantra*, Tōh 442; Zhol 7b6–7; Stog 12b2; Dunh 11b4; Fremantle 1971, v. 10cd; and Matsunaga 1978, v. 10cd.

3212. Candrakīrti, *Sgron gsal, Pradīpoddyotanaṭīkā*, Tōh 1785, 32a5–6; Chakravarti 1984, 42.

it is necessary to ascertain that the emblem signifying the mind is the samaya seal. So our holy lama Tsongkhapa explains.

[Qualm:] Why is the samaya seal indicated by the name queen and not by the name emblem?[3213]

[Reply:] The *Illuminating Lamp* teaches: "The vajra queen is wisdom."[3214] Thus it is taught that the queen is wisdom indivisible from emptiness, while the emblem signifies the mind of the Victorious One, which is the essence of the wisdom indivisible from emptiness. And from among the four seals, the samaya seal is the secret of the mind. Hence the samaya seal is referred to by the term "queen."

This being so, each of the thirty-two deities is generated by means of the four stages: (1) the seed syllable is generated; (2) from the seed syllable the emblem is generated; (3) from this emblem, the complete body of the deity is generated; (4) and then that body performs the deeds of enlightened action. [153b] This indeed[3215] is the meaning of sealing with the four seals, and therefore sealing with the four seals does not require any specific hand seal.

Here ends the section on removing uncertainties with regard to the method of generating the deity.

Examining Uncertainties Concerning the Appearance of the Deities[3216]

Formulating the Sādhana introduces this topic by means of the following qualm:[3217] "The *Compendium of Truth of All Tathāgatas*[3218] and so forth, and the *ubhaya* tantras,[3219] celebrate the fact that the deities have one face; hence, why do they appear to have three faces here?" The point raised in *Formulating*

3213. See Tsong kha pa, *Rnam gzhag rim pa'i rnam bshad*, 66b2.

3214. Candrakīrti, *Sgron gsal, Pradīpoddyotanaṭīkā*, chap. 1, Tōh 1785, 9a1–2; Chakravarti 1984, 12.

3215. Reading *nyid* for *gnyis* in our text.

3216. See Tsong kha pa, *Rnam gzhag rim pa'i rnam bshad*, 67a2–71b1.

3217. Nāgabuddhi's *Rnam gzhag rim pa*, *Vyavastholi*, chap. 3, Tōh 1809, 127b4, Tanaka 2016, 114. D and Tanaka have *gnyi ga'i* for *gnyis ka'i*. Reading *dogs pa* for *dgos pa* in our text.

3218. *De kho na nyid bsdus pa, Sarvatathāgatatattvasaṃgraha*, Tōh 479. Once more, in our text this tantra is called *De nyid bsdus pa*, but Nāgabuddhi's *Rnam gzhag rim pa, Vyavastholi*, chap. 3, Tōh 1809, 127b4; Tanaka 2016, 114, has *De kho na nyid bsdus pa*.

3219. Immediately below, Mkhas grub rje specifies that the *Rnam snang mngon byang, Mahāvairocanābhisambodhi*, Tōh 494, belongs to the category of *ubhaya* tantras. On the term *ubhayatantra* in relation to the *Mahāvairocanābhisambodhi*, see Dalton, 2005, 123 and passim.

the Sādhana is that in yoga tantras such as the *Root Tantra Compendium of Truth of All Tathāgatas*, and the *Explanatory Tantra Vajra Peak*,[3220] and in the *ubhaya* tantras, such as the *Perfect Awakening of Vairocana*,[3221] the majority[3222] of deities have but one face. What is the reason then that in the *Guhyasamāja Tantra* all the deities have three faces? Not only in the lower tantras but also in the unexcelled tantras such as the *Hevajra* and *Cakrasaṃvara* tantras, the majority of maṇḍala deities have but one face.

In reply, the vajra master of *Formulating the Sādhana* explains:

> The Blessed One himself teaches this in the explanatory tantra entitled the *Revelation of the Intention*: "The great thatness, which may be conceptualized as consisting of outer and inner and both [outer and inner] natures, is declared nondual. [Regarding the outer nature:] The fingers of the left hand called the little finger, the ring finger, the middle finger, the index finger, and the thumb denote form, sound, scent, taste, and tangibles.[3223] When [these fingers] are united indivisibly [with the objects of the senses], a perfect wisdom capable of discerning [the true meaning] arises. This is expounded as dharmakāya, suchness, or nonduality. [154a] [Regarding the inner nature:] The tathāgatas Akṣobhya, Ratnasaṃbhava, Amitābha, Amoghasiddhi, and Vairocana signify the five respective fingers of the right hand beginning with the little finger.
>
> "[Regarding both inner and outer natures:] The nature of the two joined as one is the triple refuge in the Buddha, Dharma, and Saṅgha, that are one but conceptualized as three. By joining one palm with the other, the supreme stage of Vajrasattva, the union of wisdom and method is attained. Once the palms are joined, all the buddhas are invoked. When conceptualized, the joining of the palms invokes the threefold refuge, the threefold thatness, the three bodies, the three liberations, the three faces, the three colors, the three yogas, the three supreme pledges,[3224] the three paths in the three times with the three maṇḍalas of the three

3220. *Rdo rje rtse mo, Vajraśekhara*, Tōh 480.

3221. *Rnam snang mngon byang, Mahāvairocanābhisambodhi*, Tōh 494.

3222. In his *Rnam gzhag rim pa'i rnam bshad*, 67a5, Tsong kha pa points out that these tantras also describe four-faced deities.

3223. Our text has form and so forth.

3224. The Sanskrit has *śreṣṭha* after *samaya*.

deities in the three realms. Actions such as offering supplications, making prostrations, acting for the sake of sentient beings, and satisfying the perfect buddhas are all signified by this joining of the palms. Both ordinary sentient beings and those who have become buddhas are endowed with the nature of suchness and nonduality. In the yoga of abiding with no abode all buddhas abide."[3225]

The answer to the uncertainty [about the number of faces] here is elucidated by citing these lines of the twelfth chapter of the *Revelation of the Intention*, which explains the "vajra-joining-of-the-palms"[3226] in its definitive meaning. How do these lines answer the question here? To explain each word in the passage would take too long, and therefore I will explain the main meaning in a concise and easily understood manner. [154b] The [first five verses] up to *that are one but conceptualized as three* explain the "vajra-of joining-the-palms" in the definitive meaning in relation to clear light, and the [latter five verses] explain the "vajra-of-joining-the-palms" in the definitive meaning in relation to union.

Although other tantras likewise explain that joining the palms of the hands and pressing the fingers of one hand against the fingers of the other is "vajra-of-joining-the-palms," the definitive meaning of the equivalent term in the *Guhyasamāja Tantra* is special. What makes it special? Since the left side is the aspect of wisdom, the five fingers of the left hand signify the five objects of the senses that are indicated by the term the five vajra ladies.[3227] The right is the aspect of method, and therefore the five fingers of the right hand signify the five faculties that are indicated by the term the five tathāgata families. The fingers of both hands joined together signify the consciousness that

3225. Nāgabuddhi, *Rnam gzhag rim pa*, *Vyavastholi*, chap. 3, Tōh 1809, 127b5–128a4; Tanaka 2016, 115–118. D and Tanaka have *don bshad pa'i rgyud* for *bshad pa*; in v. 1: *gyur* for *'gyur*, *rnams* for *gnas* and *'di yi* for *de yi*; in v. 2: *rab grags pa'i* for *grags pa yi*, *tha ltag* for *mtha' ltag*, *gung mo* for *gung med* and *gzung* for *bzung*; in v. 3: *dngos po* for *dngas pa* and *med pa yi* for *med sbyor bas*; in v. 4: *mthe'u chung* for *mthe chung*: in v. 5: *brtags pa* for *btags pa*; in v. 6: *sbyor ba tsam* for *sbyar ba tsam*; in v. 7: *rnam par thar gsum gyi* for *rnam par thar gsum gyis* and *mdog gsum yang* for *mdog gsum yin*: and in v. 10: *rnam par bzhugs* for *rnam par gzhug* in our text. See *Dgong pa lung ston*, *Sandhivyākaraṇa*, chap. 12, Tōh 444, 197b6–198a2 and 198b2–3. Tsong kha pa comments on these lines in his *Rnam gzhag rim pa'i rnam bshad*, 68b1–69b3.

3226. Tib. *rdo rje thal mo*, Skt. *vajrāñjali*.

3227. Rdo rje ma, Vajrā. The five vajra ladies of the five senses.

arises from the meeting of the objects of the senses with the faculties. All three, the object, the faculty, and consciousness, should enter the clear light.

[In relation to the clear light,] the meaning signified by joining the palms of the hands, pressing together the fingers of one hand against the fingers of the other, is that when the three [object, faculty, and consciousness] enter the clear light, in the wisdom of great bliss the proliferation of dualistic appearances subsides. As for the definitive meaning in relation to union,[3228] *wisdom* is the actual clear light and *method* is the conventional illusory body. *Joining the one with the other* indivisibly is the stage of the indivisible union of the two truths; this is the ultimate definitive meaning signified by "the vajra-joining-of-the-palms," *the supreme stage of Vajrasattva*. When the vajra-palms[3229]—the definitive meaning of the two truths indivisible—are joined or this union is generated in your continuum, Vajradhara, the essence of *all buddhas is invoked* or attained.

At this stage of union, the purpose of the sets of three, the threefold refuge, the threefold body, the threefold liberation and so forth, is fulfilled.[3230] [155a] In order to clarify this [the *Revelation of the Intention* speaks of]:[3231] "The threefold refuge, threefold thatness," and so forth. But how is the purpose of the three realms fulfilled? The meaning of "the three realms" is not [the three realms of the world] the desire realm and so forth, but rather, as the *Compendium of Practices*[3232] teaches: "It is synonymous with the union... constituted by the three realms."[3233]

This, then, is the meaning of joining the palms in the present context: The main cause that affects the attainment of the stage of union itself, as explained above, is the generation in your continuum of each of the two facets that are to be united—the two truths endowed with all the essential characteristics, and then the generation of these two truths in union. The cycle of the Guhyasamāja in particular, alone of all the tantras, provides explanations[3234] that

3228. The following is an interpretation of verse six cited above: "By joining the one with the other, the supreme stage of Vajrasattva, the union of wisdom and method is attained. Upon joining the palms, all the buddhas are invoked."

3229. Reading *thal mo* for *thal ma* in our text.

3230. Reading *tshang* for *cheng* in our text.

3231. These are vv. 7–8 cited above.

3232. Reading *spyod* for *spyad* in our text.

3233. Āryadeva, *Spyod bsdus, Caryāmelāpakapradīpa*, chap. 8, Tōh 1803, 92b5–7; Sanskrit, Tibetan, and English translation in Wedemeyer 2007, B: 52a; Sanskrit and Tibetan in Pandey 2000, 73–74 and 302.

3234. Reading *bton* for *bten* in our text.

emphasize all elements on this path in their entirety. To this end, all the deities meditated on during the creation and completion stages in the *Guhyasamāja Tantra* have, uniquely, three faces each, signifying ultimate and conventional truth and their indivisible union. None of the other tantras specify that all the deities have three faces each. Such is the meaning of [the lines in the *Revelation of the Intention*]. Furthermore, the right face signifies method, the conventional illusory body; the left face signifies wisdom, the ultimate clear light; and the central face uniting the two signifies the indivisible union of the two truths.

The explanations provided in other tantras do not lay particular stress[3235] on the manner of attaining the illusory body, but do they elaborate extensively, and with special emphasis, on the method of attaining the ultimate clear light? The mother tantras elaborate extensively on the wisdom of great bliss—endowed with the essential characteristics of the four and sixteen joys, in descending and ascending order—which arises from the penetration of the vital points of the body, [155b] and they elaborate also on the indivisible union [of the wisdom of great bliss] with the emptiness of the intrinsic nature of all phenomena. In such a case, having earlier attained the illusory body, complete with all its essential characteristics, and having purified this illusory body into clear light, the wisdom of great bliss arises, and it is this wisdom of great bliss that realizes emptiness directly; what it realizes is the ultimate clear light, which is one facet of the union.

However, if you attain the illusory body, but then without first habituating to the transmitted instructions on how to infuse it into clear light, you lay special emphasis solely on the practice of uniting the wisdom of great bliss—which arises from entering, abiding, and dissolving the winds into the central channel—with the ultimate emptiness of the natural state, this could be taken for the dawning of the wisdom of ārya beings whereby the wisdom of great bliss realizes emptiness directly. Yet this would merely qualify as union of bliss and emptiness and as clear light, but would be insufficient to complete all the essential characteristics of ultimate clear light as one facet of the pair in union. The reasons for this are extremely difficult to understand, but understanding them is of the greatest significance. Hence you should rigorously investigate these points so you will comprehend them in full.

Thus, now that the "vajra-joining-of-the-palms" has been explained in its definitive meaning, you should thoroughly understand why all deities of the Guhyasamāja are endowed with three faces; and unless your faculties are extremely dull and you have little merit, you should by now be wholeheartedly

3235. Reading *bton* for *bten* in our text once more.

certain that the Guhyasamāja is the most supreme tantra of all, and that the two stages of the path explained in it are greatly superior to the path expounded in any other tantra. [156a]

While none of the works of Ārya Nāgārjuna and his disciples explain specifically how to ascertain that the arms of the deities are six in number, SOME TIBETAN LAMAS say that the six arms signify the three appearances in direct order and the three in reverse order,[3236] that is to say, the six dharmas of the path. SOME say[3237] that the six arms signify the six constituents on the ground of purification: flesh, blood, and skin received from the mother, and marrow, bones, and semen received from the father.

Examining Uncertainties Concerning the Number of Deities[3238]

In *Formulating the Sādhana*: "The questioner raises the qualm: With such a variety of explanations about the placement of the deities in the maṇḍala of the *Guhyasamāja Tantra* taught by different masters in widely circulating works, how is the disciple not to be in doubt?"[3239] The *Vajrasattva Sādhana* likewise teaches: "Some maintain that the number of deities residing in the maṇḍala is thirteen, some maintain nineteen, and some assert that twenty-five deities are placed in the maṇḍala."[3240] Tathāgatarakṣita explains the meaning of this: The first maṇḍala is the heart maṇḍala with thirteen deities consisting of the five tathāgatas and the four mothers, and in addition, four fierce deities at the four doors beginning with Yamāntaka.[3241] The second is the maṇḍala with nineteen deities in the sequence found in the *Māyājāla*[3242] and so forth. The third is the maṇḍala with twenty-five deities, consisting of the nine deities of the heart

3236. The white appearance, red enhanced appearance, and approaching attainment.

3237. See Bu ston, *Mdor byas 'grel chen*, 39a1–2.

3238. See Tsong kha pa, *Rnam gzhag rim pa'i rnam bshad*, 71b1–75a5.

3239. Nāgabuddhi, *Rnam gzhag rim pa*, *Vyavastholi*, chap. 3, Tōh 1809, 128a4–5; Tanaka 2016, 118. D and Tanaka have *de ji ltar* for *ji ltar* in our text.

3240. Candrakīrti, *Rdo rje sems dpa'i sgrub thabs*, *Vajrasattva Sādhana*, Tōh 1814, 196a3–4; Luo and Tomabechi 2009, 3.10–11 and 35.16–17.

3241. The four fierce deities are Yamāntaka, Prajñāntaka, Padmāntaka, and Vighnāntaka. This maṇḍala is described in the first chapter of the *Guhyasamāja Tantra*.

3242. Tib. *Sgyu 'phrul dra ba*, Tōh 466.

maṇḍala, as explained above, surrounded by the six yoginīs from Rūpavajrā up to Dharmadhātuvajrā,[3243] and beyond them the ten fierce ones.[3244]

It is not clear which master maintains which number. [156b] EARLY LAMAS[3245] explain that these are the positions of the younger Indrabodhi,[3246] Jñānapāda, and Paṇḍita Drinsumpa,[3247] but I saw no proof of this. Jñānapāda lived after Candrakīrti,[3248] therefore Candrakīrti did not have Jñānapāda in mind; still, if someone before him had maintained as did Jñānapāda that there are nineteen deities that would be just fine.

SOME[3249] say that there are seventeen deities in the maṇḍala, because the *Secret Attainment* teaches: "Indeed, the sequence is completed with the seventeen bodhisattvas."[3250] Thus, in the system of Master Padmavajra[3251] there are seventeen deities in the maṇḍala of the Guhyasamāja. SO THEY SAY, but this is inappropriate, firstly, because if there were seventeen bodhisattvas in the maṇḍala as implied by that line, then in the maṇḍala of the Guhyasamāja according to the system of this master, there would not be room enough for five male tathāgatas and five female tathāgatas. And secondly, because in a transitional passage that explains the twenty-two deities in the opening of the

3243. These are the six vajra ladies: Rūpavajrā, Śabdavajrā, Gandhavajrā, Rasavajrā, Sparśavajrā, and Dharmadhātuvajrā. Tib. Gzugs rdo rje ma, Sgra rdo rje ma, Dri rdo rje ma, Ro rdo rje ma, Reg bya rdo rje ma, and Chos dbyings rdo rje ma.

3244. Tathāgatarakṣita, *Rdo rje sems dpa'i sgrub pa'i thabs kyi bshad pa*, *Vajrasattva Sādhana Vyākhyā*, Tōh 1835, 281a1–3. This is not a direct quotation, but a paraphrase.

3245. Rngog Āryadeva (twelfth century), *Gsang ba 'dus pa'i 'grel pa sgron ma gsal bar byed pa'i ṭīkka*, 179, maintains that according to Indrabodhi, there are thirteen deities in the Guhyasamāja maṇḍala; according to Jñānapāda, nineteen deities; and twenty-five deities according to Paṇḍita Mgrin gsum pa. Rngog Āryadeva is followed in this by Red mda' ba in his *Yid kyi mun sel*, 97b6–98a2, and Rong ston Shes bya kun rig in his *Gsang 'dus rnam bshad*, 96a2–5. See Tsong kha pa's *Rnam gzhag rim pa'i rnam bshad*, 71b6.

3246. See Indrabhūti, *Ye shes grub pa'i sgrub pa'i thabs*, *Jñānasiddhi Sādhana*, chap. 15, Tōh 2219, 53a3–b3; Sanskrit and Tibetan in Samdhong Rinpoche and Vrajvallabh Dwivedi with a team 1987, 167–168 and 214–215.

3247. Tib. Mgrin gsum pa.

3248. On Jñānapāda's dates and their relation to Candrakīrti's, see note 1051 above.

3249. See Bu ston, *Sgron gsal bshad sbyar*, 61a1–5. Our text follows here Tsong kha pa, *Sgron gsal mchan*, 52a3–6. See also his *Rim lnga gsal sgron*, 24a4–b2; English translation in Kilty 2013, 59.

3250. Padmavajra, *Gsang ba grub pa*, *Guhyasiddhi*, chap. 2, Tōh 2217, 7b3–4; Sanskrit and Tibetan in Samdhong Rinpoche and Vrajvallabh Dwivedi with a team 1987, 16 and 23.

3251. The author of the *Gsang ba grub pa*, *Guhyasiddhi*, *Secret Attainment*.

Guhyasamāja Tantra,[3252] the *Illuminating Lamp* teaches: "This very number [of bodhisattvas] completes the circle of deities,"[3253] it would follow then that in the tradition of Candrakīrti there are twenty-two [instead of thirty-two] deities in the maṇḍala of the Guhyasamāja. What then is the meaning of the line from the *Secret Attainment*? When the *Guhyasamāja Tantra* speaks of bodhisattvas,[3254] it refers to the *completed* assembly *of seventeen bodhisattvas* who heard the *Guhyasamāja Tantra* when it was first taught—rather than to the maṇḍala that is *completed* when *seventeen* deities are placed inside it.

[Replies to These Uncertainties][3255]

Formulating the Sādhana teaches: "Wonderful, wonderful, O Great Being! I will explain this using both scriptural authorities and reason."[3256] [157a] Thus the number of deities placed in the maṇḍala of the Guhyasamāja is very difficult to ascertain and is debated by many supremely learned scholars in the sacred land of India. Therefore Ārya Nāgārjuna and his disciples had to find the precise reason[3257] for the deities being thirty-two in number.

Formulating the Sādhana and the *Illuminating Lamp* teach both the scriptural authorities and the reasoning behind the number of deities, but the reasoning in this case is not direct, but reached through inference. Hence, in order to establish that thirty-two deities must be placed in the maṇḍala, it is necessary to set forth flawless evidence[3258] of the threefold criteria.[3259]

3252. In the very opening of the *Guhyasamāja Tantra*, seventeen bodhisattvas are listed, from Samayavajra to Dharmadhātuvajra, as well as five tathāgatas. See *Guhyasamāja Tantra*, chap. 1, Tōh 442; Zhol 1b3–2a3; Stog 2a3–3a3; Dunh folio missing; Fremantle 1971, 174; and Matsunaga 1978, 4.

3253. Candrakīrti, *Sgron gsal, Pradīpoddyotanaṭīkā*, Tōh 1785, 12a5; Chakravarti 1984, 17. D has *yongs su rdzogs par* for *rdzogs par* and *cig* for *gcig* in our text.

3254. *Guhyasamāja Tantra*, chap. 1, Tōh 442; Zhol 1b3–2a3; Stog 2a3–3a3; Dunh folio missing; Fremantle 1971, 174; and Matsunaga 1978, 4.

3255. See Tsong kha pa, *Rnam gzhag rim pa'i rnam bshad*, 72a1–75a5.

3256. Nāgabuddhi, *Rnam gzhag rim pa, Vyavastholi*, chap. 3, Tōh 1809, 128a5; Tanaka 2016, 119.

3257. Reading *rnyed pa la ni* for *rnyed pa ni* in our text.

3258. Tib. *rtags*.

3259. The threefold criteria (*tshul gsum, trairūpya*) consisting of: pertaining to the subject (*phyogs chos, pakṣadharmatā*), the forward entailment (*rjes khyab, anvayavyāpti*), and the reverse entailment (*ldog khyab, vyatirekavyāpti*).

In stating the evidence, LATER LAMAS[3260] of the *Guhyasamāja Tantra* think that since there are thirty-two deities in the body maṇḍala, there should be thirty-two deities in the emanated maṇḍala. This is so because the deities placed in the outer maṇḍala are generated from the drop that emanates after the deities of the body maṇḍala dissolve.

EARLIER TIBETAN LAMAS[3261] of the *Guhyasamāja Tantra* maintain: SOME explained that in the body maṇḍala, which is the cause of the emanated deities, there are thirty-two deities. Having stated this evidence, they establish that there are thirty-two deities in the emanated maṇḍala, and this, they say, is also what is meant in *Formulating the Sādhana* and the *Illuminating Lamp*. Still, when the effect is inferred by taking the cause alone in evidence, the effect cannot be ascertained. When the effect is inferred from a cause the efficacy of which is unimpeded,[3262] [the capacity for the effect] is inherent to it. For the glorious Dharmakīrti taught: "When the arising of the effect from the totality of causes [can be] inferred it is called inherent, because it does not depend on anything else."[3263]

THEY ask:[3264] [But which body maṇḍala do you take as the cause?] With regard to the number of deities placed in the body maṇḍala of the father, the *Vajra Garland Tantra* does not specify that the five vajra ladies should be placed in it,[3265] [157b] hence there are only twenty-seven deities placed there, and this number is deficient. With regard to the deities placed in the body maṇḍala of the mother, since the eight bodhisattvas are left out, only twenty-four deities remain in the maṇḍala, and again this number is deficient. With regard to the deities placed in the body maṇḍala of both father and mother,

3260. See Bu ston, *Sgron gsal bshad sbyar*, 81b4–83a1, and Red mda' ba, *Yid kyi mun sel*, 96a3–5.

3261. Reading *'dus pa po* for *'dus pa pa*. See Rngog Āryadeva, *Gsang ba 'dus pa'i 'grel pa sgron ma gsal bar byed pa'i ṭīkka*, 178–182. See also Khams pa Ro mnyam rdo rje (twelfth century), *Gsang ba 'dus pa'i rgyud kyi rnam par bshad pa dri ma med pa ye shes gyi sngang ba*, 103–105, and Mi bskyod rdo rje (thirteenth century), *Gsang ba 'dus pa'i rgyud kyi rnam par bshad pa dri ma med pa'i snang ba*, 36 and 42.

3262. Tib. *rgyu nus pa thogs med*, Skt. *apratibaddhasāmarthyakāraṇa*.

3263. Dharmakīrti, *Tshad ma rnam 'grel, Pramāṇavārttikā*, Tib. chap. 1, *Rang don rjes su dpag pa*, Skt. chap. 3, *Svārthānumāna*; Toh 4210, 95a, Miyasaka 1971–1972, v. 7; English translations in Dunne 2004, 163, n. 34, and Eltschinger 2014, 230, n. 97.

3264. See Rngog Āryadeva, *Gsang ba 'dus pa'i 'grel pa sgron ma gsal bar byed pa'i ṭīkka*, 181.

3265. *Rgyud rdo rje phreng ba, Vajramālā Tantra*, chap. 64, Tōh 445, 269b7–270b4.

there are fifty-one in all, and thus too many. If so, it is not established that the evidence pertains to the subject.[3266]

[THEY continue:] As for example, in order to beget a child, the semen and blood of the father and mother must intermingle; likewise, since the deities issue from the womb, you must consider the number of deities that are on the bodies of both father and mother. Yet there is no surplus of deities because the two sets of five tathāgatas and the two sets of four mothers that are placed on the bodies of both the father and mother form a single pure entity. Likewise, the ten fierce deities placed in the body of the father and the ten fierce female deities placed in the body of the mother form a single pure entity. Hence, these deities should not be counted twice, and at this point the number of deities amounts to nineteen.[3267] To this number are added the eight bodhisattvas placed on the father and the five vajra ladies placed on the mother, a total of thirty-two deities in all. Thus there is no error of a surplus of deities, for the number of thirty-two deities is established by scriptural authority and the primary entailment is proven by a valid cognition through the force of objective inference. This is so because the effect is certain to arise from a cause the efficacy of which is unimpeded. SO THEY SAY.

But this is unreasonable because such a statement surely goes against the meaning of the verse [of Dharmakīrti]: "When the arising of the effect from the totality of causes" and so forth. Furthermore, if YOU state in evidence that "the thirty-two deities in the body maṇḍala are the direct cause, the efficacy of which is unimpeded, for the thirty-two deities of the outer maṇḍala" then when you establish that the evidence pertains to the subject, your proposition will be proven. [158a]

But if YOU prove the relationship of entailment[3268] by stating as evidence "because the thirty-two deities are placed in the body," and you establish the entailment by arguing that the deities placed in the body must be a direct cause, the efficacy of which is unimpeded, for the emanated deities, this[3269] is no proof at all, since it would follow that after meditating on the First Yoga, it would be impossible not to meditate on the Supreme King of Maṇḍalas. If YOU merely state as YOUR primary evidence "the thirty-two deities placed in the body are in general the direct cause the efficacy of which is unimpeded," then the primary entailment will not be ascertained.

3266. Tib. *phyogs chos*, Skt. *pakṣadharmatā*, the first of the threefold criteria, *tshul gsum*, *trairūpya*.

3267. The five tathāgatas, the four mothers, and the ten fierce deities are nineteen deities.

3268. Tib. *khyab 'brel*.

3269. Reading *de nyid* for *da nyid* in our text.

In both cases YOU maintain that the number of deities in the effect is inferred from their number in the cause. Therefore your argument is annulled[3270] through direct proofs, such as both father and mother bring forth one son, as cause and effect, and likewise one seed brings forth several sprouts.

[Our Own Tradition][3271]

The subject[3272] is the celestial mansion of Guhyasamāja's Supreme King of Maṇḍalas with Akṣobhya as the principal deity. [The thesis][3273] is that the thirty-two deities are placed there. [Regarding the evidence][3274] it is in the celestial mansion where all deities of the Guhyasamāja-Akṣobhya maṇḍala are placed. The example[3275] for this is the celestial mansion of the body maṇḍala. Being stated in this way, the evidence that pertains to the subject[3276] is accepted by the opponent as well, so there is no need to prove it; and since the evidence is specified by a homologous example,[3277] there is no contradiction. There is a common basis here,[3278] for the number of deities placed in both the body maṇḍala and the emanated maṇḍala is equal. The reverse entailment[3279] is ascertained by means of indicating a valid cognition[3280] that refutes the exclusion factor.[3281] [158b]

Furthermore, the scriptural authority for the number of thirty-two deities in the body maṇḍala is established in the *Vajra Garland Tantra*: "On this body (*lus*) of the vajra master, the bodies (*sku*) of the victorious ones abide

3270. Reading *bsal* for *gsal* in our text.

3271. This is based on Tsong kha pa's paraphrasing of Nāgabuddhi's *Rnam gzhag rim pa*, *Vyavastholi*, Tōh 1809, 128a5–6; Tanaka 2016, 219, in his *Rnam gzhag rim pa'i rnam bshad*, 72a6–b5. Tsong kha pa however speaks about the body maṇḍala and not specifically the celestial mansion of the body maṇḍala.

3272. Tib. *chos can*, Skt. *dharmin*.

3273. Tib. *dam bca'*, Skt. *pratijñā*.

3274. Tib. *rtags*, Skt. *liṅga*.

3275. Tib. *dpe*, Skt. *dṛṣṭānta*.

3276. Tib. *phyogs chos*, Skt. *pakṣadharmatā*, the first among the threefold criteria (*tshul gsum*, *trairūpya*).

3277. Tib. *mthun dpe*, Skt. *sādharmyadṛṣṭānta*.

3278. Tib. *gzhi mthun*, Skt. *samānādhikaraṇa*.

3279. Tib. *ldog khyab*, Skt. *vyatirekavyāpti*, the third among the threefold criteria (*tshul gsum*, *trairūpya*).

3280. Tib. *tshad ma*, Skt. *pramāṇa*.

3281. Tib. *ldog pa*, Skt. *vyāvṛtti*.

successively," and so forth.[3282] *Formulating the Sādhana* teaches that the definite number of thirty-two deities is established by both scriptural authorities and reason.[3283] The *Illuminating Lamp* teaches the homologous example[3284] with the line: "As thirty-two deities are placed in the body maṇḍala."[3285] This treatise teaches the subject[3286] with the line: "In the emanated maṇḍala [thirty-two deities should be placed]."[3287] Then the *Illuminating Lamp* teaches both the evidence[3288] and the subject to be proved with the line: "As the body maṇḍala."[3289] Hence there is no doubt that the way to state the formal argument[3290] is as explained in this treatise.

This being so, *Formulating the Sādhana* explains why the *Guhyasamāja Tantra* does not specify the total number of deities in the maṇḍala: "However the *Guhyasamāja Tantra* does not stipulate the total number of deities in the maṇḍala so that it will not circulate without a master."[3291] And the *Illuminating Lamp* teaches this in like manner.[3292] You must rely on a master. In this path of the Vajrayāna, there are no better means for completing the accumulations than worshipping and satisfying the vajra master. Since the root of all siddhis depends on satisfying your master, you must serve and worship your master for a long time, and thereby increase your devotion and reliance on the

3282. *Rgyud rdo rje phreng ba*, *Vajramālā Tantra*, chap. 64, Tōh 445, 270a2, cited in Nāgabuddhi, *Rnam gzhag rim pa*, *Vyavastholi*, chap. 3, Tōh 1809, 128a7; Tanaka 2016, 120. Reading *'di la* for *'di las* in our text. The *Rgyud rdo rje phreng ba* (D and P) has *sku* for *lus* in the *Rnam gzhag rim pa*, while the Sanskrit, in Tanaka 2016, 120, is *kāya* twice. This line was cited above [120b]. Here and in the following verses, the *Rgyud rdo rje phreng ba*, Tōh 445, lists the thirty-two deities and their locations on the body.

3283. Nāgabuddhi, *Rnam gzhag rim pa*, *Vyavastholi*, chap. 3, Tōh 1809, 128a5; Tanaka 2016, 119.

3284. Tib. *mthun dpe*, Skt. *sādharmyadṛṣṭānta*.

3285. Candrakīrti, *Sgron gsal*, *Pradīpoddyotanaṭīkā*, Tōh 1785, 21b7; Chakravarti 1984, 27.

3286. Tib. *chos can*, Skt. *dharmin*.

3287. This is the end of the line just cited from Candrakīrti, *Sgron gsal*, *Pradīpoddyotanaṭīkā*, Tōh 1785, 21b7; Chakravarti 1984, 27.

3288. Reading *rtags* for *rtogs* in our text.

3289. This is the following line in Candrakīrti, *Sgron gsal*, *Pradīpoddyotanaṭīkā*, Tōh 1785, 21b7; Chakravarti 1984, 27.

3290. Tib. *sbyor ba*, Skt. *prayoga*.

3291. Nāgabuddhi, *Rnam gzhag rim pa*, *Vyavastholi*, chap. 3, Tōh 1809, 128a6; Tanaka 2016, 119. D and Tanaka have *lha* for *lha rnams* in our text.

3292. Candrakīrti, *Sgron gsal*, *Pradīpoddyotanaṭīkā*, Tōh 1785, 21b4–5; Chakravarti 1984, 27.

master who knows how to conjoin the root and explanatory tantras. Understand that this is why the *Guhyasamāja Root Tantra* does not specify the total number of deities in the maṇḍala.

With this, the explanation about the samādhi entitled the Supreme King of Maṇḍalas is complete. [159a]

16. The Supreme King of Deeds

Explaining the Samādhi of the Supreme King of Deeds[3293]

There are two sections here: (1) the yoga pertaining to the actual meditation session and (2) the yoga between meditative sessions.

The Yoga Pertaining to the Actual Meditation Session

There are five sections here: (1) the yoga of the subtle drop, (2) the yoga of recitation, (3) dissolving into clear light and arising in response to the invocation with a song, (4) praises, offerings, and tasting the nectar, and (5) the ritual method of dissolving the visualization.

The Yoga of the Subtle Drop

As explained before, those who have attained the three bodies for the sake of their own awakening display passionate activities for the benefit of others [yoga with the consort] and perform the deeds of the body, speech, and mind for the sake of others. Among these three deeds, the Supreme King of Maṇḍalas is the meditation that corresponds to the deeds of the body, which acts for the sake of others through various emanations. The meditation that corresponds to deeds of the mind—abiding in perfect inward rest—is the yoga of the subtle drop.

What is the purpose of meditating on the subtle drop? The meditation takes place on two occasions: during the beginner stage and after completing the coarse creation stage. The purpose of the first is primarily to eliminate laxity and excitement during the coarse yoga of the meditation on the sādhana practice in four sessions. As Vaidyapāda[3294] and others have explained, when

3293. Tib. *las kyi rgyal mchog*, Skt. *karmarājāgrīṣamādhi*.

3294. Vaidyapāda, Sman zhabs, *Yan lag bzhi pa'i sgrub thabs kun tu bzang mo'i rnam par bshad pa*, *Caturaṅga Sādhana Samantabhadrīṭīkā*, Tōh 1872, 168a2–5.

laxity is predominant, meditate on a subtle emblem on your upper nose, and when excitement is predominant, meditate on a subtle drop on your lower "nose."[3295] During this practice, meditate solely on the emblem and the drop, not on the deities themselves. Only after obtaining signs that your mind has stabilized on the emblem or the drop should you meditate on the deities, emanate them, and so forth.

Therefore, when beginners meditate on subtle objects during the sādhana practice in four sessions, the main purpose is to eliminate laxity and excitement. [159b] They meditate a while on the subtle emblem on the upper nose and then on the subtle drop on the lower "nose," alternating between them from time to time. Yogis should only engage in such a practice for a short while, however, for this is not their main meditation. After completing the coarse meditation, yogis should meditate continuously, day and night, primarily on the subtle emblem and drop. The purpose of this meditation is to attain a mind that is perfectly stable on its object, for the *Illuminating Lamp* explains: "Now, for the sake of stabilizing one's mind, [the *Guhyasamāja Tantra*] teaches the threefold[3296] subtle yoga, beginning with the word *jewel*[3297] and so forth."[3298] So long as the beginners do not attain signs of stability in the earlier stages, they should not meditate on the later stages. However, having achieved stability at an earlier stage, they should now meditate on the next stage. Therefore, once they are able to eliminate ordinary appearances and attitudes by means of the coarse yoga, they should meditate on the subtle object.

If you belong to the tathāgata family of Akṣobhya or Vajradhara, meditate on yourself as Akṣobhya or Vajradhara; and at the tip of the upper nose of your main face, meditate on a five-pronged blue vajra the size of a white mustard seed upon a solar seat, and perceive it as your own deity. Meditate until you attain stable signs of seeing and touching. Signs of stable seeing are attained when a clear appearance, much clearer than seeing directly with your eyes, arises in your mind, and that appearance remains until the end of the meditative session, without scattering for a single instant and without changing

3295. The terms "upper" and "lower noses" refer to openings of the subtle body. The "upper nose" means the nostrils or the spot between the eyebrows, while the "lower nose" is the opening of the secret place.

3296. The subtle yoga is repeated three times with increasing subtlety of son-visualization and grandson-visualization. See below.

3297. This word is found in the *Guhyasamāja Tantra*, chap. 3, Tōh 442; Zhol 7a5; Stog 11b1–2; Dunh 10b1; Fremantle 1971 v. 12; and Matsunaga 1978, v. 12.

3298. Candrakīrti, *Sgron gsal, Pradīpoddyotanaṭīkā*, chap. 3, Tōh 1785, 28b7; Chakravarti 1984, 38. D has *rnam pa gsum* for *gsam* in our text.

the form [of the object]. Signs of touching are attained when you sense that you can touch [the object] with your hands. So long as you have not attained these signs you should not emanate the vajra. Emanate it only after you have attained them.

The *Guhyasamāja Tantra* teaches: "By means of yoga, continuously and earnestly visualize a five-colored precious jewel, small as a white mustard seed, on the tip of the nose. When the jewel is stable, emanate it, but not until then."[3299] [160a] The *Illuminating Lamp* comments on this: "*Continuously*, that is day and night, meditate on the [jewel][3300] the size of a *mustard seed on the tip of your nose, by means of the yoga* of your own deity. *When the jewel is stable* and so forth means that when signs of stable seeing arise, by meditating on the vajra and so forth, you will know that your concentration is unchangeable, and you will *emanate* it for the sake of developing mastery over your meditation. *But not until then* means that while you are still practicing this meditation you should not emanate it."[3301]

Taking into account that the meditation on the subtle drop is taught in both the yoga and unexcelled tantras, the *Illuminating Lamp* explains [this meditation] in the shared level of interpretation.[3302] The great master Śākyamitra explains that when you attain signs that your mind has stabilized on the subtle emblem, you obtain mental and physical pliancy.[3303] Several great scriptures, such as the *Yogācārabhūmi*,[3304] explain these [signs of stability] as the measure of complete attainment of the defining features of mental quiescence.[3305] Since

3299. *Guhyasamāja Tantra*, chap. 3, Tōh 442; Zhol 7a5–6; Stog 11b1–2; Dunh 10b1; Fremantle 1971, vv. 123–13ab; and Matsunaga 1978, vv. 12–13ab. These lines are cited by Nāgārjuna and Āryadeva. See Nāgārjuna's *Mdor byas, Piṇḍīkrama Sādhana*, Tōh 1796, 9b4; L 200–201ab; T omits the first verse; Nāgārjuna's *Rim pa lnga pa, Pañcakrama* chap. 1, v. 11, Tōh 1802, 45b4–5; Sanskrit and Tibetan in Mimaki and Tomabechi 1994, 2; Sanskrit and French translation in Tomabechi 2006, 106–107; and Āryadeva's *Spyod bsdus, Caryāmelāpakapradīpa*, chap. 3, Tōh 1803, 67b2; Sanskrit, Tibetan, and English translation in Wedemeyer 2007, A: 16a; Sanskrit and Tibetan in Pandey 2000, 21 and 195.

3300. Candrakīrti's *Sgron gsal, Pradīpoddyotanaṭīkā*, Tōh 1785, 28b7–29a1; Chakravarti 1984, 38, explains that this jewel is an emblem such as a vajra and so forth. And since it is very precious, it is like a jewel.

3301. Candrakīrti, *Sgron gsal, Pradīpoddyotanaṭīkā*, Tōh 1785, 29a1–2; Chakravarti 1984, 38.

3302. Candrakīrti, *Sgron gsal, Pradīpoddyotanaṭīkā*, Tōh 1785, 28b7–29a5; Chakravarti 1984, 38.

3303. Śākyaśrīmitra, *Ko sa la'i rgyan, Kosalālaṅkāra*, Toh. 2503, *yi*, 154b6–155a2. Our text follows Tsong kha pa's *Sngags rim chen mo*, chap. 12, 480.

3304. Tib. *Sa sde*, Asaṅga, *Sa'i dngos gzhi, Maulībhūmi*, Tōh 4035; Bhattacharya 1957.

3305. Tib. *zhi gnas*, Skt. śamatha.

by this point in the practice all essential characteristics of mental quiescence have been attained, the tantric treatises do not teach the practice of mental quiescence apart from deity yoga.[3306]

If you also meditate on the emanation, gathering, and so forth of the bodies of the deities, of the emblems, and so forth, during this practice, you will gain special insight[3307] into all that exists.[3308] Having developed an intense understanding of emptiness, when you reach the meditation on the principal deity entering into ultimate truth and so forth, you will gain all the defining features of special insight into things as-they-really-are.[3309] [160b] And therefore, from that moment on, you will attain the complete unique defining features of the samādhi on the union of mental quiescence and special insight.[3310]

The *Illuminating Lamp* explains how you should emanate the emblem once you stabilize your mind on it: "Having stabilized your mind on the vajra, by emanating it,"[3311] and so forth. Accordingly, you should practice emanating[3312] and gathering by initially emanating the root emblem—a vajra and so forth—and from it, a second emblem similar to it, then a third and so forth, and then gather them back into the root emblem. When your mind has stabilized in this way, practice emanating and gathering of a gradually increasing number of emblems. Finally, emanate emblems to fill the sky and then gather them back.

When you have attained a mind thus stabilized, the *Illuminating Lamp* goes on to explain: "You should emanate the form of the great seal as well,

3306. In his *Lam rim chen mo*, 1997, 553, Tsong kha pa says (Cutler 2002, 94): "Moreover, the serenity explained in the tantric texts contains certain differences in methods for generating concentration and in objects of meditation, such as focusing on a divine form, on hand implements of the chosen deity, or on syllables. But apart from those, they are entirely alike in terms of the need to eliminate the five faults of concentration, including laziness and so on; in terms of the means of cultivating their antidotes, such as mindfulness and vigilance, and so on; and in terms of the achievement of the nine mental states and the ensuing occurrences of pliancy, etc. So this concentration is very widespread." Likewise, *Lam rim chen mo*, 555 (Cutler 2002, 95): "Moreover, the point at which serenity first arises, in terms of the stage of generation and the stage of completion, is during the first of these two."

3307. Tib. *lhag mthong*, Skt. *vipaśyanā*.

3308. Tib. *ji snyed pa*.

3309. Tib. *ji lta ba*.

3310. This is paraphrased in the *Sngags kyi sa lam* by Dbyangs can dga' ba'i blo gros, 4b6–5a3; English translation in Tenzin Dorjee and Russell 1995, 48–49; and in Coghlan and Zarpani n.d., 32–33.

3311. Candrakīrti, *Sgron gsal*, *Pradīpoddyotanaṭīkā*, Tōh 1785, 29a3; Chakravarti 1984, 38, commenting on the *Guhyasamāja Tantra*, chap. 3, v. 13ab.

3312. Reading *spro* for *sgro* in our text.

[as the *Guhyasamāja Tantra* teaches with the line] *the radiance of the Buddha* and so forth."[3313] Therefore you should transform the emblems into the bodies of deities and emanate and gather them as before. The *form of the great seal* is the great seal of the body of the deity.[3314] At the end of the session when you have practiced emanating and gathering in this way,[3315] gather everything you have emanated into the root sign visualized on the tip of your nose, draw it through one of your nostrils, and gather it back into the visualized subtle emblem in the heart of the jñānasattva on your heart.

When you are habituated in the meditation on the subtle object on the upper tip of the nose, you should practice meditating on a subtle object on the lower gate: At the gate of your vajra, visualize a blue drop the size of a white mustard seed upon a solar seat, with five rays of light emanating from it. Perceive it in the nature of your special deity[3316] and meditate on it until you attain signs of touching and seeing. Ratnākaraśānti,[3317] [161a] Phalavajra,[3318] Vaidyapāda,[3319] Thagana,[3320] and so forth explain that at this time, you will perceive the five signs of dissolution at death, mirage, smoke, and so forth arising as indications of a stable mind.[3321]

Having stabilized your mind on that, the *Illuminating Lamp* teaches: "When you practice conceptual yoga on this mustard seed, visualize the

3313. Candrakīrti, *Sgron gsal, Pradīpoddyotanaṭīkā*, Tōh 1785, 29a3, Chakravarti 1984, 38, commenting on the *Guhyasamāja Tantra*, chap. 3, v. 13ab. The *Guhyasamāja Tantra*, chap. 3, Tōh 442; Zhol 7a6; Stog 11b2–3; Dunh 10b1–2; Fremantle 1971, v. 13cd; and Matsunaga 1978, v. 13cd.

3314. In his *Sgron gsal mchan*, 106a6, Tsong kha pa glosses *the form of the great seal* with "the body of the deity."

3315. Reading *de ltar* for *da ltar* in our text.

3316. Tib. *lhag pa'i lha*.

3317. Ratnākaraśānti, *Gsang ba 'dus pa'i dkyil 'khor gyi cho ga'i 'grel pa, Guhyasamāja Maṇḍalavidhiṭīkā*, Tōh 1871, 83a1.

3318. Phalavajra, *Kun tu bzang po'i sgrub pa'i thabs kyi 'grel pa, Samantabhadra Sādhana Vṛtti*, Tōh 1867, 178b2–3.

3319. Vaidyapāda, *Yan lag bzhi pa'i sgrub thabs kun tu bzang mo'i rnam par bshad pa, Caturaṅga Sādhana Samantabhadrīṭīkā*, Tōh 1872, 168a6–7.

3320. Thagana, *Kun bzang sgrub thabs 'grel ba, Samantabhadra Sādhana Vṛtti*, Tōh 1868, 224b3–4.

3321. Here our text follows Tsong kha pa, *Sngags rim chen mo*, chap. 12, 480.

inanimate and animate[3322] as Vajrasattva."[3323] Thus you—visualized as the principal father-mother with your vajra and lotus united—draw forth the drop on which you have meditated earlier to the tip of the nose of the lotus of the mother. Meditate on the inanimate celestial mansion and the animate deities of the maṇḍala arising simultaneously in their entirety within this drop and fix your mind one-pointedly on this. Meditate until you attain signs of touching and seeing. This is the emanation as a son-visualization.

When your mind has stabilized on this, visualize the deities [of this son-maṇḍala, Akṣobhya and his consort], within the drop abiding in union, [and a drop arising from their union once more]. Practice emanating and gathering the assemblage of the maṇḍala deities as before within this drop until you attain the signs of a stable mind. This is the emanation as a grandson-visualization, as the *Illuminating Lamp* explains: "By means of the verse *light equal to the radiance of Buddha* and so forth the *Guhyasamāja Tantra* teaches that the maṇḍala emanates out of the bodhicitta in the manner of a son, grandson, and so forth."[3324] There are other ways of explaining the visualization of the son and grandson.

To demonstrate the meaning of this practice, the *Concise Sādhana* instructs: "Generate the entire maṇḍala consisting of thirty-two deities, with yourself at the center, and then undertake the subtle yoga."[3325] [161b] This means that while visualizing yourself as the principal deity of the maṇḍala, you should meditate on the subtle object at the tip of your nose. [The *Concise Sādhana* continues:] "Visualize a mustard seed on the tip of your nose and the animate and inanimate world within this mustard seed. Meditate on the abode

3322. Tsong kha pa glosses "inanimate and animate" with the subtle celestial mansion and the deities residing therein. See his *Sgron gsal mchan*, 149a6–b1.

3323. Candrakīrti, *Sgron gsal, Pradīpoddyotanaṭīkā*, chap. 6, Tōh 1785, 43a5; Chakravarti 1984, 56. Cited also in Tsong kha pa's *Sngags rim chen mo*, chap. 12, 477.

3324. Candrakīrti, *Sgron gsal, Pradīpoddyotanaṭīkā*, chap. 3, Tōh 1785, 29a7–b1; Chakravarti 1984, 38. D has *byung ba* for *phyung ba* in our text. Here the line of the *Guhyasamāja Tantra* is explained in the hidden level of interpretation. See *Guhyasamāja Tantra*, Tōh 442, chap. 3; Zhol 7a6; Stog 11b2–3; Dunh 10b1–2; Fremantle 1971, v. 13cd; and Matsunaga 1978, v. 13cd. See above [160b].

3325. Nāgārjuna, *Mdor byas, Piṇḍīkrama Sādhana*, Tōh 1796, 9b2–3; L 198; T 195. D has *lha ni sum cu gnyis rang bzhin* for *sum cu rtsa gnyis rang bzhin du* and *na* for *nas* in our text.

of supreme wisdom mentally created by the secret mantra."[3326] The first two lines here indicate that you should meditate on the subtle drop at the lower gate and within it visualize the maṇḍala of the celestial mansion and its deities. The third line explains the mantra-body of conceptual yoga, which should be kept secret from disciples who are unsuitable to receive these teachings.[3327] The fourth line teaches that the meditation on the subtle drop at the lower gate is indeed the *abode* or basis for the arising of the *supreme wisdom* of great bliss within the mental continuum.

Next [the *Concise Sādhana*] teaches how to meditate on the subtle object at the tip of the upper nose: "Those skilled[3328] in yoga must continuously and earnestly visualize a five-colored precious jewel the size of a white mustard seed on the tip of the nose. When the jewel is stable, they should emanate it, but so long as it is not stable, they should not emanate it. They should emanate it together with clouds of supreme excellence, equal in their light to the

3326. Nāgārjuna, *Mdor byas, Piṇḍīkrama Sādhana*, Tōh 1796, 9b3–4; L 199; T 196. D has *yi* for *yis* in our text. This verse appears in the *Guhyasamāja Tantra*, chap. 6, v. 9, Tōh 442; Zhol 9b3; Stog 15b5–6; Dunh 15b3, and in Nāgārjuna's *Rim lnga, Pañcakrama*, chap. 1, v. 10, Tōh 1802, 45b4–5; Sanskrit and Tibetan in Mimaki and Tomabechi 1994, 2; Sanskrit and French translation in Tomabechi 2006, 106–107. But while the Tibetan translation of the last two lines in the *Rim lnga* is similar to that of the *Mdor byas*, the translation in the *Guhyasamāja Tantra* is different, whereas the Sanskrit of these two lines in the *Mdor byas*, the *Guhyasamāja Tantra*, and the *Rim lnga* accord. The reading in our text, which is similar to that of the *Rim lnga*, is the version that has been translated here. The Sanskrit of the last two lines is different.

3327. Tib. *snod min*, "unsuitable vessels."

3328. Nāgārjuna, *Mdor byas, Piṇḍīkrama Sādhana*, Tōh 1796, has *rig pa* for *rigs pa*, while the *Guhyasamāja Tantra*, Zhol, 7a5–6, has *rnal 'byor gyis*.

radiance of the Buddha."[3329] The meaning of this can be understood from the earlier explanation.

[The Samādhi of Single-Mindedness and Conceptual Yoga]

What is the meaning of the samādhi of "single-mindedness"[3330] and of conceptual yoga[3331] in the creation stage,[3332] both of which are taught in the *Compendium of Practices*?[3333] The commentary on the *Compendium of Practices* explains that single-mindedness means practicing the creation stage for one moment, and conceptual yoga means practicing it for many moments.[3334] But this is unreasonable because according to the *Illuminating Lamp* the generation of Vairocana and the other deities through the five manifest awakenings is single-mindedness.[3335]

On the basis of the explanation in the eleventh chapter of the *Illuminating Lamp* that single-mindedness is the generation of Vairocana and the other

3329. Nāgārjuna, *Mdor byas, Piṇḍīkrama Sādhana*, Tōh 1796, 9b4–5; L 200–201; in T the first verse is missing and the second is no. 197. D has *lnga la* for *lnga pa*; *rig pa* for *rigs pa*; and *mnyam pa* for *mnyam pa'i* in our text. The first six lines were cited above [159b] from the *Guhyasamāja Tantra*, which is slightly different (the differences are noted below). See *Guhyasamāja Tantra*, chap. 3, Tōh 442; Zhol 7a5–6; Stog 11b1–2; Dunh 10b1; Fremantle 1971, vv. 12–13; and Matsunaga 1978, vv. 12–13. As mentioned in a note above [159b], the first verse is cited in the Nāgārjuna's *Rim lnga, Pañcakrama*, chap. 1, v. 11, Tōh 1802, which accords with the reading in our text (except for *rigs pas* for *rig pas*); and is cited with small variations in Āryadeva's *Spyod bsdus, Caryāmelāpakapradīpa*, chap. 3, Tōh 1803, 67b2; Sanskrit, Tibetan, and English translation in Wedemeyer 2007, A: 16a; Sanskrit and Tibetan in Pandey 2000, 21 and 195. Regarding the readings of the *Guhyasamāja Tantra*, Zhol has *rin chen chen po kha dog lnga* for *rin chen kha dog sna lnga la* [*pa* in our text]; *tshang tsam* for *tshod tsam*; *rnal 'byor gyis ni* for *rnal 'byor rig pa* [*rigs pa* in our text]; *yong mi spro* for *de mi spro*; *sangs rgyas 'bar ba 'dra ba'i 'od* for *sangs rgyas 'bar ba'i 'od mnyams pa'i* [*mnyams pa* in our text]; *mchog rab* for *rab mchog*; and *sprin rnams* for *sprin ni*.

3330. Tib. *dran pa gcig pa'i ting nge 'dzin*, Skt. *ekasmṛtisamādhi*.

3331. Tib. *rtog pa'i rnal 'byor*, Skt. *kalpitayoga*.

3332. Our text follows here Tsong kha pa's *Mtha' gcod*, 50a5–b1.

3333. Āryadeva, *Spyod bsdus, Caryāmelāpakapradīpa*, chap. 1, Tōh 1803, 59b4–5; Sanskrit, Tibetan, and English translation in Wedemeyer 2007, A: 5a; Sanskrit and Tibetan in Pandey 2000, 5 and 163.

3334. Śākyamitra [attributed to], *Spyod pa bsdus pa'i sgron ma'i rgya cher bshad pa, Caryāsamuccayapradīpaṭīkā*, Tōh 1834, 242b4.

3335. Candrakīrti, *Sgron gsal, Pradīpoddyotanaṭīkā*, chap 11, Tōh 1785, 78b6–7; Chakravarti 1984, 98. Our text follows Tsong kha pa's *Mtha' gcod*, 50b1, and not the *Sgron gsal*, which does not mention the five manifest awakenings in this context.

deities one by one, SOME SAY[3336] that the practice of one deity in the beginning is single-mindedness, and after becoming familiar with that, [162a] the meditation on the entire sādhana is conceptual yoga. This is inappropriate in the context of the Supreme King of Maṇḍalas, because the explanation about the generation of Vairocana and the other deities one by one refers to the meditation on the thirty-two specially visualized deities.

Hence,[3337] single-mindedness should not be understood as a single instant of mindedness of the deity, nor should it be understood as mindedness of a single deity, but rather as mindedness of the deity one-pointedly or of yourself and the deity as one.[3338] Although this characterization encompasses both subtle and coarse yogas, here the general term is applied to a specific case, hence the coarse yoga of the celestial mansion and its deities is called the yoga of single-mindedness. Likewise, even though "deity yoga imputed by conceptualization" is a general term for the creation stage, when it is applied to this case specifically, the meditation on the subtle object at the upper and lower tips of the noses is called "conceptual yoga." As the sixth chapter of the *Illuminating Lamp* explains, meditating on the subtle object is the practice of conceptual yoga.[3339]

The lines from the *Concise Sādhana* that teach this subtle yoga are explained in terms of the four levels of interpretation,[3340] but in this context only the meditation on the subtle object during the creation stage is relevant. Since the vajra recitation during the completion stage and so forth is irrelevant to the meditation on the subtle object during the creation stage, I will write no more about it here.

3336. Here our text follows Tsong kha pa's *Mtha' gcod*, 50b2–3.

3337. Here our text follows Tsong kha pa's *Mtha' gcod*, 50b3–51a2.

3338. Cited by Ngag dbang dpal ldan, *Gsangs chen rgyud chen*, 12b5–13a2; English translation in Coghlan and Zarpani 2011, 107.

3339. Candrakīrti, *Sgron gsal, Pradīpoddyotanaṭīkā*, Tōh 1785, 42b7–43b6; Chakravarti 1984, 56.

3340. Nāgārjuna, *Mdor byas, Piṇḍīkrama Sādhana*, Tōh 1796, 9b4; L 200–201ab; T omits the first verse; has only 197ab, cited above [159b]. These lines are drawn from the *Guhyasamāja Tantra*, chap. 3, Tōh 442; Zhol 7a5–6; Stog 11b1–2; Dunh 10b1; Fremantle 1971, vv. 12–13; and Matsunaga 1978, vv. 12–13. Candrakīrti explains them in three levels of interpretation, the shared, hidden, and ultimate levels. See his *Sgron gsal, Pradīpoddyotanaṭīkā*, chap. 3, Tōh 1785, 28b7–29a5; Chakravarti 1984, 38. Tsong kha pa adds the literal level of interpretation in his *Sgron gsal mchan*, 106a6–b2.

The Yoga of Recitation

There are two sections here: (1) vajra recitation and (2) voiced recitation.

Vajra Recitation

The *Sādhana Incorporating the Scripture* teaches: "Mindfully engage in vajra recitation, for the seventh chapter of the *Guhyasamāja Tantra* teaches: 'Do not recite while eating food received as alms and do not delight in begging. Recite the mantra in undivided wholeness, enjoying every object of desire.'"[3341] [162b] The explanation of these lines in the seventh chapter of the *Guhyasamāja Tantra* specifies the vajra recitation in the present context. This stanza of the *Guhyasamāja Tantra* is also found, word for word, in the *Concise Sādhana*.[3342]

The *Illuminating Lamp* explains the lines in both their interpretable and definitive meanings.[3343] The definitive meaning is that since *eating food received as alms* means adhering to wind and mantra as discrete elements, you should refrain from doing so, and instead, join wind and mantra indivisibly and practice the vajra recitation of the three syllables during the arising, entering, and abiding of the winds. This is the vajra recitation of the completion stage, but it is irrelevant in the present case.

Therefore, in the case of the creation stage, the relevant explanation lies in the interpretable meaning. The *Illuminating Lamp* explains the interpretable meaning of the verse from the *Guhyasamāja Tantra* as follows: "*Eating food received as alms* serves as an illustration, hence *do not recite* while engaging in lesser matters such as striving after things, as for example begging alms."[3344] Accordingly, you should consume food and drink to the extent that they enhance your body—the support of your faculties, and your comfort. But you should recite only after you have abandoned inner and outer distractions, such

3341. Nāgārjuna, *Mdo bsre, Sādhanasūtramelāpaka*, Tōh 1797, 14a7–b1. D has *bzlas te* for *bzla ste*, and *bya ste* for *bya la*, has *la* for *'ang* in our text. The *Guhyasamāja Tantra*, Tōh 442; Zhol 10a6; Stog 17a2–3; Dunh 17a3–4; Fremantle 1971, v. 4; and Matsunaga 1978, v. 4. Zhol has *slongs* for *slong* and *slong la'ang dga' bar mi bya'o* for *ma bslangs pa'ang chags mi bya* in our text.

3342. Nāgārjuna, *Mdor byas, Piṇḍīkrama Sādhana*, Tōh 1796, 9b5; L 202; T 198.

3343. Candrakīrti, *Sgron gsal, Pradīpoddyotanaṭīkā*, Tōh 1785, 48a2–b3; Chakravarti 1984, 62–63. See also Tsong kha pa, *Sgron gsal mchan*, 162b4–163a6 and 163b5–164a6.

3344. Candrakīrti, *Sgron gsal, Pradīpoddyotanaṭīkā*, Tōh 1785, 48a3–4; Chakravarti 1984, 63. D has *bzlas par* for *bzlos par* in our text. Mkhas grub rje follows here Tsong kha pa's *Sgron gsal mchan*, 162b6–163a6.

as farming, trade, and so forth, and begging alms as illustrated by the line *do not delight in begging.* Thus do not engage in excessive mental cravings beyond your needs, or crave the best or most plentiful things, or beg alms motivated by these cravings. This is the meaning of the first two lines. Although the *Illuminating Lamp* applies these lines to the context of *caryā*, there is nothing contradictory about applying them to the creation stage as well, and hence the *Sādhana Incorporating the Scripture* cites them here.

Regarding the meaning of the last two lines, the *Illuminating Lamp* explains: "A mantrin in a state of *undivided wholeness*, that is, at one with deity yoga, *while enjoying every object of desire should recite the mantra,* meaning the three syllables."[3345] [163a] Accordingly you should recite the three syllables while enjoying the five objects of desire through a perfect understanding of their nature, never parting with the stable divine identity of your deity. Not only while reciting the three syllables, but whatever you recite, invoke the mental continuum of the deity, at one with deity yoga and never parting from it through ordinary conceptualization.

There are two ways to recite the three syllables, voiced recitation and vajra recitation. With regard to vajra recitation [our topic here], the *Illuminating Lamp*[3346] explains the definitive meaning of these lines of the *Guhyasamāja Tantra* as vajra recitation of the three syllables during the completion stage, hence its intention must be that the interpretable meaning is applied to the vajra recitation of the three syllables during the creation stage, just as the *Sādhana Incorporating the Scripture* does.[3347] The vajra recitation during the creation stage is a soundless mental recitation without moving the tongue and lips, as cited[3348] by Phalavajra:[3349] "You should recite vajra words; vajra words are soundless."

3345. Candrakīrti, *Sgron gsal, Pradīpoddyotanaṭīkā*, Tōh 1785, 48a5–6; Chakravarti 1984, 63.

3346. See above [162b].

3347. See the citation from Nāgārjuna's *Mdo bsre, Sādhanasūtramelāpaka*, Tōh 1797, at the beginning of this section.

3348. The second line, *vajra words are soundless*, appears in various Indian works, including Candrakīrti's *Sgron gsal, Pradīpoddyotanaṭīkā*, Tōh 1785, 71b7; Chakravarti 1984, 91; the Sanskrit for soundless is *svaravarjita*. In his *Sgron gsal mchan*, chap. 10, 221a2, Tsong kha pa explains it as mental recitation.

3349. Phalavajra, *Kun bzang sgrub thabs 'grel pa, Samantabhadra Sādhana Vṛtti*, Tōh 1867, 179a4–5. D has twice *rdo rje tshig* for *rdo rje'i tshig* and *bzla bya* for *bzlas bya* in our text. Cited also in Tsong kha pa, *Sngags rim chen mo*, chap. 12, 521–522.

Voiced Recitation[3350]

The voiced recitation is explained in the *Cluster of Instructions* as fourfold:[3351] (1) samaya recitation, (2) palanquin recitation, (3) enraged recitation, and (4) fierce recitation.

[Samaya Recitation][3352]

Visualize the seed syllables on the heart [of the deities] surrounded by the heart and essence mantras.[3353] When you recite the mantras, the assembly of the deities of the maṇḍala emanate from the seed syllables and act for the sake of sentient beings. Then, through the inhaled wind, the deities enter together with their mantras, entwined like a garland into the seed syllable on the heart. As you complete the mantra recitation for each deity, that deity will emanate and be gathered back. This is the way to recite the heart and essence mantras.

Having taken this meaning into account, the *Sādhana Incorporating the Scripture* explains: "You should utter the voiced recitation as the thirteenth chapter of the *Guhyasamāja Tantra* instructs: 'While reciting, emanate the vajras, and after completing this, gather them back.'"[3354] [163b] Likewise, the *Concise Sādhana* cites these lines without alteration.[3355] In the *Illuminating Lamp*, the lines are applied to the dissolution of the maṇḍala's deities into yourself at the end of the sādhana.[3356] These two cases are not different in so far as you emanate the deities and gather them into your body. Hence, since

3350. See Tsong kha pa's *Sngags rim chen mo*, chap. 12, 522–523, and his *Rnal 'byor dag rim*, 23b6–25a2.

3351. Abhayākaragupta, *Man ngag snye ma*, *Āmnāyamañjarī*, chap. 12, Tōh 1198, 138b7–139a4.

3352. Tib. *dam tshig gi bzlas pa*. In *Sngags rim chen mo*, chap. 12, 522, Tsong kha pa points out that this is the tradition of the *Kun bzang sgrub thabs*. See Jñānapāda, *Kun bzang sgrub thabs*, *Samantabhadra Sādhana*, Tōh 1855, 34b4–6.

3353. Tib. *snying po* and *nye snying*, Skt. *hṛdayamantra* and *upahṛdayamantra*; these terms are explained below.

3354. Nāgārjuna, *Mdo bsre*, *Sādhanasūtramelāpaka*, Tōh 1797, 14b1. D has *rab tu bsdu bar bya* for *bsdu ba rab tu bya* and *zhes bya ba* for *zhes bya bas* in our text. *Guhyasamāja Tantra*, Tōh 442; Zhol 20a6; Stog 34b1; Dunh 37b3; Fremantle 1971, v. 15ab; Matsunaga 1978, v. 13ab. Zhol has *rab tu bsdu bar bya* for *bsdu ba rab tu bya* in D.

3355. These lines are cited in the context of mantra recitation in Nāgārjuna's *Mdor byas*, *Piṇḍīkrama Sādhana*, Tōh 1796, 9b6; L 203ab; T 199ab.

3356. Candrakīrti, *Sgron gsal*, *Pradīpoddyotanaṭīkā*, chap. 13, Tōh 1785, 102a7–b1; Chakravarti 1984, 125. See also Tsong kha pa, *Sgron gsal mchan*, 295b4–5.

it is regarded as proper to apply these lines on both occasions, there is no contradiction.[3357]

What is the meaning of these lines of the scripture when they are applied to the mantra recitation? Having *recited* the mantra of the voiced repetition, you should *emanate*. What should you emanate? The vajra that is the assembly of the maṇḍala deities. *Having completed this* emanation, you should *gather them back* into your heart once more. How are these lines of the scripture applied to the dissolution of the visualization at the end of the sādhana?[3358] *Reciting* means that the deities placed in the maṇḍala proceed from their respective abodes. *Emanate* means that you place them[3359] on the aggregates, the sensory spheres, and the sense bases of your body. *Having completed* means that once the goddesses you emanate complete the offerings, you *gather* them back into your heart.

Why is this called "samaya recitation"? Because you should not go beyond this method of recitation.

[Palanquin Recitation][3360]

While maintaining the divine identification with the complete sameness of all phenomena, visualize the garland mantra[3361] circling, entering your mouth, issuing from your vajra path into the lotus of the consort, then ascending through the central channel of your consort, emerging from her mouth, and entering through your mouth to your central channel. While visualizing this, calmly and freely recite the syllables of the root mantra or the garland mantra.

3357. Our text here follows Tsong kha pa, *Mtha' gcod*, 123a3–4.

3358. See Candrakīrti, *Sgron gsal, Pradīpoddyotanaṭīkā*, chap. 13, Tōh 1785, 102a7–b1; Chakravarti 1984, 125. See also Tsong kha pa, *Sgron gsal mchan*, 295b4–5.

3359. Both Candrakīrti's *Sgron gsal, Pradīpoddyotanaṭīkā*, Tōh 1785, and Tsong kha pa's *Sgron gsal mchan* have *bzhag* for *gzhug* in our text.

3360. Tib. *khyogs kyi bzlas pa*. A similar recitation, entitled fierce recitation, Tib. *khro bo'i bzlas pa*, is described by Vajraghaṇṭa, *Bcom ldan 'das bde mchog yid bzhin nor bu, Bhagavancakrasaṃvaracintāmaṇi*, Tōh 1437, 236b1–2, and *Kambala, Lwa ba pa, *Bde mchog gi sgrub thabs gtsug nor, Cakrasaṃvara Sādhana Ratnacūḍāmaṇi*, Tōh 1443, 249b5–6. See Tsong kha pa, *Sngags rim chen mo*, chap. 12, 522.

3361. Tib. *sngags phreng*.

[Enraged Recitation][3362]

Meditate on the garland mantra circling as before, but begin with the mantra entering the mouth of the consort, and recite the syllables of the garland mantra coarsely and rigidly. [164a]

[Fierce Recitation][3363]

Recite the heart, essence, and root mantras loudly so that both you and others may hear it.

Additionally, in heap recitation[3364] you recite while visualizing the mantras as though the letters were inscribed by your mind, with their heads pointing upward, drawing a circle around the seed syllable on the deity's heart, and radiating light like butter lamps.

[All the Ways of Recitation]

No matter what you recite, while visualizing all the deities of the maṇḍala reciting the mantras with you, your recitations will multiply proportionally, as explained by several of the mahāsiddhas including Vajraghaṇṭa and *Kambala.

During the meditation session itself, count the number of recitations, considering only those recited while you maintain divine identity, when your mind is not dispersed, and your recitation is uninterrupted by extra words. Recitations in other circumstances cannot compensate for the number of recitations carried out during the meditation session itself. However, there are several circumstances in which you must perform protective rituals against obstacles, purifying karma and obscurations and so forth, and therefore several scriptures such as *Cakrasaṃvara Tantra* explain the need to recite mantras during all daily activities, including defecating and urinating.

Regarding the number of mantra recitations[3365] that qualify you to perform rituals of initiation, self-entry into the maṇḍala, consecration, and so forth, the mantra of the principal deity should be recited a hundred thousand times, the mantras of each of the surrounding deities ten thousand times, the garland

3362. Tib. *khros pas bzlas pa*. See Saroruha, *Dgyes pa rdo rje'i sgrub thabs, Hevajra Sādhana*, Tōh 1218, 5b3–4; *Dhīḥ* 2003, 139–140; Sanskrit, Tibetan, and English translation in Gerloff 2017, 109–110, 126, and 143.

3363. Tib. *khro bo'i bzlas pa*.

3364. Tib. *gong bu'i bzlas pa*. See Tsong kha pa, *Rnal 'byor dag rim*, 24a5–6.

3365. See Tsong kha pa, *Bung ba'i re skong*, 27b2–3.

mantra of Vighnāntaka ten thousand times, and the mantra of the descent of wisdom a hundred thousand times. You should likewise recite an additional one tenth of the total number for each mantra and perform a fire ritual. Thus you will complete the required number of recitations. When you recite in order to attain siddhis, you should recite the mantra more than ten million times until you receive the blessings of the deity and achieve signs of attaining lesser, intermediate, or greater siddhis. [164b]

As for the mantras recited, the *Jewel Rosary* teaches that the heart mantras of the five tathāgatas and the four mothers are their mantras of sending forth[3366] without the seed syllables; and the heart mantras of the other deities are their mantras of sending forth with their seed syllables, between *oṃ āḥ hūṃ phaṭ svāhā*. The essence mantras are seed syllables alone between *oṃ āḥ hūṃ phaṭ svāhā*.[3367] But these explanations are unreliable, and their identification of the essence mantra explicitly contradicts the *Guhyasamāja Tantra*,[3368] and they are thus inappropriate. EARLY TIBETAN LAMAS explain these mantras in various ways, but their explanations seem simply untrustworthy.[3369]

Ārya Nāgārjuna and his disciples did not explain the mantras to be recited[3370] in any clear, explicit way, but Master Abhayākaragupta[3371] taught that the heart mantra is the name mantra of the respective deity with the seed syllable interspersed with the three syllables *oṃ āḥ hūṃ*.[3372] This method is the most appropriate.

Regarding the essence mantra, the *Guhyasamāja Tantra* teaches: "From his vajra body, speech, and mind [the Blessed One] brought forth this supreme innermost essence, *vajradhṛk*."[3373] Thus the essence mantra is the name mantra

3366. This is the mantra with which each of the deities is sent forth during the Supreme King of Maṇḍalas [150b3–151a3].

3367. Ratnākaraśānti, *Rin chen phreng ba, Ratnāvalī*, Tōh 1826, 71a4–b4.

3368. See the second paragraph below.

3369. See Bu ston, *Mdor byas 'grel chen*, 84b5–7, who himself refers to some Tibetan lamas.

3370. See Tsong kha pa, *Rnal 'byor dag rim*, 24b2–25a2.

3371. Abhayākaragupta, *Dkyil chog rdo rje phreng ba, Vajrāvalī Maṇḍalavidhi*, Tōh 3140, 18a1–7; Mori 2009, §10.8–9, 133–135, and his *Rdzogs pa'i rnal 'byor gyi phreng ba, Niṣpannayogāvalī*, Tōh 3141, 99b5–7; Sanskrit, Tibetan, and English translation in Lokesh Chandra and Nirmala Sharma 2015, 36–37.

3372. For example, the heart mantra of Akṣobhya is *oṃ āḥ vajradhṛk hūṃ hūṃ*. *Vajradhṛk* is his name mantra, *hūṃ* is his seed syllable, and these are preceded by *oṃ āḥ* and followed by *hūṃ*.

3373. *Guhyasamāja Tantra*, chap. 1, Tōh 442; Zhol 4a3; Stog 5b3; Dunh 4b1–2; Fremantle 1971, 182; Matsunaga 1978, 6.

only, while *oṃ āḥ hūṃ* is the heart-essence of the suchness of all deities. As for the root mantra or garland mantras,[3374] the *Guhyasamāja Tantra* teaches the garland mantra of the four mothers and the nine fierce deities,[3375] while the garland mantras of the remaining deities are taught in other tantras.[3376]

By practicing voiced recitation in this way, you take in the path the fruit of the meditation that corresponds to the enlightened speech of the nirmāṇakāya who teaches the Dharma.

Dissolving into Clear Light and Arising in Response to the Invocation with a Song[3377]

When the nirmāṇakāyas complete the actual deeds of their bodies, speech, and minds in this buddhafield,[3378] and no disciples remain to be guided by their actual bodies in the buddhafield, they pass into nirvāṇa. [165a] The meditation that corresponds to this is the entry of the principal father-mother into ultimate truth, which is termed "dissolution into suchness." Yet SOME INDIANS[3379] such as the author of the *Intense Illuminating Lamp*,[3380] maintain that, as evinced in other works, the fire of great passion dissolves the principal father-mother into a drop. THESE people do not have the least idea about the method of entering into clear light maintained by Ārya Nāgārjuna and his disciples.

In other traditions, such as the Hevajra and the school of Jñānapāda, the invocation of the one dissolved with a song corresponds to the stages of saṃsāric birth as its ground of purification. OTHER SYSTEMS maintain that the dissolution of the principal father-mother corresponds to parents on the ground of purification, and so forth. But as already explained at great length,

3374. Tib. *rtsa sngags* and *'phreng sngags*.

3375. *Guhyasamāja Tantra*, chap. 14, Tōh 442.

3376. Here too, in the two last paragraphs Mkhas grub rje follows Bu ston, *Mdor byas 'grel chen*, 84b7–85a4.

3377. See Tsong kha pa, *Rnal 'byor dag rim*, 25a2–b6.

3378. As noted above [159a], the meditation on the Supreme King of Maṇḍalas corresponds to the deeds of the body which acts for the sake of others by displaying various emanations, the meditative recitations of mantras correspond to the deeds of speech of the nirmāṇakāya teaching the Dharma, and the yoga of the subtle drop corresponds to deeds of the mind.

3379. This is based on Bu ston, *Mdor byas 'grel chen*, 86a3–4, who mentions in this context some paṇḍitas do not share the tradition of Abhayākaragupta.

3380. Bhavyakīrti, *Rab tu sgron gsal*, *Prakāśikā*, Tōh 1793.

this meditation on dissolution and arising does not correspond to the ground of purification, but to the fruit of the path itself.

There are two methods of entering into clear light in this context, gradual and instantaneous. When entering gradually into clear light,[3381] the mother dissolves into the father, the father samayasattva dissolves into the jñānasattva, the jñānasattva[3382] dissolves into the samādhisattva, the vowel sign *ū* of the samādhisattva dissolves into the *ha*, the body of the *ha* dissolves into its own head [the horizontal line of the *ha*], the head into the crescent moon, the crescent moon into the drop which dissolves into the *nāda*, and the *nāda* dissolves into clear light. In this way all parts of your body gradually gather into your heart and enter into clear light. When entering instantaneously into clear light, meditate on the triple sattvas together with the consort dissolving instantaneously into clear light. [165b]

However, the main purpose of the repeated meditation during the creation stage on the dissolution of the display of the rūpakāya into clear light is to ripen the roots for the manifestation of the innate wisdom during the completion stage, upon the dissolution of the actual and concordant illusory bodies into the actual and metaphoric clear lights. And it is the heart [into which everything dissolves during the creation stage] where the ultimate clear light of the completion stage arises. Since the dissolution during the creation stage corresponds to the meditative stages of the dissolution of the illusory body into clear light during the completion stage, the gradual method of dissolution in the present context is considered best.

To explain this, the *Concise Sādhana* teaches: "Once again mantrins should cause themselves to enter into suchness,"[3383] but these lines do not explain precisely how to enter clear light. The main purpose of the citation is to bring to mind the method for maintaining the divine identity of the dharmakāya as explained above.[3384]

When the actual bodies of the nirmāṇakāyas have no more disciples left to guide in this buddhafield, the four goddesses beyond measure invoke them once more to display the deed of awakening in other world realms. In correspondence with this, you should meditate on arising in response to the invocation with a song. The invocation by the four goddesses as the four pure qualities

3381. See Tsong kha pa, *Gsang mngon*, 68a6–b2.

3382. Reading *sems* for *sens* in our text.

3383. Nāgārjuna, *Mdor byas, Piṇḍīkrama Sādhana*, Tōh 1796, 9b6; L 204cd; T 200cd.

3384. See [96a].

beyond measure[3385] states of mind, signifies that you are conditioned by great compassion—the nature of the four qualities beyond measure. Visualize that being invoked, you arise instantaneously from the clear light as the deity body consisting of the triple sattvas. This meditation corresponds to the display of the deed of awakening in other buddhafields out of great compassion.

The four verses of invocation are "O Vajra Mind, the lord dwelling in the realm of sentient beings," and so forth.[3386] [166a] To understand the meaning of these five verses consult the commentary on the *Guhyasamāja Tantra*.[3387] I will write no more about these verses here in order not to prolong the book.

Praises, Offerings, and Tasting the Nectar

There are three sections here: (1) praises, (2) offerings, and (3) tasting the nectar.

When a nirmāṇakāya displays the deed of awakening in other buddhafields, all beings there utter with great fervor praises to the buddha who appears for the first time in a world that has never known his like; then they worship him with manifold exquisite offerings. In accepting them, the buddha becomes the recipient of offerings from the beings in that world. In correspondence, you [as the buddha] should sing the praises, make offerings to yourself, and taste the nectar.

Praises

Imagine the entire assembly of the maṇḍala deities echoing your praises and proclaiming that you have been endowed with all the qualities of the five tathāgata families. You should offer praises with the fives verses taught in the *Guhyasamāja Tantra* and cited in the *Concise Sādhana*: "Akṣobhya Vajra, endowed with supreme wisdom,"[3388] and so forth. To understand the meaning

3385. Our text here is unclear, and a suggested reading would be *tshad med ba'i rnam par dag pa'i*.

3386. See the *Guhyasamāja Tantra*, chap. 17, Tōh 442; Zhol 47a7–b5; Stog 79b7–80b2; Dunh 88a1b4; Fremantle 1971, vv. 72–75; and Matsunaga 1978, vv. 72–75; Nāgārjuna's *Mdor byas, Piṇḍīkrama Sādhana*, Tōh 1796, 9b7–10a4; L 206–209; T 202–205. Note that the Skt. is different. See also Tsong kha pa, *Gsang mngon*, 68b3–69a5.

3387. Candrakīrti, *Sgron gsal, Pradīpoddyotanaṭīkā*, Tōh 1785, 195a6–196b4; Chakravarti 1984, 224–225. See also Tsong kha pa, *Sgron gsal mchan*, 505a4–508a1.

3388. *Guhyasamāja Tantra*, chap. 17, Tōh 442; Zhol 40b5–7; Stog 68b5–69a2; Dunh beginning missing 76a1–3; Fremantle 1971, vv. 1–5; and Matsunaga 1978, vv. 1–5. Nāgārjuna, *Mdor byas, Piṇḍīkrama Sādhana*, Tōh 1796, 10a4–7; L 211–215; T 207–211, with some differences. See Tsong kha pa, *Gsang mngon*, 69b1–6.

of these five verses, consult the commentary on the *Guhyasamāja Tantra*.[3389] I will write no more about these verses here in order not to prolong the book.

Offerings

The methods of blessing and generating the offerings have already been explained.[3390] Now you should offer them to yourself while maintaining divine identity with Vajradhara or Akṣobhya. For instance, while making the five offerings to the senses of the desire realm,[3391] you should visualize Rūpavajrā[3392] holding a pure and clear mirror in her soft-as-lotus hand, gazing at you with peaceful eyes; her large heaving breasts, squeezed tightly together, are covered with dangling strings of pearls; her garments, slightly lifted, reveal her beautiful lower body. [166b] Visualize the sky realm filled with numerous such ladies. As you meditate by gazing at their bodies, a great inner bliss will be born in you, and you will develop a powerful certainty that all appearances are empty of intrinsic nature. Practice understanding that all three spheres [the offerer, the offerings, and the receiver of the offerings] arise as a display of bliss and emptiness. Likewise, you should understand how this points to the experience of the other sense-offerings.[3393]

Tasting the Nectar of the Inner Offerings[3394]

In the context of the unexcelled tantra, the inner offerings of the five meats and five nectars are purified, transformed, and set ablaze in profusion.[3395] They

3389. Candrakīrti, *Sgron gsal, Pradīpoddyotanaṭīkā*, Tōh 1785, 175a1–b3; Chakravarti 1984, 203. See also Tsong kha pa, *Sgron gsal mchan*, 462a4–463a6.

3390. See [14b–16a] above.

3391. Tib. *'dod yon lnga* or *'dod pa'i yon tan lnga*, Skt. *pañcakāmaguna*. See Āryadeva, *Spyod bsdus, Caryāmelāpakapradīpa*, chap. 10, Tōh 1803, 101b5–6; Sanskrit, Tibetan, and English translation in Wedemeyer 2007, B: 66b; Sanskrit and Tibetan in Pandey 2000, 92 and 339–340.

3392. Tib. Gzugs rdo rje ma, Eng. Vajra Lady of Forms.

3393. The four additional offerings of sounds, scents, tastes, and objects of touch are described in Āryadeva, *Spyod bsdus, Caryāmelāpakapradīpa*, chap. 10, Tōh 1803, 101b5–102a5; Sanskrit, Tibetan, and English translation in Wedemeyer 2007, B: 66b–67a; Sanskrit and Tibetan in Pandey 2000, 92–93 and 340–341.

3394. See Tsong kha pa, *Sngags rim chen mo*, chap. 12, 527–530.

3395. These terms are explained below on [170a–171a].

are offered to satisfy the deities and the lama, and then you yourself taste them as well.

[Diverse Methods for Making the Inner Offerings]

The inner offerings, as taught in most tantras and treatises of the mahāsiddhas, are indispensable. Nevertheless, individual treatises offer a great many diverse explanations about defining the five meats and five nectars, identifying them with the five male and female tathāgatas, describing the cardinal and intermediate directions within the skull at which they are generated, and the seed syllables with which they are marked.

According to the *Maṇḍala Vajra Garland*[3396] and the *Cluster of Instructions*,[3397] which clarify the view of the *Saṃpuṭa Tantra*,[3398] the seed syllables of the five meats are *hūṃ*, *bruṃ*, *āṃ*, *hrīḥ*, and *khaṃ*, and those of the five nectars are *bruṃ*, *hūṃ*, *hrīḥ*, and *tāṃ*.[3399] The *Maṇḍala Vajra Garland*, the *Cluster of Instructions*, the *Saṃpuṭa Tantra*, the *Four Chapters Tantra*,[3400] and the *Saṃvarodaya Tantra*[3401] offer no specific instructions about the cardinal and intermediate directions where they are generated.

The *Red Yamāri Tantra*[3402] explains that the five meats called *go ku da ha na*[3403] in the nature of the five tathāgatas, Vairocana and so forth, arise respectively from the seed syllables *bruṃ*, *oṃ*, *jriṃ*, *khaṃ*, and *hūṃ* and are placed in the east, south, west, north, and in the center. [167a] Then the five nectars named *bi ra śu ma me*,[3404] arising from the seed syllables *laṃ*, *maṃ*, *baṃ*, and

3396. Abhayākaragupta, *Dkyil chog rdo rje phreng ba*, *Vajrāvalī Maṇḍalavidhi*, Tōh 3140, 89a1–2; Mori 2009, §48.1.2, 494–495.

3397. Abhayākaragupta, *Man ngag snye ma*, *Āmnāyamañjarī*, chap. 34, Tōh 1198, 297a1.

3398. Abhayākaragupta, *Man ngag snye ma*, *Āmnāyamañjarī*, is a commentary on the *Saṃpuṭa Tantra*, Tōh 381.

3399. These are only four syllables, but since both the meats and nectar contain the great meat, the seed syllable of the great meat is added here. This is explained below.

3400. The *Gdan bzhi*, *Catuḥpīṭha*, Tōh 428.

3401. The *Sdom 'byung*, *Saṃvarodaya Tantra*, Tōh 373.

3402. *Gshin rje'i gshed dmar po'i rgyud*, *Raktayamāri Tantra*, Tōh 474, 203b6.

3403. This is an acronym for *go*, cow; *kukkura*, dog; *dantin*, elephant; *haya*, horse; and *nara*, human.

3404. This is an acronym for *viṭ*, excrement; *rakta*, blood; *śukra*, semen; *māṃsa*, great meat, Tib. *sha chen*; and *me* is perhaps *mu* for *mūtra*, urine, Tib. *dri chu*.

taṃ,[3405] are set clockwise in the four intermediate directions and in the center beginning from the southeast, each nectar marked with the syllable that is uttered as its name.

The *Cluster of Instructions* does not specify explicitly at which intermediate direction to generate the nectars, but it does explain that: "Those visualized as the five tathāgatas in this aspect of[3406] great wisdom are the five lamps and the five hooks,"[3407] thereby implying that the five lamps and the five hooks are the five tathāgatas, and specifically that Akṣobhya, Vairocana, Ratnasambhava, Amitābha, and Amoghasiddhi are the five hooks in sequence. It is thus evident that the five meats are generated from their first syllables.

After this generate the five meats, the great meats, and so forth, from *hūṃ*, *bruṃ*, and so forth successively, marked with these syllables in succession, beginning at the center and proceeding dextrally through the four directions. Likewise, in the four intermediate directions from southeast to northeast, generate successively the five nectars, excrement, and so forth, from the syllables *bruṃ* and so forth, marked with these syllables. Only four seed syllables are specified with respect to the five nectars, because the great meat, included in the five meats, is also one of the five nectars. This is indicated in the *Cluster of Instructions* and the *Maṇḍala Vajra Garland*.[3408]

The *Drop of Great Seal*,[3409] the *Five Deity Cakrasaṃvara Sādhana* by the Mahāsiddha Vajraghaṇṭa,[3410] and the Mahāsiddha *Kambala[3411] all explain that the five meats as well the five nectars are the five tathāgatas. The *Precious Lamp Commentary on Difficult Points in the Black Yamāri Tantra*,[3412] [167b]

3405. The letters *laṃ*, *māṃ*, *pāṃ*, and *tāṃ* are the seed syllables of the four mothers, Locanā, Māmakī, Pāṇḍaravāsinī, and Tārā respectively.

3406. As explained in the previous lines of Abhayākaragupta, *Man ngag snye ma*, *Āmnāyamañjarī*, Tōh 1198.

3407. Abhayākaragupta, *Man ngag snye ma*, *Āmnāyamañjarī*, Tōh 1198, 293b7–294a1.

3408. Abhayākaragupta, *Dkyil chog rdo rje phreng ba*, *Vajrāvalī Maṇḍalavidhi*, Tōh 3140; and *Man ngag snye ma*, *Āmnāyamañjarī*, Tōh 1198, cited above.

3409. *Phyag chen thig le'i rgyud*, *Mahāmudrātilaka Tantra*, Tōh 420.

3410. Vajraghaṇṭa, *Bcom ldan 'das bde mchog yid bzhin nor bu*, *Bhagavancakrasaṃvaracintāmaṇi*, Tōh 1437.

3411. *Kambala, Lwa ba pa, *Bde mchog gi sgrub thabs gtsug nor*, *Cakrasaṃvara Sādhana Ratnacūḍāmaṇi*, Tōh 1443.

3412. Ratnākaraśānti, *Gshin rje dgra nag po'i dka' 'grel rin po che'i sgron ma*, *Kṛṣṇayamāri Pañjikāratnapradīpa*, Tōh 1919.

Atiśa's commentary on Lūyīpāda's *Cakrasaṃvara Sādhana*,[3413] and Jayasena's *Sādhana of Ḍākārṇava*[3414] stipulate that all ten substances are generated from the first syllables of their respective names.

Thus there are two different methods with regard to the seed syllables from which the five meats and the five nectars are generated: either from the seed syllables of the female and male tathāgatas or from the respective name syllables of the ten substances. There are likewise two systems of placing the ten substances: either in five locations, four cardinal directions and their center, or nine locations, the eight cardinal and intermediate directions and their center. Regarding[3415] the latter system, there are likewise two methods of placing the substances in the nine locations: either placing the five meats in the cardinal directions and the five nectars in the intermediate directions or vice versa, placing the nectars in the cardinal directions and the meats in the intermediate directions. There are also two methods for relating the substances to the tathāgatas: either by regarding meats as male and nectars as female tathāgatas, or by regarding nectars as male and meats as female tathāgatas.

Although there is no disagreement concerning the identification of the five meats and the first four of the five nectars—excrement, urine, semen,[3416] and blood—there are many differing positions about the fifth nectar. Nāropa, Vaidyapāda, and others explain that the fifth nectar is great meat while Bhavabhadra in his *Commentary on the Four Chapters Tantra* explains that it is dry phlegm[3417] and mucus.[3418] But in the *Saṃvarodaya Tantra* the lesser fifth nectar is fat originating from meat,[3419] the intermediate is marrow and spinal fluid originating from the hollow canals [in the bones], and the best is the brain originating from the head.[3420] Synonyms of the five meats are the

3413. Dīpaṅkaraśrījñāna, *Mngon par rtogs pa rnam par 'byed pa*, *Abhisamayavibhaṅga*, Tōh 1490, 197b6. This is a commentary on Lūyīpāda, *Bcom ldan 'das mngon par rtogs pa*, *Bhagavadabhisamaya*, Tōh 1427; Sakurai 1998.

3414. Jayasena, Rgyal ba'i sde, *Mkha' 'gro rgya mtsho'i sgrub thabs padma rā ga'i gter*, *Ḍākārṇava Sādhana Padmarāganidhi*, Tōh 1516.

3415. Reading *yang* for *yar* in our text.

3416. Reading *dkar* for *dgar* in our text.

3417. Reading *lud pa* for *lung pa* in our text.

3418. Bhavabhadra, *Gdan bzhi pa'i 'grel pa dran pa'i rgyu mtshan*, *Catuḥpīṭha Smṛtinibandhaṭīkā*, Tōh 1607, 202a4. See also Szántó 2012, vol. 1, 358.

3419. Reading *tshil bu* for *tshil phu* in our text.

3420. *Sdom 'byung*, *Saṃvarodaya Tantra*, chap. 25, Tōh 373, 297a6; Stog 109a1–2; not in Tsuda 1973.

five hooks and the five lamps, because they draw forth the attainments and illuminate them.[3421]

There are four positions regarding the skull: *Kambala describes it as all of a piece, white on the outside and red on the inside.[3422] Some maintain that it consists of three parts and is white in color. [168a] Some say it is white in color but are unclear as to its components. Others are unclear about both.

There are two methods for generating the ten substances within the skull: either seating the substances on a throne or not on a throne. Those who visualize thrones for the substances meditate either on a lotus seat or a lunar seat. Some place the vowels and consonants on or around the ten substances and some do not. Some place a *khaṭvāṅga*[3423] in the space above the substances and some do not. Some place a lunar disk marked with a vajra in the space above, some place a solar disk marked with a vajra and some place no disk at all but only the syllable. So there are three methods here. Thus there are many such systems.

[The Method of the Opponents]

The *Sādhana*s of Ārya Nāgārjuna and his disciples do not teach any ritual method for the nectars. Hence, SOME TIBETAN SCHOLARS maintain that Master Abhayākaragupta's[3424] explanation based on the *Saṃpuṭa Tantra* is the generation ritual of the nectars for all three traditions of Guhyasamāja, Cakrasaṃvara, and Hevajra. Therefore they take the method of Abhayākaragupta for generating the five meats and five nectars to be the ritual method for the nectars in the Ārya tradition of the Guhyasamāja.

Their method proceeds as follows: From a yellow *ha*, a white *hoḥ*, and a blue *hrīḥ* on the substances, they generate Amitābha, Vairocana, and Akṣobhya respectively. They visualize light-rays emanating from them, gather them back, and dissolve them in the skull, thus purifying them in due order from all flaws of color, smell, and taste. [168b] Then they visualize a light-ray emanating from the *hūṃ*s on their hearts, a wind stirring, fire igniting, and the substances together with the syllables within the skull melting and boiling. Then they

3421. In other words, attain and manifest the siddhis.

3422. *Kambala, Lwa ba pa, *Bde mchog gi sgrub thabs gtsug nor*, *Cakrasaṃvara Sādhana Ratnacūḍāmaṇi*, Tōh 1443. It seems that our text here follows Tsong kha pa, *'Dod 'jo*, 173a6–175a2. Reading *nang* for *nad* in our text.

3423. A staff with a skull at the top.

3424. See Abhayākaragupta, *Man ngag snye ma*, *Āmnāyamañjarī*, chap. 34, Tōh 1198, 297a1–3. See also his *Dkyil chog rdo rje phreng ba*, *Vajrāvalī*, Tōh 3140, 89a1–4; Mori 2009, §48.1.2, 494–495.

visualize the syllable *hūṃ* rising from the steam and turning into a *khaṭvāṅga* marked with a vajra and with *hūṃ*,[3425] and the heat under the *khaṭvāṅga* melting and dissolving them inside the skull. They repeat this three times, and visualize the substances thereby turning into the nature of nectar.

Then they visualize the syllable *oṃ* over the nectar transforming into a lunar disk marked with an upside-down syllable *oṃ*.[3426] Above it they stack the syllables *oṃ āḥ hūṃ* one on top of the other. Then they emanate a light-ray from these syllables invoking the wisdom-nectar of the buddhas and bodhisattvas. They visualize this wisdom-nectar dissolving into the *oṃ āḥ hūṃ*, and thereby these three syllables melt one after the other and dissolve into the lunar disk, and the lunar disk melts and dissolves into the skull. Having recited the three syllables three times, they bless [the blend in the skull] transforming it into nectar that is splendidly clear in the nature of quicksilver. So they maintain.[3427]

But such a profusion of sundry ritual practices concerning the nectars appears to be merely a TIBETAN fabrication that does not concur with any of the tantras or Indian treatises. YOU who are deprived of transmitted instructions on how to apply the root tantra and its commentaries to the practice have no idea whatsoever on how to meditate on the ritual practice of the five meats and five nectars according to the tradition of the Guhyasamāja.

[Our Method, Which Follows the Guhyasamāja Tradition]

Although Ārya Nāgārjuna and his disciples do not give precise instructions about the five meats and five nectars, relying on the nectar from the mouth of our Vajra Master who is Bodhicittavajra, I will entrust you with the unexcelled understanding of the ritual practice of the nectars according to our tradition of the Guhyasamāja, which correctly applies the root and explanatory tantras to the practice. Attend to me and listen well![3428]

The sixteenth chapter of the *Guhyasamāja Tantra* teaches:[3429] "The wise should eat elephant[3430] meat, horse meat, and great meat and then offer it to all

3425. According to Tsong kha pa's *Sngags rim chen mo*, chap. 12, 529, the *khaṭvāṅga* is marked with a vajra.

3426. Reading *thur* for *thub* in our text.

3427. See Tsong kha pa's *Sngags rim chen mo*, chap. 12, 529–530.

3428. In the following explanations, Mkhas grub rje follows Tsong kha pa, *Mtha' gcod*, 136b4–138a3.

3429. *Guhyasamāja Tantra*, Tōh 442; Zhol 38a7–b1; Stog 64b5–6; Dunh 71a1–2; Fremantle 1971, vv. 49–50; Matsunaga 1978, vv. 37cd–39. Zhol has *bsgoms* for *bsgom* in our text.

3430. Tib. *glang po*, Skt. *hasti*, elephant or bull.

the mantras.[3431] [169a] By doing so they please the lords. They should explain the maṇḍala to their vajra disciples on a daily basis alongside the rituals of excrement, urine, and meat as well as the secret vajra words.[3432] As soon as they meditate on the syllable *oṃ* in every mantra, [the meats and nectars] are set ablaze." These verses clearly show that you yourself consume the five meats and the five nectars[3433] and offer them to each deity with the mantra. Furthermore the way to perform the rituals of the five meats and the five nectars is clearly established here: purify, transform, and set them ablaze in profusion.[3434] Having done so, you should consume them as vital to the meditation.

Hence in the explanatory *Later Tantra* the Bodhisattvas Maitreya and others ask:[3435] "How are the five nectars consumed? And what are the five powerful ones?" The tathāgatas replied:[3436] "The five impurities appear in the dharmas of ordinary bodies. When they are blessed by the five wisdoms, they are proclaimed as the five nectars. Blazing in profusion, flaming, radiating, and appearing in a perceptible form,[3437] these five nectars should be consumed by the yogis through the practice of the mantra body." The first four lines explain that the *dharmas* arising from the *body* are the five nectars. These five are *ordinary* and *impure*, but *when blessed* as the nature of *the five wisdoms, they are proclaimed as the five nectars*. This indicates that you should bless the five nectars by generating them from the seed syllables of the five tathāgatas,

3431. Candrakīrti, *Sgron gsal, Pradīpoddyotanaṭīkā*, Tōh 1785, 166a7, Chakravarti 1984, 194, glosses *mantras* with "deities."

3432. Reading *gsang* for *gsad* in our text.

3433. Candrakīrti, *Sgron gsal, Pradīpoddyotanaṭīkā*, Tōh 1785, 166b2–3, Chakravarti 1984, 194, glosses *excrement and urine* with "the five nectars" and *meat* with "the five types of meat."

3434. Tib. *sbyang rtogs sbar gsum*, the Sanskrit according to Chakravarti 1984, 194, *śodhite, prabodhite*, and *jvalati*; Nāgārjuna's *Mdor byas, Piṇḍīkrama Sādhana*, Tōh 1796, L 222, has *śodhaya, bodhaya*, and *jvālaya*. In his commentary on the later, the *Rim pa lnga'i don mdor bshad pa, Pañcakramārthaṭippaṇi*, Tōh 1813, 168a2–3, Muniśrībhadra has: Tibetan, *sbyong, rtogs*, and *rab tu 'bar bar byed pa* and Sanskrit, Jiang and Tomabechi 1996, 35, *śodhanam, bodhanam*, and *prajvālanam*.

3435. *Rgyud phyi ma, Uttara Tantra*, Tōh 443, 149a5, Matsunaga 1978, v. 19cd. D has *ci* for *ji*.

3436. *Rgyud phyi ma, Uttara Tantra*, Tōh 443, 153b5–6, Matsunaga 1978, vv. 128–129. D has *snang bar byed* for *snang bar bya* and Zhol and Stog have *gzungs snang ba* for *gzungs snang la* in our text. These and the following verses of the *Rgyud phyi ma* are also cited in Tsong kha pa's *Mtha' gcod*, 136b5–137a3.

3437. In his *Mtha' gcod*, 137b3–4, Tsong kha pa explains how each of these qualifiers "blazing, flaming, radiating, and appearing in a perceptible form" are related to steps in his *Gsang mngon*, 9b5–10b1.

that is to say, the five wisdoms, and by marking them with the seed syllables of the five tathāgatas.

How to identify the five nectars, and to which tathāgata family does each pertain? The *Vajra Garland Explanatory Tantra* teaches:[3438] "Consuming the five nectars, you attain all siddhis. [169b] How do the five supreme nectars relate to the tathāgatas? The five[3439] tathāgatas, Vairocana, Akṣobhya, Amoghasiddhi, Amitābha, and *Ratnadhvaja,[3440] are the essential nature of the five nectars. Blood is proclaimed as Lord Ratna, semen as Amitābha, Amoghasiddhi as meat, Akṣobhya as vajra water, and excrement as Vairocana. These are the five supreme nectars." This clearly shows how the five nectars pertain to the five tathāgatas, and also that the fifth nectar is great meat.

Regarding the meaning of the latter four lines in the above citation of the *Later Tantra*: "*Blazing in profusion, flaming*," and so forth: after purifying the nectars, transforming, and setting them ablaze in profusion, you *should consume* them, while maintaining the divine identity of the *practice of the mantra body* of your deity. How do you purify the nectars, transform, and set them ablaze in profusion? The *Later Tantra* explains this in detail:[3441] "Visualize a vajra rising from *hūṃ*, abiding in space." Nāropa's commentary[3442] on the *Later Tantra* explains that the vajra abides on a solar disk, Muniśrībhadra[3443] explains that the color of the vajra is white, and Ratnākaraśānti[3444] says that it is blue and upright.[3445]

The *Later Tantra* continues with the line:[3446] "Meditate on the lotus arising from *āḥ* beneath." Accordingly, you should meditate on a red lotus arising from the *āḥ* under the five nectars; or else, since it is asserted in several places

3438. *Rgyud rdo rje phreng ba, Vajramālā Tantra*, chap. 61, Tōh 445, 266a4–6. D has *bdud rtsi lnga ni* for *bdud rtsi lnga yi, lnga pa ni* for *lnga pa 'di*, and *bdud rtsi lnga ni* for *bdud rtsi lnga yi* in our text.

3439. Reading *lnga po* for *lnga pa* in our text.

3440. Rin chen rgyal mtshan.

3441. *Rgyud phyi ma, Uttara Tantra*, Tōh 443, 153b6–7, Matsunaga 1978, v. 130ab.

3442. *Yaśobhadra/Nāropa, *Gsang ba thams cad kyi sgron ma'i rgya cher 'grel pa, Sarvaguhyapradīpaṭīkā*, Tōh 1787, 224a6.

3443. Muniśrībhadra, *Rim pa lnga'i don mdor bshad pa, Pañcakramārthaṭippaṇi*, Tōh 1813, 168a2; Sanskrit, Jiang and Tomabechi 1996, 35.

3444. This is found in Tsong kha pa's *Mtha' gcod*, 137b1.

3445. Reading *'greng bar* for *'gred bar* in our text.

3446. *Rgyud phyi ma, Uttara Tantra*, Tōh 443, 153b7, Matsunaga 1978, v. 130cd.

that the lotus vessel is a skull,[3447] you may also meditate on a skull arising from the syllable *āḥ*. Both systems are taught. The *Later Tantra* continues:[3448] "At the center of the lotus place the nectar marked with *oṃ*." This indicates that you should place the five nectars at the center of the lotus inside the skull and that all five nectars are marked collectively with the syllable *oṃ*. [170a]

Nine lines further down, the *Later Tantra* teaches:[3449] "Thus you should eat the five powerful ones." Taking this line to explain the present context, *the five powerful ones* are the five meats, *thus* means that they are generated from the seed syllables of the five tathāgatas. Mark them with the seed syllables of the five tathāgatas and place them on a lotus that arises from an *āḥ*, at the center of the skull that arises from an *āḥ*. Consume them through the practice of the mantra body of your [deity], as explained with regard to the five nectars.

Which of the five meats pertains to which of the tathāgatas? Commenting on the sixth chapter of the *Guhyasamāja Tantra*,[3450] the *Illuminating Lamp*[3451] explains that yogis of the tathāgata family of Akṣobhya eat the great meat[3452] and then: "In order to clarify what the fierce families of tathāgata and so forth consume, the *Guhyasamāja Tantra* teaches 'elephant'[3453] and so forth."[3454] This then clearly identifies the five meats as the families of the five tathāgatas.

Since both the five meats and the five nectars are thus established as the five tathāgatas, in practicing this tradition it is definitely inappropriate to set the tathāgatas in the intermediate directions. This proves that you must place the

3447. *Kye'i rdo rje mkha' 'gro ma dra ba'i sdom pa*, *Hevajra Tantra II*, Tōh 418, 19a3; Snellgrove 1959, II.iii.58b, teaches that in the secret language, "lotus vessel" means skull.

3448. *Rgyud phyi ma*, *Uttara Tantra*, Tōh 443, 153b7, Matsunaga 1978, v. 130ef. D and Stog have *gzhag par* for *bzhag par* in our text.

3449. *Rgyud phyi ma*, *Uttara Tantra*, Tōh 443, 154a1–2, Matsunaga 1978, v. 133b.

3450. *Guhyasamāja Tantra*, chap. 6, Tōh 442; Zhol 10a1–2; Stog 16b1–2; Dunh 16b2; Fremantle 1971, v. 22; Matsunaga 1978, v. 23.

3451. Candrakīrti, *Sgron gsal*, *Pradīpoddyotanaṭīkā*, Tōh 1785, 45b1–2, Chakravarti 1984, 59. D as well as Tsong kha pa's *Sgron gsal mchan* have *khro bo rnams kyi* for *khro bo rnams kyis* in our text.

3452. See Tsong kha pa's *Sgron gsal mchan*, 155a4–156a5.

3453. Tib. *glang po*, Skt. *hasti*, elephant or bull.

3454. *Guhyasamāja Tantra*, chap. 6, Tōh 442; Zhol 10a1–2; Stog 16b1–2; Dunh 16b2; Fremantle 1971, v. 22; Matsunaga 1978, v. 23. Here the *Guhyasamāja Tantra* speaks of eating various meats such as elephant [or bull], horse, and dog meats. In his *Sgron gsal mchan*, 156a3–4, Tsong kha pa explains that yogis of the Vairocana tathāgata family eat elephant [or bull] meat; those of Ratnasambhava, horse meat; those of Amitābha, cow meat; and those of the Amoghasiddhi tathāgata family, dog meat.

two sets of five substances in the four cardinal directions and in the center and also proves that it is therefore preferable, as explained by Muniśrībhadra,[3455] to generate both the five meats and the five nectars from the syllables *bruṃ*, *aṃ*, *jriṃ*, *khaṃ*, and *hūṃ*.[3456]

[Blessing the Nectars]

This section consists of three steps: (1) purifying, (2) transforming, and (3) setting ablaze in profusion:[3457]

[PURIFYING]

First generate the five meats from these syllables in the four cardinal directions and in the center and mark them with their respective syllables. Then generate the five nectars from these five syllables once again in the four cardinal directions and in the center, and mark them with their syllables, and then mark all five nectars collectively with the syllable *oṃ*. [170b]

The *Guhyasamāja Tantra* does not specify that wind and fire are generated under the skull, but Nāropa elucidates the method of doing so in his commentary on the *Later Tantra*.[3458] Muniśrībhadra explains how to generate them from *hūṃ yaṃ hūṃ* and *hūṃ raṃ hūṃ*.[3459] This is appropriate since most of these explanations appear to accord with the method of generating the maṇḍalas of the four elements in individual tantras and in sādhanas of the mahāsiddhas found in other traditions as well.

After this you should ignite them. The method for doing so is imparted in the line of the *Later Tantra*: "Setting ablaze in profusion, [flaming, radiating, and appearing in a perceived form],"[3460] and so forth. A light ray from the *hūṃ* at the nave of the vajra causes the wind to stir and the fire to ignite. *Flaming* means that the fire strikes the skull, and the substances within it boil. *Radiating* is explained in detail in the following line of the *Later Tantra*: "At the

3455. Muniśrībhadra, *Rim pa lnga'i don mdor bshad pa*, *Pañcakramārthaṭippaṇi*, Tōh 1813, 168a1; Jiang and Tomabechi 1996, 35.

3456. For the following instructions, see also Tsong kha pa, *Gsang mngon*, 9a2–b5.

3457. See Tsong kha pa, *Gsang mngon*, 9b5–10b1.

3458. *Yaśobhadra/Nāropa, *Gsang ba thams cad kyi sgron ma'i rgya cher 'grel pa*, *Sarvaguhyapradīpaṭīkā*, Tōh 1787, 224a5.

3459. Muniśrībhadra, *Rim pa lnga'i don mdor bshad pa*, *Pañcakramārthaṭippaṇi*, Tōh 1813, 167b6–7; Jiang and Tomabechi 1996, 35. *Yaṃ* is the seed syllable of wind and *raṃ* of fire.

3460. *Rgyud phyi ma*, *Uttara Tantra*, Tōh 443, 153b6; Matsunaga 1978, v. 129.

center of the lotus, set the nectar marked with *oṃ*."[3461] Immediately after that, as the *Later Tantra* teaches: "By joining the vajra and lotus, [the nectar] flames and satisfies the yogi. It appears in the form of a crystal."[3462] The meaning of *appearing in a perceived form* is explained in the following line: "Nectar arising like a second sun of wisdom."[3463] Therefore the vajra in space[3464] falls into the skull called the "lotus," [stirring] the substances until they "possess a single taste."[3465] The learned Paṇḍita Muniśrībhadra explains that this is the meaning of *joining the vajra and lotus.*[3466]

Thus you should visualize the ten substances that have melted and boiled together in the nature of bodhicitta that arises from joining the vajra and lotus. By tasting this [nectar] and offering it you and all the deities are set ablaze with great bliss. The understanding of the signifier here is a quintessential point. Thus[3467] the vajra with its solar seat falls [into the skull], and stirs the substances, whereby the vajra and the substances possess a single taste and appear crystal clear. [171a] Such is the meaning of the line "The nectar appears in the form of a crystal."[3468]

[Transforming]

Then, when the syllable *āḥ* that marks the anthers of the lotus[3469] within the skull has melted, the nectar of wisdom *appears* yellow-red, in the perceived *form* of a second sun. This is what is meant by *appears in a perceived form* and *nectar arises like a second sun of wisdom.*[3470]

3461. *Rgyud phyi ma, Uttara Tantra,* Tōh 443, 153b7; Matsunaga 1978, v. 130ef. D and Stog have *gzhag par* for *bzhag par* in our text. Cited above [169b].

3462. *Rgyud phyi ma, Uttara Tantra,* Tōh 443, 153b7–154a1; Matsunaga 1978, v. 131abc.

3463. *Rgyud phyi ma, Uttara Tantra,* Tōh 443, 154a1; Matsunaga 1978, v. 131d.

3464. See above [169b].

3465. Tib. *ro mnyam par gyur,* Skt. *samarasībhūtam.*

3466. Muniśrībhadra, *Rim pa lnga'i don mdor bshad pa,* Skt. *Pañcakramārthaṭippaṇi,* Tōh 1813, 168a2; Jiang and Tomabechi 1996, 35.

3467. See Tsong kha pa, *Gsang mngon,* 10a2–3.

3468. *Rgyud phyi ma, Uttara Tantra,* Tōh 443, 153b7–154a1; Matsunaga 1978, v. 131c. Cited on [170b] above.

3469. In Tsong kha pa's *Gsang mngon,* 10a4, as well as his *Mtha' gcod,* 137b4, the lotus and the syllable *āḥ* that marks the lotus both melt.

3470. See the *Rgyud phyi ma, Uttara Tantra,* Tōh 443, 154a1; Matsunaga 1978, v. 131d.

[Setting Ablaze in Profusion]

Immediately following this line, the *Later Tantra* teaches: "Draw the nectar from the world realms in the ten directions with the finest of implements, cast it down into the skull, and consume it as food yoga."[3471] Muniśrībhadra explains the meaning of *the finest of implements* as a hook-like ray of light that emanates from the syllable *oṃ* that marks all five nectars.[3472] This explanation is correct since the meaning of this line appears to be the same in the *Guhyasamāja Tantra*, and the *Illuminating Lamp* comments on this: "As soon as the yogi meditates on the syllable *oṃ* at the beginning of every mantra, they [the five nectars] blaze."[3473]

Therefore you should visualize[3474] a hook-like ray of light emanating from the syllable *oṃ*, drawing the wisdom nectar of all tathāgatas residing in the ten directions of the world realms, and infusing the wisdom nectar into the samaya nectar,[3475] setting it *ablaze*, that is to say, "in profusion."[3476] The *Later Tantra* teaches: "Thus you should eat the five powerful ones,"[3477] and immediately after that: "You should generate them through the three seed syllables, for anything other will not bring attainments."[3478] Hence you must *generate* the [five meats and five nectars] as wisdom-nectar by purifying, transforming, and setting them ablaze in profusion through *the three syllables*. Doing *anything other* than this, as already explained, will *not bring attainments*. The *three syllables* are the *hūṃ* that marks the nave of the vajra above, the *oṃ* that marks all five nectars collectively in the middle, [171b] and the *āḥ* that marks the anthers of the lotus below. The line "through the practice of mantra body

3471. *Rgyud phyi ma, Uttara Tantra*, Tōh 443, 154a1; Matsunaga 1978, v. 132.

3472. Muniśrībhadra, *Rim pa lnga'i don mdor bshad pa, Pañcakramārthaṭippaṇi*, Tōh 1813, 168a1–4; Jiang and Tomabechi 1996, 35.

3473. *Guhyasamāja Tantra*, chap. 16, Tōh 442; Zhol 38b1; Stog 64b6; Dunh 71a1–2; Fremantle 1971, v. 50ef; and Matsunaga 1978, v. 39cd. Cited in [169a] above. Candrakīrti, *Sgron gsal, Pradīpoddyotanaṭīkā*, Tōh 1785, 166b4–5; Chakravarti 1984, 194.

3474. See Tsong kha pa, *Gsang mngon*, 10a4–b1; Tsong kha pa's *Mtha' gcod*, 137b5–6; and Muniśrībhadra, *Rim pa lnga'i don mdor bshad pa, Pañcakramārthaṭippaṇi*, Tōh 1813, 168a3–4; Jiang and Tomabechi 1996, 35.

3475. Tib. *dam tshig gi bdud rtsi*, Skt. *samayāmṛta*.

3476. Tib. *'bar bar byas ba ste mang por spel ba'o*.

3477. *Rgyud phyi ma, Uttara Tantra*, Tōh 443, 154a1–2; Matsunaga 1978, v. 133b. Cited above [170a].

3478. *Rgyud phyi ma, Uttara Tantra*, Tōh 443, 154a2; Matsunaga 1978, v. 133cd.

[of the deity]"[3479] also indicates that when you consume the food and drink blessed as the five nectars, you—visualized as the body of the deity—bless your tongue and throat and so forth.

The nectars are blessed in this way not only for the sake of the inner offerings and tormas; this method is essential in several instances, such as the empowerment of the nectar pills in this tradition as well as the empowerment of pills, essence-extracts, and the wheel of gathering[3480] taught in the *Guhyasamāja Tantra*, the *Request of the Four Goddesses*, and so forth. Therefore the blessing of the nectars is explained in detail.

Before you offer the nectars blessed in this way, as the *Root Tantra of Cakrasaṃvara* teaches: "The skillful[3481] yogi always tastes them by joining the tips of the thumb and the ring finger."[3482] Accordingly, you should join your thumb and ring fingers, and stir dextrally three times. When the primordial gods churned the ocean by using Mount Meru as their churning stick, the nectar appeared at the center. Accordingly, visualize the thumb of your left hand as Mount Meru arising from *suṃ*, and your ring finger as an ocean resting on the earth arising from *kṣuṃ*; take the essence of the nectar from the center of the swirl and offer it. Such is the explanation in the *Four Chapters Tantra*.[3483]

In which order should you offer the nectar? Offer first to the lama and then to the deities of the maṇḍala, beginning with the principal father-mother. Then join your thumb and ring finger, take some nectar, place it on the tip of your tongue and taste it, for as cited in the treatise of the Mahāsiddha *Kambala: [172a] "The wise ones taste the ritually prepared nectar. After first offering it to the lama, then to Heruka, and after that, to his consort, they themselves taste it. This is how they make offerings in order to become vajra

3479. *Rgyud phyi ma, Uttara Tantra*, Tōh 443, 153b6; Matsunaga 1978, v. 129c. Cited above [169a].

3480. Tib. *tshogs kyi 'khor lo*, Skt. *gaṇacakra*.

3481. Reading *rig pas* for *rigs pas* in our text.

3482. The version cited here is from the *Mngon brjod bla ma, Abhidhānottara*, chap. 48, Tōh 369, 337a7–b1. D has *rim pas* for *rigs pas* in our text. A similar verse appears in the *Bde mchog rtsa rgyud, Cakrasaṃvara Tantra*, chap. 1, Tōh 368, v. 12, 213a7–b1; Pandey 2002, 25.

3483. *Gdan bzhi, Catuḥpīṭha Tantra*, Tōh 428, 198b1–2; Sanskrit and English in Szántó 2012, 2.3.131–132.

holders. Through the quintessence[3484] of all yogas the substances turn into the five nectars. Through this practice they will become equal to Vajrasattva."[3485]

There is not even a speck of proof either in scripture or in reason for the claim that when you practice self-generation, you alone should taste the nectars, and that it is inappropriate to extend the inner offerings to the lamas and the deities of the maṇḍala. Since by pleasing the supreme field for accumulating merit with exquisite inner offerings you gather an astonishing store of merit with little difficulty,[3486] refuting this with such great insistence indicates that YOU have run out of reasons for your criticism.

Then, as propounded in treatises of[3487] early lamas, you should also visualize the general and specific dharma protectors, the heroes and yoginīs of the twenty-four holy sites, the eight charnel grounds and so forth, the directional guardians, the guardians of the field, the serpents and so forth, the local spirits, and all beings as deities of the maṇḍala, and offer them the nectars in order to satisfy them.

[Praises and Offerings]

The *Vajrasattva Sādhana* does not bid you to recite praises, make offerings, or taste the nectars in this context, and neither does the *Concise Sādhana*, while the *Sādhana Incorporating the Scripture* instructs only to "take care to make the offerings in accordance with the ritual method."[3488] This denotes all offerings—outer, inner, and secret offerings.

The line in the *Concise Sādhana* "Then, as the buddhas offer praises[3489] to the maṇḍala wheel and reveal the supreme secret"[3490] [172b] carried the same

3484. Reading *snying po* for *snyid po* in our text.

3485. *Kambala, Lwa ba pa, *'Khor lo sdom pa'i dka' 'grel sgrub pa'i thabs kyi gleng gzhi*, *Sādhananidānapañjikā*, Tōh 1401, 6a2–3. D has *bsgrubs pa'i* for *grub pa'i*; *rdo rje can gyis sbyor* for *rdo rje can gyi phyir*; and *snying po yis* for *snying po yi* in our text. My translation is provisional.

3486. Reading *chung* for *chud* in our text.

3487. Reading *kyi* for *kyis* in our text.

3488. Nāgārjuna, *Mdo bsre*, *Sādhanasūtramelāpaka*, Tōh 1797, 14ab4.

3489. The verb in the Tibetan translation is *bstod gsol*, while the Sanskrit has two verbs *nutvā* and *anurāgya*. Ratnākaraśānti's commentary on this work, the *Rin chen phreng ba*, *Ratnāvalī*, Tōh 1826, 75b2, has both verbs *bstod* and *rjes chags*.

3490. Nāgārjuna, *Mdor byas*, *Piṇḍīkrama Sādhana*, Tōh 1796, 10a7; L 216ab; T 212ab. D has *de nas* for *de ltar* in our text. Bu ston prefers the reading *de nas sangs rgyas kyis bstod 'khor lo rjes chags nas*, meaning: "Then the buddhas praise and delight in the maṇḍala," over the version of the *Mdor byas*, cited in our text. See Bu ston, *Mdor byas 'grel chen*, 90a7.

meaning as the line[3491] in the *Vajrasattva Sādhana* "Then [the tathāgatas] reveal the Buddha's wisdom and delight in the maṇḍala."[3492] Both are instructions on making the secret offerings at this point, and therefore you should definitely make secret offerings to the father-mother abiding in union. In making such offerings you should visualize yourself as the principal deity with your consort, joining your vajra and lotus, absorb with her in union, and thus experience great bliss. Thereupon, since all the deities of the maṇḍala, the principal and the surrounding deities, share a single mental continuum, all of them are simultaneously satiated with great bliss.

The Ritual Method of Dissolving the Visualization

The *Concise Sādhana* teaches: "The maṇḍala wheel enters into your own maṇḍala wheel, and only the lord[3493] who is in a state of great bliss remains."[3494] The first line teaches that the celestial mansion and the circle of deities dissolve into you, while the second line teaches that the principal father-mother deity is not dissolved.

The *Sādhana Incorporating the Scripture* explains how to dissolve the circle of deities: "The tenth chapter of the *Guhyasamāja Tantra* teaches: 'Meditate on a maṇḍala-array resting in the midst of the realm of space, and at its center visualize the syllable *hūṃ* in its own form. Imagine it emanating an abundance of blazing vajra rays that draw the body, speech, and mind of the buddhas to your heart. At that very moment you will become the holder of vajra body, speech, and mind.'[3495] This indicates that you must visualize the realm of space filled entirely with the syllables *hūṃ* in the nature of Vajrasattva, and then dissolve them. The *Vajrasattva Sādhana* teaches: [173a] "As

3491. Reading *gnyis po* for *gnyis pa* in our text.

3492. Candrakīrti, *Rdo rje sems dpa'i sgrub thabs*, *Vajrasattva Sādhana*, Tōh 1814, 204a6; Luo and Tomabechi 2009, 31.8 and 65.11–12.

3493. Following the reading in the Bstan 'gyur.

3494. Nāgārjuna, *Mdor byas*, *Piṇḍīkrama Sādhana*, Tōh 1796, 10a7; L 216cd; T 212cd. D has *mgon po* for the third *'khor lo*, Skt. *nātha*, and *gcig po* for *gcig pu*, Skt. *ekaḥ*.

3495. Nāgārjuna, *Mdo bsre*, *Sādhanasūtramelāpaka*, Tōh 1797, 14b4–6. D has *nam mkha'* for *nam mkha'i*; *de 'gyur ba* for *dar 'gyur ba*; and *rnam bsgoms na* for *rnam bsgom na* in our text. *Guhyasamāja Tantra*, Tōh 442; Zhol 14a5–6; Stog 24a2–4; Dunh 26a3–4; Fremantle 1971, vv. 5–7ab; and Matsunaga 1978, vv. 5–7ab. Zhol has *rdo rje'i 'od zer cher 'bar ba* for *rdo rje 'od zer rab tu 'bar*; *rnam par 'phro ba* for *rnam par 'phro bar*; *drangs par* for *snying la*; and *rnam bsgoms na* for *rnam bsgom na* in our text. Note that Dunh too has *snying* here. Regarding the Sanskrit, Fremantle 1971 and Matsunaga 1978 have *hṛtaṃ* while Candrakīrti's *Pradīpoddyotana*, in Chakravarti 1984, 91, has *hṛdayam* ākṛṣṭam.

before, visualize them entering the maṇḍala of your own body and dissolving one by one. When you recite the *hūṃ* abiding in your heart, the entire realm of sentient beings transforms into Great Vajradhara.[3496] Remain absorbed in this visualization."[3497]

The meaning of these lines is: visualize light-rays emanating from the *hūṃ* on your heart and inducing all the deities of the maṇḍala to enter your body, just as earlier the specially visualized deities dissolved into your body.[3498] All parts of the celestial mansion enter into the respective parts of your body as well, each in the particular location you first visualized when you meditated on the body maṇḍala.[3499] Following this, rays of bodhicitta light emanate from the point of union between yourself and the consort absorbed in union. The bodhicitta light empowers all sentient beings, purifies their obscurations, and transforms them into the syllables *hūṃ* that fill the realm of space, and are then transformed into Vajradharas. The light-rays of the *hūṃ* on your heart draw all these Vajradharas and induce them to enter your body. This is the ritual method for the dissolution.[3500]

The *Illuminating Lamp* applies the verses of the *Guhyasamāja Tantra* cited above[3501] to stir the heart of the meditator on the creation stage.[3502] But since it is appropriate to apply each vajra word of the *Guhyasamāja Tantra* to several topics, as explained, there is no contradiction here. The *Concise Sādhana* teaches that all sentient beings become Vajrasattva and then dissolve into you: "The yogis who have practiced the four yogas in this way visualize the world and its inhabitants in the essence of *hūṃ* and imagine all beings arising from

3496. Following the reading in the Bstan 'gyur.

3497. Candrakīrti, *Rdo rje sems dpa'i sgrub thabs*, *Vajrasattva Sādhana*, Tōh 1814, 204a6–7; Luo and Tomabechi 2009, 31.8–10 and 65.12–16. D and Luo and Tomabechi have *snying gar* for *snying khar* and *yongs su gyur par bsams nas* for *yongs su gyur ba'i gzugs zung nas* in our text.

3498. See above [89a–90b].

3499. See above [124b–125b].

3500. See Tsong kha pa, *Gsang mngon*, 73b4–6.

3501. Candrakīrti, *Sgron gsal*, *Pradīpoddyotanaṭīkā*, Tōh 1785, 4a4; Chakravarti 1984, 5, selects a topic for each chapter of the *Guhyasamāja Tantra*. The topic of the tenth chapter [a few lines from which were cited above] is "stirring the heart" or "exhorting the essence of the deity," Tib. *lha'i snying po bskul ba*, Skt. *devatāhṛdayasaṃcodana*. Or as appears at the end of the tenth chapter of the *Sgron gsal*, "stirring the heart" or "exhorting the essence of all Tathāgatas," Candrakīrti, *Sgron gsal*, *Pradīpoddyotanaṭīkā*, Tōh 1785, 76b5–6; Chakravarti 1984, 95.

3502. See also Tsong kha pa, *Mtha' gcod*, 103b4–108b1.

this *hūṃ* as Vajrasattvas.[3503] When they arise from their yoga, they perceive living beings and act accordingly." [173b]

3503. Nāgārjuna, *Mdor byas*, *Piṇḍīkrama Sādhana*, Tōh 1796, 10b1; L 217; T 213. D has *rnal 'byor pa* for *rnal 'byor pas*; *de byung* for *des 'byung*; and *sbyad par bya* for *sbyar* in our text.

17. Epilogue

The Yoga Between Meditation Sections

There are four sections here: (1) the yoga of body enhancement, (2) food yoga, (3) the yoga of sleeping and waking, and (4) the yoga of offering tormas.

The Yoga of Body Enhancement[3504]

The *Concise Sādhana* teaches: "When being absorbed in samādhi and the bodies of the mantrins become enervated, they should meditate on this yoga that will satiate body, speech, and mind. They should visualize a lunar[3505] disk just a hand-span above their heads, and an *oṃ* syllable there pouring down the five nectars. By means of this vajra practice they will become instantly radiant and attain the well-being of body, speech, and mind; of this there is no doubt."[3506] This topic was [initially] taught in chapter seventeen of the *Guhyasamāja Tantra*: "They should visualize a disk just a hand-span above their heads, with an *oṃ* syllable at its center pouring down the five nectars. By means of this vajra practice they will instantly become radiant and abide in the well-being of body, speech, and mind; of this there is no doubt."[3507]

3504. See also Tsong kha pa, *Sngags rim chen mo*, chap. 12, 525, and *Rnal 'byor dag rim*, 31b1–3.

3505. This word is not found in the Sanskrit.

3506. Nāgārjuna, *Mdor byas, Piṇḍīkrama Sādhana*, Tōh 1796, 10b1–3; L 218–220; T 214–216. D has *sngags pas* for *sngags pa*; *bskams for skams*; *bsgom par bya* for *bsgoms par bya*; *spags pa* for *dpags pa*; *dkyil 'khor bsgom par* for *zla ba brtag par*; *'bebs pa'i* for *'bab pa'i*; *bsam par* for *brtag par*; and *'di* for *de* in our text.

3507. *Guhyasamāja Tantra*, Tōh 442; Zhol 46a2–3; Stog 77b3–4; Dunh 85b2–3; Fremantle 1971, vv. 65–66; and Matsunaga 1978, vv. 65–66. Zhol has *dpags par* for *spags par* in our text. For a commentary on these lines in a fragment of the anonymous **Guhyasamājoddhṛtayāgavidhi*, see Szántó 2015.

Such are the stages of the practice:[3508] When your body becomes worn and weary because you have meditated day and night enwrapped in yoga during the four sessions, you should visualize a white syllable *wa* in space just a handspan above your head; the *wa* is transformed into a lunar disk. Beneath the lunar disk at its center, visualize a white upside down *oṃ*. Nectar in the five colors, the essences of the five tathāgatas, will pour forth from the syllable *oṃ* and the lunar disk, empowering you from head to toe. Instantly, your body will recover its well-being, strength, and radiance. [174a] If you cultivate this visualization every day you will live long, your hair will not turn white, and you will have no wrinkles.

Food Yoga

This is the food yoga taught in the *Concise Sādhana*:

> Mantrins who engage in this practice should purify [themselves and their food] and transform them in the following way. They should thoroughly purify their throats and hearts and satiate the tathāgatas. Then they should purify their food, by thoroughly *purifying* it with *hūṃ*, *transforming* it with the syllable *āḥ*, and *setting it ablaze* by condensing it with the syllable *oṃ*.[3509] For purifying the throat, they should first visualize a conch[3510] at their throat with the syllable *hrīḥ* that emanates an eight-petaled lotus; resting upon the lotus they should visualize a syllable *hūṃ* with a five-pronged great vajra rising from it and an *oṃ* on its central prong.
>
> Then, in order to make their inner fire offerings, mantrins should imagine a thunderbolt on their hearts emanating a fire with three tongues that burn the food. This occurs when wind has

3508. See Candrakīrti's *Sgron gsal, Pradīpoddyotanaṭīkā*, Tōh 1785, 191b2–3; Chakravarti 1984, 220, as well as Tsong kha pa, *Sgron gsal mchan*, 497a3–b4, and *Rnal 'byor dag rim*, 31b1–3.

3509. The three steps of purifying, Tib. *sbyang bar bya*, Skt. *śodhayet*; transforming your perception, Tib. *rtogs par bya*, Skt. *bodhayet*; and setting ablaze in profusion, Tib. *sbar bar bya*, Skt. *jvālayet*, are parallel to the blessing of the inner offerings.

3510. Our text and D in the Bstan 'gyur have *mtshams*, while the Sanskrit is *śaṅkhaṃ*. However, in his commentary on Nāgārjuna's *Mdor byas, Piṇḍīkrama Sādhana*, the *Rim pa lnga pa'i dgongs 'grel zla ba'i 'od zer, Pañcakramamatiṭīkā Candraprabhā*, Tōh 1831, 185b2, Abhayākaragupta glosses "conch," Tib. *dung*, thus indicating that he is commenting here on the word *conch*. Likewise, in his explanation below Mkhas grub rje describes a red conch inside the throat.

> been visualized igniting the fire, and the fire reaches the earth disk and brings the water there to a boil.[3511] The water disk sends all the suitable food and drink through the lotus of the mouth into the lotus of the heart, till it reached the disk of the navel. Then through the yoga of conjoining,[3512] the [food and drink] emerge through the lotus of the secret place as ashes. No old age, plague, poisoning, untimely death, and so forth can then befall the yogi who has practiced in this way, and all harm will be vanquished.[3513]

These lines indicate[3514] that when you eat, you should bless the food as you bless tormas and then purify your throat as follows: If you are a yogi of the vajra tathāgata family, meditate on yourself as Akṣobhya or Vajradhara, [174b] and within your throat visualize the form of a red conch with a *hrīḥ* inside and a red eight-petaled lotus arising from it. From the blue *hūṃ* at its center, a blue five-pronged vajra will appear with a hollow middle prong and a white *oṃ* on the tip of the vajra emanating rays of light toward the food. Then you should purify your heart by visualizing there a variegated lotus with a solar disk upon it and upon the solar disk a blue *hūṃ* blazing with three tongues of fires.

Then, imagine your right hand as the ladle of the fire offering, and a light ray emanating from the *oṃ* within your throat sending the food there. Meditate on your tongue as a five-pronged vajra arising from *hūṃ*, and food entering through its hollow middle prong. Eating thus as an offering to the *hūṃ* on your heart comprised of the assembled deities is what is meant by the inner fire offering.

Then you should visualize a wind disk arising from the *yaṃ* on the secret place, a fire disk arising from the *raṃ* on the navel, an earth disk arising from the *laṃ* on the heart, and a water disk arising from the *vaṃ* [*baṃ*] on the

3511. This translation follows the explanation below.

3512. Some commentaries on the *Mdor byas*, such as Abhayākaragupta, Tōh 1831, *Rim pa lnga pa'i dgongs 'grel zla ba'i 'od zer*, 185b2–3, explain this as "conjoining of the winds."

3513. Nāgārjuna, *Mdor byas*, *Piṇḍīkrama Sādhana*, Tōh 1796, 10b3–6; L 221–229; T 217–225. D has *sbyangs* for *sbyang* twice; *rtogs par bya* for *rtogs 'bar bya*; *tshim* for *tsham*; *rtogs* for *gtso*; *sbar* for *'bar*; *sbyang ba ba'o* for *sbyang ba'o*; *bsam* for *bsams*; *lte ba'i nang* for *padma'i steng*, Skt. *karṇikopari*; *rtse mo* for *rtse myo*; *sbyang ba'o* for *spyod pa'o*, Skt. *śodhanam*; *sprin gyi* for *'brug gi*; twice *snying gar* for *snying khar*; *rtse gsum me ni* for *gru gsum rtse mo*, Skt. *triśikhāgniṃ*; *de la spro* for *de las spro*; *bza' ba* for *bza'*; *gang* for *dag*; *gang du* for *gang nas*; *rgyu ba* for *byung ba*; *gang ci rung ba* for *gang ci'ang rung ste*; *rims nad* for *rims sogs*; *dug la sogs* for *dug sogs* and *'tshe ba* for *'chi ba* in our text. The Sanskrit for *me* in its first occurrence is *agni* and in its second occurrence is *havis*.

3514. See Tsong kha pa, *Rnal 'byor dag rim*, 30a5–b2.

throat. The wind ignites the fire that bakes the earth, and its heat boils the water. Consequently, when the food enters through the lotus of the throat and reaches the heart, the refined food satiates the deities. When the food reaches the navel, the *tummo*,[3515] the inner fire, burns it, and its waste[3516] turns into ashes, which then pass through the lotus of the secret place and emerge from the lower gate. When some food has been digested, hold the winds conjoined. Thus, practicing continuously, you will never be harmed by disease, poison, and so forth and will avert untimely death.

Furthermore, the *Enquiry of the Four Goddesses* teaches:

> Heed the inner yoga. Along the middle line of your body the four lotuses are placed [topped respectively with] fire, wind, earth, and water disks.[3517] When the wind ignites the fire, the fire moves and reaches the earth disk whereby the water heats.[3518] [175a] *Ra* is the syllable of fierce activities, *ya* the syllable of subjugation, *la* the syllable of increase, and *ba* the syllable of pacification.[3519]
>
> Visualize the syllable *kṣa* upside down on the lotus [of the throat] sending all the food and drink from the water disk [of the throat] through the lotus of the heart, and into the lotus of the

3515. Tib. *gtum mo*.

3516. Reading *snyigs ma rnams* for *brtsigs ma rnams*.

3517. According to the commentaries on the *Lha mo bzhis zhus pa*, *Caturdevīparipṛcchā Tantra*, Tōh 446, by Smṛtijñānakīrti, Jñānagarbha, and Tsong kha pa, the wind disk is on the lotus of the secret place, the fire disk is on that of the navel, the earth disk is on that of the heart, and the water disk is on that of the throat. See Smṛtijñānakīrti, *Lha mo bzhis zhus pa'i rnam bshad rgyas pa*, *Caturdevatāparipṛcchāvyākhyā*, Tōh 1915, 247a6–b2; Jñānagarbha, *Lha mo bzhis zhus pa'i rnam par bshad pa*, *Caturdevatāparipṛcchāṭīkā*, Tōh 1916, 266a1–3; and Tsong kha pa's *Bzhis zhus*, 46a5–6.

3518. My translation follows the commentaries mentioned in the previous note, as well as Nāgārjuna's *Mdor byas*, *Piṇḍīkrama Sādhana*, Tōh 1796, translated above [174a] that apparently cites this tantra. According to Smṛtijñānakīrti, *Lha mo bzhis zhus pa'i rnam bshad rgyas pa*, *Caturdevatāparipṛcchāvyākhyā*, Tōh 1915, 247b4–5, this is not the order of the disks taught in the *Lha mo bzhis zhus pa*, *Caturdevīparipṛcchā Tantra*, Tōh 446, but the transmitted instruction of lamas. Tsong kha pa, *Bzhis zhus*, 46b3, emphasizes that the water does not heat the food, rather the wind on the lotus of the secret place stirs, igniting the fire on the lotus of the navel, which heats the earth on the lotus of the heart. This heat brings the water on the throat to a boil.

3519. The four disks of the physical elements arise from the four seed syllables *raṃ*, *yaṃ*, *baṃ*, and *laṃ*, respectively.

navel.[3520] Reaching the lotus of the secret place through the yoga of conjoining[3521] they immediately turn to ashes.[3522]

The fire offering, as explained, should be carried out day and night. By eating your food in this manner unceasingly, you will attain the following in your present life: You will experience neither old age, sickness, lesions, or untimely death,[3523] and all harm will be vanquished. Bad dreams will be quelled, and you will enjoy favorable circumstances and live for eons. All sentient beings will delight in you, and the mere sight of you will stir their hearts."[3524]

These lines are cited in the *Concise Sādhana*.[3525]

The meaning of *ra is the syllable of fierce activities* and so forth is this:[3526] through the outer fire-offering, you complete the four rituals of pacification, increase, subjugation and fierce activities. Likewise, you accomplish these four rituals as you consume your food through the inner fire offering while generating the disks of the four elements from the four syllables on the four lotuses along the inner channel of the body and engaging in wind yoga. Regarding the line: *the syllable*[3527] *kṣa upside down on the lotus*, it seems that some Indian manuscripts have the syllable *kṣa* here and some do not, but the correct Indian version is according to the *Concise Sādhana*: "sends [the food] through the lotus of the mouth,"[3528] without the syllable *kṣa*.

3520. While our text has *phyi rol* and the end of the line, Jñānagarbha's commentary on this tantra, *Lha mo bzhis zhus pa'i rnam par bshad pa, Caturdevatāparipṛcchāṭikā*, Tōh 1916, 266b1, has *phyir ro*. In his own commentary, *Bzhis zhus*, 47a5–6, Tsong kha pa prefers the reading of Nāgārjuna's *Mdor byas, Piṇḍikrama Sādhana*, Tōh 1796, cited above: *phyin 'og tu*.

3521. Tsong kha pa explains that this is the conjoining of the winds. See his *Bzhis zhus*, 47b2.

3522. Tsong kha pa's commentary, *Bzhis zhus*, 47a2, has *rnam par brtag pa* for *rnam par bstan* in our text, which he glosses with *bsgom par bya*.

3523. Tsong kha pa points to the translation in Nāgārjuna's *Mdor byas, Piṇḍikrama Sādhana*, Tōh 1796, cited above, that has "untimely death and so forth." See his *Bzhis zhus*, 47b3–4.

3524. *Lha mo bzhis zhus kyi rgyud, Caturdevīparipṛcchā*, Tōh 446, 281a5–b2. D has *khyod kyis nang* for *khyod kyi nad*; *dbus su* for *dbus na*; *rlung gis me ni 'bar byas te* for *rlung gi me la spar bya ste*; *bskyod pa'o* for *bskyod pa yi*; *padmar kṣa yig kha mar lta* for *padma kṣa yi kha mar blta*; *btsud par* for *gzhug par*; *tshul gyi sbyor* for *tshul du sbyar*; *thal bar* for *thal bas*; *nyin dang nyin* for *nyin dang mtshan*; *'chi ba med* for *shi ba'ang med*; *de ni glo bur* for *de bzhin glo bur*; *'chi ba med* for *'chi ba' nag med*; and *rmi lam ngan yang* for *rmi lam ngan pa' ang*.

3525. See above [174a].

3526. In the following Mkhas grub rje follows Tsong kha pa, *Bzhis zhus*, 46b3–47a3.

3527. Reading *yig* for *yi* in our text.

3528. Cited above [174a].

If you are a yogi of another tathāgata family,[3529] you should know how to generate your tongue as a wheel, lotus, jewel, and so forth. Likewise, when you bless your tongue while tasting the inner offering, you should know how to practice in terms of each tathāgata family. [175b]

When you eat your food while[3530] engaging in the practice of the yoga of food, any amount of food and drink you may consume will earn you a vast amount of merit with little effort, as much merit as through the practice of the great maṇḍala. Likewise, no matter how many heaps of food you may consume as gifts of faith-food, you will be able to purify[3531] all the food you eat, for the *Four Chapters Tantra* teaches: "Whatever you eat and drink, small in quantity though it may be, should first be dedicated and only then consumed. The yogi who practices in this way will never be found wanting."[3532]

Dedicated means you must dedicate it to yourself, generated as a deity. If you do not dedicate your food and drink, but consume it for your own sake, not in conjunction with the yoga of food and without generating yourself as a deity and so forth, motivated solely by your craving for it, every bite of food and sip of drink you consume will be a wrongdoing that results from afflictive emotions violating your bodhisattva vow; and in the present context of mantric practice, every bite and sip will constitute an infraction of the thirteenth root downfall.[3533]

Moreover, additional flaws will accrue, as the *Saṃvarodaya Tantra* teaches: "If you drink out of craving and not in conjunction with the three deities and so forth, your drink will surely be poisonous and no mantric attainments will

3529. Our text above [174a] describes how yogis of the vajra tathāgata family meditate on themselves as Akṣobhya or Vajradhara with a blue five-pronged vajra in their throats.

3530. Reading *sgo nas* for the unclear syllable in our text.

3531. Reading *sbyong* for *sbyod* in our text.

3532. Skt. *ṛṇa*. *Gdan bzhi*, *Catuḥpīṭha*, Tōh 428, 224b2–3, at the end of *Gsang ba'i gdan gyi rab tu byed pa las rim par bye ba gnyis pa*. D and Stog have *cung zad bza' dang btung la sogs* for *gang zhig cung zad bza' btung rnams* and *rung bar* for *bsngo ba* in our text. Our text follows these lines as they are cited in Tsong kha pa's *'Dod 'jo*, 179a2–3. For a summary of Bhavabhaṭṭa's explanation of these lines, see Szántó 2012, vol. 1, 453. See also Bhavabhadra's commentary on the *Gdan bzhi*, his *Gdan bzhi pa'i 'grel pa dran pa'i rgyu mtshan*, *Catuḥpīṭhasmṛtinibandhaṭīkā*, Tōh 1607, 256b2–3, which also has *cung zad bza' dang btung la sogs* for *gang zhig cung zad bza' btung rnams* and *rung bar* for *bsngo ba*.

3533. For the thirteenth root downfall, see Tsong kha pa's *Dngos grub snye ma*, 49a1–50a3; English translation in Sparham 2005, 108–110.

arise."[3534] The *Sādhana Incorporating the Scripture* explains that you should practice food yoga as the seventeenth chapter of the *Guhyasamāja Tantra* teaches: "When you eat, always practice as Vajra Body; when you engage in other activities, practice as Vajradhara; and when you recite scriptures, practice as Vajra Dharma."[3535] [176a] The *Illuminating Lamp* explains that when you eat you should generate yourself as Vajra Body Vairocana,[3536] so whether you generate yourself as Vairocana or as the deity of your own family, either method is held appropriate.

The Yoga of Sleeping and Waking

Although the three sādhanas by Ārya Nāgārjuna and his disciples teach only these two yogas [the yoga of body enhancement and the yoga of food] between meditative sessions,[3537] you should also practice the yogas of sleeping and waking. As regards the yoga of sleeping, you should dissolve the deities of the body maṇḍala as you dissolve the specially visualized deities into clear light.[3538] Then do not let your mind wander, but focus single-pointedly on the clear light, thus falling asleep while maintaining the clear light of sleep. When you wake up, visualize the four goddesses invoking you with a song, and practice rising in the body of the principal father-mother while in the continuum of clear light.[3539]

3534. *Sdom 'byung, Saṃvarodaya Tantra*, Tōh 373, 299a2, Stog 211a3–4; Sanskrit, Tibetan, and English translation in Tsuda 1974, chap. 26, v. 23. D, Stog, and Tsuda have *bral bar* for *bral bas*; *ci ste dam tshig can gyis 'thungs* for *gal te sred ldan 'thungs gyur na*; and *mi skye'o* for *skye mi 'gyur* in our text. Once more our text follows these lines as they are cited in Tsong kha pa's *'Dod 'jo*, 178b1, with the exception of *bral ba* for *bral bas*.

3535. Nāgārjuna, *Mdo bsre, Sādhanasūtramelāpaka*, Tōh 1797, 14b7. D has *lus kyi* for *sku yi*; *rdo rje chos la rtag par ni* in the third line for *rtag par rdo rje chos su bya* in the fourth line; *sngags bton* for *mdo 'don*; and *cho ga spyad par bya* for *cho ga'i bya ba la* in our text. *Guhyasamāja Tantra*, Tōh 442; Zhol 42b4–5; Stog 72a2; Dunh 79b4–5; Fremantle 1971, v. 35; and Matsunaga 1978, v. 35. Zhol has *kha zas la* for *kha zas dang*.

3536. Candrakīrti, *Sgron gsal, Pradīpoddyotanaṭīkā*, Tōh 1785, 180a5–b2, Chakravarti 1984, 208. See also Tsong kha pa's *Sgron gsal mchan*, 473b3–474a5. While reciting scriptures the yogis should visualize themselves as Amitābha and when engaging in other activities as Vajradhara Akṣobhya.

3537. For the yoga of body enhancement, see Nāgārjuna, *Mdor byas, Piṇḍīkrama Sādhana*, Tōh 1796, 10b1–3; L 218–220; T 214–216. For food yoga see the *Mdor byas*, Tōh 1796, 10b3–7; L 221–209; T 217–225; and Nāgārjuna, *Mdo bsre, Sādhanasūtramelāpaka*, Tōh 1797, 14b7.

3538. See above [90b2–96b1].

3539. See Tsong kha pa, *Rnal 'byor dag rim*, 31a5–b1.

The Yoga of Offering Tormas

Many tantras maintain that it is important to offer tormas to worldly and transcendent deities at all times in order to pacify the interference of obstructors and attain siddhis. You should offer tormas as you complete each of the four sessions of practice, or if that is unfeasible, at least at the end of the last session.

Regarding the vessel in which tormas are offered,[3540] several tantras and Indian scriptures specify the so-called "lotus vessel," which is a skull.[3541] The *Cluster of Instructions* mentions wooden troughs and so forth as well,[3542] and the *Red Yamāri*[3543] *Tantra* names "sedan chair" vessels or brass platters too;[3544] sedan chair here means a "dish" made of cotton or leaves and so forth;[3545] while the *Maṇḍala Vajra Garland* explains that tormas can be offered in dishes or in the palm of the hand. Thus there is no definitive instruction.[3546]

Regarding the substance of the tormas,[3547] the *Maṇḍala Vajra Garland* and other scriptures list grain, rice, peas, meat, fish, beer, water, onions, [176b] garlic, porridge, pastry, milk, and so forth.[3548] If you cannot afford these, grain and water alone are said to be suitable as well. Still the *Saṃvarodaya Tantra* teaches that "A torma without intoxicants will not bring about swift

3540. Here our text follows Tsong kha pa, *Sngags rim chen mo*, chap. 12, 526.

3541. For example, the *Kye'i rdo rje mkha' 'gro ma dra ba'i sdom pa*, *Hevajra Tantra II*, Tōh 418, 19a3; Snellgrove 1959, II.iii.58b, explains that "lotus vessel" means a skull in the secret language.

3542. Abhayākaragupta's *Man ngag snye ma*, *Āmnāyamañjarī*, chap. 34, Tōh 1198, 296b6.

3543. Reading *gshed* for *gshad* in our text.

3544. *Gshin rje'i gshed dmar po'i rgyud*, *Raktayamāri Tantra*, Tōh 474, 198a1 and 203b2.

3545. Reading *yin* for *min* in our text.

3546. Abhayākaragupta, *Dkyil chog rdo rje phreng ba*, *Vajrāvalī Maṇḍalavidhi*, Tōh 3140, 66a4; Mori 2009, §18.3, 368–369. The Sanskrit for dish is *śarāva*.

3547. Here our text follows Tsong kha pa, *Sngags rim chen mo*, chap. 12, 526.

3548. Abhayākaragupta, *Dkyil chog rdo rje phreng ba*, *Vajrāvalī Maṇḍalavidhi*, Tōh 3140, 88b5–89a1, Mori 2009, §48.1.1, 493–495.

attainments. This is why the previous Buddha praised the torma so highly."[3549] Since without beer there is no swift attainment, beer is of great importance. The method of blessing the tormas is identical to the blessing of the inner offerings, as explained above.

The method for generating and inviting the worldly and transcendent guests for the tormas is taught in the *Maṇḍala Vajra Garland*: "Visualize light rays emanating from the seed syllable on your heart invoking a ten-spoked protection wheel together with the fierce deities, and at its center a celestial mansion where the [remaining] deities of the maṇḍala abide, while [outside][3550] Indra and the others[3551] abide with their circles of deities, nāgas, and all sentient beings. Indra and the others instantly dissolve into clear light and then appear as the deities of the Guhyasamāja together with their consorts."[3552]

The *Maṇḍala Vajra Garland* also instructs how to offer the tormas and the mantras with these offerings: "First place water for their feet and so forth before you. While ringing the bell and brandishing the vajra, maintain your resolve in the-mind-for-enlightenment of indivisible emptiness and compassion, and deem your tormas as having been fully purified of the three spheres. In this state call the deities one by one, starting with the lord of your own maṇḍala and up to Sumbha, with *oṃ āḥ* so-and-so vajra, and then recite their seed syllables as well. Recite the mantra: *sarva duṣṭa samaya mudrā*

3549. *Sdom 'byung, Saṃvarodaya Tantra*, chap. 32, v. 3, Tōh 373, 307b6–7; Stog 223b6; not in Tsuda 1974. No doubt our text derives from a different translation. D and Stog have *chang dang gtor ma med par ni* for *gtor ma myos byed med pa las*; *las rnams myur du 'grub mi 'gyur* for *myur du 'grub par mi 'gyur ro*, with the sequence of the last two lines reversed; and D has *sngon gyi sangs rgyas rnams kyis gsungs* for *des na sngon gyi sangs rgyas kyis* and *des na gtor ma rab bsngags te* for *gtor ma rab tu bsngags par gsungs* in our text. Once more our text closely follows the version in Tsong kha pa, *'Dod 'jo*, 173b2, the only difference being *myos byed gtor ma* for *gtor ma myos byed* in our text.

3550. This word is not found in Abhayākaragupta, *Dkyil chog rdo rje phreng ba, Vajrāvalī Maṇḍalavidhi*, Tōh 3140, but appears in Tsong kha pa's *Rnal 'byor dag rim*, 27b3, where he specifies that these deities are outside the protection wheel.

3551. These are the fifteen guardians of the directions beginning with Indra. See the torma appendix to Tsong kha pa's *Gsang mngon*, 5b4–7a2, and our text below [177a–b].

3552. Abhayākaragupta, *Dkyil chog rdo rje phreng ba, Vajrāvalī Maṇḍalavidhi*, Tōh 3140, 89a5–7; Mori 2009, §48.1.3, 495 and 497. Mori has *snying ga'i* for *snying kha'i*; *phyi rol tu dbang po la sogs pa* for *dbang po la sogs pa rnams*; *'khor dang bcas pa'i klu rnams* for *'khor dang bcas pa dang klu rnams*; once more *dbang po la sogs pa* for *dbang po la sogs pa rnams*; *shes rab ma* for *shes rab*; and *ngo bor* for *gzugs su* in our text. See also Tsong kha pa, *Rnal 'byor dag rim*, 27b2–4 and 28a6–b1.

prabhañjaka mama śāntiṃ rakṣāṃ ca kuru svāhā hūṃ."[3553] This is the mantra of the tormas for the transcendent deities. [177a] The line *call the deities one by one* and so forth means that you must recite the name mantra of each deity. The line *recite their seed syllables as well* indicates that after the name mantra you should recite the seed syllable of each deity as well. The mantra of the tormas for worldly deities according to the *Maṇḍala Vajra Garland* is *oṃ āḥ sarva tryadhvaja daśa dig loka dhātv,*[3554] and so forth. In translation this means: all those born in the three times and ten directions, and so forth.

Then the *Maṇḍala Vajra Garland* explains how to visualize the act of offering: "Visualize all the guests, starting with the lord of the maṇḍala, up to Sumbha, and then Indra and the others with their circle of deities and then the nāgas and then all sentient beings, with red single-spoked vajra-tongues that arise from *hūṃs*. Invite them to partake of the nectar through the straw-like rays of their tongues or visualize them doing so. While maintaining the single taste of intrinsic emptiness and great bliss, visualize this for as long as you wish."[3555]

The *Maṇḍala Vajra Garland* then teaches the concluding rituals: "Offer them the two kinds of water, water to refresh the mouth and water to rinse the hands, and then offer *paan* and so forth. Beg forbearance for the sake of those who endeavored to help you complete the ritual activities.[3556] Recite the hundred-syllable mantra that you recited once again,[3557] and then *oṃ yoga śuddhāḥ sarva dharmā yoga śuddho 'haṃ,*[3558] while making the lotus circle[3559]

3553. Abhayākaragupta, *Dkyil chog rdo rje phreng ba*, *Vajrāvalī Maṇḍalavidhi*, Tōh 3140, 89a7–b2; Mori 2009, §48.1.3, 495–96 and 497. D and Mori have *zhes* for *zhes bya bas* and *gtor la* for *gtor ma* in our text. See also Tsong kha pa, *Rnal 'byor dag rim*, 28b2–3 and 28b5–6.

3554. Abhayākaragupta, *Dkyil chog rdo rje phreng ba*, *Vajrāvalī Maṇḍalavidhi*, Tōh 3140, 89b2, Mori 2009, §48.1.3, 496 and 497. For the rest of the translated mantra, see Tsong kha pa, *Rnal 'byor dag rim*, 28b6–29b2.

3555. Abhayākaragupta, *Dkyil chog rdo rje phreng ba*, *Vajrāvalī Maṇḍalavidhi*, Tōh 3140, 89b5–6; Mori 2009, §48.1.3, 496–497. D and Mori have *lce hūṃ las byung ba'i rdo rje rtse gcig pa* for *hūṃ las byung ba'i lce rdo rje rtse gcig pa*; *dmar po* for *dmar po can*; *sbu gu rnams kyis* for *sbu gu rnams*; *yid kyis* for *yid kyi* in our text. See also Tsong kha pa, *Rnal 'byor dag rim*, 29b2–3.

3556. Or in reading *lhag chad* for *lhur byed*: beg forbearance for any excess or omission.

3557. See above [16b].

3558. See Tsong kha pa, *Gsang mngon*, 74a1.

3559. Tib. *pad skor*, Skt. *kamalāvartta*.

and embracing mudrā."[3560] Then: "Snap your fingers thrice and entreat the deities, Indra and so forth, to depart to their respective abodes."[3561]

Master Tsongkhapa expounds in his sādhana the colors, emblems, and so forth of the fifteen directional guardians beginning with Indra exactly as explained in the *Cluster of Instructions*.[3562] [177b] The names Vajra Weapon given to Indra, Vajra Sage[3563] to Brahmā, and so forth are explained as the secret names Vajradhara conferred on the directional deities when they entered the maṇḍala and received initiation. When the directional deities arise from clear light, they are generated as the deities of the Guhyasamāja.[3564]

If you meditate according to the elaborate sādhana, Brahmā and the Earth Goddess,[3565] who belong to the body family, should be generated as Vairocana. The Sun God,[3566] who belongs to the jewel family, should be generated as Ratnasambhava. Vajrabhairava, Vajrakrodha, and Vajranāga, who belong to the speech family, should be generated as Amitābha. The Wind God,[3567] who belongs to the karma family, should be generated as Amoghasiddhi. The remaining gods, who belong to the Akṣobhya family, should be generated as Akṣobhya.

If you meditate according to the concise sādhana, all fifteen deities should be included in the family of Great Secret Vajradhara, and hence you should generate them all as blue Vajradhara with three faces and six arms embraced by Sparśavajrā.[3568] I heard this myself from our Master Tsongkhapa.

This completes my explanation of the yoga practiced between meditative sessions. According to both the *Sādhana Incorporating the Scripture* and *Vajrasattva Sādhana*, the Supreme King of Deeds includes the steps beginning with the meditation on the subtle drop and up to this point [of offering tormas and the concluding rituals] as well as the accomplishment of manifold activities and the shared siddhis of the creation stage.

3560. Abhayākaragupta, *Dkyil chog rdo rje phreng ba, Vajrāvalī Maṇḍalavidhi*, Tōh 3140, 89b6–7; Mori 2009, §48.1.4, 497–498. Mori has *pad skor* for *pad kor* in our text. See also Tsong kha pa, *Rnal 'byor dag rim*, 29b3–6.

3561. Abhayākaragupta, *Dkyil chog rdo rje phreng ba, Vajrāvalī Maṇḍalavidhi*, Tōh 3140, 90a2–3; Mori 2009, §48.1.4, 498.

3562. Tsong kha pa, *Gsang mngon*, 11a2–12b2.

3563. Reading *mi smra* for *me smra* in our text.

3564. See [176b] above.

3565. Tib. Sa'i lha mo, Skt. Pṛthivīdevī.

3566. Tib. Nyi ma, Skt. Sūrya.

3567. Tib. Rlung lha, Skt. Vāyudeva.

3568. Tib. Reg bya rdo rje ma, Eng. Vajra Lady of Tangibles.

The Framework of the Sādhana[3569]

Now I will explain the main subdivisions of the sādhana. While there are several different frameworks for the sādhana of the unexcelled maṇḍalas, in the present case there are four primary ways of dividing the sādhana: (1) the four limbs of familiarization and achievement, (2) the four yogas, (3) the three samādhis, and (4) the forty-nine essential points. [178a]

The Four Limbs of Familiarization and Achievement

The *Later Tantra* teaches: "In all yoga tantras the yogi always praises the following: the practice of familiarization as the first limb; approaching achievement as the second limb; achievement as the third limb; and great achievement as the fourth limb."[3570] Hence there are four limbs here: (1) familiarization, (2) approaching achievement, (3) achievement, and (4) great achievement.[3571]

[THE LIMB OF FAMILIARIZATION]

The *Guhyasamāja Tantra* teaches: "You should meditate on supreme awakening—being wholly absorbed in the samādhi of familiarization."[3572] On the whole, the limb of familiarization is taught in relation to both the creation and completion stages, but here the ordinary use of the term "familiarization" in the creation stage refers to one among the four limbs of the practice. The Sanskrit equivalent of familiarization is *sevā* and its meaning is "that with which to become familiar" and "that on which to focus."[3573]

According to the *Illuminating Lamp*, the brief meaning of the term

3569. See Tsong kha pa, *Sngags rim chen mo*, chap. 12, 481–489, partially translated in Beyer 1973, 114–119, and see 118 for a comparative chart of the different frameworks of the sādhana. For a more recent translation, see Yarnall 2013, 171–186.

3570. *Rgyud phyi ma, Uttara Tantra*, Tōh 443, 154a3; Matsunaga 1978, v. 136. Zhol has *bsgrub pa yang ni* for *sgrub pa yang ni* in our text and in D.

3571. Tib. *bsnyen, nye sgrub, sgrub pa*, and *sgrub chen*; Skt. *sevā, upasādhana, sādhana*, and *mahāsādhana*.

3572. *Guhyasamāja Tantra*, chap. 12, Tōh 442; Zhol 19a5–6; Stog 32b5; Dunh 35b3; Fremantle 1971, v. 62cd; Matsunaga 1978, v. 61ab. In his explanation here Mkhas grub rje follows Candrakīrti's *Sgron gsal, Pradīpoddyotanaṭīkā*, Tōh 1785, 94b2–5; Chakravarti 1984, 115, and Tsong kha pa's *Sgron gsal mchan*, 272a3–273a1, as well as Tsong kha pa's *Sngags rim chen mo*, chap. 12, 481–482.

3573. See Candrakīrti, *Sgron gsal, Pradīpoddyotanaṭīkā*, Tōh 1785, 94a6; Chakravarti 1984, 114–115, and Tsong kha pa's *Sgron gsal mchan*, 271b2–3.

familiarization is suchness,[3574] while its extensive meaning is the mind-for-enlightenment.[3575] Consequently, familiarization is the mind-for-enlightenment that focuses on suchness, and in this[3576] familiarization the mind is absorbed in single-pointed samādhi. This is the meaning of the line in the *Guhyasamāja Tantra, absorbed in the samādhi of familiarization*. What is the manner of meditating on familiarization? Pause the mind on manifest awakening from suchness that arises from probing the meaning of the mantra of emptiness.[3577] This is what is meant by the line in the *Guhyasamāja Tantra, meditate on supreme awakening.*

Hence the actual limb of familiarization here is manifest awakening from suchness—the clear light into which the specially visualized deities have dissolved; the steps starting from the meditation on the ground of wisdom and up to gathering the specially visualized deities into the body are ancillary to the actual familiarization. This is implied by the term *wholly absorbed*[3578] in familiarization, which means "gathered within" it. Therefore the literal meaning of the term *familiarization* is the ultimate mind-for-enlightenment—or the subject [178b] that focuses on emptiness as its object, by becoming familiar with it and dissolving in it as a "single-taste."[3579]

[The Limb of Approaching Achievement]

The *Guhyasamāja Tantra* teaches: "In the supreme attainment of approaching achievement, explore the vajra sensory spheres."[3580] Regarding the meaning of the term "approaching achievement," the object toward which one

3574. Reading *de bzhin nyid* for *da bzhin nyid* in our text.

3575. The limb of familiarization appears in two consecutive verses: first in the introductory verse concerning all four limbs in the *Guhyasamāja Tantra*, chap. 12, Tōh 442; Fremantle 1971, v. 61; Matsunaga 1978, v. 60abcd, interpreted in Candrakīrti, *Sgron gsal, Pradīpoddyotanaṭīkā*, Tōh 1785, 94a6; Chakravarti 1984, 115. The following verse in the *Guhyasamāja Tantra*, chap. 12, Tōh 442; Fremantle 1971, v. 62cd; Matsunaga 1978, v. 61ab, is devoted to the limb of familiarization, interpreted in the *Sgron gsal*, Tōh 1785, 94b2–3; Chakravarti 1984, 115.

3576. Reading *de 'dra* for *da 'dra* in our text.

3577. The mantra *oṃ śūnyatā jñāna vajra svabhāvātmako 'haṃ.*

3578. Tib. *rab sbyor ba*, Skt. *saṃyoga*.

3579. Tib. *ro gcig tu*, Skt. *ekarasa*.

3580. *Guhyasamāja Tantra*, chap. 12, Tōh 442; Zhol 19á6; Stog 32b5; Dunh 35b3; Fremantle 1971, v. 63ab; Matsunaga 1978, v. 61cd. The explanation below follows Candrakīrti's *Sgron gsal, Pradīpoddyotanaṭīkā*, Tōh 1785, 94b4–7; Chakravarti 1984, 115; Tsong kha pa's *Sgron gsal mchan*, 273a2–b1; and Tsong kha pa's *Sngags rim chen mo*, chap. 12, 482–483.

approaches is the *wisdom body of saṃbhoga* made of mere wind-and-mind; and that which approaches this body is the practitioner in the *mantra body of saṃbhoga*. Thus the actual limb of approaching achievement begins with arising from clear light as a solar disk and extends to the end of the generation of the First Lord. The following steps in the sādhana up to the placing of the complete body maṇḍala on the body [of the First Lord] that has transformed into Vajrasattva's nirmāṇakāya are ancillary to approaching achievement, and therefore should be included in the limb of approaching achievement. The explanation of Karuṇaśrī that all these steps are ancillary to the limb of approaching achievement accords with the view of the *Illuminating Lamp*.[3581]

Therefore the line [in the *Guhyasamāja Tantra*:] *In the supreme attainment of approaching achievement* means that approaching achievement [is carried out] through the five manifestations of awakening. What is approached? The supreme attainment, the wisdom body of saṃbhoga. In the line *explore the vajra sensory spheres*, *vajra* means the thirty-two deities beginning with Vajra Body Vairocana up to Sumbharāja. The *sensory spheres* are the thirty-two parts of the body beginning with the form aggregate [on the crown of the head] down to the soles of the feet. *Exploring* means placing the maṇḍala on the body, by uniting the two [the thirty-two deities with the thirty-two parts of the body] as one essence. Although there is no explicit teaching here about where to place the body maṇḍala, elsewhere in the *Guhyasamāja Tantra* it is taught that you should place it on Vajrasattva's nirmāṇakāya, as explained above.[3582] [179a]

[The Limb of Achievement]

The *Guhyasamāja Tantra* teaches: "Meditating on the mantra lord during achievement is called 'invoking.'"[3583] The term *achievement* here means that your three doors [body, speech, and mind] "are achieved" [or become] indivisible from the three vajras [enlightened body, speech, and mind], and thus you yourself "achieve" or become the triple sattvas. *Mantra* in the line

3581. Karuṇaśrī, *Sgron ma gsal bar byed pa'i gsal byed dka' 'grel, Pradīpoddyotanoddyota-pañjikā*, Tōh 1790, 125a6–b3.

3582. As we saw, Mkhas grub rje objects to the position that the body maṇḍala is set on the First Lord, following Tsong kha pa, *Sngags rim chen mo*, chap. 12, 483.

3583. *Guhyasamāja Tantra*, chap. 12, Tōh 442; Zhol 19a6; Stog 32b5–6; Dunh 35b3–4; Fremantle 1971, v. 63cd; Matsunaga 1978, v. 62ab. The Sanskrit here is different.

from the *Guhyasamāja Tantra*[3584] means the syllables *oṃ āḥ hūṃ* and their *lords* are the triple sattvas. Thus, by *meditating [on the mantras oṃ āḥ hūṃ]* on the three doors of your body, emanating the three syllables and gathering them back *during achievement* of your three doors as the three vajras, you *invoke* Vairocana, Amitābha, and Akṣobhya.[3585] Therefore the limb of achievement begins with the blessing of the three doors and continues up to the empowerment with the lord of the tathāgata family.

[The Limb of Great Achievement]

The *Guhyasamāja Tantra* teaches: "During great achievement, the holders of the wisdom-vajra visualize the form of the vajra holders [arising from] their own mantras, with the lords [of the tathāgata family] on their crowns and thereby they achieve."[3586] What should be done *during great achievement*? *Visualize the form of*[3587] *the vajra holders*—the thirty-two bodies of the deities—which have emanated from *their* respective *mantras with* the *lords* of the tathāgata family on their crowns empowering them. On what basis will *they achieve*?[3588] *The [holders] of wisdom-vajra* are the mantrins endowed with deity yoga who, having united their vajras and lotuses, absorb in union *and thereby they achieve*. This indicates that the great achievement extends from seeking the consort and union with her up to the completion of the Supreme King of Maṇḍalas. According to the *Illuminating Lamp* this[3589] implies that the Supreme King of Deeds is also ancillary to the great achievement.[3590] [179b] This limb is called the great achievement because it achieves great benefit for others.

3584. See Candrakīrti, *Sgron gsal, Pradīpoddyotanaṭīkā*, Tōh 1785, 94b7–795a3; Chakravarti 1984, 115; Tsong kha pa's *Sgron gsal mchan*, 273b2–274a2; and Tsong kha pa's *Sngags rim chen mo*, chap. 12, 483.

3585. Reading *bskyod pa* for *bskyed pa* in our text.

3586. *Guhyasamāja Tantra*, chap. 12, Tōh 442; Zhol 19a6–7; Stog 32b6; Dunh 35b4; Fremantle 1971, v. 64; Matsunaga 1978, vv. 62cd–63ab. Zhol has *sgrub pa chen po* for *bsgrub pa chen po* in our text. See Candrakīrti, *Sgron gsal, Pradīpoddyotanaṭīkā*, Tōh 1785, 95a3–6; Chakravarti 1984, 115, and Tsong kha pa's *Sgron gsal mchan*, 274a2–b5.

3587. Reading *gyi* for *gyis* in our text.

3588. Reading *de gang la* for *da gang la* in our text.

3589. Reading *des* for *das* in our text.

3590. Here Mkhas grub rje follows Tsong kha pa's *Sngags rim chen mo*, chap. 12, 483.

[Comparative Conclusions][3591]

Thus in the Ārya tradition of the Guhyasamāja, the two preliminaries of merit accumulation and the protection wheel are only ancillary to the actual sādhana and do not form a part of the main sādhana. All the other yogas related to the celestial mansion and the deities are included in the four limbs of familiarization and achievement that form the framework of the sādhana. Hence, [in the Ārya tradition of the Guhyasamāja] these four limbs are not applied to the visualization of the celestial mansion[3592] alone nor to the meditation on each individual deity.

According to Jñānapāda's tradition of the Guhyasamāja, the limb of familiarization is the generation of the samayasattva; approaching achievement is the blessing of the sensory spheres; achievement is the blessing of the body, speech, and mind; and great achievement is the conferral of empowerment and the sealing with the lord of the tathāgata family. Each of the four limbs of familiarization and achievement is applied in its entirety first to the principal deity, then to the mother, and finally to the deities of the Supreme King of Maṇḍalas, called respectively the lesser, the middling, and the greater limbs.[3593]

The Four Yogas[3594]

The *Black Yamāri Tantra* teaches: "Meditate first on 'the yoga,' then in the second stage on the 'subsequent yoga,' in the third on 'the higher yoga,' and finally on 'the great yoga.'"[3595] Thus the four yogas are the yoga, the subsequent yoga, the higher yoga, and the great yoga.[3596] According to tantras outside the Guhyasamāja cycle, the framework of the four yogas encompasses the entire

3591. See Tsong kha pa's *Sngags rim chen mo*, chap. 12, 483–484.

3592. Reading *rten pa* for *brtan pa* in our text as in Tsong kha pa, *Sngags rim chen mo*, chap. 12, 483.

3593. In is commentary on Jñānapāda's *Kun bzang sgrub thabs*, *Samantabhadra Sādhana*, Tōh 1855, Vaidyapāda uses the terms lesser, middling, and greater familiarization, approaching achievement, achievement, and great achievement as a means for dividing the practice. See his *Yan lag bzhi pa'i sgrub thabs kun tu bzang mo'i rnam par bshad pa*, *Caturaṅga Sādhana Samantabhadrīṭikā*, Tōh 1872. See also Tanaka 2017, 34–37.

3594. See Tsong kha pa's *Sngags rim chen mo*, chap. 12, 484–485.

3595. *Gshin rje gshed nag po'i rgyud*, *Kṛṣṇayamāri Tantra*, Tōh 467, 150a4–5; Samdhong Rinpoche and Vrajvallabh Dwivedi with a team 1992, 250; Sanskrit on page 123.

3596. Tib. *rnal 'byor*, *rjes su rnal 'byor*, *shin tu rnal 'byor*, and *rnal 'byor chen po*; Skt. *yoga*, *anuyoga*, *atiyoga*, and *mahāyoga*.

sādhana, for the *Black Yamāri Tantra* teaches: "The completion of Vajrasattva is called the yoga. The completion of the deities that emanates through the same cause is known as the subsequent yoga. The completion of those deities that surround them are considered the higher yoga. The blessing of body, speech, and mind, as well as the divine eye and so forth, [180a] and the entry of the wisdom wheel along with extensive offerings and praises—all these are known as the great yoga."[3597]

However, Nāgārjuna in his *Concise Sādhana* teaches that the steps from the meditation on the ground of wisdom to the gathering of the specially visualized deities into the body are preliminaries to the main practice of the yoga. The actual yoga consists of the manifest awakening from suchness and from the lunar disk; while the three remaining manifest awakenings comprise the subsequent yoga. The higher yoga begins as soon as the manifest awakenings have been completed and continues until all the deities of the maṇḍala are placed on the body. The steps beginning with the blessing of the three doors until the completion of the *First Yoga*[3598] constitute the great yoga.[3599]

The latter statement follows the explanation of the *Vajra Garland Tantra*: "The yoga, the subsequent yoga, the higher yoga, and the great yoga are included in the First Yoga, which precedes the Supreme King of Maṇḍalas and the Supreme Yoga of the King of Deeds."[3600] Thus within the tripartite division—the First Yoga, the Supreme King of Maṇḍalas, and the Supreme King of Deeds—all four yogas are included in the First Yoga. Therefore, in the Ārya tradition of Guhyasamāja the four yogas pertain to the First Yoga, not to the entire sādhana. It seems inappropriate to apply explanations from other tantras on the meaning of the term "the four yogas" in the present context of the Guhyasamāja. Since there is no reliable explanation of the four yogas in the tradition of the Guhyasamāja, I will write no more about it here.

3597. *Gshin rje gshed nag po'i rgyud*, *Kṛṣṇayamāri Tantra*, Tōh 467, 150a5–6, Samdhong Rinpoche and Vrajvallabh Dwivedi with a team 1992, 250; Sanskrit on page 123. D and Samdhong Rinpoche and Vrajvallabh Dwivedi with a team 1992, 250 and 266 have *rdzogs pa yin* for *rdzogs pa ni*; *de ni rgyu* for *de yi rgyu*; *grags* for *'dod*; and *chen po dag* for *chen po ni* in our text. Our text skips the line *bdud rtsi myang ba dag dang ni*, as does Tsong kha pa, *Sngags rim chen mo*, chap. 12, 484. Samdhong Rinpoche and Vrajvallabh Dwivedi with a team 1992, 266 has *gzhugs pa* for *gzhug pa* in D and our text.

3598. Tib. *dang po sbyor ba'i ting nge 'dzin*, Skt. *ādiyogasamādhi*. This is not one of the yogas, but rather includes all four yogas. See immediately below.

3599. Yoga in vv. 37–51, subsequent yoga vv. 51–52, higher yoga vv. 53–68, and great yoga vv. 69–92.

3600. Tib. *las kyi rgyal po rnal 'byor mchog*. *Rgyud rdo rje phreng ba*, *Vajramālā Tantra*, chap. 65, Tōh 445, 272a1–2. My translation follows the explanation below.

The Three Samādhis[3601]

(1) The *Samādhi of the First Yoga*[3602] is so designated because it is the samādhi of the emanator of the deities of the maṇḍala as the *first yoga*; it is the *first*, that is to say, the initial, emanation of the deities of the maṇḍala; and it is a samādhi that yokes [*yoga*] wisdom to method indivisibly. [180b]

(2) The *Samādhi of the Supreme King of Maṇḍalas*[3603] is so designated because the visualization of the deities residing in the maṇḍala—emanated from the bodhicitta of the principal father-mother—is completed here and the deities are placed on their respective seats. Thus it is a samādhi that fully completes the wheel of deities to be placed in the maṇḍala.

(3) The *Samādhi of the Supreme King of Deeds*[3604] is so-designated because it is the samādhi in which the yogi meditates on the steps of the sādhana from the subtle drop to the attainment of manifold activities, for the most part in correspondence with the enlightened *deeds* of the body, speech, and mind of the Buddha.

This explanation refers to the Ārya tradition of the Guhyasamāja. For explanations about the framework of the three samādhis in other traditions, consult the *Stages of the Path of Mantra* of the Great Vajradhara.[3605]

The Forty-Nine Essential Points

The scripture of the *Vajra Garland Tantra* offers two explanations concerning the essential points; one enumerates thirty-eight essential points and the other forty-nine, but the latter is the system found in the authentic Indian manuscript.[3606] These essential points form the framework of the entire sādhana. Nāropa[3607] explains that this method of division into forty-nine essential points accords precisely with the viewpoint of Ārya Nāgārjuna and his disciples, and venerable master Tsongkhapa follows this division explicitly

3601. See Tsong kha pa's *Sngags rim chen mo*, chap. 12, 487–488.

3602. Tib. *dang po sbyor ba'i ting nge 'dzin*, Skt. *ādiyogasamādhi*.

3603. Tib. *dkyil 'khor gi rgyal po mchog gi ting nge 'dzin*, Skt. *maṇḍalarājāgrīsamādhi*.

3604. Tib. *las kyi rgyal po mchog gi ting nge 'dzin*, Skt. *karmarājāgrīsamādhi*.

3605. Tsong kha pa's *Sngags rim chen mo*, chap. 12, 487–488.

3606. *Rgyud rdo rje phreng ba*, *Vajramālā Tantra*, chap. 35, Tōh 445, 245a6–7. Our text follows Tsong kha pa's *Rnal 'byor dag rim*, 31b6–32a1.

3607. This is mentioned in Tsong kha pa's *Rnal 'byor dag rim*, 32a2.

in the structure of his own sādhana.[3608] To clarify the forty-nine divisions further, consult master Tsongkhapa's writings. For the sake of brevity, I will write no more about them there.

How to Habituate Your Mind to the Visualization During the Creation Stage[3609]

There are two sections here: (1) how to meditate on the sādhana during the four sessions, and (2) the actual method of maintaining the visualization.

How to Meditate on the Sādhana During the Four Sessions

The *Sādhana Incorporating the Scripture* teaches: "Habituate to deity yoga during the four sessions in order to attain the sublime for yourself as well as for others."[3610] Likewise, the *Illuminating Lamp* explains: "When you have practiced continually during the four sessions in this way, the roots of merit will ripen."[3611] Several other tantras and Indian treatises explain the practice in the four sessions. [181a] Jalandharipa clarifies what the four sessions are: "The stages called blessing in the four sessions are meditations at daybreak, noon, late afternoon, and night."[3612] Vaidyapāda describes it in this way as well,[3613] while the commentary on the *Four Hundred and Fifty* explains that the third session occurs at the end of day.[3614]

How much should you meditate on the sādhana during these sessions?[3615] Several Indian scholar-yogis explain that there are two methods: in the first, the initial and final sessions are extensive while the middle two are abridged,

3608. Tsong kha pa's *Rnal 'byor dag rim* is arranged on the basis of these forty-nine essential points, and his *Sādhana, Gsang mngon*, follows this.

3609. For this heading see above [14b].

3610. Nāgārjuna, *Mdo bsre, Sādhanasūtramelāpaka*, Tōh 1797, 14b6–7.

3611. Candrakīrti, *Sgron gsal, Pradīpoddyotanaṭīkā*, chap. 11, Tōh 1785, 80a4; Chakravarti 1984, missing.

3612. Jalandhari, *Kye rdo rje'i sgrub thabs kyi mdor bshad pa dag pa rdo rje sgron ma, Hevajra Sādhana Vajrapradīpaṭippaṇīśuddha*, Tōh 1237, 91b2–3. D has *brlab pa'i rim pas zhes pa ni* for *brlabs pa'i zhes bya ba'i rim pa ni* in our text.

3613. Vaidyapāda, *Yan lag bzhi pa'i sgrub thabs kun tu bzang mo'i rnam par bshad pa, Caturaṅga Sādhana Samantabhadrīṭīkā*, Tōh 1872, 176a1.

3614. Ratnākaraśānti, *Gsang ba 'dus pa'i dkyil 'khor gyi cho ga'i 'grel pa, Guhyasamāja Maṇḍalavidhiṭīkā*, Tōh 1871, 87a3.

3615. See Tsong kha pa, *Sngags rim chen mo*, chap. 12, 533.

while in the second method, only the first session is extensive while the other three are abridged. Hence, you should practice continuously, regardless of how much leisure time you have. However, the twelfth chapter of the *Cluster of Instructions* states that you should practice in keeping with how much leisure time you have; if you are busy, practice the first session too in its abridged form.[3616] This is the tradition you should follow.

Other traditions, such as Cakrasaṃvara and Nairātmyā, explain the extensive and abridged sādhana in several different ways; however here in Guhyasamāja tradition there are undoubtedly both extensive and abridged methods for generating the four vajras as explained above.[3617]

What is the abridged method of meditating on the sādhana? You begin with the ground of wisdom and meditate up to the divine identity of offerings at the end of the First Yoga. Then, recite the mantras while visualizing each mantra successively as it circles its respective seed syllable at the heart of each of the deities of the body maṇḍala and so forth, and chant praises, make offerings and taste the nectar. Next, dissolve the visualization by gathering the individual parts of the celestial mansion into the respective parts of your body. In this system you should have dissolved the seat of each deity in the celestial mansion as you gathered the specially visualized deities into your body earlier. [181b]

But since for beginners, accumulation, purification, and protection against interference are most crucial, they are instructed to continually make offerings to the field for accumulating merit and to meditate on the protection wheel, for this will be of great benefit to them.

The Actual Method of Maintaining the Visualization[3618]

The meditation on the creation stage during the four sessions in this way is mainly (1) a ripener for the arising of the fully perfected completion stage and (2) an antidote for ordinary appearances and attitudes.

(1) Since the creation stage serves as a ripener for the arising of the fully perfected completion stage, whether you meditate on an extensive or abridged sādhana, you should meditate on all the key points of the purifier and the ground of purification—taking birth, death, and the intermediate state as the three bodies, as already explained at length.

(2) Next is how to meditate on the celestial mansion and the deities as

3616. Abhayākaragupta's *Man ngag snye ma*, *Āmnāyamañjarī*, Tōh 1198, 140b3–4.

3617. See [12b] above.

3618. See Tsong kha pa, *Sngags rim chen mo*, chap. 12, 462–464. See also the "Short Review" by Geshe Losang Tsephel in Tenzin Dorjee and Russell 1995, 139–141.

antidotes for ordinary appearances and attitudes. As an antidote for ordinary attitudes, meditate on the celestial mansion and its deities while maintaining a most powerful pure divine identity with the resolve: "I am the actual deity so and so, endowed with a pure buddha field, with the body of the Buddha and the virtues of a mind that has abandoned all obscurations and knows all knowable objects."

In order to visualize in this way, you must maintain single-pointed stabilization, totally undistracted by peripheral matters and uninterrupted by extraneous thoughts so long as your powers of apprehension have not dimmed, for the *Sādhana Incorporating the Scripture* teaches: "Therefore beginners who have upheld their mantric vows and commitments and have received empowerment to engage in the practice are free from ordinary identities."[3619] Several other scriptures reiterate time and again that you must annul your ordinary identity. Hence, [182a] vitally important is the meditation on the divine identity of the maṇḍala—the celestial mansion and the deities—that serves as an antidote for ordinary identity. Subsidiary to this is the meditation on the appearance of the maṇḍala that serves to block ordinary appearances.

This is the way to meditate on the appearance of the maṇḍala as an antidote to ordinary appearances: At first, while meditating on the sādhana stage by stage, stabilize your mind so that it will not be distracted even slightly by other objects, and then slowly visualize each pure appearance at the right stage until a clear generic image arises in your mind. Then, after meditating on the sādhana in this way stage by stage, maintain a stabilized meditation. This is the position held by most scholar-yogis in the land of India. Accordingly, visualize the generic image of the complete maṇḍala wheel with its celestial mansion and deities, focus on it single-pointedly, systematically applying mindfulness and alertness, and then instantaneously visualize the entire maṇḍala, practicing "clear appearance" stage by stage. If you know how to maintain this, it will be exceedingly powerful.

According to the transmitted instruction of Tibetan lamas, first visualize only the father with one face and two arms and stabilize your mind on him. Being entirely focused, you should not pursue anything else that arises in your mind. This is the basic visualization and if it is unclear, you must visualize it again and concentrate on it. If one aspect of your basic visualization, like an eye or the hair-tuft between the eyebrows, is clear but the rest is not, fix your mind on the clear aspect and then meditate by gradually adding other body parts. When your mind has stabilized on the clear appearance of all body parts of the father with one face and two arms, meditate by adding the

3619. Nāgārjuna, *Mdo bsre*, *Sādhanasūtramelāpaka*, Tōh 1797, 14b6.

other faces and arms. [182b] Once the appearance of the principal deity with all his faces and arms is clear and your mind is stable, add the other deities individually, first the mother, then Vairocana, and so forth. In the final stage, meditate gradually until you attain a mind[3620] stable in the simultaneous clear appearance of the entire maṇḍala of the celestial mansion and its deities.

For some, a strong divine identity may dawn while a clear appearance of the celestial mansion and its deities does not.[3621] For some, a clear appearance dawns while a strong divine identity does not. For some, both occur and for some, neither. All four logical possibilities may occur, it seems. Moreover, due to varying mental states among disciples, the arising of divine identity and clear appearance may occur in a diversity of ways. Therefore you should choose your own way of guiding in accordance with the disciple's mental state; specifically, master the vital points of the transmitted instructions found in the great books regarding the elimination of laxity and excitement and the application of mindfulness and alertness; then meditate on the eight conditionings for abandonment.[3622]

The ordinary appearances of the world and its inhabitants that must be eliminated are not those which appear to five-sense-consciousness, but rather those which appear to the mental consciousness as the ordinary world and its inhabitants.[3623] How are these appearances and ordinary identities blocked by meditating on the creation stage? They are not blocked by eradicating the seeds, as in the elimination on the supramundane path,[3624] nor by temporarily obstructing the manifestation of ordinary appearances and attitudes whether the meditator visualizes the deity yoga or not, as in the case of eliminating afflictive emotions in the desire realm and so forth, through the mundane path, the first concentration, and so forth. Rather, unless you suffer from incidental conditions such as bad health due to an imbalance of the elements and so forth, [183a] merely by visualizing the maṇḍala wheel, it will appear

3620. Reading *sems* for *soms* in our text.

3621. See Tsong kha pa, *Sngags rim chen mo*, chap. 12, 463.

3622. Reading *'du byed* for *'du shes* in our text. Tib. *spong ba'i 'du byed brgyad*, Skt. *aṣṭaprahāṇasaṃskāra*.

3623. See Tsong kha pa, *Sngags rim chen mo*, chap. 12, 463. See also his *Lam rim chung ba*, 142a2; English translation in Wallace 1998, 150.

3624. See Tsong kha pa, *Lam rim chen mo* 1997, 550–551; English translation in Cutler 2002, 91–92, on two kinds of special insight: the mundane path of insight, which eliminates manifest afflictions, and the supramundane path of insight, which eradicates the seeds of afflictions. Tsong kha pa cites here Asaṅga's *Nyan thos kyi sa*, *Śrāvakabhūmi*, Tōh 4036, on these two paths.

to your mind clearly as a direct perception in the very same way that you visualized it; and merely by meditating on divine identity, you will maintain a genuine divine identity with the resolve: "I am actually this particular deity." Thus you will engage naturally in both [the clear appearance of the maṇḍala wheel and divine identity] without exertion until the end of the session.

In summary, merely by meditating on deity yoga, the appearances of the impure world and its inhabitants that arise in your mind, and your attitudes toward them, will be transformed into pure appearances and attitudes, clear and intense; and you will be able to keep these pure appearances and attitudes stable naturally for a very long time[3625] without exertion. This is the meaning of blocking ordinary appearances and attitudes through the creation stage.

When yogis who have developed a greater habituation to deity yoga settle in equipoise of the creation stage, objects that appear to the consciousness of the five senses are averted, but the creation stage does not annul them.[3626] Rather, since mental consciousness is more intensely engaged in its object [i.e., deity yoga], the capacity of the immediately preceding condition[3627] of consciousness to arouse the five-sense-consciousness becomes diminished. As the Lord of Reasoning, Dharmakīrti, taught: "For consciousness that is intent on something becomes incapable of apprehending another object."[3628]

Whenever you meditate on the creation stage in this way, you develop an intense understanding that every appearance of the maṇḍala wheel that arises in your mind, while appearing, is empty of intrinsic existence and thus its arising is illusion-like.[3629] Furthermore, you should train yourself to perceive these appearances as a display of bliss and emptiness whereby the objective aspect of the wisdom of great bliss, indivisible from emptiness, arises in the form of the deity and the celestial mansion. This is of crucial importance, as explained many times.[3630] [183b] Such a way of practicing deity yoga is the

3625. Reading *ngang* for *dang* in our text.

3626. See also Tsong kha pa, *Sngags rim chen mo*, chap. 12, 464. Cited also by Ngag dbang dpal ldan, *Gsang chen rgyud sde bzhi'i sa lam gyi rnam gzhag rgyud gzhung gsal byed*, 14a2–3; English translation in Coghlan and Zarpani 2011, 114.

3627. Tib. *de ma thag rkyen*, Skt. *samanantarapratyaya*.

3628. Dharmakīrti, *Tshad ma rnam 'grel*, *Pramāṇavārttika*, *Pramāṇasiddhi*, Tōh 4210, 111b6; Miyasaka 1971–1972, v. 112; English translations in Jackson 1993, 294, v. 112, and Coghlan and Zarpani 2011, 114.

3629. See also Tsong kha pa, *Sngags rim chen mo*, chap. 12, 493. Cited also by Ngag dbang dpal ldan, *Gsang chen rgyud sde bzhi'i sa lam gyi rnam gzhag rgyud gzhung gsal byed*, 15b1–16a3; English translation in Coghlan and Zarpani 2011, 124–127.

3630. See above [38a].

coarse single-mindedness mentioned above,[3631] unlike the practice of subtle conceptual[3632] yoga that was explained before.[3633]

When your identity as the principal deity becomes somewhat stabilized by practicing in this way, the apprehension of "I am a deity" will occasionally manifest. But so long as the essence of the divine identity has not faded and the capacity of your conditioning has not diminished, all bodily movements and verbal utterances that are as yet karmically indeterminate will serve to complete your accumulations of merit and wisdom, to the same extent as the mudrās and mantras do. When your habituation to deity yoga becomes stable, many of your bodily movements and verbal utterances—which may be nonvirtuous when performed by others—will help you complete the accumulations, for as the *Activities of the Yoginīs* teaches: "While abiding at the stage of Śrī Heruka, the manifold movements and utterances you perform will be equal in number to your mudrās and mantras."[3634]

Explaining the Criteria for Completing the Creation Stage Through This Practice

The criteria for completing the subtle yoga have already been explained in the relevant context above and you may consult it.[3635] Regarding the criteria for completing the coarse yoga, the *Commentary on Difficult Points in the Tantra of the Black Yamāri* teaches: "When you spontaneously see the vajra body and so forth like a fruit in the palm of your hand, you attain mastery in wisdom, without being confined to sessions and in-between-sessions."[3636] Likewise the *Pearl Rosary* teaches: "You will attain siddhis by means of a stable mind, that

3631. See above [161b–162a].

3632. Reading *rtog* for *rtogs* in our text.

3633. See [159a–162a] above.

3634. *Kun spyod, Yoginīsañcāra*, Tōh 375, 42b1–2; Sanskrit and Tibetan in Pandey 1998, 137 and 339. D and Pandey have *he ru ka dpal gzhir gnas pa'i* for *shrī he ru ka yi go 'phang gnas*; *yan lag bskyod pa ji snyed dang* for *yan lag gi ni bskyod pa dang*; and *tshig tu brjod pa* for *tshig gi rab 'byams* in our text.

3635. See above [159a–161b].

3636. Ratnākaraśānti, *Gshin rje dgra nag po'i dka' 'grel rin po che'i sgron ma, Kṛṣṇayamāripañjikāratnapradīpa*, Tōh 1919, 160a7–b1.

is, by constantly being engaged in a state whereby you spontaneously appear in the form of the deity and maintain his or her divine identity."[3637] [184a]

Accordingly when the colors and shapes of the maṇḍala wheels of both the celestial mansion and the deities, the number of faces and arms, their emblems and ornaments and so forth, the lord of the tathāgata family with his consort upon the head, the [inner subtle] deities such as Kṣitigarbha with his consort visualized within the deities' eyeballs, their colors, emblems, number of faces and arms, up to[3638] the white and black of their eyes—all these appearances arise directly and clearly to mental consciousness, all at once and unmingled, and when your meditative equipoise is likewise accompanied by a mode of apprehension of yourself transforming into the actual identity of the deity, you will gain mastery in the habituation of engaging naturally for as long as you wish without the interference of ordinary thought.

The explanation for completing the session presented above refers to criteria for attaining *a stable mind*, not for the attainment of mastery in the creation stage; nevertheless, it is essential to attain mastery in order to complete [the creation stage]. The scriptures of the system of Jñānapāda and his followers[3639] refer to four levels: the beginner level,[3640] the initial dawning of wisdom,[3641] the attainment of initial mastery of wisdom,[3642] and the attainment of perfect mastery of wisdom.[3643] When you reach the fourth level you complete the

3637. Ratnākaraśānti, *Dgyes pa'i rdo rje'i dka' 'grel mu tig phreng ba, Hevajrapañjikāmuktikāvalī*, Tōh 1189, 273b1–2; Tripathi and Negi 2001, 138. D has *nga rgyal du gzhag pa rgyun tu ngang gis 'byung ba* for *de'i nga rgyal bdag la nyi ma re re zhing rang gi ngang gis 'jug pa de* in our text. This is a commentary on the *Kye'i rdo rje mkha' 'gro ma dra ba'i sdom pa, Hevajra Tantra II*, Tōh 418, 14b6–7; Snellgrove 1959, II.ii.15. Our text follows the reading in Tsong kha pa's *Sngags rim chen mo*, chap. 12, 472.

3638. Reading *tshun chad* for *chun chad* in our text.

3639. See Dīpaṅkarabhadra, *Gsang ba 'dus pa'i dkyil 'khor gyi cho ga = Dkyil chog bzhi rgya lnga bcu pa, Guhyasamāja Maṇḍalavidhi*, Tōh 1865, 74b2–4; Bahulkar 2006, 124, vv. 133–136; and Klein-Schwind 2008, vv. 133–136. See also its commentary by Ratnākaraśānti, *Gsang ba 'dus pa'i dkyil 'khor gyi cho ga'i 'grel pa, Guhyasamāja Maṇḍalavidhiṭīkā*, Tōh 1871, 87a4–b3. See also Tsong kha pa, *Sngags rim chen mo*, chap. 12, 464–469.

3640. Tib. *dang po'i las* or *las dang po pa*, Skt. *ādikarmika*.

3641. Tib. *ye shes cung zad babs pa*, Skt. *jñāne kiñcitsamāveśī*.

3642. Tib. *ye shes la cung zad dbang thob pa* or *ye shes dbang ba cung zad 'thob pa*, Skt. *prāptajñānavaśī kiñcid*.

3643. Tib. *ye shes la yang dag par dbang thob pa* or *yang dag ye shes dbang thob pa*, Skt. *samyagjñānavaśī*.

practice of the creation stage, and only then can you proceed to practice the completion stage.[3644]

The beginner level extends from the first meditation on the creation stage and continues until you have attained the clear appearance of the coarse deities of the maṇḍala. At the second level, the maṇḍala with the coarse deities placed within appears directly and clearly to your mind and all at once, but the subtle deities, Kṣitigarbha placed on the eyes and so forth, do not appear as clearly as do the coarse deities. In order to be able to see them clearly, you must practice this meditation in stages. The third level [184b] occurs when the subtle deities too appear clearly, as described above. Since the *Great Treatise on the Stages of the Mantric Path* by the Great Vajradhara explains the system in detail, you can understand it by consulting his work.[3645]

How long must you habituate for the direct and clear appearance of the deities to arise?[3646] The *Commentary on the Compendium of Truth of All Tathāgatas* teaches: "Thus you should meditate every day until you see directly the great Vajradhātu maṇḍala. Or else, once you have completed the three samādhis[3647] you meditate either for six months or a year."[3648] Nor do other works specify that it is necessary to meditate for longer than one year. Therefore, once you have received initiation properly and adhered strictly to your vows and commitments, if you master the key points of the practice and persevere in your meditation day and night, you need not practice for a very long time.

If you rub fire sticks together, making the wood hot, and then rest a while and let the sticks cool a bit, and then rub them again and take a rest, the fire will not ignite. But if you continue to rub the sticks together when heat begins to rise, it will increase, and the fire will finally ignite. So too, if you meditate perseveringly on deity yoga, and a clear appearance begins to arise thereby, and then while the strength of your concentration subsides, your mind is distracted by other activities, whether dharmic or nondharmic, and you waver in your practice, a great many years might pass from the first to the last moment

3644. Reading *rdzogs* for *rdzags* in our text.

3645. See Tsong kha pa, *Sngags rim chen mo*, chap. 12, 465–469. Tsong kha pa relies here on the aforementioned commentary by Ratnākaraśānti, *Gsang ba 'dus pa'i dkyil 'khor gyi cho ga'i 'grel pa, Guhyasamāja Maṇḍalavidhiṭikā*, Tōh 1871.

3646. Reading *skye bar* for *skya bar* in our text.

3647. Tib. *ting nge 'dzin gsum*. These are the First Yoga, Supreme King of Maṇḍalas, and Supreme King of Deeds.

3648. Ānandagarbha, *De nyid bsdus pa'i bstod 'grel, Sarvatathāgatatattvasaṅgrahavyākhyā*, Tōh 2510, 148a6–7. See also Tsong kha pa, *Sngags rim chen mo*, chap. 12, 473. Both D and the *Sngags rim chen mo* have *nyin re zhing for nyin re bzhin* in our text.

of your practice, but you will not achieve clear appearance. Whereas, if you meditate by exerting yourself over and over to increase the capacity of each of the earlier mental moments of clear appearance and identification with the deity without letting the experience diminish, [185a] you will accomplish clear appearance swiftly, for as Āryaśūra teaches: "You should exert yourself in the practice of concentration through continuous yoga. If you rest again and again while rubbing the sticks, fire will not ignite. Similarly, you should not interrupt your practice of yoga till you achieve a special attainment."[3649]

There is no need to begin with a meditation on quiescence for a stabilized appearance of the deity to arise directly and clearly. Although things do not exist in actuality as you meditate on them, when you habituate to the objects of your meditation, they arise directly in your mental consciousness. There is no contradiction here, for the master logician, Dharmakīrti, taught: "Though unreal, [meditational objects such as] 'the loathsome'[3650] and *kṛtsna*,[3651] when manifest through the powers of meditation, are clear and nonconceptual."[3652]

Nevertheless, is it inconsistent to say that the mental continuum of a yogi who engages in conceptual meditation can thereby become nonconceptual?[3653] If this were inconsistent, however long you engaged in conceptual habituation, no clear appearance of an object could possibly arise, as the master logician, Dharmakīrti, taught: "Awareness bound up in conceptual thinking lacks a clear perception of its objects."[3654] If the appearance of the object arises clearly without any blending of time or place, yet a nonconceptual perception of the object is not attained, no line of reasoning could possibly refute the position of non-Buddhists who assert that the sense consciousnesses are conceptual.[3655]

3649. Āryaśūra, *Pha rol tu phyin pa bsdus pa*, *Pāramitāsamāsa*, Tōh 3944, 229a3–4. D has *bso* for *bsos*, and *me 'gyur* for *mi 'gyur*. Cited also in Tsong kha pa, *Sngags rim chen mo*, chap. 12, 473.

3650. Tib. *mi gtsang*, Skt. *aśubhā*.

3651. Literally, "earth-totality," Tib. *zad par sa*, Skt. *pṛthivīkṛtsna*.

3652. Dharmakīrti, *Tshad ma rnam 'grel*, *Pramāṇavārttika*, *Pratyakṣa*, Tōh 4210, 129a6; Miyasaka 1971–1972, v. 284; English translations in Dunne 2006, 516; Eltschinger 2009, 195; and Yarnall 2013, 100. D has *bsgoms* for *bsgom* and *rtog* for *rtogs* in our text. Cited also in Tsong kha pa, *Sngags rim chen mo*, chap. 11, 442.

3653. Reading *rtog* for *rtogs* in our text.

3654. Dharmakīrti, *Tshad ma rnam 'grel*, *Pramāṇavārttika*, *Pratyakṣa*, Tōh 4210, 129a6; Miyasaka 1971–1972, v. 283ab; English translations in Dunne 2006, 516; and Yarnall 2013, 99. D has *rtog* for *rtogs* and *ni* for *gang* in our text. Cited also in Tsong kha pa, *Sngags rim chen mo*, chap. 11, 442.

3655. On the differences between the Nyāya school and Dharmakīrti on this point, see Dreyfus 1997, 344–353.

If no matter how long you engage in conceptual habituation, no clear appearance of the object you habituate arises, you will have no homologous example at your disposal[3656] to serve as the basis for ascertaining the forward entailment[3657] of the correct evidence[3658] in order to prove direct yogic perception to those non-Buddhist opponents who maintain that liberation is impossible; [185b] therefore you would have to discount the significance of the line by the master logician: "Those who are deranged by desire, grief, or fear, or by dreams of thieves and so forth, see these distressing objects that are unreal as if they were right in front of them."[3659] There are a great many things that could be said about this, but I will stop here for the sake of brevity.

Yogis who complete the coarse creation stage are called "wholly devoted to mantra,"[3660] and yogis who complete the subtle yoga as well are said to be "wholly devoted inwardly."[3661] These terms are taught again and again in the tantras and their commentaries.[3662]

How Siddhis Are Attained upon the Completion of the Creation Stage[3663]

Generally, there are two types of attainable siddhis for meditators on mantra: worldly and nonworldly. Since at this point we will not consider the realization arising in the mental continuum of meditators on the completion stage,

3656. Tib. *mthun dpe*, Skt. *sādharmyadṛṣṭānta*.

3657. Tib. *rjes khyab*, Skt. *anvayavyāpti*.

3658. Tib. *rtags yang dag*, Skt. *samyakliṅga*.

3659. Dharmakīrti, *Tshad ma rnam 'grel*, *Pramāṇavārttika*; Miyasaka 1971–1972, chap. 3, v. 282, 129a5; English translations in Dunne 2006, 516; Eltschinger 2009, 193; and Yarnall 2013, 155. D has *min pa* for *min pa 'ang* in our text. Cited also in Tsong kha pa, *Sngags rim chen mo*, chap. 12, 470.

3660. Tib. *sngags la mchog tu gzhol ba*, Skt. *mantraparāyaṇa*.

3661. Tib. *nang la mchog tu gzhol ba*, Skt. *adhyātmaparāyaṇa*.

3662. See, for example, the opening of Āryadeva's *Spyod bsdus*, *Caryāmelāpakapradīpa*, chap. 1, Tōh 1803, 57a3–4; Sanskrit, Tibetan, and English translation in Wedemeyer 2007, A: 1b; Sanskrit and Tibetan in Pandey 2000, 1 and 153. See also *Yaśobhadra/Nāropa, *Gsang ba thams cad kyi sgron ma'i rgya cher 'grel pa*, *Sarvaguhyapradīpaṭīkā*, Tōh 1787, 208a4–6, 208b5, 220a5 and 233a2–3. See also Candrakīrti's *Sgron gsal*, *Pradīpoddyotanaṭīkā*, Tōh 1785, cited below [187b]. These terms appear also in Dbyangs can dga' ba'i blo gros, *Sngags kyi sa lam*, 3b2–4; English translation in Tenzin Dorjee and Russell 1995, 41, and Coghlan and Zarpani, n.d, 24.

3663. See Tsong kha pa, *Rim lnga gsal sgron*, chap. 10, 340b3–341a4; English translation in Kilty 2013, 559–560.

the siddhis available to meditators on the creation stage are of the first kind [worldly siddhis], as taught [in the *Illuminating Lamp*]: "The ritual activities of pacification and so forth and the eight attainments."[3664]

The lesser siddhis are the four activities: *pacification of* illnesses; *increase of* life, wisdom, affluence, and so forth; *subjugation of* kings, ministers, countries, consorts, fortunate disciples, and so forth; and [*fierce*] killing, banishing, and freezing of harmful beings, and so forth. The middling siddhis are the eight attainments as taught for example in the *Request of the Four Goddesses*: "I will explain the eight substances and subsidiary attainments: The siddhis of pills, of eye medicine, of subterranean travel, of swords, of flying through the sky, of invisibility, of immortality, and of overcoming illness."[3665]

What is the siddhi of pills?[3666] If, after empowering the pills as taught in the *Request of the Four Goddesses*, [186a] you steadily consume a pill a day, you will gain six advantages: your body will become radiant as light, shining as refined gold, powerful as Nārāyaṇa, you will persevere with intense delight in virtuous deeds, you will attain your aspirations to their fullest extent, and you will attain the five extrasensory perceptions,[3667] magical powers[3668] and so forth.

The siddhis of eye medicine are as explained in the *Illuminating Lamp*:[3669] By relying on empowered gray powder[3670] eye medicine, you will obtain three siddhis: the highest is invisibility, the middle is seeing treasures buried underground, and the lowest is overcoming others with a mere glance. The siddhi of subterranean travel means that meditators are able to travel in their ordinary bodies back and forth several leagues under this great earth like fish in water, and so forth. The siddhi of swords means that having empowered an object such as sword, merely by wielding it you will be able to arrive instantly wherever you wish, even the celestial realms, the summit of Mount Meru, the

3664. Candrakīrti, *Sgron gsal, Pradīpoddyotanaṭīkā*, chap. 1, Tōh 1785, 2b2; Chakravarti 1984, 2. The line of the *Sgron gsal*, Tōh 1785, ends with: "and the supreme attainment of buddhahood."

3665. *Lha mo bzhis zhus pa, Caturdevīparipṛcchā*, Tōh 446, 280a7. D has *sgrub* for *bsgrub*; *ril bu* for *ri lu*; *mig sman* for *mi snang*; *'chi ba* for *shi ba*; and *dang* for *so*.

3666. Our text follows here Tsong kha pa's commentary on this tantra, *Bzhis zhus* 43a1–3.

3667. Tib. *mngon shes*, Skt. *abhijñā*.

3668. Tib. *rdzu 'phrul*, Skt. *ṛddhi*.

3669. This is based on Candrakīrti, *Sgron gsal, Pradīpoddyotanaṭīkā*, chap. 17, Tōh 1785, 193a3–4; Chakravarti 1984, 222, but is taken from Tsong kha pa's paraphrase of this passage in his *Bzhis zhus*, 41b3.

3670. Perhaps lampblack or antimony.

No-Higher Heaven,[3671] and so forth. The meanings of the remaining siddhis are easily understood.

As explained, meditators on the creation stage who are "wholly devoted to mantra"[3672] attain these siddhis through recitations, fire offerings, the use of substances, *yantras*, and so forth; while meditators on the creation stages who are "wholly devoted inwardly" can attain any of these siddhis merely by becoming absorbed in concentration without recourse to such means. The latter can acquire the siddhis of pills and objects and so forth merely by using meditative pills and objects without the actual substances.

Mantrins who have maintained their commitments and pledges, [186b] who have reached some degree of stabilized deity yoga, and have completed a certain number of recitations and so forth, can from this stage on realize several minor[3673] achievements, such as alleviating illnesses. These meditators can attain great shared siddhis far beyond those explained in the lower tantras. Although in terms of their level, these siddhis are shared with the lower tantras, to attain them, mantrins need not practice for a long time or undergo the difficulties explained in the lower tantras. They can attain such special siddhis with little difficulty, swiftly—in as little time as seven days or less. Still, in order to attain them, those who have fully completed either the subtle or coarse creation stage must rely on one of the three postmeditative practices.[3674]

Therefore the *Guhyasamāja Root Tantra*, the *Later Tantra*, and the *Illuminating Lamp* all teach that meditators on the creation stage must engage in the three postmeditative practices. The reason for this is that if you have completed the creation stage, and without attaining the shared siddhis you engage in the meditation on the completion stage, it will be pointless to then engage in the postmeditative practices.

Mantrins who are "wholly devoted inwardly" and engage in any of the three postmeditative practices for six months can attain all the siddhis without hindrance and without relying on the practices of enhancement and arousing the deity's heart.[3675] Practitioners who are "wholly devoted to mantra" and who practice for six months yet do not attain the special siddhis as explained, must

3671. Tib. 'Og min, Skt. Akaniṣṭha.

3672. See above [185b].

3673. Reading *tshegs* for *chegs* in our text here and immediately below.

3674. Tib. *spyod pa*, Skt. *caryā*. These are elaborated practices, Tib. *spros pa dang bcas pa'i spyod pa*, Skt. *prapañcacaryā*; unelaborated practices, Tib. *spros pa med pa'i spyod pa*, Skt. *niṣprapañcacaryā*; and completely unelaborated practices, Tib. *shin tu spros pa med pa'i spyod pa*, Skt. *atyantaniṣprapañcacaryā*.

3675. Tib. *snying po bskul ba*, Skt. *hṛdaya[saṃ]codana*.

engage in the enhancements of the postmeditative practices for another six months. If they do not attain them even then, they must practice the enhancements of the postmeditative practices for six more months. If they engage in the three postmeditative practices in this way three times for eighteen months and still do not attain the special siddhis as explained, [187a] they should drive stakes into the deities, as the *Later Tantra* teaches, and arouse their hearts for seven days through the two practices of the hooks that the tenth chapter of the *Guhyasamāja Tantra* teaches.[3676] Thus meditators on the creation stage who are "wholly devoted to mantra" will surely attain the special siddhis as explained.

The *Later Tantra* explains [how to attain siddhis] in this way: "Mantrins who are able to see [what was previously explained] after meditating on the twofold practice for six months should continuously practice without failing, enjoying all objects of desire. Those who are unable to see after practicing for six months must engage in the ritual and vows three times [six months] as explained. Those who still cannot see [after eighteen months], should practice *haṭhayoga* as long as they have not achieved [a condition for] awakening. Then, as through this yoga, the wisdom siddhi arises, they should drive the vajra-stakes by means of the yoga of division into tathāgata families and afterward engage in the practices of subjugation and protection."[3677] Likewise, the tenth chapter of the *Guhyasamāja Tantra* explains this in detail from the beginning up to: "If you practice this supreme vajra method for seven days, you will attain the secret body, speech, and mind and become a holder of vajra wisdom."[3678]

Why should the deity's heart be aroused? Some mantrins endowed with special siddhis who engage in postmeditative practices in order to reach attainments swiftly attain the special ability to unite bliss with emptiness, and as a result the deities of the maṇḍala bless them directly; while mantrins endowed with different minds and faculties who engage in postmeditative practices for eighteen months [187b] but have still not been able to realize the union of bliss with emptiness will not be blessed by the deities of the maṇḍala directly and must arouse the hearts of the deities in order to be blessed by them.

3676. *Guhyasamāja Tantra*, Tōh 442; Zhol 14b1–3; Stog 24a7–b5; Dunh 26b1–27a1; Fremantle 1971, vv. 10–16; and Matsunaga 1978, vv. 10–16.

3677. *Rgyud phyi ma*, *Uttara Tantra*, Tōh 443, 155a2–4; Matsunaga 1978, vv. 160–164ab. D has *gang tshe bya ba* for *gal te byang chub*; *'byung* for *'gyur*; *srung* for *bsrung*; and *bya* for *byed* in our text. Our text follows the readings of the Zhol. Tsong kha pa explains these verses in his *Mtha' gcod*, 104b5–105b6.

3678. *Guhyasamāja Tantra*, Tōh 442; Zhol 14b2–3; Stog 24b3–4; Dunh 26b4; Fremantle 1971, v. 14; and Matsunaga 1978, v. 14.

Arousing the hearts of the deities in this way is meant for mantrins who have not yet engaged in postmeditative practices and also for those who are "wholly devoted to mantra" as we see in the *Illuminating Lamp*: "These [lines of the *Guhyasamāja Tantra*][3679] explain that when yogis who have fully engaged in habituation to the three postmeditative practices, beginning with the elaborated practice,[3680] and still do not attain siddhis must arouse the hearts of their deities."[3681] And: "When [the Blessed One] saw that the tathāgatas turned their faces away from mantrins 'wholly devoted to mantra,' [he taught] aspirants how to make themselves acceptable in the eyes of the tathāgatas so that they might receive their grace,"[3682] and so forth. To learn how to engage in these postmeditative practices, how to meditate and reflect while you practice them, how to arouse the hearts of the deities and so forth, consult the extensive explanation of our venerable master Tsongkhapa in his *Lamp to Illuminate the Five Stages*[3683] and *The Analysis of Tantra*.[3684]

It is highly recommended that meditators on the creation stage engage in each and every one of these activities through absorption in union with any of the three consorts, for the *Sādhana Incorporating the Scripture* explains: "Then, the tenth chapter of the *Guhyasamāja Tantra* teaches: 'You should meditate on all the personifications of the mantra perfected in the wisdom of the three vajras through the union of the two organs.' With these lines the *Guhyasamāja Tantra* explains the practice of all activities, pacification and so forth, through the union of the vajra and lotus."[3685] [188a] Likewise the *Vajrasattva Sādhana* teaches: "You should accomplish all your activities—outer and inner fire offerings, recitations of the three syllables, the garland mantra or [other] mantras, preparation of pills—by joining together the vajra

3679. The lines of the tenth chapter of the *Guhyasamāja Tantra*, one of which was translated in a previous paragraph.

3680. These are elaborated practices, unelaborated practices, and completely unelaborated practices.

3681. Candrakīrti, *Sgron gsal, Pradīpoddyotanaṭīkā*, chap. 10, Tōh 1785, 70b1–2; Chakravarti 1984, 89. D has *snying pos* for *snying po* in our text.

3682. Candrakīrti, *Sgron gsal, Pradīpoddyotanaṭīkā*, Tōh 1785, 72a5–6; Chakravarti 1984, 90.

3683. Tsong kha pa, *Rim lnga gsal sgron*, chap. 10, 318b3–340b4; English translation in Kilty 2013, 527–558.

3684. Tsong kha pa, *Mtha' gcod*, chap. 10, 103b4–110a4.

3685. Nāgārjuna, *Mdo bsre, Sādhanasūtramelāpaka*, Tōh 1797, 15a1–2. D has *sbyar bas* for *sbyor bas* and *bsrub pa'i* for *bsrub pa'o* in our text. Like our text the *Mdo bsre* has *gnyis ni* and not *gnyis kyi* as in the Zhol and Stog editions of the *Guhyasamāja Tantra*, Tōh 442; Zhol 14b4; Stog 24b6–7; Dunh 27a2; Fremantle 1971, v. 18; and Matsunaga 1978, v. 18.

and lotus."[3686] There are numerous explanations on this matter in the tantric scriptures.

You must thoroughly apprehend all three spheres[3687] of any activity you may practice, in whatever way you practice it and so forth, by meditating on the view of emptiness—recollecting that while things appear in various ways, they are all illusion-like and empty of intrinsic nature. Otherwise, you will not be able to accomplish these activities as explained. Therefore, in the passage leading to the fifteenth chapter, the *Illuminating Lamp* teaches: "The siddhis of the activities of pacification and so forth, whether they have been clarified or not yet clarified, cannot be attained without a complete understanding of[3688] the illusion-like samādhi."[3689] Numerous such explanations are found in the higher and lower tantras and in various authentic treatises.

Vajra recitation that unites the winds indivisibly with the mantras affords special enhancement of mantric abilities to meditators on the creation stage, and thereby assists them in swiftly accomplishing the activities, for as the fourteenth chapter of the *Guhyasamāja Tantra* teaches: "The supremely perfect and beautiful vajra king of cessation promptly summons all [deities] who arise from the three vajra wisdoms."[3690]

For mantrins who accomplish this group of activities relying on the creation stage [188b] there are eight shared variations.[3691] The first group of four variations—that relates to the "four activities"[3692]—includes variations in (1) the direction you face; (2) the time of day you engage in the practice; (3) the color of your robe according to the deity of the practice and so forth; (4) and your thoughts on the practice of each activity. The second group of four variations includes: (1) the place where you practice each activity; (2) the object

3686. Candrakīrti, *Rdo rje sems dpa'i sgrub thabs*, *Vajrasattva Sādhana*, Tōh 1814, 204b2–3; Luo and Tomabechi 2009, 32.7–8 and 66.9–12. D and Luo and Tomabechi have *sbyin sreg* for *sbyin sreg dang* in our text. The Sanskrit equivalent of *sman gyi sbyor ba* is *adhiyoga* or *saṃyoga*.

3687. Tib. *'khor gsum*: action, actor, and object acted upon.

3688. Tsong kha pa adds here "and meditating." See his *Sgron gsal mchan*, 375b5.

3689. Candrakīrti, *Sgron gsal*, *Pradīpoddyotanaṭīkā*, Tōh 1785, 136a2–3; Chakravarti 1984, 162.

3690. *Guhyasamāja Tantra*, Tōh 442; Zhol 29a4; Stog missing; Dunh 53a4; Fremantle 1971, v. 45; and Matsunaga 1978, v. 45. Zhol has *'gog pa* for *'gog pa'i* in our text. See Candrakīrti's *Sgron gsal*, *Pradīpoddyotanaṭīkā*, Tōh 1785, 131a1–4; Chakravarti 1984, 156; and Tsong kha pa's *Sgron gsal mchan*, 364b5–365a5.

3691. Our text follows Tsong kha pa, *Mtha' gcod*, chap. 14, 128b2–129a4.

3692. These are pacification, enhancement, subjugation, and fierce activities.

of your practice; (3) the food that sustains you while you accomplish each activity; (4) and the ritual you engage in to accomplish each activity. The first four are taught in the *Vajra Garland Explanatory Tantra* and are cited in the *Illuminating Lamp*, while the latter four are expounded in the *Guhyasamāja Root Tantra* and its commentary. To understand them in detail, consult these tantras. I will write no more about this here for the sake of brevity.

Prior to accomplishing any activity, it is taught that all meditators on the creation stage—whether beginners who have developed a slight habituation to deity yoga or those who have reached the end of the coarse creation stage—must complete their familiarization with all deities of the maṇḍala—the principal deity and the surrounding deities. Then, using any mantra, such as the garland mantras of the four goddesses or the garland mantras of the fierce deities, they should recite the particular mantra for accomplishing their activities one hundred thousand times. As the fourteenth chapter of the *Guhyasamāja Tantra* teaches: "Or, it is further explained, upon reciting the mantras of all the fierce deities one hundred thousand times in areas of great isolation, mantrins will [be able to] accomplish all activities."[3693]

Furthermore, the *Saṃvarodaya Tantra* teaches: "During the golden age[3694] recite once; during the second age,[3695] twice; [189a] during the third age,[3696] thrice; and during the age of degeneration,[3697] four times."[3698] Accordingly, whatever number of special recitations is taught in the practice of the activities at the end of the sādhana, nowadays each mantra should be recited four times.

Here ends the explanation on how meditators on the creation stage attain the siddhis.

This work is entitled "Ocean of Attainments: An Explanation of the

3693. *Guhyasamāja Tantra*, Tōh 442; Zhol 29a4; Stog missing; Dunh 53a4–5; Fremantle 1971, v. 46; and Matsunaga 1978, v. 46. Candrakīrti, *Sgron gsal, Pradīpoddyotanaṭīkā*, Tōh 1785, 131a4–6; Chakravarti 1984, 156, comments on this verse, and Tsong kha pa's *Sgron gsal mchan*, 365a5–b4, refers to the line of the *Sdom 'byung, Saṃvarodaya Tantra*, Tōh 373, cited immediately below.

3694. Tib. *rdzogs ldaṇ*, Skt. *satya*.

3695. Tib. *gsum ldan*, Skt. *tretā*.

3696. Tib. *gnyis ldan*, Skt. *dvāpara*.

3697. Tib. *rtsod ldan*, Skt. *kaliyuga*.

3698. The *Sdom 'byung, Saṃvarodaya Tantra*, chap. 12, Tōh 373, 280a5; Stog 196a4–5; not in Tsuda 1974. D and Stog have *rdzogs ldan dus su gcig bzlas pa* for *rdzogs ldan la ni bzlas bya gcig*; *gsum ldan dus su nyis 'gyur bzlas* for *nyis 'gyur gsum ldan la bzlas bya*; *gnyis ldan dus na sum 'gyur bshad* for *sum 'gyur gnyis ldan la rab brjod*; and *rtsod dus bzhi 'gyur du ni bzla* for *rtsod ldan bzlas pa bzhi 'gyur ro* in our text which follows Tsong kha pa's *Sngags rim chen mo*, chap. 5, 171.

Sādhana, the Method of Practicing the Creation Stage of the Guhyasamāja, the King of All Tantras." I touch my head to the lotus feet of the Venerable Great Tsongkhapa, the All-Knowing King of Dharma, master of attainment who is inseparable from Vajradhara, the lord of all the victorious ones, who has illuminated the path of the three vehicles through immaculate reasoning, unfolding every meaning of the three baskets of scriptures and the four classes of tantra. The venerable Gelek Palsangpo[3699]—fearless in the presence of the masters, who has attained the exalted stage of the leader of the flock and reached the other side of the ocean-like tenets, Buddhist and non-Buddhist—composed this work in the great temple Palkhor Dechen[3700]—the monastic school that is in a grove[3701] of fine elucidations, located in upper Nyang in Tsang—the site and source of reasoning. The scribe who carefully prepared this book,[3702] Lodrö Chökyong,[3703] studied all classes of scriptures and tantras, and led an austere life, abiding in the pure vow-observance of the Sage.

Through the merits of my composition, may all precious teachings spread far and wide and may they long endure.

3699. Dge legs dpal bzang po.

3700. Dpal 'khor sde chen.

3701. Reading *tshal* for *tshul* in our text.

3702. Reading *legs par* for *lags par* in our text.

3703. Blo gros chos skyong (1389–1463), the Fifth Ganden Tripa, assumed office in 1450.

Topic Outline

[Homage and Introduction]

I. Characteristics of the yogis, 5a2

II. The reasons yogis should meditate on the creation stage before they meditate on the completion stage, 9a6

III. Characteristics of the place of practice, 13b1

IV. The practice—how the realization is attained, 13b4

A. The scriptures on which the explanation relies, 13b4

B. The practice based on these genuine scriptures, 14b3

1. The First Yoga, 14b4

1.1. Preliminary stages of the practice, 14b5

1.1.1. The preparatory steps, 14b5

1.1.1.1. Making the preliminary tormas, 14b5

1.1.1.2. The mode of sitting, 15a5

1.1.1.3. Blessing the offerings, 15b1

1.1.1.4. Recitation of the hundred-syllable mantra of Vajrasattva, 16b1

1.1.2. Making offerings to the field for accumulating merit, maintaining vows, and so forth, to establish favorable conditions, 16b3

1.1.2.1. The sevenfold worship, 18a6

1.1.3. Meditating on the protection wheel to avert unfavorable conditions, 21b3

1.2. Explanation of the actual meditation—the First Yoga, 31b4

1.2.1. The yoga of taking death as the dharmakāya—the specially visualized deities, 31b6

1.2.1.1. Visualization of the celestial mansion—the place where you will be awakened, 32a1

1.2.1.1.1. Meditation on the ground of wisdom in correspondence with the empty eon that follows the dissolution of the previous world, 32a1

1.2.1.1.1.1. Refutation of the claim that it is not necessary to

meditate on emptiness during the creation stage, 32a2
1.2.1.1.1.2. The method of meditating on the ground of wisdom, 38b6
1.2.1.1.1.3. The purpose of the meditation on emptiness at this point of the sādhana, 41b3
1.2.1.1.2. Visualization of the vajra ground and meditating on the celestial mansion in correspondence with the evolution of the subsequent world, 43b5
1.2.1.1.2.1. Generating the vajra ground, 43b5
1.2.1.1.2.2. Meditating on the celestial mansion, 50a1
1.2.1.1.2.2.1. Measurements for drawing and meditating on the celestial mansion, 50a3
1.2.1.1.2.2.2. The essentials for drawing and meditating on the celestial mansion of the maṇḍala, 51a1
1.2.1.1.2.2.2.1. [The surroundings of the celestial mansion] between the garland of light and the portals, 51a3
1.2.1.1.2.2.2.1.1. Explanation of the area between the garland of light and the crossed vajra, 51a4
1.2.1.1.2.2.2.1.2. Explanation of the portals, 54a2
1.2.1.1.2.2.2.2. Explaining the actual celestial mansion along with the thrones, 58a6
1.2.1.2. Visualization of the deities—the indwellers of the maṇḍala who will be awakened there, 68b6
1.2.1.2.1. Placing the specially visualized deities, 69a1
1.2.1.2.1.1. How to visualize the deities and in correspondence with whom, 69a2
1.2.1.2.1.2. The reason for visualizing the deities in correspondence with the people of the first eon, 73a1
1.2.1.2.1.2.1. Refuting the system of others, 73b6
1.2.1.2.1.2.2. Establishing our own position, 76a1
1.2.1.2.1.3. The meaning of purifying the ground of purification by means of the creation stage, 80a5
1.2.1.2.1.3.1. Removing uncertainty as it pertains to the explanation of correspondence with the stages of saṃsāric evolution, 80a6
1.2.1.2.1.3.1.1. Points of uncertainty that may arise in those endowed with an inquiring mind, 80b1
1.2.1.2.1.3.1.2. Our response to these points of uncertainty, 80b6
1.2.1.2.1.3.2. Why the other parts of the sādhana are not applied in correspondence with the stages of saṃsāric evolution, 84b3

1.2.1.2.1.3.2.1. Refuting the system of others, 84b4
1.2.1.2.1.3.2.2. Establishing our own position, 86b4
1.2.1.2.2. The "deeds" of the specially visualized deities, 88a2
1.2.1.2.3. Gathering the specially visualized deities into the body, 89a3
1.2.1.2.4. Dissolution of the specially visualized deities into the ultimate maṇḍala—the method of awakening, 90b2
1.2.2. The yoga of taking the intermediate being as the saṃbhogakāya—visualizing the First Lord, 96b1
1.2.2.1. The intermediate being, the ground of purification, 96b2
1.2.2.1.1. The essential characteristics of the intermediate being and its duration, 96b3
1.2.2.1.2. Explanation of the specific intermediate being that displays awakening in Jambudvīpa after rebirth, 97b5
1.2.2.1.3. Explaining the three minds—the mind that passes into the intermediate being, the mind at the death of the intermediate being, and the mind at rebirth into new life, 98a5
1.2.2.1.3.1. Establishing our own position, 98a5
1.2.2.1.3.2. Refuting the position of others, 100a4
1.2.2.2. How to visualize the First Lord in correspondence with this ground of purification, 101a1
1.2.2.2.1. Refuting the imputation of others, 101a1
1.2.2.2.2. Establishing our own position, 103b1
1.2.3. The yoga of taking birth as the nirmāṇakāya—transforming into Vajrasattva's nirmāṇakāya, 107b3
1.2.3.1. The ground of purification—taking birth in a womb, 107b4
1.2.3.2. The meditation that corresponds to it: Which stage of the purifier corresponds to which stage in the ground of purification, 111a4
1.2.3.2.1. How the First Lord transforms into Vajrasattva's nirmāṇakāya, 111a5
1.2.3.2.1.1. Refuting the position of others, 111a5
1.2.3.2.1.2. Establishing our own system, 111b3
1.2.3.2.2. How the visualization of placing the deities on the transformed body and so forth is applied to the ground of purification, 115a5
1.2.3.3. A separate explanation of how to meditate on the body maṇḍala, 116a6
1.2.3.3.1. Refuting the systems of others, 116b1
1.2.3.3.2. Establishing our own system, 124b4
1.2.3.3.2.1. General explanation about the method for generating one's body as maṇḍala with its celestial

mansion and deities, 124b5
1.2.3.3.2.2. The specific explanation—which deity is generated from which seed syllable at which location on the body, 127a5
1.2.3.4. The blessing of the body, speech, and mind and the meditation on the triple sattvas, 131a6
1.2.3.4.1. Blessing the three doors, 131a6
1.2.3.4.1.1. Blessing the body, 131b5
1.2.3.4.1.2. Blessing speech, 133a5
1.2.3.4.1.3. Blessing the mind, 134b1
1.2.3.4.1.4. Maintaining a divine identity as Vajradhara, the indivisible three vajras, 135b5
1.2.3.4.2. Meditation on the triple sattvas, 136b2
1.2.4. Seeking and absorbing in union with the consort to demonstrate that these three bodies are attained through the dharma of passion, 139b5
1.2.4.1. Seeking the consort and blessing, 139b5
1.2.4.2. The activities of passion and offerings, 145a1
2. Explaining the samādhi of the Supreme King of Maṇḍalas, 147a3
2.1. The actual explanation, 147a3
2.2. Removing uncertainties concerning the Supreme King of Maṇḍalas, 152a6
2.2.1. Examining uncertainties concerning the sealing of the deities with the four seals, 152a6
2.2.2. Examining uncertainties concerning the appearance of the deities, 153b1
2.2.3. Examining uncertainties concerning the number of deities, 156a3
3. Explaining the samādhi of the Supreme King of Deeds, 159a1
3.1. The yoga pertaining to the actual meditation session, 159a1
3.1.1. The yoga of the subtle drop, 159a2
3.1.2. The yoga of recitation, 162a5
3.1.2.1. Vajra recitation, 162a5
3.1.2.2. Voiced recitation, 163a4
3.1.3. Dissolving into clear light and arising in response to the invocation with a song, 164b6
3.1.4. Praises, offerings, and tasting the nectar, 166a1
3.1.5. The ritual method of dissolving the visualization, 172b3
3.2. The yoga between meditative sessions, 173b1
3.2.1. The yoga of body enhancement, 173b1
3.2.2. Food yoga, 174a1
3.2.3. The yoga of sleeping and waking, 176a2

3.2.4. The yoga of offering tormas, 176a3

3.3. The framework of the sādhana, 177b5

3.3.1. The four limbs of familiarization and achievement, 178a1

3.3.2. The four yogas, 179b4

3.3.3. The three samādhis, 180a6

3.3.4. The forty-nine essential points, 180b3

4. How to habituate your mind to the visualization during the creation stage, 180b5

4.1. How to meditate on the sādhana during the four sessions, 180b5

4.2. The actual method of maintaining the visualization, 181b1

V. Explaining the criteria for completing the creation stage through this practice, 183b4

VI. How siddhis are attained upon the completion of the creation stage, 185b3

Abbreviations

D	Sde dge edition of the Bka' 'gyur and Bstan 'gyur
Dunh	Dunhuang, IOL (India Office Library), Tib. J 481 and IOL Tib. J 438
L	La Vallée Poussin 1896
Mvy	Mahāvyutpatti; *see* Sakaki 1987
P	Peking edition of the Bka' 'gyur and Bstan 'gyur
Stog	Stog Palace edition of the Tibetan Kangyur
T	Ram Shankar Tripathi 2001
Tōh	Tōhoku catalog of the Sde dge edition of the Bka' 'gyur and Bstan 'gyur
Zhol	*Gsang ba 'dus pa'i rtsa rgyud 'grel ba bzhi sbrags dang bcas pa*. Lhasa, Zhol, n.d., made from blockprints carved in 1890. This includes the *Guhyasamāja Root Tantra*, Tsong kha pa's *Sgron gsal mchan*, the *dkar chags* of the latter, and Tsong kha pa's *Mtha' gcod rin chen myu gu*.

Bibliography

Canonical Tibetan Texts

Bka' 'gyur

Abhidhānottara Tantra. See *Mngon brjod.*

Bde mchog rtsa rgyud = *Bde mchog nyung ngu*, *Cakrasaṃvara Tantra* = *Laghusaṃvara*, Tōh 368, *rgyud*, *ka*, 213b1–246b7. Sanskrit edition in Pandey 2002; English translation in Gray 2006.

Bsam gtan gyi phyi ma rim par phye ba, *Dhyānottarapaṭalakrama*, Tōh 808, *rgyud*, *wa*, 223a1–225b7.

Chos yang dag par sdud pa'i mdo, *Dharmasaṃgīti Sūtra*, Tōh 238, *mdo sde*, *zha*, 1b1–99b7.

Ḍākārṇava Tantra. See *Mkha' 'gro rgya mtsho'i rgyud.*

De kho na nyid bsdus pa = *De bzhin gshegs pa thams cad kyi de kho na nyid bsdus pa*, *Sarvatathāgatatattvasaṃgraha*, Tōh 479, *rgyud*, *nya*, 1b1–142a7. Sanskrit edition in Lokesh Chandra 1987; Partial English translation from Chinese in Giebel 2001.

Dgongs pa lung ston = *Dgongs pa lung bstan [ston] pa'i rgyud*, *Sandhivyākaraṇa Tantra*, Tōh 444, *rgyud*, *ca*, 158a1–207b7.

Dri ma med par grags pas bstan pa, *Vimalakīrti Nirdeśa.* Tōh 176, *mdo sde*, *ma*, 175a1–239b7. Sanskrit edition online at: http://gretil.sub.uni-goettingen.de/gretil/1_sanskr/4_rellit/buddh/vimkn_u.htm; French translation in Lamotte 1962; English translation (from French) in Boin 1994.

'Dul ba phran tshegs kyi gzhi, *Vinayakṣudrakavastu*, Tōh 6, *'dul ba*, *tha*, 1b1–310a7, and *da*, 1b1–333a7.

'Dul ba rnam par 'byed pa or *Lung rnam 'byed*, *Vinayavibhaṅga*, Tōh 3, *'dul ba*, *ca*, 21a1–292a7, continued in vols. *cha*, *ja*, and *nya*.

Gdan bzhi = *Rnal 'byor ma'i rgyud kyi rgyal po chen po gdan bzhi pa*, *Catuḥpīṭha Tantra*, Tōh 428, *rgyud*, *nga*, 181a1–231b5. Partial English translation in Szántó 2012.

Gsang 'dus = *De bzhin gshegs pa thams cad kyi sku gsung thugs kyi gsang chen gsang ba 'dus pa*, *Guhyasamāja Tantra* = *Sarvatathāgatakāyavākcittarahasyaguhyasamāja*, Dunhuang, IOL (India Office Library) Tib. J 481 and IOL Tib. J 438; *The Rnying ma rgyud 'bum* (Thimbu: Dingo Khyentse Rimpoche, 1973), vol. 17, 1b1–314a4; Stog, *ca*, 1b1–82a5; Tōh 442, *rgyud*, *ca*, 90a1–148a6; P. Ōtani 81, *ca*, 95b5–167b1; also in *Gsang ba 'dus pa'i rtsa rgyud 'grel pa bzhi sbrags dang bcas pa* (Lhasa: Zhol Printing House, made from blockprints carved in 1890). My notes refer to the translation found in the Zhol, Stog, and Dunhuang and not to D and P. Sanskrit editions in Bhattacharyya 1931, Bagchi

1965, Fremantle 1971, and Matsunaga 1978; English translation in Fremantle 1971; German translation in Gäng 1988.

Gshin rje gshed nag po'i rgyud, *Kṛṣṇayamāri Tantra*, Tōh 467, *rgyud*, *ja*, 134b1–151b4; Sanskrit edition in Samdhong and Dwivedi et al. 1992.

Gshin rje'i gshed dmar po'i rgyud, *Raktayamāri Tantra*, Tōh 474, *rgyud*, *ja*, 186a1–214b7. Also Tōh 475, *rgyud*, *ja*, 215a1–244b7.

Gur = *Mkha' 'gro ma rdo rje gur rgyud*, *Vajrapañjara Tantra* = *Ḍākinīvajrapañjara Tantra*, Tōh 419, *rgyud*, *nga*, 30a4–65b7; Stog 380, 149a1–201a4.

Heruka mngon 'byung = *Khrag 'thung mngon par 'byung ba*, *Herukābhyudaya*, Tōh 374, *rgyud*, *ga*, 1b1–33b7.

Hevajra Tantra. See *Kye'i rdo rje rgyud* and *Kye'i rdo rje mkha' 'gro ma dra ba'i sdom pa*.

Kun spyod = *Rnal 'byor ma'i kun tu spyod pa*, *Yoginīsañcāra*, Tōh 375, *rgyud*, *ga*, 34a1–44b5. Sanskrit and Tibetan editions in Pandey 1998.

Kye'i rdo rje mkha' 'gro ma dra ba'i sdom pa'i rgyud kyi rgyal po, *Hevajra Tantra II*, Tōh 418, *rgyud*, *nga*, 13b5–30a3. Sanskrit and Tibetan editions with English translation in Snellgrove 1959.

Kye'i rdo rje rgyud, *Hevajra Tantra I*, *Kye'i rdo rje rgyud kyi rgyal po*, Tōh 417, *rgyud*, *nga*, 1b1–13b5. Sanskrit and Tibetan editions with English translation in Snellgrove 1959.

Lag na rdo rje dbang bskur ba'i rgyud, *Vajrapāṇyabhiṣeka Tantra*, Tōh 496, *rgyud*, *da*, 1b1–156b7.

Lang kar gshegs pa'i theg pa chen po'i mdo, *Laṅkāvatāra Sūtra*, Tōh 107, *mdo sde*, *ca*, 56a1–191b7. Sanskrit edition in Nanjio 1923.

Lha mo bzhis zhus pa = *Lha mo bzhis yongs su zhus pa*, *Caturdevīparipṛcchā*, Tōh 446, *rgyud*, *ca*, 277b3–281b7.

Māyājāla Tantra. See *Sgyu 'phrul dra ba*.

Mkha' 'gro rgya mtsho'i rgyud, *Ḍākārṇava Tantra*, Tōh 372, *rgyud*, *kha*, 137a1–264b7.

Mngal gnas = *Dga' bo la mngal na gnas pa bstan pa theg pa chen po'i mdo*, *Nandagarbhāvakrānti Nirdeśa*, Tōh 57, *dkon brtsegs*, *ga*, 205b1–236b7. Tibetan edition and English translation in Kritzer 2014.

Mngal 'jug = *Tshe dang ldan pa dga' bo la mngal du 'jug pa bstan pa theg pa chen po'i mdo*, *Āyuṣman Nandagarbhāvakrānti Nirdeśa*, Tōh 58, *dkon brtsegs*, *ga*, 237a1–248a7. Tibetan edition and English translation in Kritzer 2014.

Mngon brjod = *Mngon par brjod pa'i rgyud bla ma*, *Abhidhānottara Tantra*, Tōh 369, *rgyud*, *ka*, 247a1–370a7. Sanskrit edition and partial English translation in Kalff 1979.

Ngan song thams cad yongs su sbyong ba gzi brjid, *Sarvadurgatipariśodhana*, Tōh 483, *rgyud*, *ta*, 58b1–96a3 (version A); Tōh 485, *rgyud*, *ta*, 96b1–146a7 (version B). Sanskrit and Tibetan editions with English translation in Skorupski 1983.

Phyag chen thig le'i rgyud, *Mahāmudrātilaka Tantra*, Tōh 420, *rgyud*, *nga*, 66a1–90b7.

Rdo rje mkha' 'gro rgyud, *Vajraḍāka Tantra*, Tōh 370, *rgyud*, *kha*, 1b1–125a7.

Rdo rje rtse mo, *Vajraśekhara Tantra*, Tōh 480, *nya*, 142b1–274a5.

Rdo rje snying po rgyan gyi rgyud, *Vajrahṛdayālaṅkāra Tantra*, Tōh 451, *rgyud*, *cha*, 36a1–58b3.

Rgyud phyi ma, *Uttara Tantra*, Tōh 443, *rgyud*, *ca*, 148a6–157b7. Sanskrit edition in Matsunaga 1978.

Rgyud rdo rje phreng ba, *Vajramālā Tantra*, Tōh 445, *rgyud*, *ca*, 208a1–277b3. English translation in Kittay 2011.

Rnam snang mngon byang = *Rnam par snang mdzad chen po mngon par rdzogs par byang chub pa*, *Mahāvairocanābhisambodhi*, Tōh 494, *rgyud*, *tha*, 151b2–260a7. English translation in Hodge 2003.

Sa bcu'i le'u or *Sa bcu'i mdo*, *Daśabhūmika Sūtra*, in Tōh 44, *phal chen*, *kha*, 166a6–283a7. Sanskrit edition in Vaidya 1967; English translation in Honda 1968.

Saṃpuṭa Tantra. See *Yang dag par sbyor ba'i rgyud*.

Saṃvarodaya Tantra. See *Sdom 'byung*.

Sangs rgyas mnyam sbyor, *Sarvabuddhasamāyoga Tantra*, Tōh 366, *rgyud*, *ka*, 151a1–193a6.

Sangs rgyas thod pa'i rgyud, *Buddhakapāla Tantra*, Tōh 424, *rgyud*, *nga*, 143a1–167a5. Sanskrit edition and English translation (chaps. 9–14) in Luo 2010.

Sdom 'byung = *Bde mchog 'byung ba'i rgyud*, *Saṃvarodaya Tantra*, Tōh 373, *rgyud*, *kha*, 265a1–311a6. Sanskrit and Tibetan editions with partial English translation in Tsuda 1974.

Sdong pos brgyan pa or *Sdong po bkod pa*, *Gaṇḍavyūha Sūtra*, in Tōh 44, *phal chen*, *ga*, 274b7–396a7, and *a*, 1b1–363a6. Sanskrit edition in Vaidya 1960; English translation (from Chinese) in Cleary 1993, 1135–1518.

Sgyu 'phrul dra ba, *Māyājāla Tantra*, Tōh 466, *rgyud*, *ja*, 94a1–134a7.

Thams cad gsang ba rgyud kyi rgyal po, *Sarvarahasya Tantra*, Tōh 481, *rgyud*, *ta*, 1b1–10a1. Tibetan edition and English translation in Wayman 1984.

Vajraḍāka Tantra. See *Rdo rje mkha' 'gro rgyud*.

Vajrapañjara Tantra = *Ḍākinīvajrapañjaratantra*. See *Gur*.

Vajraśekhara Tantra. See *Rdo rje rtse mo*.

Yang dag par sbyor ba'i rgyud = *Kha sbyor*, *Saṃpuṭa Tantra*, Tōh 381, *rgyud*, *ga*, 73b1–158b7. Partial Sanskrit edition in Elder 1978 and Skorupski 1996. Partial English translation in Elder 1978.

Ye shes rdo rje kun las bsdus pa, *Jñānavajrasamuccaya*, Tōh 450, *rgyud*, *cha*, 1b1–35b7.

Ye shes rdo rje kun las btus pa'i rgyud, *Vajrajñānasamuccaya Tantra*, Tōh 447, *rgyud*, *ca*, 282a1–286a6.

Bstan 'gyur

Abhayākaragupta ('Jigs med 'byung gnas sbas pa). *Dkyil chog rdo rje phreng ba* = *Dkyil 'khor gyi cho ga rdo rje phreng ba*, *Vajrāvalī Maṇḍalavidhi*, Tōh 3140, *rgyud 'grel*, *phu*, 1b1–94b4. Sanskrit and Tibetan editions in Mori 2009.

———. *'Jigs pa med pa'i gzhung 'grel* = *Sangs rgyas thod pa'i rgyud kyi rgyal po chen po'i rgya cher 'grel pa 'jigs pa med pa'i gzhung 'grel*, *Abhayapaddhati* = *Buddhakapālamahātantra rājaṭīkābhayapaddhati*, Tōh 1654, *rgyud 'grel*, *ra*, 166b1–225b3. Sanskrit and Tibetan editions in Chog Dorje 2009. Sanskrit edition and English translation (chaps. 9–14) in Luo 2010.

———. *Man ngag snye ma* = *Yang dag par sbyor ba'i rgyud kyi rgyal po'i rgya cher 'grel pa man ngag gi snye ma*, *Āmnāyamañjarī* = *Sampuṭatantrarājaṭīkāmnāyamañjarī*, Tōh 1198, *rgyud 'grel*, *cha*, 1b1–316a7.

———. *Rdzogs pa'i rnal 'byor gyi phreng ba*, *Niṣpannayogāvalī*, Tōh 3141, *rgyud 'grel*, *phu*, 94b4–151a7. Sanskrit and Tibetan editions and English translation in Lokesh Chandra and Nirmala Sharma 2015.

———. *Rim pa lnga pa'i dgongs 'grel zla ba'i 'od zer*, *Pañcakramamatiṭīkā Candraprabhā*, Tōh 1831, *rgyud 'grel*, *ci*, 180b3–203a4.

Advayavajra (Gnyis med rdo rje). *Lta ba ngan pa sel ba*, *Kudṛṣṭinirghāta*, Tōh 2229, *rgyud 'grel, wi*, 104a7–110a2. Sanskrit edition and Japanese translation in Mikkyō-seiten kenkyūkai 1988.

Alakakalaśa (Lcang lo can gyi bum pa). *Rdo rje phreng ba'i rgya cher 'grel pa zab mo'i don gyi 'grel pa, Vajramālāṭīkāgambhīrārthadīpikā*, Tōh 1795, *rgyud 'grel, gi*, 1b1–220a7.

Ānandagarbha (Kun dga' snying po). *De nyid bsdus pa'i bstod 'grel = De bzhin gshegs pa thams cad kyi de kho na nyid bsdus pa theg pa chen po mngon par rtogs pa'i rgyud kyi bshad pa de kho na nyid snang bar byed pa, Sarvatathāgatatattvasaṅgrahavyākhyā = Sarvatathāgatatattvasaṅgrahamahāyānābhisamayatantratattvālokakarīvyākhyā*, Tōh 2510, *rgyud 'grel, li*, 1b1–352a7, continued in *shi*, 1b1–317a7.

———. *Dpal mchog dang po'i 'grel pa, Paramādivivaraṇa*, Tōh 2511, *rgyud 'grel, si*, 1b1–49b2.

———. *Rdo rje 'byung ba = Rdo rje dbyings kyi dkyil 'khor chen po'i cho ga rdo rje thams cad 'byung ba, Vajrodaya = Vajradhātumahāmaṇḍalopāyikāsarvavajrodaya*, Tōh 2516, *rgyud 'grel, ku*, 1b1–50a4.

Āryadeva ('Phags pa lha). *Bdag byin gyis brlab pa'i rim pa rnam par dbye ba, Svādhiṣṭhānakramaprabheda*, Tōh 1805, *rgyud 'grel, ngi*, 112a3–114b1. Sanskrit and Tibetan editions in Pandey 1997, 169–194; English translation in Wedemeyer 1999, 383–391.

———. *Spyod bsdus = Spyod pa bsdus pa'i sgron ma, Caryāmelāpakapradīpa = Sūtakamelāpaka*, Tōh 1803, *rgyud 'grel, ngi*, 57a2–106b7. Sanskrit and Tibetan editions and English translation in Wedemeyer 2007; Sanskrit and Tibetan editions in Pandey 2000.

Āryaśūra (Slob dpon Dpa' bo). *Pha rol tu phyin pa bsdus pa, Pāramitāsamāsa*, Tōh 3944, *dbu ma, khi*, 217b1–235a5. English translation in Meadows 1986.

Asaṅga (Thogs med). *Chos mngon pa kun las btus pa, Abhidharmasamuccaya*, Tōh 4049, *sems tsam, ri*, 44b1–120a7. Sanskrit edition in Pradhan 1950; French translation in Walpola 1971; English translation (from the French) in Boin-Webb 2001.

———. *Nyan thos kyi sa, Śrāvakabhūmi*, Tōh 4036, *sems tsam, dzi*, 1b1–195a7. Sanskrit edition in Shukla 1973.

———. *Primary Ground*. See *Sa'i dngos gzhi, Maulībhūmi*.

———. *Sa'i dngos gzhi, Maulībhūmi*, Tōh 4035, *sems tsam, tshi*, 1b1–283a7. Sanskrit edition in Bhattacharya 1957. This is the first part of the *Rnal 'byor spyod pa'i sa, Yogācārabhūmi*.

———. *Theg pa chen po bsdus pa, Mahāyānasaṃgraha*, Tōh 4048, *sems tsam, ri*, 1b1–43b7. Tibetan edition and French translation in Lamotte 1938–1939.

———. *Theg pa chen po'i mdo sde'i rgyan gyi rgya cher bshad pa, Mahāyānasūtrālaṃkāra*, Tōh 4029, *sems tsam, bi*, 38b6–174a7. Sanskrit edition in Lévi 1907 and 1911.

Aśvaghoṣa (Rta dbyangs). *Bla ma lnga bcu pa, Gurupañcāśikā*, Tōh 3721, *rgyud 'grel, tshu*, 10a2–12a2. Sanskrit editions in Lévi 1929 and in Szántó 2013.

———. *Rdo rje theg pa rtsa ba'i ltung ba bsdus pa, Vajrayānamūlāpattisaṅgraha*, Tōh 2478, *rgyud 'grel, zi*, 179a6–b5.

Bhavabhadra. *Gdan bzhi pa'i 'grel pa dran pa'i rgyu mtshan, Catuḥpīṭhasmṛtinibandhaṭīkā*, Tōh 1607, *rgyud 'grel, 'a*, 137b1–264a7.

———. *Rdo rje mkha' 'gro'i rnam par bshad pa = Rgyud kyi rgyal po chen po dpal rdo rje mkha' 'gro'i rnam par bshad pa, Vajraḍāka Vivṛti = Vajraḍākamahātantrarājavivṛti*, Tōh 1415, *rgyud 'grel, tsha*, 1b1–208b7.

Bhavyakīrti (Skal ldan grags pa). *Rab tu sgron gsal = Sgron ma gsal bar byed pa'i dgongs pa rab gsal bshad pa'i ṭīkā, Prakāśikā = Pradīpodyotanābhisaṃdhiprakāśikāvyākhyāṭīkā*, Tōh 1793, *rgyud 'grel, ki*, 1b1–292a7, continued in *khi*, 1b1–155a5.

———. *Rim pa lnga'i dka' 'grel, Pañcakramapañjikā*, Tōh 1838, *rgyud 'grel, chi*, 1b1–7b7.

Bhūva (Bhu ba blo ldan). *'Khor lo bde mchog 'byung ba'i dkyil 'khor gyi cho ga, Cakrasamvarodaya Maṇḍalavidhi*, Tōh 1538, *rgyud 'grel, za*, 117b2–150a5.

Buddhaguhya (Sangs rgyas gsang ba). *Dkyil 'khor gyi chos mdor bsdus pa, Dharmamaṇḍalasūtra*, Tōh 3705, *rgyud 'grel, tsu*, 1b1–5b4. English translation in Lo Bue 1987.

Buddhaśrījñāna (Sangs rgyas dpal ye shes). See Jñānapāda.

Candrakīrti (Zla ba grags pa). *Dbu ma la 'jug pa, Madhyamakāvatāra*, Tōh 3861, *dbu ma, 'a*, 201b1–219a7. French translation in La Vallée Poussin 1907, 1910, and 1911.

———. *Rdo rje sems dpa'i sgrub thabs, Vajrasattva Sādhana*, Tōh 1814, *rgyud 'grel, ngi*, 195b6–204b6. Sanskrit and Tibetan editions in Luo and Tomabechi 2009.

———. *Mngon rtogs rgyan = Gsang ba 'dus pa'i mngon par rtogs pa'i rgyan gyi 'grel pa, Samājābhisamayālaṅkāravṛtti*, Tōh 1817, *rgyud 'grel, ngi*, 210b1–232b6.

———. *Sgron gsal = Sgron ma gsal bar byed pa'i rgya cher bshad pa, Pradīpoddyotanaṭīkā*, Tōh 1785, *rgyud 'grel, ha*, 1b1–201b2. Sanskrit edition in Chakravarti 1984.

Dārika (Dā ri ka pa). *'Khor lo sdom pa'i dkyil 'khor gyi cho ga de kho na nyid la 'jug pa, Cakrasaṃvara Maṇḍalavidhi Tattvāvatāra*, Tōh 1430, *rgyud 'grel, wa*, 203b5–219b3.

Dharmakīrti (Chos kyi grags pa). *Mngon par rtogs pa'i rgyan zhes bya ba'i 'grel pa rtogs par dka' ba'i snang ba'i 'grel bshad, Abhisamayālaṃkāravṛtti Duravabodhālokaṭīkā*, Tōh 3794, *shes phyin, ja*, 140b1–254a7.

Dharmakīrti (Chos kyi grags pa). *Tshad ma rnam 'grel, Pramāṇavārttika*, Tōh 4210, *tshad ma, ce*, 94b1–151a7. Sanskrit edition in Miyasaka 1971–72.

———. *Tshad ma rnam par nges pa, Pramāṇaviniścaya*. Tōh 4211, *tshad ma, ce*, 152b1–230a7. Sanskrit edition of chapters 1 and 2 in Steinkellner 2007.

Dīpaṅkarabhadra (Mar me mdzad bzang po). *Gsang ba 'dus pa'i dkyil 'khor gyi cho ga = Dkyil chog bzhi rgya lnga bcu pa, Guhyasamāja Maṇḍalavidhi*, Tōh 1865, *rgyud 'grel, di*, 69a4–87a3. Sanskrit edition in Bahulkar 2006 and in Klein-Schwind 2008. Sanskrit and Tibetan editions in Bahulkar 2010.

Dīpaṅkaraśrījñāna (Mar me mdzad ye shes). *Mngon par rtogs pa rnam par 'byed pa, Abhisamayavibhaṅga*, Tōh 1490, *rgyud 'grel, zha*, 186a1–202b3.

Ḍombhiheruka (Ḍo mbi he ru ka). *Bdag med ma rnal 'byor ma'i sgrub thabs, Nairātmyāyoginī Sādhana*, Tōh 1306a, *rgyud 'grel, ta*, 212b7–215a7.

Durjayacandra (Thub dka' zla ba). *Dkyil 'khor gyi cho ga'i sgrub thabs bzang po yongs su gzung ba, Suparigraha Maṇḍalavidhi Sādhana*, Tōh 1240, *rgyud 'grel, nya*, 130a3–154a7.

Indrabhūti (Indra bhū ti). *Ye shes grub pa = Ye shes grub pa'i sgrub pa'i thabs, Jñānasiddhi Sādhana*, Tōh 2219, *rgyud 'grel, wi*, 36b7–60b6. Sanskrit and Tibetan editions in Samdhong and Dwivedi et al. 1987.

Jālandhari. *Kye rdo rje'i sgrub thabs kyi mdor bshad pa dag pa rdo rje sgron ma, Hevajra Sādhana Vajrapradīpaṭippaṇīśuddha*, Tōh 1237, *rgyud 'grel, nya*, 73a2–96a1. Sanskrit and Tibetan editions and English translation in Gerloff 2017, 151–399.

*Jayabhadra or *Laṅkājayabhadra (Lang ka Rgyal ba bzang po). *Bde mchog gi dkyil 'khor bya ba'i thabs, Cakrasaṃvara Maṇḍalavidhi*, Tōh 1477, *rgyud 'grel, zha*, 80b7–116b1.

Jayasena (Rgyal ba'i sde = Rgyal sde). *Mkha' 'gro rgya mtsho'i sgrub thabs padma rā ga'i gter = Mkha' 'gro rgya mtsho'i rgyud kyi dkyil 'khor gyi 'khor lo'i sgrub thabs padma rā ga'i gter, Ḍākārṇava Sādhana Padmarāganidhi = Ḍākārṇavatantramaṇḍalacakra Sādhana Ratnapadmarāganidhi*, Tōh 1516, *rgyud 'grel, za*, 1b1–35a7.

Jñānagarbha (Ye shes snying po). *Lha mo bzhis yongs su zhus pa'i rnam par bshad pa, Caturdevatāparipṛcchāṭīkā*, Tōh 1916, *rgyud 'grel, phi*, 250a1–267a7.

Jitāri (Dgra las rnam rgyal). *Phyag rgya bzhi yi sgrub thabs, Caturmudrā Sādhana*, Narthang

Bstan 'gyur, *rgyud 'grel, phu* 143b5–144a2; and P. Ōtani 4690, *rgyud 'grel, phu,* 144b7–147a4.

Jñānapāda or Buddhaśrījñāna (Sangs rgyas dpal ye shes). *Bdag sgrub pa la 'jug pa, Ātmasādhanāvatāra,* Tōh 1860, *rgyud 'grel, di,* 52a7–62a7. According to Kawasaki 2004, 51–52, a Sanskrit ms. is kept in Lhasa.

———. *Kun bzang sgrub thabs = Kun tu bzang po'i sgrub pa'i thabs, Samantabhadra Sādhana,* Tōh 1855, *rgyud 'grel, di,* 28b6–36a5. Partial Sanskrit edition in Tanaka 1996 and in Kano 2014.

———. *Rim pa gnyis pa'i de kho na nyid bsgom pa'i zhal lung, Dvikramatattvabhāvanā,* Tōh 1853, *rgyud 'grel, di,* 1b1–17b2.

———. *Yan lag bzhi pa'i sgrub thabs kun tu bzang mo, Caturaṅga Sādhana Samantabhadrī,* Tōh 1856, *rgyud 'grel, di,* 36a5–42b5.

*Kambala (Lwa ba pa). *Bde mchog gi sgrub thabs gtsug nor = Bcom ldan 'das 'khor lo bde mchog gi sgrub thabs rin po che gtsug gi nor bu, Cakrasaṃvara Sādhana Ratnacūḍāmaṇi,* Tōh 1443, *rgyud 'grel, wa,* 243b6–251a7.

———. *'Khor lo sdom pa'i dka' 'grel sgrub pa'i thabs kyi gleng gzhi, Sādhananidānacakrasaṃvarapañjikā,* Tōh 1401, *rgyud 'grel, ba,* 1b1–78a7.

Karuṇaśrī (Thugs rje dpal). *Sgron ma gsal bar byed pa'i gsal byed dka' 'grel, Pradīpoddyotanoddyotapañjikā,* Tōh 1790, *rgyud 'grel, a,* 10b1–170a7.

Kṛṣṇa (Nag po pa). *Rdo rje sems dpa' mchod pa'i cho ga, Vajrasattva Pūjāvidhi,* Tōh 1820, *rgyud 'grel, ngi,* 258b1–261a7.

———. *Sdom pa bshad pa, Saṃvaravyākhyā,* Tōh 1460, *rgyud 'grel, zha,* 6a3–10b7.

Kṛṣṇācārya (Spyod pa nag po pa). *Bcom ldan 'das bde mchog 'khor lo'i dkyil 'khor gyi cho ga, Bhagavacchrīcakrasamvara Maṇḍalavidhi,* Tōh 1446, *rgyud 'grel, wa,* 276b7–292b7.

———. *Dpyid kyi thig le, Vasantatilakā,* Tōh 1448, D *wa,* 298b2–306b4.

———. *Gsang ba'i de kho na nyid rab tu gsal ba, Guhyatattvaprakāśa,* Tōh 1450, *rgyud 'grel, wa,* 349a3–355b7.

*Kṛṣṇasamayavajra (Nag po dam tshig rdo rje). *Rim pa lnga'i dka' 'grel, Pañcakramapañjikā,* Tōh 1841, *rgyud 'grel, chi,* 157b1–187a7. Sanskrit edition in Tomabechi, work in progress.

Lalitavajra (Sgeg pa rdo rje). *Rdo rje 'jigs byed kyi sgrub thabs, Vajrabhairava Sādhana,* Tōh 1998, *rgyud 'grel, mi,* 196b3–201b3.

Līlavajra (Lī la badzra). *Rdo rje sems dpa'i sgrub thabs kyi 'grel pa, Vajrasattva Sādhana Nibandha,* Tōh 1815, *rgyud 'grel, ngi,* 204b6–209a3.

Lūyīpāda (Lū'i pa). *Bcom ldan 'das mngon par rtogs pa, Bhagavadabhisamaya,* Tōh 1427, *rgyud 'grel, wa,* 186b3–193a1. Sanskrit edition in Sakurai 1998 and in *Dhīḥ* 2008.

*Mañjuśrīkīrti ('Jam dpal grags pa). *Gsang ba thams cad kyi spyi'i cho ga'i snying po rgyan, Sarvaguhyavidhigarbhālaṅkāra,* Tōh 2490, *rgyud 'grel, zi,* 232b2–243b3.

———. *Rdo rje theg pa'i rtsa ba'i ltung ba'i rgya cher bshad pa, Vajrayānamūlāpattiṭīkā,* Tōh 2488, *rgyud 'grel, zi,* 197b7–231b7.

Muniśrībhadra (Thub pa dpal bzang po). *Rim pa lnga'i don mdor bshad pa = Rim pa lnga'i don mdor bshad pa rnal 'byor pa'i yid kyi 'phrog, Pañcakramārthaṭippaṇī = Pañcakramārthayogimanoharāṭippaṇī,* Tōh 1813, *rgyud 'grel, ngi,* 148b4–195b6. Sanskrit edition in Jiang and Tomabechi 1996.

Nāgabuddhi (Klu'i blo). *Rim pa khongs su bsdu ba = Rim pa khongs su bsdu ba'i man ngag rab tu byed pa, Kramāntarbhāvopadeśaprakaraṇa,* Tōh 1812, *rgyud 'grel, ngi,* 147a1–148b4.

———. *Rnam gzhag rim pa = 'Dus pa'i sgrub pa'i thabs rnam par gzhag pa'i rim pa,*

Vyavastholi = *Samājasādhanavyavastholi*, Tōh 1809, *rgyud 'grel, ngi*, 121a6–131a5. Sanskrit and Tibetan editions in Tanaka 2016.

Nāgabodhi (Klu'i byang chub). *Dkyil chog nyi shu pa* = *Gsang ba 'dus pa'i dkyil 'khor gyi cho ga nyi shu pa*, *Maṇḍalaviṃśatividhi* = *Guhyasamājamaṇḍala Viṃśatividhi*, Tōh 1810, *rgyud 'grel, ngi*, 131a5–145a3. Tanaka's Sanskrit and Tibetan editions of this work are spread over a number of publications. For the fourth chapter on the measurement of the maṇḍala, see Tanaka 2004.

———. *Nor bu'i phreng ba* = *Rim pa lnga pa'i bshad pa nor bu'i phreng ba*, [No Sanskrit title] Tōh 1840, *rgyud 'grel, chi*, 14a6–157a7.

———. *Rim pa don gsal* = *Rim pa lnga'i don gsal bar byed pa*, *Pañcakramārthabhāskaraṇa*, Tōh 1833, *rgyud 'grel, ci*, 207b2–237a7.

Nāgārjuna (Klu sgrub). *Bsdus pa'i rim pa'i bsgrub thabs*, *Piṇḍīkrama Sādhana*, Ōtani 4788, P. *zhu*, 1a1–12a6.

———. *Gsang ba 'dus pa'i dkyil 'khor gyi cho ga*, *Guhyasamāja Maṇḍalavidhi*, Tōh 1798, *rgyud 'grel, ngi*, 15b1–35a7.

———. *Gsang ba 'dus pa'i rgyud kyi rgyud 'grel*, *Guhyasamājatantrasya Tantraṭīkā*, Tōh 1784, *rgyud 'grel, sa*, 1b1–324a7.

———. *Mdo bsre* = *Rnal 'byor chen po'i rgyud gsang ba 'dus pa'i bskyed pa'i rim pa bsgom pa'i thabs mdo dang bsres pa*, *Sādhanasūtramelāpaka* [*meśravaka*] = *Guhyasamājamahāyo gatantrautpādakrama Sādhanasūtramelāpaka* [*meśravaka*], Tōh 1797, *rgyud 'grel, ngi*, 11a2–15b1; P. Ōtani 2662, *gi*, 12a7–17a7.

———. *Mdor byas* = *Sgrub pa'i thabs mdor byas pa*, *Piṇḍīkrama Sādhana* or *Piṇḍīkṛta Sādhana*, Tōh 1796, *rgyud 'grel, ngi*, 1b1–11a2; Ōtani 2661, P. *gi*, 1a1–12a6, and Ōtani 4788. Sanskrit edition in La Vallée Poussin 1896 and Tripathi 2001.

———. *Rim lnga* = *Rim pa lnga pa*, *Pañcakrama*, Tōh 1802, *rgyud 'grel, ngi*, 45a5–57a1. Sanskrit and Tibetan editions in Mimaki and Tomabechi 1994 and in Tripathi 2001; Sanskrit and French translation in Tomabechi 2006.

———. *Rtsa she* = *Dbu ma rtsa ba'i tshig le'ur byas pa shes rab*, *Prajñāmūlamadhyamakakārikā*, Tōh 3824, *dbu ma, tsa*, 1b1–19a6. Sanskrit edition and English translation in Siderits and Katsura 2013; English translation (from the Tibetan) in Garfield 1995.

———. *Rtsod pa bzlog pa'i tshig le'ur byas pa*, *Vigrahavyāvartanīkārikā*, Tōh 3828, *dbu ma, tsa*, 27a1–29a7. Sanskrit edition in Yonezawa 2008; English translation in Westerhoff 2010.

Nāropa. *Rim pa lnga bsdus pa gsal ba*, *Pañcakramasaṅgrahaprakāśa*, Tōh 2333, *rgyud 'grel, zhi*, 276a7–278a7.

Padmasambhava (Padma 'byung gnas). *Dam tshig lnga pa*, *Samayapañca*, Tōh 1224, *rgyud 'grel, nya*, 26b7–28b6.

Padmasambhava or Padmākara (Padma 'byung gnas). *Gzhal yas khang gsal bar byed pa'i mngon rtogs mun sel sgron ma*, Tōh 3706, *rgyud 'grel, tsu*, 5b4–6b6.

Padmavajra (Padma badzra). *Gsang ba grub pa* = *Rgyud ma lus pa'i don nges par skul bar byed pa*, *Guhyasiddhi*, *Sakalatantrasambhavasañcodanīguhyasiddhi*, Tōh 2217, *rgyud 'grel, wi*, 1b1–28b4. Sanskrit and Tibetan editions in Samdhong Rinpoche and Dwivedi et al. 1987.

Phalavajra ('Bras rdo rje). *Kun bzang sgrub thabs 'grel pa* = *Kun tu bzang po'i sgrub pa'i thabs kyi 'grel pa*, *Samantabhadra Sādhana Vṛtti*, Tōh 1867, *rgyud 'grel, di*, 139b3–187b4.

Prajñārakṣita (Pra dznyā ra kṣi ta). *Mngon par rtogs pa'i dka' 'grel*, *Abhisamayapañjikā*, Tōh 1465, *rgyud 'grel, zha*, 34a2–45b7.

Puṇḍarīka (Avalokiteśvara, Spyan ras gzigs dbang phyug). *Dri ma med pa'i 'od = Bsdus pa'i rgyud kyi rgyal po dus kyi 'khor lo'i 'grel bshad / rtsa ba'i rgyud kyi rjes su 'jug pa stong phrag bcu gnyis pa dri ma med pa'i 'od, Vimalaprabhā = Vimalaprabhā Mūlatantrānusāriṇī Dvādaśasāhasrikā Laghukālacakraṭīkā*, Tōh 1347, *rgyud 'grel, tha*, 107b1–277a7, continued in *da*, 1b–297a7. Also Tōh 845. Sanskrit edition vol. 1 in Jagannatha Upadhyaya 1986; vols. 2–3 in Dwivedi and Bahulkar 1994.

*Rāhulaśrīmitra (Sgra gcan 'dzin dpal bshes gnyen). *Zung du 'jug pa gsal ba zhes bya ba'i dbang gi bya ba, Yugalanaddhaprakāśa-sekaprakriyā*, Tōh 1818, *rgyud 'grel, ngi*, 232b6–247a7.

Ratnākaraśānti (Rin chen 'byung gnas zhi ba or Śāntipa). *Dgyes pa'i rdo rje'i dka' 'grel mu tig phreng ba, Hevajrapañjikāmuktikāvalī*, Tōh 1189, *rgyud 'grel, ga*, 221a1–297a7. Sanskrit edition in Tripathi and Negi 2001. For the first six verses, see Isaacson 2000.

———. *Gsang ba 'dus pa'i dkyil 'khor gyi cho ga'i 'grel pa, Guhyasamāja Maṇḍalavidhiṭīkā*, Tōh 1871, *rgyud 'grel, ni*, 59a7–130a7.

———. *Gshin rje dgra nag po'i dka' 'grel rin po che'i sgron ma = Gshin rje dgra nag po'i rgyud kyi rgyal po chen po'i dka' 'grel rin po che'i sgron ma, Kṛṣṇayamāripañjikāratnapradīpa*, Tōh 1919, *rgyud 'grel, bi*, 124a1–172b7.

———. *Gshin rje'i dgra nag po'i sgrub pa'i thabs ku mu da kha bye ba, Kṛṣṇayamāri Sādhana Protphullakumudā*, Tōh 1935, *rgyud 'grel, mi*, 58b5–64b5.

———. *'Khrul pa spong ba zhes bya ba'i sgrub pa'i thabs, Bhramahāra Sādhana*, Tōh 1245, *rgyud 'grel, nya*, 189a4–194b6. Sanskrit edition in Isaacson 2002.

———. *Rin chen phreng ba = Mdor bsdus pa'i sgrub thabs kyi 'grel ba rin chen phreng ba, Ratnāvalī = Piṇḍīkṛta Sādhana Vṛtti Ratnāvalī*, Tōh 1826, *rgyud 'grel, ci*, 1b1–95a6.

———. *Thams cad gsang ba'i bshad sbyar gsang ba'i sgron ma, Sarvarahasyanibandhara-hasyapradīpa*, Tōh 2623, *rgyud 'grel, cu*, 122a5–152b1.

Ratnarakṣita (Rin chen 'tsho). *Padma can = Sdom pa 'byung ba'i dka' 'grel padma can, Padminī = Samvarodayapadminīpañjikā*, Tōh 1420, *rgyud 'grel, wa*, 1b1–101b3. Chapter 13 is about the creation stage. Sanskrit edition in Kuranishi 2016, Tanemura, Kano, and Kuranishi 2017, and Tanemura, Kano, and Kuranishi 2019.

Ratnavajra (Rin chen rdo rje). *Mi bskyod rdo rje'i sgrub pa'i thabs, Akṣobhyavajra Sādhana*, Tōh 1884, *rgyud 'grel, pi*, 144a6–162b7.

Śākyamitra (Shākya bshes gnyen). *Ko sa la'i rgyan = De kho na nyid bsdus pa'i rgya cher bshad pa ko sa la'i rgyan, Kosalālaṅkāra = Kosalālaṅkāratattvasaṅgrahaṭīkā*, Tōh 2503, *rgyud 'grel, yi*, 1b1–245a7, continued in *ri*, 1b1–202a5

———. *Spyod pa bsdus pa'i sgron ma'i rgya cher bshad pa, Caryāsamuccayapradīpaṭīkā*, Tōh 1834, *rgyud 'grel, ci*, 237b1–280b2.

Samantabhadra (Kun tu bzang po). *Snying po snye ma = Yan lag bzhi pa'i sgrub thabs kyi rgya cher bshad pa snying po snye ma, Sāramañjarī = Caturaṅga Sādhana Ṭīkāsāramañjarī*, Tōh 1869, *rgyud 'grel, ni*, 1b1–45b4. Sanskrit edition in Szántó, work in progress.

Saroruha (Mtsho skyes or Slob dpon Padma). *Dgyes pa rdo rje'i sgrub thabs, Hevajra Sādhana*, Tōh 1218, *rgyud 'grel, nya*, 1b1–7a2. Sanskrit edition in *Dhīḥ* 2003. Sanskrit and Tibetan editions with English translation in Gerloff 2017.

———. *Kye'i rdo rje'i rgyud kyi dka' 'grel padma can, Hevajratantrapañjikāpadmin*, Tōh 1181, *ka*, 126b1–173a7.

Smṛtijñānakīrti (Dran pa'i ye shes grags pa). *Gsang ldan gyi thig chog = Sgrub thabs gsang ba dang ldan pa'i thig gi cho ga*, Tōh 2585, *rgyud 'grel, ngu*, 150b1–151a1.

———. *Lha mo bzhis zhus pa'i rnam bshad rgyas pa = Lha mo bzhis yongs su zhus pa'i rnam par bshad pa man ngag rgyas pa, Caturdevatāparipṛcchāvyākhyā = Caturdevatāparipṛcchāvyākhyānopadeśapauṣṭika*, Tōh 1915, *rgyud 'grel, phi*, 217b3–249b7.

Śraddhākaravarman (Dad pa'i 'byung gnas go cha). *Dkyil 'khor gyi thig gdab pa'i mdor bsdus pa, Saṅkṣiptamaṇḍalasūtra*, Tōh 2505, *rgyud 'grel, ri*, 205b5–207b3.

———. *Dkyil 'khor gyi thig gdab pa'i mdor bsdus pa'i 'grel pa, Saṅkṣiptamaṇḍalasūtravṛtti*, Tōh 2506, *rgyud 'grel, ri*, 207b3–215b3.

Śrīdhara (Dpal 'dzin). *Gshin rje gshed dmar po'i sgrub thabs, Raktayamāri Sādhana*, Tōh 2023, *rgyud 'grel, tsi*, 88b5–95a1.

———. *Gshin rje gshed nag po'i sgrub thabs, Kṛṣṇayamāri Sādhana*, Tōh 1923, *rgyud 'grel, mi*, 1b1–8b4.

Śūraṅgavajra (Shū raṃ ga badzra). *Rtsa ba'i rgyud kyi snying po 'dus pa nges par brjod pa'i rgyud bla ma rtsa ba rtsa ba'i 'grel pa, Mūlatantrahṛdayasaṅgrahābhidhānottaratantra Mūlamūlavṛtti*, Tōh 1414, *rgyud 'grel, tsa*, 120a1–232a7.

Tathāgatarakṣita (Ta thā ga ta ra kṣi ta). *Rdo rje sems dpa'i sgrub pa'i thabs kyi bshad pa, Vajrasattva Sādhana Vyākhyā*, Tōh 1835, *rgyud 'grel, ci*, 280b2–285b4.

Tathāgatavajra (De bzhin gshegs pa'i rdo rje). *Bde mchog gi dkyil 'khor gyi cho ga, Sambara Maṇḍalavidhi*, Tōh 1511, *rgyud 'grel, zha*, 308b3–334a3.

———. *Lū yi pa'i mngon par rtogs pa'i 'grel pa'i ṭī kā khyad par gsal byed, Lūyipādābhisamayavṛittiṭikāviśeṣadyota*, Tōh 1510, *rgyud 'grel, zha*, 285a4–308b2.

Thagana (Tha ga na). *Kun bzang sgrub thabs 'grel ba = Kun tu bzang po'i sgrub pa'i thabs kyi 'grel pa, Samantabhadra Sādhana Vṛtti*, Tōh 1868, *rgyud 'grel, di*, 187b4–231a7.

Vaidyapāda or Vitapāda (Sman zhabs), *Mdzes pa'i me tog ces bya ba rim pa gnyis pa'i de kho na nyid bsgom pa zhal gyi lung gi 'grel pa, Sukusumanāmadvikramatattvabhāvanāmukhāgamavṛtti*, Tōh 1866, *di*, 87a3–139b3.

———. *Yan lag bzhi pa'i sgrub thabs kun tu bzang mo'i rnam par bshad pa, Caturaṅga Sādhana Samantabhadrīṭīkā*, Tōh 1872, *rgyud 'grel, ni*, 130b1–178b7.

Vajragarbha (Rdo rje snying po). *Kye'i rdo rje bsdus pa'i don gyi rgya cher 'grel pa, Hevajrapiṇḍārthaṭīkā*, Tōh 1180, *rgyud 'grel, ka*, 1b1–126a7.

Vajraghaṇṭa (Rdo rje dril bu or Dril bu pa). *Bcom ldan 'das bde mchog yid bzhin nor bu = Bcom ldan 'das 'khor lo bde mchog sgrub pa'i thabs rin po che yid bzhin gyi nor bu, Bhagavancakrasaṃvaracintāmaṇi = Bhagavancakrasaṃvara Sādhana Ratnacintāmaṇi*, Tōh 1437, *rgyud 'grel, wa*, 233b5–237b2.

———. *Bde mchog lhan cig skyes pa'i sgrub thabs, Sahajasaṃvara Sādhana*, Tōh 1436, *rgyud 'grel, wa*, 233a4–233b5.

———. *Dpa' bo gcig pa'i sgrub pa'i thabs, Ekavīra Sādhana*, Tōh 1226, *rgyud 'grel, nya*, 29b6–31a6.

———. *'Khor lo sdom pa'i dbang gi bya ba mdor bsdus pa, Cakrasaṃvaraṣekaprakriyopadeśa*, Tōh 1431, *rgyud 'grel, wa*, 219b3–222b5.

———. *'Khor lo sdom pa'i lus dkyil gyi mngon rtogs*, (no Sanskrit title), Tōh 1434, *rgyud 'grel, wa*, folio 227a1–227b3.

Vajrapāṇi (Phyag na rdo rje). *Mngon par brjod pa 'bum pa las phyung ba nyung ngu'i rgyud kyi bsdus pa'i don rnam par bshad pa, Lakṣābhidhānātuddhṛta Laghutantrapiṇḍārthavivaraṇa*, Tōh 1402, *rgyud 'grel, ba*, 78b1–141a2.

Vasubandhu (Dbyig gnyen). *Mdzod = Chos mngon pa'i mdzod kyi tshig le'ur byas pa, Abhidharmakośakārikā*, Tōh 4089, *mngon pa, ku*, 1b1–25a7. Sanskrit edition in Pradhan 1975; French translation in La Vallée Poussin 1971 [1926]; English translation (from the French) in Pruden 1988–90.

———. *Mdzod 'grel = Chos mngon pa'i mdzod kyi bshad pa, Kośabhāṣya = Abhidharmakośabhāṣya*, Tōh 4090, *mngon pa, ku*, 26b1–258a7, continued in *khu*, 1b1–95a7. For the Sanskrit, French, and English, see the previous entry.

Vibhūticandra (Rnam grol zla ba or Rab 'byor zla ba). *Sdom gsum 'od kyi phreng ba, Trisaṃvaraprabhāmālā*, Tōh 3727, *rgyud 'grel, tshu*, 54b2–56b7.

Virūpa (Bir wa pa). *Dbu bcad ma'i sgrub thabs, Chinnamuṇḍa Sādhana*, Tōh 1555, *rgyud 'grel, za*, 206a1–208a4.

Vīryabhadra (Brtson 'grus bzang po). *Rim pa lnga pa'i dka' 'grel don gsal ba, Pañcakramapañjikāprabhāsārtha*, Tōh 1830, *rgyud 'grel, ci*, 142b7–180b3.

*Yaśobhadra (Snyan grags bzang po). *Gsang ba thams cad kyi sgron ma'i rgya cher 'grel pa, Sarvaguhyapradīpaṭīkā*, Tōh 1787, *rgyud 'grel, ha*, 203b5–234a7 [cited in Tibetan sources as a work by Nāropa].

Yaśomitra (Grags pa bshes gnyen). *Chos mngon pa'i mdzod kyi 'grel bshad, Abhidharmakośaṭīkā*, Tōh 4092, *mngon pa, gu*, 1b1–330a7, continued in *ngu*, 1b1–333a7. Sanskrit edition in Wogihara 1989 [1936].

Tibetan Works

A khu ching Shes rab rgya mtsho (1803–1875). *Mi bskyod mgon po'i zhal lung = 'Dus pa 'phags lugs lha so gnyis pa'i lam rim pa dang po'i khrid dmigs kyi brjed byang mi bskyod mgon po'i zhal lung*. In *Collected Works, kha*, 101 folios. Ngawang Sopa: New Delhi, 1973. English translation in Jinpa 1999, unpublished.

A myes zhabs Ngag dbang kun dga' bsod nams (1597–1659/60). *Gsang 'dus chos byung = Gsang ba 'dus pa dam pa'i chos byung ba'i tshul legs par bshad pa gsang 'dus chos kun gsal ba'i nyin byed*. In *History and Explanation of the Practice of the Guhyasamāja*, work 1, 96 folios. Sakya Centre: Dehradun, 1985.

———. *Gsang 'dus dkyil 'khor sgrub thabs rnam bshad = Gsang ba 'dus pa'i dkyil 'khor 'khor lo sgrub pa'i thabs rnam par bshad pa nges don phrin las rgya mtsho'i 'byung gnas*. In *History and Explanation of the Practice of the Guhyasamāja*, work 2, 162 folios. Sakya Centre: Dehradun, 1985.

'Ba' ra ba Rgyal mtshan dpal bzang po (1310–1391). *Bskyed rim zab don 'gal du skyon med*. In *Rtsib ri spar ma, tsha*, 68 folios. Darjeeling: Kargyud Sungrab Nyamso, 1985.

Bla ma dam pa Bsod nams rgyal mtshan (1312–1375). *Lam 'bras bu dang bcas pa'i gdams ngag gi rnam par bshad pa man ngag gi mdzod*. In *Collected Works, ga*, 144 folios. In TBRC W00KG02390.

Blo gros 'byung gnas Gro lung pa (eleventh to twelfth centuries). *Bstan rim chen mo*. Mundgod, Karnataka: Khri byang bla brang dpe mdzod, 2001.

Bsod nams grags pa, Paṇ chen (1478–1554). *Gsang 'dus bskyed rim rnam gzhag = Rgyud thams cad kyi rgyal po gsang ba 'dus pa'i bskyed rim gyi rnam gzhag mkhas pa'i yid 'phrog*. In *Collected Works, tha*, 85 folios. Mundgod, Karnataka: Drepung Loseling Library Society, 1982–1990.

———. *Rgyud sde spyi'i rnam bzhag = Rgyud sde spyi'i rnam par bzhag pa skal bzang gi yid 'phrog*, 63 folios. Dharamsala: Library of Tibetan Works and Archives, 1975. English translation in Martin J. Boord and Losang Norbu Tsonawa 1996.

Bsod nams rtse mo (1142–1182). *Collected Works of the Sa skya*, vol. 2. Tokyo: The Toyo Bunko, 1968.

———. *Kyai rdo rje'i sgrub thabs mtsho skyes kyi ṭīkā*, work 9, 30 folios.

———. *Kye rdo rje'i dkyil 'khor du slob ma smin par byed pa'i cho ga dbang gi chu bu chen mo*, work 20, 55 folios.
———. *'Khor lo bde mchog dril bu pa'i gzhung gi mngon par rtogs pa*, work 24, 6 folios.
———. [*'Khor lo bde mchog dril bu pa'i gzhung gi*] *de'i dbang gi bya ba mdor bsdus*, work 25, 24 folios.
———. *Nyi ma'i 'od zer = Kyai rdo rje'i rtsa rgyud brtag gnyis kyi rnam par bshad pa nyi ma'i 'od zer*, work 6, 137 folios.
———. *Rgyud sde spyi'i rnam gzhag*, work 1, 74 folios.
Bstan pa'i nyi ma (nineteenth century). *Bskyed rim gyi zin bris cho ga spyi 'gros ltar bkod pa man ngag kun btus*. In *Klong chen snying thig gi nang sgrub rig 'dzin 'dus pa'i zin bris rig 'dzin zhal lung bde chen dpal ster*, 110 folios. Gangtok, Sikkim: Pema Thinley, 1999. English translation in Dharmachakra Translation Committee 2, 2012.
Bu ston Rin chen grub (1290–1364). *Collected Works*. New Delhi: International Academy of Indian Culture, 1967.
———. *Dril bu lus dkyil = 'Khor lo sdom pa'i lus kyi dkyil 'khor gyi mngon par rtogs pa lhun gyis grub pa'i dkyil 'khor gsal bar byed pa*, *ja*, 16 folios.
———. *Kun spyod rgyud 'grel = Rnal 'byor ma'i kun tu spyod pa'i rgyud kyi bshad pa bde mchog gi don rab tu gsal ba*, *cha*, 76 folios.
———. *Lus dkyil dbang chog = 'Khor lo sdom pa'i rang bzhin gyis grub pa'i dkyil 'khor du dbang bskur ba'i cho ga zab don gsal ba*, *ja*, 20 folios.
———. *Mdor byas 'grel chen = Gsang ba 'dus pa'i sgrub thabs mdor byas kyi rgya cher bshad pa bskyed rim gsal byed*, *ta*, 98 folios.
———. *Nag po pa'i sgrub thabs = Bde mchog Nag po pa'i sgrub thabs 'khrul pa'i dri bral*, *ja*, 18 folios.
———. *Rgyud sde spyi'i rnam par gzhag pa rgyud sde rin po che'i mdzes rgyan*, *ba*, 305 folios.
———. *Sgron gsal bshad sbyar = Gsang ba 'dus pa'i ṭīkka sgron ma rab tu gsal ba*, *ta*, 271 folios.
Dbyangs can dga' ba'i blo gros Ā kyā yongs 'dzin (1740–1827). *Gzhi sku gsum gyi rnam gzhag rab gsal sgron me*. In *Dpe cha dpar gsar 'debs pa dge*. 16 folios. Mussoorie: Shri Dalam, 1963. English translation in Lati Rinbochay and Jeffrey Hopkins 1979.
———. *Sngags kyi sa lam = Gsang ba 'dus pa 'phags lugs dang mthun pa'i sngags kyi sa lam rnam gzhag legs bshad skal bzang 'jug ngogs*. In *Collected Works*, *ka*, 23 folios. Sku 'bum: Sku 'bum par khang, 199–. English translation in Tenzin Dorjee and Russell 1995, and in Coghlan and Zarpani n.d.
Dge 'dun grub, the First Dalai Lama (1391–1474). *Mdzod ṭig thar lam gsal byed = Dam pa'i chos mngon pa'i mdzod kyi rnam par bshad pa thar lam gsal byed*. In *Collected Works*, *nga*, 227 folios. Bkra shis lhun po'i par khang, 199–. English translation of first five chapters in Patt 1993.
Dge 'dun rgya mtsho, Rgyal ba, the Second Dalai Lama (1476–1542). *Gsang bskyed = Gsang ba 'dus pa'i rim pa dang po'i lam la slob pa'i tshul*. *Collected Works*, *nya*, 44 folios. Dharamsala: Library of Tibetan Works and Archives, 2006.
Dkon mchog yan lag, the Fifth Zhwa dmar pa (1525–1583). *Bstan bcos zab mo nang don gyi gting thun rab gsal nyi ma'i snying po*. In *Collected Works*, vol. 15, 115 folios. Zi ling: Mtshur phu mkhan po lo yag bkra shis, 2006.
Dwags po Bkra shis rnam rgyal (1512–87). *Gsang sngags rdo rje theg pa'i spyi don mdor bsdus pa legs bshad nor bu'i 'od zer*. Delhi: Drikung Kagyu Publications, 2004. 184 folios. English translation in Roberts 2011, 401–620.

Go rams pa Bsod nams seng ge (1429–1489). In *Collected Works of the Sa skya*. Tokyo: The Toyo Bunko, 1969.

———. *Gsang ba 'dus pa'i sgrub thabs kun tu bzang po'i nyi 'od kyi don 'grel lam bzang gsal ba'i snang ba*, work 78, vol. 15, 71 folios.

———. *Lta ba'i shan 'byed theg mchog gnad kyi zla zer*, work 47, vol. 13, 47 folios. English translation in Cabezón and Dargyay 2007 and in Jamyang Tenzin and Pauline Westwood 2014.

Grags pa bshad sgrub (1675–1748). *Gsang bde 'jigs gsum gyi rim gnyis kyi 'khrid*. Bylakuppe: Sera-Mey Computer Project Centre, n.d.

———. *Gsang 'dus bskyed rim gnad don kun gsal = Gsang ba 'dus pa'i bskyed rim gyi rnam bshad gnad don kun gsal*, 1–70.

———. *Rdo rje 'jigs byed bskyed rim = Rdo rje 'jigs byed kyi rim pa dang po'i khrid rgyun man ngag snang brnyan kun 'char gsal ba'i me long*, 147–223.

Grags pa rgyal mtshan (1147–1216). *Rgyud kyi mngon rtogs = Rgyud kyi mngon par rtogs pa rin po che'i ljon shing*. In *Collected Works of the Sa skya*, vol. 3, work 1, 139 folios. Tokyo: The Toyo Bunko, 1968.

Gser sdings pa Gzhon nu 'od (twelfth–thirteenth century). Works included in *Rngog slob brgyud dang bcas pa'i gsung 'bum*, vol. 252. Beijing: Krung go'i bod rig pa dpe skrun khang, 2011. [A modern bounded book.]

———. *Rim lnga don bzhi ma*, 154–185.

———. *Rim lnga don lnga ma*, 186–211.

———. *Rim lnga stan gcig gi steng du sbyar te sgom pa'i man ngag 'khor lo can*, 109–153.

'Gos Khug pa lhas btsas (eleventh century). *Gsang 'dus stong thun*, 270 folios. New Delhi: Trayang, 1973.

'Jam dbyangs bzhad pa'i rdo rje (1648–1721/22). *Gsang 'dus bskyed rim khrid kyi zin bris = Rgyud thams cad kyi rgyal po dpal gsang ba 'dus pa'i bskyed rim khrid kyi zin bris rig 'dzin yongs kyi gzhung lam*. In *Collected Works*, *kha*, 55 folios. New Delhi: Ngawang Gelek Demo, 1972.

Khams pa Ro mnyam rdo rje (twelfth century). *Gsang ba 'dus pa'i rgyud kyi rnam par bshad pa dri ma med pa ye shes gyi snang ba*. In *Rngog slob brgyud dang bcas pa'i gsung 'bum*, vol. 249. Beijing: Krung go'i bod rig pa dpe skrun khang, 2011.

Ko zhul Grags pa 'byung gnas and Rgyal ba blo bzang mkhas grub. *Gangs can mkhas grub rim byon ming mdzod*. Lanzhou: Kan su'u mi rigs dpe skrun khang, 1992.

Kong sprul Yon tan rgya mtsho or 'Jam dbyangs Kong sprul blo 'gros mtha' yas (1813–1900). *Shes bya kun khyab*, 3 vols. Beijing: Mi rigs dpe skrun khang, 1982. English translation as the ten-volume *Treasury of Knowledge Series*, by The International Translation Committee Founded by the V.V. Kalu Rinpoché, and several individual translators. Snow Lion / Shambhala / The Tsadra Foundation, 1995–2012.

Kun dga' snying po, Sa chen (1092–1158). *The Complete Works of the Great Masters of the Sa-skya Sect of the Tibetan Buddhism*, vol. 1. Tokyo: The Toyo Bunko, 1968.

———. *[Mtsho skyes kyi] Mngon rtogs tshig gi bum pa*, work 54, 15 folios.

———. *Rdo rje gur las gsungs pa'i khro bcu'i srung 'khor*, work 45, 5 folios.

Lcang skya Ngag dbang chos ldan (1642–1714). *Gsang chen myur lam = Gsang ba 'dus pa'i rim pa dang po'i lam la slob tshul gyis dmigs rim 'khrul med bla ma dam pa'i zhal las byung ba zin thor bkod pa gsang chen myur lam*. In *Collected Works*, *ca*, 32 folios. Peking: nineteenth century.

Mar pa lo tsā ba Chos kyi blo gros. *Zab lam snying po Nāro'i chos drug gsang ba bdud rtsi'i chu rgyan*. In *Collected Works, Gsung 'bum chos kyi blo gros*, vol. 1, work 48, 554–580. Ser gtsug nang bstan dpe rnying 'tshol bsdu phyogs sgrig khang, 2009.

Mi bskyod rdo rje (thirteenth century). *Gsang ba 'dus pa'i rgyud kyi rnam par bshad pa dri ma med pa'i snang ba*. In *Rngog slob brgyud dang bcas pa'i gsung 'bum*, vol. 250. Beijing: Krung go'i bod rig pa dpe skrun khang, 2011.

Mkhas grub rje Dge legs dpal bzang po (1385–1438). *Collected Works*. New Delhi: Gurudeva, 1982, reproduced from the 1897 Old Zhol blocks.

———. *Bde dril bskyed rim = Bde mchog dril bu lus dkyil gyi dbang du byas pa'i bskyed rim gyi dka' gnas*, *cha*, 12 folios.

———. *Bskyed rim dngos grub rgya mtsho = Rgyud thams cad kyi rgyal po dpal gsang ba 'dus pa'i bskyed rim dngos grub rgya mtsho*, *ja*, 190 folios.

———. *Dge bshes kon ting gu[g] shri ba la phul ba*. In *Gsung thor bu*, *ta*, work 43, folios 153a1–169b1.

———. *Gnam lcags 'khor lo = Phyin ci log gi gtam gyi sbyor ba la zhugs pa'i smra ba ngan pa rnam par 'thag pa'i bstan bcos gnam lcags 'khor lo*, *kha*, 47 folios.

———. *Rgyud sde spyi'i rnam gzhag = Rgyud sde spyi'i rnam par gzhag pa rgyas par brjod*, *nya*, 94 folios. Tibetan with a partial English translation in Lessing and Wayman 1968.

———. *Rnal 'byor rol pa'i dga' ston*. In *Gsung thor bu*, *ta*, work 47, folios 195b1–258a1.

Mus srad pa Byams pa rdo rje rgyal mtshan (1424–1498). In *Sngon byon pa'i sa skya pa'i mkhas pa rnams kyi sngags skor*. Kathmandu: Sa skya rgyal yongs gsung rab slob gnyer khang, 2007.

———. *Dbang chu'i rtsod spong*, *kha*, work 2, 110 folios.

———. *Rnam bshad chu rgyun log smra'i dri ma 'khrud byed*, *kha*, work 3, 133 folios.

Ngag dbang dpal ldan (b. 1797). *Gsangs chen rgyud chen = Gsang chen rgyud sde bzhi'i sa lam gyi rnam gzhag rgyud gzhung gsal byed*. In *Collected Works*, *kha*, 51 folios. Delhi: Mongolian Lama Gurudeva, 1983. English translation in Coghlan and Zarpani 2011.

Ngor chen Kun dga' bzang po (1382–1456). *Collected Works of the Sa skya*. Tokyo: Toyo Bunko, vol. 9, 1968; vol. 10, 1969.

———. *Bya rgyud spyi'i rnam bshad = Bya rgyud spyi'i rnam par bshad pa legs par bshad pa'i rgya mtsho*, work 135, vol. 10, 142 folios.

———. *Dril bu pa'i lus dkyil gyi bshad pa*, work 184, vol. 10, 16 folios.

———. *Gsang 'dus dkyil 'khor gyi sgrub thabs dngos grub rgya mtsho = Gsang ba 'dus pa'i dkyil 'khor gyi sgrub pa'i thabs dngos grub rgya mtsho*, work 106, vol. 10, 21 folios.

———. *Lta ba ngan sel = Kyai rdo rje'i lus kyi dkyil 'khor la rtsod pa spong ba lta ba ngan sel*, work 50, vol. 9, 23 folios.

———. *Kye rdo rje'i lus kyi dkyil 'khor gyi sgrub pa'i thabs rnal 'byor snying po*. In *Sa skya'i chos mdzod chen mo* 28: 296–312. Lhasa: Bod ljongs bod yig dpe rnying dpe skrun khang, 2013.

———. *Shin tu rnal 'byor gyi khyad par sgrub thabs kyi yan lag tu bris pa*, work 107, vol. 10, 2 folios.

———. *Smra ba ngan 'joms = Kyai rdo rje'i lus kyi dkyil 'khor la rtsod pa spong ba smra ba ngan 'joms*, work 49, vol. 9, 28 folios.

———. *Spyod pa'i rgyud spyi'i rnam gzhag = Spyod pa'i rgyud spyi'i rnam par gzhag pa legs par bshad pa'i sgron me*, work 134, vol. 10, 35 folios.

———. *Zla zer = Kyai rdo rje'i sgrub thabs kyi rgya cher bshad pa bskyed rim gnad kyi zla zer*, work 55, vol. 9, 209 folios.

Nor bzang rgya mtsho, Mkhas grub (1423–1513). *Gsang ba 'dus pa'i bskyed rim gyi don gsal bar byed pa'i sgron me*. Library of Tibetan Works and Archives, number *ga* 2,9 4050, TBRC W1KG1254, 180 folios, block print, n.d.

Paṇ chen Blo bzang chos kyi rgyal mtshan (1570–1662). *Bskyed rim dngos grub rgya mtsho'i snying po = Rgyud thams cad kyi rgyal po gsang ba 'dus pa'i bskyed rim gyi rnam bshad dngos grub kyi rgya mtsho'i snying po*. In *Collected Works*, *kha*, 77 folios. New Delhi: Gurudeva, 1973. English translation in Bentor and Dorjee 2019.

'Phags pa Blo gros rgyal mtshan (1235–1280). *Gsang ba 'dus pa 'jam pa'i rdo rje lha bcu dgu'i sgrub thabs*. In *Collected Works of the Sa skya*, work 110, vol. 7, 16 folios. Tokyo: Toyo Bunko, 1968.

———. *Kyai rdo rje lus dkyil gyi sgrub*. In *Collected Works of the Sa skya*, work 51, vol. 6, 1968, 2 folios. Tokyo: Toyo Bunko.

Rang byung rdo rje, the Third Karmapa (1284–1339). *Collected Works of the Karmapas*: Karma pa sku phreng rim byon gyi gsung 'bum phyogs bsgrigs, vol. 19, *ta* [in the works of the Third Karmapa], Lhasa: Dpal brtsegs bod yig dpe rnying zhib 'jug khang, 2013.

———. *Gsang ba 'dus pa'i sgrub pa'i thabs phyi nang gzhan gsum gsal ba*, work 10, 16 folios.

———. *Lus kyi dkyil 'khor gyi 'thad pa lung sbyor*, work 19, 6 folios.

Red mda' ba Gzhon nu blo gros (1348–1412). *Bsgrub pa dpal bas zhus lan = Bla ma bsgrub pa dpal bas gsang ba 'dus pa'i bsgrub thabs mdor byas dang bsgrub thabs rnam gzhag gi rim pa rnam gnyis kyi mi 'dra ba'i khyad par zhus pa'i lan*. In *Collected Works*, *nga*, in *Spring yig gi tshogs*, 47a4–52a5. Kathmandu: Sa skya rgyal yongs gsung rab slob gnyer khang, 2009; and in *Gsung thor bu*, 302b–307a, in TBRC W1CZ1871.

———. *Yid kyi mun sel = Gsang ba 'dus pa'i 'grel pa sgron ma gsal ba dang bcas pa'i bshad sbyar yid kyi mun sel*. In *Collected Works*, *ga*, work 1, 380 folios. Kathmandu: Sa skya rgyal yongs gsung rab slob gnyer khang, 2009.

Rin chen bzang po (958–1055). *Mngon par rtogs pa'i dka' ba'i gnas bshad pa*. In *Bka' gdams gsung 'bum phyogs bsgrigs*, work 5, vol. 1, 13 folios. Khreng tu'u: Si khron dpe skrun tshogs pa / Si khron mi rigs dpe skrun khang, 2006. Tibetan edition in Kano and Kawasaki 2014.

———. *Rgyud sde spyi'i rnam bzhag = Rgyud sde spyi'i rnam par bzhag pa 'thad ldan lung gi rgyan gyis spras pa*. In *Sngon byon sa skya pa'i mkhas pa rnams kyi rgyud 'grel skor*, *ka*, 39 folios. Kathmandu: Sa skya rgyal yongs gsung rab slob gnyer khang, 2007.

Rin chen dpal = Lho pa kun mkhyen Rin chen dpal (twelfth–thirteenth centuries). *Dpal ldan Sa skya Paṇḍita'i rnam thar*. In *Lam 'bras slob bshad*, *ka*, 19 folios. Dehradun: Sakya Centre, 1983.

Rngog Āryadeva (twelfth century), *Gsang ba 'dus pa'i 'grel pa sgron ma gsal bar byed pa'i ṭikka*. In *Rngog slob brgyud dang bcas pa'i gsung 'bum*, vol. 255. Beijing: Krung go'i bod rig pa dpe skrun khang, 2011.

Rong ston Shes bya kun rig (1367–1449). *Gsang 'dus rnam bshad = Gsang ba 'dus pa'i rnam bshad byin rlabs kyi bdud rtsi rnam par rol pa'i gter*. In *Collected Works*, *kha*, 414 folios. Jyekundo (Skye dgu mdo), Gangs ljongs rig rgyan gsung rab par khang, 2004.

———. *Gsang sngags kyi spyi don slob dpon grags 'od kyi zhus lan*. In *Collected Works*, 1: 319–323. Chengdu: Si khron dpe skrun tshogs pa, 2008.

Sgam po pa Bsod nams rin chen (1079–1153). *Dmar khrid gsang chen*. In *Collected Works*, *kha*, 27 folios. Kathmandu: Khenpo S. Tenzin and Lama T. Namgyal, 2000.

Stag tshang Lo tsā ba Shes rab rin chen (1405–?). *Collected Works*, vol. 3. Beijing: Krung go'i bod rig pa dpe skrun khang, 2007. [A modern bound book.]

———. *'Dus pa zhabs lugs kyi bskyed rim rnam bshad*, 20–118.

———. *'Jam dpal rdo rje'i mngon par rtogs pa 'dod dgu rgya mtsho*, 225–278.
———. *Zhabs lugs rdzogs rim snying gi thig le*, 119–135.
Tshe tan zhabs drung. *Bstan rtsis kun las btus pa*. Xining: Qinghai People's Publishing House, 1982.
Tsong kha pa Blo bzang grags pa (1357–1419). *Collected Works*. New Delhi: Ngawang Gelek Demo, 1975–1979. 27 vols. Reproduced from an example of the old Bkra shis lhun po redaction from the library of Klu 'khyil Monastery of Ladakh.
———. *Bla ma lnga bcu pa'i rnam bshad slob ma'i re ba kun skong, ka*, 29 folios, vol. 1, work 10. English translation in Sparham 1999.
———. *Bskyed rim zin bris = Gsang 'dus bskyed rim gyi zin bris, ca*, 40 folios, vol. 9, work 2.
———. *Bung ba'i re skong = Gsang ba 'dus pa'i bskyed rim blo gsal bung ba'i re skong gnad don gsal ba, ja*, 29 folios, vol. 10, work 14.
———. *Bzhis zhus = 'Dus pa'i bshad rgyud lha mo bzhis zhus kyi rgya cher bshad pa srog rtsol gyi de kho na nyid gsal ba, ca*, 50 folios, vol. 8, work 3.
———. *Dngos grub snye ma = Gsang sngags kyi tshul khrims kyi rnam bshad dngos grub kyi snye ma, ka*, 75 folios, vol. 1, work 11. English translation in Sparham 2005.
———. *Dril dbang = Rnal 'byor dbang phyug dril bu lugs bde mchog lus dkyil gyi dbang chog rin po che'i bang mdzod, tha*, 27 folios, vol. 15, work 2.
———. *'Dod 'jo = Bcom ldan 'das 'khor lo bde mchog gi mngon par rtogs pa'i rgya cher bshad pa 'dod pa 'jo ba, ta*, 195 folios, vol. 14, work 3.
———. *Gsan yig = Rje rin po che Blo bzang grags pa'i dpal gyi gsan yig, ka*, 31 folios, vol. 1, work 8.
———. *'Jam rdor sgrub thabs = Gsang ba 'dus pa 'jam pa'i rdo rje'i sgrub thabs 'jam pa'i dbyangs kyi dgongs pa gsal ba, nya*, 22 folios, vol. 13, work 4.
———. *Lam rim chen mo = Byang chub lam rim che ba, pa*, 491 folios, vols. 19 and 20. English translation in Cutler 2000–2004. My notes refer to the edition published in Xining: Mtsho sngon mi rigs dpe skrun khang, 1997.
———. *Lam rim chung ba = Byang chub lam gyi rim pa, pha*, 219 folios, vol. 21, work 1.
———. *Mtha' gcod = Rgyud kyi rgyal po gsang ba 'dus pa'i rgya cher bshad pa sgron ma gsal ba'i dka' ba'i gnas kyi mtha' gcod rin chen myu gu, ca*, 143 folios, vol. 8, work 2.
———. *Nā ro = Zab lam nā ro'i chos drug gi sgo nas 'khrid pa'i rim pa yid ches gsum ldan, ta*, 62 folios, vol. 13, work 9. English translation in Mullin 1996.
———. *Rim lnga gsal sgron = Rgyud kyi rgyal po gsang ba 'dus pa'i man ngag rim pa lnga rab tu gsal ba'i sgron me, ja*, 344 folios, vol. 11. English translations in Thurman 2010 and in Kilty 2013.
———. *Rnal 'byor dag rim = Gsang ba 'dus pa'i sgrub thabs rnal 'byor dag pa'i rim pa, ja*, 32 folios, vol. 10, work 12.
———. *Rnam gzhag rim pa'i rnam bshad = Rnam gzhag rim pa'i rnam bshad gsang ba 'dus pa'i gnad kyi don gsal ba, Don gsal, ca*, 90 folios, vol. 9, work 4.
———. *Sgron gsal mchan = Rgyud thams cad kyi rgyal po gsang ba 'dus pa'i rgya cher bshad pa sgron me gsal ba'i tshig don ji bzhin 'byed pa'i mchan gyi yang 'grel, nga*, 521 folios, vols. 6, and 7.
———. *Slob tshul = Rdo rje 'chang gi go 'phang brnyes par byed pa'i lam la slob pa'i tshul, nya*, 22 folios, vol. 13, work 1.
———. *Sngags rim chen mo = Rgyal ba khyab bdag rdo rje 'chang chen po'i lam gyi rim pa gsang ba kun gyi gnad rnam par phye ba, ga*, 512 folios, vols. 4 and 5. My notes refer to the edition published in Xining: Mtsho sngon mi rigs dpe skrun khang, 1995.

———. *Ye rdor ṭīkā* = *Gsang ba 'dus pa'i bshad pa'i rgyud ye shes rdo rje kun las btus pa'i ṭīkā*, *ca*, 69 folios, vol. 8, work 4.

———. *Gsang mngon* = *The Sādhana* = *Gsang ba 'dus pa'i bla brgyud gsol 'debs dang bdag bskyed ngag 'don bkra shis lhun po rgyud pa grwa tshang gi 'don rgyud rje thams cad mkhyen pas zhus dag mdzad pa*, 82 folios, 17–180, n.p., n.d,. My notes refer to this publication. Published also in *The Collected Ritual Texts of the Rnam rgyal grwa tshang Phan bde legs bshad gling*. Dharamsala: Namgyel Dratsang, 1977. English translation in Engle 2019.

Modern Works

Arénes, Pierre. 1998. "Herméneutique des tantra: Étude de quelques usages du 'sens caché'." *Journal of the International Association of Buddhist Studies* 21.2: 173–226.

———. 2002. "Herméneutique des tantra: Le *Ye shes rdo rje kun las btus pa'i rgyud las 'byung ba'i rgyan bdun rnam par dgrol ba* de Śraddhākaravarman." In *Religious and Secular Culture in Tibet*, edited by Henk Blezer, 163–183. Leiden: E.J. Brill.

Bagchi, S. 1965. *Guhyasamāja Tantra or Tathāgataguhyaka*. Darbhanga: The Mithila Institute.

Bahulkar, S. S. 2006. "Śrīguhyasamājamaṇḍalavidhiḥ of Ācārya Dīpaṅkarabhadra." *Dhīḥ: Journal of Rare Buddhist Texts* 42: 109–154. Also published as a book with the Tibetan text in Rare Buddhist Texts Series no. 31. Sarnath: Central University of Tibetan Studies, 2010.

Banarsi Lal. 2001. *Luptabauddhavacanasaṅgrahaḥ (Part 2)*. Rare Buddhist Texts Series no. 25. Rare Buddhist Texts Research Unit. Sarnath: Central Institute of Higher Tibetan Studies.

Bentor, Yael. 1996. *Consecration of Images and Stūpas in Indo-Tibetan Tantric Buddhism*. Leiden: Brill.

———. 2006. "Identifying the Unnamed Opponents of Tsong-kha-pa and Mkhas-grub-rje Concerning the Transformation of Ordinary Birth, Death, and the Intermediate State into the Three Bodies." In *Tibetan Buddhist Literature and Praxis: Studies in Its Formative Period 900–1400*, edited by Ronald M. Davidson and Christian K. Wedemeyer, 185–200. Leiden: Brill.

———. 2008. "Can Women Attain Enlightenment through Vajrayāna Practices?" In *Karmic Passages: Israeli Scholarship on India*, edited by David Shulman and Shalva Weil, 123–137. New Delhi: Oxford University Press.

———. 2009a. "Do 'The Tantras Embody What the Practitioners Actually Do'?" In *Contributions to Tibetan Buddhist Literature*, edited by Orna Almogi, 351–373. Halle: International Institute for Tibetan and Buddhist Studies.

———. 2009b. "The Convergence of Theoretical and Practical Concerns in a Single Verse of the *Guhyasamāja Tantra*." In *Tibetan Rituals*, edited by José Cabezón, 89–102. New York: Oxford University Press.

———. 2015a. "Interpreting the Body *Maṇḍala*: Tsongkhapa versus Later Gelug Scholars." *Revue d'Etudes Tibétaines* 31: 63–74. Reprinted in *Trails of the Tibetan Tradition: Papers for Elliot Sperling*, edited by Roberto Vitali, 63–74. Dharamsala: Amnye Machen Institute.

———. 2015b. "Meditation on Emptiness in the Context of Tantric Buddhism." *The Journal of Buddhist Philosophy* 1 (guest editor, Kevin Vose): 136–155.

———. 2015c. "Tsong-kha-pa's *Guhyasamāja Sādhana* and the Ārya Tradition." In *Śāsanadhara: Papers in Honor of Robert A. F. Thurman on the Occasion of his 70th Birthday*, edited by Christian K. Wedemeyer, John D. Dunne, and Thomas F. Yarnall, 165–192. New York: The American Institute of Buddhist Studies at Columbia University in New York with Columbia University's Center for Buddhist Studies and Tibet House US.

———. 2015d. "Women on the Way to Enlightenment." In *From Bhakti to Bon: Festschrift for Per Kvaerne*, edited by Charles Ramble and Hanna Havnevik, 89–96. Oslo: Novus Forlag. The Institute for Comparative Research in Human Culture.

———. 2017a. "Tibetan Interpretations of the Opening Verses of Vajraghaṇṭa on the Body Maṇḍala." In *Chinese and Tibetan Esoteric Buddhism*, edited by Yael Bentor and Meir Shahar, 230–259. Leiden: Brill.

———. 2017b. "Did mKhas grub rje Challenge the Authenticity of the Sa skya *Lam 'bras* Tradition?" In *Fifteenth Century Tibet: Cultural Blossoming and Political Unrest*, edited by Volker Caumanns and Marta Sernesi, 227–248. Lumbini International Research Institute, Nepal.

Bentor, Yael, and Penpa Dorjee, trans. 2019. *The Essence of the Ocean of Attainments: The Creation Stage of the Guhyasamaja Tantra according to Panchen Losang Chökyi Gyaltsen*. Somerville, MA: Wisdom Publications.

Beyer, Stephan V. 1973. *The Cult of Tārā: Magic and Ritual in Tibet*. Berkeley: University of California Press.

Bhadanta Indra. 1997. *Sūtratantrodbhavāḥ Katipayadhāraṇīmantrāḥ*. Sarnath, Rare Buddhist Texts Series 16. Sarnath: Central Institute of Higher Tibetan Studies.

Bhattacharya, Vidhushekhara. 1957. *The Yogācārabhūmi of Ācārya Asaṅga*. Calcutta: University of Calcutta.

Bhattacharyya, Benoytosh. 1931. *Guhyasamāja Tantra or Tathāgataguhyaka*. Baroda: Oriental Institute.

Blezer, Henk. 1997. *Kar gliṅ Źi khro: A Tantric Buddhist Concept*. Leiden: Research School CNWS.

Boin, Sara. 1994. *The Teaching of Vimalakīrti*. Oxford: The Pali Text Society. (English translation from the French of Lamotte 1962.)

Boin-Webb, Sara, trans. from French. 2001. *Abhidharmasamuccaya: The Compendium of the Higher Teaching (Philosophy) by Asaṅga*. Fremont, CA: Asian Humanities Press.

Boord, Martin J., and Losang Norbu Tsonawa, trans. 1996. *Overview of Buddhist Tantra*. By Panchen Sonam Dragpa. Dharamsala: Library of Tibetan Works and Archives.

Broido, Michael. 1983. "*Bshad thabs*: Some Tibetan Methods of Explaining the Tantras." In *Contributions on Tibetan and Buddhist Religion and Philosophy*, edited by Ernst Steinkellner, 2: 15–45. Vienna: Arbeitskreis für Tibetische und Buddhistische Studien Universität.

———. 1988. "Killing, Lying, Stealing, and Adultery." In *Buddhist Hermeneutics*, edited by Donald Lopez, 71–118. Honolulu: Kuroda Institute.

Cabezón, José Ignacio, and Geshe Lobsang Dargyay. 2007. *Freedom from Extremes: Gorampa's "Distinguishing the Views" and the Polemics of Emptiness*. Boston: Wisdom Publications.

Campbell, John R. B. 2009. "Vajra Hermeneutics: A Study of Vajrayāna Scholasticism in the *Pradīpoddyotana*." PhD dissertation, Columbia University, New York.

Campbell, John R. B., Robert Thurman, et al. 2020. *The Esoteric Community Tantra with the Illuminating Lamp, Volume 1: Chapters 1–12.* New York, NY / Somerville, MA: The American Institute of Buddhist Studies and Wisdom Publications.

Cantwell, Cathy, and Robert Mayer. 2008. *Early Tibetan Documents on Phur pa from Dunhuang.* Vienna: Verlag der Österreichischen Akademie der Wissenschaften.

Chakravarti, Chintaharan. 1984. *Guhyasamājatantrapradīpoddyotanaṭīkāṣaṭkoṭīvyākhyā.* Patna, India: Kashi Prasad Jayaswal Research Institute.

Chog Dorje. 2009. *Abhayapaddhati of Abhayākaragupta: Commentary on the Buddhakapālamahātantra.* Sarnath: Central Institute of Higher Tibetan Studies.

Cleary, Thomas. 1993. *The Flower Ornament Scripture: A Translation of the Avatamsaka Sutra.* Boston: Shambhala Publications.

Coghlan, Ian, and Voula Zarpani, trans. 2011. *Principles of Buddhist Tantra: A Commentary on Chöjé Ngawang Palden's Illumination of the Tantric Tradition: The Principles of the Grounds and Paths of the Four Great Secret Classes of Tantra.* By Kirti Tsenshap Rinpoché. Boston: Wisdom Publications.

———, trans. n.d. *Stairway to the State of Union: A Collection of Teachings on Secret Mantra.* By Chöden Rinpoché. Melbourne: Awakening Vajra Publications.

Conze, Edward. 1975. *The Large Sutra on Perfect Wisdom.* Berkeley: University of California Press.

Cuevas, Bryan J. 1996. "Predecessors and Prototypes: Towards a Conceptual History of the Buddhist Antarābhava." *Numen* 43: 263–302.

———. 2003. *The Hidden History of the Tibetan Book of the Dead.* Oxford: University Press.

Cutler, Joshua W.C., editor-in-chief. 2000–2004. *The Great Treatise on the Stages of the Path to Enlightenment, Lam-rim-chen-mo.* 3 vols. Ithaca, NY: Snow Lion Publications.

Dagyab Rinpoche. 2015 [1995]. *Buddhist Symbols in Tibetan Culture.* Somerville, MA: Wisdom Publications.

Dalton, Catherine. 2019. *Enacting Perfection: Buddhajñānapāda's Vision of a Tantric Buddhist World.* PhD. Diss., University of California, Berkeley.

Dalton, Catherine, and Péter-Dániel Szántó. 2019. "Jñānapāda." In *Brill's Encyclopedia of Buddhism*, editor-in-chief, Jonathan A. Silk, 2: 264–268, Leiden: Brill.

Dalton, Jacob, 2005. "A Crisis of Doxography: How Tibetans Organized Tantra during the 8th–12th Centuries." *Journal of the International Association of Buddhist Studies* 28.1: 115–181.

Davidson, Ronald M. 1991. "Reflections on the Maheśvara Subjugation Myth: Indic Materials, Sa-skya-pa Apologetics, and the Birth of Heruka." *Journal of the International Association of Buddhist Studies* 14.2: 197–235.

Dharmachakra Translation Committee 1. 2007. *Deity, Mantra, and Wisdom.* Ithaca, NY: Snow Lion Publications.

Dharmachakra Translation Committee 2. 2012. *Vajra Wisdom: Deity Practice in Tibetan Buddhism.* By Kunkyen Tenpe Nyima and Shechen Gyaltsap IV. Boston: Snow Lion Publications.

Dhīḥ 2003. *Hevajra-sādhanopāyikā. Dhīḥ: Journal of the Rare Buddhist Texts Research Unit* 36: 133–144.

Dhīḥ 2008. Siddhācārya Lūyīpāda, *Cakrasaṃvaraherukābhisamayaḥ. Dhīḥ: Journal of the Rare Buddhist Texts Research Unit* 45: 143–159.

Doboom Tulku. 1996. "Interpreting the Tantric Maṇḍala." In *The Buddhist Path to Enlightenment: Tibetan Buddhist Philosophy and Practice*, 57–68. San Diego: Point Loma Publications.

Doniger, Wendy, and Sudhir Kakar. 2003. *Vatsyayana Mallanaga: Kamasutra*. Oxford: Oxford University Press.

Dreyfus, Georges B. J. 1997. *Recognizing Reality: Dharmakīrti's Philosophy and Its Tibetan Interpretations*. New York: SUNY.

———. 2003. *The Sound of Two Hands Clapping: The Education of a Tibetan Buddhist Monk*. Berkeley: University of California Press.

Dwivedi, Vrajavallabha, and S. S. Bahulkar, 1994. *Vimalaprabhāṭīkā of Kalkin ŚrīPuṇḍarīka on Śrī Laghukālacakratantrarāja*, volumes 2 and 3. Sarnath, Varanasi: Central Institute of Higher Tibetan Studies.

Dunne, John D. 2004. *Foundations of Dharmakīrti's Philosophy*. Studies in Indian and Tibetan Buddhism. Boston: Wisdom Publications.

———. 2006. "Realizing the Unreal: Dharmakīrti's Theory of Yogic Perception." *Journal of Indian Philosophy* 34: 497–519.

Eastman, Kenneth W. 1980. "The Dun-huang Tibetan Manuscript of the Guhyasamājatantra." *Report of the Japanese Association for Tibetan Studies* 26: 8–12. English language appended version of "Chibetto-go Guhyasamājatantra no tonkō shutsudo shahon."

Eimer, Helmut. 1997. "A Source for the First Narthang Kanjur: Two Early Sa skya pa Catalogues of the Tantras." In *Transmission of the Tibetan Canon*, edited by Helmut Eimer. Vienna: Verlag der Österreichischen Akademie der Wissenschaften.

———. 1989. *Der Tantra-Katalog des Bu ston im Vergleich mit der Abteilung Tantra des tibetischen Kanjur*. Studie, Textausgabe, Konkordanzen und Indices. Bonn: Indica et Tibetica Verlag.

Elder, George Robert. 1978. "The *Saṃpuṭa Tantra*: Edition and Translation, Chapters I–IV." PhD dissertation, Columbia University, New York.

Eltschinger, Vincent. 2009. "On the Career and Cognition of Yogins." In *Yogic Perception, Meditation and Altered States of Consciousness*, edited by Eli Franco, 169–213. Vienna: Verlag der Österreichischen Akademie der Wissenschaften.

———. 2014. *Buddhist Epistemology as Apologetics: Studies on the History, Self-Understanding and Dogmatic Foundations of Late Indian Buddhist Philosophy*. Vienna: Verlag der Österreichischen Akademie der Wissenschaften.

Engle, Artemus B., trans. 2019. *Guhyasamāja Practice in the Ārya Nāgārjuna System. Volume One: The Generation Stage*. By Lobsang Jampa, Gyumé Khensur, and Tsongkhapa. Boulder: Snow Lion Publications.

English, Elizabeth. 2002. *Vajrayoginī: Her Visualization, Rituals, and Forms*. Boston: Wisdom Publications.

Faure, Bernard. 2003. *The Power of Denial: Buddhism, Purity, and Gender*. Princeton: Princeton University Press.

Filippani-Ronconi, Pio. 1972. "La formulazione liturgica della dottrina del Bodhicitta nel 2 Capitolo de *Guhyasamājatantra*." *Annali* (Istituto Universitario Orientale di Napoli) 32.2: 187–199.

Finot, Louis. 1934. "Manuscrits Sanskrits de sādhana's retrouvés en Chine." *Journal Asiatique* 225 (July–September): 1–85.

Flood, Gavin. 2006. *The Tantric Body: The Secret Tradition of Hindu Religion*. London: I. B. Tauris.

Franco, Eli. 2017. "Introduction, Dharmakīrti." In *Encyclopedia of Indian Philosophies*, vol. 21. *Buddhist Philosophy from 600 to 750 AD*, edited by K. H. Potter, 51–136. Delhi: Motilal Banarsidass Publishers.

———. "10.1.2 *Pramāṇasiddhi*, Summary by Eli Franco." In *Encyclopedia of Indian Philosophies*, vol. 21. *Buddhist Philosophy from 600 to 750 AD*, edited by K. H. Potter, 297–354. Delhi: Motilal Banarsidass Publishers.

Fremantle, Francesca. 1971. "A Critical Study of the *Guhyasamāja-Tantra*." PhD dissertation, SOAS University of London.

———. 1990. "Chapter Seven of the Guhyasamāja Tantra." In *Indo-Tibetan Studies: Papers in Honour and Appreciation of Professor David L. Snellgrove's Contribution to Indo-Tibetan Studies*, edited by Tadeusz Skorupski, 101–114. Tring, England: The Institute of Buddhist Studies.

Gäng, Peter. 1988. *Das Tantra der verborgenen Vereinigung*. Munich: Eugen Diederichs Verlag.

Garfield, Jay L. 1995. *The Fundamental Wisdom of the Middle Way: Nāgārjuna's Mūlamadhyamakakārikā*. New York: Oxford University Press.

Garrett, Frances M. 2008. *Religion, Medicine, and the Human Embryo in Tibet*. Routledge Critical Studies in Buddhism. London: Routledge.

Gerloff, Torsten. 2017. "Saroruhavajra's Hevajra-Lineage: A Close Study of the Surviving Sanskrit Works." PhD dissertation, Hamburg University.

Gerloff, Torsten, and Julian Schott. 2020. "Towards a Reassessment of Indrabhūti's *Jñānasiddhi*." *Buddhist Studies Review* 37.2: 241–60.

Giebel, Rolf W. 2001. *Two Esoteric Sutras: The Adamantine Pinnacle Sutra and the Susiddhikara Sutra*. Berkeley: Numata Center for Buddhist Translation and Research.

Gómez, Luis O. 1977. "The Bodhisattva as Wonder-worker." In *Prajñāpāramitā and Related Systems*, edited by Lewis Lancaster, 221–261. Berkeley: Berkeley Buddhist Studies Series.

———. 2010 [2011]. "On Buddhist Wonders and Wonder-Working." *Journal of the International Association of Buddhist Studies* 33.1–2: 513–554.

Gómez, Luis O., and Paul M. Harrison. 2022. *Vimalakīrtinirdeśa: The Teaching of Vimalakīrti*. Berkeley, CA: Mangalam Press.

Guarisco, Elio, and Ingrid McLeod, trans. 2005. *Systems of Buddhist Tantra, from the Treasury of Knowledge*. By Jamgön Kongtrul, book six, part four. Ithaca, NY: Snow Lion Publications.

———. 2008. *The Elements of Tantric Practice, from the Treasury of Knowledge*. By Jamgön Kongtrul, book eight, part three. Ithaca, NY: Snow Lion Publications.

Gray, David B. 2006. "Mandala of the Self: Embodiment, Practice, and Identity Construction in the Cakrasamvara Tradition." *Journal of Religious History* 30.3: 294–310.

———. 2011. "Experiencing the Single Savior: Divinizing the Body and the Senses in Tantric Buddhist Meditation." In *Perceiving the Divine through the Human Body: Mystical Sensuality*, edited by Thomas Cattoi and June McDaniel, 45–65. New York: Palgrave MacMillan.

Harrison, Paul M. 1990. *The Samādhi of Direct Encounter with the Buddhas of the Present*. Tokyo: International Institute for Buddhist Studies.

Hayes, Richard P., and Brendan S. Gillon. 1991. "Introduction to Dharmakīrti's Theory of Inference as Presented in *Pramāṇavārttika Svopajñavṛtti* 1–10." *Journal of Indian Philosophy* 19.1: 1–73.

Heimbel, Jörg. 2017a. *Vajradhara in Human Form: The Life and Times of Ngor chen Kun dga' bzang po*. Lumbini: Lumbini International Research institute.

———. 2017b. "The Dispute Between mKhas grub rje and Ngor chen: Its Representation and Role in Tibetan Life-Writing." In *Fifteenth Century Tibet: Cultural Blossoming and Political Unrest*, edited by Volker Caumanns and Marta Sernesi, 249–289. Lumbini, Nepal: Lumbini International Research Institute.

Helffer, Mireille. 1985a. "A Typology of the Tibetan Bell." In *Soundings in Tibetan Civilization*, edited by Barbara Nimri Aziz and Matthew Kapstein, 37–41. New Delhi: Manohar.

———. 1985b. "Essai pour une typologie de la cloche tibétaine *dril-bu*." *Arts Asiatiques* 40: 53–67.

Hodge, Stephen. 2003. *The Mahā-Vairocana-Abhisambodhi Tantra with Buddhaguhya's Commentary*. London: Curzon.

Honda, Megumu. 1968. "Annotated Translation of the *Daśabhūmika-Sūtra*." Revised by Johannes Rahder. In *Studies in South, East and Central Asia* (presented to Prof. Raghu Vira), edited by Denis Sinor, 115–276. New Delhi: International Academy of Indian Culture.

Hopkins, Jeffrey, ed. and trans. 1977. *Tantra in Tibet*. London: George Allen & Unwin.

———. ed. and trans. 1981. *Yoga in Tibet*. London: George Allen & Unwin.

———, with Dorje Yudon Yuthok, trans. 1992. *Tibetan Arts of Love*. By Gedün Chöpel. Ithaca, NY: Snow Lion Publications.

———. 2008a. *Tsong-kha-pa's Final Exposition of Wisdom*. Ithaca, NY: Snow Lion Publications.

———. 2008b. *Tantric Techniques*. Ithaca, NY: Snow Lion Publications.

Hugon, Pascale. 2012. "Inherited Opponents and New Opponents: A Look at Informal Argumentation in the *Tshad ma rigs gter*." *Journal of Tibetology* 8: 26–57.

Isaacson, Harunaga. 2000. "The Opening Verses of Ratnākaraśānti's *Muktāvalī* (Studies in Ratnākaraśānti's Tantric Works II)." In *Harānandalaharī* (Festschrift Minoru Hara), edited by Ryutaro Tsuchida and Albrecht Wezler, 121–134. Reinbek: Verlag für orientalistische Fachpublikationen.

———. 2002. "Ratnākaraśānti's *Bhramaharanāma Hevajrasādhana*: Critical Edition (Studies in Ratnākaraśānti's Tantric Works III)." *Journal of the International College for Advanced Buddhist Studies* 5: 151–176.

Isaacson, Harunaga, and Francesco Sferra 2014. *The Sekanirdeśa of Maitreyanātha Advayavajra with the Sekanirdeśapañjikā of Ramapala*. Napoli: Università degli studi di Napoli "L'Orientale."

Jackson, David P. 1985. "Madhyamaka Studies among the Early Sa-skya-pas." *The Tibet Journal* 10.2: 20–34.

———. 2007. "Rong ston bKa' bcu pa: Notes on the Title and Travels of a Great Tibetan Scholastic." In *Pramāṇkīrtiḥ: Papers Dedicated to Ernst Steinkellner on the Occasion of his 70th Birthday*, edited by Birgit Kellner et al, 345–360. Vienna: Arbeitskreis für Tibetische und Buddhistische Studien, Universität Wien.

———. 2010. *The Nepalese Legacy in Tibetan Painting.* Masterworks of Tibetan Painting. New York: Rubin Museum of Art.

Jackson, Roger R. 1992. *Is Enlightenment Possible?* Ithaca, NY: Snow Lion Publications.

Jagannatha Upadhyaya. 1986. *Vimalaprabhā*. 3 vols. Sarnath: Central Institute of Higher Tibetan Studies.

Jampa Samten. Unpublished. "Ratnarakṣita (Rin chen 'tsho)'s Commentary on the *Saṃvarodaya Tantra*, entitled *Samvarodayapadminīpañjikā*." PhD dissertation, Visva Bharati University, Santiniketan, India.

Jamyang Tenzin, Khenpo, and Pauline Westwood. 2014. *Distinguishing the Views.* Kathmandu: Vajra Books.

Jiang, Zhongxin, and Tōru Tomabechi. 1996. *The Pañcakramaṭippanī of Muniśrībhadra: Introduction and Romanized Sanskrit Text.* Bern: Peter Lang.

Jinpa, Thupten. 1999. *Sacred Words of Lord Akshobya.* New York: Unpublished.

———, ed. 2017. *Science and Philosophy in the Indian Buddhist Classics: The Physical World,* vol. 1, translated by Ian J. Coghlan. Somerville, MA: Wisdom Publications.

———. 2019. *Tsongkhapa: A Buddha in the Land of Snows.* Boulder: Shambhala Publications.

Jones, J. J. 1949. *The Mahāvastu,* vol. 1. London: Luzac.

Kajiyama, Yūichi. 2000. "Buddhist Cosmology as Presented in the *Yogācārabhūmi.*" In *Wisdom, Compassion, and the Search for Understanding,* edited by Jonathan A. Silk, 183–199. Honolulu: University of Hawai'i Press.

Kalff, Martin M. 1979. "Selected Chapters from the Abhidhanottara-Tantra: The Union of Female and Male Deities." PhD dissertation, Columbia University, New York.

Kano, Kazuo. 2014. "Newly Available Sanskrit Materials of Jñānapāda's *Samantabhadrasādhana.*" *Mikkyōgakukenkū* 46: 61–73.

Kano, Kazuo, and Kazuhiro Kawasaki. 2014. "A Critical Edition of Rin chen bzang po's *Cakrasaṃvarābhisamaya* Commentary." *Kōyasandaigaku ronsō* 49: 1–36.

Kapstein, Matthew. 1998. "Pilgrimage of Rebirth Reborn: The 1992 Celebration of the Drigung Powa Chenmo." In *Buddhism in Contemporary Tibet: Religious Revival and Cultural Identity,* edited by Melvyn C. Goldstein and Matthew T. Kapstein, 95–119. Berkeley: University of California Press.

Kawasaki, Kazuhiro. 2004. "On a Birch-bark Sanskrit Manuscript Preserved in the Tibet Museum." *Journal of Indian and Buddhist Studies* 52.2: 905–903 (reverse pagination).

Kikuya, Ryūta. 2010. "Two Steps (*Dvikrama*) in the Jñānapāda School of Indian Tantric Buddhism," *The Annual Reports of Graduate School of Arts and Letters, Tohoku University* 60: 156–134.

Kilty, Gavin, trans. 2004. *Ornament of Stainless Light: An Exposition of the Kālacakra Tantra.* By Khedrup Norsang Gyatso. The Library of Tibetan Classics 14. Boston: Wisdom Publications.

———. 2013. *A Lamp to Illuminate the Five Stages: Teachings on Guhyasamāja Tantra.* By Tsongkhapa. The Library of Tibetan Classics 15. Boston: Wisdom Publications.

Kittay, David R. 2011. "Interpreting the Vajra Rosary: Truth and Method Meets Wisdom and Method." PhD dissertation, Columbia University.

Kittay, David R., with Lozang Jamspal. 2020. *The Vajra Rosary Tantra with Commentary by Alaṁkakalasha.* New York, NY / Somerville, MA: The American Institute of Buddhist Studies and Wisdom Publications.

Klein-Schwind, S., trans. 2008. *Guhyasamājamaṇḍalavidhi.* By Dīpaṃkarabhadra. Hamburg: Centre for Tantric Studies (tantric-studies.org). URL: GuSaMaVi.txt.

Kloetzli, Randolph W. 1983. *Buddhist Cosmology: Science and Theology in the Images of Motion and Light.* Delhi: Motilal Banarsidass.

Kramer, Jowita. 2008. *A Noble Abbot from Mustang: Life and Works of Glo-bo mKhan-chen (1456–1532).* Vienna: Arbeitskreis für Tibetische und Buddhistische Studien, Universität Wien.

Kritzer, Robert. 1998. "Garbhāvakrāntisūtra: A Comparison of the Contents of Two

Versions." *Notre Dame Joshi Daigaku Kirisutokyō Bunka Kenkyūjo Kiyō* [Maranata] 3.6: 3–12.

———. 2000. "*Rūpa and the Antarābhava.*" *Journal of Indian Philosophy* 28: 235–272.

———. 2014. *Garbhāvakrāntisūtra: The Sūtra on Entry into the Womb*. Studia Philologica Buddhica. Tokyo: International Institute for Buddhist Studies.

Krug, Adam. 2018. "The Seven Siddhi Texts: The Oḍiyāna Mahāmudrā Lineage in Its Indic and Tibetan Contexts." PhD dissertation, University of California, Santa Barbara.

van der Kuijp, Leonard. 1985a. "Apropos of a Recent Contribution to the History of Central Way Philosophy in Tibet: *Tsong Khapa's Speech of Gold.*" *Berliner Indologische Studien* 1:47–74.

———. 1985b. "Studies in the Life and Thought of Mkhas-grub-rje I: Mkhas-grub-rje's Epistemological Oeuvre and his Philological Remarks on Dignāga's Pramānasamuccaya I." *Berliner Indologische Studien* 1: 75–105.

———. 1985c. "A Text-Historical Note on Hevajratantra II:v:1–2." *Journal of the International Association of Buddhist Studies* 8.1: 83–89.

———. 1987. "Ngor-chen Kun-dga' bzang-po on the Posture of Hevajra: A Note on the Relationship between Text, Iconography and Spiritual Practice." In *Investigating Indian Art, Proceedings of a Symposium on the Development of Early Buddhist and Hindu Iconography held at the Museum of Indian Art Berlin in May 1986*, 173–177. Veröffentlichungen des Museums für Indische Kunst 8. Berlin: Museum für Indische Kunst und Staatliche Museen Preussischer Kulturbesitz.

———. 2007. "*Nāgabodhi/Nāgabuddhi: Notes on the *Guhyasamāja* Literature." In *Pramāṇakīrtiḥ: Papers Dedicated to Ernst Steinkellner on the occasion of his 70th birthday*, edited by B. Kellner, H. Krasser, M.T. Much, and H. Tauscher, Part 2, 1001–1022. Vienna: Arbeitskreis für Tibetische und Buddhistische Studien, Universität Wien.

Kuranishi, Kenichi. 2016. "A Study on Scholarly Activities in the Last Period of the Vikramaśīla Monastery: Quotations in Ratnarakṣita's *Padminī*." *Oriental Culture* 96: 49–61. Published by the Institute for Advanced Studies on Asia, The University of Tokyo.

Kyuma, Taiken. 2009. "Superiority of Vajrayāna—Part I: Some Remarks on the **Vajrayānāntadvayanirākaraṇa* (*rDo rje theg pa'i mtha' gnyis sel ba*) Ascribed to Jñānaśrī." In *Genesis and Development of Tantrism*, edited by Shingo Einoo, 469–485. Tokyo: University of Tokyo, Institute of Oriental Culture.

de La Vallée Poussin, Louis. 1896. *Études et textes tantriques: Pañcakrama*. Ghent, Belgium: Ghent University.

———. 1907, 1910, and 1911. "*Madhyamakāvatāra*: Introduction au Traité du Milieu de L'Ācārya Candrakīrti, avec le commentaire de l'auteur, traduit d'aprés la version tibétaine." *Le Muséon* 8: 249–317, 11: 271–358, 12: 235–328.

———. 1971 [1926]. *L'Abhidharmakośa de Vasubandhu*. Brussels: Institut Belge des Hautes Études Chinoises.

Lamotte, Étienne. 1938–1939. *La Somme du Grand Véhicule d'Asaṅga (Mahāyānasaṃgraha)*. 2 vols. Louvain: Université de Louvain, Institut Orientaliste.

———. 1962. *L'enseignement de Vimalakīrti—Vimalakīrtinirdeśa*. Bibliothèque du Muséon, vol. 51. Louvain: Université catholique de Louvain.

Langenberg, Amy Paris. 2017. *Birth in Buddhism: The Suffering Fetus and Female Freedom*. London: Routledge.

Lati Rinbochay and Jeffrey Hopkins. 1979. *Death, Intermediate State, and Rebirth in Tibetan Buddhism*. Ithaca, NY: Snow Lion Publications.

Lessing, F. D., and Alex Wayman, trans. 1968. *Introduction to the Buddhist Tantric Systems*. By Mkhas grub rje. The Hague, Mouton; reprinted: Delhi: Motilal Banarsidass, 1978 [1983].

Lévi, Sylvain. 1907 and 1911. *Mahāyāna-Sūtrālaṅkāra: Exposé de la doctrine du Grand véhicule selon le système Yogācāra*. 2 vols. Paris: Librairie Honoré Champion.

———. 1929. "Autour d'Aśvaghoṣa." *Journal Asiatique* 215: 255–263.

Li Xuezhu. 2015. "*Madhyamakāvatāra-kārikā*, Chapter 6." *Journal of Indian Philosophy* 43: 1–30.

Lo Bue, Erberto. 1987. "The *Dharmamaṇḍala-sūtra* by Buddhaguhya." In *Orientalia Iosephi Tucci Memoriae Dicata*, edited by Gherardo Gnoli and L. Lanciotti, 2: 787–818. Rome: Istituto Italiano per il Medio ed Estremo Oriente.

Lokesh Chandra. 1987. *Sarvatathāgatatattvasaṅgraha: Sanskrit Text*. New Delhi: Motilal Banarsidass.

Lokesh Chandra and Nirmala Sharma. 2015. *Niṣpanna-yogāvalī: Sanskrit and Tibetan Texts with English Translation*. New Delhi: Aditya Prakashan.

Lopez, Donald S., Jr. 1996. "Polemical Literature (*dGag lan*)." In *Tibetan Literature: Studies in Genre*, edited by José I. Cabezón and Roger R. Jackson, 217–228. Ithaca, NY: Snow Lion Publications.

Luo Hong and Tōru Tomabechi. 2009. *Candrakīrti's Vajrasattva-niṣpādana-sūtra (Vajrasattva-sādhana) Sanskrit and Tibetan Texts*. Beijing and Vienna: China Tibetology Publishing House and Austrian Academy of Sciences Press.

Luo, Hong. 2010. *The Buddhakapālatantra, Chapters 9 to 14*. Beijing: China Tibetology Publishing House and Hamburg: Centre for Tantric Studies.

———. 2010. *Abhayākaragupta's Abhayapaddhati, Chapters 9 to 14, Critically Edited and Translated*. Beijing: China Tibetology Publishing House and Hamburg: Centre for Tantric Studies.

Martin, Dan. 2001. *Unearthing Bon Treasures: Life and Contested Legacy of a Tibetan Scripture Revealer*. Leiden: Brill.

Matsunaga, Yukei. 1964. "A Doubt to Authority of the Guhyasamāja-Ākhyāna-Tantras." *Journal of Indian and Buddhist Studies* 13.2: 16–25.

———. 1978. *The Guhyasamāja Tantra: A New Critical Edition*. Osaka: Toho shuppan.

Mayer, Robert. 2004. "Pelliot 349: A Dunhuang Tibetan Text on Rdo-rje-phur-pa." *Journal of the International Association of Buddhist Studies* 27.1: 129–164.

Meadows, Carol. 1986. *Ārya-Śūra's Compendium of the Perfections*. Bonn: Indica et Tibetica Verlag.

Mikkyō-seiten kenkyūkai (Study Group of Sacred Tantric Texts). 1988. "Advayavajrasaṃgraha: New Critical Edition with Japanese Translation I." *Taishō daigaku sōgō bukkyōkenkyūjo nenpō* 10: 234–178. Tokyo: Institute for Comprehensive Studies of Buddhism Taisho University.

Mimaki, Katsumi, and Tōru Tomabechi. 1994. *Pañcakrama: Sanskrit and Tibetan Texts Critically Edited with Verse Index and Facsimile Edition of the Sanskrit Manuscripts*. Tokyo: The Centre for East Asian Cultural Studies for UNESCO.

Miyasaka, Yūsho. 1971–1972. "*Pramāṇavārttika-kārikā* (Sanskrit and Tibetan)." *Acta Indologica* 2: 1–206.

Mori, Masahide. 1997. "The Vajrāvalī of Abhayākaragupta: A Critical Study, Sanskrit

Edition of Selected Chapters and Complete Tibetan Version." PhD dissertation, SOAS University of London.

———. 2009. *Vajrāvalī of Abhayākaragupta*. Tring, England: The Institute of Buddhist Studies.

Mullin, Glenn H. 1996. *Tsongkhapa's Six Yogas of Naropa*. Ithaca, NY: Snow Lion Publications.

Ñāṇamoli, Bhikkhu. 2010. *The Path of Purification (Visuddhimagga) by Buddhaghosa*. Kandy: Buddhist Publication Society.

Nanjio, Bunyiu, 1923. *The Laṅkāvatāra Sūtra*. Bibliotheca Otaniensis series no. 1. Kyoto: Otani University Press.

Onoda, Shunzo. 1992. *Monastic Debate in Tibet: A Study on the History and Structures of Bsdus Grwa Logic*. Vienna: Arbeitskreis für Tibetische und Buddhistische Studien Universität Wien.

Pandey, Janardan. 1997. *Bauddhalaghugranthasaṅgraha: A Collection of Minor Buddhist Texts*. Rare Buddhist Texts Research Project, Rare Buddhist Texts Series no. 14. Sarnath: Central Institute of Higher Tibetan Studies.

———. 1998. *Yoginīsañcāratantram with Nibandha of Tathāgatarakṣita and Upadeśānusāriṇīvyākhyā of Alakakalaśa*. Sarnath: Central Institute of Higher Tibetan Studies.

———. 2000. *Caryāmelāpakapradīpam of Ācārya Āryadeva*. Sarnath: Central Institute of Higher Tibetan Studies.

———. 2002. *Śrīherukābhidhānam Cakrasaṃvaratantram with the Commentary of Bhavabhaṭṭa*. Sarnath: Central Institute of Higher Tibetan Studies.

Patt, David. 1993. "Elucidating the Path to Liberation: A Study of the Commentary on the Abhidharmakośa by the First Dalai Lama." PhD dissertation, University of Wisconsin, Madison.

Pecchia, Cristina. 2015. *Dharmakīrti on the Cessation of Suffering: A Critical Edition with Translation and Comments of Manorathanandin's Vṛtti and Vibhūticandra's Glosses on Pramāṇavārttika II*, 190–216. Leiden: Brill.

Perdue, Daniel E. 1992. *Debate in Tibetan Buddhism*. Ithaca, NY: Snow Lion Publications.

Pradhan, Pralhad. 1950. *Abhidharma Samuccaya of Asanga*. Santiniketan, India: Santiniketan Press.

———. 1975. *Abhidharmakośabhāṣyam of Vasubandhu*. Patna, India: K. P. Jayaswal Research Institute.

Pruden, Leo M. 1988–1990. *Abhidharmakośabhāṣyam*. Berkeley: Asian Humanities Press. (English translation from the French of La Vallée Poussin 1971.)

Ray, Reginald A. 1974. "Understanding Tantric Buddhism: Some Questions of Method." *Journal of Asian Studies* 34.1: 169–175 (review of Wayman 1973).

Roberts, Peter Alan, trans. 2011. "Light Rays from the Jewel of the Excellent Teaching: A General Presentation on the Points of Secret Mantra." By Dwags po Bkra shis rnam rgyal. In *Mahāmudrā and Related Instructions: Core Teachings of the Kagyu Schools*, 401–620. Boston: Wisdom Publications and the Institute of Tibetan Classics.

Roerich, George N., trans. 1949. *The Blue Annals*. By Gö Lotsawa Zhönnu Pel. Calcutta: Asiatic Society. Reprint, Delhi: Motilal Banarsidass, 1979.

Roloff, Carola. 2009. *Red mda' ba: Buddhist Yogi-Scholar of the Fourteenth Century*. Wiesbaden: Ludwig Reichert Verlag.

Ruegg, David Seyfort. 1981. *The Literature of the Madhyamaka School of Philosophy in India*. Wiesbaden: Otto Harrassowitz.

Sadakata, Akira. 1997. *Buddhist Cosmology: Philosophy and Origins*. Tokyo: Kōsei.

Sakaki, Ryōzaburō. 1987 [1916]. *Mahāvyutpatti, Sgra sbyor bam po gnyis pa*. Honyaku myōgi taishū. 2 vols. Tokyo: Kokusho Kankōkai.

Sakurai, Munenobu. 1998. "A Critical Study on Lūyīpāda's *Cakrasaṃvarābhisamaya*." *Journal of Chisan Studies* 47: 1–32.

Samdhong Rinpoche and Vrajvallabh Dwivedi with a team. 1987. *Guhyādi-aṣṭasiddhi-saṅgraha*. Sarnath: Central Institute of Higher Tibetan Studies.

———. 1992. *Kṛṣṇayamāritantraṃ with Ratnāvalī Pañjikā of Kumāracandra*. Sarnath: Central Institute of Higher Tibetan Studies.

Schmithausen, Lambert. 1987. *Alayavijñana: On the Origin and Early Development of a Central Concept of Yogācāra Philosophy* (2 vols.). Tokyo: International Institute for Buddhist Studies.

Seton, Gregory. 2018. "Ratnākaraśānti." In *Brill's Encyclopedia of Buddhism*, editor-in-chief Jonathan A. Silk, 2: 366–370. Leiden: Brill.

Sferra, Francesco. 2005. "Constructing the Wheel of Time: Strategies for Establishing a Tradition." In *Boundaries, Dynamics and Construction of Traditions in South Asia*, edited by Federico Squarcini, 253–85. Florence: Firenze University Press.

Shukla, Karunesha, ed., 1973. *Śrāvakabhūmi of Ācārya Asaṅga*. Patna: K. P. Jayaswal Research Institute.

Siderits, Mark, and Shōryū Katsura. 2013. *Nāgārjuna's Middle Way: Mūlamadhyamaka-kārikā*. Boston: Wisdom Publications.

Sinclair, Iain. 2016. "The Names of Nāgabodhi and Vajrabuddhi. Appendix A." In *Esoteric Buddhism in Mediaeval Maritime Asia. Networks of Masters, Texts, Icons*, edited by Andrea Acri, 389–391. Singapore: ISEAS–Yusof Ishak Institute.

Skorupski, Tadeusz. 1983. *The Sarvadurgatipariśodhana Tantra: Elimination of All Evil Destinies*. Delhi: Motilal Banarsidass.

———. 1996. "The *Sampuṭatantra*: Sanskrit and Tibetan Versions of Chapter One." In *The Buddhist Forum IV*, edited by Tadeuz Skorupski, 191–244. London: School of Oriental and African Studies.

Snellgrove, David L. 1964 [1954]. "Supreme Enlightenment." In *Buddhist Texts Through the Ages*, edited by Edward Conze et al., 221–224. New York: Harper Torchbooks. [Translation of *Guhyasamāja Tantra*, chapter 7, vv. 1–13 and 21–38.]

———. 1959. *Hevajra Tantra: A Critical Study*. London: Oxford University Press.

———. 1987. *Indo-Tibetan Buddhism: Indian Buddhists and their Tibetan Successors*. Boston: Shambhala Publications.

Sobisch, Jan-Ulrich, 2002. *Three-Vow Theories in Tibetan Buddhism: A Comparative Study of Major Traditions from the Twelfth through Nineteenth Centuries*. Wiesbaden: Ludwig Reichert Verlag.

Sparham, Gareth, trans. 1999. *The Fulfillment of All Hopes: Guru Devotion in Tibetan Buddhism*. By Tsongkhapa. Boston: Wisdom Publications.

———. 2005. *Tantric Ethics: An Explanation of the Precepts for Buddhist Vajrayāna Practice*. By Tsongkhapa. Boston: Wisdom Publications.

Steinkellner, Ernst. 1978. "Remarks on Tantristic Hermeneutics." In *Proceedings of the Csoma de Kőrös Memorial Symposium*, edited by L. Ligeti, 445–458. Budapest: Akadémiai Kiadó.

———. 2007. *Dharmakīrti's Pramāṇaviniścaya, Chapters 1 and 2*. Beijing/Vienna: China Tibetology Publishing House and Austrian Academy of Sciences Press.

Stearns, Cyrus, trans. 2011. *Treasury of Esoteric Instructions: An Explication of the Oral Instructions of the Path with the Result*. By Lama Dampa Sönam Gyaltsen. Ithaca, NY: Snow Lion Publications.

Sugiki, Tsunehiko. 2000. "Kṛṣṇācārya's Śrīcakrasaṃvarasādhana: Critical Edition with Notes." *Chisan Gakuhō (Journal of Chisan Studies)* 49: 45–62.

———. 2017. "Perfect Realization (*Sādhana*) of Vajraḍāka and His Four Magical Females: Critical Editions of the Sanskrit *Vajraḍākamahātantra* Chapters 12 and 13." *Waseda Daigaku Kōtō Kenkyūjo Kiyō (WIAS Research Bulletin)* 9: 5–31.

———. 2018. "The Structure and Meanings of the Heruka Maṇḍala in the Buddhist *Ḍākārṇava* Scriptural Tradition." A paper read at the *World Sanskrit Conference*, available on Academia.edu.

Szántó, Péter-Dániel. 2012. "Selected Chapters from the Catuṣpīṭhatantra." PhD dissertation, Balliol College, Oxford.

———. 2013. "Minor Vajrayāna Texts II. A New Manuscript of the *Gurupañcāśikā*." In *Puṣpikā: Tracing Ancient India Through Texts and Traditions*, edited by Nina Mirnig, Péter-Dániel Szántó, and Michael Williams, vol. 1, 443–450. Oxford: Oxbow Books.

———. 2015. "Minor Vajrayāna Texts III: A Fragment of the **Guhyasamājoddhṛtayāgavidhi*." In *Tibetan and Himalayan Healing: An Anthology for Anthony Aris*, edited by Charles Ramble and Ulrike Roesler, 677–685. Kathmandu: Vajra Books.

———. 2016. "Early Exegesis of the Guhyasamāja: Philological Notes on the *Vyavastholi* of Nāgabuddhi." *Bulletin de l'École française d'Extrême-Orient* 102: 437–450.

———. Work in Progress: "The *Sāramañjarī* of Samantabhadra, a Commentary to the *Samantabhadrasādhana* of Jñānapāda: Critical Edition of the 'Pāla Recension.'"

Tanaka, Kimiaki. 1996. *Indo-Chibetto mandara no kenkyū* [*Studies in the Indo-Tibetan Maṇḍala*]. In Japanese with English chapter summaries. Kyoto: Hōzōkan.

———. 1999. "Nāgabodhi's *Śrīguhyasamājamaṇḍalopāyikāviṃśatividhi* (10/11) *āvāhanavidhi*: A Romanized Text of Newly Identified Sanskrit Manuscript." *The Mikkyo Bunka* 203: 23–36.

———. 2000. "Nāgabodhi's *Śrīguhyasamājamaṇḍalopāyikā-viṃśatividhi* (12) *Śiṣyapraveśavidhi*." *The Mikkyo Bunka* 205: 68–85.

———. 2001. "Nāgabodhi's *Guhyasamājamaṇḍalopāyikā-viṃśatividhi*: Ākāśasūtrapātanavidhi." *Indogaku Bukkyōgaku Kenkyū* [*Journal of Indian and Buddhist Studies*] 50.1: 214–209.

———. 2004. "The Measurement of the Maṇḍala According to Nāgabodhi's *Guhyasamāja maṇḍalopāyikāviṃśatividhi*." *Mikkyo Zuzo* 23: 26–39.

———. 2016. *Samājasādhanavyavastholi of Nāgabodhi/Nāgabuddhi: Introduction and Romanized Sanskrit and Tibetan Texts*. Tokyo: Watanabe Publishing.

———. 2017. *Samantabhadra Nāma Sādhanaṭīkā: Introduction, Romanized Sanskrit and Translation*. Tokyo: Watanabe Publishing.

Tanemura, Ryugen. 2009. "Superiority of Vajrayāna—Part II: Superiority of the Tantric Practice Taught in the **Vajrayānāntadvayanirākaraṇa* (*rDo rje theg pa'i mtha' gnyis sel ba*)." In *Genesis and Development of Tantrism*, edited by Shingo Einoo, 487–514. Tokyo: University of Tokyo, Institute of Oriental Culture.

———. 2015. "Guhyasamāja." In *Brill's Encyclopedia of Buddhism*, editor-in-chief, Jonathan Silk, 1: 326–333. Leiden: Brill.

Tanemura, Ryugen, Kazuo Kano, and Kenichi Kuranishi. 2017. "Ratnarakṣita's *Padminī*: A

Preliminary Edition of the Excurses in Chapter 13, Part 1." *Journal of Kawasaki Daishi Institute for Buddhist Studies* 2: 34–1.
———. 2019. "Ratnarakṣita's *Padminī*: A Preliminary Edition of the Excurses in Chapter 13, Part 2." *Journal of Kawasaki Daishi Institute for Buddhist Studies* 4: 42–1.
Tenzin Dorjee and Jeremy Russell, trans. 1995. *Paths and Grounds of Guhyasamāja according to Ārya Nagarjuna*. By Yangchen Gawai Lodoe with commentary by Geshe Losang Tsephel. Dharamsala: Library of Tibetan Works and Archives.
The International Translation Committee Founded by the V.V. Kalu Rinpoché. 1995. *Myriad Worlds: Buddhist Cosmology in Abhidharma*, Kālacakra and Dzog-chen. By Jamgön Kongtrul Lodrö Tayé. Ithaca, NY: Snow Lion Publications.
Thurman, Robert A. F. 1988. "Vajra Hermeneutics." In *Buddhist Hermeneutics*, edited by Donald Lopez, 119–148. Honolulu: Kuroda Institute.
———. 1990 [1982]. "The Middle Transcendent Insight." In *Life and Teachings of Tsong Khapa*, edited by Robert Thurman, 108–185. Dharamsala: Library of Tibetan Works and Archives.
———. 1995. "Practicing the Creation Stage." In *Essential Tibetan Buddhism*, 213–247. San Francisco: HarperSanFrancisco.
———. 2010. *Brilliant Illumination of the Lamp of the Five Stages*. New York: The American Institute of Buddhist Studies, Columbia University Center for Buddhist Studies, Tibet House U.S.
Tillemans, Tom J. 1995. "Dharmakīrti and Tibetans on *Adṛśyānupalabdhihetu*." *Journal of Indian Philosophy* 23: 129–149.
———. 1999. *Scripture, Logic, Language: Essays on Dharmakīrti and His Tibetan Successors*. Boston: Wisdom Publications.
———. 2000. *Dharmakīrti's Pramāṇavārttika: An Annotated Translation of the Fourth Chapter (Parārthānumāna), Volume 1 (k. 1148)*. Vienna: Verlag der Österreichischen Akademie der Wissenschaften.
Tomabechi, Tōru. 2006. "*Étude du Pañcakrama: introduction et traduction annotée.*" PhD dissertation, University of Lausanne.
———. 2008. "Vitapāda, Śākyamitra, and Āryadeva: On a Transitional Stage in the History of Guhyasamāja Exegesis." In *Esoteric Buddhist Studies: Identity in Diversity. Proceedings of the International Conference of Esoteric Buddhist Studies, Koyasan University, Sept. 2006*, edited by Editorial Board of the ICEBS, 171–77. Koyasan: Koyasan University.
———. In progress. *Pañcakramapañjikā* by Samayavajra from the Collection of the China Tibetology Research Center, Beijing; see https://buddhanature.tsadra.org/index.php/People/Tomabechi,_T.
Tripathi, Ram Shankar. 2001. *Piṇḍīkrama and Pañcakrama of Ācārya Nāgārjuna*. Sarnath: Central Institute of Higher Tibetan Studies.
Tripathi, Ram Shankar, and Thakur Sain Negi. 2001. *Hevajratantram with Muktikāvalīpañjikā of Mahāpaṇḍitācārya Ratnākaraśānti*. Sarnath: Central Institute of Higher Tibetan Studies.
Tsuda, Shinichi. 1974. *The Saṃvarodaya-Tantra: Selected Chapters*. Tokyo: Hokuseido Press.
Tucci, Giuseppe. 1934–1935. "Some Glosses upon the Guhyasamāja." In *Mélanges chinois et bouddhiques*, 3: 339–353, reprinted in *Opera Minora*. Roma: G. Bardi, 1971.
Vaidya, P. L. 1960. *Gaṇḍavyūhasūtra*. Darbhanga: The Mithila Institute.

———. 1967. *Daśabhūmikasūtra*. Darbhanga: The Mithila Institute.

Verrill, Wayne, and Ngor Thartse Khenpo Sonam Gyatso (Hiroshi Sonami), trans. 2012. *The Yoginī's Eye: Comprehensive Introduction to Buddhist Tantra*, volume 1: *Systemization and Interpretation*. By Sonam Tsemo. Xlibris Corporation.

Vetter, Tilmann. 1984. *Der Buddha und seine Lehre in Dharmakīrtis Pramāṇavārttika. Der Abschnitt über den Buddha und die vier edlen Wahrheiten im Pramāṇasiddhi-Kapitel.* Arbeitskreis für Tibetische und Buddhistische Studien. Vienna: Universität Wien.

Viehbeck, Markus. 2014. *Polemics in Indo-Tibetan Scholasticism: A Late 19th-Century Debate between 'Ju Mi pham and Dpa' ris Rab gsal.* Vienna: Arbeitskreis für Tibetische und Buddhistische Studien. Vienna: Universität Wien.

Wallace, Alan. 1998. *The Bridge of Quiescence: Experiencing Tibetan Buddhist Meditation.* Chicago: Open Court.

Wallace, Vesna. 2001. *The Inner Kālacakratantra: A Buddhist Tantric View of the Individual.* New York: Oxford University Press.

Walpola, Rahula. 1971. *Le Compendium de la Super-Doctrine (Philosophie) Abhidharmasamuccaya d'Asaṅga.* Paris: École française d'Extrême-Orient.

Walshe, Maurice. 1995. *The Long Discourses of the Buddha: A Translation of the Dīgha Nikāya.* Boston: Wisdom Publications.

Wayman, Alex. 1962. "Buddhist Genesis and the Tantric Tradition." *Oriens Extremus* 9: 127–131.

———. 1971. "Contributions on the Symbolism of the Maṇḍala-Palace." In *Études tibétains dédiées à la mémoire de Marcelle Lalou*, 557–566. Paris: Adrien Maisonneuve.

———. 1973. *The Buddhist Tantras: Light on Indo-Tibetan Esotericism.* New York: Samuel Weiser.

———. 1974. "The Intermediate-State Dispute in Buddhism." In *Buddhist Studies in Honour of I.B. Horner*, edited by L. Cousins et al., 227–239. Dordrecht: D. Reidel Publishing Company.

———. 1977. *Yoga of the Guhyasamājatantra.* Delhi: Motilal Banarsidas.

———. 1984. "The Sarvarahasyatantra." *Acta Indologica (Indo Kotan Kenkyu)* 6: 521–569.

Wedemeyer, Christian Konrad. 1999. "Vajrayāna and Its Doubles: A Critical Historiography, Exposition, and Translation of the Tantric Works of Āryadeva." PhD dissertation, Columbia University, New York.

———. 2006. "'Tantalising Traces of the Labours of the Lotsāwas: Alternative Translations of Sanskrit Sources in the Writings of Rje Tsong kha pa." In *Tibetan Buddhist Literature and Praxis: Studies in Its Formative Period, 900–1400*, edited by Ronald M. Davidson and Christian K. Wedemeyer, 149–182. Leiden: Brill.

———. 2007. *Āryadeva's Lamp that Integrates the Practices, Caryāmelāpakapradīpa: The Gradual Path of Vajrayāna Buddhism according to the Esoteric Community Noble Tradition.* New York: The American Institute of Buddhist Studies at Columbia University in New York with Columbia University's Center for Buddhist Studies and Tibet House U.S.

Westerhoff, Jan. 2010. *Nāgārjuna's Vigrahavyāvatanī, The Dispeller of Disputes.* Oxford: Oxford University Press.

Wogihara, U. 1989 [1936]. *Sphutārtha: Abhidharmakośavyākhyā, The Work of Yaśomitra.* Tokyo: Sankibo Buddhist Book Store.

Yaita, Hideomi. 1988. "Dharmakīrti on the Person Free from Faults: Annotated Translation of the *Pramāṇavārttikasvavṛttiḥ*, Ad v. 218–223." *Journal of Naritasan Institute for Buddhist Studies* 11: 433–445.

Yarnall, Thomas F. 2013. *Great Stages of Mantra (Sngags rim chen mo): Chapters 11–12, The Creation Stage*. New York: The American Institute of Buddhist Studies at Columbia University in New York with Columbia University Center for Buddhist Studies and Tibet House U.S.

Yonezawa, Yoshiasu. 2008. "*Vigrahavyāvartanī*: Sanskrit Transliteration and Tibetan Translation." *Journal of Naritasan Institute of Buddhist Studies* 31: 209–333.

Yoshimizu, Chizuko. 1987. "The Theoretical Basis of the *bskyed rim* as Reflected in the *bskyed rim* Practice of the Ārya School." *Report of the Japanese Association for Tibetan Studies* 33: 21–33.

Zhang, Yisun (Krang Dbyi sun). 1993. *Bod rgya tshig mdzod chen mo—A Tibetan-Tibetan-Chinese Dictionary*. Beijing: Mi rigs dpe skrun khang.

Index

A

Abhayākaragupta, 192
  on fierce deities, 322
  on ground of wisdom, 366
  on jñānasattva, 597–98
  on lotuses, 631
  on mantras, 233
  on offerings, 295
  Perfected Yoga Garland, 576–77
  on protection wheel, 309, 311
  on samayasattva, 189–90
  on *uṣṇīṣa mudrā*, 633
  on Vajradhara visualization, 314
  See also *Cluster of Instructions*; *Maṇḍala Vajra Garland*
Abhidhānottara Tantra, 176, 296–98, 409, 444–45, 448, 579
Abhidharmakośa (Vasubandhu), 86, 87
  on first eon, 62, 439
  on intermediate being/state, 84n367, 145, 447, 500–502
  on three maṇḍalas (cosmology), 562n2801
Abhidharmakośabhāṣya (Vasubandhu), 81, 86, 500, 504, 531, 533
Acala, 122, 302, 321n1479, 433, 488, 575
accordant cause, 136, 138–39, 262
action consorts, 175, 555–56, 568–69
Activities of the Yoginīs, 712
afflictive emotions, 246, 549, 694, 710
  of present body, 136–37, 262, 547–48
  purifying, 219–20, 225, 493–94, 550, 633–34
  suffering of, 453
  taking in path, 611
aggregates, five, 381
  blessing of, 539–40
  in body maṇḍala, 574
  colors of, 572
  correspondences, 546
  dissolution of, 122, 485, 486–93
  as five buddhas, 101, 117, 122, 301, 479, 538–41
  variant views, 38–39
  in voiced recitation, 665
Akaniṣṭha, 157n698, 298, 449, 718
Akhu Ching Sherab Gyatso, 152, 168–69, 173, 191, 232, 246
Akṣobhya, 208, 323, 699
  blessings of, 188, 590, 591–93
  color of, 104, 387
  divine pride of, 26, 30
  emanating maṇḍala, 204, 206, 436–37
  and First Lord, variant views, 151–52, 159, 213, 536–37, 542
  hatred purified by, 219, 633–34
  initiation of, 550
  invocation of, 157–59, 320–21, 470, 481, 544, 573–74, 625–26, 703
  mantras of, 233, 633, 667n3372
  between meditation sessions, 235
  placement of, 109, 558, 559, 574
  as principal deity, 115, 649
  samādhi of, 219
  at sealing with, 114, 635
  shared seat of, 111
  in subtle drop yoga, 231, 658
  in Supreme King of Maṇḍalas, 224, 225, 226, 628–29, 634

as triple sattvas, 600–601
as Vajra Mind, 31
and Vajradhara, dissolution into, 315, 316
water element and, 543
Akṣobhya Vajra, 296, 628
all-empty, 487, 492, 493, 509, 520, 538, 539
Amitābha, 558, 559, 559n2783, 699
blessings of, 188, 587–88
color, 104, 387
dissolution, 487, 490
invoking, 703
maṇḍala size, 383n1790
passion purified by, 219, 302
placement, 432, 574
seat of, 428
as Vajra Speech, 31
Amitāyus, 208, 481
Amoghasiddhi, 208, 302, 574n2861, 699
in consort yoga, 618, 619
dissolution, 487, 491
divine identity of, 31, 188
emblem, 631
invoking, 481
maṇḍala size, 383n1790
placement, 558, 559
Amoghavajra, 104
Amṛtakuṇḍalin, 326–27, 328, 433, 575
Amyé Shap, 54, 65, 70, 98, 99, 189, 247, 248
analogies
beggars claiming to be kings, 6
dyeing cloth, 167
enemy employed to overcome that enemy, 5–6
last year's ashes and this year's fire, 461
moon's reflection, 350–51, 353
my mother is a barren woman, 274
rabbit's horns, 274
rope as snake, 17, 18
water poured into water, 29, 127, 360
Ānandagarbha, 397, 421n2066. See also *Commentary on the Compendium of Truth of All Tathāgatas*
anger, 300, 302, 529
animals, 438, 452, 502
antidotes, power of, 17–19, 304
Aparājita, 433, 575, 578, 614, 630
appearance, enhanced appearance, approaching attainment, 130, 451n2214, 492–93, 506, 507–8, 509–10, 517, 520, 644
appearances
coarse dualistic, eliminating, 73, 360–61
during dissolution, 124, 505–6
natural, variant views, 123–24
in post-meditation, 24–25
special appearances, 14, 24–27, 33–35, 61, 460
special supreme, 362
See also ordinary appearance; pure appearance
Ārya tradition, 7, 41, 42, 81, 494
creation stage dissolution in, 73
critiques of, 44
deities in, number of, 229
on external objects, 77
five manifest awakenings in, 140
Guhyasamāja sādhanas of, 51–56, 94–95, 98, 115–16
inner mansion, distinctions of, 418
jñānasattva in, 636
Madhyamaka in, 75–76, 133–36
Prāsaṅgika in, 131
seven ornaments (hermeneutics), 205
unique correspondences in, 86
Āryadeva. See *Compendium of Practices*; *Stages of Self-Blessing*
Āryaśūra, 715
Asaṅga
Abhidharmasamuccaya, 501, 502
Primary Ground, 452, 502, 503, 507, 510, 528, 533, 534
Treatise on the Grounds, 508
Yogācārabhūmi, 87, 130, 150, 447, 655
Aśvaghoṣa, *Fifty Stanzas on the Guru*, 259
Atiśa. *See* Dīpaṅkaraśrījñāna
attainments, four kinds of persons not able to reach, 270
Avalokiteśvara, 490. *See also* Lokeśvara
awakening
in intermediate state, 145–46, 483–84, 486

in present life, 139, 262–63, 447, 448, 450, 463, 485–86
See also buddhahood/enlightenment

B

Barawa Gyeltsen Palsangpo, 11, 148
basis, complete transformation of, 346–47
bhaga, 98–99
Bhavabhadra, 194, 455
Bhavyakīrti, 7
on jñānasattva, 597–98, 636
on moon orb, 131
on offerings, 295
on principal deity, 115
on seven royal treasures, 403
on triple sattvas, 192
See also *Intense Illuminating Lamp*
Bhṛkuṭi, 614
birth, 55, 466
as ground of purification, 82, 83, 85, 86, 92–93, 94, 118, 462, 465–66, 473
miraculous, 90, 91, 92, 113–14, 432, 437, 440n2165, 441, 508
stages of, correspondences with, 449–50
two stages and, 32
See also four modes of birth; womb birth
birth state, 501, 508–9, 516
Black Yamāri, 396
Black Yamāri Tantra, 261, 704, 705
blessings
with bodhicitta, 211–12
of body, 584–87
of five meats and five nectars, 680–83
of mind, 590–93
of speech, 587–90
of three doors, 30–31, 187–89, 216–17, 544–46, 583–84
bliss, 202, 211–12, 274–75, 353, 366, 372, 538, 611, 711–12, 719. *See also* great bliss
Blue Annals (Gö Lotsāwa Zhönnu Pel), 152
bodhicitta
Akṣobhyas from, 153–54, 155, 157, 158–59
blessing with, 211–12
bliss of, 99
dissolution of, 450–51
holding, 202, 611, 612
in human birth, 528
in initiation, 226, 477, 635, 636
intermediate being and, 151
light rays of, 252–53
melted, 539
mentally emitting, 621
moon orb as, 131–33, 521, 572n2851
obstacle for, 620
offering, 472
Bodhicittavajra, 116, 154–55, 208, 314, 481, 537, 676
lama as, 297
prostrating to, 301
three faces of, 204, 213–14, 215, 315, 512, 545
bodhisattvas, 114
in consort yoga, 614, 615
generated, deeds of, 225
ideal of, 4, 5, 219
last rebirth of, 147
and magicians, difference between, 25–26
placement of, 417, 554–55, 557, 564
seed syllables of, 630
See also under sense bases/faculties
body, ordinary, 216, 262, 363, 460
as cause of saṃsāra, 137
at death, 138, 463
during deity dissolution, 121
five impurities of, 677
transforming, 38–39, 215, 262–63
See also human body
body enhancement, 235, 689–90
body isolation, 85n369, 126, 279
body maṇḍala, 160, 279, 494
actual basis of, 175
body, meaning of in, 573
celestial mansion as basis, 164–65
deities, numbers of, 578–80, 647–50
deities as body parts in, variant views, 169–73
deity placement in, 554, 557–59
and gathering deities into body, distinction in, 479, 482, 568–69, 571

Geluk and Sakya disputes on, 177–84
in Guhyasamāja tradition, distinctions of, 580–81
as naturally present, 173–74, 179, 181–82
and outer maṇḍala, relationship of, 165, 166–69, 566–68
in sleep, 695
transformation in, variant views, 161–64, 168–69, 175
uncontrived basis, 176–77
uses of term, 117
variant views, 177–85, 545, 547–49, 551, 552–53, 555, 570–71, 702n3582
body of union. *See* saṃbhogakāya
Brahmā, 438, 699
brahma line, 393, 417, 418
Buddha essence, 516
Buddha Śākyamuni, 137, 258, 474, 475, 605
Buddha Skull Tantra, 267
Buddha Vehicle, 266, 277
buddhafields, 115, 232, 477
creation of, 22
displays of awakening in, 222–23, 249, 251, 475, 668, 669–70
as Mind Only, 131
Buddhaguhya, 395, 396, 424–25, 426
buddhahood/enlightenment, 360
bodily changes for, 137–38
causes for, 242n1110, 273–77
corporeal elements in, 138–39
potential for, 11
in single lifetime, 148, 149, 195
through passion, 198
vows and, 270–71
See also awakening
buddhas, 4–5
deeds of, 453, 475, 605 (*see also* enlightened deeds)
females inviting males, 584n2913
images, consecrating, 549–50
self-visualization of, 12
stupid, 180, 548
Buddhaśrījñāna. *See* Jñānapāda
Butön Rinchen Drup, 7, 45, 46, 47, 142, 147, 186, 210
on Akṣobhya and First Lord, 151–52, 155–56
on blessings of three doors, 189, 216–17
on body maṇḍala, 184, 185, 570–71
on celestial mansion, 207
on consort yoga, 203, 212, 620n3123
creation stage integration by, 82, 89
on emblems, manifest awakening from, 140–41
on First Lord's appearance, 141
on fourfold meditation, 75
on intermediate being, 130n556
on maṇḍalas, capacity for, 174
on moon orb, 131–32
on philosophy in Vajrayāna, 133
on principal deities, 94
on protection meditation, 98, 323n1494, 332n1570
on specially visualized deities, 117–18, 119, 208

C

Cakrasaṃvara cycle, 180, 184, 295, 331, 544, 597, 708
birth, purifying in, 446–47
body maṇḍala in, 161, 165, 179, 186, 564, 578
borrowings from, 160
cremation grounds in, 245
initiation in, 181
maṇḍalas of, 408, 409–10, 422
preliminaries in, 239, 241, 244
tormas in, 290
women in, 194
Cakrasaṃvara Sādhana (Lūyīpāda), 368, 446–47
Cakrasaṃvara Tantra, 268, 640, 666, 683
Candrakīrti, 53, 77, 442, 645. See also *Illuminating Lamp*; *Vajrasattva Sādhana*
caryā practices, 318, 463, 465, 603–4, 663, 718n3674
caryā tantra, 310, 352–53
celestial mansion, 87, 88, 164, 384–85, 420n2056, 711
beams, 407–8
from *bhrūṃ*, 380–81, 384

body generated as, 176–77, 184, 564–65, 569–70, 571–73, 580, 649
columns, 408–10
deities' locations in, 109
dissolution, 252
drip-like layer/ornaments, 108, 400, 414, 415, 424
eaves, 414
erroneous views on, 551–52
finial, 426–27
between garland and crossed vajra, 385–92
grounds and ceilings, colors of, 427
height, 396
macrocosmic correspondences with, 86–88, 91, 92–93, 381, 443, 519
measurements, 382–84
offering ledge, 410–11, 414, 416
outline, 373–75
panels, 404, 412, 415
parapets, 415, 416, 424
pearl strands, 412–13, 415, 424
and portals, distance between, 394–96
as purifier, 381–82
roofs of, 111, 424–25
in session breaks, 253
shape of, 426
single-mindedness in, 661
source of phenomena and, 369, 370, 371, 372
in subtle drop yoga, 658, 659
support of, 379
two- and three-dimensional depictions of, 103–8
victory banners, 108, 415–16
visualization of, maintaining, 709
walls, 404–6, 416, 427
See also inner mansion
central channel, 124, 228, 234, 485, 495, 643, 665
centripetal dissolution, 601
Changkya Ngawang Chöden, 167, 172, 173
"clear appearance" layer, 107–8
clear appearances, 26, 412n1999
arising of, 654–55
in consort yoga, 610, 611
stage by stage practice of, 35–37, 709–11
time needed for, 714–16
Tsongkhapa's view, 38
clear light
actual, 228, 523, 642
actual and metaphorical, 249, 669
in emptiness meditation, 360–61
manifestation of, 461
preparation for, 32
in sleeping and waking, 695
clear light of death, 463, 493, 506
and clear life of path, correspondence with, 507
completion stage and, 494
erroneous views of, 509–10
habituating to, 121, 125
clear-light-emptiness, 5, 64, 65, 127, 139
Cluster of Instructions (Abhayākaragupta), 239, 298
on celestial mansion, 398, 422
on intermediate being, 509
on protection wheel, 247, 312
on samayasattva, 595
on session length, 708
on specially visualized deities, 464
on torma offerings, 696, 699
on two accumulations, 365
Commentary on the Compendium of Truth of All Tathāgatas (Ānandagarbha), 714
compassion, 115, 342
emptiness and, 18n77, 244, 697
motivation of, 250, 633–34
need for, 5
refuge and, 304, 305
of three bodies, 138n590
See also great compassion
Compendium of Practices (Āryadeva), 134, 137
on bodily correspondences, 122
on Buddha's deeds, 198–99
on creation stage, 276
on dissolution, 126, 489
on indestructible drop, 506–7
on intermediate beings, 83, 85, 462–63
on mantra path, 266
on mirror-like wisdom, 488

on self-transformation, 351–52
on three modes of practice, 474
on three realms, 642
on two stages, 277, 464–65
on wisdom of dharma realm, 493–94
Compendium of Truth of All Tathāgatas, 638, 639
Compendium of Vajra Wisdom Tantra, 197, 451
completion stage, 3, 23–24, 84–85, 102, 275, 485, 523, 629
awakening in, 567
beginning practice, 277–78
clear light in, 124, 495, 497
consort yoga and, 612
culmination of, 139
historical development of, 7, 8
levels of interpretation, 205
purification by, 126, 278–79
purpose of, 32, 382
ripening for, 31–32, 134, 257–58, 276, 279, 282, 360, 520, 669, 708
source for, 83
three bodies of, 461, 462
three maṇḍalas during, 175
union requiring practice in, 625
unsuitability for, 269
winds during, 378n1769
See also body isolation; illusory body; two stages
Concentration Continuation, 352
conception (biological), 142n616, 149, 150, 154–55, 158–59, 212, 527–29, 648
conceptual yoga, 277, 657–58, 659, 660–61, 712, 715
conceptualization/conceptual thought, 19–20, 22, 344
antithesis of, 15–19
in creation stage, 5
nonapprehension of, 346
ordinary, 33, 345
overcoming conceptualization with, 9 (*see also* deproliferation)
purifying, 69, 128
Concise Sādhana (Nāgārjuna), 45, 52, 99, 156, 246, 247, 295, 471, 635, 662
on Akṣobhya, 536
on body blessing, 584–86
on body enhancement, 689
on body maṇḍala, 117, 552, 553, 557, 559, 564
on celestial mansion, 384–85
on celestial mansion as body maṇḍala, 573–75, 576
commentaries, 53, 131–32, 133, 134, 192
on consort yoga, deity placement, 614–15
on consort yoga practices, 616, 617, 618, 619
on consorts, 200, 610
on deities, bringing to suchness, 483
on dissolution, 253, 685, 686–87
on divine identity, 593
on Dveṣavajra, 309
on emblems, 631, 632
on emotions, 220
on emptiness mantra, 495
on emptiness meditation, 341
on fierce deities, 321, 322
on First Lord, 151, 520–21, 522, 524
on five manifest awakenings, 510–11, 523–24
on food yoga, 690–91, 693
on four disks, 101
on four mothers, 563–64
four yogas in, 57, 118–19, 160, 705
Guhyasamāja emptiness verse in, 61
on inner mansion, 420–21
on jñānasattva, 189, 596
on Māmakī, 637
manifest awakenings in, 140
on meditation posture, 291
on mind blessing, 590–91, 592
on name mantras, 629–30
on offerings, 684–85
preliminaries in, 237
on principal deities, 56, 94, 115, 437
on protection, 98
on samayasattva, 595
on sense offerings, 292–93
as source, 283
on space realm, 368, 374

on specially visualized deities, 113, 431, 432–33, 479
on speech blessing, 587–88, 589
on subtle yoga, 658–60, 661
on suchness, entering, 669
on Supreme King of Maṇḍalas, 224, 428, 628, 629
on twenty-five coarse elements, 123, 126
on ultimate truth, 497
on vajra ladies, 554, 555–56
on vajra stakes, 323–25, 326, 329, 330
and *Vajrasattva Sādhana*, relationship of, 284
on voiced recitation, 664
concluding practices, 249
dissolution and arising, 668–70
final dissolution, 685–87
praises and offerings, 670–71, 684–85
consciousness
aggregate of, 123–25
entering womb, 511, 528, 529–30
in joining-of-palms, 640–42
as root of phenomena, 518
at time of death, 507
See also mental consciousness; sense consciousnesses
consciousness-base-of-all, 150
consort yoga, 31, 223, 457
correspondence with fruit, 473–74
divine identity in, 618–21
emptiness view in, 612
faults in, 620–21
importance of, 720–21
passion and, 197
practices of, 608, 609
purpose of, 202–3
requirements for, 199–200
scriptural sources, 604–5
seeking consort, 606–8
uniting vajra and lotus, 616–17
visualization, 613–15
yogis' characteristics, 610–12
consorts, 302
actual and wisdom, requirements for practicing with, 200, 610–12
characteristics of, 606–8, 611, 612
erroneous views on, 471–72
heart-emanated, 200–201
See also action consorts; wisdom consorts
constituents, red and white. *See* bodhicitta
conventional existence, 63, 64
conventional truth, 98, 126, 133, 465, 514, 567
cooperative conditions, 166–68, 172–73
creation stage, 3
amount of practice needed, 279–82
body maṇḍala's effect in, 168, 179
Buddha's bodies in, 30
as cause for buddhahood, 272–77, 344
and completion stage, relationship between, 31–32, 38, 85, 136, 278–79, 447, 462, 465, 515, 567
condensed and extensive, 280–81
as contrived, 567
eight shared variations, 721–22
erroneous views of, 549–50
false sources, 284–85
goals of, 27, 33
historical development of, 7–8, 72
human birth correspondence in, 439
Indian and Tibetan perspectives on, 6–7, 9–13
levels of interpretation, 205
main path, characteristics of, 466
mental elaboration in, 20–21
overview, 4–5
practice places, 282
as preliminary, 8–9, 281
purification by, 126
purification not occurring through, 467–68
scriptural sources, 282–84
stability in, 712–13
stages of mastering, 36–37, 713–16
transformation in, 161, 212
triple sattvas in, purpose of, 191
visualization in, maintaining, 708–11
Yogācāra methods in, 75
cremation grounds, 244–45, 290, 297–98, 375, 457
crossed vajras, 106, 111, 330, 373, 378, 385, 393

body maṇḍala and, 183
colors, 103–4, 386–88
as five wisdoms, 379
formation of, 100
maṇḍalas of physical elements and, 102–3, 206, 374, 376, 377
offering ledges and, 411
size, 375, 388–92
two kinds, 386, 396–97
in vajra fence, 331
Crown Jewel Sādhana (*Kambala), 297, 331

D

Ḍākārṇava Tantra, 290, 389, 393, 409, 445n2185
Dakpo Tashi Namgyal, 70–71
Daṇḍin, 597
Dārikpa, 405
Daśabhūmikasūtra, 232
death
correspondences with, 461, 485
five dissolutions at, 487–93
as ground of purification, 81, 83, 85, 86, 92–93, 118, 462, 473
recognizing dissolution at, 494
signs at, 657
stages of, 443–44
taking on path to dharmakāya, 59, 80, 119, 121–29, 337, 463, 487
at time of ground, 506–7
two stages and, 32
wind at, 138, 506, 507
Death, Intermediate State, and Rebirth in Tibetan Buddhism (Lati and Hopkins), 122
death state, 501, 508, 509–10, 516
debate tradition, 39, 46–47, 169
definitive meaning, 205, 228, 275
deities
appearance of, uncertainties about, 228
bodily nature of, 172
heart of, arousing, 719–20
number of, uncertainties concerning, 229–30
size of, 396
in visualization, role of, 6
in visualization, variant views, 10–13
visualizing as psycho-physical constituents, 169, 170–73
womb emergence of, 530–31
See also principal deities; specially visualized deities; thirty-two maṇḍala deities
deity platform, 108, 417, 422, 425
deity yoga, 13, 238
as cause for awakening, 272
as conceptual meditation, 10
emptiness and bliss in, 711–12
erroneous views of, 549–50
habituating to, 707
inconceivability of, 12
intellectual understanding of, 494
length of practice, 37
mental quiescence in, 11, 656
perseverance in, 714–15
two Buddha kāyas in, 23–24
wind yoga and, 353n1640
deproliferation, 5–6, 9, 37, 276, 350
desire. *See* passion
Desire Realm, 147, 197, 201, 293. *See also* gods of desire realm
dhāraṇī maṇḍala, 474–75
dharmadhātu, 132, 180, 409
Dharmadhātuvajrā, 301, 645
dharmakāya
attaining, 121
in creation stage, 5
during dissolution, 493
divine identity of, 27, 28–29, 127, 360, 361, 364, 495, 497, 669
emptiness meditation and, 29–30, 82
fruit taken as path, 129
natural abode and, 298
of path, 461, 463
profound mind and, 23
and saṃbhogakāya, uniting, 146
Dharmakīrti, 10, 19, 23, 34, 144, 347, 648
Pramāṇasiddhi (chapter *Pramāṇavārttika*), 16, 17, 90, 711
Pramāṇavārttika, 15, 37, 38, 348–49, 715, 716
Pramāṇaviniścaya, 21
*Dharmasubhūti, 504

Dignāga, 21n95
Dīpaṅkarabhadra, *Maṇḍala Rituals of the Guhyasamāja*, 383, 404, 405
Dīpaṅkaraśrījñāna (Atiśa), 25, 78–80, 283–84, 361–62, 363
direct perception, 21–22, 35–37, 38, 716
directional guardians, 290–91, 327, 684, 699
disciples
  characteristics of, 264, 269, 272
  five types, 456
  jewel-like, 196, 201, 456
  unsuitable, 266
divine identity/pride, 4, 27–29, 215
  attainments of, 35
  clear appearance and, 710–11
  emptiness meditation and, 127, 128, 359–60
  genuine, maintaining, 36
  habituating to, 26
  importance of, 709
  maintaining, 512, 518, 520, 524
  in mantra recitation, 234, 666
  in offerings, 296
  of passion, 618
  purpose of, 712
  in Supreme King of Maṇḍalas, 629
  of Vajra Body, 586–87
Ḍombhiheruka, 276, 364
downfalls, 268, 270–71, 354, 694–95
Drakpa Gyaltsen, 126, 148
Drakpa Shedrup, 12, 167, 171
Drigung school, 126, 495n2441
Drinsumpa, 229, 645
Drop of the Great Seal Tantra, 267, 673
Dveṣarati, 563
Dveṣavajra, 320, 323n1497, 469
  divine identity of, 634
  in preliminaries, 238, 245, 290–91, 315, 317–18, 321, 322, 323
  samādhi of, 309
  in Supreme King of Maṇḍalas, 226, 628

E

eight conditionings for abandonment, 710
eight pure liberations, 398
eightfold noble path, 398
eighty intrinsic conceptual minds, 492–93, 505, 508, 510
Ekajaṭā, 614
Eltschinger, Vincent, 21
emblems, 224, 380, 421
  four seals and, 638
  manifest awakening from, 140–41, 524, 525
  meditation on, 101–2
  in subtle drop yoga, 656–57
  of Sumbharāja, 325
  in Supreme King of Maṇḍalas, 631–32
embryo/fetus, 159
  embryology of, 149–50
  emergence of, 215
  heart of, 507–9, 528
  phases of development, 142n616, 143–45, 484–85, 511–12, 516–17, 532–34
  purification and transformation, 188, 189, 541–43
emptiness, 538
  and appearance, unifying, 22
  and bliss, union of, 99, 202, 353, 366, 372, 611, 711–12, 719
  clinging to, 357
  in deity visualization, 6, 11–12, 13
  direct realization, 643
  forms and, 10, 13–14, 24
  and selflessness, distinctions between, 22–23
  in tantras and Mahāyāna, 199, 358
emptiness meditation, 23
  averting obstructions with, 366
  in creation stage, variant views, 24–25, 36, 77–79, 338–42, 351, 354–55
  divine identity in, 363–64
  examination-based, 71
  forceful, 66, 68, 69, 70, 71
  Gorampa's view, 62–65, 66–67
  importance of, 721
  instructions for, 342–46, 359–60
  macrocosmic context, 59–60, 72–73, 206
  microcosmic context, 59–60, 127–29
  in Pāramitā and Mantra Vehicles, differences in, 27–29, 127
  protection wheel and, 248, 309–10, 312

purposes of, 24, 25, 34, 78–80, 127–28, 361–63
Sakya view, 68–71, 72
Tsongkhapa's view, 65–66, 67
enlightened deeds, 605
and *caryā* practices, three types, 603–4
in concluding rituals, 249, 250, 251
enactment of, 204, 222–23
future, 211, 212
shared and specific, 634
three kinds, 198–99
variant views, 158
enlightenment. *See* buddhahood/ enlightenment
Enquiry of the Four Goddesses, 692–93
Entirely Secret Tantra, 398, 613
evaṃ, meaning of, 99, 371–72
excitement, 359, 653–54, 710
explanatory tantras (*Guhyasamāja*), 49–50, 51
external objects, 33–34, 74–75, 76–77, 133, 519
extremes, falling into, 39, 66

F

father tantras, 138, 258, 261
Faure, Bernard, 194
feminist theories, 197
field of accumulating merit, 242–43, 244–45, 290, 295–98, 470–71, 473, 684
first beings of eon, 82, 89–93, 114, 118, 438–41, 442–44, 458, 471, 511
First Lord, 56, 94, 193, 511
abiding as, 129
description of, 526
disputes about, 141–46, 151–54, 469, 470, 513–15, 536–37
five manifest awakenings and, 511, 521, 523, 524–25, 580
intermediate being and, 84, 86, 519, 541
nirmāṇakāya transformation, 537–41, 543–44, 546
rebirth as, 121
saṃbhogakāya and, 520
in subsequent yoga, 140–41
transformation of, 212–13
Vajradhara and, 318
visualization, 32, 130, 464, 520–21, 522
wind-and-mind body of, 132, 134, 138
First Yoga, 56–57, 118, 349, 443, 626
four yogas included in, 705
passion in, 198–99, 451–53, 474, 604
samādhi of, 706
See also consort yoga
five elements, 301
five manifest awakenings, 119, 214, 436, 437, 511, 702
correspondences with, 517–18
fetal development and, 143–45
First Lord and, 443
four yogas and, 523–24, 705
order, 139–40
single-mindedness and, 277n1250, 660
five meats and five nectars, 238–40, 671–72
in Ārya tradition, 676–80
blessing, 680–83
diverse offering methods, 672–75
fifth nectar, variant views, 674, 678, 679
opponents' methods, 675–76
order of offering, 683–84
synonyms, 674–75
Five Stages (Nāgārjuna), on illusion-like samādhi, 467
five tathāgata families
consorts and, 607, 614
correspondences, 519, 541–43
five nectars and, 678, 679–80
as five poisons, 301–3
in food yoga, 691, 694
on illusion-like samādhi, 467
in subtle drop yoga, 654–56
triple sattvas and, 596–97
vows of, 243
five tathāgatas/buddhas, 30–31, 114
blessings of, 188
colors of, 107
dissolution of, 487
divine identity of, 31, 188
and five meats and five nectars, 239, 672–74
in joining-of-palms, 640–42
mantras, 31
placement, 555, 557, 558–59
See also under aggregates, five

five wisdoms, 122, 379, 486–93, 520, 572, 677
food in first eon, 440–41
food yoga, 235, 682
  dedication, 694
  downfalls and flaws, 694–95
  inner fire offering in, 690–94
formless absorptions, 20–21
formless realm, 502
Formulating the Sādhana (Nāgabuddhi), 56, 144, 145, 215, 283, 473, 484
  on Akṣobhya, 536–37
  ambiguity of, 93
  authenticity of, 54–55
  authority of, 92, 154
  on bodhisattvas, intermediate beings of, 503–4
  on body, setting deities on, 545
  on body maṇḍala, 553, 556, 557
  on body maṇḍala as celestial mansion, 564–65, 569
  on celestial mansion, correspondences with, 468–69, 470
  on conception, purification of, 212
  on consciousness entering womb, 529
  on consort yoga, 475, 613–14
  on deities, number of, 230, 646, 647, 650
  on deities, three faces, 526, 639–41
  on deity placement, 554, 644
  on dissolution, 123
  on embryonic development, 511–12, 532
  emptiness meditation in, 73
  on fire maṇḍala, 380
  on four continents, people of, 454–55
  on four modes of birth, 429, 438
  on four seals, 637, 638
  on grounds of purification, 81
  on human womb birth, 446
  macrocosmic correspondences in, 86, 88–90, 365
  on nature of space, 61–62
  on nirmāṇakāya transformation, 146
  on people of first eon, 439
  principal deities in, 94, 115
  on specially visualized deities, 436
  on stages of birth, correspondences with, 449
  on Supreme King of Maṇḍalas, 225, 227–30
  Tsongkhapa's commentary on, 82, 83, 87
  on twenty-five coarse elements, 126
  on two purposes, 221
  on vajra overpowering all tathāgatas samādhi, 537
  Vajradhara in, 141–42, 441–42
  on womb birth, 214
  on yoga and subsequent yoga, 510, 513
four activities, 693, 717, 721–22
Four Chapters Tantra, 240, 340, 469, 672, 683, 694
four continents, 453–55, 469
four disks, 100–102, 384
  and crossed vajra, merging, 102–3, 206, 374, 376–80
  seed syllables of, 692n3519
four elements, 367
  in birth state, 508–9
  dissolution of, 122, 486–93, 505
  four mothers and, 101, 209, 225, 376, 379, 384, 553, 560–61, 574
  subtle, 562
four empty states, 194, 195, 279, 457, 487, 506, 521, 538
four extremes of intrinsic existence, 357
four joys, 195, 202, 457, 610–11
four modes of birth, 147–49, 438–39, 444–49
four mothers, 114, 160
  dissolution, 562
  mantras for, 563–64
  nature of, variant views, 101–2, 163n719
  placement, 432, 553, 555, 560–61, 574
  seats of, 109, 110–11
  seed syllables of, 576–77, 673n3405
  in Supreme King of Maṇḍalas, 224, 225
  See also under four elements
four noble truths, 21, 346–47
four proper abandonments, 398
four seals, 227–28, 228n1039, 634, 637–39

four stages/limbs of familiarization and achievement, 57, 279–81, 283, 700–704
four tantra classes, 258
deity yoga in, 13
differences between, 352–53
emptiness in, 358
three lower, gender in, 457–58
four types of specific-perfect discernment, 422
four ways of interpretation (Candrakīrti), 73–74, 75, 155n684, 205, 209–10
four yogas, 139, 214, 281
in Ārya tradition, 546, 705
in daily activities, 235–36
variant views, 55–56, 57, 118–19, 217–18, 513–14, 704–5
fruit
causes that accord with, 23–24
existing in cause, 548
taken as path, 4, 12, 29–30, 78, 625

G

Gaṇḍavyūha Sūtra, 232
Ganden monastery, 181
Gandhavajrā, 253, 432n2155, 490
Gelek Palsangpo, 723. *See also* Khedrup Jé Gelek Palsangpo
Geluk school, 218
after Tsongkhapa, 173
on body as celestial mansion, 166–69
on consorts, 201
creation stage emptiness meditation in, 72, 78
on deities as psycho-physical constituents, 171, 172–73
on inner offerings, 240–41
on natural abode, 157n698
rebirth purification in, 159
and Sakya, disputes between, 173, 177–84, 246–47, 248
tantra formation in, 44
tathāgatagarbha in, 137
triple sattvas in, 191n836
gender
development of, 441
enlightenment and, 456–58
in first eon, 440n2166
in scripture, male point of view, 194–97
in womb birth, 528, 531–32
Gendun Gyatso, Second Dalai Lama, 166
Gö Khukpa Lhetsé, 45, 46, 142, 152
on fetal development, 143
on First Lord, 513n2530
on grounds of purification, 81–82, 87–88, 89, 216
on principal deities, 94
Quintessential Elucidation of the Guhyasamāja Practice, 45
on specially visualized deities, 117–18
on three syllables, 525
Tsongkhapa's critique of, 242
on two stages, 126
goddesses
four, 106, 107, 222–23, 250, 669–70, 695
knowledge, 479
sixteen offering, 107, 411
gods of desire realm, 438, 450–51, 452–53, 502
Gómez, Luis, 25
Gorampa Sönam Sengé, 62–66, 69, 71, 72
great bliss, 31, 98–99, 202, 450–52
great compassion, 10, 115, 211, 225, 242, 257, 295, 670
Great Treatise on the Stages of the Mantric Path (Tsongkhapa), 180, 244, 706, 714
on body and constructed maṇḍalas, relationship of, 174
on causes that accord with result, 23–24
on consciousness, 150
on deity visualization, subjective and objective aspects, 13–14
on emptiness meditation, six purposes, 127–28
on maṇḍala visualization, 26, 27
on meditation, two methods of, 20
on mind, profundity and manifestation in, 22–23
on ordinary appearances, 34–35
on samādhisattva, 190
on subtle drop yoga, 230
great yoga tantras, 266, 512

ground of resources, 453, 454
grounds of purification, 86, 92, 94, 443, 467–68, 538–39
aim of purifying, 472
for blessings of three doors, 189
body maṇḍala deities and, 160, 580–81
conception as, 212
and correspondences, purposes of, 459–60, 464, 471
first beings/eon as, 89–90, 461
later steps of sādhana and, 473–75
physical world as, 381
purifiers and, 81–82, 83, 85, 87–88, 708
specially visualized deities and, 114, 118
stages of birth at, 444–49
triple sattvas and, 190–91
in two stages, 126, 464–66
Guhyasamāja maṇḍala, 245, 422–23
deities, number of, 229–30, 644–51
deities' faces in, 141, 228, 526, 639–43
deities' mantras in, 233
depictions of, 103–11
divine identity in, 30–31
familiarization with, 722
final dissolution of, 252–53, 685–87
See also thirty-two maṇḍala deities
Guhyasamāja Practice in the Ārya Nāgārjuna System (Engle), xiv
Guhyasamāja Sādhana (Tsongkhapa), 47, 56, 159, 173, 359n1673
on Akṣobhya, 157
on bliss, 155
on body maṇḍala transformation, 162–63, 168
on celestial mansion, 164, 165
on concluding rituals, 249, 250
on consorts, 200–201
on deities, withdrawing into body, 117
on deities as body parts, 170, 171–72, 173
on emanated initiation, 210
on emotions, 220
on father-mother union, 540–41, 543
on female practitioners, 193
on First Lord and Akṣobhya, relationship of, 152
forty-nine essential points in, 706–7
on four disks, 101
on gathering deities into body, 481n2347
heart mantras in, 234
on inner offerings, 240
on jñānasattva, 188, 189
preliminaries in, 238, 241, 242, 244
on principal deities, dissolution, 249
on protection wheel, 245
on samayasattva, 190
on source of phenomena, 98–99
on specially visualized deities, 113–15, 119, 477
on torma offerings, 699
on triple sattvas, 191
two types of steps in, 204
on vajra enclosures, 97–98
Guhyasamāja sādhanas, 187, 210
abridged, 708
differences between, 217
frameworks for, 56–57, 700–707
ground of wisdom in, 365–66
number and length of sessions, 223, 707–8
special qualities of, 462
transformation in, variant views, 118–19
triple sattvas in, 189–90
Guhyasamāja Tantra, 31, 116, 204, 230, 313–14, 318, 524–25, 583–84, 721
"absence of being" verse (*abhāve bhāvanābhāvo*), 60–61, 73, 338, 355–58, 365, 470
on attainments, 719
authority of, 246
on *bhrūṃ*, 380–81, 436
on bodily constituents, 38–39, 101, 122, 137
on body blessings, 187, 585, 586
on body enhancement, 689
on body maṇḍala, 159–60, 557–58, 559
on conception, 154–55
on consort yoga, 609, 616, 720
on consorts, 606–8
deities in, number of, 229–30, 644–46
deities in, three faces of, 640–43
on dissolution, 685

on divine identity, 593–94
emanation of first maṇḍala in, 206–7
on emblems, 632
emptiness mantra in, 29, 359
on fierce deities, 321, 322
five tathāgata mantras in, 31
on food yoga, 695
on four limbs of familiarization and achievement, 57, 279–81, 700, 701, 702–3
hermeneutics of, 3, 203–4, 205
on initiation, 635–36
on maṇḍala measurements, 384
mantras in, 234, 328–29, 586–87, 667–68
on meats and nectars, 676–77
meditative absorptions in, two types, 601
on mind blessing, 187, 590, 591, 592
name of, 258–59
omissions in, reasons for, 282–83, 650–51
opening line, 99, 205
oral explanation needed for, 272
postmeditative practices in, 718
on practice places, 282
praise of, 259–61
praises in, 250, 251
principal deities in, 437
samādhi: enjoying all desires, 199
samādhi: method of great passion, 198, 199, 451, 474, 604–5
samādhi: vajra lamp of wisdom, 218–19, 225, 315, 316
samādhi: vajra origination from samaya of vajra body, speech, and mind, 213, 512, 545–46
samādhi: vajra overpowering all tathāgatas, 209, 477, 511, 536, 537–41
samādhi: vajra pacifying impediments to sentient beings, 333
on sealing, 602, 637–38
on semen issued from union, 483, 484–85
on sensual pleasures, 456–57
on space vajra, 369, 370, 376
on specially visualized deities, 207–9, 433–35, 478, 482
on speech blessing, 187, 588–89
on subtle yoga, 232, 655
superiority of, 228–29, 644
on tathāgatas, slaying, 483, 485–86
translations of, xiv
on triple sattvas, 319–20, 598–99
on vajra recitation, 662
on vajra stakes, 325, 327
on voiced recitation, 664
women in, 629
Guhyasamāja Tantra tradition, 42, 49–51
guru yoga, 237, 238
gurus. *See* lamas
Gyümé Khensur Lobsang Jampa, xiv
Gyümé Monastery, xiii, 108

H

hatred, 137, 454, 550
abode of, 321, 322
purifying, 151n667, 153, 225, 633–34
tathāgata family of, 219, 316, 323
Hatred Vajra. *See* Dveṣavajra
Hayagrīva, 302, 321n1479, 423n2075, 433, 490, 575
Hearers, 198, 605
Heaven of Clear Light, 438
hells, 267, 269, 339, 438, 502
Heretical Materialistic School, 340
Hevajra cycle, 381, 544, 668
body maṇḍala in, 3, 184, 186
borrowings from, 160
Lamdré in, 187
offerings in, 239, 241
Hevajra Tantra, 183, 187, 640
on bodily constituents, 39
on deproliferation, 5, 9, 37, 276, 350
on passion, 197
on sense offerings, 293
on two stages, 274–75
homologous example, 649, 650, 716
Hugon, Pascale, 47, 227
human body, 449–50, 502–3
hungry ghosts, 438, 452, 502
Hwashang, 275

I

Illuminating Lamp (Candrakīrti), xiv, 46, 137, 232, 280, 284, 472–74, 486, 519, 664
on "absence of being" verse, 73–74, 355–58
on afflictive emotions, 633
on aggregates and buddhas, 39
on all-vajra maṇḍala, 376–77, 378, 379
on bliss during conception, 155
on body maṇḍala, 556, 557–59
on concentration, 333
on conceptual yoga, 661
on consort yoga, 617
on consorts, 607, 608, 609–10
on creation stage, fruit of, 275–76
on deities, number of, 230, 646, 647, 650
on disciples, five types, 456
on emanating first maṇḍala, 206, 207, 317–18, 321–22
on emblems, 140–41
on emptiness meditation, 341–42
on external objects, 76–77, 133, 519
on eye medicine, siddhis of, 717
on First Lord, 514, 525
on five manifest awakenings, 436
on five meats and five nectars, 679, 682
on food yoga, 695
on four limbs of familiarization and achievement, 700–701, 702
on four mothers, 101
on four sessions, 707
on four yogas, completion of, 217
on *Guhyasamāja Tantra*, 260
on heart of meditator, stirring, 686
on hearts of deities, arousing, 720
hermeneutics in, 155n684, 156n688, 205, 209–10, 211–12, 214, 220
on initiation, 316
on intermediate state, 483
on jñānasattva, subtle, 599
Later Tantra and, 311
on Lord of Secrets, 592
on Māmaki, 629, 636–37
on maṇḍalas, 384
on mantra, blessing of, 546
mantras in, 328–29
on meats and nectars, 239
on name mantras, 630–31
on *oṃ dharma dhātu svabhāva* mantra, 522–23
on overpowering all tathāgatas samādhi, levels of interpreting, 538–41
on passion in tantra, 197–98, 452
postmeditative practices in, 718
on samādhisattva, 600, 601
on sealing, 602, 638, 639
on seed syllables, 143–44
on siddhis, 721
on single-mindedness, 660
on solar disk, 584, 591
on source of phenomena, 370–71
on space element, 369, 521
on specially visualized deities, 434–35, 477, 478, 481–82
on subtle yoga, 654, 655, 656–58
on Supreme King of Deeds, 703
on Supreme King of Maṇḍalas, 219, 225, 226, 625–26
on tathāgata families, 596–97
on vajra recitation, 662, 663
on Vajra Stake, 327
on Vajradhara as three vajras, 593–94
on *vajrarati*, 302
on womb birth, 485
on women, enlightenment of, 193–94, 456–57
on yogic training, 201
illusory body, 23–24, 84, 138–39, 143, 515, 520, 521, 643
actual and concordant, 669
awakening and, 145–46
body maṇḍala and, 168
and creation stage yoga of illusion-like, distinctions between, 351–52
dissolution of, 213
emphasis on, 228–29
entry into clear light, 484
as mere wind-and-mind, 134
of path, 514
ripening for, 520, 523
immediately preceding conditions, 34, 711

indestructible drop, 102, 216n971, 379, 496, 506–7, 600n3000
Indrabhūti, *Jñānasiddhi Sādhana*, 9–10, 11, 229
Indrabodhi, 229
Indrabodhi, younger, 645
initiations, 316, 477, 550
  conferred through samādhi, 479
  four, order of conferring, 268–69
  need for, 266–67, 427–28
  in Supreme King of Maṇḍalas, 226
  vajra master, 269
  vase, 267, 268, 272–74
inner heat
  in food yoga, 690–93
  ordinary, 528
inner mansion, 417–19
  exterior, 108–9
  gates, variant views, 420–21
  interior, 110
  roof, 422–23, 425–26
inner offerings, 252
  blessing, 103, 238–41, 290–91
  tasting, 671–72, 681, 683, 684, 694
  See also five meats and five nectars
Intense Illuminating Lamp (Bhavyakīrti), 322, 325, 477, 526, 536, 576–77, 668
intermediate beings, 83–84, 94, 146, 215, 438–39, 448–49
  birth in Jambudvīpa, 443, 444, 466
  of bodhisattvas that will awaken, 503–4
  correspondences with, 143, 152, 153–54, 461, 517–18
  erroneous views of, 151–53, 154, 158–59, 447, 471, 509–10, 515–17
  evolution of, 130
  formation of, 508
  as mere wind-and-mind, 132–33, 134–35, 138, 517, 519
  role in human conception, 504, 527
  size and characteristics, 500–503
  womb entry of, variant views, 529–31, 536
intermediate state
  awakening in, 145–46, 483, 486
  correspondences with, 463, 464
  and death, simultaneity of, 508, 510
  death in, 502, 503
  as ground of purification, 82, 83, 84, 85, 86, 92–93, 118, 462, 473
  name, meaning of, 500
  taking as path to saṃbhogakāya, 129–41 (*see also* First Lord)
  two stages and, 32
interpretable meaning, 205, 214
interpretation, four levels of. *See* four ways of interpretation (Candrakīrti)
intoxicants, 236, 696–97
Iron Mountains, 332, 468–69

J

Jackson, David, 177, 183
Jalandharipa, 707
Jambudvīpa, 92, 147
  first beings in, 89–90
  intermediate beings rebirth in, 443, 444, 466
  karma in, 453–55
  miraculous birth in, 445
  saṃsāric rebirth in, 449–50, 458
  womb birth in, 448
Jamyang Khyentsé Wangpo, 148
Jamyang Zhepé Dorjé, 167, 172
*Jayabhadra, 392, 397
Jayasena, *Sādhana of Ḍākārṇava*, 674
Jewel Rosary (Ratnākaraśānti), 322, 482, 524, 526, 536, 564, 577, 615, 667
Jikmé Lingpa, 148
Jitāri, 185, 186
Jñānapāda, 7, 13, 23, 24, 645. See also *Oral Instruction of Mañjuśrī*; *Samantabhadra Sādhana*
Jñānapāda school, 14–19, 577, 597n2984
  deities in, number of, 229
  on four levels of creation stage mastery, 713–14
  four stages of familiarization in, 57, 704
  preliminaries in, 237
  on protection wheel, 309
  on sensory spheres, 301
  sevenfold worship in, 242
  song invocation in, 668
jñānasattva, 12, 214, 319
  color and appearance of, 596–98

correspondences of, 191, 546
deities merging with, 226
dissolution of, 669
entering samayasattva, 159, 188–89, 478, 529
invoking, variant views, 192–93, 598–99, 635
meaning of term, 190, 599
sequential entry by, 636
in subtle drop yoga, 657

K

Kagyü school, 78, 135
*Kambala, 331–32, 666, 673, 675, 683–84. See also *Crown Jewel Sādhana*
karma, 547–48
accumulation of, 469, 471
avoiding, 90–91
conception and, 528
ground of, 453
purifying, 493–94
shared, 87, 442
wind of, 530, 534, 535
Karmarāṭ, 432
Karuṇaśrī, 602, 702
Khagarbha, 301, 432, 487, 490, 575, 578
Khedrup Jé Gelek Palsangpo, xiv
on Akṣobhya, 154, 157, 158–59
on awakening in intermediate state, 145–46
on awakening in present body, 136
on body and constructed maṇḍalas, relationship of, 174, 175–77
on body maṇḍala, 161, 163
and Butön, misrepresenting, 185–87
on consorts, 200
on creation stage as ripener, 202
critiques by, 71, 72
on deities, number of, 229–30
on deities as body parts, 170–71, 172
on emptiness mantra, 67, 71
on emptiness meditation, 73, 78–79, 127
on four disks, 101, 102–3
on fruit, attaining, 162
on inner offerings, 239, 240
and Kunga Sangpo, relationship of, 46
on lotus ring, 100
on modes of birth, 148–49
on moon orb, 133
Playful Fest for the Yogis, 238
on preliminaries, 244–45
on principal deities, dissolution, 249
on purification, intermediate state and rebirth, 142, 143, 145
on sādhana correspondences, 87–88, 90
and Sakya scholars, disputes with, 177–84
on source of phenomena, 99
on specially visualized deities, 113, 117, 124–25
on stage of union, 228
on stage replacing rebirth, 215
on tormas, preliminary, 241
on triple sattvas, 190–91, 192–93
Tsongkhapa, admiration for, 179, 263
on *Vajrasattva Sādhana*, 54
on women, enlightenment of, 193
See also *Ocean of Attainments*
Khön family, 177
Kongtrul Yönten Gyatso, 26, 70–71, 174
Konting Gushri, 187
kriyā tantra, 310, 352–53
Kṛṣṇa, 186
Saṃvaravyākhyā, 184
Vajrasattva Offering Ritual, 576–77
Kṛṣṇācārya, 261, 332, 567n2822
*Kṛṣṇasamayavajra, 151, 152, 326, 470, 477, 536, 577, 616, 620n3120, 631
kṛtsna meditation, 20–21, 33, 37, 715
Kṣitigarbha
basis for, 175–76
dissolution, 122, 123, 124, 125, 488, 494, 495
as eye organ, 170, 171, 301
number of, 578, 579
placement, 432, 557, 564
seed syllable, 568, 574, 630
Künga Nyingpo, 68, 69, 71, 72, 128, 343n1602

L

lamas
in field of merit, 296–97, 298

genuine, recognizing, 272–73
in tantric practice, need for, 49–55
Lamdré tradition, 183, 187
Later Tantra of the Guhyasamāja, 103, 238, 247, 283
authority of, 245, 246
commentary, 247, 280, 303
on five meats and five nectars, 239–40, 677–79, 680–81, 682
on four limbs of familiarization and achievement, 57, 700
and *Guhyasamāja Tantra*, relationship of, 369–70
on *Guhyasamāja Tantra*, 259
on maṇḍalas, three kinds, 564–65
postmeditative practices in, 718
prostration verses in, 300
on protection wheel, 311, 312
on siddhis, 719
on triple sattvas, 319
laxity, 359, 653–54, 710
light garland, 110, 418, 419
Līlavajra, *Commentary on the Vajrasattva Sādhana*, 53, 283, 311, 435, 578
limbs of body, 160
in dissolution, 123, 488, 490
as fierce deities, 117, 209, 479, 554–55, 576, 614–15
number of deities on, 176–77, 578–80
lingual discernment, 588–89
Locanā, 101
blessings of, 188, 585–86
in consort yoga, 614
dissolution, 122, 123, 488
as earth, 301, 379, 480
emblem, 632
inviting, 584–85
mantra, 563
placement, 553
Lodrö Chökyong, 723
Lokeśvara, 301, 432, 487, 491, 575
Longchen Rapjampa, 41
Losang Chökyi Gyaltsen (Panchen Rinpoché), xiii, 238
on blessing of three doors, 188
Essence of the Ocean of Attainments, 218
on protection wheel, 246
on sealing, 193
lotus, 373–74
colors of, 631–32
correspondences with, 518, 520, 522
description of, 386
disputes on, 515, 516–17
ring of, 100, 104, 375
seed syllables and, 130n557
variegated, 99–100, 111
love, arts of, 201–2, 608n162, 609, 611
Lozang Rapjor, xiii
lunar disk
correspondences with, 518, 520, 522
disputes on, 135n576, 515, 516–17, 521
seed syllables and, 130n557
Lūyīpāda, 78, 161–62, 361, 448, 570, 579. See also *Cakrasaṃvara Sādhana*

M

macrocosmic events (world cycles), 55
celestial mansion and, 86–88, 90–91, 92–93, 381, 443, 519
correspondences with, purpose of, 460–61
correspondences with, variant views, 86–88
emptiness meditation and, 59–60, 72–73, 206
four disks and, 100–101, 380
ground of wisdom and, 365–66
Madhyamaka school, 7
in creation stage emptiness meditation, 59, 65–67, 72, 338–42
emptiness in, 61, 69
in Guhyasamāja systems, 75–76, 133–36
outer offerings and, 252
in Tibet, 72, 75
See also Prāsaṅgika Madhyamaka; Yogācāra-Madhyamaka
Mahābala, 302, 303, 321n1479, 433, 491, 575
Mahāyāna tradition, 115, 198–99, 258, 265, 605
Mahāyānasūtrālaṃkāra, 15
Maitreya, 122, 301, 370, 432, 488, 554, 575, 576, 630

Māmakī, 101
blessings of, 188, 590, 591, 592
in consort yoga, 614
dissolution, 489
emblem, 631
issuing forth, 629
placement, 553
seat of, 111, 428
tathāgata family of, 636–37
as water, 301, 379, 480
Mamos, 579
Maṇḍala Vajra Garland (Abhayākaragupta)
on beams, 407, 408
on crossed vajras, 388, 389, 390–91, 392
on emblems and seats, 421
on grounds and ceilings, 427
on inner mansion, 417, 418
on inner offerings, 672, 673
on maṇḍala size, 383
on platform/offering ledge, 396–97, 411
on portals, 394, 401–3
on source of phenomena, 373, 374
on torma offering, 236, 696, 697, 698
on vajra fence, 331
on vases, 429
on victory banners, 415, 416
on walls, 406
maṇḍalas, 21, 24
of all-vajra, 376–77, 378, 379
constructed, 566
emptiness of, 79–80
four elemental (*see* four disks)
four modes of entering, 478–79
as illusion-like, 25–26, 711
importance of understanding, 428
measuring cord, 374–75
mind endowed with aspect of, 19–20
outer and body, relationship of, 165, 166–69, 173–77
pure, arising of, 63, 64
purposes of meditating on, 5, 26, 35, 36
special appearances of, 24–25, 27, 30, 33, 34–35, 61, 460
square, 409–10
three kinds, 564–65
visualization of, variant views, 22–23
wisdom, 298, 316
See also body maṇḍala; Guhyasamāja maṇḍala
*Mañjuśrīkīrti, *Heart Ornament*, 293
Mañjuśrī/Mañjughoṣa, 301, 432, 490, 493, 575, 597
Mañjuvajra Guhyasamāja, 387, 417, 597
mantra body, 214n959, 447, 521, 659, 677, 678, 679, 682–83, 702
Mantra Vehicle, 258
dissolution in, 65
efficacy of, 23–24
emptiness meditation in, 360–61
entering, 266–67, 268, 427–28
as fruit vehicle, 30, 363–64
guru in, importance of, 49–55
on intermediate being, 130
as Mahāyāna, 59
merit, accumulating in, 350
offerings, attitude toward, 296
and Pāramitā Vehicle, distinctions between, 201, 350
passion in, 197–99, 450–51
sense desires in, 292–93
superiority of, 13, 14, 18, 191
two obscurations in, 163
unique feature of, 26
on wind and mind, 132
mantras, 70, 722
"absence of being" verse as, 60–61
of all tathāgatas, 213, 214, 315, 545, 586–87
concluding, 253
for divine identity of offerings, 619–21
for divine identity of passion, 618, 619–20
garland, 234, 665, 666–67, 668, 720–21, 722
heart and essence, 664, 665, 667–68
for heart of deities, arousing, 222
oṃ dharma dhātu svabhāva, 522–23
oṃ Sumbha Nisumbha, meaning of, 324–25
of sense offerings, 299, 300
svabhāva, 11, 312, 361n1682
for torma offerings, 697–98
types of, 329

See also name mantras; recitation; *śūnyatā* (emptiness) mantra
Marpa, *Elucidating the Epitome of the Five Stages*, 281
Matsunaga, Yukei, 49, 51
Māyājāla, 644
meditation on the loathsome, 21, 37, 715
meditative absorptions, 11, 20, 346, 347, 601
meditative equipoise, 79, 305, 363, 366, 713
mental consciousness, 33, 37, 88, 150, 162–64, 489, 573, 710, 711, 715
mental quiescence, 20–21, 33, 231, 655–56, 715
mere wind-and-mind, 132–34, 135, 136–39, 702
merit, 249, 350. *See also* field of accumulating merit
Meru, Mount, 87, 717
  churning ocean with, 240, 252, 683
  erroneous views on, 469
  putting in mustard seed, 232
microcosmic context, 55, 59–60, 80, 93–95, 127–29
Middle Way. *See* Madhyamaka school
mind
  and body, relationship between, 138
  in body maṇḍala, 162–64
  creative power of, 4, 6, 7
  endowed with maṇḍala, aspect of, 345–46, 347
  nonconceptual and valid, 22
  profound and sublime natures of, 15–19, 20, 21–22, 24, 33
  restricted power of, 88
  subjective and objective aspects of, 13–14
  as "wind-and-mind," 134–35
mind bound for enlightenment, 59, 266, 270, 354, 355
  familiarization limb as, 701
  five mothers as, 302
  genuine experience of, 265
  prior aspirations for, 363–64
  in torma offerings, 697
  verse for generating, 305–6
Mind Only, 7
  in hidden interpretation, 76
  as mere wind-and-mind, 132–34
  moon meditation in, 131, 519
  in *Vajrasattva Sādhana*, 54
mindfulness, 35, 125, 411, 437, 495, 607, 709, 710
mind-isolation, 85n369, 139, 142, 279, 515
miraculous powers, 398, 400, 500–501
mirror-like wisdom, 122, 123, 486, 488
modes of being, 163, 520–21, 522, 580
Moharati, 432, 561, 563
Monastic Guidelines. See *Vinayavibhaṅga*
moon orb, 520, 522
  as bodhicitta, 131–33, 521, 572n2851
  disputes on, 130–33, 135n576, 519
  as manifest awakening, 140, 518
mother tantras, 39, 183–84, 258, 261, 537
  adapting, 238, 239, 240
  body maṇḍala in, 187
  clear light in, 228
  great bliss in, 643
mundane path, 28, 710
Muniśrībhadra, 7, 11, 283–84, 317
  on First Lord, 141, 526
  on five meats and five nectars, 678, 680, 681, 682
  on moon orb, 131
  on Vajradhara visualization, 314
  on *Vajrasattva Sādhana*, 53

N

Nāgabodhi, 285, 423. See also *Twenty Maṇḍala Rituals*
Nāgabuddhi
  on body maṇḍala, 551
  on deities and body parts, relationship of, 576n2872
  on ground of wisdom correspondence, 470
  on mother and father, 512n2525
  Revelation of the Intention, 496
  See also *Formulating the Sādhana*
Nāgārjuna, 7, 42, 51–53, 77
  Concise Sādhana, 45
  on external objects, 133

Five Stages, 7, 83, 134, 271–72, 276, 353–54, 467
homage, 257
on illusory appearances, 25
Root of Wisdom, 356
See also *Concise Sādhana*; *Sādhana Incorporating the Scripture*
Nairātmyā tradition, 708
name mantras, 233–34, 563–64, 577
for sending forth, 633–34
in Supreme King of Deeds, 667–68
in Supreme King of Maṇḍalas, 627, 630–31
in torma offerings, 698
Nāropa, 280, 281n1272, 303, 319, 674, 678, 680, 706
natural abode, 157n698, 159, 298, 320, 540
negation, 28, 62, 63, 66–67, 72–73
Ngaripa Sanggyé Puntsok, 178, 185
Ngok tradition, 45, 46, 229–30
Ngorchen Kunga Sangpo, 3, 41, 44–45, 165, 210
Abolishing Wrong Statements, 184
on Akṣobhya, 152–53, 154, 157
on body maṇḍala, 117, 174, 177–86, 570–71
on constructed and body maṇḍalas, relationship of, 174
Dispelling Wrong Views, 184, 186
on emptiness meditation, 69–70
on First Lord, 141
on five manifest awakenings, 140
on four disks, 102, 379n1774, 380n1776
Khedrup Jé and, 46, 177–84, 185–86
on Nāgārjuna's Guhyasamāja works, 52–53
on protection wheel, 98, 247, 248, 332n1570, 367n1703
on source of phenomena, 373n1736
on specially visualized deities, 119
on *tathāgatagarbha*, 181
on *Vajrasattva Sādhana*, 53
nihilism, 63, 64, 67, 72–73, 339, 361
Nīladaṇḍa, 302, 321n1479, 433, 490, 575
nirmāṇakāya
First Lord's transformation, 537–41, 543–44, 546
humans as, 466
of path, 461–62
placing deities on body and, 82
saṃbhogakāya's transformation to, 142, 152, 158
transformation, occurrence in sādhana, 217–18
See also under Vajrasattva
nirvāṇa, 243, 487, 492–93, 591, 668
Buddha's deed of displaying, 222–23, 249, 475
in intermediate state, 145–46
with and without remainder, 137
No-Higher Heaven. *See* Akaniṣṭha
nonconceptual meditation, 21, 37–38, 715
nonconceptuality, sublime and profound causes, 15n59
nondual tantras, 261–62
nonmeditation, 275
"nonobservation of the suitable to appear," 144–45, 516, 550n2729
Norsang Gyatso, 28, 171, 188, 218
nose-tips, 572, 573, 654
nyāsa ("emplacement"), 161, 169

O

Ocean of Attainments (Khedrup Jé), 14
colophon, 722–23
dating, 3
homage, 257–58
polemics of, 41, 43–47
purpose of composing, 47–48, 263
sādhana structure in, 56–57
topics, 263
offering ledge, 396–97, 410–11, 414
offerings
in concluding rituals, 251
of four flowers, 378–79
maṇḍal, 238, 241
outer, 241, 251–52
preliminary, 291–93
secret, 212, 252, 685
in sevenfold worship, 299–300
suchness, 252

visualization in, 4
See also inner offerings; torma offerings
Old School of the Mantra Vehicle, 313
Oral Instruction of Mañjuśrī (Jñānapāda), 84–85, 260
ordinary appearance, 12, 362
antidote to, 26, 27, 708, 709–10
in emptiness meditation, 79
external objects and, 33–34
freedom from, 252–53, 292, 296
prior to visualizations, 310
purifying, 88, 246, 248, 278–79
Ratnākaraśānti's view of, 19–20
in session breaks, 253
as space-like, 338
variant views, 33–38, 62–66, 73
visualization and, 4–5, 60
ordinary attitudes, 339
antidote to, 26, 27, 33, 36, 708, 709–10
freedom from, 252–53, 292, 296
prior to visualizations, 310
purifying, 32, 246, 248, 251, 278–79
ordinary identity, 26, 27, 296, 710–11
Ornament of Vajra Essence Tantra, 577

P

Padmasambhava, *Five Pledges*, 270
Padmavajra, *Secret Attainment*, 260, 372–73, 645, 646
Pakpa Lodrö Gyaltsen, 107, 184, 186
Palkhor Dechen monastery, 3, 723
Pāṇḍaravāsinī (Pāṇḍārā), 101, 188, 301, 379, 480, 490, 553, 587–88, 614
Pang Lotsāwa, 401
Pāramitā Vehicle, 13, 14, 18, 258, 548
dissolution in, 65
emptiness meditation in, 60, 70, 127, 352, 359, 360
gender in, 456, 457–58
methods of, 23–24
mind for awakening in, 354
offerings in, 296
on root of phenomena, 132
passion
divine identity of, 618
erroneous views on, 668
during the fruit, 625
on path, 538, 611
practice of, 474–75, 604, 605
in tantra, role of, 197–99, 450–51
past events, 116, 188, 217, 629
in consort yoga, 604, 605
emanation of first maṇḍala, 206, 210
initiation and, 226
linkage of, 205, 220
and practices that follow them, 204, 212
samādhis as, 198, 199, 203, 316
as scriptural authority, 206
specially visualized deities and, 207–8, 479, 481, 482
Pecchia, Christina, 16
Perfect Awakening of Vairocana Tantra, 640
Phalavajra, 348, 349, 358, 657, 663
places of practice, two levels of meaning, 282
pliancy, mental and physical, 655
polemical literature, 41–43, 44, 47, 130n556, 218, 227
portals
columns supporting, 397–98
drawn, 392–93
height of, 375
layers of, 400–401
top of, 401–3
variant views, 395–97
visualized, 394–95
width, 399–400
postmeditative practices, 79, 363, 718–20
postures, 291, 429
Prajñākaragupta, 54
Prajñāntaka, 301, 321n1479, 489
prāṇa, use of term, 138n587
Prāsaṅgika Madhyamaka, 11–12, 54, 76, 77, 131
preceding state, 501
preliminaries, 704, 705
averting unfavorable conditions, 245–48
establishing favorable condition, 241–45
preparatory steps, 237–41, 289–93
three parts, 237
principal deities, 436–37
colors, changing, 82

crossed vajra and, 103–4
dissolution of, 249
divergences in, 55–56, 93–94, 114–15
as dynamic figures, 30
mantra recitation amount, 666
placement, 421
in protection wheel, 313–16
seats of, 428–29
stabilizing appearance of, 709–10
stabilizing identity as, 712
as triple sattvas, 319–20
Tsongkhapa on, 114, 208
prostrations, 300–303
protection, two types, 367
protection wheel, 97, 98, 309–10
height and width of, 331–32
principal consorts in, 317–18
principal deities in, 313–16, 319, 320
purpose of, 245, 332–34, 367, 473
shape of, 312–13
stakes, 323–29
surrounding deities, 320–23
variant views, 246–48, 310–12, 468–71
visualizing, 367–68
protective enclosures, 97–98, 111, 248. *See also* vajra enclosure meditation
Puṇḍarīka, *Stainless Light*, 9–10, 11
pure appearance, 26, 35–36, 709, 711
purification
retroactive, 91
three methods of, 467, 690n3509

R

Rangjung Dorjé, Third Karmapa, 148, 174, 210, 325n1509, 367n1703
Rasavajrā, 253, 432n2155, 491, 632
*Ratnadhvaja, 678
Ratnākaraśānti, 7, 34, 147, 348, 657, 678
Commentary on the Maṇḍala Ritual of the Guhyasamāja, 345, 407, 408
on creation stage visualization, 19–20, 21, 25
on four disks, 102
Hevajra Sādhana, 234, 363
Lotus Commentary on the Saṃvarodaya Tantra, 10, 147, 445
Pearl Rosary, 271, 712–13
on portals and columns, 398
Precious Lamp Commentary on Difficult Points in the Black Yamāri Tantra, 673–74, 712
on principal deity, 115
Sādhana of Black Yamāri, 365
on self-grasping, antidote to, 346–47
on source of phenomena, 370
on triple sattvas, 192
on walls, 405
See also *Jewel Rosary*
Ratnaketu, 208, 481, 619n3118, 636
Ratnasaṃbhava, 699
color, 104
in consort yoga, 618, 619
dissolution, 489
divine identity, 31, 188
initiation of, 550
maṇḍala size, 383n1789
placement, 432, 558, 559, 574
sealing with, 637
Ray, Reginald, 49
reasoning
in body maṇḍala, understanding, 168–69
in creation stage emptiness meditation, 70–72, 338–39, 356–57
in deity yoga, 12
on singularity and plurality, 358
in systemizing Tibetan tantra, 42, 43
tetralemma, 74
threefold criteria, 647–49
See also four ways of interpretation (Candrakīrti)
rebirth, 189
in Ārya tradition, 505–9
beginning of, 142n616, 149
body maṇḍala and, 162
correspondences with, 513–15
ending, 146
as ground of purification, 82, 83, 85, 86, 92–93, 94, 118, 150–57
taking on path to nirmāṇakāya, 146–59
transforming, 214, 215
recitation
correspondences, 668
number of, 666–67
vajra, 233, 496, 497, 662–63, 721

voiced, fourfold, 234–35, 664–66
Red Yamāri, 396, 597
Red Yamāri Tantra, 261, 672
reductio ad absurdum, 63–64
refuge, 304–5
relative truth. *See* conventional truth
Rendawa Shönu Lodrö, 45, 94–95, 142, 178
on Akṣobhya, 157–58
on fetal development, 143
on grounds of purification, 82, 87, 89
Khedrup Jé's critiques of, 182, 191, 192, 310
on protection wheel, 247, 248
Replies to Druppa Pal, 144, 156, 159
on specially visualized deities, 117–18
Tsongkhapa and, 45–46
on two stages, purification in, 126
on *Vajrasattva Sādhana*, 53, 54
Request of the Four Goddesses, 627–28, 683, 692, 717
Request of the Four Mothers, 512
Revelation of the Intention Tantra, 282, 318, 378, 379, 496, 522–23, 526, 619–20, 640–43
Rinchen Sangpo, 87, 362, 630
Rising of Heruka, 612
Riwo Gendenpa, 65
Rngog Āryadeva, 645n3245
Rongtön Sheja Kunrik, 95, 117–18, 126, 148, 178, 189
rūpakāya
accordant cause for, 138–39
arising of, 27, 28–29, 135, 142, 364
in creation stage, 5, 6, 275, 669
maṇḍala meditation and, 29–30
sublime mind and, 23
taking as path, 360
Rūpavajrā, 122, 123, 124, 432, 488, 495, 671

S

Śabdhavajrā, 432n2155, 489
Sādhana Incorporating the Scripture (Nāgārjuna), 51–52, 54, 101, 207, 284, 295, 376, 483, 536
on beginning practitioners, 709
on *bhrūṃ*, 381, 569
on body maṇḍala, 557
on consort yoga, 619, 621, 720
on consorts, 606–7, 613
on correspondences, 474
on crossed vajra, 377, 378
on deities, inviting, 583–84
on dissolution, 685
on fierce deities, 321, 322
on First Lord, 513–14, 525
on food yoga, 695
four seals in, 637–38
four yogas in, 57, 221
on intermediate being, 215
on jñānasattva, 188, 192–93, 598
on lord of tathāgata family, 602
on lunar disk, 522
on mind blessing, 590–91
on nirmāṇakāya transformation, 146
on offerings, 684
on passion, 198, 451, 604
preliminaries in, 242
principal deities in, 56, 115, 156, 437
on protection, 98, 313, 315, 327–28
on sealing, 227
as source, 283
on space element, 369
on specially visualized deities, 432, 434, 435, 436, 480
on Supreme King of Deeds, 699
on Supreme King of Maṇḍalas, 224, 625, 634
on three syllables, 589–90
on triple sattvas, 599, 600, 601
on vajra emblem, 524
on vajra recitation, 662, 663
on vajra tent, 330–31, 332
on Vajradhara, 318
on voiced recitation, 664
sakṛt, translating, 19
Śākya clan, 441
Sakya Paṇḍita, *Record of Teachings Received*, 54
Sakya school, 184
emptiness meditation in, 68–71, 72, 128
formation of coherent tantric tradition in, 44

grounds of purification in, 82
Khedrup Jé and, 71, 186–87
mere wind-and-mind in, 135
tathāgatagarbha in, 180
Śākyamitra, *Kosalālaṅkara*, 424, 426, 655
Samādhi of Direct Encounter, 131
samādhis
"delight in all desires," 199, 604, 605–6
of Dveṣavajra, 309
illusion-like, 467, 721
"method of great passion of all tathāgatas," 198, 204, 223, 257, 451, 604
powers of, 22
"supreme maṇḍala," 635
"vajra lamp of wisdom," 218–19, 225, 226, 315, 316
"vajra origination from samaya," 190, 213, 512, 545–46
"vajra overpowering all tathāgatas," 116, 154–55, 157, 209, 211–12, 477, 479, 511, 536, 537, 539–40
"vajra pacifying impediments to sentient beings," 333
samādhisattva, 214, 320, 596, 597, 598
correspondences, 191, 546
descriptions, 599–601
dissolution, 249, 669
meaning of term, 190
syllable, 189
Samantabhadra (commentator), 21–22
Samantabhadra (deity), 301, 433, 491, 575, 578–79
Samantabhadra Sādhana (Jñānapāda), 351
commentaries, 19, 21–22, 244, 349
on conceptual thoughts, 15–16, 343–44, 345–46
on emptiness, 342
on sevenfold worship, 303–6
śamatha. *See* mental quiescence
samaya wheel, 368, 422
samayasattva, 214
dissolution of, 669
jñānasattva and, 159, 189, 478, 529
meaning of term, 189–90, 595–96
role of, 12
tathāgata family of, 596
Samayavajra. *See* *Kṛṣṇasamayavajra
saṃbhogakāya, 378n1769
attaining, 136, 262
basis of, 379
deity visualization and, 82
fruitional, 134, 514, 520, 543
intermediate being and, 84, 461
natural abode and, 298
of path, 461
two bodies of, 702
Saṃkhya School, 548
Saṃpuṭa Tantra, 340, 562, 672
saṃsāra, 591
causes of, 83, 137, 462
foundation of, 134–35
as knowledge object, 548
liberation from, 16, 20, 69, 347
Mantra Vehicle and, 14
root of, 344, 347–49, 350, 611
suffering of, 345
saṃsāric evolution, 91–92, 458, 459–60, 471–72, 476
Saṃvaravyākhyā, 570
Saṃvarodaya Tantra, 39, 672
on embryos, 534
on food yoga, 694–95
on four continents, people of, 454
on gender, 531–32
on human womb birth, 446
on intermediate beings, rebirth of, 537
on lama in field of merit, 296–97, 298
on maṇḍalas, marking lines, 374
on maṇḍalas, size, 383
on mantras, number of recitations, 722
on torma offerings, 696–97
on vows, 270
on walls, 405
on womb entry, 529–30
Saroruha, 364
Hevajra Sādhana, 68, 71, 290, 342–43, 457
Padmin, 293
Sarvabuddhasamāyoga Tantra, 133
Sarvanīvaraṇavikṣambhin, 301, 433, 491–92
Śāstra of Love, 609

sealing, 193, 203, 227–28, 602, 634, 635, 637–39
seed syllables, 130, 224
  bhrūṃ, 380–81, 384, 436, 569
  in body maṇḍala, 170, 172–73, 552, 557–59, 574–75
  in consort yoga, 616
  of five meats and five nectars, 672–74, 680, 682
  four disks and, 100, 101, 376
  hūṃ, 590–91
  manifest awakening from, 140, 143–44, 523–24
  oṃ, meaning of, 324
  See also three syllables; individual deities
self-blessing stage, 83–84, 85, 462–63
self-grasping
  creation stage as antidote to, 344, 345–49, 350
  eradicating roots of, 16–18, 28
  meditation methods and, 20
  overcoming, 22–23
  purifying, 467, 468
selflessness, 16, 18, 20, 22–23, 28, 346–47, 354
sense bases/faculties
  blessing of, 539–40
  as bodhisattvas, 38, 39, 117, 122, 301, 479, 552–53, 555–56, 564, 580
  correspondences, 546
  dissolution of, 122, 485, 486–93, 495
  in emptiness meditation, 70
  in four continents, 453–55
  in joining-of-palms, 640–42
  in voiced recitation, 665
sense consciousnesses, 33, 88, 162–64, 573, 710, 711, 715
sense objects, 122, 292–93, 552–53, 640–42, 663
sensory spheres
  blessing of, 539–40
  correspondences, 546
  dissolution of, 485, 493, 495
  emptiness of, 340
  goddesses as, 117, 479
  identity of, 39
  vajra, 701–2
  as vajra ladies, 301
  in voiced recitation, 665
sentient beings
  basis of designation, 190, 539
  essence body in, 550
  in final dissolution, 686–87
  hidden interpretation of, 211–12
  as naturally present maṇḍalas, 180–81, 547–49, 566–68
  pure, 442, 595
Serdingpa Shönu Ö, 46, 148
session breaks, 689
  hundred-syllable mantra during, 293, 698
  practices during, 235–36, 253
  sleeping and waking during, 695
  See also body enhancement; torma offerings
seven features of union, 138, 262
seven royal treasures, 106, 403n1938
sevenfold worship, 242
  confession, 303–4
  mind for enlightenment generation, 305–6
  Mind Only view of, 244
  offerings, 299–300
  pledging reliance, 306
  prostrations, 300–303
  refuge, 304–5
  rejoicing and dedication, 304
  in sūtra and tantra, distinctions in, 243
  vows, maintaining past, 306–7
siddhis, 260, 678
  in creation stage, 273, 344, 699, 717–22
  of eye medicine, 717
  of pills, 717, 718
  recitation and, 667
  requesting, 238
  root of attaining, 650
  time in attaining, 718–19
  two types, 716
  unsuitable disciples and, 266, 267
  vows and, 269
  yoginīs as source of, 194
single-mindedness, 277, 280–81, 660–61, 712

skull
in inner offerings, 675, 679, 680
in torma offerings, 696
sleeping yoga, 235, 695
Smṛtijñānakīrti, *Secret Drawing Ritual*, 394–95
Snellgrove, David, 194–95
solar disk, 584
correspondences with, 518, 520, 522
disputes on, 515, 516–17, 521
seed syllables and, 130n557
solitary buddhas, 265, 352
Sönam Drakpa, Panchen, 152, 167, 246
Sönam Lhundrup, 178
Sönam Tsemo, 71, 72
on celestial mansion layers, 107
on emptiness meditation, 68–69, 70, 128, 343n1602
Khedrup Jé's critiques of, 181–82, 547n7723
on maṇḍalas, capacity for, 174
songs
concluding, 250
invocation, 668–70
source of phenomena, 98–99
color, 373
description and symbolism, 370–72
meditation on, 205, 206
purpose of meditating on, 372–73
as space element, 368–69, 374
space realm, 99, 153, 155n687, 210, 211, 313, 368–70, 374, 521
Sparśavajrā, 114, 592, 699
in consort yoga, 613, 614
dissolution of, 491–92
placement, 109, 432
in Supreme King of Maṇḍalas, 224
transformation into, 317–18, 321
special insight, 231, 656, 710n3624
specially visualized deities, 88–93, 193, 431–32, 436
deeds of, 115–16, 209–11, 477–79
dissolution, instructions for, 124–25, 494–95
dissolution, order of, 121–23, 486–93
dissolution, purpose of, 121, 349, 443, 580–81
dissolution, scriptural authority for, 122–23, 480, 483–84
and first eon beings, correspondence with, 442–44, 458, 464, 469
gathering into body, 117–19, 209, 479–82, 494
as gendered, 441
instantaneous visualization, 113–14, 208, 445, 447
placement, scriptural authority for, 433–35
placement and appearance, 432–33
as preparatory practice, 125
purpose of meditating on, 114
specific-perfect-discernment, 588n2934
speech, eight bases of, 546
Śraddha, 107
Śraddhākaravarman, 395
Śrīdhara, 297, 351
Stages of Self-Blessing (Āryadeva), 505, 506
subjective mode of apprehension, 26, 168–69
substantial cause
of body maṇḍala, 165, 166–68
definition of, 168–69
of deities as bodily constituents, 172–73
subtle body, 8, 162, 175, 191, 211–12, 228, 485
subtle drop yoga
correspondences, 472, 653, 668n3378
on lower nose, 657–59
overview, 230–33
purpose, 653–54
single-mindedness and conceptual yoga in, 660–61
stability in, 654–56
on upper nose, 656–57, 660
suchness
of deities and sentient beings, distinction in, 550–51
dissolution into, 343, 483, 668
manifest awakening from, 140, 517–18, 580, 584, 701
meditation, 349, 356
of phenomena, 339
suffering, 265, 547
antidote to, 344–45

and bodily bliss, mixed, 452
meditation's effects on, 20
source of, 15
Sumati, 276–77
Sumbharāja, 302, 319n1472, 320, 320n1475, 321n1479, 492n2424
dissolution, 493
implements and emblems, 325
placement of, 109, 110, 423, 433, 552, 575
in protection wheel, 245, 323–24, 329
variant views on, 327–28
śūnyatā (emptiness) mantra, 338, 361n1682, 495, 521, 701
in concluding offerings, 251
in dissolutions, 11–12, 66, 127
divine identity and, 28–29
meaning of, 29, 358–59, 496–97
in preliminary offerings, 292
three doors of liberation in, 342
variant views, 67–68, 70, 71
supramundane path, 28, 710
Supreme King of Deeds, 56, 57, 221, 230, 280, 699
offerings, 671
samādhi of, 706
See also recitation; subtle drop yoga
Supreme King of Maṇḍalas, 56, 57, 155n684, 158, 221, 280, 435, 543, 625–26
abiding on seat, 636–37
beginning of, variant views, 223–24
celestial mansion in, 227
consort yoga and, 202, 203, 620–21
correspondences, 653, 668n3378
deities, number of, 644–51
deities, number of faces, 639–43
erroneous views on, 472
four limbs of achievement in, 704
generation, mantras and emblems, 629–33
generation, visualization, 627–29
and King of Deeds, distinction between, 230
purpose of, 219–20, 605
samādhi of, 706
sealing deities, uncertainties about, 637–39
seven steps, 224–26, 626–27, 633–37
Supreme King of Samādhis. *See* First Yoga
Śūraṅgavajra, *Commentary on the Abhidhānottara Tantra*, 448
Sūtra on Entering the Womb, 502, 527–28, 532–33, 534–35
Śvetaketu, 450

T

Ṭakkirāja (Ṭarkvirāja), 302, 321n1479, 330, 433, 489, 575, 632–33
Tantra Requested by Indra, 371
tantras, multiple meanings in, 318, 377–78
tantric Buddhism, 6–7, 237, 242. *See also* Vajrayāna
Tārā, 101, 301, 379, 480, 491, 553, 614, 631–32
tathāgatagarbha theory, 11, 12, 137, 174, 179–80, 181–82
Tathāgatarakṣita, 53, 229, 283, 644
ten fierce deities, 108–9, 114, 301–2, 417
deeds of, 225
dissolution of, 486–93
female, in consort yoga, 614–15
mantras, 321n1479, 722
from mother's womb, drawing out, 320–21
placement, 553, 554–55
in protection wheel, 311, 313, 325–27, 368
seats of, 428
seed syllables of, 576
ten powers of Buddha, 550n2732
Tenzin Gyatso, Fourteenth Dalai Lama, 11–12
Thagana, 344, 345, 349, 657
Thekchen Chöje, 177
thirty-two maṇḍala deities, 423
arms, significance of number, 644
in body maṇḍala, 556
faces, significance of number, 639–44
generating, four stages of, 639
seats of, 110–11, 428–29
in Supreme King of Maṇḍalas, 224, 225, 661
thirty-two drops and, 626–27

three Buddha bodies
actual and similitude, 462
actualizing, 474–75
attaining, 84–85, 136–39
in creation stage, purpose of, 193
as fruit of purification, 83, 86, 92–93, 118, 466
ground, path, fruit, 461–64, 473
habituating to, 31–32
for one's own enlightenment, 603
transformation into, 56, 466
two stages and, 85–86
in *Vajrasattva Sādhana*, 56
three doors of liberation, 99, 342, 357–58
three realms, meaning of, 642
three samādhis, 56, 57, 281, 706, 714
three spheres, 721
of confession, 304
in meditation, 356–58
in offerings, 236, 251–52, 296, 671, 697
three syllables
blessing offerings with, 292, 300
correspondences with, 518, 519, 520, 522
disputes on, 515, 516–17
placement of, 248
thirty-two drops and, 627–28
vajra recitation of, 662–63
throat, purifying, 691–92
Tibetan Buddhism, 41–43, 44, 47, 246
Tibetan scholarship, 6, 7, 8–9, 10–13
Timuk Gama. *See* Moharati
torma offerings
between meditative sessions, 236, 696–99
preliminary, 241, 290–91
transference of consciousness, 125–26, 495
triple sattvas, 31, 160, 544–45, 601
achieving, 250, 702–3
correspondences, 546
dissolution, 669
invoking, 599
overview, 189–91
principal deity as, 319–20
purification of, 216
sealing by, 193, 203
variant views, 191–93
Tsongkhapa (Jinpa), xiv
Tsongkhapa Losang Drakpa, 158, 179
on Akṣobhya, 219
Analysis of Tantra, 720
on awakening in intermediate state, 145–46
on beings of first eon, 439n2164
on buddha bodies, 137, 139
on buddhahood in one lifetime, 199
Commentary on Formulating the Sādhana, 263
on consort yoga, 203, 615n3094
on creation stage dissolution, 65
on deity generation, 631n3160
on divine identity, 593n2965
on drop, melted, 621n3126
on emptiness meditation, 78, 127
on external objects and Mind Only, 76–77
on First Lord, 212–13, 224
on five manifest awakenings, 140
on food yoga, 692n3518
on four mothers, placement of, 553n2751
on four seals, 638–39
Fulfilling the Bee's Hopes, 32, 83–84, 244, 248
on grounds and correspondences, 461
on Guhyasamāja and Madhyamaka, 75–76
on Guhyasamāja system, 49–50, 52
homage, 257, 258, 723
on illusory body, 139
on intermediate beings, 501n2461, 503n2472
Khedrup Jé and, 3, 41
Lam rim chem mo, 656n3306
Lamp to Illuminate the Five Stages, xiv, 135, 720
on Locanā, 632n3177
on lords of families, 597n2982
on mere wind-and-mind, 132–36
on modes of birth, purifying, 148
on outer and body maṇḍalas, relationship of, 166, 177
Precious Sprout, 46, 239–40
on protection wheel, 247, 248

on purification, intermediate state and rebirth, 142, 143, 144
on purification, stages of, 94
on rebirth, correspondences to, 150–51
Record of Teachings Received, 46
and Rendawa, relationship of, 45–46
on sādhana correspondences, 82, 85–86, 90
on sealing, 203
Short Treatise on the Stage of the Path, 24
on stages, purifications by, 216
on Supreme Kings, correspondences, 222–23
as systematizer, 43, 47, 83, 178
on three maṇḍalas, distinctions between, 175
on tormas, 241
on two stages, 8–9, 126
Wish-Granting Cow, 164–65, 174, 180, 244
on women, enlightenment of, 194, 195–96, 197
See also *Great Treatise on the Stages of the Mantric Path*; *Guhyasamāja Sādhana*
Tsunmochen, 468–69
Tuṣita, 147, 198, 453, 474, 504, 605
Twenty Maṇḍala Rituals (Nāgabodhi), 98, 100, 377, 632
on colors, 406, 427
on gate posts, 398
on inner maṇḍala, 421, 422
on inner mansion, 418–19
on maṇḍala measurements, 374, 375, 383
on portal, 401–2
on rain gutters, 414
twenty-five coarse elements, 121–23, 126, 128–29, 487, 561–62
two accumulations, 14, 128, 242, 350, 365, 712. *See also* field of accumulating merit; wisdom
two stages, 24, 32, 148–49, 258
as clear light and illusory body, 465–66
clear light in, 129
correspondences during, importance of understanding, 142
deities body, distinctions in, 447
dissolutions, distinctions in, 669
four modes of birth and, 448
integration of, 14n55
purifications in, 93, 126
sequence of, 272–77
serenity in, 656n3306
union of, 8
See also completion stage; creation stage
two truths, 74–75, 519, 642

U

ubhaya tantras, 639, 640
ultimate truth, 20, 61, 341, 461, 483, 497, 507, 668
appearances and, 65
completion stage and, 126
death as, 465
generating, 567–68
indestructible drop and, 379
protection in, 98
unexcelled tantra, 13, 148, 260–61
awakening in, 450–51, 463
completion stage of, 352–53
deities in, 228
inner offerings in, 671–72
practitioners of, 201
sense offerings in, 252
subtle drops in, 655
swiftness of, 199
two stages in, 447
types of disciples, 456
union of no more practice, 146, 461, 463
union still requiring practice, 145–46, 463
universal monarchs, 440
Uṣṇīṣacakravartin, 111, 302, 321n1479, 492n2424
dissolution, 493
mudrā of, 633
placement of, 109, 423, 424, 427, 433, 575

V

Vaidyapāda (also Vitapāda), 17, 57n258, 84–85, 344–45, 358, 653–54, 657, 704n3593, 707
Vairocana, 208, 699
blessings of, 188, 585–86

color, 104
dissolution, 122, 123, 125, 488, 494
divine pride, 26
as form aggregate, 170, 171, 381, 580
gate of, 511, 529, 586
ignorance purified by, 219, 634
invoking, 481, 584–85, 703
maṇḍala size, 383
placement, 432, 552, 558, 559, 574
seed syllable, 381
in Supreme King of Maṇḍalas, 225, 630
as Vajra Body, 31
Vairocanavajra, 202–6
vajra and bell blessing, 238
Vajra Crown Tantra, 329
Vajra Deathless (Vajrāmṛta), 326–27
vajra enclosure meditation, 330–32, 333, 368
vajra garland[s], 110, 417, 418, 419–20, 421–22, 425, 429n2105
Vajra Garland Explanatory Tantra, xiv, 283, 329, 553, 722
on body maṇḍala, 160, 161, 168, 556
on celestial mansion, body as, 551–52, 564, 565, 569, 571–72
on channels, division of, 507
on consciousness entering womb, 530
on consorts, 607
on deities, number of, 230, 647, 649–50
on dissolution, 123, 485, 486–87, 492
on essential points, 706
on five nectars, 678
on four mothers, placement, 561
on four yogas, 705
on initiation, 267
on inner mansion, 420
on Maitreya, 576
on nose-tips, 573
offering mantras in, 299
on seats, 428
on specially visualized deities, 483–84
on stages of existence, 518
on tantra, qualities needed for, 264, 266
on three appearances, 509
on transference between lives, 506
vajra ground, 97, 183, 206, 330n1552, 337, 367–73, 473, 570
vajra ladies, 114
in consort yoga, 614, 615
deeds of, 225
in joining-of-palms, 641
placement of, 109, 417, 420, 421, 429n2105, 552–53, 554–56, 564
seed syllables, 577–78
as sensory spheres, 301
six, 645n3243
vajra masters, 259–60, 556, 649–51
Vajra Pavilion Tantra, 267–68, 350–51, 382–83
Vajra Peak Tantra, 270, 324
Vajra Queen, 99, 204, 205, 206, 371
Vajra Sky Traveler Tantra, 455
Vajra Stake (Vajrakīla), 326–27, 328
vajra stakes, driving, 323–29
Vajrabhairava, 188, 189, 699
Vajraḍāka Tantra, 194, 202, 243, 410, 567, 608–9
Vajradhara, 12, 56, 114, 259, 296, 314–15, 318, 485, 642, 699
cause of, 372
in consort yoga, 618
dissolution, 125, 253, 494–95
divine identity, 30, 31, 328
maṇḍala of, 547–48
in preliminaries, 245
as principal deity, 115, 208, 436–37, 629
as progenitor, refutation of, 441–42
purification by, 94
residence of, 371
sealing with, 193, 602
seat of, 428–29
self-visualization, 124, 214, 319
between sessions, 235
as single deity, 141–42
in Supreme King of Maṇḍalas, 226
as three vajras, 593–94
Vajradhātvīśvarī, 193, 317–18, 320, 613
Vajragarbha, 274–75, 632
Vajraghaṇṭa, 173–74, 177, 179–80, 364, 445, 447, 547, 566, 666, 673
Vajrajñānasamuccaya Tantra commentary, 49–50
vajra-joining-of-palms, 228, 526, 640–43

Vajrapāṇi, 301, 428, 432, 489, 557, 564, 574, 578, 636–37
Vajrapāṇi Initiation Tantra, 266
Vajrasattva, 30, 56, 94, 574
 blessing of, 539, 540
 entry-mode of, 477, 478, 479
 as ground of purification, 86
 nirmāṇakāya, transformation into, 129, 146, 152–53, 156, 159, 162, 165, 215, 443
 nirmāṇakāya, yogi's body as, 172, 175–76
 nirmāṇakāya as samayasattva, 190
 nirmāṇakāya father-mother, 626
 placement, 432
 as principal deity, 115, 437
 in subtle drop yoga, 658
 visualized as lama, 297
Vajrasattva meditation and recitation, 241, 293
Vajrasattva Offering Ritual, 300
Vajrasattva Sādhana, 7, 99, 207, 246, 474, 522, 577–78, 684
 on all activities, joining vajra and lotus in, 720–21
 authorship, 53–54, 248, 284
 on *bhrūṃ*, 381
 on body blessing, 586–87
 on Buddha's deeds, 198–99
 on consort yoga, 605–6, 612–13, 616, 618, 619
 on deities, number of, 229, 644
 on deities, withdrawing into body, 117
 on dissolution, 685–86
 on divine identity, 593–94
 on fierce deities, 322
 on First Lord, 318, 525
 on four disks, 101, 376, 377
 on four mothers, 561, 563
 four yogas in, 57, 118–19
 on *hūṃ*, 590–91
 on jñānasattva, 188, 192, 597
 on lord of tathāgata family, 602
 on meditation posture, 291
 on mind blessing, 590–91, 592
 on moon orb, 131
 on offerings, 295, 296
 preliminaries in, 237, 242
 on principal deities, 56, 115, 437
 on protection, 98, 314, 315, 324, 326–27
 on samādhisattva, 599–600, 601
 on samayasattva, 190, 595–96
 on seats, 428–29
 on secret offering, 685
 as source, 283
 on space element, 368, 369
 on specially visualized deities, 433–34, 435, 479
 on speech blessing, 588, 589
 on suchness, 343
 on Supreme King of Deeds, 699
 on Supreme King of Maṇḍalas, 223–24
 three Buddha bodies in, 82, 94
 on triple sattvas, 599
 on two purposes, 221–22
 on ultimate protection, 365
 on vajra enclosure, 330, 331, 332
 on Vajra Stake, 327
Vajraśekhara Tantra, 243
Vajrayāna
 emptiness meditation in, 70
 gender symmetry in, 196–97
 goals of, 8, 9
 historical development, 7–8, 131
 merit, accumulating in, 350
 pre-conditions for, 264
 suitability for, 265
 See also Mantra Vehicle
valid cognition, 23, 347–48, 648, 649
Van der Kuijp, Leonard, 183
vases, 106, 109, 403, 429
Vasubandhu. See *Abhidharmakośa*; *Abhidharmakośabhāṣya*
Vehicle of Disciples, 352
Vetālī, 555, 614
Vibhūticandra, 270–71, 407, 408
victory banners, 108, 415–16
vidyā, personification of, 204, 213, 214, 215, 219, 315, 316, 319, 514, 545
Vighnāntaka, 292, 302, 321n1479, 491, 667
Vikṣambhin, 575
Vimalakīrti Nirdeśa, xiv, 232
Vinayavibhaṅga, 81, 439, 441

virtue, foundation of, 31–32
Virūpa, 291
Vīryabhadra, *Clarifying the Meaning of Difficult Points in the Five Stages*, 271
visualization
in completion stage, 8
as conceptual, 8
in creation stage, reality of, 6
as creation stage's foundation, 179
Mahāyāna visions and, 233
in mental consciousness, 33
son- and grandson-, 231–32, 654n3269, 658
in tantric practice, role of, 4, 5–6
vows and commitments, 268
bodhisattva, 265, 694
keeping unshared, 243
maintaining, 269–71
monastic, 550
past, maintaining, 305–6
tantric, 128

W

Wayman, Alex, *The Buddhist Tantras*, 49
wind yoga, 353, 610, 612, 693
winds
in birth state, 508–9
in central channel, 643
in fetal development, 532
five basic, 560–61
life-sustaining, 491, 506, 560
and mind, indivisibility of, 518
of physical elements, 562
swift entry of, 495
ten, 491
at time of death, 138, 506, 507
vajra recitation and, 496
wisdom, 29
accumulation of, 63, 69, 78, 339
dissolution, 493–94
ground of, 61, 62, 64, 310, 355, 366, 367
nonconceptual and pure worldly, 363
wisdom and method, 23–24, 480n2331, 484, 539, 540, 639, 642
wisdom body, 214n959, 262, 447, 521
wisdom consorts, 175, 202, 569, 611, 612–13
wisdom of discernment, 453, 486, 489–90
wisdom of equanimity, 486, 488–89
wisdom of purposive acts, 486, 491
Wisdom Sūtra, 511, 537. See also *Saṃvarodaya Tantra*
womb birth, 485, 487, 494
actual emergence, 534–35
correspondences, 143, 145, 146–47, 148–49, 443, 446–48, 471, 513
death and, 92, 129, 487, 505
human, conditions for, 527–29
in intermediate being's role in, 504
in Jambudvīpa, 92, 149, 443, 448, 494
past events and, 214–15
women
as enlightened beings, 204
enlightenment of, 193–95, 197, 456–58
as jewel-like disciples, 196
wrong cognitions, 11–12

Y

Yamāntaka, 321n1479, 423n2076
basis of generating, 555
dissolution, 122, 488
emblem, 632
as ignorance, 301
jñānasattva of, 597
placement of, 109, 433, 575, 576, 578
Yamāntaka cycle, 241, 245
Yamāri cycle, 239, 396. See also *Black Yamāri Tantra*; *Red Yamāri Tantra*
Yaśomitra, 532
yoga of nondual profundity and manifestation, 13–14, 24, 27, 34, 349–51
yoga of union, 479, 482, 597
yoga tantras, 264, 292, 467, 638, 640, 655, 700
Yogācāra school, 6–7, 74–76, 131, 150
Yogācāra-Madhyamaka, 7, 346n1616
Yoginīsañcaryā Tantra, 184, 186

About the Authors

YAEL BENTOR, professor emerita at the Hebrew University of Jerusalem, is a scholar of Tibetan tantric Buddhism. Her research focuses on the crystallization of tantric traditions among Geluk scholars during the early fifteenth century in Tibet. Currently she is working on the Six Dharmas of Nāropa as presented by Tsongkhapa vis-à-vis the standpoints of Kagyü scholars. She lives in Jerusalem, Israel.

PENPA DORJEE was a professor and head librarian of Shantarakshita Library of the Central Institute of Higher Tibetan Studies, Sarnath, India. He received an acharya degree from Sampurnanand Sanskrit University in Varanasi and his PhD from the Central Institute of Higher Tibetan Studies. He has seventeen books to his credit as author, coauthor, translator, or editor. He retired as a professor in 2020. He is presently working on curriculum development for the Dalai Lama Centre for Tibetan and Ancient Indian Wisdom, Bodhgaya, India. He is also a part of the project initiated by the Dalai Lama Trust translating the Pāli Tipiṭaka into Tibetan.

Studies in Indian and Tibetan Buddhism
Titles Previously Published

Among Tibetan Texts
History and Literature of the Himalayan Plateau
E. Gene Smith

Approaching the Great Perfection
Simultaneous and Gradual Methods of Dzogchen Practice in the Longchen Nyingtig
Sam van Schaik

Authorized Lives
Biography and the Early Formation of Geluk Identity
Elijah S. Ary

The Buddha's Single Intention
Drigung Kyobpa Jikten Sumgön's Vajra Statements of the Early Kagyü Tradition
Jan-Ulrich Sobisch

Buddhism Between Tibet and China
Edited by Matthew T. Kapstein

The Buddhist Philosophy of the Middle
Essays on Indian and Tibetan Madhyamaka
David Seyfort Ruegg

Buddhist Teaching in India
Johannes Bronkhorst

A Direct Path to the Buddha Within
Gö Lotsāwa's Mahāmudrā Interpretation of the Ratnagotravibhāga
Klaus-Dieter Mathes

The Essence of the Ocean of Attainments
The Creation Stage of the Guhyasamaja Tantra according to Panchen Losang Chökyi Gyaltsen
Translated by Yael Bentor and Penpa Dorjee

Foundations of Dharmakīrti's Philosophy
John D. Dunne

Freedom from Extremes
Gorampa's "Distinguishing the Views" and the Polemics of Emptiness
José Ignacio Cabezón and Geshe Lobsang Dargyay

Himalayan Passages
Tibetan and Newar Studies in Honor of Hubert Decleer
Benjamin Bogin and Andrew Quintman

Histories of Tibet
Essays in Honor of Leonard W. J. van der Kuijp
Edited by Kurtis R. Schaeffer, Jue Liang, and William A. McGrath

How Do Mādhyamikas Think?
And Other Essays on the Buddhist Philosophy of the Middle
Tom J. F. Tillemans

Jewels of the Middle Way
The Madhyamaka Legacy of Atiśa and His Early Tibetan Followers
James B. Apple

Living Treasure
Tibetan and Buddhist Studies in Honor of Janet Gyatso
Edited by Holly Gayley and Andrew Quintman

Luminous Lives
The Story of the Early Masters of the Lam 'bras Tradition in Tibet
Cyrus Stearns

Mind Seeing Mind
Mahamudra and the Geluk Tradition of Tibetan Buddhism
Roger R. Jackson

Mipham's Beacon of Certainty
Illuminating the View of Dzogchen, the Great Perfection
John Whitney Pettit

Omniscience and the Rhetoric of Reason
Śāntarakṣita and Kamalaśīla on Rationality, Argumentation, and Religious Authority
Sara L. McClintock

Reason's Traces
Identity and Interpretation in Indian and Tibetan Buddhist Thought
Matthew T. Kapstein

Reasons and Lives in Buddhist Traditions
Studies in Honor of Matthew Kapstein
Edited by Dan Arnold, Cécile Ducher, and Pierre-Julien Harter

Remembering the Lotus-Born
Padmasambhava in the History of Tibet's Golden Age
Daniel A. Hirshberg

Resurrecting Candrakīrti
Disputes in the Tibetan Creation of Prāsaṅgika
Kevin A. Vose

Saraha's Spontaneous Songs
With the Commentaries by Advayavajra and Mokṣākaragupta
Klaus-Dieter Mathes and Péter-Dániel Szántó

Scripture, Logic, Language
Essays on Dharmakīrti and His Tibetan Successors
Tom J. F. Tillemans

Sexuality in Classical South Asian Buddhism
José I. Cabezón

The Svātantrika-Prāsaṅgika Distinction
What Difference Does a Difference Make?
Edited by Georges Dreyfus and Sara McClintock

Vajrayoginī
Her Visualizations, Rituals, and Forms
Elizabeth English

About Wisdom Publications

Wisdom Publications is the leading publisher of classic and contemporary Buddhist books and practical works on mindfulness. To learn more about us or to explore our other books, please visit our website at wisdomexperience.org or contact us at the address below.

Wisdom Publications
132 Perry Street
New York, NY 10014 USA

We are a 501(c)(3) organization, and donations in support of our mission are tax deductible.

Wisdom Publications is affiliated with the Foundation for the Preservation of the Mahayana Tradition (FPMT).